Encyclopedia of
Industrial and
Organizational
Psychology

With much love and heartfelt gratitude to my mom and dad, Jane and Joel Rogelberg

Encyclopedia of
Industrial and Organizational Psychology

2
Volume

Edited by
Steven G. Rogelberg
University of North Carolina Charlotte

A SAGE Reference Publication

SAGE Publications
Thousand Oaks ■ London ■ New Delhi

For information:

 SAGE Publications, Inc.
2455 Teller Road
Thousand Oaks, California 91320
E-mail: order@sagepub.com

SAGE Publications Ltd.
1 Oliver's Yard
55 City Road
London EC1Y 1SP
United Kingdom

SAGE Publications India Pvt. Ltd.
B-42, Panchsheel Enclave
Post Box 4109
New Delhi 110 017 India

Printed in the United States of America on acid-free paper

Library of Congress Cataloging-in-Publication Data

Encyclopedia of industrial and organizational psychology / Steven G. Rogelberg, Editor.
    p. cm.
"A Sage reference publication."
Includes bibliographical references and index.
ISBN 1–4129–2470–7 (cloth)
   1. Psychology, Industrial—Encyclopedias. 2. Organizational behavior—Encyclopedias. I. Rogelberg, Steven G.

HF5548.8.E498 2007
158.7—dc22

                        2006006930

06 07 08 09 10 10 9 8 7 6 5 4 3 2 1

Publisher:	Rolf Janke
Acquiring Editor:	Jim Brace-Thompson
Developmental Editor:	Paul Reis
Production Editor:	Sanford Robinson
Reference Systems Coordinator:	Leticia Gutierrez
Typesetter:	C&M Digitals (P) Ltd.
Indexer:	Molly Hall
Cover Designer:	Candice Harman

Contents

Editorial Board, *vii*

List of Entries, *ix*

Reader's Guide, *xv*

Entries

VOLUME I: A–L,
1–466

VOLUME II: M–W,
467–910

Appendixes, *911*

Index, *I-1*

List of Entries

Abusive Supervision
Academy of Management
Action Theory
Adverse Impact/Disparate Treatment/
    Discrimination at Work
Affective Events Theory
Affective Traits
Affirmative Action
Age Discrimination in Employment Act
American Psychological Association,
    Association for Psychological Science
Americans With Disabilities Act
Applicant/Test-Taker Reactions
Army Alpha/Army Beta
Assessment Center
Assessment Center Methods
Attitudes and Beliefs
Attraction–Selection–Attrition Model
Automation/Advanced Manufacturing
    Technology/Computer-Based Integrated
    Technology
Autonomy. *See* Empowerment

Balanced Scorecard
Banding
Behavioral Approach to Leadership
Benchmarking
Big Five Taxonomy of Personality
Biographical Data
Bona Fide Occupational Qualifications
Boredom at Work

Career Development
Careers
Case Study Method
Charismatic Leadership Theory

Civil Rights Act of 1964, Civil Rights Act of 1991
Classical Test Theory
Classification. *See* Placement and Classification
Cognitive Abilities
Cognitive Ability Tests
Comparable Worth
Compensation
Competency Modeling
Compressed Workweek
Computer Adaptive Testing. *See* Computer
    Assessment
Computer Assessment
Confidence Intervals/Hypothesis Testing/Effect Sizes
Confirmatory Factor Analysis. *See* Factor Analysis
Conflict at Work
Conflict Management
Construct
Content Coding
Contextual Performance/Prosocial Behavior/
    Organizational Citizenship Behavior
Control Theory
Core Self-Evaluations
Corporate Ethics
Corporate Social Responsibility
Counterproductive Work Behaviors
Counterproductive Work Behaviors, Interpersonal
    Deviance
Counterproductive Work Behaviors,
    Organizational Deviance
Creativity at Work
Credentialing
Criterion Theory
Critical Incident Technique
Cross-Cultural Research Methods and Theory
Customer Satisfaction With Services
Cyberloafing at Work

Data Sampling. *See* Sampling Techniques
Descriptive Statistics
Dictionary of Occupational Titles
Differential Item Functioning
Dirty Work
Distance Learning
Diversity in the Workplace
Diversity Training
Downsizing
Drug and Alcohol Testing

Electronic Human Resources Management
Electronic Performance Monitoring
Emotional Burnout
Emotional Intelligence
Emotional Labor
Emotions
Employee Assistance Program
Employee Grievance Systems
Employee Selection
Employment at Will
Employment Interview
Empowerment
Engineering Psychology
Entrepreneurship
Equal Pay Act of 1963
Equity Theory
Ergonomics. *See* Engineering
    Psychology
Ethics in Industrial/Organizational Practice
Ethics in Industrial/Organizational Research
Eustress
Executive Coaching
Executive Selection
Exit Survey (Exit Interview)
Expatriates
Expectancy Theory of Work Motivation
Experimental Designs
Exploratory Factor Analysis.
    See Factor Analysis

Factor Analysis
Family and Medical Leave Act
Feedback
Feedback Seeking
Flexible Work Schedules
Focus Groups
Frame-of-Reference Training
Free Riding. *See* Social Loafing

Gainsharing and Profit Sharing
Gay, Lesbian, and Bisexual Issues at Work
Generalizability Theory
Genetics and Industrial/Organizational Psychology
Glass Ceiling
Global Leadership and Organizational Behavior
    Effectiveness Project
Globalization
Goal-Setting Theory
Graphology
Gravitational Hypothesis
Group Cohesiveness
Group Decision-Making Quality and Performance
Group Decision-Making Techniques
Group Development
Group Dynamics and Processes
Group Mental Model. *See* Team Mental Model
Groups
Groupthink

Hardiness
Hawthorne Studies/Hawthorne Effect
High-Performance Organization Model
History of Industrial/Organizational Psychology
    in Europe and the United Kingdom
History of Industrial/Organizational Psychology
    in North America
History of Industrial/Organizational Psychology
    in Other Parts of the World
Honesty Testing. *See* Integrity Testing
Human–Computer Interaction
Human Factors. *See* Engineering Psychology
Human Relations Movement
Human Resource Management
Human Resources Strategy

Implicit Theory of Leadership
Impression Management
Incentives
Incremental Validity
Individual Assessment
Individual Differences
Industrial Relations
Inferential Statistics
Initial Screening. *See* Prescreening Assessment
    Methods for Personnel Selection
Innovation
Input–Process–Output Model of Team Effectiveness
Integrity at Work

Integrity Testing
Intergroup Relations
Interpersonal Communication
Interpersonal Communication Styles
Intrinsic and Extrinsic Work Motivation
Item Response Theory

Job Advertisements
Job Analysis
Job Analysis Methods
Job Characteristics Theory
Job Choice
Job Control. *See* Empowerment
Job Description
Job Design
Job Evaluation
Job Involvement
Job Knowledge Testing
Job Performance Models
Job Rotation
Job Satisfaction
Job Satisfaction Measurement
Job Search
Job Security/Insecurity
Job Sharing
Job Typologies
Judgment and Decision-Making Process
Judgment and Decision-Making Process:
    Advice Giving and Taking
Judgment and Decision-Making Process: Heuristics,
    Cognitive Biases, and Contextual Influences
Justice in Teams

Labor Law
Labor Unions. *See* Unions
Latent Trait Theory. *See* Item Response Theory
Layoffs. *See* Downsizing
Leader–Member Exchange Theory
Leadership and Supervision
Leadership Development
Learning Organizations
Least Preferred Coworker Theory
Lens Model
Letters of Recommendation
Life-cycle Model of Leadership
Linkage Research and Analyses
Locus of Control
Longitudinal Research/Experience Sampling
    Technique

Machiavellianism
Measurement Scales
Measures of Association/Correlation Coefficient
Meetings at Work
Mentoring
Mergers, Acquisitions, and Strategic Alliances
Meta-Analysis
Moderator and Mediator Variables
Mood
Morale
Motivational Traits
Multilevel Modeling
Multilevel Modeling Techniques
Multitrait–Multimethod Matrix

National Institute for Occupational Safety
    and Health/Occupational Safety
    and Health Administration
Naturalistic Observation
Need for Achievement, Power, and Affiliation
Need Theories of Work Motivation
Negotiation, Mediation, and Arbitration
Networking
New Employee Orientation
Nomological Networks
Nonexperimental Designs
Normative Models of Decision Making and
    Leadership
Normative Versus Ipsative Measurement

Occupational Health Psychology
Occupational Information Network (O*NET)
Older Worker Issues
Open-Ended Data Collection Approaches.
    See Content Coding
Optimism and Pessimism
Organizational Behavior
Organizational Behavior Management
Organizational Change
Organizational Change, Resistance to
Organizational Climate
Organizational Commitment
Organizational Communication, Formal
Organizational Communication, Informal
Organizational Culture
Organizational Cynicism
Organizational Development
Organizational Image
Organizational Justice

Organizational Politics
Organizational Retaliatory Behavior
Organizational Sensemaking
Organizational Socialization
Organizational Socialization Tactics
Organizational Structure
Organizational Surveys
Outsourcing

Path–Goal Theory
Performance Appraisal
Performance Appraisal, Objective Indexes
Performance Appraisal, Subjective Indexes
Performance Feedback
Personality
Personality Assessment
Person–Environment Fit
Person–Job Fit
Person–Organization Fit
Person–Vocation Fit
Physical Performance Assessment
Placement and Classification
Policy Capturing
Positive Psychology Applied to Work
Practical Intelligence
Prejudice. *See* Stereotyping
Prescreening Assessment Methods for Personnel
    Selection
Profit Sharing. *See* Gainsharing and Profit Sharing
Program Evaluation
Project A
Protestant Work Ethic
Psychological Contract

Qualitative Research Approach
Quality of Work Life
Quantitative Research Approach
Quasi-experimental Designs
Questionnaires. *See* Survey Approach

Race Norming
Rating Errors and Perceptual Biases
Realistic Job Preview
Recruitment
Recruitment Sources
Reinforcement Theory of Work Motivation
Reliability
Retirement
Rightsizing. *See* Downsizing
Role Ambiguity

Role Conflict
Role Overload and Underload

Sampling Techniques
Scientific Management
Scientist-Practitioner Model
Selection: Occupational Tailoring
Selection Strategies
Self-Concept Theory of Work Motivation
Self-Efficacy
Self-Esteem
Self-Fulfilling Prophecy: Pygmalion Effect
Self-Regulation Theory
Sexual Discrimination
Sexual Harassment at Work
Shiftwork
Simulation, Computer Approach
Situational Approach to Leadership
Situational Judgment Tests
Social Cognitive Theory
Social Exchange Theory
Social Loafing
Social Norms and Conformity
Social Support
Socialization. *See* Organizational Socialization
Socialization: Employee Proactive Behaviors
Society for Industrial and Organizational Psychology
Sociotechnical Approach
Spirituality and Leadership at Work
Standardized Testing
Statistical Power
Stereotype Threat
Stereotyping
Strategic Human Resources.
        See Human Resources Strategy
Strategic Planning
Stress, Consequences
Stress, Coping and Management
Stress, Models and Theories
Structural Equation Modeling
Succession Planning
Survey Approach
Survivor Syndrome

Team-Based Rewards
Team Building
Team Development. *See* Group Development
Team Mental Model
Teams. *See* Groups
Telecommuting

Temporary Workers. *See* Outsourcing
Terrorism and Work
Test Security
Theft at Work
Theory of Action
Theory of Reasoned Action/Theory of Planned
    Behavior
Theory of Work Adjustment
360-Degree Feedback
Time Management
Total Quality Management
Trade Unions. *See* Unions
Trainability and Adaptability
Training
Training Evaluation
Training Methods
Training Needs Assessment and Analysis
Trait Approach to Leadership
Transfer of Training
Transformational and Transactional Leadership
Trust
Turnover. *See* Withdrawal Behaviors, Turnover
Two-Factor Theory
Type A and Type B Personalities

Underemployment
Uniform Guidelines on Employee Selection
    Procedures
Union Commitment

Union Law. *See* Labor Law
Unions
Utility Analysis

Validation Strategies
Validity
Verbal Protocol Analysis
Violence at Work
Virtual Organizations
Virtual Teams

Web-Based Assessment. *See* Computer Assessment
Whistleblowers
Withdrawal Behaviors, Absenteeism
Withdrawal Behaviors, Lateness
Withdrawal Behaviors, Turnover
Workaholism
Work Ethic. *See* Protestant Work Ethic
Work–Life Balance
Work Motivation
Workplace Accommodations
    for the Disabled
Workplace Incivility
Workplace Injuries
Workplace Romance
Workplace Safety
Work Samples
Work Values

Reader's Guide

FOUNDATIONS

History

Army Alpha/Army Beta
Hawthorne Studies/Hawthorne Effect
History of Industrial/Organizational
    Psychology in Europe and the United Kingdom
History of Industrial/Organizational
    Psychology in North America
History of Industrial/Organizational
    Psychology in Other Parts of the World
Human Relations Movement
Project A
Scientific Management
Scientist-Practitioner Model
Unions

Ethical and Legal Issues

Adverse Impact/Disparate
    Treatment/Discrimination at Work
Affirmative Action
Age Discrimination in Employment Act
Americans With Disabilities Act
Bona Fide Occupational Qualifications
Civil Rights Act of 1964, Civil Rights Act of 1991
Comparable Worth
Corporate Ethics
Corporate Social Responsibility
Employment at Will
Equal Pay Act of 1963
Ethics in Industrial/Organizational Practice
Ethics in Industrial/Organizational Research
Family and Medical Leave Act
Glass Ceiling
Labor Law

National Institute for Occupational Safety and
    Health/Occupational Safety and Health
    Administration
Race Norming
Sexual Discrimination
Sexual Harassment at Work
Stereotyping
Test Security
Uniform Guidelines on Employee Selection
    Procedures
Workplace Accommodations for the Disabled

Research Methods

Benchmarking
Case Study Method
Competency Modeling
Content Coding
Critical Incident Technique
Cross-Cultural Research Methods and Theory
Experimental Designs
Focus Groups
Lens Model
Linkage Research and Analyses
Longitudinal Research/Experience Sampling
    Technique
Meta-Analysis
Naturalistic Observation
Nonexperimental Designs
Organizational Surveys
Policy Capturing
Program Evaluation
Qualitative Research Approach
Quantitative Research Approach
Quasi-experimental Designs
Sampling Techniques

Simulation, Computer Approach
Survey Approach
Verbal Protocol Analysis

Measurement Theory and Statistics

Classical Test Theory
Confidence Intervals/Hypothesis Testing/Effect Sizes
Construct
Criterion Theory
Descriptive Statistics
Differential Item Functioning
Factor Analysis
Generalizability Theory
Incremental Validity
Inferential Statistics
Item Response Theory
Measurement Scales
Measures of Association/Correlation Coefficient
Moderator and Mediator Variables
Multilevel Modeling
Multilevel Modeling Techniques
Multitrait–Multimethod Matrix
Nomological Networks
Normative Versus Ipsative Measurement
Reliability
Statistical Power
Structural Equation Modeling
Utility Analysis
Validation Strategies
Validity

INDUSTRIAL PSYCHOLOGY

Understanding and Assessing Individual Differences

Affective Traits
Big Five Taxonomy of Personality
Biographical Data
Cognitive Abilities
Cognitive Ability Tests
Computer Assessment
Core Self-Evaluations
Emotional Intelligence
Employment Interview
Genetics and Industrial/Organizational Psychology
Graphology
Gravitational Hypothesis
Hardiness

Impression Management
Individual Assessment
Individual Differences
Integrity Testing
Job Knowledge Testing
Letters of Recommendation
Locus of Control
Machiavellianism
Motivational Traits
Need for Achievement, Power, and Affiliation
Optimism and Pessimism
Personality
Personality Assessment
Physical Performance Assessment
Practical Intelligence
Protestant Work Ethic
Self-Esteem
Situational Judgment Tests
Standardized Testing
Stereotype Threat
Trainability and Adaptability
Type A and Type B Personalities
Work Samples
Work Values

Employment, Staffing, and Career Issues

Applicant/Test-Taker Reactions
Banding
Career Development
Careers
Compensation
Credentialing
Dictionary of Occupational Titles
Dirty Work
Drug and Alcohol Testing
Electronic Human Resources Management
Employee Selection
Executive Selection
Exit Survey (Exit Interview)
Expatriates
Gainsharing and Profit Sharing
Gay, Lesbian, and Bisexual Issues at Work
Human Resources Strategy
Job Advertisements
Job Analysis
Job Analysis Methods
Job Choice
Job Description
Job Evaluation

Job Search
Job Typologies
Occupational Information
     Network (O*NET)
Older Worker Issues
Person–Environment Fit
Person–Job Fit
Person–Organization Fit
Person–Vocation Fit
Placement and Classification
Prescreening Assessment Methods
     for Personnel Selection
Realistic Job Preview
Recruitment
Recruitment Sources
Retirement
Selection: Occupational Tailoring
Selection Strategies
Succession Planning
Underemployment

Developing, Training, and Evaluating Employees

Assessment Center
Assessment Center Methods
Distance Learning
Diversity Training
Electronic Performance Monitoring
Employee Assistance Program
Executive Coaching
Feedback Seeking
Frame-of-Reference Training
Leadership Development
Mentoring
Organizational Socialization
Organizational Socialization Tactics
Performance Appraisal
Performance Appraisal, Objective Indexes
Performance Appraisal, Subjective Indexes
Performance Feedback
Rating Errors and Perceptual Biases
Self-Fulfilling Prophecy: Pygmalion Effect
Socialization: Employee Proactive Behaviors
360-Degree Feedback
Training
Training Evaluation
Training Methods
Training Needs Assessment and Analysis
Transfer of Training

Productive and Counterproductive Employee Behavior

Contextual Performance/Prosocial
     Behavior/Organizational Citizenship
     Behavior
Counterproductive Work Behaviors
Counterproductive Work Behaviors,
     Interpersonal Deviance
Counterproductive Work Behaviors,
     Organizational Deviance
Creativity at Work
Customer Satisfaction With Services
Cyberloafing at Work
Innovation
Integrity at Work
Job Performance Models
Organizational Retaliatory Behavior
Theft at Work
Time Management
Violence at Work
Whistleblowers
Withdrawal Behaviors, Absenteeism
Withdrawal Behaviors, Lateness
Withdrawal Behaviors, Turnover
Workplace Incivility

Motivation and Job Design

Action Theory
Control Theory
Empowerment
Expectancy Theory of Work
     Motivation
Goal-Setting Theory
Human–Computer Interaction
Incentives
Intrinsic and Extrinsic Work Motivation
Job Characteristics Theory
Job Design
Job Involvement
Job Rotation
Job Sharing
Need Theories of Work Motivation
Path–Goal Theory
Positive Psychology Applied to Work
Self-Concept Theory of Work Motivation
Self-Efficacy
Self-Regulation Theory
Social Cognitive Theory
Telecommuting

Theory of Work Adjustment
Two-Factor Theory
Work Motivation
Workaholism

Leadership and Management

Abusive Supervision
Behavioral Approach to Leadership
Charismatic Leadership Theory
Employee Grievance Systems
Global Leadership and Organizational Behavior
   Effectiveness Project
Implicit Theory of Leadership
Judgment and Decision-Making Process
Judgment and Decision-Making Process: Advice
   Giving and Taking
Judgment and Decision-Making Process: Heuristics,
   Cognitive Biases, and Contextual Influences
Leader–Member Exchange Theory
Leadership and Supervision
Least Preferred Coworker Theory
Life-cycle Model of Leadership
Normative Models of Decision Making and
   Leadership
Reinforcement Theory of Work Motivation
Situational Approach to Leadership
Spirituality and Leadership at Work
Trait Approach to Leadership
Transformational and Transactional Leadership
Trust

Groups, Teams, and Working With Others

Conflict at Work
Conflict Management
Diversity in the Workplace
Group Cohesiveness
Group Decision-Making Quality and Performance
Group Decision-Making Techniques
Group Development
Group Dynamics and Processes
Groups
Groupthink
Input–Process–Output Model of Team Effectiveness
Intergroup Relations
Interpersonal Communication
Interpersonal Communication Styles
Justice in Teams
Meetings at Work

Negotiation, Mediation, and Arbitration
Networking
Social Exchange Theory
Social Loafing
Social Norms and Conformity
Social Support
Team-Based Rewards
Team Building
Team Mental Model
Virtual Teams
Workplace Romance

Employee Well-Being and Attitudes

Affective Events Theory
Attitudes and Beliefs
Boredom at Work
Emotional Burnout
Emotional Labor
Emotions
Eustress
Job Satisfaction
Job Satisfaction Measurement
Job Security/Insecurity
Mood
Morale
Organizational Commitment
Organizational Cynicism
Organizational Justice
Psychological Contract
Quality of Work Life
Role Ambiguity
Role Conflict
Role Overload and Underload
Stress, Consequences
Stress, Coping and Management
Stress, Models and Theories
Theory of Reasoned Action/Theory of Planned
   Behavior
Union Commitment
Work–Life Balance

Organizational Structure, Design, and Change

Attraction–Selection–Attrition Model
Automation/Advanced Manufacturing
   Technology/Computer-Based Integrated
   Technology
Balanced Scorecard

Compressed Workweek
Downsizing
Entrepreneurship
Flexible Work Schedules
Globalization
High-Performance Organization Model
Learning Organizations
Mergers, Acquisitions, and Strategic Alliances
Organizational Behavior
Organizational Behavior Management
Organizational Change
Organizational Change, Resistance to
Organizational Climate
Organizational Communication, Formal
Organizational Communication, Informal
Organizational Culture
Organizational Development
Organizational Image
Organizational Politics
Organizational Sensemaking
Organizational Structure
Outsourcing
Shiftwork

Sociotechnical Approach
Strategic Planning
Survivor Syndrome
Terrorism and Work
Theory of Action
Total Quality Management
Virtual Organizations
Workplace Injuries
Workplace Safety

PROFESSIONAL ORGANIZATIONS AND RELATED FIELDS

Academy of Management
American Psychological Association,
    Association for Psychological Science
Engineering Psychology
Human Resource Management
Industrial Relations
Occupational Health Psychology
Organizational Behavior
Society for Industrial and
    Organizational Psychology

M

MACHIAVELLIANISM

Machiavellianism is a strategy of interpersonal conduct whereby others are manipulated and deceived in the pursuit of one's own interests. In the workplace, people who are high in Machiavellianism (referred to as *high Machs*) regard coworkers as means toward personal ends. High Machs are characterized by four criteria: lack of interpersonal affect, lack of concern for conventional morality, low ideological commitment, and lack of gross psychopathology. Machiavellianism shares some common features with psychopathy (similar to antisocial personality disorder) but is more situation dependent and lacks the pathological lying and anxiety that are usually associated with psychopathic behavior patterns. Although Machiavellianism is not related to intelligence, it is arguably a component of social intelligence. Machiavellian behaviors tend to be highest in late adolescence and decline with age, suggesting that this interpersonal strategy strikes a balance between "state" and "trait."

The term itself is a reference to the 16th-century Florentine diplomat Niccolo Machiavelli, who was expelled from office and briefly imprisoned in 1512 when the de Medici family overthrew the regime he had served. Machiavelli felt passionately about Florence, and he desperately wished to restore his political career. In an effort to win favor with the new rulers, he wrote and dedicated to them *The Prince,* an openly amoral treatise on methods of acquiring and retaining political power. Although Machiavelli was unsuccessful in his own bid to regain political power, *The Prince* had a lasting impact on political ideology and its relation to morality.

During the late 1960s, a number of pioneering studies conducted by Richard Christie and Florence Geis helped to define and explore the construct. These efforts developed and validated scales used to measure Machiavellianism, namely, the Mach IV and Mach V scales. Early laboratory research established that high Machs outperform low Machs in non-zero-sum games such as the prisoner's dilemma, in which two players can either "cooperate" or "defect." Both players gain if each chooses to cooperate, but a player can gain more by defecting when the other player cooperates (the typical strategy adopted by high Machs). High Machs succeed by employing both cooperative and defecting strategies, toggling between them as opportunity arises. Additional research established that high Machs succeed in bargaining or alliance-forming games by taking advantage of opportunities for physical confrontation, lack of formal structure, and emotionally charged situations. These factors—face-to-face interaction, latitude for improvisation, and arousal of irrelevant affect—are recognized as the situational antecedents of Machiavellian behavior.

MACHIAVELLIAN LEADERS

Machiavellianism is often studied in conjunction with charismatic leadership. Charismatic leaders are characterized by outgoing, dynamic, and persuasive conduct that creates powerful motivational bonds with their followers. Both charismatic leaders and high Machs engage in impression management and regulate their emotions in high-pressure situations. One notable position of leadership that has been examined for Machiavellian behavior is the U.S. presidency. The

U.S. president holds a position of tremendous power, requiring leadership and negotiation skills in critical situations that show little semblance of structure. Retrospective research methods have demonstrated that charismatic presidents, such as Franklin Roosevelt and Richard Nixon, had greater Machiavellian tendencies than presidents with less charisma, such as William McKinley. These high-Mach leaders were also perceived as more effective presidents.

When opportunities for personal gain emerge, high Machs employ a variety of influence tactics to satisfy their own needs. In competitive group settings, for example, Machiavellian leaders may exhibit prosocial behaviors toward members of their own group and aggressive behaviors toward members of competing groups. When attempting to influence those at higher organizational levels, high Machs may be more likely to use ingratiation than low Machs. To secure the compliance of subordinates, high Machs may threaten the use of exploitive tactics to block employees from accomplishing their own goals. In the absence of situational characteristics such as face-to-face interaction, however, such conduct is less likely to occur.

ASSESSING THE IMPACT OF MACHIAVELLIANISM IN ORGANIZATIONS

Although high-Mach employees may be misperceived as possessing superior intellect by coworkers, consistent relationships between Machiavellianism and job performance have not been demonstrated. Some studies show a positive relationship, some a negative relationship, and still others no relationship at all. Surprisingly few studies in organizational settings, however, have examined the impact of situational moderators on this relationship. For example, jobs with a greater degree of job autonomy or a laissez-faire organizational culture may allow the latitude for improvisation that enables high Machs to outperform low Machs. Indeed, research suggests that high Machs may gain the upper hand in positions marked by social interaction in loosely structured environments, such as stockbroker, politician, or senior executive. Another finding of note is a consistent negative relationship between Machiavellianism and job satisfaction, such that high Machs report low job satisfaction. One explanation for this finding is that many workplaces do not offer—or did not offer in the past—a great deal of autonomy to accomplish work tasks. Thus, high Machs may be frustrated by perceived situational constraints, leading to low satisfaction but otherwise not affecting performance.

In managerial positions, high Machs are likely to use their power to the detriment of others. When subordinates disagree with the decisions of Machiavellian managers, they may be dealt with in harsh or even inhumane ways. Moreover, Machiavellianism may influence more than simply the interpersonal workings of organizations. In addition to their willingness to pursue personal gains at the expense of others, high Machs are willing to engage in ethically questionable behaviors to further the goals of the organization as well. Thus, Machiavellian leaders could conceivably commit transgressions that affect entire organizations or industries. A system of checks and balances, however, can minimize the harm done by aggressors. For example, establishing organizational norms that encourage full disclosure and documentation of work activities should thwart openly Machiavellian conduct.

—*Steven S. Russell and Erin C. Swartout*

See also Abusive Supervision; Charismatic Leadership Theory; Workplace Incivility

FURTHER READING

Christie, R., & Geis, F. (1970). *Studies in Machiavellianism.* New York: Academic Press.

Machiavelli, N. (1513/1966). *The prince.* New York: Bantam.

McHoskey, J. W., Worzel, W., & Szyarto, C. (1998). Machiavellianism and psychopathy. *Journal of Personality and Social Psychology, 74,* 192–210.

Wilson, D. S., Near, D., & Miller, R. R. (1996). Machiavellianism: A synthesis of the evolutionary and psychological literatures. *Psychological Bulletin, 119,* 285–299.

MEASUREMENT SCALES

Measurement scales refer to the types of information provided by numbers. Each scale (i.e., nominal, ordinal, interval, and ratio) provides a different type of information. Knowing which scale applies in a particular situation is necessary to accurately interpret numbers assigned to people, objects, or events. Ignorance of scales' distinguishing characteristics can lead to improper treatment of the numbers (e.g., computing incorrect statistics) and inappropriate actions toward and decisions about people.

NOMINAL SCALES

Numbers are used to name or identify people, objects, or events—for example, a social security number or driver's license number. Gender is an example of a nominal measurement in which a number (e.g., 1) is used to label one gender, such as males, and a different number (e.g., 2) is used for the other gender, females. Numbers do not mean that one gender is better or worse than the other; they simply are used to classify persons. In fact, any other numbers could be used because they do not represent an amount or quality. It is impossible to use word names with certain statistical techniques (e.g., Pearson product–moment correlation or linear multiple regression), but numerals can be used in a coding system. For example, fire departments may wish to examine the relationship between gender (where male = 1, female = 2) and performance on physical ability tests (with numerical scores indicating ability).

Other examples of nominal scales used to classify people are race (e.g., Caucasian, African American, Asian) and political party affiliation (e.g., Democrats and Republicans). Examples of nominal measurements that can be used to classify objects are test items (e.g., multiple choice, short answer, and essay) and type of physical injury suffered on the job (e.g., slip, trip, or fall). Examples of nominal measurement of events are charges of discrimination (e.g., racial, gender, age, and disability) and selection procedures (e.g., interview, paper-and-pencil test, and assessment center exercise).

ORDINAL SCALES

Numbers are used to represent rank order and indicate the order of quality or quantity, but they do not provide an amount of quantity or degree of quality. Usually, the number 1 means that the person (or object or event) is better than the person labeled 2; person 2 is better than person 3, and so forth. For example, to rank order persons in terms of potential for promotion, May might be 1, Joe might be 2, and Wong might be 3. The 1 rating assigned to May indicates that she has more potential but does not indicate how much more potential than Joe. There may be very little difference between May and Joe, but Wong may be extremely inferior to Joe. Academic journals (objects) have been rank ordered in terms of prestige. When ordinal measurement is used (rather than interval measurement), certain statistical techniques are applicable (e.g., Spearman's rank correlation).

INTERVAL SCALES

Numbers form a continuum and provide information about the amount of difference, but the scale lacks a true zero. The differences between adjacent numbers are equal or known. If zero is used, it simply serves as a reference point on the scale but does not indicate the complete absence of the characteristic being measured. For example, if an individual obtains a score of 0 on the extroversion scale of the Revised NEO Personality Inventory, the 0 score does not mean that he or she is completely unsociable. The Fahrenheit and Celsius scales are examples of interval measurement. It takes the same amount of heat to raise the temperature from 50 degrees to 60 degrees as it does to raise the temperature from 60 degrees to 70 degrees. The most powerful statistical techniques are appropriate with interval measurement.

Most measures of psychological constructs are not true interval scales, according to the strict definition. They provide information about order, but whole numbers on such a scale are not precisely equidistant from adjacent whole numbers. Moreover, the amount of difference (of the construct or trait) between numbers may be unknown. For example, the work scale of the Job Descriptive Index measures satisfaction with the work itself, separate from other aspects of the job (e.g., pay or promotion). The 18 items constituting the scale are scored 3 for favorable responses, 2 for unfavorable responses, and 0 if the respondent is undecided whether the item accurately describes the job. Although a score of 54 is three points higher than a score of 51, which is three points higher than 48, increases in the degree of satisfaction may actually be different from 48 to 51 than from 51 to 54. Although they do not adhere to the strict definition of interval scales, psychological tests (in the broad sense of the word) that have been carefully constructed can be treated as interval scales.

Before numbers can be assigned to people (reflecting a level or degree of some psychological characteristic), items (such as those on an application blank, mental ability test, or performance appraisal form) must be assigned numbers to reflect some quality, such as relevance, difficulty, or importance. Using the method of equal appearing intervals, subject-matters experts may be instructed to indicate their opinion of items by rating them on an interval scale. For example, subject-matter experts constructing a job knowledge test for firefighters may be asked to rate the importance of knowing how to use certain pieces of equipment (e.g., the jaws of life) from 1 (not important at all) to 5 (extremely important). An importance index can then be computed by averaging item ratings.

RATIO SCALES

Ratio scales have all of the characteristics of interval scales as well as a true zero, which refers to complete absence of the characteristic being measured. Physical characteristics of persons and objects can be measured with ratio scales, but most psychological characteristics (e.g., intelligence, conscientiousness, and interests) cannot. Consequently, most measures of employees' and applicants' optimal and typical performance do not use true ratio scales. Height and weight are examples of ratio measurement. A score of 0 means there is complete absence of height or weight. Ratios can also be created such that a person who is 4 feet tall is two thirds (4 divided by 6) as tall as a 6-foot-tall person; a 100-pound person is two thirds as heavy as a 150-pound person.

SUMMARY

Measurement refers to the assignment of numbers in a meaningful way. Understanding scales of measurement is important to interpreting the numbers assigned to people, objects, and events. For the most part, numbers used in the work world are nominal, ordinal, or approach interval measurements. Assuming interval measurement permits the use of statistical techniques (parametric statistics) that are more powerful than other techniques (nonparametric statistics).

—*Jo Ann Lee*

See also Inferential Statistics; Item Response Theory; Measures of Association/Correlation Coefficient; Reliability; Statistical Power; Validity

FURTHER READING

Allen, M. J., & Yen, W. M. (1979). *Introduction to measurement theory*. Monterey, CA: Brooks/Cole.

Crocker, L., & Algina, J. (1986). *Introduction to classical and modern test theory*. New York: Harcourt Brace Jovanovich.

Murphy, K. R., & Davidshofer, C. O. (2005). *Psychological testing: Principles and applications* (6th ed.). Upper Saddle River, NJ: Prentice Hall.

Nunnally, J., & Bernstein, I. (1994). *Psychometric theory* (3rd ed.). New York: McGraw-Hill.

Society for Industrial and Organizational Psychology. (2003). *Principles for the validation and use of personnel selection procedures* (4th ed.). Bowling Green, OH: Author.

MEASURES OF ASSOCIATION/ CORRELATION COEFFICIENT

In many situations, researchers are interested in evaluating the relationship between variables of interest. Such associations are important for testing theories and hypotheses in which changes in one variable are tied to changes in another. In other words, is an increase in one variable associated with a systematic increase or decrease in the other? The most frequently reported measure of association within industrial and organizational psychology is the correlation coefficient (r). Correlation is a standardized index of the extent to which two sets of scores vary together. As an index, correlation can vary between −1.00 (i.e., a perfect negative relationship) and +1.00 (i.e., a perfect positive relationship). Correlations near zero indicate the absence of a linear relationship between the variables of interest. Squaring the correlation (i.e., r^2) provides an indication of the percentage of variance in one variable that can be explained by the other variable. For example, if the correlation between height and weight is .5, then 25% of the variance in height can be explained by weight, or vice versa.

NUMERICAL REPRESENTATION OF CORRELATIONS

The correlation between two variables can be described in one of two ways: numerically or graphically. The following example illustrates how correlation is computed and what the numerical value indicates. First, assume that five individuals respond to two measures (x and y). Scores for the five individuals on x are 2, 4, 8, 6, and 5, and scores on y are 5, 7, 6,

8, and 4. Thus, the mean of x is equal to 5 (i.e., 25/5) and the mean of y is 6 (i.e., 30/5).

As a second step, deviation scores can be computed for each person on each variable by subtracting the mean of each distribution from each raw score. As a result, the deviation scores for x are $-3, -1, 3, 1$, and 0, and the deviation scores for y are $-1, 1, 0, 2$, and -2. These deviation scores can then be used to compute the standard deviation and variances for these measures.

With the current data, these values are as follows:

$$\sigma_x = 2$$

$$\sigma_y = 1.41$$

$$\sigma_x^2 = 4$$

$$\sigma_y^2 = 2$$

In addition to computing standard deviations and variances, deviation scores can also be used to construct a matrix of these data. Because there are only two variables, it will be a simple 2×2 matrix that describes all possible relationships among the data. To create the matrix, take the sums of the cross-products that are produced by cross-multiplying the deviation scores—that is x^2, y^2, and xy.

$$20 = (-3)^2 + (-1)^2 + 3^2 + 1^2 + 0^2$$

$$10 = (-1)^2 + (1)^2 + 0^2 + 2^2 + (-2)^2$$

$$4 = (-3 \times -1)^2 + (-1 \times 1) + (3 \times 0) + (1 \times 2) + (0 \times -2)$$

In matrix form, these values can be represented as shown in Table 1.

Table 1   Cross-Products Matrix

	x	y
x	20	4
y	4	10

The matrix in Table 1 can then be transformed into a variance-covariance matrix (see Table 2) by dividing

Table 2   Variance-Covariance Matrix

	x	y
x	4.0	0.8
y	0.8	2.0

the elements by the number of cases (e.g., 20/5, 4/5, 10/5).

Importantly, the covariance in this example (0.8) is a measure of association between the two variables of interest. An important consideration in using covariance as a measure of association, however, is that it is fundamentally related to the scales of measurement for both x and y and therefore unstandardized. To get the correlation matrix, divide each of the elements by the product of the standard deviations of the variables involved. For example,

$$r_{xy} = \frac{.8}{\sqrt{4}\sqrt{2}} = .28.$$

This produces a standardized variance-covariance matrix and takes care of the problem of having different scales for each variable. A covariance of 10 tells us nothing because it is dependent on the scales used to obtain it, but a correlation of .40 means the same thing across any situation. Continuing with the current example, the resulting correlation matrix is displayed in Table 3.

Table 3   Correlation Matrix

	x	y
x	1.0	0.28
y	0.28	1.0

The preceding example illustrates the basic operations that underlie the computation of correlations. In practice, correlations would be computed directly from data using either the raw score formula,

$$r_{xy} = \frac{\Sigma xy}{N(\sigma_x)(\sigma_y)},$$

or the standard score formula,

$$r_{xy} = \frac{\Sigma z_x z_y}{N},$$

where z is the standard score (z score) for each case on a particular variable.

The preceding example and formulas make several features of correlations apparent. First, an increase in the numerator will increase r. Specifically, when both z_x and z_y are large and of the same sign, they contribute more to the numerator than if one or the other is small. Correlations also take into account whether the rank order of people on both variables is maintained and their relative distances from the mean. Importantly, the preceding discussion focused on the Pearson product–moment correlation, which is computed when both variables are continuous and measured at either the interval or ratio level of measurement. When one or both variables do not have these characteristics, alternative correlations must be computed. (More information regarding these alternative correlations is presented in the last section of this entry.)

GRAPHICAL REPRESENTATION OF CORRELATIONS

Correlations can also be depicted graphically. Scatterplot diagrams are a useful and instructive way of looking at data and often reveal the extent to which violations of assumptions of correlation are present. Chief among these assumptions are linearity and homoscedasticity. Because a correlation is an index of the extent to which two variables are linearly related, the more the relationship deviates from a straight line, the lower the observed correlation. Examples of different correlations are presented in Figure 1. Panel (a) illustrates a perfect positive correlation, panel (b) illustrates no correlation between two variables, and panel (c) reflects a correlation of .50. A real problem can occur when the relationship

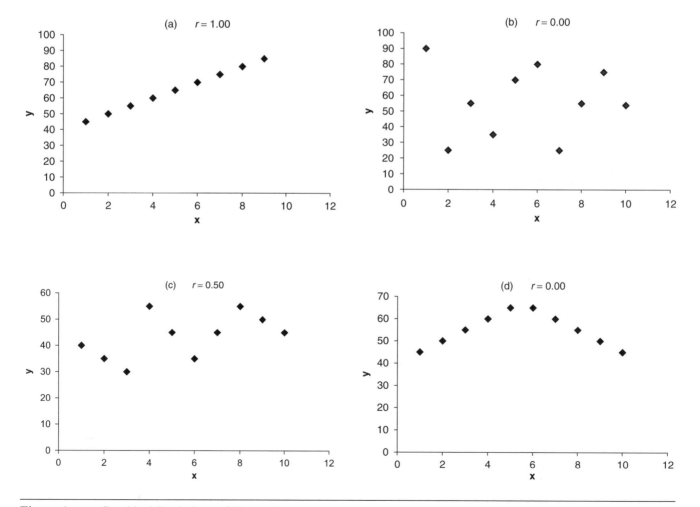

Figure 1   Graphical Depictions of Correlations

is not linear—panel (d) in Figure 1—but still systematic. Such nonlinear relationships can easily be overlooked if the scatterplot is not evaluated.

The assumption of homoscedasticity refers to the variances of either or both variables through their respective ranges. Specifically, variance is assumed to be equal throughout the range of scores. The assumption is fundamentally tied to another key assumption, the normality of both variables. When this assumption is violated, heteroscedasticity exists. Two possible causes of this include nonnormality of one or both variables, which can be the result of either the data being truly nonnormal or some data transformation. To the extent that variables are skewed and the homoscedasticity assumption has been violated, observed correlations will be reduced.

The following points should be noted with respect to correlation coefficients, scatterplots, and the preceding assumptions. First, correlations tend to be robust with respect to violations of the linearity assumption. Second, violations of homoscedasticity are more serious and, according to some reviews, more prevalent. Finally, any plotted score that is off the diagonal is not optimal in the sense of its contribution to the numerator in the preceding equations. The only situation in which a perfect correlation will be observed is that in which each person receives the same z score on both the x and y variable.

OTHER TYPES OF CORRELATIONS

Several different types of correlations can be computed depending on the scale of measurement of the two variables of interest. The following is a brief summary of some of these correlations. Although these correlations are computed differently and make different assumptions about the underlying structure of data, all range between −1.00 and +1.00 and are interpreted in the same way as the product–moment correlation discussed previously.

Spearman's rho correlation is computed when one or both variables are measured at an ordinal scale of measurement. For example, Spearman's rho would be computed if a researcher were interested in correlating SAT scores (interval-level variable) with birth order (ordinal-level variable).

The *point-biserial correlation* is computed when one of the variables is continuous and the other is truly dichotomous. A truly dichotomous variable is one for which only two scores are possible. For example, a multiple-choice item would be considered a truly

Table 4   Types of Correlations

Pearson product-moment	• Two continuous variables
Spearman's rho	• One or two ordinal variables
Point-biserial	• One continuous variable • One true dichotomous variable
Biserial	• One continuous variable • One artificially dichotomous variable
Phi coefficient	• Two truly dichotomous variable
Tetrachoric	• One or two artificially dichotomous variables

dichotomous variable insofar as an individual answers the question either correctly or incorrectly. Point-biserial correlations are used in the area of test construction, in which item responses (correct/incorrect) are correlated with total test score (interval-level variable). These item-total correlations are then used as the basis for removing items that are not strongly related to total score.

The *biserial correlation* is used in situations in which one variable is continuous and one is an artificial dichotomy. An artificially dichotomous variable is one that was originally measured with continuous scores (e.g., percentage of correct answers on an examination) but has been converted post hoc to a dichotomy (e.g., everyone scoring above 60% passes the test and everyone below 60% fails). Biserial correlations are not true product–moment correlations, and the standard error is larger than that of product–moment correlations.

The *phi coefficient* is used in situations involving two truly dichotomous variables. The correlation between gender and performance on a multiple-choice item is an example of a phi coefficient.

The *tetrachoric correlation* is used when one or both variables are artificially dichotomous. For example, tetrachoric correlation would be used when a researcher is interested in correlating performance in one class (pass/fail) with performance in another (pass/fail).

SUMMARY

Correlation is an essential statistic for researchers in the field of industrial and organizational psychology. Not only is this index important for assessing simple bivariate relationships; it also serves as the fundamental statistic on which more sophisticated analyses (e.g., multiple regression analysis, factor analysis, path analysis) are based.

—*Ronald S. Landis*

See also Factor Analysis

FURTHER READING

Cohen, J., Cohen, P., West, S. G., & Aiken, L. S. (2003). *Applied multiple regression/correlation analysis for the behavioral sciences* (3rd ed.). Mahwah, NJ: Lawrence Erlbaum.

Nunnally, J. C., & Bernstein, I. H. (1994). *Psychometric theory* (3rd ed.). New York: McGraw-Hill.

MEETINGS AT WORK

A work meeting is a gathering of employees for a purpose related to the functioning of an organization or a group (e.g., to direct, to inform, to govern, to regulate). The gathering can occur in a single modality (e.g., a videoconference) or in a mixed-modality format (mostly face-to-face with one participant connected by telephone). A meeting can be described as more formal than a chat but less formal than a lecture. A meeting is usually characterized by multiparty talk that is episodic in nature. Typically, meetings are scheduled in advance (some notice is provided), informally or formally facilitated by one of the members, involve four to eight individuals (but can contain as few as two participants), last 30 to 60 minutes, and have some specific purpose or goal (which is often made known in advance). Less commonly, an annotated transcription of the meeting activity is undertaken (minutes). There are five principal types of meetings:

- Information-giving meeting: The meeting is primarily about announcing and discussing organizational, department, unit, team, or personnel news.
- Training meeting: The meeting is primarily about receiving some type of work training.
- Recognition meeting: The meeting is primarily about recognizing and celebrating relevant events or accomplishments.
- Routine monitoring and decision-making meeting: The meeting is primarily about day-to-day problems and issues; it is called to work on issues identified previously—for example, gathering reports about progress to date, assigning tasks, coordinating activities, or making decisions.
- Special problem-solving meeting: The meeting is primarily about new or unusual issues rather than day-to-day problems and issues; it is called to discuss one or more special issues—for example, aiming for a greater understanding, a preliminary decision, a final decision, or a plan.

Impromptu meetings are those in which the gathering of individuals has not been planned in advance. They are rarer than scheduled meetings. They are usually smaller in size, less structured, more informal, and often assembled to exchange information or make decisions quickly, as in a crisis situation. Alternatively, these events may occur spontaneously to consider routine matters, as when a lunch is transformed into a quick meeting.

Besides their more formal purposes, meetings have an employee socialization, relationship-building, and networking component. In addition, meetings can serve to enforce and make clear formal and informal reporting structures and power differentials.

TIME IN MEETING

The meeting is a common organizational activity across cultures. Estimates of an individual's time spent in meetings vary widely. On the high end, the average senior manager spends approximately 23 hours per week either preparing for, attending, or following up on meetings, and middle managers spend 11 to 12 hours per week on these activities. On the low end, estimates suggest that employees spend an average of approximately 6 hours in scheduled meetings during a typical week, and supervisors spend more time than nonsupervisors in meetings. Employees in large organizations tend to have more meetings than employees in small organizations.

Recent studies suggest that the amount of meeting activity in organizations appears to be rising. One study suggested that the average executive participated in twice as many meetings in the 1980s as in the 1960s. In a survey of 1,900 business leaders, almost 72% reported spending more time in meetings than they did five years ago. In addition, more than 49% surveyed expected to be spending even more time in meetings in the future.

RESEARCH ON MEETINGS

Despite the practical importance of meetings, the meeting, as an entity in and of itself, has rarely been studied. In one of the first scholarly treatments of the meeting, anthropologist Helen Schwartzman discussed how the meeting is a neglected social form in organizational studies and how it is taken for granted because it is so commonplace and accepted by members of an organization. She further discussed how meetings have been used as a methodological tool to study other topics (e.g., small-group dynamics and group decision making) but are rarely studied empirically in their own right as a legitimate area of research.

Recently, however, there appears to be an emerging empirical literature focusing on the characteristics of meetings. For example, sit-down meetings last longer than stand-up meetings, yet there is no improvement in decision quality. Another stream of research focuses on the impact of meeting demands (e.g., the number of meetings attended) on employee attitudes and well-being. For example, the relationship between meeting demands and employee well-being was found to be moderated by an individual difference characteristic called *accomplishment striving*. Namely, for individuals with a strong desire to accomplish work goals, a negative relationship between the number of meetings in a day and daily well-being was found. Conversely, a weak positive relationship between the number of meetings in a day and daily well-being was found when striving is low—for those who are less goal-oriented, meetings may be desired, perhaps to permit social interaction or to give structure to an unstructured day.

MEETING EFFECTIVENESS

The trade literature is replete with suggestions for improving the quality of meetings. Besides the overriding suggestion to meet only when necessary, the following structural and group dynamics factors are often mentioned in the literature. For the most part, these suggestions (in relation to meeting effectiveness) have not been empirically studied.

- Provide an agenda in advance of the meeting. Have specific meeting goals and objectives. Provide relevant materials in advance of the meeting so that participants have time to reflect on them.
- Establish a set of ground rules to promote good communication processes (e.g., staying on task, not dominating the discussion, constructive conflict resolution, listening before responding to others).
- Evaluate the meeting periodically. Either midstream or at the conclusion, the group should reflect on what went well and what could be improved for the next meeting.
- Pay careful attention to time. Start the meeting on time. End the meeting on time.
- Assign someone to the role of meeting facilitator or leader to promote productive meeting practices (sticking to the agenda, not spending too much time to discuss trivial items).

—*Steven G. Rogelberg*

See also Group Decision-Making Quality and Performance; Group Decision-Making Techniques; Group Dynamics and Processes; Groups

FURTHER READING

Luong, A., & Rogelberg, S. G. (2005). Meetings and more meetings: The relationship between meeting load and the daily well-being of employees. *Group Dynamics: Theory, Research, and Practice, 1,* 58–67.

Rogelberg, S. G., Leach, D. J., Warr, P. B., & Burnfield, J. L. (2006). "Not another meeting!" Are meeting time demands related to employee well-being? *Journal of Applied Psychology, 91*(1), 83–97.

Schwartzman, H. B. (1989). *The meeting: Gatherings in organizations and communities.* New York: Plenum.

Tropman, J. E. (2003). *Making meetings work: Achieving high quality group decisions* (2nd ed.). Thousand Oaks, CA: Sage.

MENTORING

Workplace mentoring is generally described as a relationship between two individuals, usually a senior and a junior employee, in which the senior employee teaches the junior employee about his or her job, introduces the junior employee to contacts, orients the employee to the industry and organization, and addresses social and personal issues that may arise on the job. The mentoring relationship is different from other organizational relationships (e.g., supervisor–subordinate) in that the mentoring parties may or may not formally work together, the issues addressed may include nonwork matters, and the bond between mentor and protégé is usually closer and stronger than that of other organizational relationships.

MENTORING FUNCTIONS AND STAGES

Mentors provide two primary functions to their protégés. Psychosocial mentoring focuses on the enhancement of identity, competence, and effectiveness in the professional role and includes role modeling, acceptance and confirmation, counseling, and friendship. Career-related mentoring focuses on success and advancement within the organization and includes sponsorship, coaching, exposure and visibility, protection, and challenging assignments.

Mentoring relationships have been theorized to progress through four distinct stages. In the *initiation* stage, the mentor and protégé are just beginning the relationship and learning about each other. During the second phase, known as *cultivation*, the greatest amount of learning occurs and benefits are obtained. As the needs of the mentor and protégé evolve, the partnership enters the *separation* phase. During this phase, the protégé begins to assert independence, and the mentor begins to consider that he or she has no additional knowledge to share with the protégé or guidance to provide. The final phase of the mentoring relationship is referred to as *redefinition*. Redefinition occurs when the relationship transforms into one of peers or colleagues.

MEASUREMENT OF MENTORING

Two types of studies are commonly found in the literature. One type compares individuals with mentoring experience (protégés or mentors) with those without mentoring experience (nonprotégés or nonmentors) on some variable of interest. Participants are typically given a screening question that includes a definition of mentoring and classified into the experienced or nonexperienced group on the basis of their response. The second type of study examines the relationship between mentoring functions and other variables of interest. In this case, those who have mentoring experience also report on the career and psychosocial mentoring behaviors or functions provided during the course of the mentoring relationship.

MENTORING BENEFITS

Mentoring relationships are reputed to be beneficial for protégés, mentors, and organizations. Most benefits research has focused protégés. Recent meta-analytic research supports the notion that mentoring has both objective and subjective career benefits for protégés. Specifically, individuals who are mentored advance more rapidly in the organization, earn higher salaries, have greater job satisfaction, and have fewer intentions to leave the organization. Research also indicates that being mentored is related to greater career planning, career involvement, career motivation, socialization, and career self-efficacy.

Less research has focused on benefits to the mentor. Qualitative studies suggest that mentors achieve personal satisfaction from passing knowledge and skills on to others, exhilaration from the fresh energy provided by protégés, improved job performance from receiving a new perspective on the organization from protégés, loyalty and support from protégés, and organizational recognition. A few quantitative studies have yielded similar findings, indicating that mentors report that mentoring provides personal satisfaction and improved work group performance. Researchers are beginning to examine how mentoring others may relate to more tangible career benefits to the mentor, such as increased promotion rates and salary. Initial results indicate that those who have mentored others report greater salary and rates of promotion than those without any mentoring experience.

Mentoring is also said to provide benefits to the organization, but organizational benefits have been inferred primarily based on the benefits to individuals within the organization. For example, mentoring can help the organization by reducing individual employee turnover, enhancing employee productivity, and increasing the retention of women and minorities. However, there is no empirical research showing that mentoring relates to organizational-level outcomes such as firm performance.

FACTORS RELATED TO MENTORING PROCESSES

Gender

Although men and women generally report similar access to mentors, once in a mentoring relationship, the type of mentoring provided may vary by gender. Though individual study results are mixed, when gender differences are detected, the results show that women report receiving more psychosocial mentoring than men and men report receiving more career-related mentoring than women.

The gender of the mentor may also matter in terms of the type of mentoring provided and the outcomes realized. For example, female mentors have been found to provide more psychosocial mentoring than their male counterparts. Additionally, male mentors are associated with greater career outcomes (such as compensation) than female mentors. It may be that male mentors are in more powerful organizational positions and thus can better aid the career development of their protégés.

The dyadic composition of the mentoring relationship is also an important consideration. That is, it is not just the gender of the mentor or protégé that is important but the *interaction* between the two. For example, there is some evidence that greater psychosocial mentoring occurs in same-gender mentoring relationships than in cross-gender relationships.

Race

There is little evidence that minorities are less likely to have mentoring experience than are nonminorities. Additionally, there is no consistent evidence to suggest that the amount of career or psychosocial mentoring provided differs across race. However, the race of the mentor does appear to make a difference. Research has shown that Black employees with White mentors earn more compensation than do Black employees with Black mentors.

Like the findings regarding gender, research also indicates that protégés in same-race mentoring relationships report greater psychosocial support than do protégés in cross-race relationships. However, because of small samples, different minorities are often grouped together, and analyses are conducted examining minorities versus nonminorities. Thus, it is not certain to what extent the findings generalize to all minorities. Additionally, research that has focused on a single race has been almost exclusively on Black Americans.

Perceived Similarity

In addition to the impact of mentor–protégé similarity in terms of demographic characteristics such as race and gender, some research has examined perceived similarity in terms of attitudes, values, personality, interests, and work styles. Results show that protégés who perceive their mentors as similar to themselves are more satisfied with the relationship and report receiving more mentoring than do protégés who perceive their mentors as less similar to themselves. Likewise, mentors with perceived similar protégés report more high-quality mentoring relationships than do mentors with protégés who are perceived to be less similar.

Protégé Attributes

Research suggests that dispositional characteristics relate to one's likelihood of engaging in a mentoring relationship. For example, individuals with an internal locus of control and high self-monitors are more likely to initiate mentoring relationships than individuals with an external locus of control and low self-monitors. Research also indicates that individuals who are high in need for achievement are more likely to report having a mentor than individuals who are low in need for achievement.

Some research suggests that mentors look for certain attributes in the protégés they mentor. Specifically, research has found that mentors prefer protégés who possess strong potential for achievement, favorable past performance, and a willingness to learn and accept feedback.

Mentor Attributes

Several factors relate to one's propensity or willingness to serve as a mentor to others. One consistent finding is that those with previous mentoring experience, either as a protégé or as a mentor, are more willing to mentor others than those with no previous mentoring experience. There is also evidence that dispositional factors relate to the willingness to mentor others. Specifically, a prosocial personality is associated with experience as a mentor and with future willingness to mentor others.

Few studies have examined individual mentor differences in mentoring behavior. One study found that individuals higher in openness to experience reported providing more mentoring than those lower in openness to experience. In another study, the mentor's learning-goal orientation was positively linked with mentoring. Recent research has examined the motives that mentors report for mentoring others. Mentors who are motivated to mentor others for self-enhancement reasons are more likely to provide career-related mentoring, whereas mentors who are motivated by the intrinsic satisfaction that mentoring others brings are more likely to provide psychosocial mentoring.

Organizational Factors

The organizational environment can inhibit or facilitate mentoring relationships. Organizations can foster mentoring relationships by encouraging an organizational learning and development climate. Mentoring relationships are more likely to occur naturally when the organization cultivates an environment that encourages employees to actively learn from and teach one another. This can be accomplished by recognizing and rewarding the efforts of those who mentor others, providing opportunities for junior and senior employees to interact, and helping employees develop the tools needed for coaching and counseling others.

FORMAL MENTORING

Formal mentoring programs are increasingly being used as a form of employee development. Formal and informal mentoring relationships differ in two primary ways. First, formal mentoring relationships may occur through an assignment or matching process instigated by a third party within the organization, whereas informal mentoring relationships develop spontaneously through a process of mutual attraction. Second, formal mentoring relationships are typically shorter in duration than informal mentoring relationships. Informal mentoring relationships generally last three to six years, whereas formal mentoring relationships generally last for six months to one year.

Interest in formal mentoring has generated research examining differences in outcomes for protégés involved in formal versus informal mentoring relationships. Generally, the research shows that formal mentoring relationships are less effective than informal relationships but better than no mentoring. However, research also shows that the quality of the relationship matters more than the manner in which the relationship was initially formed. High-quality mentoring relationships can evolve from both formal and informal pairings.

—*Tammy D. Allen*

FURTHER READING

Allen, T. D., Eby, L. T., Poteet, M. L., Lentz, E., & Lima, L. (2004). Career benefits associated with mentoring for protégés: A meta-analytic review. *Journal of Applied Psychology, 89,* 127–136.

Dreher, G. F., & Cox, T. H. (1996). Race, gender, and opportunity: A study of compensation attainment and the establishment of mentoring relationships. *Journal of Applied Psychology, 81,* 297–308.

Kram, K. E. (1985). *Mentoring at work: Developmental relationships in organizational life.* Glenview, IL: Scott, Foresman.

Ragins, B. R., & Cotton, J. L. (1999). Mentor functions and outcomes: A comparison of men and women in formal and informal mentoring relationships. *Journal of Applied Psychology, 8,* 529–550.

Turban, D. B., & Dougherty, T. W. (1994). Role of protégé personality in receipt of mentoring and career success. *Academy of Management Journal, 37,* 688–702.

Wanberg, C. R., Welsh, E. T., & Hezlett, S. A. (2003). Mentoring research: A review and dynamic process model. In G. R. Ferris & J. J. Martocchio (Eds.), *Research in personnel and human resources management* (Vol. 22, pp. 39–124). Greenwich, CT: Elsevier Science/JAI Press.

MERGERS, ACQUISITIONS, AND STRATEGIC ALLIANCES

Mergers, acquisitions, and strategic alliances have become entrenched in the repertoire of contemporary business executives. Mergers and acquisitions have the potential to accelerate the execution of a business strategy by rapidly helping a firm expand its product or service mix, move into new regional or international markets, capture new customers, or even eliminate a competitor. In this era of intense and turbulent change involving rapid technological advances and ever-increasing globalization, mergers also help organizations gain flexibility, leverage competencies, share resources, and create opportunities that otherwise would be inconceivable.

A *merger* is the integration of two previously separate entities into one new organization, whereas an *acquisition* is the takeover and subsequent integration of one firm into another. Of course, there are many shades of gray here—there are very few "mergers of equals," and a lead firm may adopt key components of the acquired target. Mergers can be opportunities to transform companies—for example, when Canadian paper producers Abitibi-Price and Stone Consolidates combined to form Abitibi-Consolidated, the new company selected best practices from the partners and adopted new ways of doing things where required. By contrast, there is typically a clearly dominant partner in acquisitions in consolidating industries such as oil (e.g., Chevron–Texaco and Exxon–Mobil) and entertainment (e.g., Disney–ABC and General Electric–NBC).

A *strategic alliance* sidesteps the legal combination of the entities but requires a close working relationship. (Some observers liken strategic alliances to "living together" as opposed to "getting married" in a merger or acquisition.) For example, the large German pharmaceutical firm Schering entered into a strategic alliance with the small biotech firm Titan Pharmaceuticals. Titan had innovative products in development, and Schering brought marketing muscle to the relationship. Through this alliance, Schering and Titan hope to leverage each other's strengths without making a commitment to change either company's legal ownership or structure.

Despite their popularity, 75% of all mergers, acquisitions, and alliances fail to achieve their strategic or financial objectives. Many reasons have been suggested for this dismal track record, but research findings reveal that what matters most to eventual success is the human and cultural aspects of the process by which the partner companies are integrated.

THE MERGER SYNDROME

Organizational psychologists Philip H. Mirvis and Mitchell Lee Marks identified the *merger syndrome* as a primary cause of the disappointing outcomes of otherwise well-conceived mergers, acquisitions, and alliances. The syndrome is triggered by the unavoidably unsettled conditions present in the earliest days and months following the announcement of a deal and encompasses stress reactions and the development of crisis management in the companies involved.

Personal Signs of the Merger Syndrome

The first symptom of the merger syndrome is heightened self-interest—people become preoccupied with what the combination means for themselves, their incomes, and their careers. They develop a story line about the implications, but often it is a mix of fact and fantasy. No one has real answers, and if they do, the answers are apt to change. Not only do people become fixated on the combination, they also tend to focus on the costs and ignore the gains. Soon after a combination announcement, the rumor mill starts and people trade on dire scenarios.

Combination stress takes its toll on people's psychological and physiological well-being. Reports of tension and conflict increase at the workplace and at home—spouses and children worry about their fates and grow anxious, too. Rates of illness and absenteeism rise in workforces going through combinations. Interviews with executives in the early stages of a combination are colored by reports of headaches, cold and flu symptoms, sleeplessness, and increased alcohol and drug use.

Organizational Signs of the Merger Syndrome

To cope with the many tasks of combining, teams of executives in both the lead and target companies typically lurch into a crisis management mode. The experience is stressful yet exhilarating, and many liken themselves to generals in a war room. Decision making in these top groups can be crisp and decisive. However, top management is generally insulated during this period and often prepares self-defeating gambits. They cut themselves off from relevant information and isolate themselves from dissent. All of this is symptomatic of what psychologist Irving Janis terms *groupthink*—the result of accepting untested assumptions and striving for consensus without testing the possible consequences.

While the executive teams are in their respective war rooms, people in one or both organizations are adrift. Decision-making powers become centralized and reporting relationships clogged with tension and doubt. Priorities are unsettled, and no one wants to make a false move. Meanwhile, downward communications tend to be formal and unsatisfactory. Official assurances that any changes will be handled smoothly and fairly ring hollow to the worried workforce.

Cultural Signs of the Merger Syndrome

All of these symptoms are exacerbated by the clash of cultures. By their very nature, combinations produce an us-versus-them relationship, and there is a natural tendency for people to exaggerate the differences as opposed to the similarities between the two companies. First, differences are noted in the ways the companies do business—maybe their relative emphasis on manufacturing versus marketing or their predominantly financial versus technical orientation. Then, differences in how the companies are organized—say, centralization versus decentralization or differing styles of management and control—are discerned. Finally, people ascribe these differences to competing values and philosophies, seeing their company as superior and the other as backward, bureaucratic, or just plain bad.

Ironically, a fair amount of diversity in approaching work aids combinations by sparking productive debate and discussion of the desired norms in the combined organization. When left unmanaged, however, the clash of cultures pulls sides apart rather than joining them together.

MAKING MERGERS, ACQUISITIONS, AND ALLIANCES WORK

Psychologists and other professionals work with executives to minimize the unintended consequences of mergers and acquisitions and to put combinations on the path toward financial success. Some common trends are emerging that distinguish successful deals from the majority of failures:

- Managing the merger syndrome: Many firms act to raise awareness of the merger syndrome. Consultations guide executives and managers on leading their people during a difficult time. Workshops help all employees understand methods for minimizing the stress, uncertainty, and culture clash present in any combination. In addition to practical tactics, employees get a sense that leadership is acknowledging and managing their issues rather than ignoring or denying them.
- Managing culture clash: The primary method for minimizing the unintended consequences of culture clash is to establish a basis of respect for the partner cultures. This is true even if the ultimate intention is to absorb a company and assimilate its culture. Managers who display a consideration for the partner's way of doing things rather than denigrate it are likely to gain a reciprocal sense of respect for their own culture. In mergers in which a new culture is being built—either through transformation or by selecting the best from both organizations—a tone of cross-cultural consideration helps employees open up to different ways of doing things rather than tightly hold on to their ways.
- Managing the transition: The upside of a merger, acquisition, or alliance is the opportunity to generate breakthrough ways of thinking that can leverage the strengths of both partners to accelerate the achievement of a business strategy. This requires an effective

transition management structure that creates a forum in which the parties can study and test whether or how hoped-for synergies can be realized, that contributes to relationship and trust building across partners, and that involves people close to the technical aspects and key business issues implicated in the combination. Psychologists contribute to this process by facilitating transition decision-making meetings, providing credible and rigorous issue identification and decision-making processes, and accelerating the development of teamwork across typically sparring partners.

—*Mitchell Lee Marks*

FURTHER READING

Haspeslagh, P., & Jamison, D. B. (1991). *Managing acquisitions: Creating value through corporate renewal.* New York: Free Press.

Marks, M. L. (2003). *Charging back up the hill: Workplace recovery after mergers, acquisitions and downsizings.* San Francisco: Jossey-Bass.

Marks, M. L., & Mirvis, P. H. (1998). *Joining forces: Making one plus one equal three in mergers, acquisitions, and alliances.* San Francisco: Jossey-Bass.

Stahl, G. K., & Mendenhall, M. E. (2005). *Mergers and acquisitions: Managing culture and human resources.* Stanford, CA: Stanford Business Books.

META-ANALYSIS

The best way to understand meta-analysis is to begin with a review of basic statistics. There are two main areas in statistics: descriptive and inferential. The former deals with the basic organization and presentation of data, the latter with the process of deriving conclusions and generalizations (i.e., inferences) about a population based on an analysis of sample data taken from that population.

Significance testing is an older and more traditional means of making inferences about populations based on sample data. Developed by the eminent statistician Ronald Fisher during the early 1930s, significance testing focuses on the concept of the null hypothesis and involves estimating the probability that differences observed in a sample occurred entirely by chance, with no true effect in the corresponding population. The real strength of significance testing is that it constrains Type I errors (i.e., rejecting the null hypothesis when there is no true effect in the population) to the α level or less. The Achilles' heel of significance testing is that it does not have any formal control over Type II errors. Some have estimated that the average probability of a Type II error (i.e., retaining the null hypothesis when there is a true effect in the population) in the behavioral sciences is as high as 50%.

Meta-analysis is a second approach to inferential statistics. Like significance testing, its goal is to make inferences about a population based on an analysis of sample data taken from that population. However, the process by which meta-analysis makes inferences is very different. Whereas significance testing focuses on evaluating the probability of chance with a single (usually new) research study, meta-analysis seeks to mathematically combine a group of related studies that have already been conducted. In meta-analysis, the primary analysis computes the mean (often weighted by sample size) of the common test statistic that is reported or computed for each study, which represents the best available estimate of the true strength of the effect in the population.

Meta-analysis began to be formally developed during the late 1970s, pioneered independently by two camps of researchers: Gene Glass in the clinical area and Frank Schmidt and John Hunter in the industrial and organizational area. Two factors contributed to the emergence of meta-analysis. One was a growing concern about the impact of Type II errors on behavioral science research. Traditional thinking maintained that it is more important to prevent researchers from claiming false effects (i.e., making Type I errors), but some began to believe it is also (even equally) important to prevent researchers from missing real effects (i.e., making Type II errors). In psychotherapy, for example, a series of studies with Type II errors could lead to the conclusion that a particular technique is not consistently helpful, when in fact it might have at least some benefit for most clients.

The second factor that contributed to the development of meta-analysis was a realization that large numbers of studies had accumulated in some areas of behavioral science research. Employment interviews, gender differences in personality, and psychotherapy are examples of areas in which literally hundreds of independent studies are available. In these areas, it made sense to pull together these vast bodies of research to gain a better understanding of the characteristic in question.

Unfortunately, the only technique available at the time for integrating a group of studies was to have a prominent researcher look at them and present his or her impressions, a process known as a *narrative review*. Not surprisingly, narrative reviews are problematic because they are subjective and prone to personal interpretations and perspectives. Moreover, the significance testing results in the studies can be misleading because at least some of the studies retaining the null hypothesis could actually have Type II errors, leading the reviewer to underestimate the true strength or consistency of the effect or relationship. Meta-analysis provided a way to synthesize a body of literature but in a more objective and mathematical way.

In terms of methodology, meta-analysis involves five steps:

- **Step 1: Clearly specify the characteristic to be studied.** Being very specific about what is to be studied helps to focus the meta-analysis and make it more meaningful. For example, the relationship between employment interview ratings and job performance is probably too vague because interviews can vary greatly in terms of their structure, job performance can be assessed in different ways (e.g., objective, subjective), and the jobs for which the interviews were developed can vary (e.g., low, medium, or high complexity). Unfortunately, there is a trade-off in regard to specificity, at least in most cases. The more specific the focus (e.g., the validity of situational interviews for predicting subjective ratings of performance with managerial positions), the more meaningful the results tend to be. In turn, the number of available studies also tends to decrease. Thus, one must balance scientific precision with practical constraints.

- **Step 2: Search for research studies that have analyzed the characteristic.** Journals, technical reports, and dissertations are all good sources. This step can be very time-consuming, often taking several months or more. A common problem during this phase is the tendency that only studies with strong results are published in journals, a phenomenon Rosenthal referred to as the *file drawer* problem. To minimize this problem, which can result in overestimation of the true strength of the effect or relationship in the population, it is important to spend time looking for technical reports, theses, dissertations, and unpublished studies, which are not subject to publication bias.

- **Step 3: Establish a list of criteria (standards) the studies must meet before including them in the meta-analysis.** These criteria can involve the type of test used, the experimental procedure employed, the date of publication, or anything else the researcher deems important. In regard to employment interviews, for example, the researcher might want to drop studies conducted before the 1964 Civil Rights Act, which increased awareness of minority group issues and likely influenced the questions asked in most interviews. Studies in which the interviewer had test results available (e.g., mental ability) might also be dropped because they may have led to preconceived notions about the candidates. These criteria act as a filter, refining the nature of the studies and the results.

- **Step 4: For every study that meets the criteria, collapse the findings into a common test statistic.** Although t, F, r, and χ^2 are the main test statistics used in significance testing, the two main test statistics used in meta-analysis are r and d. The correlation coefficient has the distinction of being the only test statistic used in both approaches. Although it may seem as if r and d are unrelated—the former is used for variables, the latter for groups—one statistic can be converted into the other using commonly available formulas, and meta-analysis can be done either way. (With correlations, some choose to use the r-to-z transformation to prevent the distribution from becoming progressively more skewed as the magnitude increases.)

- **Step 5: Mathematically summarize the findings of the studies.** The first analysis that is typically done in a meta-analysis is to find the mean of the test-statistic values, usually weighting them by their sample size. The rationale for sample weighting is the basic notion that sampling error—the difference between the characteristics of a sample and those of the population from which it was drawn—tends to decrease as the sample size increases. The mean test-statistic value then becomes a direct estimate of the strength of the relationship or effect in the population. The next analysis typically analyzes the variability to determine whether moderator variables are present. The most common approach is the classic Schmidt and Hunter 75% rule, whereby the actual (observed) variance across the studies is computed and compared with the variance expected to occur as a result of sampling error and other sources of artifactual variance. If the latter is at least 75% as large as the former, moderator variables are assumed not to exist or, if present, to have minimal influence. Some have turned to significance tests to help assess whether a moderator variable is present. Though interesting statistically, doing so is problematic because it courts one of the main problems that meta-analysis was designed to prevent: Type II errors.

Why does meta-analysis work? The meta-analytic technique is based on two fundamental principles. First, each study included in a meta-analysis represents one sample taken from the population being studied, commonly referred to as the *target population*. Thus, if 50 studies are combined in a meta-analysis, in effect, 50 samples from the target population are used. Not surprisingly, the total sample across the studies can be quite large in a meta-analysis, which is beneficial because of the general tendency for the magnitude of sampling error to decrease as the sample size increases.

The second fundamental principle relates to sampling error itself, specifically, that sampling errors are random. Even if the studies in a meta-analysis are drawn from the same (homogeneous) population, it is unlikely their respective test-statistic values will match the true population value. Rather, each study is likely to contain some degree of sampling error, which will push the test statistic higher or lower by varying amounts.

Borrowing from classical test theory, the actual value of the test statistic in a given study can be conceptualized as comprising the population value plus or minus sampling error. For example, using the correlation form of meta-analysis, the value in the first study in the meta-analysis can be represented as

$$r_1 = \rho + \varepsilon_1.$$

The second study would then be represented as $r_2 = \rho + \varepsilon_2$, the third study as $r_3 = \rho + \varepsilon_3$, the fourth study as $r_4 = \rho + \varepsilon_4$, and do on. Note that ε represents the random error component, one that, as noted previously, can either increase or decrease the starting population value by varying amounts. Accordingly, to find the mean correlation across the studies, the following formula is used, where k is the total number of studies:

$$\bar{r} = [(\rho + \varepsilon_1) + (\rho + \varepsilon_2) + (\rho + \varepsilon_3) + (\rho + \varepsilon_4) + \ldots + (\rho + \varepsilon_k)] / k$$

Continuing, the foregoing formula can be rearranged and simplified mathematically as

$$\bar{r} = (k * \rho + \Sigma\varepsilon) / k.$$

Because the sampling errors are random, they tend to form a symmetrical distribution with a mean of zero.

Accordingly, the sum of the errors in the foregoing formula is zero, leaving the number of studies (k) times ρ divided by k, which simplifies to just ρ, the value of the correlation in the population. In short, this mathematical exercise demonstrates that the mean correlation (or effect size) in a meta-analysis is a reasonable estimate of the true strength of the effect in the target population.

Is meta-analysis a perfect technique? Absolutely not. In fact, there are three situations in which the mean value in a meta-analysis may not reflect the true effect or relationship in the target population. The first is the situation in which the test-statistic values are influenced by artifacts such as measurement error (e.g., performance criterion in validity studies) and range restriction (e.g., using only interview ratings from those hired). Fortunately, methodology exists to correct for these artifacts.

The second is the situation in which one or more moderator variables are present. A moderator is a characteristic that changes the strength of the relationship or effect in the target population. Structure, for example, moderates the validity of the employment interview, increasing it from around .20 for unstructured interviews to around .50 for highly structured interviews. There are several ways to detect the presence of a moderator variable, the most common of which is the Hunter and Schmidt 75% rule. If a moderator variable is found, then the studies should be separated according to the levels or categories of that variable and a new meta-analysis conducted for each (e.g., for low-, medium-, and high-structure interviews). Confirmation that a variable is a moderator generally occurs when the mean test-statistic values separated in terms of magnitude and artifactual variance exceeds 75% of the observed variance in the levels or categories of that variable.

In the third problematic situation in meta-analysis, only a small number of studies is analyzed, a phenomenon that is quite common in most areas of research. In these situations, there is no guarantee that the sampling errors will sum to zero, in which case the mean value could be biased. What constitutes a reasonable number of studies in a meta-analysis? Stability traditionally has been overlooked in the field. A new line of research is addressing this issue by modifying Rosenthal's original fail-safe N concept for modern use. Though highly preliminary, early results suggest that many meta-analytic results are not as stable as might be imagined.

In conclusion, meta-analysis has emerged as a method for making inferences about populations based on sample data taken from those populations. It has gained popularity not only in the behavioral sciences but also in other areas, such as the medical field. It is not uncommon for major conclusions in textbooks to reference a meta-analysis. Though the technique is not without limitations, meta-analysis has emerged as a prominent and powerful technique for data analysis.

—*Allen I. Huffcutt*

See also Descriptive Statistics; Inferential Statistics; Statistical Power

FURTHER READING

Fisher, R. A. (1932). *Statistical methods for research workers* (4th ed.). Edinburgh, Scotland: Oliver and Boyd.

Fisher, R. A. (1935). *The design of experiments.* Edinburgh, Scotland: Oliver and Boyd.

Glass, G. V. (1976). Primary, secondary and meta-analysis of research. *Educational Researcher, 5,* 3–8.

Glass, G. V., McGaw, B., & Smith, M. L. (1981). *Meta-analysis and social research.* Beverly Hills, CA: Sage.

Hedges, L. V., & Olkin, I. (1985). *Statistical methods for meta-analysis.* Orlando, FL: Academic Press.

Huffcutt, A. I., & Arthur, W. (1994). Hunter and Hunter (1984) revisited: Interview validity for entry-level jobs. *Journal of Applied Psychology, 79,* 184–190.

Hunter, J. E., & Schmidt, F. L. (1990). *Methods of meta-analysis: Correcting error and bias in research findings.* Newbury Park, CA: Sage.

Hunter, J. E., Schmidt, F. L., & Jackson, G. B. (1982). *Meta-analysis: Cumulating research findings across studies.* Beverly Hills, CA: Sage.

Rosenthal, R. (1979). The "file drawer problem" and tolerance for null results. *Psychological Bulletin, 86,* 638–641.

Rosenthal, R. (1984). *Meta-analysis procedures for social research.* Beverly Hills, CA: Sage.

Schmidt, F. L. (1992). What do data really mean? Research findings, meta-analysis, and cumulative knowledge in psychology. *American Psychology, 47,* 1173–1181.

MODERATOR AND MEDIATOR VARIABLES

Organizational researchers frequently propose and test hypotheses that involve relationships between variables. Beyond simple bivariate associations, more complex models may involve third variables that provide greater explanatory power. Two common types of explanatory mechanisms are *mediator* and *moderator* variables. Importantly, mediator and moderator variables have fundamentally different effects in causal models and must be kept conceptually and statistically distinct. A mediator variable is part of a longer causal chain. In the simplest case, an antecedent variable causes the mediator variable, which, in turn, causes an outcome variable. Alternatively, a moderator variable does not imply a particular causal sequence. A variable is said to act as a moderator to the extent that the relationship between two other variables changes depending on the level of the moderator. Because of the different nature of these variables, mediator and moderator variables are discussed separately, as well as the statistical tests typically associated with evaluating their presence.

In this discussion, x represents the predictor variable, y represents the criterion variable, and m represents either the mediator or moderator.

MEDIATOR VARIABLES

Graphically, mediation may be represented by the simple model $x \rightarrow m \rightarrow y$. In this model, m mediates the relationship between x and y. As this model illustrates, a mediator variable transmits variance between two other variables. Thus, a mediator serves as an explanatory mechanism in the model. That is, the mediator provides an explanation of how and, to some extent, why two variables are related. For example, consider a model in which a researcher believes that student learning is negatively related to class size (i.e., students in smaller classes learn more than students in larger classes). To explain this effect, the researcher includes a mediator variable (e.g., the amount of student–teacher interaction) in the model. That is, in smaller classes, teachers are expected to spend more time with each student, and that, in turn, is related to student learning. The amount of student–teacher interaction provides a mechanism through which the bivariate relationship between class size and learning can be explained.

The extent to which a variable serves as a mediator can be easily tested using a three-step process of ordinary least squares regression. In the first analysis, y is regressed on x. This step is necessary insofar as there must be a relationship for m to mediate. If x and y are unrelated, m cannot mediate a relationship that does not exist. In a second analysis, m is regressed on x. If x and m are unrelated, m cannot serve as a mediating mechanism. Finally, y is regressed on both x and m together, and the regression coefficient associated with x is compared with the regression weight computed in the first step. The extent to which m mediates the x–y relationship is defined in terms of the difference between these coefficients. If the regression weight associated with x is reduced to zero, m is said to fully mediate the relationship between x and y. In short, the effect of x on y is fully explained when m is included in the model. Evidence for partial mediation is provided to the extent that the regression weight associated with x drops but is not reduced to zero. In this case, m explains some of the variance in the x–y relationship, but there is still a direct effect of x on y. The Sobel test is often used to test for the presence of this indirect (i.e., mediated) effect.

Recently, scholars have debated the extent to which these steps are required to argue for mediation; some have argued that the relationship between x and y need not be significant in order for m to serve as a mediator variable. In this alternative process of testing for mediation, the first step is unnecessary when the x–y relationship is relatively small in magnitude or when suppression is a possibility.

MODERATOR VARIABLES

A variable is said to moderate a relationship to the extent that the relationship between x and y changes depending on the level of m. In short, moderation is fundamentally an interactive effect. Again, ordinary least squares regression may be used to test for moderation. Two steps are required to test for moderation. First, the main effects of x and m are entered in the first step of an analysis in which y is the criterion variable. In the second step, the product of x and m is entered and the change in R-squared from the first to the second model is evaluated for statistical significance. If this value is significant, evidence is provided for moderation.

When the interaction term is significant, the nature of moderation (i.e., ordinal versus disordinal interaction) can easily be illustrated in a two-dimensional graphical representation. For example, imagine a test of general reading ability (x) and college performance measured by teacher ratings (y). Assume that a researcher who is interested in evaluating whether the relationship between these variables is the same across gender (m) subgroups applies the statistical technique described in the previous paragraph and observes the following regression equation:

$$\hat{Y} = .58\ (x) + 31.03(m) + (-.24)(x)(m) + (-9.92)$$

This equation can be used to plot the regression lines for these two groups using values from both x and m.

Though conceptually distinct, mediation and moderation analyses share several common issues. For example, both analyses can be strongly influenced by multicollinearity. In the case of mediation, a strong correlation between x and m can influence the precision of estimates of regression coefficients in the final equation. In tests of moderation, given that the interaction term is directly computed as the product of x and m, this term can be strongly related to either or both of the individual predictors. To address this issue, x and m are often centered by subtracting each observed score from the corresponding mean prior to forming the interaction term.

Finally, mediation and moderation can be present within the same causal model. Mediated moderation is said to exist when the interactive effect of two variables on an outcome of interest passes through an intervening variable. Alternatively, moderated mediation is said to exist when a mediation model is stronger for one group than another.

—*Ronald S. Landis*

FURTHER READING

Baron, R. M., & Kenny, D. A. (1986). The moderator-mediator variable distinction in social psychological research: Conceptual, strategic, and statistical considerations. *Journal of Personality and Social Psychology, 51,* 1173–1182.

Cohen, J., Cohen, P., West, S. G., & Aiken, L. S. (2003). *Applied multiple regression/correlation analysis for the behavioral sciences* (3rd ed.). Mahwah, NJ: Lawrence Erlbaum.

Shrout, P. E., & Bolger, N. (2002). Mediation in experimental and nonexperimental studies: New procedures and recommendations. *Psychological Methods, 7,* 422–445.

MOOD

The late 20th and early 21st centuries have seen a dramatic increase in the study of affect in organizations. The affective realm consists of state and trait affect, and there are many types of each. *Mood* is a transitory affective state that is relatively mild and long lasting. Different from other transitory affective states (i.e., emotions), mood does not have a clear triggering stimulus or a specific object. Rather, mood is present at all times in the background of our minds (i.e., we are not void of mood at any given point in time), although we are not always aware of it. Mood is generally considered either positive or negative, whereas emotions are discrete and specific, such as anger, fear, hope, and joy. Although it is possible to talk about an angry mood, for example, this is different from the emotion of anger in that the angry mood is not related to any known stimulus, is generalized and diffused, lasts a longer time, and is characterized by an overall irritability and tendency to view external stimuli as negative.

There are several theoretical models of the structure of mood. These models describe mood according to two orthogonal and bipolar dimensions, pleasantness and activation. The interplay between these dimensions results in mood ranging from activated (e.g., aroused) to deactivated (e.g., calm); from pleasant (e.g., happy) to unpleasant (e.g., unhappy); from pleasant and activated (e.g., excited) to unpleasant and deactivated (e.g., tired); and from unpleasant activated (e.g., tense) to pleasant deactivated (e.g., relaxed). Other structural models of mood also exist.

Most research has focused on the effects of positive mood. However, there is an asymmetry between the influences of positive and negative moods, such that the effects of negative mood are not necessarily the opposite of those of positive mood. Therefore, caution must be exercised when inferring conclusions about negative mood from research conducted on positive mood, and vice versa.

METHODOLOGIES FOR STUDYING MOOD

Industrial/organizational researchers typically measure mood using self-report measures or implicit measures of mood, usually behaviors. Mood has been studied in both laboratory and field settings using experimental and nonexperimental methods. When studying mood, researchers either manipulate it or measure research participants' naturally occurring mood. Common methods for manipulating mood are movies, music, and small gifts. The induction of negative moods has been found to result in larger effects than the induction of positive moods. Films and stories are the most efficient methods of mood elicitation.

INFLUENCES ON MOOD

Because mood does not have concrete causes, it may be influenced by an infinite number and unlimited types of causes. Among the commonly studied influences are personality, external factors, and internal factors. External factors that have been found to affect mood are weather, temperature, odor, physical activity, food, and drugs; these factors affect mood through their influence on biological processes. Social influences also affect mood—for example, when people look at the mood of others as a source of information or when the moods of others affect one's own mood. Internal influences on mood include biological, physiological, and neurological determinants, such as circadian rhythms, fatigue, and arousal. Emotions can also influence mood, which becomes an aftereffect of emotion.

MOOD AND PERSONALITY

In addition to having transient positive and negative moods, people also have positive and negative personality tendencies, known as *positive* and *negative affectivity*. It is generally agreed that people who are high in positive affectivity tend to experience more positive moods, and people who are high in negative affectivity tend to experience more negative moods. However, because the correlations between state and trait affect are modest at best, trait affect is not the strongest predictor of mood. Other affective dispositions such as trait affect, also affect mood. For example, trait anxiety leads people to react with more anxiety to certain events and makes it difficult for them to differentiate between justified and unjustified anxiety. Affect intensity (the intensity of an individual's affective responsiveness) is another personality trait that affects people's tendency to experience different mood states and ability to regulate their moods.

MOOD AND COGNITION

Mood is related to the cognitive processes of memory, recall, and attention. Consistent findings show mood congruency effects, that is, a congruence between an individual's mood state, attention to information, coding of information, and retrieval of information, such that mood facilitates the processing of state-congruent materials. For example, people in a positive mood tend to perceive neutral stimuli as more positive, have more positive perceptions of others, and can better recall events that were congruent with their mood when the event occurred. Similar congruency effects have been found for negative moods.

Other robust findings refer to thought processes that are affected by mood. Specifically, people who are in a positive mood tend to use more heuristics, use broader categories to analyze and classify data, and are more cognitively flexible than people in a negative mood, who tend to go through very elaborative thought processes. These processes can lead to a *depressive realism effect,* whereby people who are slightly depressed have a more realistic grasp of reality and their control of it. People in positive mood, however, look at themselves in ways that are more positive and overestimate their abilities. Thus, there is a trade-off between the accuracy of perception and self-enhancement.

Whereas the preceding research emphasized the importance of valence in affecting cognition, other research has examined the importance of the energy dimension of mood in influencing cognition. According to this research, mood affects cognitive processes through its influence on the efficiency with which people process information. Specifically, mood affects available cognitive resources, attentional selectivity, readiness to respond, and short-term memory, such that higher arousal leads to higher availability of most cognitive resources. These results apply to some tasks, but not to others. Apparently, the relative importance of valence and the energy dimensions of mood depend on the kind of task being performed and the cognitive processes required.

MOOD AND PERFORMANCE

Mood can affect performance through its influence on cognitive processes and on motivation. It is generally assumed that people who are in a positive mood are motivated to maintain it, whereas people who are in a negative mood are motivated to repair their emotional state. These motivations sometimes lead to similar behavioral influences of positive and negative mood. At other times, behaviors will differ based on mood.

Research has found that people who are in a positive mood tend to engage in prosocial behaviors, such as helping other people and volunteering more, but only if they perceive their behaviors as affecting them positively. Under some circumstances, people in a negative mood also help others as a means of improving their own emotional state.

Mood has also been found to influence withdrawal behaviors, such as absenteeism. To the extent that the work situation is perceived as negative, withdrawal behaviors will increase. Both positive mood and negative mood have been shown to be related to absenteeism in this manner. Individuals who experience a positive mood at the workplace are less likely to be absent, whereas those who experience a negative mood at work are more likely to be absent.

As for the performance of duties required by a job, the influence of mood is related to the kind of performance that is required. That is, when flexibility, working with others, and creativity are needed, positive mood has a positive influence. For example, research has found a positive relationship between positive mood and customer service activities and between positive mood and creativity. Positive mood also positively influences negotiation and conflict resolution because people in a positive mood are better able to understand the other person's point of view and more often adopt constructive problem-solving strategies.

When attention to detail and vigilant information processing are needed, negative mood may be preferable; research has shown that negative moods influence more systematic and detailed processing of information. Still, under some circumstances, negative mood leads to less effort on cognitive processes and positive mood leads to more effort in cognitive processing. Depending on the ability of information processing to alleviate a sad mood or worsen a positive mood, and depending on the relevancy of the information, individuals use more or less effort in processing the information, depending on their mood.

Mood also has strong implications for decision making. Research has found that positive moods lead to simplification of complex tasks (which can be beneficial or harmful, depending on the task) and more efficient decision-making processes. People who are in a positive mood also tend to take fewer risks when more is at stake because they have higher sensitivity to loss, which may diminish their positive mood.

Finally, an important indicator of people's performance is their performance appraisals. Here, mood may have an indirect effect by influencing raters' tendency to be more lenient, subjected to rating biases, or affected by irrelevant information, such as affection for the individual.

MOOD AT THE TEAM LEVEL

Until now, the moods of individuals have been discussed. Recently, however, mood has also been studied as a group-level phenomenon, usually referred to as *group affect*, which is the shared affect among group members. It has been found that mood is contagious—this is one mechanism through which it transfers from one individual to others. In this way, the mood of a single individual affects the mood of the group. Other factors that have been shown to influence the convergence of group members' mood are task and social interdependence, group membership stability, mood regulation norms, and the leader's mood.

To conclude, mood plays an important role in the behavior of people and groups in organizations. It is both a result of working in organizations and a cause of people's behavior.

—*Yochi Cohen-Charash and Brittany Boyd*

See also Affective Traits; Contextual Performance/Prosocial Behavior/Organizational Citizenship Behavior; Group Dynamics and Processes; Withdrawal Behaviors, Absenteeism; Withdrawal Behaviors, Lateness

FURTHER READING

Barsade, S. G. (2002). The ripple effect: Emotional contagion in groups. *Administrative Science Quarterly, 47,* 644–675.

Forgas, J. P., & George, J. M. (2001). Affective influences on judgments and behavior in organizations: An information processing perspective. *Organizational Behavior & Human Decision Processes, 86,* 3–34.

George, J. M., & Brief, A. P. (1992). Feeling good–doing good: A conceptual analysis of the mood at work–organizational spontaneity relationship. *Psychological Bulletin, 112,* 310–329.

Larsen, R. J. (2000). Toward a science of mood regulation. *Psychological Inquiry, 11,* 129–141.

Wegener, D. T., Petty, R. E., & Smith, S. M. (1995). Positive mood can increase or decrease message scrutiny: The hedonic contingency view of mood and message processing. *Journal of Personality and Social Psychology, 69,* 5–15.

Westermann, R., Spies, K., Stahl, G. N., & Hesse, F. W. (1996). Relative effectiveness and validity of mood induction procedures: A meta-analysis. *European Journal of Social Psychology, 26,* 557–580.

Yik, M. S. M., Russell, J. A., & Barrett, L. F. (1999). Structure of self-reported current affect: Integration and beyond. *Journal of Personality and Social Psychology, 77,* 600–619.

MORALE

Employee *morale* is a term that is often used loosely by professionals and laypeople. Morale refers to employees' shared attitudes toward and identification with the elements of their job, working conditions, fellow workers, supervisors, and general management. As a group-level term, morale is akin to the affective climate of an organization. Although morale is often equated with intrinsic job satisfaction averaged across a work group, department, or organization, more technical definitions posit that morale refers to a summary evaluation of a broader range of job-related attitudes (e.g., organizational commitment, employee loyalty, job involvement, employee engagement, and employee well-being). Whereas some of the evaluations an employee expresses toward the organization are unique to himself or herself, members of one's work group may have similar views as a result of sharing common experiences at work. These shared perceptions tend to be reinforced and maintained by the group. Hence, morale is often influenced by factors present in the work environment that are common to all employees in the group or organization.

The use of employee morale surveys is a relatively common practice among businesses. Management's concern for employee morale was heightened as a result of the Hawthorn studies at the Western Electric Company from 1927 to 1932. These studies suggested that the feelings and sentiments of being a part of a special work group had a greater effect on performance than changes in physical working conditions such as illumination, incentives, work hours, and rest breaks. In addition to recognizing important social motives, these findings implied an important relationship between morale and productivity as suggested by the well-known adage of the *happy/productive worker*. Along this vein, morale is often assumed to relate to motivation in general and to intrinsic motivation and pride in one's work in particular. Although some research has demonstrated a relationship between morale and performance, the relationship may be reciprocal, such that being a member of a high-performing team actually enhances morale. On the other hand, low morale is assumed to be evidenced in high turnover, high absenteeism, tardiness, and customer complaints.

RESEARCH ON MORALE

As a result of its long history and multiple meanings, the empirical research on employee morale is difficult to summarize. For example, research claiming to examine morale has often operationalized morale as a specific attitude (e.g., job satisfaction, organizational commitment) at the individual (rather than group) level. Recently, researchers have begun to examine group-level organizational phenomena such as organizational climate. In light of this research, consideration should be given not only to workers' average scores but also to the consistency between scores (e.g., intraclass correlation coefficient, r_{wg}), which indicates the extent to which employees share a common perception of the workplace.

Although research has largely neglected the underlying structure of employee morale, some empirical evidence suggests the following five basic dimensions or patterns of attitudes:

- General management: This dimension relates to employees' relationships with general management and the organization and includes identification with the organization and a sense of security for the future. It also represents an evaluation of communication within the organization and management's competencies and concern for employee welfare.
- Immediate supervision: This dimension relates to attitudes toward immediate supervision and includes interpersonal relations and people skills, as well as the administrative aspects of supervision.
- Material rewards: This facet deals with material rewards in terms of pay and benefits.
- Fellow employees: This dimension relates to friendliness, motivation, and cohesion among employees.
- Job satisfaction: This dimension relates to the intrinsic motivation and satisfaction associated with the nature of the job. Related to this, employees feel that the job is worthwhile, provides a meaningful service, and affords opportunities for personal growth and development.

Empirical studies have found that employee morale (loosely defined) is positively associated with customer satisfaction, particularly among employees who have direct contact with customers. Research also suggests that the closeness of employee–management relations is related positively to morale and teamwork, especially when combined with feedback, incentives, and autonomy. Research further suggests that the reduced morale of survivors following an organizational downsizing may undermine any expected gains from the restructuring, presumably because it destroys trust and reduces employees' sense of empowerment.

IMPROVING MORALE

The trade literature offers several suggestions for improving employee morale. For the most part, these suggestions for improving work group morale have not been empirically examined.

- Compensation: Provide formal, fair, and accurate performance evaluations and merit systems, paying attention to shift differentials and overtime pay. Clarify the link between achievements and rewards.
- Benefits: Provide benefits such as paid holidays, vacation and sick leave, pension and retirement plans, health care coverage, and life insurance. Consideration may also be given to providing tuition reimbursement, paid parking, employee assistance and well-being programs, and child care.
- Communications: Provide employees a chance to express their opinions and concerns by forming employee committees, holding regular meetings with management, conducting attitude surveys, instituting employee recognition practices, publishing newsletters, and putting up bulletin boards. Let employees know when management has considered or implemented employee suggestions. When people work hard to complete a project, make sure their accomplishments are acknowledged.
- Respect: Make sure guidelines for staff behavior are reasonable and appropriate. Staff participation in the formulation of workplace rules can reduce management's efforts to reinforce compliance with unpopular regulations. When making a policy ruling, explain its purpose and enforce it fairly. Be tactful with discipline; reprimand should be private rather than public and should address the specific fault rather than the person's character. When they are forced to downsize, companies that provide outplacement services, training, and career counseling have a better chance of retaining the loyalty and trust of survivors.
- Conditions, facilities, and services: Provide employees with safe, clean working conditions and reasonable workloads. Work underload and overload can be equally damaging to morale.
- Personnel functions and policies: Provide an orientation and early socialization program to help employees

feel welcomed and valued by the organization. Ensure clear and fair performance appraisal systems, grievance procedures, promotion systems, and training opportunities. Hold regular work parties or company retreats. Provide family-friendly practices. Promoting from within demonstrates that management believes talent already exists within the organization.

—*Craig Crossley*

See also Attitudes and Beliefs; Job Satisfaction; Organizational Climate; Organizational Commitment

FURTHER READING

Abbott, J. (2003). Does employee satisfaction matter? A study to determine whether low employee morale affects customer satisfaction and profits in the business-to-business sector. *Journal of Communication Management, 7,* 333–339.

Griffith, J. (2001). Do satisfied employees satisfy customers? Support-services staff morale and satisfaction among public school administrators, students, and parents. *Journal of Applied Social Psychology, 31,* 1627–1658.

McKnight, D., Ahmad, S., & Schroeder, R. G. (2001). When do feedback, incentive control, and autonomy improve morale? The importance of employee-management relationship closeness. *Journal of Managerial Issues, 13,* 466–482.

Mishra, K., Spreitzer, G. M., & Mishra, A. (1998). Preserving employee morale during downsizing. *Sloan Management Review, 39,* 83–95.

Viteles, M. S. (1953). *Motivation and morale in industry.* New York: W. W. Norton.

MOTIVATIONAL TRAITS

Motivation refers to an internal set of nonability processes that channel, energize, and sustain behavior over time. Motivation influences the direction (i.e., choice of activities), intensity (i.e., amount of effort), and persistence (i.e., duration of effort) of an individual's behavior. A trait can be defined as a distinguishable feature of a person's nature that demonstrates consistency across situations and over time. Traits are often contrasted with states, which are more situation specific and change relatively quickly. That is, a trait exhibits temporal stability and has a similar effect on behavior in different situations, whereas states are much more temporary.

A motivational trait can be defined as a stable and distinguishable feature of an individual that is distinct from cognitive ability yet influences the choice of goal-directed activities, the amount of effort expended on tasks, and the duration of time activities are pursued. Furthermore, a motivational trait has a similar effect on behavior in different situations (e.g., work, recreation, social) and over time (e.g., today and in six months).

MOTIVATIONAL TRAITS AS DISTAL INFLUENCES ON WORK BEHAVIOR

Motivational traits have been shown to predict training outcomes, job performance, and organizational citizenship behaviors. Motivational traits are believed to affect behavior largely through task-specific motivation (i.e., state motivation) and self-regulation (i.e., self-management). Indeed, several studies have shown that motivational traits affect individuals' self-efficacy (i.e., task-specific confidence), goal choice, and goal commitment (i.e., strength of attachment to a goal). These more statelike motivational factors are then believed to influence performance In addition, some researchers have argued that motivational traits affect performance through task-specific self-regulatory processes, such as motivation control (i.e., keeping motivation high by creating personal rewards or challenges), emotion management (i.e., preventing worry and negative emotions from interfering with performance), mental focus (i.e., staying focused on the task), and metacognition (i.e., monitoring one's learning and progress). In sum, motivational traits are expected to affect work behaviors through task-specific motivation and self-regulation variables.

MOTIVATIONAL TRAIT CONCEPTUALIZATIONS

There is little consensus about which traits best represent dispositional motivation. As a result, several parallel streams of research have developed based on different theories of motivation. Although the particular traits differ across frameworks, many have a foundation in the long-standing distinction between approach and avoidance motivation. *Approach motivation* refers to a general sensitivity to rewarding stimuli and the tendency to seek out such stimuli. *Avoidance motivation* refers to a general sensitivity to

punishing stimuli and the tendency to move away from such stimuli. Approach and avoidance motivation are considered to be independent such that individuals can be high on both, low on both, or high on one and low on the other.

The following sections provide a brief overview of some recent and influential motivational trait conceptualizations. This overview is not intended to be comprehensive but to describe traits that are grounded in well-articulated motivation theories. This overview does not include personality traits that are very broad in focus, tapping more than motivation (e.g., conscientiousness includes the motivation variable of achievement striving, as well as nonmotivation variables such as competence, order, and dutifulness), or traits that affect motivation only in particular situations (e.g., openness to experience may yield strong motivation to explore a new city, but it may not lead to strong motivation to perform a familiar work task).

Behavioral Activation System and Behavioral Inhibition System

Jeffrey Gray developed a theory of motivation based on evidence from physiological research. This theory argues that motivational traits are captured by the *behavioral activation system* (BAS) and the *behavioral inhibition system* (BIS), which correspond to approach and avoidance motivation, respectively. High-BAS individuals tend to seek out rewarding activities and have a strong drive to attain goals. These individuals exhibit impulsivity, sensation seeking, and a tendency to experience positive emotions (e.g., hope, happiness, elation). High-BIS individuals strive to avoid threatening or punishing situations, leading to low levels of goal-directed behavior and the experience of negative emotions (e.g., fear, frustration, sadness). Measures of BIS and BAS sensitivity have been linked to distinct areas of the prefrontal lobe, supporting the biological foundation of these traits. Although the BIS–BAS framework represents perhaps the most basic model of approach and avoidance motivation, it has received no attention in the organizational research.

Goal Orientation

The concept of goal orientation was originally developed by Carol Dweck. Goal orientation refers to differences in the way people interpret and respond to achievement situations. Because it focuses on learning and achievement, this concept has become one of the most widely studied motivational trait frameworks in organizational research. Generally, individuals adopt either a *learning goal orientation* (LGO) or a *performance goal orientation* (PGO). Individuals high in LGO wish to develop their knowledge, skills, and competence on tasks and believe that ability is changeable. This orientation is considered an approach motivation trait. Individuals high in PGO seek to demonstrate their competence and ability in comparison to others and tend to believe that ability is fixed. This orientation can be divided into approach and avoidance subtraits. Individuals who are high in PGO-approach seek to prove their competence and ability in comparison to others. Individuals who are high in PGO-avoid seek to avoid displays of incompetence and negative judgments from others. Although goal orientation has been shown to predict a variety of work outcomes, there is some debate as to whether it is best conceptualized as a trait, a state, or something in between (i.e., a contextualized trait).

Motivational Traits

Ruth Kanfer and colleagues developed a theory of motivational traits based on the approach and avoidance distinction but with an emphasis on organizational applications. In addition, they developed a corresponding measure, the Motivational Trait Questionnaire, which measures individual differences in motivation across three domains: *personal mastery*, *competitive excellence*, and *motivation related to anxiety*. Personal mastery is an approach trait comprising a *desire to learn* subtrait (i.e., the need to achieve in the context of learning) and a *mastery* subtrait (i.e., the desire for continuous task improvement). Competitive excellence is made up of an *other referenced goals* subtrait (i.e., looking to others to determine how well one is performing), which is a mix of approach and avoidance motivation, and a *competitiveness* subtrait (i.e., a focus on competition and outperforming others), which is an approach trait. Motivation related to anxiety is an avoidance-oriented trait and is made up of a *worry* subtrait (i.e., worrying about being evaluated in performance contexts) and an *emotionality* subtrait (i.e., experiencing emotions in an evaluation situation). Kanfer and colleagues provided construct validity evidence for the scales, but no research has examined whether the scales predict job performance.

Action–State Orientation

Action–state orientation was first described by Julius Kuhl as part of a larger theory of action control. Action–state orientation reflects differences in the ability to manage one's goal-directed behaviors over time and comprises three dimensions: preoccupation, hesitation, and volatility. Action-oriented individuals are generally more effective than state-oriented individuals. *Preoccupation* refers to differences in one's ability to disengage from thoughts regarding failure or alternative goals and states. State-oriented individuals cannot easily disengage from negative thoughts, whereas action-oriented individuals put such thoughts out of mind and move forward with new activities. The *hesitation* dimension reflects differences in one's ability to initiate action on already chosen tasks. Action-oriented individuals are able to easily begin work on tasks, whereas state-oriented individuals have difficulty starting activities. The *volatility* dimension pertains to the ability to persist in tasks until they are completed. Action-oriented individuals finish activities, whereas state-oriented individuals stop activities before they are completed. Research has demonstrated that action–state orientation predicts job performance, classroom performance, and job attitudes.

Regulatory Focus

E. Tory Higgins and colleagues developed *regulatory focus theory*, which argues that individuals differ in their propensity to be promotion focused and prevention focused. *Promotion-focused* individuals seek to minimize differences between their actual and ideal selves (e.g., hopes, aspirations), and prevention-focused individuals seek to minimize differences between their actual and "ought" selves (e.g., duties, responsibilities). Individuals who are high in promotion focus seek out their desires and strive for personal growth. As a result, promotion-focused individuals experience eagerness when striving for goals, joy when goals are attained, and sadness when goals are not attained. Individuals who are high in prevention focus see goals as obligations and are concerned with maintaining security and avoiding losses. As a result, prevention-focused individuals tend to be cautious when striving for goals, feel relaxed when goals are attained, and experience nervousness when goals are not attained. Applications of this theory to organizational research are just beginning, with most efforts focused on theory development.

Self-Determination

Edward Deci and Richard Ryan's *self-determination theory* distinguishes between intrinsically motivated behavior (i.e., activities that are performed because they are enjoyable) and extrinsically motivated behavior (i.e., activities that are performed to receive some external reward). Self-determination theory describes three traits that are related to intrinsic and extrinsic motivation: autonomy orientation, control orientation, and impersonal orientation.

Autonomy orientation refers to differences in the extent to which individuals regulate their behavior based on personal interests and preferences. Autonomy-oriented individuals seek opportunities to satisfy their personal needs and desires. As a result, they tend to experience intrinsic motivation, feelings of competence, and task enjoyment. *Control orientation* refers to differences in the extent to which individuals regulate behavior based on external constraints and controls. Control-oriented individuals perceive that others control their behaviors. As a result, these individuals experience extrinsic motivation and little task enjoyment. *Impersonal orientation* refers to the extent to which individuals focus on information that suggests they are incompetent and will not succeed. Impersonal-oriented individuals believe that they cannot do well and therefore experience neither intrinsic nor extrinsic motivation. This lack of motivation leads to a sense of helplessness, depressed mood, and low levels of goal-directed action. Initial research on this topic has shown that these traits predict job performance and employee well-being.

SUMMARY

Motivational traits are stable, nonability characteristics that influence the direction, intensity, and persistence of individuals' goal-directed behaviors across situations. Motivational traits are thought to affect behavior through task-specific motivation and self-regulation. Several motivational trait frameworks exist, each deriving from a different theory of motivation. One avenue for future research would be to develop an integrative model of motivational traits that consolidates these approaches into a comprehensive framework.

—*James M. Diefendorff*

See also Work Motivation

FURTHER READING

Brett, J. F., & VandeWalle, D. (1999). Goal orientation and goal content as predictors of performance in a training program. *Journal of Applied Psychology, 84,* 863–873.

Brockner, J., & Higgins, E. T. (2001). Regulatory focus theory: Implications for the study of emotions at work. *Organizational Behavior and Human Decision Processes, 86,* 35–66.

Carver, C. S., & White, T. L. (1994). Behavioral inhibition, behavioral activation, and affective responses to impending reward and punishment: The BIS/BAS scales. *Journal of Personality and Social Psychology, 67*(2), 319–333.

Deci, E. L., & Ryan, R. M. (2000). The "what" and "why" of goal pursuits: Human needs and the self-determination of behavior. *Psychological Inquiry, 11,* 227–268.

Diefendorff, J. M., Hall, R. J., Lord, R. G., & Strean, M. (2000). Action–state orientation: Construct validity of a revised measure and its relationship to work-related variables. *Journal of Applied Psychology, 85,* 250–263.

Elliot, A. J., & Thrash, T. M. (2002). Approach-avoidance motivation in personality: Approach and avoidance temperaments and goals. *Journal of Personality and Social Psychology, 82*(5), 804–818.

Farr, J. L., Hoffmann, D. A., & Ringenbach, K. L. (1993). Goal orientation and action control theory: Implications for industrial and organizational psychology. In C. L. Cooper & I. T. Robertson (Eds.), *International review of industrial and organizational psychology* (Vol. 8, pp. 193–232). New York: Wiley.

Kanfer, R., & Ackerman, P. L. (2000). Individual differences in work motivation: Further explorations of a trait framework. *Applied Psychology, 49,* 470–482.

Kanfer, R., & Heggestad, E. D. (1997). Motivational traits and skills: A person-centered approach to work motivation. In L. L. Cummings & B. M. Staw (Eds.), *Research in organizational behavior* (Vol. 19, pp. 1–56). Greenwich, CT: JAI Press.

Kuhl, J., & Beckmann, J. (1994). *Volition and personality: Action versus state orientation.* Seattle, WA: Hogrefe & Huber.

MULTILEVEL MODELING

As scholars of human behavior in organizations, industrial and organizational psychologists often find themselves trying to understand phenomena that are inherently nested, hierarchical, and multilevel. From private industry to universities to the military to nearly all forms of government, organizations comprise hierarchical structures that loosely resemble pyramids (even if the structures resemble flat pyramids, they are still hierarchical).

Consider a large chain of department stores: Individual employees are nested within different departments (e.g., sporting goods, men's clothing, women's clothing), which are, in turn, nested within a store in a particular location, which is, in turn, nested within the overall organization. In this example, influences and consequences occur at the individual, department, store, and organizational levels of analysis, including relationships that cross these levels. Furthermore, the people within these units (department, store, organization) are not there randomly; rather, they share some similarities that make them distinct from other units. There are many consequences of this natural nesting, which will be described shortly. But first, let us consider the consequences of ignoring hierarchical structures in organizational research.

CONSEQUENCES OF IGNORING MULTILEVEL INFLUENCES

A number of theoretical and methodological fallacies may occur as a result of ignoring multilevel structures. This entry focuses on the following theoretical fallacies:

- Misspecification fallacies involve assigning the wrong level of theory to a construct. For example, a researcher may wish to study organizational flexibility, but using only measures of individual employee flexibility does not operationalize the construct at the appropriate (organizational) level.
- Cross-level fallacies involve inappropriately equating findings at one level to other levels. If a researcher adopts a theory of individual flexibility to understand organizational-level flexibility, he or she must show how the theory adequately explains phenomena at the organizational level or risk committing a cross-level fallacy.
- Contextual fallacies involve instances in which a researcher ignores important contextual (higher-level) influences on lower-level relationships and outcomes. This is a big one in psychology: For years, the field studied individuals as if situations did not matter. For example, if organizational flexibility constrains or enhances individual-level flexibility, then both levels should be studied to truly understand how individual flexibility relates to individual-level outcomes.

The bottom line is that ignoring multilevel relationships when they exist may lead us to inappropriate conclusions from our research. This is not a trivial issue because the validity of our science depends on adequately understanding these relationships.

PROPERTIES OF EMERGENCE

Measuring individual-level cognitions, attitudes, and behaviors is relatively straightforward. But how do such constructs manifest themselves in higher-level units such as teams and organizations? Sometimes, higher-level constructs are easy to measure (e.g., organizational size, location, or money spent on human resources). But more often then not, researchers want to understand psychological phenomena that exist at higher levels (e.g., climate, customer satisfaction, or turnover). Perhaps one of the most important theoretical advancements in recent years has been the clarification of the process of *emergence*—that is, how lower-level psychological constructs manifest as higher-level constructs. There are numerous ways this can occur, but for simplicity's sake, two extreme forms will be discussed.

First, *composition* represents similarity, consensus, or "sharedness" among within-unit observations. For example, if lower-level observations are hypothesized to be sufficiently similar to form some aggregate, higher-level construct, one is dealing with a composition model. In such a model, the higher-level construct is the unit average of within-unit members' scores. For example, organizational climate may be the average of all employees' climate perceptions within that organization. Notice what just happened: The mean scores within the organization were used to create an organization-level score based on that mean. Hence, there is no direct measure of organizational climate in this case but instead an indirect measure based on an average of employees' scores. Beyond having a strong theory to justify aggregation, one must statistically demonstrate it through indexes of agreement and consensus. A composition model, by focusing on similarity, frequently makes a claim that the lower- and higher-level constructs are reasonably isomorphic (i.e., similar in their nature).

Second, *compilation* represents dissimilarity, dissensus, or, simply put, within-unit disagreement. If it is hypothesized that the unit-level score is based on differences among unit members, then one need not justify similarity to create the aggregate-level variable. Instead, one directly estimates the amount of within-unit disagreement. For example, climate strength is a variable that is hypothesized to explain how strongly climate perceptions are held. It has been operationalized as the within-unit standard deviation in climate perceptions. The higher the within-unit standard deviation, the more disagreement there is among unit members. There are other ways of operationalizing the unit-level compilation model, but the within-unit standard deviation appears to be the most popular.

Thus, composition and compilation processes represent two forms of emergence. They are not simply different sides of the same construct; with a perfectly normal distribution, means and variances are uncorrelated. In practice, they are often correlated with each other, and the researcher must clearly justify why one or both forms of emergence are relevant in a given setting.

TYPES OF MULTILEVEL RELATIONSHIPS

At the risk of oversimplifying a detailed topic, multilevel relationships can be categorized into three types. The first relationship is single level, wherein all predictors and criteria reside within a single level of analysis. This is the dominant approach in psychology, particularly industrial psychology. The second relationship is cross-level, wherein the predictors exist at multiple levels, but the criteria exist at a single level (alternatively, the predictors exist at a single level, and the criteria exist at multiple levels). For example, one might hypothesize that organizational climate moderates the relationship between individual service provider attitudes and individual customer's satisfaction. The final relationship is homologous, meaning that the same set of relationships is found at each level of analysis. For example, individual service provider attitudes may influence individual customer satisfaction, and aggregate organizational service climate influences aggregate customer satisfaction. A variety of advanced statistical techniques are capable of modeling the multilevel relationships described here, but the real difficulty is articulating a theory that makes such statistics meaningful.

SUMMARY

Industrial and organizational research continues to shift from single-level questions to multilevel questions. This research is challenging yet ultimately necessary if we are to truly understand how the behavior of the people *within* organizations contributes to the behavior *of* organizations. Many advancements have already been made, and this is likely to be an active area of research for the next several years.

—*Robert E. Ployhart*

See also Multilevel Modeling Techniques

FURTHER READING

Bliese, P. D. (2000). Within-group agreement, non-independence, and reliability: Implications for data aggregation and analysis. In K. J. Klein & S. W. J. Kozlowski (Eds.), *Multilevel theory, research, and methods in organizations: Foundations, extensions, and new directions* (pp. 349–381). San Francisco: Jossey-Bass.

Chen, G., Mathieu, J. E., & Bliese, P. D. (2004). A framework for conducting multilevel construct validation. In F. J. Dansereau & F. Yamarino (Eds.), *Research in multilevel issues: The many faces of multi-level issues* (Vol. 3, pp. 273–303). Oxford, UK: Elsevier Science.

Hofmann, D. A., Griffin, M. A., & Gavin, M. B. (2000). The application of hierarchical linear modeling to organizational research. In K. J. Klein & S. W. J. Kozlowski (Eds.), *Multilevel theory, research, and methods in organizations: Foundations, extensions, and new directions* (pp. 467–511). San Francisco: Jossey-Bass.

Klein, K. J., & Kozlowski, S. W. J. (2000). A multilevel approach to theory and research in organizations: Contextual, temporal, and emergent processes. In K. J. Klein & S. W. J. Kozlowski (Eds.), *Multilevel theory, research, and methods in organizations: Foundations, extensions, and new directions* (pp. 3–90). San Francisco: Jossey-Bass.

Ployhart, R. E. (2004). Organizational staffing: A multilevel review, synthesis, and model. In J. Martocchio (Ed.), *Research in personnel and human resource management* (Vol. 23, pp. 121–176). Oxford, UK: Elsevier.

Von Bertalanffy, L. (1972). The history and status of general systems theory. In G. J. Klir (Ed.), *Trends in general systems theory* (pp. 21–41). New York: Wiley.

MULTILEVEL MODELING TECHNIQUES

As researchers who examine phenomena within and around organizations, industrial and organizational psychologists must deal with nested data. Consider that individuals are nested within job categories, job categories are nested within work groups, work groups are nested within departments, departments are nested within organizations, and organizations are nested within nations and cultures. Furthermore, people do not enter these jobs and organizations in random ways; rather, people choose which organizational environments to enter, and organizations choose which people to select and retain. All of this leads to the important observation that much of the data obtained in organizational settings is unlikely to be independent within units. This, in turn, carries a statistical consequence: that some key assumptions of our tried-and-true statistical methods (regression and analysis of variance, or ANOVA) are likely to be violated in most organizational research.

Recently, several theoretical, methodological, and statistical advancements have made multilevel research more feasible. This entry focuses on one particularly useful statistical advancement, *hierarchical linear modeling* (HLM). This regression-based approach is useful for testing the presence of higher-level (contextual) effects on lower-level relationships and outcomes.

STATISTICAL CONSEQUENCES OF NESTED DATA

The general linear model, which subsumes both regression and ANOVA, assumes that errors are independent and normally distributed, with a mean of zero and a constant variance. Yet when the data are nested—for example, when the behaviors and attitudes of individuals within a team are affected by teammates—this assumption is violated. This is known as *nonindependence*, and its major consequence is that standard errors are smaller than they should be, which, in turn, contributes to inflated Type I errors. There are other, more subtle effects of nonindependence that can cause problems with estimation of effect size and statistical significance; the Further Reading section contains links for more details.

Nonindependence is most frequently documented by the intraclass correlation coefficient. When nonindependence exists, the use of HLM becomes problematic; however, we now have the tools to more directly model the data in such situations.

A NONTECHNICAL INTRODUCTION TO HLM

Many references to the technical details of HLM are provided in the Further Reading section. The purpose of this entry is only to introduce the concept, and this is done through the use of figures and an example. Figure 1 shows a simple example in which organizational climate is hypothesized to influence individual job satisfaction directly, as well as the relationship between satisfaction and pay. This hypothesis can be represented in terms of two levels. In the Level 1 model, job satisfaction can be regressed on pay. One would expect a positive relationship, such that higher pay is associated with more job satisfaction. However, what if multiple organizations were sampled and it was found there are mean differences in satisfaction across organizations, as well as differences in the relationship between pay and job satisfaction? Such a situation might occur when individuals within an organization share at least some common sources of influence, hence the nonindependence of their job satisfaction scores.

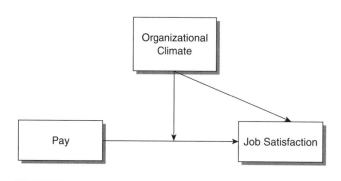

Figure 1   Graphical Example of Hierarchical Linear Modeling

The between-organization differences could be explained by organizational climate. Note that organizational climate would be considered a Level 2 predictor because the Level 1 scores are nested within organizations. Hence, one could determine whether organizational climate directly explains mean organizational differences in job satisfaction and whether the relationship between pay and satisfaction differs as a function of climate. The hypothesis might be that favorable climates enhance satisfaction and weaken the relationship between pay and satisfaction.

Thus, HLM offers the ability to link predictors at multiple levels of analysis with a dependent variable at a lower level of analysis. In the following section, some examples of research questions are provided in which HLM is most appropriate and necessary.

COMMON INDUSTRIAL AND ORGANIZATIONAL RESEARCH QUESTIONS THAT REQUIRE HLM

Hierarchical linear modeling is not necessary or even appropriate for all research questions. As reviewers and readers of the literature, we believe it is sometimes overused. In this section, examples illustrate HLM when it is most appropriate. For the sake of brevity, two major categories of applications of HLM will be considered, as well as the substantial research questions that can be addressed.

The first type of application supports a *mixed-determinants model*. This is the model described in Figure 1, which illustrates situations in which the dependent variable or criterion is at the lowest level of analysis and the independent variables or predictors are at the same or higher levels. In this case, the higher-level variable explains between-group and between-organization variance, and the lower-level variable explains within-group and within-organization variance. With regard to these models, researchers have identified four primary research questions that can be answered by HLM: (a) Does the unit in which individuals work make a difference? (b) What is the impact of individual differences across units? (c) Are individuals influenced by characteristics of the unit? and (d) Do unit properties modify individual-level relationships?

The second type of application in which HLM has proved useful is the analysis of longitudinal data. Longitudinal research questions are multilevel questions because the repeated observations within a person over time (Level 1) are nested within a person (Level 2). Such models are called *growth curve models*, and they need not occur only at the individual level; any repeated observations within a person, group, or organization can be modeled using growth models. Key questions of interest with growth models include the following: (a) Do individual differences change over time (intraindividual change)? (b) What pattern of change does the outcome variable follow over time (e.g., linear, nonlinear)? (c) Are there between-person differences in the change patterns (interindividual differences in intraindividual change)? and (d) Why are there individual differences in the change patterns? The advantage of applying HLM to these longitudinal models comes from its capability to simultaneously analyze intraindividual and interindividual differences, handle missing data and unequal measurement periods, and model correlated errors.

For example, one may want to understand how performance changes over time and the factors that explain this performance change. Suppose a researcher hypothesizes that (a) performance will follow a curvilinear pattern over time; (b) there are significant individual differences in performance change over time; and (c) personality explains these individual differences in patterns of change. In this situation, the Level 1 model has the repeated performance observations as the criterion and time as the independent variable (time may be structured in a variety of ways to test different patterns of change). Provided there are individual differences in patterns of change, we can determine whether these differences are explained by the Level 2 personality predictor.

SUMMARY

Although the origins of HLM can be traced back to decades of educational research, its applications in industrial/organizational psychology and organizational behavior have just begun to appear. Yet the timing could not be better: We now fully realize that many organizational phenomena are inherently nested and hierarchical. Hierarchical linear modeling has already been applied to such diverse topics as modeling the interaction between the individual and situation, understanding the dynamic nature of performance criteria, and illustrating the moderating effects of leadership climate, to name just a few examples. This technique is not a solution for all such questions; rather, it is most useful for questions in which the predictors exist at multiple levels and the criterion exists at the lowest level of analysis (this is true in both mixed-determinants models and growth models). These questions are frequently of great interest to organizational scholars. Therefore, HLM will likely continue to grow in application and help us to test our multilevel theories of organizational behavior.

—*Robert E. Ployhart and Adrian H. Pitariu*

See also Multilevel Modeling

FURTHER READING

Bliese, P. D. (2002). Multilevel random coefficient modeling in organizational research: Examples using SAS and S-PLUS. In F. Drasgow & N. Schmitt (Eds.), *Measuring and analyzing behavior in organizations: Advances in* measurement and data analysis (pp. 401–445). San Francisco: Jossey-Bass.

Bliese, P. D., & Ployhart, R. E. (2002). Growth modeling using random coefficient models: Model building, testing, and illustration. Organizational Research Methods, 5, 362–387.

Hofmann, D. A., Griffin, M. A., & Gavin, M. B. (2000). The application of hierarchical linear modeling to organizational research. In K. J. Klein & S. W. J. Kozlowski (Eds.), Multilevel theory, research, and methods in organizations: Foundations, extensions, and new directions (pp. 467–511). San Francisco: Jossey-Bass.

Klein, K. J., & Kozlowski, S. W. J. (2000). A multilevel approach to theory and research in organizations: Contextual, temporal, and emergent processes. In K. J. Klein & S. W. J. Kozlowski (Eds.), Multilevel theory, research, and methods in organizations: Foundations, extensions, and new directions (pp. 3–90). San Francisco: Jossey-Bass.

Ployhart, R. E., Holtz, B. C., & Bliese, P. D. (2002). Longitudinal data analysis: Applications of random coefficient modeling to leadership research. Leadership Quarterly, 13, 455–486.

Raudenbush, S. W., & Bryk, A. S. (2002). Hierarchical linear models: Applications and data analysis methods (2nd ed.). Newbury Park, CA: Sage.

MULTITRAIT–MULTIMETHOD MATRIX

In 1959, Donald T. Campbell and Donald W. Fiske published an article in the *Psychological Bulletin* that, approximately 30 years later, would become the most cited article in the history of the social sciences. By 1992, it had been cited more than 2,000 times by other authors, and a 2005 search of the Social Sciences Citation Index showed more than 4,000 citations. The subject of this article was a statistical tool known as the *multitrait–multimethod* (MTMM) *matrix*. An MTMM matrix is a matrix of correlation coefficients computed between each pair of a set of measures (the correlation coefficients indicate how strongly each pair of measures is related).

The correlation matrix is intended to evaluate psychological measures—it is used to help determine how well scores on the measures actually reflect the intended traits. For example, personality traits such as extroversion and conscientiousness are often measured by self-reports, but they could also be measured by reports from others (e.g., friends or coworkers). If all psychological measurements were perfectly accurate, we would not need to consider different methods because all would be identical. But measurements are never perfect; they can be influenced by a variety of factors in addition to the intended traits (e.g., a person's self-assessments of personality might partially reflect that person's idealized view of him- or herself instead of his or her actual personality). The MTMM matrix is designed to evaluate the extent to which measures are influenced by the intended traits versus other systematic factors, commonly referred to as *method effects*.

Industrial and organizational psychologists have made extensive use of the MTMM matrix. They have conducted large-scale reviews of MTMM studies of job affect and perceptions (using different standard surveys as methods), job performance ratings (using performance dimensions as traits and rating sources such as supervisors and peers as methods), and assessment centers (a set of exercises used to assess potential or current workers; the assessment dimensions serve as traits and the exercises serve as methods). Individual studies have focused on other topics, such as measuring personality. In many cases, the studies indicate substantial method variance—for example, job performance ratings are fairly heavily influenced by the perspective of the particular individual providing the ratings.

Computing the MTMM matrix begins with a study in which multiple traits are measured by multiple methods. This might mean that a sample of people are asked to complete a survey rating their own personality traits, and their personalities are also rated on the same survey by close friends and then again by coworkers. If, for example, five personality traits are measured by these three methods, there would be a total of 15 measures (five traits × three methods). The MTMM matrix can then be computed.

In their original paper, Campbell and Fiske described two main components of validity that, when taken together, provide information on the overall validity of the measures. One component is *convergent validity*. This means that two measures of the same trait, provided by different methods, should converge on the same conclusion. If ratings of personality are valid, then reports of extroversion by friends and coworkers should tend to agree about how extroverted the person is. A second criterion is *discriminant validity*.

This means that measures of different traits should be distinct. When rating someone's personality, a friend or coworker should distinguish between that person's extroversion and his or her conscientiousness.

Statistical evaluation of the MTMM matrix is fairly complex, and there is no consensus that there is any single best way to do it. Table 1 shows a sample matrix from Campbell and Fiske's 1959 article in which five personality traits are rated for clinical psychology students living together in teams and participating in assessment exercises. Ratings of personality were provided by staff members, teammates, and the students themselves.

Campbell and Fiske stated that convergent and discriminant validity could be evaluated using four criteria. The first criterion, intended to evaluate convergent validity, is that measures of the same traits by different methods should correlate reasonably highly. These correlations are shown in Table 1 (in the "validity diagonals") in bold. The staff–teammate same-trait, different-method correlations average .47, which seems reasonable. Convergence between self-ratings and the two other methods is lower; the mean correlations are .32 for staff–self and .30 for teammate–self. Convergent validity is therefore fairly good, at least for staff and teammate ratings.

The other three criteria are aimed at evaluating discriminant validity. The second criterion is that the same-trait, different-method correlations should be higher than the different-trait, different-method correlations that surround them (shown in Table 1 in regular font). This criterion is generally met in Table 1; same-trait, different-method correlations are almost always higher than the different-trait correlations in the same columns and rows (even for self-ratings). Third, the same-trait, different-method correlations (on the validity diagonals) should be higher than correlations for different traits measured by the same method. The different-trait, same-method correlations are shown in italics. Again, the MTMM matrix in Table 1 generally meets this criterion.

Fourth, the various sets of different-trait correlations should all show the same pattern of correlations. These sets include, for example, different-trait correlations for staff (near the top of the MTMM matrix), correlations between staff and teammates (below the staff correlations), and correlations between staff and self-ratings (below staff–teammate ratings). For example, in Table 1, all correlations between *assertive* and *cheerful* are positive, indicating that assertive people tend to be cheerful, whereas all correlations between *cheerful* and *serious* are negative, indicating a slight tendency for serious people to be less cheerful. Evaluation of this criterion is more subjective and involves comparing many correlations. Finally, the matrix in Table 1 was chosen by Campbell and Fiske because it demonstrates good convergent and discriminant validity. Many matrixes studied by industrial and organizational psychologists (and by researchers in other fields) have shown poorer results.

Recently, flaws in Campbell and Fiske's analysis procedures have been identified. For example, researchers have had to subjectively evaluate how well the criteria are met because there are no procedures for quantifying the criteria; the correlations in the matrix are influenced by how reliably the variables are measured; and there is no procedure for separating method effects from random errors of measurement. Since the publication of the original article in 1959, a variety of statistical methods have been suggested to overcome these problems. Currently, there is no consensus that there is any single best way to analyze MTMM matrixes, but one approach that has gained popularity is *confirmatory factor analysis*.

Confirmatory factor analysis provides quantitative methods for evaluating Campbell and Fiske's criteria, takes into account the reliability of the measures, and separates method effects from random errors. It deals with variation in each measure (e.g., ratings of extroversion), which simply means that some people are rated as more extroverted and others as less extroverted. This variation is conceived as a combination of three factors: (a) variation resulting from the trait (i.e., real differences in extroversion); (b) variation resulting from method effects (i.e., systematic factors unrelated to real differences—for example, a self-rater's desire to be extroverted rather than his or her actual extroversion); and (c) variation resulting from random factors (e.g., the rater's mood at the particular moment of rating).

The analysis estimates how much of the total variation results from each of the three factors. This is done separately for each measure by calculating the loadings of each measure on (a) its trait factor (e.g., a loading of an extroversion self-rating on the extroversion factor; extroversion ratings from other sources would also have loadings on this factor); (b) its method factor (all self-ratings, including the self-rating of extroversion, would load on the self method factor); and (c) a random factor (each measure has its own random factor).

Table 1 Multitrait–Multimethod Matrix Included in Campbell and Fiske's 1959 Article

		Staff Ratings					Teammate Ratings					Self-Ratings				
		A_1	B_1	C_1	D_1	E_1	A_1	B_1	C_1	D_1	E_1	A_1	B_1	C_1	D_1	E_1
Staff Ratings																
Assertive	A_1	1.00														
Cheerful	B_1	.37	1.00													
Serious	C_1	-.24	-.14	1.00												
Unshakable poise	D_1	.25	.46	.08	1.00											
Broad interests	E_1	.35	.19	.09	.31	1.00										
Teammate Ratings																
Assertive	A_1	**.71**	.35	-.18	.26	.41	1.00									
Cheerful	B_1	.39	**.53**	-.15	.38	.29	.37	1.00								
Serious	C_1	-.27	-.31	**.43**	-.06	.03	-.15	-.19	1.00							
Unshakable poise	D_1	.03	-.05	.03	**.20**	.07	.11	.23	.19	1.00						
Broad interests	E_1	.19	.05	.04	.29	**.47**	.33	.22	.19	.29	1.00					
Self-Ratings																
Assertive	A_1	**.48**	.31	-.22	.19	.12	**.46**	.36	-.15	.12	.23	1.00				
Cheerful	B_1	.17	**.42**	-.10	.10	-.03	.09	**.24**	-.25	-.11	-.03	.23	1.00			
Serious	C_1	-.04	-.13	**.22**	-.13	-.05	-.04	-.11	**.31**	.06	.06	-.05	-.12	1.00		
Unshakable poise	D_1	.13	.27	-.03	**.22**	-.04	.10	.15	.00	**.14**	-.03	.16	.26	.11	1.00	
Broad interests	E_1	.37	.15	-.22	.09	**.26**	.27	.12	-.07	.05	**.35**	.21	.15	.17	.31	1.00

499

The confirmatory factor analysis results provide information similar to that provided by Campbell and Fiske's criteria—for example, the higher the same-trait, different-method correlations, the higher the trait factor loadings will be, indicating convergent validity. The confirmatory approach removes subjectivity by using statistical significance testing to determine whether there is significant convergent validity (trait variance) and significant method variance. It also quantifies how large the trait versus method effects are. This information can be useful for determining how "good" a measure is and which measures need to be improved (generally speaking, it is desirable to have high trait effects and small method and random error effects).

The confirmatory factor analysis approach does have its shortcomings. The sources listed in the Further Reading section may be consulted for more information on this topic, as well as for other analysis methods.

—*Jim Conway*

See also Quantitative Research Approach

FURTHER READING

Campbell, D. T. (1992). Citations do not solve problems. *Psychological Bulletin, 112,* 393–395.

Campbell, D. T., & Fiske, D. W. (1959). Convergent and discriminant validation by the multitrait–multimethod matrix. *Psychological Bulletin, 56,* 81–105.

Kenny, D. A. (1995). The multitrait–multimethod matrix: Design, analysis, and conceptual issues. In P. E. Shrout and S. T. Fiske (Eds.), *Personality, research, methods, and theory: A festschrift honoring Donald W. Fiske* (pp. 111–124). Hillsdale, NJ: Lawrence Erlbaum.

Lance, C. E., Noble, C. L., & Scullen, S. E. (2002). A critique of the correlated trait-correlated method and correlated uniqueness models for multitrait–multimethod data. *Psychological Methods, 7,* 228–244.

Marsh, H. W. (1989). Confirmatory factor analyses of multitrait–multimethod data: Many problems and a few solutions. *Applied Psychological Measurement, 13,* 335–361.

Schmitt, N., & Stults, D. M. (1986). Methodology review: Analysis of multitrait–multimethod matrices. *Applied Psychological Measurement, 10,* 1–22.

NATIONAL INSTITUTE FOR OCCUPATIONAL SAFETY AND HEALTH/OCCUPATIONAL SAFETY AND HEALTH ADMINISTRATION

The U.S. Congress passed the Occupational Safety and Health Act of 1970, which resulted in the formation of two federal agencies: the National Institute for Occupational Safety and Health (NIOSH) and the Occupational Safety and Health Administration (OSHA). These agencies were established to reduce and prevent work-related injuries, illnesses, and deaths. Although both organizations focus on work-related health issues, they serve distinct purposes and are located in different branches of the U.S. government. Often, NIOSH and OSHA work together in an effort to protect worker health and safety.

NATIONAL INSTITUTE FOR OCCUPATIONAL SAFETY AND HEALTH (NIOSH)

As part of the Centers for Disease Control and Prevention in the U.S. Department of Health and Human Services, NIOSH was established to conduct research and make recommendations pertaining to work-related injury and illness prevention. Headquartered in Washington, D.C., NIOSH has offices and research laboratories in Cincinnati, Ohio; Morgantown, West Virginia; Pittsburgh, Pennsylvania; and Spokane, Washington. Although all research facilities assess occupational health, most of the NIOSH investigations on occupational stress are conducted by researchers at the Cincinnati office. In 1996, NIOSH

and more than 500 partners developed the National Occupational Research Agenda (NORA), which identified 21 priority areas (e.g., traumatic injury, work-related musculoskeletal symptoms) to guide research in the occupational safety and health community.

Organizational Composition

Of NIOSH's more than 1,400 employees, many are research staff. Researchers at NIOSH work in multidisciplinary teams, representing a wide range of disciplines, such as epidemiology, industrial hygiene, occupational medicine, psychology, ergonomics, engineering, chemistry, and statistics. The institute is organized in nine research divisions:

- *Pittsburgh Research Laboratory:* addresses the safety and health hazards of mining (e.g., coal) and disaster prevention (e.g., mine ventilation, explosives safety)
- *Spokane Research Laboratory:* addresses mine safety and health, primarily in the metal and non-metal mining sector (e.g., detection/prevention of collapse of mine roofs)
- *Division of Applied Research and Technology:* aimed at preventing occupational injury and illness; assesses intervention effectiveness; examines ergonomic and organization of work factors (e.g., psychosocial factors) in work-related illness and injury
- *Division of Surveillance, Hazard Evaluations and Field Studies:* conducts systematic, ongoing research to examine patterns of work-related illnesses, exposures, and hazardous agents in the U.S. workforce; studies the causes of work-related diseases; provides technical help on occupational safety and health issues to other organizations

- *Education and Information Division:* creates/disseminates information; makes recommendations to prevent occupational injuries/diseases; develops risk assessments
- *Division of Respiratory Disease Studies:* aims to identify, evaluate, and prevent occupational respiratory diseases (e.g., asthma); administers legislatively mandated medical services for coal miners; researches the quality of respiratory devices
- *Division of Safety Research:* takes a public health approach to occupational injury prevention (including traumatic occupational injuries); incorporates surveillance, analytic epidemiology, safety engineering, and health communication
- *Health Effects Laboratory Division:* conducts laboratory research (e.g., on causes, prevention, and control of biological health problems resulting from workplace exposure to hazardous substances); develops interventions; designs, tests, and implements communications to control and prevent workplace safety/health problems
- *National Personal Protective Technology Laboratory:* aims to prevent and reduce occupational disease, injury, and death for workers who use personal protective technologies (e.g., respirators, chemical-resistant clothing)

Mission

The mission of NIOSH is to help assure safe and healthful conditions for workers by providing research, information, education, and training in occupational safety and health. To accomplish this mission, NIOSH has three primary objectives: (a) to conduct research in an effort to reduce work-related injuries and illnesses; (b) to encourage the safety and health of workplaces through interventions, offering recommendations and building capabilities in safe work practices and conditions; and (c) to enhance workplace safety and health around the world through international collaborations.

Functions

To further its mission, NIOSH engages in both intramural and extramural programs, which are aligned to increase research in the NORA priority areas. Intramural programs include the research conducted at the nine NIOSH research divisions described previously. Extramural programs provide opportunities for researchers at other institutions to conduct quality research, receive education and training, and develop worldwide collaborations in the area of occupational safety and health. As part of its extramural program, NIOSH sponsors 16 Education and Research Centers (ERCs) and 35 Training Project Grants to enhance the training of occupational safety and health professionals and researchers. Some of the ERCs offer competitive pilot grants for doctoral students and junior faculty who conduct research related to occupational health and safety. The ERCs also provide continuing education programs for practicing professionals.

The Agricultural Centers Program also was established by NIOSH and is a national resource for agricultural health and safety problems by means of education, research, prevention, and interventions. More than 370 collaborative programs were established across the country via regional NIOSH Agricultural Centers and other regional and national agricultural agencies.

In addition, NIOSH runs state programs to enhance worker safety and health. Activities include grants and cooperative agreements to build competencies in state worker safety, evaluating hazards in the workplace and recommending solutions when requested, funding occupational safety and health research at academic institutions and other organizations, and supporting occupational safety and health training programs.

Further, the NIOSH Web site offers information on occupational health, including NIOSH publications, access to databases, and information on specific topics related to occupational safety and health. Also, NIOSH communicates occupational safety and health information in Spanish.

OCCUPATIONAL SAFETY AND HEALTH ADMINISTRATION (OSHA)

Established in 1971, OSHA is a regulatory agency for worker safety and health protection in the U.S. Department of Labor. By providing leadership and encouragement to organizations, OSHA seeks to help them recognize and understand the value of safety and health at work. Under the Occupational Safety and Health Act of 1970, OSHA is authorized to conduct workplace inspections and investigations to assess the extent to which employers comply with the standards issued by OSHA for safe and healthy workplaces. The national office is located in Washington, D.C., and 26 states also run their own OSHA state programs.

Employees and Divisions

The Occupational Safety and Health Administration has more than 2,300 employees, including more than 1,100 inspectors, complaint discrimination investigators, physicians, standards writers, engineers, and educators, as well as other technical and support staff. The agency and its state affiliates have more than 200 offices in the United States and are organized in terms of 10 directorates. Aside from the three directorates that serve primarily administrative or support functions (e.g., public affairs, technical support), the directorates include the following:

- *Directorate of Construction:* works with the construction industry on engineering issues to improve safety and health awareness and reduce fatalities, injuries, and illnesses
- *Directorate of Cooperative and State Programs:* develops, recommends, and implements policies and procedures; coordinates programs that support OSHA's cooperative efforts (e.g., compliance assistance, small business assistance)
- *Directorate of Enforcement Programs:* establishes and maintains a comprehensive occupational safety and health compliance guidance and assistance program, as well as discrimination complaint investigation programs
- *Directorate of Evaluation and Analysis:* provides advice and recommendations to the assistant secretary for occupational safety and health and OSHA program directors based on evaluations, analyses, and studies it conducts in support of OSHA activities
- *Directorate of Science, Technology, and Medicine:* provides expertise on scientific, engineering, and medical issues pertaining to occupational safety and health; provides technical assistance and support to OSHA national and regional offices
- *Directorate of Standards and Guidance:* develops workplace standards, regulations, and guidance that are feasible, addresses significant workplace risks, and considers the potential effects of standards on the economy, affected industries, and small businesses
- *Regional Administrators, Occupational Safety and Health Administration:* plans, directs, and administers a comprehensive occupational safety and health program throughout the 10 U.S. regions and U.S. territories

Mission

The mission of OSHA is to assure the safety and health of America's workers by setting and enforcing standards; providing training, outreach, and education; establishing partnerships; and encouraging continuous improvement in workplace safety and health. These strategies are authorized by the Occupational Safety and Health Act to help organizations reduce work-related illnesses, injuries, and deaths.

Functions

The primary function of OSHA is to establish standards for protection from work-related safety and health hazards, enforce those standards, and provide consultations and technical support to employers and employees. Nearly every type of worker is included within OSHA's jurisdiction, with a few exceptions (e.g., miners, transportation workers, many public employees, and the self-employed).

The agency promotes workplace safety and health through a variety of activities in pursuit of its mission (i.e., enforcement, outreach/education, and partnerships). In terms of enforcement, OSHA develops mandatory job safety and health standards and enforces them through worksite inspections, by providing assistance to employers, and by imposing citations and/or penalties. More than 39,000 federal inspections were conducted in fiscal year 2004, with more than half conducted in the construction industry. The penalty for violating an OSHA standard ranges from $0 to $70,000, depending on the likelihood that the violation could result in serious harm to employees. In addition to conducting inspections, OSHA establishes rights and responsibilities for employers and employees to reach better safety and health conditions. Further, the agency maintains a system to report and maintain records to monitor job-related injuries and illnesses.

In terms of outreach, education, and compliance assistance, OSHA establishes training programs to increase the competence of occupational safety and health professionals and to educate employers to reduce accidents and injuries. Also, OSHA supports the development of new methods of reducing workplace hazards and encourages organizations to reduce hazardous conditions (e.g., by applying new safety and health management systems or improving existing programs). Other sources of education include OSHA's Web site (www.osha.org), which offers publications and interactive e-tools to help organizations address specific hazards and prevent injuries, a hotline for workplace safety and health information and assistance, and Spanish-language services (e.g., Web page, publications).

In addition, OSHA has cooperative programs, partnerships, and alliances to promote the safety and health of workplaces. For instance, OSHA partners with states that operate their own occupational safety and health programs, and it provides a consultation service regarding workplace safety and health issues.

—Jennifer Burnfield

See also Occupational Health Psychology

FURTHER READING

National Institute for Occupational Safety and Health. (2005, June). Retrieved March 29, 2006, from http://www.cdc.gov/niosh

Occupational Safety and Health Administration. (2003). *All about OSHA: Occupational Safety and Health Administration* (OSHA 2056-07R). Washington, DC: U.S. Department of Labor. Retrieved March 29, 2006, from http://www.osha.gov/Publications/osha2056.pdf

Occupational Safety and Health Administration. (2004, December). *OSHA facts.* Retrieved March 29, 2006, from http://www.osha.gov

NATURALISTIC OBSERVATION

Observational techniques, a cornerstone of the qualitative research paradigm, can be divided into two main categories: participant and naturalistic observation. *Naturalistic observation* is a method of collecting information in a setting in which the behavior of interest occurs, typically unbeknownst to the targets of observation. Naturalistic observation is often used by ethnographers examining cultural behavior, organizational development researchers, and program evaluators. The hallmark of naturalistic observation is the lack of intrusion by the researcher into the setting and behavior of interest. An example of naturalistic observation would be a training program evaluator watching the content of the training and participant observations through closed-circuit television to assess comprehensiveness of the training program. In this example, the participants are not aware of the observer and, as such, do not shift their behavior to make a favorable impression.

Participant observation is the other broad category of observational techniques and can take one of three forms:

- *Complete participant.* The researcher conceals his or her role to more fully examine the issue of interest.
- *Observer as participant.* The role of the researcher is known to those being observed.
- *Participant as observer.* The research function performed by the observer is secondary to his or her role as a participant in the actions and behaviors.

In all of these cases, the researcher's role as an observer is overt and may influence the behaviors of those being observed.

KEY ELEMENTS FOR CONDUCTING A NATURALISTIC OBSERVATION STUDY

As with any research design, decisions regarding the specific methods and scope of the study must be made. However, a number of decisions are unique to observational research:

1. *Level of involvement* of the researcher/observer depends on the nature and sensitivity of behaviors to be observed. Naturalistic observation is better suited to settings in which a researcher's presence might change the behavior (e.g., Western Electric employees in the Hawthorne studies). Participant observation may be more suited to those situations in which actively performing the behavior of interest lends a higher level of understanding to the researcher (e.g., understanding job content in the process of job analysis).

2. *Amount of collaboration* in the coding process depends on the setting of the observation (e.g., is it feasible to involve multiple coders?). The inclusion of two or more coders allows the research team to assess the interobserver reliability of their observations.

3. *Length of time* for observation of behaviors depends on the goal of the study. There are three general sampling frames for observational research: (a) Time sampling, in which the behavior is observed for a set period of time (e.g., 3 days); (b) point sampling, in which one individual or group is observed before moving on to the next individual or group of interest (e.g., observing the training department in one plant before moving to a different plant); and (c) event sampling, in which an event is observed every time it occurs (e.g., observing the administration of annual performance appraisals).

4. *Focus and nature of the observation* depends on the specific research question. The narrower the focus, the easier it will likely be to code the behaviors reliably and efficiently using a structured approach. Broader, unstructured context examinations (e.g., narratives) may be better suited for descriptive studies in the nascent stage of a research area.

The design of a naturalistic observation study relies on clarity in goals and measurement to target the behaviors of interest to adequately address the research questions. Because the behaviors of interest are occurring in their natural context, the researcher must be able to adeptly classify and interpret only relevant behaviors. For this reason, operationalization of behaviors is critical. The creation of a comprehensive coding sheet and training on the coding of behaviors is critical to ensure that behaviors are accurately captured.

Depending on the type of data collected during the observation period, analysis remains qualitative or turns to a more quantitative approach. If structured observation was used with behavioral checklists, descriptive statistical information may be compiled (e.g., frequencies). If the focus was broader and unstructured, narrative reviews may tell the story of the behavior in context.

RELIABILITY AND VALIDITY OF NATURALISTIC OBSERVATION

Interobserver reliability is the only way to assess the consistency of behavioral coding in a naturalistic observation study. For this reason, it is critical to include multiple coders in an effort to demonstrate a lack of observer bias. However, calculation of interobserver reliability is only feasible when using structured and systematic observation. If an unstructured method is used, demonstration of consistency in observation is very difficult.

In terms of validity, naturalistic observation sacrifices internal for ecological validity. Because the behaviors observed occur in context with no interference from researchers, the extent to which the behaviors observed in this naturalistic setting mimic the "real world" is very high. However, because the observer does not interact with or participate in the context of behavior, there is no control of potentially influencing variables. To link internal and ecological validity, an observational study may be used to replicate and/or extend findings from a laboratory study on the same topic.

ADVANTAGES AND DISADVANTAGES OF NATURALISTIC OBSERVATION

The benefits of naturalistic observation research are numerous. Specifically, naturalistic observation allows researchers to examine behaviors directly in context without interference, thus providing a foundation for understanding the environmental conditions associated with the issues of interest. This is especially true when the topic under investigation is very sensitive or the presence of the researcher would likely influence behavior.

Beyond the time commitment required to conduct this type of research, the disadvantages of naturalistic observation center on three main issues: reliability, validity, and ethics. Because observation is an inherently perceptual process, bias can be introduced in the coding and interpretation of observational results in a number of ways (e.g., coding the behavior, interpreting results). Therefore, some question the accuracy of observation records (e.g., checklists, narrative reviews) and disregard their value as contextual markers.

As previously discussed, because the observer does not influence the situation, the influence of extraneous variables on the behaviors of interest cannot be assessed (e.g., no internal validity). The real-world aspect of the data may be high, but without the knowledge and/or control of influential variables affecting these behaviors, the value of the research may be limited.

Because of the unobtrusiveness of the researcher in naturalistic observation, informed consent cannot be given by participants. Under American Psychological Association (APA) guidelines, informed consent procedures do not need to be initiated when there is no expectation of harm to the participant as a result of the research.

However, the application of this standard has been controversial (e.g., R. D. Middlemist and colleagues' study of personal space invasions in the lavatory). Institutional review boards should provide guidance in the interpretation of waived informed consent for naturalistic studies.

—*Jennifer P. Bott*

See also Qualitative Research Approach

FURTHER READING

Creswell, J. W. (1994). *Research design: Qualitative and quantitative approaches.* Thousand Oaks, CA: Sage.

Denzin, N. K., & Lincoln, Y. S. (2000). *Handbook of qualitative research* (2nd ed.). Thousand Oaks, CA: Sage.

Middlemist, R. D., Knowles, E. S., & Matter, C. F. (1977). Personal space invasions in the lavatory: Suggestive evidence for arousal. *Journal of Personality and Social Psychology, 35*(2), 122–124.

Patton, M. Q. (2002). *Qualitative research and evaluation methods* (3rd ed.). Thousand Oaks, CA: Sage.

NEED FOR ACHIEVEMENT, POWER, AND AFFILIATION

The need for achievement, power, and affiliation are three primary types of motives or motivational drives that influence a broad spectrum of behavior, from how one interacts on an interpersonal level to one's choice of and/or success in an occupation. These motives can be either *implicit*—that is, developed prior to the formation of language in the developing infant—or *self-attributed,* meaning they developed as a result of social and cultural influences. With an understanding of these sources of motivation, one can predict occupational performance and managerial success; design jobs and provide incentives most suited to an employee's type of motivation; determine the contexts in which employees will be most successful; and design training programs to enhance employee performance.

Implicit motives indicate the generalized orientation of an individual's motivation, whereas self-attributed motives indicate the context or under what circumstances the motive will find expression. Implicit motives are not readily recognizable to individuals, existing on a more subconscious level of awareness, and are associated with primary emotions such as anger, sadness, love, and happiness. These motives are measured by arousing them with stimuli that are associated with each motive in the form of pictures for which an individual writes a story that describes what he or she imagines is occurring in the picture. The tool used for this purpose is referred to as the Thematic Apperception Test (TAT), consisting of a series of pictures designed to elicit the three implicit motives. Alternately, self-attributed motives or needs, referred to with the subscript *san* (for "self-attributed need"), are related to motives that one would consciously characterize oneself as having and are associated with behavior that is normative for a culture or group. They are measured best with self-report measures, because they are motives individuals would ascribe to themselves.

Implicit motives are useful for predicting long-term behavioral tendencies, whereas self-attributed motives are more useful for predicting short-term behavior that is contextually specific and more related to a conscious choice on the part of the individual. Implicit motives are more readily aroused by task incentives (i.e., a moderately difficult task for someone high in need for achievement), whereas self-attributed motives are aroused by more explicit social incentives (i.e., a task that can earn prestige for someone high in *san*Power). Measuring both types of motives together enhances the ability to predict a person's behavior beyond the individual measurement of either implicit or self-attributed motives alone.

NEED FOR ACHIEVEMENT

The *need for achievement* is defined as a continual striving for excellence, improvement in performance, and innovation. Those high in this need tend to take intermediate risks and prefer moderate challenges, ones that are not too easy yet ensure some measure of success. Individuals high in need for achievement (nAch) are more persistent in attaining goals and exert more effort when engaged in tasks than those who are low in nAch. Additionally, those high in nAch often attribute success to ability and failure to lack of effort, whereas those low in nAch attribute failure to lack of ability.

Occupationally, people high in nAch are ideally suited for entrepreneurial types of employment because of their preferences for being individually responsible for relevant outcomes, having the ability to select their own goals, the freedom to work toward their goals in a manner of their own choosing, and a desire for more immediate feedback that occurs often and is related to mastery (i.e., proficiency at completing a task). Their ability to readily obtain and use new information may also contribute to entrepreneurial success. Working environments that are less restrictive and allow greater autonomy in terms of procedures and work outcomes are contexts in which the high nAch individual will be most successful. High achievement motivation is associated with rapidity of promotions and increases in salary, in addition to future projections of income being greater for those high in nAch as compared with individuals with low nAch. Of the three motives, nAch can be increased through learning or training, with the result being increases in managerial effort, sales performance, and academic success.

Given the desirable qualities of this motive, employers may be inclined to facilitate it in employees. To do so, employers must be aware that those high in nAch are motivated by the task itself and will perform best if given a moderately challenging task with few procedural and/or organizational constraints, performance feedback, and a goal that is future oriented (i.e., one that will help them achieve a desired future goal). Those high in *san*Ach will be more responsive to a working environment that encourages achievement and provides tangible rewards for an employee's efforts. If there is no external incentive, those high in *san*Ach will demonstrate decreases in performance, whereas those high in nAch (as well as those low in nAch) will not be responsive to external incentives.

There are two paths that direct the energies of an aroused motive toward behavioral expression, and these are polar in nature. The positive path is the motive to achieve success and is theorized to have resulted from positive parental reinforcement for achievement behavior demonstrated by the developing child. The negative path is the motive to avoid failure, which is theorized to result from punishment of the developing child for lack of achievement. Both paths result in need for achievement but have different behavioral manifestations. For example, people who have high nAch tend to persist at difficult tasks when the motive to avoid failure is greater than the motive to achieve success, whereas when the motive to achieve success is greater than the need to avoid failure, people persist at easier tasks. Furthermore, those high in nAch and low in the motive to avoid failure tend to be optimistic about success, set realistic performance goals, and persist in tasks unless there is a minimal chance of success. Those who are low in nAch and high in the motive to avoid failure tend to avoid tasks that will be evaluated and choose easy tasks or ones that are so difficult, few could successfully accomplish them.

NEED FOR POWER

The *need for power* is defined as the desire to have an impact on or influence another person or situation. Those high in need for power have a strong concern for reputation and engage in activities that are highly visible and designed to garner prestige. For them, power needs to be of a direct and interpersonal nature, often legitimized by social systems. People high in need for power tend to have careers such as executives, teachers, journalists, and clergy—careers that afford one the ability to have influence over others. Often, the most successful managers and executives are characterized by a high need for power. Leaders who have high power motivation tend to create high morale in their subordinates, although they may not be generally liked by others (the need for power is negatively correlated with the need for affiliation).

The power motive, like the achievement motive, is characterized by two polarized aspects, personal power and social power. Personal power is more associated with the negative aspects of power and is characterized by aggressiveness and competitiveness, exploitation of others, excessive indulgence, relationship discord, and decreases in immune system function. Personal power is most associated with a fear of powerlessness, whereas social power is related to the motivation to influence. Social power is characterized by a concern for social, group, or organizational benefit and is less egoistic in nature. The degree to which individuals are more oriented to personal versus social power is contingent on their level of responsibility or activity inhibition. Those who have a high need for power and a high level of activity inhibition display more of the behavior associated with social power and fewer of the destructive tendencies characteristic of personal power.

NEED FOR AFFILIATION

The *need for affiliation* is defined as the desire to establish, maintain, and/or restore positive affective relationships. Those high in need for affiliation spend more time interacting with others, express more of a desire to be with others (as opposed to those low in this need), more readily learn social networks, tend to be more accommodating to others, and avoid situations that are characterized by interpersonal conflict. Individuals high in this need prefer to work with friends (rather than with experts, who are popular with those high in nAch), to have relationship-oriented feedback, and to work in supportive contexts. Compared with people low in this motive, those high in need for affiliation tend to interact more with others whom they like, like those with whom they interact more, and interact with and like those who are more similar to them in terms of values, attitudes, and beliefs. They are more likely to cooperate with and adopt the views of individuals whom they like and tend to dislike people dissimilar to themselves.

The two polar aspects of need for affiliation are a desire for inclusion and a fear of rejection. The affiliation motive has been shown to be a poor predictor of social success, because it is essentially a measure of fear of rejection. People with high need for affiliation are no better at developing and maintaining quality relationships than people low in need for affiliation. This is likely because of the need for affiliation being related to actively striving for a relationship, which could result from being unable to have meaningful or successful relationships. A new motivational conceptualization called *need for intimacy* has been shown to be a better predictor of interpersonal and social success. The need for affiliation should be viewed as a measure of anxiety related to affiliation and concern about rejection.

—*Jason R. Williams*

See also Intrinsic and Extrinsic Work Motivation; Motivational Traits; Need Theories of Work Motivation

FURTHER READING

McClelland, D. C. (1985). How motives, skills, and values determine what people do. *American Psychologist, 40*(7), 812–825.

McClelland, D. C., & Burnham, D. H. (2003). Power is the great motivator. *Harvard Business Review, 81,* 117–123.

Smith, C. P. (Ed.). (1992). *Motivation and personality: Handbook of thematic content analysis.* Cambridge, England: University Press.

Stahl, M. J. (1986). *Managerial and technical motivation: Assessing needs for achievement, power, and affiliation.* New York: Praeger.

Winter, D. G. (1996). *Personality: Analysis and interpretation of lives.* New York: McGraw-Hill.

Winter, D. G. (1998). The contributions of David McClelland to personality assessment. *Journal of Personality Assessment, 71*(2), 129–145.

NEED THEORIES OF WORK MOTIVATION

Among the best-known theories of work motivation in both academic and applied settings are models predicated on the assumption that, at root, humans are need-driven creatures, most of whose behavior can best be understood by examining their need states and identifying the goals or goal states they seek to satisfy their needs.

WHAT IS A NEED?

A variety of definitions of *need* have been offered, but the one favored by the author is attributable to Henry A. Murray. In his 1938 book *Explorations in Personality,* Murray wrote, first, that need is a hypothetical construct, not a physical entity: We cannot assess it directly or determine its color. It has no physical mass, density, or specific gravity. Second, Murray's definition also implies that a person in a state of need feels a force that activates and helps to direct him or her. Third, according to Murray, needs can be aroused by characteristics of the environment. A fourth feature of Murray's definition is that it helps us understand approach behaviors as well as avoidance behaviors. Needs are also tightly connected with emotions, although whether there are one-to-one connections between particular needs and specific emotions is still being examined by psychologists.

NEEDS AND BEHAVIOR

Perhaps the most important point in Murray's definition has to do with the connection between needs and behavior. A number of points need elaboration here. First, not all need-driven, goal-oriented behavior is successful in reaching the goals sought. The result is defined as frustration, and sometimes fantasy must suffice to quell the force generated by a need. Nevertheless, observing behavior as a means to infer a person's needs can be a tricky proposition. One reason for this difficulty is that most needs, except for the most basic biological ones, are said to be overdetermined—that is, instigated and directed by more than one motive. Hence, any behavior, such as quitting a job, may be motivated by the frustration of many needs, as well as by the attraction of an alternative job that may help to satisfy those frustrated needs and even satisfy other needs. Moreover, different people may seek the satisfaction of a common need through different behaviors. Jon may seek a leadership position in his union to satisfy power and affiliation needs, whereas Marie may coach junior hockey to satisfy her needs for power and affiliation. In short, there is a complex relationship between needs and behavior, and we frequently project our own need state or behavior state onto others, assuming that others behave the same way(s) we do when in need.

Consider the difficulty involved in making inferences about the need(s) that determine a person's behavior. First, as previously mentioned, most motivated behavior is said to be *overdetermined,* meaning that deliberately or inadvertently, behavior is driven by the force to satisfy more than one need.

For example, an employee might seek a promotion for the sake of meeting several needs (although the person may be more conscious of the importance of some of them than others). The same need may be satisfied by any of a variety of acts. So our upwardly aspiring employee may in part be seeking greater satisfaction of esteem needs. Notice that gaining a promotion is one way—but only one way—to meet esteem needs. Volunteer service after hours or becoming president of the employees' union are alternative behaviors that might be employed. In short, there is no one-to-one relationship between the force of a particular need and the type of behavior observed. To complicate matters, there is a common tendency for people to *project* their own need-behavior styles into their interpretations of the behavior. (For example, one might conclude that a friend accepted a position at the grocery store rather than a flower shop because it is closer to his or her house. Here, the mistake would be attributing to the friend a preference for short commutes to work, mostly because the person making the attribution hates to commute long distances to work!)

NEED SATISFACTION

Need satisfaction is usually thought of as the feeling of relief or reduced tension that occurs after a goal has been attained or an act has been accomplished (e.g., a funny stomach following a favorite meal). In the case of certain needs, however, satisfaction may consist more of the experience one has while in the process of *reducing* the tension. Continuing our example, satisfaction consists of both the joy of eating and the state of having eaten. Moreover, greater satisfaction can occur when more tension is reduced, so people may be motivated to deprive themselves of gratification (within safe limits) so that they can experience greater subsequent satisfaction from the process of need fulfillment. Sexual foreplay illustrates this principle, as does the notion of not eating lunch to ensure that one has a strong appetite for a special dinner.

TYPOLOGIES OF NEEDS

Much of the modern work on need theory has been devoted to making categories of needs. David McClelland, a student of Murray, spent much of his career pursuing the measurement and behavioral significance of three particular needs: power, affiliation, and achievement. Early work in this tradition suffered from problems of measurement, inasmuch as it relied heavily on the use of projective techniques to assess the strength of these needs in individuals. Nevertheless, the tradition started by McClelland and his colleagues has revealed considerable insight into the power–need profiles of effective and ineffective leaders and managers. McClelland and D. G. Winter even demonstrated in 1969 how the levels of achievement orientation in a society relate to its prosperity, and they had some success in developing achievement motivation in Third World countries, resulting in increased levels of entrepreneurial behavior in those countries.

HIERARCHICAL THEORIES

McClelland never suggested any relationships among his need categories, whereas another famous American psychologist, Abraham Maslow, did. His 1943 hierarchical theory of human motivation is among the most paradoxical approaches to work motivation. On the one hand, it is one of the most familiar theories among academics and practitioners, as noted by J. B. Miner in 2003. On the other hand, it is likely the most misunderstood and most frequently oversimplified and misrepresented. For decades after it was proposed, the theory enjoyed only mixed and poor evidence of scientific validity. But it has remained popular nevertheless.

Maslow's theory holds that there are basically five categories of human needs and that these needs account for much or most of human behavior. The needs vary in their relative *prepotency,* or urgency for the survival of the individual, arranging themselves in a hierarchical order of importance. As the most prepotent needs become reasonably satisfied, the less prepotent ones (the higher-order needs) become increasingly important for causing behavior.

The most prepotent needs in the theory are physiological in nature. They function in a homeostatic fashion, such that imbalances or deficiencies in certain physiological substances instigate behavior aimed at restoring the balance by filling the deficiencies. Hunger, sex, and thirst are three examples of such needs. Next come the physiological needs, or so-called security needs. When unfulfilled, they possess the same sort of potential for dominating a person's behavior as the physiological needs do when they are not being met. Later versions of this model have often combined these two categories into one set, arguing that need frustration or a threat is equally powerful in instigating and directing behavior, whether posed at the physiological or security level.

The *love needs* are next in importance; that is, they take on comparatively more influence in behavior as the physiological and safety needs are reasonably satisfied. The individual desires relations with other people, and he or she will feel more compelled than before to achieve such relations. Feelings of loneliness, ostracism, rejection, and friendlessness will become more acute. Maslow claimed in 1954 that the thwarting of the love needs is at the root of many cases of maladjustment. The theory claims that people need both to give and to receive love, and that social interactions need not be cordial to satisfy these needs.

The *esteem needs* are the next most prepotent category in the hierarchy. Maslow groups them into two sets: one includes desires for strength, achievement, adequacy, mastery and competence, independence, freedom, and a fundamental confidence in facing the world. The second set consists of needs for prestige and reputation—the esteem of others. It motivates people to seek recognition, praise, dominance, glory, and the attention of other people.

The esteem needs are seen as less prepotent than the highest set of needs on the hierarchy—the so-called *need for self-actualization*. In his various writings, Maslow provided differing interpretations of the meaning of this need, but the clearest and most widely accepted view is that it consists of a requirement for individuals to fulfill their potentials, to become that which they are capable of becoming. An important feature of self-actualization needs is that they express themselves in different behaviors in different people. Moreover, the satisfaction of self-actualization needs tends to *increase* their importance rather than reduce it—they become somewhat addictive. This difference between self-actualization and the other needs in the hierarchy makes it the most unusual. These are the primary elements of Maslow's theory. More detailed descriptions and interpretations of the research into the theory were given by C. C. Pinder in 1998.

EXISTENCE, RELATEDNESS, AND GROWTH

About the time Maslow completed his writings about human needs, in 1972, Harold Alderfer generated and tested an alternative to Maslow's model, the theory of *existence, relatedness, and growth*. This model has its roots in Maslow's work, as well as in the theory and research of a number of other psychologists before Maslow who had been concerned with human motivation.

The theory posits three general categories of human needs, categories similar to, and partly derived from, those in Maslow's model. All of the needs are seen as primary, meaning they are innate to human nature, rather than learned, although learning increases their strength.

The first set in the model is referred to as the *existence* needs. They correspond closely to the physiological and security needs Maslow associated with species survival. Research by Alderfer and others justifies combining them into a single category.

Similarly, the goals typically sought by people to satisfy what Maslow calls *love needs* are fundamentally the same as those that are necessary to provide for the need for prestige or the esteem of others, as well as for the interpersonal-security needs included in the second level of Maslow's hierarchy. Successful satisfaction of each of the needs identified by Maslow requires interaction with other human beings and the development of meaningful relationships with others. Moreover, each of these three varieties of social needs, on a logical level at least, seem equally important, or prepotent. Therefore, these specific Maslovian needs are combined by Alderfer as the *relatedness* needs. Alderfer's third category roughly combines Maslow's concepts of self-esteem and self-actualization into a category he calls the *growth* needs.

CURRENT ASSESSMENT OF NEED THEORIES OF WORK MOTIVATION

As mentioned, decades of research following the publication of Maslow's work were not very encouraging. It took a while even to establish the distinctiveness of the categories. Cross-cultural work by Simcha Ronen in 1994 established at least a two-level hierarchy, with evidence that the physiological and security needs do form a coherent set, whereas the other needs may be essentially of equal importance among themselves. As in the case of so many theories of work motivation, it may be that the need theories of work motivation are more valid than social scientists are capable of demonstrating, given the practical problems of measurement, manipulation (for experimentation), and generalization, not to mention the ethics of conducting internally valid research into this subject on human beings.

—*Craig C. Pinder*

See also Motivational Traits; Need for Achievement, Power, and Affiliation; Personality; Work Motivation

FURTHER READING

Alderfer, C. P. (1972). *Existence, relatedness, and growth.* New York: Free Press.

Latham, G. P., & Pinder, C. C. (2005). Work motivation theory and research at the dawn of the 21st century. *Annual Review of Psychology, 56*, 485–516.

Maslow, A. H. (1954). *Motivation and personality.* New York: Harper & Row.

McClelland, D. C., & Winter, D. G. (1969). *Motivating economic achievement.* New York: Free Press.

Miner, J. B. (2003). The rated importance, scientific validity, and practical usefulness of organizational behavior theories: A quantitative review. *Academy of Management Learning and Education, 2*, 250–268.

Murray, H. (1938). *Explorations in personality.* New York: Oxford University Press.

Pinder, C. C. (1998). *Work motivation in organizational behavior.* Upper Saddle River, NJ: Prentice Hall.

Pinder, C. C. (in press). *Work motivation in organizational behavior* (2nd ed.). Mahwah, NJ: Lawrence Erlbaum.

Ronen, S. (1994). An underlying structure of motivational need taxonomies: A cross-cultural confirmation. In M. D. Dunnette & L. M. Hough (Eds.), *Handbook of industrial and organizational psychology* (Vol. 4, pp. 241–269). Palo Alto, CA: Consulting Psychologists Press.

NEGOTIATION, MEDIATION, AND ARBITRATION

The term *negotiation* conjures up a variety of images in people's minds, most notably deal making and dispute resolution. Indeed, individuals negotiate job assignments, supplier contracts, joint ventures, and the resolution of conflict in the workplace. Whether applied to crafting deals or resolving disputes, *negotiation* refers to a joint decision-making process in which two or more parties, whose interests conflict, attempt to reach an agreement. When negotiations become difficult or impossible, and when the costs of disagreement are high, others often intervene. These third parties typically act as mediators or arbitrators as they assist negotiators in reaching agreement.

Negotiation, mediation, and arbitration are therefore distinct but related processes. An important difference among them, however, is in the degree of control individuals have over the process (i.e., *how* they come to agreement) and over the outcome (i.e., *what* agreement they reach). In negotiation, parties generally have a high degree of control over both process and outcome. For example, job candidates and recruiters work together through discussion and exchange of offers in an attempt to craft an agreement that is mutually acceptable.

When third parties become involved, however, negotiators (or disputants) relinquish some control for the sake of reaching agreement. In mediation, they give up control over the process, and in arbitration they give up control over the outcome. In other words, mediators work with the parties to help them develop and endorse an agreement, whereas arbitrators listen to the parties and impose a decision.

The study of negotiation and third-party processes has a long and somewhat fragmented history. In part, this complicated past arises from differences in the nature of the processes themselves and their objectives, as well as differences in their intellectual traditions. Not surprisingly, each has its distinct challenges; together, though, they promote processes designed to help individuals with diverse preferences work together to enhance individual and organizational effectiveness.

NEGOTIATION

Because of its link to deal making, negotiation is often conceptualized primarily in economic terms. Economists, some of the first scholars to study the topic, tend to adopt a prescriptive approach; that is, they analyze the outcomes that should result assuming that negotiators act rationally. From this perspective, negotiators are often believed to be *Olympian,* meaning that they are fully informed, having perfect information about their preferences, their counterpart's preferences, the possible outcomes, and the expected utility or value associated with those outcomes. They are also believed to be motivated exclusively by self-interest, striving to make choices that maximize their individual outcomes.

Psychologically oriented researchers have challenged this perspective, pointing out that it fails to capture the experiences of negotiators and the complexity of their motivation. In reality, negotiators rarely know their counterpart's preferences and sometimes are even unsure about their own preferences, which may shift during the course of a negotiation. Moreover, negotiators are often concerned about the other party's outcomes as well as their own, suggesting that self-interest is not the only motivation.

Other perspectives have emerged, most notably cognitive and behavioral perspectives that are primarily descriptive and emphasize negotiator aspirations, perceptions, and behavior. Unlike the traditional economic approach, these perspectives focus on conflict situations as they are understood by actual negotiators who often have incomplete and perhaps biased information, limited cognitive capacity to remember facts and imagine possible alternatives, and multiple (often conflicting) motives. Psychological approaches analyze negotiation from a negotiator's point of view and identify the main tasks of negotiation.

Cognitive and Behavioral Perspectives

To analyze negotiation from a negotiator's point of view, two important questions need to be asked. First, what is the negotiators' best alternative to a negotiated agreement (BATNA)? Figuring out a negotiator's BATNA places a boundary on the negotiation and establishes a *reservation point*, which is the point at which a negotiator is indifferent between settlement and impasse. Because negotiators are unlikely to accept offers that are less attractive than their best alternatives, it is important to know the parties' reservation points.

Second, what are the negotiators' interests? That is, what are the reasons behind the positions they take in a negotiation? Consider a job candidate who asks a recruiter for a $10,000 increase in starting salary because of a desire to pay down substantial educational loans. The candidate's interest is in paying down the loans, whereas the specific position the candidate has taken is for a $10,000 increase in starting salary. Additionally, the candidate indicates that the starting date is relatively unimportant in comparison to the financial issues. This difference in the relative importance of issues suggests certain tradeoffs or concessions the candidate might make during the negotiation.

Taken together, the assessment of the negotiators' BATNAs and interests create the structure or psychological context of the negotiation. It is within this structure that negotiators attempt to craft mutually acceptable agreements.

The Two Tasks of Negotiation

Working within this psychological context, negotiators face two primary tasks, namely *distribution* and *integration*. *Distribution* refers to the division of existing value or resources. When managers haggle over the size of their budgets, they are negotiating the division of a fixed resource or "pie." To reach a mutually agreeable settlement, negotiators generally engage in a give-and-take process and settle on a compromise. Because of the nature of the distribution task, tough bargaining tactics are commonplace, including misrepresentation, bluffing, silence, extreme positions, and threats to walk away. Distribution represents the competitive or win–lose aspect of negotiation.

Integration contrasts sharply with distribution and refers to the creation of additional value or resources. By discovering tradeoffs that meet both parties' needs, for example, negotiators increase the resource pie and create more value as a result of cooperating and working together. In general, when a negotiation involves multiple issues, which are valued differently by the parties, there is the potential for integration. For example, when organizations subsidize employee health club memberships, they are attempting to increase employee health and well-being as well as increase employee productivity, a tradeoff that is intended to create value. In general, integrative agreements that are created out of complementary interests tend to support and even strengthen long-term relationships between parties.

Although desirable, integration is not an easy task. To create integrative agreements, negotiators need to know each other's interests and be motivated to work creatively to meet each other's needs. Not surprisingly, integrative negotiations are often referred to as *joint problem solving*. Because of the nature of the integration task, cooperative bargaining tactics, including honesty, openness, information sharing, and trust, are commonplace. Integration reflects the cooperative aspect of negotiation.

Negotiations that involve both integration and distribution are called *mixed-motive* negotiations, primarily because they include both cooperative and competitive aspects. In general, most negotiations are mixed-motive. Even a negotiation such as buying an automobile, which may seem to be a purely distributive task, typically involves integration as well as distribution. For example, at some point in the negotiation, one of the parties may begin to expand the set of issues beyond price, to include such things are financing, new tires, floor mats, sound-system upgrades, extended warranty, and other issues that may be valued differently by the two parties. By adding issues to the negotiation, the resource pie increases; however, these added resources still need to be divided between the buyer and seller.

Perhaps one of the greatest challenges for disputants is to realize the integrative potential in their negotiations and to create mutually beneficial agreements. Many disputants feel uneasy about sharing information about their interests, which is an important part of identifying complementary interests and creating integrative agreements. In cases of protracted union–management negotiations, for example, the low level of trust between the parties may cripple integrative bargaining.

There are several cognitive biases that hamper effective integrative bargaining, most notably the *mythical fixed pie perception.* According to this perceptual bias, negotiators assume from the start that their interests and those of their counterpart necessarily and directly conflict. This initial win–lose bias, along with its associated tough tactics, heightens the competitive aspect of negotiation and hampers a problem-solving approach. For example, because of the mythical fixed pie perception, negotiators often misperceive shared interests as conflicting, leading them to overlook areas of mutual benefit.

WHEN OTHERS INTERVENE: MEDIATION AND ARBITRATION

When two parties run into trouble and can no longer manage their negotiation, they often turn to a neutral third party for help. For example, negotiations may become tense and difficult, creating frustration, anger, and distrust, or they may just stall because the parties lose momentum or direction, or find themselves at an impasse on critical issues. Sometimes third-party intervention is an informal process, such as when two employees turn to a respected coworker or to their manager for help in resolving a dispute. Other times it is part of an organization's formal dispute resolution system, in which case it may be either voluntary or required.

In general, third-party intervention is designed to get negotiations back on track. At a minimum, it brings negotiators back to the table and provides a cooling-off process for highly emotional negotiations. It also can reestablish and refocus communication on the substantive issues and impose or reinforce deadlines designed to keep the negotiation moving forward.

Neutral third parties may also help negotiators resolve the *substance* of their conflicts. Mediators, who take control of the process, work with the parties both to repair strained relationships and to help them develop and endorse an agreement; mediators meet with parties individually, gaining an understanding of the various issues and perspectives, and identify—and help the parties develop—possible agreements.

Arbitrators, who take control of the outcome, help negotiators primarily by providing a solution. Thus, the goal of arbitration is to design settlements. In general, the arbitrator hears each party's case and then decides the outcome; however, there are several forms of arbitration. In binding arbitration, for example, the parties agree beforehand that they will accept any resulting settlement an arbitrator designs. In final-offer arbitration, parties submit their preferred agreements, one of which is selected by the arbitrator.

Mediation and arbitration may also be combined to create hybrid processes. In some organizational dispute-resolution systems, mediation is a preliminary step leading to arbitration if an agreement is not reached. The reasoning behind this "med–arb" procedure is that if the parties cannot craft a solution themselves with the help of a mediator, then the dispute automatically goes to arbitration (i.e., the mediator becomes an arbitrator) and is resolved for them.

Another hybrid process is "arb–med," which consists of three phases. In the first phase, the third party holds an arbitration hearing and places the decision in a sealed envelope. This phase is followed by mediation, during which the arbitrator's envelope (i.e., decision) is prominently displayed. If mediation fails, the envelope is then opened, revealing the arbitrated decision. When comparing these two hybrid processes, arb–med resulted in more mediated settlements and in settlements of greater joint benefit.

Like negotiation, mediation and arbitration can be extremely effective ways of resolving disputes. As mentioned above, when negotiations are tense and emotional, or if the parties reach an impasse and cannot themselves figure out a solution, it may be wise to involve a neutral third party. It can also offer the parties a way to save face by allowing them to make concessions during mediation without appearing weak, or letting them blame an arbitrator if the settlement is unsatisfactory to a party's constituents. Research shows that it is best to involve third parties only after negotiators have made a serious effort to resolve their own conflict and when they realize that they can no longer manage their negotiation. The use of third parties is particularly helpful for managing conflicts in ongoing work relationships.

Researchers also point out some important challenges, however. Turning to third parties, especially to arbitrators, usually signals that the negotiation process has failed and that the parties could not settle their differences themselves. In the case of ongoing work relationships, this failure can be problematic. Organizations generally prefer that workers become skilled in managing their relationships, even strengthening them to benefit the organization.

Additionally, because arbitration involves imposing a settlement on the parties, there may be less commitment to the settlement than if the parties crafted an agreement themselves. The process may also inadvertently create systemic problems. For example, merely anticipating arbitration may inhibit serious negotiation, especially when both parties feel strongly about their positions and believe that a neutral third party will side with them. Such overconfidence may undermine the negotiation process and needlessly escalate conflict. It may also jeopardize the parties' acceptance of the arbitrated decision.

One of the biggest challenges for neutral third parties is being perceived as neutral by both sides. To be effective, third parties need to be acceptable to both parties and perceived to be unbiased. This may be very difficult to achieve. For example, mediators require discretion: Even when feeling strongly about one party's proposal, they risk undermining the process by appearing to side with one party. They must be careful not to systematically favor one side or they may compromise their image of fairness and impartiality.

SUMMARY

Negotiation and third-party processes are part of everyday life in organizations. Work group members negotiate task assignments and days off, and prospective employees negotiate the terms of their new jobs. When negotiation stalls, third parties often step in and assist. Mediators take control of the process, attempting to help the parties find a mutually acceptable agreement. Arbitrators, who take control of the outcome, listen to the parties and then decide on a settlement. Negotiation, as well as third-party processes, has shortcomings. However, despite these challenges, these processes serve to help individuals with diverse preferences work together to enhance individual and organizational effectiveness.

—*Susan E. Brodt*

See also Conflict Management; Judgment and Decision-Making Process

FURTHER READING

Babcock, L., & Laschever, S. (2004). *Women don't ask: Negotiation and the gender divide.* Princeton, NJ: Princeton University Press.

Brett, J. (2001). *Negotiating globally: How to negotiate deals, resolve disputes, and make decisions across cultural boundaries.* San Francisco: Jossey-Bass.

Brodt, S., & Dietz, L. (1999). Shared information and information sharing: Understanding negotiation as collective construal. *Research in Negotiation in Organizations, 7,* 263–283.

Brodt, S., & Thompson, L. (2001). Negotiating teams: A levels of analysis framework. *Group Dynamics, 5,* 208–219.

Friedman, R. A. (2000). *Front stage, back stage.* Cambridge, MA: MIT Press.

Lewicki, R., Saunders, D., & Barry, B. (2005). *Negotiation.* Boston: McGraw-Hill/Irwin.

Tinsley, C., & Brodt, S. (2004). Conflict management in East Asia: A dynamic framework and future directions. In K. Leung and S. White (Eds.), *Handbook of Asian management.* New York: Kluwer Academic.

Walton, R. E., & McKersie, R. (1991). *A behavioral theory of labor negotiations* (2nd ed.). Ithaca, NY: ILR Press.

NETWORKING

Networking refers to the development, maintenance, or use of social or professional contacts for the purpose of exchanging information, resources, or services. Networking typically occurs between two individuals but can be examined as an interaction between groups, companies, or institutions.

Industrial/organizational psychologists have been primarily concerned with how networking affects *individual* employment status and career mobility. For instance, in the context of job search, *networking* refers to contacting social and professional acquaintances, or other persons to whom the job seeker has been referred, for the purposes of gaining information, leads, or advice related to obtaining a job. Research suggests that as many as 60% to 90% of individuals find jobs by networking, as opposed to traditional job search methods, such as sending out lead inquiry résumés or responding to want ads. Similarly, networking is also used by individuals for the purposes of seeking promotion, gaining visibility, or seeking out career advice or mentoring (i.e., for the purpose of upward career mobility). In fact, research suggests that individual career mobility may be equally or more influenced by informal social relationships than by formal organizational policies and infrastructure.

Both the degree to which people engage in networking and the types of people with whom they network seem to play an important role in determining career outcomes. Although there has been relatively little research on networking behavior (e.g., the intensity with which one engages in networking), a fair amount of research (in particular, from the sociology literature) has examined the structural characteristics of individuals' current social and professional networks as predictors of career outcomes. A social or professional network can be thought of as a web or series of interconnected webs, whereby links or ties exist between focal individuals and the individuals or entities with whom they share a connection or relationship. Structural characteristics of networks include things such as the size of one's network, the strength of ties that exist between focal individuals and other individuals or entities in their network, and the diversity that exists among and between the various individuals or entities in one's network. In addition, the power and influence held by individuals in one's network may play a particularly important role in whether networking will lead to upward career mobility.

NETWORKING BEHAVIOR

Research suggests that not all individuals engage in networking to the same extent. In one of few studies

examining individual differences in networking behavior, Connie Wanberg and her colleagues examined both the intensity with which individuals engage in networking and the level of comfort (versus apprehension) individuals express about engaging in such behaviors during a job search. Results of this study suggest that individuals' reported *comfort with networking* is positively related to *networking intensity* (defined as an individual action directed toward contacting friends, acquaintances, and referrals to get job information, leads, or advice) and further, that the "Big Five" personality characteristics are all related to *networking comfort* and *networking intensity*. With the exception of neuroticism, which was negatively related, all traits were positively related to both comfort and intensity, with conscientiousness and extraversion being the strongest predictors of intensity. Finally, self-reported comfort with networking was related to networking intensity above and beyond the effects of personality.

In another recent study of networking behavior, researchers examined the extent to which several other individual differences predict networking intensity. Specifically, this study found no differences with regard to age, race, or gender when it came to the intensity with which individuals reported networking. However, proactive personality trait (the dispositional tendency toward proactive behavior across situations) was positively related to networking intensity.

STRUCTURAL NETWORK CHARACTERISTICS

Size of Network

Among structural characteristics of individual networks, the size of one's network is thought to affect access to information and leads. However, several qualifications about network size should be made. Namely, the strength of connections or ties, the diversity of contacts, and the status of contacts in one's network may have a bigger impact than network size alone.

Strength of Ties

Despite the size of one's network, dyadic relationship characteristics such as the strength of ties between individuals and their network contacts seem to be important predictors of information exchange. In a seminal piece on network ties, Mark Granovetter explored the degree to which weak versus strong network ties would lead to information exchange. The idea set forth by Granovetter was that because individuals who share close or strong relationship ties (e.g., friends and family members) often share access to the same information, focal individuals can benefit more from maintaining weak ties with multiple individuals (e.g., acquaintances) who do not share common information with them. This argument, called the *strength of weak ties,* led to a series of studies examining the structure of networks, or *network analysis,* as a means of determining the relationship between network characteristics and career-related outcomes. The conclusion of the resulting body of literature on network ties is that both weak and strong network ties can be beneficial to career outcomes.

Diversity Among Contacts

In addition to research examining strength of ties, the diversity among contacts in one's network has been examined as a predictor of information exchange and positive career outcomes. In particular, work by Ronald Burt suggested that the extent to which one's network contacts know one another will determine the amount of overlapping and redundant information they offer. Thus, diversity among and between one's contacts will provide greater opportunities to access unique and different information.

Power and Influence of Contacts

Last, but certainly not least, the power and influence held by individuals in one's network may be one of the most important factors influencing the utility of networking for career success. In particular, the occupational status of one's contacts (e.g., a high-ranking manager versus a low-ranking nonmanager) may determine their ability to exert influence on one's career outcomes (e.g., hiring or suggesting that one be hired, exposing one to challenging projects that help one gain visibility in the organization), as well as the quality of information they have and are able to exchange (e.g., access to important leads, or reliable and accurate career advice).

—*Tracy A. Lambert*

See also Career Development; Job Search

FURTHER READING

Burt, R. S. (1992). *Structural holes.* Cambridge, MA: Harvard University Press.

Granovetter, M. S. (1973). The strength of weak ties. *American Journal of Sociology, 78,* 1360–1380.

Granovetter, M. S. (1974). *Getting a job: A study of contacts and careers.* Cambridge, MA: Harvard University Press.

Lambert, T., Eby, L. T., & Payton, M. (in press). Predictors of networking intensity and network quality among white-collar job seekers. *Journal of Career Development.*

Lin, N., Ensel, W. M., & Vaughn, J. C. (1981). Social resources and strength of ties: Structural factors in occupational status attainment. *American Sociological Review, 46,* 393–405.

Wanberg, C. R., Kanfer, R., & Banas, J. T. (2000). Predictors and outcomes of networking intensity among unemployed job seekers. *Journal of Applied Psychology, 85,* 491–503.

NEW EMPLOYEE ORIENTATION

New employee orientation occurs in almost every type of organization: schools, colleges, work organizations, government agencies, social/religious/volunteer organizations, the military, and prisons. The common objective is to help newcomers make a smooth transition from outside to inside the organization.

Despite the widespread use of newcomer orientation, very little research has been conducted about it when compared with other types of staffing activities, such as interviewing, testing, and recruitment sources. Although most organizations have common objectives for newcomer orientation, the methods used vary considerably both by organization type (e.g., military versus voluntary organizations) and even within a particular type of organization (e.g., work organizations).

We begin with a definition of *newcomer orientation* by comparing it with organizational socialization. Following this comparison, seven recommended principles for conducting newcomer orientation are presented.

DEFINITION

A definition of *newcomer orientation* should address four questions: (a) Who is involved? (b) When does it occur? (c) What is learned? and (d) How is the teaching conducted? First, newcomer orientation concerns only those who are new members of an organization. It does not concern those who have been rehired, nor those who move internally, such as when a student changes his or her college major from music to business. Second, there is a loose consensus among writers that orientation almost always occurs on the first day, but less agreement exists as to how long it lasts. Most would agree that it probably does not go too much beyond the first week, as asserted John Wanous in 1992. Third, what is learned in orientation varies with both the amount of time devoted to it and the objectives to be achieved. A minimal orientation might include just the filling out of forms related to one's employment (e.g., income tax withholding and medical benefits), or it could be a tour of the organization. A typical newcomer orientation session is often limited to the presentation of factual information. Fourth, because presenting factual information is so common, the typical orientation methods and media are lecturing, videos, and brochures.

Another approach to defining *newcomer orientation* is to compare it with organizational socialization. This is because some writers do not separate them, by asserting that orientation is nothing more than the beginning of socialization. A different position is taken here. Newcomer orientation is not the same as organizational socialization, for a number of reasons.

First, orientation concerns a much shorter time period. Socialization continues well after the initial entry period. Socialization can occur years after entry, because it becomes relevant during internal transitions, such as a promotion or a move to a different functional area within the organization, as pointed out by E. H. Schein in 1971. Second, socialization typically involves a far greater number of organization members than does orientation. For example, coworkers usually are not involved in orientation. Third, the content of an orientation program is quite limited compared with socialization. Orientation concerns issues typically faced by newcomers, whereas socialization concerns all facets of one's experience in an organization. Many issues of concern in socialization do not occur until years later—learning and accepting organizational values, learning how to cope with organizational politics, understanding the performance expectations for one's own job, and so on. Fourth, the available research evidence shows that newcomers are under considerable stress resulting from organizational entry but that this stress decreases fairly rapidly.

As a result, newcomer orientation should concern how to cope with these particular stressors. Finally, orientation can be viewed as a specific event or program that is limited by both time and content, whereas socialization is considered to be a long-term process. Thus, it is much easier to conduct research on orientation than on socialization.

DESIGN OF NEWCOMER ORIENTATION PROGRAMS

Because there was no consensus about how to conduct newcomer orientation, John Wanous proposed in 1992 a new approach called Realistic Orientation Programs for new Employee Stress (ROPES). This approach was based on the idea that newcomers "need to learn the ropes" to be both effective and satisfied in a new organization. A key assumption of ROPES is that newcomers experience very high stress during their first few days. In 2000, Arnon Reichers joined with Wanous to update the ROPES model.

The ROPES approach to newcomer orientation incorporates ideas from three different areas of previously existing research: (a) both of the primary ways to cope with stress, (b) some of the principles for training developed by Arnold Goldstein and Melvin Sorcher, and (c) the stress-inoculation method described by Irving Janis and Leon Mann. With these three research areas as the foundation for ROPES, seven implementation principles were derived. Each is described below.

First, one of the two basic approaches for coping with stress has been called the *problem-focused* approach, because it concerns actions that a person can take to reduce stress by addressing its origin. Thus, newcomers need realistic information about the most likely causes of stress experienced by the typical newcomer. After being provided realistic information about the most common, important stressors, newcomers are also told about specific actions that can reduce stress. Bruce Meglino, Angelo DeNisi, Stuart Youngblood, and Kevin Williams provided an excellent example of this approach for those entering basic training with the U.S. Army. New recruits anxious about meeting new people are told that getting to know one new person is the best solution.

Second, the other basic approach for coping with stress has been called the *emotion-focused* method, because it concerns thoughts, feelings, and moods. This is an intrapsychic approach, and it is best used when taking action to reduce stress is futile. Raymond Novaco, Thomas Cook, and Irwin Sarason provided an excellent example of this approach being used for U.S. Marines entering basic training. One aspect of emotion-focused coping is to provide emotional support, through statements such as, "Everyone feels the same pressure to perform well in rifle training . . . you can help yourself by focusing on the specific task at hand." Emotional support can also be more specific: "If you can make it through the first two weeks, you can make it through basic training."

Whereas the first two principles are drawn from the stress–coping research literature, the next three are drawn from advice on training adults to master specific types of interpersonal skills, developed by Goldstein and Sorcher, including how to give praise to an average-performing employee. Thus, the third principle for newcomer orientation is to use role models as examples of how to handle stressful situations. For example, consider the experiences of international graduate students in United States universities. Many such students, particularly those from Asian countries, are uncomfortable with asking questions or making comments in the classroom. Showing a short video of a student doing this successfully is the first step toward helping them overcome this fear and also demonstrates how to participate in class successfully.

The fourth principle follows directly from the third. It is to discuss what the role model did. In the example of international students, this is important so that newcomers can learn all of the specific actions necessary to speak successfully in class. The fifth principle is to have newcomers rehearse the actions that were shown by the role model. Learning is unlikely to result from just observing a role model, as is obvious to all novice golf and tennis players.

Principle 6 is to teach newcomers how to control their own thoughts *and* feelings, as demonstrated in research by Marie Waung. This is a technique that was initially developed to help patients cope with the stress of going to the dentist or undergoing an invasive or obnoxious medical procedure. As applied to newcomer orientation, such advice might be to "listen to what your drill instructor is saying, and try to ignore the shouting that goes with it."

Principle 7 is to target certain specific stressors to particular newcomers, as originally suggested decades ago by Earl Gomersall and Scott Myers. In any group of newcomers, it is likely that they will be dispersed throughout the organization, thus reporting to different bosses. To the extent that certain specific

characteristics of different bosses can be identified, the idea is to provide newcomers with the most relevant information for their own new boss. For example, one newcomer might be told: "Richard may appear to be unfriendly, but that is just his shyness. So, be sure to start a conversation on something you might have in common. His hobbies are . . ." A different newcomer in the same orientation session might be told: "Your new boss, Susan, prefers to have you check in with her before taking a break from work."

—*John P. Wanous*

See also Organizational Socialization; Organizational Socialization Tactics; Realistic Job Preview; Training

FURTHER READING

Goldstein, A. P., & Sorcher, M. (1974). *Changing supervisor behavior.* New York: Pergamon.

Gomersall, E. R., & Myers, M. S. (1966, July–August). Breakthrough in on-the-job training. *Harvard Business Review,* 62–72.

Janis, I. L., & Mann, L. (1977). *Decision-making: A psychological analysis of conflict, choice, and commitment.* New York: Plenum Press.

Meglino, B. M., DeNisi, A. S., Youngblood, S. A., & Williams, K. J. (1988). Effects of realistic job previews: A comparison using an "enhancement" and a "reduction" preview. *Journal of Applied Psychology, 73,* 259–266.

Novaco, R. W., Cook, T. M., & Sarason, I. G. (1983). Military recruit training: An arena for stress-coping skills. In D. Meichenbaum & M. E. Jaremko (Eds.), *Stress reduction and prevention* (pp. 377–418). New York: Plenum Press.

Schein, E. H. (1971). The individual, the organization, and the career: A conceptual scheme. *Journal of Applied Behavioral Science, 7,* 401–426.

Wanous, J. P. (1992). *Organizational entry: Recruitment, selection, orientation, and socialization* (2nd ed.). Reading, MA: Addison-Wesley.

Wanous, J. P., & Reichers, A. E. (2000). New employee orientation programs. *Human Resource Management Review, 10,* 435–451.

Waung, M. (1995). The effects of self-regulatory coping orientation on newcomer adjustment and job survival. *Personnel Psychology, 48,* 633–650.

NOMOLOGICAL NETWORKS

The *nomological network* is a tool for construct validation (i.e., gathering evidence about the meaning) of psychological measures. For example, construct validation of job performance ratings by supervisors should indicate what the ratings really mean, or how accurately they reflect actual performance levels. The goal is to link observable measurements to unobservable theoretical constructs.

In 1955, L. J. Cronbach and P. E. Meehl described the nomological network as a system of intertwined laws that make up a theory and stated that the laws in the network should generate testable predictions. Laws could relate measurements to each other (e.g., linking job performance ratings to scores on ability or personality measures), theoretical constructs to observed measurements (e.g., linking a rating of some aspect of job performance, such as effort, to the construct of effort), or constructs to other constructs (e.g., linking the construct of job effort to the personality construct of conscientiousness). Building a nomological network involves thinking about what construct is (or should be) measured by an instrument, what other constructs should be related to that construct, and what other measures should be related to the instrument of interest.

Psychological constructs are generally not directly observable, so it is not usually possible to directly determine how well a measure reflects the intended construct. Research based on a nomological network can provide indirect evidence of validity by demonstrating how well the measure correlates with other measures it should theoretically relate to. Confirmation of relationships predicted by the network supports the construct validity of a measure, whereas failure to confirm predictions leads to doubt about construct validity. (Note: A complication with failures of confirmation is that they could result from poor validity of the measure or from incorrect theory in the nomological network, or both.)

An example of a nomological network involves job performance. In recent years, industrial/organizational psychologists have theorized and researched a distinction between performance on required, job-specific tasks (task performance) and performance of behaviors that are less likely to be required and not specific to particular jobs (e.g., helping coworkers; doing things that need to be done but are not assigned to particular workers); this latter type of behavior has been referred to as *organizational citizenship*. If supervisors are asked to evaluate workers on both their task performance and citizenship, we might ask whether the ratings really adequately distinguish between the two performance constructs (i.e., we might question

the ratings' construct validity); alternatively, ratings might be subject to a *halo effect*, in which a general impression of a worker forms the basis for each (supposedly) separate evaluation.

Testing predictions based on a nomological network could help determine the construct validity of the job performance ratings. The research question concerns a link between observed measures of performance and their constructs. This question can be addressed indirectly by examining links between the performance measures and measures of theoretically related constructs. It has been theorized that the task performance construct should relate more strongly to ability constructs, and the citizenship construct should relate more to personality (e.g., conscientiousness) and job satisfaction. There exist measures of ability, personality, and job satisfaction that have been linked to their theoretical constructs. These measures can be used to test predictions from the nomological network. Research has provided some but not overwhelming support for these links, which raises questions about the validity of the performance ratings and/or the theory. For examples of how nomological networks can be applied to personnel selection measures, see the sources in the Further Reading section, which follows, by G. V. Barrett and J. F. Binning.

—*Jim Conway*

See also Construct; Criterion Theory; Job Performance Models; Validation Strategies

FURTHER READING

Barrett, G. V. (1992). Clarifying construct validity: Definitions, processes, and models. *Human Performance, 5,* 13–58.

Binning, J. F., & Barrett, G. V. (1989). Validity of personnel decisions: A conceptual analysis of the inferential and evidential bases. *Journal of Applied Psychology, 74,* 476–494.

Cronbach, L. J., & Meehl, P. E. (1955). Construct validity in psychological tests. *Psychological Bulletin, 52,* 281–302.

NONEXPERIMENTAL DESIGNS

The most frequently used experimental design type for research in industrial and organizational psychology and a number of allied fields is the *nonexperiment.*

This design type differs from that of both the randomized experiment and the quasi-experiment in several important respects. Prior to describing the nonexperimental design type, we note that the entry on experimental designs in this volume considers basic issues associated with (a) the validity of inferences stemming from empirical research and (b) the settings within which research takes place. Thus, the same set of issues is not addressed in this entry.

ATTRIBUTES OF NONEXPERIMENTAL DESIGNS

Nonexperimental designs differ from both quasi-experimental designs and randomized experimental designs in several important respects. Overall, these differences lead research using nonexperimental designs to be far weaker than that using alternative designs, in terms of internal validity and several other criteria.

Measurement of Assumed Causes

In nonexperimental research, variables that are assumed causes are measured, as opposed to being manipulated. For example, a researcher interested in testing the relation between organizational commitment (an assumed cause) and worker productivity (an assumed effect) would have to measure the levels of these variables. Because of the fact that commitment levels were measured, the study would have little if any internal validity. Note, moreover, that the internal validity of such research would not be at all improved by a host of data analytic strategies (e.g., path analysis, structural equation modeling) that purport to allow for inferences about causal connections between and among variables (Stone-Romero, 2002; Stone-Romero & Rosopa, 2004).

Nonrandom Assignment of Participants and Absence of Conditions

In nonexperiments, there are typically no explicitly defined research conditions. For example, a researcher interested in assessing the relation between job satisfaction (an assumed cause) and organizational commitment (an assumed effect) would simply measure the level of both such variables. Because participants were not randomly assigned to conditions in which the level of job satisfaction was manipulated,

the researcher would be left in the uncomfortable position of not having information about the many variables that were confounded with job satisfaction. Thus, the internal validity of the study would be a major concern. Moreover, even if the study involved the comparison of scores on one or more dependent variables across existing conditions over which the researcher had no control, the researcher would have no control over the assignment of participants to the conditions. For example, a researcher investigating the assumed effects of incentive systems on firm productivity in several manufacturing firms would have no control over the attributes of such systems. Again, this would serve to greatly diminish the internal validity of the study.

Measurement of Assumed Dependent Variables

In nonexperimental research, assumed dependent variables are measured. Note that the same is true of both randomized experiments and quasi-experiments. However, there are very important differences among the three experimental design types that warrant attention. More specifically, in the case of well-conducted randomized experiments, the researcher can be highly confident that the scores on the dependent variable(s) were a function of the study's manipulations. Moreover, in quasi-experiments with appropriate design features, the investigator can be fairly confident that the study's manipulations were responsible for observed differences on the dependent variable(s). However, in nonexperimental studies, the researcher is placed in the uncomfortable position of having to assume that what he or she views as dependent variables are indeed effects. Regrettably, in virtually all nonexperimental research, this assumption rests on a very shaky foundation. Thus, for example, in a study of the assumed effect of job satisfaction on intentions to quit a job, what the researcher assumes to be the effect may in fact be the cause. That is, individuals who have decided to quit for reasons that were not based on job satisfaction could, in the interest of cognitive consistency, view their jobs as not being satisfying.

Control Over Extraneous or Confounding Variables

Because of the fact that nonexperimental research does not benefit from the controls (e.g., random assignment to conditions) that are common to studies using randomized experimental designs, there is relatively little potential to control extraneous variables. As a result, the results of nonexperimental research tend to have little, if any, internal validity. For instance, assume that a researcher did a nonexperimental study of the assumed causal relation between negative affectivity and job-related strain and found these variables to be positively related. It would be inappropriate to conclude that these variables were causally related. At least one important reason for this is that the measures of these constructs have common items. Thus, any detected relation between them could well be spurious, as noted by Eugene F. Stone-Romero in 2005.

In hopes of bolstering causal inference, researchers who do nonexperimental studies often measure variables that are assumed to be confounds and then use such procedures as hierarchical multiple regression, path analysis, and structural equation modeling to control them. Regrettably, such procedures have little potential to control confounds. There are at least four reasons for this. First, researchers are seldom aware of all of the relevant confounds. Second, even if all of them were known, it is seldom possible to measure more than a few of them in any given study and use them as controls. Third, to the degree that the measures of confounds are unreliable, procedures such as multiple regression will fail to fully control for the effects of measured confounds. Fourth, and finally, because a large number of causal models may be consistent with a given set of covariances among a set of variables, statistical procedures are incapable of providing compelling evidence about the superiority of any given model over alternative models.

—*Eugene F. Stone-Romero*

See also Experimental Designs; Quasi-experimental Designs

FURTHER READING

Cook, T. D., & Campbell, D. T. (1979). *Quasi-experimentation: Design and analysis issues for field settings.* Boston: Houghton Mifflin.

Shadish, W. R., Cook, T. D., & Campbell, D. T. (2002). Experimental and quasi-experimental designs for generalized causal inference. Boston: Houghton Mifflin.

Stone-Romero, E. F. (2002). The relative validity and usefulness of various empirical research designs. In S. G. Rogelberg (Ed.), *Handbook of research methods in industrial and organizational psychology* (pp. 77–98). Malden, MA: Blackwell.

Stone-Romero, E. F. (2005). Personality-based stigmas and unfair discrimination in work organizations. In R. L. Dipboye & A. Colella (Eds.), *Discrimination at work: The psychological and organizational bases* (pp. 255–280). Mahwah, NJ: Lawrence Erlbaum.

Stone-Romero, E. F., & Rosopa, P. (2004). Inference problems with hierarchical multiple regression-based tests of mediating effects. *Research in Personnel and Human Resources Management, 23,* 249–290.

NORMATIVE MODELS OF DECISION MAKING AND LEADERSHIP

Psychologists who have advanced normative theories of management have typically advocated highly participative processes for making decisions. The principal basis for such prescriptions is the motivational benefit that results from a leader involving group members in decision making. In spite of this advocacy, reviews of the literature suggest a much more mixed picture of the consequences of participation.

One way of reconciling the inconsistent evidence is to attempt to identify the moderating variables that regulate these different effects. Such moderating variables could then be incorporated into a contingency theory to guide managers in selecting the degree of participation appropriate to each situation. In the early 1970s, Victor Vroom, working with a graduate student, Philip Yetton, formulated a normative model of leadership style that had that objective. Expressed as a decision tree, the model distinguished five degrees of participation and eight situational factors believed to interact with participation in determining its effectiveness. The Vroom–Yetton model inspired many studies aimed at determining its validity as well as its usefulness in leadership training. The validity data, summarized 15 years later by Vroom and Jago, showed that the incidence of successful decisions was about twice as high when the decision process used was consistent with the model as when it was inconsistent. Clearly the model had promise, but the research suggested that there was much room for improvement.

In the three decades since its original publication, the Vroom–Yetton model has been substantially revised, first by Vroom and Arthur Jago in 1988 and

Deciding How to Decide

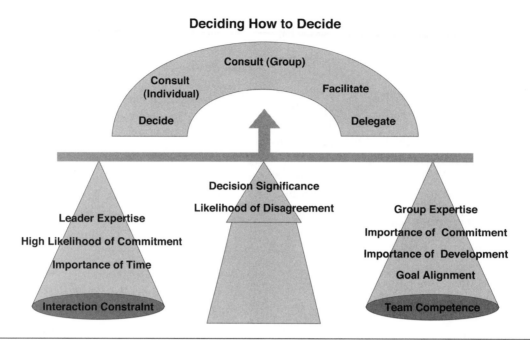

Figure 1   Scale Diagram

in 2000 by Vroom. Its current structure is shown as a balance scale in Figure 1.

The five decision processes have undergone significant modification from the Vroom–Yetton model, as have the eight situational factors, which have been expanded to 11. The factors at the left-hand side drive the recommended process toward the more autocratic end of the spectrum, whereas those at the right favor a more participative approach. Finally, the two in the center, *decision significance* and *likelihood of disagreement,* interact with those at the left or right to determine the sensitivity of the scale. For example, when a highly significant decision is combined with factors at the left, the recommended process is shifted further toward autocratic methods. When it is combined with factors at the right, it will shift further toward participation.

Of course, the scale is only a metaphor for the actual model, which is driven by a set of equations. To use the model, a manager, faced with a specific problem to solve or decision to make, is asked for judgments (typically on a five-point scale) concerning each of the 11 factors. These judgments are entered into four equations that estimate the effects of each of the five processes on the quality of the decision, its likely implementation, the time consumed in making it, and the developmental benefits resulting from the process. Finally these four consequences (quality, implementation, time, and development) receive differential weights corresponding to the manager's judgments of their importance in that problem.

Using the model sounds complicated but can be accomplished in less than one minute using a computer program called Expert System. Once the judgments are entered, the manager sees not a single recommended process (as in the Vroom–Yetton model) but a bar graph showing the relative estimated effectiveness of each of the five processes.

SCIENTIFIC IMPLICATIONS

It has been said that a theory should be evaluated not only in terms of its validity but also in terms of the questions it raises and the quality of research it stimulates. Jago has recently compiled a list of more than 100 studies in scientific journals and more than 40 doctoral dissertations dealing directly with the Vroom–Yetton–Jago models. The models have also stimulated the development of a novel measure of leadership style that has proven useful both in research and in leadership development. The measure uses a set of 30 real or realistic cases, each depicting a manager faced with a decision to make that would affect his or her team. For each case, the manager chooses from the five alternative decision processes the one that he or she would select. The cases are not selected randomly, but rather on the basis of a multifactorial experimental design in which eight principal situational factors are varied independently of one another. This property makes it possible to systematically determine how managers change their intended behavior as elements of the situation are changed.

With the advent of the Internet, it is now possible for a manager to view and respond to the cases online in one of several available languages. As an inducement to enter their choices, managers can choose two groups from a list, varying in organizational level, nationality, and industry, with whom they would like to be compared. Finally, the manager downloads a 12-page individualized report comparing his or her style with the model and with the chosen comparison groups.

The data obtained from this measure has taught us a lot about the correlates of leadership style including the influence of nationality, gender, functional specialty, and hierarchical position. Managers do vary their behavior over situations in a manner not unlike that shown in the previous figure. However, they differ from one another in two respects. The most obvious is a preference for one side of the scale or another. This is similar to what is meant by describing mangers as *autocratic* or *participative*. But it should not be thought of as a general trait, because it accounts for only 10% of the total variance in behavior. Using the metaphor of the balance scale, it can be thought of as an extra weight added to one side of the scale or the other.

The other respect in which managers differ is the specific situational factors that govern their choices among the five styles. Although the pattern shown in the figure is a reasonable approximation of that of a manager choosing the modal response on each of the 30 cases, each individual manager displays a different pattern, ignoring factors or sometimes responding to them in a manner opposite to that prescribed by the normative model.

PRACTICAL IMPLICATIONS

Apart from the impact that the Vroom–Yetton–Jago models and derivative tools have had in the science of leadership, it is safe to say that it has had an even greater impact on the practice of leadership. About 200,000 managers around the world have now been

trained in the models. Invariably, such training has included feedback on responses to sets of cases showing managers how they compare with their peers, with occupants of positions to which they aspire, and with the model. In effect, managers can compare their model of decision making and leadership with those of other groups and with the normative model.

—*Victor H. Vroom*

See also Judgment and Decision-Making Process; Leadership and Supervision

FURTHER READING

Vroom, V. H. (2000). Decision making and the leadership process. *Organizational Dynamics, 28*(4), 82–94.

Vroom, V. H. (2003). Educating managers in decision making and leadership. *Management Decision, 41*(10), 968–978.

Vroom, V. H., & Jago, A. (1988). *The new leadership: Managing participation in organizations.* Englewood Cliffs, NJ: Prentice Hall.

Vroom, V. H., & Yetton, P. W. (1973). *Leadership and decision making.* Pittsburgh, PA: University of Pittsburgh Press.

NORMATIVE VERSUS IPSATIVE MEASUREMENT

Normative and *ipsative* measurements are different rating scales usually used in personality or attitudinal questionnaires. Normative measures provide interindividual differences assessment, whereas ipsative measures provide intraindividual differences assessment. Normative measurement is very popular and prominent in the United States, and ipsative measurement is getting wider use in Europe and Asia.

NORMATIVE MEASUREMENT

Normative measurement usually presents one statement at a time and allows respondents using a five-point Likert-type scale to indicate the level of agreement they feel with that statement. Here is an example:

"I keep my spirits up despite setbacks."

1	2	3	4	5
Strongly disagree	Disagree	Neutral	Agree	Strongly agree

Such a rating scale allows quantification of individuals' feelings and perceptions on certain topics. Scoring of normative scales is fairly straightforward. Positively phrased items get a 5 when marked as *Strongly agree*, and negatively phrased items need to be recoded accordingly and get a 5 when marked as *Strongly disagree*. Despite occasional debates on the ordinal versus interval nature of such normative scales, scores of similar items are usually combined into a scale score and used to calculate means and standard deviations, so norms can be established to facilitate interpersonal comparisons. The normative scores can be submitted to most statistical procedures without violating the assumptions assuming the normative scores are accepted as interval-level measurements.

IPSATIVE MEASUREMENT

Ipsative measurement presents an alternative format that has been in use since the 1950s. Ipsative measures are also referred to as *forced-choice* techniques. An ipsative measurement presents respondents with options of equal desirability; thus, the responses are less likely to be confounded by social desirability. Respondents are forced to choose one option that is "most true" of them and choose another one that is "least true" of them. A major underlying assumption is that when respondents are forced to choose among four equally desirable options, the one option that is most true of them will tend to be perceived as more positive. Similarly, when forced to choose one that is least true of them, those to whom one of the options is less applicable will tend to perceive it as less positive. For example, consider the following:

"I am the sort of person who . . ."

    a. prefers to keep active at work.

    b. establishes good compromises.

    c. appreciates literature.

    d. keeps my spirits up despite setbacks.

The scoring of an ipsative scale is not as intuitive as a normative scale. There are four options in each item. Each option belongs to a specific scale (i.e., independence, social confidence, introversion, or optimism). Each option chosen as *most true* earns two points for the scale to which it belongs; *least true*, zero points; and the two unchosen ones each receive one point. High scores reflect relative preferences/strengths within the person among different scales; therefore, scores reflect intrapersonal comparisons.

In an ipsative questionnaire, the sum of the total scores from each respondent across all scales adds to a constant. This creates a measurement dependency problem. For example, if there are 100 items in an ipsative questionnaire with four options for each item, the total score for each participant always adds up to be 400. Because the sum adds to a constant, the degree of freedom for a set of m scales is $(m - 1)$, where m is the number of scales in the questionnaire. As long as the scores on $m - 1$ scales are known, the score on the mth scale can be determined. The measurement dependency violates one of the basic assumptions of classical test theory—independence of error variance—which has implications for the statistical analysis of ipsative scores, as well as for their interpretation.

The problem with having the total ipsative scores add to a constant could be solved by avoiding use of total scores. The measurement dependency problem is valid when the number of scales in the questionnaire is small. However, the problem becomes less severe as the number of scales increases.

Readers who are interested in the reliability, validity, and comparability of normative versus ipsative measurements might study the works listed in the Further Reading section, which follows.

—*Chieh-Chen Bowen*

See also Individual Differences; Integrity Testing; Measurement Scales; Personality Assessment

FURTHER READING

Baron, H. (1996). Strengths and limitations of ipsative measurement. *Journal of Occupational and Organizational Psychology, 69,* 49–56.

Bowen, C.-C., Martin, B. A., & Hunt, S. T. (2002). A comparison of ipsative and normative approaches for ability to control faking in personality questionnaires. *The International Journal of Organizational Analysis, 10,* 240–259.

Gordon, L. V. (1951). Validities of the forced-choice and questionnaire methods of personality measurement. *Journal of Applied Psychology, 35,* 407–412.

Hicks, L. E. (1970). Some properties of ipsative, normative and forced-choice normative measures. *Psychological Bulletin, 74,* 167–184.

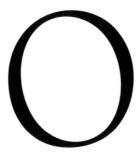

OCCUPATIONAL HEALTH PSYCHOLOGY

According to the National Safety Council, more than 5,500 workplace fatalities and 4.3 million injuries occurred in the United States in 2003. Estimates from the World Health Organization (WHO) show occupational injuries are a concern throughout the world. The WHO reports that there are approximately 268 million nonfatal workplace accidents each year causing more than three days of lost work, and roughly 160 million new cases of work-related illness. These occupational illnesses include but are not limited to musculoskeletal, respiratory, and circulatory diseases. In addition to occupational illness and injuries, occupational stress has been and still is a major concern throughout the world. This concern was evident when the 1970 Occupational Safety and Health Act (OSHA) specifically voiced the need to research occupational safety and health (OSH), including the study of psychological factors and job stresses on potential for illness, disease, or loss of functional capacity in aging adults. According to the Bureau of Labor Statistics, in 2003 the concern about stress remained justified; the OSHA *recordable* stress-related cases involving days away from work reached 5,639 in 2001. Compared with the total nonfatal injury and illness cases in 2001, stress-related cases showed higher percentages of long-term work loss (approximately 42.1% of stress-related cases involved 31 or more days away from work). The median number of days away from work was 25 for stress-related cases, which is substantially greater than that of other nonfatal injuries and illnesses.

Since 1990 concerns of human and financial losses associated with the aforementioned health issues have driven the development of a new discipline, occupational health psychology (OHP). Although the development of OHP may seem fairly recent, its roots can be traced back to the development of industrial/ organizational (I/O) psychology. This common history will be reviewed in sections that follow. It should be noted that OHP and I/O psychology share a common history. Even today, the Society of Industrial and Organizational Psychology (SIOP) notes that quality of work life is a major concern encountered by I/O psychologists in their professional work.

In his presidential address to SIOP in 1988, D. R. Ilgen voiced the aforementioned concern and reminded I/O psychologists that occupational health is a timeless concern for obvious humanitarian and utilitarian reasons. Workers' health, either physical or psychological, has an immense impact on their families, colleagues, organizations, communities, and society as a whole. The challenges associated with occupational health can provide I/O psychologists with invaluable opportunities and internal rewards while investigating the etiology of illness, injuries, behavioral maladjustment or deficiency, burnouts, or psychological disorders occurring at work. Ilgen (1990) also raised a second concern from an economic perspective. He argued that an unhealthy workforce can lead to decreases in organizational productivity and individual performance, as well as an increase in health care costs. In a recent five-year prospective study, D. C. Ganster, M. L. Fox, and D. J. Dwyer (2001) lent credence to Ilgen's statement. Their study provided convincing evidence that changing job design in an effort to improve worker health predicts decreases in health care costs five years later.

HISTORICAL ROOTS OF OCCUPATIONAL HEALTH PSYCHOLOGY

The term *occupational health psychology* was first mentioned by J. S. Raymond, D. W. Wood, and W. K. Patrick in *American Psychologist* in 1990. Although OHP has been embedded within other disciplines, psychologists such as R. L. Kahn, Arthur Konhauser, Joseph Tiffin, and Morris Viteles have taken an active role in promoting workers' psychological and physical well-being for almost a century. The beginnings of this can be traced to events in the early 1900s in the fields of I/O and human factors psychology. For example, Hugo Munsterberg (1898 president of the American Psychological Association [APA] as well as one of the "fathers" of I/O psychology) studied accident prevention and safety promotion as early as 1913. Henry Elkind applied the concept of *preventive management* in 1931 to workers in organizations in an effort to help workers improve their mental health.

Although the previously mentioned cases suggest a long history of psychologists' concern for workers' well-being, most psychologists have primarily focused on healthy lifestyles and health promotion in the general population, not the working population specifically. Given that people spend a large portion of their lives at work, and that work often has a tremendous impact on their personal as well as family lives, it seems obvious and logical for psychologists in general and I/O psychologists in particular to use their unique strengths to assist workers and management to build healthy workplaces in which people employ their talents toward maximum performance and satisfaction, as pointed out by J. C. Quick.

WHAT IS OCCUPATIONAL HEALTH PSYCHOLOGY?

According to the Society for Occupational Health Psychology, OHP is an interdisciplinary specialty that blends psychology and occupational health sciences, such as public health or preventive medicine. The ultimate goal for occupational health psychologists in this new frontier is to improve the quality of work life by developing an array of primary, secondary, and tertiary prevention programs and strategies to reduce work stress and strain; promote safe and healthy work behavior; prevent accidents, illnesses, and injuries; and enhance work and family life.

The aims of primary prevention are to identify and eliminate individual and organizational health risks.

For example, organizations can redesign jobs to eliminate unsafe practices, individuals can learn how to manage time to reduce feelings of time pressure, and organizations can provide day care or eldercare for their employees so that workers experience less family–work conflict. When primary interventions fail, secondary interventions can be used, such as establishing social support networks at work, altering organizational structures, providing organizational and individual stress management, or developing family policies. Although primary and secondary interventions are preferred and tend to fall into the realm of I/O psychologists' specialties, tertiary preventions might also be needed to help employees cope with psychological or physical distress resulting from negative feedback from an assessment, layoff, job loss, or injury.

Although emerging from a blend of behavioral and social sciences and occupational health disciplines, the domains falling within OHP are not yet agreed on by researchers and practitioners. Regardless of what these domains might be in the future, OHP is intended to be inclusive and interdisciplinary in nature. OHP applies knowledge and methodology from areas such as occupational and environmental health, organizational behavior, human factors, sociology, industrial engineering, ergonomics, and economics. Possible OHP domains or topics can be reviewed in the *Handbook of Occupational Health Psychology*, the *Handbook of Work Stress, Counterproductive Work Behavior, The Psychology of Workplace Safety*, and *Health and Safety in Organizations*.

SURVEY OF RESEARCH AND PRACTICES IN OHP

There has been progressive advancement in OHP literature involving the investigation of plausible antecedents and determinants of occupational health and its consequences. These investigations have focused on one or more of the following:

- Dispositional factors, such as Type A, negative affectivity, and optimism;
- Societal and environmental factors, including workers' compensation and public health policies;
- Organizational factors, such as job design, organizational structure and climate, work arrangement, and compensation systems;
- Management factors, including leadership and communication;

- Family issues, such as variables associated with the interface between work and family; or
- Interactions among these variables.

This trend has encouraged psychologists to take a proactive role in preventing occupational illness and injury and workplace aggression, reducing work stress, strengthening the work–family relationship, and improving physical as well as psychological well-being.

Many of the issues in OHP are considered to be *soft* issues, such as work–family conflict, stress, or health, which might be viewed as less important in organizations, compared with bottom-line issues, including productivity and turnover. Since soft criteria, although they occur often at work, are bound to be de-emphasized because they lack the clear financial implications of *hard* criteria like productivity and turnover, it is important for I/O psychologists to develop empirically supported applications to promote healthy workplaces and demonstrate that these soft applications affect organizations' bottom lines. A few exemplary applications have been documented and will be briefly presented in the following text.

J. A. Adkins (1999) described the promising economic gains, such as workers' compensation costs, health care utilization rates, and mortality rates, of an organizational health center in the United States Air Force. The ultimate goal of the program was to develop a healthy workplace through promoting physical, behavioral, and organizational health so that organizational productivity could be maximized and workers' potentials could be optimized. Quick also documented the culture of Chaparral Steel Company that valued workers as resources rather than costs, and management made efforts to engage the minds and spirits of their workers. The economic gains in productivity—man-hours per ton of steel, sales, accidents, and turnover—were phenomenal.

OHP TRAINING PROGRAMS IN NORTH AMERICA AND EUROPE

An Institute of Medicine report in 2000, *Safe Work in the 21st Century,* voiced the urgency in training qualified OSH professionals while facing the challenges of a rapidly changing workforce in the 21st century. The report further pointed out the core disciplines in which OSH professionals should be trained. These core disciplines include occupational safety, industrial hygiene, occupational medicine, ergonomics, employee

assistance, and occupational health psychology. Compared with the more established disciplines mentioned earlier, OHP has been relatively less developed.

Beginning in the 1990s, several universities in North America and Europe have developed training in OHP. As the result of a needs assessment survey from human resources management programs and schools of public health, the APA and National Institute for Occupational Safety and Health (NIOSH) conducted a pilot program for postdoctoral training between 1994 and 1998 at three universities. The main objective was to broaden the knowledge and skills of postdoctoral professionals in a range of OHP-related disciplines. Similar to the nature of the aforementioned pilot programs, postgraduate OHP programs were also developed in Sweden and the Netherlands. In addition to postdoctoral and graduate studies programs, several universities in the United States and England have developed graduate-level OHP training programs. It should be noted that most of the graduate training programs in the United States have received funding from NIOSH and have been sponsored by the APA.

Although the previously mentioned programs have different emphases on OHP training, they all share at least one common characteristic: interdisciplinary training. More specifically, it is evident when looking at these programs that diverse faculty from psychology (e.g., I/O psychology, clinical and counseling psychology, health psychology, social psychology, human factors) and other disciplines (e.g., communications, epidemiology, ergonomics, industrial engineering, management, medicine, labor relations) play important roles in OHP training. The interdisciplinary training model is critical because discipline-specific training models as well as subdiscipline-specific training models tend to employ a myopic approach that fails to capture the complexity and multilevel nature of occupational health issues. For example, fatal or nonfatal work accidents are multilevel, complex, and dynamic phenomena, which can likely be attributed to a combination of cultural, societal, environmental, economic, organizational, ergonomic, management, psychological, and family factors.

FUTURE CHALLENGES IN OHP

Similar to any new specialty, the development of OHP is dependent on continuous advancement in research and practice. The inherent nature of OHP complicates the developmental process and makes for a number of future challenges for the field. Foremost, traditional training in psychology tends to be discipline specific; OHP, however, is a blend of psychology and other occupational health sciences. Hence, I/O psychologists must step outside their comfort zones to incorporate findings and best practices from a variety of disciplines and diverse topics, such as integration of ergonomic principles, organizational support, and attitude change to promote healthy behaviors among office workers. Second, many criteria within the OHP realm present problems for research and practices. For example, if accidents, injuries, and illnesses are of interest to I/O psychologists, we must advance methodology to address issues such as low base rate, problems associated with reporting these incidents, and the delayed onset of many occupationally related illnesses. Third, it is important to point out that occupational health is more than merely the absence of injuries and illnesses at work. Hence, the traditional disease or management models (i.e., fixing symptoms or problems) would not be the best models to follow when I/O psychologists attempt to develop a healthy workplace. A new model must be created, which incorporates a more complete definition of health and can be accepted by stakeholders including governments, society, organizations, management, and workers. Finally, among the many goals to be achieved by organizations, occupational health is likely a long-term goal. This presents a problem for gaining access to organizations, which is particularly critical for advancing OHP research and practice. Given the intense competition in the business world, short-term goals will likely capture management's immediate attention; and occupational health might not be considered their first priority. As a result, I/O psychologists who are trying to gain access to organizations must seriously consider the short-term gains of occupational health interventions and, specifically, consider such things as the economic gains associated with these interventions to gain attention.

—*Peter Y. Chen, Sarah DeArmond, and*
Yueng-hsiang Huang

See also Quality of Work Life

FURTHER READING

Adkins, J. A. (1999). Promoting organizational health: The evolving practice of occupational health psychology. *Professional Psychology: Research & Practice, 30,* 129–137.

Elkind, H. B. (Ed.). (1931). *Preventive management: Mental hygiene in industry.* New York: B. C. Forbes.

Ganster, D. C., Fox, M. L., & Dwyer, D. J. (2001). Explaining employees' health care costs: A prospective examination of stressful job demands, personal control, and physiological reactivity. *Journal of Applied Psychology, 86,* 954–964.

Ilgen, D. R. (1990). Health issues at work: Opportunity for industrial/organizational psychology. *American Psychologist, 45,* 273–283.

Institute of Medicine. (2000). *Safe work in the 21st century: Education and training needs for the next decade's occupational safety and health personnel.* Washington, DC: National Academy Press.

National Safety Council. (2004). *Injury facts 2004 edition.* Itasca, IL: Author.

Occupational Safety and Health Act of 1970. (1970). Pub. L. No. 91-596, 84 Stat. 1590.

Quick, J. C. (1999). The convergence of health and clinical psychology with public health and preventive medicine in an organizational context. *Professional Psychology, 30*(2), 123–128.

Raymond, J. S., Wood, D. W., & Patrick, W. K. (1990). Psychology doctoral training in work and health. *American Psychologist, 45,* 1159–1161.

Society for Industrial and Organizational Psychology. (2005). *Brief description of the specialty.* Retrieved August 12, 2005, from http://www.siop.org/history/crsppp.htm

Society for Occupational Health Psychology. (2005). *What Is Occupational Health Psychology?* Retrieved July 15, 2005, from http://www.sohp-online.org

Viteles, M. S. (1932). *Industrial psychology.* New York: W. W. Norton.

OCCUPATIONAL INFORMATION NETWORK (O*NET)

The Occupational Information Network (O*NET) refers to the database of worker and occupational attributes that succeeds the U.S. Department of Labor's (DOL) *Dictionary of Occupational Titles* (DOT) as the primary source of information for occupations in the U.S. economy. Although the DOT had held this title for many years, numerous events—including the explosion of new occupations that accompanied the Internet and technology age, the decline in blue-collar industrial/manufacturing occupations, the dynamic nature of many of today's jobs, and theoretical and methodological advances in our understanding of work and job analysis—necessitated a new system for collecting and disseminating occupational information. The DOL responded by sponsoring the development of a computerized repository of occupational information that would permit rapid revision of the data, as well as easy access by the many individuals who wished to use the data therein.

With a strong theoretical framework, a procedure for updating content on a regular basis, an online viewer, associated career exploration tools, and links to current labor market data, O*NET offers current, diverse data on key occupations in the U.S. economy. Although no occupational information or classification system can be optimal for every purpose, O*NET provides many users with many ways of exploring the world of work.

O*NET CONTENT

Occupations

The occupational taxonomy included in O*NET products and tools differs from that used in the DOT so as to reflect the changing world of work. First, job analysts aggregated the more than 12,000 DOT occupations into a more manageable number of occupational units (OUs). The initial aggregation yielded 1,172 OUs, which have been further refined to the approximately 950 occupations that now constitute the Standard Occupational Classification System (SOC). Some DOT occupations were not aggregated and stand as SOC occupations today, whereas other SOC occupations comprise hundreds of DOT occupations. Consistent with the dynamic nature of today's world of work, new occupations continue to be added, whereas others are removed. Also contained by O*NET are crosswalks of SOC occupations to other classification systems such as the DOT and the Military Occupational Classification.

Descriptors

Second, O*NET describes occupations using an expansive set of variables drawn from a *content model*. The content model is a theoretical framework that specifies 21 types of occupational descriptors:

1. Training
2. Experience
3. Licensing
4. Generalized Work Activities
5. Work Context
6. Organizational Context
7. Occupational Knowledges
8. Occupational Skills
9. Tasks
10. Machines/Tools/Equipment
11. Labor Market Information
12. Occupational Outlook
13. Wages
14. Abilities
15. Interests
16. Work Values
17. Work Styles
18. Basic Skills
19. Cross-Functional Skills
20. General Knowledge
21. Education

These 21 classes of occupational information, in turn, can be placed into one of six broad categories:

1. Worker characteristics such as abilities and interests
2. Worker requirements including basic skills and education
3. Experience requirements such as training and licensing
4. Occupational characteristics including occupational outlook and wages
5. Occupational requirements such as work context and generalized work activities
6. Occupation-specific information including tasks and machines/tools/equipment

The variables of the content model can also be categorized according to whether they are *worker-oriented* or *job-oriented* and whether they apply to a specific occupation (*within-occupation*) or many occupations (*cross-occupation*). Worker-oriented variables that cross occupations include skills, abilities, and interests; those applicable within occupations include occupational skills and knowledge. Job-oriented

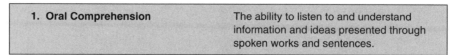

A. How **important** is ORAL COMPREHENSION to the performance of *your current job*?

*If you marked Not Important, skip LEVEL below and go on to the next activity.

B. What **level** of ORAL COMPREHENSION is needed to perform *your current job*?

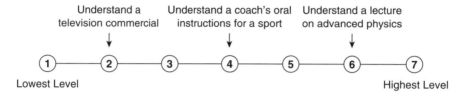

Figure 1   Sample Ability Rating Scale

variables that cross occupations include generalized work activities and organizational context; those applicable within occupations include tasks and machines/tools/equipment.

Each of the 21 classes of occupational descriptors defined by the content model comprises multiple variables on which each occupation receives ratings on appropriate scales such as importance, level, and frequency or extent. In all, the O*NET database describes each occupation using more than 275 variables. For example, there are 52 abilities that span the cognitive (oral comprehension, number facility), physical (gross body equilibrium, stamina), psychomotor (finger dexterity, speed of limb movement), and sensory (far vision, speech recognition) domains. Similarly, the 35 skills span six domains, including basic skills (mathematics, writing), social skills, (negotiation, instructing), and systems skills (systems analysis, judgment and decision making).

Each occupation receives ratings of importance, level, and frequency or extent on each of these variables. A sample ability rating scale is given in Figure 1.

Initially, trained job analysts provided ratings of each O*NET occupation, but the National Center for O*NET Development is leading an effort to augment the O*NET database with ratings from job incumbents. Occupational experts are also used for occupations having few incumbents or for which incumbents are difficult to locate, and job analysts continue to provide abilities ratings for all occupations. Incumbent data currently are added for approximately 200 occupations annually. Collectively, these data provide a rich, common language that can be used to describe occupations in the U.S. labor force.

THE O*NET SYSTEM

The O*NET database is part of the O*NET System, which also includes the O*NET OnLine viewer and O*NET career exploration tools.

O*NET OnLine

O*NET OnLine is a viewer that is available on the Internet. Hosted by the National Center for O*NET Development, the viewer affords O*NET users several options for using information provided in the O*NET database. For example, the viewer permits individuals to search for occupations via keywords or occupational codes, explore various job families, find occupations that match their skill profiles, or cross-walk occupations from other job classification systems to their counterpart SOC occupations.

Career Exploration Tools

DOL offers several vocational assessment tools that can be linked to the occupational information in the O*NET database. With an eye toward whole-person assessment, the O*NET career exploration tools (provided in both paper-and-pencil and computerized versions) allow individuals to determine their standing on abilities (Ability Profiler), vocational interests (Interest Profiler), and work values (computerized Work Importance Profiler, paper-and-pencil Work Importance Locator).

—*Rodney A. McCloy*

See also Dictionary of Occupational Titles; Job Analysis; Person–Vocation Fit; Work Values

FURTHER READING

Donsbach, J., Tsacoumis, S., Sager, C., & Updegraff, J. (2003). *O*NET analyst occupational abilities ratings: Procedures* (FR-03-22). Alexandria, VA: Human Resources Research Organization.

Levine, J., Nottingham, J., Paige, B., & Lewis, P. (2000). *Transitioning O*NET to the Standard Occupational Classification.* Raleigh, NC: National Center for O*NET Development.

McCloy, R., Campbell, J., Oswald, F., Lewis, P., & Rivkin, D. (1999). *Linking client assessment profiles to O*NET occupational profiles.* Raleigh, NC: National Center for O*NET Development.

Peterson, N., Mumford, M., Borman, W., Jeanneret, P., & Fleishman, E. (1999). *An occupational information system for the 21st century: The development of O*NET.* Washington, DC: American Psychological Association.

U.S. Department of Labor. (1991). *Dictionary of occupational titles* (Rev. 4th ed.). Washington, DC: Government Printing Office.

OLDER WORKER ISSUES

Older workers compose a growing segment of the workforce who must contend with a variety of distinctive concerns as they navigate their careers. Special concerns include physical, cognitive, and emotional changes that accompany the aging process, sources of work stress for older workers, the specter of age discrimination in employment opportunities, late career and skill maintenance concerns, and ultimately, decisions about when and how to retire from active employment. Evidence indicates that older adults are capable of maintaining high performance levels and positive attitudes toward work late into their lives.

Industrial/organizational (I/O) psychologists can use information about challenges that confront older workers to develop recruitment and retention strategies and work designs that allow older workers to maintain their performance effectiveness and to see work as a satisfying and rewarding experience.

AGE AND WORKFORCE DEMOGRAPHICS

The point at which the term *older worker* is applied in studies of workforce demographics may be as early as 40 years of age or as late as 65 years of age. Nonetheless, studies of workforce demographics all come to similar conclusions: The proportion of older adults who continue to engage in paid employment well into their 60s and 70s is growing and the proportion of our workforce that can be classified as *older* will continue to expand throughout the next decade.

Labor force participation rates generally tend to drop off beginning at about age 55 years, due primarily to early and *normal* retirements. However, labor force participation rates among those who are age 55 years and older are on the rise, with a projected labor force participation rate of 37% among those 55 and older by the year 2010. Among those ages 55 to 64 years, participation rates are expected to exceed 60%, and participation rates among those aged 65 to 74 are expected to exceed 22%. In fact, it is projected that *over 55* workers will compose approximately 17% of the total civilian labor force in the United States by the year 2010. The growth of this segment of the workforce represents the convergence of several forces, including increased health and life span, economic policies that encourage prolonged working (e.g., increases in the *standard* retirement age that qualifies an individual for full Social Security benefits), and elimination of mandatory retirement policies from most civilian occupations in the United States.

CHANGES THAT ACCOMPANY AGING

Several aspects of physical work capacity, such as aerobic capacity, strength and endurance, tolerance for heat and cold, and ability to adapt to shifts in waking and sleeping cycles, systematically decline with age. Sensory skills such as visual acuity and auditory sensitivity, and some psychomotor abilities including manual dexterity and finger dexterity, begin to decline once workers move into their 40s and beyond. Of course, the extent to which such decrements are likely to be associated with performance problems depends substantially on the nature of physical job requirements.

The most consistent finding in studies of cognitive abilities across the life span is a general slowing of response to information processing demands as adults age, particularly as they move into their 60s and beyond. In addition, recall and working memory both decline with age. Also, the manner in which learners prefer to acquire new skills differs between younger and older learners, with older learners preferring more active, experiential learning approaches and preferring to learn at a somewhat slower pace. Certain aspects of cognition are more affected by aging than others, and the rate of decline is slowed when cognitive skills are used regularly—*use it or lose it* seems to be an apt phrase in this case. Furthermore, some aspects of intellectual development—notably, those aspects of cognitive functioning that rely on expert knowledge (or *wisdom*)—continue to increase or remain stable well into the 70s.

Most personality traits are quite stable throughout the life course, but a general dampening of emotional responsiveness accompanies the aging process. There are also age-related shifts in the kinds of coping strategies that adults use to manage stressful experiences and increased skill in using such strategies.

Normal aging is also accompanied by increased frequency and severity of health concerns. Many older workers function with a variety of chronic health conditions, such as arthritis and chronic back pain, which also prompts them to carry out work duties while coping with some degree of pain or mobility impairment. All these factors have implications for physical stamina and the ability to sustain physically and mentally demanding work.

With all these changes in mind, it is important to point out two other sets of findings regarding age-related changes and characteristics. First, from life span studies, we know that the rate and extent of age-related change differs considerably among adults. This is a recurring theme of findings regarding cognitive and physical abilities, health status, and most other characteristics relevant to work functioning. Thus generalities regarding characteristics of older workers will frequently be incorrect for a particular individual worker.

Second, it is a common misconception that the changes accompanying aging will inevitably be associated with systematic declines in motivation, work attitudes, and job performance. Although it is certainly true that changes in physical and cognitive functioning that accompany the aging process provide the *potential* for reduced performance in some kinds of jobs, evidence of performance declines with aging tends to be the exception rather than the rule. There is little evidence that levels of motivation differ as a function of worker age, and studies of the relationship between age and work performance show no systematic relationship between the two. Absenteeism rates are generally low among older workers, and the frequency of accidents is actually lower among older workers than among younger workers. Furthermore, attitudes such as job satisfaction are somewhat more positive among older workers than among younger workers.

SOURCES OF WORK STRESS

Workers experience occupational stress when there is a mismatch between the demands of the job and the capabilities and resources of the worker. The changes that accompany aging provide some guidance regarding the conditions under which older workers are most likely to experience stress and the strains that accompany prolonged stress, such as performance decrements, injuries, negative work attitudes, and mental and physical health symptoms.

For example, jobs that require heavy lifting and tasks that involve external pacing and substantial time pressure produce chronic demands that may be of particular significance to older workers. Likewise, hot and cold work environments may be physically more taxing to older workers than they are to younger workers; and work schedules that require night work will be more demanding for older workers than for younger workers.

Other features of job design, such as the widespread incorporation of technology in the workplace, may produce both threats and opportunities for older workers. On the one hand, technological innovations (e.g., adjustable illumination and font sizes on computer displays and ergonomically designed chairs and workstations) can be used as a way of redesigning work to accommodate needs of older workers, thus reducing some sources of work-related stress. On the other hand, new technologies often require skill sets that many older workers have not developed. The threat of obsolescence that this raises can serve as a stressor that is particularly salient to older workers.

Older workers are also at risk from organizational sources of stress associated with their work roles. For example, time pressures and work *overload* have become a way of life on many jobs. The long-term nature of their exposure to the constant pressure of too much to do and insufficient time to accomplish it increases the likelihood that older workers will experience negative consequences, including *burnout* and reduced health and well-being.

Distinct from work design, the social environment in which work takes place exerts a variety of pressures on older workers that may be experienced as stressful, or that may reduce their ability to cope effectively with work demands. These include subtle or overt forms of age discrimination, hints about what older workers *can* and *should* do, and organizational cultures that devalue experience and *wisdom.*

AGE DISCRIMINATION

Although evidence regarding the relationship between worker age and work performance suggests that worker age is a singularly *poor* predictor of work performance, older workers encounter a variety of barriers to employment opportunities that reflect discrimination on the basis of age. Studies have documented age discrimination in many occupations with respect to hiring, promotions, salaries, and access to development opportunities. Sometimes the discrimination is fairly blatant, but at other times it represents more subtle (and often unintentional) differences in the way older workers and younger workers are treated at work.

One of the most common explanations for age discrimination is that managers and other decision makers are influenced by stereotypes that depict older workers as less capable, less energetic, less creative, more rigid, and less willing to learn than younger workers. This has the potential to put older job candidates at an unfair disadvantage when competing against younger applicants for jobs, promotions, and development opportunities. An additional unfortunate consequence of age discrimination is that it creates an environment in which older workers sometimes feel threats to their job security and, quite reasonably, experience anxiety about becoming re-employed should they lose their jobs.

To combat age discrimination in the United States, legal protections are afforded to older workers by the Age Discrimination in Employment Act. This legislation protects employees 40 years of age and older from discrimination on the basis of age in hiring, promotion, discharge, wages, and conditions of employment.

CAREER AND WORK–LIFE ISSUES

Workplace norms and expectations about appropriate career trajectories, such as the sense that an individual is *stalled* with respect to career advancement, cause considerable distress and distraction for many older workers. As organizational structures continue to *flatten,* the problem of career plateaus has become more widespread because there are fewer opportunities to continue upward movement.

Training and retraining are an important means of ensuring that older workers can continue to perform their jobs effectively and that they can move into new jobs and career paths later in their careers. Unrestricted opportunities for new skill development, support for participation in training, and training program design that incorporates the learning styles and preferences of older workers are all important to ensuring that late-career workers can continue to be effective in their work.

Among their work–life concerns, many older workers are likely to have significant responsibilities for the care of elderly adults, financial responsibility for college students, and concerns about coordinating their own plans for retirement or continued work with those of a spouse or partner. To be responsive to the work–life needs of older workers, employers need to take these kinds of concerns into account when they develop programs aimed at providing workers with options for balancing their work and personal lives.

RETIREMENT DECISIONS

As they move into their 50s and 60s, most workers devote considerable time and energy to wrestling with decisions about if and when to retire. Retirement decision making is a complex process that includes consideration of the *timing* of retirement (retire at age 55? 65? 75? Never?); the *completeness* of retirement, such as complete permanent withdrawal from the paid workforce versus alternative work arrangements such as part-time work or so-called *bridge* employment; and the *voluntariness* of retirement including feeling *pushed* out of a job or retiring for health reasons versus retiring to spend more time with family and other personal pursuits.

Personal preferences, health, and economic and social pressures to continue working or discontinue working as one nears *normal* retirement age all play important roles in this process. For example, early retirement packages offered by many organizations as a way of reducing their workforces provide opportunities for some workers to leave the workforce early or shift to new careers. Chronic health problems may speed retirement; or they may lead to the decision to delay retirement to maintain access to health care benefits. In addition, personal preferences for continued work and the financial pressures of eldercare and family education lead many older workers to continue some form of paid employment well past the age of 65 years, but it may not be in the form of traditional full-time employment. As a result, the reality of retirement is that many workers will move into and out of the workforce several times during their later years, and organizations can make best use of the talents of these workers if they design flexible work arrangements that can accommodate this kind of movement.

—*Janet L. Barnes-Farrell*

See also Age Discrimination in Employment Act; Careers; Retirement; Stereotyping; Stress, Consequences

FURTHER READING

Adams, G. A., & Beehr, T. A. (Eds.). (2003). *Retirement: Reasons, processes and results.* New York: Springer.

Barnes-Farrell, J. L. (2004). Older workers. In J. Barling, K. Kelloway, & M. Frone (Eds.), *Handbook of work stress* (pp. 431–454). Thousand Oaks, CA: Sage.

Farr, J., & Ringseis, E. (2002). The older worker in organizational context: Beyond the individual. In C. Cooper & I. Robertson (Eds.), *International review of industrial and organizational psychology, 2002 Vol. 17* (pp. 31–75). New York: Wiley.

Fullerton, H. N., & Toossi, M. (2001). Labor force projections to 2010: Steady growth and changing composition. *Monthly Labor Review, 124*(11), 21–38.

Hansson, R. O., DeKoekkoek, P. D., Neece, W. M., & Patterson, D. W. (1997). Successful aging at work: Annual review, 1992–1996: The older worker and transitions to retirement. *Journal of Vocational Behavior, 51,* 202–233.

McEvoy, G., & Cascio, W. (1989). Cumulative evidence of the relationship between employee age and job performance. *Journal of Applied Psychology, 74,* 11–17.

Sterns, H., & Huyck, M. H. (2001). The role of work in midlife. In M. Lachman (Ed.), *Handbook of midlife development* (pp. 447–486). New York: Wiley.

OPEN-ENDED DATA COLLECTION APPROACHES

See CONTENT CODING

OPTIMISM AND PESSIMISM

The terms *optimism* and *pessimism* refer to the tendencies of people to expect that good things will happen and to expect that bad things will happen, respectively. Persons who believe that their goals can be achieved despite the difficulties they might encounter are said to hold an optimistic view. They are predisposed to think that whatever problems may come their way, they will be able to manage and resolve them. Pessimism is the general tendency to expect negative outcomes. These individuals tend to view future experiences negatively. They are predisposed to think about the potential negative outcomes of whatever problems, setbacks, challenges, or difficulties are placed in their way.

In recent years optimistic and pessimistic expectations have been found to predict who will succeed. Regardless of job or level in the organization, individuals encounter many *curve balls*: changes, obstacles, difficulties, or adversities on the job. Whether it is dealing with a sudden change in procedures; an irate customer, coworker, or boss; or an accidentally deleted important e-mail, it is estimated that the average employee can face up to 23 adversities in just one day. How well employees handle these job challenges can affect how productive they are as well as their ability to learn, adapt, overcome future obstacles, meet goals, and even lead others. In sum, how successfully employees deal with adverse situations affects their success as well as the organization's success. Thus optimism and pessimism can have important ramifications for an organization in the selection, training, motivation, and work life of its employees and leaders.

BACKGROUND AND KEY ISSUES

It has only been within the past 35 or so years that we have seen a renewed interest among psychologists in understanding the constructs of optimism and pessimism and their effects on individuals' lives. Michael Scheier and Charles Carver were the pioneers of this research stream based on their studies examining generalized outcome expectancies. Martin Seligman's work on learned helplessness and more recently, positive psychology, has also provided a strong influence for sparking additional research. Today we see an explosion of studies examining the effects of optimism and pessimism on our health, physical and mental well-being, and psychological adjustment. It has generally been found that those who tend toward an optimistic perspective experience fewer physical symptoms of stress, cope more effectively with stressful events, and adjust better to important life transitions. The positive effects for optimism tend to be explained by the type of coping strategies typically embraced by those with an optimistic perspective. Optimism is related to an individual's use of adaptive, engaging coping strategies, which include rational problem solving, cognitive restructuring, expressing emotions, and seeking social support during stressful times. Conversely, pessimism is related to an individual's use of maladaptive, disengaging coping strategies, which include avoiding problems, impulsive and careless problem solving, being self-critical, and socially withdrawing from stressful situations.

Despite the potential value of optimism and pessimism, few studies have examined these important notions of optimism and pessimism in an organizational context. More research is needed. Before reviewing what we know about the role of optimism and pessimism in the workplace, a key issue in the literature centers on the measurement of optimism and pessimism and the dimensionality of these constructs.

MEASUREMENT OF OPTIMISM AND PESSIMISM

A number of different instruments have been developed to assess optimism and pessimism. The distinctions among the instruments stem mainly from the different theoretical perspectives held by the researchers. As a consequence it can be a challenge to compare and contrast the findings across studies, which have used different measures of optimism and pessimism. Therefore, it is crucial to become familiar with the measures to understand the research.

The Life Orientation Test (LOT) is probably the most popular measure used to assess optimism and pessimism. It is based on the notion that optimism and pessimism are generalized outcome expectancies; for example, "Rarely do I expect good things to happen." The

LOT was revised, resulting in the Revised Life Orientation Test (RLOT).

One debated issue in the literature deals with the dimensionality of optimism and pessimism (discussed in more detail in the following text). In short, the LOT and RLOT were developed as unidimensional measures of dispositional optimism, but there is now evidence suggesting the LOT is bidimensional. The Extended Life Orientation Test (ELOT) has added to this evidence by demonstrating that a two-factor model provided the best fit, resulting in separate scores for optimism and pessimism. Regardless, the LOT, RLOT, and ELOT tend to provide the most direct assessment of optimism and pessimism.

The attributional style questionnaire (ASQ) is also a popular measure that assesses the constructs based on an individual's tendency to explain or make attributions for positive and negative events. As a more indirect measure, respondents are given a negative or positive event and asked to indicate one major cause for the event and rate the internality, stability, and globality. Those who are labeled as having a pessimistic explanatory style believe bad things happen to them because it has something to do with them (internal) and happens frequently (stable) and across all situations (global). Individuals with an optimistic explanatory style believe positive things happen to them because of internal, stable, and global factors. The expanded attributional style questionnaire (EASQ), a revision to the ASQ, is composed of 24 negative events only. Another technique to assess explanatory style, the content analysis of verbatim explanations (CAVE), has also been developed.

Other measures of optimism and pessimism include the optimism-pessimism instrument, the defensive pessimism questionnaire (DPQ), and the Hope Scale.

DIMENSIONALITY OF OPTIMISM AND PESSIMISM

Optimism and pessimism have traditionally been considered polar opposites on a continuum. From this perspective, a person is either optimistic or pessimistic but cannot hold optimistic and pessimistic perspectives concurrently. This singular way of thinking is limiting because it could be argued that overly optimistic beliefs are not always advantageous. Consider, for example, the disastrous outcome for an individual who decides to spend forthcoming winnings after buying a lottery ticket because the person felt so optimistic about winning and thus neglected to think about the dismal odds. Consequently, more recent thinking along with supportive evidence has shown that we can hold some of both aspects and therefore, optimism and pessimism are believed to represent two independent or partially independent constructs. Notably, when treating optimism and pessimism as separate constructs, distinct results have been obtained. Interestingly, specific terms have also been coined to reflect this separateness notion such as *flexible optimism, defensive pessimism, cautious optimists,* or *strategic optimists.*

OPTIMISM AND PESSIMISM IN THE WORK SETTING

Optimism and pessimism have been examined with regard to academic performance among college freshmen and career planning and exploration in high school students. In addition, their effects on stress, coping, and effort at work have been topics of study. In general, optimism buffered against the occupational and life stress of university teachers and burnout for information technology professionals, and it led to increased effort intentions of salespeople.

Only a handful of studies have examined the effects of optimism and pessimism on job performance. Interestingly, each study used a different measure of optimism, pessimism, and job performance and also used employees in different types of jobs. In a study that used the ASQ, life insurance agents with an optimistic explanatory style sold more life insurance and reported a lower likelihood of quitting their jobs than did agents with a pessimistic style. In another study using a single overall LOT score, pessimistic call center employees reported higher levels of self-reported performance, more satisfaction, and lower turnover intent than optimists. Optimists, however, perceived lower levels of job stress and work and nonwork conflict than the pessimists. Finally, in a third study, the effects of separate measures of optimism and pessimism using the ELOT found both optimism and pessimism to be related to supervisory-rated ratings of overall job performance for production employees in a manufacturing plant. Pessimism, however, was found to remain a significant predictor after controlling for variance accounted for by selection measures such as a personality test and work skills inventory. These findings demonstrate the importance of assessing optimism and pessimism separately.

These three studies, which examined the effects of optimism and pessimism on job performance, vividly demonstrate the challenge of comparing across results in which different measures of optimism and pessimism have been used. Therefore, this area could benefit greatly from more systematic research that clearly addresses the measurement and dimensionality of optimism and pessimism.

Given the power of optimism and pessimism on our lives in general and the role of such positive and negative thinking in work situations, a number of important questions about optimism and pessimism await further research. There is relatively little work on the selection, training, and job performance of individuals in work settings. It will also be interesting to explore what those who now hold optimistic and pessimistic perspectives do when they encounter threatening, challenging, and novel situations. Although research has not tended to find gender difference with regard to optimistic and pessimistic perspectives, some cultural differences have been noted between Asian Americans and Caucasian Americans and should be further explored. From an optimistic perspective, the opportunities are endless for research; but from a pessimistic perspective, the construct issues of measurement and dimensionality of optimism and pessimism must be faced so that research in this area can advance.

—*Therese Macan*

See also Positive Psychology Applied to Work

FURTHER READING

Chang, E. C. (Ed.). (2002). *Optimism & pessimism: Implications for theory, research and practices.* Washington, DC: APA.

Macan, T. H., Heft, L., & Roberts, L. (2005). *Optimism and pessimism: Predictors of success in the workplace?* Paper presented at the 20th Annual SIOP conference, Los Angeles, CA.

Seligman, M. E., & Schulman, P. (1986). Explanatory style as a predictor of productivity and quitting among life insurance agents. *Journal of Personality and Social Psychology, 50,* 832–838.

Stolz, P. G. (2000). *The adversity quotient @ work.* New York: Morrow.

Tuten, T. L., & Neidermeyer, P. E. (2004). Performance, satisfaction, and turnover in call centers: The effects of stress and optimism. *Journal of Business Research, 57,* 26–34.

ORGANIZATIONAL BEHAVIOR

Organizational behavior (OB) can be defined as the study of human behavior in the workplace. More specifically, investigators employ the principles of the scientific method to help them understand, predict, and manage employee behavior. The knowledge that follows rigorous, systematic study is used to enhance the productivity of organizations and the quality of work life for its employees.

HISTORY

The field of organizational behavior can trace its roots back to the late 19th and early 20th centuries when many industrial efficiency experts were attempting to discover how to get people to do more work in less time. These investigations in the workplace, conducted by management forerunners such as Frederick Taylor, Frank and Lillian Gilbreth, Henri Fayol, and Max Weber, to name a few, focused mainly on the hierarchical structure of the organization, division of labor, and the management functions of planning and controlling. Then in 1924 Elton Mayo led the human relations movement by focusing on the importance of human social processes in work settings. He and his colleagues helped conduct the landmark Hawthorne Studies at the Western Electric's Hawthorne Works just outside of Chicago. The Hawthorne Studies investigated such issues as the effects of illumination, length of workday, rest breaks, method of payment, and group dynamics on employee behavior. Despite methodological flaws present in the Hawthorne Studies, an important implication of these studies followed. That is, paying special attention to the human component of an organization can affect employee behavior. Because of this focus on the social side of human behavior in the organization (i.e., rather than just investigating the physical side as was seen in the earlier efficiency studies mentioned), it is generally recognized that the Hawthorne Studies served as the catalyst to propel OB as a modern field of study.

THE SUBFIELDS OF ORGANIZATIONAL BEHAVIOR

The investigation of human behavior can occur at three levels of analysis within the organization: the individual, groups and teams of individuals, and the organization itself as a whole. As a result, there have been a plethora of diverse contributors to the academic discipline of OB. The original goal of researchers in this newly created field was to construct a uniform comprehensive body of organizational research. However, because of the different perspectives held by the contributors from the various areas of the social sciences (e.g., psychology, economics, sociology, political science, communication, and anthropology), the result was three somewhat distinct subfields of OB. These subfields mirrored the three levels of analysis of human behavior. Micro-OB mainly concerns itself with investigating the behavior of individuals within the organization. Meso-OB focuses on the behavior of groups and teams in the workplace. Finally, researchers in Macro-OB conduct investigations at the organizational level of analysis.

CURRENT TOPICS OF INTEREST IN OB

Some research topics of interest within the Micro-OB subfield deal with selecting and training employees, employee motivation, evaluating performance of individual employees, decision making, and employee satisfaction and stress. Areas of investigation within Meso-OB include group dynamics, team effectiveness, job design, and leadership, to name a few. Some main areas of investigation at the Macro-OB level are organizational culture and climate, organizational change and development, employee socialization, power and politics within the organization, conflict management and negotiation, and the interaction of the organization with its environment.

—*Robert D. Yonker*

See also Human Resource Management; Organizational Development

FURTHER READING

Fayol, H. (1949). *General and industrial management.* London: Pittman.
Mayo, E. (1933). *The human problems of an industrial civilization.* London: Macmillan.
Taylor, F. W. (1947). *Scientific management.* New York: Harper & Row.
Weber, M. (1921). *Theory of social and economic organization* (A. M. Henderson & T. Parsons, Trans.). London: Oxford University Press.

ORGANIZATIONAL BEHAVIOR MANAGEMENT

Organizational behavior management (OBM) combines the principles of B. F. Skinner's reinforcement theory with applications in work settings. It espouses the same basic tenet as reinforcement theory: Behavior is shaped and maintained by its consequences. What occurs *after* rather than before the behavior of interest is the focus, as exemplified in the principles of reinforcement and punishment. These principles, particularly positive reinforcement, are applied in the public and private sectors to motivate the members of these organizations.

OBM EMBODIES THE SCIENTIST-PRACTITIONER MODEL

Embracing reinforcement or behavior analysis principles that are used to solve problems in work settings, OBM embodies the scientist-practitioner model recommended for the study of psychology. A behavior analyst acts in the role of a practitioner, who provides professional services to the members of organizations, as well as that of a scientist, who seeks to improve the plan used to promote performance. To determine whether a given plan or intervention is effective, no number of testimonials or expert opinions substitute for the collection of data that a given result actually occurred. So strong is this belief in empirical evidence that the primary journal, the *Journal of Organizational Behavior Management (JOBM)*, was started in 1977 not by academics but by members of a consulting firm, Behavioral Systems, Inc., spearheaded by former quarterback Fran Tarkenton and led by clinical psychologist Aubrey Daniels.

Exchanges between academics and nonacademics continue to be plentiful. At the Association for Behavior Analysis conference, professors and students give papers side by side with colleagues in organizations such as Chevron and JPMorgan Chase. In the OBM network, 58% of the members are academics and 42% are nonacademics, and in *JOBM,* 31% of the articles are contributed by professionals in human service settings as well as members of behaviorally oriented consulting firms. In contrast, in the *Journal of Applied Psychology,* the affiliation of authors outside of universities is 13%.

Proactive Stance Plays a Key Role in the Direction of OBM

The aim of making the world a better place is distinctive in psychology to OBM in particular and reinforcement theory in general. Fueled by Skinner, who wrote about his vision of a utopian community in *Walden Two,* the use of reinforcement for prosocial purposes took root in the 1960s. During that era in the United States, dramatic societal changes were occurring: the passage of landmark civil rights legislation and the ending of the Vietnam War. At the same time, reports heralded the first successful applications of reinforcement theory. Children who had been diagnosed as autistic and were destined to spend the remainder of their lives within the drab walls of institutions began to communicate and help themselves when they were reinforced for successive approximations to desired behaviors. Teachers using a combination of positive reinforcement and extinction helped first graders in a disadvantaged neighborhood learn skills critical to their further achievement. At Emery Air Freight and American Airlines, as Skinner described, positive reinforcement programs were being implemented. The evening news touted the results of a token economy program in the army at Fort Ord, California. In 1968, in the first issue of the *Journal of Applied Behavior Analysis,* the field's pioneers Donald Baer, Montrose Wolf, and Todd Risley predicted that researching mental retardation, crime, mental illness, and education, to name a few, would make for a better society. Hence it was not surprising when behavior analysts went to work sites where they too actively sought to make improvements.

This desire to make a difference has made a difference. Behavior analysts do not restrict themselves to traditional areas such as productivity and absenteeism. Instead, they have tackled such subtle and elusive issues as the quality of client care, even though the definitions and measures of what staff should do to bring about the changes in their clients is a challenge. Similarly, when company presidents wanted to reduce employees' injuries, behavior analysts went beyond the conventional counts of accidents to develop new ways of appraising what workers need to do to avoid having accidents.

The kinds of performance addressed range widely. They include, among others, the following:

- Production and production-related, such as conducting building code inspections, processing student applications, and sorting and loading packages

- Attendance and punctuality necessitated by needing to have a minimum number of qualified personnel in human service settings, hospitals, and unionized manufacturing and distribution centers
- Safety and health, which includes safe and unsafe acts, such as properly lifting patients and wearing ear plugs, as well as other indexes, including housekeeping and the reduction of hazards, all of which are designed to lessen the chance of causing a disabling injury
- Care given to patients, clients, and students in community mental health centers, schools, and institutions, as well as service delivered to customers in banks, restaurants, and department stores

Productivity accounts for approximately one fifth of the studies. The second highest is attendance. Next, with 10% to 15% of the studies, are safety and service.

A BEHAVIORAL APPROACH TO APPRAISING AND MOTIVATING MEMBERS OF ORGANIZATIONS

Five Integral Steps

In the most prevalent intervention, that of positive reinforcement, behavior analysts use five steps.

1. They analyze the situation to determine what conditions might be responsible for maintaining the problem. Instead of dwelling on the characteristics of individuals such as their poor work attitudes, problematic personalities, or lower educational and experience levels, none of which can be readily changed, they examine the consequences of employees' performance, including the evaluation, compensation, and promotion practices of companies. Then, if warranted, they attempt to change not the people per se, but these personnel practices.

2. They specify desired performance, defining work practices, such as smiling at a customer or clearing walkways of spills, until the definitions meet the test of interrater reliability, in which two raters independently collect data, check for agreements, and obtain agreement scores of 90% or better.

3. They measure desired performance, going regularly to the site, recording the level or rate of performance, and conducting interrater reliability checks.

4. They provide frequent, contingent, positive consequences, such as posting scores on a graph to permit

workers to see how their scores compare with their previous record.

5. Finally, they evaluate the effectiveness of the program by using a research design (often the within-group reversal or multiple baseline), permitting the drawing of conclusions about causality with confidence, to see if the program caused the changes.

HIGHLIGHTING THE INTEGRAL STEPS OF SPECIFYING AND MEASURING PERFORMANCE

Steps two and three are critical to positively reinforce workers for jobs well done. Hence behavior analysts expend considerable time and effort ensuring the quality of *how* the information is gathered. However, *what* is measured is as important as how the data are obtained. Judith L. Komaki has identified five criteria. Given as the mnemonic SURF & C, the criteria stand for the following:

S: The target or dependent variable is sampled (S) directly rather than using a filtered or secondary source, for example, workers or the products of their work are observed firsthand instead of relying on their own or someone else's reports.

U: The target is primarily under (U) the workers' control, responsive to their efforts, and minimally affected by extraneous factors.

R: Interrater reliability (R) scores of 90% or better are obtained during the formal data collection period. Observers or raters go independently to sample workers' performance or behaviors, terms used interchangeably, rating use of the same scoring system and checking to see if they agree. They continue practicing and, in some cases, revamping the coding system until they can obtain scores of 90% or better.

F: The target is assessed frequently (F)—often and regularly—at least 20 and ideally 30 times during the intervention period. And

C: Evidence is provided showing that the target is indeed *critical* (C) to the desired result, otherwise referred to as *valid*. The evidence can be a significant correlation between the measure, such as a newly developed checklist for service, and the ultimate criterion including customer satisfaction.

The criteria of U and C are concerned with *what* is measured; the criteria of S, R, and F are concerned with *how* the information is collected.

A Nontraditional Approach to Reducing Injuries: Measuring Safety Performance

Consider an example: Lack of control is an issue with the readily available injury statistics. Workers can perform safely yet still be injured; at the same time, workers can be unsafe and still not have an accident. Hence to avoid relying on a measure over which workers cannot readily exert much control, behavior analysts have devised new measures of safety performance, such as looking at whether workers lift properly, actions that are for the most part under (U) their control. To ensure that the newly developed measure is valid, Robert A. Reber and Jerry A. Wallin (1983) collected data in different departments in a factory on injuries and the new measure of safety practices and then conducted a correlational analysis. Finding the higher the practices, the lower the injuries per department indicated that the measure was critical (C). At the same time, data are typically collected so that the S, R, and F criteria are met. Trained observers go to the site and directly sample (S) work practices. They collect information frequently (F), often at least weekly. Last, interrater reliability (R) checks are done in which two observers independently record and identify agreements between raters and calculate a percentage agreement score (number of agreements/ number of agreements and disagreements). Checklist revisions continue until agreement is reached on the scoring of checklist items almost all the time. When this criterion is achieved, then and only then are the terms considered to be acceptably defined. Reliability checks are also used in training; trainees are not considered trained until they can pass the interrater reliability test. Raters are then regularly checked to see if they are becoming stricter or more lenient during the formal data collection. These measures of safety enable the providing of positive consequences, which have the long-term impact of reducing costly and tragic injuries.

Going Beyond the Student to Assess the Behavior of the Teacher

Behaviorally based interventions have become the most prevalent approach for the treatment of children and adults with autism and developmental disabilities. Among its special features are the ways teachers are assessed. The ultimate outcome—improving client skills—is clear. To achieve this result, however, it is insufficient to focus on only the client. Instead, it is important to identify what staff members should do to enable improvements in their clients. Among the enabling practices Dennis R. Reid and his colleagues specified for teachers of the developmentally disabled were giving instructions, often verbal; guiding the student physically through the steps; and delivering rewards that are timely and contingent. To see whether these behaviors were valid, they looked to see if there was a relationship between the behaviors of students and teachers. Their analysis showed that as the appropriate use of teaching techniques increased, so did the skills of the students, indicating that the practices were critical (C). As in the preceding example, the S, R, and F criteria were met. Reid and his colleagues directly sampled (S) the teachers' implementation of the techniques, collecting data frequently (F), at least daily. The observers conducted interrater reliability (R) checks on one fifth of the observations; scores ranged between 74% and 97%.

The specification and measurement of performance enable frequent, contingent, positive consequences for desired performance. Although these steps are deceptively simple, they have resulted in far-reaching and meaningful differences at work on a variety of challenging tasks.

—Judith L. Komaki and Alicia M. Alvero

See also Reinforcement Theory of Work Motivation

FURTHER READING

Austin, J., & Carr, J. E. (Eds.). (2000). *Handbook of applied behavior analysis.* Reno, NV: Context Press.

Baer, D. M., Wolf, M. M., & Risley, T. R. (1968). Some current dimensions of applied behavior analysis. *Journal of Applied Behavior Analysis, 1,* 91–97.

Daniels, A. C. (1994). *Bringing out the best in people.* New York: McGraw-Hill.

Komaki, J. L. (1998). When performance improvement is the goal: A new set of criteria for criteria. *Journal of Applied Behavior Analysis, 31,* 263–280.

Komaki, J. L. (2003). Reinforcement theory at work: Enhancing and explaining what employees do. In L. W. Porter, G. A. Bigley, & R. M. Steers (Eds.), *Motivation and work behavior* (7th ed., pp. 95–112). New York: McGraw-Hill.

Reber, R. A., & Wallin, J. A. (1983). Validation of a behavioral measure of occupational safety. *Journal of Organizational Behavior Management, 5*(2), 69–77.

Skinner, B. F. (1983). *A matter of consequences: Part 3 of an autobiography.* New York: Random House.

ORGANIZATIONAL CHANGE

Change has been considered the most reliable constant within organizations. Yet, although the phenomenon has been recognized as important for years, organizational change is one of the least understood aspects of organization life, evidenced by numerous failed initiatives. In spite of the books and articles written about managing change, perhaps the paradox between prevalence and failure lies in the difficulty organizations have in getting a handle on change itself.

Simply put, change is the process by which an organism goes from relative stability through a period of relative instability and then back to relative stability. This is commonly represented by Kurt Lewin's three-stage model of change. The first stage is *unfreezing.* This initial stage includes the willingness of individuals to abandon the old and adopt the new and is best understood through the study of motivation. The second stage is the *change* itself where the new is put into place. This stage is associated with new routines requiring knowledge and skill acquisition. The third stage is called *refreezing,* which focuses on normalizing the new or moving from compliance to commitment. Although attention is generally placed on the second and third stages, many believe that most changes fail because the *unfreeze* stage is ineffective.

Because organizational change is fundamental to many important topics, it has not received dedicated attention sufficient to provide adequate understanding and practice. That is, change is endemic to innovation (implementing new and novel ideas); transformational leadership (taking people from point A to point B); Total Quality Management (continuous improvement); organizational development (preparing employees to identify and implement change); and, according to Peter Drucker, the basic purpose of the business enterprise itself (constantly changing to meet customers' demands).

Addressing three aspects of organizational change should prove helpful to improve understanding of this complex organizational phenomenon. First is the emerging issue of levels of analysis. Second are the major themes typically associated with organizational change. Third is explicating new ways change can be viewed.

LEVELS OF ANALYSIS

Although organizational change has typically been viewed nominally (e.g., mergers, policy change, new technology), there is an emerging view of change as cascading events beginning with the organization's external environment, down through the organizational level, to the work group level, and finally to the individual level. As such, change is characterized by different dimensions changing at different levels.

The environment consists of changes in the market, in government regulations, or in prevailing economic conditions. Organizational level change generally deals with modifications to some combination of strategy, culture, or structure. Although work groups also have structure and culture, generally focus is on goals, leadership, and work processes. Finally, individual level change typically involves the job and proximal working conditions. Therefore, understanding organizational change involves understanding how dimensions at each level affect performance at the corresponding level, and then how these dimensions affect change and performance at subsequent lower levels.

Additionally, an overlooked insight about change is that different work groups and different individuals within work groups do not experience a given organizational change in the same way. This is illustrated in the case of a jewelry company that expanded its product line to include high-end jewelry, causing a reorganization of its sales staff, a renovation of the showroom, and new skills for some employees. Thus a typical comment of employees participating in a change is "in the broad scheme of things, these were just minor adjustments to the company, but to those of us in the department, the changes were significant." Failure to recognize change in this comprehensive way results in the oversimplification of important nuances or fragmented conclusions lacking broad application.

THE THEMES OF ORGANIZATIONAL CHANGE

A review of studies of organizational change conducted in the 1990s revealed four major themes. These were content (the *what* of change), context (the *what else* of change), process (the *how* of change), and outcome (the *so what* of change).

The content of change includes variables of change such as dimensions at levels of analysis (mentioned earlier), as well as the *sign* and magnitude of change. For example, the full description of a specific *reorganization* may be expressed as an entirely new (magnitude) structure (dimension) of top management (level), which will create more opportunity for growth (favorable). Thus two different *reorganizations* should be considered different organizational changes when one or more of these four characteristics of *what changed* vary.

The context of change includes variables associated with *what else* is going on relative to the change that is outside the change itself but influences its outcome. One aspect of context deals with forces or factors that contribute to the reason for change or create significant barriers to change. Generally, these are external events of environmental influences on the organization, such as competition, government regulation, economic shifts, or geopolitical events. Another aspect of context deals with internal variables that may moderate how change is handled or experienced in the organization. This would include organizational characteristics such as climate for change, leadership style, and cultural barriers to change. A third aspect of context is the characteristics of individuals affected by organizational change. These characteristics range from distal traits, such as personality and age, to midrange states, such as general change efficacy or commitment to the organization, to change-specific individual differences in readiness for change and coping resources.

The process of change has typically been the major focus of organizational change. That is, how something is done is ultimately more important than what is done. Traditionally, *change management* has involved stage models or the proper steps to successful implementation. However, more recently change process has been viewed qualitatively. In this case, the *how* is usually characterized by the notion of procedural justice. That is, when change agents of an organization include the change participants in the process; give advanced notice and provide adequate explanations of changes; and offer an acceptable rationale for the change, those affected by the change respond more positively to the change. The process can also be characterized by the support management gives to the change. Support comes in the form of top management commitment to the change and a desire to provide adequate resources necessary for successful implementation of the change.

Finally, the outcomes of change are essentially attitudes, behavior, and performance assessed at various levels. When outcome is evaluated at the organizational or group level, typically the interest is in how the normal performance measures were affected (e.g., sales, profit, productivity). However, when individuals are the focus, there is a broad array of outcomes of interest. These outcomes could be either directly associated with the change itself, such as attitude toward the change, or a residual effect on the individual, such as stress, change in person–environment fit, job satisfaction, or organizational commitment.

Attitude toward the change has been one individual outcome of interest. It is important to note that recent research on attitude toward change has explored its multidimensional nature and the differences between it and other related constructs. Sandy Piderit posited that attitude toward the change is composed of three components: cognition, affect, and behavioral intent, none of which move in concert regarding a particular change. That is, behavioral intent to support the change would typically be more positive than beliefs about the change and emotional response to the change. This is evidenced by employees affected by a change who say, "Complaining is at an all-time high, yet work continues to be put out at an amazing pace." Distinction has also been made between acceptance and resistance. These are considered two different constructs rather than opposite ends of one continuum. That is, low acceptance is the absence of support and high resistance is the presence of negatively directed effort.

THE NATURE OF ORGANIZATIONAL CHANGE

In many areas of organizational behavior study, there are two different ways to approach a topic. One approach is to simply name a change phenomenon and build a body of knowledge around it. However, as mentioned earlier, this fragments understanding and restricts generalization. The other approach is to describe the phenomenon along one or more dimensions. That is, instead of studying *reorganizations* or *entering new markets* separately, it is possible to investigate amount of change in culture or structure occurring in either nominal change.

Pace, sequence, and linearity of change is another way to view an organizational change. Pace deals with whether there is early rapid change to overcome inertia or late rapid change following periods of *softening up* the organization, or whether change is gradual, building trust as change progresses. Sequence deals with order of importance or what needs to be changed before what else can be changed. Linearity recognizes that change may be nonlinear because of oscillations and delays caused by uncertainty and resistance.

Another issue regarding the nature of change has to do with whether change is episodic. Traditionally, change is viewed as a break in the status quo. This idea treats change as if it is a *single* disruption in an otherwise stable setting. A contrarian perspective views change more as simultaneous and cumulative, sometimes referred to as *turbulence*. This perspective posits that change does not occur in isolation of other changes, and in fact, organizations are basically in a state of flux where change is a natural state and managing change is a continual process. The success an organization ultimately has with managing change may depend on which of these two views of change applies.

Finally, an aspect that shapes how organizations view and approach change is the notion of the asymmetry of change. This involves the assumption that the motivation for and benefit of change is greater for the organization than for the individual. Although it is important for change to be a win–win experience, management cannot forget that the reality of rationale and valence of change is skewed to the organization.

—*Steven D. Caldwell*

See also Organizational Change, Resistance to

FURTHER READING

Amis, J., Slack, T., & Hinings, C. R. (2004). The pace, sequence, and linearity of radical change. *Academy of Management Journal, 47,* 15–39.

Armenakis, A. A., & Bedian, A. G. (1999). Organizational change: A review of theory and research in the 1990s. *Journal of Management, 25,* 293–315.

Burke, W. (2002). *Organization change: Theory and practice.* Thousand Oaks, CA: Sage.

McKinley, W., & Scherer, A. G. (2000). Some unanticipated consequences of organizational restructuring. *Academy of Management Review, 25,* 735–752.

ORGANIZATIONAL CHANGE, RESISTANCE TO

It has been broadly reported that change is happening at an accelerated rate in organizations. As a result, employees are constantly required to understand the changes, cope with the challenges, and ultimately adapt. In this environment, a typical employee response is to resist the change. A recent review of empirical research on reactions to change found cognitive, emotional, and behavioral aspects of resistance. The shock, anger, resistance, acceptance (SARA) model of organizational change is a pragmatic way of looking at the different stages of reactions to change. Although these reactions are not universal, nor are they necessarily linear, the point remains that organizations benefit from considering that employees may need time to work through the process of dealing with organizational change before they move to acceptance. By leaping forward too quickly, organizational leadership may bring about either direct or indirect resistance to organizational change efforts.

UNDERLYING REASONS FOR RESISTANCE TO CHANGE

Organizational change can affect individuals in a number of ways. From potential job loss to increased job opportunities, the costs and benefits of organizational changes to employees are often unpredictable. To effectively address resistance to organizational change, it is important to understand the reasons. Potential reasons why employees may resist organizational change include the following:

- Employees may not understand why the changes are occurring.
- Employees do not understand what the changes entail.
- Employees do not know how they will be affected.
- Skills may become obsolete and new skills may be required.
- Organizational structures and systems are not aligned with the change (e.g., rewards and recognition).
- There is a culture of mistrust brought on by prior ineffective changes.

These are just a sample of reasons underlying potential resistance to organizational change. At a deeper level, resistance can be brought about by feelings of fear regarding what the change may bring and lack of control of the process of change.

MODELS OF REACTIONS TO CHANGE

A variety of process models describing employee reactions to change exist. Typically, these models have been developed in a pragmatic context and have not been the subject of empirical evaluation. The SARA model has been used in a variety of contexts, including reactions to loss, organizational change, and reactions to feedback. Another widely used change model that looks at the transitions individuals go through was developed by William Bridges. This model proposes the following three stages:

Ending, Loosing, and Letting Go. During this stage, people are dealing with letting go of the way things were before the change. The general thrust is that before beginning something new, people need to let go of what had been before. The emotional reactions often resemble a grief process.

The Neutral Zone. This is the phase when the old ways have ended, but the change is not complete. The new ways of doing things are neither fully implemented nor understood. This can be a difficult time for employees because they are unsure about what is required of them and they are caught between the two, often conflicting, ways of doing things. The emotional reactions can be frustration and confusion. Guiding people through the neutral zone is a primary target of change management activities.

The New Beginning. This is the final phase of the transition process when people engage with the new ways of doing things. There is a new sense of clarity and purpose that the change has brought about. The emotional reactions often include relief and guarded excitement.

SUGGESTIONS FOR ADDRESSING RESISTANCE TO CHANGE

The management literature provides a variety of suggestions regarding how to deal with change. Whether based on theoretical models or on practical experience, several categories of suggestions are common:

Define a Communication Strategy

- Communicate why the change is occurring. The purpose of the change must be clear for employees to fully accept the change.
- Include a clear vision of the future state. This can help address fear of the unknown and inspire commitment.
- Detail the benefits to the organization and to employees. When done with regard to the future state, this can help in gaining the personal *buy in* of employees. They need to know what is in it for them.

Communicate in a Timely, Clear, and Consistent Fashion

- Inform employees as soon as possible of the change. Once it is clear what will happen, it is better that employees find out directly from management rather than from outside sources, such as public media, or from rumors building inside the organization.

- Consider the needs of the audience when communicating. Target the message at their key concerns and adapt the communication style that is used; for example, avoid jargon.
- Be consistent in the messages that are delivered. Keeping the message simple can help with consistency over time and across communications.
- Communicate honestly. Even if something is unknown about the change, it is better to share this fact directly with employees than to attempt a contrived answer.

Encourage Employee Input and Discuss Employee Reactions

- Whenever possible, involve employees in decisions that affect them. Involving employees enhances their feelings of control and reduces resistance.
- Allow opportunities for employees to share their reactions to the change, good and bad. As the SARA model suggests, employees can go through some strong emotional reactions. By allowing employees to express these feelings in an appropriate context, everyone can move on toward acceptance.
- Celebrate successes to inspire commitment to change. It is more difficult to resist a change that successfully brings about positive outcomes for the organization and employees.

Provide Training and Support for the Change

- When employees' skills may be affected, provide the necessary development support. Employees may resist changes that make their skills obsolete. Training employees to meet new job requirements reduces resistance. Some employees may see the change as an opportunity to enhance their skills.
- Ensure that reward and recognition systems are aligned to support the change. This is a common mistake and needs to be directly addressed.

—*Robert A. Schmieder*

See also Downsizing; Morale; Organizational Change; Organizational Climate; Organizational Culture; Organizational Cynicism; Organizational Development; Organizational Retaliatory Behavior; Survivor Syndrome

FURTHER READING

Bridges, W. (2003). *Managing transitions* (2nd ed.). Cambridge, MA: Da Capo Press.

Lawson, E., & Price, C. (2003). The psychology of change management [Special edition]. *McKinsey Quarterly, 2,* 30–39.

McAllaster, C. (2004). The 5 Ps of change: Leading change by effectively using leverage points within an organization. *Organizational Dynamics, 33,* 318–328.

Piderit, S. K. (2000). Rethinking resistance and recognizing ambivalence: A multidimensional view of attitudes toward an organizational change. *Academy of Management Review, 25,* 783–794.

ORGANIZATIONAL CLIMATE

The term *organizational climate* has been used in many different ways to refer to a wide variety of constructs. In recent years some consensus about what precisely should be included in the construct—and what should not be included in the construct—has begun to emerge. Research interest in climate has remained high, despite the variety of conceptualizations of the construct, because climate is generally seen as related to a variety of important organizational outcomes, including productivity (both individual and organizational), satisfaction, and turnover. More recently, climate has come to be seen as predictive of specific organizational outcomes, depending on what aspect of climate is being assessed. Thus climate continues to be seen as organizationally important, but the specific outcomes of interest seen to be affected by climate have shifted over time.

Initially, researchers used *climate* to refer to individual employee perceptions of more immediate aspects of an employee's work environment (e.g., supervision, work group characteristics, and job or task characteristics), and the climate measures that were developed and widely used reflected this orientation. However, general measures of climate began to incorporate aspects of leadership, group interaction and cohesion, job satisfaction, and other constructs, leading to questions of the uniqueness and utility of the climate construct. To counteract this tendency, researchers strategically focused the climate construct on those particular types of climates that may emerge in each particular organization. Although a recent meta-analysis by J. Z. Carr and her colleagues highlights the more molar, or broad-brush, approach to organizational climate, a more targeted approach has become dominant in the last several years.

Benjamin Schneider has long been one of the primary researchers in the area of organizational climate, and variations of the operational definition he has used are the dominant in the literature today. Specifically, Schneider has argued that organizational climate should be defined as the policies, practices, and procedures that are rewarded, supported, and expected in an organization in regard to a specific organizational domain, such as safety, innovation, customer service, and ethics. This basic definition has come to be the most commonly used conceptualization of the climate construct in the last several years.

There are two critical implications of this definition. First, by focusing on policies, practices, and procedures that are rewarded, supported, and expected, the definition implies that organizational climate is a shared perspective among organization members, rather than an individual perception. This focus on within-unit agreement places organizational climate in the category of compositional models that David Chan (1998) would call *direct consensus models,* in that the meaning of the group-level construct is based on the agreement (or consensus) among the individual units (group members or employees). Second, by focusing on specific organizational domains, the definition implies that an organization may have multiple climates operating simultaneously and may have climates that are more active in one area of the organization than in another; for example, a climate for innovation may be most salient in an R&D (research and development) division, whereas a climate for customer service may be most salient in a sales division within a single organization.

This definition is also useful because it helps clarify what organizational climate is not. Organizational climate does not refer to the *personal values* that are held by members of an organization, or shared by organization members—in general, shared values are under the umbrella of organizational culture (see Organizational Culture). Organizational climate also does not refer to individual and idiosyncratic perceptions of life within the organization; in general, these perceptions fall under the umbrella of psychological climate.

In the remainder of this entry, we first focus briefly on three examples of specific types of climates: climate for service, climate for safety, and ethical climate. We then discuss the issue of degree of agreement about climate perceptions, which is known as *climate strength*; this leads to a discussion of when it is possible to say that a climate does or does not exist.

CLIMATE FOR SERVICE

Research on organizational climate for service has flourished and considers both employee and customer perceptions of an organization's policies, practices, and procedures that are rewarded, supported, and expected for quality service in the organization. For employees, climate for service represents their experiences of the organization's emphasis on service quality. For customers, climate for service is the perceived amount of excellent service received from the organization. Research on climate for service has found links between these dual perceptions of employees' climate for service and customers' satisfaction and evaluations of the quality of service. This research is an example of linkage research because customer service perceptions are linked with important organizational outcomes, such as customer retention.

Climate for service research builds from the theory that employees emphasize service behavior to the degree that it is rewarded, supported, and expected by their employing organization. Customers of organizations that have a positive or high climate for service come to have higher satisfaction with the service they receive from the organization because of their contact and interaction with various employees, who provide consistently high levels of service. Research on the boundary conditions of this effect has begun, and initial findings suggest that higher frequency of contact between employees and customers is related to a stronger relationship between service climate and customer satisfaction. Another moderator of the climate for service and customer satisfaction relationship is the proximity of the organizational target, such as bank branches versus bank as a whole, to customers.

CLIMATE FOR SAFETY

Climate for safety has also received considerable research attention. This aspect of climate refers to employee perceptions of an organization's policies, practices, and procedures regarding safety that are rewarded, supported, and expected from employees. Several researchers have documented a consistent relationship between a positive safety climate and reduced injury rates. Dov Zohar (2003), a leading theorist in this area of research, has stressed the need to consider perceptions of actual safety practices as opposed to the safety policies and practices espoused by supervisors and top management, because the behaviors that are said to be expected and rewarded are often not the behaviors that are actually expected and rewarded. Interestingly, transformational or constructive leadership is shown to relate to lower injury rate; and this relationship is moderated by safety climate, conceptualized as perceptions of actual safety practices rather than more formalized safety policies.

ETHICAL CLIMATE

Given the many well-publicized corporate scandals of the last several years, it is hardly surprising to see that there is a sizable stream of research examining organizational ethics and ethical behavior from within an organizational climate framework. From this perspective (to use Bart Victor and John Cullen's [1987] seminal definition), ethical climate can be thought of as shared perceptions among group members regarding what constitutes ethically correct behavior and how ethical issues should be handled within an organization. This definition highlights the fact that ethical climate is not focused on *what is right or wrong* but is instead focused on the things that organization members perceive the organization to see as ethical. Thus employees might agree that when confronted with an ethical issue at work, they would be rewarded and supported by the organization if they engaged in behavior that they personally believed to be unethical.

Although ethical climate is a relatively new research area, researchers have identified several antecedents of ethical climate. Among other things, ethical climate has been shown to be affected by gender, age, ethical education, personality traits, and stage of organizational career. Victor and Cullen (1987), who are largely responsible for starting the research focus in this area, hypothesized that social norms, organizational form, and various firm-specific factors would be the dominant antecedents. Marcus Dickson, D. Brent Smith, Michael Grojean, and Mark Ehrhart (2001) addressed the literature on each of these points rather extensively. To date, there is more theory than data about the degree to which a strong organizational ethical climate is associated with individual and organizational ethical behavior and decision making.

There are many other organizational climate facets that have been investigated in the literature, including climates for sexual harassment, innovation and creativity, justice, and well-being. Of course, the climate construct could be applied to an almost unlimited range of organizational topics for which shared perceptions by group members are important.

CLIMATE STRENGTH

Recently, researchers have begun to focus on the importance of *climate strength,* which has been operationally defined as the within-group variability in member perceptions of the climate. When agreement is high, climate is strong. (Climate strength can also be conceptualized as variability in within-group perceptions, with greater variability indicating lesser strength.) Although there is not a lot of research to date that explicitly addresses climate strength, much published research has found that climate strength moderates the effects of climate itself on various outcomes of interest. For example, Jason Colquitt and colleagues (2001) found that procedural justice climate in teams predicted team effectiveness, and that the effect was greater in teams with stronger climates. Dickson and colleagues recently found that strong climates were more likely to be found in organizations with clearly distinct climates (e.g., highly mechanistic or highly organic), and that strength was typically much lower in organizations where the climate was more ambiguous. We expect to see research in this area continue to grow, because the moderating effect of climate strength will be useful in better understanding the direct effects (or lack thereof) of climate itself. Additionally, Schneider and colleagues have pointed out that there are clear implications for leadership to be found here in terms of the importance of consistent behavior in a positive direction to create maximal benefit from organizational climate.

WHEN DOES CLIMATE EXIST?

One debate in the study of organizational climate is whether there are times when there is *no climate* or whether there is always a climate, even if it is weak. This is much the same argument as that occurring in the literature on organizational culture; but given the more quantitative orientation of the climate literature over time (compared with the culture literature), the issue can become especially critical here.

Some researchers argue that unless there is some predetermined level of agreement or variability among group members, there is no climate because there is little or no evidence of a shared perspective among organizational members. This argument can be couched in terms from Chan's (1998) framework of composition models, mentioned earlier, because climate has most typically been conceptualized as a direct consensus model. In such a model, climate is considered to be the typical, or most common, response from the members of a group, *provided that there is some level of within-group agreement to justify treating the mean as a group-level variable.* In other words, if there is insufficient agreement (assessed statistically), then there is no *sharedness* in the perceptions, and thus no climate. Researchers taking this approach have sometimes used a criterion of an r_{wg} of .70 or greater (or some other statistical cutoff point), although as Harrison Trice and Janice Beyer (1993) note regarding culture strength, there is no clear answer on how to determine whether or not a climate exists. Because there is no clear point at which climate can be said to exist, other researchers have taken the perspective that climate is always present but may in many cases be weak.

This question is of practical importance when determining how to classify the units within a data set. For example, suppose that a researcher is investigating safety climate and has data from 100 organizations, including 10 organizations with r_{wg} results on the climate measure of less than .70. From one perspective, the 10 organizations showing little agreement on the safety climate measure would be dropped from the sample as having *no climate,* and of the remaining 90 organizations, the ones with r_{wg} results close to .70 would be considered to have a *weak climate.* From the alternative perspective, all 100 organizations would remain in the sample, and those with the lowest levels of agreement would be considered to have the weakest climates. At present, consensus on this issue has yet to clearly emerge. However, the approach of limiting the sample to only those organizations with a predetermined level of within-unit agreement is the more conservative approach, because that limitation serves to restrict the range on the strength variable.

CONCLUSION

Organizations tend to have as many specific climates as strategic directions, which makes organizational climate a relevant concept for organizations to consider. As Schneider (1990) notes, once a strategic direction or focus is identified for the organization, the organizational climate regarding that strategic focus can be assessed via employees. Employees' assessment of the organization's relevant policies, practices, and procedures that support the strategic focus in the organization may serve as a measure of alignment. The strategic focus of the organization needs to be clearly and consistently represented in the organization's policies, practices, and procedures. Should an assessment of the organizational climate reveal that a strategic direction of interest is not perceived in organizational practices, then policies, practices, and procedures in the organization may need to be redesigned to better align with the strategy of interest.

—*Marcus W. Dickson and Jacqueline K. Mitchelson*

See also Organizational Culture

FURTHER READING

Ashkanasy, N. M., Wilderom, C. P. M., & Peterson, M. F. (Eds.). (2000). *Handbook of organizational culture and climate.* Thousand Oaks, CA: Sage.

Carr, J. Z., Schmidt, A. M., Ford, J. K., & DeShon, R. P. (2003). Climate perceptions matter: A meta-analytic path analysis relating molar climate, cognitive and affective states, and individual level work outcomes. *Journal of Applied Psychology, 88,* 605–619.

Chan, D. (1998). Functional relations among constructs in the same content domain at different levels of analysis: A typology of composition models. *Journal of Applied Psychology, 83,* 234–246.

Dickson, M. W., Smith, D. B., Grojean, M., & Ehrhart, M. (2001). An organizational climate regarding ethics: The outcome of leader values and the practices that reflect them. *Leadership Quarterly, 12,* 197–217.

Schneider, B. (Ed.). (1990). *Organizational climate and culture.* San Francisco: Jossey-Bass.

Victor, B., & Cullen, J. (1987). A theory and measure of ethical climate in organizations. In W. C. Frederick (Ed.), *Research in corporate social performance and policy: Empirical studies of business ethics and values* (pp. 51–71). Greenwich, CT: JAI Press.

Zohar, D. (2003). Safety climate: Conceptual and measurement issues. In J. Campbell Quick & L. E. Tetrick (Eds.), *Handbook of occupational health psychology.* Washington, DC: American Psychological Association.

ORGANIZATIONAL COMMITMENT

Industrial and organizational (I/O) psychologists are interested in understanding employees' psychological reactions to their workplaces. Not surprisingly, much of this interest focuses on employees' commitment to the *organizations* for which they work. Among the several *work attitude* variables studied by I/O psychologists, only job satisfaction has received more attention than organizational commitment (OC).

CONCEPTUALIZING ORGANIZATIONAL COMMITMENT

Early definitions of OC varied considerably. Nonetheless, most scholars view OC as a psychological state characterizing an employee's relationship with the organization. This relationship influences the employee's intention to maintain a particular course of action, in this case, staying with the organization.

Beyond this, however, early OC researchers had varied views about the nature of OC and how it should be measured. For some early researchers, OC was an emotional attachment to the organization; for others, it was identification with the organization and what it represented. Some researchers described OC in terms of a reluctance to endure sacrifices, or incur costs, that voluntarily leaving the organization would entail. Still others described commitment in terms of a moral obligation to remain with the organization.

From these early one-dimensional views has emerged wide acceptance of OC as a multidimensional construct. Thus most current models propose that OC has at least two psychological bases, or components, each of which should be measured separately. Of these models, the three-component model (TCM) proposed in the 1990s has received the most theoretical and empirical attention, and it is from this perspective that the development and consequences of OC are described here.

The TCM proposes that OC has three distinct components, each of which develops via somewhat different processes. *Affective commitment* refers to the employee's emotional attachment to the organization, characterized by enjoyment of the organization and a desire to stay. Employees with strong affective commitment remain with the organization because they *want to* do so. *Continuance commitment* refers to the extent to which the employee perceives that leaving the organization would be costly. Employees with strong continuance commitment remain because they feel that they *have to* do so. *Normative commitment* refers to the employee's feelings of obligation to the organization and the belief that staying with it is the *right thing* to do. Employees with strong normative commitment remain because they feel that they *ought to* do so.

According to the TCM an employee's commitment is characterized not in terms of just one of the three components but as a profile made up of all three. Further, the model proposes that the components have interactive effects on employee behavior.

MEASURING ORGANIZATIONAL COMMITMENT

Researchers and practitioners usually assess OC using multiple-item questionnaires administered directly to employees. Typically, employees respond anonymously, thus increasing the candidness of responses. As with any such measures, it is critical that items reflect the construct they are intended to assess. Especially in early research, this was accomplished with varying degrees of success. Of particular note, however, is the 15-item organizational commitment questionnaire (OCQ). Developed in the 1970s to assess identification with, involvement in, and emotional attachment to the organization, the OCQ is a psychometrically sound measure of desire-based (affective) commitment. It has been used in hundreds of studies, contributing greatly to our understanding of the affective component of OC.

To evaluate the multidimensional model of OC outlined earlier, TCM researchers developed parallel measures of the three proposed OC components. Since then, the affective commitment scale, continuance commitment scale, and normative commitment scale (ACS, CCS, and NCS) have received considerable psychometric scrutiny and have been used extensively in research conducted in dozens of organizational and cultural contexts and with members of various occupations. Overall, the evidence shows that the measures are reliable, assess three distinct constructs, and correlate with other variables in general accordance with TCM propositions.

DEVELOPMENT OF ORGANIZATIONAL COMMITMENT

Although OC might be expected to develop on the basis of both *person* and *work experience* factors, the latter play the more important role. Some person variables (e.g., age, locus of control) are modestly related to OC, but it is what people experience at work that seems to have the most influence on OC development. With respect to affective commitment, quantitative review (or meta-analysis) suggests several work experiences that seem particularly important. Affective commitment is stronger among employees who feel that they have been supported by their organizations and who have experienced procedural, distributive, and interactional justice in the workplace. Affective commitment is also stronger among employees who experience minimal role ambiguity and role conflict at work and have leaders who adopt transformational leadership styles.

The TCM proposes that normative commitment develops on the basis of both cultural and organizational experiences that highlight expectations of mutual obligation between employees and the organization and make the reciprocity norm salient to employees. These ideas have received relatively little empirical assessment. Meta-analytic results show that some of the same variables (e.g., organizational support, role ambiguity, justice) that seem to influence affective commitment are related to normative commitment, but relations are much weaker. There is also some evidence that the impact of work experiences on normative commitment depends on employees' cultural values, such as individualism versus collectivism.

Consistent with the TCM model, continuance commitment is more strongly related than are the other two components to two sets of variables: perceived alternatives and perceived investments. Specifically, continuance commitment is stronger among employees who believe that they would have few, rather than several, viable sources of employment if they left the organization. Presumably, the costs of leaving their current organization would be quite high for such employees. Continuance commitment is also stronger among employees who believe that they made significant investments developing their skills and acquiring education that would not transfer readily to other organizations. In comparison to employees who have easily transferable skills, such employees would incur greater costs if they left the organization.

CONSEQUENCES OF ORGANIZATIONAL COMMITMENT

As previously mentioned, it is most consistent with theory to examine the consequences of OC in terms of the commitment profile (or interactions between components). Some researchers have taken this approach, but most studies have involved the examination of potential OC consequences on a component-by-component, rather than profile, basis. Outcomes that have been emphasized include employee retention, work performance, and employee well-being.

The links between OC components and employee retention are fairly straightforward. Affective, normative, and continuance commitment are all negatively related to employee intention to leave the organization voluntarily. Both affective commitment and normative commitment, but not continuance commitment, have been shown to predict actual turnover.

Just as important as retention, however, is how employees *behave* at work. Here the distinction between the three components of commitment becomes especially critical. Beyond their demonstrated link with turnover intention, affective, continuance, and normative commitment are considered, and have been shown, to have somewhat different implications for behavior.

Affective commitment is linked to several key performance indicators. Employees with stronger affective commitment are less likely to be absent from work, and this effect is stronger for absence that is under the employee's control than for involuntary absence, such as that caused by illness and emergencies. Affective commitment also predicts the job performance. Across a wide variety of jobs, both self-report ratings and supervisory ratings of required (or nondiscretionary) work performance are higher among those with stronger affective commitment. Such employees are also more likely to engage in discretionary organizational citizenship behavior (e.g., exerting extraordinary effort, helping coworkers, championing the organization) than those with weak affective commitment and, in so doing, help create a more productive and positive workplace.

Normative commitment is unrelated to employee absence. Its relations with other performance indicators, however, are positive, but effects are more modest than for affective commitment. Interestingly, meta-analytic evidence shows that relations between normative commitment and both job performance and organizational citizenship behavior are stronger in studies conducted outside North America, suggesting that cultural factors might play an important role in the behavioral expression of this component of commitment. Finally, although this has not yet been tested, it has been argued that normative commitment might influence the *tone* with which the employees carry out their work, particularly if they also have weak-to-moderate levels of affective commitment. The idea here is

that strong feelings of obligation to stay, in the absence of strong desire to stay, might create feelings of resentment, prompting such employees to carry out their duties in a competent, but more grudging, manner.

Continuance commitment is unrelated to employee absence. In contrast to affective and normative commitment, however, it is also unrelated to organizational citizenship behavior; those with strong continuance commitment are neither more nor less likely to go the extra mile. Of particular note, however, is the strong negative relation, found in meta-analytic research, between continuance commitment and required aspects of job performance. The fact that employees with strong (versus weak) continuance commitment perform more poorly has critical implications for those organizations that develop retention strategies around what employees will lose if they resign. Such organizations might well increase retention but do so at the cost of employee performance. This will be especially so if employees are given little reason to develop affective commitment to the organization and, as a consequence, feel *trapped* within it.

Finally, researchers are beginning to examine whether OC has implications for employee well-being. Presumably, most people prefer workplaces about which they feel positively. It has been argued, however, that strong affective OC might reduce well-being by causing employees to focus too much attention on their work. Thus far there is little evidence of this latter view. Instead, meta-analytic research suggests that strong affective commitment is related to reduced stress and exhaustion and greater quality of life. In contrast, however, continuance commitment is related to poorer quality of life and greater stress levels.

FURTHER RESEARCH DIRECTIONS

Despite extensive OC research, there remain many challenging issues. One such issue incorporates the idea that employees feel multidimensional commitment to numerous work-related domains or foci. These include foci both within the organization (e.g., department, supervisor, team) and beyond it (e.g., occupation, union). Although complex, a comprehensive understanding of commitment in the workplace will only come through considering, in concert, the multiple components of commitment that employees feel toward these various interconnected aspects of their workplace.

Other challenges are presented by the changing workplace. For example, researchers are just beginning to examine the effects that alternate work arrangements, such as part-time employment, temporary and contract-based work, and outsourcing, have on the development and consequences of OC. Within many workplaces, greater emphasis is being placed on the interplay (or *balance*) between work and nonwork or family; it will be important to examine how policies and practices associated with this issue will influence the development of OC. Finally, likely driven by the increasing cultural diversity in the workforce, the challenges of globalization, and the growing international researcher base, more attention is focused on the role that cultural factors may play in shaping the structure, development, and consequences of organizational commitment.

—*Natalie J. Allen*

See also Job Satisfaction; Organizational Justice; Withdrawal Behaviors, Turnover

FURTHER READING

Allen, N. J., & Meyer, J. P. (1990). The measurement and antecedents of affective, continuance, and normative commitment to the organization. *Journal of Occupational Psychology, 63,* 1–18.

Allen, N. J., & Meyer, J. P. (2000). Construct validation in organizational behavior research: The case of organizational commitment. In R. D. Goffin & E. Helmes (Eds.), *Problems and solutions in human assessment* (pp. 285–314). Norwell, MA: Kluwer Academic Publishers.

Becker, T. E., & Kernan, M. C. (2003). Matching commitment to supervisors and organizations to in-role and extra-role performance. *Human Performance, 16,* 327–348.

Meyer, J. P., & Allen, N. J. (1997). *Commitment in the workplace: Theory, research, and application.* Thousand Oaks, CA: Sage.

Meyer, J. P., & Herscovitch, L. (2001). Commitment in the workplace: Toward a general model. *Human Resource Management Review, 11,* 299–326.

Meyer, J. P., Stanley, D. J., Herscovitch, L., & Topolnytsky, L. (2002). Affective, continuance, and normative commitment to the organization: A meta-analysis of antecedents, correlates, and consequences. *Journal of Vocational Behavior, 61,* 20–52.

Wasti, S. A. (2003). The influence of cultural values on antecedents of organisational commitment: An individual-level analysis. *Applied Psychology: An International Review, 52,* 533–554.

ORGANIZATIONAL COMMUNICATION, FORMAL

Formal organizational communication is not an easily defined term. Organizational communication is a complicated phenomenon that has no clear boundaries. Several definitions attempt to conceptualize the abstract nature of organizational communication. The study of organizational communication involves the intersection of two complex and dynamic concepts: organizations and communications. An organization has three primary characteristics:

1. Social collectivity (a group of people)

2. Coordinated activities (structure)

3. Goal-oriented activities (both individual and collective)

In defining communication, most scholars agree that communication is a process that is transactional (involving two or more people interacting in context) and symbolic (placing meaning and abstractions on *things*). To formalize organizational communication means to understand how the context of the organization influences communication processes and how the symbolic nature of communication differentiates it from other forms of organizational behavior.

STUDYING FORMAL ORGANIZATIONAL COMMUNICATION

Eric Eisenberg and Harold Goodall (2004) offer a broad but usable definition of organizational communication. They suggest that there are four ways to conceptualize and study formal organizational communication:

1. Communication as information transfer

2. Communication as transactional process

3. Communication as strategic control

4. Communication as balancing creativity and constraint

Communication as Information Transfer

The traditional approach to study communication has followed the linear model of communication, also known as the *transmission model, the information engineering approach,* or the *model of information transfer.* The information transfer approach views communication as a tool that people use to accomplish goals and objectives. Clear, one-way communication is emphasized as a means of impressing and influencing others. The information transfer or linear model suggests that communication flows one way or linearly from the sender of the message to the receiver of the message. This model suggests that communication is a process whereby messages are transmitted and distributed in space for the control of distance and people.

Some scholars have suggested that communication operates in a predictable fashion; hence the information engineering approach. The information engineering approach advanced the SMCR model. This model posits that communication occurs when a sender (S) transmits a message (M) through a channel (C) to a receiver (R). The sender *encodes* an intended meaning into words and the receiver *decodes* the message when it is received. The communication as information transfer model is similar to both the linear model of communication and the information engineering approach in that communication is framed metaphorically as a pipeline through which information is transferred from one person to another. Within the organizational context, managers transfer information or directives to subordinates and subordinates do the same in their peer and superordinate interactions.

Communication theories in the information transfer approach are based on the following assumptions of transmission:

- Language transfers thoughts and feelings from one person to another person
- Speakers and writers put thoughts and feelings into words
- Words contain those thoughts and feelings
- Listeners or readers extract those thoughts and feelings from the words

There are several problems associated with the information transfer method as an approach to the study of formal organizational communication. *Information overload* is when the receiver of the message becomes inundated with information that needs to be processed. Information overload is made up of the amount of information, the rate at which the information is received, and the complexity of the information.

Another problem with the information transfer model is with communication distortion. Distortion is the processing noise that distracts the receiver from fully processing information. Communication distortion can be semantic (different meanings for sender and receiver), physical (sound distractions), or contextual (sender and receiver have different positions or perspectives that lead to miscommunication).

Ambiguity offers the third problem with the information transfer model. Ambiguity occurs when multiple interpretations of a message distort or misdirect the sender's intended meaning. Differing meanings and interpretations, based on one's worldviews, backgrounds, context of communication, and experiences, along with abstract language, may lead to ambiguity.

Communication as a Transactional Process

A second approach in the study of formal organizational communication is communication as a transactional process. Communication as transactional process asserts that in actual communication situations, clear distinctions are not made between senders and receivers of messages. This assumption contrasts with the information transfer model. Instead, in the transactional process, both communicators play both roles of encoding and decoding messages simultaneously. This model emphasizes the importance of *feedback* in communication. This model also highlights the importance of nonverbal communication, which is missing in the information transfer approach. Organizational communication as a transactional process suggests that nonverbal feedback may accompany or substitute for verbal messages. Finally, the transactional process model suggests that meanings are in people, not words, as the information transfer model assumes. How an individual receives a message and how the receiver constructs the meaning of that message is the focus of the transactional process model.

The transactional process influences contemporary leadership studies. Effective and successful leaders using this approach are better able to mobilize the meanings that followers have for what leaders say or do. This creates a transactional and fluid process between leaders and followers in organizations.

The approach of studying formal organizational communication through the transactional process approach may be problematic in its emphasis on creating shared meaning through communication. By focusing on shared meaning by means of clarity, openness, and understanding, communication as a transactional process minimizes the complexities of the human condition whereas ambiguity, vagueness, and instrumental objectives are central in some forms of formal communication in organizations.

Communication as Strategic Control

Communication as strategic control views communication as a tool for controlling the organizational environment. This approach acknowledges that clarity, openness, and understanding are not always the primary goals in interpersonal and organizational interactions caused by personal, relational, social, and political factors. Communication as strategic control assumes communicators have multiple goals or agendas in organizational situations. These agendas play out in performance evaluations, delivering or accepting bad news, asking for a promotion or raise, or in various other situations where the individual or organizational interests are at stake.

The strategic control approach to formal organizational communication suggests that individuals should not be expected to communicate in a rational or objective manner. Communication rules, clarity, and honesty may be broken or compromised when it is in the communicators' best interests to do so. Generally, strategic communicators are competent communicators. Communication competence refers to the appropriateness and effectiveness of a message. The communicating party must be *rhetorically sensitive* in that he or she must be able to recognize the constraints of the situation and adapt to the multiple goals of all parties simultaneously.

Strategic ambiguity is a common form of strategic control. Strategic ambiguity describes the ways people deliberately communicate ambiguously to accomplish their goals.

Strategic ambiguity seeks to accomplish specific goals. First, strategic ambiguity promotes unified diversity by taking advantage of the multiple meanings different people may give the same message. For example, if a supervisor directs employees to *work more as a family,* there are multiple interpretations on how this should occur.

Second, strategic ambiguity is deniable because the words may seem to mean one thing, yet under pressure, these same words can seem to mean something else. For example, if an organization has announced

a merger, organizational leaders are careful when discussing job loss because of duplication of processes, so that when job loss occurs later, their words at that time appear more abstract and less definitive.

Finally, strategic ambiguity facilitates organizational change by allowing people the interpretive room to change their activities while appearing to keep those activities consistent.

The strategic control model of formal organizational communication opposes the idea of shared meaning. The primary goal of communication in this approach is organized action. Organized action minimizes the importance of understanding and clarity and highlights working and acting in mutually satisfying ways to fulfill each party's self-interest.

Many scholars have criticized the strategic control approach for several reasons. First, this approach minimizes the importance of ethics. Although strategic ambiguity is widespread in organizations, it may be used to elude the truth and escape blame.

It is also problematic because it places all responsibility on individuals without much thought about the community implications. This model implicitly suggests that individuals are only concerned with accomplishing their individual goals, often at the expense of the organizational community or the community at large.

ADDITIONAL APPROACHES TO FORMAL ORGANIZATIONAL COMMUNICATION

There are other approaches to studying formal organizational communication. These approaches include the functional approach and the meaning-centered approach.

Functional Approach

The functional approach is a way of understanding organizational communication by describing what messages do and *how these messages move* through organizations. The functional approach conceptualizes communication as a complex organizational process that serves *messaging, organizing, relationship,* and *change functions.* This approach posits that communication transmits rules, regulations, and information throughout the organization.

Message Function. In formalizing organizational communication, it is important to recognize how communication contributes to the overall function of the organization. Messages act as a communication function for production, maintenance, adaptation, management communication, regulative, integrative, innovative, informative, task, persuasion, command, and instruction.

Organizing Function. The organizing function of formal organizational communication guides, directs, and controls organizational activity. Communication functions to organize rules and regulate the environment. These regulative and organizing functions are found in employee handbooks, policy manuals, training, newsletters, memos, and so on. The organizing function establishes what is expected at work and how individuals are required to accomplish these expectations.

Relationship Function. The relationship function of organizational communication focuses on how human interaction makes organizational functioning possible. The relationship function helps individuals define their roles and measure the compatibility of individual, group, and organizational goals. This function is particularly important because it contributes to employee morale, role in the organization, and organizational self-esteem. The relationship function establishes relationships with peers, superiors, subordinates, and customers; and it further clarifies these roles.

The relationship function is accomplished by verbal and nonverbal communication. Scholars have suggested that the informal organization, often characterized by the relational function, is more powerful than the formal organization. Relational communication ranges from the informal conversations in a break room to one's job title, office space, or cubicle to how an individual is greeted on meeting.

Change Function. The final function of formal organizational communication is its change function. The change function helps an organization adapt what they do and how they do it. This adaptation occurs in decision making, internal and external changes in the environment, organizational repositioning, and other change functions. The effectiveness of the change function of organizational communication is associated with the survival of the organization and its ability to adapt to the changing environment. Change communication is necessary for innovation and adaptation and is the process through which organizations obtain existing and new information, and how they process this information in light of the current situation and emerging trends.

Meaning-Centered Approach

The meaning-centered approach is a way of understanding organizational communication by understanding how organizational reality is constructed through human interaction. This approach describes organizational communication as a process of organizing, decision making, sense making, influence, and culture. Pamela Shockley-Zalabak (2002) offers key assumptions of the meaning-centered approach.

- *All ongoing human interaction is communication in one form or another.* A major theme in the communication discipline is that an individual "cannot not communicate." This is due in part to verbal and nonverbal cues.

- *Organizations exist through human interaction; structures and technologies result from the information to which individuals react.* This idea suggests that organizations cannot exist separate from human activity. An organization relies solely on individuals' enactment of organizing and structuring. Karl Weick (1979) offered insight to these ideas by suggesting that organizations do not exist per se but are a culmination of the ongoing human interaction surrounding events that are continually created and shaped by these interactions. The meaning-centered approach to formal organizational communication describes communicating and organizing as a parallel process.

- *Organizing and decision making are essentially communication.* This is the process of choosing from among numerous alternatives to direct behaviors and resources toward organizational goals.

- *Identification, socialization, communication rules, and power all are communication processes that reflect how organizational influence occurs.* The meaning-centered approach proposes that influence is a necessary process for creating and changing organizational events. Influence plays a role in understanding how individuals identify with their organizations, how organizations attempt to socialize members, how communication rules direct behavior, and how individuals use communication to exert power.

- *Organizing, decision-making, and influence processes describe the cultures of organizations by describing how organizations do things and how they talk about how they do things.* Organizational culture reflects the shared realities and practices in organizations and how shared realities create and shape organizational events. The culture varies from organization to organization depending on the individuals' engagement with each other and the organization's goals. Culture describes the unique sense of the organization, its practices, and how the organization describes itself.

—Shawn D. Long

See also Organizational Communication, Informal

FURTHER READING

Eisenberg, E. (1984). Ambiguity as strategy in organizational communication. *Communication Monographs, 51,* 227–242.

Eisenberg, E. M., & Goodall, H. L., Jr. (2004). *Organizational communication: Balancing creativity and constraint* (4th ed.). Boston: Bedford/St. Martin's.

Jablin, F. M. (2001). Organizational entry, assimilation, and disengagement/exit. In F. M. Jablin & L. L. Putnam (Eds.), *The new handbook of organizational communication: Advances in theory, research, and methods* (pp. 732–818). Thousand Oaks, CA: Sage.

Redding, W. C. (1972). *Communication within the organization.* New York: Industrial Communication Council.

Shockley-Zalabak, P. (2002). *Fundamentals of organizational communication: Knowledge, sensitivity, skills, values* (5th ed.). Boston: Allyn & Bacon.

Weick, K. (1979). *The social psychology of organizing* (2nd ed.). Reading, MA: Addison-Wesley.

ORGANIZATIONAL COMMUNICATION, INFORMAL

Some scholars argue that the informal organization is more powerful than the formal organization. Scholars also suggest that a great deal of communication in organizations is informal communication. Elton Mayo and his famous Hawthorne studies found that informal communication influenced the development and reinforcement of performance standards, member expectations, and values at the work group level. Informal organizational communication consists of episodes of interaction that do not reflect formally designated channels of communication. P. H. Tompkins wrote that informal organizational communication is not *rationally specified.* An organization may be formally structured with specific communication rules and patterns, such as chain of command; however, that does not mean that all activities and interactions strictly conform to the original formalized organization. A great deal of time and effort is devoted to creating an organization driven by control and predictability through formal means such as employee handbooks, rules, regulations, and procedures and standard means of practices. However, an elaborate setup of organizational mechanisms and contingencies cannot fully predict and control the dynamic and complex nature of human beings and their interactions with other individuals and the environment.

Scholars posit that in every formal organization emerges an informal organization, primarily through communication. Various groups develop their own values, norms, and practices in relation to their peers, subordinates, and supervisors. These practices construct context-specific ways of working beyond the scope of the formal organization. Rules are important in formal organizations, particularly in organizations highly characterized by hierarchy and bureaucracy. Max Weber suggested that the functioning of formal organizations is made possible by five primary characteristics.

1. There is the principle of fixed and official jurisdictional areas, which are generally ordered by rules, laws, or administrative regulations.

2. The principles of organizational hierarchy and of levels of graded authority mean a firmly ordered system of superordination and subordination in which there is a supervision of the lower offices by the higher ones.

3. The management of the formal organization is based on written documents, which are preserved in their original form.

4. When the organization is fully formalized, official activity demands the full working capacity and attention of management.

5. Management follows general rules, which are more or less stable, are more or less exhaustive, and can be learned.

The last characteristic suggests that rules should be general to have enough scope to cover a multitude of situations or contingencies. However, not all contingencies can be imagined and prepared for, and informal communication provides a solution to this problem.

FORMAL VERSUS INFORMAL ORGANIZATIONAL COMMUNICATION

The distinction between formal and informal organizational communication is unclear. Historically, scholars have made interesting theoretical and empirical distinctions between formal and informal communication. Scholars link formal communication with the organizational chart and formalized messages. Researchers also link informal organizational communication with the grapevine (addressed later) and communications not considered on the formal organizational chart. Scholars have attempted to distinguish formal and informal communication, but the lines are not clearly drawn. Conceptually, however, formal communication is viewed as *expected* communication patterns that are written, centralized, vertical, planned, imposed, and mandated. Formal communication is viewed as legitimate communication given authority by the organization. However, informal communication is viewed as *actual* communication patterns that are oral, decentralized, horizontal, unplanned and not imposed, and not mandated.

There have been several attempts to link formal organizational structure to organizational behavior. However, these attempts have produced inconclusive findings. Because of this lack of evidence, scholars have suggested that studying informal communication will contribute to our understanding of organizational behavior.

WHY STUDY INFORMAL COMMUNICATION?

Informal communication in organizations is an important area of inquiry in organizational theory and behavior. It is particularly useful when studying the role of informal communication in decision making, productivity, and organizational change.

There are three primary reasons informal organizational communication continues to thrive. First, decision making does not operate in a vacuum, and many times decisions must be made that fall outside the purview of the formal organizational design. Reacting in the moment allows immediate and flexible solutions that may not wait on a formalized process that may take a considerable amount of time to implement.

Second, unofficial norms may develop to regulate performance and productivity. For example, systematic soldering resulted from rate busting in the early industrial revolution era when a group of workers would pressure each other to keep productivity at a steady pace by not working too hard and fast or too slowly, to keep the rate of piecework pay the same. This pressure was placed on all workers by their peers through informal policing of productivity.

Finally, as the complex nature of social relations and informal status structures emerge, organizational

change provides an important backdrop for promoting informal organizational communication. Informal organizational communication develops in response to opportunities and problems posed by the environment, whereas formal organizational communication is a response to the immediate environment of the groups within it.

Organizations are influenced by factors other than the traditional organizational chart. Informal factors such as background, demographic characteristics, workers' abilities, their willingness to help others, and their degree of conformity to group norms all shape informal organizational communication.

TRADITIONAL FORMAL COMMUNICATION

Traditional scholars of organizational communication made no allowances for the role of informal communication in organizational functions and its influence on the organization. This was in part because of a reliance on the idea that all organizational messages should always exhibit the two characteristics of intelligibility and persuasion. Intelligible messages mean that the message should be clear and concise. Persuasive messages indicate that the average human needs coaxing to perform tasks in the interests of the organization. To better motivate and control the worker in the interest of the organization, the task goals should be communicated in such a way that it appears to serve the interest of the worker.

INFORMAL COMMUNICATION PERSPECTIVES

There are two predominant views on informal communication. Some scholars argue that informal communication arises when information transmitted through the formal organization is either insufficient or ambiguous. In this sense, informal communication is used for clarity. Other scholars suggest that informal communication is much more than a surrogate from an incomplete formal system. Instead, informal communication is an inherent and even necessary aspect of organizational life. Most organizational communication researchers agree that some informal communication is inevitable in organizational life, regardless of the form the organization may take.

GRAPEVINE COMMUNICATION

A great deal of the research on informal organizational communication centers on the study of grapevine communication. Grapevine communication is a metaphor for a communication system that began in the 1860s during the Civil War in America as a description for telegraph lines that were strung through trees, resembling grapevines. This early system was neither stable nor reliable, so the term was coined for any form of communication outside the purview of formalized organizational communication.

The flow of information in grapevine communication can be complex. Some organizational members who participate in the grapevine act only as receivers of the message. These participants do not relay information to other organizational members. However, there are certain organizational members who serve as both senders and receivers of a message to other organizational members.

There are five areas of study of grapevine communication:

1. *The function and extent of grapevine communication:* The grapevine emerges from the social and personal interests of employees rather than from formalized organizational communication. This approach is more *people oriented* than *task oriented.*

2. *Participants in grapevine communication:* This studies the participants and their roles in grapevine communication. Secretaries and liaisons play critical roles in grapevine communication. Managers and other organizational members play a role in informal communication.

3. *Patterns and media of grapevine communication:* Grapevine communication is generally oral and presented in interpersonal and group contexts. The communication may begin, flow, and end anywhere in the organization.

4. *Volume, speed, and reliability of information:* The diffusion of grapevine information is rapid and the information is more accurate than inaccurate. However, most grapevine communication is incomplete.

5. *Role in rumor transmission:* Three types of rumors are spread through the grapevine: anxiety rumors (associated with perceived negative change such as layoffs), wish-fulfillment rumors (associated with salary increase or promotions), and wedge-driving rumors (once a rumor is assigned credibility, events are altered to fit in with and support the rumor).

Research on grapevine communication suggests that a great deal of organizational communication occurs through the grapevine. The grapevine serves as a rumor mill; however, only a small portion of the communication consists of rumors. There are no demographic (male vs. female) or status (managers vs. employees) differences among grapevine participants.

CURRENT RESEARCH IN INFORMAL ORGANIZATIONAL COMMUNICATION

Research in the area of informal organizational communication has splintered from the traditional views of informal communication of examining grapevine communication to situating informal communication in various organizational structures. For example, the increased use of computer-mediated technology and communication systems has created research lines that compare the traditional organizational structure driven by formal communication with informal or emergent communication created by mediated communication. J. D. Eveland and Tora Bikson (1987) found that electronic mail served to augment, and in some cases complement, formal structures. Other scholars have shown that informal organizational communication that naturally emerges from communication technology in a sense is becoming more formalized as organizations attempt to extend control beyond time and spatial constraints characteristic of formal organizational communication.

Other streams of research include Pamela Hinds and Sara Kiesler's (1995) work that found that communication technologies were used as a tool for lateral communication across formal organizational boundaries. In another study, R. E. Rice (1994) found that electronic communication structures closely resembled formal organizational structures initially, but these similarities diminished over time. In sum, the current literature focuses on the advantages of informal communication to individuals and organizations.

—Shawn D. Long

See also Organizational Communication, Formal

FURTHER READING

Daniels, T. D., Spiker, B. K., & Papa, M. J. (1997). *Perspectives on organizational communication* (4th ed.). Boston: McGraw-Hill.

Eveland, J. D., & Bikson, T. K. (1987). Evolving electronic communication networks: An empirical assessment. *Office: Technology and People, 3,* 103–128.

Hinds, P., & Kiesler, S. (1995). Communication across boundaries: Work, structure, and use of communication technologies in a large organization. *Organization Science, 6,* 373–393.

Jablin, F. M., & Putnam, L. L. (Eds.). (2001). *The new handbook of organizational communication: Advances in theory, research, and methods.* Thousand Oaks, CA: Sage.

Miller, K. (1999). *Organizational communication: Approaches and processes* (2nd ed.). Belmont, CA: Wadsworth.

Monge, P. R., & Contractor, N. S. (2001). Emergence of communication networks. In F. L. Jablin & L. L. Putnam (Eds.), *The new handbook of organizational communication: Advances in theory, research, and methods* (pp. 440–502). Thousand Oaks, CA: Sage.

Rice, R. E. (1994). Relating electronic mail use and network structure to R&D work networks and performance. *Journal of Management Information Systems, 11*(1), 9–20.

Tompkins, P. H. (1967). Organizational communication: A state of the art review. In G. Richetto (Ed.), *Conference on organizational communication.* Huntsville, AL: NASA, George C. Marshall Space Flight Center.

Weber, M. (1947). *Max Weber: The theory of social and economic organization* (T. Parsons & A. M. Henderson, Eds. & Trans.). New York: Free Press.

ORGANIZATIONAL CULTURE

Although there is no universally accepted definition of organizational culture, researchers generally agree that organizational culture refers to the shared meaning, interpretations, and understanding of various organizational events among organizational members. Organizational culture serves as a guide to members to behave in ways shown to be effective over time; adds a sense of predictability and order to uncertainties in the environment; and provides a general understanding of how, when, and why members behave in certain ways.

Researchers generally agree that organizational culture is best represented as different layers along a continuum of accessibility. Denise Rousseau's description of culture suggests that the most observable layer of organizational culture is the material artifacts, such as organizational logos and office layout, found in the organization. The next layer is the behavioral patterns in which members engage. These are the routinized activities that members perform, which build coordination among members. The third layer is formed by the behavioral norms that provide predictability among members and identify acceptable and unacceptable behavior. The fourth, and less readily accessible, layer is made up of the values and beliefs of the organizational members. These values and beliefs represent preferences for various outcomes or behaviors and are generally conscious or espoused by organizational members. The deepest, and therefore least accessible, layer of culture is the basic, fundamental assumptions shared by organizational members. These assumptions exist outside of conscious awareness and as such, members are typically unaware of their content or influence.

Edgar Schein's (1992) highly influential definition of culture focused primarily on the deeper levels of culture, in that he defined organizational culture as a pattern of basic, largely unconscious assumptions that organizational members share. These basic assumptions are learned over time as those behaviors effective at solving organizational issues with adapting to the external environment or with resolving internal conflicts that have come to be internalized as the *right way to do things here.* Because these behaviors were effective in the past, new organizational members are socialized to these behavioral responses as the correct way to perceive, think, and feel in regard to external and internal issues. Ben Schneider's (1990) arguments about attraction, selection, and attrition leading to a homogeneous workforce suggest that because similar types of people enter the organization in the first place, it is often relatively easy for organization members to internalize the basic assumptions that form the organization's culture.

According to Schein's (1992) definition, organizational culture exists primarily at the level of these basic assumptions. Meanwhile, not included in his definition of organizational culture are *artifacts,* the visible structures, norms, and processes of an organization; and *espoused values,* the cognitively available and articulated strategies, goals, and philosophies of an organization. Instead, they are considered manifestations of the true, deeper culture. Other culture researchers (like Rousseau, described previously) view all these layers as various aspects of organizational culture.

MEASUREMENT OF ORGANIZATIONAL CULTURE

Generally speaking, there are two distinct ways to measure organizational culture, each with advantages and disadvantages. One approach is more anthropological in nature and emphasizes the investigators' immersion into the organizational culture. When embedded in the organization, the investigator can better interpret the basic assumptions made by the organizational members. The second approach uses more quantitative methods to assess organizational culture. Through surveys of organizational members, investigators can quantify an organization's culture, which provides a means to compare organizations or branches of an organization on predetermined cultural factors.

The more qualitative approach to the assessment of organizational culture is advocated strongly by Schein, and by the organizational anthropological community. Schein (1992) argues that the more efficient and accurate way to truly understand an organization's culture is to plunge into the organization. This vantage point provides an opportunity, with the help of motivated insiders, to better decipher the organizational members' basic assumptions and truly understand the culture. Specific methods used thus far in the literature include ethnographic techniques such as observation; interviews; structured focus groups; and large group meetings with organizational members designed to examine artifacts, espoused values, and basic assumptions. Schein even goes so far as to argue that a quantitative assessment of organizational culture is unethical, in that it fails to describe the unique ways in which various beliefs and assumptions are manifested in a given organization.

The qualitative assessment of culture depends on an iterative clinical approach, or a continual revising of cultural assessment as new information is made available. With this method, the investigator enters the organization and directly experiences the organizational culture. This entails both active and systematic observation as well as passively encountering situations that are different from what the investigator expected and attempting to understand these observations and encounters. An important step in this approach is to find a motivated insider that can help decipher the investigator's observations and interpretations. This motivated insider has to have the mental capacity to think analytically to be helpful in this important process, as well as have a vested interest in understanding the cultural issue that has initiated the organizational culture study.

With the help of the motivated insider, the investigator attempts to identify the underlying shared assumptions and continually recalibrates these assumptions to further understand the true organizational culture. The end product in a qualitative investigation of culture is a formal description of the organization's culture. This description is in no way static; but it is a perpetual work in progress, because organizational culture is dynamic and new information may reveal more basic assumptions or revisions to the prior basic assumptions.

The ability to converse with insiders of the organization is essential to fully understand the culture for two reasons. First, the investigator can easily misinterpret events and observations and needs the insider to help correct these misinterpretations. Second, the insider is usually unaware of the basic assumptions in the organization, because these assumptions have dropped from conscious awareness and are taken for granted. It is the goal of the investigator to help bring these basic assumptions to a conscious level.

These qualitative methods, although thorough and comprehensive, have many disadvantages. In some situations, it is not financially feasible to conduct one or two large group meetings at numerous organizations in many different countries. The time burden of this endeavor would cause too much time to pass for an equal comparison across organizations or countries. Further, the results of this type of research do not allow for necessary comparisons, because statistical analysis of qualitative data would be difficult, if not impossible.

Using Rousseau's five-level typology of culture as a framework, quantitative measures of culture vary from the more behavioral level to values and beliefs. Because quantitative measures of culture are limited to the more observable and measurable aspects of organizational culture, these self-report measures are necessarily limited to the shallower levels of the typology. However, it has been argued that when the organizational culture is strong, the material artifacts, behavioral patterns and norms, espoused values, and basic assumptions may all be in alignment. When this is the case, a quantitative measure of culture may effectively tap the deeper levels of organizational culture.

The quantitative approach to assessing organizational culture is through self-report surveys. A number of survey measures have been created and are classified by Neal Ashkanasy as either typing or profile surveys. Typing surveys classify organizations into mutually exclusive taxonomies or types. Once an organization is classified into a particular type, a description of behaviors and values typical of the type is provided. Through these types, organizations can be compared and organizational culture change can be monitored over time. Profile surveys assess an organization on predetermined cultural dimensions. High or low scores on the various dimensions of norms, behaviors, values, and beliefs provide a profile of the culture of an organization. These profiles can also be compared with those of other organizations, and changes can be tracked over time.

Assessing organizational culture using a quantitative measure provides a standardized means of understanding an organization's culture. This standardization of measurement is more conducive to comparing cultures of different organizations as well as different branches of the same organization. The ability to use statistical techniques is also a benefit of standardized, quantitative measures of organizational culture. Another advantage is that organizational members may be more likely to take part in later organizational change efforts because they were included in the cultural assessment. This commitment to the process could prove valuable later on.

There are a number of disadvantages to using the quantitative approach to cultural assessment. Self-report measures of organizational culture assume the respondent is aware of and can report the various aspects of an organization's culture. This approach assumes everyone surveyed is motivated and mentally capable of reporting on the behaviors, values, and beliefs of the organization as a whole. Further, quantitative measures are incapable of assessing all dimensions of culture identified to date. Using quantitative measures alone could miss those dimensions that are idiosyncratic, yet vitally important, to the functioning of a specific organization.

Quantitative measures are useful in assessing the more shallow layers of culture and may approach the deeper levels when the culture is strong. Although using qualitative measures may aid in the understanding of basic assumptions, quantitative measures provide information that is replicable and generalizable and that can reap the many benefits of statistical analysis. Because of the various advantages and disadvantages presented here, whether to use quantitative and qualitative measures should be considered carefully. A multimethod approach is recommended whenever feasible to avoid missing any vital level of information about organizational culture. In general, quantitative measures can be an efficient and valid measure of the more shallow levels of culture, and the use of qualitative measures can be considered for deeper layers of culture such as basic assumptions.

ROLE OF LEADERSHIP IN ORGANIZATIONAL CULTURE

The general assumption that is inherent in much organizational research on the relationship between leadership and culture is that *leaders create cultures.* This seems intuitive, in that organizational founders are seen as the people who create the initial culture of the organization, and in many organizations the founder's impact continues to be felt for years or decades after the founder has left the organization, or died. Schein (1992) in particular emphasizes the importance of the founder in shaping the organization's culture. Early research (e.g., Kurt Lewin, Ronald Lippitt, and Ralph White's 1939 study) and writing (e.g., Douglas McGregor's classic, *The Human Side of Enterprise*) in this area focused largely on how managerial beliefs about employees affect the behavior of those employees. Research has demonstrated that the personality traits of the CEO may be related to certain aspects of the organization's structure; and recently, Tomas Giberson and colleagues have shown congruence between CEO personality and values and the personalities and values of subordinates within the organization. Clearly, leadership plays a role in the creation of organizational culture.

However, other perspectives emphasize the role that culture plays in allowing (or preventing) people from emerging as leaders. For example, Robert Lord and colleagues focus on an information-processing approach to culture and suggest that the shared values and shared ways of conceptualizing and solving problems within an organization lead to evaluations of organizational members as being good or bad leaders, when a more accurate appraisal might be that a person is *consistent with the type of person who has been successful as a leader in the past here.* They thus argue that leadership itself may simply be an artifact of culture. The punctuated equilibrium model leads to similar conclusions: During times of calm, the people who rise to leadership positions tend to be those who do things in the same ways as the people who came before. They are likely to share the same values and perspectives, and it is only during times of crisis—when the shared values of an organization may be threatened or crumbling—that people with different leadership styles may come to be seen as leaders.

In short, leaders create cultures, and cultures yield leaders. The dynamics of this reciprocal process vary from organization to organization, from industry to industry, and from society to society. To believe the causal arrow points in only one direction, however, is to be too simplistic in our conceptualization of organizational functioning.

ROLE OF SOCIETAL CULTURE IN ORGANIZATIONAL CULTURE

Although it seems intuitively obvious that the culture of the society in which an organization emerges would affect the culture of the organization itself, until recently there has been little data available with which to assess this question. The Global Leadership and Organizational Behavior Effectiveness (GLOBE) project's analyses on this question have provided evidence suggesting that there is in fact some degree of congruence between aspects of a societal culture and of the culture of the average organization within that society. Speculating about the mechanisms by which this impact occurs, GLOBE researchers propose several possible avenues, including normative isomorphic pressures (e.g., organizations that structure themselves in certain ways and value certain things are seen as *good* within a given societal context) and cultural immersion (e.g., when an organization's founders have lived in an uncertainty-avoiding society, they are likely to have internalized that value, and would thus be more likely to create organizations that manifest uncertainty avoidance).

What remains unknown to date is whether the organizations in a society that are most effective are those that most closely represent the dominant values of the society, or those that diverge from those values in some distinct way. Additionally, the role of the industry here is unknown. For example, it seems plausible that in a conservative, risk-averse society, a bank with a culture of risk aversion could be seen as trustworthy and good, whereas a pharmaceutical or high-tech firm with a strong risk aversion could be seen as less appropriate. Research on these issues will be critical for better understanding the origins and effects of organizational culture in different societies and industries.

ORGANIZATIONAL CULTURE VERSUS ORGANIZATIONAL CLIMATE

Elsewhere in this volume, we describe the construct of *organizational climate*. Although the climate and culture constructs are clearly related, they have evolved in different ways and have come to be seen as representing different aspects of organizational functioning. Arnon Reichers and Schneider, in Schneider's *Organizational Climate and Culture* (1990), provide an extensive description of the historical evolution of the two constructs, showing how the current conceptualization of organizational climate has followed almost a direct linear path from the early work of Kurt Lewin, with his focus on the practicality of good theory, whereas the organizational culture construct has evolved more from a history rooted in anthropology. Reichers and Schneider point out the research emphasis on climate as a predictor of organizational effectiveness in some domain (which links cleanly to Lewinian practical theory), and the emphasis in culture research on descriptive, rather than prescriptive, approaches to organizational culture assessment (which links cleanly to a more anthropological, value-neutral, descriptive approach); but clearly there has been increased emphasis in recent years on the value of certain types of organizational cultures over others.

In the *Handbook of Organizational Culture and Climate* (Ashkanasy, Wilderom, & Peterson, 2000), both Schneider and Schein weigh in with their perspectives on climate and culture. Schneider argues that climate is the shared perception of the setting in which people work, *the way things are around here*, and that culture is the attributions made about why the setting is the way it is. Schein emphasizes the importance of attending to an organization's culture both as something that is a static property and as something that is a natural, constant process of building collective meaning. Both authors note the overlap between climate and culture, emphasize the separateness of the two constructs, and emphasize the value for researchers and practitioners of attending to both.

CONCLUSION

Several recent books, both popular and academic, have focused on the importance of organizational culture. For example, the best-selling books *Good to Great* (Jim Collins, 2001) and *Built to Last: Successful Habits of Visionary Companies* (Collins and Jerry Porras, 1994) both focus on aspects of organizational culture that help explain why certain organizations over time excel within their industry and relative to their competitors. Others have noted the importance of culture match in mergers and acquisitions and joint ventures (e.g., Yaakov Weber's work) and about the difficult but critical issue of organizational culture change when faced with an organizational crisis. Clearly, culture matters—it matters for the organization in its quest for effectiveness, and it matters for shareholders who want to see resources put to good use and not diverted by *people problems,* and it matters for employees who live within a system of shared values that affects their day-to-day functioning. We hope that consideration of the issues described in this entry illustrate both the utility and the complexity of organizational culture.

—*Marcus W. Dickson and Jacqueline K. Mitchelson*

See also Attraction–Selection–Attrition Model; Global Leadership and Organizational Behavior Effectiveness Project; Organizational Climate

FURTHER READING

Ashkanasy, N. M., Wilderom, C. P. M., & Peterson, M. F. (Eds.). (2000). *Handbook of organizational culture and climate.* Thousand Oaks, CA: Sage.

Deal, T. E., & Kennedy, A. A. (1982). *Corporate cultures: The rites and rituals of corporate life.* Reading, MA: Addison-Wesley.

Denison, D. R. (1990). *Corporate culture and organizational effectiveness.* Ann Arbor, MI: Aviat.

Schein, E. (1992). *Organizational culture and leadership* (2nd ed.). San Francisco: Jossey-Bass.

Schneider, B. (Ed.). (1990). *Organizational climate and culture.* San Francisco: Jossey-Bass.

Trice, H. M., & Beyer, J. M. (1993). *The cultures of work organizations.* Englewood Cliffs, NJ: Prentice Hall.

ORGANIZATIONAL CYNICISM

At some point in our working lives, most of us feel that things at work would be fine if only we were in charge. Some people feel that way most of the time. They believe that the problems they and their coworkers encounter at work could be avoided or surmounted if someone competent were in control. This tendency to find fault with the management of the workplace and criticize the efforts of others who strive for excellence, while doubting their motives, is called *organizational cynicism* by psychologists.

ORIGINS AND DEFINITIONS

The term *cynicism* originally referred to the beliefs of the Cynics, a small but influential school of ancient Greek philosophers who stressed self-control and individualism as the path to virtue. In their pursuit of virtue, the Cynics believed that rejection of social mores was preferable to material wealth and social acceptance because antisocial behaviors such as incivility, rude manners, and criticizing others freed one from society's bonds and restrictions. Rejection of social norms compels the individual to be self-reliant, and through self-reliance the individual attains a state of virtuous righteousness. In pursuing this ideal, the Cynics often took to scornful faultfinding in others. It is this sense of the word *cynic* that has come down to present-day use.

The idea that cynics direct their negativity toward past, present, *and* future events neatly captures the approach that many modern-day researchers bring to the study of organizational cynicism. An *organizational cynic* may be defined as someone who believes that workplace problems are solvable and improvements are possible but that change and improvement efforts are futile because of the failings of others and the inherent incompetence of the system.

As the pace at which companies reinvented themselves quickened during the later years of the 20th century, their employees became increasingly skeptical of yet another *flavor-of-the-month* change initiative. This is an ongoing theme of the popular *Dilbert* cartoon strip. Organizational researchers recognize that many of these initiatives (including quality circles, continuous quality improvement, six sigma, process reengineering, customer focus, etc.) require acceptance and support from employees to succeed. Indeed, employee resistance to change could doom these initiatives to failure; the belief that failure is inevitable becomes a self-fulfilling prophecy that gives smug cynics a perverse *I told you so* satisfaction.

RESEARCH ON CYNICISM

Researchers adopt a number of conceptually distinct approaches to the study of cynicism. One school of study regards cynicism as a personality trait. Usually labeled *cynical hostility,* in this view cynicism is dysfunctional primarily in the realm of interpersonal relations. Studies indicate that cynics tend to be especially sensitive to social stress and, because of this, are likely to keep their cynical views to themselves. Even their spouses may not realize how cynical they are. Cynics have more job dissatisfaction, more job stress, and greater difficulties with the social and interpersonal environment at work than their noncynical coworkers.

Perhaps the best known treatment of cynicism as a dispositional characteristic is that of Donald Kanter and Philip Mirvis (1989). They conducted a national survey of cynicism among American adults. In their view cynicism develops from three key ingredients:

1. Unrealistically high expectations of self or others

2. Disappointment and frustration with outcomes and accomplishments

3. Disillusionment and a sense of having been let down, deceived, or betrayed by others

They classified cynics into types, such as *command cynics, squeezed cynics,* and *hard-bitten cynics,* with each type having implications for how someone expresses a personal cynical worldview. In addition to negative evaluations of attempts by others to make improvements, cynicism breeds suspicion of the motives of change agents and antipathy toward those efforts. Their findings indicated that cynicism is related to distrust of management and coworkers, job dissatisfaction, and dissatisfaction with the employer. Other researchers who used the Kanter and Mirvis (1989) survey instrument found that cynics tend to have low self-esteem, but cynicism is unrelated to other personality traits such as introversion and extraversion as well as anxiety.

Some researchers approach the study of cynicism from a perspective of work and occupations. Arthur Niederhoffer (1967) pioneered the study of occupational cynicism by looking specifically at cynicism among police officers. In his view cynicism is an adaptive reaction for officers who must maintain an adversarial role toward the public they serve. Cynicism is thus a coping mechanism for dealing with frustration, which is learned through direct experience with duplicitous criminals and reinforced by a culture of cynical coworkers and supervisors.

Other researchers who followed the work of Niederhoffer identified specific targets of police cynicism, including the following:

- *Organizational cynicism*: problems will not be solved because of the bureaucratic way decisions are made
- *Work cynicism*: problems cannot be solved because of the nature of things; for example, human nature will always produce criminals
- *Cynicism toward management*: incompetent superiors
- *Cynicism about rules and regulations*: bureaucracy stymies effective action

- *Cynicism about the legal system*: criminals go free on legal technicalities
- *Cynicism about fellow citizens*: people try to get away with whatever they can

Findings showed that cynicism about specific targets relates differently to aspects of work performance, including relations with coworkers, encounters with citizens, and number of arrests made. Implications of this work are that a person can be more cynical with respect to some targets than others, and that social influences (peers, coworkers) identify acceptable targets of blame, which can vary across situations.

In this era (from the 1980s to the early 21st century) of mergers, acquisitions, downsizing, restructuring, and bankruptcies, management assurances about the future of the company fall by the wayside with the next episode of corporate drama, leaving workers with ever greater levels of distress, uncertainty, betrayal, and cynicism. Announcements of massive corporate layoffs regularly make headlines in today's American economy, usually accompanied by stories of multimillion-dollar severance packages for the executives who engineered such *success*. Another approach to the study of organizational cynicism uses a contract violation framework to argue that cynicism develops from frustration and disappointment when management breaks implicit and explicit promises to employees. Unmet expectations are the culprit, particularly when these expectations are encouraged by executives and managers who tout each flavor-of-the-month change initiative as the new best path to success.

WHAT IS ORGANIZATIONAL CYNICISM?

These various approaches to the study of cynicism contribute essential insights into its role in the psychology of the individual and as a dimension of social processes at work.

- There is a dispositional aspect to cynicism. Some people are generally more pessimistic than others, their general negative affectivity giving them a tendency to see the glass as half empty rather than half full. When they encounter frustration and duplicity, they are more likely than optimists to become cynical, expecting more of the same. It is probably negative affect that contributes to cynics' difficulties in interpersonal relations.
- Although pessimists are likely to become cynical about a broader range of issues than optimists, cynicism

nevertheless requires specific targets. If people are cynical, they have to be cynical about something. Pessimists may have many more targets of their cynicism than optimists, but given particular circumstances everyone is capable of becoming cynical about something.

- Cynicism serves a purpose. It is a psychological defense against disappointment and frustration that follows from naive credulity. Not only are cynics not as disappointed when promised benefits fail to appear, they are righteously reassured to know that their doubts were well founded.

- Cynicism is learned through direct experience and through group socialization. It is fair to say that most people begin their working lives eager to put skills acquired at school to use, learn new skills, earn a living, establish an identity, make new friends, and so on. From the outset their more experienced coworkers may try to convince newcomers that management cannot be trusted (*Listen to us if you want to know how things really work around here*), particularly in cases where the work group itself is highly cynical. However, it probably takes at least a few personal encounters with broken promises and misplaced priorities before eager anticipation turns to dejected cynicism. With experience comes wisdom and also, for many, cynicism.

- Cynicism implies behavior or, perhaps, lack of behavior. If you expect that the latest improvement program at work will fail, just like its predecessors, why bother to get involved? (Better to keep your head down until it passes.) There is some evidence, however, that cynics will become proactive if they believe their efforts can really make a difference. Cynics have been found to write more comments on employee opinion surveys than noncynics, and although the comments they wrote were negative in tone, they were also more specific about problem areas and more likely to suggest solutions than comments provided by noncynics.

ORGANIZATIONAL CHANGE AND CYNICISM

If you find yourself rolling your eyes in exasperation every time your employer announces another improvement initiative, you may be an organizational cynic. And you may be right. Research has not addressed the question of whether or not cynicism about workplace conditions is justified. We *do* know, however, that successfully implementing new processes and systems within large organizations is difficult. Most change initiatives require support and cooperation of employees to succeed. Too often, these efforts fail to live up to expectations. Sometimes they fail entirely, wasting resources and ultimately doing the company more harm than good. When they succeed, it can take years for the benefits of new approaches to become apparent.

Executives preparing to launch the next quality improvement or process reengineering program should not be surprised if they seem to be the only ones who are truly excited about it. To them, the need for change is obvious. Their company's rapidly changing external environment forces the issue (via changing markets, technologies, resource costs, customer demands and expectations, etc.). Only through constant change can their company remain competitive.

To most people, however, change is unsettling and stressful. The known is comfortable, the unknown is threatening. Change is therefore resisted, and promises of benefits of change are met with cynicism. In reality, of course, change occurs continually. The challenge for organizational researchers is to increase their understanding of organizational cynicism and to develop change management strategies that are both effective and acceptable to those who make them succeed or fail.

—Robert J. Vance

See also Organizational Change; Organizational Change, Resistance to

FURTHER READING

Dean, J. W., Jr., Brandes, P., & Dharwadkar, R. (1998). Organizational cynicism. *Academy of Management Review, 23,* 341–352.

Kanter, D. L., & Mirvis, P. H. (1989). *The cynical Americans: Living and working in an age of discontent and disillusion.* San Francisco: Jossey-Bass.

Niederhoffer, A. (1967). *Behind the shield: The police in urban society.* Garden City, NY: Doubleday.

ORGANIZATIONAL DEVELOPMENT

Organizational development (OD) is a field of professional practice focused on facilitating organizational change and improvement. The theory and practice of OD is grounded in both the social and behavioral sciences. The field originated in the 1960s and has been evolving ever since. This evolution has been influenced by a wide range of disciplines including social psychology, group dynamics, industrial/ organizational (I/O) psychology, participative management theory, organization behavior, the sociology of organizations, and even clinical psychology.

As a result, the application of OD tools and methodologies (of which there are many) are carried out by a wide range of professionals. For example, although some I/O psychologists also consider themselves OD practitioners, there are many others practicing OD with for-profit and nonprofit client organizations with educational backgrounds as diverse as education, philosophy, training, the military, and human resources. In part, this level of diversity of backgrounds is because of an initial lack of agreement and formal training regarding the nature and boundaries of the field. Today, however, formal training in the field does exist, in doctoral and master's-level programs as well as professional development curricula, including professional certification groups and training firms. In any case the value of the field of OD to continually embrace new perspectives, practitioners, and approaches is one of its defining characteristics; however, it is also a source of discussion among those currently practicing in and writing about the field.

Although there has been some debate over the last few decades as to what is and is not included under the definition of OD, many practitioners agree that the following definition captures the essence of the field: *Organizational development is a planned process for driving humanistically oriented, system-based change in organizations through the use of social science theory and behaviorally based data collection and feedback techniques.* This definition clearly reflects a number of specific assumptions. These include the importance of data and feedback to OD efforts, the notion of having a social systems perspective, and the humanistically oriented values-based nature of the field. Each assumption is described in more detail in the following text.

DATA DRIVEN

First, it is important to understand that OD is fundamentally a data-driven approach to organizational change. Although the source of that data can be quantitative or qualitative in nature, the information gathered and fed back to clients is an integral part of the OD consulting process. Unlike other types of consulting

models, the OD approach is generally not prescriptive. In other words, there is no single model, technique, or solution that is consistently provided by OD practitioners. Rather, OD consulting projects are based on a participative approach. This approach is known as *action research.*

Conceptualized by Kurt Lewin, a social psychologist who specialized in studying group dynamics in the 1940s and 1950s, action research consists of the following stages:

- Systematically gathering data (of whatever form and using any number of tools and techniques) on the nature of an organizational problem or situation
- Analyzing that information to find key themes, patterns, and insights that tell a compelling story about the problem or situation in question
- Feeding back that analysis in a summary form of the results while engaging with the client to ensure ownership of the diagnosis of the problem
- Determining the appropriate intervention together based on a shared understanding of the issues
- Taking action to drive positive change in the organization or social system

Given this framework it is easy to understand how OD practitioners can use many different types of diagnostic tools and interventions to produce helpful insights and feedback. Many of these methods are also used by other types of social scientists and practitioners. The key difference when using these methodologies in an OD context is that the interpretation of the results and the determination of the intervention required is a shared process between practitioner and client, and the emphasis is on organizational improvement. Regardless of the methodology, the basic notion of using data-based feedback to move clients from their comfort zone and create a need for change is common to most OD efforts.

SYSTEMS PERSPECTIVE

The second major assumption inherent in the definition of OD is that the field is firmly grounded in social systems theory. From this perspective, each organization is conceptualized as a system of interdependent subsystems and components (e.g., people and systems related) that both influence each other and are influenced by the external environment in which they exist. This means that OD interventions are designed and implemented with a thorough understanding of the interplay between different factors in the organization that can either help or hinder the success of the change effort.

Although there are a number of different OD models reflecting systems theory, the Burke-Litwin model of organizational performance and change is one of the more comprehensive. Reflecting a systems thinking perspective, it outlines 12 distinct factors of organizations that need to be considered when designing and implementing any large-scale change effort. These factors reflect both transformational and transactional areas.

Transformational factors are those that are likely to be influenced by the external environment. When these factors are the focus of an OD-related change effort, new thinking and behaviors are typically required on the part of the individuals in that social system. These factors include the external environment, the mission and strategy of the organization, the senior leadership and what they represent, and the nature of the organizational culture. Changes in these factors (or a lack of alignment and integration among any of these during a change effort) tend to be more strategic and long term in nature and eventually create a ripple effect that drives change in other parts of the organization.

Transactional factors, in comparison, are those that are more day-to-day and short-term focused. These include elements such as the behaviors of middle management, the formal structure reflecting how managers and employees are organized, the systems and processes that reinforce the right types of behaviors (e.g., the performance appraisal process), work group climate, level of motivation, needs and values of employees, and finally the fit between employees and the jobs they are in.

All these factors and their interaction with one another ultimately influence both individual and organizational performance. As with most systems models, performance also has a subsequent impact on the external environment of that organization (e.g., competitors, industry regulations, economic trends, technology trends), which in turn affects the organization itself. In other words the systems approach to OD work reflects a constant feedback loop.

In sum, the systems approach is a unique aspect of OD that helps differentiate it from some of the more narrowly focused theory and practice areas of I/O psychology, human resource management, and organizational behavior. It also reflects a broader perspective for facilitating organizational change than many management consulting approaches, such as those of firms that focus only on structure or technology.

VALUES BASED

The third defining characteristic of the field of OD, which is shared with I/O psychology, is the notion of a normative view to working with people and organizations. This means that the field and practice of OD is values-based in nature. Organizational development practitioners evaluate their efforts, including the choices of the clients they work with and the interventions they engage in, against a normative filter. In short, they ask this question of themselves: Will this effort result in a positive outcome for the organization and its employees?

Unlike some types of organizational consulting approaches that can be financially driven or very senior management focused, such as downsizing efforts or mergers and acquisitions, OD practitioners are particularly focused on the human relations component of their work. This means that for many, if the nature of the project will result in negative outcomes for a given set of employees, the OD practitioner is likely to turn down the project. Although counterintuitive from a business model perspective, this is one of the hallmarks of the OD profession and one of the key reasons why OD work is appealing to some people.

This emphasis on positivistic change is evident in areas such as the International OD Code of Ethics, sponsored by the Organization Development Institute, as well as described in many articles and books in the field. Although an area of debate for some, research has consistently shown that the majority of practitioners would endorse such OD values as improving the state of human dignity, democracy, honesty, integrity, and empowerment in organizations.

Overall, this normative filter helps OD practitioners balance the need for increasing organizational productivity and effectiveness (which is one of the most common reasons why an external or internal consultant would be engaged in the first place) with a humanistic values focus on helping improve the satisfaction and development of individuals in an organization.

OD CONSULTING APPROACH

Although it is important to understand the underpinnings of the field from a philosophical perspective, it is equally important to have a firm grasp of the tactical side of the OD profession. One of the best ways to do this is to understand the OD consulting model. There are seven phases to the OD consulting approach, which consist of

1. entry,

2. contracting,

3. data collection,

4. data analysis,

5. data feedback,

6. intervention, and

7. evaluation.

This seven-phase model is particularly relevant for OD because it

- reinforces the centrality of data or information as a key component for driving change,
- shows where and when data should be used to inform decision making, and
- reflects a systems approach to thinking about issues and interventions.

Each of these phases of the OD consulting approach are described in the following text.

Entry

Entry represents the first meeting between the OD practitioner and the client. If an external consulting engagement, this is usually the first exposure to the overall social system, and as a result, represents an important first step in the consulting relationship. During this phase the OD practitioner and client determine their ability to work together collaboratively, and get a shared understanding of the issues or problems at hand. The quality of the relationship established during entry will determine whether or not the OD effort will occur.

Contracting

Contracting is the phase where roles, expectations, and anticipated outcomes are agreed on between the OD practitioner and his or her client. Typically, this is where individual capabilities are reviewed and difficult questions are tested. For example, most OD consultants will discuss with their clients the difference between a symptom, such as the problem at hand that resulted in their being contacted, and a root cause including the real reason and best place for an intervention to occur.

Data Collection

Once entry and contracting are done, the OD practitioner next needs to determine a data-gathering strategy. The focus here is determining the best method, tool, or technique for gaining new insights into the issue or problem at hand. The collected data can be either quantitative or qualitative in nature, or some combination of both. Some of the most common OD-related methodologies include the following:

- Multisource or 360-degree feedback
- Organizational surveys
- Personality assessments
- Individual observations
- Interviews with key individuals
- Focus groups
- Process consultation during meetings
- Large-group interventions
- Appreciative inquiry

Data Analysis

Once the data is collected, it needs to be analyzed. The nature of the analysis and the techniques applied will depend on

- the type of data collected,
- the analysis skills and experience of the OD practitioner, and
- the receptivity and sophistication of the client.

Analysis techniques can range from reporting simple averages or content code summaries of comments or observations; to sophisticated statistical modeling of relationships among key predictors, such as leadership behaviors and employee engagement; and outcome variables including regional sales, plant safety incidents, and executive turnover. Whatever the approach used, the outcome is the same. Organizational development practitioners are focused on determining the best analysis method to produce the most useful and actionable insights to share with their clients.

Data Feedback

The next phase in the process is delivering the insights gleaned from the data collection and analysis with the client. From an OD perspective, it is important to work with the client during the feedback stage to help gain a shared understanding of the diagnosis rather than simply delivering the answer. As a result, one of the critical skills needed to be successful in the field of OD is the ability to tell a meaningful story with data. Although not delivering the answer per se, the OD practitioner does need to be able to convey the key findings from the data in a manner that brings the client along. This represents one of the unique aspects of the OD approach compared with other consulting models where the answer is clearly recommended during the feedback process. Organizational development practitioners are much more likely to suggest ideas and work together with their clients through the issues as a part of the feedback process. The focus here is delivering a compelling story that creates a need for change and a direction for that change. The discussion during the feedback stage is what leads to the selection of the appropriate intervention.

Intervention

The intervention phase involves determining together the appropriate solution based on the data fed back and a shared understanding of its implications. The important point to remember here is that regardless of what intervention is chosen, the determination should be based on the issues identified in the data, and what the practitioner and client think will result in the most impact. This shared approach drives client ownership and commitment, which is critical to ensuring success of the OD change effort.

Evaluation

The last stage of an OD effort is a formal evaluation process. Although often overlooked by many consultants, it is a crucial step for both the client and the practitioner. From the client's perspective, it is helpful toward quantifying the successful outcome of the effort. From the OD practitioner's perspective, it represents both a measure of success and a key source of learning and development.

SUMMARY

In sum, the theory and practice of OD represents a data-driven, systemic thinking, and values-based approach to helping improve organizations and the people that work in them. Fundamentally, the OD consulting model is collaborative in nature and grounded in data-based information.

—Allan Church

See also Human Resource Management; Organizational Behavior

FURTHER READING

Burke, W. W. (1994). *Organization development: A process of learning and changing* (2nd ed.). Reading, MA: Addison-Wesley.

Cummings, T., & Worley, C. (1997). *Organization development and change* (6th ed.). St. Paul, MN: West.

French, W. L., & Bell, C. H., Jr. (1998). *Organization development: Behavioral science interventions for organization improvement* (5th ed.). Englewood Cliffs, NJ: Prentice Hall.

Waclawski, J., & Church, A. H. (Eds.). (2002). *Organization development: A data-driven approach to organizational change*. San Francisco: Jossey-Bass.

ORGANIZATIONAL IMAGE

Organizational image refers to people's global impressions of an organization; it is defined as people's loose structures of knowledge and beliefs about an organization. Organizational image represents the net cognitive reactions and associations of customers, investors, employees, and applicants to an organization's name. Accordingly, it serves as a template to categorize, store, and recall organization-related information.

It should be noted that there is no such thing as *the* organization's image because an organization typically has multiple images. These multiple images result from various groups (also known as stakeholders or corporate audiences) holding different images of the same organization. At least, one might distinguish among the following organizational images. First, investors and executives hold an image of an organization as an economic performer. These investors typically rely on factual economic figures as a basis of their beliefs about the organization. Second, there is the image of an organization as a social performer in the general society (also known as corporate social performance). Third, customers or clients hold an image of an organization as a provider of goods and services. Fourth, each organization has an image as an employer among current employees and (potential) applicants (also known as company employment image or employer image). This is the image that is assessed in rankings such as *Fortune* magazine's "The

100 Best Companies to Work For." These multiple organizational images might not always coincide. For example, the firm's image as an employer as held by either employees or job seekers might be different from its image as a provider of goods and services in the minds of customers or clients.

Organizational images typically develop over longer periods of time. They result from, among other things, media coverage, individual or group sensemaking, and communication on the part of the organization (as reflected in an organization's advertising, sponsorships, and publicity). However, it should be clear that organizational images are not static. Specifically, organizations often audit their images. In these image audits, the aim is to carefully determine which factors make up the image among various stakeholders. Next, organizations aim to strategically modify the image held by these stakeholders. For example, this might be done by increasing an organization's exposure or by highlighting specific attributes in advertising campaigns.

COMPONENTS OF IMAGE

Generally, two components can be distinguished in an organization's image. First, people typically associate some objective attributes with an organization. These attributes might vary from factual or historical aspects of organizations to organizational procedures and policies. For example, in terms of a company's image as an employer, research has confirmed that applicants might have some knowledge about the attributes of the organization and the job that they might consider applying for. Examples include size, location, level of centralization, pay, benefits, type of work to be performed, advancement opportunities, and career programs.

A second part of people's general impressions of an organization refers to trait-related inferences. Trait inferences about organizations are different from the aforementioned objective company-related information for two reasons. First, trait inferences describe the organization in terms of subjective, abstract, and intangible attributes. Second, they convey symbolic company information in the form of imagery that people assign to organizations. For example, in terms of a company's image as an employer, research has discovered that applicants reliably and meaningfully ascribe traits to organizations. They refer to some employing organizations as trendy, whereas other employing organizations are seen as prestigious.

Similar results have been found in research on consumers' image of the organization as a provider of products and services.

CONSEQUENCES OF ORGANIZATIONAL IMAGE

An organization's image plays a central role because what various stakeholders know about an organization considerably influences how they respond to the organization. In fact, an organization's image might have various potentially favorable consequences for the organization and its main stakeholders.

First, there might be effects on investment decisions. Specifically, firms with a good image might have a competitive leverage in terms of attracting and keeping new investors. Second, it has been found that an organization's image exerts effects on consumers' product choices. In this context, an organization's image might serve as a signal of product quality and might enable an organization to distinguish itself from its main competitors. Third, an organization's image seems to affect people's attraction to an organization as a place to work. This is especially the case in early recruitment stages as potential applicants have only a rudimentary knowledge of the key job and organizational attributes. Hence, potential applicants mainly rely on their general impressions of the firm (i.e., image) when deciding to apply for a job. The general effect is that employer image influences the quantity and quality of the applicant pool of an organization in that organizations with a good image are able to attract more and better applicants. Apart from these general effects on applicant quantity and quality, applicants' view of the image of an employer also has long-lasting effects on other recruitment stages. Specifically, impressions of an organization as an employer measured in early recruitment stages are strong predictors of applicants' attraction measured in later recruitment stages, such as after a campus interview, which in turn is related to applicants' final job acceptance decisions. A fourth group of studies have examined the consequences of organizational image on employees' attitudes and behaviors toward their organization. For example, employees also uses an organization's image as a mirror of how others are judging them. Moreover, an organization's image has been found to be important to employees' sense of self. If an employee holds the company in low regard, the person has lower job satisfaction and a higher probability of leaving the organization. Conversely, if the company is held in high regard by the employee and others, job satisfaction is higher and turnover intention is lower. In this case an employee also wants to be associated with the positive image of the organization and feels proud to belong to that organization. Finally, there is evidence that firms on the best 100 list enjoy organizational performance advantages over the broad market and a matched sample of firms. In other words, organizational image seems to enhance the competitive ability of the firm.

RELATED CONSTRUCTS

Organizational image is closely related to other constructs such as organizational reputation and organizational identity. However, there are also some differences. In particular, organizational reputation refers to people's beliefs about the general public's affective evaluation of the organization. Organizational reputation differs from organizational image in that reputation entails an affective component (a loose set of feelings associated with an organization), whereas image is mainly cognitively oriented (a loose set of knowledge and beliefs about an organization). Another difference is that reputation refers to people's assessment of how others (the general public) feel about the organization, whereas image deals with a person's own beliefs.

Another related construct is an organization's perceived identity. The key difference between an organization's identity and its image is that an organization's identity is what insiders in the organization (employees) perceive to be the organization's central, enduring, and distinctive characteristics. Conversely, image and reputation deal with outsiders' (applicants, customers) views and feelings.

—*Filip Lievens*

See also Person–Organization Fit; Self-Concept Theory of Work Motivation

FURTHER READING

Arnold, J., Coombs, C. R., Wilkinson, A. J., Loan-Clarke, J., Park, J. R., & Prest, D. (2003). Corporate images of the United Kingdom National Health Service: Implications for the recruitment and retention of nursing and allied health profession staff. *Corporate Reputation Review, 6,* 223–238.

Cable, D. M., & Turban, D. B. (2001). Establishing the dimensions, sources and value of job seekers' employer knowledge during recruitment. In G. R. Ferris (Ed.), *Research in personnel and human resources management* (pp. 115–163). New York: Elsevier Science.

Collins, C. J., & Han, J. (2004). Exploring applicant pool quantity and quality: The effects of early recruitment practices, corporate advertising, and firm reputation. *Personnel Psychology, 57,* 685–717.

Fulmer, I. S., Gerhart, B., & Scott, K. S. (2003). Are the 100 best better? An empirical investigation of the relationship between being a "great place to work" and firm performance. *Personnel Psychology, 56,* 965–993.

Lievens, F., & Highhouse, S. (2003). The relation of instrumental and symbolic attributes to a company's attractiveness as an employer. *Personnel Psychology, 56,* 75–102.

ORGANIZATIONAL JUSTICE

Organizational justice refers to individual or collective judgments of fairness or ethical propriety. Investigations of organizational justice tend to take a descriptive approach. As such, an event is treated as *fair* or *unfair* to the extent that one believes it to be so. In other words, justice research is concerned with identifying the antecedents that influence fairness judgments, as well as the consequences once such an evaluation has been made. Notice that this descriptive approach does not tell organizations what really is fair, only what people believe to be just. This empirical perspective complements the normative frameworks beneficially employed by philosophers whose prescriptive approach typically attempts to ascertain what is objectively right or wrong by using reasoned analysis.

The sense of justice has a strong impact on workers' behavior and attitudes. For example, perceived fairness promotes such benefits as organizational commitment, effective job performance, and increased organizational citizenship behavior. Justice also helps alleviate many of the ill effects of dysfunctional work environments. For example, perceived fairness reduces workplace stress, vindictive retaliation, employee withdrawal, and sabotage.

DIFFERENT TYPES OF JUSTICE

Generally speaking, judgments of fairness can be said to have three targets:

1. Outcomes: distributive justice

2. Allocation processes: procedural justice

3. Interpersonal treatment: interactional justice

Distributive Justice

Research suggests that distributive justice is distinct from outcome favorability. Although these two variables are correlated, the latter is an appraisal of personal benefit, whereas the former concerns moral appropriateness. Individuals decide whether a given allocation decision is fair by examining the actual result in light of some idealized standard. Three standards or allocation rules have been most widely discussed: equity (allocations based on contributions or performance), equality (equivalent allocations for all), and need (allocations based on demonstrable hardship). Each of these rules may engender a sense of distributive justice for some people under some circumstances. For example, an equity allocation rule is more likely to be seen as appropriate when the participants are North Americans, when the goal is to maximize performance, and when the divided benefit is economic. An equality allocation rule, however, is more likely seen as appropriate when the participants are East Asian, when the goal is to maximize group harmony, and when the benefit that is being divided is socioemotional.

An interesting line of research suggests that equity and equality allocation rules can engender distinct organizational climates. For example, when resources are divided based on individual performance, there is a greater disparity between the top and bottom income brackets and a relative lack of cooperation. When resources are divided based on equality, there is obviously less income disparity; along with this comes greater social harmony and more intergroup cooperation.

To employ each allocation rule, an individual needs to evaluate the relative gains (or losses) of at least two individuals. These cognitive operations are facilitated by the existence of a *referent other* that can serve as a sort of baseline standard. For example, someone seeking equality can expect uniform earnings among everyone in a group. This correspondence can best be ascertained with knowledge of others' profits. Equity is even more cognitively complex, so it is necessary to calculate earnings relative to contributions and to compare this ratio to the ratio of the referent. The intriguing result of these cognitive operations is that

distributive justice may not be absolute. If a referent changes, a person's distributive fairness judgments may also change, even when the actual allocation remains constant. For example, when female workers are underpaid relative to their male counterparts, they will see this as distributively unfair when the more highly paid men are their referent. However, if they use other underpaid women as their referent, they sometimes perceive less injustice.

Procedural Justice

Especially important to the study of organizational fairness is work on procedural justice. Procedural justice researchers agree that workers are interested in the outcomes they receive (that is, in distributive justice). However, they add that employees also attend to the process by which these outcomes are assigned. Procedural justice is an especially strong predictor of such outcomes as organizational citizenship behavior, organizational commitment, trust, and so on. Generally speaking, processes are likely to be judged as fair if they have some combination of the following attributes: They are accurate, consistently applied, free from bias, representative of all concerned, correctable when mistakes are made, and consistent with prevailing ethical standards. Other research suggests that fair procedures should provide advance notice and not violate privacy concerns.

A large body of research has investigated the design of human resource systems in light of procedural justice considerations. This work has examined personnel procedures pertaining to performance evaluation, affirmative action programs, workplace drug testing, staffing, family-leave procedures, layoff policies, compensation decisions, conflict resolution procedures, and so on. Generally speaking, this work suggests that fair procedures can bring benefits to organizations, in the form of more effective job behaviors and more positive work attitudes.

Interactional Justice

In addition to an outcome and a formal process, scholars have also found that the interpersonal treatment that an individual receives is an important part of his or her justice perceptions. This notion of interactional justice was identified more recently than distributive or procedural justice, but it now has been well established as an important workplace variable in its own right. Researchers have divided interactional justice into two parts: informational justice and interpersonal justice. Informational justice is based on the presence or absence of explanations and social accounts. A transparent promotion decision would likely be seen as informationally fair. Interpersonal justice is concerned with the dignity that people receive. Interpersonally fair treatment is respectful, honest, and considerate of others' feelings. A racist remark during a job interview would likely be seen as interpersonally unfair.

Interactional justice is an important predictor of such variables as supervisory commitment, citizenship behavior, and job performance ratings. In addition, individuals are much more accepting of misfortunes such as downsizing when the process is implemented in an interactionally fair fashion. Given this practical value, attempts have been made to train decision makers to show more interactional justice. Such efforts have shown some success, and evidence suggests that training in interpersonal fairness can create a more effective work unit.

To date there remains less than complete consensus as to the structure of interactional justice. Because the informational and interpersonal components are correlated, some scholars treat them as manifestations of a single construct. More recently, others have separated interactional justice into these constituent parts, treating informational and interpersonal fairness as separate constructs. This new model has four factors: distributive, procedural, informational, and interpersonal. This model is promising, but the empirical evidence is as yet limited.

STUDYING JUSTICE: MAIN EFFECTS AND INTERACTIONS

The three manifestations of justice can be studied in terms of either their main effects or their interactions. Main effect studies compare the impact of one type of justice beyond the effect of another. Interaction studies explore how different types of justice work together to influence employee attitudes and behaviors.

Main Effects of Justice

Especially prominent in this regard is the two-factor model. The two-factor model maintains that distributive justice, when compared with procedural justice, better predicts individual reactions to specific allocation decisions. For example, the distributive justice of a person's compensation will be correlated with pay satisfaction. Procedural justice, however, tends to be the more efficacious predictor of reactions to organizations as a whole. For example, procedural justice will be correlated with organizational commitment. Data in support of the two-factor model lead many scholars to propose that procedural justice, when compared with distributive justice, is especially important for maintaining loyalty to institutions.

The multifoci model provides a similar main effect comparison. Multifoci researchers agree that reactions to organizations are best predicted by procedural justice. However, they add that interactional justice demonstrates an especially strong association to supervisory commitment and behaviors targeted to benefit a person's immediate boss. In this regard interactional justice tends to engender high-quality leader–member exchange relationships, as well as helpful citizenship behaviors directed toward supervisors.

Interactions Among Justice Types

Scholars also have examined the interactions between different types of justice. Generally speaking, individuals appear to be reasonably tolerant of a distributive injustice if the allocation procedures are viewed as fair. Likewise, they seem reasonably tolerant of a procedural injustice if the outcome is deemed to be appropriate. However, when both the outcome and the process are simultaneously unjust, worker reactions are especially negative. Put differently, distributive justice strongly predicts work-relevant attitudes and behaviors when the procedure is unfair; it is a weaker predictor of attitudes and behaviors when the procedure is fair. Research has also documented a similar two-way interaction between distributive and interactional justice. Specifically, individuals can accept a poor outcome if it is assigned via a fair interaction. Conversely, they can accept a poor interaction if it yields fair outcomes. However, employees become distressed when both things go poorly at once.

Recent research has begun to consider the interaction among all three types of justice together. Investigations of the resulting three-way interaction have been quite promising. This line of inquiry finds that the aforementioned two-way interaction between distributive and procedural justice is only significant when interactional justice is low. To state the matter in a different way, reactions are most negative when individuals experience all three types of injustice at the same time. Only a few studies have been conducted, but so far all have supported the existence of this three-way interaction.

WHY PEOPLE CARE ABOUT JUSTICE

It is not intuitively obvious why workers would care about justice, as opposed to their pecuniary benefits. Several models have been proposed and tested, but it is important to recognize that these are not mutually exclusive. Most experts believe that employee responses to injustice are influenced by multiple considerations. Here we will consider the best known accounts, including economic self-interest, the control model, the group-value model, social exchange theory, and deontic justice.

Economic Self-Interest

One early and still influential proposition is that the concern for justice is motivated by a sense of economic self-interest. The *fairest* system, according to this framework, is the one that maximizes long-term benefits. Even if a single decision is not personally beneficial, long-term payouts are apt to be greater if the individual can rely on fair distribution systems and procedurally just policies. There is evidence in favor of the self-interest model. For example, high performers tend to prefer equity allocations (presumably because their payment will be higher when based on contribution), whereas lower performers tend to prefer equality allocations (presumably because their payment will be higher when everyone earns equivalent amounts). Despite such evidence, self-interest does not seem to be the only motive for justice. For example, if a process is fair individuals tend not to derogate decision makers, even when their outcomes are less than favorable.

The Control Model

Another early framework for understanding justice is the control model. According to the control model, justice matters because it provides people with some means of influencing decisions. This control could be exercised at the decision stage (somewhat akin to distributive justice) or at the process stage (often

interpreted as procedural justice, and especially voice). Based on this, research has found that individuals will report some measure of fairness if either decision or process control is present. When they lose both forms of control, of course, people tend to report less justice. The control model was originally formulated within the context of legal proceedings. It has been especially influential in research pertaining to conflict management, plea bargaining, and employee involvement in decision making.

The Group-Value Model

An especially popular approach is the group-value (also called the relational) model of justice. According to the group-value model, individuals are concerned with their social status or standing within important social groups. Injustice in this respect is perceived as a lack of respect on the part of authority figures, and an individual does not feel like an esteemed member of the organization or community. Fairness, and especially procedural fairness, is desirable because it signals that a person is valued by the group and is unlikely to be mistreated. This model makes intuitive sense and evidence supports it. For example, research suggests that procedural justice is a better predictor when it comes from groups with whom individuals closely identify, and it is a less efficacious predictor when it comes from groups not identified with as closely. This is consistent with the group-value model, because standing should be of greater consequence within an important group and of less consequence within an unimportant one.

Social Exchange Theory

Social exchange theory provides an interpersonally oriented understanding of justice but does so in a somewhat different fashion than the group-value model. According to this framework, employees often have economic exchange relationships with their employers and coworkers. These relationships are *quid pro quo,* with clearly delineated responsibilities for each party. Fair treatment, especially procedural and interactional justice, can create social exchange relationships. These higher-quality relationships tend to involve emotional attachments, a sense of obligation, and open-ended responsibilities to the other party. Justice, therefore, improves performance; furthermore, it engenders citizenship behavior by improving the quality of the relationships among employees, between employees and their supervisor, and between employees and the organization as a whole. There is also solid evidence supporting this model. For example, the impact of procedural and interactional justice on work behavior seems to be at least partially mediated by the quality of interpersonal relationships.

Although the group-value model and social exchange theory both highlight the importance of relationships, they emphasize somewhat different mechanisms. Notice that the group-value model maintains that justice is based on a fear of exclusion from a desirable social group, as well as worries about exploitation from powerful decision makers. Social exchange theory, however, is based on a sense of obligation and a desire to help the other party.

Deontic Justice

An interesting feature of both the economic approach and the group-value model is the assumption that justice ultimately reduces to self-interest; it is less clear whether the control model and social exchange theory make this same assumption. For clarity, we define a self-interested concern as one based on achieving a personal benefit or benefits. These benefits may be financial (as in the case of the economic self-interest model) or social (as in the case of the group-value and relational models). The deontic model of justice breaks with this tradition by proposing that justice matters for its own sake. This approach emphasizes the importance that at least some people tend to place on their moral duty to do the right thing.

The deontic model is unique in proposing that individuals care about justice even when there are no concerns with financial gain and group status, and there is evidence for this. For example, studies suggest that individuals will forgo money to punish an act of injustice. Research has also shown that participants will sometimes sacrifice earnings even without material benefits for doing so and when it is unlikely that the participants identify with the relevant social group. Findings such as these suggest that neither economic gain nor social standing provides a full account of organizational justice. Research on deontic justice is important for another reason as well. By emphasizing moral duty, it builds bridges between empirical work on fair perceptions and normative work on business ethics.

CONCLUSION

As illustrated, organizational justice refers to perceptions of fairness in terms of outcomes, processes, and interactions. Research to date has concerned itself with identifying antecedents that influence these perceptions and the resulting attitudes and behaviors once these judgments have been made. However, it is important to keep in mind that these perceptions are subject to change, especially with a change in the referent, the standard, by which fairness is assessed. Considering what each possible framework has to offer can develop a more complete sense of the dynamics involved in any study of organizational justice and its effects.

—*Russell Cropanzano and Sharon M. Discorfano*

See also Social Exchange Theory

FURTHER READING

Brockner, J., & Wiesenfeld, B. M. (1996). An integrative framework for explaining attractiveness of decisions: The interactive effects of outcomes and processes. *Psychological Bulletin, 120,* 189–208.

Cohen-Charash, Y., & Spector, P. E. (2001). The role of justice in organizations: A meta-analysis. *Organizational Behavior and Human Decision Processes, 86,* 278–321.

Colquitt, J. A., Conlon, D. E., Wesson, M. J., Porter, C. O. L. H., & Ng, K. Y. (2001). Justice at the millennium: A meta-analytic review of 25 years of organizational justice research. *Journal of Applied Psychology, 86,* 425–445.

Cropanzano, R., Byrne, Z. S., Bobocel, D. R., & Rupp, D. E. (2001). Moral virtues, fairness heuristics, social entities, and other denizens of organizational justice. *Journal of Vocational Behavior, 58,* 164–209.

Cropanzano, R., Rupp, D. E., Mohler, C. J., & Schminke, M. (2001). Three roads to organizational justice. In G. R. Ferris (Ed.), *Research in personnel and human resource management* (Vol. 20, pp. 1–113). Greenwich, CT: JAI Press.

Folger, R., & Cropanzano, R. (1998). *Organizational justice and human resource management.* Beverly Hills, CA: Sage.

ORGANIZATIONAL POLITICS

The term *organizational politics* refers to the informal ways people try to exercise influence in organizations through the management of shared meaning. As such, politics should be viewed as neither an inherently bad nor good phenomenon but rather one to be observed, analyzed, and comprehended to gain a more informed understanding of organizations and how they operate. Theory and research on organizational politics has fallen into essentially three categories. One area concerns itself with the nature of actual political behavior, types of tactics and strategies, and their consequences. A second category focuses on *perceptions* of politics in work environments by individual employees, the antecedents of such perceptions, and their consequences. The third, and most recent, category of research on organizational politics emphasizes the construct of political skill, and demonstrates the role it plays in organizational behavior.

POLITICAL BEHAVIOR

Research in the domain of political behavior has been widespread and largely disconnected, being categorized in a number of distinct ways. Some of these include influence tactics, impression management, power, and social influence. Essentially, no matter the categorization, all these behaviors reflect attempts to influence someone or some outcome. These behaviors are generally considered to be self-serving in nature and employed to achieve some benefit for the influencer. The success of the influencing attempt depends on a multitude of factors including appropriateness and uniqueness of the attempt, readiness of targets, personal characteristics of both influencer and target, and the context. Influencing tactics have been studied singularly and in combinations or strategies of tactics such as ingratiation as a single tactic or shotgun as a combination of many tactics.

Researchers have examined political behaviors as antecedents, outcomes, and moderators of a myriad of organizational phenomena. Furthermore, both the antecedents and consequences of political behaviors have been studied. Although there have been numerous studies of work-related outcomes of influence attempts, many have found mixed results. The specific attempts of ingratiation and rationality have demonstrated the strongest relationships with work outcomes. Nonetheless, these mixed results suggest a need to examine whether the influence tactics are successful or unsuccessful.

PERCEPTIONS OF ORGANIZATIONAL POLITICS

Although the study of actual political behavior is important, many researchers consider the perception of

organizational politics of equal importance. It can be argued that individuals' perceptions of organizational politics may be just as influential on individual and organizational outcomes as the actual political behaviors occurring in the organization. People react to their perceptions of reality. Because people cannot see into the minds of others to determine the motive (e.g., self-serving or not) behind influencing attempts, they must rely on their perceptions of the attempts. The investigation of these perceptions is important, even if they differ from the actual reality of the organization.

Perceptions of organizational politics are individuals' subjective attributions of the extent to which behaviors occurring in the organization are of self-serving intent. There are three broad categories, which may influence individuals' perceptions of politics: personal influences such as personality factors, job environment influences such as autonomy and variety, and organizational influences such as organizational structure.

Several reactions to organizational politics have been investigated in the literature. Individuals perceiving a political environment could withdraw from the environment or have decreased job satisfaction, increased job anxiety, and even increased job involvement. With few exceptions, politics perceptions have been related to negative individual and organizational outcomes, such as decreased job satisfaction and increased actual turnover. Furthermore, researchers have found that politics perceptions can be viewed as a stressor causing strain reactions such as job anxiety.

However, these negative outcomes may not always occur. Specifically, there may be personal and environmental moderators of the perception–outcome relation. For example, if both supervisors and subordinates are striving toward the same goals, the impact of politics perceptions on important work outcomes is lessened. Furthermore, control and an understanding of the work environment lessens the extent to which organizational politics affects important work outcomes. Individual differences also affect the relationships between politics perceptions and negative outcomes, with some individuals working quite effectively in political environments.

POLITICAL SKILL

It is commonly held that organizations are inherently political. However, despite the negative consequences of politics perceptions, some individuals seem to manage or even thrive in these environments. Political skill, which encompasses a skill set individuals use to understand the environment, choose the appropriate political behaviors, and act them out in ways that appear earnest, might explain how some individuals not only endure but are able to succeed in political environments. It accounts for individual influencing style. Political skill is seen as partly dispositional and partly learned.

Recent work has identified four dimensions of political skill:

1. Social astuteness

2. Interpersonal influence

3. Networking ability

4. Apparent sincerity

Social astuteness is an understanding of the environment and the actors involved in the environment. Interpersonal influence enables politically skilled individuals to chose and implement the correct influencing behaviors for a given situation. Networking ability refers to politically skilled individuals' abilities to garner and use social networks of people to their advantage. Finally, apparent sincerity involves coming across as honest without ulterior motives. Political skill is different from other social variables, such as social skill, and has been shown to be an important coping mechanism in stressful and political environments.

SUMMARY

In conclusion, organizational politics is a vast area of organizational study that spans many literatures and many decades of research. Several conclusions can be drawn through this brief introduction to the politics literature. It is important to examine not only political behavior but also individual subjective evaluations of organizational environments. Furthermore, when examining political behaviors, it is necessary to account for the style of the influencing technique as well as the success of the technique. This information will help bring consistency to the findings of political behavior studies.

Although organizational politics and perceptions of organizational politics largely have been related to negative personal and organizational outcomes, this negative relationship is avoidable. Political skill,

although partly inherent, can be taught to train individuals to thrive in organizational environments that they deem political.

—*Gerald R. Ferris and Robyn L. Brouer*

See also Person–Environment Fit

FURTHER READING

Ferris, G. R., Adams, G., Kolodinsky, R. W., Hochwarter, W. A., & Ammeter, A. P. (2002). Perceptions of organizational politics: Theory and research directions. In F. J. Yammarino & F. Dansereau (Eds.), *Research in multi-level issues: Vol. 1. The many faces of multi-level issues* (pp. 179–254). Oxford, UK: JAI Press/Elsevier Science.

Ferris, G. R., Hochwarter, W. A., Douglas, C., Blass, R., Kolodinsky, R. W., & Treadway, D. C. (2002). Social influence processes in organizations and human resources systems. In G. R. Ferris & J. J. Martocchio (Eds.), *Research in personnel and human resources management* (Vol. 21, pp. 65–127). Oxford, UK: JAI Press/Elsevier Science.

Ferris, G. R., Treadway, D. C., Kolodinsky, R. W., Hochwarter, W. A., Kacmar, C. J., Douglas, C., & Frink, D. D. (2005). Development and validation of the political skill inventory. *Journal of Management, 31,* 126–152.

Kacmar, K. M., & Baron, R. A. (1999). Organizational politics: The state of the field, links to related processes, and an agenda for future research. In G. R. Ferris (Ed.), *Research in personnel and human resources management* (Vol. 17, pp. 1–39). Stamford, CT: JAI Press.

Witt, L. A. (1998). Enhancing organizational goal congruence: A solution to organizational politics. *Journal of Applied Psychology, 83,* 666–674.

ORGANIZATIONAL RETALIATORY BEHAVIOR

Organizational retaliatory behavior refers to actions taken by disgruntled employees in response to perceived injustice at work. Organizational retaliatory behavior can take many forms, including withholding effort or citizenship behaviors, intentionally performing tasks incorrectly, purposely damaging equipment, taking supplies or materials, taking longer breaks than allowed, calling in sick, spreading rumors about people at work, refusing to help others at work, failing to report problems so they get worse, attending to personal matters while at work, purposely wasting time, sabotaging projects, and ignoring or verbally abusing people at work.

Although many behaviors that are classified as organizational retaliatory behavior may also be called counterproductive work behavior, workplace aggression, or employee deviance, organizational retaliatory behavior is distinct in at least two ways. First, organizational retaliatory behavior places a stronger emphasis on the situational context in which the behavior occurs as the main catalyst. In contrast, employee deviance implies an underlying dispositional tendency to engage in negative behaviors at work. Employee deviance also refers to behavior that violates organizational norms regarding what is proper and acceptable behavior. Therefore, to the extent that retaliation is common and accepted behavior in the workplace, it may or may not be considered deviant.

Second, organizational retaliatory behavior refers specifically to behaviors that are provoked by unfair treatment at work and implies a singular motive: to restore justice or equity; counterproductive work behavior and workplace aggression take a broader perspective regarding the motives or intentions driving behavior. For example, counterproductive work behavior is defined as behavior that has the potential to harm an organization or individuals at work; and while it may be driven by malicious intent, employees may perform counterproductive work behaviors as a means of coping with job stress, as a reaction to unfairness, or out of ignorance or boredom. Workplace aggression, however, refers to behavior by employees that intends to harm; and the general aggression literature has identified two primary motives behind aggression. Aggression can be either reactive or *hot*, such as when an angry employee yells at a coworker, or aggression may be proactive or *cold*, such as when an employee spreads damaging rumors about a coworker to better personal chances of receiving a promotion. Thus although all organizational retaliatory behavior is considered workplace aggression and all workplace aggression is considered counterproductive work behavior, not all counterproductive work behavior or workplace aggression is considered organizational retaliatory behavior.

Organizational retaliatory behavior can be understood using justice theory and social exchange theory. Each of these frameworks is briefly discussed in the following text.

JUSTICE THEORY

Justice theory is the theoretical framework most commonly associated with organizational retaliatory behaviors. Organizational justice refers to the perceived fairness of interactions between individuals and organizations. Researchers have discussed justice in terms of its three forms:

1. *Distributive justice*: the perceived fairness of outcomes received from an employer

2. *Procedural justice*: the perceived fairness of the processes and decisions that determine organizational outcomes independent of the fairness of the actual outcomes received

3. *Interactional justice*: the quality of interpersonal treatment received during the enactment of organizational procedures

According to justice theory, when employees experience some form of injustice or inequity, they will be motivated to restore justice. Any effort to balance the justice equation would be considered a retaliatory behavior.

All three forms of justice have been shown to independently contribute to employee retaliation. However, procedural and interactional justice may be more important determinants of retaliatory behavior than distributive justice. Studies have shown that the negative effects of low distributive justice can be mitigated by the presence of high levels of either procedural or interactional justice. In other words, employees are less likely to retaliate for receiving fewer rewards if the procedures that determine those rewards are fair and if the employees are treated with dignity and respect throughout the reward distribution process. Employees, therefore, appear to place greater emphasis on the fairness of the procedures and how well they are treated as individuals than on the absolute level of outcomes received when deciding to retaliate.

Because organizational retaliatory behaviors are assumed to be motivated by an employee's desire to restore justice, retaliatory behavior is more easily legitimized in the eyes of the performer: "I had to do something. I couldn't let him just get away with treating me like that." Hence a valuable contribution of this construct is the recognition that employees may perform these behaviors out of a desire to punish the offender and correct some wrong. Also, unlike counterproductive work behavior, workplace aggression, or employee deviance, which assume that the consequences of these behaviors are negative, no such assumption is made regarding the outcome of retaliatory behavior. In fact, it is possible that retaliation may lead to positive outcomes because there are two ways to balance the justice equation. For example, if employees feel that their supervisor is treating them unfairly, they can balance the equation by treating their supervisor unfairly in return, such as delaying actions on projects that are important to that supervisor; or they may balance the equation by demanding fairer treatment from their supervisor by confronting the supervisor directly or by complaining to a higher-level manager. Although both actions result in a more balanced justice equation, the former case has negative implications for the supervisor and organization, and possibly for the employee to the extent that job performance is affected, whereas the latter case may lead to positive outcomes if the supervisor changes behavior to treat the employee more fairly. Therefore, an important contribution of the organizational retaliatory behavior construct is that it recognizes the possibility that seemingly negative behaviors may be performed as a means to a more productive or prosocial end.

SOCIAL EXCHANGE THEORY

Organizational retaliatory behavior can also be understood within the framework of social exchange theory. According to social exchange theory, employees define their relationships with their organization and their supervisor in terms of social exchange using the norm of reciprocity. Thus employees engage in retaliatory behaviors to reciprocate unfavorable treatment received from the supervisor or organization. If employees believe the organization is looking out for their best interests or is fairly providing them with valued rewards, they will respond in kind by performing positive actions such as organizational citizenship behaviors. However, if employees believe the organization or supervisor is withholding rewards or punishing them unfairly, they will reciprocate by reducing actions that benefit the organization or by performing actions that directly injure the organization.

A related theory, leader–member exchange theory, is also useful for understanding employee retaliatory behavior, particularly when that behavior is directed toward a leader. According to leader–member exchange theory, individual, group, and organizational outcomes are affected by the quality of the relationships that employees have with their leaders. Employees who have a high-quality relationship with their leaders are more trusted by their leaders and are given more autonomy and decision-making input. Those employees are more likely to be high performers and exhibit more citizenship behaviors as well. However, employees who have low-quality exchange relationships with their leaders are managed more closely and provided with less support from their leaders, and they are more likely to perform retaliatory behaviors in return.

Although justice theory and social exchange theory take slightly different approaches to understanding retaliation, both emphasize the importance of the relationship that employees have with their organizations and the people in them as antecedents to the performance of retaliatory behaviors.

PREVENTION

Because organizational retaliatory behaviors refer specifically to actions taken by employees in response to some perceived injustice or inequity, to prevent retaliatory behaviors organizations should identify ways to increase employee perceptions of fairness at work. According to both justice and social exchange theories, the quality of employees' relationships with their supervisors is an important determinant of retaliatory behavior; therefore organizations should carefully select managers and screen out those with a history of interpersonal conflict or other unethical behavior. Furthermore, organizations should make managers aware of the importance of treating all employees fairly and provide training to managers to equip them with the knowledge and skills necessary to provide employees with fair and just treatment, including suppressing personal biases, basing decisions on accurate information, administering policies consistently, giving employees a voice in the decision-making process, allowing for corrections to be made, behaving ethically, being truthful and honest with employees, and respectfully interacting with employees. Additionally, organizational policies and procedures should be reviewed and revised if necessary so they reflect the organization's commitment to fair treatment of all employees. If employees have confidence in their ability to redress a perceived injustice using formal channels, they may feel less of a need to perform retaliatory behaviors or otherwise take matters into their own hands.

On the employee side, there is some evidence suggesting that individual differences in personality are related to the performance of retaliatory behaviors. At least one study found that individuals high in negative affectivity or low on agreeableness were more likely to perform retaliatory behaviors when they experienced low justice. Thus organizations should modify their selection and screening processes to identify individuals with a greater propensity to perform retaliatory behaviors or who have a history of performing retaliatory behaviors in past jobs.

—*Lisa M. Penney*

See also Counterproductive Work Behaviors; Leader–Member Exchange Theory; Organizational Justice; Social Exchange Theory; Workplace Incivility

FURTHER READING

Folger, R., & Skarlicki, D. P. (2004). Beyond counterproductive work behavior: Moral emotions and deontic retaliation versus reconciliation. In P. E. Spector & S. Fox (Eds.), *Counterproductive work behavior: Investigations of actors and targets.* Washington, DC: American Psychological Association.

Greenberg, J. (1993). Stealing in the name of justice: Informational and interpersonal moderators of theft reactions to underpayment inequity. *Organizational Behavior and Human Decision Processes, 54,* 81–103.

Leventhal, G. S., Karuza, J., & Fry, W. R. (1980). Beyond fairness: A theory of allocation preferences. In G. Mikula (Ed.), *Justice and Social Interaction.* New York: Plenum Press.

Skarlicki, D. P., & Folger, R. (1997). Retaliation in the workplace: The roles of distributive, procedural, and interactional justice. *Journal of Applied Psychology, 82,* 434–443.

Townsend, J., Phillips, J. S., & Elkins, T. J. (2000). Employee retaliation: The neglected consequence of poor leader–member exchange relations. *Journal of Occupational Health Psychology, 5*(4), 457–463.

ORGANIZATIONAL SENSEMAKING

Organizational sensemaking is not an established body of knowledge; it is a developing set of ideas drawn from a range of disciplines (e.g., cognitive psychology, social psychology, communication studies, and cultural analysis) concerning a particular way to approach organization studies. Central to the sensemaking perspective is the notion that explanations of organizational issues cannot be found in any form of organizational structure or system but in how organizational actors see and attribute meaning to things. From this perspective, strategies, plans, rules, and goals are not things that exist in an objective sense within (or external to) the organization. Rather, their source is people's way of thinking. Moreover, from a sensemaking perspective, the issue of whether someone's view of the world is *correct* is not meaningful and the correctness of a decision is contingent on the point of view that is being used for evaluation. The basic idea of sensemaking is that reality is an ongoing accomplishment that emerges from efforts to create order and understanding from complex environments. Sensemaking allows people to deal with uncertainty and ambiguity by creating rational accounts of the world that enable action.

Various definitions of organizational sensemaking have been presented. For some, sensemaking is an interpretive process; for others, it is a metaphor for interpretation. Some define it as interpretation coupled with action. Others divide perception into noticing and sensemaking, whereby noticing has to come before sensemaking so that there is something available to be made sense of. Still others define it as structuring the unknown or as a recurring cycle that uses retrospective accounts to explain surprises. The introduction of a sensemaking perspective into organization studies has, however, largely arisen from the work of Karl E. Weick, who defines sensemaking, at its simplest, quite literally as making sense. By this, Weick means that organizational actors not only come to an understanding of their environments but also create those same environments. The term *enactment* is used to capture the active role that organizational members play in creating such environments. By way of example, it is on the basis of their subjective perceptions of their occupational environment (their job role, manager, employment conditions, and so forth) that employees will take action and make a range of decisions, such as whether to come to work in the morning, and if so, whether they will do so on time, the decision as to what degree of effort and enthusiasm to invest, and ultimately, the decision whether or not to leave the organization. To differing degrees, each decision will influence individual, team, department, and organizational performance and productivity. Hence, how these individuals come to understand their environments provides the basis for action, ultimately shaping this same environment (at least in part).

SEVEN PROPERTIES OF ORGANIZATIONAL SENSEMAKING

Organizational sensemaking is inherently complex (described by some as semi-inscrutable). Weick has, however, attempted to systematically organize and explain this multifaceted concept by distilling seven key properties most often mentioned in the sensemaking literature. Although there is some debate as to whether Weick construes this concept in an overly narrow fashion, this synthesis provides the best statement currently available.

1. *Retrospective*: All sensemaking processes involve some variation on the theme of retrospection or reflection on experience, which provides rationality and clarity to any outcome. This supports the notion that organizational strategic planning often involves the ability to write the story that fits recent history. Of note, although there is a consensus of opinion that it is primarily by examining history that we make sense, some scholars conclude that sensemaking is also prospective and that it is the act of envisioning the future that supplies the impetus for action.

2. *Plausible rather than accurate*: Meanings are constructed on the basis of reasonable explanations rather than through scientific discovery. Although filtered information will almost certainly be less "accurate," it will undoubtedly be more understandable.

3. *Focused on and extracted by cues*: In organizational life we attend to and extract certain elements, which form the material of the sensemaking process. However, although only partial knowledge is extracted from a mass of complex information, sense will be made of the whole on the basis of this subset. What is actually extracted and how it is made sense of is complex and dependent on a variety of issues, including context and goals.

4. *Enactive of sensible environments*: By taking action organizations create (enact) their own environments (i.e., by doing something that produces some kind of outcome, constraints are then placed on what that person or organization does next).

5. *A social process*: Sense is made in organizations through conversations, communications, and the exchange of ideas, and it is influenced by the actual, implied, or imagined presence of others. That is how sense becomes organizational.

6. *Ongoing*: Sensemaking is an ongoing, constantly negotiated process. The implication of this insight for organizational sensemaking is that organizations are always in the middle of complex situations, which they try to disentangle by making and then revising provisional assumptions. Viewed as systems of sensemaking, a key organizational goal is to create and identify events that recur to stabilize their environments and make them more predictable.

7. *Grounded in identity construction*: The process of figuring out what is going on is a product of and a process based on who the sensemaker is and is becoming. In other words, how an organization (individual or group) identifies itself (who the sensemaker is) will define what it sees *out there*. Simultaneously, this will influence identity (who the sensemaker is becoming).

THE PROCESS OF ORGANIZATIONAL SENSEMAKING

Sensemaking is a critical organizational activity. For top managers sensemaking activities such as environmental scanning and issue interpretation are key tasks that significantly influence organizational decisions and strategic change. Sensemaking activities are particularly important in dynamic and turbulent contexts, where the creation of coherent understandings is crucial.

There is no formal model for organizational sensemaking, but the basic process is found in Weick's sensemaking *recipe*. This is a sequence of enactment, selection, and retention.

- In enactment, people actively construct the environments, which they attend to by bracketing, rearranging, and labeling portions of the experience, thereby converting raw data from the environment into equivocal data to be interpreted.

- In selection, people choose meanings that can be imposed on the equivocal data by overlaying past interpretations as templates to the current experience. Selection produces an enacted environment that is meaningful in providing cause–effect explanation of what is taking place.

- In retention, the organization stores the products of (what it sees as) successful sensemaking (enacted or meaningful interpretations) so that they may be retrieved in the future.

As one property of sensemaking is that it is an ongoing process, there is no beginning point or end to this sequence.

Some view sensemaking as always being a conscious process, coming into play at times of shock or surprise or other particular occasions, for example in times of perceived environmental uncertainty or turbulence. Others believe that, although much of organizational life is routine and unsurprising and as such does not demand our attention, nonetheless we make sense in those habitual situations via the assimilation of subtle cues over time.

Organizational sensemaking can be driven by beliefs or by actions. In belief-driven processes, people start from an initial set of beliefs that are sufficiently clear and plausible and use them as nodes to connect more and more information into larger structures of meaning. People may use beliefs as expectations to guide the choice of plausible interpretations; or they may argue about beliefs and their relevancy to current experience, especially when beliefs and cues are contradictory. In action-driven processes, people start from their actions and grow their structures of meaning around them, by modifying the structures to give significance to those actions. People may create meaning to justify actions that are visible or irreversible.

RESEARCH IN ORGANIZATIONAL SENSEMAKING

A considerable amount of research has focused on strategic issue processing and making sense of the competition. Some researchers have concluded that strategic competition is essentially a product of the tendency of competitors to construct some shared interpretation of a competitive arena within which strategic thinking and action become meaningful. Such studies have provided invaluable insight not only into the identification of industry competitors and the bases on which they compete but also into why competitive industry structures in industries and markets come to develop in the first place. This is exemplified by the work carried out by Joseph F. Porac and his colleagues in the Scottish knitwear industry.

The sensemaking approach has also facilitated an understanding of organizational process, action, and structure in a range of contexts. Notable studies include those of Jane E. Dutton and her colleagues regarding issue and agenda formation and how stakeholders preserve their organization's image; and the

work of Dennis A. Gioia and his associates, who have investigated various aspects of change management, including top management teams' perceptions of identity and image under conditions of change. Additional contexts include technology diffusion and various aspects of organizational socialization and organizational crisis. Weick's concept of sensemaking has been further formulated by researchers who have coined the term *sensegiving* to the process by which managers attempt to influence sensemaking and meaning construction of others toward a preferred definition of organization reality.

—*Gail P. Clarkson*

See also Group Dynamics and Processes; Organizational Socialization

FURTHER READING

Maitlis, S. (2005). The social processes of organizational sensemaking. *Academy of Management Review, 48,* 21–49.

Porac, J. F., Thomas, H., & Baden-Fuller, C. (1989). Competitive groups as cognitive communities: The case of Scottish knitwear manufacturers. *Journal of Management Studies, 26,* 397–416.

Porac, J. F., Thomas, H., Wilson, F., Paton, D., & Kanfer, A. (1995). Rivalry and the industry model of Scottish knitwear producers. *Administrative Science Quarterly, 40,* 203–227.

Weick, K. E. (1979). *The social psychology of organizing* (2nd ed.). Reading, MA: Addison-Wesley.

Weick, K. E. (1995). *Sensemaking in organizations.* Thousand Oaks, CA: Sage.

Weick, K. E. (2001). *Making sense of the organization.* Oxford, UK: Blackwell Business.

ORGANIZATIONAL SOCIALIZATION

Organizational socialization (OS) is the process through which a newcomer to an organization transitions from outsider to integrated and effective insider. This longitudinal process includes the acquisition or adjustment of shared values, attitudes, skills, knowledge, abilities, behaviors, and workplace relationships. Organizational socialization occurs whenever an employee crosses an organizational boundary. The OS research mainly focuses on transitions across the organizational boundary; but OS also occurs for functional and hierarchical transitions, such as lateral moves, promotions, and international transfers.

PROCESS APPROACHES TO ORGANIZATIONAL SOCIALIZATION

Organizational Actions

John Van Maanen and Edgar Schein (1979) developed a model of OS tactics, based on the premise that newcomers' learning is dependent on the process as much as the content. They outlined six tactics that organizations use to influence newcomers to adopt certain role orientations. The six tactics, each of which is bipolar, are

1. Collective–individual
2. Formal–informal
3. Sequential–random
4. Fixed–variable
5. Serial–disjunctive
6. Investiture–divestiture

These tactics have also been categorized as institutionalized (collective, formal, sequential, fixed, serial, and investiture) or individualized (their opposites). Institutionalized tactics are associated with a range of positive outcomes including lower role ambiguity, role conflict, intent to quit, and anxiety; and higher levels of job satisfaction, organizational commitment, and task mastery.

PREENTRY ORGANIZATION SOCIALIZATION

Preentry or *anticipatory* socialization occurs during selection procedures in which applicants are exposed to certain aspects of the employing organization. This allows applicants to develop more realistic expectations of working life in the organization. Realistic job previews (RJPs) have been proposed as one formal method by which to effectively achieve preentry OS.

Insider Actions

Newcomers regard organizational insiders such as managers and peers as more useful sources of knowledge and support than formal orientation programs.

Insiders help newcomers to adjust by providing information, feedback, role models, social relationships, and support, as well as access to broader networks and other work-relevant resources.

Newcomer Actions

As part of the OS process, newcomers experience surprises where their expectations are not matched by reality. Surprises may be in relation to their actual role through to the organizational environment. These surprises require newcomers to employ sensemaking strategies, with this research developing from models of employee information seeking, with evidence for newcomers using a range of strategies including overt feedback requests and covert monitoring. Seeking information more frequently overall is related to positive outcomes. Further, newcomers show relatively stable information seeking behaviors over time and choose strategies and sources according to the type of information sought, but observation is the most common strategy.

CONTENT APPROACHES TO ORGANIZATIONAL SOCIALIZATION

Newcomer Learning

Recently, researchers appear to agree that learning is the key element underlying OS. To date, five information-based models of OS content have been developed, with associated measures. The domains included in these models have included task, role (or performance), group processes (also defined as a social or people domain), organization (sometimes broken down further into aspects including history and language), interpersonal resources (or coworker support), training, and future prospects.

Proximal and Distal Outcomes

A number of outcomes have been proposed as reflecting OS success. The most common outcomes have been distal and measured at the individual level and include greater job satisfaction and organizational commitment, reduced anxiety and stress, and a lower intention of leaving. In the last decade researchers have increasingly focused on proximal outcomes that more directly reflect socialization itself, rather than its effects.

These outcomes include various types of knowledge (see Newcomer Learning earlier in this entry), task mastery, role clarity, social integration, and performance.

INDIVIDUAL DIFFERENCES AFFECTING ORGANIZATIONAL SOCIALIZATION

The OS research in the last decade has begun to investigate the influence of individual differences. Research has found that newcomers with high self-efficacy and behavioral self-management tend to use more independent strategies and have better OS outcomes. Further, extraversion and openness to experience are associated with higher levels of proactive socialization behavior, such as feedback seeking and relationship building; and proactive personality leads to more positive proximal outcomes such as task mastery and social integration.

A few studies have looked at newcomers' values during OS and found that those with better objective value fit showed quicker and better adjustment outcomes. The small amount of research on sociodemographic variables has shown minimal effects: Work experience is associated with better outcomes; female newcomers report lower self-efficacy, higher self-punishing behavior, and poorer treatment by colleagues relative to male newcomers.

—*Helena D. Cooper-Thomas and Neil Anderson*

See also Feedback Seeking; Group Development; New Employee Orientation; Socialization: Employee Proactive Behaviors

FURTHER READING

Cooper-Thomas, H. D., & Anderson, N. (2002). Newcomer adjustment: The relationship between organizational socialization tactics, information acquisition and attitudes. *Journal of Occupational & Organizational Psychology, 75*(4), 423–437.

Cooper-Thomas, H. D., & Anderson, N. (2005). Organizational socialization: A field study into socialization success and rate. *International Journal of Selection and Assessment, 13*(2), 116–128.

Morrison, E. W. (2002). Information seeking within organizations. *Human Communication Research, 28*(2), 229–242.

Van Maanen, J., & Schein, E. H. (1979). Toward a theory of organizational socialization. In B. M. Staw (Ed.), *Research in organizational behavior* (Vol. 1, pp. 209–264). Greenwich, CT: JAI Press.

ORGANIZATIONAL SOCIALIZATION TACTICS

Organizational socialization refers to the process whereby new employees move from being organizational *outsiders* to becoming functioning organizational *insiders*. Socialization has been called the process of *learning the ropes* of being an effective employee. Organizational socialization tactics are the ways that organizations socialize new employees. These tactics vary on a number of dimensions that range from formal to informal in nature.

Successful socialization should lead to an effective employee who feels confident, has limited role conflict and role ambiguity, and feels accepted by his or her coworkers. These positive *accommodation* factors should then lead to enhanced job satisfaction, organizational commitment, job performance, decreased stress, enhanced job and organizational fit, and lowered turnover. Unsuccessful socialization can be identified by poor performance, poor fit, and more rapid turnover. Research generally supports these relationships.

More specifically, research has shown that the process of socialization is not solely caused by the actions of the newcomer, nor is it solely based on the attempts of organizational insiders to socialize the new employee. Rather, the process of socialization refers to the intersection of both of these forces acting on one another.

Socialization includes learning about three important factors of organizational life:

1. Task information: "How do I do this job well?"

2. Social information: "Do I fit in with my coworkers and feel accepted?"

3. Cultural information: "Do I understand the norms and expectations of this organization?"

Research has shown that significant changes take place for newcomers at a number of delineations such as prior to entry (typically referred to as the anticipatory socialization stage), after three months on the job to around six months on the job (typically referred to as the accommodation stage), and after nine months on the job (typically referred to as the role management stage). After this point, newcomers and *old-timers* seem more similar than not. Longitudinal research that follows newcomers across time has found that early indicators of socialization are predictive of later outcomes. Outcomes include adjustment variables (acceptance by the group, learning the task, forming psychological contracts) and more distal outcomes such as stress, performance, organizational commitment, job satisfaction, turnover intentions, turnover, and person–job fit.

Much work on organizational socialization tactics stems from the work of John Van Maanen and Edgar Schein (1979), who delineated six tactics that vary on a number of dimensions:

1. Level of interaction with other newcomers (ranging from formal to informal)

2. Number of newcomers within a given cohort (ranging from collective to individual)

3. Order in which socialization takes place (ranging from sequential to random)

4. Identification of whether or not there is a specific time frame for socialization (ranging from fixed to variable)

5. Identification of how newcomers are trained (ranging from serial to disjunctive)

6. Identification of whether newcomers are stripped of their old identity or not (ranging from investiture to divestiture)

Subsequent research has shown that these organizational socialization tactic dimensions developed by Van Maanen and Schein (1979) can be thought of as representing a continuum that ranges from highly institutionalized approaches to socialization (e.g., new army recruits going through boot camp) to more individualized approaches (e.g., a new college professor during the first term). To illustrate the differences between these two types of tactics, think first of a new recruit in boot camp in the army. This individual is in a collective situation with other recruits, undergoing a sequential process of physical demands, following a strict timetable of events, learning tasks serially, and being stripped of any individual identity during the process in favor of a collective identity with the army. However, a new college professor might be one of the only or few new hires for a given year; undergoing a random sequence of learning things independently; undergoing no set time frame for socialization other than tenure, which is some years away; learning tasks

in a disjunctive fashion; and valued for expertise and training at the individual level. The recruit is undergoing a classic case of institutionalized organizational socialization tactics with a high degree of routinization, and the college professor is undergoing a classic case of individualized organizational socialization tactics with a relatively *loose* structure and indoctrination. This may be because of the norms that are indoctrinated in professors as they earn their doctoral degrees so that less direction is needed once they begin in the profession.

Tactics that are highly institutional tend to be preferred by new employees, perhaps because the definite nature of these tactics helps to orient new employees and decrease ambiguity about what they should be doing. However, the potential downside of these tactics is a decrease in innovation and creativity. This is a dilemma that organizations need to approach carefully.

Organizations vary hugely in terms of how they employ these tactics. Research has shown that institutionalized tactics are negatively related to self-efficacy but positively related to organizational commitment, job satisfaction, and intentions to remain. Since that time, research on organizational socialization tactics has continued and has been associated with diverse outcomes.

For example, research studying psychological contract breach for newcomers found that those who perceived breaches were more likely to experience an informal socialization process. Additionally, newcomers' perceptions of fit are related to tactics that are fixed and serial. Researchers also found that institutionalized tactics were significantly related to newcomers' relations with organizational insiders as well as negatively related to role conflict and that serial and investiture tactics were negatively related to subsequent turnover for newcomers working at large financial services organizations.

In addition to organizational tactics, organizational insiders also influence new employee socialization. Two categories of these insiders exist: supervisors or leaders who oversee the newcomer and coworkers or peers who work with the new employee. A major goal of organizational socialization is to understand one's role in relation to these organizational insiders as well as to feel accepted by them. Newcomers who are able to do this are much more likely to become successfully socialized and integrated into their new organization. Research has also shown that newcomer personality interacts with leadership to affect adjustment and relate to turnover. A study that examined new executives across four years found that those who were introverted and formed strong leadership ties were less likely to turn over than those introverts who did not form these ties. For extraverts, leadership relationships made no difference.

As mentioned earlier, newcomers also employ tactics to learn about their new jobs, coworkers, and organizations. These tactics usually revolve around information and feedback acquisition. Newcomers vary on many dimensions, but a key dimension is their proactive personality. Those who are very proactive will seek out information, ask for feedback, and initiate ways to learn about the job, coworkers, and organization. Their less proactive colleagues will be less likely to engage in these behaviors and therefore will be more susceptible to the organization's influence.

Information seeking is related to the outcomes of socialization, by increasing knowledge regarding role expectations and by increasing confidence to accomplish personal goals. In other words information seeking should be positively related to self-efficacy and negatively related to role ambiguity. Furthermore, by voicing questions and seeking information and feedback, individuals deal with conflicting information coming from different sources, leading to reduced role conflict. Finally, information seeking may facilitate social interactions and signal to others that the individual is motivated to do a good job, leading to acceptance by peers.

Several studies have found that information seeking plays an important role in newcomer socialization. Seeking and acquiring information is key to understanding one's roles, the norms of the group and organization, and the expectations and interconnections among colleagues and functional areas. However, seeking too much information can be costly to newcomers who might come across as *not getting it*. Timing may be the key to understanding when newcomers should seek information as well as understanding how to do it and from whom. Further, information seeking has been shown to relate to distal outcomes such as satisfaction, job performance, and intentions to remain, depending on the type and source of information obtained.

Another factor that should matter in new employee socialization is personality. Some newcomers are proactive in terms of their personalities, and these individuals should approach the socialization

process differently than newcomers who are not as proactive. Similarly, newcomers who are introverted need to establish strong interpersonal relationships to help them navigate the organization, whereas more extraverted newcomers are able to learn from multiple sources.

In summary, organizational socialization tactics seem to matter for newcomer organizational socialization. What remains to be seen is the relative impact it will have on the process and whether or not outcomes mediate the relationship between tactics and more distant outcomes.

—*Talya N. Bauer*

See also New Employee Orientation; Socialization: Employee Proactive Behaviors; Training Methods

FURTHER READING

Bauer, T. N., Bodner, T., Erdogan, B., Truxillo, D. T., & Sommers, J. (2005). *A meta-analysis of the socialization literature.* Academy of Management Annual Conference, Honolulu, HI.

Bauer, T., Morrison, E. W., & Callister, R. (1998). Organizational socialization: A review and directions for future research. In G. R. Ferris (Ed.), *Research in personnel and human resources management* (Vol. 16, pp. 149–214). Greenwich, CT: JAI Press.

Fisher, C. D. (1986). Organizational socialization: An integrative review. In K. M. Rowland & G. R. Ferris (Eds.), *Research in personnel and human resources management* (Vol. 4, pp. 101–145). Greenwich, CT: JAI Press.

Kim, T., Cable, D. M., & Kim, S. (2005). Socialization tactics, employee proactivity, and person–organization fit. *Journal of Applied Psychology, 90,* 232–241.

Morrison, E. W. (1993). Newcomer information seeking: Exploring types, modes, sources, and outcomes. *Academy of Management Journal, 36,* 557–589.

Van Maanen, J., & Schein, E. H. (1979). Toward a theory of organizational socialization. In B. M. Staw (Ed.), *Research in organizational behavior* (Vol. 1, pp. 209–263). Greenwich, CT: JAI Press.

ORGANIZATIONAL STRUCTURE

Organizational structure refers to the formal and informal manner in which people, job tasks, and other organizational resources are configured and coordinated. Although organizational *structure* sounds like a singular characteristic, it is composed of a number of dimensions, because there are multiple ways the employees within an organization and the job tasks that are carried out can be structured. The most commonly studied aspects of organizational structure include *formalization, centralization,* and *complexity.*

FUNDAMENTAL ELEMENTS OF ORGANIZATIONAL STRUCTURE

Formalization refers to the extent to which organizational policies, practices, and ways of completing tasks are standardized. Specifically, highly formalized organizations are those in which rules for expected behavior are clearly articulated and followed. Conversely, organizations that exhibit *low levels* of formalization have few standardized practices or rules. Formalization is often conveyed through formal means and documents such as job descriptions, but it need not be. Informal activities, such as practices that are reinforced through group norms or informal conversations with other members of the organization, also serve to reinforce the level of formalization.

Centralization refers to the distribution of decision-making authority, information, and power throughout an organization. In some organizations all or most decisions are made by a small group of individuals, often the top management team. Such organizations are considered *highly centralized* because power is maintained by a select few individuals, for example, when decisions are made by a central group of individuals. Conversely, in *highly decentralized* organizations, power and decision making are spread across individuals throughout the organization. Individual employees in these organizations have the opportunities and authority to make day-to-day decisions and other important decisions that affect their work. The centralization of power in an organization may be dictated and described in formal rules, policies, and job descriptions. It is also common, however, that centralization occurs informally through the behaviors and norms introduced and reinforced by those in power, such as a leader who purposefully limits access to key information.

Complexity has represented a number of different aspects of organizational structure throughout history (additional historical background is presented in a later section). Among the structural aspects that have been labeled *complexity* are *specialization, interdependency, span of control,* and *height.* Although each is somewhat unique, they all share the recognition that the organization of workers and work processes can range in design from simple to complex. *Specialization* refers to the extent to which job tasks require highly specific (i.e., specialized) work skills or, conversely, can be successfully carried out by individuals who possess more broadly available knowledge, skills, and abilities. Research- and development-based organizations are examples of organizations that are likely to be highly specialized because such activities often require unique content knowledge and skills. *Interdependency* (also called integration) refers to the integration of tasks and activities across different workers. Highly integrated organizations require the cooperation and collaboration of many different employees to get work done. Nonintegrated organizations are composed of individuals who work largely on their own and do not require assistance or products from other employees. *Span of control* refers to the number of subordinates who report to a single manager. The size of the managerial span is often associated with the varying levels of the hierarchy within an organization (height). Large spans of control are associated with *flatter* organizations, such as those with fewer layers between entry-level positions and top management); small spans typically correspond with tall hierarchical organizations in which there are many levels from the bottom to the top.

Structural dimensions receiving less attention include *departmentalization* and *physical dispersion. Departmentalization* refers to the existence of formal and informal divisions within an organization. These divisions are often, but not always, created by grouping subsets of jobs, and often comprise similar (or related) jobs. Highly departmentalized organizations are those that have created many internal divisions, whereas highly nondepartmentalized organizations have few. *Physical dispersion* refers to the extent to which organizational members are physically spread apart from one another. This may refer to the dispersion of individuals within a single building or, in highly dispersed organizations, the spread of employees across numerous locations throughout the world.

FACTORS RELEVANT TO THE ELEMENTS OF ORGANIZATIONAL STRUCTURE

There is convincing evidence that no one structure is best for all organizations. Because there are many factors that determine the structure most effective for any given organization, researchers have adopted an approach called *contingency theory.* Contingency theory in this context refers to the idea that relevant circumstances must be considered before applying a specific organizational design. A number of contingencies determine structure; *environment, technology, strategy,* and *size* are among the most influential.

Environment is the total of the factors that occur outside of the organization but are relevant to the decision making of the management of the organization. These external forces include social and cultural norms, governmental regulations, economic conditions, market competition, the relevant labor pool, availability and nature of raw materials, and industry type.

Technology represents one aspect of the environment affecting an organization. Because of its importance historically (see the brief description of the seminal Woodward studies that follows) and strong impact on modern organization, technology is often separated out for special consideration in its effect on organizational structure. Although in 2006 technology is often considered interchangeable with computerization, technology in its broadest sense may be defined as the knowledge necessary to process raw material. Depending on the organizational product or service, the raw material might be objects or people. Further, technological processes can be categorized as routine or nonroutine. Routine processes are well understood and standardized. Routine technology typically leads to more traditional organization structure with higher levels of centralization and formalization.

When taken together, environmental factors are often categorized by their complexity. Complexity here refers to the heterogeneity and incompatibility of the various elements of environment enumerated earlier. Large organizations often face more complex environments because of the sometimes conflicting objectives of the various stakeholders, such as governmental regulations and resource acquisition costs, found in the environment. Generally, the more complex the environment, the more complex the organizational structure to accommodate that environmental complexity.

Environmental factors can also be categorized as stable or volatile based on an overall assessment of the predictability of change in the environment. To meet the demands of these two types of environments, organizations may be said to employ two primary approaches to structure themselves: *mechanistic* and *organic.* Mechanistic models of structure are denoted by high specialization, rigid departmentalization, strong centralization and formalization, and narrow spans of control with clear authority lines. In contrast, the organic model has decentralized authority and decision making,

low standardization, and formalization with self-directed teams or work groups as the primary departmentalization strategy. It should be noted that the two classifications, mechanistic and organic, might be considered as ends of a continuum rather than definitive categories; for example, few organizations use all elements of a strictly mechanistic or organic structure but instead use some combination of the two.

To survive, an organization must have a *strategy* for providing its products or services. The strategy of an organization will differ relative to the target customer market and industry type within which the organization functions; but within these constraints, an organization can select from many types of strategy with *innovation* and *imitation* strategies representing classic types. Innovation strategies emphasize being the leader in the industry in introducing new products or services. Organizations that choose the imitation strategy do not produce new products or services until another organization has demonstrated that those products and services are in demand. A subtype of imitation strategy is minimizing costs in an effort to generate high profits with lowered risk. The implications of different organizational strategies—innovation or imitation—lead to structures that vary along the continuum of the mechanistic and organic models described previously. Innovation strategies are more likely to require organic types of structure, whereas imitation (and cost minimization) strategies are more apt to lead to mechanistic models of organizational structure.

Size of organization is most often represented by the number of employees but may alternatively be represented by the number of plant locations or offices, net assets (manufacturing), gross sales (manufacturing or service industries), or number of units that can be produced or people who can be served. Number of employees correlates more strongly than other indicators to structural features, and the size of an organization has a strong impact on resulting structure. Large organizations have more specialization in job types, more standardization of rules and formalization of procedures, and often more decentralization of decision making.

HOW MODERN CONCEPTUALIZATIONS OF ORGANIZATIONAL STRUCTURE DEVELOPED

How to organize the people and the tasks of work has been of interest from the earliest of times. Although concerns for structure can be dated to the Roman legions, modern interest among management theorists stems most directly from Henri Fayol's prescriptions for management in the early 1900s. In his principles of management, Fayol recommended specialization, centralization, clear lines of authority with one superior for each employee, and unity of direction. *Unity of direction* refers to the proposal that all effort within a group be directed toward recognized organizational goals and is inherent in the hierarchical structures of many organizations.

Another pioneer in defining organization structure was sociologist and economist Max Weber. In the early 1900s Weber conceptualized the ideal *bureaucracy* as an organization with a hierarchical division of labor in which explicit rules were applied objectively to employees. This organizational design is widely used today and is characterized by high levels of specialization, strong formalization, functional departmentalization, narrow spans of control, and centralized authority and decision making, for example, following the mechanistic model noted earlier. Since Weber's original work, the term *bureaucracy* has also come to be used as a pejorative reference to the constraints incumbent in the rules governing organizational life.

In the 1950s Joan Woodward studied 100 manufacturing firms in England and categorized, from simple to complex, the technical complexity of their operations into three types: unit production, mass production, and continuous processing. She determined that the type of operating process an industry used determined the best structure for an organization; her findings brought to an end the search for one best structure and heralded the start of the contingency approach noted earlier. During the 1960s Paul R. Lawrence and Jay W. Lorsch continued the study of environment–structure fit and concluded that the contingencies of the environment were critical to selecting a suitable organizational configuration. More specifically, they found that organizations with stable environments were most successful if they used traditional hierarchical (i.e., mechanistic) structures; organizations with organic structures were more successful in volatile environments.

Among the best known and longest running (approximately 40 years, starting in the 1950s) studies of organizational structure are those that emanated from the University of Aston group in England. A collection of researchers headed by Derek S. Pugh examined a wide range of organizations and codified and developed measures of such concepts as centralization, specialization, and formalization described previously. Their work bridges the early modern era with the current era.

EMERGING ISSUES OF ORGANIZATIONAL STRUCTURE

The globalization of work and expansion of multinational firms has provided one element of the environment that has fomented changes in prevailing organizational structures. In addition, the rapid changes brought about by the widespread use of computers and other elements of information technology have especially had a large impact on the functioning of organizations. These changes are expected to force changes in organizational structure. In fact, information technology has already influenced organizational structure. Large-scale users of information technology tend to have more decentralized and less formalized structures and more flexibility in responding to the challenges of a volatile environment. Further, with the globalization of work and markets, some organizations have capitalized on the advances of information technology to implement new structural forms. The *boundaryless* (also called virtual, network, shadow, barrier-free) organization may have only a small number of core employees and, in its most extreme case, no physical location beyond that needed to house the small cadre of management employees. Production or services that constitute the core of the organization's mission may be outsourced completely to sites around the globe with information technologies serving as the primary communication links.

THE ROLE OF STRUCTURE IN ORGANIZATIONS

A key role of organizational structure is its relationship to organizational strategy. Depending on an organization's strategy, certain structures will be more or less effective. Therefore, matching structure and strategy is important. Ultimately, a recursive relationship exists whereby the effective implementation of strategy creates an appropriate matching structure that, in turn, produces outcomes and processes that support the intended strategy. For example, an organization that has *innovation* as a core strategy would likely produce a structure with low levels of formalization and high levels of decentralization, among other characteristics. Individuals who work in such a structure experience greater autonomy, freedom, and flexibility in carrying out their work tasks and, as a consequence, are likely to emerge as an innovative workforce. Thus structure and strategy should reinforce each other. Mismatch between structure and strategy often leads to organizational failure.

Structure is also important because of the direct and meaningful impact it may have on valued individual outcomes. A number of studies have demonstrated that organizational structure affects important individual worker attitudes including job satisfaction, work alienation, role ambiguity, role conflict, perceptions of justice, motivation, and job involvement. Structure has also been shown to affect employee behaviors such as performance, turnover, and organizational citizenship. Although some relationships are direct (i.e., increased formalization is associated with lower levels of role ambiguity), most require consideration of individual characteristics and other contextual factors to understand their impact.

Environmental demands such as changing technology and globalization have heightened the importance of organizational flexibility in many industries. Basic structural characteristics such as centralization, formalization, and complexity directly influence an organization's capacity to respond quickly to changes in the environment. One response to the demand for flexibility has been the increased dependence on self-guided teams. Further, formally hierarchical structures have become much flatter, resulting in greater decentralization, generally less formalization, and, in many cases, increased departmentalization.

SUMMARY

Organizational structure is the way people and the work to be accomplished within organizations are configured and coordinated. The primary elements of structure are centralization, formalization, and complexity. These elements are affected by forces outside the organization as well as by organizational size. Information technology and globalization are especially potent factors likely to alter the future of organizational structures. Meaningful relationships exist between organizational structure and organizational strategy, performance, and individual attitudes and behaviors.

—*Janet L. Kottke and Mark D. Agars*

See also Groups; Organizational Culture; Organizational Climate; Organizational Communication, Formal; Organizational Communication, Informal

FURTHER READING

Dibrell, C. C., & Miller, T. R. (2002). Organization design: The continuing influence of information technology. *Management Decision, 40*(5/6), 620–627.

Hall, R. H. (1991). *Organizations: Structure, processes, and outcomes* (5th ed.). Englewood Cliffs, NJ: Prentice Hall.

James, L. R., & Jones, A. P. (1976). Organizational structure: A review of structural dimensions and their conceptual relationships with individual attitudes and behavior. *Organizational Behavior and Human Performance, 16,* 74–113.

Mintzberg, H. (1979). *The structuring of organizations.* Englewood Cliffs, NJ: Prentice Hall.

Pugh, D. S. (Ed.). (1998). *The Aston Programme, Vols. I–III. The Aston Study and its developments.* Burlington, VT: Ashgate.

ORGANIZATIONAL SURVEYS

Organizational surveys are also known as employee opinion surveys or employee attitude surveys. Most experts prefer to call them organizational surveys to clarify that the sponsor and user of such surveys is almost always the organization. Further, the people asked to complete such surveys may be employees at any or all levels, including top executives. Recent estimates conclude that about 75% of all medium- to large-sized firms conduct organizational surveys, typically every year or two. Surveys are also used extensively within the United States federal government, including the armed forces.

PURPOSE AND HISTORY

The size and content of such surveys may vary widely, reflecting the different purposes to which organizational surveys are put. These purposes range along a continuum, so surveys can be seen as tools for assessment and change. Historically, surveys have been used for assessment, much like taking a broad-scale annual medical examination to see *how we are doing.* In recent decades the emphasis has been more on stimulating and measuring change in specific areas of strategic value, such as product quality, work–life human resource initiatives, or customer satisfaction.

The survey is a popular methodology for conducting research in many areas of industrial and organizational psychology. Catherine Higgs and Steve

Ashworth noted that surveys can be used for several types of research. In early stages they can be merely exploratory and later move on to be fully descriptive of the phenomena measured. At the highest level, they can be used to test causal relationships. It is quite common to see journal articles that have used surveys to collect data. Practitioners often learn or borrow survey methodology from allied fields such as sociology.

The typical content of the organizational surveys has changed since the early popularity of employee surveys in the 1930s and 1940s. That was an era of concern for employee morale and emotional adjustment, often as desirable ends in themselves and sometimes to prevent unhappiness that might cause unionization. Typically, survey questions asked about the individual employee's contentment with different aspects of work, management, and pay. They even asked about environmental issues such as parking lots, cafeterias, and lighting. Both interviews and questionnaires were used.

In the 1950s and 1960s the emphasis shifted to the individual's job satisfaction because of presumed links of satisfaction to better organizational productivity. Typical surveys were based on paper-and-pencil questionnaires. In the 1970s and 1980s attempts were made to link employee satisfaction to organizational outcomes like turnover, absenteeism, and stress. The worker's job level and part of the organization were seen as important moderators. The technology for doing surveys also evolved to the use of self-administered, standardized, scannable forms.

Since the early 1990s an extraordinarily different view of surveys has taken hold in most organizations. Behind the change is a set of assumptions linking employee opinions and perceptions to the achievement of strategic organizational goals. In service-dominated industries, employee behaviors are now seen as directly influencing customers' reactions and loyalties and thus spilling over to bottom-line measures like financial growth, profit, and product success. Set against an increasingly competitive global marketplace, the emphasis in surveys is to capture employee views, perceptions, and reports of how their organizations work, with the aim of achieving more productive teams, better quality products and services, and more satisfied customers.

This view of surveys has led to several conceptual models, some with names like the *service-profit chain*. Still others are known as *linkage research* models. They help describe to organization management just why the surveys measure the concepts they do, and show how they are linked to important outcomes. Several recent studies seem to support this way of viewing and using survey results. The relationship between employee views and organizational outcomes at the unit level (rather than the individual level) have proved to be more powerful than previously believed by a few meta-analytic studies, which distill the relationships found in many studies.

METHODOLOGY

Survey questions may cover a wide variety of issues. Closed-ended questions are typically written as Likert-type items, to be answered on a five-point scale of satisfaction or agreement.

- An example of the first type would be "How satisfied are you with the recognition you receive for doing a good job?" Possible answers: 1. Very satisfied; 2. Satisfied; 3. Neither satisfied nor dissatisfied; 4. Dissatisfied; 5. Very dissatisfied.
- An example of the agreement type would be "I like the kind of work I do." Possible answers: 1. Strongly agree; 2. Agree; 3. Neither agree nor disagree; 4. Disagree; 5. Strongly disagree.

Most surveys also include one or more open-ended questions that ask respondents to write in their response. Questions may be very general, such as, "Any other comments?" Or they may be very specific, such as, "What kind of training would help you to be more effective?" To encourage frank and honest responses to all questions, strict confidentiality is almost always promised by the survey sponsor.

In the last decade, organizational surveys have been administered largely by computers, using e-mail and the Internet. This has made astonishing changes in the administration, collection, and use of survey data. Surveys can now be sent electronically to eligible samples, avoiding the physical effort and expense of postal or other distribution systems. Surveys are cheaper and much more flexible once the infrastructure is available. Although printing a large survey might take weeks, an electronic version can be changed at the last minute (and even during a survey if a major crisis has occurred). These surveys can also use *branching* techniques, so respondents answering certain questions unfavorably can be offered more detailed follow-up items to help in diagnosis. Write-in comments are keyed in by respondents, avoiding the laborious transcription needed in paper-and-pencil surveys.

In most ways, the electronic version of organizational surveys is quite superior to earlier versions. Careful studies show no distortion of replies versus paper-and-pencil versions, except that write-in comments are typically twice as long. Still, computer programs make write-in comments much easier to analyze and report than in the past. In general, reporting survey data has been shortened from many weeks to a few days. Reports to managers can also be made via computer, giving managers a chance to receive reports sooner and in more flexible formats.

RESPONSE RATES

However, electronic surveys may create problems because surveys now seem quite easy to do. Many groups in a firm launch their own internal surveys, often of dubious quality. Along with this are employee cries of *oversurveying,* and a decline in response rates. In the past it was common to survey all of a firm's population to do a census survey. Recently, many firms have shifted to doing more frequent surveys, or *pulse* surveys, often of small samples of respondents.

Typical response rates are hard to pin down with certainty. It is believed that census surveys of employees typically get response rates of anywhere from 30% to 95%, averaging about 65%. Sample surveys seem to get 10% to 15% lower response rates. Poor response rates undermine the credibility of survey results. Some recent research, however, suggests that nonrespondents are mostly people who have other priorities and are not actively opposed to the survey or its topics. Still, it would be wise to weight any subgroups that respond at higher or lower rates than typical, to properly represent each subgroup in the firm. Of course, survey researchers should always compare a sample's demographics with the known population demographics to be sure the sample is representative.

Most experts believe that the size and content of a survey questionnaire will influence the response rates. Surveys with clear, well-written questions on topics that are obviously important to the individual and organization will gain more participation. Respondents will be *turned off* by surveys they think are overly long. In prior decades, it was not unusual for paper-and-pencil surveys to have more than 200 questions. Recent electronic surveys typically have

from 40 to 75 items and can be completed in 10 to 20 minutes. This, too, reflects the competitive, fast-moving business climate in many firms.

NORMATIVE DATA

Management getting survey reports often ask how they compare with other firms. Different consortiums of companies have been born from this desire. The granddaddy of survey consortiums is the Mayflower Group (www.mayflowergroup.org), a group of roughly 40 large firms that ask the same two dozen core items in their respective surveys and share the normative data with other member firms under strict confidentiality. There is also the Information Technology Survey Group (www.itsg.org), made up of 18 high-technology firms, that operates in a similar way. The representatives of the consortium's member firms meet twice a year and share what they believe are *best practices* in doing organizational surveys. In addition, several survey vendors offer data norms based on their client data sets, or based on specially collected national data sets.

Other types of norm data are those that represent cultural or national differences. With many large firms now truly global organizations, some international data is available for norm comparisons. Basic advances in the social sciences are also helped through such data. Three decades ago the Dutch organizational scholar Geert Hofstede used the international survey data from the IBM Corporation to lay out several cross-cultural dimensions, such as the tendencies of people in different countries to be oriented toward the group, or collective (as in Asia), or toward the individual (as in the United States).

ORGANIZATIONAL DEVELOPMENT AND ACTION TAKING

The most important outcome of surveys is meaningful and responsive action. This is also the most elusive aspect of the organizational survey process. But experts in organizational development, working with survey researchers, have developed some excellent techniques. They recognized that survey data can be energizing and motivational. Naturally, meaningful action requires a supportive top management that is knowledgeable about the overall process. They must be advocates and champions of the organizational survey. Survey practitioners responsible for doing the organization's survey must educate all levels of management; they must provide the training and infrastructure for data to be collected, analyzed, and reported and then track the actions taken.

Some experts favor reporting survey data first to top management, then letting the data *cascade* down to lower levels, with top management acting as role models for how to discuss and act on the data. Other experts prefer having the data *bubble up,* with lower levels seeing it first and then reporting their findings and action plans to higher levels. Over the years detailed protocols have been developed to *feed back* the survey results to respondents; and this is seen as a critical step to good survey practice. Recent research, however, has made it clear that action taking, not data feedback, is the critical ingredient for success. In fact, providing employees with survey data feedback and no action causes more unfavorable consequences than giving no feedback at all.

Companies that have described their experiences make it clear that the critical factor is to ensure that managers must act. It may even be best to focus on only one or two high priority areas to work on. Many firms use survey results, and improvements or declines, as the basis for performance appraisals, incentive bonuses, and promotions. If the topics measured in the survey are truly important to the organization, rewards and punishment for their achievement seem quite appropriate.

Organizational surveys have been used for many purposes in recent years. These include topics as different as managing the progress of mergers and acquisitions, improving a climate of diversity, reducing employee turnover, reinvigorating an organization after a business turndown, and coordinating practices in a large global organization. Surveys have also been modified to provide multisource feedback (360-degree feedback) for management development purposes. The organizational survey is a powerful tool for many purposes and seems destined for continuing use and influence.

—*Allen I. Kraut*

See also Feedback; Organizational Development; 360-Degree Feedback

FURTHER READING

Church, A. H., & Waclawski, J. (2001). *Designing and using organizational surveys: A seven step process.* San Francisco: Jossey-Bass.

Kraut, A. I. (Ed.). (1996). *Organizational surveys: Tools for assessment and change.* San Francisco: Jossey-Bass.

Kraut, A. I. (Ed.). (2006). *Getting action from organizational surveys: New concepts, methods and applications.* San Francisco: Jossey-Bass.

OUTSOURCING

Outsourcing is typically the domain of trade economists, whereas nonstandard work arrangements are the province of labor economists. Temporary work is one aspect of nonstandard work arrangements just as are part-time work, contract work, and other work forms. Although there are many polemics on the positive and negative results of outsourcing and nonstandard work on productivity and personal well-being, industrial/organizational (I/O) psychologists have paid scant research attention to either.

In the early 1980s outsourcing referred to the situation in which firms expanded their purchases of products (such as automakers buying car seat fabrics) rather than making them themselves. By 2004 outsourcing had taken on a different meaning. It referred to the specific segment of the growing international trade in services. This segment consists of arm's length or long-distance purchase of services abroad. Thus X-rays made in Boston can be transferred to Bombay for reading, and call centers in Deli can serve customers in Denver. This move is accompanied by the debate about whether the United States is weakening its economic power by *shipping jobs abroad.*

All in all, outsourcing is a growth industry and takes many forms. Some firms have partnered with competitors in some fashion for decades. Among the reasons firms team up with competitors are to secure sophisticated, cost-driven contracts; to fend off threats from other industries; to evaluate a partner's suitability for long-term joint ventures; to set industry standards for product compatibility in hopes of expanding markets for everyone; and so on. One study of a company's outsourcing partners found that approximately 50% were with competitors. One observer noted, "In today's complex, intertwined economy, the business-as-war, winner-take-all mind-set doesn't cut it. Better get a piece of the pie than no portion at all." In war, outsourcing cuts it. Outsourcing has been done in every war the United States has fought. In the second Gulf War, the U.S. military outsourced everything from feeding troops to providing heavy machinery. Both the numbers and types of *coopetitions* are rising.

Partnering has a number of advantages and disadvantages. Some operational benefits accrue from partnering. Partners can teach new things, perhaps through access to best-of-class processes. Perhaps partnering competitors can learn technology secrets from one another. Where industry benchmarks aren't well-known, partnering with a competitor can offer insights on a company's productivity, quality, and efficiency.

But there are also obvious disadvantages. Lack of control is a critical disadvantage. If a U.S. oil company operating in a foreign environment outsources security to an in-country organization, and the in-country security force comes in contact with drug traders, it can start a war that the United States will then have to deal with. The demise of ValuJet, for example, happened because the company outsourced cargo handling to a company where they could not control quality standards. In another form of outsourcing, competitors learn from each other's operations, which may be detrimental to one or more partners. Or a coopetition may self-destruct before the renewal option dates arrive. A new company board for one of the partners may not approve of the other partner. The strategic aims of partners may change midstream, causing failure. These are just some of the reasons for outsourcing failures.

The current trend is to export international outsourcing as a source of cost saving, particularly in service-related industries. International outsourcing takes a number of forms: *outtasking* or subcontracted exportation of particular tasks or function to a foreign enterprise; a partial exportation of a task; *the foreign-local subsidiary model* that relies on a foreign enterprise to support a foreign subsidiary of the U.S. customer; a jointly owned subsidiary to provide shared services to affiliates; and global multilateral outsourcing that relies on a multinational enterprise to support a multinational customer's operations in multiple countries.

Outsourcing has a number of advantages and disadvantages. Among the advantages are price and cost reductions, the ability to expand contract programs in short periods of time, enhanced service benefits, finding and using new talent, and lower turnover rates when outsourcing is from the United States to non-U.S. countries. This latter is generally because the kinds of jobs outsourced from the United States are not as attractive as are other jobs to U.S. employees.

Risks are also involved in outsourcing. When outsourcing is done from the United States to other countries, political instability may be a factor. Companies also run the risk of losing their core competencies to their outsourced partners. Unemployment backlashes are another risk.

TEMPORARY WORK

Contingent labor is one of the fastest growing industries in the United States. The temporary work revolution is not limited to the United States. In Europe it grew 18% in 1997 alone. Although the number of contingent jobs is growing, the types of these jobs are changing. Health care and technology jobs are two of the fastest growing job sectors. For temporary workers nearly all the traditional human relations functions—recruitment, administration, and so on—have shifted from the work organization to temporary work agencies. Users of temporary workers are afforded considerable labor flexibility and reduced obligation to these workers. In addition to flexibility, rationales for hiring temporary workers are labor cost savings, increased global competition, new technology, and the need to respond quickly to changing conditions. Despite the increased use of temporary workers, human relations contemporary textbooks offer the area scant or no coverage.

Current research in the area of temporary and contingent employment addresses the demographic characteristics of the workforce and the evolution of organizations leading to their use. In 1998 the National Association of Temporary and Staffing Services (now called the American Staffing Association) conducted a demographic survey about the state of temporary employment. This survey counted 2.8 million Americans as a part of the temporary workforce. Forty-one percent of these people had at least a two-year college degree, and another 19% currently attended college. Twenty-one percent of *temps* recently finished high school or college and viewed temporary work as a means of entry into the workforce. Clerical and administrative positions counted for 40.5% of all temporary jobs, a decrease in the types of positions available through staffing agencies. Technical and professional positions accounted for 25% of available openings, but health care positions decreased by 2.2%. An earlier survey by the same organization reported that 80% of all temps were women.

Other research addresses how organizations use temps, individual consequences of temping, and individual responses to temping. Organizations with high variability in their product lines have increased need for temps, but they are also used when permanent employees leave their positions (e.g., vacation, long-term disability leave, maternity leave). Client companies reduce their training costs by hiring specialized temps. Because companies view temps as resources, temps see themselves as alienated and have little or no commitment to the organization. Individual responses to temping include developing coping strategies to reduce feelings of alienation. Temps may seek autonomous, mentally challenging work, or control the pace of work to exert some control over their environment. Temps often look for long-term assignments to counter isolation. Existing research does not explain the motivational processes in which individuals engage while temping, despite the fact that motivation is one of the most frequently researched areas in I/O psychology.

Temps come in two types. There are those seeking permanent employment, or temporary temps, and those not seeking permanent employment, or permanent temps. About one third of both groups enjoy the variety of temporary jobs and the quality of job assignment. Temporary temps are more likely than permanent temps to use temporary employment to find job leads and develop networks. Permanent temps are more likely to feel they do not have time for permanent jobs and are more likely to value the flexibility of temporary work.

SUMMARY

Outsourcing and temporary work are both given short shrift in I/O research. In the early 2000s outsourcing came to mean the arm's length or distance purchase of services abroad. Outsourcing is a growth industry, and there are many forms of partnering that have a number of advantages and disadvantages.

Temporary work is one part of the contingent labor force and is growing dramatically. Existing research addresses the demography and organizational uses of temps. It also addresses individual consequences of and individual responses to temping and why people seek temporary work. Sadly lacking is research on the motivational aspects of temporary work.

—*Karlene H. Roberts and Daniel S. Wong*

FURTHER READING

Davis-Blake, A., & Uzzi, B. (1993). Determinants of employment externalization: A study of temporary workers and independent contractors. *Administrative Science Quarterly, 38,* 195–223.

Greaver, M. F. (1998). *Strategic outsourcing: A structural approach to outsourcing decisions and initiatives.* New York: AMACOM AMA Publications.

Housman, S., & Osawa, M. (2003). *Nonstandard work in developed economies: Causes and consequences.* Kalamazoo, MI: W. E. Upjohn Institute for Employment Research.

National Association of Temporary and Staffing Services. (1998). *Who are temporary workers? You may be surprised to learn.* Alexandria, VA: Author.

Wheeler, A. R., & Buckley, M. R. (2001). Examining the motivation process of temporary work employees: A holistic model and research framework. *Journal of Managerial Psychology, 16,* 339–354.

P

PATH–GOAL THEORY

The path–goal theory of leadership is a situational theory of leadership and is closely aligned with expectancy theory. The theory holds that the major function of the leader is to enhance subordinates' instrumentalities, for example, perceived degree of relationship between behavior and outcome; expectancies, such as perceived relationship between effort and behavior; and valences including feelings regarding attractiveness of outcome to increase subordinate force such as motivational effort. Thus, although the theory is a leadership theory, it relies heavily on the work motivation literature.

Path–goal theory was originally contrived as a dyadic theory of leadership concerning relationships between appointed supervisors and subordinates, but it has been expanded to include supervisor and unit relationships. It is generally concerned with how formally appointed supervisors influence the motivation and attitudes of their respective subordinates. It is not concerned with organizational leadership, emergent leadership, leadership strategy, or leadership during times of organizational change; it is concerned with job task leadership. In more concrete terms, path–goal theory proposes that the primary function of a leader is to increase individual employee gains, rewards, and other positive outcomes for work goal attainment by creating a more easily traversed path to goal attainment (i.e., removing obstacles, clarifying goals, increasing job satisfaction). Whether the leader can do so effectively depends heavily on various contextual and situational factors and subordinate characteristics. Thus according to the theory, effective leaders streamline work processes by complementing the characteristics of the environment and subordinates. If such situational affordances are present, leaders can increase subordinate motivation, job attitudes, and performance.

LEADER BEHAVIORS

The theory further states that a leader might display four different types of leadership styles, depending on the situation, to maximize employee effectiveness. Some researchers state that more effective leaders simultaneously incorporate all four styles because of the unique effects of each style across varying work tasks and conditions. The four styles are as follows:

1. **Directive Leadership:** Effective leaders should provide specific guidance of performance, set acceptable standards of performance, and provide explicit performance expectations to subordinates. Generally, this approach is best when work is unstructured and complex and the subordinates are inexperienced. Such an approach tends to increase subordinates' sense of security and control.

2. **Supportive Leadership:** Effective leaders should be friendly to subordinates and demonstrate concern for each subordinate's well-being by considering each individual's needs. Generally, this approach is best when work is stressful, boring, and hazardous.

3. **Participative Leadership:** The effective leader consults with subordinates by soliciting ideas and suggestions from subordinates, soliciting participative decision making affecting subordinates, and valuing and considering subordinate suggestions.

Generally, this approach is best when the subordinates are experts and their advice is necessary for achieving work goals.

4. **Achievement-Oriented Leadership:** Effective leaders set moderately difficult and challenging goals, continuously emphasize work performance improvements, and expect subordinates to achieve high levels of performance. Generally, this approach is optimal for complex work, but research suggests it is important across all types of work.

SITUATIONAL MODERATORS

Path–goal theory also contends that leadership effects on subordinates are moderated by two general classes of boundary conditions:

1. **Environmental Characteristics:** task structure and demands, role ambiguity, work autonomy, task interdependence, and task scope

2. **Subordinate Characteristics:** cognitive ability, dependence, locus of control, goal orientation, and authoritarianism

Using one of the four styles of leadership just described and considering situational factors, leaders try to influence employee perceptions and motivate them toward goal attainment by clarifying roles, expectancies, satisfaction, and performance standards.

SUPPORT FOR THE THEORY

Although path–goal theory can be classified as one of the *major triumphs* for leadership theory, empirical support for many of its mechanisms is lacking. The theoretical crux of the theory was motivation: Motivation was posited as a mediator between leader behavior and subordinate behavior and outcomes such as satisfaction and performance. However, the major pitfall of research on path–goal theory was the lack of integration of motivation into empirical assessments of the theory. Empirical assessments have focused on the direct effects of leader behavior on subordinate behavior and outcomes. This was a major problem in most leadership and work motivation research until the early 1990s. Additionally, empirical studies on path–goal theory were quite restrictive in the variety of leader behaviors examined, the outcomes studied, and the situational and person moderator variables examined. For example, nearly all empirical work on path–goal theory has focused on only two leader behaviors: directive leadership behavior and supportive leadership behavior. These two classes of behavior have generally been examined in light of task structure, task and job performance, and facets of satisfaction (e.g., job, intrinsic, extrinsic satisfaction), and results are mixed. Because of these shortcomings, the original theory has been recast to encourage researchers to reexamine the theory by including more leadership behaviors, motivational influences, and subordinate and work unit outcomes.

REFORMULATED PATH–GOAL THEORY (1996)

The increasing use of teams and other more structurally and socially defined units in organizations has forced organizational researchers to modify their way of thinking about organizational behavior and consequently the way we conduct organizational research. This change, among others, forced path–goal theory to adapt. In 1996, the theory was recast to be more inclusive of recent theoretical advancement and more readily testable. The reformulated theory concerns work-unit leadership and is not limited to dyadic relationships. This is partly because of the transition of organizations to more team-based structures. The theory is now driven by mechanisms aimed at enhancing empowerment and motivation of all subordinates within a work unit and how such empowerment influences work unit effectiveness via motivation.

SUMMARY

When comparing leadership theories, path–goal theory has stood the test of time, even with the lack of empirical support, which is easily attributable to the lack of appropriate empirical investigations. It is a theory that has helped direct the leadership area by expanding theoretical thinking and has given rise to many important leadership theories such as transformational leadership. It has done so by incorporating two important areas of industrial/organizational (I/O) psychology: motivation and power. Overall, and as with many other I/O theories, more research is needed, especially in testing the reformulated theory. The theory is certainly worthy of future attention.

—J. Craig Wallace

FURTHER READING

Bass, B. (1985). *Leadership and performance beyond expectations*. New York: Free Press.

Evans, M. G. (1996). R. J. House's "A path–goal theory of leader effectiveness." *Leadership Quarterly, 7,* 305–309.

Georgopoulos, B. S., Mahoney, T. M., & Jones, L. W. (1957). A path–goal approach to productivity. *Journal of Applied Psychology, 41,* 345–353.

House, R. J. (1996). Path–goal theory of leadership: Lessons, legacy and a reformulated theory. *Leadership Quarterly, 7,* 323–352.

PERFORMANCE APPRAISAL

Performance appraisal refers to the systematic measurement and evaluation of employee work behaviors as part of an organization's performance management system. Performance appraisals typically focus on employee behaviors or performance dimensions that are required of the position and tend not to include discretionary employee behaviors. Reflecting social, political, and organizational changes, performance appraisal systems continue to evolve to serve many different individual and organizational purposes.

BRIEF HISTORY

Performance appraisals began to grow in popularity with the industrial revolution of the early 20th century. World War II fueled this interest as industrial psychologists were given the tasks of classifying and placing individuals in positions to increase the effectiveness of the military. Performance appraisals research continued following World War II and today remains a major focus of research in industrial/organizational (I/O) psychology. Performance appraisal research has gone through many phases throughout its history. The 1960s and 1970s were largely devoted to research on rating formats, the 1980s and early 1990s largely investigated issues related to rater cognitive processes, and recent research is devoted largely to 360-degree feedback or multirater systems. One constant challenge for researchers and practitioners has been the difficulty of defining and measuring job performance given its dynamic and multidimensional nature.

VARIATIONS IN APPROACHES

Appraisals generally are classified into objective (e.g., sales volume) or subjective (e.g., supervisory ratings) measures, with the vast majority of performance appraisal systems using subjective measures of performance. Elements of the appraisal system that may differ across contexts or organizations include variations in rating purpose, rater sources, rating content and formats, and system characteristics.

Appraisal Purpose

Performance appraisals may be used for a variety of purposes, which may be classified into three categories: within-person, between-person, and system maintenance purposes. Within-person purposes involve identifying an employee's strengths or weaknesses to provide developmental feedback to the employee, set employee goals, or suggest particular training or development programs. Between-person purposes are used to make comparisons between employees and may be used to identify who should be promoted, administer merit pay increases, or decide which employees should be terminated. System maintenance purposes include using the appraisals to validate personnel selection assessments, identify organizational training needs, or document information pertaining to personnel decisions. Research indicates that the organizations often use performance appraisals for multiple purposes simultaneously, and the observed ratings and user attitudes differ as a function of rating purpose. Appraisal purpose is an important consideration given that it will direct how an organization's performance management system is developed, implemented, and maintained.

Rater Source

Supervisors are the most widely used source of performance appraisal information. Recent changes in how organizations are structured and function (e.g., flatter and more decentralized, organized around team-based work) have led many organizations to collect performance information from nonsupervisory sources. These rater sources may include peers, subordinates, or customers. Research indicates that different rater sources provide different information, and a more comprehensive assessment of work behaviors may be obtained by collecting information from multiple sources.

Rating Content and Format

Virtually any aspect of employee behavior, such as specific behaviors or outcomes, and any level of performance, whether individual or group, may be appraised. Early performance appraisal systems tended to focus on evaluating traits, whereas the current focus is on evaluating job-related behaviors. Performance appraisals generally evaluate past performance, but some forms may require raters to make predictions about potential or future performance. Rating formats may also differ across situations such that, for example, some formats requiring ratings and other formats require raters to rank-order employees.

System Characteristics

Additional features of the performance appraisal system that may differ across contexts include the frequency of appraisals; the mode by which information is collected, such as paper-and-pencil versus electronically; whether the raters are anonymous; and whether the evaluations are confidential or public.

SUMMARY

The evaluation of employee work behaviors continues to be an integral part of most organizations' performance management systems. Performance appraisal research has addressed a myriad of topics expected to influence the effectiveness of the performance appraisal system, such as rater training programs and user attitudes. Research suggests that the effectiveness of performance appraisal systems is improved when they are based on a thorough job analysis, participants are involved in its design, and raters and ratees are trained to use the system effectively. Despite some research suggesting that the task of evaluating employee performance remains one of managers' least favorite activities, an appropriately designed and implemented system has the ability to improve individual and organizational decision making and effectiveness.

—*Gary J. Greguras*

See also Criterion Theory; Job Analysis; Performance Appraisal, Objective Indexes; Performance Appraisal, Subjective Indexes; 360-Degree Feedback

FURTHER READING

Borman, W. C. (1991). Job behavior, performance, and effectiveness. In M. D. Dunnette & L. M. Hough (Eds.), *Handbook of industrial and organizational psychology,* (2nd ed., Vol. 2, pp. 271–326). Palo Alto, CA: Consulting Psychologists Press.

Bretz, R. D., Jr., Milkovich, G. T., & Read, W. (1992). The current state of performance appraisal research and practice: Concerns, directions, and implications. *Journal of Management, 18,* 321–352.

Murphy, K. R., & Cleveland, J. N. (1995). *Understanding performance appraisal: Social, organizational, and goal-based perspectives.* Thousand Oaks, CA: Sage.

Smither, J. W. (1998). *Performance appraisal: State of the art in practice.* San Francisco: Jossey-Bass.

PERFORMANCE APPRAISAL, OBJECTIVE INDEXES

Industrial/organizational (I/O) psychologists (and organizational managers) are interested in knowing how well employees perform their jobs. Such information can help make administrative decisions about employees (e.g., promotions, terminations), provide feedback to employees to help them improve their performance, and evaluate human resource procedures such as selection and training. There are two general types of indexes that provide information about employee performance. *Subjective* (or *judgmental*) *indexes* are based on evaluations or judgments of others concerning employee effectiveness. *Objective indexes* refer to measures of performance that are countable, or directly observable, and comparable for different employees.

TYPES OF OBJECTIVE PERFORMANCE INDEXES

Objective performance indexes are grouped in two categories: *production measures* and *personnel data.* Production measures are related to the amount of acceptable work (products or services) resulting from employee effort. Examples are production output, sales volume, and time required to complete a task. Personnel data do not directly assess an employee's work but are important to the overall performance of an employee. Personnel data are typically maintained in employee personnel files and include information related to absence, accidents, grievances, awards, disciplinary actions, and turnover.

Production Measures

Employers are concerned that their employees are productive and efficient in performing their job duties. Production measures are often considered to be the *gold standard* of job performance indexes, because they are linked to an organization's profitability. They also usually have greater credibility than subjective performance indexes because they do not appear to rely on human judgments. The label *objective* suggests that the measures are accurate, unbiased, and reliable; but the label can be misleading.

Objective production measures exist for many jobs, especially those jobs in which tasks are well-structured and frequently performed, such as the manufacture or assembly of established products or the provision of standard customer services. There are many possible production measures, some applicable to numerous jobs but others specific to a narrow range of jobs. Objective performance measures should be selected following a thorough *job analysis* that has identified the job's critical duties and responsibilities.

The most commonly used type of production measure is related to *quantity of work,* a count of the volume of work produced by employees. Specific examples are the number of lines of computer code written per hour by programmers, number of phone calls made per day by telemarketers, number of arrests per month made by police officers, percentage of standard time required to complete repairs by auto mechanics, and number of patent applications filed by research engineers.

Although also measuring work quantity, indexes that assess performance in sales jobs occur frequently and some specific examples are warranted. Most straightforward are simple indexes that count for some time period the number of sales of products or services or tabulate the value of such sales. More fine-grained sales measures include number of new customers, percentage of past customers who make new purchases, number of potential customers contacted, and sales of newly introduced versus *older* products or services.

Another type of production index assesses quality of work. These measures count the number of errors committed or assess the number of unacceptable or damaged items produced. Specific examples include the dollar value of scrapped raw material for manufacturing employees, number of shortages and overages in cash balances for bank tellers, errors by catalog sales clerks in processing customer orders, rate of errors for data entry personnel, and cost of dishes and glassware broken by restaurant servers.

Primarily in occupations requiring employee–customer interactions using telecommunications systems, such as call center operators and telemarketers, organizations have developed automated approaches to performance measurement. These *electronic performance monitoring* systems can accurately measure the amount of time an employee requires to answer customer questions, process orders, or present marketing information. The frequency and amount of time that employees are not connected to the telecommunication system can also be measured. Questions have been raised about whether such performance monitoring is invasive of employee privacy or reduces employee trust in the organization. Research indicates that employees are more accepting of electronic monitoring when measured behaviors are clearly job related, employees have input into the design of the monitoring procedure, and employees have some control over when monitoring occurs. Electronic performance monitoring should increase as technological advances lead to more assessment capabilities with decreased costs.

Personnel Data

Measures of *absence* are the most common personnel data. The importance of absenteeism is evident: Employees cannot meet performance goals if they are absent. Although total days absent in a time period seems like a useful measure, several problems are masked by its apparent simplicity. First, employees are absent from work for many reasons, including personal illness, the illness of family members, transportation problems, and weather conditions. These varied reasons suggest that some absences are more justified than others, but decisions about absence justification may be unclear. Second, various patterns of absence result in differential impact on the organization or are linked to different causes. For example, if Mary is absent all week and Bill is absent on either Monday or Friday for five consecutive weeks, both are absent for a total of five days. Mary's absences may be caused by illness, whereas Bill's absence pattern suggests job dissatisfaction or poor work motivation. Finally, its many causes lead to inconsistent levels of absence for individual employees over time. These problems have led to the development of absence indexes that attempt to account for different reasons that absence occurred. Some measure the amount of time lost because of specific causes, whereas others count the number of periods of absence (i.e., Mary's five consecutive days absent count as one absence period, whereas Bill's five days absent count as five absence periods).

Another type of personnel data measures *employee accidents,* usually in terms of lost work time or direct financial costs that result from the accidents. As with absence, not all accidents reflect equally on employee performance. Usually distinctions must be made in terms of the primary cause or causes of an accident and whether the accident could have been avoided if the involved one or more employees had behaved differently. Accident rates are often inconsistent unless they are based on time periods of several months or more. Research suggests that the frequency of unsafe behaviors of employees may yield more useful information than accident rates. Many unsafe behaviors do not lead to an actual accident, but reducing the amount of unsafe behavior should reduce the number of accidents. Unfortunately, it is more difficult to count unsafe work behaviors than accidents.

Turnover is another form of personnel data. Turnover can be defined as whether a particular employee is still employed by the organization at some point in time (often one year) following hiring. Turnover can also be defined as the percentage of employees in a job title whose employment ends during some time period (again, often one year). Often organizations attempt to distinguish between causes of turnover. Commonly used categories are voluntary (the employee quit) and involuntary (the employee was fired), but often these distinctions are ambiguous. Not all employees who leave an organization are equally valuable, so organizations may attempt to categorize leavers as effective or ineffective and calculate separate turnover rates for each group.

Effectiveness of Objective Performance Indexes

Objective indexes seem like valuable ways to measure job performance, but they also have less apparent limitations. Useful objective indexes are virtually nonexistent for many jobs (especially managerial and professional) and rarely exist for all important duties and responsibilities of *any* job. As examples, it is difficult to measure well a manager's effectiveness with motivating employees or developing creative solutions to problems by simply counting something. A performance index that does not measure all important parts of the job is termed *deficient.*

Another serious limitation of many objective performance indexes is that the scores are affected by situational factors not controlled by employees. For example, assigned patrol areas affect the number of arrests made by police officers, tool quality affects the dollar value of scrapped material and products, customer questions affect the time required to process an order, and work stress from understaffing may increase employee absences. Performance measures affected by factors outside employee control are termed *contaminated.* Often attempts are made to minimize contamination of the index, such as by measuring officers' arrests relative to other officers in the work unit.

Another limitation of objective indexes is that they often provide unhelpful performance feedback, because they assess the results of behavior and not the behavior itself. Informing an employee that too few products were sold does not provide the employee with information about what job behaviors, if any, are ineffective. Objective indexes that are based on counts of specific job behaviors such as number of customers called per month and number of sales of new products may provide more useful feedback.

Although objective performance indexes usually assess individual employee performance, they are often better measures of work group performance. When employees work together closely, countable measures of individual contributions are often lacking, but quantity and quality of the group's output can be assessed. Also, employees may conceal negative behaviors, such as theft or sabotage, but missing or damaged supplies and equipment can often be assessed at the group level.

Research has investigated how strongly objective and subjective measures of performance are related. The average relation can be described as moderate in strength. Although both objective and subjective indexes are measuring job performance, it is clear that each also assesses other factors. One type is not a substitute for the other.

CONCLUSIONS

Objective performance indexes are not well named. Judgments are typically required when establishing these performance measures. Commonly required judgments include the time period over which performance is assessed, the breadth of behaviors or results included in the index, and adjustments to the index to account for situational factors affecting performance.

Objective indexes can be useful measures of job performance when they assess behaviors that employees control and address a job's important duties. Objective measures are better suited for use in administrative decisions about employees and evaluation of human resource programs than for providing feedback to employees. They often provide better assessments of work group performance than of individual employees.

—*James L. Farr*

See also Job Analysis; Performance Appraisal, Subjective Indexes

FURTHER READING

Bommer, W. H., Johnson, J. L., Rich, G. A., Podsakoff, P. M., & MacKenzie, S. B. (1995). On the interchangeability of objective and subjective measures of employee performance: A meta-analysis. *Personnel Psychology, 48,* 587–605.

Campion, M. A. (1991). Meaning and measurement of turnover: Comparison of alternative measures and recommendations for research. *Journal of Applied Psychology, 76,* 199–212.

Landy, F. J., & Farr, J. L. (1983). *The measurement of work performance: Methods, theory and applications.* Orlando, FL: Academic Press.

Levy, P. E. (2006). Criterion measurement. In *Industrial/ organizational psychology* (2nd ed., pp. 86–111). Boston: Houghton Mifflin.

PERFORMANCE APPRAISAL, SUBJECTIVE INDEXES

Employee work behaviors or job outcomes may be measured and evaluated using a variety of different methods. Although employee performance may be measured with either objective (e.g., sales volume) or subjective (e.g., supervisory ratings) methods, the overwhelming majority of appraisals require raters to make subjective judgments about the performance of the ratee. These subjective judgments may be either ratings or rankings and may be collected using a variety of different rating formats.

APPRAISAL METHODS

Graphic Rating Scales

Graphic rating scales are the most widely used format for appraising performance. Graphic rating scales require raters to evaluate employee performance along a continuum of response categories or anchors that convey information about the meaningfulness of the various points along the continuum. For example, a rater may be asked to evaluate an employee's performance using a scale ranging from 1 (fails to meet expectations) through 5 (exceeds expectations). Another example requires the rater to evaluate the employee's performance by placing a check mark on a line anchored from poor to excellent. These evaluations or ratings can then easily be converted into numerical scores for the purposes of making comparisons between employees or across performance dimensions. The specificity of both the anchors and the aspect of performance being evaluated vary across scales. The simplicity and ease with which graphic rating scales may be developed likely explain their widespread use. However, this simplicity is also a limitation. The anchors of the scales and the aspect of behavior being evaluated are often ambiguously defined, which may lead to inconsistencies or disagreements among raters using the same scale. It is precisely this ambiguity of the anchors and items that served as the impetus for the development of more specifically defined scales.

Behaviorally Anchored Rating Scales

Behaviorally anchored rating scales (BARS) are a type of graphic rating scale that defines the anchors and levels of performance in specific behavioral terms. The behavioral anchors are stated in terms of expectations such as, "This employee could be expected to . . ." because it is possible that the rater may not have had the opportunity to observe the exact behavior listed on the form. This specificity in defining the behaviors and levels of performance, as well as favorable rater and ratee reactions to BARS, likely explain much of their popularity in the 1960s and 1970s. As with any approach, BARS have several limitations: The scale development process is time-consuming and costly, raters often disagree about the ordering of behavioral examples along the continuum, raters often have difficulty seeing the link between the behavioral example and the performance dimension being evaluated, and the scales often do not generalize from one setting to another. The research on the utility and effectiveness of BARS has produced inconsistent results, leading some to argue that the costs associated with developing BARS cannot be justified from a data quality perspective.

Mixed Standard Scales

Mixed standard scales (MSS) are a derivation of BARS. Consistent with BARS, MSS use behavioral anchors to define the type and level of performance being evaluated. However, instead of listing the behavioral anchors for a particular dimension along a continuum and requiring the rater to choose the anchor that most closely describes the ratee's performance, MSS require raters to evaluate each behavioral example. Generally, three items are written for each performance dimension to reflect low, medium, and high levels of performance. Items from all performance dimensions are randomly mixed together and presented to the rater. The rater then indicates whether the ratee performs at, above, or below the level of performance described for each behavioral item. These judgments are then combined to produce separate scores for each performance dimension. One advantage of this approach is that there are several judgments made for each performance dimension (i.e., each behavioral anchor serves as an item), and therefore internal reliability estimates may be calculated for each performance dimension. Similarly, raters who rate inconsistently can easily be identified and can be recommended to receive additional training. Likewise, items or performance dimensions that are inconsistently evaluated across raters can be identified for refinement. Because MSS are conceptually similar to BARS, many of the limitations noted earlier with BARS also apply to these scales. A derivation of the MSS is the behavioral observation scale (BOS), which requires raters to report the frequency, rather than favorability, of the behaviors being evaluated.

Forced-Choice Scales

Forced-choice scales require raters to choose from among a set of statements the one that best describes the ratee. Both the favorability, or social desirability, and discriminability, the degree to which the statement distinguishes between good and poor performers, of an item are considered in the development of a forced-choice scale. Statements or items are grouped so that they are relatively equal on the favorability index but differ on the discriminability index. As such, all items appear equally desirable, but only some of the items discriminate between good and poor performers. Rater responses to the items may be differentially weighted in an algorithm used to derive the overall score on a particular performance dimension, or the number of items chosen with high discriminability indexes may be summated to represent the ratee's score on that particular dimension. Forced-choice scales were designed primarily to reduce rater bias by forcing raters to choose from among a list of equally desirable descriptors. Raters who wish to intentionally distort their ratings have difficulty doing so because all items appear equally favorable and the raters likely cannot discern which items have high discriminability indexes. Research suggests that rater errors such as leniency are decreased with forced-choice scales; however, some raters react negatively to the forced-choice format because it is not directly apparent to them how they are evaluating the levels of their employees. Because of the disguised nature of the scoring, raters may also react negatively because it may be difficult for them to provide feedback to the ratees. The forced-choice rating scale is similar to the mixed standard scale in that the scale continuum or actual rating level given to the ratee is not readily apparent to the rater.

Employee Comparison Methods

All the aforementioned scales or methods required raters to make judgments about a particular ratee. In contrast, employee comparison methods require raters to evaluate ratees relative to one another. The three most common employee comparison methods include paired comparisons, ranking, and forced distribution methods.

Paired Comparisons. In contrast to the forced-choice method, which requires raters to choose from among statements for a single ratee, paired comparison methods force raters to choose between two ratees. With this method, the supervisor chooses the one employee in the comparison who performs at a higher level or more favorably on the aspect of performance being evaluated. Typically, all possible comparisons are made among employees such that there are $N(N-1)/2$ total comparisons where N is the number of employees to be evaluated. For example, if a supervisor is responsible for evaluating 10 employees, the paired comparison method would require the supervisor to make 45 paired comparisons. Once all comparisons have been completed, the rank ordering of employees may be identified by summing the number of times an employee was chosen. One limitation of this approach is that the number of comparisons required of a rater may be quite large and the task may become time-consuming as the number of ratees and the number of rated dimensions increase. Another potential difficulty of using the paired comparison method deals with the nature of the task. Generally, raters are required to choose the employee in the pairing whose overall performance is better. Raters may have difficulty with this task because a certain employee may perform better than a different employee on one dimension but not another. To overcome this limitation, raters could evaluate specific performance dimensions, rather than overall performance. Rating performance dimensions, instead of overall performance, would increase the feedback value of the ratings to the employee but would add to the complexity (i.e., number of comparisons) of the task.

Rank Ordering. Rank ordering of ratees is another type of employee comparison method and requires raters to create a list of ratees from the best to the worst employee. This rank-ordering method is much less tedious and simpler in terms of comparisons than the paired comparison method. Although it is often easy for raters to identify individuals who should be at the top or bottom of the list, the task may become increasingly difficult in the middle of the list where ratees may be very similar. Raters are often instructed to use an alternating ranking approach: They first select the best person in the group, then the worst person in the group, then the second best person from the group, and so on until all ratees have been ranked. With both the paired comparison and rank-ordering methods, an ordered list of employees is created, but this listing provides no information about the absolute level of performance of any particular individual; for example, there is no way of knowing how far apart the best and worst employees are in terms of performance. Another limitation of this approach is that it is difficult to compare ratees from different lists or groups because the rankings are dependent on who is included in each of the different groups.

Forced Distribution. The forced distribution approach requires raters to place a certain percentage of employees into various performance categories. For example, raters may be required to place 20% of the ratees in the poor performance category, 60% of the ratees in the average performance category, and 20% of the ratees in the good performance category. This method requires less detailed distinctions between ratees because the rater is merely placing them into general categories instead of rank ordering them. One difficulty with the forced distribution approach is that the size of the performance categories that is forced on raters may not reflect the actual distribution of performance of the ratees. Although this approach may simplify the rater's task, especially when the number of ratees is large, both raters and ratees may be less accepting of this appraisal approach if the forced distribution does not accommodate the actual level of performance among ratees.

Additional Approaches

The approaches previously reviewed represent the most commonly used techniques to appraise employee performance. There are, however, numerous derivations and alternative techniques that could be used. For example, narrative approaches require raters to provide written statements that reflect their evaluations and descriptions of employee performance. Although this approach has several limitations, such as amount of time and the rater's ability to effectively communicate in writing, research suggests that narrative comments are effective in improving the performance of the ratees and generally are viewed quite favorably. Other examples of approaches include behavioral diaries, weighted checklists, management by objectives, critical incidents checklists, and behavioral checklists.

SUMMARY

A variety of different performance appraisal approaches exist for measuring and evaluating employee work behaviors. Which approach is best? Comparisons of the different approaches usually involve comparing the rater errors or rating accuracy associated with the various rating approaches. Results comparing different rating formats have generally been inconsistent, and the effect sizes of rating format on rating quality have been quite small. Research has yet to produce a rating format that is clearly superior to the others. Many have suggested that rating format has little impact on data quality or appraisal effectiveness in contrast to individual, social, and organizational factors that influence performance appraisal systems.

—*Gary J. Greguras*

See also Criterion Theory; Critical Incident Technique; Frame-of-Reference Training; Performance Appraisal; Performance Appraisal, Objective Indexes

FURTHER READING

Bernardin, H. J., & Beatty, R. W. (1984). *Performance appraisal: Assessing human behavior at work.* Boston: Kent Publishing Company.

Borman, W. C. (1991). Job behavior, performance, and effectiveness. In M. D. Dunnette & L. M. Hough (Eds.), *Handbook of industrial and organizational psychology* (2nd ed., Vol. 2, pp. 271–326). Palo Alto, CA: Consulting Psychologists Press.

Feldman, J. M. (1986). Instrumentation and training for performance appraisal: A perceptual-cognitive viewpoint. In K. M. Rowland & G. Ferris (Eds.), *Research in personnel and human resources management* (Vol. 4). Greenwich, CT: JAI.

Landy, F. J., & Farr, J. L. (1980). Performance rating. *Psychological Bulletin, 87,* 72–107.

Murphy, K. R., & Cleveland, J. N. (1995). *Understanding performance appraisal: Social, organizational, and goal-based perspectives.* Thousand Oaks, CA: Sage.

Smith, P. C., & Kendall, L. M. (1963). Retranslation of expectations: An approach to the construction of unambiguous anchors for rating scales. *Journal of Applied Psychology, 47,* 149–155.

PERFORMANCE FEEDBACK

Feedback is a subset of the available information in the work environment that indicates how well individuals are meeting their goals. Thus feedback guides, motivates, and reinforces effective behaviors while simultaneously discouraging ineffective ones. Feedback is a complex stimulus entailing a process in which a sender conveys a message to a recipient regarding personal behavior at work. The presence of feedback triggers psychological processes that precede behavioral responses. Daniel R. Ilgen and colleagues outlined how psychological processes, such as recipients' perceptions of feedback, acceptance of feedback, desire to respond to feedback, and intended responses are influenced by such factors as the recipient's own characteristics, such as individual differences; characteristics of the source, including credibility; and characteristics of the feedback message, for example positive or negative sign.

Feedback has three primary uses in organizations. First, it can be used for employee development. Feedback can be used to communicate information to employees regarding their performance strengths and weaknesses so that they can be recognized for what they are doing well and can focus their efforts on areas that need improvement. A second use of feedback is for personnel decisions. For example, data from formal feedback sessions such as performance appraisals can be used to make decisions regarding who gets promoted, fired, or laid off. Finally, feedback can be used for documentation of organizational decisions. In particular, feedback records can be used to track employees' performance patterns over time; and these records can be used to protect organizations from lawsuits. These uses for feedback can be integrated into a comprehensive performance management system, which can be used to develop, motivate, and document employee behaviors.

Although feedback has traditionally been examined within the context of how it influences individual behaviors, more dynamic approaches have been recently adopted. In the following paragraphs, we review some of these perspectives to provide a more complete understanding of feedback processes in organizations.

FEEDBACK SEEKING BEHAVIOR

Moving beyond the view of the feedback target as a passive recipient of information, feedback has been conceptualized as an individual resource that people are motivated to actively seek. Originating in the work of Susan J. Ashford and Larry L. Cummings, this perspective portrays the workplace as an information environment in which individuals engage in feedback seeking behavior (FSB), enacting such strategies as monitoring the environment for feedback cues or making direct inquiries of actors in the environment in an effort to obtain personally relevant information.

A number of motivating factors can prompt an individual to engage in FSBs. First, feedback can reduce the uncertainty individuals experience regarding their roles or performance. Feedback can also serve an error corrective function and facilitate the attainment of competence or goal achievement. Furthermore, feedback has implications for self-evaluation and impression management. Individuals' desires to bolster their egos through obtaining positive feedback or, on the contrary, protect their egos by avoiding negative feedback can drive FSB. The greater the perceived value of feedback, the more proactive individuals will be in seeking it.

The costs perceived to accompany FSB can also affect the frequency of feedback seeking and the manner in which individuals pursue feedback. Costs of FSB are generally construed in terms of how much effort is necessary to acquire feedback information, concerns about image or loss of face, and the degree of inference required to make sense of feedback messages. Monitoring the feedback environment tends to necessitate less effort and invokes fewer image concerns than direct inquiry strategies. A trade-off exists between the accuracy and clarity of feedback and the effort and risk entailed in obtaining such feedback. Individuals desiring highly accurate feedback may forego the *safer* monitoring strategy in favor of inquiry. However, because feedback interpretation can be colored by such factors as recipient motives and expectations, even clearly communicated feedback messages can be misunderstood.

MULTISOURCE FEEDBACK

Multisource feedback, sometimes referred to as 360-degree feedback, is defined as feedback gathered about the target from two or more rating sources. These sources may include the self, supervisor, peers, direct reports, and customers. Multisource feedback can be used for a variety of purposes, including communicating performance expectations, setting developmental goals, establishing a learning culture, and tracking the effects of organizational change. In general, the benefits of a multisource as opposed to a traditional feedback system are predicated on five important assumptions:

1. Each of the rating sources can provide unique information about the target.

2. These multiple ratings will provide incremental validity over individual sources.

3. Feedback from multiple sources will increase the target's self-awareness and lead to behavioral change.

4. Feedback from multiple sources reduces idiosyncrasies of individual raters.

5. Ratees appreciate being involved in the process and tend to react favorably to this opportunity.

Research supporting the benefits of multisource feedback remains incomplete. Specifically, researchers need to clarify the aspects of multisource feedback requiring employee attention, the performance goals set by employees receiving multisource feedback, how employees react to discrepancies between multisource feedback and their performance goals, and how employees react to discrepancies between self-evaluations and multisource feedback. In addition, the individual differences and organizational conditions that determine when multisource feedback will be most beneficial are not well understood.

However, the literature has provided some suggestions for improving the effectiveness of multisource feedback. First, ratings should be made anonymously. Multisource feedback is more threatening to raters and ratees when ratings are not anonymous. Second, although multisource feedback is often used for evaluative purposes, it seems to garner the best response from employees when it is used for the purpose of employee development. However, there are benefits associated with using multisource feedback for administrative decisions; for example, multiple sources of feedback allow decisions to be based on more information. Another recommendation is that organizations should evaluate the effectiveness of multisource feedback programs and not simply assume that such programs are beneficial.

IMPLICATIONS OF FEEDBACK FOR PERFORMANCE: FEEDBACK INTERVENTION THEORY

A common assumption is that feedback yields consistent performance improvements. However, the literature indicates that feedback does not always result in large, across-the-board improvements in performance. In some conditions feedback improves performance, in other conditions it has no apparent effects on performance, and in certain circumstances it is actually detrimental to employee performance. To explain these inconsistencies, Avraham N. Kluger and Angelo S. DeNisi (1996) put forth the feedback intervention theory (FIT), which detailed specific conditions that help determine the effectiveness of feedback for improving employee performance.

Built largely around the notion of the feedback-standard comparison process that is the basis of control theory, FIT posits that feedback is used by individuals to evaluate their performance on some goal or standard. This comparison process indicates whether the individual's performance is above or below the standard, which has implications for subsequent performance. When performance, as informed by the feedback intervention, differs from the standard, feedback recipients can either alter their efforts, abandon the standard, alter the standard, or reject the feedback message altogether.

Because feedback has serious implications for the self, FIT posits that feedback interventions regulate behavior by changing the locus of attention to either the self or the task. According to FIT, feedback that directs attention toward the self can have a detrimental effect on performance because such feedback often depletes cognitive resources and generates affective reactions. An interesting implication of this is that feedback interventions containing praise can impede task performance because such interventions likely draw attention to the self rather than the task.

On the whole FIT suggests that there are three characteristics of feedback interventions that determine the effects of feedback on performance. First, the cues of the feedback message are important because they determine whether attention is drawn to the self or the task. Feedback interventions that contain information solely regarding performance outcomes have been shown to be detrimental to performance because they likely direct attention to the self. However, this pattern has not been displayed by feedback interventions that contain process information, which draws attention to the task. Therefore, Kluger and DeNisi (1996) suggested that the effectiveness of feedback is maximized when it directs attention to task motivation and learning processes and when the solution to the problem at hand is provided. Second, the nature of the task, such as task complexity, should be considered. In particular, feedback often improves motivation. However, improved motivation does not increase the amount of cognitive

resources available to complete a task. As such, motivation improves performance mostly when the task requires few cognitive resources. Finally, situational (e.g., the presence of goal-setting interventions) and personality variables (e.g., self-esteem) can moderate the effects of feedback interventions.

CONTEMPORARY PERSPECTIVES: PERSON–ENVIRONMENT ASPECTS OF FEEDBACK PROCESSES

Consistent with recent trends in industrial/organizational (I/O) psychology, feedback has been described as a dynamic process involving an interaction between characteristics of the individual and situation. In particular, employees' feedback orientations and the social context in which feedback is embedded have been identified as important determinants of rater and ratee behavior and reactions to feedback. Manuel London (2003) has recently identified these aspects of the person and the situation as important elements of what has been termed the organization's feedback culture. In particular, London suggested that organizations may create more global psychological settings—feedback-oriented cultures—by enhancing the quality of feedback given in the organization, emphasizing its importance, and supporting its use by employees. In such cultures, feedback is easily accessible and salient, and thus it is likely to influence employee beliefs and behaviors on a day-to-day basis.

Feedback orientation refers to a multidimensional construct that determines an individual's overall receptivity to feedback, guidance, and coaching. According to London, feedback orientation involves liking feedback; a behavioral propensity to seek feedback; a cognitive propensity to process feedback mindfully and deeply; sensitivity to others' view of oneself and to external propensity; a belief in the value of feedback; and feeling accountable to act on feedback. Individuals who have more favorable feedback orientations will believe that feedback is more useful, will feel accountable to use the feedback, and will be more likely to seek feedback from their work environments. In general, feedback orientation is likely to be more positive when the social context of the organization is more supportive of learning and development.

Recently, Paul E. Levy and his colleagues have provided a framework for understanding the social context of feedback processes in organizations.

According to this framework, distal variables such as organizational goals, legal climate, and competition; proximal process variables including organization's policies regarding feedback, feedback environment, and rater accountability; and proximal structural variables, for example purpose of feedback and feedback system features are each important aspects of the organizational environment for feedback. Although all these aspects of the social context influence feedback processes, the extent to which the workplace encourages and supports the use of feedback for the purposes of improving work performance has been identified as an element of the social context, which is especially important to feedback processes in organizations. In this vein Levy and his colleagues have started to examine the feedback environment, which is defined as contextual characteristics of organizations that support informal, day-to-day feedback processes.

The feedback environment goes beyond the formal presentation of feedback such as performance appraisal and includes information regarding how supervisors and coworkers mention and discuss feedback on a day-to-day basis. The following seven facets of the feedback environment have been identified:

1. Source credibility
2. Feedback quality
3. Feedback delivery
4. Favorable feedback
5. Unfavorable feedback
6. Source availability
7. Promotion of feedback seeking

Organizations that have more favorable feedback environments are also likely to have more effective feedback processes and communicate more information to employees that helps guide their behavior at work. Furthermore, there is evidence that the feedback environment is related to a variety of positive employee outcomes, such as increased affective commitment, job satisfaction, and citizenship behaviors, as well as decreased absenteeism. Therefore, to the extent that organizations develop favorable feedback environments, they will foster positive feedback orientations from employees. These factors will serve to develop feedback-oriented cultures and maximize the effectiveness of feedback processes in organizations.

CONCLUSION

The early feedback literature focused on feedback in a relatively narrow context. Feedback was traditionally viewed as a stimulus to which employees respond. More recently, researchers have taken a more dynamic approach, which includes examinations of active feedback seeking behavior, multisource feedback, feedback's relationship to performance, and an investigation of individual and situational variables that are associated with feedback-oriented cultures. Finally, researchers have started to focus on the feedback orientation of employees and contextual aspects of the feedback process that are associated with the provision, acceptance, and use of feedback in organizations.

—*Paul E. Levy, Christopher C. Rosen,
and Alison L. O'Malley*

See also Control Theory; Feedback; Feedback Seeking; Performance Appraisal; 360-Degree Feedback

FURTHER READING

Ashford, S. J., & Cummings, L. L. (1983). Feedback as an individual resource: Personal strategies of creating information. *Organizational Behavior and Human Performance, 32,* 370–398.

Ilgen, D. R., Fisher, C. D., & Taylor, M. S. (1979). Consequences of individual feedback on behavior in organizations. *Journal of Applied Psychology, 64,* 349–371.

Kluger, A. N., & DeNisi, A. (1996). The effect of feedback interventions on performance: A historical review, meta-analysis, and a preliminary feedback intervention theory. *Psychological Bulletin, 119,* 254–284.

Levy, P. E., & Williams, J. R. (2004). The social context of performance appraisal: A review and framework for the future. *Journal of Management, 30,* 881–905.

London, M. (2003). *Job feedback: Giving, seeking, and using feedback for performance improvement* (2nd ed.). Mahwah, NJ: Lawrence Erlbaum.

London, M., & Smither, J. W. (2002). Feedback orientation, feedback culture, and the longitudinal performance management process. *Human Resource Management Review, 12,* 81–100.

PERSONALITY

Despite the fact that many scholars have offered formal definitions of personality for almost 100 years, no consensus on any single definition has been achieved. In fact, a survey of 50 textbooks devoted to the study of personality would quite likely result in 50 distinct definitions of the term. Perhaps the reason that scholars have not agreed on a single definition is because of the broad scope encompassed by the notion of human personality. Clyde Kluckhohn and Henry A. Murray have suggested that human personality can be addressed at three distinct levels:

1. How we are like all other people

2. How we are like some other people

3. How we are like no other people

At the broadest level, Kluckhohn and Murray's framework suggests that there are some aspects of behavior that are common to all members of the human species. Murray, for example, in his classic taxonomy of needs, included a set of viscerogenic needs that are shared by all people. This category of needs, representing those things that humans need to survive, includes the need for air, the need for water, and the need for heat avoidance. Likewise, Abraham Maslow, in his specification of the hierarchy of needs, suggested that an individual's psychological needs could not be addressed unless the basic physiological (e.g., food, water) and safety (e.g., security, avoidance of pain) needs were met.

At the second level—the way we are like some other people—Kluckhohn and Murray suggested that, when considering specific aspects of personality, individuals will share similarities with some but not all people. Within contemporary personality psychology, this level of personality description is where the notion of personality traits resides. Traits can be defined as characteristic behaviors, thoughts, and feelings of an individual that tend to occur across diverse situations and are relatively stable over time. A trait, once identified, is something that all people possess, but to differing degrees. For example, although all people can be described in terms of their extroversion, some people are outgoing and social, whereas others tend to be more introverted and reserved. Thus in a trait we can be said to be like some other people.

At the third level of personality description is how we are like no other people. This level of explanation includes those aspects of our personality that make us unique individuals. As such, this level includes the experiences we have had in our own histories that

have shaped the way we think, feel, and act. In his writings about this level of personality description, Daniel P. McAdams has suggested that the goal of studying personality at this level is to understand individuals in the context of their personal life stories.

IDIOGRAPHIC VERSUS NOMOTHETIC SCIENCE

A debate has existed among personality scholars about the best approach for studying personality. Many scholars have argued that personality is best studied at the third level of Kluckhohn and Murray's framework. Science at this level is idiographic, and knowledge of personality is gained through in-depth studies of particular individuals. However, other scholars have argued that personality is best studied at Kluckhohn and Murray's second level. Science at this level is nomothetic, involving the study of general principles through the examination and comparison of many individuals. The debate over which of these approaches yields better information about the nature of human personality has, at times, been quite hostile. Although the debate has largely been argued in terms of methodological issues (i.e., the benefits and limitations of idiographic and nomothetic science), the heart of the argument is about the most appropriate level at which to understand personality. As such, the debate is in many ways pointless, because information from both levels of personality is necessary to develop a full understanding of the complexities of human personality.

LEVELS OF PERSONALITY DESCRIPTION AND INDUSTRIAL/ ORGANIZATIONAL PSYCHOLOGY

All three of Kluckhohn and Murray's levels of description are important for understanding human behavior in workplace contexts. For example, if a person's basic needs are not being met, we might come to understand why the individual no longer appears to be driven for success at work. Likewise, if we were to know an individual's personal history, we might better understand the person's problems with authority from a supervisor. However, despite the applicability of the first and third levels of personality description, almost all applications of personality to industrial/organizational (I/O) psychology are associated with the second level of personality description (i.e., how we are like some other people), and more specifically, with the notion of personality traits.

What Is a Trait?

There are two perspectives on the concept of personality traits. A first perspective is that traits are internal mechanisms that cause behavior. From this perspective, agreeableness, for example, is something within an individual that causes the person to behave in an agreeable manner. Hans J. Eysenck's theory of extroversion is an example of this perspective. Specifically, he theorized that introverts have a higher baseline level of arousal than do extroverts. When placed in a social situation with considerable stimulation, the introvert (with an already high level of arousal) would be predicted to become easily overaroused. In an attempt to reduce that overarousal, the introvert would engage in introverted behaviors, such as withdrawing from the situation. In contrast the extrovert, with a lower level of baseline arousal, would behave in an extroverted manner to obtain stimulation from the environment, thereby increasing the level of arousal (i.e., so as to avoid underarousal). According to Eysenck, then, the trait of extroversion is an internal biological process that causes behavior. Data have provided support for this internal mechanism approach to personality traits. Additionally, behavior genetic research, which has found that approximately 50% of variation in many traits can be explained by genetic influences, also points to a causal mechanism behind trait-related behavior.

A second perspective, typified by the act-frequency approach, is that personality traits are nothing more than descriptive categories of behavior. As such, a trait is a label for a set of related behaviors or acts. Acts that fall into the trait of sociability include talking to a stranger on an elevator, calling friends just to say hello, talking to coworkers in the hallway, or having a conversation with a clerk at a store. There could be hundreds of acts falling within this trait classification. A person with a high standing on this trait engages in this class of acts across situations more often than do other people. This approach is completely descriptive; there is no statement about the psychological processes that lead persons to behave the way they do. Although the acts people engage in may be caused by internal causal mechanisms, the act frequency approach does not specify those mechanisms.

The Structure of Personality Traits

Personality researchers have sought to develop a structure of personality traits for nearly 100 years. Much of this work has been based on studies of words in the English language, the so-called lexical hypothesis. The central idea of this hypothesis is that important aspects of human behavior will be encoded in the language. As such, it has been reasoned, a comprehensive understanding of personality traits can be derived from an examination of a language. The culmination of studies of the English lexicon is a structure of personality known as the Big Five. The Big Five taxonomy of personality is a hierarchical representation of the trait domain, with five broad traits representing the highest level of the classification structure. These five traits include the following:

1. **Neuroticism:** Anxious, temperamental, nervous, moody versus confident, relaxed, unexcitable

2. **Extroversion:** Sociable, energetic, active, assertive versus shy, reserved, withdrawn, unadventurous

3. **Openness:** Intellectual, innovative, artistic, complex versus unimaginative, simple, unsophisticated

4. **Agreeableness:** Trusting, trustful, helpful, generous versus cold, harsh, rude, unsympathetic

5. **Conscientiousness:** Organized, neat, thorough, systematic, efficient versus careless, undependable, haphazard, sloppy

Although adversaries of the Big Five remain and have raised notable criticisms, the Big Five is the dominant perspective on the organization of personality traits within contemporary personality psychology.

It is expected that sets of more narrowly defined traits lie under each of these broad traits. For example, it has been proposed that the broad trait of conscientiousness can be broken down into more narrowly defined traits of dependability and achievement striving. Personality researchers, however, are far from reaching consensus on the precise number or nature of these narrowly defined traits at the next level of the hierarchy.

COMPOUND TRAITS

Behavior is clearly complex, and many behaviors, especially those relevant to I/O contexts, are not a function of any single trait. Consistent with this line of thinking, more than one trait is often found to relate to particularly important work-related behaviors. In these cases researchers have proposed the notion of compound traits, which involve the combination of fundamental personality variables into a new personality variable that is capable of predicting a particular criterion. Perhaps the best known example of a compound personality variable is that of integrity. Research has demonstrated that scores on integrity tests—designed to be predictive of counterproductive employee behaviors—are notably related to the Big Five traits of conscientiousness, agreeableness, and (negatively) neuroticism. Thus the trait of integrity can be thought of as, at least in part, the confluence of these three Big Five dimensions. Other compound personality variables include customer service orientation and managerial potential. A unique aspect of compound personality traits is that they tend to result in criterion-related validities that are higher than those of the fundamental personality traits that compose them. Meta-analyses have shown, for example, that integrity tests tend to have greater predictive validity than do the individual traits of conscientiousness, agreeableness, or neuroticism.

Trait Personality and I/O Psychology

The role of personality within I/O psychology has had a rather tumultuous history. Today, however, personality is a topic of notable interest to both researchers and practitioners.

RESEARCH

Much of the research on personality in I/O contexts has sought to identify whether and which personality traits are related in meaningful ways to important organizationally relevant behaviors. Primary research and subsequent meta-analyses have demonstrated that personality traits are related to such organizational behaviors as task performance, contextual performance, performance in training, job choice, leadership, job satisfaction, and perceptions of organizational justice, among others. This research has led to a better understanding of the personal characteristics associated with important work behaviors. For example, by studying how personality traits are associated with leadership, a better understanding of those individual characteristics associated with effective leadership has been developed.

Most research (and application) involving personality within I/O psychology is associated with the act-frequency approach to personality traits. A relationship between a personality trait and a criterion, as interpreted from an act-frequency perspective, suggests only that the behaviors associated with the trait classification are also important for the criterion. By way of example, an act frequency interpretation of a relationship between extroversion and leadership would suggest that some of the acts associated with the trait of extroversion are also associated with effective leadership. Although this research is certainly useful and informative, it is descriptive in nature; there is no identification or explication of the mechanisms through which personality traits cause organizationally relevant behavior.

APPLICATION

The primary application of personality in I/O contexts is the assessment of personality traits for purposes of personnel selection. The goal of preemployment testing is to make inferences about an individual's future behaviors in the workplace. Most assessments of personality traits for personnel selection are done through self-report questionnaires, but other methods can also be used to assess traits. If an applicant were to complete a self-report assessment of the trait of conscientiousness and receive a high score, an employer could surmise that this individual tends to engage in conscientious behaviors across situations and make the inference that the person will do so in the workplace as well. If the job requires behaviors that are associated with conscientious acts, this applicant could be desirable for the position. Meta-analytic research has shown that personality trait assessments can be predictive of job performance for a number of occupational groupings and across a range of performance criteria, with the strongest findings for the trait of conscientiousness.

When attempting to predict work-related behavior with personality trait assessments, care must be taken when choosing an appropriate criterion measure. The trait-situation debate taught personality researchers a great deal about what makes an appropriate criterion. The trait-situation debate arose when scholars began to argue that there was no consistency in behavior across situations. Research had shown, for example, that when children were put into various situations where they could behave honestly or dishonestly, the children did not behave in the same ways across situations. More specifically, a child who cheated on a test in one situation may turn in a lost dollar in another. This lack of observed consistency in trait-related behaviors across situations led these scholars to argue that traits were *convenient fictions,* and that situations were the stronger determinant of behavior. In further support of their point, these situationists argued that scores on personality trait assessments were not strongly related to observed behaviors. Although it took personality psychologists some time to respond to these arguments, they finally found their voice in the principle of aggregation. The principle of aggregation suggests that if behavior is considered across many situations, consistencies will emerge. These consistencies were interpreted as providing evidence in support of the existence of traits. Likewise, personality researchers argued that if behavior is aggregated across situations, scores from assessments of personality traits will be predictive of that aggregated behavior and will, in fact, account for as much variability in behavior as situations.

The lesson learned from the trait-situation debate and the resulting principle of aggregation is important for I/O psychology. Specifically, for personality to be predictive of organizationally relevant behaviors, those behaviors must be aggregated across situations. It will not be possible, for example, to predict whether an employee will be late next Tuesday on the basis of the conscientiousness score. It should be possible, however, to make a prediction regarding this person's tendency to be late over the course of a year. In short, personality does not predict specific instances of behavior well, but it can predict lawful patterns of behavior. This is a point that I/O researchers and practitioners must keep in mind. There are several cases in the published literature where researchers have used a single instance of behavior as a criterion, and have, not surprisingly, failed to find the expected association between personality trait scores and the criterion measure.

Although personality trait assessments for purposes of personnel selection were traditionally administered in a paper-and-pencil format, it is becoming increasingly common for preemployment personality tests to be computer administered. Many companies are even beginning to use Web-based administrations, where a test taker can complete the test in an unproctored environment. Although research evaluating this mode of test administration is still emerging, initial evidence suggests that mean scores are similar between proctored and unproctored environments and that the criterion-related validity of the assessments is similar.

SUMMARY

Personality is a broad field within psychology that has been studied at various levels, from single individuals to groups of people to people in general. Within I/O psychology, almost all work on personality has focused on personality traits, or stable tendencies to behave in certain ways. Personality traits have been found to relate to a wide variety of employee behaviors at work. An emerging notion is that of compound traits, or broad personality dimensions that are associated with several more fundamental personality dimensions and are predictive of important work-related behaviors. The primary application of personality to I/O contexts is preemployment testing, where scores on personality tests are used to make predictions about people's future behaviors at work. When attempting to predict behavior from personality traits, it is essential for the I/O researchers and practitioners to keep in mind the principle of aggregation.

—*Eric D. Heggestad*

See also Big Five Taxonomy of Personality; Individual Differences; Personality Assessment

FURTHER READING

Barrick, M. R., & Mount, M. K. (1991). The Big Five personality dimensions and job performance: A meta-analysis. *Personnel Psychology, 44,* 1–26.

Buss, D. M., & Craik, K. H. (1983). The act frequency approach to personality. *Psychological Review, 90,* 105–126.

Guilford, J. P. (1959). *Personality.* New York: McGraw-Hill.

Hough, L. M., & Ones, D. (2001). The structure, measurement, validity, and use of personality variables in industrial, work, and organizational psychology. In N. Anderson (Ed.), *Handbook of industrial, work, and organizational psychology* (Vol. 1, pp. 233–277). Thousand Oaks, CA: Sage.

McAdams, D. P. (1995). What do we know when we know a person? *Journal of Personality, 63,* 365–396.

PERSONALITY ASSESSMENT

Personality assessment is the process of gathering information about an individual to make inferences about personal characteristics including thoughts, feelings, and behaviors. Raymond B. Cattell identified three primary sources of obtaining such personality information: life-data, information collected from objective records; test-data, information obtained in constructed situations where a person's behavior can be observed and objectively scored; and questionnaire-data, or information from self-report questionnaires. Each type of data is used to make assessments of personality within contemporary industrial/organizational (I/O) psychology. Common forms of life-data might include information contained in a résumé or an application blank and examinations of court, financial, or driving records in background checks. Test-data would include scores on personality-based dimensions derived from the assessment center method. However, by far the most common form of personality data in I/O psychology is questionnaire-data.

Self-report measures of personality can be divided into two broad categories: clinical and nonclinical. Self-report clinical measures, such as the Minnesota Multiphasic Personality Inventory (MMPI), have been used for some workers, such as airline pilots and police officers, to ensure that a potential employee does not suffer from an underlying psychological disorder. These clinical measures are generally given along with an interview (life-data) in the context of an individual assessment. Decisions to use these clinical evaluations for personnel selection, however, must be made carefully, because there is a notable possibility of violating the Americans With Disabilities Act.

Nonclinical self-report personality assessments, which are much more widely used than clinical assessments, are typically designed to assess personality traits. Personality traits are characteristic behaviors, thoughts, and feelings of an individual that tend to occur across diverse situations and are relatively stable over time. A trait that has been particularly important in the context of I/O psychology is conscientiousness, which is associated with a tendency to be organized, thorough, systematic and efficient. Assuming that these characteristics are desirable in an employee, a self-report questionnaire may be administered to make inferences about the conscientiousness of individuals within an applicant pool.

CONTENT VERSUS EMPIRICAL SCALE DEVELOPMENT

Although there are numerous approaches to constructing a personality assessment, two broad approaches can be identified. By far the more common approach to scale development is the content approach. In this approach items are written based on a theory of the construct the set of items is intended to measure. By way of example, an item such as *I enjoy the company of others* might be written for a sociability scale. Once written, the items are then typically empirically evaluated using principles of construct validation. As factor analysis is frequently used to evaluate items, this approach is also commonly referred to as the *factor analytic approach.*

As P. E. Meehl (1945) pointed out, however, interpreting an individual's response to such an item requires certain assumptions. For example, it must be assumed that all respondents have interpreted the item in the same way, that people are aware of and can report their own behavior, and that people are willing to tell you about their behavior. Some personality measurement theorists felt these assumptions were untenable and suggested a different approach to personality test construction, the empirical keying approach. According to this approach, a personality item is useful to the extent that responses to it accurately differentiate two groups. For example, an item would be included on a depression scale if, and only if, depressed people responded to the item differently from nondepressed people. In the classic empirical keying approach the content of the item is irrelevant; whether the item appears theoretically related to the construct does not matter. Because the response to the item is considered to be the behavior of interest, interpretation of scores from an empirically keyed measure does not require the assumptions associated with the content approach. Although the empirical keying approach was the basis for such well-known measures as the MMPI and the California Psychological Inventory, the vast majority of personality assessments in use today are based on the content approach to scale development.

NORMATIVE VERSUS IPSATIVE ASSESSMENT

Most personality assessments given in I/O contexts provide normative scores. Normative scores result when the responses to one item are independent from responses to other items. The common Likert-type rating scale, in which the respondents use the scale to place themselves along the trait continuum as represented by a single item, will result in normative scale scores. Ipsative scores, in contrast, result from response formats in which respondents choose, rank order, or otherwise indicate preference among a set of statements presented in an item. The Myers-Briggs Type Indicator is a well-known measure that provides ipsative scores.

Normative and ipsative scores result in different inferences about a person's trait standing. Normative scores allow for inferences regarding the amount of a trait that an individual possesses *compared with other people*. Ipsative scores, in contrast, support inferences about the amount of a trait possessed by the individual *compared with the other traits assessed by the measure*. Thus, a high score on a particular scale in an ipsative measure does not suggest that the respondent has a high standing on that trait, but suggests rather that the respondent has a higher standing on that trait than on any of the other traits assessed by the measure. Ipsative measures, therefore, are useful for identifying a person's particular strengths and weaknesses (i.e., intraindividual differences) and may be particularly useful in vocational guidance contexts. In many I/O contexts, however, the explicit desire is to compare the scores from a set of people (i.e., interindividual differences), as in personnel selection. When comparing people is the goal, ipsative scores are inappropriate and such measures should not be used.

ORIGINS OF PERSONALITY ASSESSMENT IN I/O PSYCHOLOGY

Applications of personality assessment within I/O psychology began as early as 1915 with the creation of the Division of Applied Psychology and the Bureau of Salesmanship Research at the Carnegie Institute of Technology. In addition to developing technologies for the selection of salesmen, this group of researchers also sought to develop measures of personality (or temperament/character as it was referred to at that time). Personality assessment gained further acceptance during World War I when United States military researchers developed the Woodworth Personal Data Sheet to identify individuals who might be susceptible to *war neuroses*. With the development of several multitrait assessment tools, the popularity of personality testing grew through the 1940s and 1950s. For example, a survey of more than 600 American

companies conducted in 1953 indicated that nearly 40% of those companies used measures of personality or vocational interests in their selection systems.

Three factors led to a marked decline in the popularity of personality testing in applied contexts during the 1960s and 1970s. First, two influential literature reviews were published that suggested that there was little evidence for the criterion-related validities of personality measures for the prediction of job performance. Second, the trait-situation debate dominated personality psychology over this period of time. On the situationist side of the debate, led by Walter Mischel, it was argued that aspects of the situation, not personal characteristics, were the driving force behind behavior. Third, Title VII of the Civil Rights Act of 1964 brought increased legal responsibilities to the use of assessments in the context of personnel decisions. Based largely on these factors, many organizations decided to forgo personality assessments in their selection systems, opting to avoid possible legal issues resulting from the administration of these tests.

Personality testing was given new life in applied contexts during the 1980s and early 1990s. Personality theorists finally found their voice in the trait-situation debate, effectively arguing that personal characteristics can predict behavior. The heart of the argument was the principle of aggregation, which suggests personality generally does not predict single instances of behavior well, but it does predict lawful patterns in behavior across diverse situations. But the biggest boon to personality assessment in I/O contexts was the emergence of the Big Five and subsequent meta-analyses demonstrating the criterion-related validities of some of these broad traits.

CRITERION-RELATED VALIDITY AND UTILITY OF PERSONALITY ASSESSMENT

One reason for the lack of strong criterion-related validity findings for personality assessments in the 1950s was the *broadside approach* taken by researchers. This tendency to correlate every available personality test score with all available performance measures was said to have resulted in large numbers of small criterion-related validity coefficients, many of which would have been expected, on the basis of theory, to be small. With the emergence of the Big Five trait taxonomy in the 1980s, conceptual links between the traits and the criterion variables could be drawn. A result of this better predictor-criterion linkage was stronger evidence for the criterion-related validities of personality assessments. To date, numerous meta-analyses on the relationships between personality test scores and measures of work performance have resulted in positive findings. The strongest findings have been associated with the conscientiousness trait, which seems to be associated with most job-related criteria (i.e., performance, training, attendance, etc.) across almost all jobs. However, the criterion-related validities remain modest, even after the corrections typically employed in meta-analytic procedures. For example, one of the most widely cited meta-analyses reported corrected criterion-related validities for conscientiousness in the range of .20 to .22 across performance criteria and occupational groups.

Many personality assessments frequently used in I/O settings were not created explicitly for applied use. That is, the questionnaires were created to provide a general assessment of personality; and as such, the items in these measures tend to be very general and do not typically convey information about any specific situational context. When responding to such acontextual items, respondents may consider their behaviors across a wide range of social situations, such as at home with family, at a gathering with friends, at a public event, or at work. Research has found, however, that when the item content was contextualized in a work setting, for example by adding the phrase *at work* to the end of each item, the criterion-related validity of the test was higher than when acontextual items were used. Thus, by including work-based situational cues within personality items, the criterion-related validity of personality scores can be enhanced.

Despite the improved validity associated with the contextualization of personality items, the criterion-related validity of personality assessments is clearly lower than that of many other available selection tools, such as ability tests, assessment centers, and work samples. Despite the lower criterion-related validities, personality assessment can still be of value in selection contexts. First, the correlations between personality test scores and scores from cognitive ability tests tend to be small, suggesting that personality tests can improve prediction of performance above and beyond cognitive ability test scores. Second, personality test scores tend not to show the large mean differences between racial groups that are found with cognitive ability tests. Third, these tests can often be administered quickly and typically are relatively inexpensive.

IMPRESSION MANAGEMENT AND FAKING

A major issue facing the application of personality assessment is the possibility of impression management, which is also known as socially desirable responding or faking. Impression management occurs when an individual changes a response to a personality item to create a positive impression. Consider a situation in which a person would, under normal circumstances, respond to the item *I am a hard worker* with a response of *neutral* on a five point Likert-type scale. If that same person were presented with the same item when applying for a job and responded with *agree completely* to increase the chances of being hired, then the individual would be engaging in impression management.

The precise effects of faking on the criterion-related validity of personality measures is still being debated, but it would appear that the effect is rather small. However, impression management does appear to negatively influence the quality of selection decisions. Although this may seem contradictory, it must be recognized that the validity coefficient takes into account the full range of personality test scores, whereas selection is generally concerned only with scores over a certain portion, usually the high end, of that distribution. In a top-down selection context, the quality of selection decisions appears to be negatively affected by the fact that a number of low performing people will rise to the top of the personality test distribution, increasing their chances of being selected. Researchers are currently examining the precise impact of faking on selection and are working on ways to deal with faking to maintain the usefulness of personality assessments.

SUMMARY

Personality assessment is the process of gathering information about a person to make an inference about the individual's characteristic ways of behaving. Although there are numerous methods for assessing personality, the most common form of assessment in I/O psychology is the self-report questionnaire. Meta-analyses have shown that these self-report measures can provide information that is valid for predicting various organizational outcomes. Further, that criterion validity may be enhanced by writing items that are contextualized in workplace settings. Finally, although personality assessments can provide useful information for making personnel decisions, intentional response distortion on the part of the respondent may lessen the usefulness of those scores in applicant contexts.

—*Eric D. Heggestad*

See also Big Five Taxonomy of Personality; Impression Management; Individual Assessment; Normative Versus Ipsative Measurement; Personality; Reliability; Validity

FURTHER READING

Barrick, M. R., & Mount, M. K. (1991). The Big Five personality dimensions and job performance: A meta-analysis. *Personnel Psychology, 44,* 1–26.

Guion, R. M., & Gottier, R. F. (1965). Validity of personality measures in personnel selection. *Personnel Psychology, 18,* 135–164.

Kanfer, R., Ackerman, P. L., Murtha, T., & Goff, M. (1995). Personality and intelligence in industrial organizational psychology. In D. H. Saklofske & M. Zeidner (Eds.), *International handbook of personality and intelligence* (pp. 577–602). New York: Plenum.

Meehl, P. E. (1945). The dynamics of structured personality tests. *Journal of Clinical Psychology, 1,* 296–303.

Mueller-Hanson, R., Heggestad, E. D., & Thornton, G. C., III. (2003). Faking and selection: Considering the use of personality from a select-in and a select-out perspective. *Journal of Applied Psychology, 88,* 348–355.

Schmit, M. J., Ryan, A. M., Stierwalt, S. L., & Powell, A. B. (1995). Frame-of-reference effects on personality scale scores and criterion-related validity. *Journal of Applied Psychology, 80,* 607–620.

PERSON–ENVIRONMENT FIT

Person–environment (PE) fit refers to the degree of match between individuals and some aspect of their work environment. The concept of PE fit is firmly rooted in the tradition of Kurt Lewin's maxim that $B = f(PE)$; behavior is a function of both person and environment. The early interactional psychologists emphasized Lewin's perspective and developed a perspective that individuals' behaviors and attitudes are determined jointly by personal and environmental conditions. On the person side, characteristics may include interests; preferences; knowledge, skills, and abilities (KSAs); personality traits; values; or goals. On the environment side, characteristics may include vocational norms, job demands, job characteristics, organizational cultures and climates, and company or group goals. Various synonyms have been used to describe fit, including congruence, match, similarity, interaction, correspondence, and need fulfillment.

The basic premise of PE fit research is that for each individual there are particular environments that are most compatible with that person's personal characteristics. If a person works in those environments, positive consequences including improved work attitudes and performance, as well as reduced stress and withdrawal behaviors, will result. Although the premise is straightforward, research on PE fit is one of the most eclectic domains in organizational psychology. In part this is because of the wide variety of conceptualizations, content dimensions, and measurement strategies used to assess fit. Questions about what we mean by the term *fit*, what characteristics constitute fit, and how to best assess fit are addressed in the following text.

WHAT DO WE MEAN BY *FIT?*

Although terms such as *congruence* or *match* seem to imply similarity, multiple conceptualizations of PE fit have been discussed in the literature. *Supplementary fit* exists when the individual and the environment are similar on a particular characteristic. The underlying mechanism is one of similarity-attraction, such that people tend to like interacting with other people and with environments that are similar to themselves in some way. Alternatively, *complementary fit* occurs when individuals' characteristics fill a gap in the current environment or the environment meets a need in the person. Complementary fit is based on the underlying process of need fulfillment, resulting in positive attitudinal and behavioral outcomes.

Research on stress and coping, which describes fit as adjustment, has elaborated on two distinct forms of complementary fit. The first is needs-supplies fit, which exists when a person's needs are met by the resources in the environment. The second is demands-abilities fit, which generally focuses on individuals' KSAs meeting environmental demands.

FIT ON WHAT?

PE fit research has generally concentrated on matching the individual to one of four levels of the environment:

1. Vocation

2. Job

3. Organization

4. Group

Each of these subtypes of PE fit emphasizes different person and environment characteristics as relevant to fit. Each type is briefly reviewed in the following text.

Person–Vocation Fit

The broadest form of PE fit is the fit between individuals and their vocations or occupations, generally labeled person–vocation (PV) fit. Vocational choice theories, such as those by John L. Holland, René Dawis, and L. H. Lofquist fall into this category. Holland proposed in 1985 that the RIASEC typology (people and vocations are characterized as realistic, investigative, artistic, social, enterprising, or conventional) suggests that people will be most satisfied if they pursue careers that are compatible with their interests. Fit is defined by the degree of match between an individual's interests and those of others who generally make up the person's chosen vocation. Dawis and Lofquist's theory of work adjustment posits that individuals and careers are compatible to the extent that personal traits (including skills, abilities, needs, and values) correspond with the requirements imposed by the environment, and personal needs are simultaneously met by the environment.

Reviews of the PV literature generally report moderate positive correlations between PV congruence and individual measures of well-being such as job and career satisfaction, stability, and personal achievement. Correlations are higher when focusing on the congruence with specialty areas within vocations. Consistent negative relationships have been found between fit and mental distress, somatic symptoms, changing vocations, and seeking satisfaction through leisure activities unrelated to work.

Person–Job Fit

A second type of fit concerns the relationship between an individual and a specific job. Labeled person–job (PJ) fit, this includes the match between a person's KSAs and the demands of a job (demands–abilities fit), or the person's needs and interests and the resources provided by the job (needs–supplies fit). Traditional notions of personnel selection, which began during World War II with the selection of soldiers into specific positions in the army, emphasized the importance of hiring people who possessed the requisite KSAs for particular jobs. Thus, PJ fit was defined from the organization's perspective, such that the most appropriately qualified people would be hired.

PJ fit from the needs-supplies perspective was the emphasis of work done by J. R. P. French, Jr., and colleagues on stress and adjustment. Their research presented a model that described psychosocial stress as the outcome of a discrepancy between the subjective environment and the subjective person (i.e., subjective PE fit), which in turn was the result of the fit between the objective environment and objective self. Thus, fit was equated to adjustment. PJ fit is also assessed in early definitions of job satisfaction, which emphasized satisfaction as the result of personal needs being met by a job. Over time scholars have separated job satisfaction (the affective outcome) from fit (the objective or perceived match that leads to the outcome). Yet because of the close relationship, PJ fit and job satisfaction are generally found to have a moderate to strong positive relationship. Other outcomes associated with PJ fit include organizational commitment, intent to quit, task performance, and strain.

Person–Organization Fit

Person–organization (PO) fit, defined broadly as the compatibility between people and organizational characteristics, is a third type of PE fit. Benjamin Schneider popularized this approach to fit with the attraction–selection–attrition (ASA) model, used to explain how homogeneity naturally results from organizational recruitment and selection processes. Although the ASA model emphasizes the antecedents and consequences of homogeneity at the organizational level, Jennifer Chatman proposed a model that emphasized PO fit from the individual's perspective. This interactive model of PO fit emphasizes the objective fit between individuals' values and those that senior management believe best represent the organization. Many researchers have used the notion of value congruence to assess PO fit but have followed French and colleagues' approach of emphasizing subjective or perceived fit, rather than objective fit. PO fit has also been assessed using personality traits, goals, and needs. Meta-analytic estimates demonstrate that

PO fit is most strongly associated with feelings of attachment to the organization, such as organizational commitment and intent to quit. Additional influences on contextual performance, or extrarole behavior, and turnover have been found.

Person–Group Fit

Finally, a fourth type of PE fit is the match between individuals and members of their immediate work groups. Most of the emphasis on person–group (PG) or person–team fit has been on demographic variables. The concept of relational demography suggests that individuals' attitudes and behaviors are influenced by the demographic similarity among teammates or coworkers. However, more recent studies have moved beyond demographic similarity to examine fit on deeper, less directly observable characteristics, including personality traits, goals, and KSAs. Outcomes most strongly associated with PG fit are group-level attitudes, including cohesion and satisfaction with coworkers, as well as contextual performance.

HOW CAN FIT BE MEASURED?

Debate over how to measure PE fit reflects the diversity of approaches outlined earlier. Each of the following strategies has been used to assess or infer PE fit.

Statistical Interactions

Traditional methods relied heavily on the use of statistical interactions, where the effect of the environment was moderated by the characteristics of the person, or vice versa. There was no requirement in such approaches that the dimensions of person and environment be commensurate (i.e., using the same dimensions), just that they were theoretically related. Fit was assumed to be supported if the interaction term explained significant variance in the outcomes, beyond the main effects of person and environment. This method captures objective, or actual, fit because person and environment are measured separately and fit is determined algebraically as the multiplicative interaction of the two terms.

Direct Measures

A second measurement strategy involves directly asking individuals whether they believe that a good PE fit exists. For example, people may be asked to assess how well their vocation or job satisfies their personal needs (PV and PJ fit respectively), how well their KSAs meet job requirements (PV fit), how compatible their values are with their organizations' (PO fit), or whether they share their coworkers' goals (PG fit). This type of assessment captures holistic assessments of subjective or perceived fit, because the individuals are asked to mentally calculate fit using whatever internal standards they wish to apply.

Indirect Measures

An alternative method for assessing subjective or perceived fit is to use indirect methods, in which person and environment variables are reported separately. This could be by the same person (perceived fit) or from two unique sources (objective fit). The actual calculation of fit is done by a researcher making an explicit comparison of these two descriptions. How these two are compared can be further differentiated into two categories:

Difference Scores. The primary means of indirect fit assessment has been the use of profile similarity indexes or difference scores. These methods assess the algebraic difference between the person and environment variables. Despite their popularity they have been heavily criticized because of the inability to determine whether person and environment contribute equally to the outcome and the loss of information on the absolute level of characteristics and the direction of differences, as well as overly restrictive statistical constraints. These limitations may result in inappropriate conclusions about the nature of the fit relationships under investigation.

Polynomial Regression. In response to the concerns over difference scores, J. R. Edwards and colleagues proposed polynomial regression as an alternative way to assess PE fit. At its core, this approach avoids using a single term to capture fit. Instead, both person and environment, and associated higher-order terms (P^2, $P \times E$, and E^2), are included as predictors in a regression. The relationship between these variables is then graphed in three-dimensional surface plots, which can be visually inspected, or characteristics of the surface (i.e., slopes and curvatures) can be statistically evaluated to determine whether a fit relationship is supported. This method requires large sample sizes and assesses fit on single dimensions (i.e., on one value) rather than across a set of dimensions (i.e., across a value profile). It provides a precise depiction of the relationship between person and environment variables but does not result in an effect size attributable to fit.

SUMMARY

Research on PE fit remains one of the most eclectic domains of organizational psychology. However it is conceptualized, operationalized, or assessed, results consistently demonstrate that people's perceptions of, and actual fit with, their environment has important consequences for work-related attitudes and behaviors.

—*Amy L. Kristof-Brown*

See also Careers; Individual Differences; Person–Job Fit; Person–Organization Fit; Person–Vocation Fit

FURTHER READING

Chatman, J. A. (1989). Improving interactional organizational research: A model of person–organization fit. *Academy of Management Review, 14,* 333–349.

Dawis, R. V., & Lofquist, L. H. (1984). *A psychological theory of work adjustment.* Minneapolis: University of Minnesota Press.

Edwards, J. R. (1991). Person–job fit: A conceptual integration, literature review, and methodological critique. In C. L. R. I. T. Cooper (Ed.), *International review of industrial and organizational psychology* (Vol. 6, pp. 283–357). Chichester, England: Wiley.

Edwards, J. R. (1994). The study of congruence in organizational behavior research: Critique and a proposed alternative. *Organizational Behavior and Human Decision Processes, 58,* 51–100.

Holland, J. E. (1985). *Making vocational choices: A theory of careers.* Englewood Cliffs, NJ: Prentice Hall.

Kristof, A. L. (1996). Person–organization fit: An integrative review of its conceptualizations, measurement, and implications. *Personnel Psychology, 49*(1), 1–49.

Kristof-Brown, A. L., Zimmerman, R. D., & Johnson, E. C. (2005). Consequences of individuals' fit at work: A meta-analysis of person–job, person–organization, person–group, and person–supervisor fit. *Personnel Psychology, 58,* 281–342.

Lewin, K. (1935). *A dynamic theory of personality.* New York: McGraw-Hill.

Schneider, B. (1987). The people make the place. *Personnel Psychology, 40,* 437–453.

PERSON–JOB FIT

Person–job (PJ) fit is defined as the compatibility between individuals and the job or tasks that they perform at work. This definition includes compatibility based on employee needs and job supplies available to meet those needs, as well as job demands and employee abilities to meet those demands. In the past, the term *PJ fit* has been used to describe fit with occupations or vocations as well, but more recently it has been distinguished from this broader form of fit.

Based firmly in interactional psychology, the underlying premise of PJ fit is that characteristics of the person and the job work jointly to determine individual outcomes. There are many theories that involve joint influence of person and job characteristics, but fit is a specific domain in which commensurate measurement is generally considered essential. Commensurate measures assess the person and job along the same content dimensions, thus allowing an assessment of fit or match to be determined. Often the combined effects of conceptually related person and job measures such as the need for achievement and job complexity are interpreted as PJ fit; however, because they employ noncommensurate measures they do not fall within the fit domain, as strictly defined. In the following text, further discussion on the various conceptualizations of PJ fit and their consequences is presented.

TWO CONCEPTUALIZATIONS OF PERSON–JOB FIT

Needs–Supplies Fit

Two primary conceptualizations characterize research on PJ fit. The first is the correspondence between employee needs or desires and the supplies that a job provides. Alternately labeled needs–supplies or supplies–values fit, this is the most commonly investigated form of PJ fit. Much of the research in this domain is based on Lyman Porter's need satisfaction questionnaire, or similar measures, which ask people to describe how much their current job provides (actual) of a particular characteristic and also how much of that characteristic is desired (ideal).

The basic notion of needs–supplies fit is that negative consequences result when job supplies fall short of personal needs, whereas positive consequences are maximized when environmental supplies exactly match personal needs. The theories imply, but often do not directly test, that negative consequences also result when there is an excess of supplies (i.e., the job provides more than what the individual wants or needs). Research by John R. P. French, Jr., Robert Caplan, and R. Van Harrison was some of the first to explicitly examine outcomes associated with conditions of both deficiency and excess. Their research, which spanned much of the 1960s and 1970s, emphasized the psychological and physiological strain that results from a mismatch between the subjective environment and person (that is, the environment as it is perceived by the individual, and the person as perceived by self).

In the mid-1990s Jeff Edwards elaborated on areas of *misfit,* suggesting four possible processes that can occur when job supplies do not correspond with individual needs. When excess supplies exist, individuals will benefit if they can either carry over these supplies to fulfill other needs, or conserve the excess to fulfill a later need. Alternatively, when excess supplies hinder the future fulfillment of needs (depletion) or interfere with fulfilling other needs, individuals will suffer from greater strain. Edwards proposed an advanced analytic strategy labeled polynomial regression and three-dimensional surface plot analysis to allow for closer inspection of misfit and fit relationships. These techniques were specifically proposed as alternatives to the commonly used algebraic difference scores or direct measures of the discrepancy between desired and actual job attributes.

Demands–Abilities Fit

The second conceptualization of PJ fit considers fit from the perspective of the organization rather than the individual. Demands–abilities fit occurs when the individual possesses the abilities (skills, knowledge, time, energy) to meet job demands. When environmental demands exceed personal abilities, strain and negative affective consequences are likely to result. When personal abilities exceed environmental demands, the four processes described previously (carryover, conservation, depletion, and interference) could also apply. The concept of demands–abilities fit is the basis for traditional selection techniques that seek to find qualified applicants to fill job vacancies. Research by David Caldwell and Charles O'Reilly III operationalized this approach by using a profile comparison process to examine the match of individual

abilities to specific task requirements. However, techniques such as polynomial regression could also be used to assess this conceptualization of fit.

CONSEQUENCES OF PERSON–JOB FIT

Person–job fit has been found to have the strongest positive correlations with job satisfaction and intent to hire, followed by moderate to strong positive correlations with organizational attraction, organizational commitment, and satisfaction with coworkers and supervisors. Moderate negative correlations exist with intent to quit and strain. With regard to behaviors, PJ fit is moderately correlated with overall performance and tenure (positive) and weakly associated with turnover (negative). For all outcomes, needs–supplies fit is a better predictor than demands–abilities fit, but for strain the effects are almost equivocal. In general, direct and indirect measures of perceived fit have stronger relationships with criteria than do measures of actual or objective fit. This is in keeping with French and colleagues' perspective that fit between the subjective person and environment is more proximal to outcomes than fit between the objective person and environment.

SUMMARY

Research on PJ fit has been popular since the early 1960s. In the beginning much of the PJ fit research was combined with research on person–vocation fit (see that entry in this volume) and was conducted under the rubric of need fulfillment or need satisfaction. More recently the trend has been to distinguish PJ fit from other forms of fit and to focus on areas of both fit and misfit as predictors of affective, behavioral, and physiological outcomes.

—*Amy L. Kristof-Brown*

See also Person–Environment Fit; Person–Organization Fit; Person–Vocation Fit

FURTHER READING

Caldwell, D. F., & O'Reilly, C. A., III. (1990). Measuring person–job fit with a profile comparison process. *Journal of Applied Psychology, 75,* 648–657.

Caplan, R. D. (1987). Person–environment fit theory: Commensurate dimensions, time perspectives, and mechanisms. *Journal of Vocational Behavior, 31,* 248–267.

Edwards, J. R. (1996). An examination of competing versions of the person–environment fit approach to stress. *Academy of Management Journal, 39*(2), 292–339.

French, J. R. P., Jr., Caplan, R. D., & Harrison, R. V. (1982). *The mechanisms of job stress and strain.* London: Wiley.

French, J. R. P., Jr., Rogers, W., & Cobb, S. (1974). Adjustment as person–environment fit. In D. A. H. G. V. Coelho & J. E. Adams (Eds.), *Coping and adaptation.* New York: Basic Books.

Porter, L. W. (1961). A study of perceived job satisfactions in bottom and middle management jobs. *Journal of Applied Psychology, 45,* 1–10.

PERSON–ORGANIZATION FIT

Person–organization (PO) fit is defined as the compatibility between people and organizations, which occurs when at least one entity provides what the other needs; they share similar fundamental characteristics; or both. This definition includes examples of mutual need fulfillment, value congruence between individuals and organizations, personality similarity between individuals and other members of the organization, and shared individual and organizational goals. PO fit has also been called person–culture fit.

Based in the interactionist perspective, in which both personal and environmental characteristics interact to predict individual outcomes, PO fit gained greatest prominence in the early 1990s. Since that time more than 100 studies have been conducted that emphasize the match between individuals and organizational cultures, not just the jobs within those organizations. In the text that follows, a brief history of the concept and its theoretical underpinnings, antecedents, and consequences are described.

A HISTORY OF PERSON–ORGANIZATION FIT

In 1958 Chris Argyris proposed that organizations were characterized by particular types of climates, which played an important role in the attraction and selection of organizational members. This view that companies hire the *right types* suggests that there is differential compatibility of individuals and organizations. In 1987 Benjamin Schneider elaborated on these ideas in what has become one the most

respected theories of interactionist psychology—the attraction–selection–attrition (ASA) framework. At its core the ASA framework proposes that the three aforementioned processes result in organizations characterized by homogeneous members, and structures, systems, and processes that reflect the characteristics of the people who *make the place.* Although principally concerned with predicting organizational-level outcomes and characteristics, the ASA framework has become the theoretical cornerstone for much of the research on PO fit.

In the late 1980s and early 1990s PO fit gained further prominence in the organizational psychology literature. This was in part because of the growing recognition of the importance of organizational cultures. Jennifer Chatman changed the focus from the ASA model that predicted organizational-level consequences to PO fit, because it affected individuals' attitudes and behaviors at work. Her definition of PO fit as individual/organizational (I/O) value congruence became the commonly accepted definition of the concept. This was coupled with the introduction of a measurement tool, the organizational culture profile, by Chatman and her colleagues Charles O'Reilly and David Caldwell, which has become the most widely used tool for operationalizing PO fit. In 1993 an *Academy of Management Executive* article by David Bowen and colleagues articulated the importance of selecting applicants for PO fit, as well as the traditional person–job (PJ) fit based on skills. In my review of the literature in 1996, I proposed the comprehensive definition that begins this entry to integrate the research on PO value congruence with other types of PO interaction such as need fulfillment, personality similarity, and goal congruence.

THEORETICAL UNDERPINNINGS OF PO FIT

There are two fundamental processes underlying PO fit. First, there is the concept of need fulfillment. As in other theories of person–environment (PE) fit, psychological need fulfillment represents a complementary perspective on fit, in which fit is determined by the extent to which the person's needs are met by the organizational environment or the organization's needs are met by the capabilities of the individual. Theories of need fulfillment suggest that dissatisfaction results when needs go unmet, and may also be the consequence of *overfulfillment,* depending on the need. The second theoretical tradition in PO fit research is the concept of I/O congruence, a supplementary approach to fit. Theoretically, congruence affects attitudes and behaviors because people are more attracted to similar others. Similarity facilitates communication, validates choices, and socially reinforces personal identities. Taken together, these mechanisms provide alternative, but not competing, explanations for why PO fit influences individual outcomes at work.

ANTECEDENTS OF PERSON–ORGANIZATION FIT

Research has emphasized recruitment, selection, and socialization as antecedents to PO fit. These processes closely mirror the three components of the ASA framework: attraction, selection, and attrition. During recruitment, organizations seek to convey particular images of themselves to applicants. In turn, job applicants draw inferences about organizational culture based on all available information, including features of the compensation system, interactions with current employees, and recruitment materials. There is evidence that both job applicants and organizational recruiters consider PO fit during selection decisions, placing it only slightly behind fit with the job in terms of importance. Socialization mechanisms, both formal and informal, are then used to convey the values and other key characteristics of the organization.

CONSEQUENCES OF PERSON–ORGANIZATION FIT

Person–organization fit has been found to have the strongest positive correlations with organizational commitment and organizational satisfaction, followed by moderate positive correlations with job satisfaction, trust, and satisfaction with coworkers and supervisors, and moderate negative correlations with intent to quit and strain. With regard to behaviors, PO fit is weakly correlated with task performance (positive) and turnover (negative), but moderately correlated with contextual performance or extrarole behaviors (positive). For all outcomes except tenure, direct measures of perceived fit have the strongest relationship with criteria, followed by indirect measures of the fit between personal characteristics and perceived organizational attributes, and then by indirect measures of the person and objective measures of the organization.

SUMMARY

Research on PO fit has proliferated since the early 1990s. Despite debates over complementary versus supplementary conceptualizations, values versus other content dimensions, and how to best measure PO fit (see Person–Environment Fit for a more in-depth discussion of these issues), there is compelling evidence that individuals are differentially compatible with various organizations, and that this compatibility has important consequences.

—*Amy L. Kristof-Brown*

See also Person–Environment Fit; Person–Job Fit; Person–Vocation Fit

FURTHER READING

Cable, D. M., & Edwards, J. R. (2004). Complementary and supplementary fit: A theoretical and empirical integration. *Journal of Applied Psychology, 89,* 822–834.

Chatman, J. A. (1989). Improving interactional organizational research: A model of person–organization fit. *Academy of Management Review, 14,* 333–349.

Chatman, J. A. (1991). Matching people and organizations: Selection and socialization in public accounting firms. *Administrative Science Quarterly, 36,* 459–484.

Kristof-Brown, A. L., Zimmerman, R. D., & Johnson, E. C. (2005). Consequences of individuals' fit at work: A meta-analysis of person–job, person–organization, person–group, and person–supervisor fit. *Personnel Psychology, 58,* 281–342.

Schneider, B. (1987). The people make the place. *Personnel Psychology, 40,* 437–453.

PERSON–VOCATION FIT

The idea that sparked person–vocation (PV) fit came from Frank Parsons, one of the earliest figures in vocational psychology, who believed that people need a clear understanding of themselves and the environment in which they work to be happy in their jobs and careers.

PV fit is the relationship between individuals and their vocations or occupations. PV literature has generally reported positive correlations between PV congruence and individual measures of well-being such as job and career satisfaction, stability, and personal achievement.

A number of theories either directly or indirectly have relevance for understanding PV fit. Some of the more prominent of these are detailed in the following text.

HOLLAND'S THEORY

John Holland's theory of vocational personality types, first presented in 1959, is one of the most influential and researched theories in psychology. Holland proposed a typology that divided interests and work environments into six types. He organized the types spatially around the six points of a hexagon. The types are as follows:

1. Realistic (likes hands-on tasks)
2. Investigative (analyzes ideas)
3. Artistic (creative and original)
4. Social (helps people)
5. Enterprising (takes on leadership role)
6. Conventional (follows rules and orders)

The main premise of the theory is that individuals search for work environments that allow them to express their vocational interests and associate with other people with similar interests. Furthermore, the interaction between the person's interests and the work environment's requirements is likely to influence job satisfaction and tenure. For example, if Jane is interested in the artistic domain, then she would be most likely to find satisfaction in work that has a large creative component. If, however, Jane's work environment is incongruent with her interests, say she is working in a conventional environment that does not allow her to do creative work, then she may express dissatisfaction with her job.

Holland based his theory of vocational types on empirical data derived from correlational and factor analytic studies. A plethora of research studies provide evidence of validity for the major tenets of Holland's theory for Western societies. Recently, research on the evidence of validity for Holland's theory for non-Western cultures has begun to appear in the literature. A benefit of Holland's theory is the ease with which the propositions and constructs can be applied to a career counseling setting. For example, understanding how the six vocational types relate to one another helps a person to match interests with the work environment. Moreover, the scale development of all major interest inventories has been influenced by Holland's theory, and instruments such as the Strong Interest Inventory and the Self-Directed Search include scales constructed to measure the six vocational types.

THEORY OF WORK ADJUSTMENT

The theory of work adjustment (TWA) was developed at the University of Minnesota by René Dawis and Lloyd Lofquist. Like Holland's theory, TWA proposes that a person will stay in a job longer if there is congruence, or correspondence in the TWA terminology, between the person and the work environment. Specifically, TWA postulates that if a person's abilities, needs, and values match the analogous workplace environment components (i.e., ability requirements and reinforcers), then job satisfaction and satisfactoriness occur. Tenure, or longevity on the job, in turn, is a result of the individual's satisfaction and satisfactoriness. In other words, the individual is satisfied if the work environment matches the person's values and needs, and the environment deems the individual satisfactory if the person's abilities or skills meet the requirements of the job. Values, an important aspect of the TWA, are grouped into six categories:

1. Achievement
2. Comfort
3. Status
4. Altruism
5. Safety
6. Autonomy

Ability also is an important consideration.

In some situations, an individual's flexibility may help that person to compensate for a lack of correspondence. In other words, people who are flexible can tolerate noncorrespondence more than individuals who are inflexible.

The Theory of Work Adjustment has been applied in areas such as career counseling, career assessment, and selection. Several instruments, such as the Minnesota Importance Questionnaire (MIQ) and the Minnesota Satisfaction Questionnaire (MSQ), have been developed to measure TWA variables.

PERSON–ENVIRONMENT FIT THEORY OF STRESS

The person–environment (PE) fit theory of stress comes from the field of occupational health psychology. Robert Caplan, John French, and R. Van Harrison contributed to the PE fit theory of stress, which developed from the perspective of PE misfit instead of the PE correspondence view of TWA. According to the theory, PE misfit causes some disturbance in the person both psychologically and physically. The theory first makes a distinction between the person and the environment and their reciprocal relationship. Then, person and environment are divided into both objective and subjective components. Subjective refers to the perception of a person's characteristics or environment. Objective refers to the personal characteristics and physical and social environment of an individual that can be observed or assessed by others.

The theory states that if PE misfit surfaces, two sets of outcomes may occur. Psychological, physical, and behavior strains compose the first set of outcomes. These negative consequences eventually lead to poor health and unresolved PE misfit. The second set of outcomes includes coping and defensive behaviors, which are used to resolve the PE misfit. Some coping strategies, used to find ways to balance the current misfit, come from objective PE fit. One such strategy is adapting to the environment. Defensive coping strategies, such as denial, provide a means for enhancing subjective PE fit. The PE fit theory of stress also suggests that outcomes of subjective misfit can be reduced by shrinking objective misfit, and vice versa.

ATTRACTION–SELECTION– ATTRITION MODEL

In the field of industrial/organizational (I/O) psychology, Benjamin Schneider's attraction–selection-attrition (ASA) model looks at organizational behavior from the person-oriented side. The model proposes that an organization is defined by the *collective characteristics* of the people who work there, which are hypothesized to develop through three steps:

1. Employee attraction to the job

2. Employer selection of employees

3. Departure by employees who are not congruent with the work environment

In other words, when people are attracted to an organization by its characteristics, their personalities are implicitly congruent with the organization's characteristics. Then, the organization chooses whom to hire based on whether the individual's attributes match what the organization wants. If the individual does not fit well with others in the organization, this person is asked to leave. As a result, characteristics of the employees will match the objectives of the organization; and ideally, people within the organization will get along because they are similar to one another. Some researchers, however, argue that adding diversity to an organization may bring more creativity and better problem-solving skills to the workplace than does a homogeneous working population.

The ASA model's main premise is that the attributes of people define the organization. Therefore, Schneider suggests that when changes need to occur in an organization, the process should begin with changes in personnel rather than with changes in the structure and processes of the organization itself.

—*Jo-Ida C. Hansen and W. Vanessa Lee*

See also Attraction-Selection-Attrition Model; Careers; Person–Environment Fit; Person–Organization Fit; Person–Job Fit; Theory of Work Adjustment

FURTHER READING

Brown, D., & Brooks, L. (Eds.). (2002). *Career choice and development* (4th ed.). San Francisco: Jossey-Bass.

Cooper, C. L. (1998). *Theories of organizational stress.* New York: Oxford University Press.

Schneider, B., Goldstein, H. W., & Smith, D. B. (1995). The ASA framework: An update. *Personnel Psychology, 48,* 747–773.

PHYSICAL PERFORMANCE ASSESSMENT

Physically demanding occupations, such as manual materials handling and public safety, require the use of a variety of physical abilities to perform the job tasks. Because of the need for workers to meet the physical requirements of arduous jobs and the potential for injury, employers use physical performance tests to determine an individual's physical capabilities to meet the job requirements. The physical abilities assessed by the tests are based on the essential tasks and functions, working conditions, and ergonomic parameters associated with a job. These abilities are defined in the following text:

- Muscular strength is the ability to exert force to lift, push, pull, or hold objects. The amount of force generated by a muscle contraction is dependent on the size of the muscles (cross-section) involved and muscle fiber type such as a fast twitch.
- Muscular endurance is the ability to exert force continuously over moderate to long time periods. The length of time a muscle can contract is dependent on the size of the muscles involved, the chemical composition of the muscle tissue, and the muscle fiber type such as a slow twitch.
- Aerobic capacity or cardiovascular endurance is the ability of the respiratory and cardiovascular systems to provide oxygen to the body systems for medium- to high-intensity tasks performed over a moderate time period. Aerobic tasks require continuous oxygen consumption.
- Anaerobic power is the ability to complete high-intensity, short-duration (e.g., 5–90 seconds) tasks. Anaerobic tasks are performed using stored energy in the form of adenosine triphosphate (ATP).
- Flexibility involves the range of motion at the joints including knees and shoulders to bend, stoop, rotate, and reach in all directions with the arms and legs. Flexibility at the joints is dependent on the extensibility of the ligaments, tendons, muscle, and skin.
- Equilibrium is the ability to maintain the center of gravity over the base of support such as feet. Equilibrium involves maintaining and recovering to a balanced position when outside forces, including gravity and slipping on ice, occur.

Combinations of different levels of these abilities are needed for all tasks in which muscular contraction, oxygen consumption, and energy expenditure are required. For example, low levels of muscular strength and muscular endurance in the abdominal and back muscles are required to sit in a chair. However, high levels of these two abilities are required to lift and carry thirty 70-pound boxes. Performance of arduous job tasks typically requires all six abilities, but to different extents. Lifting ten 90-pound boxes from a table and carrying them 100 yards to another table requires high levels of muscular strength and muscular endurance in the arms, legs, and torso, but only low levels of flexibility. The level of equilibrium needed is moderate because gravity is pulling downward as the box is carried forward. Similarly, to avoid falling over when picking up a weighted object, the base of support must be adjusted or widened, for example. This task also requires a moderate level of aerobic capacity because of the weight of the boxes, the distance they are carried, and the duration of the task. Therefore, the physical abilities interact at varying levels throughout performance of all arduous job tasks. The specificity of an ability can be determined through direct physiological measurement such as oxygen consumption, ergonomic measurement including force to torque bolts, or questionnaire data.

Physical performance tests are developed, validated, and implemented for purposes of applicant assessment, incumbent assessment and retention, and worker assessment for return to work after an injury. Physical tests are used for arduous jobs in the public (e.g., law enforcement, firefighter, emergency medical service), private (e.g., warehouse, manufacturing, longshoring, telecommunications, railroad, trades, electric, natural gas), and military sectors. Use of physical performance tests in the selection setting provides several benefits. First, individuals whose physical ability is commensurate with the demands of the job are identified. Second, physically qualified individuals have fewer injuries, which leads to lower worker compensation costs, increased productivity, and reduced turnover. Research in this area has shown reductions in injury rates of 10% to 20% for new hires who successfully completed a physical test screening when compared with individuals who did not take the test. Further, when workers were injured, those who passed the physical test had significantly lower injury costs than those who were not tested, for example, $4 million versus $12 million.

TYPES OF TESTS

There are numerous physical performance tests used by organizations to assess physical capabilities. However, these tests can be placed into one of two categories: basic ability tests and work/job simulations. Basic ability tests assess an individual's physical ability including muscular strength and flexibility. Tests such as sit-ups (muscular endurance), the step test (aerobic capacity), arm ergometry (muscular endurance), and sit and reach (flexibility) are basic ability tests. Basic ability tests measure an ability required to perform job tasks.

Work/job simulation tests include components of the job being evaluated such as dragging a hose and climbing stairs. Work simulations require individuals to perform simulated job tasks or components and may require equipment or tools used on the job. A test requiring an individual to lift boxes and place them on shelves of various heights is considered a work simulation test. Law enforcement tests that simulate pursuing and restraining a suspect are also work simulation tests.

Organizations have used basic ability, work simulation, and a combination of both test types to assess candidate and incumbent physical capabilities. Both types of test have substantial validity that ranges from 0.45 to 0.85, depending on the type of criterion measure used in the validation study. However, regardless of the type of test used, significant gender differences in performance are typically present. These differences are attributed to the physiological differences between men and women such as larger muscle mass and greater lung volume.

DEVELOPMENT AND VALIDATION OF PHYSICAL PERFORMANCE TESTS

Both basic ability and work simulation tests must match the job in terms of the physical abilities or the job tasks being assessed. Job analysis data provides the input to select or design basic ability tests or to identify essential tasks that can be safely simulated. Ergonomic parameters (e.g., weights of tools and objects, forces to loosen nuts and bolts, distances walked, heights) and working conditions (e.g., temperature, surface, surface incline) related to the essential job tasks should be incorporated into the test development plan. In addition, when developing or selecting physical performance tests, the safety of the examinees must be considered; their health status and fitness level is usually unknown, and their age can range from 20 to 60 years old.

Design or selection of basic ability tests should include consideration of the tasks that require the abilities, and not just the relevant abilities. For example, if the job requires lifting 35-pound boxes to heights of 50 to 60 inches, a test of upper body muscular strength may be more appropriate than a lower body strength test. Similarly, if a job requires performing arduous tasks such as climbing stairs while wearing a protective nonbreathable suit with a respirator, a step test or treadmill test of aerobic capacity may be more appropriate than a bicycle test. Further, the duration of a basic ability test, such as muscular endurance, can be determined based on the time it takes to complete a physically demanding task or a series of tasks.

Consideration of these parameters will result in a testing process that is more specific to the job demands.

For work simulation tests, the job's essential tasks are reviewed to determine which tasks are frequently performed and which tasks best represent the essence of the job demands. These tasks are evaluated to select which tasks can be simulated without using equipment or procedures that require on-the-job training. Use of working conditions and ergonomic parameters in the test development stage increases test fidelity. For example, a frequent and important task for firefighters is dragging a hose. This task can be safely simulated and requires no prior training, except for a demonstration of how to hold the hose. To increase the fidelity of this test component, ergonomic data such as the distances that hoses are dragged, size of the hose used, and use of assistance are evaluated to select hose size and distance parameters that are performed by one person. Other parameters related to the condition of the hose (e.g., filled with water or no water) are also examined. An example of a drag parameter that may not be included because it requires training would be opening the hose and spraying water at a target. Finally, the job analysis and working conditions information are used to ensure accurate ordering of test components, proper equipment usage, and appropriate durations for the test and its components.

The linking of job analysis and ergonomic parameters to test components provides the basis for establishing construct validity for basic ability tests and content validity for work simulations. Once the tests meet the conditions described earlier, a criterion-related validity approach can also be used to empirically establish the test validity and passing score(s).

SUMMARY

Arduous jobs are found in numerous private (e.g., electric, telecommunications, natural gas, railroad, freight, warehousing) and public (e.g., fire, police) sector organizations. Identifying the demands of essential job tasks is paramount to development or selection of basic ability or work simulation tests. The ergonomic and working conditions parameters should be incorporated into the test development or selection to ensure that the test accurately represents the physical demands of the job. Careful attention to the details of the job task demands will ensure that the test is content or construct valid and will identify individuals who can perform arduous job tasks. Although design of physical performance tests involves different strategies than cognitive test development, most of the developmental and testing principles are similar.

—Deborah L. Gebhardt and Todd A. Baker

See also Prescreening Assessment Methods for Personnel Selection

FURTHER READING

Gebhardt, D. L. (2000). Establishing performance standards. In S. Constable & B. Palmer (Eds.), *The process of physical fitness standards development—State of the art report.* Wright-Patterson AFB, OH: Human Systems Information Analysis Center (HSIAC-SOAR).

Jackson, A. S. (2000). Types of physical performance tests. In S. Constable & B. Palmer (Eds.), *The process of physical fitness standards development—State of the art report.* Wright-Patterson AFB, OH: Human Systems Information Analysis Center (HSIAC-SOAR).

Myers, D. C., Gebhardt, D. L., Crump, C. E., & Fleishman, E. A. (1993). The dimensions of human physical performance: Factor analyses of strength, stamina, flexibility, and body composition measures. *Human Performance, 6*(4), 309–344.

Rayson, M. P., Holliman, D., & Belyavin, A. (2000). Development of physical selection procedures for the British Army. Phase 2: Relationship between physical performance tests and criterion tasks. *Ergonomics, 43,* 73–105.

Sothmann, M. S., Gebhardt, D. L., Baker, T. A., Kastello, G. M., & Sheppard, V. A. (2004). Performance requirements of physically strenuous occupations: Validating minimum standards for muscular strength and endurance. *Ergonomics, 47*(8), 864–875.

PLACEMENT AND CLASSIFICATION

Selection is a personnel decision whereby an organization decides whether to hire individuals using each person's score on a single assessment, such as a test or interview, or a single predicted performance score based on a composite of multiple assessments. Using this single score to assign each individual to one of multiple jobs or assignments is referred to as placement. An example of placement is when colleges assign new students to a particular level of math class based on a math test score. Classification refers to the situation in which each of a number of individuals is assigned to one of multiple jobs based on their scores on multiple assessments. Classification refers to a complex set of personnel decisions and requires more explanation.

A CONCEPTUAL EXAMPLE

The idea of classification can be illustrated by an example. An organization has 50 openings in four entry-level jobs: Word processor has 10 openings, administrative assistant has 12 openings, accounting clerk has 8 openings, and receptionist has 20 openings. Sixty people apply for a job at this organization and each completes three employment tests: word processing, basic accounting, and interpersonal skills.

Generally, the goal of classification is to use each applicant's predicted performance score for each job to fill all the openings and maximize the overall predicted performance across all four jobs. Linear computer programming approaches have been developed that make such assignments within the constraints of a given classification situation such as the number of jobs, openings or quotas for each job, and applicants. Note that in the example, 50 applicants would get assigned to one of the four jobs and 10 applicants would get assigned to *not hired.*

Using past scores on the three tests and measures of performance, formulas can be developed to estimate predicted performance for each applicant in each job. The tests differ in how well they predict performance in each job. For example, the basic accounting test is fairly predictive of performance in the accounting clerk job, but is less predictive of performance in the receptionist job. Additionally, the word processing test is very predictive of performance in the word processor job but is less predictive of performance in the receptionist job. This means that the equations for calculating predicted performance for each job give different weights to each test. For example, the equation for accounting clerk gives its largest weight to basic accounting test scores, whereas the receptionist equation gives its largest weight to interpersonal skill test scores and little weight to accounting test scores. Additionally, scores vary across applicants within each test and across tests within each individual. This means that each individual will have a different predicted performance score for each job.

One way to assign applicants to these jobs would be to calculate a single predicted performance score for each applicant, select all applicants who have scores above some cutoff, and randomly assign applicants to jobs within the constraints of the quotas. However, random assignment would not take advantage of the possibility that each selected applicant will not perform equally well on all available jobs. Classification takes advantage of this possibility. Classification efficiency can be viewed as the difference in overall predicted performance between this univariate (one score per applicant) strategy and the multivariate (one score per applicant per job) classification approach that uses a different equation to predict performance for each job.

A number of parameters influence the degree of classification efficiency. An important one is the extent to which predicted scores for each job are related to each other. The smaller the relationships among predicted scores across jobs, the greater the potential classification efficiency. That is, classification efficiency increases to the extent that multiple assessments capture differences in the individual characteristics that determine performance in each job.

CLASSIFICATION IN THE U.S. MILITARY

With regard to most organizations and their personnel decisions, classification is much more of an idea than a practice. Although large organizations will apply classifications at a localized level, such as when staffing a new facility, most often an organization is considering a group of applicants who have applied for one particular job; that is, most personnel decisions are selection rather than classification. The armed services are a notable exception. Although their practice only approximates conceptual discussions of classification, the individual armed services (i.e., Army, Air Force, Navy, Marine Corps, and Coast Guard) constitute the best real-world example. On an annual basis, the services must select and assign a large number of inexperienced individuals to a large number of entry-level jobs. The situation requires use of classification principles.

Prospective armed service applicants complete a battery of tests. The tests an applicant completes are used to first determine whether the person qualifies for military service and second to assign the individual to one of many jobs. Qualification for military service is a selection decision. The methods the services use to narrow the range of jobs for selected individuals use ideas from classification.

The armed services hire approximately 180,000 new persons annually and need to fit them into roughly 800 entry-level jobs. Historically, the military was the first organization of any type to use large-scale testing for selection and job assignment, starting in about 1916. In 1976 a version of the current battery was put into use—the Armed Services Vocational Aptitude Battery (ASVAB). Although the ASVAB has gone through restructuring, renorming, and regular revision, it is the current official mental testing battery used by each service for entry and for job assignment on acceptance. The current ASVAB is a battery of nine operational tests:

1. general science (GS),
2. arithmetic reasoning (AR),
3. word knowledge (WK),
4. paragraph comprehension (PC),
5. mathematics knowledge (MK),
6. electronics information (EI),
7. auto information (AI),
8. shop information (SI), and
9. mechanical comprehension (MC).

Selection and Assignment

Before individuals are assigned to a job, they must meet minimal criteria to join the armed services. One of these is a cut score on a composite of four ASVAB tests (WK, PC, AR, and MK) referred to as the Armed Forces Qualification Test (AFQT). Other criteria include age, education, passing a physical examination, and meeting background and moral character requirements.

AFQT is used only to determine overall service eligibility and is not used to determine whether someone is qualified to be trained in a specific job. Each individual service uses the tests somewhat differently to make job assignments. The rest of this discussion tracks examples of applications used by the U.S. Army. A significant contributor to the assignment decision in the Army is the individual's score on each of nine scores of uniquely weighted composites of the ASVAB tests. Each entry-level job in the Army is associated with one of these *aptitude area composites*. The weights for each aptitude area were developed to predict training performance in Army jobs. For example, some entry-level Army jobs are assigned to the mechanical maintenance (MM) aptitude area. The weights for calculating the MM composite score emphasize the AI, SI, MC, and EI tests. Every Army job has a minimum cut score on its composite that an applicant must meet to be eligible for that job. There are many factors that determine to which job an applicant is assigned. Only one is whether the applicant's aptitude area composite score satisfies the job's minimum score. Other factors include current job openings, the Army's priorities, when applicants choose to begin their term of service, and which job applicants prefer.

This job assignment process is only an approximation of the conceptual classification decision model described previously. First, the goal was not to assign applicants to jobs in a way that maximizes overall predicted performance but rather to assign applicants to jobs to

- meet minimum aptitude requirements for each job,
- fill current openings,
- satisfy applicant preferences, and
- meet other constraints.

Additionally, it is difficult to satisfy the pure version of the classification model when personnel decisions are made in real time rather than in large batches that allow classification efficiency advantages associated with optimizing assignments across a larger number of applicants. Although assignments made this way are not likely to achieve the level of classification efficiency that a model closer to the conceptual description of classification would produce, the Army application is still a substantial improvement over what would be realized by selection and unguided assignment.

THE FUTURE

Although the Army example presented is not classification in the strictest sense, it is a good large-scale approximation of classification and is frequently discussed in the literature. Nonetheless, the Army is working on potential improvements to its assignment system that would improve classification efficiency. The Army is currently considering adding applicants' actual predicted score for each aptitude area to the decision process. That is, among other considerations, an applicant could choose or be assigned to a job for which the applicant's predicted score is higher than others among those for which the applicant meets

minimum qualifications. Another consideration is the possibility of using projections of the likely scores of applicants during a time period so that the assignment takes place in the context of a large batch of applicants rather than only those applying at that particular time. Finally, the Army is actively conducting research into potential additions to the ASVAB that could increase its classification efficiency. Measures of constructs in the areas of temperament, spatial and psychomotor aptitudes, and situational judgment are being examined.

—*Roy C. Campbell and Christopher E. Sager*

See also Army Alpha/Army Beta; Employee Selection; Project A; Selection Strategies

FURTHER READING

Campbell, J. P. (1991). Modeling the performance prediction problem in industrial and organizational psychology. In M. D. Dunnette & L. M. Hough (Eds.), *Handbook of industrial and organizational psychology* (pp. 687–732). Palo Alto, CA: Consulting Psychologists Press.

Rosse, R. L., Campbell, J. P., & Peterson, N. G. (2001). Personnel classification and differential job assignments: Estimating classification gains. In J. P. Campbell & D. J. Knapp (Eds.), *Exploring the limits in personnel selection and classification* (pp. 453–506). Mahwah, NJ: Lawrence Erlbaum.

Waters, B. K. (1997). Army Alpha to CAT-ASVAB: Four-score years of military personnel selection and classification testing. In R. F. Dillon (Ed.), *Handbook on testing* (pp. 187–203). Westport, CT: Greenwood Press.

POLICY CAPTURING

Policy capturing has its roots in activities central to industrial/organizational (I/O) psychology. Its origins lie in the work of the Personnel Research Laboratory at Lackland Air Force Base in the 1950s, and it achieved prominence in the broader field of psychology with the publication in 1960 of Paul Hoffman's *Psychological Bulletin* paper, "The Paramorphic Representation of Clinical Judgment." Although policy capturing is not derivative of Egon Brunswik's probabilistic functionalism, scholars in the Brunswikian tradition have been attracted to policy capturing as a method to address certain research questions.

This attraction is based on the practice in good policy capturing research of faithfully representing the situation to which generalization is aimed. Hence, policy capturing is often loosely associated with social judgment theory, which is the contemporary manifestation of Brunswikian theory.

TASKS

Many cognitive tasks require decision makers to make inferences or decisions based on multiple, often conflicting, pieces of information. Such tasks include performance assessment and salary assignments, employment interviewing, investment decisions, medical diagnosis and prognosis, evaluation of charges of discrimination, assessment of the desirability of employment contracts, and even the selection of the most appropriate bullet for use by an urban police force—the list is endless. Such tasks abound in organizations! Policy capturing is used to investigate what factors influence the decision maker, and how heavily each is weighted. Environmental outcomes are not part of the policy capturing procedure.

DATA COLLECTION

The essence of the data-gathering procedure is to have an individual respondent make a substantial number of judgments on multiattribute bundles, often paper-and-pencil or computer-presented profiles, but the judgments can be made on actual people, files, or abstracts of files or anything that can be represented by a set of quantitative variables. Typically, the attributes and the judgments are treated as interval scales, although dichotomous data such as gender are often found among quantitative variables including age, length of experience, or rating scales. The phrase *individual respondent* was not an accident, in that policy capturing entails an idiographic analysis, which may be followed by nomothetic analyses of the idiographic indexes describing the individual respondents.

DATA ANALYSIS

The appropriate data analysis depends on a number of factors, including the level of measurement of the predictors and the judgments, the function forms relating predictors to judgments, predictor intercorrelation, the presumed aggregation rule, and so forth. The common default procedure is multiple regression, but mathematical models that reflect noncompensatory rules such as conjunctive or disjunctive decision rules might also be used. Given that multiple regression is the most commonly used analytic procedure, we'll concentrate on it.

Multiple Regression

Given a sufficient number of multiattribute judgments, the investigator can use ordinary least squares regression to ascertain the degree to which each attribute accounts for variance in the judgments. Doing so requires the usual assumptions underlying regression, some of which can be violated without affecting the investigator's inferences too severely. For example, if the linear function form assumed in the regression algorithm does not correspond exactly to that used by the judge but is monotonically related thereto, the model misspecification tends to be inconsequential. Furthermore, appropriate cross-validation within subjects provides some sense of the consequences of violations of assumptions.

PERFORMANCE INDEXES

Standard multiple regression indexes are used to describe the judgment policy. The multiple correlation, or R_s, is crucial; if it is not substantial, the investigator cannot claim to have learned much about the judgment policy of the person without further analysis. One possible reason for a low R_s, other than the ever-present unreliability of judgment, is that the function forms relating the judgments to the attributes may be nonlinear. A second is that the judge's aggregation rule may be nonadditive, and the assumption of additivity has resulted in model misspecification. These first two possibilities can be subjected to some data snooping, such as inspecting the scatterplots for nonlinearities, fitting quadratic and multiplicative terms, and so forth.

These possibilities may be illustrated by a favorite class exercise: having the class design a policy-capturing study to select a mate, serve as subjects, and analyze the data. "A malevolent deity has sentenced you to spend 10 years alone on an island. In a last-minute moment of benevolence, the deity has offered to create a mate according to your preferences as assessed via policy capturing." The students develop the attributes, but gender and age, ranging from 2 to 72 years, must be among them. Assuming linearity, the weight for age will likely be trivial, but inspection of the scatterplot of desirability on age will show radical nonlinearity and implicate an important source of judgment variance. If gender is key, the regression of desirability on, say, physical attractiveness will reveal a strange-looking array, with half the points sitting in a straight line across the bottom of the scatterplot and the other half forming a typical envelope of points.

Other reasons for a low R_s include systematic shifts in importance weights as a result of doing the task, inattention caused by fatigue, and the like. One way of obtaining information about whether the judge is systematic is including reliability profiles and assessing test-retest reliability (r_{tt}). If both R_s and r_{tt} are low, it is unlikely the judge can be modeled.

Suppose R_s is high? Then we can predict the judge's responses from the attributes, assuming linearity and additivity. We can predict a new set of judgments via cross validation of a holdout sample, mitigating concerns about capitalization on chance. But this high R_s should not be taken to mean that the judge is in fact using a linear additive model; the predictive power of the linear model is all too well-known. But the weights do give us significant information about what attributes are important to the judge. Comparing the weights of different judges who have provided judgments on the same data set may reveal sources of conflict or reveal underlying sources of agreement in situations marked by conflict.

TYPICAL RESULTS

People are remarkably predictable in judgment tasks. If R_s is not more than .70 or so, even after taking nonlinearities and nonadditivities into account, do not place much faith in the results. It is not uncommon for expert judges in consequential tasks to have R_s values of .90 or more. An important finding is that judges often believe that they are taking many attributes into account, even though relatively few attributes control virtually all the systematic variance in the judgments.

OTHER DECISION MODELS

There are many approaches to the study of multiattribute judgment, decision making, and decision aiding. Some require the decision maker to decompose the decision intuitively, such as the MAUT (multiattribute utility theoretic) model of Ward Edwards and

his colleagues. Others, like policy capturing, have the decision maker make multiple holistic judgments and employ computer decomposition, such as the ANOVA approach of information integration theory. Judgment analysis is important to mention in this article because it is often confused with policy capturing. It uses the same statistical machinery as policy capturing but refers to the situation where environmental outcomes are available, and the full power of the lens model can be brought to bear on exploring the relation between the judge and the environment.

—*Michael E. Doherty*

See also Lens Model

FURTHER READING

Brehmer, A., & Brehmer, B. (1988). What have we learned about human judgment from thirty years of policy capturing? In B. Brehmer & C. R. B. Joyce (Eds.), *Human judgment: The SJT view* (pp. 75–114). Amsterdam: Elsevier Science Publishers B. V. (North-Holland).

Cooksey, R. W. (1996). *Judgment analysis: Theory, methods, and applications.* San Diego: Academic Press.

Hoffman, P. J. (1960). The paramorphic representation of clinical judgment. *Psychological Bulletin, 57,* 116–131.

Roose, J. E., & Doherty, M. E. (1978). A social judgment theoretic approach to sex discrimination in faculty salaries. *Organizational Behavior and Human Performance, 22,* 193–215.

POSITIVE PSYCHOLOGY APPLIED TO WORK

POSITIVE PSYCHOLOGY

The roots of inquiry into what is good about human nature and optimal human functioning can be traced back to Aristotle. Indeed, the initial impetus of modern psychology was to gain an understanding of transcendent experience. This objective was echoed in humanistic psychology's interest in the self-actualizing potential of human beings. However, following World War II psychology's emphasis shifted to a predominant attention to pathology, prevention, and human malfunctioning. In 1998 the president of the American Psychological Association (APA), Martin Seligman, made the clarion call for a new psychological emphasis that he termed *positive psychology.*

Positive psychology was aimed at redirecting the focus of psychology to positive individual traits and subjective experience. The purpose of positive psychology is to shift the focus away from human weakness, vulnerability, and pathology to an emphasis on strengths, resilience, and wellness. However, unlike other trends in popular psychology, positive psychology insists on the application of sound scientific theory and research to provide a social and behavioral scientific understanding of optimal functioning. The field has many levels of analysis including individual subjective experience, for example, well-being, happiness, optimal experience, hope, and optimism; positive individual traits, such as courage, forgiveness, spirituality, the capacity for love, aesthetic sensibility, perseverance, and wisdom; and beneficial group and institutional characteristics, including civic virtues that inspire good citizenship, altruism, civility, tolerance, responsibility, and transcendent performance.

Most of the processes and states that are the scholarly focus of positive psychology are not new. However, positive psychology does provide new ways of looking at old phenomena. It offers a broad conceptual framework for linking theories in several psychological fields. It is based on the assumption that happiness, goodness, and excellence are authentic states that can be analyzed by science and achieved in practice. Over the last 10 years positive psychology has generated a significant literature in the areas of clinical, counseling, community, educational, social, health, and industrial/organizational (I/O) psychology.

POSITIVE ORGANIZATIONAL PSYCHOLOGY

Industrial/organizational psychology has always been interested in the relationship between worker well-being, such as satisfaction, and performance. However, more than 40 years of research has shown that happy workers are not necessarily productive workers. By redefining what is meant by well-being, positive psychology has influenced the debate concerning the relationship between satisfaction and productivity. Subjective well-being is typically measured by two variables: happiness and satisfaction. Happiness refers to an emotional state and indicates how people feel (pleasant moods and emotions) about their work, their life, and themselves in reaction to their lives. Satisfaction consists of more global evaluative and judgmental processes about the acceptability of various aspects of work and life and as such is a more cognitive process. I/O psychology has tended to exclusively focus on judgments (satisfaction) in determining worker well-being, and ignored the affective component (happiness). Yet each is an important, but separate, characteristic of subjective well-being.

Positive organizational psychology can be defined as the application of psychological theory and research to understanding the positive, adaptive, and emotionally fulfilling elements of work. It focuses on studying both the statelike characteristics of work and how they affect subjective well-being, engagement, and transcendent performance. The emphasis on statelike characteristics is an important distinction between positive organizational psychology and positive psychology. Fred Luthans, one of the main proponents of positive organizational scholarship, believes that the field should emphasize three basic characteristics:

1. The positive constructs studied should be measurable.

2. The focus should be on statelike concepts that can be developed, as opposed to traitlike or dispositional characteristics.

3. Psychological capacities can be effectively managed to optimize performance in the workplace.

Positive Subjective States

Positive organizational psychology studies positive constructs such as confidence or self-efficacy, hope, optimism, resiliency, and subjective well-being (or happiness). Research on these characteristics has shown that they are capable of being measured and are related to effective leadership, high performance, goal attainment, perceived control, effective functioning, and positive affect. Developing people's talents has been linked to increases in employee engagement, performance, and subjective well-being.

One important subjective state that has emerged from the positive psychology literature on work is *flow*. *Flow* was a term first coined by Mihalyi Csikszentmihalyi to denote an optimal experience of intense engagement and effortless action, where personal skills match required challenges. Research on the experience of flow in athletes, popularly referred to as *being in the zone*, has also indicated that flow is associated with transcendent or optimal performance. Flow has several conceptual sources. For example, flow is seen as a state of intrinsic motivation where the individual is engaging in some activity for its own sake without any regard for external rewards. Flow is also a form of work engagement. Engagement is defined as a positive, fulfilling, work-related state of mind that is characterized by vigor, dedication, and absorption. Although engagement and flow appear to be similar, they are treated as distinct constructs in the literature. Flow refers to a more acute, short-term experience specifically associated with a particular task or activity, whereas engagement is a more stable and persistent state of mind that is associated with work in general. Research on flow indicates that many work tasks provide opportunities for experiencing a state of well-being.

Positive Institutions

Positive organizational psychology also focuses on characteristics of positive organizations. It addresses issues such as the development of virtuous organizations and the creation of healthy work environments. Specifically positive organizational scholarship has begun to investigate how organizations can effectively support and nurture both their employees and the customers they serve. This line of research emphasizes organizational virtuousness. Virtuous organizations (organizations that express virtues such as compassion, forgiveness, and gratitude) have a positive effect on personal improvement and experienced meaningfulness. Work that allows for the expression of positive emotions and the exercise of individual strengths is associated with knowledge creation and higher levels of organizational functioning. Positive psychology has also broadened the concept of transformational leadership to include authentic leadership. Authentic leaders transcend their own self-interest and are guided by end values that primarily benefit the interests of their constituency. They rely more on moral power than on coercion or rational persuasion. Characteristics associated with authentic leaders include optimism, integrity, honesty, high personal efficacy, future orientation, and resilience. Such leaders give priority to empowering followers and fostering positive deviance. There is also some theoretical and empirical evidence to suggest that transformational leadership influences employee well-being by increasing worker self-efficacy, trust in management, the meaningfulness of work, and occupational and organizational identity.

Both the individual and organizational levels of analysis have provided insights into designing optimum work environments. The aim of redesigning the workplace is to increase worker involvement, improve individual happiness, and promote optimal performance. Research on work design has identified several features of the work environment that maximize subjective well-being at work and encourage active engagement in the job. The elements associated with positive workplaces include the following:

- **Variety:** the degree to which the job requires a variety of different activities. People like to learn new skills and appreciate opportunities to challenge themselves and personally grow.
- **Significance:** the degree to which the job has a substantial impact on the lives or work of other people. Work from which people can derive a sense of purpose and meaning generates higher levels of satisfaction.
- **Autonomy:** the degree to which the job provides an opportunity for control and substantial discretion in scheduling the work and determining the procedures to be used in carrying it out. The opportunity to make decisions about the process and outcomes of a person's job is associated with the development of a sense of competence.
- **Realistic goals:** specific and difficult goals with feedback lead to optimal performance. Both flow and satisfaction are associated with having clear, challenging goals that provide opportunities to use skills.
- **Feedback:** the degree to which the activities of the job provide the individual with direct and clear information about the effectiveness of the worker's performance. Feedback is a crucial component of engagement in learning.
- **Social networks:** the opportunity to work in groups or teams and establish interpersonal contacts. Research in a variety of contexts has shown that group work is associated with better individual well-being. Social networks on the job provide the worker with companionship and social support.
- **Transformational leadership:** a form of positive leadership that contributes to individual well-being. Transformational leadership has been shown to facilitate followers' commitment to organizational goals, enhance workers' feelings of self-efficacy, nurture personal growth, and produce superior levels of performance.

SUMMARY

Positive organizational psychology is an area of scholarship and scientific study that is influenced by positive psychology's emphasis on strengths and virtues. Its aim is to identify those measurable characteristics of individuals, organizations, and work environments that can be developed and promote active engagement, enhance subjective well-being, facilitate transcendent performance, and lead to positive organizational outcomes.

—Clive Fullagar, Ronald G. Downey,
Andrew J. Wefald, and Disha D. Rupayana

See also Intrinsic and Extrinsic Work Motivation; Job Design; Job Involvement; Transformational and Transactional Leadership

FURTHER READING

Cameron, K. S., Dutton, J. E., & Quinn, R. E. (Eds.). (2003). *Positive organizational scholarship: Foundations of a new discipline.* San Francisco: Berret-Koehler Publishers.

Csikszentmihalyi, M. (1990). *Flow: The psychology of optimal experience.* New York: Harper & Row.

Luthans, F. (2002). The need for and meaning of positive organizational behavior. *Journal of Organizational Behavior, 23,* 695–706.

Seligman, M. E. P., & Csikszentmihalyi, M. (2000). Positive psychology: An introduction. *American Psychologist, 55*(1), 5–14.

Sivinathan, N., Arnold, K. A., Turner, N., & Barling, J. (2004). Leading well: Transformational leadership and well-being. In P. A. Linley & S. Joseph (Eds.), *Positive psychology in practice* (pp. 241–255). Hoboken, NJ: Wiley.

Turner, N., Barling, J., & Zacharatos, A. (2002). Positive psychology at work. In C. R. Snyder & S. L. Lopez (Eds.), *Handbook of positive psychology* (pp. 715–728). New York: Oxford University Press.

Warr, P. (1999). Well-being and the workplace. In D. Kahneman, E. Diener, & N. Schwarz (Eds.), *Well-being: The foundations of hedonic psychology* (pp. 392–412). New York: Russell Sage.

PRACTICAL INTELLIGENCE

The concept of practical intelligence reflects the idea that there might be some ability besides general mental abilities (*g*), some *street smarts* or *common sense* that predicts how successfully individuals handle situations in their actual lives in the form of appropriate responses, given facts and circumstances as they are discovered, and considering a person's short- and long-range goals.

This definition of practical intelligence is in some ways different from the usual conception and measurement *g.* First, unlike tasks assessing *g,* tasks for practical intelligence aim at the individual's own long- and short-range goals and are usually of the individual's own intrinsic interest, rather than being formulated by others. Second, the task is encountered during a situation connected to the individual's ordinary experience; and, because it is quite uncommon in classic assessments of *g* but rather ordinary in real life, those *facts of the situation as they are discovered* may not suffice to make well-informed decisions and may change during exposition to the problem at hand. Finally, although the situation is oftentimes not well-defined, there is more than one possible correct answer and more than one method of correct solution.

APPROACHES TO PRACTICAL INTELLIGENCE

Given the rather wide and situation-specific definition of practical intelligence, the construct has been addressed via different approaches, namely practical know-how, practical mathematics, practical planning, practical presupposition, social judgment, and prototypes of practical intelligence.

Practical know-how refers to solving tasks such as repairing machines or navigating the ocean without *appropriate* information such as formal education, technical manuals, or specialized tools. The most prominent form of practical know-how is tacit knowledge, practical know-how that usually is not openly expressed or stated and must be acquired in the absence of direct instruction. Frequently, tacit knowledge is further classified by its focus (i.e., how to handle oneself, others, and one's task), but measures addressing these different foci usually load onto a common factor.

Practical mathematics refers to *street mathematics,* that is, mathematical calculations undertaken in everyday life that differ from the abstract mathematics formally taught in schools and that are oftentimes conducted in forms of mental shortcuts, such as when searching for the *best buys* in supermarkets or filling orders of different quantities with minimal waste.

Practical planning refers to how people organize their everyday activities and reorganize when something goes wrong. Thus although everyone will have a routine of getting up in the mornings and getting ready to work, the effectiveness of different strategies used to react to problems, such as a failed alarm clock, may differ.

Practical presupposition refers to concept learning in everyday situations that allows individuals to discover regularities in their environment, such as general ideas about the likely preferences, decisions, and actions of individuals from different groups.

Social judgment can also be treated as an aspect of practical intelligence. Given the social nature of our lives, practical intelligence may be reflected in the attainment of transactional goals and in the individuals' adaptation to their social environments, that is, their success at meeting the requirements of diverse social roles.

Prototypes of practical intelligence refers to a conceptualization introduced by Ulric Neisser, who argued that it was not possible to define intelligence as any one thing. Instead, he suggested defining practical intelligence as the extent to which an individual resembles a prototypical person who would be an ideal exemplar of the target concept.

RESEARCH AND MEASUREMENT

Given the somewhat idiosyncratic nature of practical intelligence, much research has been done in the form of case studies showing how practically intelligent individuals improvise to complete their task by adapting whatever resources are at hand (practical know-how); handle problems arising in their daily routines (practical planning); or solve mathematical problems easily when undertaken in a context with which they are familiar (demanding the right amount of money when selling a certain number of coconuts, each of which costs a certain amount) but not, however, when presented with the same problem in an abstract form, such as "How much is 4 times 35?"

Some of these approaches have also made use of John Flanagan's critical incident technique (CIT), which allows the identification of the strategies that individuals actually use when performing specific tasks and the specific, situationally relevant aspects of this behavior. A frequent measurement approach, however, uses simulations (sometimes based on CITs). These simulations can exhibit high fidelity, that is, they try to replicate the represented situation as realistically as possible and require individuals to respond as if they were in the actual situation, such as

assessment centers, group discussions, and to a certain degree in-basket tests. Yet most prominent, particularly for the assessment of tacit knowledge, are low-fidelity simulations that present a situation to individuals orally or in writing. Individuals have to either describe how they would react in the situation, as in situational interviews, or rate the quality of diverse possible reactions, including situational judgment tests. A special kind of situational judgment test frequently used to assess tacit knowledge is the tacit knowledge inventory; these tests have been developed for management, sales, military leadership, college studies, and academic psychology. These inventories usually use longer and more elaborate scenario descriptions than most situational judgment tests. They are scored by giving points for answers that were more common among experts than novices, by judging the degree to which participants' responses conform to professional rules of thumb, or by computing the (oftentimes squared) difference between participants' responses and an expert prototype. Finally, practical intelligence, particularly involving practical presuppositions, has been tested in the laboratory, such as by giving individuals descriptions of a person (e.g., a father of four versus a student) and a target (e.g., a car with specific features) that was congruent, irrelevant, or incongruent to the person. Participants should indicate how much the person would like the target. In another study children performed considerably worse at predicting the movement of geometric forms on a computer screen with the help of a cursor than when the same algorithm was used in a computer game in which the geometric forms were birds, bees, and butterflies and the cursor a net.

CONCERNS AND DIRECTIONS FOR FUTURE RESEARCH

The concept of practical intelligence has not gone unchallenged. Although some proponents of practical intelligence argue that practical intelligence is different from and superior to g, some authors, such as L. S. Gottfredson and colleagues in 2003, conceptually and empirically discredit this argument on the basis that practical intelligence and g correlate, and it appears that practical intelligence demonstrates incremental validity above g only for tasks that are both simple and well learned—conditions under which the influence of g is reduced, anyway.

Consequently, other authors have argued that practical intelligence is nothing else but job knowledge. Finally, research by M. A. McDaniel and colleagues on situational judgment tests suggests that what is measured in practical intelligence may be a function of *g*, job knowledge, and different personality factors such as emotional stability, agreeableness, and conscientiousness.

Besides further analysis of the nomological network of practical intelligence, the use of practical intelligence in personnel selection merits further research. Although practical intelligence tests may have little incremental validity over and above cognitive ability tests, their obvious task-relatedness may increase their face validity to applicants; hence their acceptance.

—*Ute-Christine Klehe*

See also Assessment Center; Cognitive Abilities; Critical Incident Technique; Job Knowledge Testing; Situational Approach to Leadership

FURTHER READING

Gottfredson, L. S. (2003). Dissecting practical intelligence theory: Its claims and evidence. *Intelligence, 31*(4), 343–397.

McDaniel, M. A., Morgeson, F. P., Finnegan, E. B., Campion, M. A., & Braverman, E. P. (2001). Predicting job performance using situational judgment tests: A clarification of the literature. *Journal of Applied Psychology, 80*(4), 730–740.

Neisser, U. (1976). General, academic, and artificial intelligence. In L. B. Resnick (Ed.), *The nature of intelligence.* Hillsdale, NJ: Lawrence Erlbaum.

Schmidt, F. L., & Hunter, J. E. (1993). Tacit knowledge, practical intelligence, general mental ability, and job knowledge. *Current Directions in Psychological Science, 2,* 8–9.

Sternberg, R. J., Forsythe, G. B., Hedlund, J., Horvath, J. A., Wagner, R. K., Williams, W. M., et al. (2000). *Practical intelligence in everyday life.* New York: Cambridge University Press.

Wagner, R. K. (2000). Practical intelligence. In R. J. Sternberg (Ed.), *Handbook of intelligence* (pp. 380–395). New York: Cambridge University Press.

PREJUDICE

See STEREOTYPING

PRESCREENING ASSESSMENT METHODS FOR PERSONNEL SELECTION

Given that most organizations have many more job applicants than they have job openings, employers must be able to quickly and efficiently screen out those applicants who not only fail to meet the minimum qualifications but are also unlikely to be successful on the job if hired. Prescreening assessment methods provide cost-effective ways of selecting out those applicants who are unlikely to be successful if hired. Thus, these methods take a different approach from the more detailed and involved personnel selection methods that focus on identifying the most highly qualified candidates.

Prescreening assessment methods, also referred to as *initial screenings, preemployment inquiries,* or *background evaluations,* encompass a wide range of popular procedures used at the beginning stages of the personnel selection process. Common prescreening assessment methods include application forms, résumés, weighted application blanks (WABs), training and experience evaluations (T&Es), reference checks, letters of recommendation, honesty and integrity testing, and drug testing. An underlying rationale across prescreening assessment methods is that past behavior is the best predictor of future behavior. Thus the assumption is that if applicants have done it in the past, they are likely to repeat it in the future. These behaviors can range from negative or deviant behaviors, such as engaging in illegal drug use or stealing from former employers, to prosocial or positive behaviors, such as taking on leadership roles or assisting coworkers with assignments before being asked.

PRESCREENING ASSESSMENT METHODS

U.S. employers screen more than 1 billion résumés and applications each year. Unfortunately, most organizations fail to employ systematic procedures to evaluate the information obtained from résumés and applications, negating much of the usefulness of these prescreening methods. However, sophisticated practitioners have developed several procedures, including T&Es and WABs, to systematically evaluate and weight the various background information provided on application blanks. Because these weights are optimal for a given applicant pool, however, they must be cross validated on a new sample to ensure that they will still be effective when used with future job applicants. Weighted application blanks and T&Es have demonstrated modest relationships with later job performance and thus show some promise as efficient and effective prescreening tools, particularly when the job involves long and costly training, there is high job turnover, and the initial applicant pool is very large. More detailed methods of assessing background information, such as biographical questionnaires, however, typically go beyond mere prescreening. Thus they would be classified as substantive personnel selection, because their primary goal would then become to select the best qualified candidates into the organization, rather than selecting out the weakest candidates, which is typically done with WABs and T&Es.

Reference checks and letters of recommendation are also sometimes used as prescreening devices. Such evaluations typically cover employment and educational history, the personality or character of the applicant, and statements regarding job performance abilities. However, they can be expensive to use in the early stages of the personnel selection process when there are still many more applicants than job openings. Letters of recommendation tend to suffer from leniency bias because applicants predictably choose letter writers who provide a positive evaluation. Some researchers have suggested that letters of recommendation actually tell you more about the letter writer than the applicant. In addition, there is little evidence that they are predictive of later job performance. Checking references of past employers is essential for many jobs, if only to verify the validity of past employment claims. Unfortunately, past employers are often reticent to provide additional evaluative information for fear of an accusation of defamation of character. Nevertheless, prospective employers can be sued for negligent hiring if they knowingly (or unknowingly) select a job applicant who later engages in illegal or inappropriate behavior at work. As a result, many organizations will at least attempt to contact previous employers and others who know the job applicant to verify information provided or clarify inconsistencies in the application materials.

Billions of dollars are lost each year in the retail industry because of employee theft. In addition, scores of employees are injured at work or endanger the public and their coworkers because of illegal drug use. Thus honesty and integrity tests and drug tests are often used as prescreening assessment methods to screen out applicants who are likely to either steal from the organization or engage in illicit drug use. Honesty tests typically take one of two forms. Overt honesty tests assess applicants' attitudes toward theft and admissions of theft. Alternatively, personality based honesty tests evaluate counterproductive work behavior in general, of which theft is just one part. As a result, overt integrity measures are typically clear purpose tests; applicants administered personality based integrity measures, however, rarely know what the test is assessing. Although use of overt integrity measures may increase perceptions of invasion of privacy, such concerns may be diminished by the greater face validity of these measures. Although both forms of honesty tests have shown some promise in predicting future job performance, their effectiveness in reducing inventory loss is still largely unknown.

Meanwhile, most research on the effectiveness of drug testing has focused on the accuracy of the tests themselves (i.e., reducing false positive or false negative test results) or applicants' reactions to issues of invasion of privacy and procedural justice (i.e., applicants' perceptions of how the drug testing is implemented), rather than how well the tests predict job performance or reduce job-related accidents, illnesses, or sick time. As a result, the effectiveness of drug screening procedures to improve workplace performance or reduce illicit drug use among those employees who are eventually hired is still unclear.

Reducing Misinformation

Because most of the information provided on preemployment screening methods is self-report (i.e., provided directly by the job applicants themselves), embellishment, if not outright falsification, of information is common. Thus employers must take steps to make sure that the information provided by applicants is as accurate as possible. How can they best achieve this? One option is to have applicants sign a statement that all the information they provide is accurate to the best of their knowledge and that knowingly providing false information will immediately eliminate them from further consideration for the job. Additionally, using reference and background checks (as discussed earlier) can also help to verify information by providing others' assessments, in addition to the job applicant's own assessment. The extent to which the organization requests verifiable and objective information, such as degrees earned or GPA, versus unverifiable and subjective information, including how an applicant felt about the college experience, can also reduce falsification of self-reported application information. Sometimes just the written or oral threat that the organization will follow up on the information provided in the application materials is enough to significantly reduce falsifications and embellishments. Some employers have even gone so far as to include *lie scales* in their weighted application blanks and training and experience evaluations. Such scales typically include bogus job skills or experiences that would identify the applicant as lying if they report having that bogus skill or experience.

Legal Issues

Even though prescreening assessment methods focus more on selecting out the poorly qualified candidates, as opposed selecting in the best candidates, they are still required to meet state and federal fair employment guidelines and laws. As a result, development and use of any prescreening assessment method should follow established professional guidelines, such as the *Uniform Guidelines on Employee Selection Procedures* and the *Principles for the Validation and Use of Personnel Selection Procedures*. This would typically entail conducting a job analysis and a study to determine the validity of using certain prescreening methods for a given job. The validity of a prescreening measure will rely not only on the type of information gathered but also on the scoring method used to examine that information. Researchers have determined, for example, that the validity of T&Es can vary widely based on the scoring procedure used. Further, given the job-specific nature of many prescreening measures, it is possible that the composition and validity of these measures may be less generalizable across jobs or organizations than selection methods such as structured interviews or cognitive ability tests. These unique characteristics of prescreening measures further reinforce the need for conducting thorough validation studies prior to implementation.

Failure to follow recommended validation procedures will make it difficult to defend the use of any prescreening assessment procedure that is challenged in a court of law as being discriminatory. Thus employers must determine if their prescreening devices result in adverse impact, for example, whether some protected groups are hired at a significantly lower rate than other groups because of use of a given prescreening procedure. In addition, employers should determine whether a given procedure is predictive of success on the job, can be justified as needed for business necessity, or results in an invasion of privacy. Only in doing so will employers be on solid legal footing when the need to justify and defend their use of a given prescreening assessment method is challenged in court. Unfortunately, most studies of organizational application forms find that most employers, both private and public, continue to include some illegal or inappropriate items in their prescreening measures. Among the most frequently assessed inappropriate items are inquiries into gender, race, age, disability, marital status, and arrest record.

Although receiving less research attention than other personnel selection measures, prescreening assessment methods continue to be popular because of their ease of administration, widespread acceptability by applicants, and utility for eliminating unqualified applicants. In an age in which organizations can successfully and cost-effectively boost the size of their applicant pools through use of Internet-based recruitment and application procedures, the use of prescreening selection tools may become increasingly necessary. Hence, additional research and continued monitoring of the legality, validity, and practical utility of using prescreening assessment methods is clearly warranted given both their current prominence and future potential to advance the overall selection process.

—*Kenneth S. Shultz and David J. Whitney*

See also Biographical Data; Employee Selection; Employment Interview; Integrity Testing; Letters of Recommendation; Selection Strategies; Uniform Guidelines on Employee Selection Procedures

FURTHER READING

Berry, L. M. (2003). Applications and other personal history assessments. In *Employee selection* (pp. 254–287). Belmont, CA: Wadsworth/Thomson Learning.

Cascio, W. F., & Aguinis, H. (2005). Initial screening. In *Applied psychology in human resource management* (6th ed., pp. 277–307). Upper Saddle River, NJ: Prentice Hall.

Gatewood, R. D., & Feild, H. S. (2001). Application forms, training and experience evaluations, and reference checks. In *Human resource selection* (5th ed., pp. 407–470). Fort Worth, TX: Harcourt College Publishing.

Heneman, H. G., III, & Judge, T. A. (2006). External Selection I. In *Staffing organizations* (5th ed.). Boston: Irwin McGraw-Hill.

PROFIT SHARING

See GAINSHARING AND PROFIT SHARING

PROGRAM EVALUATION

Historically, program evaluation has been used as a tool for assessing the merits of educational and governmental programs, where public funding demands a demonstration of accountability. The basic tenet underlying program evaluation that makes it so useful in this context is its reliance on methods that integrate science and practice to produce reliable and actionable information for decision makers. During the past decade, program evaluation has also become increasingly recognized as a useful tool for helping for-profit organizations implement and enhance human resource (HR) programs to achieve key business outcomes. Successful companies understand that survival and growth in the marketplace cannot occur without programs that are designed to improve competitive performance and productivity, engage employees in the organization's mission, and create an environment where people want to work. Recognizing the impact that HR programs have on employees and the company's bottom line, organizations need practical tools to accurately and efficiently evaluate program quality, so they can take the necessary actions to either improve or replace them.

The field of program evaluation is based on the commonsense notion that programs should produce demonstrable benefits. Evaluation is a discipline of study that concentrates on determining the value or merit of an object. The term *program* in this article refers to the object of the evaluation and includes such organizational functions as recruitment and staffing, compensation, performance management, succession planning, training, team building, organizational communications, and health and work–life balance.

Evaluations can help organizations identify how a program can be improved on an ongoing basis or examine its overall worth. The first approach, called *formative evaluation,* is usually conducted while the program is being formed or implemented and will generally lead to recommendations that focus on program adjustments. The specific findings might be used to identify program challenges and opportunities and provide strategies for continuous improvement. Formative evaluations seek to improve efficiency and ensure that the program is responsive to changing organizational needs.

An evaluation that is conducted to examine a program's overall worth is called a *summative evaluation* and will generally be performed when an organization is attempting to determine if the program should be replaced, rather than modified. This approach focuses on the program's outcomes and their value to the organization. The specific findings are used to address accountability or the overall merits of the program. Some decisions to replace a program or major parts of the program are easy because of major program deficiencies. However, most such decisions will be more difficult because of the need to weigh multiple strengths and weakness of the program as well as other considerations such as resource constraints such as budget, staff, and time.

A SIX-PHASE APPROACH TO PROGRAM EVALUATION

There are a variety of approaches for conducting an evaluation, but most proceed through a similar sequence of steps and decision points. We have grouped these steps and decision points into a six-phase approach for executing a successful evaluation:

1. Identifying stakeholders, evaluators, and evaluation questions

2. Planning the evaluation

3. Collecting data

4. Analyzing and interpreting the data

5. Communicating findings and insights

6. Using the results

Although other approaches and actual HR program evaluations may over- or underemphasize some steps within these phases or accomplish a step in an earlier or later phase, any evaluation will need to address the activities covered within each of the six phases.

Deviations from these six phases may be related to the nature of the specific HR program being evaluated, characteristics of the organization, composition of the evaluation team, or a variety of resource considerations.

Phase 1: Identify Stakeholders, Evaluators, and Evaluation Questions

Phase 1 requires three major sets of decisions that will have implications throughout the HR program evaluation. The identification of stakeholders is a critical first step toward ensuring that the evaluation is appropriately structured and that the results will be relevant. Stakeholders are those individuals with a direct interest in the program, because either they depend on or are directly involved in its execution in some way. An organization's leaders, the HR and legal departments, as well as other internal groups are often important stakeholders in an HR program evaluation. External stakeholders such as stockholders and customers might also need to be considered because of their potential investment in the targeted program. Accounting for stakeholders' different perspectives from the start of a program evaluation can bring two important benefits: increased buy-in to the process and decreased resistance to change. Sometimes representative groups of stakeholders also serve on an advisory panel to the evaluation team to provide guidance throughout the process and assist with needed resources.

Another decision to be made in phase 1 involves identifying the evaluators. Although a single evaluator can conduct evaluations, we and other professionals generally recommend that a team be formed to plan and execute the evaluation process. A team approach speeds up the process and increases the likelihood that the right combination of skills is present to generate valid findings and recommendations. Using a single evaluator may limit the choice of evaluation methods to those that feel most comfortable, rather than identifying the most appropriate methods. Also, more than one explanation can often be given for a finding, and the ability to see patterns and alternative interpretations is enhanced when a team conducts an evaluation.

Identifying evaluation questions constitutes a third type of critical decision made in phase 1. An essential ingredient to valid findings and recommendations is identifying well-focused, answerable questions at the beginning of the project that address the needs of the stakeholders. The way the evaluation questions are posed has implications for the kinds and sources of data to be collected, data analyses, and the conclusions that can be drawn. Therefore, the evaluation team must arrive at evaluation questions that not only address the needs of the stakeholders but that are also answerable within the organizational constraints that the team will face.

In many cases, stakeholder groups, evaluators, and evaluation questions will be obvious based on the nature of the HR program and the events that led to its evaluation. Any number of events can precipitate a decision to conduct an HR program evaluation. These events can vary from a regularly scheduled review of a program that appears to be working properly, such as a review of the HR information system every three years, to the need for a program to be certified, which could be a safety inspection in a nuclear power plant, to a major revamping of a program caused by a significant or high-visibility event such as a publicized gender discrimination case.

Phase 2: Plan the Evaluation

Phase 2 focuses on designing the HR program evaluation, developing a budget, and constructing the timeline to accomplish the steps throughout the next four phases of the evaluation. A good evaluation design enhances the credibility of findings and recommendations by incorporating a sound methodological approach, minimizing time and resource requirements, and ensuring stakeholder buy-in. A well-executed evaluation requires a good deal of front-end planning to ensure that the factors likely to affect the quality of the results can be addressed. Failure to spend the time necessary to fully plan the evaluation can result in a good deal of rework, missed milestones, unmet expectations, and other problems that make findings and recommendations difficult to *sell* to upper management and other stakeholders.

An often-overlooked aspect of the planning phase is the need to develop a realistic budget that is reviewed and approved by the sponsors of the evaluation. The evaluation team's budget should include, among other things, staffing, travel, special equipment, and space requirements. The extent of the evaluation plan will depend on the size and scope of the HR program being evaluated and the methods used in the analysis. The goal is to obtain credible answers to the evaluation questions through sound methodology and by using only those organizational resources that are absolutely required.

Phase 3: Collect Data

In most HR program evaluations, data collection will require more time than any other phase. The credibility of the evaluation's conclusions and recommendations rests largely with the quality of the data assembled, so a good deal of attention needs to be paid to *getting it right*. It is critical that this phase be carefully planned so that the data adequately answer the evaluation questions and provide the evidence needed to support decisions regarding the targeted program.

The tasks performed for this phase are concentrated on four primary sets of overlapping activities, which include

- ensuring that the proper data collection methods have been selected to properly evaluate the HR program,
- using data collection strategies that take into account organizational resource limitations,
- establishing quality control measures, and
- building efficiency into the data collection process.

A program evaluation will only be as good as the data used to evaluate its effectiveness. The ultimate goal is to deliver the most useful and accurate information to key stakeholders in the most cost-effective and realistic manner.

In general, it is wise to use multiple methods of data collection to ensure the accuracy, consistency, and quality of results. Specifically, a combination of quantitative methods such as surveys and qualitative methods such as interviews will typically result in a richer understanding of the program and more confidence in the accuracy of the results.

Phase 4: Analyze and Interpret Data

Statistical data analyses and interpretation of the results are an integral part of most HR evaluation programs. The evaluation plan and goals should dictate the types of statistical analyses to be used in interpreting the data. Many evaluation questions can be answered through the use of simple descriptive statistics, such as frequency distributions, means and medians, and cross-tabulations. Other questions may require more sophisticated analyses that highlight trends and surface important subtleties in the data. The use of advanced statistical techniques may require specialized professional knowledge unavailable among the evaluation team members. If so, the team may need to obtain outside assistance. The evaluation team is ultimately responsible for using statistical procedures that will generate practically meaningful interpretations and address the evaluation questions.

Simpler is often better in choosing statistical procedures because the evaluation team must be able to explain the procedures, assumptions, and findings to key stakeholders who are likely to be less methodologically sophisticated than the team members. The inability to explain and defend the procedures used to generate findings—particularly those that might disagree with a key stakeholder's perspective—could lead to concerns about those findings, as well as the total program evaluation effort.

Phase 5: Communicate Findings and Insights

Phase 5 focuses on strategies for ensuring that evaluation results are meaningfully communicated. With all the information produced by an evaluation, the evaluation team must differentiate what is essential to communicate from what is simply interesting and identify the most effective medium for disseminating information to each stakeholder group. Regardless of the group, the information must be conveyed in a way that engenders ownership of the results and motivation to act on the findings.

Each stakeholder group will likely have its own set of questions and criteria for judging program effectiveness. As such, the evaluation team needs to engage these groups in discussions about how and when to best communicate the progress and findings of the evaluation. Gaining a commitment to an ongoing dialogue with stakeholders increases ownership of and motivation to act on what is learned. Nurturing this relationship throughout the project helps the evaluation team make timely and appropriate refinements to the evaluation design, questions, methods, and data interpretations.

The extent and nature of these information exchanges should be established during the planning phase of the evaluation (i.e., phase 2). Thereafter, the agreed-on communication plan, with timelines and milestones, should be followed throughout the evaluation.

Phase 6: Use the Results

In reviewing the literature on program evaluation, the chief criticism that emerges is that evaluation reports frequently go unread and findings are rarely used. Although credible findings should be enough to drive actions, this is rarely a sufficient condition. Putting knowledge to use is probably the most important yet intransigent challenge facing program evaluators. Furthermore, the literature on both program evaluation and organizational development indicates that planned interventions and change within an organization are likely to be met with resistance. The nature and source of this resistance will depend on the program, stakeholders involved, and culture of the organization. By understanding that resistance to change is a natural state for individuals and organizations, the program evaluation team can better anticipate and address this challenge to the use of program evaluation results.

Decisions about whether to implement recommendations (e.g., to adjust, replace, or drop an HR program) will be driven by various considerations. Ideally, the nature of the stakeholder questions and the resulting findings heavily influence how recommendations are formulated. In addition, the evaluation approach, such as formative versus summative, will influence which recommendations are implemented. A primary consideration in the adjust–replace–drop decision is cost. In most cases, the short-term costs will probably favor modification of the existing program, and the long-term costs will probably favor replacement. It should be noted that replacing an HR program is almost always more disruptive than adjusting an existing system. In these situations it is not uncommon for program staff members, users, and other key stakeholders to take a short-term perspective and prefer work-arounds and other program inefficiencies instead of the uncertainty that comes with a replacement program.

The Joint Committee on Standards for Educational Evaluation (founded by the American Educational Research Association, the American Psychological Association, and the National Council on Measurement in Education in 1975) published a set of standards organized around the major tasks conducted in a program evaluation. Anyone embarking on a program evaluation would benefit from a review of these standards. Other useful readings on the subject are listed in the reference section.

—*John C. Scott, Nambury S. Raju, and Jack E. Edwards*

AUTHOR'S NOTE: The opinions expressed in this entry are those of the authors and do not necessarily reflect the views of the U.S. Government Accountability Office—of which the third author is an employee—or the federal government.

See also Compensation; Organizational Communication, Formal; Organizational Communication, Informal; Recruitment; Succession Planning; Team Building; Training; Work–Life Balance

FURTHER READING

Davidson, E. J. (2004). *Evaluation methodology basics: The nuts and bolts of sound evaluation.* Thousand Oaks, CA: Sage.

Edwards, J. E., Scott, J. C., & Raju, N. S. (Eds.). (2003). *The human resources program-evaluation handbook.* Thousand Oaks, CA: Sage.

Joint Committee on Standards for Educational Evaluation. (1994). *The program evaluation standards: How to assess evaluations of educational programs* (2nd ed.). Thousand Oaks, CA: Sage.

Morris, L. L., Fitz-Gibbon, C. T., & Freeman, M. E. (1987). *How to communicate evaluation findings.* Beverly Hills, CA: Sage.

National Science Foundation. (1993). *User-friendly handbook for project evaluation: Science, mathematics, engineering and technology education* (NSF 93-152). Arlington, VA: Author.

Patton, M. Q. (1996). *Utilization-focused evaluation* (3rd ed.). Thousand Oaks, CA: Sage.

Rose, D. S., & Davidson, E. J. (2003). Overview of program evaluation. In J. E. Edwards, J. C. Scott, & N. S. Raju (Eds.), *The human resources program-evaluation handbook* (pp. 3–26). Thousand Oaks, CA: Sage.

Rossi, P. H., & Freeman, H. E. (1993). *Evaluation: A systematic approach* (5th ed.). Newbury Park, CA: Sage.

Scriven, M. (1991). *Evaluation thesaurus* (4th ed.). Beverly Hills, CA: Sage.

Wholey, J. S., Hatry, H. P., & Newcomer, K. E. (Eds.). (1994). *Handbook of practical program evaluation.* San Francisco: Jossey-Bass.

PROJECT A

Project A was the name applied by the U.S. Army to its contribution to the Joint-Service Job Performance Measurement/Enlistment Standards (JPM) Project sponsored by the Department of Defense (DoD) in 1982. Lasting until 1989, Project A—which now also comprises the follow-on Career Force project (examining performance during soldiers' second tours of duty and spanning 1990–1994)—is arguably the largest selection and classification project ever conducted. Results from Project A continue to shape the way the Army selects, assigns, trains, and promotes its soldiers. Project A data remain a rich storehouse of information about individual differences and job performance. Project results and data have also had an impact on the field of industrial/organization (I/O) psychology at large, having sparked theoretical developments regarding models of job performance (contextual performance, determinants of relevant variance), a resurgence in interest regarding personality tests as selection tools, and development of models for setting recruit enlistment standards.

THE JOINT-SERVICE JOB PERFORMANCE MEASUREMENT/ ENLISTMENT STANDARDS PROJECT

The JPM Project was a congressionally mandated multimillion-dollar effort that spanned 1982 to 1994. The impetus for JPM was the discovery of a scoring error that inflated the scores of lower-aptitude recruits on the Armed Services Vocational Aptitude Battery (ASVAB). This miscalibration of ASVAB scores led to the enlistment of approximately 250,000 individuals who otherwise would not have qualified for entrance, and increased congressional concerns about recruit quality.

In response to the miscalibration, the DoD initiated the JPM Project. A primary goal of JPM was to determine if *hands-on* job performance could be measured. If so, the DoD could set enlistment standards on the basis of that job performance information. Previous standards were tied to training success rather than job performance, and the ASVAB was validated against training performance but not against performance on the job in the field.

The DoD encouraged each branch of the armed forces to conduct its own research for JPM. The U.S. Army Research Institute (ARI) sponsored the Army's effort. The Army's approach was ambitious, expanding the predictor and criterion domains by developing new entry-level selection and performance measures. The selection project was named *Project A* to distinguish it from the classification research effort *Project B*.

STUDY DESIGN

Project A included both concurrent and longitudinal validation samples. The concurrent validation (CV) cohort included soldiers who enlisted during the 1983 and 1984 fiscal years. These soldiers completed the new selection and performance measures at the same time, approximately two years into their first tours of duty (CVI sample). Those soldiers who reenlisted were eligible to complete measures of second-tour (supervisory) performance (CVII sample). Soldiers in the longitudinal validation (LV) cohort enlisted during the 1985 and 1986 fiscal years. They received the Experimental Battery during their first two days in the Army (LVP sample), measures of training performance at the end of technical training for their jobs (LVT sample), and measures of job performance once in their units approximately two years after enlistment (LVI) and during their second tours (LVII).

The project collected data on soldiers from 21 military occupational specialties (MOS). The full complement of performance measures (written test of job knowledge and hands-on tests, in particular) was developed for 10 of these, which were deemed *Batch A MOS*. They tended to be high-density jobs of central importance to Army functioning such as infantryman, light wheel mechanic, and medical specialist. The other 11 *Batch Z MOS* reflected more specialized, lower-density occupations, including ammunition specialist, utility helicopter repairer, and intelligence analyst; they did not have hands-on measures developed for them.

CRITERION MEASURES

To determine whether ASVAB scores predicted job performance, the Army developed numerous performance measures to serve as criteria for its validation and performance modeling studies. Selection studies are only as meaningful as the criteria used, and Project A addressed the traditional criterion problem head-on. This approach of obtaining multiple measures of multiple job behaviors broke with conventional notions that viewed job performance as unitary, hypothesizing instead that job performance was not a single entity but was instead a complex variable to study.

Two broad categories of criterion content were considered: performance elements that are specific to a particular job (assessed by MOS-specific measures), and performance elements that are relevant to all jobs (assessed by Army-wide measures). Criteria were also categorized as *can-do* measures (assessing how well soldiers are able to perform) and *will-do* measures (assessing how well soldiers typically perform from day to day). The criteria included written tests of MOS-specific job knowledge, hands-on performance tests (also known as *work samples*), various anchored rating scales (MOS-specific performance for Batch A and performance on Army-wide dimensions for all MOS), and data from administrative files such as letters of commendation and counseling statements.

PREDICTOR MEASURES

In addition to evaluating whether ASVAB scores predicted job performance, the Project A research team investigated the degree to which measures of other individual differences could increase the predictive power of this test battery. Measures of spatial ability, perceptual speed and accuracy, psychomotor ability, temperament, vocational interests, and work values—collectively denoted the Trial Battery (CV sample) and Experimental Battery (LV sample)—were developed, administered to thousands of soldiers, and correlated with the various criterion measures. Results were obtained for the Army as a whole and by subgroups of interest (MOS, race/ethnicity, gender).

MAJOR FINDINGS

Results from Project A research and their implications for personnel psychology have filled journals and books. Nevertheless, some of the major findings from the project include the following:

- ASVAB is a valid predictor of performance across Army jobs and across subgroups (race and ethnicity, gender). Soldiers with higher aptitude perform better than lower-aptitude soldiers on many types of performance measures.
- Measures of other ability constructs such as spatial ability, perceptual speed or accuracy, and psychomotor ability also predict performance across jobs but provide little incremental validity to the ASVAB.
- Performance is not unidimensional but is instead a complex multidimensional construct.
- ASVAB scores predict maximal performance (can-do criteria) better than they predict typical performance (will-do criteria).
- Measures of noncognitive constructs, such as temperament, collected under research conditions predict will-do criteria better than ASVAB, and they provide substantial incremental validity to ASVAB.
- Criterion-related validity of ASVAB scores assessed longitudinally was very similar for first- (LVI) and second-tour (LVII) soldiers. Noncognitive measures, however, tended to show declining correlations over time.

- The elements of performance are similar as the soldier gains experience, but leadership emerges as a performance element in the second tour.
- First-tour performance provides more incremental validity than ASVAB when predicting leadership and effort during the second tour, but it provides less incremental validity for can-do performance criteria.

—*Rodney A. McCloy*

See also Job Performance Models; Selection Strategies; Validation Strategies; Work Samples

FURTHER READING

Campbell, J. P., & Knapp, D. J. (Eds.). *Exploring the limits in personnel selection and classification.* Mahwah, NJ: Lawrence Erlbaum.

Project A: The U.S. Army selection and classification project. (1990). *Personnel Psychology, 43*(2), 231–378.

Zook, L. M. (1996). *Soldier selection: Past, present, and future.* Alexandria, VA: U.S. Army Research Institute for the Behavioral and Social Sciences.

PROTESTANT WORK ETHIC

The notion of the *Protestant work ethic* has its roots in Max Weber's *The Protestant Ethic and the Spirit of Capitalism*, in which he espoused the idea that the success of capitalism and economic growth throughout Western Europe and North America was partly the consequence of Puritanical values such as a calling to one's work and frugality with one's resources. Today, psychologists use the term *Protestant work ethic* (PWE) to refer to the extent to which individuals place work at the center of their existences, abhor idleness, and value accomplishment. Although there are several measures of the PWE, the most commonly used measure asks respondents the extent to which they agree or disagree (typically using a 1–7 response range) with statements such as the following: "The credit card is a ticket to careless spending," "Most people who do not succeed in life are just plain lazy," and "Our society would have fewer problems if people had less leisure time."

The psychological study of the PWE has centered on two primary questions:

1. What are the antecedents of PWE endorsement?

2. What are the consequences of PWE endorsement?

Research has tended to focus more on the second of these two questions, the one more likely to be of interest to an industrial/organizational (I/O) psychologist. But before examining the consequences of PWE endorsement, we briefly examine its antecedents.

ANTECEDENTS OF PWE ENDORSEMENT

Endorsement of the PWE is related to a general conservative ideology. Indeed, one consistent research finding is that PWE endorsement in the United States is positively correlated with extent of identification with the Republican Party. In addition, PWE endorsement is related to values such as accomplishment, salvation, obedience, and self-control. However, PWE endorsement is distinct from other forms of conservatism. For example, social dominance orientation is the belief in a societal hierarchy of groups based on some group-level characteristic such as ethnic background. Right-wing authoritarianism consists of displaying high degrees of deference to established authority, acting aggressively toward societal outgroups when authorities permit such aggression, and supporting traditional values when authorities endorse those values. The PWE is related more to the notions of ambition, delay of gratification, and equitable distribution of rewards. Thus although PWE endorsement has its roots in conservative ideology, it is distinct from general conservative orientation and other forms of conservatism.

CONSEQUENCES OF PWE ENDORSEMENT

It has been reported that hiring managers placed more emphasis on a potential employee's attitude toward work than aptitude for work, and that job interviews are in part intended to gain a sense of a candidate's attitude toward work. In another survey more than half of those managers queried believed that people's attitudes toward their work were more important than even native intelligence! Thus a number of studies have investigated the relationship between PWE endorsement (as a proxy for work attitudes) and work-related variables. In large part, these studies tend to buttress the importance of one's attitude toward work. For example, several studies indicate that PWE endorsement is positively correlated with work motivation, job-growth satisfaction, job involvement, organizational commitment, organizational citizenship behaviors, persistence in a task, and conscientiousness.

In addition to beneficial work-related outcomes, several studies have indicated that PWE endorsement is positively related to psychological well-being across different operationalizations of psychological well-being. However, two cautions of this replicated result are warranted. First, it is less clear if this finding is applicable to individuals is non-Western cultures. Second and related, there is minimal evidence for why PWE endorsement is positively correlated with psychological health. It may be that because hard work is a traditional Western and certainly American value, adhering to the pervasive cultural norm is the *third variable* responsible for this finding. Evidence for this contention comes from one study in which it was found that among overweight women, PWE endorsement was predictive of lower levels of psychological health, presumably because being overweight carries with it a stigma of being lazy. Thus although PWE endorsement has been found to be predictive of greater psychological health, there appear to be certain boundaries on this result. Employees who endorse the PWE, but are not performing up to their own or their supervisor's standards, may be at risk for reduced levels of psychological well-being.

It is also important to note that PWE endorsement also appears to be related to prejudice against groups of people who violate the core value of PWE endorsement, that is, hard work. Indeed, if an employee who strongly endorses the PWE is working with fellow employees who are not *pulling their weight,* we might expect major impediments in such professional relationships. Likewise, for supervisors with strong PWE orientations, it might be particularly irksome to perceive that some employees are not offering their best efforts in the workplace. Even if the work itself is at least satisfactory, PWE-oriented supervisors may be biased against such employees in terms of performance appraisals and the distributions of other rewards.

WHAT DO WE NEED TO KNOW ABOUT PWE ENDORSEMENT?

Much like the constructs of *intelligence* and *extraversion,* there is wide interindividual variation in PWE endorsement. Interestingly, research strongly suggests physiological differences in why some individuals are more intelligent or more extraverted than others. Might there be a physiological disposition for PWE endorsement? The answer to this question might foster research on the PWE from investigators in a variety of disciplines.

Most of this entry is based on research that has tended to treat the PWE as a unifaceted construct. However, as several researchers have demonstrated, existing measures of the PWE construct are in fact multifaceted, much as Max Weber himself conceived of the PWE. In an extensive analysis of the seven existing PWE scales, Adrian Furnham found that they tended to operationalize five different facets of the PWE. Specifically, they tapped into the importance of hard work in one's life, antileisure attitudes, religion and morality, independence from others, and asceticism. Research within personality psychology has found utility in examining smaller, more precise facets of personality as opposed to larger, more general facets of personality. Future research in the PWE arena might benefit from similarly addressing how different facets of PWE endorsement are differentially predictive of the outcomes summarized in this chapter. A relatively new measure of different PWE facets might greatly facilitate such investigations.

—*Andrew N. Christopher*

See also Work Motivation; Work Values

FURTHER READING

Christopher, A. N., & Mull, M. S. (2005). *Conservative ideology and ambivalent sexism.* Manuscript submitted for publication.

Feather, N. T. (1984). Protestant ethic, conservatism, and values. *Journal of Personality and Social Psychology, 46,* 1132–1141.

Furnham, A. (1990). A content, correlational, and factor analytic study of seven questionnaire measures of the Protestant work ethic. *Human Relations, 43,* 383–399.

Miller, M. J., Woehr, D. J., & Hudspeth, N. (2002). The meaning and measurement of work ethic: Construction and initial validation of a multidimensional inventory. *Journal of Vocational Behavior, 60,* 451–489.

Quinn, D. M., & Crocker, J. (1999). When ideology hurts: Effects of belief in the Protestant work ethic and feeling overweight on the psychological well-being of women. *Journal of Personality and Social Psychology, 77,* 402–414.

PSYCHOLOGICAL CONTRACT

A psychological contract is a belief based on commitments expressed or implied, regarding an exchange agreement between two parties, as commonly used, between an individual and an employer. People typically are motivated to fulfill the commitments they have made to others, consistent with their own understanding of what those commitments entail. In employment, psychological contracts can vary considerably across workers and between firms. They can be as limited to highly economic or transactional terms, such as an hourly wage for a temporary worker who ships packages over the holidays, or as complex and broad as the generous support and mutual investment characteristic of high involvement work. Employers in turn have their own psychological contracts with individual workers.

FEATURES OF THE PSYCHOLOGICAL CONTRACT

The dynamics of the psychological contract are shaped by its defining features.

Voluntariness

Psychological contracts motivate people to fulfill their commitments because they are based on the exchange of promises in which the individual has freely participated. Commitments made voluntarily tend to be kept. A worker who agrees to work for a firm for a set time period is likely to be internally conflicted on receiving an outside offer shortly after being hired. That worker is more likely to decline the offer than a colleague who had made no such commitment to the employer.

Perceived Mutuality

An individual's psychological contract reflects the person's own understanding of the commitments made with another. Individuals act on that subjective understanding as if it were mutual, regardless of whether that is the case in reality.

Incompleteness

At the outset of employment, initial psychological contracts tend to be incomplete and need to be fleshed out over time. Neither worker nor employer can spell out all the details of an employment relationship that will last a period of time. Because of bounded rationality, neither party can recall all relevant details to be shared with another. Moreover, changing circumstances mean that not all contingencies can be foreseen. As a result, psychological contracts tend to become more elaborate and detailed over the course of the employment relationship.

Multiple Contract Makers

A variety of information sources shape how workers interpret their psychological contract with an employer. Employers are represented by several parties including the top management team; human resource representatives; and in particular, a worker's immediate superior, often the most influential agent in shaping employee psychological contracts. Informal sources such as coworkers can influence how individuals interpret the terms of their psychological contract as well as the extent to which the contract has been fulfilled. Human resource practices such as development programs and performance appraisal systems can signal promised benefits and required contributions. In particular, early experiences with an employer, from recruitment to early socialization and initial assignments to particular bosses and coworkers, can have pervasive effects over time on worker psychological contracts. When contract makers convey different messages, they erode the mutuality of the psychological contract.

Reliance Losses

When a party relies on the psychological contract as a guide to action, losses result if the other party fails to fulfill its anticipated commitments. Losses mean that benefits a party has relied on failed to materialize; and they are the basic reason why psychological contract violation and change generate adverse reactions, including anger, outrage, termination, and withdrawal of support. Efforts that both workers and employer take to manage their psychological contract with the other typically focus on fulfilling commitments as well as on managing losses when existing commitments are difficult to keep. Psychological contracts are a subset of a broader array of beliefs and expectations workers and employers may hold, where expectations that are not promise based are not relied on to the same extent as more general expectations regarding worker and employer behavior. Non-promise-based aspects of employment that workers find satisfying, such as the quality of their workspace or the camaraderie of colleagues, can eventually be viewed as part of the promised status quo—and generate negative reactions comparable to contract violations.

Automatic Processes

Once a psychological contract is formed, it creates an enduring mental model of the employment relationship. This mental model provides a stable understanding of what to expect in the future and guides efficient action without a lot of need to be refreshed or practiced. Having a psychological contract as a mental model of the employment relationship helps employer and worker function despite having incomplete information regarding the other party's intentions or expectations. Subsequent information tends to be interpreted in light of the preexisting psychological contract. For the most part, this is functional because new performance demands can be incorporated into existing understandings of a person's work role. But when existing psychological contracts are in conflict with new employment conditions, a more elaborate change process is required.

TYPES OF PSYCHOLOGICAL CONTRACTS

Psychological contracts can take many forms depending on the nature of the worker's job, the employer's human resource strategy, and the motives the worker has in contracting with a particular employer. Promises can be very limited in nature, as in the case of the simple economic transaction temporary work entails. Or promises workers and the employer make to each other can involve a host of relational commitments including loyalty and mutual concern. Although the myriad details of a psychological contract can be as unique as each individual, there are general patterns that differentiate how workers and employers behave toward each other.

A relational psychological contract includes such terms as *loyalty*, worker and employer commitment to meeting the needs of the other, and *stability*, an open-ended commitment to the future. Workers with relational contracts are more likely to willingly work overtime, whether paid or not, to help coworkers on the job, and to support organizational changes their employer deems necessary. Although workers with a relational contract are likely to be particularly upset when it is violated, the commitment to their employer created by such contracts often manifests in worker attempts to seek redress or remedy to maintain the relationship. Failure to remedy the situation typically leads to turnover or, should the employee remain, to reduced contributions and erosion of the employment relationship. Employers with relational contracts absorb more of the risk from economic uncertainties, often protecting workers from economic downturns. An archetypal employer with a relational contract might keep workers employed during severe economic downturns. Employers in turn offer the individual workers they particularly value more relational contracts than they do other workers who contribute less.

A transactional psychological contract includes such terms as *narrow duties* and *limited* or *short-term duration.* Workers with transactional contracts are likely to adhere to its specific terms and seek employment elsewhere when conditions change or when the employer fails to live up to the agreement. Transactional contracts characterize workers whose contributions are less critical to the firm's comparative advantage and employers operating in highly unstable markets such as entertainment and fashion. Both worker and employer are likely to immediately terminate a transactional arrangement that fails to meet their needs. Transaction contracts assign more risk to workers from the economic uncertainties the employer faces because the worker often has fewer alternatives (being less able to seek credit for future services). With transactional contracts workers tend to perform in ways consistent with the contributions they are paid to make. Employers receive a specific level of contribution and incur no future obligations to these workers. Such arrangements work well when workers are individual contributors, whose performance deliverables can be explicitly established and monitored, and where there is little need to coordinate with others. Transactional contracts are less functional when they are a by-product of violation of or poorly managed change in relational contracts where either worker or employer has lost trust in the other, resulting in a warier, arms'-length arrangement.

The emergence of a hybrid (*balanced*) form of psychological contract in recent years combines the open-ended time frame and mutual concern of relational agreements with the performance demands and renegotiation of the transactional contract. Balanced contracts state commitments on the part of the employer to develop and provide career advantage to workers, in the firm as well as in future employability elsewhere if need be, while anticipating flexible contributions and adjustment to changing economic conditions on the part of workers. Balanced contracts entail shared risk between worker and employer and anticipate renegotiation over time as economic conditions of the firm and worker interests and needs change.

Psychological contracts are related to, yet distinct from, objective conditions of work such as employment status (e.g., full-time, temporary). Part-time workers and newcomers can have highly relational agreements with an employer, and many full-timers and veterans report only limited commitments between themselves and their employer. It is necessary to drill down into the beliefs workers and managers hold and the information sources they rely on (their manager, coworkers, and events they witnessed) rather than relying on general assumptions regarding broad job categories.

Mutuality is important to the effective functioning of an employment relationship. A major feature of a psychological contract is the individual's belief that an agreement is mutual, and a common understanding exists binding the parties involved to a particular course of action. Agreement between worker and employer on what each owes the other is critical to the employment relationship's success from each party's perspective. Psychological contracts are more likely to be kept when the parties agree as to their terms. Creating mutuality is the gold standard in employment relations. When both parties agree on their joint obligations, worker attitudes and job performance are higher than where their beliefs are mismatched. Nonetheless, parties tend to have different perceptions of how well each fulfills their side of the bargain. Employers tend to rate themselves more highly on fulfilling their end of the deal than workers rate their employer. Similarly, workers rate themselves on average as having fulfilled their end of the bargain to a greater degree than their employer has. This pattern conforms to the well-established availability bias, where parties to a relationship are better able to recall their own contributions than they are those of their partners. Biases in perceptions of contributions do create problems in an important aspect of mutuality: agreement on what workers owe the employer in payback for the employer's contributions to them.

Violation where an employer or worker believes that the psychological contract has been willfully breached by the other generates a long list of dysfunctional outcomes. Anger, quitting, and lower performance, particularly in terms of discretionary contributions such as citizenship behavior, are the more overt manifestations of psychological contract violation. More subtle can be the mistrust, emotional withdrawal, and sabotage that also accompany violation, particularly in circumstances where the violated party continues in the relationship. In such cases erstwhile relational contracts can turn transactional as the aggrieved party monitors each interaction for signs of exploitation or abuse. Although more relationally oriented employment relations may withstand threats to the psychological contract, breaches of significant important or drastic changes that are poorly managed can create a cycle of escalating violation over time. Incidents that fundamentally breach valued conditions of employment can form the basis of contract violation (e.g., where worker health and safety are affected or employers fail to support workers in providing quality care to clients or service to customers). In the aftermath of violation or poorly managed change, the process of restoring trust can require the formation of a new relationship, finding ways for veterans to begin feeling like newcomers to a new relationship.

But by far the most important aspect of the *employer's side* is the role managers play. Managers, both immediate supervisors and higher-ups, play the central role in shaping a worker's psychological contracts. The presence of a supportive immediate manager can serve to amplify or downplay messages sent by the firm's HR practices regarding the nature of the employment relationship. An individual manager's own psychological contract itself influences the contracts that manager in turn creates with workers.

Actions individual workers take can influence their own psychological contracts. First, their career goals influence the kinds of commitments individuals believe they make to the employer. Second, worker personality plays a role in psychological contracts with more conscientious workers having more relational contracts. Individual workers can negotiate special arrangements with their employer unavailable to their coworkers, resulting in distinct psychological contracts with the employer.

—*Denise M. Rousseau*

See also Withdrawal Behaviors, Turnover

FURTHER READING

Dabos, G. E., & Rousseau, D. M. (2004). Mutuality and reciprocity in the psychological contracts of employee and employer. *Journal of Applied Psychology, 89,* 52–72.

Raja, U., Johns, G., & Ntalianis, F. (in press). The impact of personality on the psychological contract. *Academy of Management Journal.*

Robinson, S. L., & Morrison, E. W. (1995). Organizational citizenship behavior: A psychological contract perspective. *Journal of Organizational Behavior, 16,* 289–298.

Robinson, S. L., & Rousseau, D. M. (1994). Violating the psychological contract: Not the exception but the norm. *Journal of Organizational Behavior, 15,* 245–259.

Rousseau, D. M. (1990). New hire perspectives of their own and their employer's obligations: A study of psychological contracts. *Journal of Organizational Behavior, 11,* 389–400.

Rousseau, D. M. (1995). *Psychological contracts in organizations: Understanding written and unwritten agreements.* Newbury Park, CA: Sage.

Simon, H. A. (1997). *Administrative behavior* (4th ed.). New York: Free Press.

QUALITATIVE RESEARCH APPROACH

Qualitative research is an approach to inquiry that refers to a broad umbrella domain of various research traditions and investigative and analytic practices employed by researchers in a wide range of subject disciplines. One way of understanding the variety is to understand qualitative inquiry from the perspective of three broad philosophical paradigms that represent various worldviews composed of values, beliefs, and methodological assumptions and that bring into focus different domains of study. These can be characterized as modernist, interpretive, and postmodern. Practiced from within the modernist paradigm, qualitative inquiry identifies the facts and causes of particular phenomena to test or develop theory in the context of the real world of work; for example, collecting accounts of the circumstances under which people choose to leave their jobs to theorize voluntary turnover. From the perspective of the interpretive paradigm, however, researchers are interested in understanding the relationship between people's subjective reality and their work-related behaviors—that is, what do objects and events mean to people, how do they perceive what happens to them, and how do they adapt their behavior in light of these understandings and perceptions. For example, researchers may explore people's subjective interpretation of competence at work, developing an understanding of how those subjective interpretations affect performance. From the perspective of a postmodern worldview, qualitative inquiry offers the possibility to examine and challenge the realities in which people live and work and the things they take for granted, including the assumptions of the researcher. For example, researchers may surface implicit gendering reflected in research and theorizing about leadership.

In addition to the variety generated by paradigmatic orientations, qualitative research is also practiced from many different traditions. Within these, research takes a slightly different shape and pursues different outcomes. Consider just a few. For example, researchers doing ethnographic research focus on the detailed examination of social phenomena in a small number of settings; typically, ethnography is carried out in just one social setting. Within that setting the ethnographic researcher simultaneously participates in and observes daily life to learn about its mundane and routine habits of mind and behavior. Action researchers, by comparison, aim to both provide practical advice and acquire knowledge about the dynamics of change in organizations; their research subjects are active participants in the research process. Case study researchers typically gather a variety of data, which can include both qualitative and numerical observations; and they write up a case history of the social systems studied.

Although there is considerable variety in the orientations and traditions of qualitative research, its operational practices are relatively consistent. As a set of operational practices, qualitative inquiry is distinguished by the following conditions in the practice of sampling, the practice of gathering observations, and the practice of analysis. Regardless of data-gathering modes chosen, sampling in qualitative research follows a distinct logic. Generally speaking, qualitative inquiry focuses in depth on relatively small samples that are selected purposefully. The logic and power of purposeful sampling is founded on deliberately searching out and selecting settings, people, and events that will provide rich and detailed information regarding the research question. For example, a researcher interested in understanding how ethically pioneering decisions are made might seek out research sites where such decisions are common, perhaps a biotechnology firm, and within that setting focus on the decisions surrounding the development and marketing of a new product, perhaps a genetic profiling product, whose ethical implications are unclear. In its selective pursuit of information-rich settings and subjects, purposeful sampling is distinct from probabilistic sampling.

In terms of observation, qualitative inquiry typically takes place in natural settings where researchers are present to the social situations and phenomena they are studying. They focus their attention on ordinary situations, events, and experiences; this access to life at work as it unfolds and as it is experienced by organization members allows researchers to gain an understanding of and theorize everyday realities in the workplace. This is achieved through various data-gathering techniques, which are intensive and time-consuming.

Gathering data through participant observation, researchers enter and become a part of the actual context in which people pursue their work, learning first-hand how they accomplish their work on a daily basis; how they talk, behave, and interact; and how they understand and experience their work. Prolonged engagement with the research site is typical, because researchers often remain present for an annual cycle within the social system they are studying, spending sufficient time there to understand and learn how to conduct themselves according to the norms of the setting. Observations are logged and converted into field notes on a daily basis. Interviews provide another avenue for gaining observations, and these vary in the extent to which they are structured and formalized. For example, interviews can be organized through highly structured and standard interview protocols or semiformal conversation guides; or they can be free-flowing, informal exchanges. Interviews can be one-off events, or subjects can be interviewed multiple times to gain their stable and changing perspectives on events as they unfold. Through interviews, researchers collect people's accounts of their work lives, actions, experiences, perceptions, opinions, and feelings. As a matter of practice, interviews are usually tape-recorded and transcribed verbatim. Documents of

various types, such as e-mails, memos, policy statements, reports, photographs, drawings, and audio and video materials, are also important data sources to understand how work is organized. Within any particular study, researchers often incorporate a number of data-gathering modes to gain a better understanding of the phenomena in which they are interested. For example, although a researcher's primary data-gathering strategy may be participant observation, such as being a participant observer to an organization's product development process, they are also likely interviewing people to gain their perspective on the events observed in, say, a product development meeting, and they may collect any organizational documents relevant to that product's development.

In the act of analysis, qualitative researchers typically work with verbal language (and occasionally visual images) rather than quantitative language as indicators of the phenomenon of interest. Consistent with the outlined data gathering modes, these verbal language texts include field notes, verbatim interview transcripts, diaries, conversation records, and organizational documents of various types. It is not usual for a data set for a given study to amount to more than 1,000 pages of unstructured text to be analyzed. With the involvement of the computer in qualitative research, researchers are able to draw on a number of software packages that aid in the management and organization of their data.

Data analysis typically overlaps with data gathering, and analysis strategies roughly fall into two main groups: categorizing strategies such as coding and thematic analysis and contextualizing strategies such as narrative analysis and case studies. Coding is the main categorizing strategy; through this strategy the data set is fractured and arranged into categories so that similarities and differences between data fragments can be recognized and identified. Through these categories, data are conceptualized, and the conceptual categories are integrated into a theoretical framework. Another form of categorizing analysis progresses by sorting data into broader themes and issues. Coding categories vary in the extent to which they draw on existing theory. In contextualizing strategies, instead of fracturing the data set into discrete elements and developing categories for them, researchers attempt to understand the data in context using various procedures to identify different relationships among elements in the text. For example, through narrative analysis researchers examine the data for relationships that organize statements and events into a coherent whole. In addition, practices such as displaying data and memoing are central to and support analysis regardless of whether researchers follow categorizing or contextualizing strategies.

A majority of qualitative studies are open-ended in their initial design, and they place minimum theoretical constraint on their data analysis and the expected outcomes of the research. This results in a research process characterized by emergence and flexibility. The term *funnel shaped* is often used to characterize this approach to design in which researchers begin with a general research question and then narrow and refine their paths of inquiry in the course of their study. This means that the activities of collecting and analyzing data, conceptualizing it, and refining research questions are in play simultaneously, influencing each other. Accordingly, data analysis is pursued in a nontheoretically constrained way; this is typical, for example, in the grounded theory approach in which data are analyzed and codes are developed by researchers through the analytic process. This process is challenging because researchers can be overwhelmed by the ambiguities and uncertainties associated with assigning meaning to hundreds of pages of words.

By contrast, some qualitative studies are more deductive in their orientation. Studies are designed and researchers pursue data collection and analysis with predetermined theoretical questions in mind and conceptual categories that they plan to elaborate and refine. For example, the form of analysis practiced in content analysis relies on existing theory to derive coding categories; these preestablished defined categories are applied to the data, and frequency counts of data fragments representing these defined categories can form the basis for quantitative analysis.

Generally speaking, qualitative inquiry results in the development of dynamic process-oriented models explaining how and why things happen as they do. Qualitative researchers' ability to be present to action as it unfolds, whether to developing work team norms or changing team behaviors, allows them to identify precisely how organization members understand their situations; the actions that flow from this understanding; what events lead to what consequences; and to the underlying contextual influences on behavior and events.

—*Karen Locke*

See also Case Study Method; Content Coding; Focus Groups; Verbal Protocol Analysis

FURTHER READING

Krippendorf, K. (2004). *Content analysis: An introduction to its methodology.* Thousand Oaks, CA: Sage.

Maxwell, J. A. (2005). *Qualitative research design: An interactive approach* (2nd ed.). Thousand Oaks, CA: Sage.

Patton, M. Q. (2002). *Qualitative research and evaluation methods* (3rd ed.). Thousand Oaks, CA: Sage.

Schwandt, T. A. (2001). *Dictionary of qualitative inquiry* (2nd ed.). Thousand Oaks, CA: Sage.

Seale, C., Giampietro, G., Gubrium J. F., & Silverman, D. (2004). *Qualitative research practice.* Thousand Oaks, CA: Sage.

QUALITY OF WORK LIFE

Discussed since the 1950s, quality of work life (QWL) has been identified as a personal reaction to the work environment and experience such as perceptions of control, satisfaction, involvement, commitment, work–life *balance,* and well-being in relation to someone's job and organization, with no one generally accepted definition of the term. As such, it has been criticized for being a vague *catchall* concept.

Early on, little to no responsibility was placed on the organization for facilitating or hindering QWL. As industrial and organizational researchers began to identify links between employee perceptions of QWL and important organizational level outcomes such as absenteeism, turnover, and in some cases performance, things started to change and organizational interventions began to be designed specifically to improve QWL. Thus the term was popularized in the 1970s and 1980s, because many QWL interventions at the time had a general goal of improving individuals' organizational perceptions and a secondary goal of improving productivity.

These interventions were focused on changes in the objective work environment that improve employees' overall work attitudes. QWL interventions were aimed at empowering workers by increasing control and autonomy, providing increased recognition and rewards in an effort to improve overall well-being and overall positive reactions to work. Types of interventions varied from the provision of employee counseling services to team building and quality circles in the

1970s and job design and enrichment in the late 1970s and 1980s. These interventions further evolved in the 1990s into the provision of alternative work schedules and family-friendly workplace supports such as paid family leave and dependent care support (e.g., the provision of on- or off-site child care). Thus we can see that QWL interventions are aimed at having an impact on individual employees' perceptions of the work environment as being positive, rewarding, and ultimately having an impact on enhanced well-being.

A primary outcome of QWL is job satisfaction. In addition, QWL interventions are expected to have an impact on the objective work context in terms of working conditions that are safe, secure, and provide adequate pay and benefits, leading to improved employee attitudes.

Here we discuss what we see as important outcomes of QWL. When a high QWL exists, we expect to see employees who are satisfied with their jobs; feel valued by their organization; are committed to the organization; and have low levels of conflicts between their work and family roles and a corresponding high level of enrichment, or positive spillover, between work and family. Furthermore, in addition to positive job attitudes and possibly job behaviors, we want to extend the outcomes to general health and well-being. In fact, recent research demonstrates positive relationships between such characteristics as job control and job demands and cardiovascular disease. Other research demonstrates relationships between work–family conflict and depression. Still other research demonstrates improved overall health when employees are happy on the job. Thus although positive job attitudes and behaviors are important, we urge researchers and practitioners not to forget about also improving our understanding of the link between QWL and enhanced physical and psychological health.

These ideas coincide with more recent attention given to the concept of the *healthy workplace*. In fact, the American Psychological Association (APA) has begun to recognize such organizations as *healthy* when they focus on employee well-being through the provision of supportive cultures and climates that value the importance of providing employees with low-stress work environments that contribute to employee health and well-being. The focus of the healthy workplace has moved away from the corporate bottom line toward viewing employees as the most valued resources. Furthermore, efforts by the APA and the National Institute for Occupational

Safety and Health (NIOSH) have led to the development of a new interdisciplinary field that integrates occupational health disciplines and psychology and that is primarily concerned with improving the QWL for employees. Specifically, occupational health psychology is focused on the prevention of stress, injury, and illness in the workplace and the promotion of safety, health, and well-being of workers. Thus it appears that efforts in the science and professional realm have led to further developments in understanding QWL, while the term itself has lost much of its popularity. Rather, more contemporary concepts such as healthy workplaces, health promotion, work–life balance, and organizational well-being are characteristics of what we traditionally know as QWL.

In sum, although the term *QWL* is not commonly used today, the meaning is inherent in many aspects of organizational psychology. QWL is now more explicitly studied and discussed within the specific organizational structures and interventions that positively influence employee attitudes, health, and well-being.

—*Leslie B. Hammer and Diana Sanchez*

See also Empowerment; Job Satisfaction; Occupational Health Psychology; Stress, Consequences; Work–Life Balance

FURTHER READING

Loscocco, K. A., & Roschelle, A. R. (1991). Influences on the quality of work and nonwork life: Two decades in review. *Journal of Vocational Behavior, 39,* 182–225.

Mirvis, P. H., & Lawler, E. E. (1984). Accounting for the quality of work life. *Journal of Occupational Behaviour, 5*(3), 197–212.

Nadler, D. A., & Lawler, E. E. (1983). Quality of work life: Perspectives and directions. *Organizational Dynamics, 11*(3), 20–30.

QUANTITATIVE RESEARCH APPROACH

Quantitative research approaches increase our knowledge by gathering data that can be manipulated mathematically. This allows us to answer questions about the meanings of psychological concepts, as well as to determine their levels and variability as well as the relationships among them. Quantitative research approaches may be contrasted with qualitative approaches, which tend to collect data expressed in nonmathematical, symbolic representations sometimes referred to as *thick descriptions,* and place less focus on estimating the strength and form of relationships.

The data associated with quantitative approaches can result from simple measurement operations such as counts or categorizations, or from more complex operations that may involve the creation of measurement scales that function as *psychological yardsticks.* For example, quantitative research approaches have allowed industrial/organizational (I/O) psychologists to develop self-report measures of a construct called job satisfaction (JS), to determine that JS has a variety of different aspects or facets (such as satisfaction with pay, supervisor, or work setting), and to study its relationships with conditions such as organizational culture or leadership that make its general level higher or lower.

A basic tenet of any science is that scientists must collect and analyze data in a manner that can be replicated by others and is open to public inspection and criticism. Really, I/O psychologists are no different; they rely heavily on a wide range of quantitative methods to pursue two broad endeavors. The first of these is to accurately *measure* psychological variables of interest, such as performance, personality, intellectual capacity, work attitudes, and many more aspects of the world of work. The second endeavor consists of the systematic and theory-driven *search for relationships* among variables. Typically, the search for relationships involves testing theory-based hypotheses, the results of which allow for scientific inferences about the presence or absence of the relationships of interest. Next, we briefly describe quantitative approaches to measurement, the rationale for significance testing, and quantitative techniques for assessing relationships.

QUANTITATIVE TECHNIQUES ADDRESSING MEASUREMENT ISSUES

Psychological measurement consists of developing rules that either allow us to classify objects into meaningful categories or identify where aspects of those objects fall on a numerical scale. Importantly, measurement is best when it is theory driven.

Two important characteristics of measures, often addressed using quantitative methods, are reliability and validity. Reliability may be defined in various

ways; however, they all address the extent to which the same (or presumably equivalent) measurement procedures will yield the same results, if repeated. A variety of statistical techniques estimate reliability—including classic test theory–based procedures, such as test–retest correlation and coefficient alpha—and more recently developed methods such as generalizability theory. Closely related are indexes of agreement, which tell us the extent to which multiple observers rate the same object in the same way.

In contrast, validity addresses the issue of whether measures capture the true essence of the intended psychological construct. Again, a variety of quantitative approaches can be used to assess validity. Construct validity questions are often addressed with factor analytic techniques, which help us better understand the patterns of interrelatedness among measures and thus the number and nature of underlying constructs or latent variables. Exploratory factor analysis (EFA) is primarily inductive, providing empirical guides to the dimensionality of a set of measures. Each separate dimension suggests the presence of a different underlying construct; and EFA also estimates the extent to which specific items or measures appear to be influenced by a common underlying factor. Confirmatory factor analysis (CFA) allows a more deductive approach, because the researcher can prespecify a hypothesized latent factor structure. It also permits tests of how well a given factor model fits the data and allows comparisons of alternative models.

Another extremely useful quantitative approach is item response theory (IRT), which relates test item responses to levels of an underlying latent trait such as cognitive ability. This technique helps distinguish good test items that discriminate well between people high or low in a trait from poor items that do not. The IRT technique also enables the development of adaptive tests, allowing researchers to assess an individual's standing on a trait without having to administer the entire measure.

WHY SIGNIFICANCE TESTS ARE USED

Psychological data typically contain a lot of *noise* because measurements generally reflect not only the level of the desired variable but also other extraneous influences such as misunderstandings or impression management attempts by research participants, temporary fluctuations in mood or alertness, and random variability. Focal variables often account for as little as 5% to 10% of the observed variability in responding. This frequent condition of small to moderate effect sizes means variability caused by the focal variables is not much larger than that possibly expected from sampling error. Statistical significance testing helps researchers determine whether observed differences or associations should be attributed to the variables of interest or could simply be an artifact of sampling variability. Significance tests typically pit two mutually exclusive and exhaustive hypotheses against each other, with the desired result being to find evidence that leads one to reject a *null hypothesis* of no effect.

QUANTITATIVE TECHNIQUES ADDRESSING RELATIONSHIP ISSUES

The quantitative techniques used by I/O psychologists were primarily developed in the late 1800s, 1900s, and into the present century. Research design and quantitative analysis were closely intertwined in their development. We describe some of the most commonly used techniques, which are appropriate when the dependent variable is at least an interval level measurement. These techniques have tended to rely on least-squares estimation procedures and have linear and fixed-model assumptions.

The experimental method is particularly powerful because it allows causal inference. Experiments are studies in which the researcher systematically manipulates conditions in groups that have been created by random assignment and then compares the effects of those manipulations. Variations of experimental methods, called *quasi-experiments,* attempt to preserve at least some of the characteristics of experimental designs while acknowledging that researchers cannot always use random assignment or manipulate key variables.

The most common statistical approach for experimental data analysis is the analysis of variance (ANOVA) model; it was first developed by Sir Ronald A. Fisher, who was interested in studying differences in crop yields associated with different agricultural practices. In general, ANOVA involves the comparisons of mean levels of a dependent variable across different groups created by experimental manipulations. There are many subtypes of ANOVA models, which incorporate mixed and random effects, allow analysis of incomplete design matrices, and control for covariates, among other variations.

There is also a strong tradition of survey and questionnaire research in I/O psychology. Although this approach makes causal inference more difficult, at least some researchers argue that this drawback is compensated for by better generalizability and construct richness. In fact, there are many interesting research questions where experimental designs are impractical or impossible because of ethical or practical issues.

Correlation and regression analysis, as well as related but more complex path and structural equation modeling approaches, are commonly used to analyze survey and questionnaire data. Sir Francis Galton and Karl Pearson were instrumental in developing correlation and regression. Correlation indicates the extent and direction of association between two variables. For example, a positive correlation between job satisfaction and organizational commitment indicates that employees who are more satisfied with their jobs tend to be more committed. Regression analysis determines whether predictor variables such as grade point average (GPA) and personality linearly relate to a criterion such as job performance, and estimates the proportion of variance in the criterion explained by the predictors. Ironically, given the sharp distinction made historically between ANOVA and regression techniques, in the 1950s statisticians began to recognize that they were in fact subtypes of an umbrella statistical model called the general linear model (GLM). The GLM also subsumes other important techniques such as canonical correlation, discriminant analysis, and multivariate analysis of variance.

Finally, important developments in a set of quantitative techniques called meta-analysis have led to advances in many areas of study over the past 25 years. These techniques allow researchers to cumulate the results from multiple studies of a given relationship. Meta-analysis thus more definitively addresses the question of whether a relationship is nonzero, and better estimates its *true* effect size.

CURRENT TRENDS

Quantitative research techniques are becoming increasingly sophisticated and are simultaneously easier to implement with specialized computer software. Researchers are beginning to work more with techniques appropriate for dynamic, nonlinear, and longitudinal models; increase their use of robust or assumption-free statistics and alternative estimation methods; and critically reexamine aspects of the null hypothesis statistical testing paradigm.

—*Rosalie J. Hall and Hsien-Yao Swee*

See also Descriptive Statistics; Experimental Designs; Factor Analysis; Generalizability Theory; Inferential Statistics; Item Response Theory; Measurement Scales; Structural Equation Modeling

FURTHER READING

Bobko, P. (1995). *Correlation and regression: Principles and applications for industrial/organizational psychology and management.* New York: McGraw-Hill.

Drasgow, F., & Schmitt, N. (Eds.). (2002). *Measuring and analyzing behavior in organizations: Advances in measurement and data analysis.* San Francisco: Jossey-Bass.

Harlow, L. L., Mulaik, S. A., & Steiger, J. H. (1997). *What if there were no significance tests?* Mahwah, NJ: Lawrence Erlbaum.

Nunnally, J. C., & Bernstein, I. H. (1994). *Psychometric theory* (3rd ed.). New York: McGraw-Hill.

Rogelberg, S. G. (Ed.). (2002). *Handbook of research methods in industrial and organizational psychology.* Malden, MA: Blackwell.

Shadish, W. R., Cook, T. D., & Campbell, D. T. (2002). *Experimental and quasi-experimental designs for generalized causal inference.* New York: Houghton Mifflin.

QUASI-EXPERIMENTAL DESIGNS

One of the three basic experimental design types used in empirical research in industrial/organizational (I/O) psychology and related disciplines is quasi-experimentation. Quasi-experimental designs are different from both randomized experimental designs and nonexperimental designs (see relevant entries in this volume). In the process of describing the nature of quasi-experimental designs, we make reference to a number of issues having to do with the validity of inferences stemming from research. These issues are covered in the entry on experimental designs in this encyclopedia.

ATTRIBUTES OF QUASI-EXPERIMENTAL DESIGNS

Quasi-experimental designs have a number of features. Taken together they serve to differentiate such designs from designs of the experimental and nonexperimental varieties.

Types of Quasi-experimental Designs

There are five major varieties of quasi-experimental designs, as noted by W. R. Shadish, T. D. Cook, and D. T. Campbell (2002). They differ from one another in terms of the use of comparison conditions, the use of pretests, and the degree to which they are time-series based. The term *comparison conditions* is used here to refer to either a no-treatment control condition or a condition that has a different level of the independent variable than the focal condition.

Single-Group Designs Without a Control Condition. In terms of single-group designs without a control condition, the weakest ones, with respect to the criterion of internal validity, have only a posttest, for example the one-group posttest-only design. Slightly stronger designs have both a pretest and a posttest, such as the one-group pretest–posttest design. Even stronger designs have multiple pretests and posttests. For designs of the latter type, internal validity can be enhanced through such means as introducing treatment at one time period and removing it at a later period as in the removed treatment design. This process can be repeated several times, as with the repeated-treatment design.

Designs With a Control Condition but No Pretest. A second type of quasi-experimental study uses a control condition but no pretest. One example of such a design is the posttest-only design with a nonequivalent control condition. In general, internal validity is quite problematic with studies that use this design because the researcher typically has no knowledge about any pretreatment differences on a host of variables, making it difficult, if not impossible, to attribute posttest differences to the treatment.

Designs With Control Conditions and Pretests. A third type of quasi-experimental design uses both pretests and posttests. The simplest example of this is the untreated control condition design with both pretest and posttest measures. The addition of pretests in the treatment and comparison conditions serves to improve internal validity, such as by ruling out selection as a rival explanation of posttest differences on the dependent variable.

Time Series Designs. A fourth type of quasi-experimental design uses time series data to assess how the introduction of a treatment affects measures of dependent variables. For time series designs there must be a large number of observations, such as 50 or more, of such variables prior to and following the introduction of a treatment. In some cases time series designs involve both the introduction of a treatment and its subsequent removal. Internal validity is enhanced to the degree that these changes have expected effects on the dependent variables and the changes cannot be attributed to such confounds as history-based fluctuations. In addition, internal validity can be further enhanced through the addition of a nonequivalent control condition to the basic time series design.

Regression Discontinuity Designs. A fifth type of quasi-experimental design is the regression discontinuity design. In the most basic of such designs, the researcher uses scores on a pretest to assign individuals in a single group to treatment and control conditions. Individuals who have pretest scores at or above a given level are assigned to one condition, such as treatment, and those with scores below that level are assigned to the other condition, such as control. After the treatment, posttest scores are regressed on pretest scores. The effect of the treatment is indexed by a discontinuity in the regression lines for the treatment and control groups.

MANIPULATION OF VARIABLES

In quasi-experiments the values of independent variables $(X_1, X_2, \ldots X_j)$ are manipulated by the researcher. This is important in terms of the criterion of internal validity. More specifically, the fact that the manipulations precede the measurement of dependent variables serves to strengthen inferences about the effects of the manipulated variables on one or more dependent variables.

The simultaneous manipulation of several independent variables is common in randomized experiments that are of the factorial variety. However, it is rare to encounter quasi-experiments with more than one independent variable. This is, at least in part, a function of the fact that most quasi-experiments are conducted in non–special purpose settings (see the Experimental Designs entry for more on setting-related issues). Relative to special purpose settings, in non–special purpose settings, researchers typically have relatively little control over the number and nature of manipulations to which units, such as individuals or groups, are exposed. In addition, it is often difficult to deliver treatments to units in a uniform manner, reducing statistical conclusion validity. What's more, because individuals other than the experimenter, for example managers, have control over many features of the settings in which quasi-experiments are conducted, the same individuals may behave in ways that serve to reduce the construct validity of treatments. For example, to lessen research-related inequalities, managers may deliver desirable *treatments* of their own to units in study conditions that are scheduled to receive less desirable research-related treatments than others. This can lead to compensatory equalization-based threats to the construct validity of the study's independent variable(s).

NONRANDOM ASSIGNMENT OF UNITS TO CONDITIONS

A key characteristic that differentiates quasi-experimental designs from randomized experimental designs is that in the case of the former, there is no capacity to randomly assign units to treatment conditions. Rather than being randomly assigned to conditions by the experimenter, the units may be routed to treatment and control conditions through such means as self-selection or assignment by an administrator such as a manager. An important implication of this is that, in most cases, it is difficult, if not impossible, to rule out both selection as a threat to internal validity and selection by treatment interaction as a threat to external validity.

MEASUREMENT OF DEPENDENT VARIABLES

As is true of all other experimental design types, in quasi-experiments, dependent variables are measured. A number of techniques can be used for this purpose (see the Experimental Designs entry for examples). However, it should be added that because most quasi-experiments are conducted in non–special purpose settings, the experimenter often has diminished control over the timing of measurement and the conditions under which it takes place. In addition, many quasi-experiments use data from archival records such as those of the organizations participating in a study. As a consequence, there are often problems with the construct validity of measures of dependent variables.

CONTROL OVER CONFOUNDING OR EXTRANEOUS VARIABLES

As noted earlier, in the case of quasi-experimental research, there is no capacity to randomly assign units to treatment conditions. As a result, there may be pretreatment differences between or among the conditions on variables that are related to the dependent variables of a study. For example, consider a hypothetical study in which a researcher tested the effects of job enrichment on job satisfaction in an organization having two geographically separate production facilities. Individuals in one facility experienced job enrichment, whereas workers in the other served as no-treatment controls. Because workers were not randomly assigned to these facilities in advance of the quasi-experimental study, they might have differed from one another at the pretreatment period on such variables as age, tenure, pay, and job satisfaction, reducing the study's internal validity.

In quasi-experimental research, assumed confounds are controlled through statistical means. For example, in a study using an untreated control condition and a pretest, a researcher might regress posttest scores on pretest scores and measures of a set of assumed confounds. Regrettably, the statistical controls used in quasi-experimental studies are typically a poor substitute for the control that can be achieved in randomized experiments, as noted by Shadish and colleagues (2002) and Eugene F. Stone-Romero (2002).

—*Eugene F. Stone-Romero*

See also Experimental Designs; Nonexperimental Designs

FURTHER READING

Cook, T. D., & Campbell, D. T. (1979). *Quasi-experimentation: Design and analysis issues for field settings.* Boston: Houghton Mifflin.

Shadish, W. R., Cook, T. D., & Campbell, D. T. (2002). *Experimental and quasi-experimental designs for generalized causal inference.* Boston: Houghton Mifflin.

Stone-Romero, E. F. (2002). The relative validity and usefulness of various empirical research designs. In S. G. Rogelberg (Ed.), *Handbook of research methods in industrial and organizational psychology* (pp. 77–98). Malden, MA: Blackwell.

QUESTIONNAIRES

See SURVEY APPROACH

R

RACE NORMING

Race norming is the practice of converting individual test scores to percentile or standard scores within one's racial group. In the process of race norming, an individual's percentile score is not calculated in reference to all persons who took the test; instead, an individual's percentile score is determined only in reference to others in the same racial group. After norming scores by percentile in separate racial groups, the lists are combined to make selection decisions. By norming within racial groups, the same raw score for Whites and Blacks can be converted to different percentile scores based on the distribution of scores for each racial group.

For example, suppose that a White candidate and a Black candidate each earn a raw score of 74 points on a test. If the White candidate's test score is converted to a percentile only in reference to other White candidates and the Black candidate's test score is converted to a percentile only in reference to other Black candidates, then the percentile scores earned by the two candidates may not be equal even though they attained the same raw test score. Perhaps the 74-point raw score for the White candidate may be at the 60th percentile of the White distribution of scores, whereas the 74-point score for the Black candidate may be at the 65th percentile of the Black distribution of scores. When the White and Black percentile scores are combined into a common list and selection decisions are made, the candidates who scored the same 74 raw points on the test might be treated very differently. For example, if the organization decides to hire only persons who scored at the 65th percentile and above, then the Black candidate would be selected and the White candidate would not. In another circumstance, the organization could decide to hire persons with the highest percentile first, which would mean that the Black candidate would be selected prior to the White candidate.

As this example demonstrates, when test scores are race normed, the score required to reach a particular percentile score for a member of one group may be different from the score required for a member of another group to reach that percentile. In effect, the use of separate norms based on race can add points to the scores of persons from a particular racial group. The Civil Rights Act of 1991 made approaches to adjusting test scores based on race illegal.

The adjustment of scores using within-group norming procedures or other techniques is a common practice in work organizations. For example, many civil service exams call for bonus points to be awarded to veterans. Despite the prevalence of score adjustment, the concept of adjusting scores based on race (e.g., race norming) became controversial during the 1980s. At the time, the United States Employment Service (USES) made extensive use of the General Aptitude Test Battery (GATB) for hiring purposes. Research has demonstrated that Whites significantly outperform Blacks and Hispanics on the GATB; therefore, the USES race normed the data by converting test scores to percentiles within racial groups. During the mid-1980s, this practice was challenged by the U.S. Department of Justice, and it eventually became a key issue addressed in the Civil Rights Act of 1991. The act makes it unlawful to adjust or alter the scores of an employment test or to use different cutoff scores based on race, color, religion, sex, or national origin.

The ramifications of this provision, both intended and unintended, have generated much discussion, and experts continue to debate how the provision should be interpreted and implemented.

—*Harold W. Goldstein*

See also Affirmative Action; Civil Rights Act of 1964, Civil Rights Act of 1991

FURTHER READING

Gottfredson, L. S. (1994). The science and politics of race-norming. *American Psychologist, 49*(11), 955–963.

Sackett, P. R., & Wilk, S. L. (1994). Within-group norming and other forms of score adjustment in preemployment testing. *American Psychologist, 49*(11), 929–954.

RATING ERRORS AND PERCEPTUAL BIASES

The appraisal and management of performance is an important concern in organizations. Although interest in and the use of performance appraisals has increased during the last 30 years, the practice of formally evaluating employees has existed for centuries. Despite its widespread use, the performance appraisal process continues to be plagued by both technical and nontechnical problems that reduce its effectiveness. Rating errors and perceptual biases in performance ratings are two such problems.

Performance ratings—quantifiable yet subjective assessments of an individual's performance made by supervisors, peers, or others who are familiar with the employee's work behavior—are frequently used to assess work performance. However, performance ratings do not always accurately represent an employee's true level of performance. Differences between an employee's true, veridical, objective level of performance and the performance ratings that he or she receives, which are believed to be caused by perceptual biases, are referred to as *rating errors*. Although such differences are sometimes the result of intentional manipulation of the performance appraisal system because of political or interpersonal motivations, the term *rating errors* generally refers to the unconscious and unintentional biases that influence the rating task. Biases and rating errors can be classified into several categories; the following sections describe

these types of biases and errors, their consequences, and possible remedies.

TYPES OF BIASES AND RATING ERRORS

Distributional Errors

It is not uncommon to find that 80% to 90% of all employees rated by a single rater receive an above-average rating. This often indicates a *distributional error,* wherein the rater misrepresents the distribution of performance across persons they are evaluating. In other words, these errors occur when the distribution of assigned ratings differs from the (assumed) distribution of actual job performance of the group of employees being rated. Such misrepresentations can occur both in terms of the mean level and the variability of ratings provided. The three most common types of distributional errors are leniency/severity, range restriction, and central tendency errors.

Leniency/severity errors occur when the mean of the ratings of all employees rated by a particular supervisor differs substantially from the midpoint of the rating scale. For example, if the mean ratings for all employees rated by a supervisor are very low, then the rater is thought to be overly severe; when the mean ratings are very high, he or she is thought to be overly lenient. This error can be caused by (a) raters having inaccurate or unreasonable frames of reference or expectations for performance; (b) the rater's desire to be liked, hence his or her unwillingness to give negative feedback; or even (c) expectations that other raters will also inflate their ratings. Recent research has shown that rating severity/leniency is a relatively stable characteristic of the rater and can be related to his or her personality. Specifically, individuals who score higher on agreeableness tend to provide more elevated ratings, whereas individuals who score higher on conscientiousness tend to provide lower ratings.

It is also possible for a rater to fail to make adequate distinctions among multiple ratees when rating their performance, an error referred to as *range restriction.* For example, consider a group of employees who vary widely in their levels of performance on one dimension, quality of work. If all of the supervisor's ratings on this dimension are clustered within a small range of scores, the variance of the supervisor's ratings will be lower than the variance of the actual performance levels of the ratees, and hence, range restriction is said to occur. Raters who commit this error fail to distinguish among ratees on individual performance dimensions, either because of a lack of opportunity to observe the employees or a conscious desire to avoid differentiating among ratees.

A *central tendency error* is a special form of the range restriction error, wherein ratings tend to cluster near the midpoint of the rating scale. This is the most common and perhaps the most harmful type of error found in organizations, as it tends to inflate the ratings of low performers and underestimate those of high performers. This type of error may be caused by a rater's unwillingness to justify high or low ratings to the organization or to the ratee or a rater's desire to treat all employees equally and avoid hostility among ratees.

Although these distributional errors are typically assumed to reduce the accuracy of performance ratings, such a conclusion may be premature, for several reasons. First, the implicit assumption behind distributional errors is that the true underlying distribution of performance is known, which is rarely the case. Second, organizations expend considerable effort through their selection and training systems to ensure that the distribution of performance is, in fact, skewed (e.g., more high performers than low), in which case observed leniency or range restriction may not be an error but a reflection of the actual performance of employees. Thus, comparison of raters based on such errors should be undertaken only after the relevant contextual factors affecting each group of raters and ratees have been considered.

Correlational/Halo Errors

It is not uncommon to find that raters give similar evaluations across multiple performance dimensions when evaluating one employee, even when those dimensions are clearly distinct. This is referred to as a *halo error*, and it is based on the rater's tendency to let the overall evaluation or the evaluation of one dimension color ratings on other dimensions. Consider, for example, an employee who is outstanding in his ability to convince delinquent customers to pay up but performs poorly in terms of identifying new customers and expanding his market. In such a situation, halo error would occur if his excellence in the area of delinquent accounts caused his manager to rate him highly on the other performance dimensions as well. Thus, halo errors occur when raters fail to differentiate between performance on different dimensions. (Halo errors wherein a negative rating on one dimension adversely affects ratings on other dimensions are sometimes referred to as *horn effects*.) Halo errors are typically caused by the confirmatory biases of raters (wherein raters form initial impressions based on certain performance dimensions and tend to look for confirmation rather than disconfirmation of their judgments in the evaluation of other aspects of performance), the discounting of inconsistent information, or the lack of adequate information about the ratee when making evaluations.

However, like the other errors reviewed here, the existence of halo error should be interpreted with caution. Halo effects may be a function of the actual conceptual similarity among the dimensions being rated (true halo) rather than cognitive biases and errors by raters (illusory halo). It is also possible that all of the dimensions on a performance appraisal scale relate to overall performance, so they are unlikely to be seen as completely independent by raters. In such cases, observed halo may be a reflection of actual performance rather than error.

Other Errors and Biases

Performance appraisal ratings can also be plagued by other specific errors and biases. The *similar-to-me error* refers to the tendency of some raters to rate those who resemble themselves more highly than they rate others. The *first-impression error* occurs when the rater allows early experiences with a ratee to color or distort later information when making performance judgments. *Contrast effects* refer to the tendency of a rater to evaluate ratees relative to others rather than against objective rating standards. For example, if Jane is a stellar performer and her supervisor tends to rate other employees using Jane as the comparative standard, then other employees are likely to be rated lower than they deserve.

The *recency effect* describes the tendency of minor events that have occurred recently to influence ratings more than other events that occurred during the appraisal period. Such errors typically occur when the rater does not keep formal records of performance or critical incidents involving each ratee. The tendency to attribute performance failings to factors that are under the control of the individual and performance successes to external causes is known as *attribution bias*. For example, if a supervisor attributes the successes of her subordinates to her leadership skills but their failures to their own lack of ability, her performance ratings are affected by attribution bias. Finally, *stereotyping* refers to the tendency to generalize across groups and ignore individual differences. For example, consider Bob, a salesman who is quiet and reserved but whose sales record is one of the best in the company, in contrast to the stereotypical salesman. If his supervisor has an implicit belief that extroverted, outgoing behavior is a prerequisite for being a good salesman, he may rate Bob's performance lower because of that stereotype.

These errors can sometimes occur together in practice, or one error may be the cause of another observed error. For example, the contrast effect error, wherein employees are compared to one stellar employee, could result in observed severity errors.

CONSEQUENCES OF RATING ERRORS

Several negative consequences may befall performance appraisal and management systems characterized by the errors just described. For example, elevated ratings (i.e., the leniency error) reduce the funds available to recognize and reward stellar performance (because the funds must be shared among a larger number of employees), and therefore employees may become dissatisfied with both performance management and reward systems. Besides being a mechanism for allocating rewards, performance appraisals are also used to provide feedback. Employees whose supervisors fail to give them accurate information about performance deficiencies have little motivation (or guidance) to improve. As a result, such employees are likely to be passed over for opportunities they might have had if they had been honestly confronted with the need for change. Employees who receive inflated yet inaccurate ratings may be placed in a situation they are unable to handle, causing them to experience failure. Short-term kindness on the supervisor's part may result in long-term harm to the employee.

Elevated or otherwise inaccurate ratings also make it difficult to substantiate termination decisions, not only in court (if the decision is contested) but also to the remaining employees, who may question the fairness and meaningfulness of performance ratings. Equity theory suggests that individuals are concerned not only with their own situation in an absolute sense ("How much money am I making?") but also with the way their situation compares with others in the organization ("How does the ratio of my input in the job to the output/reward that I receive compare with that of others?"). A good performer, observing that a lackluster coworker is receiving the same appraisal ratings—and thus the same organizational rewards for a far lower contribution—perceives his or her situation as unfair. Equity theory suggests that as a result of such comparisons, the good performer will act to make the situation equitable by reducing his or her effort or even leaving the organization.

REMEDIAL MEASURES

Approaches to avoiding these rating errors and perceptual biases depend on the format of the rating instrument used. Forced-choice instruments ask the rater to select one item (from a list of four or five statements) that best describes the employee's performance. Because the statements are all similar in desirability (yet differ in their relation to job performance), this format is designed to eliminate the tendency of raters to be lenient, thus minimizing bias. Forced-distribution performance appraisal systems attempt to impose a normal distribution on the ratings by forcing the rater to assign a certain percentage of employees to each performance category. Similarly, paired comparison performance rating methods force raters to make distinctions among ratees by comparing each ratee to every other one, producing an overall rank order of employees. Finally, a commonly used format is the behaviorally anchored rating scales (BARS), which specifies poor, average, and good performance levels using anchors of behavioral exemplars for each performance dimension. This ensures that each employee's performance ratings on different dimensions are accurately rated and differentiated from one another. Although each of these different rating formats has its advantages, each also comes with a corresponding set of disadvantages.

A more recent (and arguably more effective) approach to dealing with rating errors is to train raters in performance appraisal rating methods. For example, rater error training (RET) focuses specifically on reducing errors by making raters aware of them and their possible causes. Despite its effectiveness in reducing rater errors, research has found that RET can actually decrease the accuracy of ratings (recall that errors do not always equal inaccuracy). As a result of using RET, raters seem to replace an erroneous rating strategy (e.g., lenient or haloed ratings) with an invalid rating bias (avoid rater errors). Thus, merely avoiding rater errors does not seem to ensure accuracy.

The best-known rater training program with the goal of increasing accuracy is frame-of-reference (FOR) training. In FOR training, raters discuss the performance dimensions used in the evaluation system and the behaviors that represent different effectiveness levels on each performance dimension; they also practice making ratings and receive feedback on the accuracy of their practice ratings. Research suggests that FOR training is the single most effective training strategy for improving rater accuracy.

—Deidra J. Schleicher and Vijaya Venkataramani

See also Performance Appraisal; Performance Appraisal, Objective Indexes; Performance Appraisal, Subjective Indexes

FURTHER READING

Borman, W. C. (1991). Job behavior, performance and effectiveness. In M. D. Dunnette & L. M. Hough (Eds.), *Handbook of industrial and organizational psychology* (2nd ed., Vol. 3, pp. 271–326). Palo Alto, CA: Consulting Psychologists Press.

Cooper, W. (1981). Ubiquitous halo. *Psychological Bulletin, 90,* 218–244.

Murphy, K. R., & Cleveland, J. N. (1991). *Performance appraisal: An organizational perspective.* Boston: Allyn & Bacon.

Murphy, K. R., Cleveland, J. N., Skattebo, A. L., & Kinney, T. B. (2004). Raters who pursue different goals give different ratings. *Journal of Applied Psychology, 89*(1), 158–164.

Schleicher, D. J., & Day, D. V. (1998). A cognitive evaluation of frame-of-reference rater training: Content and process issues. *Organizational Behavior and Human Decision Processes, 73*(1), 76–101.

Smither, J. W. (1998). *Performance appraisal: State of the art in practice.* San Francisco: Jossey-Bass.

Woehr, D. J., & Huffcutt, A. I. (1994). Rater training for performance appraisal: A quantitative review. *Journal of Occupational and Organizational Psychology, 67,* 189–205.

REALISTIC JOB PREVIEW

The primary method of realistic recruitment is the *realistic job preview* (RJP). The RJP is the presentation of realistic, often quite negative information about an organization to a job candidate. This information is given to job candidates during the selection process to help them make an informed job choice, should a job offer be made. Another realistic recruitment strategy is the use of certain recruitment sources (e.g., employee referrals) that communicate realistic information to job candidates while avoiding others that do not (e.g., newspaper ads). Finally, four selection methods that communicate realistic information to job candidates are briefly discussed here; their primary intended purpose is selection rather than recruitment.

The RJP contains accurate information about job duties, which can be obtained from interviews with subject-matter experts or from a formal job analysis. The RJP also contains information about an organization's culture, which can be obtained from surveys, interviews with current employees, and exit interviews. There are four criteria for selecting information for the RJP: (a) It is important to most recruits; (b) it is not widely known outside the organization; (c) it is a reason that leads newcomers to quit; and (d) it is related to successful job performance after being hired. Because it is necessary to tailor the RJP to both the job and the organization, the RJP is not so much a specific technique but a general approach to recruitment. Furthermore, organizations may differ in the particular means used to present realistic information to job candidates; for example, organizations may use a brochure, a discussion during the job interview, or a video. Sometimes, a combination of these three specific techniques is used; combining the latter two is probably the best approach.

One important purpose of the RJP is to increase the degree of fit between newcomers and the organizations they join. Two types of fit are affected: (a) the person–job fit and (b) the person–organization fit. Good person–job fit typically results in better newcomer performance and indirectly increases retention. Good person–organization fit typically results in reduced quitting and indirectly increases job performance. To the extent that an RJP affects candidates' job choices, also known as self-selection, it can improve either or both types of fit.

The information in the RJP is communicated to job applicants *before* they enter the organization. Realistic information disseminated after organizational entry is defined as newcomer orientation, which is different from the RJP in several ways. The most important difference is that the primary purpose of newcomer orientation is to help new hires cope with both a new job and a new organizational culture. Thus, newcomer orientation teaches solutions to common newcomer adjustment problems during organizational entry. In contrast, the RJP presents adjustment problems without solutions, as one purpose of the RJP is to discourage job candidates who are likely to be misfits with the job or organizational culture.

For a long time, the RJP was thought to affect newcomer retention more than job performance, as reported in a 1985 review by Steve Premack and John Wanous. However, a 1998 review by Jean Phillips found a stronger effect of the RJP on job performance while affirming the same effect on the retention of new hires. As of this writing, the Phillips review is the most recent study available.

Some RJP methods are more effective than others. Specifically, the best RJP technique for hiring better performers is the video, in which recruits are shown a role model performing critical job duties successfully. Role models are an effective way to demonstrate the interpersonal and physical skills that are part of most entry-level jobs.

The best RJP method for increasing new hire retention is a two-way conversation between the job candidate and a job interviewer during the job interview. Explaining why this is the case is more complicated. There are four hypotheses. First, the information provided in the RJP helps job candidates choose more effectively among job offers. This process of self-selection is believed to increase person–organization fit. Furthermore, research on cognitive dissonance suggests that when job candidates feel free to accept or reject the job offer, they are more likely to be committed to the choice. Second, the RJP can "vaccinate" expectations against disappointment after organizational entry because the most dissatisfying job and organizational factors have already been anticipated. Third, the information in the RJP can help newcomers cope more effectively with the stress of being in a new environment, called "the work of worry" by Irving Janis. Finally, the RJP can enhance the perceived trustworthiness or supportiveness of the organization to job candidates, increasing their initial commitment to the organization. Support for any one of these hypotheses does not necessarily mean that others are refuted, however; all are viable explanations.

Several guidelines for designing and using the RJP can be derived from the reviews of Phillips and Wanous, which use sophisticated quantitative methods. First, self-selection should be explicitly encouraged. That is, job candidates should be advised to carefully consider whether to accept or reject a job offer. This is best done during the job interview, and this may be an important reason why it is the best method for increasing new hire retention. Second, the RJP message must be credible. Credibility can be achieved by using actual employees as communicators, whether in a video or a job interview. This may explain why using only a brochure is the least effective of all the methods. Third, the way that typical employees feel about the organization, not just sterile facts, must be part of the RJP. Again, employee feelings are best provided in a video or a job interview. Fourth, the balance between positive and negative information should closely match the realities of the job itself. This requires careful data collection and analysis before developing the RJP. Finally, the RJP should normally be done before rather than after hiring, but not so early that the information is ignored. (An exception might be to position the RJP at the end of executive recruitment, although there is no research on executives.)

Research continues to identify the boundaries of the RJP. First, if the retention rate for new hires is very low, the job is probably so undesirable that an RJP will have no effect on job survival. For example, one study of newly hired self-service gas station attendants revealed that not one of the 325 new hires lasted as long as nine months. In fact, many quit by the end of the first month. In organizations with very high retention, the RJP may not be able to improve on that already high level. Therefore, the RJP is probably most effective when the one-year job retention rate for newcomers is in the range of 50% to 80%. For an organization with a 50% job retention rate (for the first year after being hired), use of the RJP is estimated to increase job retention 56% to 59%.

Second, if the labor market has relatively few job openings, the RJP will have little effect on a job candidate's job choice because the chance of obtaining multiple job offers is low. Furthermore, a very tight labor market means that new hires tend to stick with a job even if they would prefer to leave it. Third, the RJP appears to be more effective when job candidates have some previous job knowledge or work experience because they can better understand the information that is provided. Fourth, both Phillips and Wanous found that the RJP is more effective at increasing newcomer retention in business organizations than in the military. The primary reason for the difference in job survival rates is that there are restrictions on attrition from the military.

The impact of the RJP can be translated into dollar terms (utility analysis) by calculating the difference between the number of new hires needed without using RJP versus the number needed when using RJP. Consider an organization that wants to hire and retain 100 new employees. If the job retention rate for the first year is 50%, the organization will need to hire 200 new employees to retain the target goal of 100. If the RJP increases job retention 50% to 56%, the organization would have to hire only 178 people. If the RJP increases job retention 50% to 59%, the organization would have to hire only 169 new people. For fast-food chain restaurants (e.g., McDonald's, Wendy's, Burger King, Pizza Hut) that typically hire more than 100,000 newcomers corporation-wide at a cost of $300 to $400 per hire, the dollar savings in recruitment and hiring can be in the tens of millions of dollars.

The RJP may also be relevant for other aspects of human resource management. It could easily be used to prepare managers for international assignments. Although it is intuitively appealing, there is no rigorous research on this topic—a puzzling gap, as the cost of failure in international assignments for executives is far greater than the cost of lower-paying, entry-level jobs, which typify most studies of the RJP.

REALISTIC RECRUITING SOURCES

Besides the RJP, there are other ways that realistic information can be communicated to job candidates. One recruitment strategy is to hire from sources that have higher job retention rates and higher job performance. A rigorous review of this research by Michael Zottoli and John Wanous found that inside sources (referrals by employees and rehires) had significantly better job retention rates than those from outside sources (newspaper ads and employment agencies). Furthermore, inside sources produced better job performers, although the effect on performance was less than that on retention. However, the effects of recruitment source on retention and performance are both significant. Their usefulness in dollar terms can be estimated in the same way as the RJP. Although there are fewer recruitment source studies (25) than RJP studies (40), there seems to be enough evidence that the results of recruitment source research can be taken seriously. Unfortunately, no study has yet examined organizations that combine the RJP with inside recruitment sources. Thus, the effect of combining these realistic recruitment methods is unknown at present.

Six hypotheses have been offered to explain the link between recruitment source, job survival, and job performance. First, inside recruits have more accurate information, which results in less disappointment among newcomers. Second, having accurate information enables job candidates to make better job choices. Third, inside recruits fit better with the organization because those who referred them know what it takes to succeed. Fourth, candidates from employment agencies or newspaper ads may know more about the full range of job possibilities and thus have higher turnover than candidates referred by other sources. Fifth, source differences may be the result of systematic differences in the types of candidates attracted from each source. Sixth, candidates referred by friends may be treated better by experienced employees and thus have higher retention than other new hires.

A second recruitment source strategy is to set up a company Web site that communicates realistic information to potential job candidates. Unfortunately, there is no rigorous research on real organizational Web sites as of this writing. Studies of students responding to fictitious Web sites are just now beginning to be published. However, the trustworthiness of research using college students reacting to fictitious Web sites has yet to be established.

The Web site of Texas Instruments (TI, www.ti.com) provides one example of how a Web site can be used for realistic recruitment. Job seekers are directed to a section in which a self-scored survey can be taken. The purpose of the survey is to assess both person–job fit (14 questions) and person–organization fit (18 questions), which TI refers to as "job content fit" and "work environment fit," respectively. Job seekers are asked to rate certain items on a five-point scale ranging from *strongly agree* to *strongly disagree*. After responding to the 32 items, the job seeker is then given an overall score. The score is a simple dichotomy: The candidate either fits or does not fit in at TI. In addition to overall fit, the job seeker is also shown TI's "best answer" to each of the questions. The company is careful to remind job seekers that TI's best answers are not right or wrong—rather, they indicate TI's best estimate of its typical work content and organizational culture. Unfortunately, the company does not indicate how these best answers were determined.

REALISTIC SELECTION METHODS

Although RJP and recruitment sources are the two major concerns in realistic recruitment, there are four selection methods that may also communicate realistic information, complementing the use of the RJP and inside recruitment sources. These methods include (a) probationary employment, (b) structured job interviews (i.e., the situational interview and the behavior description interview), (c) work sample tests (both verbal and motor skills tests), and (d) assessment centers. Research on these four methods has focused on job performance rather than retention. Because these techniques are primarily selection rather than recruitment methods, a detailed analysis is beyond the scope of this entry. As predictors of job performance, however, their validity and utility are both fairly well established.

—*John P. Wanous*

See also Job Advertisements; Organizational Socialization; Recruitment; Recruitment Sources

FURTHER READING

Janis, I. L. (1958). *Psychological stress: Psychoanalytic and behavioral studies of surgical patients.* New York: Wiley.

Meglino, B. M., DeNisi, A. S., & Ravlin, E. C. (1993). Effects of previous job exposure and subsequent job status on the functioning of a realistic job preview. *Personnel Psychology, 46,* 803–822.

Phillips, J. M. (1998). Effects of realistic job previews on multiple organizational outcomes: A meta-analysis. *Academy of Management Journal, 41,* 673–690.

Popovich, P., & Wanous, J. P. (1982). The realistic job preview as a persuasive communication. *Academy of Management Review, 7,* 570–578.

Premack, S. L., & Wanous, J. P. (1985). A meta-analysis of realistic job preview experiments. *Journal of Applied Psychology, 70,* 706–719.

Thornton, G. C. (1992). *Assessment centers in human resource management.* Reading, MA: Addison-Wesley.

Wanous, J. P. (1992). *Organizational entry: Recruitment, selection, orientation, and socialization of newcomers* (2nd ed.). Reading, MA: Addison-Wesley.

Wanous, J. P., & Reichers, A. E. (2000). New employee orientation programs. *Human Resource Management Review, 10,* 435–451.

Zottoli, M. A., & Wanous, J. P. (2000). Recruitment source research: Current status and future directions. *Human Resource Management Review, 10,* 353–382.

RECRUITMENT

The term *recruitment* refers to a set of organizational activities and practices that are intended to attract new hires to an organization. The goal of recruitment is to generate applicants who are qualified for employment, who will accept employment offers, and who will ultimately succeed on the job. Recruitment is an important complement to employee selection. Recruitment generates a pool of applicants from which organizations can select new employees and influences the likelihood that the most desirable candidates will accept the organization's offer of employment.

Effective recruitment is essential to organizational success. In recent years, scholarly research and the business press have documented the importance of human capital to organizational performance; recruitment is the process by which human capital is drawn to the organization. Indeed, the search for qualified employees is frequently referred to as a *war for talent,* a phrase that clearly conveys the importance of recruitment. Recent research suggests that recruitment can have significant impact on applicant quality, which, in turn, can lead to significant productivity advantages for the hiring organization.

Recruitment has important implications for individual job seekers as well. The hiring process is a two-way street: Employers attempt to attract qualified employees, and individuals attempt to find satisfying work. Ideally, recruitment leads individuals to make job choices that meet their personal needs.

Recruitment is a process that unfolds over time. It comprises three phases. First, the organization must generate applicants. It must identify a pool of potential employees and persuade a reasonable number of individuals in that pool to apply for work in the organization. Second, it must maintain applicant interest as the candidates proceed through the organization's (sometimes lengthy) screening processes. Finally, the organization must persuade the most desirable applicants to accept job offers.

Recruitment outcomes also unfold over time. In the short run, organizations might assess what are known as *prehire outcomes,* such as the quantity, quality, and diversity of applicants or the length of time required to fill a position. In the longer term, organizations might assess long-term or *posthire outcomes,* such as the performance and longevity (retention) of the recruits. Similarly, individual job seekers initially might attend to whether or how quickly they obtained employment; later, they might focus on how satisfying the employment is.

GENERATING APPLICANTS

Some have argued that the first phase of recruitment, the generation of applicants, is the most important phase. If the right individuals are not in the applicant pool to begin with, then no amount of attention to maintaining applicant interest or persuading successful candidates to join the organization will result in the right hires. Certainly, this phase requires the organization to make a number of critical strategic decisions, including where to search for applicants and how to communicate with potential applicants. Fortunately, there is a reasonable body of research evidence to support these strategic decisions.

RECRUITING SOURCES: WHERE TO LOOK

One of the most frequently studied aspects of recruitment is source selection. Applicants may be sought from a variety of sources, both formal and informal. Formal sources typically involve a third-party intermediary that assists in the recruitment process, such as an employment agency, a college placement office, or a newspaper or online advertisement service. Informal sources typically involve direct contact between the potential employee and the employer and include such techniques as direct applications and referrals.

A significant body of research on recruitment source effects has accumulated over the years. The most consistent finding of this research is that informal sources (referrals in particular) tend to have positive effects on posthire outcomes. Specifically, individuals who are hired by means of referral from existing employees tend to have greater longevity in their new positions than those who are hired from other sources. Two theoretical frameworks have been proposed to explain these effects. First, it has been suggested that different recruiting sources yield individuals with different characteristics. These individual differences then translate into different posthire outcomes. Second, it has been proposed that applicants recruited from different sources have access to different information. Individuals with greater advance knowledge may be better positioned for long-term success on the job. Unfortunately, research testing the power of these two models has been somewhat inconclusive.

EARLY RECRUITMENT COMMUNICATIONS

Once an applicant pool has been identified or targeted, the organization must communicate with potential applicants to persuade them to apply. Quite often, this initial communication comes in the form of advertisements, flyers, or brochures. More recently, employer Web sites have become an important aspect of early recruitment. For each of these areas, research has investigated the role of design as well as the role of content in attracting applicants.

Design of Materials

In terms of printed material, research suggests that applicants are attracted to firms whose recruitment materials are informative, and both the amount and the specificity of the information seem to make a difference. In most cases, applicants seem to devalue positions about which important information is not made available. One explanation for this reaction is that the failure to provide sufficient information may be seen as a signal of undesirable organizational attributes. Firms that provide less informative materials may be seen as less concerned about applicants' (and by attribution, employees') needs.

Recruitment materials are also more effective when they are distinctive and vivid. To attract attention, materials need to stand out from the group in some way, either through physical representation or the presentation of unusual information. For example, materials that promise uncommon benefits (such as pet insurance) may be more effective than materials that promise more conventional benefits.

Content of Materials

Research on the portrayal of specific job or organization attributes in early recruitment communication has demonstrated that applicant preferences (and reactions to specific content in ads) vary as a function of their personal characteristics. Rather than specifying absolute or universal rules about desirable attributes, studies in this area have demonstrated that applicants respond to attributes through the lens of their own values and preferences. In other words, a person–organization or person–job fit perspective prevails. For example, individual differences in demographic characteristics, values, and personality have been shown to predict attraction to job attributes such as pay system, work system (i.e., individual versus team based), and diversity policies (affirmative action versus equal employment opportunity).

Internet Recruitment

Although most research on early recruitment communications has focused on traditional (usually print) media, the impact of Internet-based recruitment has not been ignored. Studies of applicant reactions to employer Web sites reached similar conclusions to those for print media—that is, both content and design matter. Applicants prefer Web sites that provide useful information and that are easy to navigate. In addition, the interactive nature of Web sites allows applicants to more easily identify the extent to which specific positions and organizations match their personal qualifications and needs.

ORGANIZATIONAL IMAGE

Applicants sometimes have knowledge of an organization even before the organization begins its targeted recruitment. In particular, large organizations may be familiar to many individuals. It is common for individuals to have loosely structured general impressions of a company—in other words, to hold some image of what the company is like. These general impressions or organizational images may be formed by corporate advertising, the way the firm is depicted in the media, personal experience with the company or its products, and many other factors. A number of studies have documented the impact of organizational image on applicant attraction. In particular, several studies suggest that firms that are viewed as socially responsible are attractive to potential applicants. What is less clear is whether organizations actively manipulate their images in an effort to be attractive to prospective employees.

MAINTAINING STATUS

In many cases, there is a significant time lapse between a candidate's initial application and the organization's decision whether to hire that applicant. The goal of recruitment during this phase is to maintain the applicant's interest in the organization while the screening process runs its course. Every interaction between the applicant and the organization during this period can influence the applicant's interest and, as a result, has important recruitment aspects. In this section, the impact of recruiters and interviewers, as well as applicant reactions to other selection devices, are reviewed.

Recruiters

In many hiring processes, the initial application is followed by an interview. In most cases, the first interview has a dual nature: It serves as a selection device but also provides an opportunity for recruitment. Most existing research on the role of the early interview in recruitment focuses on the characteristics and qualities of the individual conducting the interview (i.e., the recruiter).

Research has consistently demonstrated that applicants prefer recruiters who are warm and informative. Furthermore, they form more favorable views of the organization and are more attracted to its jobs when recruiters are warm and informative. Two theories have been proposed to explain the impact of reactions to recruiters. First, the interview is, to a great extent, an opportunity for recruiters to convey information about the organization, and warm and informative recruiters may simply do a better job of communicating with applicants. Second, recruiters may serve as signals for unobserved organizational characteristics. Applicants may presume that the recruiter is representative of the organization and its employees—that is, organizations whose recruiters are warm are likely to have a friendly, collegial culture; organizations whose recruiters are informative have a culture that respects employees' need for information.

Research has also attended to the demographic characteristics of recruiters, but here the results are more ambiguous. Recruiter gender, age, experience, and functional area were found to have significant effects on applicant attraction in some studies but no effects in others. Likewise, the degree of demographic similarity between the recruiter and the applicant was found to have an impact in some studies but no impact in others.

Applicant Reaction to Selection Devices

Because the recruitment and selection processes occur simultaneously, an organization's approach to selection will likely influence how an applicant feels about the organization and its methods, and therefore it is likely to influence whether the applicant will accept the job if one is offered. Two rationales have been offered to explain these reactions. First, applicant reactions may be a function of privacy concerns; some selection techniques, such as drug testing and certain psychological tests, may be viewed as overly intrusive. Second, applicants may respond based on their desire for and perceptions of justice; some techniques are seen as more fair, either in process or outcome, than others.

Literature in this area has focused primarily on the question of justice. Rather than identifying lists of techniques that are viewed as just or unjust, most research has focused on aspects of the selection process that may be perceived as just or unjust. The timeliness of feedback, the job-relatedness of the selection device, and the degree to which procedures are explained to applicants are examples of elements that enhance the perceived justice of selection techniques and thus are likely to lead to maintenance of applicant status. It is also clear that the context in which selection and recruitment occur can make a difference. For example, the impact of specific selection techniques on attraction to the organization can vary as a function of job type, characteristics of the organization, and applicant characteristics (in particular, race).

Realism

During the maintenance phase of recruitment, organizations supplement their initial recruitment communications with additional information. Decisions regarding the nature of the information that is added are critical. One of the most frequently studied aspects of recruitment is the impact of realistic communications. Organizations can use realistic job previews (RJPs) to present a balanced and true representation of the job and the organization. Such previews are carefully designed to include both positive and negative aspects of the work. This approach can be contrasted with the more traditional sales-oriented approach, in which organizations strive to present jobs in a uniformly positive light.

Numerous theories have been developed to support the realistic approach. The first is the *met-expectations theory,* which suggests that providing realistic information prevents applicants from developing inflated expectations of what the job is like and therefore makes them less likely to suffer disappointment on the job. Second, the *ability-to-cope perspective* suggests that giving applicants advance notice of negative aspects of the job gives them time to develop coping strategies. Third, RJPs may create an atmosphere of honesty that is appreciated by applicants. Finally, RJPs may operate through self-selection: Candidates who react negatively to the unattractive aspects of the job can remove themselves from consideration.

The cumulated evidence suggests that RJPs are associated with positive posthire outcomes. In particular, applicants who receive realistic recruitment communications exhibit lower turnover and higher performance. These effects are moderated, however, by design factors such as timing (when the realistic information is provided) and medium (the method used to communicate—for example, written versus verbal).

CLOSING THE DEAL: INFLUENCING JOB CHOICE

During the final phase of recruitment, organizations must persuade their most attractive applicants (those to whom job offers have been made) to join the company. This stage is critical because significant investments in both recruitment and selection processes are lost if candidates reject offers. Unlike the other two phases of recruitment, research on this final phase focuses on the thought processes of applicants as they make decisions about which job to choose. Substantially less research has focused on the activities of the organization at this final stage.

Job Choice Research: Content Issues

One of the most significant debates in the job choice literature focuses on what content is attended to in job choice—that is, which characteristics or attributes of jobs and organizations are most likely to lead to a positive job choice outcome. By and large, this debate has centered on the validity of two methods of assessing attribute preference: direct estimation and policy capturing. In the *direct estimate* technique, applicants are provided with a list of job attributes (e.g., high pay, opportunities for advancement, pleasant working conditions) and asked to rate or rank the importance of each of these factors. The underlying assumption is that more important attributes will play a greater role in job choice. However, this approach has been criticized as lacking in context. For example, it does not allow for variation in levels or for trade-offs among attributes. In addition, the direct estimation technique has been faulted for requiring more self-insight than applicants might have.

Policy capturing provides a methodological alternative to direct estimation. In policy-capturing studies, applicants are provided with a set of job descriptions across which attribute levels are systematically varied.

They are then asked to rate the attractiveness of the job. Statistical regression is used to identify the degree to which specific attributes influenced attraction to the job.

It has become increasingly clear that, methodological issues aside, neither of these approaches is likely to yield a single set of universally attractive attributes. Instead, research using both techniques has identified differences in attribute preferences as a function of demographic status, individual values, and personality traits.

Job Choice: Process Issues

Research on the job choice process offers consistent support for expectancy-based decision-making models. The expectancy perspective suggests that applicants will estimate the probability of obtaining certain outcomes if a specific job is chosen (e.g., attributes such as good benefits or pleasant coworkers), weight those probabilities by the value or attractiveness of each attribute, sum across attributes, and then select the job that obtains the highest total weighted attribute score.

Consistent findings notwithstanding, some have argued that job choice is not as rational as the expectancy model suggests. For example, some recent research suggests that interactions that occur during the final job offer negotiations can have an impact on job choice, above and beyond their impact on attribute levels (e.g., through their effect on perceptions of justice). However, relatively little research on this topic has been conducted.

—*Alison E. Barber*

See also Job Advertisements; Job Choice; Job Search; Realistic Job Preview; Recruitment Sources

FURTHER READING

Barber, A. E. (1998). *Recruiting employees: Individual and organizational perspectives.* Thousand Oaks, CA: Sage.

Breaugh, J. A. (1992). *Recruitment: Science and practice.* Boston: PWS-Kent.

Breaugh, J. A., & Starke, M. (2000). Research on employee recruitment: So many studies, so many remaining questions. *Journal of Management, 26*(3), 405–434.

Carlson, K. D., Connerly, M. L., & Mecham, R. L. (2002). Recruitment evaluation: The case for assessing the quality of applicants attracted. *Personnel Psychology, 55*(2), 461–490.

Phillips, J. M. (1998). Effects of realistic job previews on multiple organizational outcomes: A meta-analysis. *Academy of Management Journal, 41*(6), 673–690.

Ryan, A. M., & Ployhart, R. F. (2000). Applicants' perceptions of selection procedures and decisions: A critical review and agenda for the future. *Journal of Management, 26*(3), 565–606.

Rynes, S. L. (1991). Recruitment, job choice, and post-hire consequences: A call for new research directions. In M. D. Dunnette & L. M. Hough (Eds.), *Handbook of industrial and organizational psychology* (2nd ed., Vol. 2, pp. 399–444). Palo Alto, CA: Consulting Psychologists Press.

RECRUITMENT SOURCES

Recruitment sources are one of the most frequently studied aspects of employee recruitment. Recruitment sources are the avenues that organizations use to reach applicants. Evidence suggests that the choice of recruitment source(s) is a strategic decision, in the sense that there are relationships between recruitment sources and employment outcomes. However, the exact nature and reasons for those effects remain ambiguous.

Traditional recruitment sources include employee referrals, employment agencies (including campus placement offices and executive search firms), newspaper and radio advertisements, employee referrals, and unsolicited applications (known as walk-ins). Newer recruitment sources that are growing in popularity include job or career fairs and Internet-based recruitment through electronic job boards or the organization's own Web site.

Recruitment sources can be either formal or informal. Formal sources typically involve a third-party intermediary that assists in the recruitment process, such as an employment agency, a college placement office, or a newspaper or online advertisement service. Informal sources typically involve direct contact between the potential employee and the employer and include such techniques as direct applications, referrals, and the rehiring of former employees.

INITIAL RESEARCH ON RECRUITMENT SOURCES

A significant body of research on recruitment source effects has accumulated over the years. Initial research was primarily descriptive in nature and explored the relationship between recruitment sources and posthire outcomes such as employee satisfaction, retention, and absenteeism. The most consistent finding of this research is that informal sources (referrals in particular but also walk-ins and the rehiring of former employees) tend to have positive associations with posthire outcomes: lower turnover and, in some cases, better work attitudes and job performance.

Recruitment scholars soon began to propose and test explanations for these findings. The two most commonly studied explanations are the *individual differences hypothesis* and the *realistic information hypothesis.*

First, regarding individual differences, it has been suggested that different recruitment sources yield individuals with different characteristics. These individual differences ultimately lead to different posthire outcomes. For example, employee referrals might be an effective hiring source because employees choose to refer only individuals who, in their judgment, would be effective employees. This method of screening would produce a group of applicants that is superior to other groups on important job qualifications.

Second, regarding realistic information, it has been proposed that applicants recruited from different sources have access to different information. In particular, individuals recruited through informal sources may have access to more extensive, more specific, or more accurate information about the new job. Having that information might provide greater role clarity and more realistic expectations for those applicants, which, in turn, could lead to better adjustment and therefore better posthire outcomes.

Research on the validity of these explanations has yielded mixed support. In support of the individual differences hypothesis, associations have been found between recruitment sources and individual characteristics such as age, education, experience, and physical abilities. In support of the realistic information hypothesis, informal sources have been associated with greater amounts of realistic information. However, these findings are not universal. Furthermore, relatively few studies have been able to verify that the relationship between recruitment sources and posthire outcomes is mediated by these intervening variables. Some studies found only a modest, if any, relationship between recruitment sources and posthire outcomes.

CONTINGENCY PERSPECTIVES ON RECRUITMENT SOURCE EFFECTS

The inability of the most popular explanations of recruitment source effects to fully explain the relationship between recruitment sources and employment outcomes has led to speculation about contingency factors. Based on a limited number of studies, there appears to be some merit to the argument that the proposed processes hold in some cases or situations but not in others. For example, one study found differences in source effects across racial and ethnic lines: Employee referrals were associated with lower turnover for White applicants, but employment agencies yielded the lowest turnover among Blacks. Another study found that the use of employee referrals in Mexico was associated with higher turnover, the opposite of the effect observed in U.S.-based research. A full range of contingency factors for recruitment source effects has not yet been specified.

RECRUITMENT SOURCES AND DIVERSITY

Despite the observed advantages of informal recruiting sources, heavy reliance on these sources does raise concerns. Several studies found differences in recruitment source use by gender and by race and ethnicity, with White males more likely to use informal recruitment sources than are women or people of color. Therefore, organizations that rely on informal recruitment to reduce turnover may be trading opportunities to diversify their workforce. A complete assessment of recruiting source effectiveness should incorporate a variety of recruiting goals, something that is not always done in recruiting source research.

THE INTERNET AS A RECRUITMENT SOURCE

A recruiting source that is growing in popularity and in research attention is the Internet. Descriptive research suggests that Web sites are already among the most commonly used recruitment sources across a wide variety of jobs, and their use is expected to grow. Recruiters cite perceived benefits of online recruitment that include low cost and high speed. It is also possible through Web-based recruiting to provide rich, detailed information that is comparable to the information that applicants recruited through informal sources might receive.

A disadvantage of Web-based recruiting is that the large quantity of applications generated may not be particularly high in quality. Also, because of the "digital divide" in access to computers by race and ethnicity, it has been suggested that this source may have negative implications for diversity.

In fact, recent research suggests that Internet-based recruiting may provide a compromise between formal and informal sources. One study indicated that online recruiting yields applicants who are more diverse than those recruited through informal means (but less so than those recruited by formal means) and is more successful in recruiting qualified applicants than traditional formal methods (but less so than informal recruitment sources).

—*Alison E. Barber*

See also Job Search; Realistic Job Preview; Recruitment

FURTHER READING

Barber, A. E. (1998). *Recruiting employees: Individual and organizational perspectives.* Thousand Oaks, CA: Sage.

Carlson, K. D., Connerly, M. L., & Mecham, R. L. (2002). Recruitment evaluation: The case for assessing the quality of applicants attracted. *Personnel Psychology, 55*(2), 461–490.

Chapman, D. S., & Webster, J. (2003). The use of technologies in the recruiting, screening, and selection processes for job candidates. *International Journal of Selection and Assessment, 11*(2/3), 113–120.

Linnehan, F., & Blau, G. (2003). Testing the impact of job search and recruitment source on new hire turnover in a maquiladora. *Applied Psychology, 52*(2), 253–271.

McManus, M. A., & Ferguson, M. W. (2003). Biodata, personality, and demographic differences of recruits from three sources. *International Journal of Selection and Assessment, 11*(2/3), 175–183.

REINFORCEMENT THEORY OF WORK MOTIVATION

The *operant conditioning* or *reinforcement theory* of B. F. Skinner is one of the major psychological theories concerned with motivation at work. Unique in the social sciences, it identifies two of its major concepts according to the time at which they occur: (1) antecedents, such as communicating company policy, providing training, and setting goals, which typically precede the targeted behavior; and (2) consequences that take place after performance, such as compliments for a job well done, acknowledgment of the receipt of work, feedback on the quality of the task done, and graphs showing performance plotted over time, as well as the avoidance of such distasteful events as unwarranted criticism, punching in on a time clock, or the processing of complaints or grievances.

The action that occurs (or does not occur) *after* the behavior of interest is considered the driving force in motivation.

HISTORY

Although Skinner had formulated the basic principles of operant conditioning by the 1940s, they were not widely applied outside university laboratories until the 1960s. Initially, reinforcement theory, also referred to as *applied behavior analysis,* was used in the wards of institutions for the mentally retarded. Behavior analysts designed programs for use with patients and, soon thereafter, with staff.

The same principles were used regardless of whether the setting was a school or a package delivery company. After truck drivers and dockworkers at Emery Air Freight, for example, were positively reinforced, they worked together more efficiently and harmoniously. During boot camp at Fort Ord, California, a token-economy program was introduced in which soldiers could exchange points for such coveted backup reinforcers as early dismissal and time off with pay. As a result, the soldiers not only maintained their morale but also met the rigorous standards of their superiors.

Industrial and organizational psychologists such as Walter R. Nord and Lyman W. Porter identified the behavioral approach as an innovative advance in the understanding of motivation during the early 1970s. Since then, hundreds of studies have been conducted in work settings and published in the *Journal of Applied Psychology, Organizational Behavior and Human Decision Processes, Academy of Management Journal,* and *Journal of Applied Behavior Analysis,* as well as the *Journal of Organizational Behavior Management.* Conducted by authors at the universities of Kansas, Florida State, and Western Michigan, as well as members of organizations in the public and private sectors, these experiments encompass multiple aspects of performance—productivity, attendance, safety, and service—with individuals, groups, and entire organizations.

USING REINFORCEMENT THEORY TO PROMOTE SUBSTANTIAL AND SUSTAINED IMPROVEMENTS AT WORK

Consequences Are Primary

The basic tenet of reinforcement theory is that behavior is shaped and maintained by its consequences. In planning a program aimed at increasing safety, for example, behavior analysts identify what consequences *follow* the behavior of interest. They ask a number of questions: What happens when workers behave safely? Do coworkers applaud safe acts, behaviors, or performance? (The terms are used interchangeably here.) Does management recognize workers for performing as desired? Similar queries are made about the undesired consequences: What happens when workers perform unsafely? Do employees incur injuries? Are there penalties for acting unsafely? In other words, what are the consequences of safe and unsafe acts? When consequences are found to be sparse, rarely favorable, and at times unrelated to the desired behavior—not an atypical situation in many organizations—behavior analysts arrange for positive, contingent, and frequent consequences to follow the desired performance.

Evidence of the Effectiveness of Positive Reinforcement

Reviews of the literature (e.g., Johnson, Redmon, & Mawhinney, 2001; Stajkovic & Luthans, 1997) attest to the efficacy of positive reinforcement, the most prevalent organizational change strategy. Judith L. Komaki and her colleagues examined the literature from 1969 to 1998 and found successful improvements in a variety of work settings. Of a total of 72 meticulously controlled experiments, 58 studies supported positive reinforcement, 10 showed mixed support, and only 4 did not show any support—a success rate of 93%. The changes, on average, were not ephemeral; almost half of the studies lasted 26 weeks or longer, and in over 40%, the longest intervention was at least 12 weeks or longer.

Types of Positive Consequences Used in Work Settings

In setting up a positive reinforcement program, behavior analysts typically use one or more of the following consequences:

- *Organizational:* Events that are indigenous to work settings, such as promotions, bonuses, and special training opportunities, are offered. For example, benefits such as free gasoline and free monthly passes on the bus system were made available as incentives for reducing accidents among workers in a regional transportation authority. Letters of recommendation

were among the consequences successfully used by advisers to reinforce master's degree students' progress toward completing their theses.
- *Activity:* Another class of consequences is derived from the Premack principle (named after researcher David Premack), which states that any higher-frequency activity can be used as a positive consequence for a lower-frequency activity. For example, when calls to renewal customers were found to have a higher frequency than calls to new customers, the former were made contingent on the latter. Making the opportunity to sell five renewal contracts dependent on the higher-frequency activity resulted in more new sales calls.
- *Generalized:* Generalized consequences derive their potency from the fact that they can be exchanged for backup reinforcers. Examples include cash, frequent flyer coupons, and trading stamps. The latter, exchangeable for household and recreational items, were given to miners who had not suffered a lost-time injury during the month. In another instance, coupons were traded in at a job-training center for the opportunity to select a clerical assignment.
- *Social:* Typically expressed by individuals, social consequences include commendations, compliments, criticism, reviews, and recognition for a job well done. For example, a hospital supervisor commented to a staff member, "I'm pleased to see you interacting with clients, but I'm sure Mary is even more pleased."
- *Informational:* As the name suggests, information is provided about performance. This information can be conveyed in notes to employees written by supervisors, in the form of a graph of baseline and intervention levels, or by listing, as one Louisiana official did, what had been done after a hurricane: "We're feeding more people. . . . We're recovering more people. . . . We're clearing more roads. . . . We're building more power lines. . . . Every day, more victories."

Antecedents Play a Secondary Role

Confronted with problems involving the workforce, the most common recommendation is "to inform or exhort," both of which are antecedents. Although antecedents serve valuable educational or cuing functions (e.g., clarifying expectations for performance, specifying the relationship between behavior and its consequences, and signaling occasions on which consequences are likely to be provided), when they are used alone, the evidence for their efficacy is meager. Field experiments addressing how consequences add to the effectiveness of antecedents consistently show that antecedents alone do not result in substantial and sustained improvements in ongoing behaviors, and only when consequences accompany antecedents do they occur. Because of the essential role of consequences in motivation, the delivery of one or more consequences is the mainstay of virtually all reinforcement programs.

EXPLANATORY POWER OF REINFORCEMENT THEORY

Illuminating Why We Do What We Do

Reinforcement theory also clarifies why people sometimes do the perplexing, often paradoxical things they do—for example, why managers who purportedly believe in merit promote based on seniority, or why professors who profess about the importance of education neglect their teaching.

Normally, positive reinforcement is exercised in a constructive, planned way. But it can also be used, often inadvertently, to produce unwanted results. For example, the head of a public relations firm could not understand why her staff kept postponing work. Yet the year before, when the staff had been under pressure to produce an anniversary report, she had given permission to set all other work aside and hire temporary staff at company expense. When the report was finally completed, she gave everyone a bonus. Despite the agency head's well-meaning intentions, she may have inadvertently reinforced her staff for procrastinating. Positive reinforcement may explain why some professors spend less time on teaching than research: because their promotion depends heavily on what appears in journals rather than in the classroom.

The principle of *negative reinforcement,* which involves escaping from or avoiding negative or aversive consequences, such as nagging, censure, or litigation, may explain why a manager would promote someone with only an adequate record rather than an exemplary employee with less seniority—to avoid complaints of favoritism or bias. The same principle sheds light on why people often remain quiet in the face of corruption—to avoid censure—and why some lieutenants choose to remain at their rank—to avoid the increased scrutiny, responsibility, and restrictions that come with being promoted to captain.

The consequences for performing as desired sometimes can be punishing. For example, the head of a major research laboratory bemoaned the lack of creativity of the engineers in his group. When asked about the consequences, however, he could readily point to a host of inherently negative consequences— their time-consuming, seemingly fruitless literature searches; difficulty communicating concepts that were, as yet, incomprehensible to their peers; and inordinate amounts of time expended before having anything to show for their efforts. All of these aversive events helped to explain why some engineers shunned such endeavors, preferring the tried and true.

The principle of *punishment by removal,* technically called *response cost,* wherein a positive reinforcer is withdrawn as a consequence of a behavior, sheds light on how some preferred behaviors can be unintentionally discouraged. For example, even when their lives are in danger, fighter pilots are often reluctant to call for help. Such an admission, as Tom Wolfe graphically points out in his book *The Right Stuff,* triggers a very public chain of events, some punishing— fire trucks trundling out to the runway, incoming flights being held up, the bureaucracy gearing up to investigate—and at least one punishment by removal—the pilot's peers questioning the pilot's mettle and hence dampening the idea that the pilot had "the right stuff."

Although punishment or negative reinforcement are not recommended as the primary way of changing behavior, decision makers need to be sensitive to their use of these consequences, eliminating the punishing ones whenever possible and redesigning the flow of the work to enable naturally or specially arranged favorable consequences.

Shedding Light on What Effective Leaders Do

The theory of operant conditioning has inspired the challenging but rarely researched question of what effective leaders really do to motivate others. Komaki predicted in her operant model of effective supervision that first-rate managers are more likely to provide consequences. Because consequences must be related to what employees actually do, she conjectured that effective supervisors frequently monitor or inquire about performance, particularly by directly sampling the work. The original rationale was a logical one: Managers who monitor are more likely to have dependable and up-to-date information with which to provide contingent consequences. Later, she found that supervisors who monitor are more likely than those who provide antecedents to have subordinates who discuss their performance, which, in turn, increases the likelihood of back-and-forth exchanges between the two.

In every one of seven field studies, Komaki and her colleagues found that effective managers monitor, provide consequences, or do both. The consequences may be as brief as a simple "thanks," or even an "okay" while sampling the work. Neutral consequences (e.g., "Yep. That's all right," or as an officer handed a sergeant a report, "You need a statement from the driver to complete that report.") separated effective police sergeants from lackluster ones in a study by Neil Brewer and colleagues. Investment bankers, identified as exemplary in motivating others, actually thanked the bearer of bad news, acknowledging employees for bringing thorny issues to their attention. Furthermore, top-notch sailboat skippers were found to use a particular sequence during races in which monitors routinely precede consequences in what is referred to as an *AMC sequence,* where A stands for an antecedent (an order or instruction), M for monitor, and C for consequence. Exemplary leaders can perform these AMC sequences quickly.

Besides inspiring a leadership model and providing a way of explaining why people do what they do, reinforcement theory shows how a judiciously arranged set of consequences can result in enhanced performance from day to day and season to season.

—*Judith L. Komaki*

See also Organizational Behavior Management

FURTHER READING

Brewer, N., Wilson, C., & Beck, K. (1994). Supervisory behavior and team performance amongst police patrol sergeants. *Journal of Occupational and Organizational Psychology, 67,* 69–78.

Johnson, C. M., Redmon, W. K., & Mawhinney, T. C. (Eds.). (2001). *Handbook of organizational performance: Behavior analysis and management.* New York: Haworth.

Komaki, J. L. (1998). *Leadership from an operant perspective.* London: Routledge.

Komaki, J. L., Coombs, T., Redding, T. P., & Schepman, S. (2000). A rich and rigorous examination of applied behavior analysis research in the world of work. In C. L. Cooper & I. T. Robertson (Eds.), *International review of industrial and organizational psychology 2000* (pp. 265–367). Sussex, UK: Wiley.

Porter, L. W. (1973). Turning work into nonwork: The rewarding environment. In M. D. Dunnette (Ed.), *Work and nonwork in the year 2001* (pp. 113–133). Monterey, CA: Brooks/Cole.

Skinner, B. F. (1978). *Reflections on behaviorism and society.* Englewood Cliffs, NJ: Prentice Hall.

Stajkovic, A. D., & Luthans, F. (1997). A meta-analysis of the effects of organizational behavior modification on task performance, 1975–95. *Academy of Management Journal, 40*(5), 1122–1149.

RELIABILITY

Reliability can be defined as the extent to which scores of a measure are free from the effect of measurement error. Measurement error is reflected in random deviations of the scores observed on a measure from respondents' true scores, which are the expected values of respondents' scores if they completed the measure an infinite number of times. Mathematically, reliability is quantified as the ratio of true score variance to observed score variance or, equivalently, the square of the correlation between true scores and observed scores. Based on these indexes, reliability can range from zero (no true score variance) to one (no measurement error).

Reliability is important for both practical and theoretical purposes. Practically, it enables estimation of the standard error of measurement, an index of accuracy of a person's test score. Theoretically, reliability contributes to theory development by allowing researchers to correct for the biasing effect of measurement error on observed correlations between measures of psychological constructs and by providing researchers with an assessment of whether their measurement process needs to be improved (e.g., if reliability is low).

SOURCES OF MEASUREMENT ERROR

Multiple sources of measurement error can influence a person's observed score. The following sources are common in psychological measures.

Random Response Error

Random response error is caused by momentary variations in attention, mental efficiency, or distractions within a given occasion. It is specific to a moment when a person responds to an item on a measure. For example, a person might provide different answers to the same item appearing in different places on a measure.

Transient Error

Whereas random response error occurs within an occasion, transient error occurs across occasions. Transient errors are produced by temporal variations in respondents' mood and feelings across occasions. For example, any given respondent might score differently on a measure administered on two occasions. Theoretically, such temporal differences are random, and thus not part of a person's true score, because they do not correlate with scores from the measure completed on other occasions (i.e., they are occasion specific).

Specific Factor Error

Specific factor error reflects idiosyncratic responses to some element of the measurement situation. For example, when responding to test items, respondents might interpret item wording differently. Theoretically, specific factors are not part of a person's true score because they do not correlate with scores on other elements (e.g., items) of the measure.

Rater Error

Rater error arises only when a person's observed score (rating) is obtained from another person or set of persons (raters). Rater error arises from the rater's idiosyncratic perceptions of a ratee's standing on the construct of interest. Theoretically, idiosyncratic rater factors are not part of a person's true score because they do not correlate with ratings provided by other raters (i.e., they are rater specific).

TYPES OF RELIABILITY COEFFICIENTS

Reliability is indexed with a reliability coefficient. There are several types of reliability coefficients, and they differ with regard to the sources of observed score variance that they treat as true score and error variance. Sources of variance that are treated as error variance in one type of coefficient may be treated as true score variance in other types.

Internal Consistency

This type of reliability coefficient is found most frequently in psychological research (e.g., Cronbach's alpha, split-half). Internal consistency reliability coefficients, also known as *coefficients of equivalence,* require only one administration of a measure and index the effects of specific factor error and random response error on observed scores. They reflect the degree of consistency between item-level scores on a measure. Because all items on a given measure are administered on the same occasion, they share a source of variance (i.e., transient error) that may be unrelated to the target construct of interest but nonetheless contributes to true score variance in these coefficients (because it is a shared source of variance across items).

Test–Retest

Test–retest reliability coefficients, also known as *coefficients of stability,* index the effects of random response error and transient error on observed scores. Test–retest coefficients reflect the degree of stability in test scores across occasions and can be thought of as the correlation between the same test administered on different occasions. Because the same test is administered on each occasion, the scores from each occasion share a source of variance (i.e., specific factor error) that may be unrelated to the target construct of interest but nonetheless contributes to true score variance in these coefficients (because it is a shared source of variance across occasions).

Coefficients of Equivalence and Stability

Coefficients of equivalence and stability index the effects of specific factor error, transient error, and random response error on observed scores. These coefficients reflect the consistency of scores across items on a test and the stability of test scores across occasions; they can be thought of as the correlation between two parallel forms of a measure administered on different occasions. The use of different forms enables estimation of specific factor error and random response error, and the administration on different occasions enables estimation of transient error and random response error. Therefore, this coefficient can be seen as a combination of the coefficient of equivalence and the coefficient of stability. Hence, the coefficient of equivalence and stability is the recommended reliability estimate for most self-report measures because it appropriately accounts for all three sources of measurement error, leaving none of these sources of variance to contribute to the estimate of true score variance.

Intrarater Reliability

Intrarater reliability coefficients—a type of internal consistency coefficient that is specific to ratings-based measures—index the effects of specific factor error and random response error on observed score variance. These coefficients reflect the degree of consistency between items rated by a given rater on one occasion. Because the items are rated by the same rater (intrarater) on the same occasion, they share two sources of variance (i.e., rater error and transient error) that may be unrelated to the construct of interest but nonetheless contribute to true score variance in these coefficients (because they are shared sources of variance across items).

Interrater Reliability

Like intrarater reliability coefficients, *interrater reliability coefficients* are also specific to ratings-based measures. However, interrater reliability coefficients index the effect of rater error and random response error on observed score variance. They reflect the degree of consistency in ratings provided by different raters and can be thought of as the correlation between ratings from different raters using a single measure on one occasion. Because the same ratings measure is administered to different raters (interrater) on the same occasion, the ratings share two sources of variance (i.e., specific factor error and transient error) that may be unrelated to the target construct of interest but nonetheless contribute to true score variance in these coefficients (because they are a shared source of variance across raters).

ESTIMATING RELIABILITY COEFFICIENTS

Methods for estimating the coefficients just described are provided by two psychometric theories: *classical test theory* and *generalizability (G) theory*. Researchers who adopt a classical test theory approach to the estimation of coefficients often calculate Pearson correlations between elements of the measure (e.g., items,

raters, and occasions) and then use the Spearman-Brown prophecy formula to adjust the estimate for the number of items, raters, or occasions across which observations on the measure were gathered. Conversely, researchers who adopt a G-theory approach focus on first estimating components of the reliability coefficients (i.e., true score variance, or *universe score variance* in G-theory terms, and error variance) and then form a ratio with these estimates to arrive at an estimated reliability coefficient (generalizability coefficient in G-theory terms).

FACTORS AFFECTING RELIABILITY ESTIMATES

Several factors can affect the magnitude of reliability coefficients that researchers report for a measure. Their potential impact on any given estimate must be considered in order for an appropriate interpretation of the estimate to be made.

Measurement Design Limitations

The magnitude of a reliability coefficient depends partly on the sources of variance that are treated as error. Unfortunately, not all measurement designs allow estimation of all types of reliability coefficients. Thus, even though a researcher may wish to consider a source of variance in his or her measure as error, it may not always be possible to account for it in the measurement design. For example, researchers cannot index the amount of transient error variance in observed scores if the measure (or at least parts of it) was not administered on multiple occasions. In such a case, the researcher may have to report a reliability coefficient that overestimates the true reliability of the measure.

Constructs Being Measured

Items measuring different constructs may be differentially susceptible to sources of measurement error. For example, items for broader constructs (e.g., conscientiousness) are likely to be more strongly affected by specific factor error than items for narrower constructs (e.g., orderliness). Similarly, items measuring stable personality constructs (e.g., the Big Five) may be less susceptible to transient error than items measuring affect-related constructs.

Heterogeneity of the Sample

It is well-known that range restriction attenuates correlations between variables. Because reliability coefficients can be interpreted as the square of the correlation between observed scores and true scores, they, too, are subject to range restriction. Reliability estimates tend to be higher when they are obtained from a sample of persons who vary greatly on the construct being measured and lower if the persons in the sample do not vary greatly on the construct.

Test Length

Scores on a measure are typically formed by summing or averaging responses across items. Because specific factor errors associated with items are uncorrelated, their contributions to the observed score variance when summed or averaged diminish in proportion to the number of items included in the measure. Hence, all else being equal, the more items on the measure, the higher its reliability.

—Huy Le and Dan J. Putka

See also Classical Test Theory; Generalizability Theory; Validity

FURTHER READING

Feldt, L. S., & Brennan, R. L. (1989). Reliability. In R. L. Linn (Ed.), *Educational measurement* (3rd ed., pp. 105–146). New York: American Council on Education.

Nunnally, J. C., & Bernstein, I. H. (1994). *Psychometric theory* (3rd ed.). New York: McGraw-Hill.

Schmidt, F. L., & Hunter, J. E. (1996). Measurement error in psychological research: Lessons from 26 research scenarios. *Psychological Methods, 1,* 199–223.

Schmidt, F. L., Le, H., & Ilies, R. (2003). Beyond alpha: An empirical examination of the effects of different sources of measurement error on reliability estimates for measures of individual differences constructs. *Psychological Methods, 8,* 206–224.

Traub, R. E. (1994). *Reliability for the social sciences: Theory and applications.* Thousand Oaks, CA: Sage.

RETIREMENT

Retirement is a general term that has traditionally referred to older adults' disengagement from the workforce. As an area of research inquiry, it is a broad concept that has been studied by a number of disciplines, including economics, gerontology, and organizational behavior, as well as developmental and industrial and organizational psychology. Appropriately, these fields have offered many different perspectives on the concept of disengagement. Some frame it in terms of the amount of participation in the workforce (i.e., the number of hours worked), whereas others frame it in terms of the receipt of pensions as a source of income rather than paid work. Still other fields focus on disengagement as a form of commitment to and reliance on work as a source of personal identity and fulfillment. These differing viewpoints—and the theoretical perspectives that underlie them—are all valuable because each provides important insights into the concept and process of retirement. However, such divergent perspectives can make the systematic study of retirement challenging for students and researchers.

RETIREMENT TRENDS

Increasing interest in the topic of retirement on the part of researchers, students, policymakers, organizational decision makers, and the general public has been fueled by at least three demographic trends. The first and most notable of these trends is the gradual aging of the nearly 80 million people born between 1946 and 1964, commonly known as the baby boomers. At present, this group represents approximately 50% of the U.S. population in the prime working years (between ages 25 and 64). As this cohort continues to age over the next decade, the percentage of adults between 55 and 64 (when retirement is a realistic option) will increase by approximately 65%. As a result, the baby boomers will no doubt redefine the concept of retirement, as they have so many other concepts as they have moved through their life course.

The second demographic trend is the decline in workforce participation of older adults, namely men, during the second half of the 20th century. The workforce participation rate for men between the ages of 55 and 64 was 87% in 1950 but just 67% in 2000. For men over the age of 65, the workforce participation rate dropped from 46% in 1950 to a mere 17% in 2000. However, this decreasing trend appears to have leveled out somewhat since approximately 1985. For women between the ages of 55 and 64, workforce participation rates increased from 27% in 1950 to 52% in

2000. The workforce participation rate for women over the age of 65 also increased, from 8% in 1950 to 11% in 2000. Similar trends have been observed in most developed countries. As a result, the divergent trends for men's and women's late-life workforce participation rates will no doubt redefine the concept of retirement for generations to come.

The third demographic trend is the increasing longevity of the population in developed countries. In 1950, for example, the average 65-year-old could expect to live 13.9 more years; however, by 2002, that number had increased to 18.2 years (approximately 22% longer). Given this trend toward increased longevity, the way we define and study retirement will need to change to accommodate the fact that we may now spend upwards of one third of our lives or more in retirement.

Taken together, these trends indicate that more workers will be experiencing retirement and will do so for a longer period of time than ever before. The sheer magnitude of this phenomenon raises a number of social, organizational, and individual concerns. At the societal level, the most prominent issue is the looming strain that will be placed on public (e.g., Social Security) and private pension systems by the large number of retiring baby boomers. Thus, public policymakers will need to make many difficult yet crucial decisions in the near future about how we can best address the projected shortfalls in pension systems, particularly Social Security.

At the organizational level, both public- and private-sector employers will be faced with the loss of well-trained, highly experienced employees and, in some sectors, potential labor shortages as the massive baby boomer cohort begins to retire in earnest in 2010. Thus, employers will be faced with the decision of where and how to spend depleted resources. Should they work to retrain older workers? Provide incentives to keep older, more experienced workers from contemplating retirement? Develop mentoring programs to tap the wisdom of older workers who are quickly approaching retirement? Restructure jobs to make them more appealing and accommodating to older workers? Choosing among these options will be challenging for organizational decision makers.

RETIREMENT AND THE INDIVIDUAL

For individuals, the questions center predominantly on deciding whether and when to retire, how to finance retirement, and quality of life after retirement. These highly personal decisions are becoming more and more complex for those approaching retirement.

Research on decisions about whether and when to retire shows that these choices appear to be influenced by a number of factors. At the individual level, demographic variables such age, health, and wealth show some of the most consistent relationships with the decision to retire. Older workers, those whose health limits their ability to work, and those who can financially afford to stop working (because they are eligible to receive Social Security or private pension income) are more likely to retire.

Familial variables and gender are also related to retirement decisions. For example, married couples generally tend to coordinate the timing of their retirements. Those having higher quality of marital and family life appear to find retirement more attractive. Gender is also related to retirement decisions, but this relationship is more complex and likely influenced by the presence of dependents (including a spouse or aging parents) in the home. For example, women tend to retire when there are dependents in the home, presumably to engage in caregiving, whereas men tend to continue working, presumably to meet the financial demands created by having dependents in the home. In addition to these factors, lower commitment to aspects of the work role and a positive attitude toward retirement are also related to the decision to retire.

Research on quality of life after retirement suggests that, contrary to the once-popular belief, most retirees do not experience retirement as a stressful crisis. Rather, most retirees adjust to retirement fairly well. Studies examining adjustment to retirement suggest that it is influenced by many of the same factors that influence the retirement decision. For example, those with better financial situations and better health tend to be more satisfied with retirement. Those who have engaged in more retirement planning also tend to have higher satisfaction with retirement. With regard to gender, men and women with similar circumstances appear to experience retirement similarly. However, when their circumstances differ, there are often important differences between the sexes. For example, women may have fewer financial resources, and therefore they are less able to afford the retirement lifestyle they prefer. Beyond these factors, people with more social contacts and social support are more likely to experience a higher quality of life in retirement. Contrary to popular belief, less than 10% of retirees move out of state, presumably to warmer climates and more affordable locations, after retiring.

EVOLVING CONCEPTIONS OF RETIREMENT

At one point in time, retirement meant a complete disengagement from the workforce. However, recent trends suggest this definition of retirement is inaccurate. Indeed, in 2000, 38% of men and 33% of women receiving income from private pensions were also employed. In one survey of adults between the ages of 36 and 54, 55% reported that they planned to work part-time and 32% planned to work full-time after they retire. This continued paid work during retirement is sometimes referred to as *bridge employment, phased retirement,* or *blurred retirement.* This transitional phase between full-time work and complete retirement allows older workers to try out retirement and determine whether it is a good fit for them. Given the trend toward increased longevity, this transition phase is likely to become more prevalent and lengthen considerably over time. However, as past research has shown, not all individuals (particularly less-educated and minority workers) have equal opportunity to engage in such a transitional phase. Thus, policymakers need to consider how best to provide transitional retirement to as many individuals as possible, regardless of their means or demographic background.

Retirement is a rapidly evolving phenomenon. We must keep in mind that retirement is a continuous process of preparation, transition, and adjustment. Demographic factors are altering the way we define, view, and experience retirement. The idea that an individual can work for the same company for 30 to 40 years and then retire at age 65 with a gold watch and enjoy a life of leisure is quickly becoming extinct, if it ever really existed at all. Instead, we are seeing what scholars refer to as the "widening trajectory" of the life course. That is, we are observing a wider array of what is considered normative in terms of retirement. As a result, scholars, researchers, and students will be challenged in studying the retirement concept and experience.

Organizational decision makers will be challenged to determine how best to meet staffing and training needs. Policymakers must also determine how best to meet the needs of the public, and individuals on the front lines may be at a loss as to how to determine when, how, or even whether they should retire, given the increasing lack of normative standards to rely on. Only through continued diligent scholarship, study, and research will we be able to keep pace with the moving target that is known as retirement.

—*Gary A. Adams and Kenneth S. Shultz*

FURTHER READING

Adams, G. A., & Beehr, T. A. (Eds.). (2003). *Retirement: Reasons, processes, and results.* New York: Spring.

Beehr, T. A. (1986). The process of retirement: A review and recommendations for future investigation. *Personnel Psychology, 39,* 31–55.

Feldman, D. C. (1994). The decision to retire early: A review and conceptualization. *Academy of Management Review, 19,* 285–311.

Henretta, J. C. (2001). Work and retirement. In R. H. Binstock & L. K. George (Eds.), *Handbook of aging and the social sciences* (5th ed., pp. 255–271). San Diego: Academic Press.

Kim, J. E., & Moen, P. (2001). Moving into retirement: Preparation and transition in late midlife. In M. E. Lachman (Ed.), *Handbook of midlife development* (pp. 487–527). New York: Wiley.

Moen, P. (1996). A life-course perspective on retirement, gender, and well-being. *Journal of Occupational Health Psychology, 1,* 131–144.

Talaga, J. A., & Beehr, T. A. (1989). Retirement: A psychological perspective. In C. L. Cooper & I. T. Robertson (Eds.), *International review of industrial and organizational psychology* (pp. 185–211). Chichester, UK: Wiley.

RIGHTSIZING

See DOWNSIZING

ROLE AMBIGUITY

Role ambiguity, or the extent to which one's work responsibilities and degree of authority are unclear, is one of the most widely studied variables in the field of occupational stress. Because it represents a subjective judgment of one's work situation, role ambiguity is typically assessed using employees' self-reports. Some researchers refer to role ambiguity by its polar opposite, *role clarity.*

Employees who experience role ambiguity feel uncertainty about which behaviors are and are not appropriate. They may wonder, for example, whether they are engaging in inappropriate work behaviors. On the other hand, they may wonder whether they are failing to engage in appropriate work behaviors. Most employees find both of these situations distressful.

Much of the research on occupational stress has focused on identifying work stressors; role ambiguity and a related variable, called *role conflict* (i.e., the extent to which an employee faces incompatible work demands), are the most commonly studied stressors. A *stressor* is any aspect of the work environment that requires an employee to adapt and has the potential to cause poor health. In addition to role ambiguity, other stressors include having a heavy workload or being mistreated by a supervisor. The negative health consequences produced by a stressor, such as depression, anxiety, or physical symptoms, are called *strains*.

Role theory provides the theoretical basis for the study of role ambiguity. According to role theory, each employee has a unique set of rights and responsibilities within the organization. Formal roles are the set of official behaviors that employees perform as part of their job description and are maintained by organizational policies. The formal role of a teacher, for example, includes grading tests and assigning homework. In addition, informal roles develop as part of the everyday social dynamic of the organization. Although these roles are not enforced by written policies, they are maintained by informal social interactions. For teachers, for example, informal roles might include planning and organizing staff parties. Role ambiguity is generally operationalized as uncertainty concerning formal roles.

CAUSES OF ROLE AMBIGUITY

According to leadership theories, good leaders help employees clarify their responsibilities and then create situations in which those responsibilities can be effectively executed. By this standard, effective leaders create work situations for their subordinates that are free of role ambiguity. When role ambiguity does arise, effective leaders work to minimize it. Leadership theories also suggest that effective leaders show concern for the personal welfare of their subordinates. To the extent that supervisors care about employee well-being, they are likely to work toward reducing role ambiguity and other stressors.

Empirical evidence supports the notion that effective leader behavior is associated with low levels of role ambiguity. Leader initiating structure (i.e., the extent to which leaders engage in behaviors aimed at clarifying employee responsibilities) and leader consideration (i.e., the extent to which leaders show concern for employees), for example, are two leadership variables that are associated with low role ambiguity. Furthermore, employees are likely to experience little role ambiguity when their leaders provide opportunities for employee participation and create a formalized work environment. In short, role ambiguity is indicative of poor management practices. Indeed, many survey items measuring role ambiguity make specific reference to one's supervisor.

In addition to the negative behaviors of supervisors, employees who report high levels of role ambiguity generally report having unfavorable work environments. Some of the environmental factors associated with role ambiguity are lack of autonomy, feedback, and task identity. In other words, role ambiguity is most likely to occur in simple, unenriched jobs. Furthermore, employees who report high levels of role ambiguity also generally report high levels of role conflict.

Individual differences may predispose individuals to experience role ambiguity. Individuals who have an external locus of control (i.e., those who believe they have little control over their lives), who are high in neuroticism, who are high in need for clarity, or who have low self-esteem, for example, are especially likely to report high levels of role ambiguity.

CONSEQUENCES OF ROLE AMBIGUITY

Perceptions of uncertainty are at the core of many workplace stressors, and role ambiguity is no exception. Uncertainty can result in many negative consequences. Indeed, several studies have shown that role ambiguity is related to manifestations of poor mental and physical health. For example, role ambiguity is associated with anxiety, burnout, depression, and physical illness.

In addition to these negative health consequences, role ambiguity is associated with both negative employee attitudes and ineffective job behaviors. Meta-analyses, for example, have found that role ambiguity is associated with the following attitudes:

- Overall job dissatisfaction
- Dissatisfaction with work tasks
- Dissatisfaction with supervision

- Dissatisfaction with coworkers
- Low organizational commitment
- Low job involvement
- High turnover intention
- Absenteeism

The correlation between role ambiguity and dissatisfaction with supervision is especially strong, suggesting that employees perceive management as the source of role ambiguity.

Important methodological issues surround the study of role ambiguity. Most of the research examining the causes and consequences of role ambiguity has used cross-sectional designs. This makes it difficult to draw strong conclusions about the causal relationships between role ambiguity and its potential causes and consequences.

TREATMENTS FOR ROLE AMBIGUITY

Organizations have several options at their disposal for treating role ambiguity. Because ineffective leadership is a root cause of role ambiguity, the most promising treatments are likely to involve leaders. These treatments may include the following actions:

- Training managers to identify when their own behaviors might lead to role ambiguity and encouraging them to modify these behaviors
- Selecting managers who are likely to engage in high levels of initiating structure and consideration
- Redesigning jobs to be more complex
- Introducing efforts aimed at reducing role conflict

Given the negative consequences associated with role ambiguity, one might expect that organizations would be highly motivated to minimize the levels of role ambiguity experienced by their workers. However, as organizations focus more on the bottom line, unfavorable working conditions and their negative effects on employees are often overlooked.

—*Nathan A. Bowling*

See also Role Conflict; Role Overload and Underload; Stress, Consequences; Stress, Coping and Management; Stress, Models and Theories

AUTHOR'S NOTE: The author wishes to thank Terry A. Beehr for his helpful suggestions concerning earlier versions of this entry.

FURTHER READING

Beehr, T. A., Walsh, J. T., & Taber, T. D. (1976). Relationship of stress to individually and organizationally valued states: Higher order needs as a moderator. *Journal of Applied Psychology, 61,* 41–47.

Fisher, C. D., & Gitelson, R. (1983). A meta-analysis of the correlates of role conflict and ambiguity. *Journal of Applied Psychology, 68,* 320–333.

Jackson, S. E., & Schuler, R. S. (1985). A meta-analysis and conceptual critique of research on role ambiguity and role conflict in work settings. *Organizational Behavior and Human Decision Processes, 36,* 16–78.

Kahn, R. L., & Byosiere, P. (1992). Stress in organizations. In M. D. Dunnette & L. M. Hough (Eds.), *Handbook of industrial and organizational psychology* (2nd ed., Vol. 3, pp. 571–650). Palo Alto, CA: Consulting Psychologists Press.

Katz, D., & Kahn, R. L. (1978). *The social psychology of organizations.* New York: Wiley.

ROLE CONFLICT

Role conflict occurs when employees experience incompatible work demands. It is a widely studied variable in the occupational stress literature, where it is considered to be a stressor. A *stressor* is any part of the work environment that requires an adaptive response from employees and has the capacity to produce poor health. In addition to role conflict, other stressors include role ambiguity (i.e., the extent to which one's role requirements are unclear), mistreatment at work, and unreasonable workload. The negative health outcomes produced by stressors, such as anxiety, depression, and physical symptoms, are called *strains.* Role conflict is associated with a number of strains.

Role theory provides the theoretical basis for the study of role conflict. According to role theory, each employee has a unique set of work roles. Each role has its own unique rights and responsibilities. Employees simultaneously occupy multiple roles, both within and outside the organization. A midlevel manager who is married, for example, would have the roles of supervisor, subordinate, and spouse. Role conflict is especially likely to exist among individuals who occupy several different roles.

TYPES OF ROLE CONFLICT

Researchers have distinguished several forms of role conflict. One form of conflict occurs when employees experience incompatibility between their values and their job responsibilities. For example, a convenience store employee who personally objects to gambling but sells lottery tickets as part of his or her job experiences this form of conflict. A second type of role conflict involves incompatibility between employees' job responsibilities and their abilities, time, and resources. Examples of this form of conflict include not having enough time to complete one's work tasks or not having the training or equipment necessary to complete one's work. Similar situations are sometimes referred to as role overload (i.e., having too much work or work that is too difficult) and organizational constraints (i.e., any aspect of the work environment that interferes with job performance).

These two types of conflict are examples of *intrarole conflict,* which occurs when incompatibility exists within a single role. On the other hand, *interrole conflict* occurs when two or more roles are incompatible with each other. One form of interrole conflict occurs when individuals must behave in a particular way in one role that is inconsistent with the way they must behave in another role. For example, a business executive might be required to act authoritatively toward subordinates, but would be expected to act differently when socializing with friends. Conflict between work and family life is another form of interrole conflict.

WORK–FAMILY CONFLICT

Work–family conflict is a form of interrole conflict that occurs when the role requirements of work and family are incompatible with each other. Researchers further distinguish between work-to-family conflict and family-to-work conflict. Work-to-family conflict occurs when one's work roles interfere with the successful execution of one's family roles. If a mother misses her son's school play because she has to attend a work meeting, for example, she experiences family-to-work conflict. Family-to-work conflict, on the other hand, occurs when one's family role interferes with the successful performance of one's work role. This occurs, for example, when a father consistently misses work to care for an ill child. Of these two forms of conflict, work-to-family conflict is likely to produce greater health consequences.

Work–family conflict researchers also distinguish between time-based, strain-based, and behavior-based conflict. Time-based conflict occurs when the amount of time needed to satisfy the role requirements of one

domain do not allow enough time to meet the role requirements of another domain. For example, working excessive hours can prevent employees from spending sufficient time with their families. Strain-based conflict occurs when the demands of one role produce illness that interferes with performance in another role. Caring for a sick spouse, for example, might produce high levels of stress, making it difficult to perform effectively at work. Finally, behavior-based conflict occurs when work roles and family roles require behaviors that are inconsistent with each other. For example, a bill collector is expected to act aggressively at work when interacting with debtors but must act nurturing when caring for his or her children.

WORK–SCHOOL CONFLICT

Individuals who attend school while working often experience an additional form of role conflict: work–school conflict. Work–school conflict occurs when one's work and school responsibilities conflict with each other. An employed student, for example, might spend time working instead of studying for an exam. A further distinction is made between work-to-school conflict and school-to-work conflict. Work-to-school conflict occurs when work responsibilities interfere with school responsibilities, whereas school-to-work conflict occurs when school responsibilities interfere with work responsibilities. Workload and number of hours worked are likely to be positively associated with work–school conflict. In addition to producing the negative consequences discussed later, work–school conflict is also likely to have a negative impact on school performance.

CAUSES OF ROLE CONFLICT

Role conflict is largely the result of ineffective managerial behaviors. Research has found, for example, that leader consideration (i.e., the extent to which supervisors care about the well-being of their subordinates) and leader initiating structure (i.e., the extent to which supervisors clarify employees' roles) are both negatively associated with role conflict. Role conflict is also likely to be high when supervisors fail to provide employees with opportunities for participation.

Ineffective organizational policies are a direct cause of some forms of role conflict. Indeed, some survey questions measuring role conflict specifically refer to incompatible organizational guidelines.

Conflict can arise, for example, from incompatible requests from supervisors or from differing and incompatible performance standards across supervisors. Such forms of conflict are most likely to occur when organizational policies allow employees to report to multiple supervisors.

Role conflict is also likely to occur in simple, unenriched jobs. Specifically, the following job characteristics are negatively associated with role conflict:

- Feedback
- Task identity (i.e., the extent to which a job requires one to complete an entire piece of work, such as assembling a product from start to finish)
- Skill variety (i.e., the extent to which a job requires one to use a variety of different skills)

Finally, role conflict is likely to result from any situation that causes one to simultaneously occupy several roles, both within and outside the workplace. Being employed with multiple jobs, having a family, and being a student can all result in one having many roles.

CONSEQUENCES OF ROLE CONFLICT

Most workplace stressors include a component of uncertainty. Role conflict likely leads employees to feel uncertain about their ability to effectively satisfy their role requirements. This uncertainty leads to a number of negative consequences. Indeed, research has found that role conflict is associated with several indicators of mental and physical health. Some of the negative health consequences potentially produced by role conflict include depression, anxiety, burnout, and physical symptoms. In addition, role conflict is linked with a number of negative job attitudes and ineffective work behaviors:

- Overall job dissatisfaction
- Dissatisfaction with work tasks
- Dissatisfaction with supervision
- Dissatisfaction with coworkers
- Dissatisfaction with pay
- Dissatisfaction with promotional opportunities
- Low organizational commitment
- Low job involvement
- Turnover intention
- Poor job performance

However, most of the research examining the causes and consequences of role conflict has used cross-sectional designs. Thus, it is difficult to draw firm conclusions concerning causal relationships in this research.

TREATMENTS FOR ROLE CONFLICT

Because role conflict is largely the result of ineffective leadership behaviors, many of the treatments for role conflict require the involvement of supervisors. Supervisors, for example, could be trained to identify behaviors that encourage role conflict and could be trained to modify those behaviors. Likewise, one form of role conflict occurs when employees receive incompatible demands from two or more supervisors. This type of conflict could be eliminated by requiring employees to report to only one supervisor.

Some forms of role conflict are the direct result of organizational policies. Not having the required training or equipment to effectively satisfy one's role requirements, for example, might be the result of organizational policies. Changing such policies could eliminate these forms of role conflict. Some role conflict occurs because employees' personal values are incompatible with the role requirements of their jobs. This type of conflict speaks to the importance of hiring only job applicants who have a good fit with the job requirements.

Given that role conflict is associated with a number of negative outcomes, one might suspect that organizational leaders would adopt many of these suggestions in an effort to reduce role conflict. This has not been the case, however, as organizations have given more attention to treating the symptoms than to the causes of role conflict.

—*Nathan A. Bowling*

See also Occupational Health Psychology; Role Ambiguity; Stress, Consequences; Stress, Coping and Management; Stress, Models and Theories

AUTHOR'S NOTE: I wish to thank Terry A. Beehr for his helpful suggestions concerning earlier versions of this entry.

FURTHER READING

Greenhaus, J. H., & Beutell, N. J. (1985). Sources of conflict between work and family roles. *Academy of Management Review, 10,* 76–88.

Jackson, S. E., & Schuler, R. S. (1985). A meta-analysis and conceptual critique of research on role ambiguity and role conflict in work settings. *Organizational Behavior and Human Decision Processes, 36,* 16–78.

Kahn, R. L., & Byosiere, P. (1992). Stress in organizations. In M. D. Dunnette & L. M. Hough (Eds.), *Handbook of industrial and organizational psychology* (2nd ed., Vol. 3, pp. 571–650). Palo Alto, CA: Consulting Psychologists Press.

Karkel, K. S., & Frone, M. R. (1998). Job characteristics, work-school conflict, and school outcomes among adolescents: Testing a structural model. *Journal of Applied Psychology, 83,* 277–287.

Kossek, E. C., & Ozeki, C. (1998). Work-family conflict, policies, and the job-life satisfaction relationship: A review and directions for organizational behavior-human resources research. *Journal of Applied Psychology, 83,* 139–149.

ROLE OVERLOAD AND UNDERLOAD

In any organizational setting, a role represents a set of behavioral expectations that are assigned to one organizational member. In typical organizations, it is rarely the case that each employee has one clearly defined role that is recognizable and distinct from the roles of other organizational members. Rather, in most organizations, employees may hold multiple roles, the roles of different employees may overlap and occasionally conflict, and roles may change from time to time.

Because of the complexity of organizational roles, they can be a source of stress for employees. In fact, much has been written in the stress literature about role conflict and role ambiguity. Much less has been written, however, about the sheer amount of role demands that an employee may have. This entry will focus on two role stressors that have to do with the amount of role demands an employee possesses. *Role overload* occurs when employees simply have too much to do—in other words, their roles become too big. *Role underload,* on the other hand, occurs when employees have too little to do—in other words, their roles become too small.

HOW DO ROLES DEVELOP?

To understand role overload and underload, it is helpful to consider how roles develop in organizations. Most people enter organizations with at least some idea of what their role will be. People may be hired to be teachers, bank tellers, college professors, or tax accountants, and based on their knowledge of these jobs, they are likely have some idea of what the role responsibilities will entail. In addition to these expectations, new employees often receive formal job descriptions and communicate with their immediate supervisor regarding role and performance expectations. Other employees (both peers and subordinates) may also communicate their expectations regarding a new employee's role.

All of the sources of role-related information for an employee are known as that person's *role set.* Within an employee's role set, some members are obviously more important than others (e.g., supervisor), but an employee must pay attention to all members. In an ideal world, the members of an employee's role set would regularly meet to discuss the messages they are conveying and to make sure they are reasonable. Organizations, however, are not ideal, so it is possible that an employee may receive too many or too few role demands, or the demands of different members of the role set may be in conflict. The focus here will be role demands that are too big or too small.

ROLE OVERLOAD: WHY DO ROLES BECOME TOO BIG?

Role overload occurs when an employee's role simply becomes too demanding or too big. What exactly does it mean when a role becomes "too big" for the person occupying it? Role overload may occur in a strictly quantitative sense. That is, the person who occupies a role may simply have more items on his or her to-do list than can be accomplished in the available period of time. Most people, either at work or at home, feel overloaded in this fashion from time to time.

It is also possible for role overload to occur in a more qualitative sense. In this case, an employee may have enough time to accomplish his or her tasks, but the tasks may be too difficult to handle. One example of qualitative overload has to do with the inability to perform any task that is even remotely mechanical. For example, if something in the house is broken and needs to be repaired, one might become qualitatively overloaded.

From a role theory perspective, there are several different explanations for role overload. In many cases, there is little or no communication between the members of an employee's role set. An employee's supervisor, coworkers, subordinates, and in some cases, customers all make demands on an employee without necessarily knowing the demands of other members of the role set. This is particularly true when members of an employee's role set exist both within and outside the organization.

Another reason may have to do with the role itself. Some roles are inherently bigger than others regardless of what organizations do. In most organizations, roles that involve the supervision of others tend to be larger than roles that do not have any supervisory responsibilities. Likewise, roles that require employees to regularly interact with people outside the organization (called boundary-spanning roles) tend to be bigger than roles in which all of the members of the role set are located within the organization.

Temporary circumstances may also lead to role overload. Suppose, for example, that a work group consists of four employees, and one employee quits. In most organizations, the departing employee will eventually be replaced, but this typically takes some time. In the meantime, other members of the work group may be asked to pick up the slack and take on the work left by the departing employee. When organizations conduct layoffs, it is typical for the roles of layoff survivors to become larger than they were before the layoff.

A final reason that role overload may occur is poor organizational or job design. For example, an organization may assign one clerical person to a work unit consisting of 25 people. It is almost inevitable that the clerical person in this scenario will experience at least some form of role overload.

CONSEQUENCES OF ROLE OVERLOAD

The vast majority of research on role stress has focused on role conflict and role ambiguity. In fact, there is so much research on these role stressors that more than one meta-analysis has been conducted to summarize the literature. What these meta-analyses have shown is that both role stressors are associated with negative psychological (e.g., job dissatisfaction, anxiety), physical (e.g., self-reported symptoms, sick days), and behavioral (e.g., decreased performance, increased absenteeism) outcomes.

The little research that has focused on role overload mirrors the findings for role conflict and role ambiguity. The differences are in the areas of physical symptoms

and performance. On balance, role overload is more strongly related to physical symptoms and physical exhaustion than are other role stressors. This makes a great deal of sense, considering the nature of role overload and the fact that most research has measured role overload from a quantitative perspective.

The other difference is that, in contrast to other role stressors, role overload may be *positively* related to performance in some cases. In many cases, those who are the most competent and skilled are asked to take on more tasks and responsibilities than others within the organization. It may also be a result of the nature of the job in some cases. A person selling real estate, for example, will be much busier and overloaded during periods in which his or her sales commissions are highest.

When considering the effect of role overload, it is important to consider that the impact of role overload may vary from employee to employee. People who manage their time very well, those who have a great deal of help and support from others, and those who simply do not view being overloaded as negative probably do not respond to this stressor as negatively as others. Admittedly, though, more research needs to be done on individual difference moderators of the effect of role overload and other stressors.

WHAT ABOUT ROLE UNDERLOAD?

Little research has examined role overload, and even less has examined role underload. Intuitively, though, it makes sense that if people can have too much to do, they can have too little to do as well. Like role overload, role underload can likely be viewed from both a quantitative and a qualitative perspective. An employee who is experiencing quantitative underload simply has too few tasks to do, and thus may experience periods of idleness or boredom on the job. Though many workers may wish they occasionally had a day when they had too few tasks to accomplish at work, most would probably become bored if this were the case every day.

When an employee is qualitatively underloaded, he or she has enough things to do, but the nature of the work tasks are below his or her capabilities. Most people have experienced qualitative underload at some point in their working lives. Many college students, for example, hold part-time or summer jobs at which they are required to perform tasks (e.g., washing dishes, waiting tables) that are likely far below their intellectual capabilities. It is also the case that when the job market is tight, workers are often forced to accept jobs for which they are overqualified, and thus they may be subject to some degree of qualitative role underload.

As the examples in the previous paragraph suggest, role underload may be attributable to circumstance in some cases. It is also possible, however, that organizations may deliberately design jobs to be as simple as possible, and these jobs have high potential for role underload. Research on job design has shown that simplifying jobs may increase efficiency and decrease an organization's labor costs because skill requirements are reduced.

What is the impact of role underload? Though there is little research on role underload, research on job design suggests that in general, it should result in negative affective reactions such as job dissatisfaction. For example, employees who hold low-complexity jobs (very similar to role underload) tend to report much lower job satisfaction than employees who hold more complex jobs. However, responses to role underload may differ from employee to employee. Some people may find it very difficult to have too little to do, whereas others may be less bothered or even enjoy it. Readers can probably think of people they know who vary on this dimension.

SUMMARY AND CONCLUSIONS

This entry has described two important sources of stress in organizational settings—role overload and role underload. Both of these stressors have been studied far less than other role stressors, but there is some evidence that they may lead to negative outcomes for employees. Employees, however, may vary as to how they respond to role overload or underload. Given the causes of both stressors, organizations can take steps to reduce them through job redesign and job enrichment.

—*Steve M. Jex*

See also Empowerment; Job Characteristics Theory; Job Satisfaction; Occupational Health Psychology; Role Ambiguity; Role Conflict; Stress, Models and Theories

FURTHER READING

Barling, J., Kelloway, E. K., & Frone, M. R. (Eds.). (2005). *Handbook of work stress.* Thousand Oaks, CA: Sage.

Beehr, T. A., Jex, S. M., Stacy, B. A., & Murray, M. A. (2000). Work stressors and coworker support as predictors of individual strain and job performance. *Journal of Organizational Behavior, 21,* 391–405.

Parker, S., & Wall, T. (1998). *Job and work design: Organizing work to promote well-being and effectiveness.* Thousand Oaks, CA: Sage.

Shirom, A., Westman, M., Carel, R. S., & Shamai, O. (1997). Effects of work overload and burnout on cholesterol and triglyceride levels: The moderating effects of emotional reactivity among male and female employees. *Journal of Occupational Health Psychology, 2,* 275–288.

Sparks, K., Cooper, C., Fried, Y., & Shirom, A. (1997). The effects of hours of work on health: A meta-analytic review. *Journal of Occupational and Organizational Psychology, 70,* 391–408.

Stellman, J. (Ed.). (1997). *Encyclopaedia of occupational health and safety.* Geneva, Switzerland: International Labour Office.

S

SAMPLING TECHNIQUES

For describing or testing hypotheses about a population, sampling a small portion of the population is often preferable to taking a census of the entire population. Taking a sample is usually less expensive and less time-consuming than taking a census and more accurate because more effort and care can be spent ensuring that the right data are gathered in the right way. Data collected appropriately can be used to make inferences about the entire population.

Sampling techniques can be categorized into nonprobability samples and probability samples. A *probability sample* is selected in a way such that virtually all members of a population have a nonzero probability of being included, and that probability is known or calculable. A *nonprobability sample* is gathered in a way that does not depend on chance. This means that it is difficult or impossible to estimate the probability that a particular unit of the population will be included. Moreover, a substantial proportion of the population is typically excluded. The quality of the sample, therefore, depends on the knowledge and skill of the researcher.

In general, probability samples are preferable to nonprobability samples because results can be generalized to the entire population using statistical techniques. Such generalization is typically invalid with nonprobability samples because the exclusion of portions of the population from sampling means the results are likely to be biased. People who volunteer to participate in a study, for example, may be different from those who do not; they may differ in age, gender, occupation, motivation, or any number of other characteristics that may be related to the study. If the study concerns attitudes or opinions, volunteer participants may have different and often stronger feelings about the issues than nonparticipants.

Nonprobability samples, however, have their advantages and uses. They are relatively easy and inexpensive to assemble. They can be valuable for exploratory research or when the researcher wants to document a range or provide particular examples rather than investigate tendencies or causal processes. Moreover, techniques have recently been developed for obtaining unbiased results from certain kinds of nonprobability samples.

Two concepts are important to sampling in general: the target population and the sampling frame. The *target population* is the population to which the researcher wants to generalize the findings. One important characteristic of the population is the kind of entities its members are, known as the *unit of analysis*. The cases in the sample correspond to this unit of analysis. Examples of a unit of analysis are the individual, the organizational department, the organization, or some geographical unit, such as the state. The unit of analysis is characterized by a set of attributes on which the researcher gathers data. These are the variables the researcher scores for each case in the sample. For example, a researcher might explore individual characteristics such as age or years of education. Usually, the target population is circumscribed by some characteristic or combination of characteristics. It may be employees of a particular firm, or there may be a geographical limitation, such as residents of a particular city. Constraints on gender, ethnicity, age-group, work status, or other characteristics may be specified as well. A target population, for example, might be permanent, full-time female employees of a particular company.

The *sampling frame* is the complete list of all units from which the sample is taken. For the target population of permanent, full-time female employees, for example, the sampling frame might be a list of permanent, full-time female employees from all of the company's locations. For telephone surveys, a list of phone numbers is a typical sampling frame, perhaps for particular area codes or in conjunction with block maps.

PROBABILITY SAMPLES

Sample Designs

For probability samples, there are four common designs: the simple random sample, the systematic sample, the stratified sample, and the cluster sample. A *simple random sample* is drawn in such a way that every combination of units of a given size has an equal probability of being drawn. If there are n individuals in the sample and N in the population, for example, each individual's probability of being included is n/N. The simple random sample is optimal for estimating unbiased population characteristics as precisely as possible. The most commonly used statistical techniques assume and work best with simple random samples. A simple random sample can be drawn by applying a table of random numbers or pseudorandom numbers generated by a computer to the sampling frame. Unfortunately, for many target populations, it is difficult and costly to draw a simple random sample. Hence, researchers use sample designs that approximate simple random samples.

One such design is a *systematic sample,* which is drawn in such a way that every unit in the target population has the same probability of being selected, but the same is not true for every combination of units of a given size. A systematic sample might be used when the sample frame is a long, noncomputerized list. To carry it out, determine a sampling interval (I) based on the desired sample size (n): $I = N/n$. Choose at random a starting case, from the first through the Ith units in the list. Then from that starting case, select every Ith unit. A systematic sample will approximate a simple random sample unless there is some sort of periodicity in the sampling frame, which then will lead to bias in the results.

A more controlled sampling design is the *stratified sample,* which is undertaken to ensure a specified proportional representation of different population groups in the sample. If the target population is 10% Hispanic, for example, a simple random sample drawn from the population may be more or less than 10% Hispanic. A stratified sample ensures that 10% of the sample—or some other desired proportion, say 20%—will be Hispanic. Stratified samples may be classified into proportionate and disproportionate samples. A *proportionate* stratified sample ensures that the composition of the sample mirrors the composition of the population along some variable or combination of variables. To carry it out, divide the target population into subgroups according to the desired aspect—Hispanic and non-Hispanic, for example. Then take a simple random sample from each subgroup, with the same probability of selection for each subgroup.

In a *disproportionate* stratified sample, the proportion of different subgroups in the sample is set to differ from that in the target population. Typically, the composition of the sample overrepresents subgroups that form only a small proportion of the population. The purpose is to improve estimates for that subgroup and improve comparison between subgroups. For example, suppose the sample size is to be 500 and the target population is 5% Hispanic. A simple random sample would include about 25 Hispanic individuals, which is too small to obtain precise estimates for that subgroup. If better estimates are desired, the proportion of Hispanics in the sample can be raised, say to 20%, which will ensure that 100 Hispanic individuals are selected, thus producing more precise estimates for the subgroup and allowing Hispanic and non-Hispanic individuals to be compared more accurately. Analysis of the entire sample should be conducted using weights to adjust for the overrepresentation of some subgroups, a simple option in most major statistical packages for computers.

Cluster sampling is a common method for face-to-face data collection such as surveys. The data are gathered from a small number of concentrated, usually spatially concentrated sets of units. A few departments of an organization may be sampled, for example, or a few locations if an organization has multiple locations. Cluster sampling may be chosen to reduce costs or because there is no adequate sampling frame from which a simple random sample or systematic sample could be drawn.

Sample Size

One question that commonly arises in research is how large a sample is necessary. Collecting data is costly, and it may be better to concentrate on gathering higher-quality data from a smaller sample, if possible. Several methods for estimating the necessary sample size exist. One method is simply to use sample sizes that approximate those of other studies of high quality. Some references contain tables that give appropriate sample sizes.

Two formulas may be of assistance. Let p denote the proportion of the population with a key attribute; if the proportion is unknown, $p = .5$ (which assumes maximum variability) may be used. Let e denote the sampling error or level of precision, expressed as a proportion. Thus, $e = .05$ means $\pm 5\%$ precision. Finally, suppose a confidence level of 95% is desired. The sample size, n_0, may be estimated by

$$n_0 = \frac{1.96p(1-p)}{e^2}.$$

If the key variable takes on more than two values, the best method may be to dichotomize it—that is, transform it into a variable that takes two values—and then estimate p. Otherwise, $p = .5$ may be used, which gives a conservative estimate of sample size. For smaller populations (in the thousands, for example), wherein population size is denoted by N, the formula

$$n_0 = \frac{N}{1 + e^2 N}$$

may be used.

Other considerations may also affect the determination of the necessary sample size. If the researcher wishes to analyze subgroups of the target population separately or compare subgroups, then the sample must be large enough to represent each subgroup adequately. Another concern is nonresponse. Inevitably, not all units in the selected sample will provide usable data, often because they refuse or are unable to participate but also because of respondent error. Here, too, the sample must be large enough to accommodate nonresponses and unusable responses. Finally, money and time costs are a constraint in sampling and should be considered in planning the study so that the sampling can be completed as designed.

NONPROBABILITY SAMPLES

Haphazard, convenience, quota, and purposive samples are the most common kinds of nonprobability samples. *Convenience samples* comprise units that are self-selected (e.g., volunteers) or easily accessible. Examples of convenience samples are people who volunteer to participate in a study, people at a given location when the population includes more than a single location, and snowball samples. A snowball or respondent-driven sample is one in which the researcher begins with certain respondents, called "seeds," and then obtains further respondents through previous respondents. A *quota sample* is one in which a predetermined number of units with certain characteristics are selected. For a *purposive sample,* units are selected on the basis of characteristics or attributes that are important to the evaluation. Many focus groups are samples of this kind.

Recently, advances have been made in obtaining unbiased results for populations from which probability samples cannot be drawn directly, typically because no adequate sampling frame is available. A *hypernetwork method* can be applied to a target population of objects or activities that are linked to people—for example, art objects or arts-related activities. A probability sample of the individuals can then be used to obtain a probability sample of organizations providing those objects or activities. Another method again uses the techniques of social network analysis to obtain unbiased estimates from respondent-driven samples. This method is especially helpful in estimating characteristics of hidden populations, such as the homeless or drug users in a particular location.

—*Joseph M. Whitmeyer*

See also Descriptive Statistics; Experimental Designs; Focus Groups; Inferential Statistics; Longitudinal Research/ Experience Sampling Technique; Nonexperimental Designs; Quantitative Research Approach; Quasi-experimental Designs; Statistical Power

FURTHER READING

Cochran, W. G. (1977). *Sampling techniques.* New York: Wiley.

Kish, L. (1965). *Survey sampling.* New York: Wiley.

McPherson, M. (2001). Sampling strategies for the arts: A hypernetwork approach. *Poetics, 28,* 291–306.

Miaoulis, G., & Michener, R. D. (1976). *An introduction to sampling.* Dubuque, IA: Kendall/Hunt.

Salganik, M. J., & Heckathorn, D. (2004). Sampling and estimation in hidden populations using respondent-driven sampling. *Sociological Methodology, 34,* 193–240.

SCIENTIFIC MANAGEMENT

Scientific management is the umbrella term for practice and research that advocates making organizations more efficient by systematically working to improve the efficiency of workers. The work of individuals associated with this movement, such as Frederick Winslow Taylor, Frank and Lillian Gilbreth, and Henry Gantt, lives on in the current management approaches of statistical process control and Total Quality Management. Because scientific management arose at the same time as the field of industrial and organizational psychology—during the first decades of the 20th century—there was competition between the disciplines (as noted in critiques by Kurt Lewin, Charles Myers, and Morris Viteles). This entry approaches the scientific management school of thought from four points: (a) the genesis and growth of the school, (b) the key concepts of scientific management, (c) the role of scientific management in shaping the history and trajectory of industrial and organizational (I/O) psychology, and (d) the field's current status and importance in the world of work. Although Taylor's work often dominates the discussion of scientific management, the role of other researchers—especially the Gilbreths—should be acknowledged to avoid bias and to better show the linkages to I/O psychology.

GENESIS AND GROWTH OF SCIENTIFIC MANAGEMENT

Frederick Winslow Taylor is considered the founder and dominant figure in this school of thought, which is often referred to as Taylorism. Considered alongside his collaborators and contemporaries, Taylor looms large. Arthur Bedaeian and Daniel Wren, based on an order of merit ranking procedure, credited Taylor with the most influential management book of the 20th century, *Principles of Scientific Management,* although multiple books from the human relations movement make the list. Edwin Locke and others have provided flattering treatments. Taylor's treatment in his *Principles* viewed management as systematic process and moved the field beyond the familial and craft leadership that was predominant in American industry. The

scientific management approach offered stability in an era when traditional methods and assumptions were changing as a result of the confluence of progress, immigration, engineering, and education. Historian Robert Wiebe described the interval between 1877 and 1920 as a time in which many individuals and movements sought order in a country that was buffeted in a choppy sea of forces, such as industrialization and urbanization. The bureaucratic worldview coincided with a concept called *psychotechnology* in Europe.

Taylor blazed a trail as a consulting engineer and offered insights to industrialists and managers, much as Walter Dill Scott offered insights to advertising executives. After earning an engineering degree at Stevens Institute of Technology (site of the Taylor archives), he worked at the Midvale Steel Company, where he formulated his thinking. The expression of scientific management theory in *Shop Management* in 1903 and *Principles of Scientific Management* in 1911 earned Taylor widespread praise from factory owners but condemnation from trade unionists. Misunderstanding flourished on both sides. Taylor's biggest success was achieved at Bethlehem Steel, where his methods claimed to achieve a 200% increase in productivity after two years with only a 50% increase in wages. Careful historiographic research by Charles Wrege and his colleagues, however, shows problems with some of Taylor's claims about "Schmidt the laborer" (see Further Reading).

KEY CONCEPTS OF SCIENTIFIC MANAGEMENT

Taylor and his contemporaries advocated the study of the way workers perform tasks (most notably, time studies), collection of the informal job knowledge possessed by workers (i.e., knowledge management), and investigations aimed at improving the way tasks are performed in order to increase efficiency (defined as reductions in time). The next step is to convert the results of these studies into new methods of performing tasks with written, standardized work rules and operating procedures. Some attention is paid to the selection of workers, so that they have the skills and abilities to match the needs of the task, and to training, so that workers can perform their tasks according to the established rules and procedures. Taylor also addressed the need to establish a fair or acceptable level of performance for each task and to develop a pay system that provides higher rewards for performance above the acceptable level.

Although the two approaches are often treated synonymously, Taylor's time studies were not the same as motion studies. Time studies do not include the discrete movements that the Gilbreths labeled "Therbligs" and included in their motion studies. Although there were later attempts to connect motion study to time study, Gilbreth pointed out that Taylor conducted no motion studies. The discipline of industrial engineering integrated the techniques of the early giants as codified in a handbook prepared by H. B. Maynard.

The key concepts of this paradigm include *soldiering* or restriction of output (at two levels), conducting time studies of workers to study and improve work processes, creating "functional foremen," cost accounting, and paying the person rather than the position. Soldiering is a term used for workers completing no more than the amount of work that the informal work group enforces through social rules (i.e., no rate busting—rates are established and enforced by formal organizational work rules). A goal of scientific management is to find the most efficient rate and structure the work so that any and all minimally qualified workers can meet the established rate. Time-study rate systems are based on the fastest worker for each job in the organization. This worker's movements on the job are systematically examined, unnecessary movements eliminated, and a rate established for the job based on this time study. All workers are made accountable to the established rate.

The concept of the *functional foremen* was posited in opposition to the military management model, with supervision focusing on some aspect of work rather than the supervision (i.e., discipline) of people. Functional foremen were the forerunners of the production expediter and quality control or assurance clerk positions. Cost accounting is also known as task management, in which time clocks and time cards are the most salient feature and routing cards are used to track associated work products. Such a system allows the cost of labor per product to be tracked, archived, reported, and used for reward systems. Paying the person and not the position is the basis for pay-for-performance and per-piece rate pay systems.

ROLE OF SCIENTIFIC MANAGEMENT IN SHAPING I/O PSYCHOLOGY

The role of scientific management was a counterfoil to early I/O psychology, although it did provide a legacy of an objective, measurement-driven framework with an emphasis on the economic bottom line.

Hugo Munsterberg, among others (such as Harold Burtt and Viteles), advocated fitting the worker to the work and focusing scientific methods on the appropriate design of each. The success of scientific management in some organizations provided the impetus in business for I/O psychologists to focus on field application versus basic laboratory science. The human relations movement and basic research findings in social psychology offered counterarguments to a strictly applied focus (e.g., scientific management principles) for the young field. Kurt Lewin's critique of Taylorism in 1920 argued that psychologists and efficiency experts should work together to make work both more productive and more satisfying. Steven Hunt's recent critique asked rhetorically whether organizational citizenship behaviors would detract from performance in Taylorist jobs—a question that may be countered, how many jobs are Taylorist?

CURRENT IMPACT OF SCIENTIFIC MANAGEMENT

Current management disciplines, tools, and approaches influenced by the school of scientific management include statistical process control in production techniques, Total Quality Management methods, program evaluation and review technique charting methods, critical path method, benchmarking, and business process redesign. Workforces within U.S. government entities (e.g., military, bureaucracies) continue to *not* be influenced by scientific management, and little progress in this direction is anticipated in the future.

—*Scott A. Davies and James T. Austin*

See also Hawthorne Studies/Hawthorne Effect; History of Industrial/Organizational Psychology in North America; Human Relations Movement

FURTHER READING

Hunt, S. T. (2002). On the virtues of staying "inside of the box": Does organizational citizenship behavior detract from performance in Taylorist jobs? *International Journal of Selection and Assessment, 10,* 152–159.

Kanigel, R. (2005). *The one best way: Frederick Winslow Taylor and the enigma of efficiency.* Cambridge: MIT Press.

Maynard, H. B. (Ed.). (1956). *Industrial engineering handbook.* New York: McGraw-Hill.

Taylor, F. W. (1911). *Principles of scientific management.* New York: Harper & Brothers.

Wiebe, R. (1967). *The search for order, 1877–1920* (Reprint ed.). Westport, CT: Greenwood Press.

Wrege, C. D., & Hodgetts, R. M. (2000). Frederick W. Taylor's 1899 pig iron observations: Examining fact, fiction, and lessons for the new millennium. *Academy of Management Journal, 43,* 1283–1291.

SCIENTIST-PRACTITIONER MODEL

According to the scientist-practitioner model, psychologists are both practitioners who apply knowledge and scientists who base their activities on sound research in the profession. Some individuals may function more fully as scientists, conducting research and publishing their findings, whereas others may devote their lives to its application, but each has a keen respect for the other. The scientist-practitioner model is an aspirational goal for psychologists as well as a prescription for how psychologists should be trained.

The model can be traced back to the end of World War II, when the Veterans Administration (VA) and the United States Public Health Service (USPHS) encouraged the training of mental health professionals to work with returning veterans. At the same time, more people were seeking graduate education in psychology to meet this need. This put quite a strain on the small number of psychology departments that were training clinical psychologists. Throughout the 1940s, small working groups within the American Association of Applied Psychology (AAAP) addressed these issues, primarily under the direction of David Shakow, and developed outlines for training programs for doctoral-level clinical psychologists. The early drafts recommended that students first gain a sound grounding in scientific psychology, followed later by coursework and internships in more applied practice skills. The hope was to upgrade the skills of future clinical psychologists as well as the reputation of psychology.

The AAAP merged with the American Psychological Association (APA), and with encouragement from the VA and the USPHS, a committee was formed to address the training of psychologists, including standards for educational institutions. This committee visited doctoral training institutions to accredit those that met the standards. To address many remaining concerns, a conference was held during the summer of 1949, when 73 psychologists and key stakeholders from the VA and USPHS gathered in Boulder, Colorado. By the end of the meeting, several resolutions had been adopted that defined psychologists as people who are trained in both scientific research and practice. The conference had another lasting impact: Programs that adhere to the scientist-practitioner model are often identified as "Boulder model" programs. Even today, the APA accreditation standards insist that training programs reflect the principle that the practice of psychology is based on the science of psychology; in turn, the practice of psychology influences the science of psychology.

Although the Boulder conference primarily focused on clinical training, the scientist-practitioner model soon found its way into other applied areas. When the Industrial and Business Section of the AAAP became Division 14 of the APA, its first two goals were to (a) ensure high standards of practice and (b) promote research and publication in the field. Many years later, when Division 14 incorporated to become the Society for Industrial and Organizational Psychology, its mission statement prominently included promoting both the science and practice of industrial and organizational psychology. Later, the guidelines for education and training at the doctoral level focused on producing students who could be both generators of knowledge and consumers of knowledge. To this end, most, if not all, doctoral students take coursework in research design and statistics, in addition to classes in specific industrial and organizational topics, and their program of study culminates with a significant research project, the dissertation.

Although the scientist-practitioner model is pervasive, it is not universally accepted as either a standard for training or a description of the activities of most psychologists. Some graduates of psychology programs believe training overemphasizes research at the expense of practice. These concerns were voiced in 1973 at a conference in Vail, Colorado, leading to the development of an alternative model: the scholar-professional. In this view, psychologists are highly trained practitioners who are consumers rather than generators of research. Programs that adopt the Vail model often grant a PsyD degree in lieu of the PhD.

—*William D. Siegfried, Jr.*

See also American Psychological Association, Association for Psychological Science; Society for Industrial and Organizational Psychology

FURTHER READING

Baker, D. B., & Benjamin, L. T. (2000). The affirmation of the scientist-practitioner: A look back at Boulder. *American Psychologist, 55*(2), 241–247.

Ellis, H. C. (1992). Graduate education in psychology: Past, present, and future. *American Psychologist, 47*(4), 570–576.

Society for Industrial and Organizational Psychology. (1999). Guidelines for education and training at the doctoral level in industrial-organizational psychology. Retrieved March 9, 2006, from http://www.siop.org/phdguidelines98.html

SELECTION: OCCUPATIONAL TAILORING

The most effective and appropriate selection procedures vary for different types of work and in different types of organizations. Two major considerations should guide this occupational tailoring. The first consideration is the work behavior of the people hired: What is required by the work itself, and what work-related outcomes does the organization want to achieve with the selection procedures? This consideration addresses the effectiveness of the selection procedure at bringing about desired work behaviors. The second consideration is the fit of the selection procedures with other human resource (HR) processes and systems and with the organization's culture. This consideration addresses the extent to which selection procedures complement existing HR processes and systems and are consistent with the organization's culture when it comes to the treatment of job candidates and employees.

These two considerations are often separate and independent. For example, highly technical work usually implies selection procedures that gauge acquired technical knowledge through degree and grade point average requirements and job knowledge assessment. In contrast, an organization may have a culture and recruiting strategy that emphasizes close recruiting relationships with selected technical schools and relies on faculty referrals to identify technically skilled candidates. In such a setting, a job knowledge test may be an inappropriate selection procedure even if it is the most effective procedure for ensuring that the organization hires candidates with the required level of technical skill. The tailoring of selection procedures requires a careful evaluation of both sets of considerations.

CONSIDERATIONS OF WORK BEHAVIOR

The evaluation of work behavior should begin with a consideration of the work behavior outcomes that the organization wants to achieve with the selection procedure. The organization's desired work outcomes may have a direct bearing on the information about the work that is relevant to the choice of selection procedures. Continuing the example of highly technical work, if an organization is satisfied with the technical expertise of its new hires but wants to select more loyal employees who will stay with the company, the analysis of the work would focus less on technical content and more on work context that influences employees' decisions to leave or stay.

Organizations may have any number of desired outcomes, including productivity, helpfulness, schedule adherence, retention, customer satisfaction, accountability, creativity, safety and security, and dependability. In general, the organization's desired outcomes can be organized into two major categories: work proficiency and contextual behavior. *Work proficiency* refers to the extent to which employees perform their work tasks quickly, accurately, and consistently and achieve the desired objectives of the work activity. *Contextual behavior,* on the other hand, refers to employee behavior that is valued by the organization but is not considered a specific task or element of the work itself. Examples include helping others, staying in the organization, showing up on time, not stealing, and being accountable for results.

The distinction between an organization's interest in work proficiency and its interest in contextual behavior is important to occupational tailoring because, with few exceptions, any selection procedure is likely to be more relevant to one type of interest than the other. To understand the relationship between selection procedures and organization interests, selection procedures may be classified into five major categories: (a) ability and aptitude; (b) personality, disposition, and temperament; (c) values, interests, and attitudes; (d) acquired skills and knowledge; and (e) work-related experience, training, and education.

Contextual Behavior

In organizations that place high value on contextual behavior, the selection procedures that are most likely to help create these outcomes assess personality, disposition, and temperament (Category 2) and values, interests, and attitudes (Category 3). The particular attributes that are most likely to create the desired outcome may be understood through an evaluation of the context surrounding the work and the organization. For example, staying in a customer service job with significant time pressure, highly repetitive volume, and rule-bound job procedures may require personality attributes associated with optimism and dependability. In contrast, staying in a sales job that requires many self-initiated customer contacts with a high percentage of negative outcomes but with significant payoffs for positive outcomes may require high levels of achievement orientation and independence. In general, with the exception of conscientiousness, the effectiveness of attributes in Categories 2 and 3 depends on the specific contextual features of the work. Conscientiousness is, by far, the most generally effective personality attribute and leads to a wide range of positive work behaviors across many types of work.

An important contextual consideration is the extent to which the work situation is a strong determiner of employee work behavior. When the work context is strong, there is little opportunity for personal interests, values, dispositions, and motives to influence work behavior, at least within the range of ordinarily acceptable behavior. For example, telemarketing work often requires that employees adhere to carefully worded scripts, spend closely monitored amounts of time on calls, and leave their desks at prescribed times and durations. Under those strong conditions, attributes such as creativity are unlikely to have much impact on demonstrated work behavior. In general, in order for selection procedures in Categories 2 and 3 to affect desired contextual behaviors, the work situation must be weak enough to enable the targeted attributes to influence the employee's behavior. The implication for occupational tailoring, particularly as it relates to contextual behavior, is that different selection procedures are likely to be effective for strong and weak situations.

Work Proficiency

In organizations that emphasize the importance of work proficiency, the most effective selection procedures assess some combination of ability and aptitude (Category 1), acquired skills and knowledge (Category 4), and work, training, and education experience (Category 5). In this case, a thorough analysis of the work content may be necessary to identify the particular selection procedures that are most likely to be effective.

A major consideration in the maximization of work proficiency is that some relevant attributes are highly work specific, such as acquired skills and knowledge (Category 4) and physical and psychomotor abilities (a subset of Category 1), whereas the relevance of general mental ability (GMA, a subset of Category 1) is not work specific but is effective at maximizing proficiency across a wide range of types of work. One of the most well-established results in industrial and organizational psychology is that GMA is an important determiner of work proficiency across virtually all types work. Only the cognitive complexity of the work has much influence on the effectiveness of GMA. The more complex the work, the more effective GMA is at enabling work proficiency.

An analysis of work content should indicate the extent to which work-specific acquired skills and knowledge are required for early work proficiency. Therefore, it is important to design some component of the selection procedure to evaluate the target acquired skills and knowledge. Almost always, these selection procedures should be tailored to the work. The same is true for work requirements relating to physical and psychomotor abilities. An appropriate analysis of the work content should identify the specific physical or psychomotor abilities required for work proficiency.

In the design of selection procedures intended to maximize work proficiency, a major decision point is whether GMA assessments will be used, and if so, whether tailoring the GMA assessment will have any benefit for the effectiveness of the selection procedure. To be sure, there is a wide variety of mental ability tests ranging from the most general, measuring abstract reasoning, complex problem solving, and mechanical aptitude, to the most specific, measuring arithmetic facility, clerical coding speed, and spelling and vocabulary. Whatever combination of GMA procedures is used for whatever type of work, the most effective GMA-based selection procedures assess a broader composite of mental abilities. This can be achieved by assessing one or two general abilities (such as abstract reasoning or problem solving) or by assessing three or four narrow mental abilities and relying on a composite of those narrow assessments. Often, the tailoring decision is based on the organization's interest in having the selection procedure appear reasonable and job-relevant to candidates.

Overlap Between Work Proficiency and Contextual Behavior

The overlap between considerations of contextual behavior and work proficiency should be evaluated. When successful work proficiency and desired contextual behavior have the same underlying determinants, the same selection procedure may be effective at achieving both purposes. For example, an organization's interest in minimizing turnover may be addressed by the use of a selection procedure designed to maximize work proficiency if the primary cause of turnover is poor work proficiency. However, other than the broadly beneficial effects of conscientiousness, the attributes that are most likely to affect contextual behavior tend to be different from the attributes that are most likely to affect work proficiency.

CONSIDERATIONS OF ORGANIZATION FIT

In addition to considerations of the work itself, appropriate selection procedures should be tailored to fit two aspects of the organization: (a) existing HR processes and systems and (b) the organization's culture relating to the treatment of job candidates and employees.

Existing HR Processes and Systems

Training and recruiting processes are closely connected to selection processes. In most cases, recruiting creates a candidate pool that completes the selection procedures. A recruiting process that focuses on identifying candidates with certain attributes, such as degrees or grade point averages, minimizes the need for a selection process designed to assess precisely the same acquired knowledge. In general, it is unnecessarily inefficient for both recruiting processes and selection processes to target the same attributes among candidates.

New hire training processes rely on new hires having certain sets of attributes. For example, training may assume some amount of preexisting job knowledge or job experience. Selection procedures should be tailored to be consistent with the assumptions made by the new hire training process. Of course, optimal planning would consider both together and determine the most cost-effective manner for the organization to achieve the level of acquired skills and knowledge among new hires. In general, training is likely to be more expensive per new hire than selection. This

tends to produce HR strategies that maximize the scope of selection to minimize the cost of training. However, organizations that have unique requirements for acquired skills and knowledge, such as a product line that is unique to the industry, may find that selection procedures are simply not cost-effective when the target skill or knowledge is rare. In this case, training may take on the role of developing the needed, unique skills and knowledge.

Organizational Culture

Finally, some attention should be paid to a frequently overlooked consideration in the tailoring of selection procedures. Many organizations have strong cultures relating to the treatment of employees and job candidates. The design of selection procedures should carefully consider the imperatives of the organization's culture. For example, an organization may place very high value on enabling employees to realize job progression through successful job performance. In such an environment, a selection procedure that governs employee progression and assesses the personal attributes, abilities, or skills and knowledge related to successful performance may not be consistent with a culture that values demonstrated work performance as the key to progression. Other cultures, such as highly entrepreneurial, risk-seeking environments, may have a built-in disdain for standardized practices associated with selection procedures, particularly testing. In such environments, selection procedures are sustainable only if they do not significantly inhibit the self-reliance of hiring managers. In general, selection procedures represent a strong culture for making crucial people decisions. They should be tailored to match the overarching organizational culture that shapes other HR processes and systems.

—*Jerard F. Kehoe*

See also Employee Selection; Selection Strategies

FURTHER READING

Kehoe, J. F. (Ed.). (2000). *Managing selection in changing organizations: Human resource strategies.* San Francisco: Jossey-Bass.

Tippins, N. (2002). Issues in implementing large-scale selection programs. In J. W. Hedge & E. D. Pulakos (Eds.), *Implementing organizational interventions: Steps, processes, and best practices.* San Francisco: Jossey-Bass.

SELECTION STRATEGIES

SELECTION AND ASSESSMENT CONSULTING

Selection strategies differ from organization to organization in any number of ways. Some rely mostly on tests, others on interviews. Some are computer or Web based, others paper-and-pencil tests. Some automatically select candidates out, whereas others inform decisions that select candidates in—and so on. Selection strategies are the result of many design decisions, and it is safe to say that no two strategies are the same.

The purpose of this entry is to describe different selection strategies and evaluate the effectiveness of those strategies in different employment situations. These descriptions and evaluations will be limited to the manner in which information from the selection procedures is used to make selection decisions. This entry will not address strategies relating to delivery methods or types of assessment procedures. Rather, the focus will be on describing and evaluating the different strategies that organizations use to make selection decisions.

FRAMEWORK

This entry is organized into two major sections. The first section will identify and describe the most common types of selection decision-making strategies. This section is primarily descriptive and highlights key differences among the strategies. The second section will evaluate these strategies based on their fit with each of several types of employment context. The employment context is defined based on three considerations: (a) employment volume (high/low), (b) mode of employment processing (continuous/episodic), and (c) the organization's culture for accountability (systems accountability/manager accountability). The decision-making strategies will be evaluated based on their fit with each of the eight combinations of volume, mode, and accountability. Although this approach is somewhat artificial—actual employment contexts are not likely to be exact invariant combinations of volume, mode, and accountability—it has the advantage of being systematic and reveals key principles that can be applied to any employment context.

This essay will not evaluate strategies based on considerations of legal risk. Certainly, legal risk is an important consideration in the design of any selection strategy. The primary means of controlling legal risk is the documentation of validation evidence. However, legal risk can also be influenced by the extent to which selection decisions are not precisely prescribed and uniformly applied to all candidates. Although the latter considerations certainly relate to decision-making strategies, legal risk often depends on subtle and nuanced aspects of the situation and the particular charge, making it difficult to offer general guidelines beyond the principles of validity, adverse impact, and consistency of application, which may be applied to any decision-making strategy.

SELECTION DECISION-MAKING STRATEGIES

Some of the strategies described here are typically mutually exclusive, such as multiple hurdles and compensatory scoring, whereas others are not, such as compensatory scoring and profile matching. The descriptions offered here summarize the relationships among the most commonly used strategies. The first two strategies, *multiple hurdles* and *compensatory scoring,* are typically viewed as mutually exclusive, although hybrid strategies are beginning to emerge. The third and fourth strategies, *cut scores* and non-cut-score-based *judgment methods,* are deliberately defined as mutually exclusive to clarify their most important differences. The fifth strategy, *banding,* is a class of methods introduced primarily to manage legal risk in certain types of situations but not equally applicable in all employment contexts.

Multiple Hurdles

A major consideration in designing a selection strategy is the cost-effective management of candidate flow. One common approach to this issue is the strategy of multiple hurdles. According to this strategy, selection procedures are administered in sequential steps. After each selection procedure is administered, it is then scored. At each step, candidates whose scores fall below an established threshold are eliminated. Candidates who are not eliminated proceed to the next step, where the next selection procedure is administered and scored and additional candidates are eliminated.

Two methods of multiple hurdles can be considered. The first and most common method, the *independent method,* eliminates candidates based only on scores from the selection procedure administered at the current step in the series. The second method, the *accumulative method,* eliminates candidates at each step based on scores from all of the previously administered procedures and the current procedure. For example, consider a multiple hurdles strategy in which Step 1 is a problem-solving test, Step 2 is a work sample exercise, and Step 3 is an employment office interview. At Step 2, the independent method would eliminate candidates based solely on scores from the work sample exercise, whereas the accumulative method would eliminate candidates based on some combination of both the problem-solving score and the work sample score.

The primary advantage of the multiple hurdles strategy is that it minimizes administration cost and time by not administering later selection procedures to candidates who performed poorly on earlier procedures. Typically, this advantage is maximized by administering the selection procedures in order of cost from lowest to highest. Its primary disadvantage is that it sacrifices some predictive accuracy at each decision step by considering information from only some (usually one) of the selection procedures that the organization views as relevant to the job. The accumulative method mitigates this disadvantage somewhat.

Compensatory Scoring

When organizations prefer to maximize the predictive power of each selection decision, all candidates are administered a common set of selection procedures. A composite score is then created for each candidate that combines information from the entire set of selection procedures. This composite score is then used in some decision method to select among the candidates.

In virtually all applications of compensatory scoring, only one composite of selection procedures is used as the basis for making selection decisions. This common practice reflects an assumption that there is only one model or type of successful employee. All selection decisions seek to choose employees who fit that particular model of success. In contrast, some organizations recognize that different employees are successful and valued in different ways. Some employees may be successful because they are accurate and fast producers; others may be successful because they are able to engage others in achieving objectives. Still others may be successful because they are reliable employees who show up every day, perform well enough, and are loyal to the organization. An organization that

values different models of success may prefer to use more than one composite of the same predictors and choose candidates who are predicted to be successful by at least one of the valued models. Little research has examined this possibility of simultaneous, separate composites to determine how much gain could be realized compared with the standard practice of a single, presumably optimal composite.

Compared with multiple hurdles, compensatory scoring is more expensive but has somewhat more predictive accuracy. There is no general conclusion about the actual trade-off between cost and accuracy. This trade-off depends on the actual costs and predictive validities of each of the selection procedures. However, it is common for cost differences between types of selection procedures to be very large, sometimes 500% to 1,000%, though the incremental accuracy that the second procedure adds to the first is often slight, say 10%. Of course, a 10% increase in predictive accuracy may actually have more dollar value than the cost of administering the second procedure to all candidates.

Cut Scores

The use of cut scores can be combined with any of the other strategies described here. In fact, some strategies, such as multiple hurdles and banding, invariably rely on cut scores as part of the decision-making process. However, it is useful to describe cut scores as a distinct strategy, perhaps a substrategy, and to provide information about specific methods for determining and using them.

A cut score is a particular score on a selection procedure or composite of selection procedures that serves as a threshold value for determining which candidates are excluded or included. There is no law or professional standard that requires cut scores to be either low or high. Generally, it is acknowledged that the hiring organization may consider a variety of factors, including expected work proficiency, cost of employment, labor market conditions, and efforts to avoid discriminatory employment practices, in determining a cut score that optimizes the organization's value for its new hires.

Because many factors may influence cut scores, there are many methods for setting cut scores. Some methods rely primarily on the judgment of experts, whereas other methods rely on quantitative analyses of desired outcomes. Some methods focus on the probability that hired candidates will be successful employees, whereas other methods focus on the probability that people who will be successful employees will be hired. In any case, no cut score can be set without some form of value judgment being made on behalf of the organization. All cut scores rely on some judgment about the outcomes the organization values and desires from its selection strategy.

More than one cut score may be used to enable selection decisions. In the simplest decision process, a single cut score is used to determine that candidates who score at or above the cut score will be hired. More complex decision processes may use multiple cut scores to create ranges of scores that distinguish the most qualified candidates from the next most qualified, and so on. In all cases, a cut score defines a boundary line between candidates who are treated in different ways.

The primary advantage of cut scores is that they simplify the selection decision process. The primary disadvantage is that the use of cut scores ignores potentially useful information both above and below the cut score. For example, by relying on a single cut score set at the 75th percentile of candidate scores, the organization treats the highest-scoring candidates the same as candidates scoring at the 75th percentile. Both are hired. This process can be disadvantageous to the organization if it only needs to hire a small percentage of the candidates. For example, suppose an organization only needs to hire 5% of the available candidates but has adopted a cut score that 25% of the candidates satisfy. In this situation, the organization is losing value from its selection strategy because the cut score does not allow it to choose just the top 5% of all candidates. Of course, in such a case, the organization may change the cut score to be closer to the 95th percentile so that it does not lose useful information.

Judgment Methods

For convenience, the term *judgment methods* is used to refer to methods of making selection decisions that are not based on cut scores to determine automatic decisions. Judgment methods include all methods for using quantitative information from the selection procedures to inform the judgment of the person making the hiring decision. Certainly, there are innumerable such methods. The two most common types of judgment methods will be described here: expectancy methods and profile-matching methods.

Expectancy methods convert the score results from the selection procedures into quantitative predictions or expectations about outcomes of interest to the organization. This conversion requires quantitative analysis that relates the scores on the selection procedures to scores on outcome measures. One method, *probability of success,* converts each selection procedure score into a probability of success. This, of course, requires the organization to define what level of outcome result corresponds to success and to provide a measure of this outcome in some study sample of employees that can be used to define the conversion. For example, suppose the organization is interested in making selection decisions to minimize the number of new hires who leave during the first 12 months. Success is defined as staying on the job for 12 months or longer. To convert scores on the selection procedure into a probability of staying for 12 months or longer, retention would need to be tracked for candidates who had taken part in the selection procedures in question. Based on an analysis of the results of such a study, for each candidate, the person making the hiring decision would be provided with a measure of the probability that the candidate will stay for 12 months or longer, as predicted by the selection procedure. The decision maker could then make an informed hiring decision based on this information and whatever other information might be available about the candidate.

Similarly, another expectancy method, *predicted performance,* provides predicted levels of performance rather than probability of success. The same types of data and analyses are required to produce this type of information, although it is no longer necessary for the organization to define success.

A second judgment method, *profile matching,* provides a different type of quantitative information to the person making the hiring decision. According to this method, the information describes the extent to which the candidate's selection procedure scores are similar to the selection procedure scores of people who have demonstrated success on the job.

Consider a sales organization, for example. Suppose this organization is implementing new selection procedures to assess achievement orientation, independence, intelligence, sociability, and integrity. As part of the study of this new process, the organization administers selection procedures to its current salespeople. Suppose that the top sellers are different from average sellers on achievement orientation, independence, and intelligence but no different on sociability and integrity. In addition, top sellers score very high on achievement orientation, moderately on independence, and moderately high on intelligence. This profile of a top seller becomes the ideal pattern of scores on these three selection procedures and distinguishes top sellers from average sellers. Each new candidate's profile of achievement orientation, independence, and intelligence scores is compared with this ideal profile. In some fashion, usually graphically or quantitatively, the decision maker is shown the extent to which each candidate's score profile is similar to the ideal profile. Like expectancy methods, the profile method provides quantitative information to decision makers as the basis for making a hiring decision but generally does not trigger any automatic decision.

Banding Methods

During the early 1990s, banding methods were introduced as a technique for selecting candidates so as to equalize the hiring rates among different groups of candidates. Although these methods were designed to minimize group selection rate differences, they also have broader applications. Banding methods all separate the full range of scores on the selection procedure of interest into several bands. The essential feature of banding is that each band of scores is defined as a range within which the organization is indifferent to the highest- and lowest-scoring candidates. Some banding methods define the indifference bands based on the reliability of differences between scores on the selection procedure; other methods define the indifference bands based on differences between predicted outcomes. Regardless of the method used to define the bands, the selection decisions are made by first considering the candidates in the top band, choosing among them, and, if any vacancies remain, moving to the next highest band and repeating the process until all vacancies are filled.

The primary advantage of banding methods is that they provide an explicit definition of the organization's indifference to the highest- and lowest-scoring candidates within a band. This enables organizations to base selection decisions on other considerations because they can be confident that candidates within bands are similarly qualified with respect to the attributes assessed by the selection procedures. The primary disadvantage of banding is that it is most effectively applied only when the whole set of candidates is known before any selection decisions are made.

EVALUATION OF STRATEGIES

Eight employment contexts are listed in Table 1. For each context, the selection strategies most likely to fit with the demands of that context are shown, as well as the most significant considerations in choosing among the selection strategies. This evaluation is presented in a table format for ease of comparison and use.

The distinction between high and low volume is not based on absolute numbers of vacancies or candidates. Rather, high volume exists when the number of candidates or vacancies to be filled stretches the capacity of the regular employment process.

Mode of employment refers to the continuity of recruiting and screening processes. Continuous-mode operations manage ongoing recruiting to maintain an available pool of candidates to be ready when vacancies occur or to support continuous vacancies. Continuous employment processes include processes that are modulated from time to time but maintain ongoing recruiting and screening processes. A common example of continuous employment is the process used by retail sales organizations that need to maintain fully staffed sales clerk positions in the face of typically high turnover rates. In contrast, episodic employment processes stop and start over time. Typically, they start when a batch of new vacancies is to be filled or a batch of new candidates is to be recruited. Once the batch of vacancies or candidates is completed, the process stops. A common example of episodic employment is public-sector employment for police and firefighter jobs, which are frequently managed as periodic episodes of employment.

The culture for accountability is perhaps the least well-prescribed context feature. It refers to the organization's tendency to place high accountability on either its systems or its managers, especially with regard to human resource processes and systems. For example, some organizations manage annual performance management and compensation processes largely as a matter of inputting performance results into a system and then following that system's rubrics for performance assessment and compensation decisions. In contrast, other organizations rely entirely on managers to make performance management decisions and compensation decisions with little, if any, systematic structure or guidelines.

—*Jerard Kehoe*

Table 1   The Fit Between Employment Contexts and Selection Strategies

Employment Context			*Good-Fitting Strategies* • *Preferred strategies* ○ *Primary considerations*
Volume	*Mode*	*Accountability*	

High	Continuous	Systems	• Multiple hurdles
			  ○ Cut scores
			  ○ Minimized potential for high costs
			  ○ Rapid, automatic decisions

High	Continuous	Manager	• Compensatory scoring
			• Early-stage cut scores
			• Late-stage judgment methods
			  ○ Reduce volume to managers
			  ○ Tolerate potential for high costs
			  ○ Enable managers' rapid decisions and reduce workload

High	Episodic	Systems	• Banding
			• Cut scores
			• Compensatory scoring
			  ○ Higher risk of scrutiny
			  ○ Tolerance of higher costs
			  ○ Explicit decisions
			  ○ Rapid, automatic decisions
			  ○ Automatic control of group selection rates

High	Episodic	Manager	• Compensatory scoring
			• Early-stage cut scores
			• Late-stage judgment methods
			  ○ Reduce volume to managers
			  ○ Tolerate potential for high costs
			  ○ Enable managers' rapid decisions

Low	Continuous	Systems	• Compensatory scoring
			• Banding with systematized decision rules and small number of bands (two or three)
			• Cut scores at early stage, representing minimum qualifications
			  ○ Little potential for high cost, so maximum predictive accuracy
			  ○ Automated decision rules (banding) using complete information

Low	Continuous	Manager	• Compensatory scoring
			• Cut scores at early stage, representing minimum qualifications
			  ○ Little potential for high cost, so maximum predictive accuracy
			  ○ Exclude the least competitive candidates to reduce manager workload

Low	Episodic	Systems	• Cut scores
			• Compensatory scoring
			  ○ Automatic decisions
			  ○ Little potential for high cost, so maximum predictive accuracy

Low	Episodic	Manager	• Compensatory scoring
			• Judgment methods
			  ○ Little potential for high cost, so maximum predictive accuracy
			  ○ Enable manager's effective use of complete selection information

See also Employee Selection; Executive Selection; Prescreening Assessment Methods for Personnel Selection; Selection: Occupational Tailoring; Uniform Guidelines on Employee Selection Procedures

FURTHER READING

Aguinis, H. (Ed.). (2004). *Test score banding in human resource selection.* Westport, CT: Praeger.

Kehoe, J. F. (Ed.). (2000). *Managing selection in changing organizations: Human resource strategies.* San Francisco: Jossey-Bass.

Kehoe, J. F., Dickter, D. N., Russell, D. P., & Sacco, J. M. (2005). E-selection. In H. G. Gueutal & D. L. Stone (Eds.), *The brave new world of eHR: Human resources management in the digital age.* San Francisco: Jossey-Bass.

Kehoe, J. F., & Olson, A. (2005). Cut scores and employment discrimination litigation. In F. J. Landy (Ed.), *Employment discrimination litigation: Behavioral, quantitative, and legal perspectives.* San Francisco: Jossey-Bass.

Schmitt, N., & Borman, W. C. (Eds.). (1993). *Personnel selection in organizations.* San Francisco: Jossey-Bass.

Tippins, N. (2002). Issues in implementing large-scale selection programs. In J. W. Hedge & E. D. Pulakos (Eds.), *Implementing organizational interventions: Steps, processes, and best practices.* San Francisco: Jossey-Bass.

SELF-CONCEPT THEORY OF WORK MOTIVATION

The study of work motivation centers on why employees initiate, terminate, or persist in specific work behaviors in organizations. Most traditional theories of work motivation are built on the premise that individuals act in ways that maximize the value of exchange with the organization. However, the nature of an individual's work motivation may also involve an internal, individually rooted need or motive—for example, to enhance one's self-esteem, to achieve, or to affiliate. These motives are assumed to be part of the unique, internal core of a person's self-concept.

STRUCTURE OF SELF-CONCEPT

Current theories purport that self-concept is a multidimensional knowledge structure that helps individuals organize and give meaning to memory and behavior. Indeed, psychologists have argued that attaching an object or event to the self gives it special meaning (e.g., *my* car versus *a* car). Self-concept may be seen as consisting of attributes related to individual self-perception, including traits, competencies, and values. For example, individuals may use trait terms such as *ambitious* and *dependable* to describe their essential character or hold perceptions of the competencies they possess (e.g., "I am a good leader").

The *working self-concept* (WSC) is the highly activated, contextually sensitive portion of the self-concept that guides action and information processing on a moment-to-moment basis. The activation of the components of the WSC varies depending on the cues in one's current context. For example, one's self-concept may include several roles, such as being a parent, a spouse, and an employee. These alternative self-concepts are associated with different social contexts, which become activated when the right social cues are present.

The WSC can be viewed as consisting of three components: *self-views,* or one's perceived standing on salient attributes, and two types of comparative standards—*current goals,* which are short-term and narrowly focused, and *possible selves,* which are long-term and future focused and provide much broader comparative standards. These three components combine to create control systems that regulate motivation. Furthermore, a control system may involve any two of the three components, so that one component provides the standard and the other the source of feedback. Researchers have proposed that combinations of the three components have very different motivational consequences on work behavior.

Finally, self-concept also has different focal levels that are composed of personal and social identities. Personal identity refers to self-categorization based on comparisons to others that emphasize one's own uniqueness. Social identity is based on self-definition through relations with others or through group membership, and thus it emphasizes one's similarities and connectedness. These identities are active at different times, creating a personal WSC or, alternatively, a social WSC.

RELATIONSHIP BETWEEN SELF-CONCEPT AND WORK MOTIVATION

The self-concept is a source of work motivation in that individuals are motivated to maintain and enhance an internalized view of the self. Specifically, the meaning that individuals attribute to information is often a function of the strength of their self-perceptions and their need to affirm their self-concept. In an organizational setting, employees make choices among behavioral alternatives, set and accept work goals, take on projects, and generally direct effort toward obtaining task and social feedback that is consistent with their self-concept. In addition, when there is conflict between the self-concept and social or task feedback, employees may engage in a number of adaptive strategies to achieve congruence between their self-concept and performance feedback (e.g., increasing effort, changing feedback).

Whether work goals are tied to current self-views or possible self-views has important implications for work motivation. When work goals are tied to current self-views, more proximal motivation mechanisms may be engaged, creating an overriding performance orientation that accentuates self-enhancement. Alternatively, when work goals are connected to possible selves, more distal motivational processes predominate that are rooted in the need for uncertainty reduction and consistency and the ability to predict and control the environment.

Possible selves normally reflect ideals toward which individuals strive, but they can also represent feared selves that individuals attempt to avoid. The contribution of these two motivational components changes with one's perceived proximity to each, with the more proximal source generally having a greater impact. For example, studies show that feared selves are powerful sources of motivation, particularly for individuals who perceive themselves to be close to the feared self. These findings have implications for work motivation: Organizational leaders may need to understand that both feared and desired selves serve as regulatory standards for employees. Consequently, for an employee who is close to the feared self, articulating a vision of an ideal may not have much motivational impact, but framing work tasks in terms of the feared self may serve as a powerful motivator. Conversely, for an individual who is close to ideal and far from the feared self, explaining how the employee can avoid the feared self may have minimal effects, but linking work activities to the ideal self may be very motivating.

Consistent with the distinction between personal identity and social identity, work motivation may also be internally or externally based. Work motivation is internally based when a personal WSC is activated by cues in the work environment. In this situation, the employee may set internal standards that become the basis of the possible self. Furthermore, the individual may tend to use fixed rather than ordinal standards of self-measurement as he or she attempts to first reinforce perceptions of competency and later achieve higher levels of competency. Employees for whom a personal WSC is chronically activated will likely have a high need for achievement and be highly motivated by task feedback. It is important to these individuals that their efforts are vital in achieving work outcomes and their ideas and actions are instrumental in performing a job well.

Work motivation is externally based when a social WSC is activated and the individual is primarily other-directed. In this case, the possible self is derived by adopting the role expectations of the reference group, leading to ordinal standards of self-evaluation. When a social WSC is chronically activated, the individual is motivated to behave in ways that meet the expectations of others and elicit social feedback that is consistent with self-concept perceptions. The individual may behave in ways that satisfy reference group members, first to gain acceptance and, after achieving that, to gain status.

Recent studies show that core self-evaluations, a concept that overlaps to a great extent with self-concept, are predictive of work motivation. Core self-evaluations refer to fundamental assessments that people make about their worthiness, competence, and capabilities. Findings suggest that individuals who choose goals that are concordant with their ideals, interests, and values are happier than those who pursue goals for other (e.g., extrinsic) reasons. Further, self-concordant goals are likely to receive sustained effort over time and be more attainable and more satisfying.

In sum, the theories and findings related to self-concept and work motivation suggest that individuals are motivated to behave in ways that are consistent with their existing self-concepts. Thus, theories based on the assumption that individuals have a fundamental need to maintain or enhance their self-concept may be useful in expanding our understanding of motivated behavior in the workplace.

—Heather MacDonald and Douglas Brown

See also Job Involvement; Work Motivation

FURTHER READING

Judge, T. A., Bono, J. E., Erez, A., & Locke, E. A. (2005). Core self-evaluations and job and life satisfaction: The role of self-concordance and goal attainment. *Journal of Applied Psychology, 90,* 257–268.

Leonard, N. H., Beauvais, L. L., & Scholl, R. W. (1999). Work motivation: The incorporation of self-concept-based processes. *Human Relations, 52,* 969–998.

Lord, R. G., & Brown, D. J. (2004). *Leadership processes and follower self-identity.* Mahwah, NJ: Lawrence Erlbaum.

SELF-EFFICACY

Albert Bandura defined self-efficacy as a person's belief in his or her capability to successfully perform a particular task. Together with the goals that people set, self-efficacy is one of the most powerful motivational predictors of how well a person will perform at almost any endeavor. A person's self-efficacy is a strong determinant of his or her effort, persistence, and strategizing, as well as subsequent training and job performance. Besides being highly predictive, self-efficacy can also be developed to harness its performance-enhancing benefits. After outlining the nature of self-efficacy and how it leads to performance and other work-related outcomes, the measurement and sources of self-efficacy will be discussed. We conclude by considering whether it is possible to have too much self-efficacy.

NATURE OF SELF-EFFICACY

Because self-efficacy pertains to specific tasks, people may simultaneously have high self-efficacy for some tasks and low self-efficacy for others. For example, a manager may have high self-efficacy for the technical aspects of his or her role, such as management accounting, but low self-efficacy for other aspects, such as dealing with employees' performance problems.

Self-efficacy is more specific and circumscribed than self-confidence (i.e., a general personality trait that relates to how confidently people feel and act in most situations) or self-esteem (i.e., the extent to which a person likes himself or herself), and therefore it is generally more readily developed than self-confidence or self-esteem. Self-efficacy is a much stronger predictor of how effectively people will perform a given task than either self-confidence or self-esteem.

HOW SELF-EFFICACY AFFECTS PERFORMANCE AND WELL-BEING

A high degree of self-efficacy leads people to work hard and persist in the face of setbacks, as illustrated by many great innovators and politicians who were undeterred by repeated obstacles, ridicule, and minimal encouragement. Thomas Edison, believing that he would eventually succeed, reputedly tested at least 3,000 unsuccessful prototypes before eventually developing the first incandescent lightbulb. Abraham Lincoln exhibited high self-efficacy in response to the numerous and repeated public rebukes and failures he experienced before his eventual political triumph. Research has found that self-efficacy is important for sustaining the considerable effort that is required to master skills involved in, for example, public speaking, losing weight, and becoming an effective manager.

When learning complex tasks, high self-efficacy prompts people to strive to improve their assumptions and strategies rather than look for excuses, such as not being interested in the task. High self-efficacy improves employees' capacity to collect relevant information, make sound decisions, and take appropriate action, particularly when they are under time pressure. Such capabilities are invaluable in jobs that involve, for example, dealing with irate customers when working in a call center or overcoming complex technical challenges in minimal time. In contrast, low self-efficacy can lead to erratic analytical thinking, which undermines the quality of problem solving—a key competency in an increasingly knowledge-based society.

In a dynamic work context, in which ongoing learning and performance improvement are needed, high self-efficacy helps individuals react less defensively when they receive negative feedback. In areas in which self-efficacy is low, people often see a negative outcome as confirming the incompetence they perceive in themselves. This can set up a vicious circle whereby ambiguous results are considered evidence of perceived inability, further lowing an individual's self-efficacy, effort, and subsequent performance. When people have low self-efficacy, they tend to blame the situation or another person when things go wrong. Denial of any responsibility for poor performance inhibits the chance that an individual will learn how to perform more effectively in the future.

People are inclined to become anxious or depressed when they perceive themselves as unable to manage aversive events or gain what they value highly. Thus, self-efficacy is related to the experience of stress and occupational burnout. Specifically, low self-efficacy can readily lead to a sense of helplessness and hopelessness about one's capability to learn how to cope effectively with the challenges and demands of work. When this occurs, low self-efficacy can be distressing and depressing, preventing even highly talented individuals from performing effectively.

MEASUREMENT OF SELF-EFFICACY

Because self-efficacy is task specific, there is no single, standardized measure of self-efficacy. Rather, measures must gauge an individual's self-assessed capacity to either (a) achieve a certain outcome on a particular task (*outcome self-efficacy*) or (b) engage in the processes likely to lead to a certain desired outcome (*process self-efficacy*). For example, an outcome self-efficacy scale in the domain of job search might include items such as "I believe that I can get a new job within four weeks" or "I believe I can get a new job with a starting salary of at least $65,000," with response anchors ranging from "not at all confident" to "extremely confident." Alternatively, a process self-efficacy scale for job search would focus on items such as "I believe I can network effectively to at least six people during the next four weeks" or "I believe that I can send out 15 résumés during the next four weeks," with response anchors similar to the outcome self-efficacy scale. The key point is that measures of self-efficacy are most informative, predictive, and useful when addressing areas in which self-efficacy is lacking or when they are highly focused on specific behaviors, tasks, or objectives.

SOURCES OF SELF-EFFICACY

There are three key sources of self-efficacy. The most powerful determinant of self-efficacy is *enactive self-mastery,* followed by *role modeling,* and then *verbal persuasion.*

Enactive self-mastery is achieved when people experience success at performing at least portions of a task. It serves to convince them that they have what it takes to achieve increasingly difficult accomplishments of a similar kind. Self-mastery is best achieved through progressive mastery, which is attained by breaking down difficult tasks into small steps that are relatively easy in order to ensure a high level of initial

success. Individuals are then given progressively more difficult tasks in which constructive feedback is provided and accomplishments celebrated before increasingly challenging tasks are attempted. Building self-efficacy through enactive self-mastery entails structuring situations that bring rewarding success and avoid the experience of repeated failure. For example, a person who is learning to pilot an aircraft may be given many hours to develop skill and confidence in the separate component skills before attempting to combine them by actually flying solo. Initial flying lessons are designed so that trainee pilots are challenged but also experience efficacy-building successes during each session. For employees to develop self-efficacy through enactive self-mastery, managers need to provide challenges in which individuals regularly encounter and celebrate successes as they develop their proficiency at work tasks.

Role modeling occurs when people observe others perform a task that they are attempting to learn or vividly visualize themselves performing successfully. Role modeling can provide people with ideas about how they could perform certain tasks and inspire their confidence so that they can act in a similarly successful manner.

Effective role models approach challenging activities as an opportunity to learn and develop their knowledge, skills, and effectiveness rather than as a test of how talented they are. They respond to setbacks by exploring what can be done differently in the future. In short, good role models demonstrate the development of skill, persistence, and learning rather than the defensiveness and blaming that cause mistakes to recur and subsequent performance to decline.

Models are most effective at raising self-efficacy when they are personally liked and seen as having attributes (e.g., age, gender, or ethnicity) similar to those of the individuals who observe them. One implication is that managers should think carefully before assigning mentors, especially without the input of those being mentored. Individuals may learn and become more confident from observing both the successes and failures of others, as long as they feel confident that they can avoid repeating the errors they observe.

Verbal persuasion builds self-efficacy when respected managers encourage and praise individuals for their competence and ability to improve their effectiveness. Positive self-talk can also raise self-efficacy. Regardless of its source, verbal persuasion is most likely to increase self-efficacy when it is

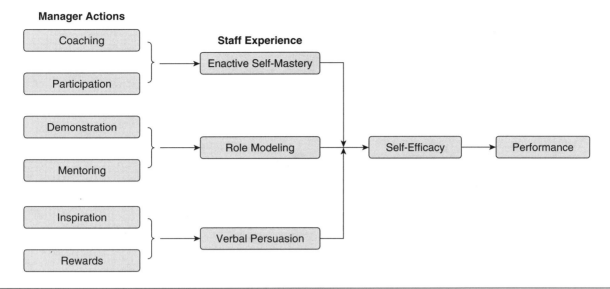

Figure 1   Managerial Actions That Improve Employees' Performance by Building Their Self-Efficacy

SOURCE: Adapted from Heslin (1999).

perceived as credible and emphasizes how success results from devoting sufficient effort to mastering acquirable skills rather than depending on inherent talent. Efficacy-raising feedback highlights how consistent efforts have enabled substantial improvements, as well as the progress made, rather than involving peer comparisons or making reference to how far individuals have to go until their ultimate objective is achieved. Effective verbal persuasion is reinforced with corresponding actions. For example, telling individuals that they are capable but not assigning them any challenging tasks tends to erode both employees' self-efficacy and the manager's credibility. In contrast, having individuals draw up a progress chart before complimenting them on their genuine progress can be a potent way of raising employees' sense of what they can achieve.

UNDERMINING SELF-EFFICACY

These approaches contrast with the subtle, though common, messages that individuals have low ability, which erode self-efficacy beliefs. Such signals include consistently being assigned unchallenging tasks, receiving praise for mediocre performance, being treated indifferently for faulty performance, or being offered unsolicited help. Faultfinding and personal criticism are particularly destructive because these actions undermine motivation to explore and experiment, whereby individuals discover what they are

actually able to achieve. Although encouraging messages can raise self-efficacy, attempts at building self-efficacy through verbal persuasion may easily degenerate into empty sermons unless they are supported by efficacy-affirming experiences (i.e., enactive self-mastery).

Figure 1 illustrates the types of managerial initiatives that build employees' self-efficacy. Table 1 provides a self-assessment of how frequently efficacy-building behaviors should be engaged in.

TOO MUCH OF A GOOD THING?

Extremely high self-efficacy can lead to excessive risk taking, hubris, and dysfunctional persistence, though in most cases, the resulting failures that people experience soon recalibrate their self-efficacy to a more realistic level. In general, the many benefits of high self-efficacy make it a worthwhile attribute to cultivate. This is best done through the simultaneous and systematic application of enactive self-mastery, role-modeling, and verbal persuasion.

—*Peter A. Heslin and Ute-Christine Klehe*

See also Social Cognitive Theory

FURTHER READING

Bandura, A. (1986). *Social foundations of thought and action.* Englewood Cliffs, NJ: Prentice Hall.

Table 1   Self-Assessment: How Frequently Do You Build Employees' Self-Efficacy?

Rate how often you exhibit the following behaviors using the following scale:

1. Rarely
2. Occasionally
3. About half the time
4. Regularly
5. Often

Manager Actions	*To what extent do you . . .*	*Rating*
Coaching	• Provide clear, broad objectives for your employees to work toward? • Break complex tasks down into components to enable employees to experience success? • Provide feedback about behaviors rather than personal style? • Deal with "silly" questions or suggestions by tactfully helping employees to explore their implications?	
Participation	• Enable your employees to establish or at least participate in the determination of their goals? • Encourage participation in decision making, where feasible? • Actively engage employees in solving problems that they experience? • Seek input before making changes that will affect your employees?	
Demonstrate	• Personally model struggling to overcome challenges? • Walk the talk—do what you ask others to do? • Express enthusiasm, persistence, and not taking yourself too seriously?	
Mentoring	• Provide opportunities that may result in your employees having more expertise than yourself in certain areas? • Express interest in the learning experiences of your employees? • Make yourself available as a sounding board?	
Inspiration	• Establish a clear and exciting vision that your employees are inspired to strive toward? • Leave your employees feeling stronger and more capable after spending time with you? • Have and demonstrate a genuine concern for the welfare of your employees?	
Rewards	• Reward employees by making encouraging comments and publicly acknowledging their efforts and achievements? • Provide each employee with rewards that they value? • Make employees feel safe and supported when they have made mistakes?	

Add up your scores to obtain an approximate estimate of how much you build the self-efficacy of your employees. How would your employees rate you on these questions? Why not reevaluate yourself one month from now to gauge your improvement at raising the self-efficacy of your employees?

NOTE: This exercise is intended as a self-development activity illustrating efficacy-building behaviors rather than as a tool for assessing managers to make selection, performance appraisal, or promotion decisions.

Bandura, A. (1997). *Self-efficacy: The exercise of control.* New York: Freeman.

Heslin, P. A. (1999). Boosting empowerment by developing self-efficacy. *Asia Pacific Journal of Human Resources, 37*, 52–64.

Wood, R., & Bandura, A. (1989). Social cognitive theory of organizational management. *Academy of Management Review, 14*, 361–384.

SELF-ESTEEM

Self-esteem (SE) is the overall value that one places on oneself as a person. Few topics have received more attention in psychology than SE, and indeed, a search of the PsycINFO database in 2005 identified more than 25,000 articles with *self-esteem* as a keyword. There are several reasons for the enduring interest in SE. First and foremost, most people are inherently curious about SE because it encompasses important information about the self, such as how worthy, competent, and well-liked one is. In that sense, possessing self-knowledge necessitates understanding ones' SE, and few can be indifferent to this kind of information. Second, researchers and practitioners alike have assumed that high SE has many positive outcomes, and in fact, much of the research on SE has been focused on exploring what enhances SE. Third, SE has been shown to be related to many important variables of interest, such as subjective well-being, job satisfaction, performance, competition, causal attribution, achievement, and helping. Therefore, understanding SE appears to enhance knowledge in many other areas of psychology. Because SE seems to have such major importance to researchers, practitioners, and people in general, it is not surprising that more than 150 articles are published every month on SE. Despite this proliferation of studies and decades of empirical research, the topic is not free of controversies, and there is no universal agreement about some aspects of the validity of the construct and its effects.

THEORETICAL AND MEASUREMENT ISSUES

Because SE involves an evaluation of how worthy one is as a person, by definition, it seems that people with high SE should have positive self-regard and those with low SE should have negative self-regard. However, though it is true that people with high SE have positive, well-defined views of the self, people with low SE do not necessarily hold negative views of themselves. Instead, low-SE individuals tend to evaluate themselves neutrally, and their self-views tend to vary considerably from situation to situation.

This neutrality and variability in evaluations of the self raises several important theoretical, methodological, and practical questions that have not been clearly answered in the SE literature. For example, it is not completely clear why people with low SE have variable views of themselves; several incompatible theoretical explanations may account for this phenomenon. On one hand, it is possible that people with low SE lack a clear notion of who they are, and therefore they describe themselves in noncommittal, middle-of-the-road terms. Indeed, people with low SE exhibit less stability of self-evaluations and tend to

give inconsistent responses to questions asking them to describe themselves (compared with those with high SE). Thus, according to the *self-concept clarity* explanation, low-SE individuals are confused and ambivalent about who they are and therefore tend to be variable and noncommittal in their self-views.

On the other hand, it is also possible that people with low SE are actually more accurate in their self-evaluations than high-SE individuals. In this sense, the neutrality and inconsistency of self-evaluations associated with low SE actually represent a more accurate perception of the self that truly varies across situations and circumstances. Because we sometimes act as worthy and capable individuals and sometimes do not, people with low SE may be correct in their self-descriptions, and those with high SE may be positively biased and even detached from reality. Indeed, there is some evidence to suggest that people with high SE consistently exaggerate their positive views of the self. For example, several studies have shown that people with high SE overevaluate how much other people like them, and some researchers have even claimed that the interpersonal success of high-SE individuals exists only in their own minds. Indeed, high SE has often been equated with narcissism.

These two theoretical explanations of SE have opposite practical implications. If, in fact, people with low SE have variable and neutral self-views because they lack a clear notion of who they are, then the goal of practitioners should be to enhance SE. However, if those with low SE are actually more accurate and those with high SE are self-deceivers who tend to be narcissistic, then enhancing SE may be counterproductive. These two theoretical explanations also raise some methodological difficulties: If SE represents either a lack of self-concept clarity (on the low end) or narcissism and self-deception (on the high end), then how does SE differ from these constructs, and what is its distinctive contribution as a concept? Is it a unitary concept at all? The literature on SE is not clear on this point; therefore, theories that account for SE as a self-reported descriptor have some difficulty explaining the concept and its uniqueness.

Perhaps a better approach is to look at the behavioral patterns of people with high and low SE and explain the psychological processes that underlie these behavioral patterns. The SE literature clearly shows that people with high SE are much less plastic in their behavior than people with low SE. For example, people with low SE are more reactive to external social cues and therefore more susceptible to negative feedback and more accepting of it than high-SE individuals. Low-SE individuals are also more susceptible to attempts to influence, more sensitive to anxiety-causing stimuli, and prone to be influenced by self-focus and expectancy manipulations. This tendency to be "behaviorally plastic" may be especially important in performance situations—performance has been shown to be influenced by expectancies and self rather than task-focused manipulations.

Two underlying psychological motives may explain the behavioral plasticity pattern of low-SE individuals. On one hand, individuals want to feel good about themselves and feel that they are worthy, capable, and likable; therefore, one motive that drives people is self-enhancement. On the other hand, people also desire to be self-consistent and protect their self-conceptions from change. In other words, people are driven by the desire to predict and control important life experiences and to tell themselves a consistent story about who they are. For those with positive SE, self-consistency and self-enhancement operate in concert, but for people with negative self-views, these two drives operate in opposite directions. Low-SE people want to maintain their negative self-view in order to maintain self-consistency, but at the same time, they want to think better of themselves. Because they have contradictory motives, they look outside for cues to who they are and rely on social information to determine their future actions. For example, when people with high SE encounter negative information about themselves in the form of failure or negative feedback, they tend to reject it and do not let the information affect their expectancies or behaviors. In contrast, those with low SE often accept the information and let it influence their behaviors.

Methodologically, SE presents other difficulties. A recent analysis of the relationship between SE, neuroticism, locus of control, and generalized self-efficacy found very strong correlations among all of these constructs, which are essentially representing the same underlying construct. The discriminant validity of SE as a unique construct is therefore open to debate.

CONTRIBUTIONS

Despite these issues, research on SE has made some significant contributions. First, measures of SE are highly correlated with each other and generally show high reliabilities. In particular, the Rosenberg

Self-Esteem Scale, named for Morris Rosenberg, seems to be content- and face-valid, and it is reliable and unitary and therefore can be used with confidence.

Second, meta-analytic research has shown some of the relationships between SE and important variables of interest in industrial and organizational psychology to be quite significant. For example, SE has been shown to be an important predictor of job satisfaction ($r = .26$). People with high SE actually attain more challenging jobs, and even in jobs that are not particularly complex, they see more challenges and therefore are more excited about their jobs than people with low SE. People with high SE also have higher subjective well-being ($r = .47$) and cope better with stressful situations. Self-esteem is significantly correlated with job performance ($r = .26$), and the relationship is actually stronger than the usual relationship between conscientiousness and performance, which is considered the strongest personality predictor of job performance. Another major variable of interest in the organizational literature is leadership—indeed, several studies have shown that SE is a good predictor of leadership behavior and efficacy. In addition, a recent large-scale study showed that people with high SE exhibit more "voice behavior" in organizations and therefore are less susceptible to groupthink. Overall, despite the theoretical and methodological controversies, SE has been shown to be a valuable variable of interest in industrial and organizational psychology.

—*Amir Erez*

See also Core Self-Evaluations

FURTHER READING

Baumeister, R. F., Campbell, J. D., Kruger, J. I., & Vohs, K. D. (2003). Does self-esteem cause better performance, interpersonal success, happiness, or healthier lifestyle? *Psychological Science in the Public Interest, 4,* 1–44.

Brockner, J. (1988). *Self-esteem at work: Research, theory, and practice.* Lexington, MA: Lexington Books.

Campbell, J. D., & Lavallee, L. F. (1993). Who am I? The role of self-concept confusion in understanding the behavior of people with low self-esteem. In R. F. Baumeister (Ed.), *Self-esteem: The puzzle of low self-regard* (pp. 3–20). New York: Plenum Press.

Judge, T. A., & Bono, J. E. (2001). Relationship of core self-evaluations traits—self-esteem, generalized self-efficacy, locus of control, and emotional stability—with job satisfaction and job performance: A meta-analysis. *Journal of Applied Psychology, 86,* 80–92.

Judge, T. A., Erez, A., Bono, J. E., & Thoresen, C. J. (2002). Are measures of self-esteem, neuroticism, locus of control, and generalized self-efficacy indicators of a common core construct? *Journal of Personality and Social Psychology, 83*, 693–710.

La Ronde, C., & Swann, W. B. (1993). Caught in the crossfire: Positivity and self-verification strivings among people with low self-esteem. In R. F. Baumeister (Ed.), *Self-esteem: The puzzle of low self-regard* (pp. 147–166). New York: Plenum Press.

SELF-FULFILLING PROPHECY: PYGMALION EFFECT

The *Pygmalion effect* is a special case of the self-fulfilling prophecy in which raising a manager's expectations for worker performance in fact boosts performance. The Pygmalion effect first appeared in educational psychology when psychologists experimentally raised elementary schoolteachers' expectations for a randomly selected subsample of pupils, producing significantly greater achievement gains among those pupils than among control pupils. Subsequent research has replicated this phenomenon among adult supervisors and subordinates in military, business, industrial, and service organizations and among all four cross-gender combinations—that is, both men and women lead male and female subordinates to greater success when they expect more of them. Interpersonal expectancy is inherent in most leader–follower interactions, and the Pygmalion effect undoubtedly characterizes many manager–worker relationships.

Several theories have been proposed to explain why raising leader expectations boosts subordinate performance. Common to all explanations is a causal chain that begins with the impact of the leader's expectations on and his or her *own* behavior toward subordinates, which, in turn, arouses some motivational response on the part of the subordinates and culminates in subordinate performance that accords with the leader's expectations. Self-efficacy has emerged as the key motivational mediator in this process. Self-efficacy is an individual's belief in his or her ability to execute the behaviors needed to perform successfully. Ample research shows that self-efficacy is a major determinant of performance. When individuals believe they have what it takes to succeed, they

try harder. Conversely, those who doubt they can succeed refrain from exerting the effort to apply the ability they do have and end up accomplishing less than is possible.

The *Pygmalion-at-work model* posits that having high expectations moves the leader to treat followers in a manner that augments their self-efficacy, which, in turn, motivates subordinates to expend greater effort, culminating in enhanced performance. Thus, the Pygmalion effect is a motivational phenomenon initiated by the high performance expectations held by a leader who believes in his or her followers' capacity for success. In a largely unconscious interpersonal process, leaders with high expectations lead their followers to success by enhancing their self-efficacy.

The self-fulfilling prophecy is a double-edged sword: As high expectations boost performance, low expectations can depress performance in a negative process dubbed the *Golem effect*. The word *golem* means "oaf" or "dumbbell" in Hebrew and Yiddish slang. Managers who expect dumbbells get dumbbells. Experiments have shown that Golem effects can be mitigated by informing supervisors that subordinates with relatively low qualifications have high potential to succeed.

Another variant of the self-fulfilling prophecy is the *Galatea effect*. Named for the statue sculpted by the mythical Pygmalion, this is an intrapersonal expectancy effect involving only the worker. Self-starters fulfill their own prophecies of success; believing in their own capacity to excel, they mobilize their internal motivational resources to sustain the effort needed for success even without any external source (e.g., a supervisor) of high expectations. However, Galatea effects can also be Golem-like. Individuals who harbor a negative self-image expect to fail; they refrain from using their skills and abilities, thereby needlessly but unintentionally fulfilling their own gloomy prophecy.

Finally, research shows group-level expectancy effects in which a manager's high expectations for a whole group, distinct from expectations toward particular individuals, culminate in the group exceeding the performance of control groups. This is an especially important phenomenon in team sports as well as in the teamwork that has emerged as a defining feature of modern organizations.

A fascinating but elusive aspect of interpersonal self-fulfilling prophecies involves the communication of expectations. Some of this communication is verbal and conscious, but much of it is not. Managers exhibit many nonverbal behaviors by which they convey their expectations, whether high or low, to subordinates. When managers expect more, they unwittingly nod their heads affirmatively more often, draw nearer physically, maintain eye contact, speak quickly, and show greater patience toward those they are supervising. These nonverbal behaviors serve to "warm" the interpersonal relationship, create a climate of support, and foster success. Other ways in which leaders favor those whom they expect more from include providing them with more input, more feedback, and more opportunities to show what they can do, whereas those whom managers expect less of are left neglected "on the bench."

Fortunately, the high expectations that motivate enhanced performance also augment subordinate satisfaction. In every successful Pygmalion experiment in which satisfaction was measured, it was significantly increased. Satisfaction is not a surprising by-product. High expectations and the resulting superior performance are satisfying because, by and large, employees want to succeed, and they are more satisfied when they do. Thus, all the news is good news as far as the Pygmalion effect is concerned.

Meta-analyses have confirmed that the magnitude of the Pygmalion effect in management is medium to large. The Pygmalion effect research is unique in organizational psychology because it is entirely based on field experimentation, lending it extraordinary internal and external validity. Experimental design confirms the flow of causality from leader expectations to follower performance, and the field settings confirm its generalizability. What remains to be shown is the practical validity of the Pygmalion effect. Although replications have produced the effect in organizations, attempts to get managers to apply it through managerial training have been less successful. Managers' prior acquaintance with subordinates appears to be a barrier to widespread application. Virtually all of the successful replications occurred among newcomers whose managers had not known them previously. Familiarity apparently crystallizes expectations because managers do not expect their subordinates to change much. Therefore, the most effective applications may be made among managers and new subordinates.

Organizational innovations and other deviations from routine that unfreeze standard operating procedures are particularly conducive to Pygmalion effects.

Organizational development programs or profound changes in organizational structure or function resulting from, for example, mergers and acquisitions or personnel transitions open a window of opportunity. Savvy managers piggyback on these unsettling events and raise expectations to promote successful change and productive outcomes. In one classic industrial example, the introduction of simple job rotation and job enrichment produced significant improvements in productivity when accompanied by information that raised expectations from the new work procedures, but neither innovation improved productivity when expectations were not raised.

The practical upshot is clear: Change—any change—presents managers with an opportunity to create productive Pygmalion effects. It is incumbent on those who want to lead individuals, teams, and organizations to success to convey high expectations whenever the opportunity presents itself. Conversely, cynical expressions of doubt about reorganizations, innovations, or developmental interventions condemn them to failure. Thus, the practical agenda for managers is twofold: They must counteract any manifestations of contrary expectations, and they must implant high expectations.

The essence of the Pygmalion effect is that managers get the workers they expect. Expect more and you will get more. However, the converse is true, too: Expect less and you will get less. All managers should strive to play a Pygmalion role by cultivating high expectations of their subordinates' potential and by communicating those expectations to foster high self-expectations among subordinates regarding their own potential for success. High expectations are too important to be left to chance or whim; they should be built into all manager–worker relationships and should be part of all managerial training and development programs.

—*Dov Eden*

See also Leadership and Supervision; Training

FURTHER READING

Eden, D. (1992). Leadership and expectations: Pygmalion effects and other self-fulfilling prophecies in organizations. *Leadership Quarterly, 3,* 271–305.

Eden, D. (2003). Self-fulfilling prophecies in organizations. In J. Greenberg (Ed.), *Organizational behavior: The state of the science* (2nd ed., pp. 91–122). Mahwah, NJ: Lawrence Erlbaum.

Eden, D., Geller, D., Gewirtz, A., Gordon-Terner, R., Inbar, I., Liberman, M., Pass, Y., Salomon-Segev, I., & Shalit, M. (2000). Implanting Pygmalion leadership style through workshop training: Seven field experiments. *Leadership Quarterly, 11,* 171–210.

McNatt, D. B. (2000). Ancient Pygmalion joins contemporary management: A meta-analysis of the result. *Journal of Applied Psychology, 85,* 314–322.

Merton, R. K. (1948). The self-fulfilling prophecy. *Antioch Review, 8,* 193–210.

SELF-REGULATION THEORY

The term *self-regulation* refers to a complex and dynamic set of processes involved in setting and pursuing goals. It is commonly used to refer to a broad set of theories that seek to describe, explain, and predict these goal-directed processes. Although many theories of self-regulation exist, each proposing some unique characteristics, researchers generally agree on several fundamental features of self-regulation.

GOALS AND GOAL SETTING

The most fundamental aspect of self-regulation theory is the idea that much of human behavior is directed toward accomplishing goals. Indeed, it is the pursuit of goals that forms the focus of much of self-regulation theory. The term *goal* takes on a fairly broad meaning in this context, referring to desired future states that individuals wish to attain.

Goals can differ from one another in many ways. For example, they may be assigned by others (e.g., by one's supervisor), they may be self-set by the individual, or they may be determined by some combination of the two (e.g., participatively set). Goals can vary in both difficulty and specificity, as well as content. They can be near-term (proximal) goals or long-term (distal) goals. Goals can even vary in the extent to which one is consciously aware that the goal is guiding behavior. All of these characteristics have important influences on cognition, affect, and behavior.

One of the most consistent findings (although it is not without exception) is that difficult, specific goals often result in high levels of performance. Although this finding has great practical benefit by itself, self-regulation theorists seek to understand precisely how, when, and why such goal-setting effects are obtained. This increased understanding of goal-related processes

provides valuable information about how motivational interventions can best be implemented.

FEEDBACK AND SELF-MONITORING

Feedback plays a critical role in self-regulatory processes. In this context, feedback refers to information concerning an individual's progress toward attaining a goal. By comparing feedback to goals, an individual can determine the level of success he or she is having in pursuing the goal. If the feedback indicates that he or she is not making sufficient progress, then changes are often undertaken, such as investing more effort, trying different approaches to meet the goal, or even abandoning the goal altogether.

Feedback need not come from outside sources (e.g., one's supervisor)—indeed, such external feedback is often unavailable. Thus, individuals often rely on *self-monitoring* to evaluate their progress toward achieving their goals. Unfortunately, individuals are notoriously flawed in making such self-evaluations, typically perceiving their progress to be better than it really is. As a result, without sufficiently frequent and specific external feedback, individuals often make poor decisions in the pursuit of their goals, such as investing less time and effort than is truly necessary for success and persisting with ineffective strategies.

GOAL HIERARCHIES

Most theories of self-regulation propose that goals are arranged hierarchically in a series of means–ends relationships. For example, a car salesperson may have a goal to obtain a pay raise. To accomplish this goal, the individual must get a positive performance evaluation from his or her supervisor during the annual performance appraisal. To get a positive evaluation, he or she must sell at least eight new cars per month, and so on.

The importance of goals higher up in the hierarchy can determine how committed individuals are to particular goals lower in the hierarchy. For example, if a student is seeking an A grade in a psychology course because he or she sees it as a necessary step toward fulfilling a lifelong dream of getting into graduate school, his or her commitment to obtaining the grade is likely to be very high.

Goal hierarchies are highly complex. Rather than having a strict one-to-one relationship between higher-level and lower-level goals, a higher-level goal, or end, can often be obtained by achieving several alternative, lower-level goals, or means (i.e., equifinality—"all roads lead to Rome"). Likewise, a given lower-level goal or means can often serve many higher-level goals or ends (i.e., multifinality—"kill two birds with one stone"). Goal hierarchies are also highly individualized. Each individual's hierarchy may be distinct and change over time. Some theorists postulate that an important determinant of individual personality is the goals that exist (or the relative importance of such goals) near the top of their hierarchy.

APPROACH VERSUS AVOIDANCE GOALS

Up to this point, goals have been described as future states that individuals wish to attain. Such goals are often referred to as *approach goals* because individuals seek to move toward these states. However, *avoidance goals* are also powerful influences on behavior, representing undesired future states that individuals wish to avoid. For a variety of reasons, the self-regulatory processes resulting from approach and avoidance goals differ in subtle but very important ways.

One important way in which approach and avoidance goals differ is in the affect (i.e., emotions) that arises from successful and unsuccessful pursuit. In short, success at an approach goal often leads to excitement or elation, whereas success at an avoidance goal often leads to relief or relaxation. Failure at an approach goal often leads to sadness or depression, whereas failure at an avoidance goal often leads to anxiety or nervousness. Because emotions can have important influences on the way individuals perceive and react to the world around them, the distinction between approach and avoidance self-regulation is of great practical importance.

SUMMARY

Despite the vast insights and many practical applications that have emerged from the research on self-regulation, researchers are only just beginning to understand all of the implications of this complex, dynamic, and individualized process. Nonetheless, it appears clear that the implications are many, and increased understanding in this area will likely yield further improvements in effectiveness in the workplace and beyond.

—*Aaron M. Schmidt*

See also Feedback; Goal-Setting Theory; Path–Goal Theory

FURTHER READING

Carver, C. S., & Scheier, M. F. (2000). On the structure of behavioral self-regulation. In M. Boekaerts, P. R. Pintrich, & M. Zeidner (Eds.), *Handbook of self-regulation* (pp. 41–84). San Diego: Academic Press.

Donovan, J. J. (2001). Work motivation. In N. Anderson, D. S. Ones, H. K. Sinangil, & C. Viswesvaran (Eds.), *Handbook of industrial, work, and organizational psychology* (Vol. 2, pp. 53–76). Thousand Oaks, CA: Sage.

Locke, E. A., & Latham, G. P. (2002). Building a practically useful theory of goal setting and task motivation: A 35-year odyssey. *American Psychologist, 57,* 705–717.

Shah, J. Y. (2005). The automatic pursuit and management of goals. *Current Directions in Psychological Science, 14,* 10–13.

Vancouver, J. B. (2000). Self-regulation in industrial/ organizational psychology: A tale of two paradigms. In M. Boekaerts, P. R. Pintrich, & M. Zeidner (Eds.), *Handbook of self-regulation* (pp. 303–341). San Diego: Academic Press.

SEXUAL DISCRIMINATION

Sexual discrimination occurs when individuals are treated differently or receive different outcomes solely because they are men or women. Title VII of the Civil Rights Act of 1964 made sexual discrimination illegal in the American workplace. Specifically, Title VII prohibits discrimination against any employee or applicant for employment because of his or her sex with regard to hiring, termination, promotion, compensation, job training, or any other condition or privilege of employment. Title VII prohibitions also include sexual harassment and pregnancy discrimination. Although Title VII protects both sexes, women are systematically more likely than men to be victims of sexual discrimination.

Legally, sexual discrimination is identified as manifesting itself in one of two forms: disparate treatment and disparate impact. *Disparate treatment* refers to the differential treatment of an individual intentionally and specifically because that individual is a man or a woman. This includes discrimination predicated on assumptions about the abilities, traits, or performance of individuals on the basis of sex. Examples of disparate treatment are asking men and women different questions during a job interview, offering a lower starting salary because the recruit is a woman, or exhibiting reluctance to hire a woman for a job that requires long hours and travel.

Disparate impact constitutes a broader definition of gender discrimination and is more complex. Disparate impact results when a particular group is systematically and adversely affected by a company's policy. Although the policy may not have been created with the intent of discrimination, it may nonetheless disproportionately exclude individuals on the basis of sex for reasons that are not job related. For example, requiring applicants to take a selection test that involves lifting 100 pounds, even though 30 pounds is the maximum a person would need to lift on the job, might unnecessarily screen out qualified female applicants.

EVIDENCE OF SEXUAL DISCRIMINATION

Women have made substantial gains in the last several decades in the work domain: They now compose nearly half the U.S. labor market and had a labor force participation rate of 46.5% in 2003. In addition, women are closing the education gap, earning more bachelor's and master's degrees than men and increasing their representation in business, law, and medical schools. Given the strides that women have made, coupled with the illegality of sexual discrimination, is sexual discrimination really a problem in the modern workplace? If so, what is its prevalence?

According to many sources of data, it is clear that sexual discrimination remains a concern in the work domain. One piece of direct evidence is the sheer number of sexual discrimination charges filed with the Equal Employment Opportunity Commission (EEOC), a key federal agency responsible for the enforcement of Title VII. In 2004, the EEOC received 24,249 charges of sex-based discrimination, an increase of 12% over the last decade. Moreover, these data are unlikely to capture the whole picture. Many women do not challenge the discriminatory practices they encounter in the workplace for fear of losing their jobs, and others are deterred by the personal and financial costs associated with submitting a claim.

By examining the general topography of the U.S. workforce and the way women fit into it, a clearer picture of gender inequity emerges. For example, although women make up nearly half of the U.S. workforce, they continue to be concentrated in occupations that are traditionally considered female—often support roles that are low in status and pay. In 2003, the top five occupations held by women were administrative assistant (96.3% female), registered nurse (90.2%), nursing, psychiatric, and home health aide (89%), elementary and middle school teacher (80.6%), and cashier (75.5%). Meanwhile, women remain decidedly underrepresented in roles that are traditionally considered male—roles that are often highest in authority, responsibility, and prestige in organizations.

This seemingly impenetrable barrier to women's entrance into the highest echelons of organizations is often referred to as the *glass ceiling*. Indeed, the higher up in the organizational hierarchy one looks, the more scarce women become. For example, in 2003, despite occupying 50.5% of the managerial and specialty positions overall, in Fortune 500 companies, women made up only 15.7% of corporate officers and 13.6% of board members, and only eight women were CEOs. Not surprisingly in light of these figures, only 5.2% of the Fortune 500 top earners were women.

Gender inequities are also evident in the way women are compensated; women continue to be paid less than men. In 2003, for every dollar earned by a man, a woman earned 75.5 cents on average. Differences in the jobs and occupations held by men contribute somewhat to this discrepancy; however, even after controlling for factors such as education, job training, work experience, and occupation, more than half of the gap in earnings remains unexplained. Consider this: According to the U.S. Department of Labor, women in 1997 earned less than men in 99% of all occupations.

Despite the significant advances that women have made over the past few decades, sexual discrimination continues to be a problem in organizational life. Women are consistently employed in lower-status jobs and earn less than men. This begs the question, why? In considering the causes of sexual discrimination in the workplace, gender stereotypes frequently are designated as the culprit.

ANTECEDENTS OF SEXUAL DISCRIMINATION
Gender Stereotypes

The belief that women and men are different is widely shared in our culture; in fact, research suggests that men and women are often viewed as polar opposites. Men are thought to be rational, independent, decisive, and assertive, whereas women are described as illogical, dependent, indecisive, and passive. Men and women are also described differently with respect to the qualities of warmth and expressiveness, with women rated more favorably. Yet the traits associated with men and women are not only different but valued differently. Although each sex is credited with desirable traits, it is generally argued that male traits are more highly valued in Western culture than those associated with women. That is, the achievement-oriented traits typically ascribed to men have been shown to be more highly valued than the nurturing and affiliation-oriented traits typically ascribed to women; this is particularly true with respect to the work domain.

How do these stereotypes translate into discrimination in the workplace? The answer to this question lies not only in the stereotypes about women but also in conceptions of what is required to effectively handle jobs that are considered to be male. Taken together, these elements determine performance expectations—expectations that ultimately become the precursor to sexual discrimination.

Expectations about how successful or unsuccessful an individual will be when working at a particular job are determined by the fit between the perceived attributes of the individual and the perceived attributes required for success at that particular job. If the fit is good, then success will be expected; if the fit is poor, then failure will be expected. These fit-derived performance expectations, whether positive or negative, play a key role in evaluation processes because individuals have a tendency to perpetuate and confirm them. Once an expectation has been formed, it becomes a lens through which information is filtered, including what is attended to, how it is interpreted, and whether it is remembered and recalled when making critical decisions.

Applying this reasoning to women in organizations, the lack of fit between the stereotype-based perceptions of women's attributes and the perceptions of many job requirements leads hiring managers to conclude that women are ill-equipped to handle certain types of work—namely, work that is considered to be male sex-typed—and the expectation that women are unlikely to succeed in traditionally male roles. These performance expectations are powerful in their impact: They create a tenacious predisposition to view women in a way that that is consistent with the expectation, thereby detrimentally affecting the way they are regarded and the way their work is evaluated. The behavioral consequence is sexual discrimination.

From Expectations to Discrimination

Research has demonstrated that the expectation of failure for women often permeates the entire process of women's careers. In personnel selection, there is a tendency for men to be preferred over women of similar qualifications when the job is one traditionally held by men. For example, researchers have found that for managerial positions, the same résumé is rated more favorably when it is believed to belong to a man rather than a woman. Women are also placed in positions that seem more appropriate for their attributes—ones in which the fit seems good. Thus, women tend to be placed in staff rather than line jobs, where they can provide support and assistance, something they are thought to be well-equipped to do.

When women do attain jobs that are considered to be male sex-typed, the effects of negative expectations deriving from perceptions of lack of fit persist. Men and women producing identical work are often evaluated differently, with women's work regarded as inferior. Even when a woman's successful performance is indisputable, evaluators may attribute it to some factor other than the woman herself, be it another person (if she has worked in a group), the ease of the task, or some transient factor such as luck. If it is impossible to dismiss her role in her success and she is acknowledged as competent in a male sex-typed role, then she seems to be disliked. There are many "shoulds" attached to gender stereotypes that, when violated, have negative consequences. Thus, assertive behavior that is seen as tough and decisive when acted out by a man may be seen as "bitchy" when done by a woman.

These findings have obvious implications not only for entry-level access to organizations but also for advancement opportunities such as training programs, promotions, and career trajectories in organizations. These individual processes, at an aggregate level, account for macro-level discrimination: the discrepancies in the types of roles women occupy, the roles they don't, and the compensation they receive for their work.

SUMMARY

Despite being made illegal by the Civil Rights Act of 1964, discrimination on the basis of sex continues to be a problem in today's work organizations. At the root of this problem are gender stereotypes and the expectations they produce, which ultimately result in the differential treatment of men and women on the basis of their sex.

—*Michelle C. Haynes and Madeline E. Heilman*

See also Adverse Impact/Disparate Treatment/Discrimination at Work; Civil Rights Act of 1964, Civil Rights Act of 1991; Glass Ceiling; Sexual Harassment at work; Stereotyping

FURTHER READING

Dipboye, R. A., & Colella, A. (Eds.). (2005). *Discrimination at work: The psychological and organizational bases.* Mahwah, NJ: Lawrence Erlbaum.

Heilman, M. E. (1995). Sex stereotypes and their effects in the workplace: What we know and what we don't know. *Journal of Social Behavior and Personality, 10*(6), 3–26.

Heilman, M. E. (2001). Description and prescription: How gender stereotypes prevent women's ascent up the organizational ladder. *Journal of Social Issues, 57*(4), 657–674.

SEXUAL HARASSMENT AT WORK

Psychologists generally describe sexual harassment at work as offensive, degrading, or harmful verbal or nonverbal behaviors that are of a sexual or gender-targeted nature. A variety of behaviors can be viewed as constituting sexual harassment. Examples include repeated requests for a romantic date despite rejection, as well as violent behaviors such as attempted or completed rape. Although women are more commonly victims of sexual harassment, men may be harassed as well. In the case of both female and male victims, men tend to be the most common perpetrators.

Sexual harassment is often viewed as a significant source of stress for victims. Indeed, victims may experience psychological, physical, and behavioral problems, many of which can be problematic for organizations. Sexual harassment has received a considerable amount of attention worldwide in the media, among lawmakers, and among organizational researchers. Many organizations have instituted policies and practices intended to prevent such harassment and to provide support for its victims.

To better understand workplace sexual harassment, this entry provides an overview of (a) forms of sexual harassment and how they are commonly measured by organizational researchers, (b) sexual harassment and the law, (c) causes of sexual harassment, (d) consequences of sexual harassment, and (e) how sexual harassment compares with other types of aggression in the workplace.

FORMS OF SEXUAL HARASSMENT AND THEIR MEASUREMENT

Louise F. Fitzgerald and her colleagues have played a pivotal role in advancing our knowledge of the manifestations of sexual harassment and how they can be measured. These researchers describe three forms of sexual harassment: *gender harassment, unwanted sexual attention,* and *sexual coercion.*

Gender Harassment

Gender harassment refers to verbal and nonverbal behaviors that are not aimed at sexual cooperation but convey insulting, hostile, and degrading attitudes toward a person's gender. In other words, this form of sexual harassment constitutes putting someone down on the basis of their gender. Examples of such behaviors include making crude sexual remarks, displaying or distributing sexually offensive material, and making sexist comments. Compared with the two other forms of sexual harassment described here, gender harassment is likely the most widespread.

Unwanted Sexual Attention

Unwanted sexual attention denotes verbal and nonverbal behavior that is offensive, unwanted, and unreciprocated. Unwanted sexual attention is distinguishable from gender harassment in that it indicates an inappropriate and unwelcome come-on as opposed to a putdown. Behaviors that may constitute unwanted sexual attention include attempts to discuss sex, leering, and repeated requests for drinks or dinner despite rejection, as well as physical behaviors such as touching someone in a way that makes him or her feel uncomfortable or attempting to stroke or fondle another person. Attempted or completed rape can be viewed as an extreme form of unwanted sexual attention.

Sexual Coercion

Sexual coercion is the extortion of sexual cooperation in return for job-related considerations such as job security, promotions, and compensation (e.g., salary, bonuses). Behaviors exemplifying this form of sexual harassment include making subtle bribes, making subtle threats, and making a person afraid of poor job-related treatment if he or she does not agree to provide a sexual favor.

Although gender harassment, unwanted sexual attention, and sexual coercion have been proposed as conceptually distinct forms of sexual harassment, they tend to be highly correlated because they often co-occur in the same organizational contexts. For example, victims of sexual coercion virtually always report having experienced unwanted sexual attention and gender harassment in the same context.

Measuring Sexual Harassment

Fitzgerald and her colleagues developed a questionnaire, the Sexual Experiences Questionnaire (SEQ), to measure how frequently employees believe they have been the target or victim of each of the three forms of sexual harassment. In the questionnaire, individuals are presented with a series of statements (items) describing behaviors that denote each of the three forms of sexual harassment and are asked to rate the frequency with which they have been the target of such behaviors over a given time period. Though some scholars have encouraged further refinement of the SEQ, it remains the most widely known and studied measure of sexual harassment.

SEXUAL HARASSMENT AND THE LAW

A number of countries have laws in place intended to curb the occurrence of sexual harassment. For example, the United States, Canada, Australia, Denmark, Ireland, New Zealand, Sweden, and the United Kingdom all have equal opportunity laws that address sexual harassment. For example, the United States considers sexual harassment to be a form of sex discrimination that violates Title VII of the Civil Rights Act of 1964. According to the U.S. Equal Employment Opportunity Commission (EEOC), unwelcome sexual advances, requests for sexual favors, and other verbal or physical conduct of a sexual nature constitute sexual harassment when submission to or rejection of this conduct explicitly or implicitly affects an individual's employment, unreasonably interferes with an individual's work performance, or creates an intimidating, hostile, or offensive work environment. By this legal definition, all three forms of sexual harassment may be recognized by

the EEOC as unlawful sexual harassment. However, it should be noted that the SEQ does not necessarily capture behaviors that courts recognize as unlawful. One may feel sexually harassed, psychologically speaking, without having been the target of unlawful behavior.

According to the EEOC, sexual harassment can occur in a variety of circumstances, including but not limited to the following:

- The victim as well as the harasser may be a woman or a man; the victim need not be of the opposite sex.
- The harasser may be the victim's supervisor, an agent of the employer, a supervisor in another area, a coworker, or a nonemployee.
- The victim does not have to be the person harassed but could be anyone affected by the offensive conduct.
- Unlawful sexual harassment may occur without economic injury to or discharge of the victim.
- The harasser's conduct must be unwelcome.

The EEOC notes that it is helpful for the victim to inform the offender that the conduct is unwelcome and must stop. The victim should use any employer complaint mechanism or grievance system available.

In investigating allegations of sexual harassment, the EEOC considers the circumstances, such as the nature of the sexual advances, and the context in which the alleged incidents occurred. A determination is made from the facts on a case-by-case basis. However, it is often difficult to prove that sexual harassment has taken place, especially if no objective evidence is provided. Moreover, many victims feel that making a formal complaint is worse than saying nothing at all. Not surprisingly, many victims choose not to make formal accusations. Considering the challenges associated with the legal pursuit of sexual harassers, as well as the interests of potential victims and their employing organization (the organization can suffer financially from a tarnished reputation, poor employee morale, and financial damages), it is clearly desirable to prevent the occurrence of sexual harassment in the first place. Knowing the likely causes of sexual harassment provides a roadmap for such prevention.

CAUSES OF SEXUAL HARASSMENT

The small body of empirical research conducted on potential predictors of workplace sexual harassment focuses largely on aspects of the organizational or work context and on the personal characteristics of offenders.

Work Context

Many organizations have implemented policies or practices intended to curb the occurrence of sexual harassment. Some research suggests that these policies may be beneficial. For example, both female and male employees are more likely to experience sexual harassment when they perceive their organization as being more tolerant of sexual harassment. Clearly communicating and applying policies against sexual offenders gives employees the impression that sexual harassment is not tolerated. In addition, male employees are less likely to sexually harass women when they believe that such behavior will be punished by the organization.

Another contextual factor that has been studied is the extent to which the workplace is dominated by one gender. For example, some research shows that female employees are more likely to report sexual harassment in work contexts that they view as male dominated.

Offender Characteristics

Although research on offender characteristics is limited and has focused exclusively on male offenders, it suggests that men's past sexual experiences and current beliefs and attitudes toward the sexual harassment of women are related to their self-acknowledged propensity to sexually harass women. Specifically, men are more likely to sexually harass women when they have had more sexual experience, have been the victims of childhood sexual abuse, are more easily accepting of interpersonal violence against women, and hold beliefs regarding the sexual harassment of women that tend to blame the victim.

CONSEQUENCES OF SEXUAL HARASSMENT

Psychologists conceptualize sexual harassment as a significant source of stress for targets. Thus, much of the research investigating the consequences of sexual harassment has tested whether the experience of sexual harassment relates to psychological, physical, and behavioral manifestations of stress, many of which can be problematic for the effective functioning of organizations. The primary limitation of most of this research, however, is that sexual harassment and its consequences are measured at the same point in time, thereby precluding any cause-and-effect conclusions from being drawn.

Psychological Consequences

Studies show that the more people report having experienced sexual harassment, the more they are likely to report reduced job satisfaction (a commonly measured work attitude), reduced satisfaction with life in general, and increased psychological distress (e.g., anxiety, depression, fear, and hopelessness about the future). It is also possible that victims psychologically avoid feelings of stress by denying (to themselves and to others) that the harassment ever took place.

Physical Consequences

Research suggests that the more people report having been sexually harassed at work, the more they are likely to complain of physical ailments such as severe headaches, shortness of breath, and exhaustion with no apparent cause. Such ailments are likely a response to the stress experienced as a result of sexual harassment.

Behavioral Consequences

Employees who experience sexual harassment are more likely to neglect their job tasks, be absent from work, and feel a desire to quit their job. These types of behaviors and behavioral intentions exemplify how some targets of sexual harassment choose to avoid the context in which the stressful event occurred, namely, their job or organization. Other responses to sexual harassment can be exhibited by victims, including confronting the offender directly (relatively rare), social coping (i.e., getting support from colleagues, friends, or family members), and advocacy seeking (i.e., bringing the alleged harassment to the attention of organizational authorities). Unfortunately, few victims seek such advocacy out of fear of individual or organizational retaliation, which may explain why organizational policies intended to reduce sexual harassment are not always effective.

SEXUAL HARASSMENT AND OTHER TYPES OF AGGRESSION AT WORK

Much of the research on workplace sexual harassment has progressed independently of research on other types of aggressive behavior at work, such as general incivility or nonsexual bullying. Recently, some scholars have argued that sexual harassment is only one of many types of workplace aggression. Despite general conceptual similarities, little is known about how sexual and nonsexual types of workplace aggression differ in terms of their causes or consequences.

A recent quantitative review of studies investigating nonviolent forms of workplace aggression revealed that nonsexual aggression generally shares a stronger relationship with reduced overall job satisfaction among female victims than does sexual aggression. This difference may be explained by reports that nonsexual aggression happens more frequently than sexual aggression, and therefore victims view it as more of an organizational problem than sexual aggression; that organizations rarely have policies in place to curb nonsexual aggression, making the victims of aggression more likely to be dissatisfied at work; and that targets generally view nonsexual aggression as a more severe form of aggression by targets than sexual aggression. Clearly, more research is needed to elucidate the unique causes and consequences of sexual versus nonsexual workplace aggression.

—*Laurent M. Lapierre*

FURTHER READING

Dekker, I., & Barling, J. (1998). Personal and organizational predictors of workplace sexual harassment of women by men. *Journal of Occupational Health Psychology, 3,* 7–18.

Fitzgerald, L. F., Drasgow, F., Hulin, C. L., Gelfand, M. J., & Magley, V. J. (1997). Antecedents and consequences of sexual harassment in organizations: A test of an integrated model. *Journal of Applied Psychology, 82,* 578–589.

Fitzgerald, L. F., Gelfand, M. J., & Drasgow, F. (1995). Measuring sexual harassment: Theoretical and psychometric advances. *Basic and Applied Social Psychology, 17,* 425–445.

Lapierre, L. M., Spector, P. E., & Leck, J. D. (2005). Sexual versus non-sexual workplace aggression and victims' overall job satisfaction: A meta-analysis. *Journal of Occupational Health Psychology, 10,* 155–169.

Lim, S., & Cortina, L. M. (2005). Interpersonal mistreatment in the workplace: The interface and impact of general incivility and sexual harassment. *Journal of Applied Psychology, 90,* 483–496.

Lim, S., & Howard, R. (1998). Antecedents of sexual and non-sexual aggression in young Singaporean men. *Personality and Individual Differences, 25,* 1163–1182.

Wasti, S. A., & Cortina, L. M. (2002). Coping in context: Sociocultural determinants of responses to sexual harassment. *Journal of Personality and Social Psychology, 83,* 394–405.

SHIFTWORK

Shiftwork is a term used to describe an arrangement of working hours that differs from the standard daylight working hours (i.e., 8:00 a.m. to 5:00 p.m.). Organizations that adopt shiftwork schedules extend their normal working hours beyond the traditional eight-hour shifts by using successive teams of workers. Notable examples of organizations that adopt shiftwork schedules include hospitals, fire stations, and police stations. However, forces such as industrialization, new technologies, and the increasing global economy have contributed to the creation of a society that operates 24 hours a day. This 24-hour society has led to an increase in the need for shiftwork. In fact, it is currently estimated that 15% to 30% of all workers in industrialized societies are involved in some type of shiftwork. Although shiftwork remains more common in certain occupations (e.g., process-control industries, emergency services, transport), the growth of shiftwork systems is expected to continue at a rapid pace.

The types of shiftwork systems that organizations adopt differ on a wide array of characteristics, such as the number and length of shifts. For example, one organization may adopt two 12-hour shifts, whereas another may adopt three 8-hour shifts. Shiftwork systems can also differ in the direction and speed of shift rotation. Shift systems that rotate employee schedules from morning shifts to evening shifts to night shifts have a forward rotation, whereas shifts that rotate counterclockwise (i.e., night to evening to morning) have a backward rotation. With regard to the speed of rotation, shift systems fall into three major categories: (a) permanent shift systems (e.g., permanent night shift); (b) slowly rotating shift systems (e.g., weekly rotating); and (c) rapidly rotating shift systems (e.g., an employee works the morning shift on Monday, the evening shift on Tuesday and Wednesday, and the night shift on Thursday and Friday).

A recent review of shift systems produced five general recommendations regarding the design of shiftwork systems. First, it seems that night work should be reduced as much as possible; however, if this is not possible, an organization should adopt a rapidly rotating system. Second, long shifts (e.g., 9 to 12 hours) should be avoided. Third, flexible work arrangements should be integrated with shift systems. Fourth, shift changes within the same day should be avoided, and the number of consecutive days worked should be limited. The final recommendation suggests that forward rotation is most preferable.

Although shift systems remain highly popular with employees on the front end because they seem to provide a degree of flexibility, research investigating shiftwork has found that such schedules have primarily negative effects for both individuals and organizations. The problems associated with shift systems fall into three broad categories: disturbance of circadian rhythms, physical and psychological ill health, and social and domestic disruption.

DISTURBANCE OF CIRCADIAN RHYTHMS

A great deal of research has investigated the impact of shiftwork on individual circadian rhythms. In general, humans have evolved over thousands of years as a species that habitually sleeps during the night and is awake during the day. The rotation of the earth around the sun creates a 24-hour cycle of light and dark, which is internalized by humans and forms a natural internal body clock. All human circadian rhythms normally show a fixed-phase relationship. For example, body temperature peaks around 8:00 p.m., and all other circadian rhythms reach their maximum at the appropriate time, allowing us to eventually fall asleep at night.

Problems occur for shiftworkers as a result of the mismatch between environmental time cues and the internal timing system. Although the natural light–dark cycle, the clock time, and other social cues may remain the same, the timing of shiftworkers' work and sleep is delayed. Evidence suggests that adjustments to the shiftworkers' body clock are slow, if they occur at all. This mismatch between the environment and the internal body clock has been linked to negative outcomes such as sleep deprivation.

PSYCHOLOGICAL AND PHYSICAL ILL HEALTH

Most of the early work on the psychological outcomes of shiftwork focused on the exploration of shiftworkers' attitudes, such as job satisfaction. This research suggests that, in general, although workers welcome the idea of shift systems up front, they are typically less satisfied with their work than nonshiftworkers. Additionally, the research generally shows that psychological and emotional distress accompanies shiftwork; however, these effects are often small. Some studies failed to find any psychological differences between shiftworkers and nonshiftworkers. For example, two recent studies found no differences between shiftworkers and nonshiftworkers in variation of mood and depressive symptoms. Thus, in general, though evidence suggests that shiftworkers are generally less satisfied with their jobs, other emotional and psychological outcomes, such as depression, are hardly affected.

Much more research has explored the physical consequences of shiftwork. Research has found sleep to be extremely disrupted by shiftwork. In general, many bodily functions are at their highest level of activity during the day. Thus, it is often difficult for individuals to sleep during the day because they are attempting to sleep at a time that is not natural for their circadian rhythm. The most prominent outcome of this lack of quality sleep is chronic fatigue.

Chronic fatigue is linked with greater incidence of physical injury. In general, a greater number of serious job-related injuries occur among employees who work night shifts. Additionally, night shift workers are more likely to be involved in automobile accidents on the drive home from work than day shift workers. Thus, the increased risk of injury seems clear. However, several potential confounds must be considered—for example, night shift workers are often less experienced and work with less supervision.

By far, the most prevalent health complaint associated with shiftwork is gastrointestinal problems. According to a recent study, 20% to 75% of night and shiftworkers complain of gastrointestinal problems such as irregular bowel movements and constipation, compared with 10% to 25% of nonshiftworkers. Although some research has found no difference between day and shiftworkers in gastrointestinal disease, the consensus is that these types of disorders are more prevalent in shift- and night-working populations. One explanation for the increase is that shiftworkers have less regular eating schedules and may have less access to healthful foods.

The relationship between cardiovascular disease and shiftwork has also been explored. Though there has been much debate, recent studies all seem to support a relationship between shiftwork and cardiovascular disease. Many characteristics of shiftworkers are considered predictors of cardiovascular disease (e.g., poor eating habits, gastrointestinal disorders, sleeping disorders, less favorable working conditions). Thus, the risk of cardiovascular disease should be a concern for shiftworkers.

Aside from chronic fatigue, injury, digestive disorders, and cardiovascular disease, shiftwork has additionally been shown to have negative effects on the reproductive cycle of women (e.g., increased menstrual pain and lower rates of pregnancy) and to influence drug activity and effectiveness. The latter point suggests that persistent shift or night work may be incompatible with the efficacious treatment of disease.

SOCIAL AND DOMESTIC DISRUPTION

In addition to the psychological and physical effects, shiftwork is related to several social and domestic variables. For example, although organizations may believe that it is advantageous to operate on a 24-hour schedule, estimates place the cost of shiftwork among U.S. companies at $70 billion per year. Research has shown higher rates of absenteeism among shiftworking populations. Thus, the $70 billion cost results in part from lost productivity because of absenteeism and higher medical bills because of increased injury and accidents. Not only are many of these job-related accidents harmful to the company and dangerous for the worker, but also these careless accidents can have detrimental societal consequences. Additionally, shiftwork is associated with a decreased ability to balance work and nonwork responsibilities. In fact, divorce rates for shiftworkers are up to 60% higher than those for day workers.

INDIVIDUAL DIFFERENCES AND SOCIAL SUPPORT

Several individual difference variables have been shown to be important to the relationship between shiftwork schedules and outcomes. Several of these individual difference variables involve individual circadian types. For example, morningness, or a preference for going to bed early and rising early in the morning, is moderately associated with difficulty adjusting to night work. Additionally, sleep flexibility (i.e., the ability to sleep at unusual times) and vigor (i.e., the ability to overcome drowsiness) predict an individual's level of tolerance for shiftwork.

In addition to differences in circadian type, age and personality are frequently investigated individual differences. With regard to age, the older an employee is, the less tolerance he or she will have for shiftwork. Over the age of 50, it becomes increasingly difficult for individuals to alter their sleep–wake cycles. In addition, many physical ailments increase with advancing age, and this increase in physical problems affects older individuals' ability to adjust to shiftwork. In general, it is recommended that shiftwork be voluntary after the age of 40. With regard to personality, it has been found that introverts are generally more morning oriented than extroverts, making it more difficult for them to adjust to shiftwork. Neuroticism has also been linked to lower levels of shiftwork tolerance. However, some evidence suggests that neuroticism is an outcome of prolonged shiftwork exposure. Thus, the exact role that neuroticism plays in shiftwork tolerance is not yet understood.

Another individual difference variable that has been explored is the amount of social support an individual experiences. In general, results suggest that supervisor support is extremely important in buffering the negative effects of work stress, and the positive effects of support seem to be particularly important for shiftworkers. Thus, it is extremely important to encourage supervisors to take an active interest in the well-being of their shiftworkers.

SUMMARY

Research suggests that shiftwork has negative effects for individuals, organizations, and society. These effects are many and serious. However, this does not mean that shiftwork should be abandoned. For many organizations, shiftwork is a necessity. These organizations need to understand not only how individual differences affect shiftwork tolerance but also, perhaps more importantly, how to design a shiftwork system that is minimally detrimental to employees. Although some research has been conducted, researchers should focus their attention on designing optimal shiftwork systems.

—*Boris B. Baltes and Lindsey M. Young*

See also Flexible Work Schedules

FURTHER READING

Costa, G. (1996). The impact of shift and night work on health. *Applied Ergonomics, 27*(1), 9–16.

Knauth, P. (1996). Designing better shift systems. *Applied Ergonomics, 27*(1), 39–44.

Parkes, K. R. (2003). Shiftwork and environment as interactive predictors of work perceptions. *Journal of Occupational Health Psychology, 8*(4), 266–281.

Schmieder, R. A., & Smith, C. S. (1996). Moderating effects of social support in shiftworking and non-shift-working nurses. *Work and Stress, 10*(2), 128–140.

Smith, C. S., Folkard, S., & Fuller, J. A. (2003). *Shiftwork and working hours.* In J. C. Quick & L. E. Tetrick (Eds.), *Handbook of occupational health psychology* (pp. 163–183). Washington, DC: American Psychological Association.

Taylor, E., Briner, R. B., & Folkard, S. (1997). Models of shiftwork and health: An examination of the influence of stress on shiftwork theory. *Human Factors, 39*(1), 67–82.

SIMULATION, COMPUTER APPROACH

The word *simulation* refers to any procedure that is meant to imitate a real-life system. Simulations are especially useful in examining situations that are too complex, too difficult, or too costly to explore in the real world. The computer is often used for this purpose because it is able to efficiently model systems and process data. The phrase *computer simulation* is a broad rubric for a range of different types of methodologies; the following are their general forms.

MONTE CARLO SIMULATION

In a Monte Carlo simulation, values for uncertain variables are generated by the computer to reproduce information found in the real world. Named for the city of Monte Carlo, Monaco (where the primary attractions are games of chance at gambling casinos), a Monte Carlo simulation generates data pseudorandomly to explore hypothesized models. Much like the random behavior in games of chance, a Monte Carlo simulation selects values at random to simulate a variable. For example, when you roll a die, you know that a number from one to six will come up, but you don't know what number will come up for any particular roll. In much the same way, a Monte Carlo simulation works by first defining the possible values that simulated data can take as the same values found in the real world and then using that definition to generate random numbers. In this way, any number of variables that have a known range of values but an uncertain value for any particular time or event (e.g., interest rates, staffing needs, stock prices, inventory, phone calls per minute) can be modeled. In a typical Monte Carlo simulation, behavioral processes are entirely simulated by the computer.

MICROWORLD SIMULATION

Microworld simulations have a higher level of realism. Microworld simulations are complex, computer-generated situations used in controlled experiments that are designed to study decision making. Microworld simulations represent a compromise between experimental control and realism and enable researchers to conduct experimental research within a dynamic, complex decision-making situation. In a typical microworld simulation, the situation is generated with a moderate degree of fidelity and behavioral processes are examined as humans navigate through it. The simulation is typically only unidimensional—that is, participants are instructed to make decisions that are cognitively complex but that do not invoke a range of senses (e.g., visual, aural, olfactory, tactile, and proprioceptive).

VIRTUAL REALITY SIMULATION

At the most realistic level, a virtual reality (VR) simulation is defined as a computer-simulated, multisensory environment in which a perceiver—the user of the VR computer technology—experiences *telepresence.* Telepresence is defined as feeling present in an environment that is generated by a communication medium such as a computer. In the context of VR, telepresence occurs when the VR user loses awareness of being present at the site of the human–computer interface and instead feels present or fully immersed in the VR environment. Thus, a successful VR simulation reproduces the experience of reality with a high degree of accuracy so that behavioral processes can be examined as humans navigate through the simulated environment. The simulation is typically multidimensional—that is, the best VR simulations attempt to invoke the full range of participants' senses (i.e., visual, aural, olfactory, tactile, and proprioceptive).

EXAMPLES FROM THE LITERATURE

Computer simulations have been used to explore a multitude of real-world situations. What follows are a number of examples, broken down by simulation type, which may help to make the exposition more concrete.

Monte Carlo Simulations

Monte Carlo simulations have been used to investigate such phenomena as faking on personality inventories, the effect of forced distribution rating systems on workforce potential, adverse impact in selection, statistical properties of various indexes, and withdrawal behaviors, to name just a few.

Microworld Simulations

Microworld simulations have been used to study a number of situations, including a sugar production factory, a fire chief's job, a beer game, and a water production plant. These microworlds vary along four dimensions: (a) dynamics, that is, the system's state at time t depends on the state of the system at time $t - 1$; (b) complexity, or the degree to which the parts interconnect, making it difficult to understand or predict system behavior; (c) opaqueness, or the invisibility of some parts of the system; and (d) dynamic complexity, or the effect of feedback structures on a decision maker's ability to control a dynamic system.

Virtual Reality Simulations

Virtual reality simulations have been used to create virtual environments to assess large-scale spatial abilities; to model responses to a fire; and to prepare trainees for job experiences that normally would have high costs (e.g., flying an airplane), the risk of costly damage to equipment (e.g., landing a plane on an aircraft carrier), or the potential for injuries to the trainee (e.g., training in a race car).

ADVANTAGES AND DISADVANTAGES OF COMPUTER SIMULATIONS

There are trade-offs with any methodology. The major advantage of computer simulations is that they are particularly well-adapted for situations in which it would be difficult, because of cost, safety, or validity, to examine a particular phenomenon in a real-life situation. With a computer simulation, any one of a number of naturally occurring parameters can be manipulated in a controlled laboratory setting many times without endangering participants, spending large sums of money, or resorting to correction formulas for participants who drop out.

The major disadvantage of computer simulations is their lack of external generalizability—that is, the degree to which the results of the computer simulation apply to actual situations and behavior in real life. However, external generalizability can be enhanced in several ways:

- When conducting Monte Carlo studies and designing microworlds, choose parameter estimates sensibly (e.g., from prior empirical studies).
- When conducting VR simulations, ensure that VR environments invoke maximal vividness and interactivity.

—*Chet Robie and Shawn Komar*

See also Human–Computer Interaction; Judgment and Decision-Making Process; Quasi-experimental Designs; Virtual Organizations; Virtual Teams

FURTHER READING

Gamberini, L., Cottone, P., Spagnolli, A., Varotto, D., & Mantovani, G. (2003). Responding to a fire emergency in a virtual environment: Different pattern of actions for different situations. *Ergonomics, 46,* 842–858.

Gonzalez, C., Vanyukov, P., & Martin, M. K. (2005). The use of microworlds to study dynamic decision making. *Computers in Human Behavior, 21,* 273–286.

Scullen, S. E., Bergey, P. K., & Aiman-Smith, L. (2005). Forced distribution rating systems and the improvement of workforce potential: A baseline simulation. *Personnel Psychology, 58,* 1–32.

Seitz, S. T., Hulin, C. L., & Hanisch, K. A. (2000). Simulating withdrawal behaviors in work organizations: An example of a virtual society. *Nonlinear Dynamics, Psychology, and Life Sciences, 4,* 33–65.

Waller, D. (2005). The WALKABOUT: Using virtual environments to assess large-scale spatial abilities. *Computers in Human Behavior, 21,* 243–253.

SITUATIONAL APPROACH TO LEADERSHIP

The situational approach to leadership asserts that there is no one best way to lead others and emphasizes that a leader's style and behavior should depend on the characteristics of his or her followers. Specifically, the *situational approach to leadership model* provides leaders with insight regarding the most effective leadership style to demonstrate based on the readiness of their followers. This approach contends that a leader will elicit maximum performance from his or her followers when the leader's behaviors are tailored to the followers' ability, willingness, and level of confidence.

Known previously as the life-cycle model of leadership and situational leadership theory, the situational approach to leadership has been revised several times, and the terminology has been modified with each revision.

Research examining the behavioral approach to leadership has demonstrated that leaders engage in both directive behaviors and supportive behaviors (also recognized as task and relationship behaviors). Directive behavior refers to one-way communication that clearly explains each needed detail to the follower to ensure the completion of the task. Supportive behavior is two-way communication with an interpersonal focus that demonstrates the leaders' desire to build and maintain relationships. The situational approach to leadership suggests that effective leaders practice both directive and supportive behaviors, yet their use depends on the developmental level of their followers (previously termed *maturity*).

FOLLOWER DEVELOPMENT LEVEL

Two follower factors make up the follower development level. The first is competence—it asks the question, "Does the follower have the skills and knowledge to successfully complete the task?" Competence refers to learned job-related abilities, knowledge, and skills gained from education or experience (earlier versions of the model referred to this as *job maturity*). The second determinant, commitment, asks, "Does the follower possess the motivation and self-assurance to successfully complete the task?" Commitment refers to the follower's motivation and self-confidence (earlier versions of the model referred to this as *psychological maturity*).

The combinations of competence and commitment can be divided into four categories, which indicate the four levels of development (D1–D4) that followers may possess:

- D1—Not committed and not competent; not developed or developing
- D2—Committed but not competent; low to moderate development
- D3—Not committed but competent; moderate to high development
- D4—Committed and competent; developed

When the followers' developmental level is determined, an appropriate leadership style can be identified. The four leadership styles are *directing, coaching, supporting,* and *delegating*.

LEADERSHIP STYLES

Directing (Telling)

The directing leadership style (S1), previously referred to as *telling,* is used when followers are at the lowest developmental level (D1). The directing style of leadership involves relaying information to the follower in a very clear, specific manner. The directing style primarily consists of one-way, top-down communication. The follower's roles and assigned tasks are explicitly and specifically stated so that the follower is clear about how, where, and when to do the tasks. In the directing style, the leader solves the problems and makes the decisions.

For example, the directing leadership style is appropriate when a new engineering graduate (follower) walks into the office on her first day. The new employee has a foundation of engineering principles from the classroom setting, but she is unaware of the practices and principles under which her new employer operates. If her boss (leader) directs her as to what to work on and when, her performance will increase because she has the requisite skills to do the tasks, but she probably does not know what needs to be done.

The directing style is also appropriate in extreme situations requiring rapid decision making and action. For example, the leader of an electrical power line maintenance crew who sees lightning nearby is likely to tell his crew to descend from the electrical poles immediately and without question.

Coaching (Selling)

The coaching leadership style (S2), previously referred to as *selling,* is linked with the second level of development (D2). Within this leadership style, the leader's supportive behavior increases to a higher level, allowing two-way communication, and directive behaviors remain high. The leader still provides much direction to the follower, but the leader listens to the follower and allows the follower to grasp and understand the explanations and reasoning behind the leader's decisions. In the coaching leadership style, final decisions are still made by the leader.

For example, a track coach (leader) might provide detailed instruction to a novice hurdle jumper (follower). The coach explains how to jump hurdles and provides encouragement to the jumper. The jumper begins running down the track and clears three out of five hurdles. The coach praises the jumper for jumping the three hurdles, and the jumper asks the coach for further guidance on how to improve (i.e., clear all five hurdles). The jumper is developing both the competence and commitment to jump and improve her abilities. Her performance will increase as the coach continues to encourage and support her efforts while providing guidance and direction on how to perform the task more effectively.

Supporting (Participating)

The supporting leadership style (S3), previously referred to as *participating,* is practiced at the third level of development (D3). The leadership style is low on directive behaviors, but supportive behaviors remain high. At this stage, the leader and follower engage in two-way communication and joint decision making. The leader's words and actions need to be encouraging and convey support for the follower's decisions to help facilitate confidence and motivation in the follower.

Take, for example, a skilled and well-trained nurse (follower) with many years of experience. The nurse understands what tasks and duties need to be performed on a daily basis and stays abreast of current medicines and treatments. The nursing supervisor (leader) does not need to tell the nurse what to do in a step-by-step manner—in fact, such actions would likely be perceived negatively by the nurse. However, as the nurse completes his daily activities, he will need to inform his supervisor of the patients he has seen and their ailments. The nurse will also need the supervisor's support and input on decisions. The nurse has the skills and training to perform the job, but at times may feel unsure of the decisions he is making to treat his patients. Therefore, the nurse's performance will increase if the leader actively listens to the nurse while encouraging and praising the nurse's work.

Delegating

The final leadership style, delegating (S4), is used when the follower is both committed and competent (level D4). At the delegating stage, the leader removes himself or herself even further, resulting in low directive behaviors and low supportive behaviors. The follower is now at a developmental stage that allows autonomy and requires only general supervision from the leader. The leader has little need to provide support because the follower is confident and motivated to take on the responsibility of the assigned tasks. This leadership style is appropriate for peak performers.

Consider, for example, a follower who has worked in the marketing field for more than 20 years and has continually landed projects leading to substantial profits for the company. She does not need a leader who tells her what to do; she already knows the processes and required tasks. She has the skills and abilities to do the job. She possesses the willingness and confidence to take initiative. Supporting behaviors from her boss (leader) may not decrease her performance on the job, but she requires only minimal support. Her performance will increase if her boss delegates projects to her while keeping her apprised of organizational goals and the big picture. Her boss should be available for consultation and should praise and reward her successes.

EXTENSIONS AND APPLICATIONS OF THE MODEL

The situational approach to leadership offers some general suggestions relating to the leader's span of control (the number of followers the leader is responsible for supervising). Specifically, the model advises that the number of direct reports a leader can effectively lead is a function of the developmental level of the individual followers. That is, the span of control of a leader who is supervising followers at the D4 level can be larger than a leader who is managing a group of people who are all at the D1 level.

The model has been extended and applied to the leadership of work groups and teams. In this application, the readiness of the group or team is determined by the alignment of the followers toward a common goal. A group in the forming stage is at the D1 level, a group in the storming stage is at the D2 level, a group at the norming stage is at the D3 level, and a group at the performing stage is at the D4 level. The leadership styles (defining, clarifying, involving, and empowering) used in this group-level adaptation are analogous to those described previously.

MEASURES AND USES

The situational leadership model is a training model that is intended to enhance leader–follower communications. The training provides the leader with the information needed to adapt to the various situations that he or she and the followers may encounter. Although little is known about the validity of the situational approach to leadership model, it is frequently used in corporate America. The most current instruments used to measure competence and commitment (the manager rating scale and the staff rating scale) originated from the Center of Leadership Studies.

—*Mark C. Frame and Taylor P. Drummond*

See also Leadership Development

FURTHER READING

Blanchard, K. H., Zigarmi, P., & Zigarmi, D. (1985). *Leadership and the one minute manager: Increasing effectiveness through situational leadership.* New York: Morrow.

Graeff, C. L. (1997). Evolution of situational theory: A critical review. *Leadership Quarterly, 8*(2), 153–170.

Hersey, P., & Blanchard, K. H. (2000). *Management of organizational behavior: Utilizing human resources* (8th ed.). Upper Saddle River, NJ: Prentice Hall.

Vecchin, R. P. (1987). Situational leadership theory: An examination of a perspective theory. *Journal of Applied Psychology, 72*(3), 444–451.

SITUATIONAL JUDGMENT TESTS

Many work situations require the job incumbent to make a judgment about aspects of the situation and respond to the practical situational demands. An effective response to the practical demands of a situation may require the appropriate use of some combination of one's abilities and other personal attributes. Situational judgment tests (SJTs) are psychometric tests that are specifically designed to assess individual differences in this overall ability to make effective judgments or responses to a wide variety of situations.

Situational judgment tests are typically administered in a paper-and-pencil mode, although they may be implemented in other modes, such as video-based items and interview questions. The SJT is made up of several situations, each presenting a hypothetical critical incident and several courses of action in response to the situation. The instructional and response format is dependent on the specific SJT. In many SJTs, respondents are required to rate each possible course of action on a five-point effectiveness scale or indicate the best and worst action among the alternatives provided. In other SJTs, respondents are asked to rate each possible action in terms of the likelihood that they would adopt it or indicate their most likely and least likely actions among the possible actions provided.

DEVELOPMENT OF SITUATIONAL JUDGMENT TESTS

Most modern versions of SJTs derive from the work of Stephen Motowidlo and his colleagues, which builds on Robert Sternberg's concept of *tacit knowledge* (i.e., job-relevant knowledge needed to accomplish everyday tasks that are usually not openly stated or part of any formal instruction) and improves the measurement of the concept by using job analyses to identify the types of judgments made on a specific job and to improve their content and face validity. The development process usually involves the identification of a set of work-related constructs that are targeted in an SJT. Job incumbents are asked to generate critical incidents or situations that require ability or expertise related to these constructs. Other job incumbents provide a set of possible actions that could be taken to resolve or improve the situations, and a third group, usually subject-matter experts, provide effectiveness ratings of each solution and judgments about the best and worst of the solutions. These ratings and judgments are analyzed and used to develop a final item and scoring key that is applied to the items. (Detailed examples of the SJT development process are provided in the references listed in Further Reading.)

Probably as a result of the job-relevant features of the test development process, studies have shown that respondents tend to have more favorable perceptions of SJTs compared with other types of employment tests, such as cognitive ability and personality tests, because they believe the tests are relevant to work situations and valid in predicting job performance. In addition to the evidence on the face validity of SJTs, there is increasing evidence that SJTs can produce substantial zero-order and incremental criterion-related validities. However, unlike cognitive ability and personality measures, which have an extensive literature and large database, the empirical evidence on SJTs is much less established, and the theoretical or conceptual underpinnings of SJTs are much less understood.

CRITERION-RELATED VALIDITY OF SITUATIONAL JUDGMENT TESTS

In a meta-analysis of the criterion-related validities of SJTs, Michael McDaniel and his colleagues found that the average observed validity of 102 validity coefficients was .26, a figure that increased to .34 when it was corrected for criterion unreliability. However, there was substantial unexplained variability (55%) in coefficients around this population value, suggesting that the validity of an SJT is likely to be moderated by many variables. Moderator analyses indicated that measures developed as the result of job analyses yield larger validity coefficients than those that are not based on job analyses, but the results of other moderator analyses were inconclusive because of the small number of studies or small total sample size in one or more of the groups of studies formed by the moderator variable.

Several primary studies involving employees in a wide variety of jobs conducted since Motowidlo et al. revived interest in the SJT method have produced validities similar to the averages reported by McDaniel et al. In addition, several studies found that SJTs produce validity increments (in predicting job performance) over cognitive ability, personality, job knowledge, and experience measures.

The criterion-related validity of SJTs in predicting performance seems well-established. Although SJTs appear to be related to cognitive ability and, in some studies, to personality measures as well, incremental validity of SJTs over and above personality and cognitive ability has been reported in multiple studies. The substantial variability in correlations may result because different constructs are being measured depending on the types of situations included on the SJT. When the situations require cognitive-based constructs such as planning, organizational ability, and analytical problem solving, SJT scores correlate highly with cognitive ability test scores compared with situations that require constructs associated with interpersonal or leadership skills, for example, which are more personality based.

CONSTRUCT VALIDITY OF SITUATIONAL JUDGMENT TESTS

In contrast to the emerging evidence on the criterion-related validity of SJTs, research on the construct validity of SJTs is in its infancy. The bulk of the studies on SJTs are not explicitly designed to examine the nature of the constructs assessed by SJTs, and therefore the construct validity evidence available to date is indirect, at best. The constructs underlying SJTs are likely related to the concepts of adaptability, contextual job knowledge, and practical intelligence, but the precise nature of the test constructs is inextricably tied to the specific content of the SJT items.

Efforts to conduct factor analysis on SJT items typically produce little support for a priori factors that researchers have tried to incorporate into their items. The first factor in these analyses usually accounts for two to three times the variance of the second factor, but unless the scale comprises a large number of items, internal consistency (coefficient alpha) reliabilities are typically low. One explanation for these results is that responses to a single SJT item with its varied options may be the result of a variety of individual difference constructs, including both ability and motivational or personality constructs. This is consistent with empirical findings indicating that SJTs are correlated with a variety of variables, including cognitive ability and personality traits.

Given the nature of SJTs and the extant research findings, it is unlikely that SJTs measure any single unidimensional construct, even though it may be legitimate to use an overall SJT score to represent the composite (multifaceted) ability or effectiveness in situational judgment. Like interviews and many paper-and-pencil tests, SJTs may be better construed as a method of measurement that can be adapted to measure a variety of job-related constructs in different situations. However, some types of situational judgment constructs are almost inherently assessed in typical SJTs. That is, SJTs may be construed as a method of testing that constrains the range of constructs measured.

Like the interview, SJTs have dominant constructs (though they are different in nature from those in the interview method) that are readily or almost inherently assessed. Primary dominant constructs include *adaptability constructs,* which are likely a function of both individual difference traits and acquisition through previous experiences, and *contextual knowledge constructs,* which may be gained through experience in real-world contexts. Collectively, these SJT-dominant constructs can be represented by the global construct called *practical intelligence.* However, unlike the interview, SJT-dominant constructs are not associated with the structural format of the SJT (i.e., candidates are presented with a problem situation followed by the requirement to generate, endorse, or rate a series of response options). Instead, the dominant constructs are associated with the core characteristics of the test content of typical SJTs.

The details of these construct validity issues are beyond the scope of this entry. Interested readers may refer to works by David Chan and Neal Schmitt (1997, 2002, 2005), which elaborate three distinct but interrelated core characteristics of SJT content (i.e., practical situational demands, multidimensionality of situational response, and criterion-correspondent sampling of situations and response options in test content development) and relate them to SJT performance as well as job performance.

There is emerging evidence on the face validity and criterion-related validity of SJTs, but studies that directly address the fundamental issue of construct validity are lacking. Research on the construct validity of SJTs could help to identify the boundary conditions for the criterion-related validity of SJTs. Such research would also clarify the SJT constructs and increase our understanding of the nature of SJT responses and their relationship to job performance and other work-relevant variables.

—*David Chan*

See also Critical Incident Technique; Practical Intelligence; Selection Strategies; Validity

FURTHER READING

Chan, D., & Schmitt, N. (1997). Video-based versus paper-and-pencil method of assessment in situational judgment tests: Subgroup differences in test performance and face validity perceptions. *Journal of Applied Psychology, 82,* 143–159.

Chan, D., & Schmitt, N. (2002). Situational judgment and job performance. *Human Performance, 15,* 233–254.

Chan, D., & Schmitt, N. (2005). Situational judgment tests. In A. Evers, O. Smit-Voskuijl, & N. Anderson (Eds.), *Handbook of personnel selection* (pp. 219–242). Oxford, UK: Blackwell

McDaniel, M. A., Morgeson, F. P., Finnegan, E. B., Campion, M. A., & Braverman, E. P. (2001). Use of situational judgment tests to predict job performance: A clarification of the literature. *Journal of Applied Psychology, 80,* 730–740.

Motowidlo, S. J., Dunnette, M. D., & Carter, G. W. (1990). An alternative selection procedure: The low-fidelity simulation. *Journal of Applied Psychology, 75,* 640–647.

Weekly, J. A., & Jones, C. (1999). Further studies of situational tests. *Personnel Psychology, 52,* 679–700.

SOCIAL COGNITIVE THEORY

Social cognitive theory explains human accomplishments and well-being in terms of the interplay between individuals' attributes, their behavior, and the influences operating in their environment. According to this view, people are *contributors* to their life circumstances, not just the products of them. They are characterized by a number of basic capabilities. These include cognitive, vicarious, self-regulatory, and self-reflective capabilities that play a central role in human self-development, adaptation, and change.

SYMBOLIZING CAPABILITY

People's extraordinary cognitive capacity provides them with a powerful means for understanding the workings of their environment and for shaping and managing it in ways that touch virtually every aspect of their lives. Cognitive factors, which constitute people's symbolic nature, partly determine which aspects of the environment are attended to among the myriad activities, what meaning is conferred on them, what emotional impact and motivating power they have, and how the information they convey is organized for future use.

Through the medium of symbols, people transform information from transient experiences into cognitive models that serve as guides for reasoning and action. They transcend time and place in communicating with others at any distance. By symbolizing their experiences, people give coherence, direction, meaning, and continuity to their lives. The other distinctive human capabilities draw heavily on this advanced capacity for symbolization.

VICARIOUS CAPABILITY

Psychological theories traditionally emphasize learning through its positive and negative effects on one's actions. Learning would be exceedingly laborious, not to mention hazardous, if people had to rely solely on direct experience to tell them what to do. Direct experience is a toilsome, tough teacher. Fortunately, humans have evolved an advanced capacity for observational learning that enables them to expand their knowledge and competencies through the power of social modeling.

Much human learning relies on the models in one's immediate environment. However, a vast amount of knowledge about styles of thinking and behaving, as well as the norms and practices of social systems, is gained from the extensive modeling in the symbolic environment of the electronic mass media. A special power of symbolic modeling lies in its tremendous reach, speed, and multiplicative power. Unlike learning by doing, which requires shaping the actions of each individual laboriously through repeated consequences, in observational learning, a single model can simultaneously convey new ways of thinking and behaving to countless people in widely dispersed locales. Observers can now transcend the bounds of their immediate environment. Electronic systems that feed off telecommunications satellites are rapidly diffusing new ideas, values, and styles of conduct worldwide.

Modeling is not merely a process of response mimicry, as is commonly believed. Modeled judgments and actions may differ in specific content but embody the same principle. For example, a model may deal with moral conflicts that differ widely in the type of predicaments but apply the same moral standard to them. Observers learn the principles underlying the modeled activity rather than the specific examples. Such abstract modeling enables them to construct new versions of the behavior that go beyond the particular examples they see.

Modeling can also promote creativity, in several ways. Modeled unconventional modes of thinking increase innovativeness in others. Creativeness rarely springs entirely from individual inventiveness; rather, it usually involves synthesizing existing knowledge into new ways of thinking and doing things. People adopt useful modeled elements, improve on them, synthesize them into new forms, and tailor them to their particular circumstances. In these ways, selective modeling serves as the mother of innovation.

FORETHOUGHT CAPABILITY

Another distinctive human characteristic is the capability of forethought. Most human behavior, being purposive, is regulated by thought projected into the future. People anticipate the likely consequences of prospective actions, they set goals for themselves, and they plan courses of action that are likely to produce the desired outcomes and avoid detrimental ones. Through the exercise of forethought, people motivate themselves and guide their actions anticipatorily. Future events, of course, cannot be the cause of current motivation and action because they have no actual

existence. However, through cognitive representation, visualized futures are brought into the present to serve as current motivators and regulators of behavior.

Human behavior is extensively regulated by its effects. These effects may take the form of material costs and benefits, social approval or disapproval, or self-evaluative positive and negative reactions. Behavior patterns that produce positive outcomes are readily adopted and used, whereas those that bring unrewarding or punishing outcomes are generally discarded. But external consequences are not the only outcomes that influence human behavior; people also profit from the successes and mistakes of others, as well as from their own experiences. As a general rule, people do things they have seen succeed and avoid those they have seen fail. However, observed outcomes exert their influence through perceived similarity—the belief that one is likely to experience similar outcomes for similar courses of action and that one possesses the capabilities to achieve similar performances. People also influence their own motivation and behavior by the positive and negative consequences they produce for themselves. This mode of self-regulation will be discussed next.

SELF-REGULATORY CAPABILITY

People are not only planners and forethinkers. They are also self-reactors with a capacity for self-direction. Successful development requires the gradual substitution of internal regulation and direction for external sanctions and mandates. Once the capability for self-direction is developed, self-demands and self-sanctions serve as major guides, motivators, and deterrents. In the absence of personal standards and self-sanctions, individuals would behave like weathervanes, constantly shifting direction to conform to whatever momentary influence happened to impinge on them.

The self-regulation of motivation, affect, and action operates partly through personal standards and evaluative reactions to one's own behavior. The anticipated self-satisfaction gained from fulfilling a valued standard provides one source of incentive motivation for personal accomplishments. Self-dissatisfaction with substandard performance serves as another incentive for enhanced effort. The motivational effects do not stem from the standards themselves but from the fact that people care about their self-regard and respond evaluatively to their own behavior.

In activities that involve achievement and the cultivation of competencies, the personal standards selected as a mark of adequacy are progressively raised as knowledge and skills are acquired and challenges are met. In many areas of social and moral behavior, however, the personal standards that serve to regulate conduct have greater stability. People do not change from week to week what they regard as right or wrong or good or bad. After they adopt a standard of morality, their self-sanctions for actions that match or violate their personal standards serve as a regulatory influence. People do things that give them self-satisfaction and a sense of self-worth. They refrain from behaving in ways that violate their moral standards because it will bring self-disapproval. Thus, self-sanctions keep conduct in line with internal standards.

Moral standards do not function as fixed internal regulators of conduct. Self-regulatory influences do not operate unless they are activated, and there are many processes by which moral self-sanctions can be selectively disengaged from harmful conduct. The disengagement may center on sanctifying harmful conduct by portraying it as serving worthy purposes. It may focus on downplaying one's role in given activities by diffusing and displacing responsibility so that perpetrators do not hold themselves accountable for the harm they cause. It may involve minimizing, distorting, or even disputing the harm that flows from detrimental actions. And the disengagement may include dehumanizing and blaming the recipients of the maltreatment. Through the selective use of these means, otherwise considerate people can perpetrate illegalities and inhumanities.

SELF-REFLECTIVE CAPABILITY

The capability to reflect on oneself and the adequacy of one's thoughts and actions is another distinctly human attribute that figures prominently in social cognitive theory. People are not only agents of action but also self-examiners of the quality of their own functioning. Effective functioning requires reliable ways of distinguishing between accurate and faulty thinking. In verifying the adequacy of thought by self-reflective means, people generate ideas and act on them or predict occurrences from them. They then judge from the results the accuracy and functional value of their thinking and use this information to improve their thinking if necessary.

Among the various types of self-referent thoughts, none is more central or pervasive then people's beliefs in their capability to exercise influence over their own functioning and events that affect their lives. Beliefs about personal efficacy are the foundation of motivation and accomplishment. Unless people believe they can produce desired results by their actions, they have little incentive to act or to persevere in the face of difficulty. Whatever other factors serve as guides and motivators, they are rooted in the core belief that one can make a difference by one's actions.

Beliefs about personal efficacy regulate human functioning through four major types of processes: cognitive, motivational, emotional, and decisional. A major function of thought is to enable people to predict events and develop ways to exercise control over them. People of high efficacy show greater cognitive resourcefulness, strategic flexibility, and effectiveness in managing their environment.

Efficacy beliefs play a central role in the self-regulation of motivation. Most human motivation is cognitively generated by goal aspirations and by the material, social, and self-evaluative costs and benefits anticipated for different courses of action. People of high perceived efficacy set motivating goals for themselves, expect their efforts to produce favorable results, view obstacles as surmountable, and figure out ways to overcome them. The functional belief system in difficult undertakings is realism about tough odds but optimism that, through self-development and perseverance, those odds can be beaten.

People's beliefs in their coping efficacy also affect how much stress, anxiety, and depression they experience in threatening or taxing situations. Those who believe they can manage threats and adversities view them as less inimical and act in ways that reduce their aversiveness or change them for the better. People have to live with a psychic environment that is largely of their own making. Many human distresses result from failures of control over perturbing thoughts. Beliefs about coping efficacy facilitate the exercise of control over perturbing and dejecting ruminations.

People also have a hand in what they become through the types of activities and environments they choose. Beliefs about personal efficacy can, therefore, play a key role in shaping the course of one's life by influencing the choices made at key decision points. In self-development through choice processes, destinies are shaped by selecting activities and environments that are known to cultivate valued potentialities and lifestyles.

People can also have a hand in what they become by the types of activities and environments they choose. Beliefs of personal efficacy can, therefore, play a key role in shaping the courses lives take by influencing the choices made at key decision points. In self-development through choice processes, destinies are shaped by selecting activities and environments known to cultivate valued potentialities and lifestyles.

People do not live their lives in isolation. They work together to secure what they cannot accomplish on their own. People's shared beliefs in their collective ability to produce desired outcomes is a crucial ingredient of group attainments. Such beliefs influence the type of futures that people seek to achieve through collective action, how well they use their resources, how much effort they put into group endeavors, their staying power when collective efforts fail to produce quick results or meet forcible opposition, and their vulnerability to the discouragement that can beset those taking on tough problems that are not easily changeable.

SOCIAL COGNITIVE THEORY IN CULTURAL CONTEXT

Cultures are dynamic and internally diverse systems, not static monoliths. They are no longer insular; global connectivity is shrinking cross-cultural uniqueness. Transnational interdependencies and global market forces are restructuring national economies and shaping the political and social life of societies. Advanced telecommunications technologies are disseminating ideas, values, and styles of behavior transnationally at an unprecedented rate. The symbolic environment, which feeds off communication satellites, is altering national cultures and producing intercultural commonalities in some lifestyles. The growing role of electronic acculturation is fostering a more extensive globalization of culture. People are becoming increasingly enmeshed in a cyberworld that transcends time, distance, place, and national borders. In addition, the mass migration of people and the high global mobility of entertainers, athletes, journalists, academics, and employees of multinational corporations are changing cultural landscapes. These intermixing social forces are homogenizing some aspects of life and fostering cultural hybridization.

One must distinguish between inherent capacities and the way culture shapes these potentialities into diverse forms. For example, modeling, which figures prominently in social cognitive theory, is essential for self-development and functioning regardless of the culture in which one resides. Modeling is a universal human capacity. But what is modeled, how modeling influences are socially structured, and which purposes they serve vary in different cultural milieus. Similarly, a resilient sense of efficacy has generalized functional value regardless of whether one resides in an individualist-oriented culture or a collectivist-oriented one. Being immobilized by self-doubt and belief in the futility of effort has little adaptive advantage. But the way efficacy beliefs are developed and structured, the way they are exercised, and the purposes to which they are put vary cross-culturally. In short, there is a cultural commonality in basic capacities and mechanisms of operation but diversity in the culturing of these inherent capacities. In this dual-level analysis, universality is compatible with manifest cultural plurality.

AGENTIC MANAGEMENT OF FORTUITY

There is much that people do purposefully to exercise some measure of control over their self-development and life circumstances. But there is a lot of fortuity in the courses people's lives take. Indeed, some of the most important determinants of life paths occur through the most trivial of circumstances. People are often inaugurated into new life trajectories, marital partnerships, and occupational careers through fortuitous circumstances. Consider the following example: An individual enters a lecture hall as it is rapidly filling up and seizes an empty chair near the entrance. He ends up marrying the woman who happened to be seated next to him. With only a momentary change in time of entry, seating constellations would have altered, and this intersect would not have occurred.

Most fortuitous events leave people untouched, whereas others have some lasting effects, and still others launch people into new trajectories of life. Fortuitous influences my be unforeseeable, but having occurred, the conditions they create contribute to causal processes in the same way that prearranged ones do. Fortuity does not mean uncontrollability. People can bring some influence to bear on the fortuitous character of life. They can make chance happen by pursuing an active life that increases the number and type of fortuitous encounters they will experience. Chance favors the inquisitive and venturesome who go places, do things, and explore new activities. People also make chance work for them by cultivating their interests, enabling beliefs, and competencies. These personal resources enable them to make the most of opportunities that arise unexpectedly. Louis Pasteur put it well when he noted that "chance favors only the prepared mind." By these means, people can exercise some influence on the way they play the hand that fortuity deals them.

—*Albert Bandura*

See also Goal-Setting Theory; Self-Efficacy

FURTHER READING

Bandura, A. (1986). *Social foundations of thought and action: A social cognitive theory.* Englewood Cliffs, NJ: Prentice Hall.

Bandura, A. (1997). *Self-efficacy: The exercise of control.* New York: Freeman.

Bandura A. (2005). The evolution of social cognitive theory. In K. G. Smith & M. A. Hitt (Eds.), *Great minds in management* (pp. 9–35). Oxford, UK: Oxford University Press.

Locke, E., & Latham, G. (1990). *A theory of goal setting and task performance.* Englewood Cliffs, NJ: Prentice Hall.

Rosenthal, T. L. (1984). Cognitive social learning theory. In N. S. Endler & J. M. Hunt (Eds.), *Personality and the behavioral disorders* (2nd ed., Vol. 2, pp. 113–145). New York: Wiley.

Schwarzer, R. (Ed.). (1992). *Self-efficacy: Thought control of action.* Washington, DC: Hemisphere.

SOCIAL EXCHANGE THEORY

Social exchange theory is one of the most influential conceptual paradigms for understanding behavior. Over the years, differing perspectives on social exchange have evolved, bridging disciples such as anthropology, sociology, organizational theory, and social psychology. As a result, social exchange theory cannot be thought of as a single theoretical model. Rather, it is a general framework or conceptual point of view about how resources are valued and exchanged. Thus, there is no single social exchange *theory* but many different social exchange *theories,* each meaningfully elaborating on the general paradigm.

Theories of social exchange view social life as a series of transactions. Social exchange transactions involve the exchange of some resource, broadly defined, between two or more parties (individuals or institutions). These exchanges are viewed as interdependent in the sense that the behavior of one party is contingent on the actions of another. A basic tenet of social exchange is that an offer of a benefit generates an obligation to reciprocate in kind. In time, a series of interdependent transactions will generate trust, loyalty, and mutual commitments. Although theories of social exchange differ on particulars, they highlight three central principles:

- Interdependent transactions are defined by rules or norms of exchange.
- Social exchange quality is defined by the attributes of the resources being exchanged.
- Social exchanges evolve into relationships among the parties involved.

EXCHANGE RULES AND NORMS

Exchange rules and norms define the expectations or attributes of transactions. In this way, parties of exchange use rules to guide behavior. Over time, these rules may become social norms, or moral standards of behavior. Both exchange rules and norms define how parties should behave and be treated. Within the organizational sciences, the most commonly accepted rule is reciprocity. However, other rules are also important for understanding social exchange.

Reciprocity

Reciprocity involves repaying like with like. By and large, most social exchange research focuses on the *positive reciprocity norm,* meaning that individuals expect to return a benefit for a benefit. However, exchanges may also involve a *negative reciprocity norm,* meaning that individuals may avenge a harm. Indeed, these felt obligations can be quite strong. For example, in some cultures, individuals will refuse valuable gifts so as to avoid expensive repayment. Likewise, the desire to punish a wrong can cause one to retaliate—even when it is economically costly and there is no hope of future deterrence. Therefore, it is not surprising that human beings have been labeled *homo reciprocus.* Some scholars have gone so far as to argue that reciprocity is an evolutionarily driven predication, whereas others contend that this tendency is learned through socialization.

The give-and-take principles of reciprocity motivate much of human behavior. For example, a tit-for-tat tactic, which begins with unilateral concessions, can defuse serious conflicts. This tactic works because one's concession tends to prompt parallel concessions in the other disputant. Similarly, individuals tend to reciprocate self-disclosing statements. This process of positive reciprocal exchange generally builds closer relationships.

Although reciprocity strongly influences human interactions, not everyone shares this propensity to the same degree. In other words, individuals differ in how strongly they endorse the norm of reciprocity or an *exchange ideology* (sometimes termed *reciprocation ideology*). The more strongly an individual endorses an exchange ideology, the more likely he or she is to "keep score" of what was exchanged and to expect the return of a good deed. For example, just treatment at work tends to have a stronger effect on work attitudes among those who are high in exchange ideology and a weaker effect among those with lower scores. In fact, those who do not strongly endorse an exchange ideology may not care whether obligations are reciprocated.

Other Rules of Exchange

Although most research emphasizes reciprocal exchanges, other models exist as well. For example, negotiated rules require the parties engaging in joint decision processes to outline exchange arrangements. Negotiated rules differ from reciprocity in that they are explicitly stated. That is, within reciprocal exchanges, individuals tend to coordinate their behavior implicitly and without formal discussion. Within negotiated exchanges, coordination is formally delineated in advance. A good deal of research has compared negotiated exchanges to reciprocal exchanges. Negotiated exchanges tend to be more concrete and have a stricter definition of terms. One specific benefit (e.g., an hourly wage) is exchanged for another (e.g., a certain unit of work completed). In contrast, reciprocal exchanges tend to be more open-ended and flexible. Generally speaking, reciprocal exchanges tend to lead to closer interpersonal relationships, engendering trust, commitment, and equality between the parties.

Other models of exchange rules have also been developed, mainly in the disciplines of anthropology and sociology. These models emphasize rules other than reciprocity and negotiation. At their core, these rules serve to identify the general goal of the exchange. Though a thorough review of this literature

is beyond the scope of this summary, it is noteworthy to mention that exchanges can also be based on principles of community (e.g., exchanges based on the common good of a group), rationality (e.g., exchanges based on self-interest), altruism (e.g., exchanges that benefit another), status or authority ranking (e.g., exchanges based on formal or informal position), and market (e.g., exchanges based on market value).

TYPES OF RESOURCES

Exchange resources include worthy possessions or capabilities. Thus, exchange resources are thought of as potential benefits to the other party. The most common typology divides these benefits into two types: financial and material benefits and socioemotional benefits. Financial and material benefits have economic or direct pecuniary value (e.g., wages, access to company vehicles). Socioemotional benefits hold symbolic value and convey standing or dignity to the recipient (e.g., friendliness, loyalty, invitations to lunch).

Both sets of resources are important, though in some cultures, they are not exchanged by the same rules. For example, American managers prefer to assign financial and material benefits based on performance, whereas socioemotional benefits tend to be assigned equally. An interesting feature of these two types of resources is that successful exchanges of one may lead individuals to exchange the other. Specifically, many workplace relationships begin with simple transactions for financial and material goods (e.g., pay for work). Over time, the involved individuals may build trust by exchanging socioemotional benefits, which builds closer interpersonal attachments.

INTERPERSONAL RELATIONSHIPS

One of the most popular components of social exchange theory used by management scientists involves the importance of workplace relationships. Accordingly, social exchanges provide for the development of interpersonal connections, referred to as *social exchange relationships*. This research tradition can be traced primarily to the seminar work of Gary Blau. According to Blau, individuals engage in two different types of exchange relationships: economic exchange and social exchange.

Economic exchange relationships are quid pro quo arrangements that emphasize short-term financial and material benefits. The benefits exchanged are clearly specified and bound by contractual obligations. In contrast, social exchange relationships are open-ended and mutually beneficial. The benefits exchanged in social exchange relations are generally socioemotional in nature. As a result, social exchange relations involve stronger emotional ties between participants. According to Blau, money is only one motivator of effective work behavior. When workers are in social exchange relationships, they tend to have more positive work attitudes and engage in more positive behaviors.

Because social exchange relations involve unspecified exchanges, people in these relationships do not know whether the other party will reciprocate in the long run. Therefore, social exchange relations may initially involve vulnerability and risk. Understandably, this means that social exchange relations are far more risky than economic exchange relations and, as a result, social exchange relations involve a certain level of trust. Mutual, balanced, and beneficial exchanges ultimately enhance trust and build loyalty and commitment among the parties involved. Employers that engender trust are seen as not taking advantage of their employees and caring about their employees; employees who feel their employers take care of them reciprocate by way of positive consequences. In this way, only social exchange relationships create enduring social patterns; economic exchange relations do not.

Indeed, much research has demonstrated the benefits of social exchange relationships. For example, researchers have found that high-quality social exchanges generate higher levels of performance and even encourage employees to perform above and beyond their formal job tasks (e.g., staying late hours, helping others, improving knowledge and skills to help the organization), called *organizational citizenship behaviors* (OCBs). Furthermore, high-quality social exchanges heighten feelings of organizational commitment (or close membership to the organization). These positive attitudes yield beneficial outcomes for organizations, such as higher levels of performance, OCB, and job satisfaction and lower levels of turnover.

Research suggests that employees may form social exchange relationships with their direct supervisor (e.g., leader–member exchange relationship), their work teams (e.g., team support), or their employing organization as a whole (e.g., organizational support). Consistent with the principle of reciprocity, individuals tend to tailor their behavior to benefit the entity with which they have a social exchange relationship. For example, those with close ties to their immediate supervisor tend to target their OCBs so as to benefit that supervisor (e.g., voluntarily assisting the supervisor until late hours), whereas those with close ties to their employing organization direct OCBs so as to benefit the firm as a whole (e.g., promoting the organization to outsiders). Research has produced similar results in terms of social exchange benefits within work teams.

CONCLUSION

Social exchange theory has become one of the most influential paradigms for understanding the nature of human interaction. Within organizational science alone, social exchange theory has been integrated into theories of organizational justice, psychological contracts, commitment, OCB, support, leader–member exchange, and networks. In this way, social exchange theory provides a powerful framework for understanding workplace exchanges and relationships. Its explanatory value relies on the basic tenet that social exchanges comprise actions that are contingent on the rewarding reactions of others. Implied is a mutual process whereby transactions or exchanges may foster quality relationships. In sum, social exchanges create interlocking status duties that ultimately initiate, maintain, and stabilize social behaviors both within and outside organizations.

—*Russell Cropanzano and Marie S. Mitchell*

See also Contextual Performance/Prosocial Behavior/Organizational Citizenship Behavior

FURTHER READING

Blau, P. M. (1964). *Exchange and power in social life.* New York: Wiley.

Coyle-Shapiro, J. A. M., & Conway, N. (2004). The employment relationship through the lens of social exchange theory. In J. Coyle-Shapiro, L. M. Shore, M. S. Taylor, & L. E. Tetrick (Eds.), *The employment relationship: Examining psychological and contextual perspectives* (pp. 5–28). New York: Oxford University Press.

Gouldner, A. W. (1960). The norm of reciprocity: A preliminary statement. *American Sociological Review, 25,* 161–178.

Molm, L. D. (2003). Theoretical comparisons of forms of exchange. *Sociological Theory, 21,* 1–17.

Shore, L. M., Tetrick, L. E., Taylor, M. S., Coyle-Shapiro, J. A. M., Liden, R. C., McClean Parks, J., Wolfe Morrison, E., Porter, L. W., Robinson, S. L., Roehling, M. V., Rousseau, D. M., Schalk, R., Tsui, A. S., & Van Dyne, L. (2004). The employee-organization relationship: A timely concept in a period of transition. In J. J. Martocchio (Ed.), *Research in personnel and human resources management* (Vol. 23, pp. 291–370). Amsterdam: Elsevier.

SOCIAL LOAFING

Many tasks at work are designed to be performed by a group of employees, with the expectation that groups are more efficient and effective than individuals. Yet group performance is not always synonymous with great performance. One reason is that some group members do not work as hard as they should. In these cases, *social loafing* or *free riding* is said to occur.

Although a number of definitions of social loafing are available, the one proposed by Steven Karau and Kipling Williams is arguably the most complete. These authors define social loafing as the reduction in motivation and effort that occurs when individuals work on a collective task as opposed to coactive or individual tasks. Collective tasks are those that most people would intuitively call a *group task*. In collective conditions, individuals work with other group members toward a single goal. Thus, individual performance is pooled to produce the group's total performance. Conversely, individuals working in coactive conditions work in the presence of others, but each individual's work remains separate from that of others at all times. People working individually do not work in the presence of others, and their work remains separate from that of others.

Free riding is similar to social loafing, and the terms are often used interchangeably. The term *free riding* is often employed by sociology and economics scholars, whereas psychology and management scholars tend to employ *social loafing* to refer to the tendency to withhold effort in group work. The main distinction between these two constructs is the amount of effort withheld, as well as the existence of a group benefit or reward that cannot be denied to any group member (e.g., all qualifying employees are entitled to health benefits regardless of whether they were involved in negotiating the insurance plan). Thus, free riding involves withholding all effort because one can reap the benefits regardless of one's contribution to the group. Conversely, social loafing involves withholding some (but not all) effort toward the group output; the existence of a public reward has not typically been studied.

Early research on social loafing primarily explored physical tasks (e.g., rope pulling or shouting). Recent research has replicated the basic social loafing effect with evaluative (e.g., rating the quality of writing samples), vigilance (e.g., detecting random signals on a computer screen), creative (e.g., brainstorming or thought listing), and work-related (e.g., completing an in-basket exercise) tasks. In addition, social loafing has been found to occur in both laboratory and field research (including some research conducted in organizations), though the effect size tends to be larger for laboratory studies. The substantial evidence accumulated since the publication of the first modern study on social loafing in 1974 makes it a topic of great interest to both scientists and practitioners—though interestingly, social loafing had already been demonstrated almost a century earlier by Max Ringelmann.

CONSEQUENCES OF SOCIAL LOAFING

Social loafing is detrimental to group performance and costly to organizations. However, there are also less apparent consequences to social loafing. When individuals are aware that a capable coworker is loafing, they will often respond by reducing their own task-related effort to avoid being taken advantage of (an occurrence termed *retributive loafing*). However, in some situations, coworkers might increase their own efforts to compensate for loafing. When group members are aware that the coworker in question does not possess the abilities required for adequate task performance, group members will typically maintain high effort and motivation. Similarly, when the task is meaningful to them, nonloafers will work harder to compensate for a loafer's poor performance (a phenomenon called *social compensation*). Still, compensating for an underperforming or unskilled group member causes a disproportionate increase in the nonloafers' workload. In time, this increased workload may be detrimental to their own task performance and may strain interpersonal relationships.

REDUCING SOCIAL LOAFING

Initially, social loafing was presumed to occur because of the coordination problems that often characterize groups. However, research has clearly shown that social loafing is a question of motivation and effort. Given the negative consequences of social loafing, it is not surprising that substantial research has focused on identifying the conditions under which individuals working in collective group settings are less likely to loaf.

Ringelmann first observed that as group size increases, social loafing also increases. This finding is consistent with social impact theory, an early explanation for social loafing, which proposes that individuals are sources or targets of social influence (e.g., when a supervisor urges individuals to work hard). Collective conditions allow for social influence to be diluted across individuals, whereas individual or coactive conditions do not. The relationship between group size and loafing is not linear: Above a certain group size, the addition of members has little influence on loafing.

Loafing is more pronounced when individual performance can be identified or evaluated, either by other group members or by a person in a supervisory position (e.g., a boss or experimenter). Thus, individuals are less likely to loaf when they perceive their efforts or productivity to be highly visible to others. In addition, regardless of whether others can evaluate individual contributions to group performance, simply allowing group members to evaluate their own input (e.g., through the provision of individual or group-level standards) reduces social loafing. The *evaluation potential* or *identifiability model* proposes that loafing occurs because collective situations diminish the possibility that individuals' effort and performance will be clearly distinguishable from their coworkers' effort and performance. Thus, it is difficult for individuals to be punished for poor performance or rewarded for good performance.

Social loafing is less likely to occur in collective tasks that are highly valued, meaningful, or personally involving. Recall that working on meaningful tasks can even prompt group members to compensate for lost productivity resulting from loafing. In addition, intrinsic involvement in a work task moderates the relationship between employees' perceptions that their on-the-job efforts are visible to supervisors and the likelihood that they will loaf, such that this relationship is stronger when intrinsic involvement is low. Individuals' propensities to engage in social loafing are also lower when group members are working on a difficult or complex task compared to a simple task. Finally, social loafing is less likely to occur when each group member has the opportunity to make a unique contribution to the group outcome compared to tasks in which group members make redundant contributions. Thus, loafing is likely to occur when effort is perceived to be dispensable.

Other notable findings show that loafing is less likely if group members perceive that their individual efforts will lead to individual performance, individual effort will lead to group performance, and group performance will lead to group outcomes. In addition, social loafing is less likely to occur when group cohesiveness is high compared to when it is low and when group members are friends rather than strangers. Finally, organizational field studies show that the presence of rewards that are contingent on good performance is negatively associated with social loafing, whereas the presence of noncontingent punishment is positively related to loafing. This research suggests that social loafing is negatively correlated with perceived altruism in the group and affective organizational commitment and positively correlated with role ambiguity.

COLLECTIVE EFFORT MODEL

Although many social loafing models (e.g., social impact, evaluation potential, dispensability of effort) have been proposed, none are truly integrative models, and none accounts for more than a few conditions in which loafing is reduced. To fill this theoretical gap, Karau and Williams developed the *collective effort model* (CEM). The CEM proposes that social loafing is best understood by combining the motivational principles of the expectancy theory of work motivation with principles drawn from self-evaluation theory. The central tenet of the CEM is that individual motivation and effort in collective contexts will be unaffected provided that a number of contingencies are satisfied.

Following expectancy theory, individuals need to feel that their effort leads to individual performance. For example, employees are unlikely to be motivated if they believe they will be unable to reach satisfactory performance regardless of the effort exerted. Additionally, individual performance must lead to group performance. In collective settings, individuals are unlikely to be motivated to exert effort if their individual effort does not help the group to attain high performance (e.g., if individual effort is redundant with others' work). Next, motivation will be sustained if group performance is directly related to group outcomes, which must, in turn, be related to individual outcomes. The CEM proposes that group outcomes can take the form of group evaluation, group cohesiveness, or extrinsic rewards. Similarly, individual outcomes can take the form of self-evaluation, feelings of belongingness to the group, intrinsic rewards, and extrinsic rewards. Finally, motivation and effort are sustained when outcomes are valued. Drawing on self-evaluation theory, the CEM proposes that outcomes are most likely to be valued if tasks are important and meaningful to the individual and the rewards are meaningful. Furthermore, some individual differences, such as culture or gender, increase the valence of some outcomes. In sum, extensive empirical and theoretical work indicates that not all collective settings necessarily give rise to social loafing.

—*Silvia Bonaccio*

See also Expectancy Theory of Work Motivation; Group Dynamics and Processes; Groups

FURTHER READING

George, J. M. (1995). Asymmetrical effects of rewards and punishments: The case of social loafing. *Journal of Occupational and Organizational Psychology, 68,* 327–338.

Ingham, A. G., Levinger, G., Graves, J., & Peckham, V. (1974). The Ringelmann effect: Studies of group size and group performance. *Journal of Experimental Social Psychology, 10,* 371–384.

Karau, S. J., & Hart, J. W. (1998). Group cohesiveness and social loafing: Effects of a social interaction manipulation on individual motivation within groups. *Group Dynamics: Theory, Research, and Practice, 2,* 185–191.

Karau, S. J., & Williams, K. D. (1993). Social loafing: A meta-analytic review and theoretical integration. *Journal of Personality and Social Psychology, 65,* 681–706.

Karau, S. J., & Williams, K. D. (1995). Social loafing: Research findings, implications, and future directions. *Current Directions in Psychological Science, 4,* 134–140.

Shepperd, J. A., & Taylor, K. M. (1999). Social loafing and expectancy-value theory. *Personality and Social Psychology Bulletin, 25,* 1147–1158.

SOCIAL NORMS AND CONFORMITY

Social norms are implicit and explicit rules of behavior that develop through interactions among members of a given group or society. Essentially, norms are prescriptions for how people should act in particular situations. All groups have established norms that tell members what they should and should not do under certain circumstances. When agreed to and accepted by the group, norms act as a means of influencing the behavior of group members with a minimum of external control. Group members desire acceptance by the group, and because of this desire, they are susceptible to conforming to group norms. There is ample research evidence that groups can place strong pressures on individual members to change their attitudes and behaviors to conform to the group's standard.

Because the workplace context is social and requires interpersonal interaction, work behavior is affected by shared social norms. Formalized norms are written up in organizational manuals that set out rules and procedures for employees to follow, but by far, most norms in organizations are informal. Norms in organizations cover a wide variety of circumstances; however, there are certain classes of norms that seem to crop up in most organizations and affect the behavior of members. Some of the most common organizational norms include the following:

- Dress norms: Social norms frequently dictate the kind of clothing people wear to work
- Reward-allocation norms: Norms that dictate how rewards such as pay, promotions, and informal favors are allocated in organizations
- Performance norms: The performance of organizational members might be as much a function of social expectations as it is of inherent ability, personal motivation, and technology

Individuals are members of many groups in domains such as family, friendship, work, and community, and each overlapping group has norms that may be similar or different. Some or all of these norms may influence an individual's behavior, and some norms apply to essentially everyone, whereas others apply only to certain members within a specific context. For example, norms against incest and cannibalism are widely held in nearly all cultures. Other norms, such as those regulating greetings and nonverbal behavior, vary among cultures or even within cultural subgroups. The norms that are salient at any particular time vary as a function of group and setting, and social norms become more salient when the situation calls attention to group membership.

Individuals obey social norms for several reasons. First, compliance is the simplest, most direct motive for conformity to group norms. It occurs because members wish to acquire rewards from the group and avoid punishment. Compliance is characterized by a change in observable behavior to match the social norm while maintaining a private lack of acceptance of the norm itself. Second, identification occurs when individuals conform because they find other supporters of the norm attractive. Identification as a motive for conformity is often revealed by an imitation process in which established members serve as models for the behavior of others. For example, a newly promoted executive might attempt to dress and talk like her successful, admired boss. Third, individuals may conform to a norm because they have truly and wholly accepted the beliefs, values, and attitudes that underlie it. Conformity occurs because the norm is seen as right, not because it achieves rewards, avoids punishment, or pleases others. That is, conformity is the result of internal rather than external forces.

TYPES OF NORMS

Descriptive and injunctive norms function at the group level of analysis, whereas subjective and personal norms operate at the individual level of analysis.

Descriptive norms are concerned with what individuals actually do and develop from watching the actions of other group members in certain situations. The more that target group members behave similarly in a given situation, the more the observer will tend to view their behavior as appropriate. When individual group members believe that the group supports a certain behavior, they are more likely to exhibit this behavior themselves.

Injunctive norms refer to attitudes toward certain behavior or what individuals feel is "right" based on morals or beliefs. They are specific guidelines about behavior in certain situations (i.e., reciprocity norms) and develop through normative influence or when group members conform to receive social approval. Rather than describing appropriate and inappropriate behavior, injunctive norms prescribe it.

Subjective norms are group members' perceptions about what important and influential individuals (e.g., leaders) think about a certain behavior. Thus, they are subjective in the sense that there are variations between individuals as to who is considered important. The *theory of reasoned action* suggests that the main influence on individual intentions is subjective norms. This may be one reason it is common practice for people to consult others before making decisions.

Rather than treating norms as a defining workplace characteristic (i.e., a shared moral understanding among members of the organization), *personal norms* allow the recognition that individuals in the same workplace may vary in their expectations. Personal norms are located within the self. For example, someone may have a long-held belief that it is important to help others, and thus his or her behavior reflects a personal norm to behave altruistically. Personal norms are generally less affected by social context, although some have argued that they may be influenced by group norms.

NORM FORMATION

Norms are more likely to be established when they facilitate group survival and task accomplishment. Moreover, insofar as the perceptual, emotional, and cognitive dispositions responsible for adherence to norms are innate, compliance with social norms must be beneficial to human adaptation. Norms can be beneficial because they (a) keep the group intact and protect the group by punishing behaviors that threaten the group; (b) provide regularity and predictability to the behaviors expected of group members, thereby helping group members predict and anticipate the actions of peers; (c) help the group avoid embarrassing interpersonal problems and ensure that no group member's self-image is damaged; and (d) express the central values of the group and clarify what is distinctive about its identity.

Some norms are actively transmitted (e.g., explicit statements and rituals), whereas others are passively transmitted (e.g., nonverbal behaviors and imitation). Norms, if they are written down, become formal rules of proper conduct, but in most instances, norms are adopted implicitly as people align their behavior until consensus in action emerges. Muzafer Sherif's classic analysis of this process suggests that this gradual alignment of action reflects the development of frames of reference for behaviors. Upon forming a group, individuals rapidly structure their experiences until they conform to a general standard. Individuals may not actively try to conform to the judgments of others, but instead they use the group consensus to revise their opinions and beliefs.

Norm formation involves consensus formation and group decision making. *Social influence network theory* suggests that norms are formed through a process of interpersonal influence in which members' attitudes toward an issue change as they revise weighted averages of the influential positions of other members. Leaders may influence the discussion that is a part of norm formation because they are likely to direct other team members' activities and influence subordinate behavior to facilitate goal achievement. Moreover, leaders often direct the discussion process or serve an integrative function within the group.

The process of *socialization* explains how established norms become institutionalized. Even though the individuals who originally fostered the norms are no longer present, their normative innovations remain a part of the organization's traditions. When new employees discover and learn their organization's standards and expectations, they are experiencing socialization. In most instances, it is the individual who assimilates the group's norms, values, and perspectives. At times, however, socialization can generate changes in norms as the group accommodates to fit the newcomer's needs. Sometimes a staunch, unyielding individual can shift the group's norms, provided he or she maintains the appearance of consistency and objectivity.

Once established, norms give rise to obligations, which form the basis of each person's agreement with his or her peers. However, because norms are often informal and emerge naturally in groups, they may not support the larger strategic goals of the group. By debating and establishing formal norms, some groups are better able to proactively determine behaviors that are tailored to their needs. The negotiation of common expectations about how each group member should behave represents a proactive stance toward dealing with group problems and may contribute to overall group performance.

ABERRANT BEHAVIOR

Upon being assigned to a group, people appear automatically to think of that group as better for them than any alternative group. This can lead to increased attraction of in-group members and devaluation and possible mistreatment of out-group members. According to social identity theorists, a common normative belief in most social groups is that their group is desirable and members are superior to nonmembers. This belief occurs because groups are motivated to keep a positive self-image. This self-image consists of both a personal identity and a social identity, and any action or thought that elevates a social identity tends to elevate self-image.

Research suggests that norm misperceptions can occur, and misperceptions predict behavior. A meta-analysis of 23 studies of norm misperceptions (described as *self–other differences*) found that misperceptions of injunctive norms were greater than misperceptions of descriptive norms. The meta-analysis reported that misperceptions were greater as social distance increased, whereas the influence on the behavior of closer or more salient social groups was stronger.

A norm often becomes salient to interactions only after it is violated. If normative behavior is defined as the typical choice that others would make in a given context, then counternormative behavior or deviance is *not* the typical choice that others would make. A person may deviate in desirable ways (e.g., display extrarole behavior) or in undesirable ways, and thus deviance may bring either praise or criticism.

By conforming to group norms, idiosyncrasy credits can be earned, and if enough idiosyncrasy credits are earned, the person can, on occasion, breach norms (deviate in undesirable ways) without retribution from the group. Individuals who breach norms but cannot provide an acceptable explanation for their violation are often evaluated negatively and may experience peer aggression, violence, and lesser forms of mistreatment.

Often, punishments for not complying with norms come from social networks as opposed to formal systems established by the organization. Not everyone who breaches a norm receives the same punishment; peer reaction depends on the magnitude of the discrepancy, the importance of the norm, and the characteristics of the person violating the norm. Not conforming to social norms and values is likely to make followers quickly perceive a leader as incompetent and not deserving of that position, regardless of his or her personal achievements. On the other hand, for most individuals, small breaches that reflect personal idiosyncrasies, if kept private, will likely be overlooked.

Individuals may obey norms to fulfill their own expectations about proper behavior. Individuals often feel duty bound to adhere to norms because, as responsible members of the group, they accept the legitimacy of the established norms and recognize the importance of supporting these norms. Individuals who breach norms that they accept may experience a range of negative emotional consequences, such as extreme self-consciousness, embarrassment, guilt, and shame.

The consequences of norm breaches vary by context. For example, cultures that are high in uncertainty avoidance tend to be intolerant of ambiguity and thus likely to be distrustful of new ideas or behaviors. They stick dogmatically to norms, which, in the extreme, become inviolable to reduce uncertainty. Breaches upset uncertainty-reducing activity, so organizations in these cultures may adopt structural formalization and centralization, thus reducing the degree of sharing of important information and decision making with subordinates. In contrast, people from low-uncertainty-avoidance societies are more tolerant of deviations from social norms.

SUMMARY

Norms simplify behavioral choices, provide direction and motivation, and organize social interactions. Most people attend to cues that convey information about social norms and try to comply with norms they believe are in force and feel distress if they act out of compliance. In general, the more consequential the norm, the swifter the social response if it is breached.

—*Simon Taggar and Heather MacDonald*

FURTHER READING

Ajzen, I., & Fishbein, M. (1980). *Understanding attitudes and predicting social behavior.* Englewood Cliffs, NJ: Prentice Hall.

Axelrod, R. (1986). An evolutionary approach to norms. *American Political Science Review, 80,* 1095–1111.

Elster, J. (1989). *The cement of society: A study of social order.* Cambridge, UK: Cambridge University Press.

Forsyth, D. R. (1990). *Group dynamics.* Pacific Grove, CA: Brooks/Cole.

Johns, G., & Saks, A. M. (2005). *Organizational behaviour: Understanding and managing life at work* (6th ed., pp. 204–236). Toronto: Pearson/Prentice Hall.

Lodzinski, A., Motomura, M. S., & Schneider, F. W. (2005). Intervention and evaluation. In F. Schneider, J. Gruman, & L. Coutts (Eds.), *Applied social psychology: Understanding and addressing social and practical problems* (pp. 55–72). Thousand Oaks, CA: Sage.

Moreland, R. L., & Levine, J. M. (1982). Socialization in small groups: Temporal changes in individual-group relations. In L. Berkowitz (Ed.), *Advances in experimental social psychology* (Vol. 15, pp. 137–192). New York: Academic Press.

Sherif, M. (1936). *The psychology of social norms.* New York: Harper & Row.

SOCIAL SUPPORT

Workplace *social support* refers to the availability or actual receipt of assistance provided to an employee by one or more individuals. It is generally examined as a means of coping with occupational stress. An important distinction concerns the sources of social support. Support may be provided by individuals within the organization—for example, supervisors, subordinates, coworkers, or even customers—or by individuals outside the organization, such as family or friends. Research shows that social support provided by individuals within the organization, particularly support provided by supervisors, has the greatest implications for employee well-being.

Another important distinction delineates *structural support* and *functional support.* Structural support refers to the size of an individual's social network, whereas functional support refers to whether the individuals in a person's social network actually provide helpful behaviors. Empirical evidence suggests that structural support and functional support are relatively independent. Thus, having a large social network does not guarantee that one will actually receive support in times of trouble. Furthermore, individuals may receive adequate support even if they have relatively small social networks. This might happen, for example, when a person receives high levels of support from one or two individuals.

Functional support can be further divided into *instrumental support* (i.e., tangible support) and *emotional support.* Instrumental social support involves the receipt of concrete assistance from others. An office employee who helps an overworked coworker clean her office, for example, is providing instrumental social support. Emotional social support, on the other hand, involves showing sympathy and concern for others. Whereas instrumental support usually involves doing, emotional support often involves listening and talking. An employee who listens and gives encouragement to a coworker who is in danger of being fired, for example, is providing emotional social support.

Although instrumental and emotional social support are related to each other, empirical evidence supports the distinction between them. Furthermore, the two forms of support may have different effects. Some research suggests that emotional support is more strongly related to employee well-being than instrumental support.

Research further distinguishes between different forms of emotional social support. Terry A. Beehr and his colleagues, for example, identified three types of conversations that people might have at work, each representing a different form of emotional support:

- Conversations about positive aspects of the workplace (e.g., talking about how one's supervisor is a great leader)
- Conversations about negative aspects of the workplace (e.g., talking about how poorly one is paid)
- Conversations about non-work-related events and activities (e.g., talking about how one spent last weekend)

Of these three forms of emotional social support, conversations about the negative aspects of work are most unlike other kinds of support. Indeed, even though people commiserating with each other and agreeing that the situation is bad is a logical form of support, research suggests that this type of support does not have the favorable effects associated with other forms of support.

DISTINCTION BETWEEN SOCIAL SUPPORT AND SIMILAR CONSTRUCTS

Social support has some resemblance to other variables that are of interest to industrial and organizational psychologists. Organizational citizenship behaviors (OCBs), employee friendship, and leader consideration all have some conceptual overlap with social support. For example, OCBs represent prosocial workplace behaviors that involve going above and beyond the responsibilities of one's official job description to help the organization or its members.

Talking favorably about one's employer to organizational outsiders or helping a coworker who has a heavy workload are both examples of OCBs. The first example is an OCB that is directed at assisting the organization, whereas the second example is an OCB that is directed at assisting an individual employee. Because it involves providing assistance to a particular individual, the latter is similar to social support. Important distinctions, however, exist between social support and OCBs. On one hand, OCBs are generally studied from the perspective of the individual performing the behavior. For example, a focal person is asked to report how often he or she personally performs OCBs, or the focal person's supervisor is asked to report the frequency of such behavior. On the other

hand, social support research also measures the extent to which the target individual is a recipient of helpful behaviors from others. Thus, much more is known about recipients' perceptions of social support given than is known about the givers of social support. Another important difference between social support and OCBs is that OCBs are typically regarded as a form of job performance, whereas social support is not considered an aspect of job performance.

Friendship among coworkers, which has attracted some attention from industrial and organizational psychologists, has some conceptual similarity to social support. Whereas friendship implies a helpful relationship between two or more people at work that develops over time, social support can represent a onetime helpful behavior performed by a stranger. It is likely that almost all friends provide social support, but not all individuals who provide social support are necessarily friends. A customer who helps a waiter clean up a spilled drink, for example, is providing instrumental social support but probably not friendship.

Leader consideration is another variable that is conceptually similar to social support. Consideration is the extent to which a leader displays concern for subordinates' well-being and shows appreciation for their efforts. Whereas social support can be provided by anyone within or outside the organization, leader consideration is necessarily a quality of the behavior performed by a supervisor. Thus, some of the behaviors described as consideration are unique to individuals in leadership positions and are not likely to be performed by nonleaders.

ANTECEDENTS OF SOCIAL SUPPORT

Because social support can prove useful as a treatment for occupational stress, it is important to understand the factors that contribute to the amount of social support one receives. Once the factors contributing to social support are understood, organizations will be in a better position to develop interventions to increase support among organizational members. Despite the attention social support has received in the literature, researchers have only recently examined the antecedents of social support. For example, research suggests that reciprocity plays an important role in determining the amount of social support one receives. Specifically, employees are likely to receive the most social support when they give social support to others.

CONSEQUENCES OF SOCIAL SUPPORT

Much more attention has been paid to the effects of social support than to its causes. This research has primarily examined the effects of social support on stressors and strains, as well as the moderating effects of social support on the stressor–strain relationship. Workplace stressors are aspects of the work environment that require an adaptive response on the part of the employee and have the potential to cause ill health. Examples of workplace stressors include having a heavy workload, being exposed to abusive customers, and having to work on tasks that are highly repetitive. Strains, on the other hand, are the negative health consequences produced by stressors, such as depression, anxiety, and physical illness.

Social support is related to both stressors and strains. For example, one recent meta-analysis found that social support is negatively associated with several forms of workplace stressors, such as role ambiguity (having unclear work responsibilities), role conflict (having multiple work responsibilities that interfere with each other), and underutilization of skills. The same meta-analysis found that social support is negatively associated with a number of strains, such as poor mental and physical health, life dissatisfaction, and burnout. In sum, those who report high levels of social support generally report relatively fewer workplace stressors and better mental and physical health.

Much of the attention given to social support has focused on the *buffering effect* (i.e., moderating effect) of social support. Indeed, many researchers agree that the buffering effect is the most important hypothesis about social support. The buffering effect occurs when the relationship between stressors and strains is weaker for individuals who receive high levels of social support than for individuals who receive little or no social support. The following are two examples of the buffering effect:

- The amount of workload one has is strongly associated with anxiety for individuals who receive little social support, but it is only weakly related to anxiety for individuals who receive a great deal of social support.
- Being abused by a supervisor produces serious physical health symptoms for individuals who are low in social support, whereas abuse by a supervisor produces little or no physical health symptoms for individuals who are high in social support.

However, most studies have failed to support the buffering effect. If fact, evidence for the buffering effect is so inconsistent that many current researchers prefer to conduct exploratory analyses regarding the moderating effects of social support rather than actually hypothesize the buffering effect. Perhaps the most common finding is that social support has no effect on the relationship between stressors and strains. In other words, the magnitude of the relationship between stressors and strains is similar regardless of the amount of social support one receives.

Some studies have even found evidence of a *reverse buffering effect,* which occurs when the stressor–strain relationship is stronger rather than weaker for individuals who receive high levels of social support compared to individuals who receive little social support. The reverse buffering effect is counterintuitive, and little evidence exists to explain when and why it might occur. One possibility is that some forms of social support (e.g., conversations about the positive aspects of work) may produce the buffering effect, whereas other forms of support (e.g., conversations about negative aspects of work) may produce the reverse buffering effect. Another possibility is that social support produces a buffering effect only when the social support and the stressor come from different sources. Support from coworkers but not from supervisors, for example, may buffer the relationships between workload (a stressor presumably caused by the supervisor) and strains.

On the other hand, a reverse buffering effect may occur when social support and stressors come from the same source. This may occur because it is distressful to interact with the source of stressors even when that source is providing support. Another possibility is that under some conditions, people feel uneasy when they must consistently depend on the support of others, and this uneasiness may exacerbate the negative effects of stressors.

ORGANIZATIONAL SUPPORT

So far, support provided by particular individuals, such as supervisors or coworkers, has been discussed. In addition to the supportive behavior of individuals, employees generally develop perceptions about whether their employing *organization* is supportive or unsupportive. Organizational support represents the extent to which employees perceive that their employing organization cares about their personal welfare, values their contributions, and is committed to them. Unlike social support, organizational support represents a global perception of one's organization rather than a perception of particular individuals.

ANTECEDENTS OF ORGANIZATIONAL SUPPORT

Social support provided by one's supervisor is one possible antecedent of organizational support. Immediate supervisors are the organizational representatives whom employees have the most direct exposure to; thus, employees are likely to infer organizational support based on the support provided by their supervisor. The favorability of one's working conditions is also likely to contribute to employee perceptions of organizational support. Both intrinsic job conditions (e.g., having work tasks that are stimulating) and extrinsic job conditions (e.g., availability of promotions) likely affect perceived organizational support, as do workplace stressors (e.g., role ambiguity and conflict).

CONSEQUENCES OF ORGANIZATIONAL SUPPORT

Research suggests that when employees perceive that their organization supports them, they will reciprocate by showing support for the organization. When employees perceive that their organization is supportive, for example, they will generally feel indebted to the organization and manifest attitudes and behaviors that express their gratitude toward the organization.

Organizational support has been examined as a predictor of several employee attitudes and behaviors. Job satisfaction, organizational commitment, job involvement, attitude toward management, and turnover intention, for example, are all attitudes that may be influenced by organizational support. Behaviors related to organizational support include job performance and organizational citizenship behaviors. Like social support, organizational support has been examined as a predictor of employee strains. Organizational support, for example, is negatively associated with burnout, fatigue, job tension, and somatic symptoms.

—*Nathan A. Bowling*

AUTHOR'S NOTE: The author wishes to thank Terry A. Beehr for his helpful suggestions concerning earlier versions of this entry.

See also Interpersonal Communication; Occupational Health Psychology

FURTHER READING

Beehr, T. A. (1995). *Psychological stress in the workplace.* London: Routledge.

Bowling, N. A., Beehr, T. A., & Swader, W. M. (2005). Giving and receiving social support at work: The roles of personality and reciprocity. *Journal of Vocational Behavior, 67,* 476–489.

Cohen, S., & Wills, T. A. (1985). Stress, social support, and the buffering hypothesis. *Psychological Bulletin, 98,* 310–357.

Eisenberger, R., Huntington, R., Hutchison, S., & Sowa, D. (1986). Perceived organizational support. *Journal of Applied Psychology, 71,* 500–507.

Visweswaran, C., Sanchez, J. I., & Fisher, J. (1999). The role of social support in the process of work stress: A meta-analysis. *Journal of Vocational Behavior, 54,* 314–334.

SOCIALIZATION

See Organizational Socialization

SOCIALIZATION: EMPLOYEE PROACTIVE BEHAVIORS

An employee starting a new job is confronted by the challenge of adapting to a new organizational culture and a new social setting. These roles carry many expectations for appropriate behavior. Information about how to behave is encoded in a sometimes bewildering array of contextually bound communications. To facilitate the transmission of this cultural information to organizational newcomers, most organizations invest a great deal of effort in the creation of orientation programs. There are, however, limits to what an organization can do. Effect sizes for most of the relationships between organizational socialization efforts and newcomer adjustment are small or modest. After years of studying organizational tactics, researchers began to recognize the omission of the newcomer's own agency in most socialization models.

There are many reasons why organization-level socialization may not be especially effective without newcomer effort in the process. Although organizations may provide a great deal of cultural information, if newcomers discount or ignore this information, it will not affect their behavior. Organizational orientation sessions for many workers do not include job information because task demands are likely to be too specific to be covered on an organization-wide basis. Moreover, for many newcomers, learning how to fit in socially requires developing one-on-one relationships with coworkers. Even if coworkers and supervisors are available to newcomers, these established organizational members may no longer understand what it is like to be a new entrant. They may, therefore, neglect to provide critical information without prompting from the newcomer. In other words, newcomers need to get involved in the process of learning. The most important contribution of the proactive concept of newcomer entry is the examination of an *active* process of adjustment.

To facilitate an understanding of how newcomers proactively influence their own organizational adjustment, three major questions must be answered: (a) What proactive behaviors are newcomers most likely to engage in? (b) What makes a newcomer more or less likely to engage in certain proactive behaviors? (c) What is the relationship between newcomer proactivity and the social environment at work? A standard taxonomy for considering proactive socialization considers the strategy used to find information (e.g., actively searching, asking questions, or passively observing), the target of the action (e.g., supervisors or coworkers), and the type of information being sought (e.g., organizational values, social information, or performance feedback). A comprehensive examination of proactive socialization should take all of these factors into account.

NEWCOMER PROACTIVE BEHAVIOR

One of the most important activities for newcomers is actively seeking information from knowledgeable coworkers about task procedures. This might range from simply asking for guidance on how to complete procedures to more detailed questions regarding the relative importance of tasks. Newcomers may be reluctant to directly ask coworkers how to complete tasks, and so they may prefer to actively observe coworkers as they perform task-related behaviors and then copy these models. Finally, policy and procedure manuals can be an additional source of information.

Besides learning about work tasks, newcomers engage in other forms of proactive socialization related to the social environment. Social acceptance may be facilitated by organizational newcomers directly asking role incumbents about work group norms and acceptable behavior. Newcomers can also engage in relationship building by initiating conversations and participating in social activities with coworkers. Newcomers also seek information about the authority and reward structure of their new organization.

Not all proactive newcomer behavior relates to fitting in to an established role. Some research suggests that newcomers who are especially confident and have a strong desire for control will actively negotiate job tasks and redesign their work. For organizations that are engaged in highly competitive fields, such changes are crucial for enhancing innovation and avoiding stagnation. This process of role innovation can be encouraged by organizational efforts to engage in investiture socialization, whereby a newcomer is given positive messages regarding his or her unique worth and resources to facilitate new methods of work. Role innovation of this nature requires the newcomer to be willing to risk changing expectations and challenging social conventions in the workplace.

Studies show that proactive newcomer activities are related to superior socialization outcomes such as role clarity, task knowledge, and social integration. Comparison of effect sizes across studies suggests that these proactive activities are at least as important as organizational programs. The general story of adjustment that emerges from repeated measures of organizational newcomers suggests that most newcomers move attitudinally from a state of comparative ignorance of the organization's culture and work demands toward a more stable conception of how they fit in with the job and organization. Individuals who engage in more proactive behaviors appear to be most likely to move quickly to a state of relative adjustment. Those who do not make this progress toward greater commitment over time engage in another form of proactive behavior: They quit. Research demonstrates that turnover rates among newcomers are much higher than turnover rates among established employees.

PERSONALITY AND ADJUSTMENT

To predict proactive socialization, researchers typically examine personality. On a practical level, if personality is a major component of the socialization process, then selection systems should emphasize traits that are necessary for learning how to perform well in a particular job. On a theoretical level, the relationship between proactive behavior and personality may explain why satisfaction levels are consistent for individuals across multiple job changes.

The most important personal characteristics related to newcomer adjustment relate to personal agency. Confident and personally active newcomers are more likely to engage in proactive behaviors because they believe their efforts will succeed. Empirical studies show a positive relationship between self-efficacy and active information seeking, the use of problem-focused coping strategies, and better work adjustment among organizational newcomers. Research also shows that an individual disposition toward proactive behavior (which is closely related to achievement motivation) is an important predictor of a number of important work-related outcomes, including objective career success, task mastery, role clarity, and social integration across a variety of settings. Most of these relationships are mediated through proactive socialization behaviors.

There are relationships between five-factor model personality variables and newcomer adjustment as well. Openness to experience and extroversion are significantly related to positive work outcomes for organizational newcomers and mediated through information acquisition and relationship building. Although studies show strong relationships between work attitudes and personality for conscientiousness and emotional stability, neither of these variables has yet been empirically linked to proactive socialization behaviors in the literature. The extensive debate regarding the importance of emotional stability (i.e., trait negative affectivity) and work attitudes suggests that there is a dispositional tendency toward dissatisfaction and poor adjustment among some individuals, but the behavioral consequences of emotional stability in the adjustment process have not yet been demonstrated.

INTERPERSONAL SOURCES OF SOCIALIZATION

During adjustment, newcomers must build a repertoire of contextually based knowledge to adequately understand how to fit into a new job. Researchers have proposed that interpersonal interactions or "guides" help newcomers understand the context of most organizations. The interpersonal perspective has opened the door for subsequent research investigating symbolic interactionism and other forms of information exchange. Interactions between members of a work group are important in the development of shared meaning and attitudes because newcomers interpret their environment through the lens of their interactions with others. Unlike organizational socialization, these interactions involve the newcomers' reactions to the social environment. The small-group socialization perspective of Richard Moreland and John Levine deemphasizes the organization and focuses on how individuals come to identify with those occupying similar roles. Organizations understand the importance of interpersonal interactions in the socialization process and take steps to enhance these interactions.

Mentoring, whereby a higher-ranking organizational member takes a new employee under his or her wing and provides guidance on how to adapt to an organizational role, is an important source of interpersonal socialization. Supervisory efforts to provide role clarification, social support, and encouragement are conceptually similar to mentoring and have many of the same positive outcomes for organizational newcomers. There is considerable empirical evidence that mentoring and supervisory socialization efforts are associated with significantly higher levels of work role integration and job satisfaction, although effect sizes are modest. Although mentoring is typically conceptualized as a relationship initiated by a higher-ranking member of an organization, employees with higher levels of proactive personality and locus of control are more likely to have mentors. This suggests that either some individuals are selected for mentoring relationships because they are more proactive or that some individuals proactively initiate mentoring relationships.

Studies show that newcomers who actively engage their coworkers are likely to be better adjusted to their new workplaces. Coworkers may be seen by newcomers as having particular expertise in how to behave appropriately because they are in similar roles to newcomers. Coworkers also play an important role in transmitting important information about task completion by providing feedback for processes that cannot be picked up in prior training or education. Coworkers are one of the most significant sources of information regarding knowledge of the work group, and some newcomers report that they are more comfortable seeking social information from peers than from supervisors. Consistent with these observations, research has shown that those who successfully build relationships with coworkers are more satisfied and more committed and report greater intentions to remain.

SUMMARY

The literature on organizational socialization has historically been marked by claims that socialization occurs primarily because of organizational efforts. Research now demonstrates the importance of the newcomer's point of view as an important element in the adjustment process.

—John D. Kammeyer-Mueller

See also Organizational Socialization

FURTHER READING

Chan, D., & Schmitt, N. (2000). Interindividual differences in intraindividual changes in proactivity during organizational entry: A latent growth modeling approach to understanding newcomer adaptation. *Journal of Applied Psychology, 85,* 190–210.

Kammeyer-Mueller, J. D., & Wanberg, C. R. (2003). Unwrapping the organizational entry process: Disentangling multiple antecedents and their pathways to adjustment. *Journal of Applied Psychology, 5,* 779–794.

Miller, V. D., & Jablin, F. M. (1991). Information seeking during organizational entry: Influences, tactics, and a model of the process. *Academy of Management Review, 16,* 92–120.

Moreland, R. L., & Levine, J. M. (2001). Socialization in organizations and work groups. In M. E. Turner (Ed.), *Groups at work: Theory and research* (pp. 69–112). Mahwah, NJ: Lawrence Erlbaum.

Morrison, E. W. (1993). Newcomer information seeking: Exploring types, modes, sources, and outcomes. *Academy of Management Journal, 36,* 557–589.

Saks, A. M., & Ashforth, B. E. (1997). Organizational socialization: Making sense of the past and present as a prologue for the future. *Journal of Vocational Behavior, 51,* 234–279.

SOCIETY FOR INDUSTRIAL AND ORGANIZATIONAL PSYCHOLOGY

The Society for Industrial and Organizational Psychology (SIOP) is the primary professional membership organization for professionals engaged in the application or study of psychology in business, industry, and public service. Although industrial psychologists were involved in applied professional organizations as early as the founding of the American Psychological Association (APA) in 1892, the SIOP in its current form was incorporated as Division 14 of the APA in 1982. The SIOP is also an organizational affiliate of the Association for Psychological Science (APS).

The SIOP is governed by 13 elected members of the Executive Committee, which meets three times per year. The society currently has 10 standing committees that carry out the functions of the SIOP (e.g., awards, job placement, workshops), as well as several ad hoc committees that address issues that are pertinent to the SIOP community.

The SIOP president appoints committee chairs and approves membership in all standing committees. Committee chairs must be fellows or full members of the SIOP, but associate members may serve on committees.

MEMBERSHIP

The SIOP's membership is diverse, with more than 6,500 members representing all 50 states in the United States, as well as 42 countries. There are two main categories of membership: professionals and students. More than 3,700 of the SIOP's members are classified as professionals (more than 2,700 of whom are considered full members), and approximately 2,900 are students.

Professional membership types include member, associate member, international affiliate, and fellow. Applicants for full membership must meet several requirements: First, they must be dues-paying members of the APA, the APS, or the industrial and organizational division of the Canadian Psychological Association. Most of the professional members (more than 80%) are affiliated with the APA, and more than 24% are affiliated with the APS (some are affiliated with both organizations).

Members must have a doctoral degree based on a psychological dissertation awarded by a recognized graduate school, be engaged in study or professional work that is primarily psychological in nature, and be involved in professional activities (research, teaching, or practice) related to the purpose of the SIOP. Associate member applicants must be associate members of the APA or the APS, have completed two years of psychology graduate study or have a master's degree in psychology or a related field, and be engaged in professional or graduate work related to the SIOP's purpose. Undergraduate and graduate students may apply for either student or student international affiliate membership.

The SIOP's membership includes both academics and practitioners, and many members engage in both areas. Currently, approximately 33% of professional members are primarily academics, 29% are primarily consultants, 15% work in industry, and 5% are in the government or military (18% did not indicate their primary employer).

MISSION

The mission of the SIOP is to increase the well-being and performance of workers by supporting the study and practice of industrial and organizational (I/O) psychology. To achieve this mission, the SIOP has several guiding objectives:

- To support SIOP members in the study, application, and teaching of I/O psychology methods and principles
- To provide opportunities to discuss and exchange research findings, information, and perspectives pertaining to the science, practice, and teaching of I/O psychology
- To identify opportunities to advance the field of I/O psychology
- To identify and address challenges in organizational and work settings regarding the understanding and practice of I/O psychology
- To encourage the education and training of current and future I/O psychologists
- To support public awareness of I/O psychology

FUNCTIONS

The SIOP provides a wide variety of services in pursuit of its mission. It offers distinct programs targeted toward its many constituents, including the media, those seeking consultants, job seekers and employers, graduate students or prospective students, and specific groups within the society (e.g., new members, academics, practitioners). Many of these services and functions are detailed on the SIOP's Web site, http://www .siop.org.

The SIOP offers a quarterly publication, the *Industrial-Organizational Psychologist,* which is available free with membership. This journal contains information about current topics that are relevant to SIOP academic and professional members, international affiliates, and student affiliates. Topics include addressing legal issues, surviving graduate school, teaching I/O psychology, and planning career advancement, as well as calls for manuscripts and conference submissions. The SIOP produces a number of other publications that are freely available on its Web site (e.g., *Guidelines for Education and Training at the Master's and Doctoral Level* and *The Principles for the Validation and Use of Personnel Selection Procedures*). The SIOP also sells selected books written by SIOP members and has a link to the PubHub service, which lists other I/O books that can be purchased through the Web site.

The SIOP's JobNet program allows employers to post job openings in I/O psychology and job seekers to post résumés and search available positions. A resource for employment in I/O psychology is the compensation information obtained from the SIOP salary survey. Every three years, the SIOP sponsors a salary survey within the field of I/O psychology, the results of which are available online.

The SIOP also provides resources for those in academic settings. For example, an instructor's guide with ready-to-use lectures is available for those who teach introductory I/O psychology. An important service for students is the Graduate Training Program Listing. More than 200 graduate training programs in I/O psychology and related fields (e.g., organizational behavior) are posted, with relevant information regarding program focus and admission statistics (e.g., number of students applied and accepted, average GRE scores of accepted students, level of assistantship support). Other documents are available to aid prospective students in their selection of a graduate program (e.g., articles regarding program rankings).

The SIOP provides resources to get people connected with others the field. The Member-2-Member program links new members with established members to facilitate integration into the SIOP community during the member's first two years in the society. A listing of I/O-related professional organizations (e.g., local communities) is also available on the SIOP Web site.

Another important function of the SIOP is to disseminate information about the field to the public, as well as to those who may be in need of the services of an I/O psychologist. The media resources service is designed to help those in the media locate I/O psychologists with expertise in a given area. This listing includes more than 1,700 psychologists, and recent press releases are also posted on the site. Another service, the Consultant Locator, is a database that the public can search for firms or SIOP professional members with expertise in specific technical areas who provide consulting services.

The major endeavor of the SIOP is its annual conference, which is held each spring. The conference features intensive workshops on cutting-edge topics, special seminars on selected topics, symposia and poster sessions, panel and roundtable discussions, and education forums that present the latest I/O research and practice. The conference also offers a placement center where job seekers have access to available positions and employers can access the résumés of potential candidates; on-site interviews are conducted at the conference. Finally, the conference offers ample opportunities for networking and social activities to connect members of the field of I/O psychology.

—*Jennifer Burnfield*

See also Academy of Management; American Psychological Association, Association for Psychological Science

FURTHER READING

Koppes, L. L. (2000). *A brief history of the SIOP.* Retrieved March 9, 2006, from http://www.siop.org/history/history.htm

SOCIOTECHNICAL APPROACH

The sociotechnical approach to organizational structure was developed in England during the late 1940s by Eric Trist and his colleagues at the Tavistock Institute of Human Relations. These researchers conducted seminal studies on the coal mining industry, where the introduction of new technology had shifted the social patterns of work so profoundly that productivity and job satisfaction were negatively affected. In response, managers and workers fundamentally reorganized their work patterns, returning to the small-team, collaborative process that had prevailed before the mechanization of the industry.

In these and subsequent studies across a variety of work settings, Trist and his colleagues found that technical changes in an industry (e.g., increased automation) consistently produce profound changes in the social aspects of work as well. They became convinced that work must be conceptualized as a joint social and technical process and that the so-called self-regulating work group is the essential building block of effective organizations.

Following the initial Tavistock studies, further experiments in the design of work according to sociotechnical principles proceeded slowly in the United Kingdom, India, and Europe during the 1950s. Support for the approach was bolstered in the early 1960s, when the government of Norway supported a labor and management effort to introduce Trist's principles of "industrial democracy" into industry there. Highly publicized early examples of work designed around sociotechnical principles in the United States include the General Foods plant in Topeka, Kansas, and the Procter & Gamble plant in Lima, Ohio. In the years since those early efforts, sociotechnical principles have been widely applied in a variety of work settings. The approach is commonplace today and has come to be viewed as a major category of organizational theory.

Although there are no universally accepted defining principles and assumptions of the sociotechnical approach, the following ideas are commonly identified with this approach:

- Organizations are open systems. They exist as animate entities in an environment of customers, competitors, suppliers, regulators, technology, stakeholders, and the broader economy. They must scan that environment, exchange with it (receive inputs and produce outputs), and anticipate and react to environmental changes in adaptive ways. The Tavistock group was strongly influenced by general systems theory as it was articulated in the physical sciences by Ludwig von Bertalanffy during the 1940s and 1950s. Fred Emery, a noted member of the Tavistock team, brought von Bertalanffy's work to the attention of Trist and the rest of the Tavistock group, and it became a pillar of the sociotechnical approach.
- Change is the norm in the environment of work. The business environment is aptly described as turbulent and uncertain, connoting that change can be sudden, extreme, and largely unpredictable. Turbulence disrupts previously stable patterns of interaction and requires a rethinking and redesign of work.
- Joint optimization is essential. Because work is, by its very nature, an intertwined technical and social process, both aspects need to be integrated into the

design of work to achieve the critical objective of improved productivity and quality of work life.

- Equifinality, a notion diametrically opposed to Frederick Winslow Taylor's concept that there is only one road to success, prevails. In all living systems, there are many possible ways to achieve the same outcome. Thus, there are many possible work designs that can achieve the joint goals of productivity and quality of work life.
- Work must be designed for flexibility. Because the environment is constantly changing, no hardwired design, no matter how well adapted to current conditions, will continue to fit the evolving demands of the environment. The organization must be designed—and continually redesigned—for flexibility. The design process is never completed. No design is ever final.
- Design with minimum critical specification. Work designers should specify only what absolutely must be specified in terms of technical and social job design parameters and allow the organization the flexibility to specify the rest for itself.
- Stakeholder input is critical. Employee participation at multiple levels is essential in creating a sociotechnically designed organization and operating it daily. High levels of employee empowerment are central to the sociotechnical philosophy.
- Teams do the work. Teams are the universal, most visible end product of sociotechnical design. The primary production unit is the self-directed work team (also known as the self-managing, self-regulating, semiautonomous, or high-performance team). Team members are usually expected or even required to acquire broader skills and more business knowledge so that they can take on a higher level of decision-making ability and authority. Internal controls gradually supplant external controls. Teams have access to much more information than workers in traditionally structured organizations. Continual learning and growth is expected. Thus, in practice, such multi-skilled teams commonly complete a whole, meaningful unit of work rather than a subcomponent only. They absorb some functions traditionally provided by support departments, such as managing quality, setting production goals, tracking performance and productivity, and making process improvements. Self-managing teams are the embodiment of the sociotechnical systems approach.
- As teams become more capable of self-direction and less reliant on daily supervisory control, they are allowed to manage the bulk of their daily work internally. Management is then able to step out to the boundaries of the team—to focus more strategically on keeping the team linked with other teams and other parts of the organization and helping to build and manage such structures as pay-for-skill and gain-sharing programs, which support the team concept.
- When problems occur, they should be handled at the source by those who directly encounter them. Thus, quality variances are detected and addressed promptly by line employees who are trained in quality as well as production.

There is a moderate amount of field research on the effectiveness of the sociotechnical approach. However, because applications vary widely, it is not always easy to determine what was done and which parts of the design or redesign may have been effective. And there certainly are reports in the literature of failed or minimally effective sociotechnical design efforts. Still, the bulk of the evidence from studies that meet the standard criteria of research excellence points to substantial increases in productivity—increased throughput, reduced rejects or scrap, decreased cycle time, and decreased machine downtime. Effects on employee satisfaction and quality of work life, measured directly through opinion surveys or indirectly through data on absenteeism, grievances, and job bid-outs, are also generally positive.

The huge body of anecdotal evidence is also strongly positive, showing productivity improvements in the 25% to 45% range and greatly improved employee satisfaction. Such gains, touted in the practitioner literature and lore, are sufficient to keep the approach prominent in contemporary practice.

Critics of the sociotechnical systems approach observe that applications commonly accept the technical work process as a given and focus largely on social redesign. Furthermore, despite such guiding principles as equifinality, the social redesign always results in the same solution—the self-managing team. A further criticism is that the classical sociotechnical design process, which relies on steering committees and design teams to do the analysis and design, is very slow (24 to 36 months being a common time frame) and costly. However, there are alternatives, such as the "future search" methodology, that compress the timeline for work redesign.

The sociotechnical systems philosophy and approach to the design of work continues to spread. The approach forms a central part of the philosophical base of the popular contemporary high-performance organization model.

—John Kello

See also High-Performance Organization Model; Quality of Work Life

FURTHER READING

Campbell, J. P., & Campbell, R. J. (1988). *Productivity in organizations: New perspectives from industrial and organizational psychology.* San Francisco: Jossey-Bass.

Cummings, T. G., & Worley, C. G. (2005). *Organization development and change* (8th ed.). Mason, OH: Thomson/South-Western.

Lawler, E. (2001). *Organizing for high performance: Employee involvement, TQM, re-engineering, and knowledge management in the Fortune 1000.* San Francisco: Jossey-Bass.

Pasmore, W. A. (1988). *Designing effective organizations: The sociotechnical systems approach.* New York: Wiley.

Trist, E. L. (1981). The sociotechnical perspective: The evolution of sociotechnical systems. In A. H. Van de Ven and W. F. Joyce (Eds.), *Perspectives on organization design and behavior* (pp. 19–75). New York: Wiley.

SPIRITUALITY AND LEADERSHIP AT WORK

A significant change is taking place in the personal and professional lives of leaders as they aspire to integrate their spirituality with their work. Most leaders agree that this integration is leading to positive changes in their relationships and effectiveness. Furthermore, there is evidence that workplace spirituality programs not only lead to beneficial personal outcomes, such as increased positive human health and psychological well-being, but also improve employee commitment, productivity, absenteeism, and turnover. Recent studies have shown that companies perform better when they emphasize workplace spirituality through both people-centered values and a high-commitment model of attachment between the company and its employees. There is mounting evidence that a more humane workplace is not only more productive but also more flexible and creative and a source of sustainable competitive advantage.

Advocates of workplace spirituality propose that people bring unique and individual spirits to the workplace, and they are highly motivated by the spiritual need to experience a sense of transcendence and community in their work. Spiritual leadership involves motivating and inspiring workers through a transcendent

vision and a culture based on altruistic values to produce a more motivated, committed, and productive workforce. In such an organization, when employees' spiritual needs are met and aligned with organizational objectives, this higher motivation, commitment, and productivity has a direct impact on organizational processes and outcomes that, in turn, influences customer satisfaction and, ultimately, organizational performance (see Figure 1).

WORKPLACE SPIRITUALITY

Although research is still in the early stages of theory building and testing, the role of spirituality in the workplace is receiving increasing attention. In particular, workers who view their work as a called vocation are likely to approach work very differently than employees who see work primarily as a means of paying bills. Most importantly to management and leadership, there is emerging evidence that spirituality provides competitive advantage through its impact on organizational performance. Workplace spirituality incorporates values that lead to a sense of transcendence and interconnectedness of all life, so that workers experience personal fulfillment on the job. This sense of transcendence—having a calling through one's work (vocationally)—and the need for membership, community, and social connection provide the foundation for a theory of workplace spirituality. Hence, workplace spirituality must be framed within a holistic or system context of interwoven cultural, organizational, and personal values. To be of benefit to leaders and their organizations, workplace spirituality must demonstrate its utility by influencing performance, turnover, productivity, and other relevant effectiveness and performance criteria.

Finally, to gain a systemic understanding of how workplace spirituality affects organizational effectiveness—through transcendence and value congruence among organizational, team, and individual values—a focus on the interconnectedness and interplay across these levels is required. Leaders who seek to transform the organizational culture from materialistic to altruistic values that are more idealistic and spiritual must address value congruence across all levels of the organization.

RELIGION AND WORKPLACE SPIRITUALITY

The study of workplace spirituality so far has been relatively free of denominational politics and the

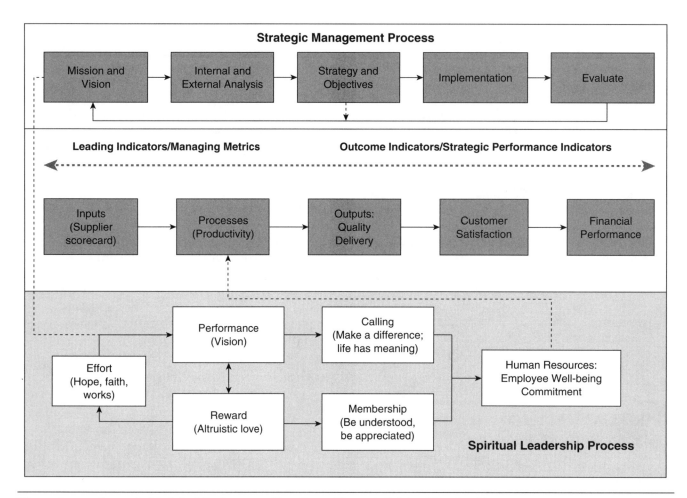

Figure 1   Strategic Model of Performance Excellence Through Spiritual Leadership

"faith blanket" in which such arguments are frequently cloaked. In fact, religious ideology has been virtually disregarded. The issues that have surfaced regarding workplace spirituality avoid any mention of a comparatively right or wrong ideology. Viewing workplace spirituality through the lens of religious traditions and practice can be divisive because, to the extent that a given religion views itself as the only path to God and salvation, it excludes those who do not share that particular denominational tradition. Thus, religion can lead to arrogance that a company, faith, or society is better, morally superior, or worthier than another. Translating religion of this nature into workplace spirituality can foster zealotry at the expense of organizational goals, offend constituents and customers, and decrease morale and employee well-being.

The Dalai Lama, among others, makes a distinction between spirituality and religion, noting that religion is concerned with faith in the claims of one faith tradition or another and connected with systems of belief, ritual prayer, and formalized practices and ideas. Spirituality, on the other hand, is concerned with qualities of the human spirit, including positive psychological concepts such as love and compassion, patience, tolerance, forgiveness, contentment, personal responsibility, and a sense of harmony with one's environment. Spirituality is found in the pursuit of a vision of service to others; through humility, or the capacity to regard oneself as an individual equal in value to other individuals; through charity, or altruistic love; and through veracity, which goes beyond basic truth telling to engage one's capacity for seeing things exactly as they are, free of subjective distortions.

The common bridge between spirituality and religion is altruistic love—regard or devotion to the interests of others. In this respect, the basic spiritual teachings of the world's great religions are remarkably similar. In religion, this is manifest in the Golden Rule, also called the *rule of reciprocity*—do unto others as you would have them do unto you—which is common to all major religions. From this perspective, spirituality is necessary for religion, but religion is not necessary for spirituality. Consequently, workplace spirituality can be inclusive or exclusive of religious theory and practice.

SPIRITUAL LEADERSHIP

Spiritual leadership is a causal theory based on an intrinsic motivation model that incorporates vision, hope, faith, and altruistic love; theories of workplace spirituality; and spiritual survival and well-being. Spiritual leadership, as a model for organizational development and transformation, can guide the evolution of positive organizations in which human well-being and organizational-level performance can not only coexist but also be optimized.

Spiritual leadership taps into the leader's and the follower's fundamental need for spiritual survival and well-being through calling and membership; creates vision and value congruence across the individual, empowered team, and organization levels; and ultimately fosters higher levels of organizational commitment and productivity. Operationally, the spiritual leadership process comprises the values, attitudes, and behaviors that are necessary to intrinsically motivate one's self and others and to have a sense of spiritual survival through calling and membership (see Figure 1). This entails two actions:

1. Creating a vision wherein leaders and followers experience a sense of calling in that their life has meaning and makes a difference

2. Establishing a social and organizational culture based on the values of altruistic love, whereby leaders and followers have a sense of membership, feel understood and appreciated, and have genuine care, concern, and appreciation for *both* self and others

Spiritual leadership theory explores the concept of positive human health and psychological well-being through recent developments in workplace spirituality, character ethics, positive psychology, and religion. These areas provide a consensus on the values, attitudes, and behaviors necessary for spiritual leadership and ethical and spiritual well-being.

Ethical well-being is defined as authentically living one's values, attitudes, and behavior from the inside out and creating a principled center that is congruent with the universal, consensus values inherent in spiritual leadership theory. Spiritual well-being incorporates transcendence of the self in pursuit of a vision, purpose, or mission in service to key stakeholders that satisfies one's need for calling and membership. Individuals who practice spiritual leadership at the personal level have more joy, peace, serenity, and overall life satisfaction. Not only is their psychological well-being greater, but also spiritual leaders have better physical health. Specifically, spiritual leaders have a high regard for themselves and others, quality relationships with others, a sense that life is meaningful, the ability to effectively manage their surrounding world, the capacity to follow inner convictions, and a sense of continuing personal growth and self-realization.

WORKPLACE SPIRITUALITY, SPIRITUAL LEADERSHIP, AND PERFORMANCE EXCELLENCE

The field of performance excellence has established the need to go beyond reporting financial metrics to include nonfinancial predictors of financial performance such as customer satisfaction and organizational outputs such as quality and delivery, process or internal operating measures, and employee commitment and growth (see Figure 1). Moreover, key performance indicators reported in these areas are derived from the firm's strategic plan and have quantifiable performance objectives. Of these performance categories, employee commitment is the central and leading indicator of the other performance categories; in other words, a high degree of workplace spirituality and spiritual leadership, as a driver of organizational commitment and productivity, is essential to optimizing organizational performance.

In Figure 1, the strategic management process begins with the development of a vision and mission, followed by an internal and external analysis, which results in strategic action plans and objectives. These objectives provide the basis for strategy implementation and determine key performance indicators and outcomes. Furthermore, performance indicators may be either leading or lagging measures. For example, a firm's outputs, which include quality (service or product) and on-time delivery, are leading indicators of customer satisfaction, which, in turn, affect financial performance. Internal processes in an organization, such as best practices, determine whether the outputs are excellent. Internal processes are affected by inputs (e.g., late delivery from a supplier can result in a late delivery to the customer), as well as employee well-being and commitment.

SUMMARY

Developments in strategic scorecards, performance measurement, and quality (e.g., Baldrige Award criteria and strategy maps) point to the pivotal role that employee well-being and performance play in predicting other key strategic performance indicators. The strategic model of performance excellence through spiritual leadership, depicted in Figure 1, provides a process for influencing customer satisfaction and financial performance by fostering the motivation and leadership required to drive both human well-being and excellent operational performance.

Workplace spirituality and spiritual leadership research is in the initial concept and elaboration stage of development. A 2003 special issue of *Leadership Quarterly* revealed that research in this area has used novel methods to develop and test new theory. Three themes emerged: What is required for workplace spirituality is an *inner life* that nourishes and is nourished by *calling or transcendence of self* within the context of a *community* that is based on the values of altruistic love. Satisfying these spiritual needs in the workplace positively influences human health and psychological well-being and forms the foundation of the spiritual leadership paradigm. By tapping into these basic and essential needs, spiritual leaders produce the follower trust, intrinsic motivation, and commitment that is necessary to optimize organizational performance and human well-being. This is the fundamental proposition that should be tested in future research—that spiritual leadership is necessary for the transformation and continued success of learning organizations—and the organizational paradigm that is necessary for performance excellence in the 21st century.

—*Louis W. Fry*

See also Leadership and Supervision; Leadership Development

FURTHER READING

Baldrige National Quality Program. (2004). *Criteria for performance excellence.* Washington, DC: U.S. Department of Commerce, National Institute of Standards and Technology.

Fry, L. W. (2003). Toward a theory of spiritual leadership. *Leadership Quarterly, 14,* 693–727.

Fry, L. W. (Ed.). (2005a). Toward a paradigm of spiritual leadership [Special issue]. *Leadership Quarterly, 16*(5).

Fry, L. W. (2005b). Toward a theory of ethical and spiritual well-being and corporate social responsibility through spiritual leadership. In R. A. Giacalone & C. L. Jurkiewicz (Eds.), *Positive psychology in business ethics and corporate responsibility.* Greenwich, CT: Information Age.

Giacalone, R. A., Jurkiewicz, C. L., & Fry, L. W. (2005). From advocacy to science: The next steps in workplace spirituality research. In R. F. Paloutzian & C. L. Park (Eds.), *Handbook of psychology and religion* (pp. 515–528). Thousand Oaks, CA: Sage.

STANDARDIZED TESTING

Since the early 20th century, the United States has been the foremost developer and consumer of testing technology in the world. Tests have been used widely by the U.S. military, government and civilian employers, and educational institutions to improve selection, placement, and promotion decisions. However, the pervasiveness of testing in American life, starting as early as age six, has called into question the purported benefits of testing, led to intense scrutiny of organizational decisions, and raised concerns about the general impact of testing on society. Although some of these criticisms are certainly justified, standardized tests, the most common targets of public rebuke, are among the best assessment devices available and, in our view, do not deserve the bad rap they have been given in the popular press.

The term *standardized tests* originally referred to tests using uniform administration procedures. Over time, the term has evolved to describe tests that measure constructs related to academic achievement and aptitude, that are administered to a very large number of examinees on a regular basis (usually in a group format), and that have a variety of normative information available for interpreting scores. Today, all modern standardized tests are (a) constructed, validated, and normed using large and diverse samples, (b) routinely updated to reflect changes in curricula and social context, (c) administered under uniform conditions to eliminate extraneous sources of variation in scores, and (d) examined using advanced psychometric methods (e.g., item response theory) to detect and eliminate measurement and predictive bias. All of these features help make standardized tests reliable and valid assessments of the constructs they are intended to measure. The tests are continuously being improved and revised to incorporate advances in psychometric theory, substantive research, and testing technology.

Standardized tests can be roughly grouped into three general types: (a) educational achievement and aptitude tests, (b) military and civil service classification tests, and (c) licensure and certification exams. Each type of test has a different purpose, but the main psychometric features are similar. In the sections that follow, a brief overview of each test type is provided, followed by a discussion of the important issues regarding standardized test use and future development.

EDUCATIONAL ACHIEVEMENT AND APTITUDE TESTS

By far, large-scale educational assessments constitute the largest portion of standardized tests. These include instruments designed to measure student achievement in primary and secondary schools, as well as those developed to assess a student's academic aptitude to perform successfully at a university (both undergraduate and graduate levels). The most well-known primary and secondary school test batteries are the Iowa Test of Basic Skills, the Metropolitan Achievement Test, and the Comprehensive Test of Basic Skills. Each of these instruments aims to provide a thorough and integrative coverage of major academic skills and curricular areas and contains subtests covering different topics (i.e., reading, science) and grade ranges. The advantage of these batteries over earlier objective achievement tests is that their subtests have been normed on the same sample of students, which allows for relatively straightforward comparisons within and across individuals and groups. Collectively, these tests are referred to as *achievement tests,* emphasizing the retrospective purpose of the assessment. Their main goal is to gain information about a student's learning accomplishments and to identify deficiencies as early as possible.

College admission tests, on the other hand, are often called *aptitude tests* because their main purpose is to make predictions about future academic performance. The two most widely taken exams are the Scholastic Aptitude Test (SAT) and the ACT assessment (American College Testing Program), which are used mainly for undergraduate university admissions. Tests for admission to graduate and professional programs include the Graduate Record Examination (GRE), the Graduate Management Aptitude Test (GMAT), the Law School Admission Test (LSAT), and the Medical College Admissions Test (MCAT).

The GRE, SAT, GMAT, and LSAT all measure basic verbal, mathematical, and analytical skills acquired over long periods of time; however, good performance on these tests does not depend heavily on recently acquired content knowledge. On the other hand, the ACT, MCAT, GRE subject tests, and the SAT II tests do require knowledge in specific content areas, and thus they are much more closely tied to educational curricula. Consequently, it has been argued that, despite their prospective use, tests such as the ACT are more appropriately referred to as *achievement* tests. Yet, as many researchers have noted, the distinction between aptitude and achievement is a fine and perhaps unnecessary one. So-called aptitude and achievement test scores tend to correlate about .9 because individuals high in general ability also tend to acquire content knowledge very quickly. On the whole, it is safe to say that all of these tests measure an examinee's current repertoire of knowledge and skills related to academic performance.

MILITARY AND CIVIL SERVICE CLASSIFICATION TESTS

Military classification tests are the earliest examples of standardized tests developed in the United States. As part of the World War I effort, a group of psychologists developed and implemented the Army Alpha and Army Beta exams, which were designed to efficiently screen and place a large number of draftees. High-quality multiple aptitude test batteries, such as the Army General Classification Test (AGCT), emerged during World War II and were instrumental in the area of aviation selection.

The most prominent successor of the AGCT, the Armed Services Vocational Aptitude Battery (ASVAB), is now widely used to select and classify recruits into hundreds of military occupational specialties. This is accomplished, in part, by using 10 subtests—covering general science, arithmetic reasoning, word knowledge, paragraph comprehension, numeric operations, coding speed, auto and shop information, mathematics knowledge, mechanical comprehension, and electronics information—to measure an array of specific skills rather than a few broad dimensions. The primary difference between these general aptitude tests is that the ASVAB has a stronger mechanical-spatial emphasis and a unique speeded component that enhances its usefulness in predicting performance in technical and clerical jobs.

In the civilian sector, the General Aptitude Test Battery (GATB) was developed by the U.S. Department of Labor in 1947 for screening and referral of job candidates by the United States Employment Service. The GATB uses 12 subtests to measure three general abilities (verbal, numerical, spatial) and five specialized factors, which include clerical perception, motor coordination, and finger dexterity. Like the ASVAB, the inclusion of these subtests, in addition to measures of math, verbal, and general mental ability, makes the GATB predictive of performance in a diverse array of occupations, ranging from high-level, cognitively complex jobs to low-level, nontechnical positions.

LICENSURE AND CERTIFICATION EXAMS

Licensure and certification exams represent the third type of standardized tests. These tests are similar to achievement tests in that they assess examinees' knowledge and skills, but their main purpose is to determine whether examinees meet some minimal level of professional competency. Whereas achievement test scores are generally interpreted with respect to normative standards (e.g., a large representative group of examinees who took the test in 1995), licensure and certification exam scores are meaningful only in relation to a *cut score* that is tied directly to performance through a standard-setting procedure.

The most popular standard-setting procedure is the Angoff method (named for William H. Angoff), whereby subject-matter experts are asked to indicate the probability that a minimally competent professional would correctly answer each item. This information is combined across items and experts to determine the cut score used for licensure and certification decisions. The key is that scores are interpreted with respect to a defined set of skills that must be mastered. Consequently, in any given year, it is possible that all or no examinees will pass the test. In practice, however, passing rates are often similar from year to year because the average skill level of examinees and

educational curricula are slow to change and because test developers may make small adjustments to passing scores to correct for rater effects and to ensure a steady flow of professionals into the field.

Although many licensure and certification exams still contain a number of multiple-choice items similar in form to those on traditional educational tests, some recently revised exams, such as the Architect Registration Examination (ARE) and the American Institute of Certified Public Accountants Exam (the CPA exam), also include some innovative simulation-type items that are designed to mimic the actual tasks performed by professionals in the field. For example, items might require examinees to locate information in an Internet database, enter values and perform calculations using a spreadsheet, design a structure or mechanical system, or write a narrative report conveying a problem and proposed solution to a client. These types of items not only increase the realism and face validity of the tests but also enhance the measurement of integrative, critical-thinking skills, which are difficult to assess using traditional items.

CURRENT AND FUTURE ISSUES IN STANDARDIZED TESTING

For discussion purposes, standardized tests have been divided into three groups, but there are important issues that cut across domains. The greatest overall concern in standardized testing is fairness. Criticisms of standardized tests are fueled by differences in test scores across demographic groups. The popular belief is that these differences result from measurement bias (i.e., a psychometric problem with the instruments). However, most studies suggest that these differences do not result from bias but rather *impact,* a "true" difference in proficiency across demographic groups. For example, a recent study that examined the relative contributions of bias and impact to observed score differences on the ACT English subtest found that test bias (i.e., differential test functioning) was associated with only .10 of the observed total 12.6 raw score point difference across groups of Black and White examinees. Thus, impact, not bias, poses the biggest problem for college admissions decisions. To the extent that these findings are generalizable, it seems that fairness concerns are best addressed by devoting more attention to the motivational and educational factors influencing test performance rather than searching for a fundamental flaw in the assessment devices.

An issue that is closely connected with bias and fairness is test validity. Many critics have argued that standardized tests do not predict academic or on-the-job performance, and so other types of assessments should be used. However, predictive efficacy is complicated by measurement artifacts (e.g., range restriction and unreliability) that limit the size of the correlations between standardized test scores and performance criteria. Meta-analytic studies, which attempt to correct for these artifacts, have demonstrated that standardized tests are valid predictors of a wide array of outcomes. Four-year grade point averages and work samples do provide comparable validities, but they involve observation over a much longer period of time and, more importantly, make normative comparisons difficult when examinees come from very different backgrounds. On the other hand, tests such as the GRE and SAT make it possible to assess thousands of examinees in a single testing session and provide a common yardstick for comparing examinees from urban schools and community colleges to the most prestigious and selective institutions.

Another issue in standardized testing that has received considerable attention among researchers and test developers is the desire to make exams more accessible to test takers while maintaining a reasonable level of test security. Historically, most standardized tests were offered only a few times per year in a proctored group session format. Security was handled by coordinating testing sessions nationally, using at least one new form per administration, and limiting the public disclosure of items and answers. If, for some reason, a test taker missed or knew in advance that he or she would not be able to attend a testing session, he or she typically had to wait several months for the next opportunity. Needless to say, examinees viewed such timing constraints unfavorably.

Fortunately, advancements in computer technology and psychometric theory now offer many solutions to this problem. Perhaps the most promising development is the widespread availability of computerized adaptive tests (CAT), which allow each examinee to receive a unique sequence of items chosen from a large item pool; items are selected individually or in groups, in real time, to provide near-maximum information about an examinee's estimated proficiency level. Because the number of items in the testing pool is usually very large (sometimes in the thousands) and item-selection algorithms incorporate stochastic features that provide exposure control, it is unlikely that

an examinee would encounter overlapping items upon retesting. Hence, unless there is a substantial coordinated effort among test takers to expose the pool, test security can be maintained reasonably well while offering exams on a more frequent, flexible basis than was possible with paper-and-pencil formats. A related benefit is that scores can be given to examinees immediately upon test completion. Examples of standardized tests that now use some variation of CAT technology are the GRE, ASVAB, and CPA exams.

The last concern in standardized testing is the emerging desire to broaden the scope of aptitudes and skills measured by standardized tests. This effort is being driven largely by organizations that use test score information to make important personnel or admissions decisions. The use of innovative simulation-type items, such as those in the ARE and CPA exams, seems to allow for the assessment of skills that are difficult, if not impossible, to measure using traditional multiple-choice items.

In addition, some testing programs (e.g., military) are seeking to augment cognitive test batteries with subtests measuring noncognitive variables, such as personality and vocational interests, in order to improve not only the prediction of performance but also outcomes such as retention, organizational loyalty, and group cohesion. Of course, making these variables a fundamental part of the decision-making process is not easy because noncognitive assessments are notoriously susceptible to several forms of response distortion (e.g., faking). However, given the number and quality of studies currently being conducted to address this issue, the day when noncognitive subtests become a key component of standardized test batteries may not be far away.

CONCLUSION

Standardized tests play an important role in American society. The information provided by these tests facilitates the diagnosis, screening, and classification of large numbers of examinees from diverse backgrounds. Standardized tests were created with the aims of test precision, efficiency, and predictive efficacy in mind, and many researchers and practitioners argue these ideals are embodied and represented well, particularly in comparison to other types of psychological assessments. Although this entry has focused on standardized testing in the United States, other countries will certainly experience similar issues as global competition demands more efficient screening and placement of individuals in emerging economies.

—*Stephen Stark and Oleksandr S. Chernyshenko*

See also Prescreening Assessment Methods for Personnel Selection

FURTHER READING

Drasgow, F. (2002). The work ahead: A psychometric infrastructure for computerized adaptive tests. In C. N. Mills, M. T. Potenza, J. J. Fremer, & W. C. Ward (Eds.), *Computer-based testing: Building the foundation for future assessments* (pp. 1–35). Hillsdale, NJ: Lawrence Erlbaum.

Kuncel, N. R., Hezlett, S. A., & Ones, D. S. (2001). A comprehensive meta-analysis of the predictive validity of Graduate Record Examinations: Implications for graduate student selection and performance. *Psychological Bulletin, 127,* 162–181.

Murphy, K. R., & Davidshofer, C. O. (2005). *Psychological testing: Principles and applications* (6th ed.). Upper Saddle River, NJ: Prentice Hall.

Schmidt, F. L., & Hunter, J. E. (1998). The validity and utility of selection methods in personnel psychology: Practical and theoretical implications of 85 years of research findings. *Psychological Bulletin, 124,* 262–274.

Stark, S., Chernyshenko, O. S., & Drasgow, F. (2004). Examining the effects of differential item/test functioning (DIF/DTF) on selection decisions: When are statistically significant effects practically important? *Journal of Applied Psychology, 89,* 497–508.

Thorndike, R. M. (2005). *Measurement and evaluation in psychology and education* (7th ed.). Upper Saddle River, NJ: Prentice Hall.

STATISTICAL POWER

Statistical power (SP) refers to the probability of rejecting a null hypothesis (a hypothesis of no difference) when it is actually false. When an organizational researcher retains (fails to reject) a false null hypothesis, he or she is likely to conclude, for example, that the organizational intervention did not positively affect productivity or that a selection test does not validly predict future job performance. Because an erroneous decision can have important practical implications, researchers would like to have adequate SP in order to be able to reject the null hypothesis when it is false. The amount of SP present when testing, say, the difference between two means or the relationship of two sets of values, is influenced by three factors: (a) the alpha level (α, or probability value) adopted for the statistical test, (b) the size of the sample used to obtain the means or correlation, and (3) the effect size (ES; or the magnitude of the difference or relationship). Before discussing these factors, a few words must be said about Type I and Type II errors in hypothesis testing.

TYPE I AND TYPE II ERRORS

Figure 1 shows the interplay of accepting or rejecting a null hypothesis when it is actually true or false. A Type I error occurs when a null hypothesis (e.g., two variables that are *not* related or two subgroups that are *not* different) is rejected as being true, but it is actually true. A Type II error occurs when a null hypothesis is retained as being true, but it is actually not true. The probability of Type I error is denoted by alpha (α), and the probability of Type II error is denoted by beta (β). Statistical power—the probability of rejecting the null hypothesis when it is false—is equal to 1 minus the probability of a Type II error ($1 - \beta$).

In a statistical analysis, the likelihood that a Type I versus a Type II error will occur can be manipulated by adjusting the probability, or α level, for the statistical test. The most typical α value is .05. When α = .05, the rate of committing a Type I error is five times per 100 independent samples that might be compared. If a smaller value for α (e.g., .01) is chosen, the likelihood of committing a Type I error decreases, but the likelihood of a Type II error increases. Similarly, by increasing α (to a value greater than .05), we decrease the probability of a Type II error.

FACTORS AFFECTING STATISTICAL POWER

As noted previously, α, sample size, and ES play important roles in determining SP. According to Figure 1, SP is the converse of the probability of Type II error (SP = $1 - \beta$). One way to decrease the likelihood of a Type II error is to increase α. Although there is nothing sacred about the commonly used α levels, one should be careful about increasing the α levels excessively. There are very few organizational interventions in which the treatment effect is truly zero; many treatments may have small effects but rarely zero effects. According to null hypothesis testing, Type I errors can only occur when the treatment effect is zero. Therefore, raising the α level without a good rationale is not recommended because the higher the

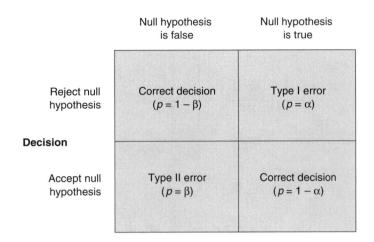

Figure 1   Type I and Type II Errors in Hypothesis Testing

α, the less rigorous the test of an effect, and the greater the chance of making a Type 1 error.

All else being equal, the bigger the sample size, the greater the SP. Therefore, one should obtain as big a sample as possible within prevailing practical constraints to ensure detection of a significant effect. Typically, obtaining a bigger sample is more time-consuming and costly. If the population correlation is .10, one would need a sample of 1,000 cases to have enough SP (say, SP = .80, which is generally considered acceptable) to detect it with α = .01, or a sample of more than 600 cases with α = .05.

Effect size is a way of quantifying the effectiveness of an organizational intervention. The bigger the ES, the greater the SP for detecting a significant organizational intervention effect for a given sample size and α level. A commonly used ES is the standardized mean difference, d, which can be calculated by dividing the mean difference (between the intervention and comparison groups) by the pooled standard deviation. Another commonly used ES is the correlation coefficient, r, which can be converted to d. According to the prevailing convention, ds of .20, .50, and .80 are considered to be small, medium, and large ESs, respectively. Similarly, rs of .10, .30, and .50 are considered to be small, medium, and large ESs, respectively.

There are statistical formulas for estimating the sample size, α, SP, or ES when the other three factors are known. (There are also tables for estimating required sample sizes for given values of α, SP, and ES.) For example, prior to implementing a new organizational intervention or a new selection test, a researcher may want to know what size sample would be needed to detect a given level of significant difference.

To use this formula, the researcher might conclude that α = .05 and SP = .80 would be adequate. An assumption that the intervention should result in a smaller ES requires a larger sample for the given set of SP and α values. Conversely, an assumption that the intervention will result in a larger ES requires a smaller sample size. Often, the temptation is to assume a large ES and thus a smaller sample size estimate. If the assumed ES is smaller than expected, the researcher may not be able to detect a significant difference when it actually exists. Information from previous investigations or meta-analyses is helpful when estimating the ES for a given condition.

We have reviewed the major factors affecting SP and its role in designing a study. Additional information about SP and its estimation can be found in the citations given in Further Reading.

—*Nambury S. Raju, John C. Scott, and Jack E. Edwards*

FURTHER READING

Cohen, J. (1988). *Statistical power analysis for the behavioral sciences* (2nd ed.). Hillsdale, NJ: Lawrence Erlbaum.

Cohen, J. (1994). The earth is round ($p < .05$). *American Psychologist, 49,* 997–1003.

Kraemer, H. C., & Thiemann, S. (1987). *How many subjects?* Newbury Park, CA: Sage.

Murphy, K. R. (1990). If the null hypothesis is impossible, why test it? *American Psychologist, 45,* 403–404.

Murphy, K. R., & Myors, B. (1998). *Statistical power analysis: A simple and general model for traditional and modern hypothesis tests.* Mahwah, NJ: Lawrence Erlbaum.

STEREOTYPE THREAT

The concept of *stereotype threat* was originally proposed by Claude M. Steele and Joshua A. Aronson in 1995. It is the risk that an individual will confirm a widely known, negative stereotype about his or her group when placed in a situation in which that stereotype is made salient. Concern about making an unfavorable stereotype believable to others outside one's group or to oneself can cause individuals to exhibit decreased performance in these situations.

Stereotype threat was initially offered as an explanation for the performance gap between African Americans and European Americans on tests of cognitive abilities such as the SAT (Scholastic Aptitude Test), GRE (Graduate Record Examination), and LSAT (Law School Admission Test). The difference in mean score of European Americans on tests of cognitive abilities has been reported to be as much as one standard deviation higher than that of African Americans. The size of this difference varies based on sample type, test type, subtest type, education level, employment status, and the complexity of the job being assessed.

Steele and Aronson reasoned that when an African American enters a standardized testing environment, he or she is faced with the threat that his or her behavior will serve as evidence for the validity of stereotypes concerning the intellectual abilities of African Americans. This fear causes the individual to redirect attentional resources from performing well on the test toward disconfirming negative stereotypes about the mental capabilities of African Americans, thereby lowering his or her score. Understanding this theory is important for individuals in educational and employment settings who administer and interpret tests of cognitive abilities because the significance of the decisions based on these tests is great.

Steele and Aronson established several boundary conditions that must be met in order for a person to experience stereotype threat. First, the task being performed must be one to which a specific negative stereotype is attached (e.g., lower performance on tests of cognitive abilities for African Americans in comparison to European Americans). The individual need not internalize the negative generalization, but he or she must be aware that a stereotype exists about his or her group for that particular situation. The domain being measured also must be important to the self-image of the person being evaluated. Finally, the individual must identify himself or herself as a member of the stigmatized group. According to stereotype threat theory, when these three conditions are satisfied, the performance of the individual is deflated.

EMPIRICAL EVIDENCE

Steele and Aronson's first study provided preliminary support for the existence of stereotype threat. These researchers examined the performance of high-achieving African American and European American college students on a test comprising difficult items from the verbal portion of the Graduate Record Examination. Two separate conditions were created to manipulate the situational aspects of the test. Participants in the stereotype threat condition were told that the test was intended to diagnose their intellectual ability, thus evoking the racial stereotype of African American intellectual inferiority in the minds of the African American students and generating fear of endorsing the stereotype. The non-stereotype-threat participants were not told that the test was an indicator of verbal ability—instead, they were instructed that they were completing a problem-solving task created by the researcher.

The results showed that African American participants in the diagnostic condition performed significantly worse than the African Americans in the nondiagnostic condition and worse than the European Americans in both conditions. Although the performance of African Americans in the nondiagnostic condition was not equal to that of the European American participants, the performance gap between the two groups was larger in the stereotype threat condition than in this condition. These findings support the notion that the incidence of stereotype threat leads to a performance decrement in the minority group, and reducing the relevance or salience of the stereotype in question will lessen the effects of stereotype threat.

Other studies have shown that any group about which negative stereotypes exist may experience stereotype threat, including women and older Americans.

STEREOTYPE THREAT AND EMPLOYMENT SETTINGS

Although tests that measure intelligence have been shown to be valid predictors of job performance for most occupations, psychologists are concerned that their use may create adverse impact for protected groups. Stereotype threat has been examined as one method of understanding and alleviating the differences in performance between African Americans and European Americans on personnel selection tests. Several empirical studies have investigated the generalization of stereotype threat to tests administered in the applied setting. Researchers in these studies failed to find the typical stereotype threat effect of lower performance for African Americans in the control condition.

UNDERLYING MECHANISMS

Although researchers have provided support for the existence of stereotype threat across a range of groups and settings, we still do not have a clear understanding of how stereotype threat negatively affects performance processes such as anxiety, stereotype endorsement, and self-handicapping. Some of these processes have been tested, but none has been identified as the means by which stereotype threat affects test performance.

—*Lela Strong*

See also Race Norming; Stereotyping

FURTHER READING

Mayer, D. M., & Hanges, P. J. (2003). Understanding the stereotype threat effect with "culture-free" tests: An examination of its mediators and measurement. *Human Performance, 16*(3), 207–230.

Sackett, P., Henderson, C., & Cullen, M. (2004). On interpreting stereotype threat as accounting for African American–White differences on cognitive tests. *American Psychologist, 59*(1), 7–13.

Steele, C., & Aronson, J. (1995). Stereotype threat and the intellectual test performance of African Americans. *Journal of Personality and Social Psychology, 69*(5), 797–811.

Steele, C., & Aronson, J. (2004). Stereotype threat does not live by Steele and Aronson (1995) alone. *American Psychologist, 59*(1), 47–48.

STEREOTYPING

In a social or organizational context, *prejudice* refers to an attitude, usually negative, toward a person or a group of people because of their group membership. When this attitude is expressed behaviorally, the result is discrimination. At the core of prejudice are stereotypes and stereotype-based assumptions.

THE STEREOTYPING PROCESS

Although researchers have debated the precise definition of a *stereotype,* the term generally refers to a set of beliefs about the characteristics, attributes, and behaviors of members of a certain group. Stereotypes about groups of people are a by-product of categorization processes. Just as we categorize cars and foods, we also categorize people. Once categorized, generalizations about what we believe to be the defining features of a category (e.g., cars have four wheels) are assumed to characterize individual category members. When applied to individuals, generalizations based on categorization are called *social stereotypes.* Though people can be categorized along innumerable dimensions, distinctions are commonly made based on highly visible characteristics such as sex, ethnicity, and age.

Research evidence suggests that stereotyping serves multiple functions. First, social stereotypes can be cognitively useful. Because human processing is limited, categorizing people into groups and extrapolating about them on that basis can be functional by allowing us to simplify complex situations. Furthermore, because stereotypes create expectations, they allow us to make inferences about people's characteristics that are more remote and abstract and serve a preparatory function. Second, stereotypes can serve a variety of social motivations, including self-enhancement needs. For example, social identity theory argues that humans have a need to belong to an in-group with a positive identity, and negatively stereotyping members of other groups may help bolster that positive identity.

The categorization of individuals and the social stereotypes that categorization produces serve multiple functions. Irrespective of its purpose, however, one of the most remarkable features of categorization is how rapid and automatic a process it can be. Another remarkable feature is how powerful and tenacious the resulting stereotypes can be. Once an individual is categorized and stereotypes are in play, we tend to process information about that individual based on generalized knowledge and expectations about the group he or she is a part of, not based on his or her unique individuality. Consequently, social stereotypes, which are inherently overgeneralizations, can become the basis of faulty reasoning and, ultimately, result in prejudice.

IMPACT ON INFORMATION PROCESSING

Several processes that result from stereotypes can lead to biased judgments and decisions. These same processes also serve to maintain and perpetuate social stereotypes by insulating them from potentially disconfirming information.

Perception

Stereotypes can influence the extent to which information is attended to. For example, individuals have a tendency to recognize stereotype-consistent information and process it faster than stereotype-inconsistent information, which sometimes is ignored altogether. Additionally, stereotypes promote a confirmation bias. If an individual is trying to understand why a particular outcome occurred, once that individual finds information that is consistent with his or her stereotype-based expectation, the information search is halted.

Causal Attribution

When stereotype-inconsistent information is not ignored, it is often causally attributed in a manner that is consistent with the stereotype. For example, research has documented that although stereotype-consistent information is often attributed to stable dispositional attributes, stereotype-inconsistent information is often attributed to temporary elements of the situation. Therefore, the inconsistent information is written off as a fluke.

Interpretation

Stereotypes influence the manner in which individual actions are interpreted. For example, the same behavior performed by people from differing social groups may be interpreted through a different lens. For example, the same work demeanor may be seen as "relaxed" when an employee is White but as "lazy" when an employee is Black. This suggests that potentially individuating information, which is often contrary to the stereotype, is assimilated into it and consequently disregarded.

Memory

Stereotypes have been shown to influence what people remember about a particular individual. Typically, memory is biased in the direction of expected stereotype-consistent attributes—what fits the stereotype is remembered more completely and more accurately than what does not fit the stereotype. There is also documentation of a tendency to "remember" stereotype-consistent events and behaviors even when they did not actually happen.

ORGANIZATIONAL FACTORS THAT MODERATE STEREOTYPE USE

The impact of stereotypes, although powerful, is not inevitable or invariable. Many organizational factors can promote or inhibit the activation or use of stereotypes in the evaluation process.

Contextual Salience

Only when it is salient does a feature of an individual become the basis of categorization. Though certain highly visible features such as sex or race are often the basis of categorization, contextual elements such as uniqueness or scarcity can highlight their visibility. Thus, a woman's sex is more likely to stand out when she is in the company of nine men than when she is with five men and four other women. More balanced proportional representations reduce stereotype use in evaluations.

Ambiguity in Performance Outcome

Stereotypes prevail in ambiguous circumstances. To the extent that a performance outcome is ambiguous in its implications and inference is required to interpret it, stereotypes will play a greater role in its evaluation. When information about performance is definitive, the output is objectively measurable, or there is broad consensus about its quality, the impact of stereotypes will be attenuated and the distortion they create avoided.

Ambiguity in Evaluation Methods

Ambiguity in the decision-making process can prompt the use of stereotypes. In the absence of explicit criteria to attend to, evaluators often selectively attend to different aspects of information, such that the information processed is congruent with stereotyped expectations. Structured decision making can preclude the use of stereotypes by forcing the consideration of multiple sources of information about an individual, requiring attention to explicit criteria, and ensuring that the same attributes are assessed and weighted equally for everyone.

Ambiguity About the Source of Performance

Stereotypes are likely to predominate when it is unclear who is responsible for a performance outcome—for example, when an individual is working in a group, with a partner, or under the tutelage of a mentor. In such situations, the stereotyped individual is apt to be seen as making less of a contribution to a successful outcome than others, a situation that can be avoided if work situations are structured so that individual inputs are clear and indisputable.

Motivation of the Perceiver

The motivation of the perceiver is a critical determinant of whether stereotypes are used. The more motivated an individual is to be accurate in his or her impression formation, the less likely he or she is to rely on stereotypes. Instances that are likely to be motivating are those in which the perceiver has a personal stake in the outcome of a decision, such as having to work with the person selected, or those in which the perceiver is accountable for his or her decisions and must justify them to a third party.

SUMMARY

Social stereotypes are the result of the human tendency to categorize people, places, and things. They create a powerful tendency to distort information to conform to stereotype-based expectations, and they are highly resistant to change. Despite the force of stereotypes, their effects are not inevitable; organizational conditions can both facilitate and hinder their use and the prejudice they promote.

—*Madeline E. Heilman and Michelle C. Haynes*

See also Adverse Impact/Disparate Treatment/Discrimination at Work; Affirmative Action; Civil Rights Act of 1964, Civil Rights Act of 1991; Diversity Training; Sexual Discrimination

FURTHER READING

Fiske, S. T. (1998). Stereotyping, prejudice, and discrimination. In D. T. Gilbert, S. T. Fiske, & G. Lindzey (Eds.), *The handbook of social psychology* (4th ed., Vol. 2, pp. 357–411). New York: McGraw-Hill.

Fiske, S. T. (2004). Intent and ordinary bias: Unintended thought and social motivation create casual prejudice. *Social Justice Research, 17*(2), 117–127.

Heilman, M. E. (2001). Description and prescription: How gender stereotypes prevent women's ascent up the organizational ladder. *Journal of Social Issues, 57*(4), 657–674.

Hilton, J. L., & von Hippel, W. (1996). Stereotypes. *Annual Review of Psychology, 47*, 237–271.

STRATEGIC HUMAN RESOURCES

See HUMAN RESOURCES STRATEGY

STRATEGIC PLANNING

Strategic planning is a process by which organizations put business plans into action in the marketplace. This process differs from the annual planning process in which most organizations engage in that it is typically geared toward a longer-term planning horizon. Most organizations today consider the duration of a strategic plan to be anywhere from three to five years. However, in rapidly changing industries, strategic planning timelines may be shorter.

The purpose of developing a strategic plan is to determine the long-term direction of the organization and to set it up to succeed in its endeavors. In the business world, this often means identifying "white space" in the marketplace—that is, areas in which there are few or no competitors—and identifying areas of competitive advantage for the organization. When it is crafted properly, a strategic plan can be used as a framework for decision making, provide a basis for more detailed planning, explain the purpose and goals of the business to others, engage and motivate others, and facilitate benchmarking.

In broad terms, the development of a strategic plan is typically based on a rigorous analysis of the competitive landscape in which the organization operates or wants to enter. This analysis examines competitors and competitor activity, identifies existing and emerging consumer trends, identifies market opportunities, and forecasts the growth potential of entering a particular area of the market.

Although there are many ways to approach the strategic planning process, these can all be broken down into three basic steps: (1) an analysis of the current state and resources, (2) an explication of the desired future state, and (3) a description of the steps needed to reach the future state.

STEP 1: ANALYSIS OF THE CURRENT STATE

The analysis of the current state and resources consists of conducting an internal and external environmental scan to assess the organization's goals, resources, and competitors. Many organizations conduct what is known as a *SWOT analysis* during this phase. A SWOT analysis is a form of competitor analysis that is characterized by an in-depth look at the organization's strengths, weaknesses, opportunities, and threats for the purpose of understanding how it fares against competitors in a particular industry, market space, or even market segment.

According to Michael Porter, a renowned strategist and Harvard professor, a sophisticated competitor analysis is essential to a well-conceived strategy because, without it, faulty and dangerous assumptions about competitors can creep into management thinking. For example, senior leadership may make invalid assumptions about a competitor's plans or activities based on prior knowledge and experience that may no longer be relevant. In addition, Porter recommends conducting an industry analysis. This entails examining five essential factors: rivalry, supplier power, buyer power, threat of substitutes, and barriers to entry. Both types of analyses help to ensure that an organization's strategic plan is based on a thorough understanding of its external environment, its competitors, and its own resources.

STEP 2: DEFINITION OF THE FUTURE STATE

In this step, most organizations construct a vision and a mission statement that describe what the future of the organization should look like. This phase often follows the environmental scan. The development of these statements, which are really guiding principles, is done by a small group—usually the company's senior management team. The purpose of the vision statement is to identify the ideal future toward which

the organization will move as a result of the implementation of its strategic plan. The mission statement typically indicates the purpose of the organization—the reason it exists. Mission statements generally contain a mixture of components that describe the company's essence, either now or aspirationally in the future. For example, the business's purpose, its key products and services, customers, markets, competitive advantage, philosophical underpinnings, and key organizational values are all likely to be found in a mission statement. In combination, these documents help to keep the organization on course as it implements its strategy. The idea is that the strategy should always support and guide the organization toward the achievement of its vision and mission.

Once the vision and mission are in place, detailed strategy formulation can begin. This entails using data gathered from the environmental scan and competitive and industry analyses to form a plan of attack for key products or markets.

STEP 3: IMPLEMENTATION OF THE STRATEGIC PLAN

The final step is focused on the activation and evaluation of the strategic plan. As a rule, in large organizations, those who are involved in crafting the plan are not the people who implement it. Therefore, it is essential that the plan is communicated in sufficient detail to ensure that it is carried out correctly. Moreover, careful monitoring and evaluation of progress is essential to the long-term viability of the strategy. As business conditions and competitor actions shift, the plan must be modified. For these reasons, many organizations dedicate a great deal of time, energy, and resources to the strategic planning process.

—*Janine Waclawski*

FURTHER READING

Porter, M. E. (1980). *Competitive strategy: Techniques for analyzing industries and competitors.* New York: Macmillan.

STRESS, CONSEQUENCES

Work-related stress can negatively affect individual employees as well as entire organizations. Many organizations are negatively affected by the economic costs associated with stress-related workers' compensation claims, employee absenteeism, and turnover. In 2001, for example, the U.S. Bureau of Labor Statistics documented 5,659 cases of anxiety, stress, and neurotic disorder involving days away from work. Rates declined 25% between 1992 and 2001, from 0.8 per 10,000 full-time workers in 1992 to 0.6 in 2001. In 2001, most cases involved workers who were ages 25 to 54 (78.3%), female, and White non-Hispanic (64.8%). Two occupational groups accounted for more than 63% of all anxiety, stress, and neurotic disorder cases in 2001: technical, sales, and administrative support (39.9%) and managerial and professional specialty occupations (23.6%).

OCCUPATIONAL STRESSORS

A wide variety of work-related environmental conditions and occupational stressors affect the well-being of employees. These work-related factors trigger a stress response characterized by the activation of the body's physiological systems that prepare it for fight or flight. Some occupational stressors may be intrinsic to the job, such as excessive workload and work pace, abnormally long work hours, shiftwork, or harmful environmental and ergonomic conditions.

Role stressors refer to the lack of clarity or ambiguity in the way that job expectations are communicated to employees and the necessity of dealing with many, often conflicting, job responsibilities. Job insecurity resulting from downsizing, layoffs, and reengineering is a common stressor. Interpersonal stressors include workplace violence, sexual harassment, discrimination, mobbing, and other forms of workplace incivility. Many employees experience conflict between work and family. Work–family conflict exists when the role pressures of the work and family domains are mutually incompatible. Prolonged exposure to these occupational stressors has been linked to harmful physiological, psychological, and behavioral outcomes.

PHYSIOLOGICAL CONSEQUENCES

Physiological stress response affects the musculoskeletal system, the autonomic nervous system, and the hormone secretion and immune systems. Excessive work-related stress has been linked to negative changes in cardiovascular, hormonal, and immune system functioning. Stress affects the biochemical processes in the body by triggering hormone secretion. For example, an increase in levels of the hormone cortisol has been associated with chronic occupational stress. Employees in stressful occupations experience higher blood pressure than employees in other types of jobs. Stress also tends to exacerbate the metabolic and hemostatic risk factors, such as increased serum cholesterol levels, associated with coronary heart disease. High levels of stress are detrimental to individuals' immune functioning through changes in the number of white blood cells and antibodies in the blood. Individuals under stress report more muscle tension, accelerated muscle fatigue, and discomfort that is associated with these symptoms. As a consequence, employees exposed to work-related stress are at risk of developing musculoskeletal disorders of the back and upper extremities.

PSYCHOLOGICAL AND EMOTIONAL CONSEQUENCES

Job dissatisfaction or a negative emotional state associated with one's job situation is a common psychological reaction to adverse job conditions. Job dissatisfaction is consistently and positively correlated with work stress. Negative changes in other job attitudes are also associated with work-related stressors. For example, employees who experience chronic occupational stressors are less committed to the organization and more likely to think about quitting. Stressors are also associated with a variety of mood disturbances such as depression, psychosomatic complaints, disturbed sleep, and anxiety. Burnout, a common response to prolonged stress, is characterized by emotional exhaustion, depersonalization or job alienation, and reduced feelings of personal accomplishment. Burnout is also associated with such dysphoric symptoms as fatigue, loss of self-esteem, and depression. Job stress may also lead to increased feelings of hostility, irritability, and negativity.

Statistics on occupational illness and injury indicate a link with organizational stressors. Stressful work conditions are believed to interfere with workplace safety and lead to workplace injury. Stress has a negative influence on the predominate antecedent of safety behavior, the safety climate of the organization. Under stressful conditions, the perceived importance of safety decreases. As a consequence, occupational injuries become more frequent.

BEHAVIORAL CONSEQUENCES

In laboratory settings, reduced performance is often observed in stressful situations. In many field studies, the relationship between stressors and performance found mixed support. Some stressors, such as situational constraints, may impede work performance. Stressors may also indirectly affect performance by decreasing motivation, impairing cognitive functioning, and increasing fatigue. However, overall job performance does not always suffer. A stronger relationship has been found between stressors and contextual performance, a type of performance that is not formally required of employees. This pattern indicates that in stressful situations, employees assign a higher priority to formally required tasks and are more likely to neglect discretionary behaviors.

Moreover, to elevate the tension that is caused by stressful work conditions, employees sometimes engage in counterproductive coping behaviors such as cigarette smoking or alcohol and drug abuse. These behaviors exacerbate the harmful effects of stress. Stressors are also associated with counterproductive behaviors such as sabotage, interpersonal aggression, and hostility. Stressful work conditions lead to costly organizational outcomes such as turnover intentions and actual turnover.

FACTORS INFLUENCING STRESS REACTIONS

Several individual and organizational factors are known to influence the strength and severity of stress reactions. Personality and dispositional characteristics such as negative affectivity and type A personality have been found to exacerbate the detrimental effects of stressors. Individuals who are predisposed to negative emotionality and self-concept and those who are generally hostile and impatient tend to report stronger reactions to occupational stressors.

Conversely, some individual factors are associated with less severe stress response. Individuals who believe that they control important aspects of their lives have an internal locus of control. These individuals experience fewer negative stress reactions compared with those who have an external locus of control. Self-esteem or favorable self-appraisal has been found to moderate the relationship between role stressors and health outcomes, such that individuals who have high self-esteem are less vulnerable to stress. The individual characteristic of hardiness is a combination of commitment, control, and readiness to respond to challenges. People who are high on hardiness appear to report fewer negative effects of workplace stressors.

Some studies suggest that organizational factors, such as work control or the extent to which employees have the potential to influence their tasks and work environments, may have a buffering effect on stress reactions, such that employees who exercise considerable work control experience less strain in response to stressors than do those who are in high-stress, low-control jobs. This relationship appears to be influenced by individual differences. For example, self-efficacy, or one's level of self-confidence in carrying out the appropriate strategy in a given job situation, influences an individual's ability to benefit from work control. Individuals who lack self-efficacy demonstrate negative reactions to highly demanding jobs despite high control levels.

Social support has also been found to buffer some of the effects of occupational stress. Specifically, the relationship between stressor and strain is thought to be stronger for individuals who lack social support. However, there is only partial empirical support for the mediating effect of social support on the stressor–strain relationship.

—*Olga L. Clark*

See also Emotional Burnout; Empowerment; Job Satisfaction; Occupational Health Psychology; Stress, Coping and Management; Stress, Models and Theories

FURTHER READING

Barling, J., Kelloway, E. K., & Frone, M. R. (Eds.). (2005). *Handbook of work stress.* Thousand Oaks, CA: Sage.

Jex, S. M. (1998). *Stress and job performance: Theory, research, and implications for managerial practice.* Thousand Oaks, CA: Sage.

Nelson, D. L., & Burke, R. J. (Eds.). (2002). *Gender, work stress, and health.* Washington, DC: American Psychological Association.

Sonnentag, S., & Frese, M. (2003). Stress in organizations. In W. C. Borman, D. R. Ilgen, & R. J. Klimoski (Eds.), *Handbook of psychology: Industrial and organizational psychology* (Vol. 12, pp. 453–491). New York: Wiley.

Stellman, J. (Ed.). (1997). *Encyclopaedia of occupational health and safety.* Geneva, Switzerland: International Labour Office.

Sulsky, L., & Smith, C. (2005). *Work stress.* Belmont, CA: Thomson/Wadsworth.

STRESS, COPING AND MANAGEMENT

A considerable amount of research has been devoted to the manner in which individuals cope with stressful situations in daily organizational life. Coping efforts can either mitigate feelings of stress, have no impact on felt stress, or exacerbate felt stress when coping efforts fail. During the last two decades, as coping research has evolved, some researchers have focused on the trait-like aspect of coping, emphasizing the stable coping styles of individuals. Others have taken a state or situational approach, emphasizing the dynamic features of coping and viewing it as a process. Still others have taken the middle ground, treating coping patterns as stable, situation-specific styles that individuals develop over time and deploy in stressful situations.

One of the first models of stress, labeled the *general adaptation syndrome,* posits that, under stress, an individual senses alarm and either flees or adapts to the situation. Focusing on how individuals adapt to stress, R. S. Lazarus and his colleagues provided perhaps the most studied model of coping, often referred to as the *appraisal* or *transactional model* of stress. According to this model, coping comprises behavioral, cognitive, and emotional efforts aimed at managing external and internal demands, thereby managing felt stress and restoring an individual's sense of equilibrium. The transactional model of the stress process includes both a primary appraisal of the stressor and a secondary appraisal of the coping mechanisms available to the individual.

The primary appraisal of a stressor will differ among individuals because perceptions of a particular stressor can vary given personality characteristics (e.g., negative affectivity, optimism, locus of control), knowledge of a stressor, or experience with a stressor. For example, a new graduate who is hired to prepare complex tax returns by the April 15 deadline will likely perceive the seasonal volume of work to be more threatening than does an experienced tax preparer who is familiar with the laws, required forms, and recurring deadline. An individual with high self-efficacy within a specific domain will perceive stressors within that domain differently than an individual who feels less efficacious and less in control. Finally, individuals with an external locus of control may perceive

that sources of stress at work are beyond their control (e.g., organizational policies) and withdraw more quickly from a source of stress than an individual with an internal locus of control who is actively engaged in influencing his or her outcomes. Individuals' reactions to stressors also differ given their perceptions of the coping choices available within the organizational context, relationships with a supervisor, and other organizational resources. In sum, individuals assess the means by which they can regain control of the situation that is generating negative feelings of stress. A large body of literature suggests that perceptions of greater control aid in reducing felt stress.

Lazarus and his colleagues argue that strain results when a person feels unable to cope with an identified threat. In other words, not every potential stressor becomes a source of strain for an individual. In the appraisal model, individuals assess whether events in the work environment have implications for their well-being. Those deemed irrelevant have no bearing on well-being. Events that could affect well-being trigger a secondary appraisal in which individuals determine the adequacy of their coping resources. In a related approach, the *cybernetic model* of stress and coping proposes that the discrepancy between the individual's current state and desired state affects psychological well-being and activates coping as the individual seeks to restore well-being directly or alter the source of stress. Feelings of stress spur individuals to find a method of coping that restores a sense of cognitive and emotional balance.

COPING STRATEGIES

Coping strategies have been defined and operationalized in a variety of ways. Different coping strategies serve different functions, such as avoiding a stressor, confronting a stressor, or analyzing a source of stress. In general, styles of coping fall into one of two categories: emotion-focused (sometimes referred to as *avoidant* or *escapist* coping) or problem-focused (sometimes referred to as *instrumental* or *control* coping). Emotion coping efforts focus on improving the feelings experienced, whereas problem-solving coping refers to proactive actions and cognitive reappraisals that are take-charge in tone. For example, running five miles after work may make one feel better after a long day at the office (emotion-focused coping), whereas making a priority list or asking for additional help from a coworker (problem-focused coping) may alter the source of the felt stress. Thus, emotion coping, in contrast to problem-solving coping, excludes any efforts to change or adapt to the stressor but instead engages in wishful thinking or avoids the stress-inducing situation through passive behavioral, cognitive, and emotional responses.

Coping efforts are also context specific, and therefore, a coping strategy may be effective or ineffective, generating different consequences in different situations. Nevertheless, the preponderance of research on coping choices has focused on individual differences, such as personality types (e.g., negative affectivity), perceptions of skills (e.g., self-efficacy), and gender, as antecedents of coping strategies. Far less research has directly assessed the relationship between situational factors and individuals' choice of coping strategies. This is an important omission, for not only do individuals perceive and interpret potentially stressful cues from the environment differently; context may also determine which coping strategy works best for individuals given the immediate situation. For example, are coworkers available, able, and willing to help?

Individuals also assess the reactions of others in coping with stress. Will a supervisor react negatively to the coworker stepping in to help? Will a coping approach be acceptable to others in the workplace or tarnish one's reputation? Given cultural influences on the appropriateness of emotional expressiveness among males and females, it is probable that in the United States, female employees feel much more comfortable expressing their anxiety in the workplace through conversations with coworkers, whereas male employees feel compelled to maintain an image of being strong and in charge.

In sum, individuals deploy specific coping strategies to assess and react to stressful situations. Different coping strategies carry different costs and benefits, including time invested, likelihood of success, risks of failure, and others' perceptions of coping behavior in the work setting. A particular coping strategy becomes attractive when the benefits outweigh the costs.

Although individuals often have a preferred coping style, they use both problem-solving and escapist forms of coping. Some researchers have argued that, in general, emotion-focused coping is not as effective at reducing experienced stress as problem-focused coping because such efforts do not alter the source of stress. For example, avoiding one's supervisor or

having a drink after work may minimize one's felt stress for a few hours, but inevitably, the negative emotions return as the effects of alcohol fade and the source of the stress remains unchanged.

An overreliance on emotion or escapist strategies can eventually have a negative influence on one's self-image, self-confidence, and job performance. Some evidence suggests that individuals who rely exclusively on avoidant or escapist strategies report higher levels of negative consequences, including burnout, job dissatisfaction, physical symptoms, and intentions to quit. However, within limits, escapist coping is not necessarily a negative strategy. For example, exercise and relaxation techniques are helpful in the overall coping process. Additionally, cognitive approaches to escapist coping may be valuable in situations in which the individual is not ready to actively undertake the problem or the situation is resistant to change. Finally, at least one form of emotion-focused coping, seeking and receiving emotional support, appears to provide a buffer against job burnout.

SOCIAL SUPPORT

Social support influences the way individuals cope and adapt to challenges. Social relationships increase an individual's confidence in facing stressful situations, or alternatively, they may provide the information one needs to solve a stressful problem. Evidence suggests that individuals with more social support experience less strain and greater well-being. For example, sales clerks who perceive more support from their supervisors in dealing with difficult customers or a greater willingness of coworkers to take a shift for them experience less anxiety and strain when an unexpected conflict prevents them from reporting to work on time. Alternatively, social support can simply show employees that others understand their difficulties. Research suggests that individuals with greater social support experience higher levels of arousal without the negative effects associated with high-strain jobs. Because arousal, or positive stress, can motivate individuals to accomplish tasks more quickly, social support may be key to an individual's interpretation of stressors as challenges and opportunities rather than threats.

The relationship between support and strain needs further examination. The exact nature of the support–strain relationship (antecedent, mediator, or moderator) continues to be debated, as does the importance of the source and content of support. In a series of studies, T. A. Beehr and his colleagues investigated the content of social support and identified three types of affective communication among workers: non-work-related, negative work-related, and positive work-related communications. Results indicate the content of social support expressed through conversations among coworkers appears to significantly influence the outcomes of felt stress. When workers gather at lunch to engage in gripe sessions, the "support" received may exacerbate one's feelings of stress. Alternatively, engaging in conversations at work regarding hobbies, common interests, or the activities of one's children may provide momentary relief from a stressor, thus allowing a worker to return to work calm and ready to reassess the problem and search for a solution. Conversations that imply others at work simply care about an individual's well-being may also provide the necessary calming influence to allow workers to think more clearly about possible solutions.

Level of perceived social support has been linked to individual coping styles. Individuals with supportive family networks tend to use more active, problem-focused coping strategies than do individuals with less social support, who are more likely to engage in avoidant coping strategies. Personality traits also appear to influence the seeking and receiving of social support. For example, the extroversion trait may cause some individuals to consistently seek out more support, thereby influencing the amount of support received. Further work is needed to investigate how personality characteristics affect the amount of support received in the workplace.

IMPROVING COPING AT WORK

Increasingly, organizations are attempting to train their employees to be more proactive in coping with workplace stress and thereby reduce the psychological and physical health problems that accompany chronic stress. Training programs vary from online courses to multiday comprehensive programs. Approaches that focus on the individual include stress management techniques (e.g., yoga, exercise, diet), time management skills, mandatory breaks and vacations, and wellness programs.

However, situational conditions created by the organization's goals, culture, processes, or compensation packages can significantly influence employees' coping

strategies. Therefore, some organizations are assisting in employees' coping efforts by focusing on the job itself. Stress management at the organizational level includes job rotation, ergonomic solutions, task or work redesign, increased staffing, and role clarification.

A growing number of organizations have adopted family-supportive work policies and programs such as flexible scheduling. Providing employees with alternative work schedules can reduce the strain arising from competing work and nonwork obligations. The success of such programs largely depends on managerial support for employee use of such programs. For example, employees are more likely to use a policy that allows them to arrive at work late in order to resolve a problem at a child's school if they are confident that their manager supports such a program. Many organizations with family-friendly policies leave the implementation to the discretion of managers, who operate on a case-by-case basis. Such an approach may leave some employees vulnerable to the whims of a manager and inequitable treatment of employees within the same organization.

The stressor–strain relationship unfolds over time—that is, it is a process. The appraisal model of stress provides for a feedback loop, positing that an individual chooses a coping technique and subsequently assesses one's feelings. If the felt stress remains, an individual may continue coping with the same technique or opt to try another technique. Although it is widely recognized that the experience of workplace stress and coping is a process, there are few published longitudinal studies. There is a critical need for more longitudinal studies to better understand the choice of a coping strategy and the decision to change strategies.

Given the economic costs of long-term job strain and its influence on productivity and turnover, organizations have a strong incentive to identify factors in the organizational environment that contribute to employees' perceptions of stressors, influence coping choices, and generate chronic strain.

—*Kelly L. Zellars*

FURTHER READING

Beehr, T. A. (1985). The role of social support in coping with organizational stress. In T. A. Beehr & R. S. Bhagat (Eds.), *Human stress and cognition in organizations: An integrated perspective* (pp. 375–398). New York: Wiley.

Edwards, J. R. (1992). A cybernetic model of stress, coping, and well-being in organizations. *Academy of Management Review, 17,* 238–244.

Fenlason, K. J., & Beehr, T. A. (1994). Social support and occupational stress: Effects of talking to others. *Journal of Organizational Behavior, 15,* 157–175.

Lazarus, R. S. (1999). *Stress and emotion.* New York: Springer.

Lazarus, R. S., & Folkman, S. (1984). *Stress, appraisal, and coping.* New York: Springer.

Perrewé, P. L., & Ganster, D. C. (Eds.). *Research in occupational stress and well being.* Oxford, UK: JAI Press/Elsevier.

Zellars, K. L., & Perrewé, P. L. (2001). Affective personality and the content of emotional social support: Coping in organizations. *Journal of Applied Psychology, 86,* 459–467.

STRESS, MODELS AND THEORIES

Occupational stress research refers to the study of the negative impact of organizational environments on employees. In the last half century, occupational stress has become an important topic within the field of industrial and organizational psychology, and there is no reason to believe this will change in the near future. In this entry, some of the most common models and theories that have guided occupational stress research are described.

Before providing an overview of the models and theories, it is important to define these two terms. In science, a *model* is a replica or abstraction of some phenomenon or process. A *theory* is very similar to a model; the difference, however, is that a theory is more abstract. Specifically, a theory presents a set of ideas and propositions about something, whereas a model represents a detailed description of how those ideas fit together to explain some process or phenomenon.

In the social and behavioral sciences, models and theories are useful to both researchers and those who apply research findings in real settings. For researchers, models and theories help to guide investigations and serve as benchmarks by which research findings can be evaluated. Many research studies are either direct tests of models or theories or use models and theories to set them up. It is common to evaluate research findings on the basis of whether they are or are not consistent with some model or theory.

OCCUPATIONAL STRESS MODELS AND THEORIES

Before describing the specific models and theories used in occupational stress research, the manner in which they are used in this field of study must be discussed. Like other areas of industrial and organizational psychology, models and theories are used to guide occupational stress research and evaluate research findings. Unlike researchers in other areas, however, few occupational stress researchers conduct direct model tests (one notable exception will be described later). The most likely reason is that models and theories in occupational stress are generic, and thus they are hard to use to directly derive testable hypotheses.

In describing models and theories, a distinction can be made between *generic frameworks, general models,* and *testable theories.* Generic frameworks are general theories or theoretical propositions that guide research but cannot be empirically tested. General models represent a higher level of specificity than generic frameworks in that they describe specific steps in the stress process. Though general models can be tested, they rarely are, either because the components of such models are so general or because the models are very complex. Testable theories are the most concrete and, in that sense, represent the only truly testable hypotheses in the field of occupational stress.

Generic Frameworks

Most readers who have had any exposure to the field of occupational stress have heard of Hans Selye, whom many acknowledge as the "father of stress." Selye, a medical researcher, was studying sex hormones when he noticed that the reactions to adverse physical conditions of the animals he used in his research tended to follow a similar pattern. From these observations, he came up with the *general adaptation syndrome* (GAS) as a response to stressors, and this has become a common generic framework in stress research.

According to the GAS, when faced with a stressor, an individual will progress through three stages: *alarm, resistance,* and *exhaustion.* In the alarm stage, the body's physiological systems react to a stressor or threat in the environment. This is represented by increased heart and respiration rates, as well as increased production of adrenal hormones; in a sense, the body is preparing for battle. In the resistance stage, the body continues to fight the stressor threat using the same mechanisms that kicked into action in the alarm stage. In some cases, the effort that the body puts forth in the resistance stage is enough to mitigate or at least neutralize the stressor or threat. If this is not the case, the body can only hold out so long, and if the stressor persists, it will ultimately reach the third stage, exhaustion. In this final stage, the mechanisms the body uses to fight the stressor will wear down and sustain damage; in the animals Selye observed, the exhaustion stage often ended in death.

Although the GAS cannot be directly tested in organizational settings, it can be an important lens through which to understand the stress process. Consider, for example, an employee who works for an abusive, rude supervisor. When this employee first encounters the supervisor's abusive behavior, the stressor is likely to evoke a number of physiological and psychological reactions, which could be considered alarms. If the abusive behavior continues over time, the employee will attempt to cope with the situation in some way, perhaps by trying to reason with the supervisor, fighting back, or simply trying to interact with him or her as little as possible—all of these responses could be considered forms of resistance. Over time, however, if these efforts do not reduce the abusiveness of the supervisor, the employee may develop emotional or physical problems or perhaps leave the organization altogether, which would represent exhaustion.

Another notion that is prevalent in occupational stress research and may be considered a generic framework is that of *person–environment fit*. The basic idea of person–environment fit, which certainly could be applied to many areas of psychology, is that people tend to be happier and adapt better when they fit into the environment they are placed in. Organizational research—and occupational stress research in particular—has focused on the skill and ability requirements of jobs and the skills and abilities possessed by job incumbents. As one might imagine, the most stressful work situations are those in which an employee lacks the skills and abilities to perform his or her job. It may also be problematic if an employee possesses skills and abilities that are far above those required by the job that he or she is performing.

Though early work on person–environment fit focused on skills and abilities, more recent work has expanded the concept to other areas, such as the fit between organizational culture and an individual's personality, the fit between work content and an individual's interests, and the fit between specific types of work organization (e.g., team-based work) and an employee's skills and preferences. In general, research has supported the basic notion of person–environment fit.

General Models

By far, the most popular general model of occupational stress was developed by researchers at the Institute for Social Research (ISR) at the University of Michigan during the early 1960s. The *ISR model,* as it is known, was developed to serve as a guide for one of the first large-scale studies of occupational stress funded by the National Institute for Occupational Safety and Health.

The ISR model proposes that all employees in organizations encounter objective characteristics of the work environment, such as the amount of work they are assigned. These objective characteristics of the work environment are perceived or appraised by the employee, and based on this appraisal, there is some short-term reaction that may be psychological, physical, or behavioral in nature. If an employee exhibits these short-term reactions for a long period of time, his or her response may ultimately lead to poor mental or physical health.

In addition to describing the process by which stress leads to mental and physical health problems, the ISR model proposes that each step in this process may be affected by characteristics of the individual (e.g., demographic characteristics, personality traits), as well as the interpersonal relations within the individual's work environment. This aspect of the model has become very important, particularly in recent years, because much occupational stress research has focused on how individual differences influence the stress process.

Although occupational stress researchers have not focused on testing the ISR model, its importance to the field of occupational stress cannot be overstated. Its focus on the psychological interpretation of the work environment, in particular, has influenced the way researchers measure stressors. Specifically, most occupational stress researchers assess work-related stressors by using employees' perceptions of stressful aspects of the work environment. Unfortunately, however, this focus on perceptions led researchers to pay too little attention to the objective environment—a criticism often leveled at occupational stress research conducted by social and behavioral scientists.

The other general model of occupational stress that has influenced a great deal of research was described by Terry Beehr and John Newman in an extensive review published in 1978. According to this model, characteristics of the individual interact with characteristics of the work environment through perceptual or appraisal processes. Based on the precise nature of this interaction, there may be consequences for both the individual employee and the organization in which he or she works. For the individual, these consequences may include health problems, whereas the organizational consequences may include decreased productivity and increased health care costs. The final step in the model is represented by adaptive responses on the part of both the individual and the organization. This simply represents actions that people and organizations take to mitigate the effects of stress when they are recognized.

The final component of Beehr and Newman's model, which cuts across all other components, is time. This component simply recognizes that all of the steps in the stress process are embedded in a temporal framework. For example, in some cases, stressful conditions at work may occur suddenly—an unexpected layoff or a violent incident, perhaps. In other cases, stressful conditions take much more time to manifest themselves—a relationship with a coworker deteriorates over time, or physical working conditions gradually deteriorate. Employee and organizational responses to these conditions will likely be much different.

Readily Testable Models

Over the past 25 years, the most tested occupational stress model has been the *demands-control model* developed by Robert Karasek during the late 1970s. The basic idea put forth in this model is very straightforward: The most stressful situations are those in which employees are subjected to high work demands yet have low control over decisions concerning their work. Another way to look at the demands-control model is that demands and control interact in such a way that job demands are related most strongly to strain when control is low. Many blue-collar jobs fit this high demand–low control pattern; that is, employees are expected to do or produce a great deal, yet have little say in how they do their jobs or how the organization operates.

Since Karasek proposed the demands-control model in the 1970s, the model has been modified based on research findings. Specifically, research has shown that the demands-control interaction is stronger among employees who lack high levels of social support from others. Thus, it has become common for researchers to refer to Karasek's model as the *demands-control-support*, or DCS, model. A small number of empirical studies have shown that the interaction is stronger among individuals with high self-efficacy. Self-efficacy refers to an individual's belief that he or she is capable of carrying out some task or course of action; individuals with low self-efficacy are less likely than their high-self-efficacy counterparts to derive the benefits of high control. As yet, however, self-efficacy has not been included as a part of the demands-control model by most researchers.

Support for the demands-control model has been quite mixed, for a number of reasons. Perhaps the most important reason is that there is no agreement as to exactly what constitutes support for the model. According to Karasek, minimum support for the model is represented by the additive effects of job demands and control, even if the interaction between the two is not supported. By this criterion, the model has received abundant support. Some, however, view the true test as the interaction between demands and control. If this criterion is applied, support is much more modest.

The other model that is quite testable—though it has not been tested as extensively as the demands-control model—is the *effort-reward-imbalance model* developed by Johannes Siegrist in Germany. According to this model, people evaluate their work situation in terms of the effort they put into it relative to the rewards they derive. In stressful situations, employees feel as though they are putting a great deal into their job or doing a great deal for their organization, yet they feel as though they are not receiving rewards that are commensurate with these efforts.

A final model proposed relatively recently (1992) is the *cybernetic model* developed by Jeff Edwards. Edwards proposed that employees compare their current work situation with what they desire their work situation to be. If this comparison results in a negative discrepancy, or if the current situation is not what the employee wants it to be, the employee experiences the job as stressful. The model goes further, however, and describes the process by which employees attempt to change this negative discrepancy. Although Edwards's theory is complex, it is also much better at describing the stress process in real time than many other stress theories. As yet, this theory has not been explicitly tested, but in the future, it has a great deal of potential in occupational stress research.

—*Steve M. Jex*

See also Emotional Burnout; Empowerment; Occupational Health Psychology; Role Overload and Underload; Stress, Consequences; Stress, Coping and Management

FURTHER READING

Barling, J., Kelloway, E. K., & Frone, M. R. (Eds.). (2005). *Handbook of work stress*. Thousand Oaks, CA: Sage.

Beehr, T. A. (1995). *Psychological stress in the workplace.* London: Routledge.

Cooper, C. L., & Dewe, P. (2004). *Stress: A brief history.* Oxford, UK: Blackwell.

Edwards, J. R. (1992). A cybernetic theory of stress, coping, and well-being in organizations. *Academy of Management Review, 17,* 238–274.

Jex, S. M. (1998). *Stress and job performance: Theory, research, and implications for managerial practice.* Thousand Oaks, CA: Sage.

Siegrist, J. (2002). Effort-reward imbalance at work and health. In P. Perrewé & D. Ganster (Eds.), *Research in occupational stress and well-being: Vol. 2. Historical and current perspectives on stress and health* (pp. 261–291). Boston: JAI.

Sulsky, L., & Smith, C. (2005). *Work stress.* Belmont, CA: Thomson/Wadsworth.

STRUCTURAL EQUATION MODELING

Structural equation modeling (SEM) refers to the use of a general framework for linear multivariate statistical analysis that includes as special cases less general models, such as linear regression, factor analysis, and path analysis. Researchers can use SEM in a hypothetico-deductive context to test complex hypotheses or in an inductive context to estimate parameter values (effect sizes). For example, one might test a model of job performance or assume such a model to estimate effect sizes of different explanatory variables. Somewhat more controversially, researchers can also use SEM as an exploratory method for hypothesis generation. Structural equation modeling applies equally well to experimental, quasi-experimental, and passive observational research designs. Like other statistical models, SEM can facilitate causal inference, although nothing inherent to SEM requires a causal interpretation. It does require a clear understanding on the part of the researcher as to what models do and do not entail, specialized software, and reasonably large samples. In general, SEM analysis supports useful, substantive conclusions in proportion to the firmness and precision of the substantive theory brought to the analysis.

STATISTICAL MODELING WITH SEM

The prototypical structural equation model includes several *latent* (unobserved) continuous variables, each measured by several *manifest* (observed) continuous variables. The latent variables typically serve as *common factors* for their manifest indicators. The factor loadings and the regression weights connecting the latent variables together account for the observed patterns of association between the manifest indicators. For example, several latent job competencies, each measured by several continuous items, might predict several job performance dimensions, each similarly measured. Structural equation modeling allows the expression of all of these relationships within one inclusive model rather than requiring the researcher to break up the relationships into a series of discrete hypotheses tested by separate analyses.

Like other latent variable models, SEM also allows researchers to estimate effect sizes controlling for measurement error. In the previous example, the regression weight connecting a latent job competency to a latent job performance dimension will generally exceed (in absolute value) the regression weight connecting two manifest measures of these constructs in a model without latent variables. This difference occurs because of measurement error in the manifest measures.

Multiple regression constitutes a special case of SEM with one manifest endogenous variable and several correlated manifest exogenous variables. *Path analysis* generalizes regression to multiple endogenous variables by combining a system of equations into one model. *Confirmatory factor analysis* limits itself to the effects of latent variables on manifest variables but allows the latent variables to covary. *Multiple indicator, multiple cause* models allow manifest exogenous variables to affect latent endogenous variables, measured by endogenous manifest variables. For example, a researcher might use such a model if he or she has multiple measures of job performance but not each job competency and wants to predict latent job performance from observed competency measures.

Latent growth curve models model individual variation in change over time in terms of latent slopes and intercepts. For example, employees may vary in how their job performance changes over time, some starting at different levels than others and some growing at different rates than others. *Recursive* models contain no loops, whereas *nonrecursive* models do. For example, if job motivation affects job knowledge, job knowledge affects job performance, and job performance affects job motivation, this forms a loop.

Model Specification

Structural equation modeling analysis typically proceeds from model specification to parameter estimation to assessment of fit to model interpretation. Model specification involves selecting the manifest variables for analysis, specifying the latent variables, and specifying the parameters (effect coefficients and residual variances) that connect them. For example, a simple regression involves specifying one dependent variable, one or more independent variables, regression weights, and a residual term. Users can do this with algebraic equations (such as regression equations) or *path diagrams* in which boxes and circles represent manifest and latent variables, single-headed arrows represent effects, and double-headed arrows represent covariation. Path diagrams differ from *directed graphs* in that they explicitly represent all of the statistical parameters in the model, allowing most software programs to accept path diagrams instead of program syntax as input.

Model specification may involve specifying *free* parameters for estimation, *fixed* parameters with user-specified values, and *constrained* parameters set equal to a free parameter or restricted to some range of values. Fixing a parameter to zero corresponds to omitting the parameter from the model. For example, a regression weight of zero indicates no effect. Model specification involves many untested and sometimes untestable assumptions guided by substantive theory. For example, SEM typically assumes residual variances that are uncorrelated with predictor variables and assumes that no nonzero effects are omitted from the model.

Parameter Estimation

In additional to meeting the statistical assumptions discussed previously, a model must allow for the statistical identification of all of its parameters to permit parameter estimation. For example, one cannot freely estimate all of the factor loadings and the variance of the common factor because the same patterns of association can be reproduced by increasing the variance and decreasing the loadings or vice versa. This follows the familiar principle requiring more equations than unknowns to solve a set of equations. A *just-identified* model will always have zero degrees of freedom (*df*), an *overidentified* model will always have positive *df*, but an *underidentified* model may have positive, zero, or negative *df*. Textbooks provide various rules of thumb for identification. Structural equation modeling software typically provides a choice of specialized methods for estimating the values of the parameters, and these methods differ in their statistical assumptions.

Parameter estimation requires fewer assumptions than the statistical tests used in SEM. However, SEM classically assumes that the data follows a multivariate normal distribution and comprises independent observations from the same population distribution. Every endogenous manifest variable (e.g., competency and performance measure) should have a normal distribution for each combination of values of the other variables. For example, skewed performance rating distributions would violate this assumption. Furthermore, the values of the variables for one employee should not depend on the values for any other employee—a situation that might result from using supervisor ratings when some employees share the same supervisor but others do not. Researchers and software developers have maintained a relentless assault on these classical restrictions, extending SEM to include statistical interactions, multiple groups, some categorical variables, partially missing data, clustered data, and more.

Model Fit

Just-identified models, like regression models, always fit the data perfectly. Overidentified models, however, seek the best possible fit within the constraints imposed by model specification. For example, SEM software allows the user to run a regression analysis with the regression weights constrained to equal one another. If the weights differ in the population, then the constrained model will not fit perfectly. Estimation will select a compromise value estimated for both regression weights that maximizes the fit of the model to the data. The more parameters the researcher can fix or constrain, the greater the *df* and the more risky the test of the model, all else being equal.

Software provides an ever-expanding selection of fit measures. *Fit statistics* (e.g., chi-square, root mean square error of approximation) have statistical distributions and allow for probability values and statistical tests, whereas *fit indexes* (e.g., comparative fit index, normed fit index) do not. However, different statistics and indexes measure different aspects of fit, making it preferable to consider some combination of them. One can multiply certain indexes by a *parsimony ratio* to get a measure of fit that adjusts for the flexibility to fit different patterns of data afforded by free parameters. Some indexes, such as information criterion indexes, adjust for the number of estimated parameters instead.

Poor fit typically results from some combination of *sampling error* and model *misspecification.* Misspecification can result from the omission of parameters, incorrectly constrained or fixed parameter values, or the violation of statistical assumptions. Misspecification can produce both biased parameter estimates and biased statistical tests.

Model Interpretation

Effect parameters generally have the same rate-of-exchange interpretation as in regression or factor analysis. If job knowledge predicts job performance, for example, then the regression weight gives the change in job performance per unit change in job knowledge. Typically, SEM provides unstandardized estimates (such as regression weights) but can also provide standardized estimates (such as beta weights in regression). Effect parameters describe effect direction and size. Effect, variance, and covariance parameters typically come with individual standard errors for use in confidence intervals or statistical tests. However, one can also conduct statistical tests by comparing a sequence of *nested models* produced by adding constraints to an initial model. As noted previously, it only makes sense to interpret parameters for correctly—or nearly correctly—specified models.

CAUSAL MODELING WITH SEM

Typically, SEM holds the most substantive interest when the statistical effects carry a causal interpretation. In the previous example, one may want to model the job

competencies as causes of job performance, not just predictors. Some methodologists favor assuming an accurate statistical model and asking whether it supports a causal interpretation, whereas others favor assuming a causal interpretation and asking about the statistical and causal accuracy of the model. Theories differ as to how best to characterize causal relationships, some seeking a more general characterization than others. Some, but not all, seek a sense of causation that applies to both experimentation and passive observation. Most agree that typical applications remain uncomfortably vague about causation. Different causal interpretations can have different implications for research design.

As noted earlier, one can use SEM to analyze experimental data while controlling for measurement error in both the manipulation and outcome variables. However, the overwhelming majority of applications involve passive observation. Using time-ordered data rather than cross-sectional data can help to establish causal order among the variables and reduce the chances of misspecification.

The model fit aspect of SEM allows for the testing of causal models. For example, a model in which job knowledge affects job motivation and job motivation affects job performance will not fit the same data patterns as a model in which job motivation affects job knowledge and job knowledge affects job performance. As a result, poor fit can rule out certain causal models.

Generally, however, more than one model will fit any given data pattern. For example, a model in which job motivation affects both job knowledge and job performance will fit the same data as a model in which job knowledge affects job motivation and job motivation affects job performance. *Statistically equivalent* models fit the same data and thus require additional information to choose between them. This information can take the form of additional variables or theoretical considerations, such as time order or plausible causal mechanisms. Just-identified models will fit any data, and thus all just-identified models bear statistical equivalence to one another. For example, all models of the foregoing three variables with three recursive effects, as well as all models in which two correlated variables affect the third variable, fall into this category.

SEM RESOURCES AND ALTERNATIVES

Resources

The many books on SEM basically break down into three categories: general introductory texts, texts introducing specific software, and edited collections of current work. Reviews in methods journals, particularly *Structural Equation Modeling,* provide current information about available books. Web pages of SEM software developers provide current information about software capabilities and related developments. Most also provide free student versions of software that anyone considering a purchase should download first. Edward Rigdon's SEMNET e-mail list provides a friendly and supportive forum for questions about SEM.

Alternatives

Researchers with categorical latent and manifest variables might consider latent class analysis as an alternative to SEM. Those concerned with the measurement of a continuous latent variable by categorical indicators might consider item response theory. Multilevel modeling offers an alternative to latent growth curves. Partial least squares offers an alternative to SEM that is useful for exploratory modeling and smaller samples. Finally, TETRAD offers an alternative for exploratory applications, and exploratory factor analysis remains a useful alternative to the confirmatory factor analysis available through SEM.

—*Keith A. Markus*

See also Construct; Experimental Designs; Factor Analysis; Item Response Theory; Moderator and Mediator Variables; Multilevel Modeling; Multitrait–Multimethod Matrix; Nomological Networks; Nonexperimental Designs; Quantitative Research Approach; Quasi-experimental Designs; Reliability; Statistical Power; Survey Approach; Validity

FURTHER READING

Bollen, K. A. (1989). *Structural equations with latent variables.* New York: Wiley.

Bollen, K. A., & Long, J. S. (1993). *Testing structural equation models.* Thousand Oaks, CA: Sage.

Glymour, C., & Cooper, G. F. (1999). *Computation, causation, and discovery.* Menlo Park, CA: AAAI Press.

Hoyle, R. H. (1995). *Structural equation modeling: Concepts, issues, and applications.* Thousand Oaks, CA: Sage.

McKim, V. R., & Turner, S. P. (1997). *Causality in crisis? Statistical methods and the search for causal knowledge in the social sciences.* Notre Dame, IN: University of Notre Dame Press.

Sosa, E., & Tooley, M. (1993). *Causation.* Oxford, UK: Oxford University Press.

West, J. (2000, August 19). *Structural equation modeling.* Retrieved March 9, 2006, from http://www.gsm.uci.edu/%7Ejoelwest/SEM/index.html

SUCCESSION PLANNING

Succession planning, the process by which an organization makes sure that it will have the right leaders in the right place at the right time, has always been one of the most important accountabilities of the chief executives and top leaders of organizations. However, the importance of succession planning to business success has never been greater or more widely recognized than it is now—a result of the globalization of industry, demographic and generational shifts, and the ever-changing challenges of leadership in today's organizations. In fact, corporate boards have become more actively involved in CEO succession and are holding CEOs accountable for making sure that succession planning is in place below them.

The term *succession planning,* along with the scope and primary focus of this managerial function, has evolved over the last half century. During the 1950s and 1960s, the economies of developed nations were growing and a lean Depression generation was rising through the leadership ranks. The focus was on *replacement planning,* in which key positions were targeted and slates of candidates were identified as possible backups in case the current incumbent retired, was promoted, or was "hit by a bus." The impetus was the realization that there were not a lot of candidates to fall back on, especially as the postwar economic expansion began to heat up, resulting in the need for more leaders to manage growing businesses.

Human resources (HR) practitioners had few tools in these years, but assessment center methodology, created during the late 1930s and first applied to business during the 1950s in the AT&T Managerial Progress Study, laid the scientific foundation for the major contribution of industrial and organizational (I/O) psychology to the practice of succession planning: the definition of managerial competencies and the prediction of managerial success.

During the 1970s and 1980s, the process evolved into *succession management.* As the baby boom generation bulged its way through organizations, the focus was on figuring out a way to select and develop the right people from a plethora of possibilities so that the best would rise to the top—not by accident or good fortune, but by plan. The goal was no longer to just identify replacements for key positions at the top to minimize risk but also to develop a robust pipeline of leaders at all levels of the organization to ensure its continued growth and success. Included in this process at each major level (frontline, middle, and executive leadership) was the identification of high-potential individuals, appraisal of their strengths and skill and experience gaps, and plans for their development. Especially at the executive level, the people in this pipeline of future leaders came to be called *corporate assets* because they were valuable leadership resources of the whole company, not just the particular function or business unit in which they were based.

Companies such as AT&T, IBM, General Electric, and Exxon were on the leading edge in creating and using this kind of system. Industrial and organizational psychologists at these companies and in consulting firms serving a wide spectrum of companies were busy developing assessment centers, administering cognitive tests and personality inventories to screen for leadership potential, gathering observations of on-the-job performance and estimates of future potential through multiperspective interviews, and conducting in-depth behavioral interviews to help companies get data for promotion decisions and individual development planning. Today, General Electric is still touted as a leading example of succession management, with its Session C review of A, B, and C players, multilevel management curriculum, and decades-long dedication to building such a rich leadership pool that it has been able to "export" CEOs to other companies.

Despite auspicious progress in the field, there was so much change and churn in corporations during the 1980s and 1990s as a result of massive downsizing, major technological breakthroughs, and considerable merger and acquisition activity that many companies found themselves rebuilding their knowledge base around their key people and rediscovering or reinventing their expertise in managing succession during these decades.

Now, in the early 21st century, we are seeing the next stage in this evolution emerging—*strategic talent management*—which is marked by a broadening of the corporate view of global talent management and a keener awareness that leaders are critical, but there are other pivotal talent pools (e.g., as diverse as global account managers and Disney World's street sweepers) that must be acquired, developed, and managed proactively to achieve and sustain competitive advantage in a dynamic, global economy. In fact, a whole new HR decision science is beginning to emerge that provides theory and tools for tying business strategy to talent pool identification, development, and investment.

Succession planning began as a very secret process; charts were often placed on the walls of a locked "war room," and people were not told that they were on them. In smaller, entrepreneurial companies, planning was frequently ad hoc, and plans were often sketched on the back of an envelope. In large corporations, succession plans were carefully compiled and elaborately detailed in heavy binders. The irony is that these plans were rarely used for real decision making. When the time actually came to pass the baton, the name on the replacement chart or key talent pool might no longer be seen as high potential, or the individual might no longer be available, interested, or willing to move.

The reasons were many: The needs of business were changing rapidly, and most plans were out of date almost as soon as the ink was dry. Unlike previous generations, the personal priorities and career aspirations of employees at this time were not always in sync with the corporation's plans for them. Wars for talent were beginning to erupt, especially in the technology sector; the managers of high potential employees tended to hoard them because they were not willing to give up their power, privilege, and precious talent to submit to someone else's plans for them. And executive leaders just didn't trust the evaluations of performance, potential, and readiness that were served up by lower levels.

The key components of a comprehensive process have been evolving over time to cover the essential aspects of the succession or leadership continuity solution, including the following:

- Business review: An update of the current state of business strategies and priorities; clarifying the implications of the business strategy and vision for leadership roles and pivotal talent pools
- Talent needs forecast: An estimate of the number and kinds of talent needed to fill roles in a defined future time frame, including outlines of the performance challenges, competencies, and selection criteria for key positions and pivotal roles
- Talent inventory: Identification and appraisal of key position candidates and high-potential pools in terms

of their performance, potential, and readiness for advancement; sometimes summarized in an overall estimate of bench strength at key leadership levels

- Talent review: A review, discussion, and documentation of key position plans and development plans for key individuals and talent pools by a representative group of organization leaders (usually the top management team for the business unit or a special committee or board established for this purpose)
- Follow-up and progress review: A process for regular review, update, and oversight of the execution of succession and development plans

At the heart of the talent inventory are four key decisions about people:

- Who are proven *performers* who deliver the right results in the right way?
- Which of these has the *potential* to grow into positions at a higher level?
- What do they need to get *ready for promotion,* and how fast will they be ready?
- Which candidate is the best all-around *fit* for a particular role or opening?

Companies address these four questions in different ways. Some use simple managerial input, whereas others use more rigorous methodologies, but most rely on performance observations and appraisals that are not calibrated across the organization and provide necessary but not sufficient input for predicting success at higher levels. As any good I/O psychologist knows, current performance is a good predictor of future performance only if the context of performance (level, scope, challenges, competency requirements) is similar. This is where I/O psychology has the most to offer—defining the performance requirements of key jobs, measuring peoples' current capabilities and future capacity, and accelerating the development of individuals and groups.

Starting with the definition of performance requirements in terms of the position responsibilities and the person capabilities to match them, I/O psychology has well-developed expertise and tools for job analysis. The terms currently in use are *job modeling* or *strategic performance modeling,* which recognize the highly dynamic nature of today's organizations and the need to constantly reshape the critical roles within them.

In the domain of assessment, I/O psychologists provide tools and processes for in-depth and comprehensive assessments of leadership capability that can be used to supplement or check insiders' observations, predictions, and plans. The lenses that internal managers look through are foggy, at best, and misleading, at worst. The I/O psychologist's tools (e.g., measures of cognitive and personality traits that predict leadership potential, multimethod assessments of current leadership capability and readiness for more responsible roles) add significant value, especially when an individual's capabilities are not well-known by decision makers, when he or she hasn't been in situations that approximate the challenges of the target role, or when cultural and individual biases have a significant effect on organizational decisions.

Psychologists in the field of learning design and organizational development have additional wisdom and methodologies to offer succession management practitioners. These include powerful techniques such as intensive individual coaching, action learning methods, multilevel curriculum design, and process consultation.

Companies that are successful at managing succession embed the expertise of I/O psychology into their processes and follow several basic principles:

- Make it an ongoing, integral business process. Succession planning must be an ongoing process, not a onetime or annual event, with business and people plans refreshed and discussed on a regular basis.
- Link succession planning to the vision, values, and strategy of the business. People plans should support the business strategy, especially the core competencies and values of the corporation that give it its distinctive, sustainable competitive advantage. These should be reflected in the performance requirements and selection criteria for all key roles.
- Use credible, valid data for talent assessment. The right tools and processes should be designed to provide credible and accurate data that is objective and calibrated so that comparisons of people can be made across business units and geographies. Data must also be updated to capture critical transitions and changes in capabilities.
- Invest in active and systematic talent development. It must include not only identification of potential and assessment of current strengths and development needs but also proactive and systematic strategies for accelerating the development and measuring the growth of key individuals and talent pools.
- Provide incentives for developing. People identified as "high potentials" should be given no guarantees of a promotion or a specific position, but they should know they are valued by the company and will be

supported and rewarded if they are willing to take on stretch assignments that entail significant personal risk. In addition, talent builders (managers who sacrifice their own status and comfort to grow and promote others) should be made heroes and provided incentives to continue this work on behalf of the company.

- Make sure succession planning is owned by the line but facilitated by a strong HR function. The process must be owned by line managers and sponsored and directed by the chief executive of the business unit, but it must be supported by a strong, skilled, and credible HR function.

Industrial and organizational psychology has a lot to offer, not only in providing accurate data for decision making and powerful tools to accelerate development but also in providing guidance for designing and managing the entire process. However, to be effective sources of expertise in this domain, I/O psychologists must become interdisciplinary in their research and practice and skilled in tapping into and connecting different specialty areas to create the multifaceted and systemic solutions required. They also need to do a better job of explaining and marketing their expertise, so that they don't leave the field of succession management to the fads and fancies of the constantly changing marketplace.

—Elaine B. Sloan

See also Executive Selection; Selection Strategies

FURTHER READING

Berger, L. C., & Berger, D. R. (Eds.). (2004). *The talent management handbook: Creating organization excellence by identifying, developing, and promoting your best people.* New York: McGraw-Hill.

Boudreau, J. W., & Ramstad, P. M. (2005). Talentship, talent segmentation, and sustainability: A new HR decision science paradigm for a new strategy definition. *Human Resource Management, 44*(2), 129–136.

Bray, D. W., Campbell, R. J., & Grant, D. L. (1974). *Formative years in business: A long-term AT&T study of managerial lives.* New York: Wiley.

Byham, W. C., Smith, A. B., & Paese, M. J. (2002). *Grow your own leaders: How to identify, develop, and retain leadership talent.* Upper Saddle River, NJ: Prentice Hall.

Charan, R., Drotter, S., & Noel, J. (2001). *The leadership pipeline: How to build the leadership-powered company.* San Francisco: Jossey-Bass.

Eastman, L. J. (1995). *Succession planning: An annotated bibliography and summary of commonly reported organizational practices.* Greensboro, NC: Center for Creative Leadership.

Fulmer, R. M., & Congers, J. A. (2004). *Growing your company's leaders: How great organizations use succession management to sustain competitive advantage.* New York: AMACOM Books.

Hogan, R., Curphy, G. J., & Hogan, J. (1994). What we know about leadership: Effectiveness and personality. *American Psychologist, 49*(6), 493–504.

Howard, A., & Bray, D. W. (1988). *Managerial lives in transition: Advancing age and changing times.* New York: Guilford.

Levit, R. A., & Gikakis, C. (Eds.). (1994). *Shared wisdom: Best practices in development and succession planning.* New York: Human Resources Planning Society.

Mahler, W. R., & Drotter, S. J. (1986). *The succession planning handbook for the chief executive.* Midland Park, NJ: Mahler.

McCall, M. W., Jr. (1998). *High flyers: Developing the next generation of leaders.* Boston: Harvard Business School Press.

Rothwell, W. J. (2001). *Effective succession planning: Ensuring leadership continuity and building talent from within* (2nd ed.). New York: AMACOM Books.

Schippman, J. S. (1999). *Strategic job modeling: Working at the core of integrated human resources.* Mahwah, NJ: Lawrence Erlbaum.

Schmidt, F. L., & Hunter, J. E. (1998). The validity and utility of selection methods in personnel psychology: Practical and theoretical implications of 85 years of research findings. *Psychological Bulletin, 124,* 262–274.

Sloan, E. B., Hazucha, J. F., & VanKatwyk, P. T. (2003). Strategic management of global leadership talent. In W. H. Mobley & P. W. Dorfman (Eds.), *Advances in global leadership* (Vol. 3, pp. 235–274). New York: JAI/Elsevier Science.

SURVEY APPROACH

A survey can be broadly defined as a detailed investigation of a topic. Although interviews and focus groups are often included under this broad umbrella, the term *survey* has become synonymous with a questionnaire approach to research. Surveys are arguably the most common approach to data collection in organizations, primarily because of their broad applicability. They can be used to gather information both inside and outside the organization. Surveys can be used to assess employee attitudes, gauge readiness for organizational change efforts, gather performance feedback, or measure customer satisfaction. To gather accurate information for any of these purposes, certain steps need to be followed; however, users often underestimate the time necessary to do a survey properly. The critical steps of planning, designing, communicating, administering, analyzing, and addressing the results of a survey are a serious undertaking for any organization.

DEFINING THE PURPOSE AND GOALS OF THE SURVEY

Before any survey project can begin in earnest, the goals and expected outcomes of the project must be clearly defined. The goals will drive the content to cover, the questions to ask, the people to ask, and the format to use. Therefore, the researcher needs to determine whether the survey is intended to take the pulse of the organization, identify necessary action to take, or explore new products, policies, or other changes. The researcher also needs to include key stakeholders in the planning process. Organization members who will be asked to address the results of the survey must be included at the earliest stages of the process. This is also a good time to gather the support of senior management, not to mention union officers, if applicable. Without the buy-in of the people at the top of the organization, a survey project can easily be subverted.

Once support from key players has been obtained, the process of identifying the information to be gathered can begin. This process is driven by how the information will be used. If retention of key talent is the goal, for example, employee satisfaction surveys need to address topics that influence employee engagement (supervision, the work itself, coworkers, growth opportunities). Customer satisfaction surveys must address key products and services and how they are delivered. The goal of any survey is to gather information that will help to improve the organization.

DESIGNING THE SURVEY

Designing the Instrument

Some initial decisions need to be made about the type of questions that will be asked. First, the balance of open-ended (i.e., write-in) versus closed-ended (Likert-type) questions must be considered. Open-ended questions provide a wealth of information but also take significantly longer to code and interpret.

Open-ended questions also provide an opportunity for respondents to ramble, so the questions need to be very specific to prevent unintended or uninterpretable responses. Closed-ended questions are much easier to summarize but don't provide respondents with any real opportunity for elaboration. Closed-ended questions present different problems, though, in terms of their construction. In an attempt to gather more information, survey designers often create unintentionally double-barreled questions that ask for two separate pieces of information (e.g., asking respondents in one question to rate their pay *and* benefits). Post hoc interpretation is impossible because the focus of the respondents is not clear (e.g., did they rate pay or benefits or both?). Questions need to address issues that respondents know about, avoid jargon or acronyms that respondents may not know, and use the simplest language possible. Always put the most sensitive questions toward the end of the survey to avoid losing potential respondents before they really begin.

To ensure that questions ask what is intended, a brief pretest of items can prevent headaches later. Ask a small group to review the questions to ensure that they are worded properly. You also want to test how long the survey takes (so your invitation letter doesn't lie about the time required) and skip patterns to ensure respondents see the right questions. The flow and naturalness of the question order can also be assessed during the pretest. For online surveys, URLs and hyperlinks must be tested to ensure the survey tool does what you hope it will and that the final survey looks the way it should.

Deciding How to Administer

Before the survey can be administered, several additional decisions need to be made. Will the survey go to all employees or a smaller sample of them? Will the survey be done online or using paper and pencil? If paper surveys are used, will they be administered by mail or in group administrations at work locations? Are incentives for participation needed? When is the best time to administer?

The decision to do a census or sample survey is related to other stages of the survey process. If the survey is intended to harness commitment to further action or change, then the entire organization should be included. If results will be shared within every department in the organization (with the expectation that department-level action will be taken), a census is required. If the survey is intended to take the pulse of how the organization as a whole feels about an issue (or issues), then a sample may be sufficient. Sample surveys allow the organization to survey more often without running the risk of survey fatigue. Sample surveys may raise suspicion about why and who was actually invited, however, and they may be easier for the respondent to ignore because everyone around them is not taking it as well. Sample surveys require support from human resources (and potentially information technology) to be able to identify eligible employees and then select them randomly. If results will be broken down into smaller groups (e.g., by divisions, geographic regions, or demographic groups), a stratified sampling approach may be needed to ensure valid results for relevant subgroups.

COMMUNICATING THE SURVEY

The next step in administering the survey is communicating that it will be happening. Response rates suffer if the survey is not communicated well. The level of communication needed is a function of the survey culture of the organization. In companies that have not done surveys before, extensive communication before the survey is needed to indicate why the survey is being done, why responses are critical, how the results will be used, and how the organization is committed to action. In organizations that have had negative experiences with surveys in the past, the communication needs to focus on how things will be different this time. The medium of communication will vary from company to company. E-mails from senior managers may be enough, whereas public addresses may be needed in other organizations. The medium of communication that is usually used in the organization to communicate important events should be used for the survey as well.

ADMINISTERING THE SURVEY

The medium by which the survey is administered is a critical decision. If all employees have access to the Internet or an e-mail system, an online or network survey may be advisable. Online surveys allow for easier tracking of response rates and remove the need for the data entry involved with paper surveys. As a result, online surveys are generally more cost-effective compared to other approaches. However, online surveys can fall prey to network problems and suspicions that responses are not truly anonymous. Online surveys also require that access to the survey be controlled. If the workforce does not have ready access to the Internet or company network, then paper surveys may be required. Paper surveys are what most people think of automatically, and thus there is some comfort with this format. They also allow for group administration, which can help to increase response rates. Voice-response surveys can be done by phone but typically require the survey to be very short and not very complex. Fax-based surveys are still used but have faded in popularity.

Incentives for participation are usually less of a concern for internal employee surveys because people are expected to participate. However, for external surveys (e.g., customer satisfaction surveys), incentives may help boost response rates. Research continues on the most effective incentives, but lotteries based on responses seem to actually reduce responses below levels with no incentive at all. More immediate incentives appear to be more effective. The promise of sharing results can also motivate some respondents.

Finally, the timing of the survey is critical. Organizations should avoid exceptionally busy times (April for accountants, November and December in retail) or times when many employees are expected to be away (summertime or holidays). Organizations need to provide employees with enough time to respond and must accommodate individual travel, vacations, and leave. Having a survey available for only one week may cause employees to miss the opportunity to respond. Two weeks is a short administration period, and two months is relatively long. Of course, online surveys may require a shorter window, and mail surveys need to allow time for postal service. Similarly, the timing of survey action planning must be considered. The survey should be timed so that immediate communication of results and preliminary follow-up action can be taken shortly after the survey is complete and results have been analyzed.

ANALYZING THE SURVEY RESULTS

There are as many ways to analyze survey results as there are questions to be asked. The analysis approach must be geared to the audience that will be receiving the information. Although regression analyses and other higher-level statistics may provide very useful information, they are not appropriate for every audience. Generally, the percentage of favorable responses to individual questions or groups of questions is summarized. The mean values of items or groups of items may also be compared. For example, categories or questions with relatively high mean values identify areas of strength and categories or questions with relatively low mean values represent opportunities for improvement.

PRESENTING THE SURVEY RESULTS AND TAKING ACTION

The culture within an organization influences how survey results are fed back to employees. Some organizations share results at the department level and then move up the hierarchy, with senior management actually receiving lower-level results last. Other organizations ask for results to be presented at the top first, and then results are rolled out from the top to the bottom of the organization. The direction of the rollout is another opportunity for the company to communicate the importance of the survey and where they expect action to occur.

The results shared depend on the audience and should focus on "what's in it for them." Therefore, the results shared with a frontline department will be very different from those shared with the senior management team. Departments want to know how the group felt, where they are up and where they are down, and how they compare with other groups (or the rest of the chain of command). Senior managers want to know which parts of the organization are working well and which require their immediate attention. They also want to know how the results of the organization compare with industry (or competitor) norms.

This raises the important question of whether the focus of analysis and interpretation should be internal or external to the organization. For a first survey, external norms may be an unnecessary distraction when analysis should focus on internal strengths and weaknesses. After initial internal baselines are established, making comparisons to benchmark norms on subsequent surveys can be useful. Once again, the purpose of the survey drives the organization's focus.

When improvement areas are identified, the organization (or department) must decide where to begin—it cannot necessarily take on every challenge. At this point, commitment from senior management (or department management) is critical. Those who need to make the changes will not be on board unless they believe they will have the needed resources and support. (Other entries in this encyclopedia provide more detail on taking action in organizations.)

SUMMARY

Surveys are a popular tool in organizations but suffer from the fate that nearly everyone believes that he or she can conduct a survey well. Unfortunately, it is very easy for a survey to be done poorly. By following the steps outlined here, some of the key pitfalls in survey research can be avoided and the benefits of an effective survey can be achieved.

—*Peter D. Bachiochi*

See also Job Satisfaction; Linkage Research and Analyses; Organizational Surveys; Quantitative Research Approach

FURTHER READING

Church, A. H., & Waclawski, J. (1998). *Designing and using organizational surveys: A seven-step process.* San Francisco: Jossey-Bass.

Kraut, A. I. (1996). *Organizational surveys: Tools for assessment and change.* San Francisco: Jossey-Bass.

Rogelberg, S. G., Church, A. H., Waclawski, J., & Stanton, J. M. (2002). Organizational survey research. In S. G. Rogelberg (Ed.), *Handbook of research in industrial and organizational psychology* (pp. 141–160). Malden, MA: Blackwell.

Stanton, J. M., & Rogelberg, S. G. (2001). Using Internet/intranet Web pages to collect organizational research data. *Organizational Research Methods, 4,* 199–216.

SURVIVOR SYNDROME

Downsizing is the planned elimination of jobs and positions in order to decrease the number of workers employed by an organization; it is often a response to changing technology, market demands, and institutional pressures. Downsizing occurs in a large number of organizations, and it is increasingly being accepted as a legitimate management tool even in economically healthy organizations. The effects of downsizing extend beyond employees who lose their jobs. Downsizing alters the work environment of the workers who remain in the organization, who are described in the literature as *survivors*. Downsizing can alter the conditions of survivors' jobs and change their perceptions of the organization. Some studies show that after downsizing, survivors become narrow-minded, self-absorbed, and risk averse. Furthermore, morale sinks, productivity drops, and distrust—especially toward management—increases. This constellation of symptoms is termed *survivor syndrome.*

There are many definitions of survivor syndrome. In general, this syndrome relates to the negative effects experienced by the remaining workforce after a major organizational change. It also refers to the way survivors react when many of their friends are forced to terminate their employment in the organization. Survivor syndrome is described as a mixed bag of emotions exhibited by employees following organizational downsizing—a set of attitudes, feelings, and perceptions. These symptoms can be broken down into four clusters of feelings: (1) fear, insecurity, and uncertainty; (2) frustration, anger, and resentment; (3) sadness, depression, and guilt; and (4) injustice, betrayal, and guilt. These psychological states can affect survivors' work behavior (e.g., motivation, performance) and attitudes (satisfaction, commitment).

Survivors experience apathy, disengagement, distrust, powerlessness, and loss of motivation, morale, and commitment. Their feelings of powerlessness and the uncertainty of their job security can cause severe stress reactions. Furthermore, the high increase in workload following the downsizing may lead to burnout and decreased performance. In situations in which downsizing is perceived as merely a cutback in personnel, commitment and loyalty to the organization among survivors decreases significantly. Survivors feel they have to cope with an additional role while getting little or nothing in return.

Researchers suggest several explanations for survivor syndrome. Some focus on increased job insecurity, perceptions of procedural and distributive injustice, and diminishing intrinsic motivation of the job. Others point to violation of the psychological contract, perceptions of unfairness on the part of the organization, and the organization's lack of future vision. Two concepts are core to the survivor syndrome phenomenon: psychological contract and distributive and procedural justice.

The *psychological contract* refers to the unwritten reciprocity of the relationship between the employer and the employee. It is voluntary, subjective, and informal, and it evolves with time. The essence of the old psychological contract was that the employee gives his or her compete loyalty and trust to the organization, and the organization takes care of the employee for life. When downsizing occurs, employees feel the psychological contract has been violated by management. Thus, employees feel their psychological contract with the employer has been broken, and they blame management for breaking the contract. Blame among survivors may be a projection defense mechanism that helps them cope with their guilt over surviving the cutback.

Distributive justice refers to the perceived fairness of the way resources are distributed among people. One approach to distributive justice, *equity theory,* proposes that individuals strive to ensure that their own outcome/input ratios are equal to the outcome/input ratios of others to whom they compare themselves. When downsizing occurs, survivors compare themselves to those who have been laid off and experience inequity.

Procedural justice refers to perceptions of the fairness of the procedures used to determine outcomes. In the case of downsizing, it relates to perceptions of the fairness of the procedures used to lay off employees. Studies show that when procedural justice is perceived—fairness in implementing the layoff process—it minimizes survivors' guilt and blame.

Thus, research shows that the following are antecedents of survivor syndrome and decreased performance: downsizing through attrition, leading to skill shortage; no overall work reduction in the organization; inappropriate elements in the reward and appraisal system; and pursuing downsizing without quality improvement programs and redesign.

Several studies have focused on the outcomes of survivor syndrome. A field study investigating the impact of repeated layoffs showed that organizational commitment is negatively related to the severity of the layoff. In a survey of senior managers after downsizing, most reported that their employees had low morale, feared future cutbacks, and distrusted management. Lack of communication before and during cutbacks causes low morale, loss of trust in the organization, and increased stress. Low morale and lack of trust have a ripple effect on all dimensions of activity: Research shows that after layoffs, most survivors have diminishing future expectations, indicating low commitment.

Some researchers have found an inverted-U relationship between the job insecurity of survivors and their work efforts. Positive relationships have been found among survivors whose economic need to work is high. Laboratory experiments demonstrate that regardless of whether a layoff is accompanied by job insecurity, it elicits an increase in performance among survivors. Survivors who experience job insecurity work harder because they believe that by doing so, they can reduce the threat of layoff. Survivors who do not experience job insecurity work harder to alleviate their feelings of survivor guilt produced by positive inequity.

Findings concerning survivors' coping demonstrate that they cope in ways that are not good for them or their organization. They are reluctant to take personal and organizational risks and demonstrate reduced innovation and productivity. They distance themselves from the layoff victims or, when they identify with them, distance themselves from the organization. Though some survivors try to reduce their feelings of guilt over their peers' layoffs by increasing their output, others redress their feeling of inequity by convincing themselves that those who were laid off were poor performers. Thus, in some cases, the job insecurity of survivors leads to temporarily heightened productivity, but in most cases, it is accompanied by low morale.

Another defense mechanism found among survivors coping with feelings of uncertainty and threat is *identification with the aggressor syndrome:* Some survivors cope with their impotence by identifying with the executive, the perceived aggressor. This enhances their self-esteem by creating a kind of merger with the powerful figure, making them feel like winners and reinforcing their distance from the layoff victims. They feel equity and legitimacy in scapegoating the victims, the losers.

Longitudinal studies following survivors show that wounds do not seem to heal and symptoms intensify with time. Findings from several studies indicate that some procedures can reduce the negative reactions of survivors. These include giving clear explanations of the reasons for the downsizing and providing information about the compensation given to leavers, as well as the fairness of the organization's decisions (procedural justice), the way management breaks the news, and the level of job insecurity. One recommendation is to treat leavers fairly to prevent survivor syndrome. Managers in downsizing organizations must realize that survivors have experienced a traumatic event that they have little or no control over; therefore, they need reassurance if they are to maintain their commitment to the organization. Managers must realize the need for human resource policies to cope with the effects of downsizing. Organizations should find ways to nurture confidence in organizational support and to make the employees believe the organization cares about their well-being. Organizational support can be fostered by redesigning jobs using job enrichment procedures and implementing employees' empowerment strategies. Creating a future vision that survivors can identify with is also recommended.

—*Mina Westman*

See also Downsizing; Psychological Contract

FURTHER READING

Brockner, J., Grover, S., Reed, T., & Dewitt, R. (1992). Layoffs, job insecurity, and survivors' work effort: Evidence of an inverted-U relationship. *Academy of Management Journal, 35,* 413–425.

Brockner, J., Wiesenfeld, B., Stephan, J., Hurley, R., Grover, S., Reed, T., DeWitt, R., & Martin, C. (1997). The effects of layoff survivors on their fellow survivors' reactions. *Journal of Applied Social Psychology, 10,* 835–863.

de Vries, K., & Balazs, K. (1997). The downside of downsizing. *Human Relations, 30,* 11–50.

Sahdev, K. (2004). Revisiting the survivor syndrome: The role of leadership in implementing downsizing. *European Journal of Work and Organizational Psychology, 13,* 165–196.

T

TEAM-BASED REWARDS

Rewards for performance are commonly used to maximize work output and productivity. With the increased use of team-based work, a variety of team-based reward systems have been developed, with the intent of maximizing performance and satisfaction in work teams. A *team-based reward* is commonly defined as any formal incentive provided to a work team or at least one of its individual team members. Rewards may be based on organizational, team, or team member performance or other outcomes (e.g., sales, customer satisfaction, and profit).

Rewards provided to teams can be categorized as monetary or nonmonetary. Monetary team-based rewards include one-time cash bonuses, permanently increased base salary, and variable pay (i.e., earning a specified percentage of base salary). Nonmonetary team-based rewards include achievement awards, time off work, and special dinners. Team-based rewards can be distributed equally across team members, so that all members receive the same reward (e.g., amount of money, recognition award), or nonequally, either based on individual performance within the team (i.e., equitably) or in proportion to individual base salary.

There are seven major categories of team-based rewards:

- *Team gainsharing/profit sharing.* Team rewards are tied to organizational outcomes; rewards are generally cash in nature and shared equally among all teams in the organization. With profit sharing, the organizational outcome is financial in nature (e.g., organizational profit); *gainsharing* refers to nonfinancial organizational outcomes (e.g., overall company customer satisfaction, improvements in organizational productivity or quality).

- *Team goal-based rewards.* The organization (often in conjunction with the team) formulates goals or targets for each team that are believed to reflect effective short- or long-term performance outcomes (e.g., predetermined production objectives, customer service goals). When the team meets its goal(s), it earns predetermined reward(s).

- *Team discretionary rewards.* Also known as *spot rewards*, these team-based rewards, like goal-based rewards, evaluate team outcomes (e.g., customer satisfaction, team productivity) when determining whether a specific team should be provided with incentives. Unlike in goal-based systems, however, the team is not provided with a predetermined performance standard that will guarantee the receipt of a specific predetermined reward. Instead, when the organization determines a team has done an outstanding job, the team is provided with a reward.

- *Team skill rewards.* Teams are rewarded for acquiring valued skills (e.g., collaboration, cooperation, interpersonal understanding) regardless of team outcomes, following the rationale that if such skills improve, desired outcomes will eventually be achieved. Skills are generally evaluated by supervisors.

- *Team member skill rewards.* Individual team members are rewarded for acquiring team-related skills (e.g., adaptability, communication, leadership, initiation of ideas). Skills are generally evaluated by other team members and/or supervisors.

- *Team member goal-based rewards.* Individual team members are rewarded when they achieve predetermined performance goals, often in conjunction with quarterly or annual formal performance evaluations.

- *Team member merit rewards.* Individual team members are rewarded when they make an outstanding contribution to the team, as determined by other team members and/or supervisors.

RESEARCH ON TEAM-BASED REWARDS

Research on team-based rewards has generally lagged behind other categories of work team research. Although much additional research is required, existing work suggests that team-based rewards may have greater impact on the productivity of lower-performing team members. Additionally, highest-performing employees appear to prefer individually based rewards. An accumulating body of evidence suggests that as team interdependence increases, team-based rewards are most effective when based on equal rewards for team members; otherwise, group cohesiveness and performance may be negatively affected.

TEAM-BASED REWARD EFFECTIVENESS

To date, practical experience suggests that several factors need to be considered when choosing a team reward system. As noted above, the majority of these guidelines have not been the target of substantial research.

- *Team interdependence.* High within-team interdependence (e.g., need for cooperation in performing tasks and meeting team goals) suggests the need for equal distribution of rewards among team members. Current research does not clearly support the belief that such reward systems encourage slacking among team members. Equitable reward systems may be more useful for less interdependent teams. To the extent team cooperation is required throughout the organization (i.e., high between-team interdependence), profit-sharing systems may be most effective.
- *Full- versus part-time teams.* Full-time work teams may benefit most from clear, predetermined performance targets. Skills incentive systems may be useful for these teams, as they encourage team members to learn one another's tasks. When tenure on a work team is part-time and temporary, an important consideration is ensuring that team-based rewards are not so enticing that they conflict with other (non-team) job responsibilities.
- *Line-of-sight.* As the basis for reward is further outside of the team's immediate control (commonly termed

the *line-of-sight problem*), reward systems may become less effective. This is a particular concern in large organizations, where individual teams may perceive little direct control over organizational outcomes as a whole (e.g., organizational profit).

- *Measurable performance standards.* It is important to ensure that it is possible to measure aspects of performance that are the basis for rewards. This may be particularly critical when it is necessary to assess contributions of team members relative to team outcomes; otherwise, rewards may be perceived as unjust.
- *Additional factors.* Other factors that influence team-based reward effectiveness may include team composition (same or mixed gender; same or mixed occupation teams); organizational context factors (e.g., type of industry, size of organization); and team pressures (e.g., time pressure, stress), to name a few.

—Jody Hoffman

See also Compensation; Gainsharing and Profit Sharing; Group Cohesiveness; Groups; Incentives; Intrinsic and Extrinsic Work Motivation; Performance Appraisal; Social Loafing

FURTHER READING

Beersma, B., Hollenbeck, J. R., & Humphrey, S. E. (2003). Cooperation, competition and team performance: Toward a contingency approach. *Academy of Management Journal, 46*(5), 572–590.

Hoffman, J. R., & Rogelberg, S. G. (1998). A guide to team incentive systems. *Team Performance Management, 4*(1), 23–32.

Jenkins, G. D., Mitra, A., & Gupta, N. (1998). Are financial incentives related to performance? A meta-analytic review of empirical research. *Journal of Applied Psychology, 83*(5), 777–787.

Johnson, D. W., Maruyama, G., Johnson, R., Nelson, D., & Skon, L. (1981). Effects of cooperative, competitive, and individual goal structures on achievement: A meta-analysis. *Psychological Bulletin, 89,* 47–62.

Rynes, S. L., Gerhart, B., & Parks, L. (2005). Personnel psychology: Performance evaluation and pay for performance. *Annual Review of Psychology, 56,* 571–600.

Stoneman, K. G., & Dickinson, A. M. (1989). Team member performance as a function of group contingencies and group size. *Journal of Organizational Behavior Management, 10,* 131–150.

Wageman, R., & Baker, G. (1997). Incentives and cooperation: The joint effects of task and reward interdependence on group performance. *Journal of Organizational Behavior, 18,* 139–158.

TEAM BUILDING

Teamwork has always been an important feature of successful organizations, but the use of teams as a business strategy and structure was relatively rare until the 1980s. Now, in the 21st century, work teams have become a common feature in many manufacturing and product development organizations, service organizations, and government agencies. They range from ongoing work teams on the floor of a manufacturing plant, to white collar teams, teams of managers or executives, problem-solving committees, project-based teams, or task forces that exist only for the duration of a given problem.

Although the effectiveness of these teams varies considerably from organization to organization, teams work best when they are composed of employees who have interdependent jobs and the best subject matter knowledge of the work to be accomplished, and when the leadership of the organization plays an active role in establishing and supporting them.

People often equate team building with trust building or relationship building, but that is only half of what is needed to develop a group of individuals into a highly functioning team. Teams exist to perform, to accomplish something for the organization. Thus, team building must also include knowledge of business objectives and the development of goals, roles, and procedures needed to get the job done. Team-building efforts must be task-oriented as well as relationship-oriented.

How teams are built will be, to some extent, a function of the type of team being implemented, but all team-building efforts need to include the following characteristics:

- Alignment around goals
- Clarification of roles
- Establishment of policies and procedures
- Building effective working relationships
- Working with the environment, including support systems

Team building can be done within the team, or at the organizational level, where multiple teams, or even a team-based organization, is desired. Team building can also be done within the team itself.

ORGANIZATIONAL LEVEL

Organizational team building generally begins with a steering committee composed of the leadership of the organization (at the local level). For example, a steering committee in a manufacturing plant would typically be composed of the operating committee of that plant, as well as the local union leadership in unionized plants. (In unionized settings, the authors strongly recommend bringing the union in at the beginning of any team-development effort.) The steering committee would determine the following framework for the teams:

- *Goals.* Often established with a charter or mission statement. Why is the organization developing and launching teams? What are goals for having teams in the organization?
- *Roles.* How teams would be structured. Within functions? Cross-functionally? How many teams? How many members for a given team? How will we deploy and use talent? To whom do the teams report? Are there leaders on each team? Will members be expected to learn one another's jobs and rotate among the jobs? Who is to make which decisions?
- *Policies and procedures.* How are members and leaders selected? How are team meetings conducted? What kinds of issues can the team address on its own? Are team decisions to be made by consensus?
- *Relationships.* How do we ensure that the teams function effectively? How will the teams manage conflict? How will we reinforce good team behavior?
- *Environment.* How will the various organizational systems (e.g., finance systems, personnel systems, communications systems, rewards systems) support the teams?
- *The plan for rolling out teams in the organization.* What will be the timing? Will the teams process be piloted in some areas of the plant?

Once the steering committee has established this framework, the organization can begin the actual implementation of its teams. Implementation will consist of preparing the organization, providing training in the necessary skills, management of the relevant support systems, and the actual launching of the teams. The steering committee/leadership team will also have to provide ongoing direction and support to the teams. Direction may be in the form of policy deployment, in which business goals are established for each team. Support will be ensuring that the team is able to get its issues resolved and its ideas implemented. Direction and support from leadership is absolutely critical in any successful organizational team-building effort.

Launching of the teams may well begin with one or more pilots of the proposed team structure. Pilots are often helpful, particularly in brownfield sites (usually underused or abandoned commercial/industrial property that may also be environmentally contaminated), where the organization or plant has been in operation with the same employees over a period of time without teams. Pilots enable the steering committee to test its strategy for its teams and to see what adjustments it should make before rolling out teams throughout the entire organization. Pilots are also a confidence builder for the organization (including management, the union, and employees generally), proving that it has a workable and successful process. Teams should be implemented at a pace that is supportable by the organization. Launching teams that fail, because they are not supported or because they lack direction or skills, will substantially impede the overall team implementation process.

Preparing the organization consists generally of communication to midlevel management and other employees—answering their questions about the teams' process and addressing their concerns. Questions can be expected to include how a given employee's job will change when the teams are implemented (i.e., What will my new job look like? Will I need to learn new skills?).

Selection of team members and team leaders is important. Often teams will be composed of the existing employees of the organization. If new members are being brought in, selection procedures should support teamwork. Selection procedures should also be established to ensure that new team leaders have good people skills and also will work to help the organization achieve its goals.

Skill development—of both team members and leaders—is also critical. Generally, new or additional skills are required for team members to perform effectively. These skills usually cluster into three groups:

- Technical skills (to get the job done)
- Teamwork skills (the interpersonal and facilitative abilities needed to help people work and solve problems together)
- Business skills (understanding of business metrics, how the organization functions regarding quality, timing and material flow systems, and the computer systems relevant to team members' jobs)

Ensuring systems support for teams is also critical. Team efforts in some organizations are hindered by some of the systems already in place in the organization. (Systems to monitor in a manufacturing plant would be the engineering, finance, information, and human resource systems.) For example, if the finance systems in a plant discourage team development by penalizing teams for meetings, training, implementation of ideas, and so on, organizational leadership will need to manage this, or the teams' process will continually be swimming against the current. If major support systems are congruent with the team-building effort, they will aid considerably in the long-term health of the teams.

The final piece of organizational team building is evaluation (and adjustment where required). Teams should be evaluated on a regular basis to ensure they are using the right processes and that they are achieving anticipated results. If teams are not achieving the goals set out for them, leadership needs to ask why and to take the actions required to help the teams become more successful.

TEAM LEVEL

Team building within the team will also be critical. Generally, this team building will be ongoing rather than a one-shot session and will be composed of training and discussion specific to that team. Also, team-building training, as opposed to training for skill development, is conducted with the entire intact team, rather than with individuals. Topics might include the following:

- *Goals.* Training/discussion may be focused on how to set clear goals. Many organizations insist on teams negotiating a team charter between the team and responsible mangers (and union leaders) to empower the team to accomplish things on behalf of the organization.
- *Roles.* It is important that each member of the team understand the roles and responsibilities he or she is expected to fulfill for this team to succeed. An understanding of the talent that exists on the team, and how best to use it, allows members to understand why clear roles are important. Group dynamics roles should be clarified in addition to task-related roles.
- *Procedures.* Training/discussion should be focused on how to identify and resolve problems, how to reach consensus decisions, and how to conduct effective and efficient meetings. Time may also be dedicated to the establishment of specific work task procedures. This standardization of work may be especially important if the team members are

expected to learn one another's jobs and to rotate among positions on the team.

- *Relationships.* Training/discussion may be focused on improving communication skills (especially effective listening and providing constructive feedback) and how to enhance conflict resolution skills. Sessions may also be dedicated for team members to get better acquainted, in the hope that this will lead to greater trust among members. (An area that probably deserves more research is to investigate whether these bonding activities actually lead to greater performance or whether greater performance of a team leads to increased bonding among team members.) Regardless of the causal relationship between these elements, it is generally thought that respect, trust, and embracement of the benefits of diversity are key dimensions of the relationship side of team development.

- *Environment.* Teams are not closed systems. It is critical that they interact effectively with their external environments. Teams need good diplomatic relationships with key managers, union officials, other teams, and the functions that affect their performance. Team members must feel free to disagree with each other during team meetings but should present a united, positive front to the rest of the organization.

Virtually all teams experience times when they feel stuck. This can occur if teams have resolved the easy problems and are now confronted by more complex problems. Teams can become snagged on political issues. Also, teams are often changed by the introduction of new members or the loss of some old members. It is important to monitor the health of teams and take steps to intervene to help them stay viable. These steps may include revisiting the team-building steps described earlier in this chapter and especially asking the team to revisit its charter. Teams should be asked to apply the problem-solving and planning skills they have learned in their team-building sessions to the problems underlying their own performance.

SUMMARY

Team building can be done at the organizational level and within the team itself. All team-building efforts will address goals, roles, policies and procedures, relationships, and the environment. Team building at the organizational level will also require preparation of the organization, skills development, management of support systems, and evaluation of the teams.

—*Lee O. Sanborn and Gregory E. Huszczo*

See also Group Cohesiveness; Group Development; Group Dynamics and Processes; Groups

FURTHER READING

Cohen, S. G., & Bailey, D. E. (1997). What makes teams work: Group effectiveness research from the shop floor to the executive suite. *Journal of Management, 23,* 239–290.

Hackman, J. R. (2002). *Leading teams: Setting the stage for great performance.* Boston: Harvard Business School Press.

Huszczo, G. E. (2004). *Tools for team leadership: Delivering the X-factor in team excellence.* Palo Alto, CA: Davies-Black.

Katzenbach, J. R., & Smith, D. K. (2002). *The wisdom of teams: Creating the high-performance organization.* New York: Harper Business Essentials.

Shonk, J. H. (1982). *Working in teams: A practical manual for improving work groups.* New York: AMACOM.

Weldon, E., & Weingart, L. R. (1993). Group goals and group performance. *British Journal of Social Psychology, 32,* 307–334.

TEAM DEVELOPMENT

See GROUP DEVELOPMENT

TEAM MENTAL MODEL

The notion of a team mental model was introduced in 1990 to account for the fluid, implicit coordination frequently observed in effective teams and to advance the understanding of how teams function in complex, dynamic, and ambiguous situations. For example, the seemingly effortless execution of a blind pass in basketball illustrates a well-known situation in which team members correctly predict the positioning and readiness of other team members on the court. In contrast, postincident investigations of many catastrophic aviation incidents reveal breakdowns in teamwork, as well as ambiguity with respect to who is responsible for specific tasks. Therefore, both team successes and failures speak to the necessity of being "on the same page" with respect to what to do, with whom, and when to do it.

Team mental models are thus defined as team members' shared, organized understanding and mental representation of knowledge about key elements of the team's relevant environment. The general thesis of this emerging literature is that team effectiveness will improve if team members are mentally congruent and have an adequate shared understanding of the task, team, equipment, and situation. Teams whose members share mental models of both task and team variables are expected to have more accurate expectations of team needs and be better positioned to anticipate the actions of other members, as compared with teams whose members do not have a shared mental model.

THE IMPORTANCE AND FUNCTION OF TEAM MENTAL MODELS

At the most basic level, a *mental model* is a cognitive structure or network of associations between concepts in a person's mind. The information stored in mental models, which helps to explain and predict events, enables individuals to interact more efficiently with their environment. Having built its foundation on this earlier individual-level research, the current mental model literature has been expanded to incorporate cognitive processes at the team level, thus helping to account for team actions and behaviors. Although cognition is normally thought of at the individual level of analysis, the existence of group-level cognitive structures is receiving widespread acceptance because of the increasing emphasis on teams in research and in organizations.

Team mental models bring explanatory power to team performance by directly affecting team processes and enabling members to formulate accurate teamwork and task work predictions. Individuals involved in teams must devote their efforts not only to completing the task at hand but also to synchronizing their efforts with other team members. Thus, team mental models fulfill multiple purposes, including description, prediction, and explanation. Not surprisingly, team mental models are especially crucial to team functioning in emergency situations because of the way in which they allow team members to anticipate and initiate the exchange of information and required resources when there is not enough time for explicit communication.

THE NATURE OF TEAM MENTAL MODELS

The studies of mental model type and mental model similarity have been at the forefront of some of the earliest work in the team mental model literature. Team members develop multiple mental models to represent their environment, but researchers have primarily focused on two types of mental models. Whereas task-focused mental models include representations of the equipment, procedures, and performance requirements, team-focused models include information about the interpersonal interaction requirements and skills of other team members.

Mental model similarity is defined as the level of congruence across team members' mental models. Rather than being dichotomous in orientation, mental model similarity is generally measured along a continuum. At one end, team members hold incongruent mental models, in that their mental representations of people, places, and things related to the task at hand are strikingly different from one another's. At the other end of the continuum, the mental models of each team member are seemingly identical. It is worth noting, however, that the optimal level at which information should be shared among team members remains a prominent focus of the team mental model literature. At present, the consensus seems to be that the degree of information overlap needed for effective team functioning depends on a number of factors, including the nature of the task and the type of mental model in question.

THE MEASUREMENT OF TEAM MENTAL MODELS

The concept of team mental models is undoubtedly complex. It is further complicated by the fact that various researchers have measured the construct in different ways. One of the most common measurement techniques collects relatedness ratings from participants by asking them to provide quick, intuitive judgments regarding the similarity between concept pairs. These judgments, which are individually analyzed via a computerized scaling program, are then graphically transformed to represent the way in which elements are organized within each individual's mind. The similarity of element structures among each of the team members can then be compared by means of statistical indexes.

Concept mapping, another team mental model measurement technique, requires individuals to select prelabeled concepts that best depict their actions during a task, and then place these concepts in the appropriate rows on a concept map. Respondents are also asked to indicate which concepts depict the actions of their teammates during a task. Given the complexity and multidimensional nature of team mental models, researchers propose that multiple measures are often necessary for thorough assessment.

RESEARCH ON TEAM MENTAL MODELS

Empirical work on team mental models has substantially lagged behind conceptual development. Nevertheless, the team mental model literature has seen a flurry of activity and research in the last decade. Although many of the studies have engaged team members in computer-based flight/combat simulations, more recent work has begun to investigate how mental models converge in organizational teams performing actual tasks. As this research is still in its formative stages, there is a need for continued conceptual development of the construct and empirical support linking team mental models to antecedents and outcomes.

ANTECEDENTS

Research from several studies has provided evidence to suggest that team members can be trained to mentally organize incoming performance-relevant information in such a way as to facilitate the development of mental models that are shared among the majority of team members. Shared mental model training interventions (e.g., self-correction training, computer-based instruction) have shown promise, owing in large part to their ability to foster various teamwork skills, such as monitoring and backup behaviors that allow team members to observe one another's needs. In addition, team planning has been shown to increase mental model similarity among team members. Because little work has focused on antecedents, researchers have called for more studies to investigate the individual-, team-, and organizational-level variables that contribute to the development of team mental models.

OUTCOMES

The construct of a team mental model was developed to help explain performance differences between teams. Therefore, a common theoretical assumption is that they are precursors to effective team performance. Indeed, several studies have demonstrated that both shared teamwork and task-work mental models relate positively to team processes and performance. When team members share similar mental models, their interpersonal interactions appear more effective, thus enabling them to perform more successfully.

Although most of the research has been devoted to the degree of sharedness among team member mental models, the quality of teammates' mental models is another concept that has been examined. Researchers have argued that team mental model similarity alone does not ensure success. They have pointed out that certain mental models may in fact be inaccurate, thus leading to potentially more detrimental (rather than successful) performance. Consequently, most researchers have concluded that highly convergent mental models, in combination with those that are of high quality, will yield the greatest performance benefits for teams.

SUMMARY

As a result of an increasingly global marketplace, the formation of teams whose members are often separated, temporally and/or geographically, has instigated a renewed interest in identifying the keys to successful team performance and effectiveness. Given the promising results from a number of team mental model studies, researchers have become increasingly confident that at least one of these keys lies within the team mental model domain. They have argued, first and foremost, that we cannot begin to understand team actions and behaviors until we begin to understand team cognitive processes. Thus, despite its relative infancy, the construct of team mental models has the potential to advance our understanding of work teams, therefore warranting further investigation in coming years.

—*Susan Mohammed and Lori Ferzandi*

See also Group Dynamics and Processes; Groups; Team-Based Rewards; Team Building

FURTHER READING

Cannon-Bowers, J. A., Salas, E., & Converse, S. A. (1993). Shared mental models in expert team decision making. In N. J. Castellan Jr. (Ed.), *Current issues in individual and group decision making* (pp. 221–246). Hillsdale, NJ: Lawrence Erlbaum.

Klimoski, R., & Mohammed, S. (1994). Team mental model: Construct or metaphor? *Journal of Management, 20*(2), 403–437.

Mathieu, J. E., Heffner, T. S., Goodwin, G. F., Cannon-Bowers, J. A., & Salas, E. (2005). Scaling the quality of teammates' mental models: Equifinality and normative comparisons. *Journal of Organizational Behavior, 26,* 37–56.

Mathieu, J. E., Heffner, T. S., Goodwin, G. F., Salas, E., & Cannon-Bowers, J. A. (2000). The influence of shared mental models on team process and performance. *Journal of Applied Psychology, 80,* 191–195.

Mohammed, S., & Dumville, B. (2001). Team mental models in a team knowledge framework: Expanding theory and measurement across disciplinary boundaries. *Journal of Organizational Behavior, 22,* 89–106.

Mohammed, S., Klimoski, R., & Rentsch, J. (2000). The measurement of team mental models: We have no shared schema. *Organizational Research Methods, 3*(2), 123–165.

Smith-Jentsch, K. A., Campbell, G., Milanovich, D. M., & Reynolds, A. M. (2001). Measuring teamwork mental models to support training needs assessment, development, and evaluation: Two empirical studies. *Journal of Organizational Behavior, 22,* 179–194.

TEAMS

See GROUPS

TELECOMMUTING

The idea for *telecommuting* started in the early 1970s. A scientist stuck in Los Angeles traffic reasoned that a good deal of time and stress could be saved by moving the work to the employee instead of always moving the employee to the work. Since that time, communication technologies (e.g., fax, mobile phones, e-mail, the Internet, and instant messaging) and information technologies (e.g., the personal computer) have become more common. Subsequently, work has begun to move out of the traditional work space. Employees have become freed of time and place constraints to work whenever and wherever they choose.

Telecommuting and *teleworking* are often used interchangeably when referring to working outside of an organization. However, *telework* is usually considered the more general term and refers to any use of communication or information technologies to substitute for work-related travel. Virtual teams of coworkers who are scattered around the world can be considered teleworkers even if all of them work within an office.

Telecommuters are a subset of teleworkers. These are employees who work outside of a main office. There are four main types of telecommuters. The first, and most well known, are telecommuters who work from their homes. These telecommuters may have a dedicated home office space or may simply set up their laptop on the kitchen table. Although some home-based telecommuters work from their home every day, most do not. Some telecommute from home only one or two days a week, and some only once a month.

The second type of telecommuter is found in satellite offices that are located outside the home and outside the main office. Satellite offices provide an organizational location convenient to customers or to the employees, but it is still considered a type of telecommuting because even though employees may be close to other employees of their organization, they may be separated from their primary coworkers and teams.

A third type of telecommuter works in a neighborhood office. This telecommuting arrangement is similar to the satellite office except that the office is not dedicated to one organization. Instead it is occupied by employees from several different organizations. Thus, telecommuters interact with other employees, but not necessarily ones from their own organization.

Mobile workers are the final type of telecommuter. These employees work on the road in their car, hotels, and airplanes. These employees have no dedicated work location and no colleagues with whom they regularly interact while working.

Home-based telecommuting is the most common form of telework. In 2004, 24.1 million employees engaged in home-based telecommuting at least one day per month. An additional 20.3 million self-employed workers can also be classified as telecommuters. That means that nearly 20% of the workforce works at home at least part-time. It is expected that the number of home-based telecommuters will grow as technology improves and it becomes more acceptable for employees to work outside of an office.

How do employees become telecommuters? Telecommuting programs are either informal or formal. Informal telecommuting occurs when employees irregularly work away from the office. Employees and their managers may decide that the employees should work at home occasionally to focus on a particular project or to save commuting time for specific personal obligations (e.g., a doctor's appointment).

Formal telecommuting programs involve an arrangement between the employees and their human resources department. A formal program may mean changing the employees' classification to signal to other employees their telecommuting status, providing training on setting up a home office, and creating monetary allowances for purchasing home office supplies.

Historically, telecommuting was offered primarily to high-performing, trustworthy employees. Managers were more likely to grant their best employees the benefit of working without immediate supervision. Many organizations made it clear that telecommuting was not for employees who just wanted the convenience of working at home. The arrangement had to be mutually beneficial to the organization and the employee.

However, as telecommuting becomes more common, employees of all types are starting to work outside the office. Additionally, a new generation of employees with significant experience and comfort with technology is coming on the market. Organizations may offer telecommuting to these employees as a competitive hiring perk. Managers may soon be faced with a growing number of employees with whom they do not have regular face-to-face contact.

ADVANTAGES AND CHALLENGES TO TELECOMMUTING

As telecommuting becomes more common, we are learning about the advantages and challenges it brings to working. Telecommuting can offer many benefits to the individual employee, the organization, and society. For the individual, telecommuting can be less stressful. Telecommuters have more autonomy and flexibility in how they structure and conduct their work. Telecommuters can work in a comfortable work environment (e.g., their home) with fewer distractions. They are often less involved in the normal office politics, a source of stress for many traditional employees.

One of the most common perceived benefits for telecommuters is the ability to balance their work and family obligations. By reducing their commuting time, they are able to spend more time with their family. Eliminating a 40-minute one-way commute allows telecommuters an additional 6.5 hours a week to spend with their families or working at home.

Additionally, telecommuters' flexibility allows them to schedule their work around family obligations—for example, starting work early in the morning so they can stop work early to attend a daughter's soccer match. Overall, telecommuters are more satisfied than traditional employees.

Organizations also benefit from telecommuting. Organizations report a higher quality and a greater quantity of work from their telecommuters. Telecommuters report that they work better because of the fewer interruptions they experience by working at home compared with at the office. Additionally, telecommuters benefit their organization with lower turnover and lower absenteeism. Telecommuters are less likely to call in sick to stay at home when they are already working at home.

Telecommuting also reduces the overhead that organizations have to spend on housing their employees. Estimates are that organizations save $5,000 per year on every employee who telecommutes full-time. Some organizations have even implemented wide-scale telecommuting programs as part of an effort to reduce their costs.

Society benefits by the reduction in commuting time and the number of commuters on the road. Less pollution and traffic congestion benefit everyone and are the main reasons why many traffic-dense urban communities support telecommuting initiatives. Some communities also believe that when employees work at home, it makes neighborhoods safer and residents more active in community life.

Telecommuting is not, however, without its challenges. Telecommuting can isolate employees both socially and professionally. Socially, telecommuters lose their informal interactions with their coworkers, often known as *water cooler talk*. Although these informal interactions can be considered interruptions to work, they serve as important conduits of social, political, and organizational knowledge. Without these interruptions, telecommuters may work more productively, but they know less about the norms and culture of their coworkers and the organization. They are out of the loop with the rest of the organization and may become less committed and attached to the organization.

Professionally, telecommuters have less access to mentoring and other developmental relationships at work. Telecommuters might actually work with managers and coworkers whom they have never met face-to-face. Career development may be impeded because telecommuters are "out of sight and out of mind" when managers consider promotions and additional job responsibilities.

Managers' control over the employee and their efforts at performance management and monitoring are more challenging. Managers who are used to seeing their employees working hard at their desks may feel uncomfortable at the thought of supervising an absent employee. Managers of telecommuters have to move to a results-oriented style of management; they have to learn to focus more on outcomes and project completion than on effort.

Teleworkers also have to change their work style. They must become more proactive and take charge of their job responsibilities. They have to become more structured in managing their days and their work to be effective.

Telecommuting may be particularly challenging for teams. The lone telecommuting member of a team may be less influential. Work coordination is particularly a problem if employees do not have adequate technology at their home. Broadband Internet is an essential technology for employees who need to share data and files and use the standard business communication technologies. The use of broadband Internet at home is increasing from 4.4 million telecommuters in 2003 to 8.1 million in 2004. However, this number still represents only around one-fourth of home-based telecommuters. Therefore, team members of telecommuters without broadband still face challenges sharing their work.

Ironically, work–family balance is also a challenge for the home-based telecommuter. Whereas telecommuting's flexibility and autonomy can help telecommuters meet their family needs, this same flexibility can make balancing work and family obligations difficult. If family members are home during regular work hours, telecommuters may struggle to ensure that young children, spouses, and even neighbors understand that they are really working. Telecommuters may also feel pressure to complete household chores during paid work time when they see a kitchen full of dirty dishes or laundry in the hamper. If telecommuters do combine their work, domestic, and child-care responsibilities during work hours, they may have to extend the amount of time they work to accommodate all of these roles.

Additionally, employees who work at home never get to leave work. Because all their work information and communication technologies are at home,

telecommuters may feel more pressure to answer the work phone or check their work e-mail outside their paid work hours. Pressure may also come from knowing that with their reduced visibility, they need to compensate by being available to their colleagues at any time.

Telecommuters who work with global teams may be expected to be available at odd hours of the day and night. Although this is true for all global team members, telecommuting team members are particularly susceptible because they have access to their work communication technologies 24 hours a day. For example, a telecommuter on the East Coast of the United States may need to be available for early morning meetings with coworkers in western Europe and late evening meetings with coworkers in Australia. Thus, telecommuters may work longer hours than the traditional office-bound employee.

Interestingly, some research doesn't support the idea that telecommuters work more hours than traditional employees. It may be that telecommuters perceive that they are working more hours because signs of work are constantly visible. They may also report working more hours to justify the flexibility they have for working at home.

FUTURE CONCERNS

As telecommuting becomes a more popular work option, employees and organizations will have to pay attention to important emerging issues. One important concern is ensuring that the home environment is conducive for work. Some organizations require that telecommuters arrange day care for their young children. Other organizations encourage telecommuters to have a dedicated work space (e.g., a separate room with a door) to provide physical as well as psychological boundaries from the rest of the house. For example, a shared space near the family's living area is not as conducive to work as a dedicated office space in an isolated part of the house. These physical and psychological boundaries are important to maintaining work–family balance and to keep work from overtaking the home and vice versa.

Technological support will also be important. Although broadband use is increasing, it is still at a level much lower than the number of telecommuters. Additionally, as work technology at home becomes complicated, organizations will need to determine how to support home workers when these technologies are upgraded or inevitably break down. Organizations will need to focus on distributed training as well as providing help desks that can assist with the unique configurations of telecommuters.

The lack of informal communication with coworkers continues to be a problem. Currently, no communication technology can replace water cooler talk. Organizations and managers may need to pay particular attention to including social small talk with their work communications to keep telecommuters informed about and connected to the organization.

Finally, new employees who start as telecommuters will be a challenge. Employees who never work face-to-face with others may not adequately be socialized into the organization's culture. They may operate as free agents with little commitment to the organization and a higher likelihood of turnover. As telecommuting and teleworking rates increase in our workforce, organizations may need to focus on ensuring that these employees participate as full-fledged members of the organization.

—*Anita Blanchard*

See also Job Design; Organizational Communication, Informal; Virtual Organizations; Virtual Teams; Work–Life Balance

FURTHER READING

Cooper, C. D., & Kurland, N. B. (2002). Telecommuting, professional isolation and employee development in public and private organizations. *Journal of Organizational Behavior, 23*(4), 511–532.

Golden, T., & Viega, J. (2005). The impact of extent of telecommuting on job satisfaction: Resolving inconsistent findings. *Journal of Management, 31*(2), 301–318.

Hill, E. J., Ferris, M., & Martinson, V. (2003). Does it matter where you work? A comparison of how three work venues (traditional office, virtual office and home office) influence aspects of work and personal/family life. *Journal of Vocational Behavior, 63*(2), 220–241.

Kurland, N. B., & Bailey, D. E. (1999, Autumn). Telework: The advantages of working here, there, anywhere, everywhere. *Organizational Dynamics*, 53–67.

Madsen, S. R. (2003). The effects of home-based teleworking on work-family conflict. *Human Resources Development Quarterly, 14*(1), 35–58.

Raghuram, S., Wiesenfeld, B., & Garud, R. (2003). Technology enabled work: The role of self-efficacy in determining telecommuter adjustment and structuring behavior. *Journal of Vocational Behavior, 63*(2), 180–198.

TEMPORARY WORKERS

See Outsourcing

TERRORISM AND WORK

On September 11, 2001, in the largest terrorist attack in history, four passenger planes were commandeered by terrorists and flown into the office buildings of the World Trade Center Twin Towers and the Pentagon, killing an estimated 3,000 people and injuring another 250. This tragic event was an extreme example of the many acts of terrorism that have been targeted at workplaces. Workplaces may be particularly attractive targets of terrorism for several reasons. A large number of people congregate in workplaces and are present at predictable times during the day, providing a social address where a targeted individual or group can be accessed. Attacks on workplaces are also likely to gain significant public attention. In addition, workplaces may be perfect targets from an ideological perspective, as certain workplaces may be selected because they represent an ideology to which the terrorists are opposed.

Given that there is a great deal of variation in the targets of terrorism, the nature of terrorist organizations, and the strategies used by terrorists, *terrorism* has been defined in a number of different ways. However, common to the majority of these definitions are the notions that terrorism involves intentional violence or aggression, is motivated by a political agenda, focuses attention on the cause or ideology underlying the attack, and is conducted for the purpose of creating fear among a populace, wherein this fear is leveraged to achieve a particular goal. Terrorism can be distinguished from other forms of organizational violence by the fact that one of the main motivations of acts of terrorism is the creation of fear.

POSTTERRORISM RESEARCH FINDINGS: THE INDIVIDUAL AND THE ORGANIZATION

Research suggests that organizations may be greatly affected by terrorism both as an immediate result of the attack itself and in the aftermath of an attack. As a direct and immediate result of a terrorist attack, an organization may suffer the loss of employees,

employees may sustain injuries, and physical structures and resources may be damaged or destroyed. Employee and organizational suffering may continue in the aftermath of a terrorist attack. Employees may suffer clinical or subclinical psychological trauma. A number of studies have suggested that people who are victimized by terrorist attacks may develop clinically significant symptoms severe enough for a diagnosis of posttraumatic stress disorder or clinical depression. The likelihood of developing clinical symptoms has been found to be heightened with increasing proximity to the location where a terrorist attack took place and with increasing extremity of the attack. Although clinical psychological diagnoses are common following a terrorist attack, subclinical symptoms are even more widespread. In the aftermath of terrorism, one frequent response is a heightened feeling of personal vulnerability and lack of safety. For instance, following the September 11 terrorist attacks, studies found that people continued to fear future attacks as long as six months after the attacks. An increase in somatic ailments such as headaches and sleep disruptions can also be associated with the strain of having experienced a terrorist attack. Although most of the research to date on the aftermath of terrorism has focused on the general populace, rather than employees of targeted organizations, it is reasonable to assume that the effects on the populace are fewer than the effects on members of a targeted organization.

One organizational outcome of the grief, bodily injury, and psychological and physical symptoms resulting from the stress and fear of terrorism is an increase in employee absenteeism. There may be a number of reasons why employees want to stay away from their workplace. Employees may be afraid to return to work, concerned about the possibility of another attack. Employees may also be grieving the loss or harm of coworkers and may need time to recover from their grief before facing the workplace. Employees may also be physically incapable of returning to work as a result of sustaining injuries during an attack, or because they are coping with the strain from the attack. Although absenteeism has negative implications for organizations in terms of lost productivity and the disruption of routine, following a terrorist attack, absenteeism might have some positive benefits, as a period of employee absenteeism may ultimately prevent turnover resulting from the accumulation of stress that can lead to chronic depression or disability.

Another organizational outcome of terrorism is that the work environment is likely to be disorganized, and role ambiguity may result. If coworkers have been killed or injured, if the resources required to perform one's job have been destroyed, or if the workplace itself has been destroyed, employees' routines may be completely disrupted. Under these circumstances, individuals may be unsure how to go about performing their normal job-related tasks. Lacking job clarity can impair people from accomplishing their job-related goals, and individuals' job performance may suffer.

As a result of a terrorist attack, organizations may incur a number of financial costs, as physical structures and resources may need to be rebuilt or replaced. Organizations may also lose employees through death, injury, or turnover, making it necessary for them to hire, socialize, and train new employees. Organizations may also need to assist workers with medical or psychological treatments. This may involve the use of in-house employee assistance programs or may involve making payments for these services to external treatment centers. These financial costs to the organization may lead to other organizational problems, to the extent that the attention of the organization is diverted from other workplace issues. Finally, as a result of absenteeism and the loss of people, resources, and the ability of employees to focus on their job tasks, an organization's productivity may suffer greatly, which can contribute to the extensive financial costs that may be incurred from a terrorist attack.

One unique outcome of terrorist attacks is that an individual does not have to work for the targeted organization to experience psychological distress or a disruption of work following an attack. For instance, some people may work in organizations that are similar to the one targeted for attack. People in these organizations may feel an increased level of vulnerability and fear. Other people work in occupations that force them to deal with the aftermath of a terrorist attack. Such is the case for occupations such as investigators, emergency service personnel, and body handlers. Following the terrorist bombing in Oklahoma City in 1995, there was an increase in alcohol consumption and physical ailments among people whose job was to handle the bodies of the victims.

IMPLICATIONS FOR ORGANIZATIONAL PRACTICE AND POLICY

The organization plays a critical role in facilitating recovery of a devastated workforce and the future of the organization. A variety of organizational responses may be required, and the best strategies for implementing these responses may be to have the necessary infrastructure in place prior to a terrorist attack and to have an existing plan for a response to such an event. Developing an emergency response plan may also help employees to retain or regain a sense of personal control before, during, and following a terrorist attack. Training people how to maximize their safety and how to help others in need may help increase chances of escape from potentially dangerous situations. These formal responses to emergency situations can give employees reason to feel that their organization is supportive of their needs, and this perceived support may in turn encourage employee loyalty to the organization.

Formal organizational responses to terrorism might include the use of employee assistance programs (EAPs). Following a terrorist attack, EAPs may provide employees with easily accessible counseling and support, help diagnose serious distress or psychopathology among employees, and provide treatment or referrals for employees suffering trauma. In conjunction with EAPs, organizations can help to identify people who may be at higher risk for subsequent strain following a terrorist attack, such as people who sustained injury or who were close with people who suffered or died. Outreach services may also be a vital conduit for accessing at-risk populations. Although the efficacy of EAPs following a terrorist attack has yet to be established definitely, the utility of these programs has been confirmed in studies examining other stressors.

Should an act of terrorism occur, workplaces are responsible for providing on-site intervention. Immediate and short-term responses often include Critical Incident Stress Debriefing (CISD) that can be administered through their EAPs. Critical Incident Stress Debriefing is a structured group meeting facilitated by a trained team and involving only the personnel directly affected by the critical incident. The purpose of the debriefing is to mitigate acute stress resulting from trauma and accelerate the normal recovery of ordinary people who are suffering through typical but painful reactions to an abnormal event. Critical Incident Stress Debriefing is typically conducted 24 hours after the event by a trained mental health professional. It is an early response intervention and not intended to act as a stand-alone intervention. It is important to note that recent meta-analytic results indicate that caution should be exercised in using CISD as a routine response to organizational crisis and disasters.

Ongoing, supportive organizational practices can have a great impact on employees during periods of stress. Empathic leaders can buffer the strain resulting from devastating organizational events. In fact, it is during times of crisis that leaders can exert their greatest influence. Leaders can provide compassion and social support, reduce role ambiguity, and communicate a vision for the future of the organization. Organizations and their representatives can also provide a variety of instrumentally supportive functions, such as providing psychological or economic counseling or holding blood drives. Organizations can also offer informational support, keeping employees up-to-date on new developments as events unfold. Communication networks within the organization and between the organization and community can facilitate timely information exchange.

Overall, although workplaces are often targets of terrorism, they also have an important role to play in the protection of employees and the recovery efforts. Some of the most important roles organizations can play are in the provision of social, instrumental, and informational support.

—*Michelle Inness and Julian Barling*

See also Workplace Safety

FURTHER READING

Byron, K., & Peterson, S. (2002). The impact of a large-scale traumatic event on individual and organizational outcomes: Exploring employee and company reactions to September 11, 2001. *Journal of Organizational Behavior, 23,* 895–910.

Ryan, A. M., West, B. J., & Carr, J. Z. (2003). Effects of the terrorist attacks of 9/11/01 on employee attitudes. *Journal of Applied Psychology, 88,* 647–659.

Van Fleet, E. W., & Van Fleet, D. D. (1998). Terrorism and the workplace: Concepts and recommendations. In R. W. Griffin & A. O'Leary-Kelly (Eds.), *Dysfunctional behavior in organizations: Violent and deviant behavior* (Vol. 23, Part A, pp. 165–201). Greenwich, CT: Elsevier Science/JAI Press.

TEST SECURITY

Tests and other forms of assessment give important insight into key human characteristics that drive performance. These tools are used widely in both business and educational settings, with the goals of their use ranging from low stakes (such as personal insight and development) to extremely high stakes (such as selection or promotion into coveted job positions). The fairness and accuracy of tests are critical to enable valid inferences about human behavior and to protect examinees from the misuse of test results. For this reason, psychologists have a professional and ethical obligation to ensure the security of these processes and materials at all times. *Test security* in this context refers to the continuous maintenance and control of all test material within a testing program by only those individuals who are qualified and/or designated to have access to them. *Test material* is used broadly throughout this discussion to include any document, device, or process used to assess human characteristics (psychometric tests, behavioral simulations, structured interview protocols, etc., are all included under this definition).

Psychologists are concerned with test security because of the strong impact that a breach of security can have on the standardization of the test, the integrity of the results, and the long-term value of the test itself. If the data collected from a test do not accurately reflect the examinee characteristics that the test was designed to measure, then the inferences that can be made from it may be meaningless. Proper interpretation and use of test results thus relies on the assumption that test security was maintained throughout the assessment process—that, simply stated, the test questions, answers, and/or scoring protocols were not known to any of the examinees prior to the point of assessment.

COMMON FORMS OF SECURITY BREACH

Individuals or organizations willing to breach test security may do so for any number of reasons, ranging from a single test taker's efforts to be hired for a job to an organized attempt to profit from the unauthorized release of high-stakes test material. Breaches of test security come in many forms; some common examples include the following:

- Unauthorized removal of test materials from a test site
- Posting of test answers over the Internet
- A test taker asking another person to take the test in his or her place
- Unauthorized copying of copyrighted test materials
- Hacking into data storage locations to gain access to test results

Steps should be taken to identify the potential threats to test security for any operational testing program.

CONSEQUENCES OF SECURITY COMPROMISE

Breaches in test security not only affect measurement integrity and reliability; they also diminish the potential financial and social benefits associated with testing. Several significant risks associated with a poorly secured testing program are elaborated as follows.

- *Decreased validity and reliability.* Security breaches in test content and scoring affect validity and reliability. Test scores affected by a breach of security may not reflect the target construct of the assessment; this impinges on the ability to draw inferences between other constructs and outcomes and restricts the ability to measure consistently over time.
- *Ineffective selection procedures.* Reduced validity in testing processes can have a significant impact on the effective selection of examinees into organizational settings; as validity declines, the number of selection errors increases.
- *Decreased organizational performance.* Ineffective selection procedures may further affect organizational performance outcomes and eliminate any advantage provided by the use of well-constructed assessments.
- *Lowered confidence in psychological assessment.* High-profile cases of cheating and pirating of copyrighted content may also have an impact on social perceptions of the overall fairness of specific testing applications or even of the testing industry in general.

Although these risks may differ in the level of importance for different test applications and user groups, they each represent significant concerns that can arise when test security is not maintained.

ENSURING THE SECURITY OF TEST MATERIALS

Several practical challenges in securing test content, processes, and data exist. Threats to test security may be thought of as a series of factors that interact to influence test responses, test reliability, and validity. These factors include the following:

- The physical and electronic security of testing sites, content, and data
- Appropriate qualification levels of test users and administrators
- Differences in delivery technology (e.g., paper-and-pencil, interactive voice response, and computer-based)
- Differences in stakes (e.g., educational admissions vs. self-development)
- Cultural values within which the tests are administered

Although this list is not exhaustive, each item can have some influence over the need to monitor and protect test materials.

To maintain security, test publishers and users follow several sets of guidelines and recommendations that help both to directly protect testing-related property and information and to guide safer practices. The *Standards for Educational and Psychological Testing* includes suggestions for maintaining safe and secure testing protocol and content. The Society for Industrial and Organizational Psychology provides guidance for maintaining the security of tests and assessments used within personnel selection systems in the *Principles for the Validation and Use of Personnel Selection Procedures*. Similarly, the International Testing Commission (ITC) has developed standards for test security through their *International Guidelines for Test Use*. The ITC has also issued guidelines that are specific to computer-based tests (the *International Guidelines on Computer-Based and Internet Delivered Testing*); these guidelines make several suggestions regarding test administration, data storage, and ensuring test-taker authenticity.

METHODS FOR SECURING TESTING PROGRAMS

Psychologists and other test users have devised several methods for protecting testing material and procedures, including developing alternate/parallel test forms; proctoring testing sites; physically and electronically securing locations of test materials and results; monitoring and analyzing test response data for abnormal response patterns; regularly searching the Internet for test content and test preparation materials; and copyrighting all testing materials. Advances in testing procedures and electronic security software work toward enhancing our ability to protect tests, test materials, and information. For example, the expanded use of computer adaptive testing (in which examinees with different ability levels are likely to receive different test questions) will help to reduce opportunities for cheating by limiting the number of times a test question is presented to examinees. Although these methods can be effective at controlling for some loss of materials and content, ways to circumvent test protection are often found when the stakes associated with the assessment are high. In these cases, psychologists and other testing professionals may take legal action to protect the security of a testing process (e.g., by asserting and defending the copyright on testing materials).

One of the most challenging threats to test security arises when a party to a legal or regulatory action requests test materials. Psychologists may be asked to provide, to lawyers and other individuals, confidential results, test content, and scoring keys as evidence or support for a case. However, the individuals who request the information may not be ethically or legally required to maintain test security. Test materials may then become part of a public record, thereby putting the test materials and examinee information at risk. In these situations, psychologists may ask that the requested material be delivered only to other qualified psychologists who are ethically and legally obligated to maintain the confidentiality of the material. If this is not an option, psychologists may ask that the materials be covered under a protective order and that the materials be returned directly to the psychologist following litigation.

Social awareness of test security issues will also help to enhance test security and discourage individuals or groups from obtaining testing materials for the purpose of compromising the usefulness of an assessment process. One sign of the growing importance of test security is the emergence of specialists who can assist those who are responsible for testing programs with the development of policies and practices that facilitate test security.

Over time, test security may be enhanced by the continued development of the knowledge base surrounding security issues. Research in this area can help build an understanding of the factors that contribute to the likelihood of a security compromise, as well as the factors that help maintain the quality of a test under conditions in which security compromise may be likely, such as when a test is provided over the Internet. Advances in test security are also directly related to innovations in the techniques used to monitor and analyze test data for aberrant or unlikely patterns in test data, so that security breaches can be identified quickly.

SUMMARY

The security of testing material has both a direct and an indirect impact on the validity of the inferences that can be made from a test result. However, test security is a concern not only because of the impact a security breach may have on the psychometric qualities of a test and its proper interpretation, but also because of the financial and social implications that compromised assessment processes can have within organizations and the public. As the use of testing increases in organizational settings, across international borders, and through an increasingly technology-based delivery framework, careful attention to the enhancement of security has become more critical than ever before.

—*Doug Reynolds and Joseph Jones*

See also Ethics in Industrial/Organizational Practice; Selection Strategies; Standardized Testing; Validity

FURTHER READING

American Educational Research Association, American Psychological Association, and National Council on Measurement in Education. (1999). *Standards for educational and psychological testing.* Washington, DC: Author.

American Psychological Association. (1999). Test security: Protecting the integrity of tests. *American Psychologist, 54,* 1078.

American Psychological Association. (2002). Ethical principles of psychologists and code of conduct. *American Psychologist, 57,* 1060–1073.

International Testing Commission. (2000). *International guidelines for test use.* Stockholm, Sweden: Author.

International Testing Commission. (2005). *International guidelines on computer-based and Internet delivered testing.* Retrieved March 29, 2006, from http://www.intestcom.org/guidelines

Naglieri, J., Drasgow, F., Schmit, M., Handler, L., Prifitera, A., Margolis, A., et al. (2004). Psychological testing on the Internet: New problems, old issues. *American Psychologist, 59,* 150–162.

Schroeder, L. (1996). Examination security. In A. H. Browning, A. C. Bugbee, & M. A. Mullins (Eds.), *Certification: A NOCA handbook* (pp. 125–147). Washington, DC: The National Organization for Competency Assurance (NOCA).

Society for Industrial and Organizational Psychology. (2003). *Principles for the validation and use of personnel selection procedures.* Bowling Green, OH: Author.

THEFT AT WORK

Employee theft refers to the wrongful taking of money, goods, or property by an organization member. The target is most commonly the organization itself, but the definition would also encompass stealing from coworkers or customers. The psychological literature on employee theft focuses on money and physical goods, although the definition would also encompass intellectual property.

Theft is one example of a broader phenomenon, commonly known as *counterproductive work behavior* (CWB). Counterproductive work behavior includes any intentional behavior by an organization member that is viewed by the organization as contrary to its legitimate interests. Theft, sabotage, misuse of time and resources, unsafe behavior, drug and alcohol use at work, physical violence, and sexual harassment are all examples of CWB. After a long history of examining each of these separately, recent research documents a consistent pattern of positive correlations among CWB. Thus there is value in examining common antecedents and common interventions; for example, tests designed to predict theft have been found to also predict a range of CWB.

MEASUREMENT OF THEFT

Perhaps the most critical feature of employee theft is that it is difficult to detect. It is clearly undertaken by employees with the intent of going undetected and thus stands in contrast with most other organizational phenomena of interest to the industrial/organizational psychologist. This problem of detection has widespread implications for research and practice. One issue is that it makes it difficult to even document the extent of the problem. The proportion of employees caught stealing is generally very small. For example, a common strategy for test validation is to test applicants, put them on the job, measure the behavioral outcome of interest, and then examine the relationship between test scores and outcomes. When this is done with theft as the outcome of interest, rates of detected theft over the first year of employment among typical populations (e.g., entry-level retail workers) are in the 1% to 3% range. Although there is general agreement that some theft goes undetected, there is no agreement as to the proportion. Published estimates of the extent and cost of the employee theft problem reflect untested assumptions about the rate of undetected theft.

A second implication of the difficulty-of-detection problem is that it makes research on employee theft hard to interpret. For example, in trying to document psychological characteristics of employee thieves, one faces the question of whether detected thieves constitute a random sample of all thieves, or whether those caught are different in important ways from those who steal and are not caught. Organizations using selection systems, for example, hope to screen out individuals prone to theft, not merely those prone to get caught while stealing. Another research implication is that the statistical tools used to examine the relationship between psychological variables and employee theft (e.g., the correlation coefficient) cannot be interpreted in the normal manner when a variable under study is highly skewed. The maximum value of a correlation drops as the proportion caught/not caught stealing departs from 50%. At a 98%-to-2% split, the maximum possible correlation is .39, rather than the expected 1.0, and thus correlations with theft need to be interpreted relative to this maximum value.

There are two common alternatives to reliance on detected theft in studying employee theft. The first is the use of self-report. Such measures are approximations to the true state of affairs, as respondents may perceive themselves to be at risk in admitting theft, even in situations in which anonymity is assured. Some settings are more conducive to accurate responding than others: An anonymous survey conducted by a university-based researcher is likely to be viewed differently than a survey conducted by one's current employer. A useful recent development is the use of techniques for ensuring anonymity, known as *randomized response techniques*.

The second alternative to detected theft measures is the use of aggregate measures, such as store-level sales, inventory valuation, or unaccounted losses (commonly known as *shrinkage*). Using time-series designs, monthly financial measures are tracked as a theft intervention is implemented. Such designs require the inference that change is caused by theft reduction, and thus care must be taken to ensure that the theft intervention is not confounded with other changes.

ANTECEDENTS OF EMPLOYEE THEFT

Antecedents of employee theft can be grouped into two main categories: person and situation antecedents. Although these categories reflect different perspectives, they are not necessarily in opposition. That is, situational characteristics, such as strong norms regarding theft or tight surveillance of employees, will probably affect the likelihood of theft. At the same time, regardless of the strength of any situation, employees will differ in their beliefs about the consequences of theft, the desirability of those consequences, the existence of norms about theft, and motivation to comply with perceived norms. So, within the same situation, individual differences will cause some employees to be more prone to steal than others. Therefore, to fully understand what causes theft, the optimal approach is one recognizing the interaction between person and situation variables. Keeping this in mind, it is still useful to understand the person and situation variables that covary with theft. The most widely cited research findings relating to the two broad categories are outlined below.

Person Antecedents

The most common within-person approach to prediction of theft is that of measuring individual differences in integrity. *Integrity* is best conceptualized as a compound trait mostly reflecting the Big Five personality traits of conscientiousness, agreeableness, and emotional stability. Integrity is typically measured via commercially marketed self-report instruments called *integrity tests* that contain items dealing either with admissions of theft and attitudes toward theft, or more personality-like constructs such as dependability, conscientiousness, social conformity, thrill seeking, trouble with authority, and hostility. A long line of criterion-related validity evidence, including extensive meta-analyses, supports the use of integrity tests for predicting theft.

Various demographic factors have also been shown to covary with theft. For instance, employees who are young; new to their jobs; work part-time; have low-paying, low-status positions; or abuse drugs or alcohol are more likely to steal. It is difficult to interpret such demographic factors, though. For instance, are younger employees more likely to steal because of their youth, or because they may hold less satisfying jobs?

Situation Antecedents

The most commonly cited situational antecedents of theft are organizational justice, organizational culture and norms, and control systems. In terms of organizational justice, there is considerable evidence demonstrating that employees are more likely to steal when there is inequitable distribution of rewards or punishments, formal procedures are unfair, or interpersonal treatment is poor. Concerning organizational culture and norms, research has shown that things such as strong company codes of ethics, average honesty level in the organization or work group, punitiveness of an organization toward theft, and informal understandings about acceptability of theft among work-group members are related to the occurrence of theft. Finally, concerning control systems (physical or procedural entities within the workplace, meant specifically to diminish theft occurrence through providing alternatives to, increasing the risk of, or increasing penalties for theft), despite the intuitive appeal of their relationship with theft, there is little empirical evidence for their effectiveness. As the opportunity to steal is reduced, though, some effect on the occurrence of theft should be expected.

THEFT INTERVENTIONS

Given that employee theft is caused by person and situation variables, it follows that two ways to reduce theft are to change the persons or change the situation.

Person-Oriented Interventions

The first way to attempt to reduce theft by changing the employees is to change the types of persons that are hired. That is, selection systems can be designed to select applicants with traits that covary with reduced likelihood of theft. Given the relationship between integrity test scores and theft, an organization wishing to reduce theft could hire employees based on their integrity test scores. This would create a workforce predisposed to integrity and would likely result in an organizational culture and norms of integrity.

The second way to attempt to reduce theft by changing the employees is through training and development. Ethics programs are probably the most common form of such training. Ethics programs are designed to create organizational cultures that sensitize employees to behaviors considered inappropriate (such as theft) and to discourage employees from engaging in them. The content of ethics programs generally varies, but training programs designed to help employees understand ethical issues are common. There is very little empirical evidence that ethics programs reduce the incidence of theft, but preliminary evidence has been supportive.

Situation-Oriented Interventions

Another way in which to reduce the likelihood of theft is to change the situation in ways known to covary with the incidence of theft. Person-oriented ethics training, as discussed above, is commonly accompanied by situation-oriented features, such as formal codes of ethics, ethics committees, disciplinary practices, violation-reporting mechanisms, and ethics officers. These ethics programs are one form of control system; other types of control systems aimed at theft reduction include security systems (e.g., audits, surveillance); environmental design; posting signs reporting the amount missing or stolen in the past week; rewarding whistleblowers; and providing employees the opportunity to take merchandise that is dated or partially damaged or cannot be sold. There is little empirical evidence of the effectiveness of such control systems. Finally, because employee perceptions of injustice affect the likelihood of theft, interventions aimed to decrease injustice perceptions may have some effect on theft. Organizational justice perceptions can be broken down into three areas: distributive, procedural, and interpersonal justice. If distributive justice is suspected to be a cause of theft, the organization may address whether the allocation of rewards and punishments is equitable. If procedural justice is a concern, the organization may consider if changing the unfair procedure would have an effect on theft. If interpersonal justice is a cause of theft, attempting to create more positive interactions with employees may be an effective theft intervention.

—*Paul R. Sackett and Christopher M. Berry*

See also Counterproductive Work Behaviors

FURTHER READING

Greenberg, J. (1990). Employee theft as a reaction to underpayment inequity: The hidden cost of pay cuts. *Journal of Applied Psychology, 75,* 561–568.

Hollinger, R. C., & Clark, J. P. (1983). *Theft by employees.* Lexington, MA: D. C. Heath.

Murphy, K. R. (1993). *Honesty in the workplace.* Belmont, CA: Brooks/Cole.

Sackett, P. R., & DeVore, C. J. (2001). Counterproductive behaviors at work. In N. Anderson, D. Ones, H. Sinangil, & C. Viswesvaran (Eds.), *International handbook of work psychology.* Thousand Oaks, CA: Sage.

Sackett, P. R., & Wanek, J. E. (1996). New developments in the use of measures of honesty, integrity, conscientiousness, dependability, trustworthiness, and reliability for personnel selection. *Personnel Psychology, 47,* 787–829.

THEORY OF ACTION

Chris Argyris and Donald Schön's theory of action is a descriptive and normative framework that explains and prescribes behavior at the individual, group, and organizational levels. The intellectual roots of the theory of action are John Dewey's theory of inquiry and Kurt Lewin's formulations of action research. In particular, the theory of action aspires to the Lewinian ideal of contributing simultaneously to basic knowledge of human behavior and practical action in everyday life. In so doing, the theory of action integrates science and application to an extent that is unparalleled in the organizational behavior literature.

ESPOUSED THEORY VERSUS THEORY-IN-USE

At its core, the theory of action maintains that, for virtually everyone, there is a discrepancy between what people say and believe is motivating their actions and what is actually motivating their actions. The former is termed *espoused theory,* and the latter is termed *theory-in-use.* In other words, there is a gap in awareness between the explanations people have for their own actions (espoused theory) and the cognitive structures that actually govern their actions (theory-in-use). This gap exists not only at the individual level, but at the group and organizational levels, as well (i.e., the cognitive structures that govern individual behavior give rise to interpersonal structures that regulate group behavior).

Theory-in-use must be inferred from people's actual behavior and not from their descriptions of that behavior. Over decades of research with thousands of participants from a wide variety of cultures, Argyris and Schön have found overwhelming evidence of an implicit cognitive structure, or theory-in-use, that is common to most everyone; the authors refer to this theory-in-use as *Model I.* Model I is the result of socialization early in life. Specifically, from an early age, virtually all people in modern industrial societies are socialized to (a) individually define the task at hand and the purposes to be achieved, rather than work interdependently to develop mutual definitions of task and purpose; (b) maximize winning and minimize losing; (c) suppress negative feelings; and (d) be rational and minimize emotionality. These socialized tendencies are referred to as the *governing variables* of Model I.

Model I socialization carries a behavioral imperative in which the underlying strategy is unilateral control over others and the environment. Based on their extensive research, Argyris and Schön concluded that people vary greatly in the way they attempt to control others and the environment but that the attempt to do so is nearly invariant. Because this behavioral strategy does not produce valid feedback from others, it leads individuals to be defensive and closed. At the group and organizational levels, this strategy leads to defensive relationships that reduce the production of valid information and reduce free choice among organizational members. In general, the consequences of Model I behavior in organizations are poor decision making, low commitment, wasted resources, unproductive conflict, and limited learning/change on the part of organizational members.

Automatic Nature of Model I Actions

According to Argyris and Schön, most people are unaware of the fact that their theory-in-use conforms to Model I. This means that the Model I strategy of unilateral control tends to be highly automatic (in the sense that it operates outside of conscious awareness). In fact, not only are implementations of this strategy automatic, they are often very sophisticated. The difficulty is that most people have little awareness of how and when they implement this strategy. Consequently, people's actions tend to remain consistent with the strategy of unilateral control—even when they say and believe otherwise. Especially when facing difficult human relations problems, people often unknowingly act in ways that are inconsistent with their words. That is, on the surface people may know—and espouse to others (i.e., espoused theory)—that unilateral control is a counterproductive strategy when attempting to resolve such problems, yet when they themselves are immersed in such a problem, they blindly implement this very strategy to some degree. Moreover, the higher the stakes, and especially in the midst of stress, threat, or embarrassment, the more strongly the strategy of unilateral control is activated and the more it interferes with the ability to work effectively with others.

According to Argyris and Schön, this automatic Model I programming is *the* primary source of the toughest and most persistent problems of organizational behavior (e.g., low morale, withdrawal from work, poor group decision making and problem solving, dysfunctional behavior in teams, employee–management strife, and ineffective leadership). Thus, to begin resolving these problems, organizational members must first become aware of their Model I programming and the ways in which it causes organizational problems. Then, after gaining this awareness, the existing program must be unlearned over time and replaced with a more useful and self-aware action model. Argyris and Schön advocate a replacement model they simply call *Model II,* and the primary focus of their work has been to disseminate this model while helping others learn how to assimilate and practice it.

Model II

The governing variables of Model II are to (a) maximize the use of valid information for solving problems, (b) maximize free and informed choice in solving problems, and (c) maximize internal commitment to problem solutions and the monitoring of solutions over time. In contrast to the Model I strategy of unilateral control, Model II requires *mutual control* if its principles are to be realized. Therefore, the action strategies of Model II involve creating shared purposes, expressing one's own views openly while sharing the reasoning behind those views, inviting challenge from others while inquiring into one another's views, designing ways to publicly test differences in views, and holding one another accountable. Not surprisingly, the organizational consequences of Model II are very different from those of Model I. These consequences are effective decision making, high commitment, faster adaptation to change, strong working relationships (characterized by high trust and openness), and mutual learning.

The transition from Model I to Model II requires what Argyris and Schön call *double-loop,* as opposed to *single-loop,* learning. Single-loop learning occurs when an individual learns new actions that are consistent with the core principles of his or her operative action model (e.g., Model I). Double-loop learning, by contrast, involves learning new core principles (e.g., Model II) and new actions that are consistent with those new principles. In numerous longitudinal studies, Argyris and Schön have found that the transition from Model I to Model II is generally neither fast nor easy, even for people who are highly committed to making the transition, because Model I actions tend to be highly automatic and deeply ingrained.

PRACTICING THE THEORY OF ACTION

The theory of action is unique because it is both a theory and a form of practice. As a form of practice, the theory of action has two key features: It is practiced both publicly and in real time. That is, groups of practitioners are brought together by a theory of action interventionist to inquire openly into their own work behavior and to identify whether Model I principles may be motivating their behavior and inhibiting organizational effectiveness. If Model I is found to be counterproductively operative, the interventionist then coaches the participants to behave consistently with Model II. With enough coaching and practice, the participants eventually learn to practice Model II on their own while becoming less and less dependent on the interventionist.

The theory of action approach stands in sharp contrast to the mainstream approach in organizational science. In the mainstream approach, organizational behavior is treated as an object of study separate from individuals' immediate actions. The goal of the mainstream approach is to learn as much as possible about this object of study and create a bookshelf of knowledge from which practitioners can presumably draw for guidance. Argyris and Schön essentially argue that, although this mainstream approach has generated many noteworthy findings, the separateness of those findings inevitably limits their applicability. In their theory of action approach, the generation of bookshelf knowledge is a secondary goal. The primary goal is to generate firsthand, *actionable* knowledge for the practitioners involved—that is, knowledge of the automatic Model I actions being produced, how those actions lead to unintended and counterproductive outcomes, and alternative Model II actions that are more likely to resolve difficult organizational problems.

—Paul W. Paese

See also Organizational Change; Organizational Change, Resistance to; Organizational Development

FURTHER READING

Argyris, C. (1993). *Knowledge for action: A guide to overcoming barriers to organizational change.* San Francisco: Jossey-Bass.

Argyris, C., & Schön, D. A. (1974). *Theory in practice: Increasing professional effectiveness.* San Francisco: Jossey-Bass.

Argyris, C., & Schön, D. A. (1978). *Organizational learning: A theory of action perspective.* Reading, MA: Addison-Wesley.

Argyris, C., & Schön, D. A. (1996). *Organizational learning II: Theory, method, and practice.* Reading, MA: Addison-Wesley.

THEORY OF REASONED ACTION/ THEORY OF PLANNED BEHAVIOR

The theory of reasoned action and theory of planned behavior have been influential cognitive models for understanding and predicting social behavior across a variety of domains. Both focus on the question of how to determine the likelihood that an individual will engage in a specific behavior. The theory of reasoned action examines determinants of volitional behavior, or behavior that falls under a person's individual control, whereas the theory of planned behavior provides an extension of the previous model to examine determinants of behavior over which individuals do not exert complete control. The theory of reasoned action and theory of planned behavior arose in response to discrepant findings in the social psychological literature regarding the relationship between attitudes and behavior. During this time, contrary to the common assumption of attitudes guiding behavior, there was increasing evidence that people's attitudes did not in fact predict their actions. The theories of reasoned action and planned behavior attempted to reconcile these findings by examining additional determinants of behavior and identifying specific conditions under which attitudes would guide behavior.

THEORY OF REASONED ACTION

The theory of reasoned action was developed by Martin Fishbein and Icek Ajzen with the aim of identifying determinants of behavioral decisions that are volitional, or under an individual's control. The theory posits that attitudes, subjective norms, and intentions combine to determine the likelihood of an individual performing a specific action.

Attitudes are the evaluative beliefs surrounding the target behavior (i.e., Does one feel positively or negatively toward engaging in this behavior?). They are based on *behavior beliefs,* which are beliefs about the outcomes associated with doing a behavior. Additionally, attitudes are determined by the person's evaluations of the outcomes. Therefore, a positive attitude toward a behavior will occur when a person believes that a behavior results in a positive outcome and that outcome is one that is valued by the individual.

Subjective norms are perceived social pressure to perform a behavior. They are based on *normative beliefs,* which are beliefs about whether important others approve or disapprove of one engaging in a particular behavior. Additionally, the strength of the subjective norms is determined by how motivated a person is to comply with other people's wishes. Thus, for subjective norms to be strong, an individual must not only believe that others approve of him or her engaging in a behavior but must also consider it important to comply with the wishes of others.

In this model, it is suggested that rather than having a direct influence on behavior, attitudes and subjective norms will influence behavior indirectly, through their impact on *intentions,* people's motivations or willingness to engage in a particular action. Intentions are identified as the most immediate antecedent of behavior. If intentions to engage in a behavior are strong, it is more likely that an individual will actually perform the behavior; conversely, if intentions are weak, it is less likely that one will engage in the specified behavior.

In sum, the theory of reasoned action suggests a general sequence in which attitudes and subjective norms jointly determine behavioral intentions, which then determine actual behavior. If attitudes toward a behavior are favorable, an individual will have stronger intentions, consequently resulting in greater likelihood of engaging in the behavior. On the other hand, if attitudes are unfavorable, individuals will have weaker intentions to engage in the behavior and will therefore be less likely to carry out the behavior. Similarly, if subjective norms are high (others indicate approval of the behavior and one is motivated to comply with their wishes), an individual will express stronger intentions and will consequently be more likely to actually engage in the behavior; if subjective norms are low (others disapprove of the behavior and/or one does not care about complying with others' wishes), an individual will have weaker intentions and be less likely to perform the behavior.

Application of the Theory of Reasoned Action

To provide an example, the theory of reasoned action could be used in an organizational setting to predict whether workers in a high-risk occupation will follow workplace safety regulations. The theory predicts that attitudes toward the safety regulations (beliefs about whether following these regulations is good or bad) and subjective norms toward the regulations (beliefs about whether important others would want one to follow the regulations) will both determine a worker's intentions to engage in these safe behaviors in the workplace. For instance, if people believe that following regulations at work will keep them safe, and they value this outcome, they will have a positive attitude toward engaging in safe workplace behaviors. Further, if they believe that it is important to their families and coworkers that they engage in these safe behaviors, and they want to comply with the wishes of these important others, they will have strong subjective norms surrounding the behavior. These positive attitudes and subjective norms will then translate into intentions, or motivation and willingness to follow the safety regulations, which will then determine actual behavior.

Limitations of the Theory of Reasoned Action

One important limitation of the theory of reasoned action is that it does not consider impeding or facilitating factors that might influence one's ability to engage in a behavior. The theory assumes that if a person is motivated to engage in a behavior, that particular action will be carried out. However, many behaviors require certain skills, resources, opportunities, or the cooperation of others to be carried out. For instance, individuals who are employed in high-risk jobs might have positive attitudes and subjective norms with regard to workplace safety (i.e., they are motivated to engage in behaviors that will keep them safe in the workplace); however, there may be external constraints, such as lack of funding, understaffing, or limited safety equipment,

that exert a strong influence on their ability to carry out specific safety behaviors. Although the presence or absence of such factors should influence how easy or difficult it is for individuals to carry out behavior, the impact of these factors on behavior is not examined in the theory of reasoned action.

THE THEORY OF PLANNED BEHAVIOR

The theory of planned behavior was developed by Ajzen as an extension of the theory of reasoned action to examine factors outside of one's control that might also exert influence on intentions and behaviors. Specifically, the theory of planned behavior asserts that if a behavior is less volitional in nature, it is important to consider the degree to which various factors either impede or facilitate an individual's ability to engage in that behavior. This determinant of behavior is referred to as *perceived control,* and it is examined in addition to the attitude, subjective norm, and intention components included in the theory of reasoned action. Perceived control is based on an individual's perceptions of how likely facilitating or constraining factors are to occur and to what degree these factors will influence the ease or difficulty of engaging in the behavior. Greater perceptions of perceived control lead to stronger intentions, resulting in greater likelihood of actually engaging in the behavior; less perceived control leads to weaker intentions and a lower likelihood of engaging in the behavior. Moreover, unlike attitudes and subjective norms, which are proposed to influence behavior only indirectly through their influence on intentions, perceived control is thought to exert a direct influence on behavior, as well as an indirect influence through its impact on intentions.

In summary, the theory of planned behavior asserts that attitudes, subjective norms, and perceived control will combine to influence intentions, which will then determine behavior. The theory of planned behavior differs from the theory of reasoned action, in that it examines the role of perceived control and therefore applies to a wider array of behaviors that are not fully under an individual's control. Additionally, in this model both intentions and perceived control exert a direct influence on behavior.

PREDICTING AND EXPLAINING BEHAVIOR

The theories of reasoned action and planned behavior have generated a large magnitude of research, the majority of which has focused on the prediction and explanation of behavior. Typically, researchers have measured attitudes, subjective norms, and perceived control in relation to a specific behavior and then used these constructs to either explain existing intentions and behavior or predict future intentions and behavior. Meta-analyses indicate that the theories of reasoned action and planned behavior constructs account for up to 40% of the variance in behavior and intentions. Moreover, inclusion of the perceived control construct accounts for significant variance beyond that accounted for by attitudes and subjective norms. Of these constructs, subjective norms appear to be the weakest predictor of intentions and behavior.

The theories of reasoned action and planned behavior have predicted behavior across many domains. In the context of the workplace, these theories have been applied to explain and predict behavior related to diversity training, workplace technology, occupational safety and health, occupational deviance, and career decision making. Although the primary body of research generated by these theories has focused on predicting and explaining existing behavior, more recent work has applied these models to develop interventions designed to modify behavior.

—*Jennifer L. Welbourne*

See also Attitudes and Beliefs; Judgment and Decision-Making Process; Occupational Health Psychology

FURTHER READING

Ajzen, I. (1985). From intentions to actions: A theory of planned behavior. In J. Kuhl & J. Beckman (Eds.), *Action control: From cognition to behavior* (pp. 11–39). Berlin: Springer.

Ajzen, I. (1991). The theory of planned behavior. *Organizational Behavior and Human Decision Processes, 50,* 179–211.

Ajzen, I., & Fishbein, M. (1980). *Understanding attitudes and predicting social behavior.* Englewood Cliffs, NJ: Prentice Hall.

Armitage, C., & Conner, M. (2001). Efficacy of the theory of planned behavior: A meta-analytic review. *British Journal of Social Psychology, 40,* 471–499.

Conner, M., & Armitage, C. (1998). Extending the theory of planned behavior: A review and avenues for further research. *Journal of Applied Social Psychology, 28*(15), 1429–1464.

Fishbein, M. (1980). The theory of reasoned action: Some applications and implications. In H. E. Howe Jr. &

M. M. Page (Eds.), *Nebraska Symposium on Motivation, 1979* (Vol. 27, pp. 65–116). Lincoln: University of Nebraska Press.

Fishbein, M., & Ajzen, I. (1975). *Beliefs, attitudes, intentions, and behavior: An introduction to theory and research.* Reading, MA: Addison-Wesley.

THEORY OF WORK ADJUSTMENT

The theory of work adjustment (TWA) describes how and explains why workers adjust to their work environments. It depicts adjustment as the interaction of person (P) with environment (E). *Interaction* refers to P and E acting on as well as reacting to each other. P and E interact because, to begin with, each has requirements that the other can fill, and each has capabilities to fill the other's requirements. So long as each is satisfied with the outcomes, the interaction will be maintained. But when one or both are dissatisfied with the outcomes, adjustment will be attempted. The theory of work adjustment asserts that satisfaction and work adjustment depend not so much on P variables or E variables, but on the particular combination of P and E variables (TWA calls the combination *P–E correspondence*). Thus, in TWA, work adjustment is described and explained by two psychological propositions: (a) Satisfaction drives behavior, and (b) satisfaction is a function of P–E correspondence. (Here, *satisfaction* extends to dissatisfaction and *correspondence* to discorrespondence.)

In TWA, P and E are described in parallel and complementary terms. P requirements are called *needs,* and E requirements are called *tasks.* Needs are requirements for specific reinforcers, such as compensation and opportunity to achieve. Tasks are response requirements to produce a product or perform an action. Needs differ in degree of importance, whereas tasks differ in degree of difficulty. P has response capabilities, called *skills,* to meet E tasks, and E has reinforcement capabilities, *reinforcers,* to meet P needs. Furthermore, TWA posits latent dimensions as underlying needs, called *values,* and latent dimensions as underlying skills, called *abilities.* To summarize, in TWA, P is described as having needs and skills, or values and abilities, whereas E is described as having reinforcers and tasks (but see the next paragraph).

To measure P–E correspondence requires that both P and E be described in the same terms. P needs are defined as reinforcer requirements, which allows them to be compared with E reinforcers. E tasks can be redefined in terms of their *skill requirements,* which can then be compared with P skills. Thus, two P–E correspondences can be calculated: E reinforcer to P need (reinforcer requirement) correspondence, and P skill to E skill requirement correspondence. Two other P–E correspondence measures can be calculated by using P values and P abilities. This would require that latent dimensions be determined for E reinforcers and E skill requirements, which dimensions can be called *reinforcer factors* and *ability requirements,* respectively. These two P–E correspondences will therefore be E reinforcer factor to P value correspondence and P ability to E ability requirement correspondence.

Satisfaction is the affective evaluation of a situation. In TWA, P is satisfied when P needs are reinforced by E, and E is satisfied when E tasks are accomplished by P. To avoid confusion and to keep the focus on P, TWA calls E satisfaction *P satisfactoriness.* (*P satisfaction* extends to P dissatisfaction, and *P satisfactoriness* extends to P unsatisfactoriness.) P satisfaction and P satisfactoriness lead to *tenure* (length of stay on the job). For TWA, satisfaction, satisfactoriness, and tenure are the indicators of work adjustment in P.

In TWA, P satisfaction is predicted from P(need)–E(reinforcer) correspondence, or also from P(value)–E(reinforcer factor) correspondence. P satisfactoriness is predicted from P(skill)–E(skill requirement) correspondence, or from P(ability)–E(ability requirement) correspondence. Tenure is predicted from the P satisfaction–P satisfactoriness combination. Satisfaction in P and E results in *maintenance behavior,* whereas dissatisfaction in P and/or E leads to *adjustment behavior.* P dissatisfaction may eventually lead to P quitting the job, whereas P unsatisfactoriness may lead to P getting demoted or fired by E.

To improve prediction, TWA has recourse to moderator variables, in the use of which the prediction correlation increases with higher values in the moderator variable. Three moderator variables are used by TWA: P satisfactoriness, P satisfaction, and *P–E style correspondence.* P satisfactoriness moderates the prediction of P satisfaction from P(need)–E(reinforcer) correspondence or from P(value)–E(reinforcer factor) correspondence—prediction is better for more satisfactory than for less satisfactory Ps. P satisfaction moderates the prediction of P satisfactoriness from P(skill)–E(skill requirement) correspondence or from P(ability)–E(ability requirement) correspondence—prediction is better for more satisfied Ps. P–E style correspondence moderates the prediction of both P satisfaction and P satisfactoriness from their respective P–E correspondence predictors—prediction is better when P–E style correspondence is higher. *P style* refers to distinctive characteristics of P's manner of responding and is described by four variables: *celerity* (response latency), *pace* (response intensity), *rhythm* (response pattern), and *endurance* (response duration). *E style* can be described by four parallel variables, which would then allow P–E style correspondence to be assessed.

The theory of work adjustment describes the work adjustment process further by introducing the concept of *adjustment style,* the distinctive characteristics of adjustment behavior. P's adjustment style can be described by four variables: *flexibility,* which refers to the amount of P–E discorrespondence P is typically willing to tolerate before initiating adjustment behavior; *activeness,* or P's tendency to act on E to change E to reduce P–E discorrespondence; *reactiveness,* or P's tendency to react to E by changing self to reduce P–E discorrespondence; and *perseverance,* or how long P typically continues adjustment behavior before either giving up or leaving E. To change E means changing E reinforcers and/or E skill requirements, whereas to change P (self) means changing P needs and/or P skills. The purpose, then, of adjustment behavior is to change P–E discorrespondence to P–E correspondence or, at the cognitive level, to change dissatisfaction to satisfaction. When P–E correspondence or satisfaction is attained, P and E return to maintenance behavior.

Whereas the above explication of TWA is written with the focus on P, it is also possible to view work adjustment with the focus on E—that is, TWA can view P and E as symmetrical. In this symmetrical view, E would have the kind of requirements and capabilities that P has, and vice versa. That is, E would have reinforcer requirements (E needs and E values) and response capabilities (E skills and E abilities) in addition to response requirements and reinforcement capabilities, whereas P would additionally have reinforcement capabilities (P reinforcers and P reinforcer factors) and response requirements (P skill requirements and P ability requirements). There would also be E satisfaction, E satisfactoriness, and E adjustment style (E flexibility, E activeness, E reactiveness, and E perseverance). The possibility of E style (E celerity, E pace, E rhythm, and

E endurance) has already been noted in the discussion of P–E style correspondence. And finally, for E, just as for P, (a) satisfaction drives behavior, and (b) satisfaction is a function of P–E correspondence.

—Rene V. Dawis

See also Person–Environment Fit; Person–Job Fit; Person–Organization Fit; Person–Vocation Fit

FURTHER READING

Dawis, R. V. (1996). The theory of work adjustment and person-environment-correspondence counseling. In D. Brown & L. Brooks (Eds.), *Career choice and development* (3rd ed., pp. 75–120). San Francisco: Jossey-Bass.

Dawis, R. V. (2002). Person–environment correspondence theory. In D. Brown (Ed.), *Career choice and development* (4th ed., pp. 427–464). San Francisco: Jossey-Bass.

Dawis, R. V. (2005). The Minnesota theory of work adjustment. In S. D. Brown & R. W. Lent (Eds.), *Career development and counseling* (pp. 3–23). Hoboken, NJ: Wiley.

Dawis, R. V., & Lofquist, L. H. (1984). *A psychological theory of work adjustment.* Minneapolis: University of Minnesota Press.

Lofquist, L. H., & Dawis, R. V. (1969). *Adjustment to work.* New York: Appleton-Century-Crofts.

360-DEGREE FEEDBACK

The term *360-degree feedback* refers to an appraisal and feedback system in which an employee (typically someone in a managerial or supervisory position) is evaluated by one or more supervisors, peers, and subordinates. These systems, sometimes called *multisource appraisals,* are generally expensive, and the ratings produced by them should be used as a feedback tool only. That is, numerous scholars have recommended that 360-degree ratings not be used for any decisions often associated with appraisals; yet there is a fair amount of evidence that these ratings are often used for making decisions about merit pay raises and promotions.

Considerable research had led to proposals for 360-degree systems, and several papers have critically analyzed their use in practice. Most of these papers have focused only on the reasons why 360-degree feedback may not be as effective as organizations would prefer, but very little research has actually evaluated the effectiveness of this feedback by using a strong research design.

THE DEVELOPMENT OF 360-DEGREE FEEDBACK SYSTEMS

The development of these systems grew out of research that tried to establish the construct validity of traditional performance appraisals. These studies compared ratings from appraisals generated by supervisors with ratings from appraisals generated by peers and subordinates, using a framework known as the *multitrait–multimethod matrix.* This framework examines ratings of common traits provided by raters who have different relationships with the ratee (e.g., peers and supervisors), as well as ratings of these common traits by raters who have the same relationship with the ratee. This approach also considers ratings of different traits provided by raters who have the same relationship with the ratee as well as those provided by raters who have different relationships with the ratee. Subsequent analyses of ratings search for convergence among ratings of common traits, provided by different sources as evidence of construct validity (as well as divergence among ratings of different traits provide by different groups of raters). But in many cases, the researchers failed to find the convergence that was critical for the demonstration of construct validity, which suggested that these ratings may not be valid at all.

Fortunately, some scholars argued that the failure to find convergence among ratings from different sources could be attributed to these different groups of raters observing different behaviors and interpreting those behaviors differently, based on the relationship they had with the ratee. This would suggest that each type of rating had some validity in its own right, but that each of these different ratings actually provided somewhat unique information about the ratee's performance. This suggestion was a major impetus for the development of 360-degree feedback. In addition, multisource feedback was used in several organizational change interventions as a tool to "unfreeze" the managers and make them more accepting of the need to change.

Eventually, these sets of efforts led to the fairly widespread use of 360-degree feedback systems in organizations in the United States. These systems grew in popularity, both in the United States and around the world, and were the subject of many books and articles in the popular and practitioner literature, but the academic community paid little attention to them. Slowly, the academic community began investigating 360-degree feedback systems and began raising questions about potential problems. The practitioner community also became more critical of these systems, especially noting their use in decision making, despite the recommendations that they be used for feedback purposes only. Because these systems remain popular, it is important to understand the potential problems and limitations involved in their use and how to best use 360-degree feedback systems to minimize the problems and maximize the advantages.

TYPICAL 360-DEGREE SYSTEMS

The exact form of 360-degree feedback systems varies from organization to organization, but several aspects of these programs are common across most settings. The process usually begins with the target manager, or ratee, providing self-evaluations in all the areas to be covered. In many cases, the manager is then asked to nominate peers, subordinates, and possibly even superiors who would be asked to provide the additional evaluations. In other cases, someone in charge of the process selects random peers and others; in yet other cases, all the peers, subordinates, and supervisors are asked to provide ratings. In most situations, each rater is asked to provide evaluations in all areas under consideration, although, in some cases, the raters are told to provide ratings in some areas and not others, or are told to provide ratings only in areas where they feel competent to do so.

Once the ratings are collected and tabulated, the ratee is given a feedback report. In each area rated, she or he is provided with the self-evaluation, followed by the average ratings received from each of the other groups of raters. There is typically some form of notation indicating ratings that are significantly above or below the self-ratings. The target manager is then either left to sort out this information or provided with a coach who helps interpret the feedback and determine a plan for future development.

ADVANTAGES AND PROBLEMS

The major advantage attributed to 360-degree feedback systems is that the target managers receive feedback about their performance from a variety of perspectives. This type of multisource feedback provides much more information to target managers, and the nature of that information is often much richer. Ideally, the managers will use this information to develop much more accurate insights into their behavior, which, especially with the help of a coach, will allow them to improve in areas where they are weak.

But, in fact, there is little unambiguous data to support the effectiveness of 360-degree feedback relative to other types of feedback. Several studies have found mixed results when examining change following 360-degree feedback, other studies have found improvement but suffer from a variety of methodological problems, as reviewed by Seifert, Yukl, and McDonald (2003), and very few studies have actually compared the effectiveness of feedback from multiple sources with feedback from a single source. In addition, several conceptual papers have suggested that there might also be psychometric issues with these ratings and problems with the effectiveness of the feedback as a result of the multiple sources employed in this process.

An additional problem can stem from the use of 360-degree ratings for decision making rather than simply for feedback. The problems come from the fact that ratings from different sources in the process typically don't agree—and aren't really supposed to agree. But when ratings from different sources are used to make a single decision, it is not clear how to deal with this inconsistency.

Ideally, an organization should determine which rating source would be best able to evaluate a manager in each area, and either ask for ratings only from the best source or only consider those ratings in forming an overall evaluation. For example, perhaps peers would be the best judges of "cooperation," whereas subordinates would be best to evaluate "delegation," and a supervisor best to evaluate "meets deadlines." Then, it would be possible to obtain ratings in these areas only from the source best able to evaluate the area. This would make interpretation simple, and it would be easy to combine these ratings into a single overall evaluation, but the logistics of putting together a rating instrument that reflected this would be significant. Alternatively, all three sources could rate the manager in all three areas (which is actually more typical), and the evaluator could consider separately the peer rating of cooperation, subordinate rating of delegation, and supervisory rating of meeting deadlines, and then combine these ratings to form an overall evaluation.

Unfortunately, in many cases, feedback from all sources is provided to the target manager, but only the ratings from the supervisor are used for decision making. In such cases, one would expect the manager being rated to pay more attention to the rating from the supervisor, which might negate the whole purpose of multisource evaluations. Of course, as noted earlier, the original proposers of 360-degree feedback suggested that these ratings be used for feedback only—partly because of the problems just discussed and partly because they believed the raters would be more honest if the ratings were not to be used for decision making.

EVALUATION OF 360-DEGREE FEEDBACK SYSTEMS

What, then, is the bottom line regarding the effectiveness of 360-degree feedback? As noted earlier, there have actually been very few rigorous tests of the effectiveness of these systems. What tests have been conducted have produced inconsistent results, although there is slightly more evidence that upward feedback (i.e., feedback from subordinates to their supervisors) is effective in improving performance. Furthermore, in no case has a 360-degree feedback system been directly compared with an alternative feedback delivery system. Clearly, there is the need for further evaluation, but even without additional data, there are some potential advantages that 360-degree systems can offer.

First, the fact that feedback is provided from so many different sources (and there are even feedback systems that add feedback from customers or clients) means that the manager can get a picture of how she or he is viewed that simply cannot be gained in any other way. Second, if the manager is provided with a coach to help interpret the feedback, it should be possible to get feedback in critical areas from the very best sources of that feedback. Thus, with some guidance, a manager can get critical information from the person or persons in the best position to provide that information. Third, by comparing feedback from different sources with self-ratings, the target manager can gain even more insight into him- or herself, and especially learn about those areas where the manager's self-perceptions are simply not shared by anyone else. This kind of feedback can have excellent potential for aiding in one's development both as a manager and as a person.

Therefore, the key to successful applications of 360-degree feedback systems is to develop ways to gain these advantages without incurring some of the problems that may exist with these systems. Clearly, assigning coaches to help managers to interpret and act on the feedback they receive is one way to help maximize the effectiveness of 360-degree feedback. Problems that might derive from inconsistent feedback messages could be resolved by such a coach, who could help managers determine which feedback messages they should attend to.

There have long been calls for maintaining two separate rating processes within organizations—one for decision making and one for developmental feedback. Given the fact that 360-degree ratings were proposed for use as feedback tools only, and given that ratings are usually more honest when they are not going to be used for decision making, it would be useful if the results from the 360-degree process were used only for feedback. That would require a separate set of appraisals for decision making, and it would also require that the target manager be allowed to keep the results of the 360-degree feedback confidential if desired.

Finally, there have been several recommendations regarding any feedback intervention that would apply to 360-degree feedback as well. For example, feedback tends to be more effective when the recipient can see improvements over time. Hence, once an organization begins using 360-degree feedback, it should continue to do so over time to maximize the potential benefits of the ratings. Goal setting has also been found to be a useful addition to any feedback intervention, and so organizations should make sure that any 360-degree feedback is accompanied by specific, difficult goals that help serve higher-level organizational goals as well.

CONCLUSIONS

Systems employing 360-degree feedback have been quite popular in organizations based in the United States for at least the past 10 to 15 years. Furthermore, firms in other parts of the world are beginning to adopt 360-degree systems as well. Yet, there really is little compelling evidence that they are any more effective than alternative systems in improving performance. Nonetheless, 360-degree feedback offers a richness of feedback that is not available through other means, and so these systems *may* be justified from a broader perspective. For now, though, there is still a need for research to determine the relative effectiveness of 360-degree feedback. Until the final word on effectiveness is available, organizations that wish to convey rich feedback information to employees (especially managers) may choose to use 360-degree systems, but they should be aware of the potential issues and establish procedures to maximize the usefulness of the feedback provided, while minimizing the problems these systems can cause.

—*Angelo S. DeNisi*

See also Multitrait–Multimethod Matrix; Performance Appraisal; Performance Feedback

FURTHER READING

Dalessio, A. T. (1998). Using multisource feedback for employee development and personnel decisions. In J. S. Smither (Ed.), *Performance appraisal: State of the art in practice* (pp. 278–330). San Francisco: Jossey-Bass.

DeNisi, A. S., & Kluger, A. N. (2000). Feedback effectiveness: Can 360-degree appraisals be improved? *Academy of Management Executive, 14,* 129–139.

Ilgen, D. R., Fisher, C. D., & Taylor, M. S. (1979). Consequences of individual feedback on behavior in organizations. *Journal of Applied Psychology, 64,* 349–371.

Kluger, A. N., & DeNisi, A. S. (1996). The effects of feedback interventions on performance: Historical review, a meta-analysis, and a preliminary feedback intervention theory. *Psychological Bulletin, 119,* 254–284.

Lawler, E. E. (1967). The multitrait-multirate approach to measuring managerial job performance. *Journal of Applied Psychology, 51,* 369–381.

London, M. L., & Smither, J. W. (1995). Can multi-source feedback change perceptions of goal accomplishment, self-evaluations, and performance-related outcomes? Theory-based applications and directions for research. *Personnel Psychology, 48,* 803–839.

Seifert, C. F., Yukl, G., & McDonald, R. A. (2003). Effects of multi-source feedback and a feedback facilitator on the influence behavior of managers towards subordinates. *Journal of Applied Psychology, 88,* 561–569.

Tornow, W. W. (1993). Perceptions or reality? Is multi-perspective measurement a means or an end? *Human Resource Management, 32,* 221–230.

TIME MANAGEMENT

The term *time management* became familiar in the 1950s and 1960s as referring to a tool to help managers make better use of available time. The tool was based on practical experience, in the form of dos and don'ts. The term appears to indicate that time is managed, but actually activities are managed over time. Time management is self-management with an explicit focus on time in deciding what to do; on how much time to allocate to activities; on how activities can be done more efficiently; and on when the time is right for particular activities. Much of the advice on time management concerns the standardization and routinization of activities to increase efficiency. The time gained with this increased efficiency can be used for other activities, deliberately chosen as worthwhile, rather than activities that serve only as means to achieve less worthwhile goals, so-called time wasters. In other words, time is gained for activities that deserve it, and full concentration can be devoted to these activities for a longer period of time.

Similar to self-management, time management is focused on solving problems. Examples of common problems are feeling overwhelmed by the workload; planning too optimistically; being unable to deal with distractions; deadline pressure; and procrastination. The core of time management is to prevent these problems by preparation and planning. Many scheduling techniques can be used that aim at obtaining an overview of tasks, subtasks, and actions and methods to remember them—for example, making a to-do list, organizing it according to priority based on importance (relevant to effectiveness) and urgency (relevant to timeliness), and scheduling tasks to months, weeks, and days.

In addition, time management may be seen as a way to stay on track in dynamic conditions. As such, it is more than planning, and it involves a cycle of goal setting, planning, keeping track of progress (monitoring), and the evaluation of goal achievement. In dynamic conditions, if–then rules help to quickly decide courses of action when situations change. For example, if a coworker requests to do a task unexpectedly, then there are four options, based on the judgment of importance and urgency. If it is both important and urgent, act on it immediately. If it is important, but not urgent, try to find out whether it may be done at a later time that suits your schedule. If it is urgent, but not important to your own priorities, try to delegate it to someone else. If it is neither urgent nor important, then do not do it at all. It is clear that apart from these decision rules, some social skills related to assertiveness are needed in dealing with such requests.

RESEARCH ON TIME MANAGEMENT

Despite the worldwide popularity of time management training, the research on time management has been relatively scarce. That is, although several studies have been conducted among students about study behavior and, to a lesser extent, among individuals in a work setting, there are only a few study results to substantiate the claims of time management to increased efficiency and better performance.

Therese Hoff Macan proposed a model of time management in which time management behaviors such as goal setting and organizing result in perceived control of time, which leads to outcomes such as increased performance and less tension. Research that investigated this model established the relationship between perceived control of time and tension several times. However, the relationship between certain types of behavior and control of time, and between control of time and performance, resulted in inconsistent research outcomes.

Apart from this model, the approach to time management has been largely atheoretical, focused on personal skills, without consideration of why the problems arise and why they are so common. Not much is known about the work context, which may play an important role in the pressures on and the enhancement of the use of time. A more comprehensive theoretical framework of time management than presented so far would have to involve task content and social influences, as well. Relevant issues, for example, are as follows: does a person have the autonomy to self-manage activities over time, to delegate activities, or to say no to certain requests? How heavy is the person's workload?

Some authors proposed that time management may be seen as an individual difference variable, and there are several indications that some people are more planful and attentive to time than others. Examples of these individual differences are time urgency (the degree to which a person is hurried and focused on time); polychronicity (the preference to handle several activities simultaneously); and time use efficiency. In the next section, procrastination is presented as one of these variables.

PROCRASTINATION

Procrastination may be seen as a specific time management problem that involves the delay of activities, even though the person is aware that they are important and urgent. The moral undesirability of this phenomenon may aggravate the problem, and many self-help books and tools are devoted to conquering it.

Procrastination may be studied as a state—in effect, as delay at particular moments. Discounting delayed outcomes offers a good explanation as to why everyone engages in procrastination at least once in a while. That is, people generally prefer short-term outcomes over long-term outcomes. This may explain why impulsive reactions to short-term activities (time-pressing, urgent matters) may be more common than planful execution of longer-term goals, even if these are more important than the urgent matters. Both the avoidance of unpleasant tasks and the approach to appealing tasks may motivate procrastination, and training self-control may be seen as central to overcoming procrastination.

Most of the research on procrastination has devoted attention to the trait perspective, in which procrastination is seen as a generalized tendency to repeatedly engage in this type of behavior. Within the trait perspective, the overarching Big Five factor model of personality may be used. In this model, the factor *conscientiousness* refers to discipline, order, and achievement motivation. It is highly negatively related to trait measures of procrastination. *Neuroticism,* a factor that includes anxiety and depression, is a positively related factor, but it is only moderately related. *Self-efficacy* is also negatively related to procrastination.

The degree to which procrastination is common and influenced by the context at work has not been studied extensively. Most of the research results are students' self-reports, and a general bias in the self-perception of individuals who admit they procrastinate that generalizes to other traits may not be ruled out. Another point of discussion in the literature is whether procrastination is caused by deeply rooted psychological motives that need to be dealt with in therapy.

—Wendelien van Eerde

See also Goal-Setting Theory; Self-Regulation Theory

FURTHER READING

Claessens, B. J. C., Van Eerde, W., Rutte, C. G., & Roe, R. A. (in press). A review of the time management literature. *Personnel Review.*

Koch, C. J., & Kleinmann, M. (2002). A stitch in time saves nine: Behavioural decision-making explanations for time management problems. *European Journal of Work and Organizational Psychology, 11,* 199–217.

Macan, T. H. (1994). Time management: Test of a process model. *Journal of Applied Psychology, 79,* 381–391.

Van Eerde, W. (2003). A meta-analytically derived nomological network of procrastination. *Personality and Individual Differences, 35,* 1410–1418.

TOTAL QUALITY MANAGEMENT

Total quality management (TQM) is an organizational activity that has received many labels since its widespread introduction to the American workplace in the early 1980s. It has been labeled as a comprehensive approach to management, a managerial philosophy, a set of tools for improving quality and customer focus, and an organizational development (OD) intervention that can affect both the business and the people side of operations. It is practiced by statisticians and engineers, psychologists and other behavioral scientists, and by CEOs, general managers, and HR professionals. Total quality management has been praised as the panacea for business competitiveness and survival, and it has been maligned as nothing more than a passing fad that has failed to deliver. Clearly, it is difficult to provide a comprehensive, unified definition of TQM that would inspire consensus from the wide range of academics, managers, and consultants who are invested in such a definition.

However, it is possible to identify the primary architects of TQM and to summarize the principles and assumptions that can be extracted from their work. It is widely agreed that the founders of TQM are W. Edwards Deming, Joseph Juran, and Kaoru Ishikawa. The assumptions of their collective work have been summarized as follows: (a) Quality (of goods and services) is essential for organizational survival; (b) the key to quality is through people, who inherently want to contribute to quality and will do so when trained and supported; (c) because organizations are systems comprising interdependent parts, quality improvement efforts should focus on cross-functional processes; and (d) quality must be driven from the top, by senior managers who are committed to and responsible for quality. From these assumptions flow several important principles, including the use of structured problem solving, data-driven decision making, SPC (statistical process control) tools, and employee involvement and development. From this, the essence of TQM can be distilled as a top-down commitment to quality, achieved through employee involvement in continuous process improvement.

THE EVOLUTION OF TQM

The proliferation of quality and process improvement techniques and programs that preceded and followed TQM has resulted in confusion about what is and is not TQM. Predecessors include American-born quality of work life (QWL) interventions, the industrial-democracy movement in Europe, and the quality revolution in Japan, from which quality circles emerged. It is widely agreed that these quality improvement and employee involvement initiatives of the 1960s and 1970s provided the foundation on which TQM was built. A combination of factors converged in the late 1970s and early 1980s that would cause TQM to surpass all of these in its scope and impact. These included the quality crisis in American industry, unprecedented global competition, the demands of workers for involvement and empowerment, and the adaptation of quality principles for the nonmanufacturing sector.

The legitimacy of TQM was established in 1987 when Congress established the Malcolm Baldrige National Quality Award (MBNQA). This annual award recognizes quality excellence in business, health care, and education in the areas of strategic planning; leadership; customer and market focus; measurement, analysis, and knowledge management; human resources focus; process management; and business results. Although the MBNQA has helped to provide a common framework for assessing the implementation of quality practices and has contributed greatly to the growth of TQM, it has not resulted in conceptual clarity. One major source of conceptual muddiness is the relationship between TQM and employee involvement (EI), Six Sigma, and business process reengineering (BPR).

TOWARD CONCEPTUAL CLARITY: TQM, EI, SIX SIGMA, AND BPR

As defined above, the major purpose of TQM is to improve the quality of goods and services. To do this systematically, an organization must fully engage all employees in the effort, which makes TQM a vehicle for employee involvement (EI). This places TQM into the broad category of programs known collectively as *EI interventions.* Employee involvement interventions attempt to increase employees' input into decisions that affect performance and satisfaction. They are operationalized by the downward movement and diffusion of power, information, knowledge, and rewards. Formal EI approaches include older interventions such as quality circles, job enrichment, and sociotechnical systems. Two newer interventions, Six Sigma and business process reengineering (BPR), have also raised definitional confusion about how they differ from TQM. These boundaries are discussed below.

Six Sigma

Six Sigma is a particular approach to total quality management that emerged in the late 1980s from the quality improvement efforts at Motorola. Like TQM, it is a vehicle for employee involvement through structured quality improvement activities. Also like TQM, it has been embraced by companies around the world as a comprehensive framework for business management. Because it emerged from TQM, it shares the same assumptions described above. But it also has unique aspects that have made it the most popular form of TQM today. These include the use of a standardized improvement model (DMAIC, define–measure–analyze–improve–control), an extensive training program to prepare employees for varying levels of involvement, and the use of colorful terminology for these various levels. All employees receive Green Belt training, which prepares them to become members of Green Belt project teams. Green Belts are assisted by Black Belts, who are dedicated resources to support their organization's quality efforts and who receive extensive training in group dynamics, DMAIC, and SPC tools. Some organizations also have intermediate levels of involvement called Yellow Belts.

Business Process Reengineering

Business process reengineering was popularized in the 1993 best seller by Michael Hammer and James Champy, who first coined the phrase *reengineering.* They defined reengineering as the fundamental rethinking and radical redesign of business processes to achieve dramatic results. Business process reengineering and TQM are similar in that they both target

work processes for quality improvements; however, they differ in two very fundamental ways. The first difference is that TQM, as described previously, relies on employee involvement as a central tenet, whereas BPR often lacks this feature. Instead, employees may be passive recipients of BPR-mandated changes. The second difference is the magnitude of the change produced. Although TQM targets existing work processes for incremental and continuous improvements, BPR attempts to radically redesign these processes, often through the use of information technology. Once work processes have been redesigned, it is often necessary to restructure the organization to support the new processes. This often alters the shape and size of the organization through the use of teaming, delayering, and downsizing. These latter outcomes have led to criticism, which is often backed up by claims that many reengineering efforts do not produce the dramatic results that are hoped for.

IMPLEMENTATION OF TQM

Although implementation steps and timetables will be unique to each organization, the following steps are considered essential to a successful program.

1. *Senior management commitment and training.* Total quality management is a top-down approach that depends on the commitment and knowledge of senior-level leaders, who must champion the program and lead the culture change that it requires. Thus, they must receive formal training in quality principles and tools, allocate adequate resources to its successful implementation, and demonstrate their commitment to quality.

2. *Employee training.* Total quality management depends on employee involvement in quality improvement and requires extensive training to prepare employees for their role. Although training formats and time frames vary (ranging from two weeks to two years), all employees are expected to receive some minimal level of formal classroom training. Training content includes structured problem solving (using such tools as Six Sigma's DMAIC), quality tools (histograms, flowcharts, control charts, and Pareto charts), and team dynamics.

3. *Initiate quality improvement/Six Sigma projects.* Quality activities occur through quality improvement (or Green Belt) projects, which are ideally undertaken by teams of employees who share a common work process. However, some projects are undertaken by

individual employees working alone. Projects focus on mapping and measuring existing processes, and the application of quality methods to improve the processes (e.g., reduce the number of steps required) and their output (e.g., reduce variability). Deviations from targeted quality standards are monitored by the team via product control charts and customer satisfaction measures.

4. *Monitor progress and reward results.* Besides internal monitoring of process improvements, TQM also requires measurement against external standards. This usually involves benchmarking with "best-in-class" organizations, which are targeted as quality standard-bearers. Internal improvement efforts are designed to close the gap between the organization and its external benchmark. Management and employees may be rewarded for quality improvements through gainsharing or bonuses. Some organizations have tied involvement in quality projects to performance appraisals, although most programs rely most heavily on intrinsic rewards. A major reward for many employees is the opportunity to improve or streamline a faulty work process, which makes their job easier or more satisfying.

IMPLEMENTATION OF BPR

1. *Preparation and planning.* Because of the transformational nature of the change desired, extensive preimplementation planning and preparation is required. Preparation includes a thorough understanding of strategic direction and supporting work processes as well as the competitive environment. The diagnosis attempts to identify the core business processes that support the desired strategic direction and targets them for reengineering. This step also builds commitment to the intervention as organizational leaders communicate the need for radical change.

2. *Fundamentally rethink how work gets done.* During this phase, core business processes are analyzed, using the same tools used during the *analyze* phase of a TQM or Six Sigma project. Process mapping shows all the current steps in the process and produces an as-is map of the targeted process. Performance metrics for each key process are also examined, and dramatic improvement goals, often derived from benchmarking, are then set. Finally, new work processes are engineered that will produce these dramatic results. In the most extreme approach to this phase, old work processes are completely eliminated and a blank slate is used to design new, streamlined processes. A common theme to eliminating

steps and increasing value-adding activities is the use of information technology.

3. *Restructure the organization to support the new processes.* Although the structure must be aligned to support the specific aspects of the reengineered processes, some common characteristics include a change from functional departments to a process-based structure; flatter, leaner hierarchies; and the use of teams rather than individual jobs in allocating work. A systems approach must be taken to ensure the proper alignment of all human, managerial, information, and measurement subsystems.

RESULTS OF TQM AND BPR

It is estimated that about 75% of Fortune 1,000 firms have implemented some form of TQM. Survey results indicate that 87% feel their TQM experience has been positive. Results claimed attributed to TQM include improved financial performance, employee relations, product quality, and customer satisfaction. A study of 54 companies using TQM reported that they outperformed a similar group of organizations not using TQM. The study reported the performance gains resulted from employee involvement benefits rather than the tools and techniques of TQM. A comprehensive examination of popular management techniques, including TQM and BPR, reported that organizations using these programs did not enjoy better economic performance than other organizations. However, organizations using these programs were more admired, were perceived to be more innovative, and were rated higher in management quality than other organizations. Despite these positive results, it should be acknowledged that there are companies using TQM and BPR that do not reap these benefits, and there are many instances of organizations terminating their programs.

—*Kim K. Buch*

See also Organizational Development; Training

FURTHER READING

Buch, K., & Rivers, D. (2001). TQM: The role of leadership and culture. *Leadership and Organization Development Journal, 22*(2), 365–372.

Cummings, T. G., & Worley, C. G. (2005). *Organization development and change.* Mason, OH: Thomson/South-Western.

Deming, W. E. (1986). *Out of the crisis*. Cambridge, MA: MIT Press.

Hackman, R. J., & Wageman, R. (1995). Total quality management: Empirical, conceptual, and practical issues. *Administrative Science Quarterly, 40,* 309–342.

Hammer, M., & Champy, J. (1993) *Reengineering the corporation: A manifesto for business revolution.* New York: HarperCollins.

Juran, J. (1974). *Quality control handbook.* New York: McGraw-Hill.

Lawler, E. E., III. (1992). *High involvement management: The ultimate advantage.* San Francisco: Jossey-Bass.

TRADE UNIONS

See UNIONS

TRAINABILITY AND ADAPTABILITY

Modern organizations are faced with dynamic pressures such as changing technologies, global competition, and organizational restructuring. Such demands require workers to be adaptable and demonstrate the capacity to quickly learn. To address these issues, researchers and practitioners in industrial/organizational psychology and related fields have sought to define, measure, and build interventions around the psychological concepts of *trainability* and *adaptability*. *Trainability* can be generally defined as the capacity to learn and be trained, and *adaptability* can be thought of as an effective response or change to meet demands of the environment, an event, or a new situation. Both trainability and adaptability can be considered from two different perspectives. First, we can consider how trainability and adaptability can be behaviorally manifested and measured in terms of demonstrated task or job performance. Second, we can investigate the underlying characteristics of people, such as their abilities, personality, and motivation, that make them more or less trainable or adaptable.

TRAINABILITY, ADAPTABILITY, AND PERFORMANCE MEASUREMENT

In terms of behavioral or observed evidence of trainability, trainability has been measured via the use of work samples. A work sample is a simulation of actual training or job content in which individuals are assessed in terms of their ability to effectively perform a given set of tasks. As an example, consider a work sample in which candidates for a construction job have to learn via a short course how to interpret a specific type of blueprint or construction plan and then demonstrate use of this knowledge during an actual construction task. There is convincing research evidence that individuals who can perform well on a representative sample of training will improve more during an actual, full-scale training program. Thus, an individual's ability to acquire knowledge and learn job tasks can be observed and measured to some extent directly.

When looking at adaptability, initial research evidence suggests that various types (or dimensions) of adaptive performance can be identified, including (a) solving problems creatively, (b) dealing with uncertain or unpredictable work situations, (c) learning new tasks, technologies, and procedures, (d) demonstrating interpersonal adaptability, (e) demonstrating cultural adaptability, (f) demonstrating physical adaptability, (g) handling work stress, and (h) handling emergencies or crisis situations. Furthermore, researchers have demonstrated that such dimensions of adaptive performance can be measured directly by using behavioral scales that tell observers what to look for on the job to ascertain whether someone is performing adaptively. In addition, it may be possible to measure adaptive performance using the same type of work samples and simulations mentioned for measuring trainability.

TRAINABILITY, ADAPTABILITY, AND INDIVIDUAL DIFFERENCES

Although the concepts of trainability and adaptability can be measured in terms of observed task or job performance, as discussed previously, a more fundamental question is, What are the underlying characteristics of people—the individual differences—that enable some individuals to train or adapt more quickly or more effectively? Although these are still active areas of research, with much that remains to be discovered, a number of underlying individual differences have been linked to both trainability and adaptability.

First, it has been demonstrated that individuals with higher levels of general cognitive ability (i.e., intelligence) demonstrate greater training performance or trainability. This relationship is also characteristic of adaptability, in that cognitive ability has been linked to greater adaptive performance.

Second, noncognitive characteristics such as personality, motivation, and experience may also play a role in both trainability and adaptability. For example, research suggests that variables such as self-efficacy (belief that one can do the job or tasks at hand), conscientiousness (a sense of responsibility for one's own learning), and motivation to learn may be predictive of trainability and success in training. Similarly, adaptability may be related to personality factors such as achievement motivation (one's desire to overcome obstacles, achieve results, and master tasks), cooperativeness (ability to work effectively with others toward a common purpose), and willingness to learn.

In addition, an individual's capacity to learn and adapt may relate to past experience and prior knowledge. Specifically, past experience and prior knowledge may provide a foundation that allows an individual to draw on past lessons learned in facing new training or adaptability challenges.

An important area for future research is determining the extent to which different types of individual differences predict different types of trainability and adaptive performance. A wealth of research in industrial/organizational psychology has demonstrated that job performance can often be defined in terms of multiple dimensions (e.g., technical versus interpersonal performance). Similarly, specific dimensions of trainability and adaptive performance may be better predicted by individual differences that are more conceptually aligned. For example, in looking at more cognitive training tasks or an element of adaptive performance such as solving problems creatively, cognitive ability may be the most important individual characteristic. In contrast, personality characteristics may play a more prominent role in demonstrating trainability for tasks involving interpersonal skills or for demonstrating interpersonal adaptability.

Another important challenge for trainability and adaptability research is understanding the extent to which trainability and adaptability can be trained. That is, can someone learn how to learn, or train to become more adaptive? For years, educational psychologists have focused on improving strategies for learning and providing individuals with tools for presumably improving trainability. Similarly, organizational practitioners have developed experience-based approaches for training individuals to be more adaptive. This type of adaptability training often involves the use of training tools such as critical incidents, case studies, or simulations. Additional research is needed to clarify the effectiveness of and expected gains from such training efforts, especially in light of the fact that some determinants of trainability and adaptability, such as cognitive ability, may be stable traits of individuals that are not amenable to substantial change.

SUMMARY

As organizations are faced with an increasing array of environmental demands and aspects of change, the psychological concepts of trainability and adaptability have and will continue to receive attention. Researchers and practitioners have attempted to define, measure, and develop interventions around both trainability and adaptability. These efforts have highlighted ways in which trainability and adaptability can be assessed more directly, in terms of measures of task or job performance. In addition, individual differences have been identified that may be underlying determinants of trainability and adaptability, including abilities, personality characteristics, and motivational components. New areas for research and development include evaluating the extent to which trainability and adaptability can be learned or trained.

—David W. Dorsey

See also Individual Differences; Job Performance Models; Training; Training Evaluation; Training Needs Assessment and Analysis

FURTHER READING

Colquitt, J. A., LePine, J. A., & Noe, R. A. (2000). Toward an integrative theory of training motivation: A meta-analytic path analysis of 20 years of research. *Journal of Applied Psychology, 85,* 678–707.

Pulakos, E. D., Arad, S., Donovan, M. A., & Plamondon, K. E. (2000). Adaptability in the work place: Development of a taxonomy of adaptive performance. *Journal of Applied Psychology, 85,* 612–624.

Pulakos, E. D., Schmitt, N., Dorsey, D. W., Hedge, J. W., & Borman, W. C. (2002). Predicting adaptive performance: Further tests of a model of adaptability. *Human Performance, 15*(4), 299–323.

Ree, M. J., Carretta, T. R., & Teachout, M. S. (1995). Role of ability and prior job knowledge in complex training performance. *Journal of Applied Psychology, 80,* 721–730.

Robertson, I. T., & Downs, S. (1989). Work sample tests of trainability: A meta-analysis. *Journal of Applied Psychology, 74,* 402–410.

TRAINING

Training is the systematic process by which employees learn the knowledge, skills, and/or attitudes (KSAs) necessary to do their jobs. Because training is systematic, it is distinct from other ways in which employees acquire new KSAs, such as through experience or serendipitous learning.

Training is different than employee development. Training addresses KSAs in one's current job, whereas developmental efforts enable employees to target KSAs that may be useful in some future job. This distinction, though, is sometimes fuzzy. A training course on basic supervisory skills may be both a training experience for new supervisors and a developmental experience for entry-level employees seeking promotion.

Training is ubiquitous. Whenever a new employee is hired, that individual is likely to go through some form of orientation, formal training on core job responsibilities, and informal training to learn the ropes from a supervisor or more proficient coworkers. All of these activities are considered training. Several professional organizations, including the American Society for Training and Development (ASTD), publish periodic reports on training-related activities by U.S. employers. According to their reports, the average number of hours of formal learning by employees ranges from 25 to 30 for smaller organizations to 35 to 40 for larger organizations. These organizations typically spend about $800 to $1,300 per employee (depending on the size of the organization).

TRAINING ACTIVITIES

Classic models of training development generally include four steps in the training process:

- *Needs assessment.* During this step, the organizational need and support for training is identified and the training content is defined.
- *Training development.* During this step, the training content is determined and decisions are made about the appropriate training method (e.g., how should material be conveyed? How long should the training last?).
- *Training delivery.* During this step, trainees complete the training program. Training may be on-the-job, in a classroom, online, or through workbooks, or offered in some other format.

- *Training evaluation.* During this step, the organization evaluates the effectiveness of the training program during training and/or back on the job.

VALUE OF TRAINING

Recently, several researchers have begun to investigate the impact of various human resource practices, including training, on financial indicators of organizational performance. The financial impact of training was the focus of a recent multiyear study by ASTD of more than 2,500 organizations. Organizational effectiveness was assessed by total shareholder return (TSR)—a composite of change in stock price and dividends issued. Their study offered strong support for the impact of training, reporting the following findings:

- When firms were ranked on training expenditures, firms in the upper half had a TSR 86% higher than firms in the lower half, and 45% higher than the market average.
- When firms were ranked on per-employee expenditures, firms in the upper fourth of the distribution had higher profit margins (by 24%) and higher per-employee income (by 218%) than firms ranked in the lower fourth.

Although more research is necessary to establish causal relationships between organizational performance and investments in training or training quality, research to date demonstrates the value of training to organizations.

TRAINING EFFECTIVENESS

Given preliminary evidence that training works, it is important that training be designed to maximize employee learning of job-related KSAs. Psychological research over the years has resulted in a number of principles related to effective training. These include the following:

- *Ensure trainees are motivated.* Trainees who are motivated to learn become more active learners, actively processing new information to ensure that it is efficiently stored and more easily recalled. Trainees are likely to be motivated when they perceive the training content as relevant to their jobs or career development. The trainer's expertise, charisma, or instructional style can enhance trainee motivation. An uncomfortable setting or poorly designed Web site can undermine trainee motivation.

- *Provide constructive feedback.* The impact of feedback on performance improvement is well documented in many areas of psychology and applies to training contexts, as well. Feedback should be timely and relevant, and it should address both positive and negative aspects of training performance.
- *Provide opportunities to practice.* It is important that trainees have the opportunity to practice new skills in training, before enacting them on the job. Practice works best when the training context resembles the work environment, at either a surface or structural level. Surface-level fidelity occurs when the equipment or work space in training closely resembles that in real life. For example, a successful chain of gas station/convenience stores requires that employees spend a week of training in a completely operational replica of an actual store before starting work. Structural fidelity occurs when the problems, issues, or performance–outcome contingencies in training resemble real life. The navy once conducted aircrew coordination training on a transport ship by having team members sit in folding chairs surrounding a plunger that served as the "ship's" throttle. Although the surface fidelity of this training was low, the crew practiced responding to simulated emergencies drawn from real-life events.
- *Prepare trainees to transfer.* Transfer of training occurs when trainees apply what they've learned successfully to their jobs. Transfer can be enhanced by preparing trainees for posttraining obstacles to transfer. For example, a computer technician may attend training to learn new strategies for diagnosing customers' computer malfunctions. However, when she returns to her job at a technical support center, a month passes before she receives a call that allows her to use this new strategy, or she begins to use pretraining strategies when her supervisor complains that she is not handling calls as quickly as she had in the past. Trainees can be prepared by telling them what challenges await and providing contingency plans for when obstacles are encountered.

Transfer, and hence, training in general, is more likely to be successful when the training is embedded in a supportive environment. This means that training is perceived as beneficial, sufficient resources are allocated to plan and administer effective training programs, and trainees return to supportive environments that allow them to implement and refine newly acquired skills. Given evidence of the potential impact of training, it makes good sense for organizations to offer strong support for training initiatives.

—*Kurt Kraiger*

See also Diversity Training; Training Evaluation; Training Methods; Training Needs Assessment and Analysis

FURTHER READING

Arthur, W., Bennett, W., Jr., Edens, P., & Bell, S. (2003). Effectiveness of training in organizations: A meta-analysis of design and evaluation features. *Journal of Applied Psychology, 88,* 234–245.

Bassi, M. V., Ludwig, J., McMurrer, D. P., & Van Buren, M. (2004). *Profiting from learning: Do firms' investments in education and training pay off?* Washington, DC: ASTD.

Colquitt, J., LePine, J. A., & Noe, R. A. (2000). Toward an integrative theory of training motivation: A meta-analytic path analysis of 20 years of research. *Journal of Applied Psychology, 83,* 654–665.

Kraiger, K. Training in organizations. In W. C. Borman, D. R. Ilgen, & R. J. Klimoski (Eds.), *Comprehensive handbook of psychology: Vol. 12. Industrial and Organizational Psychology* (pp. 171–192). New York: Wiley.

TRAINING EVALUATION

Training evaluation is the process used to determine the effectiveness and/or efficiency of training programs. *Training effectiveness* refers to the extent to which trainees (and their organization) benefit as intended from training. *Training efficiency* refers to the ratio of training-related benefits to training-related costs; thus, efficiency takes into account the resources used to design, develop, and administer the training. Training evaluation may also involve collecting data that do not directly address current levels of effectiveness or efficiency but are used to subsequently improve them.

There is a broad knowledge base relevant to training evaluation. There are relevant academic literatures in educational psychology, educational measurement, human resource development, and the emerging discipline of program evaluation. There is also a substantial trade literature specific to evaluating workplace training. Because evaluation is at its core a research process, industrial/organizational (I/O) psychologists have made their own contributions to this literature.

The evaluation process typically involves the following steps: (a) Determine the *purpose* of the evaluation, (b) decide on relevant *outcomes,* (c) develop outcome *measures,* (d) choose an evaluation *strategy,* (e) plan and execute the evaluation, and (f) use evaluation data and results as suggested by the purpose of the evaluation. This entry will cover key distinctions in the areas of purpose, outcomes, measures, and strategy.

PURPOSE

There are many reasons to evaluate training, most of which can be classified into three primary categories: (a) to provide feedback to designers, trainers, and trainees; (b) to provide input for decision making about training; and (c) to provide information that can be used to market the training program.

Decisions about outcomes, measures, and strategy should be based on the evaluation purpose. Following from the three purposes, an evaluation model proposed by Kurt Kraiger suggests three primary targets of evaluation: (a) training content and design, which can be assessed to provide feedback to designers and trainers; (b) changes in learners, which can be gauged to provide feedback to learners and to make decisions about training; and (c) organizational payoffs, which can be collected and used for all three purposes. Each evaluation target offers multiple outcomes that can be assessed, and evaluators must decide not only the outcome of interest but also the method by which this outcome will be measured. For example, to provide feedback to training designers that can be used to improve training, an evaluator might question learners and subject matter experts about the on-the-job relevance of training materials. These questions can be asked via survey or interview, or inferred from observation of learners interacting with materials and attempting to apply those materials to their job.

Although most training evaluation occurs after a program is fully designed, evaluating training while it is being designed is often desirable. Such evaluation, called *formative* or *process* evaluation, is useful for providing feedback to designers so they can improve the program as it is being developed. As examples of this type of evaluation, an evaluator could assess whether the intended training objectives are consistent with the organization's business strategy by having managers and customers review the objectives and provide feedback.

OUTCOMES

The most widely cited model of training outcomes was developed by Donald Kirkpatrick, who outlined four levels at which training can be evaluated. Level 1 evaluation assesses reactions, which ask how well trainees liked training. Level 2 evaluation assesses learning, assessing what knowledge was gained from the training. Level 3 evaluation assesses behavior, determining job-related behavior change that resulted from the training. Level 4 evaluation assesses results, examining tangible results of the training in terms of reduced cost, increased sales, improved quality, and so on.

The Kirkpatrick model provides some useful guidelines for evaluation, but it has been criticized in both the academic and trade literatures. Consequently, at least four major refinements to the model have been offered. The first improvement in the model has been that research has clarified the nature of trainee reactions, expanding on Kirkpatrick's original presentation. Kirkpatrick's earliest work was unclear as to what types of reaction questions should be asked and how they should be used. Applications of the model have varied considerably in the number of dimensions or facets of reactions that have been measured, from as few as 1 (overall satisfaction) to as many as 10 (program objectives and content, program materials, delivery methods and technologies, instructor or facilitator, instructional activities, program time or length, training environment, planned action or transfer expectation, logistics administration, and overall evaluation).

Recent research suggests that most reactions measures are indeed multidimensional. In addition, recent research suggests that a useful way to conceptualize reactions is hierarchically, with a global satisfaction construct underlying reactions to specific aspects of training. Both the facet reactions and the overall satisfaction measure may be useful, albeit for different reasons. Asking trainees about specific elements of the training can be useful for diagnosing problems with specific aspects of the training experience, and examining overall satisfaction may be useful for detecting motivation or attention problems with learners.

The second improvement in the model has been to clarify the multidimensional nature of learning. Kirkpatrick's treatment of learning was essentially unidimensional, proposing the use of knowledge tests to examine knowledge gained. In contrast, research suggests that learning is multidimensional and can be captured in different ways. Kraiger, J. Kevin Ford, and Eduardo Salas, in particular, suggest a tripartite model of learning: cognitive, skill-based, and affective.

Cognitive learning refers to the acquisition of different types of knowledge, including declarative knowledge, structural knowledge, and cognitive strategies. In addition to traditional tests, these outcomes can be measured with techniques such as asking trainees to draw out relationships among key concepts and testing whether trainees' beliefs about relationships are similar to experts' beliefs. *Skill-based learning* includes both compilation, which is the development of procedural knowledge that enables effective performance, and *automaticity,* which is performance without the need for conscious monitoring. Skill-based learning can be assessed with role plays and simulations. *Affective learning* includes changes in attitudes, such as attitudes about learning or the training content, and motivation, such as self-efficacy and goals. This model expands the Kirkpatrick perspective on learning and provides a wide array of options for evaluating learning outcomes based on research in cognitive and educational psychology.

Third, the perspective on organizational results has become more sophisticated since Kirkpatrick's earliest work. As part of an effort to refine the use of results as an outcome, some authors suggest there is a Level 5 evaluation, which calculates the return on investment (ROI) for training expenditures. Return on investment is an efficiency measure, as it incorporates not just the benefits for the organization, the way Level 4 evaluation requires, but also the costs of training. A number of different approaches are now available to calculate results outcomes, including basic benefits analysis, utility analysis, return-on-investment analysis, and net present value. Each technique varies in the degree to which costs are carefully considered and the method by which training benefits and costs are assigned monetary value. The most commonly used method by I/O psychologists is utility analysis. However, calculating net present value is a more sophisticated approach, because it involves appropriate financial discounting of future costs and, if relevant, cost savings. Whichever approach is used, this type of evaluation is resource-intensive, because it requires estimates of the performance difference between trained and untrained groups and of the monetary value of this difference. Consequently, this outcome is measured much less often than others.

Finally, basic assumptions of the Kirkpatrick model have been questioned, particularly the assumptions about a causal chain across levels and about the relative value of evaluations at each level. Kirkpatrick's work has been interpreted to suggest a causal chain across levels (positive reactions lead to learning, which leads to behavioral change, etc.) and a bias toward higher-level evaluations as providing the most informative data. Current thinking does not support these assumptions. Meta-analyses suggest that correlations among the levels are not as high as would be suggested by the presumed causal model. Moreover, it has been argued that each level provides different information, not necessarily better information. Depending on the purpose of the evaluation effort, different outcomes will be more or less useful.

MEASURES

Once decisions about purpose and outcomes have been made, evaluators must decide how to measure the desired outcomes. This involves deciding where to get the data and how to collect it. Most evaluations consider the target of evaluation to be learners. However, as suggested by the Kraiger model, the possibilities are much broader, including trainees' managers, trainers, experts (subject matter, work group, and instructional), and customers. In particular, when the purpose of the evaluation is to determine organizational payoffs, learners' managers and customers are valuable sources of data. Ultimately, the selection of where to collect the data should be driven by the purpose of the evaluation as well as by practical constraints.

Evaluation data can be collected in many different ways, such as with paper surveys, computer surveys, interviews, observations, or archival records. Each type of data collection method has strengths and weaknesses. For example, computer surveys are convenient to administer but only convenient for respondents who have ready access to computers and are comfortable using them. In addition, if poorly designed, surveys may fail to collect important information from the respondent. Interviews are more time-consuming than surveys to administer and interpret, but they yield richer data and are more likely to capture important information. Evaluators should consider these trade-offs when deciding which measures to adopt; the measures should be reliable and valid indicators of the outcomes being measured.

STRATEGY

Drawing on the seminal work of Thomas Cook and Donald Campbell, many training textbooks describe in detail the research designs that can be used to measure the impact of training on learners. These include experimental (with randomization of subjects into different training conditions), quasi-experimental (no randomization but some measure of control over competing explanations for training effects), and preexperimental (difficult to interpret because of limited control) designs. The most commonly used designs in organizations are posttest only and pre-post test designs, both of which are preexperimental designs. These designs are generally considered inadequate for controlling common threats to internal validity, including history, selection, and maturation. Nevertheless, these designs may be useful if the evaluator is primarily concerned that trainees reach a certain level of proficiency. For example, if training is intended to ensure that assembly line employees catch all products with a troublesome manufacturing defect, then improvement from pre- to posttest is less critical than having all trainees capable of identifying the defect.

Preexperimental designs may also be useful if the evaluator is familiar with the evaluation setting and critically examines competing explanations for the observed outcomes. An example of this type of critical examination is offered in the internal referencing strategy. This strategy requires testing trainees on concepts that are relevant to the training objectives and materials, and on concepts that are irrelevant. If training causes improvement in trainees' knowledge, then they should demonstrate improved understanding of relevant but not irrelevant concepts. Thus, this strategy rules out some common competing explanations for improvement in training outcomes.

Commonly used quasi-experimental designs include pre-post test designs with a control group, time series, and Solomon four-group design. Such designs require more time and resources than preexperimental designs but provide greater confidence that the obtained results can be interpreted as effects from training. When random assignment is possible, these evaluation strategies become true experimental designs, and they offer even greater confidence in the conclusions that can be drawn.

SUMMARY

When evaluating training, I/O psychologists have to make decisions about why they are evaluating as well as what to measure and how. Deciding the purpose of the evaluation is the essential first step, because it should influence all subsequent decisions.

—*Kenneth G. Brown*

See also Quasi-experimental Designs; Training; Training Methods; Training Needs Assessment and Analysis; Utility Analysis

FURTHER READING

Alliger, G. M., Tannenbaum, S. I., Bennett, W., Traver, H., & Shotland, A. (1997). A meta-analysis of the relations among training criteria. *Personnel Psychology, 50,* 341–358.

Brown, K. G., & Gerhardt, M. W. (2002). Formative evaluation: An integrated practice model and case study. *Personnel Psychology, 55,* 951–983.

Kirkpatrick, D. L. (1996). Great ideas revisited. *Training and Development, 50,* 54–59.

Kraiger, K., Ford, J. K., & Salas, E. (1993). Application of cognitive, skill-based, and affective theories of learning outcomes to new methods of training evaluation. *Journal of Applied Psychology, 78,* 311–328.

Noe, R. A. (2005). *Employee training and development* (3rd ed.). Boston: Irwin.

Sackett, P. R., & Mullen, E. J. (1993). Beyond formal experimental design: Toward an expanded view of the training evaluation process. *Personnel Psychology, 46,* 613–627.

TRAINING METHODS

Training is the systematic process by which employees learn the knowledge, skills, and/or attitudes (KSAs) necessary to do their jobs. All forms of training use one or more methods or processes by which these KSAs are conveyed to employees. In other words, training is effective when trainees learn. *Training methods* are the techniques used to facilitate learning.

It is challenging to provide a rational taxonomy of training methods, because these may be either broad approaches (e.g., classroom training) or specific activities (e.g., providing opportunities for practice). This entry begins with very broad distinctions and moves to more specific activities that enhance learning in training and transfer back to the job.

INFORMAL TRAINING

One important distinction is between formal and informal training methods. Formal training methods are described in more detail in the following paragraphs. Although most of the training research has focused on formal methods, it is not clear whether most corporate training is this structured. As much as half of actual organizational training may be informal in nature. Employees also learn new skills through trial and error, through developmental experiences and mentoring, and through the most common type of informal training: on-the-job training (OJT). *On-the-job training* simply refers to assigning employees to jobs and encouraging them to learn by observation or direction from supervisors or more experienced incumbents. For example, a new employee is required to wear protective clothing to handle hazardous waste materials. He or she is told to ask a senior employee to demonstrate the proper technique for donning the clothing.

Most of us have gone through OJT at some point in our careers. There was a time near the beginning of the 20th century when nearly all training was on the job (conducted by the foreman). Because of OJT's unstructured nature, it is difficult to estimate how frequently OJT actually occurs in modern organizations. For example, even if an organization knows that 50% of an employee's first week on the job is spent learning on the job, there will probably be numerous undocumented times in the next year that the employee asks a supervisor for advice or observes a more experienced worker performing a task more efficiently.

Tracking OJT is also difficult because learning might not always be taking place during those times designated as OJT. On-the-job training is sometimes referred to as training by "following around old Joe." However, it is not always clear whether old Joe is motivated or prepared to offer sound instruction. Despite the fact that there has been little research done on the frequency or effectiveness of on-the-job training, it is believed that the same principles of training effectiveness that apply to formal job training apply to OJT, as well. These include preparing for instruction by understanding the key steps and preparing equipment, materials, and so forth; explaining the training objectives; demonstrating the task and explaining the key elements of the task; having the trainee perform part or all of the task (depending on complexity); praising successful efforts and correcting unsuccessful ones; and providing opportunities for practice.

FORMAL TRAINING

In contrast to OJT, formal training methods are more structured, in the sense that there may be an a priori needs assessment, specific instructional objectives, and a formal lesson plan that prescribes learning activities designed to aid in the acquisition of desired KSAs. Formal training methods generally fall into one of three classifications: other-directed, self-directed, and technology-assisted instruction.

Other-Directed Instruction

Other-directed instruction refers to training methods in which one or more trainers assumes responsibility for all instructional processes. Instructor-led training remains the most common instructional method used in industry today. Much of the training content is covered through lectures but may be augmented by discussion and/or question-and-answer periods.

Lectures. Just as most of us have gone through some form of OJT, most of us have sat through lectures, either in corporate training programs or higher education. Accordingly, most of us can appreciate both the primary advantages and disadvantages of this method. Lectures provide one of the best means for communicating a large amount of information in a short amount of time; they are beneficial for knowledge-based outcomes or for explaining complex procedures. On the other hand, learners tend to be very passive during lectures and may not receive sufficient opportunity to practice new skills. Lectures are often supplemented with more active learning methods, such as business case studies, videos, role playing, and simulations. It is interesting to note, however, that although there are many critics of the lecture as an instructional method, there is little empirical evidence that suggests that trainees learn less from this method than from other, more active methods.

Case Studies and Role Plays. There are additional methods of other-directed instruction, including videos or television, business games, case studies, and role plays. Two of the more common methods are case studies and role plays.

Case studies provide detailed background information on an organizational problem. Working individually or collectively, training participants diagnose the problem, offer solutions, and discuss alternatives. Case studies encourage thoughtful diagnosis of realistic problems and the opportunity to think through potential actions.

Role plays constitute a type of living case study. Participants are given background information (usually less detailed than in case studies), as well as a unique role to enact. For example, one participant may play the part of a staff supervisor, and the other the part of a line supervisor, and each is given instructions to persuade the other to change his or her position on the handling of a problem employee. As participants interact, the scenario evolves, and the demands on the participants change. Role plays can be particularly useful for training in interpersonal skills.

Self-Directed Instruction

Self-directed instruction occurs when learners assume primary responsibility for their learning, principally through the use of readings, workbooks, and correspondence courses. Workbooks remain one of the most common forms of training in organizations today. Workbooks typically target specific skills or knowledge relevant to the job. For example, seasonal hires in a department store can be provided workbooks that describe the stock, how to work the cash register, and procedures for handling returns.

A workbook can provide self-assessment tools so that employees can determine their baseline knowledge or skills. Readings, exercises, and discussions in the workbook build on what employees know, allowing them to study at their own pace. Self-pacing is a primary advantage of workbooks, as is the opportunity for employees to do self-assessment (of knowledge and skills) or self-evaluation (of learning progress). Workbooks can also be kept and referenced as job aids. The primary disadvantages of workbooks are lack of support when employees cannot understand workbook material and the lack of accountability for completing the workbooks or learning as much as possible when going through them.

Technology-Assisted Instruction

Various forms of technology-assisted instruction are becoming increasingly popular training methods. Data from the American Society of Training and Development show that the use of technology-assisted instruction has more than doubled between 2000 and 2004 and is expected to continue to increase in coming years.

Technology-assisted instruction includes elements of both other-directed and self-directed instruction. The defining characteristic of technology-assisted instruction is the use of computer hardware and software to deliver learning. There are a variety of forms of technology-assisted instruction, including computer-based training, electronic support systems, and virtual reality training. This entry focuses on the most flexible method of technology-assisted instruction: computer-based training.

The two most common methods of computer-based instruction are intelligent tutoring and hypermedia systems. Intelligent tutoring follows a cognitive task analysis that breaks down tasks into a sequence of known steps. Using this sequence as an expert model, the software guides the learner toward task mastery. The learner must perform the task as intended by the program but can move forward quickly or drop back for remedial work depending on his or her ability to master the content. Intelligent tutoring systems are more popular in organizations such as the military, in which there is a prescribed or single best method for accomplishing tasks. For example, the air force uses intelligent tutoring systems to train electronics technicians in procedures for isolating, identifying, and repairing dysfunctional circuits. Users are sometimes resistant to these systems, because there are no shortcuts; learners must complete all phases of the training.

In hypermedia systems, trainees assume more control for their learning. They interact with learning systems through hyperlinked portals that allow them to choose the content and instructional methods (e.g., reading text, watching streaming videos, or solving problems). Web-based instruction, an increasingly popular instructional method, is a variant of hypermedia training in which instructional materials do not reside on the workstation but are distributed over the Internet. For example, a fast-food restaurant might develop a hypermedia training system to train its employees in customer service techniques. Once logged in to the system, trainees can choose topics (e.g., greeting customers or handling complaints) and either watch videos or read text on preferred methods for providing quality customer service.

The primary advantage of these systems is the capability of individual learners to tailor the content and delivery to their own needs and preferences. This capability is also the primary disadvantage. More knowledgeable employees may be trusted to make good decisions about what and how to learn; for them, hypermedia systems (particularly Web-based instruction) not only provide immediate access to necessary information but also grant the opportunity to explore interesting topics in greater detail. However, less knowledgeable or less intelligent workers may make bad decisions about learning content and delivery. In effect, they don't know what they don't know. The cost of developing either form of computer-based training is high, and it would be cost-prohibitive for most organizations to develop both intelligent tutoring and hypermedia training systems. However, it is easy to imagine a context in which one system is more appropriate for some employees in one type of job, and the other system is more appropriate for other employees in other types of jobs.

Other Instructional Methods

There are several other instructional methods that are more difficult to classify. These are discussed in the following paragraphs.

Simulations. Simulations are appropriate for jobs with complex tasks or those that require employees to operate sophisticated or expensive equipment. Learning through simulations may be less costly or less threatening then practicing on the job. Examples of simulation-based training range from navy pilots flying fighter craft, to customer service representatives fielding practice calls using actual databases on the computer. Although the primary advantage of simulations is the opportunity to practice on realistic equipment in a safe environment, research shows that even low-fidelity simulators (e.g., video games) can be useful for teaching job skills. Virtual reality training represents an emerging form of simulation training.

Team Training. Team-based work systems are becoming increasingly popular in modern organizations. To maximize the effectiveness of work teams, organizations should provide team training. Team training consists of two types of content: task-related knowledge and skills (task work) and team-related knowledge and skills (teamwork). Task-work training can be accomplished using the same methods used for training individuals. At issue is whether team members train individually or as a team. In some situations—for example, air traffic control teams—it may be difficult or impractical to train all team members simultaneously. When it is possible to train team members together on a task, the more interdependent

the work, the more necessary it is to train team members together.

Team members should train together when learning teamwork; teamwork skills are those that help team members work together, regardless of the task. These include coordination, shared situational awareness, and performance monitoring and feedback. Teamwork skills can be learned in low-fidelity situations. Some strategies for training teamwork skills include cross-training (training team members on more than one role), prebriefings (instructing team leaders in how to prepare teams for assignments), and posttraining reviews (training teams how to review and self-correct following task performance).

Cross-Cultural Training. Cross-cultural training involves the preparation of expatriates for work in a different culture. Cross-cultural training can include language training, knowledge of local culture and customs, and strategies for adapting and adjusting to expatriate life. An important component of cross-cultural training is providing feedback to trainees about their levels of ethnocentricity with respect to cultural values and mores. With this self-awareness, employees may be more open to different customs and practices in other countries. One common cross-cultural training tool, the cultural assimilator, prepares expatriates through the use of mini case studies—brief scenarios that require trainees to assign attributions for the actions of characters acting in the host culture. By reading whether they were correct or not in their choice of attributions, trainees learn more about the operant values of the host culture.

Characteristics of Effective Training Methods

Regardless of the training method, there are several core principles for designing training to be maximally effective. Although some of these principles are easier to incorporate into some methods than others, training designers should try to build these principles into all forms of training. These principles include the following:

- *Clarify what is to be learned and how this information will be useful to trainees.* This can be accomplished through advanced organizers—outlines, diagrams, or anecdotes that alert trainees to information to be covered in training.

- *Link new training content to preexisting knowledge or job experiences of employees.* Advanced organizers should be personally relevant to trainees. For example, at the beginning of a team training program for military pilots, trainees observed a video of a fatal helicopter crash in which the helicopter pilot and copilot showed poor communication and communication skills.

- *Chunk or organize relevant information.* New knowledge is acquired not only when it is linked to existing knowledge but also when it is presented in a way that facilitates organization in memory by learners. For example, the tones on a musical staff can be presented using the expression "Every Good Boy Does Fine" (EGBDF).

- *Provide trainees with opportunities to practice new skills.* Practice works best if it varies in difficulty and provides different cues for eliciting the desired behavior. For example, a supervisor who is learning participatory goal-setting techniques can practice with two confederates—one easy to work with and one difficult.

- *Provide constructive feedback.* Trainees need to know when they are doing things correctly and should also be told what they are doing wrong and how to do it right.

- *Provide opportunities to observe others performing new skills.* Through open discussions or practicing in public settings, trainees can learn by watching others. Trainers sometimes have the disadvantage of knowing the content too well; another trainee who acquires new knowledge or skills more rapidly can help other trainees bridge the gap between what they know and the training standard.

- *Provide opportunities for trainees to form social networks with other trainees.* Surveys show that, particularly for higher-level positions, one of the top benefits of attending training is the opportunity to form new or stronger working relationships with peers also attending training. These newly formed networks can provide support during transfer of training and offer new developmental opportunities in the future.

—Kurt Kraiger

See also Distance Learning; Diversity Training; Leadership Development; Team Building; Training; Transfer of Training

FURTHER READING

Arthur, W., Bennett, W., Jr., Edens, P., & Bell, S. (2003). Effectiveness of training in organizations: A meta-analysis of design and evaluation features. *Journal of Applied Psychology, 88,* 234–245.

Cannon-Bowers, J. A., Tannenbaum, S. I., Salas, E., & Volpe, C. E. (1995). Defining competencies and establishing team training requirements. In R. A. Guzzo & E. Salas (Eds.), *Team effectiveness and decision making in organizations.* San Francisco: Jossey-Bass.

Noe, R. A. (1999). *Employee training and development* (3rd ed.). New York: McGraw-Hill/Irwin.

Noe, R. A., & Colquitt, J. A. (2002). Planning for training impact: Principles of training effectiveness. In K. Kraiger (Ed.), *Creating, implementing, and managing effective training and development: State-of-the-art lessons for practice* (pp. 53–79). San Francisco: Jossey-Bass.

Rothwell, W. J., & Kazanas, H. (1994). *Improving on-the-job training.* San Francisco: Jossey-Bass.

TRAINING NEEDS ASSESSMENT AND ANALYSIS

Training needs assessment is a process used to determine how an organization should allocate resources toward training and related human performance improvement interventions. Compared with other related areas of study in industrial/organizational (I/O) psychology, most notably training design and training evaluation, this process has received considerably less research attention. Nevertheless, needs assessment is vitally important to ensure training effectiveness and efficiency. Organizations that do not conduct needs assessments are more likely to do too little or too much training, or to develop training programs that do not benefit employees and the organization as a whole.

Full-scale needs assessments require collecting data on organization, task, and person characteristics (described in more detail below). This broad array of data is necessary for determining what training is needed by which employees so the organization can effectively pursue its strategic goals. In an ideal world, organizations conduct needs assessments routinely and begin with an organization analysis. Then, task and person analyses are conducted, often simultaneously because they require similar types of data from the same sources (potential trainees and their managers).

ORGANIZATION ANALYSIS

Organization analysis involves determining the appropriateness of training given the organization's strategic goals, environment, resources, and characteristics. The organization's strategy is relevant to decisions about training because different strategies demand different amounts and types of training. Organizations that seek to differentiate themselves from their competitors with excellent service, for example, would likely benefit from service-related training courses. The same training courses might be less beneficial to an organization seeking a competitive advantage by minimizing costs. Organizations may also differ in the extent to which they invest in employees via training; some organizations pursue a human resources strategy of hiring the best possible employees. These organizations expend considerable resources on recruiting and selecting and may spend fewer resources on training. Assessors must understand the competitive pressures facing the organization and its strategic goals to recommend training that helps the organization effectively pursue those goals.

Organization analysis also requires an understanding of the environment within which the organization functions. Many facets of the environment, including the technical and legal, influence the type of training that an organization should offer. The technical environment includes the current and forthcoming technologies that employees will use to perform their work. For example, if an organization is planning to upgrade its computer systems, it will need to plan for training to assist in the transition and alter its existing courses to be consistent with the new systems. The legal environment includes both legislation and regulatory mandates. Although some industries and organizations are more affected by regulations than others (e.g., utilities more than services), all organizations should be aware of how training assists in compliance and reduces litigation risk. As one example, U.S. courts have determined that the degree of an organization's liability for discrimination depends on whether managers were trained in nondiscriminatory hiring practices. Consequently, managerial training covering laws related to discrimination are useful for organizations covered by employment laws such as the Civil Rights Act and the Americans With Disabilities Act. Organization analysis should determine which laws are applicable and require training for compliance.

Organization analysis also measures work environment characteristics, such as the degree to which the organization generally supports transfer of training. Such organizations are considered to have a positive transfer-of-training climate and to have employees who are more likely to use learned skills back on the job. If trainees will be returning to a work environment that is not supportive of new skills, they should be prepared in training with strategies that help them overcome barriers to transfer. Thus, data collected during the organization analysis helps to determine both what training programs are appropriate and, to some degree, how that training should be designed.

TASK ANALYSIS

Task analysis involves identifying the tasks performed by trainees and the knowledge and skill necessary to perform them effectively. Task analysis is a form of job analysis and involves different methods depending on the task being analyzed. The most common process for obtaining task analysis data involves (a) panels of job incumbents developing lists of the tasks performed; (b) assessors grouping tasks into clusters based on similarity; (c) panels of managers generating knowledge, skill, and ability (KSA) statements for each task cluster; and (d) surveys validating the task, task cluster, and KSA lists. To avoid bias in the data collection, it is generally suggested that multiple panels and multiple assessors be involved. Research supports the concern over bias with regard to surveys. For example, when it comes to accurately rating the frequency with which particular tasks are performed, research suggests that incumbents who have not performed the task for long are more accurate at recalling frequency than observers and performers who have performed the task for longer periods of time. As a result, a good source for frequency and related task information can be found in recent hires who have performed the tasks but have not attained expert status.

Two increasingly important task analysis techniques are cognitive task analysis and team task analysis. Cognitive task analysis is an examination of the goals, decisions, and judgments that employees make on the job. Whereas traditional task analysis focuses on observable tasks and behaviors, cognitive task analysis delves into the thought processes that underlie effective performance. To assess thought processes, verbal protocol analysis, card sorts, or other elicitation techniques are typically used. For example, to determine how computer technicians troubleshoot computers, expert technicians could be asked to think out loud while they solve different computer problems. Team task analysis, on the other hand, is a simultaneous examination of the task and coordination requirements of a group of individuals working together toward a common goal. Research on nuclear power plant operations, as one example, indicates that operating teams must exchange information and hand off key tasks to one another to perform effectively. Isolating the knowledge and skills that underlie these exchanges ensures that training will focus on that knowledge and those skills as well as the required technical skills.

Whatever the nature of the task analysis, its primary output is a list of objectives for the training program(s). Effective objectives specify what the trainee should be able to do at the conclusion of training, including a criterion for how well the trainee will perform and a description of conditions under which this performance will occur. An example of an effective objective for an assertiveness training program would be, "Trainee will, with 100% accuracy and no help from reference material, list the steps of the assertive communication process."

PERSON ANALYSIS

Person analysis involves determining (a) whether training or other solutions are necessary to ensure that employees can perform tasks effectively; (b) if training is needed, who needs training; and (c) whether trainees are ready for training.

First, person analysis should determine whether training is appropriate by determining the underlying causes of employees' current performance levels. If employees lack the knowledge and skill, required for performance, then training is an appropriate intervention. There are, however, many other reasons why employees may not perform effectively, including a lack of feedback about performance or lack of necessary equipment. With such causes for poor performance, training would be wasted. Consequently, an effective person analysis identifies nontraining needs as well as training needs and can be used to determine if some performance intervention other than training is appropriate. For example, person analysis might determine that, to increase their work output, office workers need faster computers rather than software training.

Second, to determine who needs training, a number of different methods can be employed. Two of the most common, examining existing employee records and soliciting self-assessed needs, suffer from potential bias. Employee records may not be sufficiently detailed or may gloss over skill deficiencies because of legal concerns over keeping records of poor performance. Self-assessed needs are influenced by person characteristics that may or may not be related to actual knowledge and skill needs. In particular, employees who have performed the relevant tasks for longer

periods of time may be unable to articulate what type of training would help novices attain their level of expertise. Because of the limitations of each method, multiple methods should be used if possible.

Third, assessors must determine if trainees are ready for training. To do this, assessors should conduct an audit of the basic skills, abilities, and motivations of potential trainees. Research strongly suggests that individuals with the prerequisite basic skills, higher levels of cognitive ability, and higher levels of motivation are more likely to benefit from training. This does not mean that training should be offered only to those who fit this profile. Training would, however, be more successful if an audit were used to identify who requires remedial basic skills training, as well as to design training to appropriately match the cognitive ability and motivation of trainees. As one example, an outsourced call center (i.e., employees in another country fielding calls from the United States) might develop two different training programs for employees with different levels of English language skills. Employees with lower English language skills may require a course that covers basic terminology and English phone etiquette before being trained on the company-specific phone protocol. Assessing the basic language skills of employees would be necessary to ascertain whether these language skill differences exist and to help assign employees to the proper training.

CONNECTION BETWEEN EVALUATION AND NEEDS ASSESSMENT

Evaluation and needs assessment are closely connected. Needs assessments establish the objectives of training, which should be used to evaluate whether training is or is not effective. For example, if one training objective is for new sales trainees to list benefits of the company's key products, then evaluation of the program should include a recall test. End-of-training evaluations also can be used to collect information relevant to selecting and designing future training programs. At the conclusion of a training program, for example, participants can be asked to rate the usefulness of various topics. Future training programs can shift their emphasis toward topics that employees believe most useful.

REACTIVE NEEDS ASSESSMENT

When applied thoroughly, the analyses discussed in the preceding sections are useful for proactively determining how an organization should allocate training resources. The organization–task–person model is less useful when it comes to reacting to a specific human performance problem, such as high turnover or poor sales. A thorough needs assessment relevant to this problem may prove inefficient; moreover, it would assume that some form of training is required to solve the problem. An alternative model has been offered to deal with these situations. It is a problem-solving process that begins with problem definition and then moves to root-cause identification and intervention design. This model is known as the human performance intervention (HPI) process or human performance technology (HPT). Although relatively neglected in I/O psychology research, this approach resonates with the consulting approach increasingly used by professionals in the human resource management and organizational development fields.

—*Kenneth G. Brown*

See also Job Analysis; Job Analysis Methods; Training; Trainability and Adaptability; Training Evaluation

FURTHER READING

DuBois, D. A., Levi, K. R., Shalin, V. L., & Borman, W. C. (1998). A cognitively oriented approach to task analysis. *Training Research Journal, 3,* 103–141.

Ford, J. K., & Wroten, S. P. (1984). Introducing new methods for conducting training evaluation and for linking training evaluation to program redesign. *Personnel Psychology, 37,* 651–665.

Noe, R. A. (2005). *Employee training and development* (3rd ed.). Boston: Irwin.

Ree, M. J., Carretta, T. R., & Teachout, M. S. (1995). Role of ability and prior knowledge in complex training performance. *Journal of Applied Psychology, 80,* 721–730.

Richman, W. L., & Quiñones, M. A. (1996). Task frequency rating accuracy: The effects of task engagement and experience. *Journal of Applied Psychology, 81,* 512–524.

TRAIT APPROACH TO LEADERSHIP

The trait approach to leadership was one of the earliest theories of leadership. Although it is not a fully articulated theory with well-developed hypotheses, the trait approach formed the basis of most early leadership research. This approach focuses on the personal attributes (or traits) of leaders, such as physical and personality characteristics, competencies, and values. It views leadership solely from the perspective of the individual leader. Implicit in this approach is the assumption that traits produce patterns of behavior that are consistent across situations. That is, leadership traits are considered to be enduring characteristics that people are born with and that remain relatively stable over time.

EARLY RESEARCH ON THE TRAIT APPROACH

Early trait researchers studied the personality attributes that they believed were related to leadership effectiveness, rather than researching exceptional historical figures (i.e., the *great man* approach to leadership). Many early researchers viewed leadership as a unidimensional personality trait that could be reliably measured and was distributed normally throughout the population (i.e., an individual difference variable).

Most of the early empirical work on the trait approach focused on the systematic investigation of the differences between leaders and followers. It was reasonable to assume that individuals in higher-level positions would possess more leadership traits than those in lower-level positions. Concurrently, a large number of studies were conducted in an attempt to develop reliable and valid measures of leadership traits.

Researchers discovered, however, that only a few traits appeared to distinguish between leaders and followers. Leaders tended to be slightly higher on traits such as height, intelligence, extraversion, adjustment, dominance, and self-confidence as compared with nonleaders. The small differences between leaders and nonleaders were attributed to errors in leader selection, errors in measuring leadership traits, or the failure to measure critical attributes.

Many early trait researchers had assumed that, no matter what the situation, there was a set of characteristics that made a leader successful. These researchers believed that the same leadership traits would be effective, for example, in both the boardroom and on the battlefield. However, the differences between leaders and followers were found to vary widely across different situations—researchers had underestimated the impact of situational variables on leadership effectiveness.

LEADERSHIP TRAITS

Trait researchers often developed lists of characteristics that they believed were related to successful leadership. In creating such lists, some researchers mixed together very different attributes. For example, lists included some leadership traits that were aspects of behaviors and skills, in addition to other traits that were related to temperament and intellectual ability. These lists of traits typically included characteristics such as self-confidence, intelligence, ambition, perseverance, assertiveness, emotional stability, creativity, and motivation. The lists, however, were not exhaustive and typically omitted some important leadership attributes.

Today, many popular books on leadership continue the tradition of providing lists of traits that are thought to be central to effective leadership. The basic idea remains that if an individual possesses such traits, she or he will be a successful leader in any situation. In 1989, John W. Gardner published a study of a large number of leaders and concluded that there are some attributes that appear to make a leader successful in any situation. These traits included the following:

- Physical vitality and stamina
- Intelligence and action-oriented judgment
- Eagerness to accept responsibility
- Task competence
- Understanding of followers and their needs
- Skill in dealing with people
- Need for achievement
- Capacity to motivate people
- Courage and resolution
- Trustworthiness
- Decisiveness
- Self-confidence
- Assertiveness
- Adaptability/flexibility

One of the concerns about such lists is that the attributes typically associated with successful leaders are often perceived as "male" traits. Reportedly, when men and women are asked about the other gender's characteristics and leadership qualities, significant patterns emerge, with both men and women tending to see successful leaders as male.

PROBLEMS AND LIMITATIONS OF THE TRAIT APPROACH

As discussed previously, many early researchers found no differences between leaders and followers with respect to their leadership characteristics—some even found that individuals who possessed these traits were less likely to become leaders. Researchers also found very small relationships between these traits and leadership effectiveness. Because so few of the traits clearly differentiated between effective and ineffective leaders, their efficacy in selecting individuals for leadership positions was severely limited. There were too many leadership variables with low reliabilities, and no rationale for selecting specific variables to include in a study. This approach has been called "dustbowl empiricism" at its worst.

Additionally, there has been little systematic research on the processes by which individuals acquire the capacity for leadership. If leadership is indeed an individual difference variable, then very little is known about the origin of these differences.

RECENT RESEARCH ON THE TRAIT APPROACH

As the trait approach fell out of favor in industrial/organizational psychology, researchers began to develop new situational approaches to leadership. They also began to focus their attention on leader behaviors, which led to the emergence of behavioral theories of leadership. Many modern researchers adopted a contingency approach to leadership, which posits that leaders who posses certain traits will be more effective in some situations than in others.

Recently, however, there has been somewhat of a resurgence in research on the trait approach to leadership, especially with the emergence of the five-factor model of personality. Recent research has attempted to correct some of the methodological shortcomings of the earlier research on leadership traits. For example, researchers have developed conceptual models linking leadership attributes to organizational performance. Additionally, they have begun to highlight consistent patterns of relationships between traits and performance measures. Rather than simply studying what combinations of traits would be successful in a particular situation, researchers are now linking clusters of personality traits to success in different situations.

SUMMARY

In general, the trait and situational approaches have resulted in only limited advances in the understanding of leadership. Although early studies highlighted the importance of situational considerations in leadership, there still is no situational theory of leadership. Most leadership researchers, therefore, have abandoned the pure situationist approach.

Researchers have concluded that successful leadership is the result of the interaction between the traits of the leader and the situation itself (i.e., the contingency approach to leadership). They have realized that the interaction between the leader and the situation is key to understanding leadership, along with the specification of important trait and situational variables.

—*John W. Fleenor*

See also Behavioral Approach to Leadership; Leadership and Supervision; Situational Approach to Leadership

FURTHER READING

Gardner. J. W. (1989). *On leadership.* New York: Free Press.

Muchinsky, P. M. (1983). *Psychology applied to work: An introduction to industrial and organizational psychology.* Homewood, IL: Dorsey Press.

Porter, L. W., Lawler, E. E., & Hackman, J. R. (1975). *Behavior in organizations.* New York: McGraw-Hill.

Vroom, V. H. (1976). Leadership. In M. Dunnette (Ed.), *Handbook of industrial and organizational psychology* (pp. 1527–1551). New York: Wiley.

Zaccaro, S. J., & Klimoski, R. J. (Eds.). (2001). *The nature of organizational leadership.* San Francisco: Jossey-Bass.

TRANSFER OF TRAINING

Businesses are spending an increasing amount of money on training and developing their workforce to increase competitiveness and to improve services. For example, the military trains new recruits for a career specialty. A manufacturing company trains an experienced worker on a new technology being introduced on the shop floor. A service organization trains a team of employees on problem-solving strategies to address customer needs. A state agency trains its leaders on how to develop and implement a strategic plan. In all these cases, the trainees are placed into a learning context such as a formal training program with the ultimate goal being that the training affects organizational efficiency and effectiveness. For example, it is hoped that a safety training program for machinists leads to greater enactment of safe behaviors

on the job (e.g., not picking up a hot object, lifting with one's legs, not one's back), resulting in fewer accidents on the job. The examination of what happens on the job after training is called the *transfer of training.*

DEFINING TRAINING TRANSFER

The commonsense notion of training transfer is that we want trainees to apply the knowledge and skills gained through a formal training program to improve individual, team, and organizational effectiveness. At the individual trainee level, *transfer* has typically been defined as the extent to which the knowledge and skill acquired in a training setting are maintained, generalized, and adapted in the job setting by the trainee. First, *maintenance* issues focus on the changes that occur in the form or level of knowledge, skills, or behaviors exhibited in the transfer setting, as a function of time elapsed from the completion of the training program.

Second, trainees must not only acquire but maintain and even enhance the level of knowledge or skills obtained through training. *Generalization* involves more than mere mimicking of responses to events that occurred in training. It requires trainees to exhibit new behaviors on the job in response to settings, people, and situations that differ from those presented in training. For example, a salesperson might be trained on how to be assertive but not aggressive in conducting a sales meeting with a client. The situations or issues that arise, as well as the types of clients that can be demonstrated and practiced in the training program, cannot match the range of situations or the diversity in clients one would actually face on the job. Instead, the training can provide demonstration and practice on key principles and skills over a few situations and types of clients, and these must then be applied by the trainee in the appropriate way on the job with a diverse set of settings and people.

Third, for many jobs today, trained individuals must not only deal with routine situations and issues but must also adapt to novel or nonroutine situational demands. With *adaptability,* trainees are able to adjust or build upon knowledge and skills to generate new approaches and strategies to meet the demands of the novel situation. For example, a highly adaptable individual might see that the steps to being assertive are not working for certain types of individuals and switch to a slower and more nuanced approach to sales for these individuals.

Organizations' concerns about investing in training often revolve around training transfer issues and the benefits or return the organization can expect to obtain for its investment in training activities. This concern over the so-called transfer problem has led researchers and practitioners to study the factors that can affect training transfer and, based on this understanding, to develop strategies that enhance the likelihood of acquired knowledge and skills being used on the job.

FACTORS AFFECTING THE TRANSFER OF TRAINING

Promoting transfer is a complex process requiring attention to a variety of factors such as trainee characteristics, training design and delivery, and the workplace environment. Identifying, measuring, and understanding the factors that encourage or discourage transfer of training are an important part of any major training implementation. A necessary condition for transfer is that the trainees must first learn the material that is trained. Therefore, much research has focused on learning principles, instructional events, and training delivery mechanisms that can be incorporated into the plan of instruction and guide training design to positively affect trainee learning. For example, traditional learning approaches explicitly instruct trainees on the complete task to be learned in terms of concepts, rules, and task strategies. In this case, the delivery or the quality of instruction can play a large role in how well the trainees acquire the necessary knowledge and skills. A more inductive approach to learning occurs through guided discovery, in which the learners explore and experiment with the training tasks to infer and learn the rules, principles, and strategies for effective performance. Guidance can come in the form of providing the learner with leading questions or in providing prompts without giving solutions. Guided discovery may lead to higher levels of knowledge and skill acquisition through increased trainee motivation to learn, because trainees are actively engaged in the learning process. From this perspective, learning (knowledge and skill acquisition) is a necessary but not sufficient condition for transfer to occur.

Researchers and practitioners have also recognized that learners differ in their motivation to learn and their capability to succeed in particular types of learning programs. Research has focused on personality characteristics, self-efficacy, and ability for their impact on knowledge and skill acquisition as well as the link to training transfer. For example, researchers have examined the issue of trainee readiness—that is, whether individuals have the aptitude, background experiences, and motivation necessary to be successful in the training program. The findings from studies support the notion that personality traits such as the level of conscientiousness of the trainee can affect skill and knowledge acquisition and transfer of training through their effect on the individual's motivation to learn. Other research has focused on tailoring a set of instructional goals, methods, and material to fit an individual's learning style. For example, high-ability individuals tend to learn well in low-structure environments (e.g., guided discovery), whereas lower-ability individuals tend to learn better in high-structure environments.

Regardless of how well designed the program or how ready the trainees are to learn, many programs fail because of organizational barriers to training transfer. Training research has noted the importance of the immediate job context that surrounds the employees as they return to the job from training as a critical factor for transfer. Work environment factors such as supervisory support, transfer climate, and the adequacy of existing tools, equipment, and supplies have been identified as affecting the extent to which the acquired knowledge and skills are applied on the job. For example, research has shown that employees in a climate favorable to the skills being trained (e.g., managers being supportive of safe work behaviors as safety training is being offered) are more likely to apply new knowledge and skills to the work setting. In addition, the extent to which skills are transferred is affected by how much opportunity trainees are given to actively obtain work experiences relevant to the tasks for which they were trained soon after completing the training course.

STRATEGIES FOR ENHANCING TRAINING TRANSFER

Training effectiveness evaluates whether or not the training achieved its intended outcomes. From an organizational perspective, training is worthless if it does not result in the intended changes in behavior and performance on the job. Strategies for enhancing training transfer have been developed for before, during, and after training.

Pretraining interventions for enhancing transfer include providing proper orientation for supervisors so they can support the training once it is begun. Other strategies involve providing time and resources for trainees to complete pretraining preparatory assignments, providing a realistic preview of training for the trainees, and highlighting the expected benefits of the training for the individual and the organization.

Strategies for enhancing transfer while the training is ongoing include providing realistic work-related case studies and practice activities. In addition, trainers can answer the "what's in it for me" question that trainees have about the expected value of the training, as well as create varied opportunities for active practice and give appropriate feedback. Trainers can also provide trainees with job performance aids and help the learner plan for addressing any barriers to transferring knowledge and skills to the job.

Following training, supervisors can help the trainees develop an implementation plan for applying the knowledge and skills gained in training to the job and provide the opportunities for trainees to immediately engage in tasks that require the new knowledge and skills to be used. In addition, coaches can be assigned to help the trainee find or create opportunities to use the new knowledge and skills on the job. Regular refresher courses can also be offered to allow the trainee to maintain and even enhance the knowledge and skills that were originally trained.

—*J. Kevin Ford*

See also Trainability and Adaptability; Training; Training Evaluation; Training Methods; Training Needs Assessment and Analysis

FURTHER READING

Baldwin, T. P., & Ford, J. K. (1988). Transfer of training: A review and directions for future research. *Personnel Psychology, 41,* 63–103.

Barnett, S. M., & Ceci, S. J. (2002). When and where do we apply what we learn? A taxonomy for far transfer. *Psychological Bulletin, 128,* 612–637.

Ford, J. K., & Kraiger, K. (1995). The application of cognitive constructs to the instructional systems model of training: Implications for needs assessment, design, and transfer. *International Review of Industrial and Organizational Psychology, 10,* 1–48.

Ford, J. K., & Weissbein, D. (1997). Transfer of training: An updated review and analysis. *Performance Improvement Quarterly, 10,* 22–41.

Horton, E., & Baldwin, T. P. (2003). *Improving learning transfer in organizations.* San Francisco: Jossey-Bass.

Yelon, S., & Ford, J. K. (1999). Pursuing a multidimensional model of training transfer. *Performance Improvement Quarterly, 12,* 58–78.

TRANSFORMATIONAL AND TRANSACTIONAL LEADERSHIP

Transformational leadership is a form of influence based on a developmental relationship that elevates others to higher levels of moral and professional development, promotes adaptability and change, and results in performance beyond expectations. Transactional leadership is a form of influence based on an exchange relationship in which the leader provides direction and rewards in exchange for a follower's delivery of agreed-upon performance. Together, these leadership styles can foster adaptability and responsiveness to changes in markets, broaden collective skill sets for generating more creative solutions to problems, and challenge and develop people more fully. Such processes are necessary for productivity and profitability in organizations.

Research on transformational-transactional leadership was originated by James MacGregor Burns as a way to differentiate outstanding leaders who change people, groups, organizations, and nations (transformational leaders) from mundane leaders who simply maintain efficient operations in social, organizational, and political systems (transactional leaders). Bernard Bass and Bruce Avolio and their colleagues have expanded on Burns's seminal work by studying transformational-transactional leadership theory with leaders from military, industry, and nonprofit sectors from all continents except Antarctica. This stream of research has contributed much to what we know about leadership styles within transformational-transactional leadership theory; characteristics of individuals who display these styles; effects of these styles on individuals, groups, and organizations; and the conditions that are most favorable for these styles.

FORMS OF LEADERSHIP WITHIN TRANSFORMATIONAL-TRANSACTIONAL LEADERSHIP THEORY

According to Bass and Avolio, leaders have a repertoire of leadership behaviors that they can display in various frequencies depending on their mental model of leadership. There are five leadership behaviors, ranging from the more passive and ineffective avoidant or corrective styles to the active and effective constructive and transformational styles:

- *Laissez faire (LF).* This is a nontransactional form of "leadership" that involves highly passive and ineffective behavior, such that the leader avoids leadership and abdicates responsibility for tasks. The leader takes a lazy approach toward responsibilities and often is absent when needed.
- *Passive management-by-exception (MBE-P).* This is a somewhat more effective corrective transactional leadership behavior in which the leader focuses on mistakes only after they have occurred and patches problems. The leader waits for things to go wrong before taking action.
- *Active management-by-exception (MBE-A).* This is a more active and effective corrective transactional leadership behavior in which the leader searches for what is done wrong, not what is done right. The leader closely monitors work performance for errors to solve problems before they occur, as in "micromanagement."
- *Contingent reward (CR).* This is a constructive and generally more active and effective transactional leadership behavior in which the leader develops well-defined roles and expectations to achieve desired performance levels. The leader uses goals and "carrots and sticks" (i.e., rewards and punishments) to shape the behavior of followers.
- *Four I's of transformational leadership.* The most effective leaders add the following behaviors to transactional CR leadership to get their followers to perform beyond expectations. *Inspirational motivation (IM)* involves articulating a future desired state (i.e., vision) and a plan to achieve it. *Idealized influence (II)* involves gaining trust, respect, and confidence from followers and setting and role modeling high standards of conduct for self and others. *Intellectual stimulation (IS)* seeks to question the status quo and promote continuous innovation and process improvement, even at the peak of success. *Individualized consideration (IC)* energizes followers to develop and achieve their full potential through mentoring and appreciation of diversity.

Research indicates that leaders who spend more time displaying the more active transformational and transactional CR behaviors and less time displaying the more passive or corrective leadership behaviors are associated with the highest levels of individual, group, and organizational performance.

CHARACTERISTICS OF TRANSFORMATIONAL LEADERS

Research on traits of transformational leaders indicates that they have positive attitudes. They are intelligent and energetic, open to learning and change, and feel that they are in control of events. They adapt well to new situations and search for opportunities for development. They possess people-oriented traits such as extraversion, nurturance, and humor. They are emotionally and socially intelligent individuals who, through their understanding of their feelings and effects on others, are able to build developmental relationships with followers.

Research on life biographies of transformational leaders depicts them as more satisfied with life, as better performers in high school and college, as recognized for their achievements, and as positive about their prior work experiences. Their parents showed interest in their development, displayed high moral standards of behavior, and provided strong, supportive homes. They were popular and active in high school and liked teachers who were hard graders. They also were bothered by people's lack of initiative, were active in clubs and communities, attained high goals in their work, and engaged in religious activity a few hours a week.

On average, women are perceived as displaying more transformational and transactional CR behaviors, and less MBE-A, MBE-P, and LF behavior, than men. It appears that women have the ability to perform very well as transformational leaders in organizations because success often depends on teaming, professional and strategic networking, and providing excellent products and services. Teaming is an outcome of IM, networking is an outcome of both IM and IC, and advocating quality is an outcome of IS.

MOTIVATIONAL EFFECTS OF LEADERSHIP STYLES ON FOLLOWERS

When a leader displays LF behavior by avoiding his or her leadership responsibilities, followers typically become demotivated and dissatisfied and perform poorly. Followers generally exert work effort in a manner that is consistent with what they see demonstrated by their leader. When a leader role models laziness, followers typically follow suit. Although such equitable disengagement on the part of followers is common, it is also possible for highly motivated professional followers to pick up the slack of the laissez faire leader by substituting for the leadership not provided by the LF leader.

When a leader displays MBE-P or MBE-A behavior by focusing on correcting mistakes, followers typically are motivated through intimidated compliance that can stifle creativity and innovation. Such leadership instills fear in followers, who are treated like children who cannot be trusted and must be monitored to conform to standards. As a result, followers pay careful attention to maintaining the status quo in the fear of reprimands from the leader.

More positive motivational effects are achieved when a leader displays CR behavior. The goals set through CR behavior establish an expectation of the receipt of a reward by followers for meeting a specified performance target. Followers see that their compliance with the leader is instrumental to their attaining valued rewards. Such extrinsic motivation can be particularly effective in sales organizations. However, some followers may feel manipulated by leaders who use only carrots and sticks as a means of motivation.

Even more positive motivational effects on followers can be achieved by leaders who display transformational leadership. When a leader displays IM, an increased sense of optimism and intrinsic motivation (i.e., action aroused by innate enjoyable or meaningful aspects of tasks/visions) is stirred in followers. Through appropriate role modeling (II), a leader can arouse followers to identify with the leader or the vision and to internalize the leader's values and beliefs. When a leader displays IS and IC, followers become motivated because they are encouraged to be creative and use their unique knowledge, skills, and abilities.

OUTCOMES OF TRANSFORMATIONAL/ TRANSACTIONAL LEADERSHIP

Transformational and transactional CR leadership can have a variety of positive outcomes. Such leadership makes followers feel satisfied with their leader, empowered, and self-motivated, and leads them to do more than what is included in their job descriptions. As a result, followers often report earning promotions. Such leadership motivates followers to exert extra effort and be more creative and effective in their jobs. It also helps to reduce followers' stress and burnout.

For groups, transformational leadership produces enhanced collective confidence, morale, and cohesion.

It results in enhanced group productivity, effectiveness, and creativity, and satisfaction with the leader and task. It can also build *shared leadership,* defined as "leadership *by* the team," in which leadership functions are distributed among members.

Organizational outcomes that result from transformational leadership include innovation, retention, organizational commitment, business unit goal attainment, unit financial performance, market share and customer satisfaction, and occupational safety.

CONDITIONS THAT FOSTER TRANSFORMATIONAL LEADERSHIP EFFECTIVENESS

Certain environmental conditions promote the effectiveness of transformational leadership. Organizations with strategic plans that encourage adaptation and boundary spanning support transformational leadership's focus on promoting change and making connections with customers and suppliers. Flat organizations that possess a simple rather than a complex structure, unstructured tasks, or a clan or collectivistic culture and mode of organizational governance support transformational leadership's emphasis on collaboration and interdependence. Environmental turbulence and crises, in which followers look to a leader to make sense of the situation and articulate a vision of a brighter future, also promote transformational leadership effectiveness.

DEVELOPING TRANSFORMATIONAL LEADERSHIP

The transformational leadership literature offers a plethora of suggestions for improving organizational effectiveness. The following are several empirically validated recommendations:

- Use a combination of transformational *and* transactional CR leadership to satisfy both the higher-order (e.g., recognition, personal growth) and lower-order (e.g., safety, security) needs of followers and promote organizational effectiveness.
- Allow time for followers to accept messages of change and identify with the vision of the transformational leader to produce organizational effects.
- Implement research-based training to develop transformational and transactional leadership. Training programs should collect leadership ratings from the

leader, superior, subordinate, and peer levels, and provide development plans, feedback, and follow-up coaching.

- Select candidates for training who are emotionally and socially intelligent, ethical, effective as communicators, and willing to change their behavior.
- Build transformational and transactional cultures through organizational development so that leadership can be shared through collaboration and shared values.

—*John J. Sosik*

See also Charismatic Leadership Theory; Leadership Development; Life-Cycle Model of Leadership; Team Building

FURTHER READING

Avolio, B. J. (1999). *Full leadership development: Building the vital forces in organizations.* Thousand Oaks, CA: Sage.

Bass, B. M. (1985). *Leadership and performance beyond expectations.* New York: Free Press.

Burns, J. M. (1978). *Leadership.* New York: Harper & Row.

Sosik, J. J., Avolio, B. J., & Kahai, S. S. (1997). Effects of leadership style and anonymity on group potency and effectiveness in a group decision support system environment. *Journal of Applied Psychology, 82,* 89–103.

TRUST

Trust is commonly described as a leap of faith one takes in the face of incomplete information. More specifically, trust is a psychological state involving positive expectations about another's actions despite vulnerability to the other's actions. Studies have supported theoretical assertions that trust is not related to gullibility, but rather to the ability to take appropriate risks. Thus, trust within organizations is associated with a number of favorable organizational outcomes and is considered a desirable state.

TYPES OF TRUST

There are five primary levels of trust within organizations, which vary according to the party being trusted (i.e., the *referent*):

- *Organizational trust.* Trust placed in the system that the organization represents

- *Trust in management* (also *trust in leadership or superiors*). Trust placed in the collective people that are near the top of the hierarchy within an organization
- *Trust in supervisor* (also *trust in leader*). Trust that focuses on a one-to-one interaction between an employee and his or her direct supervisor
- *Coworker trust* (also *trust in peers or teammates*). Trust placed in an employee's same-level peers, typically ones with whom she or he interacts regularly
- *Trust in subordinates.* Trust placed in people the employee directly manages

Global factors are expected to influence trust in higher-level referents, whereas more specific factors are expected to influence trust in lower-level referents. For example, organizational-level constructs, such as perceptions of organizational justice, are more likely to be associated with trust in organizations, whereas more specific constructs, such as perceptions of supervisor integrity, are more likely to be associated with trust in supervisor.

Another broad categorization of types of trust is *rational* or *relational* trust. Overall, rational trust (also *cognitive-based* or *conditional* trust) is based on expectancy theory, which suggests that individuals weigh risks and outcomes to determine the appropriate level of trust. In contrast, relational trust (also *affective-based* or *unconditional* trust) is based more on social identity theory, which emphasizes the interpersonal component of trust: being in a trusting relationship is a pleasant affirmation of shared values.

OUTCOMES OF TRUST

Trust is expected to reduce the costs associated with transactions between the person doing the trusting and the party being trusted. Recent studies have demonstrated that trust within organizations is directly related to a number of outcomes, such as increased satisfaction, increased commitment, decreased intentions to quit, and improved performance. In keeping with the notion that trust is associated with appropriate risk-taking behavior, trust within organizations has been shown to be predictive of extra-role behaviors related to change, citizenship, and innovation. Finally, trust has been shown to facilitate certain relationships. For example, only when there is high trust in teammates does individual motivation lead to group performance. In low-trust situations, individual motivation is directed toward individual goals instead.

FORMATION AND EVOLUTION OF TRUST

A handful of models exist describing the initial formation of trust, often with an aim of explaining employees' tendencies toward high initial trust. What these models have in common is that trust arises based on a variety of individual, interpersonal, and situational factors. In general, proximal factors based on experience with the party being trusted are weighted more strongly in the formation of trust, but in the absence of these experiences, more distal factors, such as word-of-mouth accounts of trustworthiness, are more likely to be influential.

At the individual level, personality has been shown to influence individuals' level of trust within organizations and presumably operates independent of referent. Studies suggest that individuals' predisposition to trust others serves as a source of trust within organizations. Individuals also draw on their previous interpersonal experiences to determine their level of trust. Past experiences with organizational change (e.g., restructuring, downsizing) may erode trust, whereas experiences with transformational leaders may build trust. In addition, trust may be determined in part by what others' experiences have been, whether those experiences have been witnessed or just recounted.

At the situational level, another source of trust is the affiliation of the party being trusted. For example, just knowing the referent is a member of a particular trustworthy group provides some source of trust in that individual member of the group. Also at the system level is the expectation an individual has of the role of the party being trusted. For example, one could expect that a supervisor would help one maximize performance output, increasing trust that the supervisor would not deliberately sabotage performance efforts. Finally, organizational rules and policies also serve as a system-level source of trust. Some argue that rules and policies remove the vulnerability required for true trust to exist, but others maintain that individuals may choose to obey or break those rules. Assuming a certain level of individual freedom, organizational rules and policies against a certain harmful behavior would lead an employee to trust that parties within the organization would not engage in those types of behaviors.

Some theorists have advanced theories of the evolution of trust over time. In general, these models propose that trust is episodically reevaluated based on experienced outcomes of trusting behavior. Thus, favorable interaction with the party being trusted serves to deepen trust.

DISTRUST AND THE DISSOLUTION OF TRUST

There remains some debate regarding the relationship of distrust (or mistrust) and trust. Some assert these constructs are at opposite ends of the same continuum, implying that one cannot simultaneously trust and mistrust a referent. However, a theory advanced by Roy Lewicki, Daniel McAllister, and Robert Bies suggests that trust and distrust are separate dimensions. In their classification, trust is characterized by hope, whereas distrust is characterized by fear. Thus, an individual could be hopeful about the outcome (high trust) but also fearful (high distrust), in which case the individual would engage in protective behaviors such as verification. This classification reflects the separation of the definition of trust into its two major components: positive expectations (trust) and feelings about vulnerability (distrust).

The dissolution of trust has been described from different theoretical perspectives, including symbolic interactionism, psychological contract theory, and stress/coping theory. Trust dissolution theories focus either on the robustness of the trust itself or on the betrayal of the party that was trusted. When trust itself is robust, dissolution of trust is more difficult. In fact, one of the positive outcomes of trust is that those who are trusting tend to give the party being trusted the benefit of the doubt when expectations are not met. However, that leniency is also dependent on the importance of the expectations, as well as the intent behind the betrayal.

—*Lisa M. Kath*

See also Organizational Cynicism; Organizational Justice; Psychological Contract

FURTHER READING

Kramer, R. M. (1999). Trust and distrust in organizations: Emerging perspectives, enduring questions. *Annual Review of Psychology,* 569–598.

Kramer, R. M., & Tyler, T. R. (1996). *Trust in organizations: Frontiers of theory and research.* Thousand Oaks, CA: Sage.

Lewicki, R. J., McAllister, D. J., & Bies, R. J. (1998). Trust and distrust: New relationships and realities. *Academy of Management Review, 23*(3), 438–458.

Mollering, G., Bachmann, R., & Lee, S. H. (2004). Understanding organizational trust—Foundations, constellations, and issues of operationalisation. *Journal of Managerial Psychology, 19*(6), 556–570.

Rousseau, D. M., Sitkin, S. B., Burt, R. S., & Camerer, C. (1998). Not so different after all: A cross-discipline view of trust. *Academy of Management Review, 23*(3), 393–404.

TURNOVER

See WITHDRAWAL BEHAVIORS, TURNOVER

TWO-FACTOR THEORY

Before the mid- to late 1950s, it always made sense to most people who thought about it that the opposite of employee job satisfaction was job dissatisfaction and that the opposite of job dissatisfaction was job satisfaction. The more a person had one of these on the job, the less he or she had of the other—they were opposite concepts, experiences at two extremes of a common continuum.

Then, in 1957, Frederick Herzberg, a psychiatrist from Pittsburgh, and his colleagues did a thorough review of the literature of job attitudes and came forth with a new hypothesis that they tested later in an empirical study of 200 engineers and accountants, asking them to recall events that made them especially happy or unhappy about their jobs. Herzberg, Bernard Mausner, and Barbara Bloch Snyderman published a book, based on those findings, that revolutionized thinking about employee attitudes and, subsequently, considerable management policy and practice. Herzberg and his colleagues proposed that job satisfaction and job dissatisfaction were *not* the opposite ends of a single continuum; rather, they claimed that that they are orthogonal constructs, each caused by different antecedent conditions and resulting in different consequences. Job content factors, the *motivators* (so called because the results indicated that people performed better after events involving these factors), were necessary to make people happy at their jobs, but not sufficient. On the other hand, the *hygienes*—which were elements of the job context, such as employer policies, work relationships, and working conditions—had to be in place to prevent job dissatisfaction but, by themselves, could not create job satisfaction, and, consequently, work motivation.

Tremendous controversy ensued among academics during the 1960s and early 1970s, mostly because of the empirical methods employed. It was alleged that the results of the research, and therefore the major tenets of the theory, were artifacts of the critical incident technique employed in the research. Tests of the theory, using other research methods, frequently failed to support the two-factor, orthogonal conclusion of the new model. The basic thrust of these criticisms, predicated on attribution theory, was that, naturally, people would attribute "felt-good" experiences to events during which *they* had a role, whereas events that had caused dissatisfaction had to have been caused by external factors.

In addition, there had been considerable overlap between the hygienes and the motivators in felt-good and felt-bad stories. In fairness, these overlaps were noted in the 1959 book in which Herzberg and colleagues reported their findings. For example, failure to receive recognition for good work (recognition being categorized as a motivator) was the principal cause of 18% of the felt-bad episodes. There was similar (although not as strong) association reported between instances of job dissatisfaction and two other motivators—work itself and advancement. Therefore, the empirical distinctions between the two categories of work factors and instances of job satisfaction/dissatisfaction were neither total nor definitive.

Just the same, both scientific and popular interpretations of the theory tended to overlook the overlaps and the acknowledgment by Herzberg and his colleagues of the existence of the overlaps. As is so often the case in the histories of theories of work motivation, caveats, exceptions, boundary conditions, and exceptions to the rule are overlooked as science carries on and practical applications are produced and sold to consumers, as noted by C. C. Pinder both in 1988 and in a forthcoming publication. Pinder wrote in 1977 that the commercial desire for a new, innovative model propelled the two-factor theory into classrooms and boardrooms for many years, caveats notwithstanding. It is one of the most known and recognized theories of management today, as noted by G. P. Latham and Pinder in 2005 and by J. B. Miner in 2003.

The theory has proven invaluable in the evolution of thought on work motivation theory, despite the controversies. Subsequent models of job design and redesign (e.g., by J. R. Hackman and G. R. Oldham in 1980) featured many of the major parameters of Herzberg's motivators in how to make jobs satisfying and, indeed, motivating. Designing jobs that provide the possibility of achievement gratifications is known to be wise. Providing recognition for work well done is an age-old bromide that still pays dividends for both the achiever and those who care to watch or supervise. Providing responsibility is the essence of *empowerment,* a concept that was named years after Herzberg's work but that is in vogue today. Self-determination theory, as noted by Marilye Gagne and Edward Deci in 2005, owes some of its origins to the early work.

So much for the things that motivate people. What about the two-factor theory's hygiene factors? Intelligent management these days knows that it must provide company policies to meet people's fundamental needs, else they lose good people. Indeed, failure to provide certain contextual factors in the workplace is a mistake; they may not motivate people, but they can build commitment and staying power. The list of company-sponsored provisions (such as day care for employees' children, gyms, time-sharing arrangements, flextime, profit sharing, sabbaticals, and employee assistance packages) affirm the wisdom of the Herzberg model, at least in part. Whether these provisions attract, retain, and motivate employees is more important than the nuances of the scientific battles that occurred during the years following the release of the Herzberg model. For all its scientific shortcomings, the two-factor theory provided the edge of a wedge to new thinking and practice in Western management.

—*Craig C. Pinder*

See also Job Satisfaction; Job Satisfaction Measurement

FURTHER READING

Gagne, M., & Deci, E. L. (2005). Self-determination theory and work motivation. *Journal of Organizational Behavior, 26,* 331–362.

Hackman, J. R., & Oldham, G. R. (1980). *Work design.* Reading, MA: Addison-Wesley.

Herzberg, F., Mausner, B., Peterson, R. O., & Capwell, D. F. (1957). *Job attitudes: Review of research and opinion.* Pittsburgh, PA: Psychological Service of Pittsburgh.

Herzberg, F., Mausner, B., & Snyderman, B. B. (1959). *The motivation to work.* New York: Wiley.

Latham, G. P., & Pinder, C. C. (2005). Work motivation theory and research at the dawn of the 21st century. *Annual Review of Psychology, 56,* 485–516.

Miner, J. B. (2003). The rated importance, scientific validity, and practical usefulness of organizational behavior theories: A quantitative review. *Academy of Management Learning and Education, 2,* 250–268.

Pinder, C. C. (1977). Concerning the application of human motivation theories in organizational settings. *Academy of Management Review, 2,* 384–397.

Pinder, C. C. (1998). *Work motivation in organizational behavior.* Upper Saddle River, NJ: Prentice Hall.

Pinder, C. C. (in press). *Work motivation in organizational behavior* (2nd ed.). Mahwah, NJ: Lawrence Erlbaum.

TYPE A AND TYPE B PERSONALITIES

Type A and type B personality is one of the most researched personality constructs in relation to health and work behavior. In contrast to its type B counterpart, the type A personality is characterized by specific behavioral dispositions, such as aggressiveness, competitiveness, lack of patience, and excessive striving for achievement. Type A individuals tend to try to accomplish as much as possible in little time, set high expectations for themselves, and are very self-critical.

Although the type A individual is often negatively portrayed (e.g., as easily angered, hostile, and impatient), the personality construct is actually dichotomous, comprising both desirable and undesirable components. The first component, *achievement striving,* refers to positive characteristics such as being hardworking and active and taking work seriously. The second component, *impatience–irritability,* consists of more negative characteristics, including impatience, irritability, hostility, and an obsession with time. Some research has found these two components to be unrelated to each other. Other research has shown a low but positive correlation, suggesting that the components are related but not identical. The differential relationships of each of the two components to other variables do suggest that they are distinct.

TYPE A PERSONALITY AND HEALTH

Type A individuals are more vulnerable than type B individuals to poor health. Type A individuals are more likely to experience, for instance, depression, increased frequency of nightmares, respiratory infections, and migraine headaches. One major health issue for which type A personality has been most implicated is coronary heart disease (CHD). In the Western

Collaborative Group Study, which was the first study to examine the relationship between type A personality and CHD, researchers found that, among nearly 3,200 men without CHD symptoms at the beginning of the study, those categorized as type A were twice as likely as those categorized as type B to develop symptoms within 8.5 years. Data from autopsies of participants who died during the course of the study showed that type A personality was positively related to CHD.

Although these early studies suggested a relationship between CHD and type A personality, many other studies have yielded nonsignificant findings. Given such inconclusive findings, some researchers have proposed that the relationship between type A personality and CHD is weaker than suggested by the early findings. More recent research has shown, however, that the reason for any nonsignificant findings may be that type A personality has often been assessed as an overall construct. Studies that have examined the construct as the two separate components of achievement striving and impatience–irritability have found stronger and more consistent relationships between the latter component and CHD.

Two explanations, both of which are related to suppressed immunity, may account for the relationship between type A personality and ill health. First, type A individuals are more likely than type B individuals to perceive and experience stress. To the extent that psychological stress reduces immune competence, the immune systems of type A individuals may be suppressed enough to increase their vulnerability to illness. The second explanation is the fact that chronic hyperactivity may compromise the immune system. As type A individuals are chronically hyperactive in their impatience and attempt to accomplish many things in less time, their immune systems may be compromised, thereby possibly facilitating various illnesses.

TYPE A PERSONALITY AND WORK-RELATED VARIABLES

Next to health-related consequences, type A personality has been most frequently examined in regard to its relationship to work-related variables. Individuals categorized as type A tend to exhibit higher performance and productivity than their type B counterparts. Specifically, type A employees work longer and more overtime hours. In the academic arena, a difference in performance is also seen between type A versus type

B students, in that the former tend to earn higher grades. Faculty members who are categorized as type A individuals are more productive researchers than type B individuals.

However, because the type A personality comprises both a positive and negative component (i.e., achievement striving and impatience–irritability, respectively), there exists a double-edged sword in regard to the personality's implications for work-related consequences. Specifically speaking, although type A individuals exhibit higher performance because of their excessive need to strive for achievement, their tendency to be hostile and impatient may also mean they lack effective interpersonal relationships because they are more likely to be poor listeners and abrasive. Furthermore, type A individuals also experience more somatic complaints and greater perceived stress. Therefore, hiring employees on the basis of positive type A behaviors and traits may also mean inadvertently employing individuals who harbor the less desirable characteristics.

In addition to performance, type A personality has also been found to be related to other work-related variables. Specifically, research has suggested that type A individuals are more satisfied with their jobs than their type B counterparts; however, such a positive relationship is dependent on whether the employee perceives a sense of control. For those who do not feel control over their work, type A employees are likely to feel more dissatisfied. For type A employees who perceive high control, however, their satisfaction with their jobs is greater than that experienced by type B employees. Research has also suggested that type A employees respond more negatively to jobs that are high in complexity. Over time, type A employees who have highly complex jobs are more likely than type B employees to develop symptoms of cardiovascular illness.

SUMMARY

Type A personality is a multidimensional construct, with both health- and work-related consequences. Further understanding of this construct will benefit both the individual and the organization. For the individual, knowledge of where one stands on this personality construct may help provide guidance in career-making decisions. Type A individuals may, for instance, want to avoid jobs high in complexity and in which they have little control, as such jobs have been found to be related to dissatisfaction and cardiovascular illness. Organizations should also take heed of where employees stand in terms of type A personality, as this may help provide guidance in selecting employees and designing jobs that would most enhance employee–job fit.

—*Alexandra Luong*

See also Person–Job Fit; Personality; Stress, Consequences; Stress, Coping and Management; Time Management

FURTHER READING

Adler, N. (1994). Health psychology: Why do some people get sick and some stay well? *Annual Review of Psychology, 45,* 229–259.

Day, A. L., & Jreige, S. (2002). Examining type A behavior pattern to explain the relationship between job stressors and psychosocial outcomes. *Journal of Occupational Health Psychology, 7,* 109–120.

Ganster, D. C., Schaubroeck, J., Sime, W. E., & Mayes, B. T. (1991). The nomological validity of the type A personality among employed adults. *Journal of Applied Psychology, 76,* 143–168.

Kircaldy, B. D., Shephard, R. J., & Furnham, A. F. (2002). The influence of type A behavior and locus of control upon job satisfaction and occupational health. *Personality and Individual Differences, 33,* 1361–1371.

Lee, C., Ashford, S. J., & Bobko, P. (1990). Interactive effects of "Type A" behavior and perceived control on worker performance, job satisfaction, and somatic complaints. *Academy of Management Journal, 33,* 870–881.

Schaubroeck, J., Ganster, D. C., & Kemmerer, B. E. (1994). Job complexity, "Type A" behavior, and cardiovascular disorder: A prospective study. *Academy of Management Journal, 37,* 426–439.

UNDEREMPLOYMENT

Underemployment refers to employment that is inadequate, inferior, or low quality, relative to some standard. All researchers agree that there is a small handful of distinct types of underemployment, but there is less agreement on exactly what counts as underemployment and how many types there are. Nevertheless, the following experiences are regularly classified as underemployment:

- *Overqualification:* These workers possess surplus formal education; work experience; or knowledge, skills, and abilities (KSAs) relative to the job demands or requirements.
- *Involuntary educational mismatch:* Workers who are employed in a field outside their area of education because they cannot find employment that better matches their education. This is a distinct category from overqualification in that these employees are *differently qualified,* rather than overqualified.
- *Involuntary part-time or temporary employment:* Workers who are employed in part-time or temporary jobs because they cannot find full-time or permanent positions.
- *Underpayment:* The workers' wages are significantly less than a certain standard. Standards include workers' wages from previous jobs, typical wages for workers' educational backgrounds, and a livable wage.

Other types of work experiences occasionally identified as underemployment include unemployment, intermittent (un)employment (workers who either have experienced recent periods of both employment and unemployment or work on jobs that are seasonal or otherwise sporadic), subemployment (workers who are not currently employed and have ceased the job search process because they do not believe that jobs are available), and status underemployment (workers who receive less occupational prestige from their jobs than expected based on their background).

UNDEREMPLOYMENT AS INVOLUNTARY MISMATCH

In general, a key prerequisite for defining a work situation as underemployment is that it be involuntary. For example, an individual who moves from full-time work to part-time work as part of a transition to retirement is not underemployed, whereas someone who would prefer a full-time job but can only find a part-time job is underemployed. This is an important distinction, because researchers have begun to show that employees who voluntarily choose a given work situation such as part-time work experience more positive job attitudes than employees who find themselves in the same work situation despite preferring something more, for example, full-time work.

Each type of underemployment, by definition, represents a discrepancy between the actual work situation and an alternative situation that is preferred by the employee. Recognizing this, researchers are beginning to use person–job fit and related models to frame underemployment research and generate hypotheses. In essence, each type of underemployment can be viewed as an instance of poor person–job fit. For example, overqualification reflects poor fit between worker abilities and job demands, whereas underpayment reflects poor fit between worker needs and job supplies.

MEASUREMENT

Researchers may measure underemployment by using either personnel data or self-report measures. For example, overqualification may be assessed by comparing someone's level of education and experience (as stated on a résumé or job application) to a job description. Alternatively, the employee could be asked to complete a questionnaire with items designed to tap perceptions of overqualification. In addition to these strategies, some researchers measure underemployment by culling data from databases containing labor statistics, such as the National Longitudinal Survey of Youth (NLSY). Importantly, self-report measures have the advantage of accounting for whether one's current work situation is voluntary or involuntary. Unfortunately, well-established, valid self-report measures of the various types of underemployment do not yet exist.

PREVALENCE AND DEMOGRAPHIC CORRELATES

Estimates vary, but it appears that roughly one in five U.S. workers currently experience underemployment in one form or another. Note that this rate is significantly higher than the typical unemployment rate. Not surprisingly, the proportion of individuals who may be classified as underemployed fluctuates along with the status of the economy, with the experience being more common in times of economic recession. This also means that rates of unemployment and rates of underemployment tend to display similar trends over a given period of time.

Several groups of workers are particularly likely to experience underemployment. In the United States, researchers consistently find that women and ethnic minorities (particularly African Americans and Latin Americans) are underemployed at higher rates than males and Caucasians. Because cultural norms place the primary responsibility for child care and eldercare on women, women often must choose jobs that are flexible over those that may best use their education or offer the greatest career opportunities. Discrimination, language and cultural barriers, and lower educational attainment may each contribute to underemployment among ethnic minorities. There is no consistent finding in terms of age, but recent college graduates (who are highly educated but often have little work experience) and older white-collar workers (who are among the most common victims of downsizing) commonly experience underemployment.

CONSEQUENCES

Researchers have consistently hypothesized a variety of negative consequences associated with underemployment, from dissatisfaction with one's job, to higher rates of absenteeism and turnover, to poor physical and psychological health. Managers tend to avoid hiring applicants who appear overqualified because of similar predictions. Unfortunately, as compared with the large literature on the effects of unemployment, there is little existing research on underemployment and its outcomes.

JOB ATTITUDES

Underemployed individuals generally report lower levels of job satisfaction than individuals who are not underemployed, particularly for facets of satisfaction that are relevant to the type of underemployment. For example, overqualified workers seem most unhappy with the work itself but are not necessarily dissatisfied with their coworkers or supervisor. There is also some evidence that underemployment may also be associated with a relatively weak emotional attachment to the organization (affective commitment). No consistent relationship has been found between underemployment and other types of commitment, such as commitment based on the costs of leaving the organization (continuance commitment), or a sense of obligation to the organization (normative commitment).

JOB PERFORMANCE

Researchers have posited that, because of a lack of motivation or commitment, underemployed workers may perform their tasks at a lower level and engage less in organizational citizenship behaviors (such as working late to help a coworker finish a project). In some cases, however, the reverse could be true. For example, temporary workers who would prefer to have a permanent work arrangement with the organization may be highly motivated to perform at a higher level or engage in citizenship behaviors, to maximize the chances that they will be offered a permanent position. Unfortunately, there are practically no data on the relation between underemployment and either type of job performance.

EMPLOYEE WITHDRAWAL

There is some early evidence to suggest that underemployment is associated with higher rates of absenteeism, intentions to quit one's job, and job search behavior. However, at this time, we have no data to test the proposition that underemployment will predict actual turnover behavior. This is surprising, because researchers and managers commonly predict that the underemployed (particularly overqualified workers) are particularly likely to search for more adequate employment and leave their present jobs.

PSYCHOLOGICAL AND PHYSICAL WELL-BEING

It is well-established that being out of work has negative psychological and behavioral effects, such as low self-esteem, stress, substance abuse, health problems, and depression. In what is probably the most extensive research program on underemployment, David Dooley and Joann Prause (2004) demonstrated that underemployment (which they call inadequate employment) has similar deleterious effects on the worker's psychological and physical well-being. In other words, being underemployed may be as traumatic and damaging as being unemployed. They also presented evidence that, in some cases, the relationship between underemployment and mental health may be bidirectional, with factors such as low self-esteem placing the individual at greater risk for underemployment, which then may produce further negative psychological effects. It is important to note that Dooley and Prause did not investigate the effects of all types of underemployment but instead focused on involuntary part-time employment, underpayment, and intermittent unemployment.

CONCLUSION

Underemployment, or employment that is insufficient relative to a standard, takes several forms, including overqualification, involuntary educational mismatch, involuntary part-time or temporary employment, and underpayment. The most consistent findings are that underemployment is associated with job dissatisfaction, low affective commitment, and poor psychological health, but the causal mechanisms involved in these relationships are still not well understood.

In general, given how common underemployment is, there is a surprising lack of research on this experience, its antecedents, and its consequences.

Empirical work is particularly scant with regard to overqualification and involuntary educational mismatch and on the effects of underemployment on employee performance and withdrawal behaviors. Finally, what we know about underemployment is limited to workers in the United States, because there is little published research on underemployment from other countries or cultures.

—*Douglas C. Maynard*

See also Job Satisfaction; Organizational Commitment; Person–Job Fit; Quality of Work Life; Withdrawal Behaviors, Turnover

FURTHER READING

Burris, B. H. (1983). *No room at the top: Underemployment and alienation in the corporation.* New York: Praeger.

Dooley, D. (Ed.). (2003). Underemployment and its social costs [Special issue]. *American Journal of Community Psychology, 32*(1–2).

Dooley, D., & Prause, J. (2004). *The social costs of underemployment: Inadequate employment as disguised unemployment.* Cambridge, UK: Cambridge University Press.

Ellingson, J. E., Gruys, M. L., & Sackett, P. R. (1998). Factors related to the satisfaction and performance of temporary employees. *Journal of Applied Psychology, 83,* 913–921.

Feldman, D. C., Leana, C. R., & Bolino, M. C. (2002). Underemployment and relative deprivation among re-employed executives. *Journal of Occupational and Organizational Psychology, 75,* 453–471.

Maynard, D. C. (1998). *Underemployment in the selection process: Managerial perceptions and policies.* Unpublished doctoral dissertation, Bowling Green State University, Bowling Green, Ohio.

Thorsteinson, T. J. (2003). Job attitudes of full- and part-time employees: A meta-analytic review. *Journal of Occupational and Organizational Psychology, 76,* 151–177.

UNIFORM GUIDELINES ON EMPLOYEE SELECTION PROCEDURES

The Uniform Guidelines on Employee Selection Procedures (Guidelines) were published in August 1978 as the result of a joint effort involving the governmental organizations responsible for enforcing equal employment opportunity laws: the Equal

Employment Opportunity Commission (EEOC), Department of Labor (including the Office of Federal Contract Compliance Programs [OFCCP]), Civil Service Commission, and Department of Justice. The Guidelines define discrimination in the context of employment selection procedures, which include tests, interviews, simulations, minimum requirements, or other tools used to make employment decisions. The Guidelines outline the validity and adverse impact evidence that the enforcement agencies would consider when evaluating a discrimination claim under Title VII of the Civil Rights Act of 1964, and Executive Order 11246. The Guidelines apply to all public and private employers covered by these two laws.

This review provides an overview of the Guidelines, including their purpose, major topics covered and not covered, and conclusions and implications. This review should not be construed as legal advice or a recommended interpretation of the Guidelines. Although this review takes into account some of the developments occurring since the original 1978 publication date, a comprehensive summary of such developments is not possible. In addition, certain topics that are no longer relevant or that the Guidelines address only tangentially have been excluded from this review. A Further Reading section is provided listing sources for more detail about topics within the Guidelines and for information about relevant events occurring since the Guidelines' publication.

PURPOSE

The stated purpose of the Guidelines is to codify a single set of standards to aid organizations in complying with federal laws prohibiting employment discrimination based on race, sex, or ethnicity. They are designed to provide a framework for determining the proper use of employment selection procedures. The Guidelines are not designed to apply to other forms of discrimination (e.g., age-based, disability-based).

TOPICS COVERED BY THE GUIDELINES

Definition and Documentation of Adverse Impact

The Guidelines define discrimination as an employer's use of a selection procedure that has an adverse impact on members of any race, sex, or ethnic

group. Discrimination in this form would require an employer to produce appropriate validation evidence. That is, validation evidence, although valuable for other purposes, is not required by the Guidelines if adverse impact does not exist. The Guidelines also advocate reasonable efforts to consider adverse impact while comparing alternative selection procedures that are of approximately equal validity.

The Guidelines recommend that employers collect and retain documentation regarding selection procedures' impact on different race, sex, and ethnicity groups. Federal enforcement organizations (e.g., EEOC, OFCCP) provide current guidance about specific methods for gathering this information. The Guidelines also introduce the *four-fifths* rule of thumb regarding adverse impact. Under this rule, adverse impact exists if the selection rate for a particular race, sex, or ethnic group is less than 80% that of the group with the highest selection rate.

General Standards for Validity Studies

The Guidelines espouse a three-component model of validity: criterion-related, content, and construct. More recent documents such as the 2003 Principles for the Validation and Use of Personnel Selection Procedures (Principles) and the 1999 Standards for Educational and Psychological Testing (Standards) instead view validity as a unitary concept incorporating numerous sources of evidence to justify interpretation of a selection procedure's results. Despite this discrepancy, most of the Guidelines' standards for validity studies retain relevance and are reviewed in the following text.

The Guidelines define suitable criterion-related validity evidence as data demonstrating that a selection procedure has a statistical relationship with job performance. Content validity evidence should demonstrate overlap between the content of the procedure and the content of the job. The Guidelines define construct validity as evidence that a selection procedure measures characteristics that have in turn been linked to successful job performance. However, because the Principles and Standards no longer recognize construct validity as a distinct form of evidence, it is excluded from the remainder of this review.

Key design features of acceptable validity studies under the Guidelines include adequate documentation of validity, accuracy and standardization, and correspondence between methods used during the validity research and those used operationally. The Guidelines also promote the concepts of setting cutoff scores based on acceptable proficiency, avoiding selection procedures that focus on characteristics learned during a brief orientation program, and avoiding in most circumstances the use of selection procedures to evaluate an applicant's suitability for a higher-level job. The Guidelines also outline the conditions necessary to use a selection procedure in an interim manner pending validation data collection and the importance of periodically reviewing validation studies for currency.

Alternative Validation Strategies

The Guidelines outline several circumstances in which alternative validation strategies are possible, and the standards that these strategies must nonetheless meet. The Guidelines suggest that formalizing and quantifying a selection procedure can allow a user to conduct appropriate validity research. They also advocate elimination of adverse impact as a primary objective, even if a formal validity study is not technically feasible.

The Guidelines state that validity studies conducted by other users or test publishers may provide acceptable validity evidence, but the ultimate responsibility for adhering to the Guidelines resides with the end user. They also outline conditions (i.e., validity evidence, job similarity, and fairness evidence) necessary to transport this external validity evidence to a new setting. A recurring theme is the careful consideration of variables that may substantially affect validity when relying on other studies. Examples include differences in work behaviors, criterion measures, and experience levels.

The Guidelines propose multiorganization studies as an approach to meet validation standards that an individual organization could not otherwise fulfill. They describe unacceptable forms of validity evidence such as nonempirical information obtained from an external test provider. The Guidelines also convey a stance regarding professional supervision of validation activities: Such supervision is encouraged, but it does not alleviate the need for documented validity evidence. They also clarify that employment agencies retain responsibility for following the Guidelines as a developer and a user of selection procedures.

Technical Standards for Validation Studies

Given the level of detail within the Guidelines for this topic, a thorough review is not possible. Rather, key concepts for each subtopic are briefly described. This topic comprises four subtopics, one for each of the Guidelines' three forms of validity: criterion-related, content, and construct, as well as a preceding section emphasizing the importance of a job analysis regardless of the specific validation approach chosen. As noted earlier, construct validity is no longer considered a distinct validation approach and is omitted from this review.

For criterion-related validity studies, the Guidelines outline several design considerations: technical feasibility (e.g., sample size), job analysis–based and uncontaminated criterion measures, sample representativeness, and the general (albeit not exclusive) suitability of a .05 significance level for evaluating selection procedure–performance relationships. However, the Guidelines eschew stating a minimum acceptable magnitude for these relationships, and recommend also considering adverse impact in the final choice of a selection procedure. The Guidelines define *fairness* as a selection tool's ability to predict job performance equally well regardless of race, sex, or ethnic group; several considerations for conducting fairness studies are also summarized.

The Guidelines emphasize that a content validation approach should be limited to selection procedures that provide a representative sample of the job's content. A core feature of the Guidelines' standards on this topic is use of job analysis to delineate core knowledges, skills, and abilities (KSAs), and compilation of evidence linking both the selection procedure and job content to these KSAs. Additional content validity considerations include reliability of the selection procedure, justification of prior training or experience requirements, and evidence that higher selection procedure scores are linked to higher performance prior to use of a rank-order method for comparing applicants.

Documentation of Impact and Validity Evidence

The Guidelines provide a detailed description of documentation requirements, adverse impact of selection procedures in most cases, and criterion-related or content validity evidence if adverse impact is detected. The Guidelines also propose documentation requirements for the alternative validation strategies noted earlier. Because a comprehensive summary of documentation requirements is not possible in this review, referral directly to the Guidelines on these issues is recommended.

TOPICS NOT COVERED BY THE GUIDELINES

It is important to recognize that the Guidelines do not address several important topics that were either nonexistent or insufficiently advanced when the guidelines were published; each of these topics *is* reviewed within both the Principles and the Standards. One set of such topics comprises alternative validation approaches: validity generalization, synthetic or job component validity, and meta-analysis. Other absent topics deal with sources of validity evidence: internal structure, response process, consequences of testing, and convergent or discriminant validity. The Guidelines' definition of fairness is also limited to prediction bias and does not include other forms of bias, such as differential item functioning between groups. Finally, the Guidelines do not cover utility analysis as a broader approach for evaluating the potential usefulness of a particular selection procedure.

CONCLUSIONS AND IMPLICATIONS

Along with the Principles and Standards, the Guidelines represent one of three primary documents with direct implications for employment practice and litigation related to selection procedures. However, as the earliest of these documents, the Guidelines omit certain developments in employment selection as noted previously; they have also been subject to more than 25 years of interpretation within the courts. Recent reviews also suggest that direct references to the Guidelines within recent civil rights cases have been rare, and their influence on litigation may more commonly be indirect by means of interim court decisions. Therefore a degree of caution is recommended to avoid overreliance on the Guidelines without consideration of intervening case law or the more recent developments incorporated by the Principles and Standards. Despite these cautions, the Guidelines nonetheless represent the current official standpoint of the agencies charged with enforcing Federal employment laws regarding adverse impact, validity, and other issues

relating to employment selection. As such, the Guidelines retain prominence as an important reference document in the area of employee selection.

—*Evan F. Sinar*

See also Adverse Impact/Disparate Treatment/Discrimination at Work; Civil Rights Act of 1964; Civil Rights Act of 1991

FURTHER READING

American Educational Research Association, American Psychological Association, & National Council on Measurement in Education. (1999). *Standards for educational and psychological testing*. Washington, DC: American Psychological Association.

Equal Employment Opportunity Commission, Civil Service Commission, Department of Labor, & Department of Justice. (1978). Uniform guidelines on employee selection procedures. *Federal Register, 43*(166), 38295–38309.

Gatewood, R. D., & Field, H. S. (1994). *Human resource selection* (3rd ed.). Toronto, Canada: Harcourt Brace.

Guion, R. M. (1998). *Assessment, measurement, and prediction for personnel decisions*. Mahwah, NJ: Lawrence Erlbaum.

Jeanneret, R. (2005). Professional and technical authorities and guidelines. In F. J. Landy (Ed.), *Employment discrimination litigation: Behavioral, quantitative, and legal perspectives* (pp. 47–100). San Francisco: Jossey-Bass.

Society for Industrial and Organizational Psychology. (2003). *Principles for the validation and use of personnel selection procedures* (4th ed.). College Park, MD: Author.

UNION COMMITMENT

Like many constructs in this field, union commitment was introduced with a measure of the construct. As a corollary of organizational commitment, Michael E. Gordon and colleagues (1980) defined union commitment as a member's identification with and involvement in a particular union, and operationalized the definition in terms of three related components:

1. A strong desire to remain a member of the union

2. A willingness to exert high levels of effort on behalf of the union

3. A definite belief in and acceptance of the values and goals of the union

Confirmed with factor analysis, a four-factor union commitment scale was developed with the intent of identifying predictors and outcomes of commitment. Research studies using variants of the union commitment scale have continued to the present. Union commitment research is viewed as broadening the interest of unionists in psychological aspects of union life and sparking a new generation of studies by organizational psychologists, drawing on earlier work by Ross Stagner, Hjalmar Rosen, Arthur Kornhauser, Theodore V. Purcell, and other industrial psychologists.

The factors of the union commitment scale were defined and labeled as *union loyalty,* a member's pride in being associated with the union and in the union's ability to satisfy the needs of its members; *responsibility to the union,* a member's willingness to fulfill the basic duties of membership to protect the interests of the union; *willingness to work for the union,* a member's willingness to expend extra energy in the service of the union above and beyond the call of duty; and *belief in unionism,* a member's general belief in the concept of unionism.

FACTOR CONTROVERSY

Factor solutions based on confirmatory analyses have produced a lack of consensus about the underlying dimensionality of the union commitment construct. All the following potentially conflicting interpretations of the nature and structure of the construct have been suggested: The factors are orthogonal (independent) and replicable across samples of nonprofessional and professional workers. The factors are parsimoniously defined by two oblique (nonindependent) factors, one that describes union attitudes and opinions (union loyalty and belief in unionism) and one that depicts pro-union behavioral intentions (i.e., responsibility to the union and willingness to work for the union). The factors are identifiable in an oblique four-factor solution and show stability over time.

Indexes for closeness of fit between a hypothesized factor model and an observed model (i.e., fit indexes) have produced some clarity about the dimensionality of the construct. All the following potentially revealing, albeit disparate, results have been reported: Fit indexes for an oblique four-factor solution are significantly better than one-factor, two-factor, or higher-order factor solutions. Belief in unionism is a methodological (artifactual) factor caused by negatively worded items. Belief in unionism is related to

work commitment rather than to union commitment. Belief in unionism is the most stable of the commitment factors and influences union loyalty and responsibility to the union. Fit indexes for an oblique three-factor solution are improved with deletion of belief in unionism items. An oblique three-factor solution based on union loyalty, responsibility to the union, and willingness to work for the union shows that stability of items across factors (measurement invariance) can be assumed between men and women members, and to some extent between longtime and new members, but cannot be assumed between rank-and-file members and stewards. Fit indexes for an oblique three-factor solution are improved with controls for similarity of scores within local unions (with controls for nonindependent observations), highlighting the need to adjust individual-level results by unit-level (contextual) variation.

PREDICTOR-OUTCOME MODELS

Models of union commitment have indicated multiple predictors and outcomes of commitment. A sustaining idea is that union commitment is part of a socialization process that begins with union perceptions and ends with union participation. Research studies focusing on socializing influences have identified links from pre-union and early union experiences to general union attitudes and specific union beliefs, from union attitudes and beliefs to union commitment factors, and from commitment factors to union participation. Notable pre-union experiences linked to union attitudes and beliefs among high school and undergraduate students include perceptions of parent's union attitudes and perceptions of parent's union participation. Notable early experiences linked to union attitudes and beliefs among new members include perceptions of informational orientation programs and perceptions of stewards' individual consideration and charismatic leadership.

The results of meta-analyses on models of predictors and outcomes of union commitment are inconclusive. In particular, models based on meta-analytically derived data show fit indexes below acceptable standards. Identification of a best-fitting model based on nested comparison tests (tests that examine whether models are subsets of one another) shows that the relationship between job satisfaction and union commitment is partially mediated by organizational commitment. *Union instrumentality* (a member's perception of the impact of the union on wages, benefits, and work conditions that define the employment relationship) as a predictor of union commitment is partially mediated by union attitudes. Moreover, results show that union attitudes are the strongest predictor of union commitment, but the relationship is moderated by type of commitment measure (whether a measure represents one of four commitment factors or overall commitment). Union commitment is a predictor of union participation, but the relationship is also moderated by type of commitment measure.

The results of longitudinal studies with measures of union commitment and union participation at both time 1 and time 2 show that later participation is predicted by early commitment. With an 8-month time lag, union commitment predicts formal union participation (participation in scheduled or structured activities that benefit the union, akin to contracted or in-role behaviors). With a 10-year time lag, union commitment predicts informal union participation (participation in unscheduled or unstructured activities, akin to citizenship or extra-role behaviors). These results do not show reverse and reciprocal relationships (that later commitment is predicted by early participation).

EXCHANGE THEORY

How economic and social aspects of exchange theory relate to union commitment, and subsequently to union participation, has prompted both debate and data. Because members pay unions in the form of union dues to benefit themselves economically, union instrumentality should reflect economic aspects of an exchange relationship (in exchange for services rendered, a member feels committed and engages in in-role behaviors like paying union dues). In contrast, *perceived union support* (a member's belief that the union values the contribution of and considers the needs and well-being of its members) should reflect social and emotional aspects of an exchange relationship (in exchange for socioemotional support, members feel committed and engage in extra-role behaviors like helping others to file grievances). With union participation as the predictive outcome of union commitment, a *union participation model* (a service model) suggests that union instrumentality mediates the relationship between perceived union support and union commitment. An *organizational support model* (an organizing model) suggests that perceived union support mediates the relationship between union

instrumentality and union commitment. An *alternative third model* suggests that union instrumentality and perceived union support are nonindependent predictors of union commitment. To date, with union loyalty and overall union participation (participation not differentiated for in-role and extra-role behaviors) representing commitment and participation in the models, fit indexes based on nonnested comparisons favor a union participation model and suggest an intervention direction for union loyalty aimed at union instrumentality.

—*Steven Mellor*

See also Attitudes and Beliefs; Industrial Relations; Organizational Commitment; Organizational Socialization; Unions

FURTHER READING

Barling, J., Fullagar, C., & Kelloway, E. K. (1992). *The union and its members: A psychological approach.* New York: Oxford University Press.

Bayazit, M., Hammer, T. H., & Wazeter, D. L. (2004). Methodological challenges in union commitment studies. *Journal of Applied Psychology, 89,* 738–747.

Fullagar, C. J., Gallagher, D. G., Clark, P. F., & Carroll, A. E. (2004). Union commitment and participation: A 10-year longitudinal study. *Journal of Applied Psychology, 89,* 730–737.

Gordon, M. E., Philpot, J. W., Burt, R. E., Thompson, C. A., & Spiller, W. E. (1980). Commitment to the union: Development of a measure and an examination of its correlates. *Journal of Applied Psychology, 65,* 479–499.

Purcell, T. V. (1960). *Blue collar man: Patterns of dual allegiance.* Cambridge, MA: Harvard University Press.

Stagner, R., & Rosen, H. (1965). *Psychology of union-management relations.* Monterey, CA: Brooks/Cole.

UNION LAW

See LABOR LAW

UNIONS

Unions—or more specifically, labor or trade unions—are found throughout the world and can be broadly defined as associations of workers, the purpose of which is to represent the working interests of their members with respect to wages, hours, grievance procedures, and working conditions, through collective bargaining with the employer. Collective bargaining is a process of negotiation between union and management representatives about the terms and conditions of employment, and the rights and responsibilities of the union. There are two main types of union: craft unions and industrial unions. Craft unions are historically the oldest form of union and consist of workers who possess a particular skill. Today, most craft unions represent members from a variety of occupations and skills, often unrelated to the original founding craft. Craft unions derive their power by controlling the supply of skilled labor. Industrial unions are composed of all workers in a given industry or group of industries, regardless of skill, craft, or occupation. The power of industrial unions lies in the size of their memberships, and their focus is on building unity and solidarity among workers.

In most countries unions have a legal status that entitles them to collectively negotiate with employers over wages, working conditions, and other terms of employment. Often when negotiations fail or these rights are curtailed, unions will engage in collective activities, such as strikes and boycotts, aimed at pressurizing employers to engage in some form of negotiation. In addition to strike actions, unions can use their membership numbers to lobby for legislation that protects the rights of workers and restricts the power of management.

THE HISTORY OF UNIONS

Consistently across the world, labor unions have had to struggle to establish themselves and their legal rights. In most countries, the formation of unions has been illegal at some point in their history, with workers penalized for attempting to organize or joining unions. Despite this persecution, unions have survived and developed sufficient political and economic power to enable labor legislation that legalizes the organization of unions, protects the rights of their members, and formalizes the relationship between employers and employees. Many of the rights have generalized to both union and non-union workers.

The earliest forms of labor organizations can be found in the guilds of Western Europe that began to be formed in the Middle Ages (around the 11th century). These guilds were associations of craft workers that established working standards and wages, protected the craft or profession from competition and skill dilution, and established the social status of their members. Union growth was accelerated by the Industrial Revolution in the 19th century. During this time industry shifted from centering on cottage crafts to concentrating on machines. Poor working conditions, rising production expectations, low wages, and increased work hours forced workers to form worker associations that represented the interests of workers in different trades and industries. These associations eventually became labor unions. Because of fear of worker uprisings after the French Revolution, unions were banned by law in both France and Great Britain. It was only in the 1860s, with the vigorous organization of the textile and mine workers, that the Trade Union Act of 1871 was passed in Great Britain. This was the first of several legislative acts that provided unions with legal status and recognition.

In most European countries labor organizations are affiliated to, or synonymous with, political parties. In the Third World, labor organizations also play an active political role and have been instrumental in overthrowing colonial regimes and establishing political independence. Unions in many Asian, African, and Latin American countries continue to provide workers with an influential political voice.

THE HISTORY OF UNIONS IN AMERICA

In the United States, the first *trade societies* or unions were formed by craftspeople (such as shoemakers, printers, and cabinetmakers) soon after the American Revolution in the late 18th century. As the American economy expanded, these craft unions of like-skilled laborers gave way to the growth of national unions. In 1866 the National Labor Union was formed and organized both skilled and unskilled workers. It was the National Labor Union that first realized the political potential of unions and supported the creation of local unions of workers. It advocated an eight-hour workday, abolishing convict labor, restricting immigration, and organizing African Americans. However, as the National Labor Union's political activity grew, its effectiveness as a national union diminished and it collapsed in 1872.

In 1886 several established craft unions joined together to form the American Federation of Labor (AFL) under the leadership of Samuel Gompers. Representing solely the interests of skilled labor, the

AFL fought for standard hours and wages, fair working conditions, collective bargaining rights, and the collection of union strike funds. It was the AFL that initiated a business union approach to the management of unions (bread-and-butter unionism) where the primary purpose of unions was to represent the economic, rather than the political, interests of their memberships. The AFL fought for labor's participation in decision-making processes through collective bargaining.

The depression of the 1930s encouraged the growth of industrial unions in America. Disenchanted with the craft-based unionization of the AFL, industrial workers led by John L. Lewis formed the Congress of Industrial Organizations (CIO). The CIO encouraged and organized industrial unions as well as promoting the unionization of women, immigrant, and African American workers. With strong labor support, Franklin D. Roosevelt was elected as president in November 1932. The Roosevelt administration facilitated the growth of unions and protected the rights of unions by the passage of labor legislation such as the National Labor Relations (Wagner) Act of 1935 and the Fair Labor Standards Act in 1938. Union membership expanded from 3 million workers in 1935 to 15 million in 1947.

THE DECLINE OF LABOR UNIONS

The number of workers who are members of unions varies considerably both within and across countries. In Western Europe and Northern America, union density is higher in the public sector than in the private sector. Since the 1980s the percentage of workers who belong to a union has declined throughout the world with a few exceptions: Denmark, Norway, Turkey, South Africa, and Chile. Perhaps nowhere has this decline been steeper than in the United States. In 1960 approximately 33% of the nonagricultural labor force belonged to a union. By 2003 this proportion had dropped to less than 13%.

This global decline in unionization is corroborated by other statistics. During this time period there was a severe drop in strike activity, increases in the number of successful decertification elections and collective bargaining outcomes antithetical to workers' interests, and reductions in the perceived legitimacy of organized labor in the political and public domains. There are many explanations for the decline of unions:

- Cyclical economic forces, such as unemployment and inflation levels that affect the bargaining power of unions
- Structural changes, such as the shift away from union-dense manufacturing industries to union-sparse service and knowledge industries
- Global economic restructuring that brought about greater international competition and eroded the power of trade unions
- Rapid growth in sectors of the labor force that were underrepresented in unions and less favorable to unionization (e.g., women and white-collar workers)
- Diminished resources and declining efforts of unions to expand union membership and recruit new workers
- Increased employer resistance to unions and corporate political lobbying efforts to pass legislation that weakens unions
- The promotion of international trade legislation that weakened the rights of workers to organize by establishing agreements with countries that did not enforce basic labor rights
- The replacement of blue-collar work with automation, technology, and outsourcing
- A decline in pro-union attitudes among workers, and cultural and attitudinal changes that were antithetical to organized labor
- Organizational activity and redesign that substituted for union activities

Although private sector unions have suffered the most drastic decreases in membership and density levels, public sector unions have grown in numbers and maintained their membership levels. The growth of public sector unions can be attributed to two trends. First, changes in legislation gave government and federal employees the right to join unions and to negotiate nonwage and fringe benefit issues. Second, changes in the economic environment led to the expansion of the public sector and the growth of government and a climate more favorable to union organizing efforts.

WHAT DO UNIONS DO?

Although union density levels vary considerably between industries, the private and public sectors, and countries across the world, millions of workers still belong to labor unions; and they still constitute an important part of industrial life. Unions have a substantial impact on the working lives of both unionized and nonunionized workers. Unions have played a crucial role in establishing the workplace laws and regulations that constitute labor and industrial relations policies throughout the world. A substantial body of research indicates that the protections and benefits that all workers enjoy can be attributed in large part to unions. Unions reduce wage inequality, set pay standards, and establish fringe and health benefits that are enjoyed by unionized and non-unionized workers alike.

Apart from negotiating better wages and benefits for their members, unions engage in collective bargaining to ensure that workers are treated fairly and equitably. In unionized workplaces there is usually an agreed-on grievance procedure for resolving workplace conflicts and violations of worker rights. Unions also give workers a voice in workplace decisions that affect their lives. The collective bargaining process allows unions to negotiate a contract with their employer that enables workers to participate in shaping workplace policies.

INDUSTRIAL/ORGANIZATIONAL PSYCHOLOGY AND UNIONS

Unions continue to play an important role in industry and have a substantial impact on organizational functioning. Yet industrial/organizational (I/O) psychology has largely chosen to ignore unions, both in terms of its research focus and its exclusion of union-related topics in popular textbooks. There are two main reasons for this neglect, as noted by Julian Barling, Clive Fullagar, and E. Kevin Kelloway (1992). First, many I/O concepts (e.g., job analysis, performance appraisal, and union avoidance) are antithetical to the interests of organized labor, and I/O psychology has, from its inception, been affiliated with management. Second, unions have never had the financial resources to sponsor psychological research on union issues that are beneficial to organized labor or to employ I/O psychologists. However, the little psychological research that has been done on unions has investigated why workers join unions, their commitment to the union, and their participation in union activities.

WHY DO WORKERS JOIN AND GET INVOLVED WITH UNIONS?

One of the main trigger mechanisms that causes workers to join unions is dissatisfaction with their jobs. Specifically, workers who are dissatisfied with their pay and working conditions are more likely to join a union. Although dissatisfaction with the extrinsic characteristics of the job have been found to be the most important predictor of unionization, dissatisfaction with intrinsic factors, such as the amount of job control and trust of management, have been found to be important correlates of unionization in professional samples.

Just being dissatisfied with a job is an insufficient reason to join a union. Workers also have to believe that the union will be instrumental in redressing these dissatisfactions. Union instrumentality beliefs, then, mediate the relationship between job dissatisfaction and voting for or joining a union. Not only are specific beliefs about the effectiveness of a person's own union important predictors of unionization; so, too, are attitudes about unions in general. Research would suggest that workers join unions for both instrumental and ideological reasons. Furthermore union instrumentality beliefs and general union attitudes are also important predictors of why workers leave and decertify unions.

Another thread in the research on unions is the question of how workers become committed to unions. Commitment is a construct that has occupied a central role in the literature on attachment to labor unions. Union commitment has consistently been found to consist of three components:

1. Loyalty to the union, which denotes a pride in the union, an affective identification with the union, and a desire to remain a member of the union

2. A sense of responsibility to the union to engage in the day-to-day duties of a member

3. A willingness to work for the union and engage in extra-role activities beyond those normally required for membership

Socialization practices seem to be important determinants of union commitment. Personal interaction with established members of the union is the primary means whereby new members internalize the norms of the union and develop commitment. Attitudinal variables that are associated with union commitment include intrinsic and extrinsic job dissatisfaction, beliefs about union instrumentality, and positive attitudes toward unions in general. Some structural characteristics have also been identified as having an important effect on union commitment. Specifically, the size of the union, the span of control of its officers, the extent of decentralization of collective bargaining, overall accessibility to union activities by the rank and file, and the voluntary nature of the labor union have all been found to be associated with attachment to unions.

One of the reasons that union commitment has become a focus of research attention is that it is predictive of participation in several union activities, including propensity to strike, activism within the union, support for political action, endorsement of political candidates, and turnover within unions. Union participation can be categorized into participation in formal and informal activities. Formal participation refers to involvement in such activities as voting in elections, meeting attendance, familiarity with the collective agreement, grievance filing, and serving as an officer or on a union committee. In other words formal participation is engaging in behaviors that are necessary for the union to operate effectively and democratically. Informal participation refers to engagement in such organizational citizenship behaviors as helping other members learn about the union, talking up the union, reading the union's publications, and helping another member file a grievance. These behaviors reflect support for the union but are unnecessary for its survival. Participation in union activities is believed to have several beneficial consequences such as preventing union oligarchies, unifying the membership, and generally facilitating the representative purpose of labor organizations. There is also some research evidence to suggest that participating in union activities, especially strikes, is extremely stressful.

One issue that has been of continuing concern to researchers is whether workers can be loyal to both the union and the employing organization. The results of this research have been equivocal, with some studies indicating a positive correlation between union and company loyalty, others finding no relationship, and still others suggesting a negative association between the two constructs. One important moderator of this relationship is the nature of the industrial relationship climate. When union–management relations are favorable and cooperative, company and union commitment are positively related. When union–management relations are strained and hostile, negative correlations occur. The type of union also seems to play a role. In more aggressive unions, whose membership consists of more alienated and disenfranchised workers, there is a greater tendency toward unilateral allegiance to the union. By contrast, in protective unions, whose memberships consists of more empowered workers who form unions to protect their jobs, there is more likelihood of dual allegiance.

SUMMARY

Labor unions have played an important worldwide role in industrial relations for more than 200 years. Today, millions of workers are members of unions. These unions have a significant effect on the working lives of their members, affecting their wages, job security, working conditions, productivity and performance, turnover, absenteeism, job satisfaction, work stress, and perceptions of social justice. Consequently, any scientific field that has as its aim the study of people in the workplace must acknowledge the influence that unions have on organizational behavior. Knowledge of organizational behavior and unions can be enhanced by an understanding of the impact that each has on the other.

—Clive Fullagar

See also Union Commitment

FURTHER READING

Barling, J., Fullagar, C., & Kelloway, E. K. (1992). *The union and its members: A psychological approach.* New York: Oxford University Press.

Freeman, R. B., & Medoff, J. L. (1985). *What do unions do?* New York: Basic Books.

Shostack, A. B. (1991). *Robust unionism: Innovation in the labor movement.* Ithaca, NY: ILR Press.

UTILITY ANALYSIS

Utility analysis is a tool for decision making. It is the determination of institutional gain or loss (outcomes) anticipated from various courses of action, after taking into account both costs and benefits. For example, in the context of human resource management, the decision might be which type of training to offer or which selection procedure to implement. When faced with a choice among alternative options, management should choose the option that maximizes the expected utility for the organization across all possible outcomes.

We consider alternative methods for assessing the utility of employee selection as well as employee training. In the context of selection, the utility of a selection instrument or battery of instruments is the degree to which its use improves the quality of the individuals selected beyond what would have occurred had that instrument or battery of instruments not been used. Quality, in turn, may be defined in terms of the proportion of individuals in the selected group who are considered successful, the average standard score on some job performance criterion for the selected group, or the dollar payoff to the organization resulting from the use of a particular selection procedure.

The first definition of quality is used in the Taylor-Russell model of utility, originally developed in 1939. The second definition of quality is used in the Naylor-Shine model of utility, originally developed in 1965. The third definition of quality is used in the Brogden-Cronbach-Gleser model of utility, developed in the 1950s and 1960s. The next section considers each of these utility models, along with its assumptions and data requirements, in greater detail.

TAYLOR-RUSSELL MODEL

If we define utility in terms of the percentage of selected applicants who are successful (known as the success ratio), H. C. Taylor and J. T. Russell showed that it depends on consideration of more than just a validity coefficient. In the Taylor-Russell model, the overall utility of a selection device is a function of three parameters: the validity coefficient (the correlation between a predictor of job performance and a criterion measure of job performance), the selection ratio (the proportion of applicants selected), and the base rate (the proportion of applicants who would be successful without the selection procedure). This model convincingly demonstrates that even selection procedures with relatively low validities can increase substantially the percentage successful among those selected when the selection ratio is low.

Whenever there is a limit on the number of applicants that may be accepted, the selection ratio (SR) is a major concern. As the SR approaches 1.0 (all applicants must be selected), it becomes high or unfavorable from the organization's perspective. Conversely, as the SR approaches zero, it becomes low or favorable; the organization can afford to be selective. As noted earlier, if the SR is low and if an organization needs to choose only the cream of the crop, even predictors with very low validities can be useful.

Conversely, given high selection ratios, a predictor must possess very high validity to increase the percentage successful among those selected.

It might appear, therefore, that given a particular validity, organizations should strive always to decrease the SR (become more selective). Unfortunately, the optimal strategy is not this simple, because lowering the SR forces recruiters to expand the recruiting and selection effort. Thus, to select 10 new hires, an SR of 0.5 means that 20 must be recruited. However, if the SR decreases to 0.1, 100 must be recruited. In practice, this strategy may be costly to implement.

Utility, according to Taylor and Russell, is also affected by the base rate (the proportion of applicants who would be successful without the selection measure). To be of any use in selection, the measure must demonstrate incremental validity by improving on the base rate. That is, the selection measure must result in more correct decisions than could be made without using it. As Taylor and Russell demonstrated, selection measures are most useful when the base rate is about 0.50.

Taylor and Russell (1939) published a series of tables illustrating the interaction of the validity coefficient, the selection ratio, and the base rate on the success ratio. The success ratio, then, serves as an operational measure of the value or utility of a selection device, when used in conjunction with methods presently used to select applicants.

Note that the validity coefficient referred to by Taylor and Russell is based on present employees who have already been screened using methods other than the new selection procedure. The selection ratio is applied to this population. It is assumed that the new procedure will simply be added to a group of selection procedures used previously, and it is the incremental gain in validity from the use of the new procedure that is most relevant.

The Taylor-Russell approach also makes three other assumptions. First, it assumes fixed-treatment selection; that is, individuals are chosen for one specified treatment or course of action that cannot be modified. Second, the Taylor-Russell model does not take into account the percentage of rejected individuals who would have been successful if hired (erroneous rejections). Finally, the model classifies accepted individuals into successful and unsuccessful groups. All individuals within a group are regarded as making equal contributions.

Under these circumstances the SR tells us that more people are successful, but not *how much more* successful. When it is reasonable to assume that the use of higher predictor scores will lead to higher levels of average job performance by those selected, the Taylor-Russell tables will underestimate the actual gain to be expected.

NAYLOR-SHINE MODEL

The Naylor-Shine index of utility is defined in terms of the increase in average criterion score to be expected from the use of a selection measure with a given validity and selection ratio. In contrast to the Taylor-Russell utility model, however, the Naylor-Shine approach assumes a linear relationship between validity and utility. That is, given any arbitrarily defined cutoff on a selection measure, the higher the validity, the greater the increase in the average criterion score for the selected group over that observed for the total group. This model assesses the gain in validity from the use of the new selection procedure *over and above* that which is presently available using current information. The basic equation underlying the Naylor-Shine model is

$$\bar{Z}_{yi} = r_{xy}\, \frac{\lambda_i}{\phi_i}, \tag{1}$$

where
$\bar{Z}_{yi}$ = mean criterion score (in standard-score units) of all cases above the predictor cutoff,
r_{xy} = validity coefficient,
λ_i = ordinate of the normal distribution at the predictor cutoff, Z_{xi} (expressed in standard-score units), and
ϕ_i = selection ratio.
Equation 1 applies whether r_{xy} is a zero-order correlation coefficient or a multiple regression coefficient.

Using Equation 1 as a basic building block, J. C. Naylor and L. C. Shine present a series of tables that specify, for each selection ratio, the standard (predictor) score corresponding to that selection ratio, the ordinate of the normal curve at that point, and the quotient λ_i/φ_i. The tables can be used to answer three important human resource questions:

1. Given a specified selection ratio, what will be the average performance level of those selected?

2. Given a desired selection ratio, what will $\bar{Z}_{yi}$ be?

3. Given a desired improvement in the average criterion score of those selected, what selection ratio and predictor cutoff value (in standard-score units) should be used?

Note that "average criterion performance" is expressed in terms of standard (z) scores. Standard scores are more difficult to interpret than are outcomes more closely related to the specific nature of a business, such as dollar volume of sales, units produced or sold, or costs reduced. The Brogden-Cronbach-Gleser model addresses those issues specifically.

BROGDEN-CRONBACH-GLESER MODEL

If we assume that n workers are hired during a given year and that the average job tenure of those workers is t years, the dollar increase in productivity can be determined from Equation 2. Admittedly, this is a *cookbook recipe,* but the formula was derived more than 50 years ago and is well established in applied psychology:

$$\Delta U = (N)(T)(SD_y)(r_{xy})(\bar{Z}_x) - (N)(C_y), \tag{2}$$

where
ΔU = increase in productivity in dollars,
N = number of persons hired,
T = average job tenure in years of those hired,
r_{xy} = the validity coefficient representing the correlation between the predictor and job performance in the applicant population,
SD_y = the standard deviation of job performance in dollars (roughly 40%–60% of annual wage, depending on the complexity of the job in question), and
$\bar{Z}_x$ = the average predictor score of those selected in the applicant population, expressed in terms of standard scores.

When Equation 2 was used to estimate the dollar gains in productivity associated with use of the Programmer Aptitude Test (PAT) to select computer programmers for federal government jobs, given that an average of 618 programmers per year are selected, each with an average job tenure of 9.69 years, the payoff per selectee was $64,725 over his or her tenure on the job. This represents a per-year productivity gain of $6,679 for each new programmer. Clearly, the dollar gains in increased productivity associated with the use of valid selection procedures (the estimated true validity of the PAT is .76) are not trivial, even after correcting them to account for corporate taxes and variable costs, and discounting future cash flows to express their present value.

With respect to the variability of job performance in dollars (SD_y in Equation 2), a number of alternative procedures have been proposed for estimating it. A review of 34 studies that included more than 100 estimates of SD_y concluded that differences among alternative methods for estimating it are often less than 50%, and may be less than $5,000 in many cases.

All utility analyses are plagued by uncertainty and risk. By taking uncertainty into account through break-even analysis (described in the following text), anyone of the SD_y estimation methods may be (and often is) acceptable because none yields a result so discrepant as to change the decision in question.

BREAK-EVEN ANALYSIS

Break-even analysis is an additional tool that can aid in the assessment of the relative usefulness of competing selection systems. Instead of estimating the *level* of expected utility, suppose decision makers focus instead on the *break-even value* that is critical to making the decision? In other words, what is the smallest value of any given parameter that will generate a positive utility (payoff) of the new selection technique over random selection?

For example, the minimum value of SD_y that will justify the use of a selection procedure with a given validity may be computed by setting $\Delta U = \$0.00$. That value of SD_y guarantees that the costs of the new selection procedure will be matched by equivalent benefits—no more, no less. Thus the term *break-even analysis*.

Break-even analysis seems to provide two important advantages:

1. It allows practicing managers to appreciate how little variability in job performance is necessary before valid selection procedures begin to pay positive dividends.

2. Even if decision makers cannot agree on an exact point estimate of SD_y, they can probably agree that it is higher than the break-even value.

THE UTILITY OF TRAINING AND DEVELOPMENT ACTIVITIES

In the Brogden-Cronbach-Gleser model, the only difference between the basic equation for calculating selection utility (Equation 2) and that for calculating utility from training and development programs (or any other type of organizational intervention) is that the term d_t is substituted for the product $r_{xy} \times \bar{Z}_x$ (i.e., the validity coefficient times the average standard score on the predictor achieved by selectees). The resulting utility formula is therefore

$$\Delta U = (N)(T)(d_t)(SD_y) - C,$$

where

ΔU = gain to the firm in dollars resulting from the program,

N = number of employees trained,

T = expected duration of benefits in the trained group,

d_t = true difference in job performance between the trained and untrained groups in standard deviation units,

SD_y = standard deviation of dollar-valued job performance among untrained employees, and

C = total cost of training N employees.

The parameter d_t is the *effect size*. Like a correlation coefficient, it describes the degree of departure from the null hypothesis. In the case of training and development programs, the null hypothesis is that training had no effect—that is, after training, the job performance of the trained group is no different from that of the untrained group.

How is d computed? It is simply the difference between the mean job performance of the trained and untrained groups in standard (Z)-score units. Thus

$$d = \bar{X}_t - \bar{X}_u / SD_y,$$

where

d = effect size,

$\bar{X}_t$ = average job performance score of the trained group,

$\bar{X}_u$ = average job performance score of the untrained group, and

SD_y = standard deviation of the job performance scores of the total group, trained and untrained.

To enhance managerial acceptance of utility estimates, one approach that has proven successful is to present the utility model to senior managers, acknowledging that it incorporates fallible but reasonable estimates, *before* the actual application and consideration of the model in a decision-making context.

—Wayne F. Cascio

FURTHER READING

Boudreau, J. W. (1991). Utility analysis for decisions in human resource management. In M. D. Dunnette & L. M. Hough (Eds.), *Handbook of industrial and organizational psychology* (2nd ed., Vol. 2, pp. 621–745). Palo Alto, CA: Consulting Psychologists Press.

Boudreau, J. W., & Ramstad, P. M. (2003). Strategic I/O psychology and the role of utility analysis models. In W. Borman, D. Ilgen, & R. Klimoski (Eds.), *Handbook of psychology* (Vol. 12, pp. 193–221). New York: Wiley.

Brogden, H. E. (1949). When testing pays off. *Personnel Psychology, 2,* 171–185.

Cascio, W. F. (2000). *Costing human resources: The financial impact of behavior in organizations* (4th ed.). Cincinnati, OH: Southwestern.

Cascio, W. F., & Ramos, R. A. (1986). Development and application of a new method for assessing job performance in behavioral/economic terms. *Journal of Applied Psychology, 71,* 20–28.

Cronbach, L. J., & Gleser, G. C. (1965). *Psychological tests and personnel decisions* (2nd ed.). Urbana: University of Illinois Press.

Naylor, J. C., & Shine, L. C. (1965). A table for determining the increase in mean criterion score obtained by using a selection device. *Journal of Industrial Psychology, 3,* 33–42.

Raju, N. S., Burke, M. J., & Normand, J. (1990). A new approach for utility analysis. *Journal of Applied Psychology, 73,* 3–12.

Taylor, H. C., & Russell, J. T. (1939). The relationship of validity coefficients to the practical effectiveness of tests in selection. *Journal of Applied Psychology, 23,* 565–578.

VALIDATION STRATEGIES

In the broadest sense, validation refers to the process of establishing the truth, accuracy, or soundness of some judgment, decision, or interpretation. In industrial and organizational psychology, validation generally focuses on the quality of interpretations drawn from psychological tests and other assessment procedures that are used as the basis for decisions about people's work lives. Before discussing validation specifically, it is necessary to clarify some concepts that are integral to the process of decision making based on psychological testing.

DEFINING THE FOCUS OF VALIDATION

It is important to realize that validity is not a characteristic of a test or assessment procedure but of the inferences and decisions made from test or assessment information. Validation is the process of generating and accumulating evidence to support the soundness of the inferences made in a specific situation. Logically, therefore, to examine the concept of validation, it is important to specify (a) the types of inferences involved in applied assessment situations and (b) the nature of evidence that can be used to support such inferences. Different validation strategies reflect different ways to gather and examine the evidence supporting these important inferences.

Applied psychological assessment involves a series of professional activities. A general characterization of these activities includes the following steps: (a) analysis of a work setting to determine (b) the important task and organizational behaviors (and subsequent

outcomes) composing a performance domain, which then guide (c) the selection or development of certain assessment procedures (predictors), which make possible (d) predictions about the likelihood that assessees will exhibit important behaviors, and then subsequently (e) measuring individual work behavior using some operational criterion measure. This process implies a conceptual framework, which is presented in Figure 1.

This framework comprises the following inferences:

Inference 1. The analysis of the work setting yields an accurate description of performance.

Inference 2. The construct domains tapped by the predictor overlap with the performance domains.

Inference 3. The predictors are adequate samples of relevant psychological construct domains.

Inference 4. Predictor scores relate to operational criterion measurements.

Inference 5. The operational criterion measures adequately sample from the performance domains.

Inference 6. The predictors relate to the performance domains.

The analysis of a work setting generates a conception of *desired performance,* or a performance domain. Performance domains are clusters of work activities and outcomes that are especially valued by an organization. Selection decisions based on psychological assessment represent attempts to identify regularities in work behavior—but only those behaviors that are identified by the organization as relevant for goal attainment. Personnel selection, then, is the

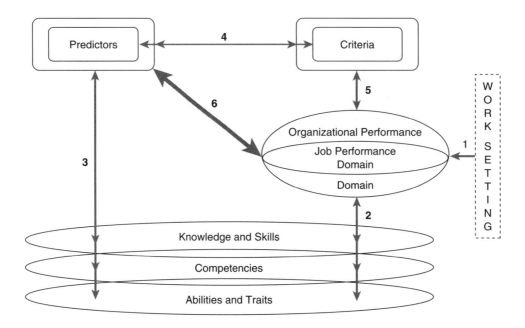

Figure 1   A Conceptual Framework Detailing the Inferences Involved in Validation

SOURCE: Adapted from Binning and Barrett (1989).

process of identifying and mapping predictor samples of behavior to effectively overlap with performance domains. Validity can be described as the extent to which the predictor sample meaningfully overlaps with the performance domain.

Validation is the process of generating evidence that the inferences drawn from assessment information are accurate. Inference 6 is the keystone inference in applied decision making because it represents whether a specific assessment process yields information that makes possible the prediction of important organizational outcomes. Inference 6 cannot be tested directly because it links predictor measurements with performance domains that are *hypothetical* domains of idealized work behavior. However, Inference 6 is tied in closed logical loops to other inferences in the framework, and therefore these other inferences play a role in validation. If certain inferences (which will be discussed in the next section) can be substantiated with sufficient evidence, then Inference 6, by implication, is substantiated. To put it another way, validation is the process of generating evidence to support Inference 6, and this involves supporting the other inferences in the framework.

Of course, many specific forms of Inference 6 may occur in a given decision situation, and the evidence needed to validate each may differ. For example, the Minnesota Multiphasic Personality Inventory (MMPI) could be administered to police candidates to predict who is more likely to possess antisocial tendencies on the job. This form of Inference 6 would require different validity evidence than if the MMPI were used to predict who is likely to experience debilitating anxiety on the job. Regardless of the specific nature of the decisions being made, there are three general approaches to generating validity evidence, and within each approach, there are specific strategies for generating and interpreting this evidence.

THREE GENERAL APPROACHES TO VALIDATION

There are three broad categories of validity evidence, often labeled *criterion-related, construct-based,* and *content-based* strategies. This trilogy of validity terms was first articulated in the *Technical Recommendations for Psychological Tests and Diagnostic Techniques,* published by the American Psychological Association, American Educational Research Association, and National Council of Measurement Used in Education in 1954. This trilogy can be usefully viewed as three broad strategies for generating validity evidence.

Criterion-Related Validation Strategies

One general approach to justifying Inference 6 would be to generate direct empirical evidence that predictor scores relate to *accurate* measurements of job performance. Inference 4 represents this linkage, which historically has been of special pragmatic concern to selection psychologists because of the allure of quantitative indexes of test–performance relationships. Any given decision situation might employ multiple predictors and multiple criterion measures, so numerous relationships can be specified.

The most common form of criterion-related validity evidence is correlational. This type of evidence is generated by statistically correlating predictor scores with criterion scores. The size and direction of predictor–criterion correlation coefficients are statistical indexes of the relationship between the predictor and the criterion. However, this correlation supports Inference 6 only if the criterion measure adequately taps the relevant performance domain. To have complete confidence in the validity of Inference 6, both Inferences 4 and 5 must be justified. An examination of Figure 1 shows that validating Inferences 4 and 5, by implication, validates Inference 6 because they complete a closed logical loop.

Criterion-related validity evidence is generally correlational because selection decisions are generally based on individual differences that are not amenable to experimental manipulation. This evidence is generally collected from current employees through a *concurrent* validation study or from job applicants through a *predictive* validation study, and many specific methodological variations exist for collecting the predictor and criterion data. Other strategies for generating empirical data relevant to Inferences 4 and 5 include experimental and quasi-experimental research. For example, identifying specific groups of applicants who are expected to differ on some predictive characteristic, then determining whether meaningful criterion differences exist, is an alternative to classic correlational research. Some predictive characteristics can be manipulated in field or laboratory experiments, and this research can also provide criterion-related validity evidence.

Construct-Based Validation Strategies

What selection psychologists have traditionally implied by the label *construct validity* is tied to Inferences 2 and 3. It can be assumed that if Inferences 2 and 3 can be supported by sound evidence, then one can confidently believe Inference 6 to be true—again, because they form a closed logical loop. If it can be shown that a test measures a specific psychological construct (Inference 3) that has been determined to be critical for job performance (Inference 2), then inferences about job performance from test scores (Inference 6) are logically justified. Of course, in any given decision situation, multiple psychological constructs may be thought to underlie performance (variations of Inference 2) and subsequently may be assessed (variations of Inference 3), and each of these requires validity evidence.

How does a selection psychologist support Inferences 2 and 3? Evidence supporting Inference 3 primarily takes the form of empirically demonstrated relationships and judgments that are both convergent and discriminant in nature. *Convergent evidence* exists, for example, when (a) predictor scores relate to scores on other tests of the same construct, (b) predictor scores from people who are known to differ on the focal construct also differ in other predictable ways, or (c) predictor scores relate to scores on tests of other constructs that are theoretically expected to be related. *Discriminant evidence* exists when predictor scores do not relate to scores on tests of theoretically independent constructs. The process of developing and researching measures of psychological constructs, then refining them to ensure that they are measuring the constructs we think they are measuring, is a scientific process that is central to the development of psychological theories of individual differences.

Because it links two hypothetical behavioral domains, Inference 2 cannot be examined empirically, at least not in the form of actual behavioral measurements. Rather, informed judgments about performance domains and psychological construct domains are required. Inference 2 must be justified theoretically and logically on the basis of accumulated scientific knowledge of relationships between performance domains and psychological construct domains. A common basis for linking these two is systematic job analysis or competency modeling, which produces job specifications in the form of knowledge, skill, ability, and other constructs required for job performance.

Inference 2 involves the translation of work behavior into psychological construct terms. This is often done in a relatively unstructured way, relying heavily on the work analyst's qualitative judgments about performance domain–psychological construct relations.

However, some job analysis and competency modeling methods explicitly structure the specification of behaviors in the performance domain and the overlap with psychological construct domains. Regardless of how Inference 2 is substantiated, the extent to which this process is viewed as professionally and scientifically credible, and whether it accompanies sound evidence for Inference 3, the validity of Inference 6 is enhanced.

Content-Based Validation Strategies

A third general approach to justifying Inference 6 involves demonstrating that the predictor samples behavior that is isomorphic with the behaviors composing the performance domain. This line of reasoning is particularly defensible when one realizes that predictor tests are always samples of behavior from which we infer something about behavior on a job. The behaviors sampled may be dissimilar (e.g., scores from the Rorschach inkblot test) or similar (e.g., scores from a work sample simulation test) to the work behaviors being predicted. If an applicant performs behaviors as part of the assessment phase that closely resemble behaviors in the performance domain, then logically Inference 6 is better justified. This line of reasoning underlies the type of evidence that is traditionally labeled *content validity.* Specific procedures for analyzing the degree of isomorphism between predictors and criteria have been proposed, but the same basic logic underlies each.

Content-related evidence of validity involves justifying Inference 6 by examining the manner in which the predictor directly samples the performance domain. Here, the predictor is examined as a sample from the performance domain rather than a sample from an underlying psychological construct domain. As in statistical sampling theory, if a predictor sample is constructed in congruence with certain principles (e.g., ensuring representativeness as well as relevance of the sample), one can assume that scores from that sample will accurately estimate the universe from which the sample is drawn. Therefore, when a selection psychologist can rationally defend the strategy for sampling the performance domain used in a given testing situation, content validity evidence supports the inference that scores from the test are valid for predicting future performance (i.e., Inference 6).

The logical assumption of content-based validation is that if a job applicant performs desired behaviors at the assessment phase, he or she can perform those behaviors on the job. Of course, many predictive difficulties arise when one considers the complexity of human motivation in this context. Evidence that someone *can* perform behaviors in one situation does not necessarily indicate that he or she *will* perform them in a particular work situation. These complexities notwithstanding, judgments and data that are relevant to whether a predictor domain directly maps onto the performance domain are the core of content-based validation strategies.

Many specific methodologies exist to guide judgments about behavioral domain overlap. Some of these methods involve having subject matter experts systematically examine performance domains and individually rate the extent to which each predictor element is relevant to the performance domain. Such structured and quantitative content-based methods can yield credible evidence about whether a predictor is likely to predict performance.

VALIDATION STRATEGIES AS PREDICTOR-DEVELOPMENT PROCESSES

Thus far, the concepts of construct-based, content-based, and criterion-related evidence have been discussed as general strategies that can be used to justify decision validity. However, the implications of differences among the three can be traced back in the decision-making process. By doing so, their differences can be more clearly appreciated.

Selection decision making involves two fundamental phases: (a) constructing the predictor as a sample of some behavioral domain and (b) using this behavioral information to make predictions about future job behavior. This latter data combination phase is the immediate precursor to employment decisions and therefore has received considerable legal and professional scrutiny. Yet the data-collection phase, which involves specifying the behavioral database, has equally important implications for validity.

To briefly review Figure 1, the development of any personnel-selection system begins with the delineation of the relevant performance domain. From this delineation of desirable job behaviors and outcomes, selection psychologists determine which construct domains should be sampled by the predictors. There are three routes from the performance domain to predictor development: The construct-based approach involves identifying psychological construct domains that overlap significantly with the performance domain (Inference 2) and then developing predictors that adequately sample these construct domains (Inference 3). The content-based approach involves developing predictors that directly sample the performance domain. The criterion-related approach involves developing some operational measure of behaviors in the performance domain (Inference 5) and then identifying or developing predictors that will relate empirically with the operational criterion measure (Inference 4). Of course, all of these depend on the accuracy with which the performance domain has been delineated (Inference 1).

There is a fundamental difference between the criterion-related approach and the other two approaches. A criterion measure is merely an operational sample of the performance domain. Predictor–criterion relationships must result from either the operation of psychological constructs or the sampling of behaviors that are especially similar to those in the performance domain. From this perspective, the construct-based and content-based approaches represent the two fundamental predictor sampling strategies. *Construct-based* implies that predictor sampling is guided by evoking a psychological construct domain. *Content-based* implies that predictor sampling is guided by evoking a performance domain. To the extent that the two domains are derived differently and relations between the two are not well understood, construct- and content-based approaches can lead to substantive differences in predictor development and decision validity. In contrast to the construct-and content-based approaches, the criterion-related approach is best characterized as a general research strategy for empirically assessing the quality of the two fundamental predictor sampling strategies. Judgments of validity are tantamount to judgments about the adequacy of behavior sampling (construct- and content-based) or direct empirical indexes of such adequacy (criterion-related).

VALIDATING EMPLOYMENT DECISIONS

Recall that validation is the process of generating and accumulating evidence to support the soundness of the inferences made in a specific situation. Three general approaches to compiling evidence have been discussed, as well as their relative strengths and weaknesses. The convenience of discussing these strategies separately should not cloud a very important point: *Validity is a unitary concept.* Specific decisions or

uses of psychological test information are either valid or not, and there are different forms of evidence relevant to the determination of validity.

The validity of a decision can be reasonably compared to the guilt or innocence of a defendant in a court case. When a trial begins, we generally do not know whether the defendant is guilty or innocent. The trial unfolds as a forum for presenting evidence collected during an investigation. Some evidence is direct and very compelling, whereas other evidence is circumstantial and open to skepticism. Some attorneys are better able to communicate the evidence, and juries are more or less able to grasp the complexities of the evidence. Validation parallels this characterization. We seldom know whether a selection decision (derived from a specific assessment process) is valid at the time it is made. However, we can anticipate needing to justify the decision process, so we *investigate* the situation and gather evidence of various forms, direct and circumstantial, to support a claim of validity. Ultimately, our validation efforts are reviewed by people who judge their credibility and deem the process to be sufficiently valid or not.

CONCLUSION

Validation, as a systematic process of generating and examining evidence, is the essence of scientific research and theoretical development, and its goal is to more fully understand and explain human functioning in work settings. There is no inherent superiority of one type of validity evidence over other lines of evidence. From this perspective, all validity evidence may be relevant to determining decision quality. Competently conducted validation efforts are ones that comprehensively generate credible information about all of the inferential linkages that compose the current framework and focus appropriate attention on predictor content, psychological constructs, and empirically demonstrated relationships.

—*John F. Binning*

See also Construct; Criterion Theory; Validity

FURTHER READING

Binning, J. F., & Barrett, G. V. (1989). Validity of personnel decisions: A conceptual analysis of the inferential and evidential bases. *Journal of Applied Psychology, 74,* 478–494.

Cronbach, L. J. (1988). *Five perspectives on validity argument.* In H. Wainer & H. Braun (Eds.), *Test validity* (pp. 34–35). Hillsdale, NJ: Lawrence Erlbaum.

Cronbach, L. J., & Meehl, P. E. (1955). Construct validity in psychological tests. *Psychological Bulletin, 52,* 281–302.

Equal Employment Opportunity Commission. (1978). Uniform guidelines on employee selection procedures. *Federal Register, 43*(166), 38295–38309.

Guion, R. M. (1998). *Assessment, measurement, and prediction for personnel decisions.* Mahwah, NJ: Lawrence Erlbaum.

Hoffman, C. C., Holden, L. M., & Gale, K. (2000). So many jobs, so little "N": Applying expanded validation models to support generalization of cognitive test validity. *Personnel Psychology, 53,* 955–992.

Lawshe, C. H. (1975). A quantitative approach to content validity. *Personnel Psychology, 28,* 563–575.

Lubinski, D. (2000). Scientific and social significance of assessing individual differences: Sinking shafts at a few critical points. *Annual Review of Psychology, 51,* 405–444.

Messick, S. (1981). Constructs and their vicissitudes in educational and psychological measurement. *American Psychologist, 89,* 575–588.

Messick, S. (1995). Validity of psychological assessment: Validation of inferences from persons' responses and performances as scientific inquiry into score meaning. *American Psychologist, 50,* 741–749.

Nunnally, J. C., & Bernstein, I. H. (1994). *Psychometric theory* (3rd ed.). New York: McGraw-Hill.

Sussmann, M., & Robertson, D. U. (1986). The validity of validity: An analysis of validation study designs. *Journal of Applied Psychology, 71,* 461–468.

VALIDITY

Validity refers to the correctness of the inferences that one makes based on the results of some kind of measurement. That is, when we measure something, we need to ask whether the measurements we have taken accurately and completely reflect what we intended to measure. For example, inferences about individual differences in people's height based on the observed scores generated from the use of a (normal) tape measure or ruler are highly valid. When used appropriately, the application of the tape measure will generate observed measurements (e.g., inches, millimeters, feet) that correspond closely to actual differences in height.

COMMON MISCONCEPTIONS

It is common to hear people refer to the "validity of the test," which might give the impression that validity is a property of the measurement device. However, this is incorrect. Validity is not a property of any assessment device; rather, it is a property of the inferences that you—the test user—make. For example, consider once again the tape measure. We might be tempted to say that "the tape measure has validity." However, if we made inferences about differences in intelligence based on that same set of measurements rather than differences in height, those inferences would likely be highly incorrect. Nothing has changed about the tape measure or the set of measurements generated from its application. What has changed is the inference about what is being measured.

Although this might seem an absurd example (presumably no one would use a tape measure to measure intelligence), it demonstrates that validity is not a property of the measurement instrument but of the inference being made. The phrase "the test has validity," though technically inappropriate, is often used because there is a general assumption about which inferences are (and are not) to be made from the use of a well-known measurement device. For example, testing experts may say, "The Wonderlic has good validity." On the surface, this may seem profoundly inaccurate; however, it should be understood that this statement actually means (or at least, should mean), "Inferences regarding individual differences in general mental ability, and inferences regarding the probability of future outcomes such as job performance, are generally appropriate by relying on observed scores generated from the appropriate use of the Wonderlic." That we sometimes use shorthand to abbreviate such a long statement should not be taken to imply that validity is a property of the test. Rather, it should be interpreted as suggesting there is reliable and verifiable evidence to support the intended set of inferences from the use of a given measurement device.

The second common misconception is that there are different types of validity. Instead, validity is best thought of as a unitary concept addressing how completely and accurately a measure measures what it is intended to measure. However, no single method or strategy can provide all the evidence needed to make accurate or confident inferences. Thus, multiple strategies exist for generating such evidence; often, these strategies—or more aptly, the evidence generated from these strategies—are referred to as *types of validity*. This is an unfortunate choice of words because it often leads to the misconception that validity is many different things and that some types of validity are more or less useful than other types. Validity is a single, unitary idea: It concerns the degree to which the differences we observe in measurements can be used to make accurate and confident inferences about some unobservable phenomenon.

TYPICAL APPROACHES TO GENERATING VALIDITY EVIDENCE

Industrial and organizational (I/O) psychologists are often concerned with whether a given measurement device can be confidently relied on for making accurate decisions about hiring and promotion. To do this, I/O psychologists attempt to correlate a measure of some job-required knowledge, skill, or ability (identified from a job analysis) with a measure of some identified job demand or criterion. However, this process requires many different inferences to be made, which, in turn, requires substantial evidence to support them. For example, it is necessary to ensure that the predictor and criterion measures accurately and completely reflect the job requirements and job demands they are intended to reflect. It is also necessary to gain evidence to show that the two measures are systematically related and that the relation is not the result of some extraneous factor that was unintentionally assessed. To gain the evidence needed to support such a large set of inferences, I/O psychologists typically use three general approaches: (a) content validity, (b) criterion-related validity, and (c) construct validity.

Content Validity Inferences

The term *content validity* typically refers to inferences regarding the degree to which the content on a measurement device adequately represents the universe of possible content denoting the targeted construct or performance domain. There are a variety of methods or strategies that are useful for generating evidence to support content validity inferences; however, to establish the relevance of any evidence, it is first necessary to clearly define the performance domain or construct of interest and to identify the specific objectives for the assessment tool's use (i.e., develop test specifications). These two activities circumscribe the universe of relevant content and constrain the set of inferences that one hopes to support.

Criterion-Related Validity Inferences

Criterion-related validity refers to the degree to which the observed scores can be used to make useful inferences (i.e., accurate predictions) about future behavior or outcomes. Typically, evidence for criterion-related validity comes from correlations between the predictor measure and the criterion measures. Of course, to support useful inferences of criterion-related validity, one must first identify theoretically meaningful criterion constructs (i.e., what types of future behaviors or outcomes should be associated with or influenced by the construct denoted by the predictor measure), as well as ensure that there are measures of criterion constructs for which there is strong content validity evidence.

Construct Validity Inferences

The attempt to establish evidence for construct validity inferences is tantamount to theory testing. Construct validity encompasses a wide set of inferences regarding the nature of the psychological construct and its place in a larger nexus of constructs. In a sense, all validity inferences are part of construct validity. For example, strong support for content validity inferences can be used to support claims concerning the construct that is being measured by the assessment device. Criterion-related validity evidence is useful, too; a content-valid measure of a given construct should be related to (content-valid measures of) other constructs nearby in the nomological network and should not be related to (content-valid measures of) constructs that are far removed from the nomological network. Often, this type of evidence is referred to as *convergent* and *discriminant validity*, respectively. It is in this sense that construct validity is similar to theory testing. The definition of the construct and its relation to other constructs is in fact a mini-theory that produces specific hypotheses regarding the results of the measurement process. If most or all of those hypotheses are supported, we can be confident in the assessment device's utility for generating observed scores, which, in turn, can be used to make a limited set of accurate inferences.

—Charlie L. Reeve

See also *See also* Construct; Criterion Theory; Incremental Validity; Multitrait–Multimethod Matrix; Nomological Networks; Validation Strategies

FURTHER READING

Binning, J. F., & Barrett, G. V. (1989). Validity of personnel decisions: A conceptual analysis of the inferential and evidential bases. *Journal of Applied Psychology, 74,* 478–494.

Crocker, L., & Algina, J. (1986). *Introduction to classical and modern test theory.* New York: Holt, Rinehart & Winston.

Cronbach, L. J., & Meehl, P. E. (1955). Construct validity in psychological tests. *Psychological Bulletin, 52,* 281–302.

Kane, M. T. (1992). An argument-based approach to validity. *Psychological Bulletin, 112,* 527–535.

VERBAL PROTOCOL ANALYSIS

Verbal protocol analysis (VPA) is a qualitative, process-tracing technique whereby participants think aloud while engaging in a task, arriving at a decision, or making a judgment. Verbal protocols are typically content coded or examined in terms of the cognitive processes used. Although the use of VPA is quite rare in industrial and organizational (I/O) psychology, some have argued that its absence is a detriment to our science. This is especially apparent because its use has substantially increased the understanding of interesting phenomena in a number of other fields, such as cognitive science, education, and human factors psychology.

CONDUCTING VERBAL PROTOCOL ANALYSIS

Like any data-collection or -analysis technique, there is no best way to conduct VPA; however, the following general principles likely apply to most uses.

- *Collect concurrent data.* Research strongly suggests that data collected in real time are superior to those collected after the fact; therefore, whenever possible, have participants vocalize their thoughts as they engage in the task.
- *Record the data.* Early forms of VPA relied on the experimenter's notes because recording equipment was not readily available. However, the ubiquity of analog and digital recording equipment makes recording protocols simple and cost-efficient.

- *Transcribe the data.* Although qualitative data are never easy to manage, computer programs are available to provide assistance, but only when data are fully transcribed.
- *Plan your work.* Have an idea of what you are looking for before you immerse yourself in the data. As with any research technique, this means drawing from relevant theory, making specific predictions about what you expect to find, and specifying defensible ways to determine whether your predictions were met.

USES IN THE ORGANIZATIONAL SCIENCES

Although VPA is certainly considered an unorthodox research method among most organizational scientists, it is not completely unheard of. A handful of studies have used VPA in an organizational context, and in most cases, it has helped to answer questions that are firmly rooted in traditional organizational science domains but require information that traditional methods simply cannot provide.

A good example is the use of VPA to investigate the processes that individuals use when deciding whether to apply for a given job. The researcher could use more traditional techniques, such as self-report, by asking participants what information they *think* they typically pay attention to while reading job ads, or a type of policy-capturing methodology to elicit similar information. However, VPA is likely a better choice because it allows the researcher to directly assess the real-time reports of participants' strategies, a benefit that few methodologies offer. Other examples of the use of VPA in the organizational sciences include examining the thought processes that job seekers use to evaluate potential employers' reputations and assessing the construct validity of the organizational culture profile through VPA alone, which brings up an interesting point regarding the potential use of VPA as a psychometric aid.

USES IN THE ORGANIZATIONAL SCIENCES

Traditional psychometric assessment devices are necessary for the further development of quality measurement systems, but they may not be entirely sufficient. This is especially true when assumptions are made regarding the cognitive processes that individuals use when responding to a given instrument. The importance of this sentiment—often referred to as *cognitive process validity*—was recently recognized by the Society of Industrial and Organizational Psychology, which argued that such assumptions should be empirically tested before instruments are used in applied contexts. Verbal protocol analysis provides one possible means of doing this.

Traditional psychometric tools provide little information as to *why* specific items are behaving poorly. Thus, psychometricians are often left with a difficult choice: (a) blindly rewrite the items in question, retest the entire scale, and rerun the analyses; or (b) throw out the problematic items. Not surprisingly, many psychometricians often choose the second option. However, a small amount of verbal protocol data gathered from participants while they are completing an instrument may allow researchers to pinpoint the precise cause of the unexpected item performance. For example, VPA may indicate that some of the items are confusing, some terms are unknown to the target sample, some questions lack important situational context, or the scale is too long and participants become bored and careless toward the end. These are all insights that are typically not available with traditional psychometric assessment tools—but, of course, there are some caveats.

CAUTIONS AND LIMITATIONS

The primary critiques of VPA can be boiled down to two arguments: (a) Verbalizations show only a moderate relationship to actual behavior, and (b) verbalizing one's thoughts fundamentally alters the cognitive processes that are typically used while engaging in a task. These claims are certainly not without merit; a number of studies show at least partial support for them. However, counteranalyses also show that these limitations are not attributable to VPA as a data-collection tool per se; rather, they may be the result of sloppy data-collection procedures. That is, the use of VPA does not guarantee good or bad data; instead, the quality of the data is determined mainly by the quality of the procedures used to gather them. If caution, common sense, and rigorous data-collection methods are used, there is no specific reason why quality verbal protocol data cannot be used to examine a host of interesting phenomena.

Although VPA certainly has the potential to be a useful tool in the organizational sciences, it is by no means a silver bullet. Like any form of data, it is most effective when it is used in conjunction with data from a variety of sources. Researchers who are interested in

using VPA should be forewarned that the resulting data are not necessarily easy to manage. Not only is it almost always necessary to transcribe the data before engaging in qualitative analyses; it is also often necessary to enter quantitatively coded data into a traditional statistics package such as SAS or SPSS so that basic analyses can be conducted. Finally, data collection tends to be quite slow because the data are generally collected one person at a time; therefore, it often takes days or even weeks to get a sample size as large as those that can be easily obtained by most quantitative techniques in one session.

SUMMARY

Verbal protocol analysis is an underused but potentially valuable qualitative data-collection tool whereby participants think aloud while engaging in a task or behavior. It has been shown to provide unique and valuable insight into the cognitive processes that individuals used in a variety of settings. Though it is certainly not without its critics, this technique has stood up to the majority of critiques, and it is now considered a relatively orthodox tool in a variety of fields. Though it will certainly never replace any traditional organizational research tool, it does have the potential to bolster claims about the cognitive processes that individuals use while engaging in relevant behaviors. Similarly, it may also be a useful psychometric assessment tool; however, further research is required in this area before any firm conclusions can be reached about its actual incremental value over and above traditional techniques.

—*Rustin D. Meyer*

See also Content Coding; Qualitative Research Approach

FURTHER READING

Barber, A. E., & Roehling, M. V. (1993). Job postings and the decision to interview: A verbal protocol analysis. *Journal of Applied Psychology, 78*, 845–856.

Ericsson, K. A., & Simon, H. A. (1993). *Protocol analysis: Verbal reports as data* (2nd ed.). Cambridge, MA: MIT Press.

Green, A. (1995). Verbal protocol analysis. *The Psychologist, 8*, 126–129.

Messick, S. (1995). Validity of psychological assessment: Validation of inferences from persons' responses and performances as scientific inquiry into score meaning. *American Psychologist, 50*, 741–749.

Nisbett, R. E., & Wilson, T. D. (1977). Telling more than we can know: Verbal reports on mental processes. *Psychological Review, 84,* 231–259.

VIOLENCE AT WORK

Every year, approximately 600 individuals in the United States are murdered at work, and 1.7 million individuals are the victims of nonfatal violence. Members of the public commit the vast majority of workplace homicides and assaults. Workplace violence perpetrated by the public can be categorized into two main types based on the perpetrator's relationship to the victim. In Type I violence, the assailant does not have a legitimate relationship with the victim and enters the work environment to commit a criminal act (e.g., robbery). Employees working in the retail, security, transportation, and service industries are at high risk for this type of violence because they have frequent contact with the public, handle cash, work alone or in small numbers, work late at night, and guard valuables (e.g., jewelry).

Type II violence is enacted within the context of a legitimate work relationship. The perpetrator of Type II violence commits an act of violence while he or she is being served by the victim (e.g., a patient assaults a nurse). Industries reporting high rates of Type II violence include social services, health care, and education. Providing service, care, advice, or education can put employees at increased risk for Type II violence, especially if clients, inmates, or patients are experiencing frustration or stress. Other potentially risky job-related tasks include interacting with unstable, volatile, or cognitively impaired populations. Having the authority to deny the public a service or request may also place employees at increased risk for Type II violence.

PREVENTING TYPE I VIOLENCE

Strategies aimed at preventing Type I violence focus on increasing the risks, reducing the rewards, and increasing the effort associated with robbery. A criminal is unlikely to rob a particular target if engaging in the act offers few rewards, requires significant effort, and has a high risk of getting caught. Three principles underlie most robbery-reduction strategies: increasing visibility, reducing rewards, and hardening targets.

Increasing visibility deters would-be robbers by increasing their perception of risk. The presence of surveillance cameras, one method of increasing visibility, has successfully decreased incidents of violence in the transportation industry. For example, in both Perth (Australia) and Toronto (Canada), surveillance cameras in taxicabs have significantly reduced the number of assaults against drivers. Besides using surveillance cameras, at-risk industries (e.g., retail) can increase visibility by keeping windows clear of signs (e.g., advertisements), allowing passersby to see inside. Good internal and external lighting may also increase visibility.

Reward-reduction strategies may make committing a robbery less appealing. Because money is the most frequent motive for robberies, at-risk industries could establish cash-handling practices, such as keeping minimal amounts of cash in registers. Obviously, organizations must post signs informing the public of their cash-handling practices in order for them to be effective at deterring crime. The transportation industry could reduce the risk of robbery by requiring passengers to pay their fares with credit cards or vouchers.

Target-hardening strategies make committing a robbery more difficult. They may also reduce the likelihood that employees will be injured during the commission of a robbery. For example, research suggests that protective screens reduce the number of assaults experienced by taxi drivers. Bullet-resistant barriers also reduce the risk for robbery in retail establishments. Making it difficult for would-be robbers to flee the scene of the crime by using speed bumps in parking lots, for example, may also deter robbery. Revolving doors at store exits may also influence would-be robbers' choice of target.

Although no research has been conducted on the efficacy of employee training on workplace violence, training employees in high-risk industries to anticipate and respond to robberies may decrease the possibility that they will be injured during a robbery. Because there is evidence that employees who cooperate with robbers are less likely to be injured than employees who resist, employee training should stress cooperation with robbers. Employees should also be taught not to make any sudden moves during a robbery and to inform perpetrators of what they are doing at all times. If there are silent alarms at their place of employment, workers should be told to activate them only when it is safe to do so. Taxi drivers should be made aware that they may be able to avoid random attacks by keeping their car doors locked when the car is idle.

PREVENTING TYPE II VIOLENCE

There are three main approaches to preventing or dealing with Type II violence: environmental, organizational and administrative, and behavioral and interpersonal. Environmental strategies focus on physical risk factors related to building layout or design. Organizational and administrative approaches involve developing policies and practices that specifically address workplace violence. Behavioral and interpersonal approaches involve training employees to anticipate and respond to workplace violence.

Some of the environmental strategies for reducing the risk of Type II violence are identical to those for reducing the risk of Type I violence. For example, surveillance cameras can be used in organizations such as hospitals, schools, and social service establishments. Other environmental strategies include installing metal detectors at front entrances, as well as surrounding reception areas with bullet-resistant glass. Card-controlled entrances and security checks for identification could also be used to limit public access to restricted areas. Waiting areas should be designed with safety in mind: They should be sparsely accessorized to limit the number of makeshift weapons that can be used against employees. Furniture should be lightweight and have few sharp edges. When employees must meet one-on-one with members of the public (e.g., in a patient care setting), meeting rooms should be equipped with phones, panic buttons, and two exits.

At-risk industries should have policies and practices in place to prevent aggression. A written policy should outline what constitutes unacceptable behavior in the workplace, and employees and the public (e.g., clients) should be informed of the policy. Organizations should also have detailed plans for dealing with violent attacks if and when they occur. Organizations should develop procedures to ensure that information about aggressive individuals (e.g., patients, inmates) is shared among employees so that they can take the necessary precautions to avoid being victimized. Employees should be prohibited from working alone, especially during late-night and early-morning shifts, when there are fewer potential witnesses who could assist during a violent situation.

Training specific to workplace violence can provide employees with the necessary knowledge, skills, and confidence to deal with potentially dangerous situations. Employee training targets the client population served, and employees are taught how to resolve conflicts, recognize escalating anger, and manage and respond to aggressive behavior. Follow-up training is also necessary if employees are to maintain their skills and confidence.

Members of the public perpetrate the majority of workplace homicides and assaults. Risk factors for violence differ among industries and workplaces, making no single prevention strategy appropriate for all organizations. Prevention strategies must be tailored to individual workplaces, and they should be regularly evaluated to determine whether they remain appropriate and effective.

—*Manon Mireille LeBlanc*

See also Abusive Supervision; Counterproductive Work Behaviors; Workplace Safety

FURTHER READING

Casteel, C., & Peek-Asa, C. (2000). Effectiveness of crime prevention through environmental design (CPTED) in reducing robberies. *American Journal of Preventive Medicine, 18,* 99–115.

Castillo, D. N., & Jenkins, E. L. (1994). Industries and occupations at high risk for work-related homicide. *Journal of Occupational Medicine, 36,* 125–132.

LeBlanc, M. M., Dupré, K. E., & Barling, J. (2006). Public-initiated aggression. In E. K. Kelloway, J. Barling, & J. J. Hurrell (Eds.), *Handbook of workplace violence.* Thousand Oaks, CA: Sage.

LeBlanc, M. M., & Kelloway, E. K. (2002). Predictors and outcomes of workplace violence and aggression. *Journal of Applied Psychology, 87,* 444–453.

Runyan, C. W., Zakocs, R. C., & Zwerling, C. (2000). Administrative and behavioral interventions for workplace violence prevention. *American Journal of Preventive Medicine, 18,* 116–127.

VIRTUAL ORGANIZATIONS

Virtual organizations are composed of employees spread across different locations who perform different jobs and may also have different cultural identities. These dispersed and diverse employees are joined together by communication technologies such as the telephone, fax, e-mail, Internet, and instant messaging. Some employees of virtual organizations may work alone, functioning essentially as telecommuters. Others, however, may work clustered together in traditional offices. In either case, the virtual organization is spread out over multiple geographic locations.

There are two important characteristics of virtual organizations: (a) They depend on teams, and (b) they have a very fluid structure. Virtual organizations use teams to conduct most of their work. This means that employees must depend on each other to complete their work. Additionally, teams form and disperse frequently and easily. Thus, the organizational structure changes often as teams reorganize to meet the organization's needs.

Although the concept of a virtual organization in which employees never interact face-to-face is intriguing, such purely virtual organizations are very rare. Instead, many organizations have *degrees* of virtuality, that is, some aspects of the organization are traditional but others are considered virtual. Virtuality can vary along four dimensions:

1. Space: The physical location of the employees—are they colocated or dispersed in different places?

2. Time: The time zone in which the employees work—are they working the same business hours or are they dispersed across time zones?

3. Culture: The employees' culture—are employees from the same culture or country or from different ones?

4. Boundary: The organizational dispersion of work—do the organizational processes stay with the organization or are they outsourced?

Organizations vary in their virtuality. At one end of the continuum are organizations such as Amazon.com: Although Amazon.com is a very successful retail organization, there are no Amazon.com stores in which customers can buy books. Instead, customers buy books, music, and many other items through the Internet. Amazon.com's employees rarely interact with the customers. They do, however, interact with each other face-to-face and through technology at several offices around the United States and the world.

At the other end of the continuum are traditional organizations with a worldwide presence. For example, IBM has offices across the world. It also has a significant number of telecommuters and employees located in customers' offices. Employees work together as teams, which may interact completely face-to-face, completely through technology, or through some combination of the two. The teams may be located in the same time zone or spread around the world. Thus, IBM and other large multinational organizations may have components that are very much like traditional organizations and other components that are very much like virtual organizations.

ELECTRONIC COMMUNICATION

One of the most important features of all virtual organizations is that they depend on communication through technology. Although research on virtual organizations is in the developmental stage, we do have a great deal of knowledge about communication through technology and its effects on organizations and their employees.

An Efficient but Cold Medium

Technological communication, particularly electronic communication such as e-mail, differs significantly from face-to-face communication. First, it is considered a colder medium that filters out nonverbal cues such as facial expressions, tone of voice, and physical movements such as nodding one's head in agreement. As a result, electronic communications can be misinterpreted, and a message sent through electronic communication may be perceived as less friendly than the same message delivered in face-to-face communication.

However, electronic communication can also reduce communication bias and improve understanding in certain instances. For example, saved e-mail messages contain an exact history of the communication. Research and experience also suggest that electronic communication can be very efficient and precise with factual information. Additionally, once communication partners have established a relationship and a history of communication, it can also be used for more complicated and social communication with less fear of misinterpretation.

One issue, though, is that it takes longer for communication partners to establish a relationship with each other through electronic communication than through face-to-face communication. Because fewer communication cues travel in the electronic messages, communication partners must exchange more messages over a longer period of time to gather enough information about each other to establish a reliable impression.

Problems With Working Virtually

Some tasks are more easily performed face-to-face than through electronic communication. For example, decision making that requires consensus building is much more efficiently accomplished through face-to-face communication. Electronic communication, on the other hand, is very good for dispersing information and can take the place of some information-sharing meetings.

Traditional organizations have the ability to decide whether they can conduct a task face-to-face or through technology, whereas virtual organizations may have no choice but to rely on communication through technology. This can make the timely and successful completion of these tasks more challenging.

Flatter Structure With More Communication Partners

Communication through technology tends to flatten organizational structure, making it more horizontal than vertical. One reason is that it is so easy for people at all levels of the organization to communicate with each other. Although this is often considered good for power distribution in the organization, it can drastically increase the number of pieces of communication to which employees have to respond. For example, when everyone can e-mail everyone else, the volume of e-mail may become overwhelming.

Norms of Technology Use

To be effective, groups must develop norms for using electronic communication. Sometimes, these norms are as basic as simple "netiquette," which includes such rules as not typing in all capitals (to avoid the appearance of shouting) and refraining from "flaming" (using e-mail to send inappropriately severe and harsh comments that would not be shared face-to-face). The norms may also include more organizationally specific norms, such as whether and when to include one's manager in the correspondence, how to effectively use the subject line to identify the topic of the communication, whether to acknowledge receipt of a job request through e-mail, and how formal grammar should be (e.g., using salutations and closings) in communications. As these norms develop

within specific groups and organizations, they form a communication culture in which communication becomes quicker and deviations from the norms take on meanings of their own.

CHALLENGES TO VIRTUAL ORGANIZATION

As organizations develop their virtuality, managers and researchers are identifying important challenges to their effectiveness and success.

Building Trust

One of the most important concerns in virtual organizations is the development and maintenance of trust between employees. Trust is an essential ingredient for teams to be effective. Team members must trust each other to perform work that is completed on time and of high quality. The same issue applies to managers of virtual employees. Trust is most effectively developed when employees have a history of working with each other, work that traditionally has taken place face-to-face. However, virtual organizations tend to form and disperse teams frequently, and team members may not have worked with each other before.

Therefore, virtual organizations may rely on *swift trust*. Swift trust is the willingness to suspend doubt about whether the "strangers" on the team can be counted on to do the job and to believe that the end result will benefit everyone. Swift trust develops and is maintained by high responsiveness and activity, often through electronic communication. Examples include returning voice mail and e-mail messages, performing tasks on time, and responding to the content and tone of communications.

Additionally, virtual organizations can increase trust by establishing positive and strong norms of communication through technology, strong business ethics, and a culture of trustworthiness.

Maintaining Cohesion, Identity, and Commitment to the Virtual Organization

Another critical concern for virtual organizations is ensuring that virtual employees develop attachment and commitment to the organization. Employees in virtual organizations may feel more isolated and decrease their social relationships with their coworkers, managers, and team members. These isolated employees may lose their cohesion, identity, attachment with, and commitment to the virtual organization. This is a concern for organizations because a great deal of research shows the importance of employees' organizational commitment and organizational identification to the effectiveness of the organization. Early research indicates that having at least some regular face-to-face interaction between employees is important and helps employees feel that their coworkers and managers support them and their work.

Managing Human Resources

Finally, virtual organizations present a particular set of challenges for human resources. Some employees may not be suited to virtual employment and thus have poor person–virtual organization fit. One current model proposes that in order to be successful, virtual employees must highly value autonomy, flexibility, and diversity. They must be trustworthy and willing to trust others. Additionally, they must be able to govern themselves in both time management and the ability to work on their own.

Productivity may vary among virtual employees. Some research suggests that virtual employees' evaluations of their own self-efficacy are very important to their ability to work well. These evaluations are particularly important in regard to their previous virtual work experience and training, the best practices they have seen modeled by their managers, and their own technology fears and capabilities.

Purely virtual organizations are quite rare. Nonetheless, as communication technologies develop, more organizations will increase their virtuality. Benefits and challenges will continue to evolve as organizations take advantage of the capabilities of their technological communication.

—*Anita Blanchard*

See also Organizational Commitment; Organizational Communication, Informal; Telecommuting; Virtual Teams

FURTHER READING

DeSanctis, G., & Monge, P. (1999). Introduction to the special issue: Communication processes for virtual organizations. *Organization Science, 10*(6), 693–703.

Jarvenpaa, S. L., & Leidner, D. E. (1999). Communication and trust in global virtual teams. *Organization Science, 10*(6), 791–815.

Kasper-Fuehrer, E. K., & Ashkanasy, N. M. (2001). Communicating trustworthiness and building trust in interorganizational virtual organizations. *Journal of Management, 27,* 235–254.

Shin, Y. (2004). A person-environment fit model for virtual organizations. *Journal of Management, 30*(5), 725–743.

Wiesenfeld, B. M., Raghuram, S., & Garud, R. (2001). Organizational identification among virtual workers: The role of need for affiliation and perceived work-based social support. *Journal of Management, 27,* 213–229.

VIRTUAL TEAMS

A virtual team is a group of individuals who work interdependently, are located at a distance from each other, and conduct most of their collaboration through communications technology (rather than face-to-face). A "pure" virtual team is one in which each member is geographically distant from each other member, but more often, at least some of the members are likely to be colocated.

As organizations become more global and outsource more of their work, and as trends such as hot desking and telecommuting become popular in some professions, more and more business is being conducted across geographic distance. In many organizations today, it is not possible to locate everyone at the same site. This fact, in combination with the recent proliferation and improvement of communications technology, means that the use of virtual teams is likely to become more common.

Despite the dispersion of team members in virtual teams, organizations want to benefit from bringing together employees with diverse expertise without spending too much on travel. Although some travel is still likely to be necessary, the aim is to allow these geographically dispersed individuals to work together while they are apart. This work typically takes place through communications technologies such as e-mail, the telephone (including audioconferences), voice mail, instant messaging, video conferencing, shared desktops, intranet sites, and other interactive computer-based tools. Although traditional colocated teams may make use of some of these technologies, virtual teams rely on them more heavily because they cannot easily arrange face-to-face contact.

LITERATURE ON VIRTUAL TEAMS

Empirical research on virtual teams is in its infancy, but more information is emerging all the time. Until recently, much of the literature was either theoretical and speculative or based on experimental findings with ad hoc or student project teams rather than teams within organizations. Nevertheless, the literature reveals a range of interesting issues.

Technology Mediation

One area of interest is the use and impact of communications technologies. The level of use of different types of technology depends on the resources available, the type of task, the level of interdependence required for the task, and the collaborators' preferences. The literature suggests that more complex tasks requiring a high level of interdependence, tasks in which misunderstandings are possible, and tasks in which emotions are involved benefit most from communications media that allow the transmission of more communication and social cues (i.e., rich media). The richest media enable the transmission of visual and verbal cues that aid understanding (e.g., nods, verbalizations such as "uh-huh") and provide immediate feedback (i.e., the nod occurs immediately after the communicator's comment, indicating the point has been understood). The richest media, therefore, are face-to-face communications; video conferencing offers a possible alternative, although problems with sound and visual synchronization can make this technology less rich.

Text-based media such as e-mail are generally considered among the least rich technologies because many social and communication cues are missing and feedback (in the form of a reply) is typically delayed. These less rich media are more suitable when tasks are routine and less interdependent and when there is less danger of emotions or misunderstandings escalating. Research also suggests, however, that when such communications technologies are used for a longer period of time, people are able to transmit more complex information through them. For example, the rocket engine design team that Anne Majchrzak and colleagues (2000) studied was able to adapt to less rich media and use them for some complex and ambiguous tasks (such as generating and critiquing new ideas, learning about unfamiliar concepts, and understanding the design concerns of other team members) because there was a high level of shared understanding among team members that had been developed through previous face-to-face meetings.

Shared Understanding and Knowledge Exchange

Another key area of concern in the literature is the concept of *shared understanding,* which appears to be central to the success of virtual teams. The team needs to have a shared view of its task, goals, roles (i.e., who should be doing what), and processes. This is crucial in virtual teams because the coordination of work is more difficult when members rarely meet. However, the dispersion of team members means that it is more difficult to establish shared understanding in virtual teams because of poor communication, little exchange of social cues, and lack of direct contact or experience of each others' contexts. Furthermore, dispersed members are likely to be more diverse: They may live and work in separate contexts, where different local constraints, goals, and expectations influence their behavior and understanding. They may also face national, professional, or functional language barriers. Therefore, it is important that members be aware of each other's different backgrounds and perspectives to avoid misunderstandings. Without a shared understanding, team members may think they have understood each other, but in fact, their understanding is based on completely different frames of reference and is actually at cross-purposes. This can lead to misunderstandings and sometimes conflict within virtual teams, jeopardizing working relationships and performance. Unfortunately, the literature suggests that such contextual information is rarely exchanged or remembered by virtual team members.

There is also some interest in dispersed expertise and knowledge within virtual teams, which can have both negative and positive implications. When a team is dispersed and does not share the same physical context, it can be harder to know who has particular knowledge or expertise. This is exacerbated by the fact that teams have a tendency to focus on commonly held information, overlook unique data, and assume that everyone knows the same information. On the positive side, the higher diversity that is typically found in virtual teams can lead to higher levels of novel and nonredundant knowledge because people from different locations and backgrounds are likely to have access to different types and sources of knowledge. This wider knowledge pool can bring huge benefits to virtual teams, but only if they are able to overcome the inherent difficulties of bringing it all together.

Relationships

Relationship issues such as conflict, cohesion, and trust have also received attention in the literature. It is often assumed that virtual teams will experience more conflict than colocated teams because of the increased likelihood of misunderstandings. However, evidence for this assumption is mixed. Nevertheless, research suggests that a remote colleague is more likely to be blamed if things go wrong than a colocated colleague. This is the result of an attribution error, whereby the distant person's context is much less salient than the colocated person's context. A team member is much more likely to be aware of the situational constraints of a colocated person and take these into account, whereas without knowledge of the remote colleague's context, the person is likely to be the focus of attention, and so the colleague will be blamed without consideration of his or her situation.

Research has found that virtual teams are less cohesive than traditional colocated teams because they lack face-to-face interaction. However, other research suggests that in some circumstances, virtual teams are actually more cohesive than colocated teams. Studies using experimental, ad hoc virtual teams whose members are visually anonymous to each other and know very little about each other have shown that extremely high attraction and team identity can develop very quickly. When cues about individuals are not available, a group identity will be inferred from whatever cues remain (e.g., they are all students). This effect is thought to enhance the attraction to other group members.

Similarly, it is often assumed that trust will be lower in virtual teams than in colocated teams because of their lack of close contact, but the research on this is inconclusive. Some research suggests that although trust may be lower in the early stages of virtual team formation, over time, it becomes equivalent after repeated interactions demonstrating trustworthiness. Still others have suggested that trust may be immediate based on stereotypical representations of the virtual collaborators (e.g., that people in certain professions are automatically trustworthy). However, this type of trust is assumed rather than evidence based, and so it may not be justified over time.

RECOMMENDATIONS

Many researchers and practitioners have made recommendations on how to get the most out of virtual teams. These suggestions include the following:

- Have an initial face-to-face meeting to develop a shared understanding of the team's goals, roles, and processes and its different contexts, expertise, and other aspects of diversity.
- Explicitly exchange contextual information (e.g., about culture, ways of working, expectations, national holidays) and explicitly identify the range of expertise within the team. Ensure that everyone on the team is made aware of this information.
- Use technology appropriately for the task at hand and have face-to-face meetings at important project junctures when richer media are required (e.g., when tasks are complex, interdependent, and involve emotions, and when shared understanding is low).
- Emphasize a common group identity (to foster cohesion), but also be aware of differences (to aid shared understanding and knowledge exchange).

—Carolyn Axtell and Steven Fleck

See also Telecommuting; Virtual Organizations

FURTHER READING

Axtell, C. M., Fleck, S. J., and Turner, N. (2004). Virtual teams: Collaborating across distance. In C. L. Cooper & I. T. Robertson (Eds.), *International review of industrial and organizational psychology* (Vol. 19, pp. 205–248). Chichester, UK: Wiley.

Duarte, D. L., & Snyder, N. T. (2001). *Mastering virtual teams* (2nd ed.). San Francisco: Jossey-Bass.

Gibson, C. B., & Cohen, S. G. (Eds.). (2003). *Virtual teams that work: Creating conditions for virtual team effectiveness.* San Francisco: Jossey-Bass

Hinds, P. J., & Kiesler, S. (Eds.). (2002). *Distributed work.* Cambridge, MA: MIT Press.

Lipnack, J., & Stamps, J. (2000). *Virtual teams: People working across boundaries with technology* (2nd ed.). New York: Wiley.

Majchrzak, A., Rice, R. E., King, N., Malhotra, A., & Ba, S. L. (2000). Computer-mediated inter-organizational knowledge sharing: Insights from a virtual team innovating using a collaborative tool. *Information Resources and Management Journal, 13,* 44–53.

WEB-BASED ASSESSMENT

See COMPUTER ASSESSMENT

WHISTLE-BLOWERS

Whistle-blowing occurs when a member of an organization reports practices, under control of the organization, that are perceived to be illegal, immoral, or in some way illegitimate. Whistle-blower reports of organizational wrongdoing are increasingly making news headlines (e.g., fraud, corruption, and other unethical acts in organizations like Enron, WorldCom, Arthur Andersen, and Tyco). Such reports are more frequently made by members of the accused organization such as employees, board members, or internal auditors, rather than by external auditing agencies. These individuals, referred to as whistle-blowers, risk retaliation both by their organization (via job loss, demotion, or harassment) and sometimes even by the public (character assassinations, accusations of being spies or *squealers*) in their efforts to expose perceived transgressions.

Although whistle-blowers typically have access to both internal (supervisor, internal affairs investigator, human resources director) and external (external auditing agency, news media, lawyer) channels by which to report an organizational transgression, nearly all of them initially attempt to report wrongdoing through internal channels. Although this means of whistle-blowing is less threatening to the organization (external reports often result in great public scrutiny or legal intervention), whistle-blower reports are frequently buried or ignored. When appropriately handled, whistle-blowing can be beneficial to the organization, especially when it results in the cessation of practices that would otherwise harm employees and consumers or negatively affect the reputation of the organization.

PREDICTORS AND CORRELATES OF WHISTLE-BLOWING

Three categories of variables are relevant to the whistle-blowing process and may serve as predictors of whistle-blowing actions: whistle-blower characteristics, whistle-blowing context, and aspects of the wrongdoing and wrongdoer.

Whistle-blower Characteristics Associated With Whistle-blowing

A variety of personal characteristics related to the decision to engage in whistle-blowing have been examined and include whistle-blower demographics (age, sex, level of education, level of job held, etc.), personality variables (i.e., locus of control), morality (i.e., ethical judgment), and other characteristics, such as job performance, organizational commitment, role responsibility to blow the whistle, and approval of whistle-blowing. Although results seem to differ slightly across studies, the results of a recent meta-analytic review of the extant literature suggest whistle-blowers (as compared with inactive observers) appear to be male, have good job performance, be more highly educated, hold higher-level or supervisory positions, score higher on tests of moral reasoning, and value whistle-blowing in the face of unethical behavior. Whistle-blowers are also more likely to report a role-related responsibility or obligation to blow the whistle. Age and organizational tenure as predictors of whistle-blowing have yielded mixed results.

Contextual Factors Associated With Whistle-blowing

Compared with the personal characteristics of whistle-blowers, contextual variables appear to better predict whistle-blowing decisions. Relevant variables may include supervisor and coworker support, organizational climate, threat of retaliation, and organization size. Potential whistle-blowers who perceive a threat of retaliation by the organization, immediate supervisors, or coworkers are much less likely to blow the whistle than those who do not perceive a retaliatory climate; perceptions of supervisor or top management support are instrumental in the decision to blow the whistle. Whistle-blowing also occurs more frequently in organizations where whistle-blowing is valued and where the whistle-blower and organization are value congruent.

Characteristics of Wrongdoing or Wrongdoer Associated With Whistle-blowing

Evidence suggests that characteristics of the wrongdoing, such as perceived severity of the wrongdoing, evidence of wrongdoing, or characteristics of the wrongdoer, such as the likability of the wrongdoer, may have significant implications in whistle-blowing decisions. Potential whistle-blowers also seek to gather solid evidence of the transgression before taking any action. Whistle-blowing occurs more frequently when the whistle-blower has been personally affected by the wrongdoing. External claims are especially likely when the organization depends on the continuation of the wrongdoing.

PREDICTORS AND CORRELATES OF RETALIATION AGAINST WHISTLE-BLOWERS

Retaliation against a whistle-blower may take many forms, ranging from attempted coercion of the whistle-blower to withdraw accusations to outright exclusion from the organization. Other retaliatory acts may include organizational attempts to undermine the complaint process, isolation of the whistle-blower, character defamation, imposition of hardship or disgrace on the whistle-blower, exclusion from meetings, elimination of perquisites, and other forms of discrimination or harassment. Retaliation may be motivated by the organization's desire to silence the whistle-blower completely, prevent a full public knowledge of the complaint, discredit the whistle-blower, or discourage other potential whistle-blowers from taking action.

Organizational response to whistle-blower action (retaliation, reward, no action) depends in part on whether management agrees with the merit of the claim and the whistle-blower's right to take action. Organizations that value the perceived ethicality of their practices and those that value report of unsanctioned practices are more likely to reward than retaliate against a whistle-blower. Under circumstances wherein an organization is dependent on the continuation of the wrongdoing or when it is not dependent on the whistle-blower, the organization is likely to both retaliate and continue the wrongdoing.

Importantly, retaliation is not always initiated by organizational top management. Sometimes acts of retaliation are initiated by a supervisor or coworker with or without the approval of top management. Supervisors may be motivated to retaliate against whistle-blowers for many reasons, but they frequently do so out of fear that a whistle-blowing claim signals their inability to maintain order and compliance within their departments or the fear that valid complaints will result in the restriction or cessation of their own operations or influence. Potential predictors of retaliation against whistle-blowers may relate to characteristics of the whistle-blower, actions taken by the whistle-blower, contextual variables associated with the climate in which the transgression occurred, and characteristics of the wrongdoing.

Characteristics of the Whistle-blower Associated With Retaliation

Whistle-blower characteristics potentially predictive of retaliation include age, education level, job level, role responsibility to report transgressions, and value congruence with the organization. Demographic characteristics of whistle-blowers are thought to be less predictive of retaliation than are contextual variables. Research suggests, however, that individuals who blow the whistle because it is their job to do so, because of an audit or role responsibility, are less likely to be retaliated against and are more likely to be successful in stopping the transgression. Similarly, older whistle-blowers are more likely to be retaliated against than are younger whistle-blowers. Research suggests whistle-blowers who are valuable to their organization (because of age, experience, education, job level) are more likely to be retaliated against than are their *less valuable* counterparts. Finally, whistle-blowers whose values regarding right and wrong are incongruent with those of the organization are more likely to be retaliated against, presumably because top management does not deem the act to be as severe as is perceived by the whistle-blower.

Actions Taken by the Whistle-blower Associated With Retaliation

Specific actions taken by a whistle-blower during the process of making a claim may also influence whether and to what extent retaliation occurs. Such actions may include whether the whistle-blower used an internal or external channel to report wrongdoing, whether the whistle-blower attempted to remain anonymous, how successful the whistle-blower was in ultimately curbing the wrongdoing, and whether others in the organization ignored the wrongdoing. Research suggests that when a whistle-blower reports wrongdoing through external channels, he or she is more likely to receive retaliation; and such retaliation is likely to be more severe than when internal channels are used. Similarly, whistle-blowers who unsuccessfully attempted to remain anonymous during the whistle-blowing process are more likely to experience retaliation. Inconsistent results have been reported regarding the effectiveness of the whistle-blower in curbing wrongdoing and experience of retaliation; however, the preponderance of research suggests that the majority of whistle-blowers are unsuccessful in exacting desired changes.

Contextual Variables Associated With Retaliation

Contextual variables examined in relation to retaliation include top management, supervisor, and coworker support, as well as organizational climate for whistle-blowing. Lack of support by supervisors and top management is predictive of retaliation

against whistle-blowers. Similarly, in organizations where whistle-blowing is not sanctioned, coworkers are typically less willing to give the whistle-blower support or protection from retaliation, thus contributing to its occurrence.

Characteristics of the Wrongdoing Associated With Retaliation

Aspects of the wrongdoing potentially associated with retaliation include the frequency of the wrongdoing, its severity, and the whistle-blower's evidence of wrongdoing. When wrongdoing is widespread within the organization or when the organization is dependent on its continuation, top management is more likely to lash out at the whistle-blower. When a whistle-blower's report cites multiple incidents of wrongdoing, multiple individuals involved in the wrongdoing, or multiple sources of evidence, potential for retaliation is reduced.

SUMMARY

Whistle-blowing on organizational wrongdoing has become increasingly publicized, and its potential to positively affect the organization and its constituents has been highlighted. Whistle-blowing assists organizations and federal agencies in halting practices that would otherwise harm employees and consumers. Unfortunately, many whistle-blowers fear and even suffer retaliation after reporting organizational transgressions. Organizations may do well to actively encourage whistle-blowing claims on unsanctioned and illegitimate practices through the following actions:

- Reaffirming the organization's commitment to ethical practices
- Promising protection from retaliation
- Enumerating the protocol for issuing whistle-blowing claims
- Communicating the process by which claims are investigated
- Reviewing the types of activities or practices considered by the organization to be unethical or unsanctioned
- Issuing an overt request that unsanctioned practices be reported

To be effective, however, the organization must ensure that these espoused ethical values are consistent with the values enacted on a daily basis and that internal reporting channels are both *free from leaks* and staffed by trustworthy individuals.

—*Jessica R. Mesmer-Magnus and*
Chockalingam Viswesvaran

See also Corporate Ethics; Corporate Social Responsibility; Counterproductive Work Behaviors; Integrity at Work; Organizational Justice

FURTHER READING

Dozier, J. B., & Miceli, M. P. (1985). Potential predictors of whistle-blowing: A prosocial behavior perspective. *Academy of Management Review, 10*(4), 823–836.

Dworkin, T. M., & Baucus, M. S. (1998). Internal vs. external whistle-blowers: A comparison of whistle-blowing processes. *Journal of Business Ethics, 17,* 1281–1298.

Mesmer-Magnus, J. R., & Viswesvaran, C. (in press). Whistle-blowing in organizations: An examination of the correlates of whistle-blower intentions, actions, and retaliation. *Journal of Business Ethics.*

Miceli, M. P., & Near, J. P. (1988). Individual and situational correlates of whistle-blowing. *Personnel Psychology, 41,* 267–281.

Near, J. P., & Miceli, M. P. (1996). Whistle-blowing: Myth and reality. *Journal of Management, 22*(3), 507–526.

Sims, R. L., & Keenan, J. P. (1998). Predictors of external whistle-blowing: Organizational and intrapersonal variables. *Journal of Business Ethics, 17,* 411–421.

WITHDRAWAL BEHAVIORS, ABSENTEEISM

Absenteeism (alternatively, absence) is an individual's lack of physical presence at a given location and time when there is a social expectation for that person to be there. An absence is a behavioral outcome or state rather than a behavior itself, because many different actions can make up an absence, such as lying on the beach if at the same time a person is expected to conduct a face-to-face meeting with employees. Moreover, attendance and absence should not be thought of as straightforward opposites. An individual can be absent from many settings simultaneously if groups or individuals from each of those settings have contradicting expectations. In the same way, a person can be in attendance at one location (such as work) while being absent from another (such as home), as long as different social referents generate role conflict about

attendance. However, an individual can attend only one setting because attendance is merely physical presence there.

For decades researchers have often ascribed many causes to absence, leading to distinctions between involuntary and voluntary absences. Such attributions are problematic, especially when they are applied to absence measures. Those attributions can be made only on the basis of empirical relationships between absences and other variables and on solid estimates of the proportions of observed variance because of latent voluntary or involuntary factors.

Absenteeism is a narrowly defined construct. Some researchers have suggested that absence be entrenched in a broader psychological construct such as avoidance of work, withdrawal from the work role, or adaptation to the work environment. Studying absence as an isolated phenomenon is likely to undermine the practitioners' focus on prediction, because of an absence's high proportions of specific, dynamic, and random variance. By combining many related behaviors (e.g., lateness, grievance filing, sabotage) into a broader construct or behavioral family, the combination might be characterized by more common variance and could be more readily predictable.

Widening the scope of the construct in which to embed absence might improve its predictability. Nevertheless, abandoning the study of absence in favor of the study of work role withdrawal and adaptation is premature. One reason is that those constructs, especially the latter, might be overly broad. Job adaptation could comprise almost any work-related behavior. Another reason is that the terms themselves imply causes for the constructs, and that the purported determinants of the constructs are often part of their stated definitions. That is, the behavioral constructs have been described as responses to negative work attitudes.

Virtually all absence research has been based on variance theories. A variance theory is one that states that X is a necessary and sufficient condition for the outcome Y. In other words, Y is completely determined by X. As such, variance theories of absence suggest that the underlying mechanisms that drive absence are mechanistic. (Remember, in conventional ordinary least squares [OLS] regression, R^2 has a maximum value of 1.0 and unexplained variance is determined by the equation $1 - R^2$.) Thus absence researchers have constructed theories with the prime objective of maximizing the variance explained in the dependent variable by the independent variables, and random variance is considered error.

Researchers should not always evaluate the merits of a theory solely on percentage of variance explained. First, conceptual parsimony may be more preferable than maximization of explained variance if the latter comes with the cost of ambiguity. Second, it is possible to find statistically significant results on the basis of chance alone.

Some have challenged the convention that a *good* theory of absence explains all the variance by arguing that stochastic or process theories may be better suited for explaining absence than variance theories. Essentially, a process theory tells a little story about how something comes about; but to qualify as a theoretical explanation of recurrent behavior, the manner of the storytelling must conform to narrow specifications. A process theory is defined as follows:

- X is a necessary condition for Y, but not a sufficient condition.
- X will cause Y stochastically (using a random variable).

That is, whether X causes Y depends on some probabilistic process. Thus process theories, unlike variance theories, leave residual uncertainty by construction.

A prominent process theory of absence suggests that absence reflects the dynamic operation of a set of motives, all of which are time varying. Thus to explain the timing of absence and attendance, consider the changing strength of motives to attend work and motives to engage in activities that require absence from work. Unfulfilled motives increase in strength with time, and this changing motive strength can be modeled as a set of differential equations. Thus if all motives were internal, there were not external constraints on time allocation, and a person could act on motives without cost, the individual could construct a deterministic model of time allocation and fully explain the timing and duration of activities. However, random events such as work stoppages, accidents, and illness impose external constraints on time allocation.

The notion of process theories highlights the probability of many possible constructs that could be causes or consequences of absenteeism. However, different sets of researchers have sliced out different sets of explanatory constructs and investigated them using simple hypotheses, all based on variance theories.

The most prominent simple hypothesis is the work attitude–absence hypothesis, in which absenteeism results from negative work attitudes, which are a function of aversive work environments or dissatisfying work experiences. This is the benchmark hypothesis studied since the early 1950s and subject to more investigations than any other hypothesis about absenteeism. Meta-analyses show that work attitudes typically are not strong predictors of absenteeism. Attitude theory suggests that for there to be a relationship between an attitude and behavior or occurrence, both must correspond in terms of their levels of specificity. Job satisfaction, organizational commitment, and job involvement are general attitudes; and absence is a specific behavior. Thus we do not necessarily expect a strong relationship.

Some researchers have argued that absence reflects inherent and long-standing personality characteristics that account for the moderate stability of absence over time and situations. *Absence proneness* emerged as the explanatory concept. However, unlike most other personality characteristics, which are measured through conventional psychological scales, absence proneness has been inferred through less conventional methods. For example, some researchers have inferred absence proneness from the relationship between prior absence and subsequent absence, arguing that those who tend to be absent more in a given period will continue to be absent more in later periods.

Absence can be influenced by factors outside an individual's control, including weather conditions, transportation modes and routes, and personal health. Further, perceived control over attendance may also be an important determinant of work absences, more so perhaps than actual control. Albert Bandura's social cognitive theory provides a basis for the relationship between perceived control and behavior. Perceptions of control over attendance may be a function of past attendance experiences and structural interferences or role conflict between the demands of the work setting and the demands of other settings.

Some theorists have attempted to combine some of the simple theories for integrative theories. However, most are completely inductive integrations, and their usefulness depends on their fit to future data. Others are more properly called frameworks than theories because they specify collections of variables rather than relations between well-defined constructs. To be tested completely, these theories require the operationalization of large numbers of variables in consort. These frameworks have serious flaws, not the least of which is that they all posit relations between extremely broad explanatory constructs and a very narrow dependent construct.

Perhaps absence-specific attitudes, social pressures, perceived environmental constraints, and work morals or ethics can all be modeled as part of an absence or participation decision process. Many researchers have implicitly espoused a decision-making perspective on absenteeism. Despite the potential for overcoming past limitations and integrating diverse findings, only a few investigations of absence have explicitly used a decision-making approach.

Some researchers have maintained that absenteeism is a differentiated phenomenon based on causes attributed to each absence occurrence by the absentee. Potential absence-inducing events should be classified by the freedom those events provide an individual in deciding whether or not to stay away from work. For example, a variety of employees were in home interviews asked to make attributions of their prior absences as well as potential future absences. The vast majority of individuals attributed prior and potential future absence to factors beyond personal control, such as illness, rather than to events within their own control, such as leisure activities. Attributing absence to medical illness is consistent with evolving social beliefs about what constitutes acceptable reasons for absence in a particular context. This conclusion is consistent with research demonstrating that medical absence was systematically related to work and nonwork motives.

Research has found additional factors related to a decision to be absent from work. Using an expectancy theory framework, some researchers have hypothesized that hobby and leisure time, kinship responsibilities, and personal illness influence absence decisions. Others found that absence was related to the value of nonwork hours, which supports the view that absence is a function of motivation processes extant in work and nonwork domains. One set of authors used a policy capturing design to model individual decisions to be absent based on the factors previously reviewed. Employees responded to hypothetical scenarios describing factors that might contribute to their decisions to be absent on a particular day. The relative importance of the antecedents of absence decisions varied substantially across individuals. With the exception of personal illness, which was a significant factor for all employees, some factors that resulted in significantly higher estimated absence for some individuals led to significantly lower estimated absence

for others—including hobby or leisure activities, work demands, and day of the week. Although these studies suggest several factors relating to absence decisions, this area of research is largely in an exploratory stage.

One notable development in absence research has been a growing awareness of the importance and mistreatment of time. Some researchers have argued that the ordering of relationships, in time, should prompt researchers to work through their conceptual schemes and methodological choices more deeply and increase the yield of future studies. Slightly more than half used a postdictive design, which seems to be roughly the same proportion overall. This state of affairs raises serious questions about the true sequence of absenteeism's origins and outcomes. For example, job satisfaction is the affective variable most often connected with absenteeism, in an approach that treats absences as responses to aversive work environments. However, in studies designed to evaluate the reverse ordering, both postdictive and predictive correlations are roughly the same size.

—*Joseph J. Martocchio*

See also Withdrawal Behaviors, Lateness; Withdrawal Behaviors, Turnover

FURTHER READING

Harrison, D. A., & Martocchio, J. J. (1998). It's time for absence: A 20-year review of origins, offshoots, and outcomes. *Journal of Management, 24,* 305–350.

Hulin, C. L. (1991). Adaptation, persistence, and commitment in organizations. In M. D. Dunnette (Ed.), *Handbook of industrial and organizational psychology* (2nd ed., pp. 445–505). New York: Wiley.

Hulin, C. L., Henry, R., & Noon, S. (1990). Adding a dimension: Time as a factor in the generalizability of predictive relations. *Psychological Bulletin, 107,* 328–340.

Johns, G. (1997). Contemporary research on absence from work: Correlates, causes, and consequences. In C. L. Cooper & L. T. Robertson (Eds.), *International review of industrial and organizational psychology* (Vol. 12, pp. 115–173). New York: Wiley.

Martocchio, J. J., & Harrison, D. A. (1993). To be there or not to be there? Questions, theories, and methods in absence research. *Research in Personnel and Human Resources Management, 11,* 259–329.

Steel, R. P. (1990). Psychometric theory and the problem of relating prior and subsequent absences. *Journal of Organizational Behavior, 11*(5), 407–411.

Steel, R. P., & Rentsch, J. R. (1995). Influence of cumulation strategies on the long-range prediction of absenteeism. *Academy of Management Journal, 38*(6), 1616–1634.

WITHDRAWAL BEHAVIORS, LATENESS

In organizational research employee lateness can be considered the orphan of behavioral outcomes. Compared with absence and turnover, the two other commonly studied withdrawal behaviors in the field, investigations of lateness and its correlates are much fewer in number; and perhaps more important, they are not anywhere as rich in theoretical explanations of the underlying construct. In organizations with set time schedules, lateness has traditionally been defined as arrival after the beginning of the workday. Both the individual and the organization suffer from employee lateness. An individual coming late may be docked some pay or, if it continues at an unabated rate, may be asked to leave. Because time can be translated into money, an employee, such as a worker on an assembly line or a salesperson in a department store, who does not arrive at work at the scheduled time may have a negative impact on the firm's performance. At the simplest level, this can be seen in the loss of work hours. A late arrival, particularly if the function performed at work is critical, may disrupt an organization's production schedule. Even when the employee is part of a service-oriented organization, the individual's lateness may affect the quality or quantity of service offered, especially when fellow workers or consumers depend directly or indirectly on the latecomer's presence.

CHARACTERISTICS OF LATENESS

In common with absenteeism and other organizational behaviors such as poor performance, employee lateness may have an element of neglect and disrespect toward work associated with it. In most cases its *psychological* message to others is negative. When some employees are tardy, morale and work motivation within the organization are likely to deteriorate. Thus a coworker who sees a colleague constantly arriving late, particularly if sanctions are not clearly defined or apparent, may start to think along the same lines and begin to change behavior.

Nevertheless, lateness differs from most other organizational behaviors in that it is often partially or entirely *invisible* from view. As compared with absence and turnover, lateness is less apparent and more readily hidden. Absences are relatively prominent as both supervisors and coworkers are aware when they have occurred. Similarly, turnover, an employee leaving one job and going to work somewhere else, is difficult to hide. Moreover, depending on the employee's position in the organization and the relevant policy, a late arrival may or may not be noted in personnel files. Absences, however, are nearly always recorded in an individual's file. This difference between the quality of the data collected may largely explain the fact that the literature contains many more empirical studies of absence and turnover than lateness.

CONCEPTUALIZING EMPLOYEE LATENESS

Although there are some suggestions in the literature that absence and tardiness are unrelated or even negatively related, the weight of the empirical evidence indicates that at least a moderate positive association should be expected. One popular notion in the field is that lateness is the first stage of a withdrawal sequence. In such a scenario, lateness is perceived as a more moderate response, which may continue until a stage of voluntary leaving, the most extreme expression of withdrawal, is attained. The assumption here is that an underlying mechanism exists, gradually leading a person to engage in more severe forms of withdrawal. Accordingly, an increase in perceived work problems will lead to more extreme behaviors. Attitudes such as dissatisfaction with the job or with the working conditions may very well serve as the underlying cause or so-called problem leading employees to arrive late.

Antecedents of Lateness

If one assumes that the outcome measure of lateness is a volitional act chosen by an employee, it is possible to posit three levels of variables that play a role here: personal, group or organizational, and extraorganizational. The first type of variable includes attitudinal measures and personality. Without a doubt, the two attitudinal indicators, job satisfaction and organizational commitment, have been the focus of a majority of the studies in the field. Findings have generally shown a moderately negative correlation between these antecedents and lateness. Recently, organizational researchers have started to consider variables other than attitudes and, in particular, personality indicators as possible predictors. The latter had been neglected or rejected for decades; but because of new instruments such as the Big Five dimensions (in particular, conscientiousness and emotional stability), moderate personality–lateness associations have been observed. Some investigators have argued that the role of personality is more likely to be seen as a moderator than as a direct predictor.

One particular personality measure, punctuality, has been found in some cases to be associated with lateness. Interestingly, this measure has wider applications than just work-related lateness. Unlike the other common withdrawal behaviors, lateness has clear counterparts in non-work-related activities. An individual chronically late for work may also be tardy when meeting friends, getting to a wedding or other celebration, or starting out on a vacation.

The group and organizational variables are said to exist within a specific work environment where common policies, norms, and work values differ significantly from those held among other groups or in other organizations. The basis for many of these antecedents is management policy, leadership style, organizational culture, organizational learning, reward, and formal or informal intraorganizational communication. Such policy may include the type of sanctions meted out for lateness or the degree of tolerance for some type of lateness behavior conveyed by management. It is very likely that within-group homogeneity will be accompanied by other shared attitudes and behaviors.

The next level of antecedents includes extraorganizational variables. The variables of interest here are those that neither the individual nor the organization can control. The most blatant examples in the literature include national culture, values, environment, and even international considerations. In the larger society, values, common beliefs, and assumptions help form certain norms that influence attitudes and behavior. The concepts of work time, leisure time, and lateness behavior vary considerably across nations. More specifically, time perceptions have been shown to be at least partially related to cultural contexts. In some societies arriving one minute after the start of a meeting would be frowned on, whereas in others, lateness of as much as one hour would not be considered inappropriate behavior.

In conclusion, a few words about a relatively new and promising variable seem in order here. By broadening the whole notion of organizational antecedents, job embeddedness provides a construct that is actually composed of personal-, organizational-, and extraorganizational-level variables. It includes three major dimensions:

1. Perceptions of fit with job, organization, and community

2. Links with job, organization, and community

3. Sacrifices entailed by leaving the job

An individual who is high on this measure may very well find it difficult to manifest any type of organizational withdrawal behavior.

LATENESS AND THE NEW WORK ENVIRONMENT

At this point a word or two about recent changes in the work environment and their impact on withdrawal research, in general, and lateness, in particular, is warranted. Definitions and pertinent measures may need to be revised. For example, is lateness or absence still a legitimate concept in an organization that allows employees to work at home rather than at the office or headquarters (i.e., telecommuting)? Similarly, does flextime allow the manager to calculate lateness for each employee? Perhaps most important, an expansion and consideration of other forms of lateness or *work* withdrawal are needed. One broad change might include missing work any time of the day, not only at the beginning. Workers who do not put in a full day of work even though they arrived *on time* can be placed into this new category. This expansion of the lateness concept allows us to study many situations that occur frequently in the modern organization. Thus workers who spend an inordinate amount of time surfing the Internet for personal reasons, leave the office for long lunch breaks, or leave early would all be subsumed in the new and broader category of lateness.

Future Directions

Again, it will be important, theoretically and practically, to understand the relationship between the classical definitions of lateness, the new concept of hours missed any time during the workday, and the new work environments. At present, the various types of missed work hours are just too difficult to gage, and employers do not have any objective or systematic way of recording such behavior. Nevertheless, it goes without saying that organizations, although becoming more open to different types of working environments, must consider the various forms of lateness and develop policies for monitoring and, if need be, sanctioning such misbehaviors.

SUMMARY

Management has a clear and present need to control all types of lateness, classical as well as the new kind. Through an understanding of the process, controlling or at least minimizing the negative effects of withdrawal may be attainable. Moreover, if there is a sequential component involved here, it may be more effective to deal with lateness at the beginning of the process rather than at a later stage when the costs become greater. Employee lateness is not unidimensional, in its antecedents or its outcome, and the awareness of this fact allows for a greater understanding of the whole phenomenon.

—*Meni Koslowsky*

See also Attitudes and Beliefs; Withdrawal Behaviors, Absenteeism; Withdrawal Behaviors, Turnover

FURTHER READING

Adler, S., and Golan, J. (1981). Lateness as a withdrawal behavior. *Journal of Applied Psychology, 5,* 544–554.

Blau, G. J. (1994). Developing and testing a taxonomy of lateness behavior. *Journal of Applied Psychology, 79,* 959–970.

Furnham, A. (1992). *Personality at work.* London: Routledge.

Koslowsky, M., Sagie, A., Krausz, M., & Dolman, A. (1997). Correlates of employee lateness: Some theoretical considerations. *Journal of Applied Psychology, 82,* 79–88.

Landy, F. J., Rastegary, H., Thayer, J., & Colvin, C. (1991). Time urgency: The construct and its measurement. *Journal of Applied Psychology, 76,* 644–657.

Mobley, W. H., Griffeth, R. W., Hand, H. H., & Meglino, B. M. (1979). Review and conceptual analysis of the employee turnover process. *Psychological Bulletin, 86,* 493–522.

WITHDRAWAL BEHAVIORS, TURNOVER

In its simplest form, turnover refers to whether an employee stays or leaves. Refinements in the measurement and definition of turnover have led researchers to consider the *voluntariness, avoidability,* and *functionality* of turnover. Voluntary turnover refers to situations in which employees have an opportunity to remain with their employer but choose to leave. Involuntary turnover refers to situations where employees do not have a choice concerning continued employment, such as employer-initiated termination. Turnover has been conceptualized as avoidable when the reasons for leaving are related to the organization, including low pay and long hours, and unavoidable when reasons are not work related, such as spouse relocation and family demands. Finally, turnover that benefits the organization, such as when high performers stay and low performers leave, has been termed functional turnover, whereas the opposite pattern is thought to reflect dysfunctional turnover. Although these three dimensions are defined by their extremes, they are perhaps better captured along a continuum in practice.

KEY MODELS AND CRITICAL ANTECEDENTS

Content Models

Content models attempt to specify antecedent variables that help predict employee turnover. At least 50 different predictors have been examined in previous research including demographic variables, work attitudes, intentions and cognitions related to quitting, and job search activities. Meta-analysis procedures have been used to summarize the strength of the relationships that have been found in previous research between these antecedents and turnover behaviors. In general, these results reveal modest effects. In absolute terms, few relationships exceed .30, and most are less than .20.

As a class, demographic variables such as education, marital status, and age are only weakly related to turnover. For other demographic variables such as race, gender, and cognitive ability the average correlation is near 0. There are two notable exceptions to this general pattern of findings. Turnover tends to be greater for employees with children and employees with longer tenure, but these effects are fairly small.

Work attitudes have a long history of research in the turnover literature. In particular, low to moderate negative relationships have been found between job satisfaction and turnover, and between organizational commitment and turnover. Weaker associations have been found for specific facets of satisfaction, such as satisfaction with a supervisor, coworkers, pay, promotion opportunities, and work content. Perceived organizational support (POS), which involves employee beliefs about how much their organization values and supports them, has been found to correlate negatively with turnover intentions and actual turnover. Research on organizational justice supports the contention that perceived unfairness is associated with greater levels of employee turnover. In particular, justice dimensions (i.e., procedural, distributive, interactional) have shown negative relationships with intentions to quit and turnover, suggesting that employees who feel they are treated fairly in terms of outcome allocations, procedures, and interpersonal treatment are more likely to remain with the organization.

Perhaps the strongest predictor of turnover is the employee's reported intentions to quit. Similarly, withdrawal cognitions and thinking of quitting are positively related to actual turnover, as are job search intentions and behaviors. As a class, cognitions and intentions related to quitting along with job search activities represent the best predictors of turnover to date. Although also positively related to turnover, perceptions of available alternatives and comparisons of these alternatives with one's present job tend to show somewhat weaker associations.

Other variables that have been studied in relation to turnover include actual pay, stress, lateness, absenteeism, and job performance. Weak, positive effects have been found for stress-related variables, lateness, and absenteeism. Weak, negative effects have been found for pay and job performance. Overall, content models of turnover help identify *what* variables predict quitting behavior on the part of employees. Process models, which are reviewed next, conceptually organize these variables to help understand *how* employees make these decisions.

Process Models

One of the earliest process models emphasized the importance of two factors in explaining turnover behavior: the perceived desirability of movement and the perceived ease of movement. Put forth in the late 1950s, the basic idea of the model is that employees will quit when they are unhappy with their jobs and when they feel that there are alternative employment opportunities available. Thus, desirability of movement has been assessed through measures of job satisfaction, whereas ease of movement has been captured through some measure of alternative job opportunities. Empirical tests of this two-factor approach have revealed fairly weak relationships with turnover. As a result, many of the later models have expanded the

network of antecedent variables and have offered new perspectives on the causal sequencing of these dimensions. These approaches have been called *intermediate linkage models* and reflect the growing complexity of turnover models that have dominated the literature since the 1970s. The logic of this perspective is that job dissatisfaction prompts employees to think about quitting and evaluate the costs and benefits of searching for another job. At that point employees may develop intentions to search for another job, actually carry out the search, and evaluate the alternatives that are found. If these alternatives are more favorable than the current job, employees will develop intentions to quit, followed by actual turnover. Variations on this basic model have appeared in the literature, and as a class, the intermediate linkage models have received modest empirical support. Meta-analysis data revealed the strongest support for a reduced linkage model that included only the linkages between dissatisfaction, withdrawal cognitions, and turnover.

Given the generally low predictive power of earlier models, new approaches to the study of turnover processes have emerged since the 1990s. The unfolding model of employee turnover represents one of these recent advancements and draws from basic research in decision making and social psychology. The approach suggests that multiple decision paths underlie turnover, and some of these do not involve much thought or planning on the part of the employee. The model introduces the notion of *shocks to the system,* or a particular jarring event that initiates deliberate judgments by employees concerning their employment relationship. Examples include receiving unsolicited job offers, experiencing a merger, and spouse relocation. These shocks are said to prompt different script-driven actions, which may or may not lead to a search for alternatives, lower job satisfaction, and actual quitting. The model is more complex than previous approaches and emphasizes the timing and sequencing of events to explain when, why, and how employees leave. In particular, four paths are specified by the model to explain the different ways in which employees leave their jobs. The first path is characterized by a shock to the system in combination with a plan for leaving. For example, employees may accept a position with full knowledge that they will quit once some period of time passes or they earn a specific amount of money. Once the shock occurs (e.g., three months have passed), the employee quits. It is important to note that traditional antecedents of turnover such as dissatisfaction and search for alternatives do not enter the process. The second path also involves a shock to the system but does not include a specific plan or script concerning alternative jobs. For example, some employees may quit spontaneously after receiving a harsh review, learning of an ill family member, or being given new, unwanted job responsibilities. The third path in the model is more gradual in that the shock leads to minor dissatisfaction and a search for alternatives. As an example, employees who receive unsolicited job offers (i.e., a shock to the system) may begin to contemplate their satisfaction relative to the new alternatives, and eventually quit after thoughtful deliberation. The fourth and final path is characterized by dissatisfaction compounded over time, which may or may not be coupled with an active search for alternatives. For example, employees may decide that after several years of work, the job falls short of their expectations. In response, some employees will quit without an alternative in hand, whereas others will leave on finding an alternative that is more attractive. Note that this final path is most closely associated with the traditional approach of the intermediate linkages model that dissatisfaction leads to intentions to leave and actually leaving. There is some empirical support for the paths outlined in the unfolding model, although additional research is certainly needed to refine the model and replicate these effects.

It is also important to note the existence of a wide range of economic models that help explain turnover. These approaches emphasize labor market conditions such as the availability of alternatives or the supply and demand of labor. Because these models tend to focus on factors unrelated to the individual, they are not reviewed here.

NEW DIRECTIONS

Over time, approaches to the study of turnover have become more complex. The unfolding model of turnover is one approach that pushes turnover theory and research in new directions. Research has also shown that simple correlational designs can oversimplify relationships between antecedent variables and turnover. Studies that account for interactions among antecedents reveal that simple additive relationships may be insufficient for explaining turnover behavior. In addition, researchers have found support for nonlinear effects in some instances.

Another avenue of inquiry that holds promise concerns the study of those factors that promote retention of employees. Although on the surface one might expect that the same set of factors would be responsible for both turnover and retention, researchers have shown that there may be subtle but important differences in the processes underlying these phenomena. Researchers have proposed the construct of *job embeddedness* to capture the broad set of factors that cause individuals to remain with their employer. The concept builds on earlier turnover models that included both work and nonwork factors to explain why employees quit. The components of job embeddedness include the following:

- Links to others within and outside the organization
- Employees' perceptions of fit with their work and community
- Assessments of what employees would have to sacrifice if they left their jobs

Empirical evidence shows that job embeddedness explains incremental variance in both turnover intentions and actual turnover beyond work attitudes and job alternatives.

Finally, there is recent research that synthesizes research on both turnover and attachment processes and proposes a set of eight motivational forces that can help explain intentions and decisions related to quitting or staying with an organization. These forces and a description of each are in the following list:

1. *Affective:* Reflects the emotional responses toward the organization; emotional comfort motivates attachment, while discomfort motivates quitting.

2. *Calculative:* Reflects a rational assessment of the probability of attaining goals within the organization in the future; favorable assessments motivate attachment, whereas unfavorable assessments motivate quitting.

3. *Contractual:* Reflects a response to norms of reciprocity based on psychological contracts; fulfillment of obligations motivates staying, whereas perceived violations motivate quitting.

4. *Behavioral:* Reflects the actual and perceived costs of quitting; higher costs motivate staying, whereas lower costs motivate quitting.

5. *Alternative:* Reflects self-efficacy toward finding an alternative opportunity; low self-efficacy motivates staying, whereas high self-efficacy motivates quitting.

6. *Normative:* Reflects motivation to comply with perceived expectations of others concerning turnover

decisions; high motivation to comply with expectations to remain motivates staying, whereas high motivation to comply with expectations to leave motivates quitting.

7. *Moral and ethical:* Reflects a desire to maintain consistency between values and beliefs about turnover; values that emphasize persistence motivate staying, whereas values that emphasize change or variety motivate quitting.

8. *Constituent:* Reflects the degree to which employees feel attachment toward others within the organization; high attachment to constituents motivates staying, while low attachment motivates quitting.

Overall, the model of motivational forces provides a parsimonious taxonomy of the array of factors that lead employees to quit. Further, they also fill a gap in the literature by specifying the conceptual processes that link antecedent variables such as work attitudes with turnover and retention outcomes. Like the unfolding model, the motivational forces also offer an opportunity to account for changing relationships among variables over time. Empirical research that tests the value of these proposed advantages is needed.

PRACTICAL RECOMMENDATIONS

Given the costs often associated with turnover, a number of suggestions for reducing and managing turnover have been suggested in the academic and practitioner literatures. Most follow from empirical research, but many of the techniques themselves have yet to be subjected to rigorous empirical evaluation.

- *Identify the nature and extent of turnover:* Find out where turnover is greatest and identify the extent to which it is functional versus dysfunctional; ensure that retention efforts are targeting the right people.
- *Enrich the job:* Look for ways to improve the job itself; consider ways to restructure the job to reduce monotony and improve employee motivation.
- *Train supervisors:* Many employees leave supervisors, not the job; provide supervisors with continuous training and updating in management skills; use feedback from direct reports, peers, supervisors, and other constituents to help supervisors gain perspective.
- *Promote fairness in the workplace:* Communicate difficult decisions with respect and concern for those affected; allow employees to participate in decisions that will affect their jobs; enforce rules and procedures consistently across employees.

- *Monitor employee attitudes:* Implement regular employee opinion surveys and act on the findings; consider including measures of job satisfaction, organizational commitment, and organizational fairness.
- *Provide incentives to stay:* Tie rewards to tenure; consider awarding perks that enhance embeddedness in the organization and community.
- *Offer realistic previews of the job:* Employees may quit because of a mismatch between their expectations and the reality of what the job involves; provide a reasonable perspective on both the positive and negative aspects of the job.
- *Attend to nonwork needs:* Consider employees' needs outside the work domain; some companies have responded by providing services and programs such as flexible work arrangements, on-site child care, fitness facilities, tuition reimbursement, concierge services, and eldercare benefits.

—*John P. Hausknecht*

See also Withdrawal Behaviors, Absenteeism; Withdrawal Behaviors, Lateness

FURTHER READING

Griffeth, R. W., Hom, P. W., & Gaertner, S. (2000). A meta-analysis of antecedents and correlates of employee turnover: Update, moderator tests, and research implications for the next millennium. *Journal of Management, 26,* 463–488.

Hom, P. W., Caranikas-Walker, F., Prussia, G. E., & Griffeth, R. W. (1992). A meta-analytical structural equations analysis of a model of employee turnover. *Journal of Applied Psychology, 78,* 890–909.

Lee, T. W., & Mitchell, T. R. (1994). An alternative approach: The unfolding model of voluntary employee turnover. *Academy of Management Review, 19,* 51–89.

Maertz, C. P., Jr., & Campion, M. A. (1998). 25 years of voluntary turnover research: A review and critique. *International Review of Industrial and Organizational Psychology, 13,* 49–81.

Maertz, C. P., Jr., & Griffeth, R. W. (2004). Eight motivational forces and voluntary turnover: A theoretical synthesis with implications for research. *Journal of Management, 30,* 667–683.

Mitchell, T. R., Holtom, B. C., Lee, T. W., Sablynski, C. J., & Erez, M. (2001). Why people stay: Using job embeddedness to predict voluntary turnover. *Academy of Management Journal, 44,* 1102–1121.

Mobley, W. H. (1977). Intermediate linkages in the relationship between job satisfaction and employee turnover. *Journal of Applied Psychology, 62,* 237–240.

Trevor, C. (2001). Interactions among actual ease-of-movement determinants and job satisfaction in the prediction of voluntary turnover. *Academy of Management Journal, 44,* 621–638.

WORKAHOLISM

Workaholism is a popular term used to describe individuals who are captivated by work. The term *workaholic* was first coined more than 30 years ago to refer to an individual whose increased need to work hinders one or more life functions. Over the years it has become a colloquial term used increasingly in the popular press, on Web sites, and in the scientific literature. The philosophy of squeezing more of everything into a single 24-hour day has become an accepted way of life. In fact, working excessive hours is often seen as a prerequisite for success. As a result it appears that some individuals may find it extremely difficult to release themselves from work, even when they are given the opportunity to do so.

DEFINITIONAL ISSUES

Although the term *workaholism* has become commonplace, unfortunately, there has been little empirical research (and consensus) examining what it means when someone is referred to as a workaholic. The modest amount of existing research has been done in a fragmentary manner; without a common definition, it becomes challenging to develop a holistic picture of workaholism. Definitional issues pertaining to workaholism are summarized in the following text.

A commonly held perspective is that workaholism is simply an extreme form of job involvement. Although the two constructs have been considered synonymous in the practitioner literature, job involvement is clearly distinct from workaholism in that job involvement has an attitudinal component regarding work, whereas workaholism refers to behavioral patterns and an overall outlook on work. High job involvement does not necessarily relate to workaholism in that workers might be highly engaged in their jobs and consider work as a key element in their lives; but they may not be workaholics (e.g., they can still leave work at the end of an eight-hour day and not think about it until returning to work the next day). Hence, workaholism is not merely an extreme case of job involvement.

In an attempt to define workaholism, some researchers have placed a quantitative requirement on its borders in that the total number of hours worked per week determines workaholic tendencies. Surprisingly, the literature has generally shown that hours worked alone do not indicate a workaholic. Many external reasons, such as the need for money or the organizational climate (i.e., overall atmosphere of the organization), may account for the long work hours. Therefore, perhaps workaholics are (in part) those individuals who are intrinsically motivated to work long hours because of an inability to disengage from work.

Other researchers have highlighted the opposite end of the continuum such as attitudes and value-based characteristics of workaholism. These researchers conceptualize workaholism in terms of the attitude of the worker in regard to the job including enthusiasm, commitment, and involvement. Another emergent body of literature has defined workaholism as consisting of three behavioral tendencies:

1. Spending discretionary time in work activities

2. Thinking about work when not at work

3. Working beyond organizational or economic requirements

Despite the plethora of definitions considered to describe workaholism, Janet Spence and Ann Robbins's instrument is by far the most frequently used self-report measure of workaholism. Similar to other recent conceptualizations of workaholism, their scale consists of three factors that constitute workaholism:

1. Excessive work involvement

2. Drivenness to work

3. Lack of work enjoyment

Work involvement refers to the extent to which individuals constructively use their time (both on and off the job) and dedicate themselves to productivity at work. Drivenness to work reflects an individual's internal drive to work. Work enjoyment is the degree to which an individual derives pleasure from work.

WHY SHOULD WE CARE?

Workaholism is detrimental to individual well-being, causing stress, burnout, anxiety, and health complaints.

Additionally, workaholics are more prone to such secondary addictions as alcoholism and overeating. Workaholism may also affect the lives of the people with whom the workaholic employee is associated. Excessive engagement in work is likely to disrupt work–life balance, such as balancing both personal and family needs with work demands, and may hinder interpersonal relationships. In fact, spouses and children of workaholics feel lonely, unloved, and emotionally or physically abandoned; workaholism puts a strain on marital relations and is a leading cause of divorce. Finally, workaholism results in negative organizational outcomes (e.g., absenteeism, turnover). In fact, the high (and likely unrealistic) standards set by workaholic managers could lead to resentment, conflict, and low morale among coworkers. The excessive costs of workaholism to the self, the family, and the organization itself warrant that individuals pay closer attention to this crucial concept.

WORKAHOLISM SYNDROME

In the medical field, a syndrome refers to a cluster of symptoms occurring on a regular basis and thus constituting a disease to which some particular name is applied. The concept of a syndrome has been used in psychological research to characterize, among many other areas, burnout, effects of physical abuse in women, and posttraumatic stress. For example, burnout is characterized as a syndrome of emotional exhaustion, depersonalization, and reduced personal accomplishment. Hence, people who experience burnout feel these characteristics in tandem.

Similarly, the workaholic is portrayed by a set of distinct characteristics. In this sense workaholism is also conceptualized as a multifaceted syndrome in that a set of key components characterizes the workaholic. Employees who experience high work involvement, high drive to work, and low work enjoyment in conjunction with each other are more likely to be workaholics than those who just experience a subset of the symptoms. For workaholism to truly be a syndrome, each of the three components is a necessary (though not sufficient) condition for somebody to be classified as a workaholic.

A large stream of research has found that typical variables associated with workaholism include job involvement, work stress, and work–life imbalance. The empirical literature has also shown that workaholics experience less job and life satisfaction than nonworkaholics. To create effective intervention programs, it is imperative that both the correlates and symptoms of workaholism be taken into account by mental health professionals and career counselors. A dimensional focus enables practitioners and their clients to examine specific correlates of workaholism instead of the global construct. For example, in terms of work–life balance, it is imperative that workplace standards be more supportive of balanced priorities and healthier lifestyles to encourage those workaholics who strive to make behavioral changes.

—*Shahnaz Aziz*

See also Work–Life Balance

FURTHER READING

Harpaz, I., & Snir, R. (2003). Workaholism: Its definition and nature. *Human Relations, 56,* 291–319.

McMillan, L. H. W., Brady, E. C., O'Driscoll, M. P., & Marsh, N. V. (2002). A multifaceted validation study of Spence and Robbins' (1992) Workaholism Battery. *Journal of Occupational and Organizational Psychology, 75,* 357–368.

Mudrack, P. E., & Naughton, T. J. (2001). The assessment of workaholism as behavioral tendencies: Scale development and preliminary empirical testing. *International Journal of Stress Management, 8,* 93–111.

Spence, J. T., & Robbins, A. S. (1992). Workaholism: Definition, measurement, and preliminary results. *Journal of Personality Assessment, 58,* 160–178.

WORK ETHIC

See PROTESTANT WORK ETHIC

WORK–LIFE BALANCE

Work and family are considered the primary domains in a person's life. The interface between the work and family domains of life is studied across psychology subfields (e.g., clinical, developmental, social) and by other disciplines (e.g., anthropology, sociology, family studies, economics, women's studies). Industrial/organizational (I/O) psychologists are interested primarily in how interactions between work life and family life, or more broadly the *nonwork* aspects of one's life, influence important individual and organizational outcomes. *Work–life* or *work–family balance* refers to the extent to which an individual is able to meet the often competing demands associated with work and nonwork roles. The terms *work–family* and *work–life* are often used interchangeably; but *family* sometimes refers more specifically to familial roles (e.g., spouse, parent), whereas *life* may refer more broadly to familial roles and other nonwork roles (e.g., church member, community volunteer). Because most research has focused on the interface between work and family roles, the term *work–family* is used here. The term *balance* is sometimes criticized in the literature because it implies an *equal* investment in work and family that may not be sought or required to achieve harmony among work and other life roles. Research shows that some individuals report greater balance when investments in work and family roles are unequal.

MODELS OF THE WORK–FAMILY INTERFACE

Traditionally the work–family interface has been conceptualized in terms of several different models, including segmentation, compensation, spillover, and conflict. The *segmentation* model holds that the work and family domains are largely separate and have little interaction in an individual's life. The *compensation* model contends that the domains can serve a complementary function in that deficiencies a person experiences in one domain can be made up for in the other (e.g., a happy home life may compensate for a dissatisfying job). The *spillover* model assumes that a person's experiences in one domain seep over into the other, acknowledging that the spillover may be either positive or negative. Having an argument with a coworker and then being impatient at home with children is an example of negative work-to-family spillover. Enjoying a relaxing weekend with family followed by a productive Monday at work is an example of positive family-to-work spillover.

WORK–FAMILY CONFLICT

It is the *conflict* model that has dominated theory and research on the work–family interface in I/O psychology. The basic premise of the conflict perspective is that work and family roles are incompatible; they compete with and interfere with one another for an individual's limited resources. Thus researchers most often study the nature of conflict or interference between work and family roles, the predictors of such conflicts, and the consequences of work–family conflict. Early research considered work–family conflict in general, but research on the topic has evolved to specify the direction of conflict, both work interference with family and family interference with work. Research shows that individuals experience greater work interference with family than family interference with work. Compared with work boundaries, family boundaries are considered more permeable, and the family domain is more accommodating of work demands than the reverse.

In addition to the directionality of conflict, research also considers conflict's dimensionality. Typical forms of work–family conflict include time-based, strain-based, and behavior-based conflicts. *Time-based* conflicts occur when time devoted to one role makes it difficult to meet responsibilities of another role. For example, working late may interfere with picking up children from school. *Strain-based* conflicts happen when the strains associated with one role interfere or infringe on another role. For example, marital strife may interfere with concentration at work. And finally, *behavior-based* conflicts result when behaviors required in one role are incompatible or inconsistent with behaviors required in another role. For example, a supervisor may find that giving direct orders gets things accomplished at work, but the same tactic produces negative results at home. Each form of conflict can occur in both directions; for example, time-based work interference with family and time-based family interference with work.

Antecedents of Work–Family Conflict

Numerous antecedents of work–family conflict have been studied. Research shows that work stressors, lack of control or unpredictability in work routines or scheduling, long work hours, high work demands, and job stress are all associated with greater work–family conflict. Work–family conflict also tends to be greater for those who have more children, younger children, high caregiving demands such as elderly parents or chronically ill children, little family support, and high family stress. Often, however, antecedents do not have simple direct effects on work–family conflict. For example, although long work hours are generally associated with greater work–family conflict, this is especially the case when an individual is required to work more hours than desired.

In terms of individual differences, higher levels of negative affectivity and neuroticism and lower levels of extraversion, self-monitoring, and proactive personality are associated with greater work–family conflict. Research regarding gender differences in the experience of work–family conflict is mixed. Although some research suggests that women experience more work–family conflict than men, other research shows no gender differences. It is clear in both the scientific literature and popular press that work–family conflict is not solely a women's issue. Both men and women are concerned about the work–family interface, and research suggests that the opportunity to achieve work–family balance is a high priority for both men and women; it is among the employment features that people are least willing to trade off.

Consequences of Work–Family Conflict

Considerable research has been devoted to the consequences of work–family conflict. Industrial/organizational psychologists have focused the greatest attention on job-related attitudes as work outcomes. Work–family conflict is negatively related to job satisfaction, organizational commitment, organizational citizenship behavior, and job performance. Work–family conflict is positively linked to work stress, poor health indicators such as depression or substance abuse, turnover intentions, and actual turnover. Although not the focus of most I/O research, some research has considered the influence of work–family conflict on family-oriented attitudes and outcomes. Work–family conflict has been negatively linked to life satisfaction, marital satisfaction, family satisfaction, and family role performance.

REDUCING WORK–FAMILY CONFLICT

Research has examined the impact of employers' family-friendly initiatives on employees' work–family conflict, job attitudes, and outcomes. Many family-friendly policies focus on creating greater flexibility in work schedules, including reduced or part-time hours, flextime, compressed workweeks, and job sharing. Other programs potentially provide opportunity for meeting family demands and balancing work and family, including sick leave, maternity and paternity leave, lactation programs, child care and eldercare, telework, concierge services, and informational resources and referrals.

Family-friendly benefits vary in their scope, availability, and focus. Scope refers to which employees are eligible for the benefits. Although some benefits have the potential to apply to all employees (e.g., flextime), other benefits may only be relevant for a subgroup of employees (e.g., lactation programs). Moreover, even when a benefit is relevant, it may not be equally available to all employees. For example, telework programs may be limited to employees with certain job specifications, and on-site child care may be available only to those who can afford it. Family-friendly benefits also vary in terms of their focus. Some programs focus on employee or family health and well-being. Some are designed to increase the likelihood that employees will be present at work. Others are aimed at increasing productivity, regardless of location.

There is some question as to whether or not family-friendly benefits actually help families. Part of the concern is that the existence of family-friendly benefits may limit individual choice. For example, if an organization offers sick child care, do parents still have the option to stay home and care for an ill child themselves? Many family-friendly programs are intended to ensure that employees are present at work and to give employees more time to engage in work activities. Finally, organizationally sponsored programs may be overly focused on family interference with work, whereas research shows that work interference with family is more prevalent.

Nonetheless, employees generally appreciate family-friendly benefits and are attracted to employers that offer them, regardless of whether or not they are personally eligible for the benefits. Family-supportive policies are associated with reduced work–family conflict, enhanced organizational commitment, and organizational citizenship behavior. Family-friendly benefits also have been positively linked to share prices, especially in industries that are high-tech and those where women are concentrated.

There is substantial evidence, however, that family-friendly benefits are underused for several reasons. First, employees are often unaware of the benefits their employers offer and their eligibility for them. Second, employees may be afraid of the negative career consequences of using family-friendly benefits. Third, even when formal family supportive policies exist, the organizational culture and climate may not support their use. Family-friendly benefit use is greater when the organizational culture and climate are generally supportive of family. Employees are more likely to use family-friendly benefits when they are encouraged to do so by supervisors and coworkers.

In addition to encouraging benefit use, organizational insiders such as supervisors, coworkers, and mentors offer informal support that is instrumental in alleviating work–family conflict. Informal support is also linked to greater individual accommodations for family. Often because of the lack of formal policies, and sometimes despite them, many work accommodations for family are negotiated on an individual case-by-case basis between the employee and immediate supervisor. Coworkers likewise offer affective and instrumental support on an individual basis.

Although men and women both experience work–family conflict, women make more work role adjustments to accommodate family than men. For example, women are more likely than men to use employer-sponsored family-friendly benefits. Women are also more likely than men to restructure their work to meet family demands. Although both men and women take advantage of work schedule flexibility, women are more likely than men to use that flexibility to meet family needs. This type of gender difference manifests itself early in career decision making. As young women consider career options, they are influenced by the type of family life they desire and envision. Young men, in contrast, tend to focus more exclusively on their interests when making educational and career decisions.

INDUSTRIAL/ORGANIZATIONAL RESEARCH LIMITATIONS

Industrial/organizational work–family research has a number of limitations. Much of the work in this area relies on cross-sectional survey research methods. More longitudinal work is needed, and a greater variety of research methods (e.g., daily diaries, participant observation) is desirable. Although some research considers the experiences of couples, most of the research is conducted at the individual level. Work–family interface issues tend not to be examined at the family unit level or at the work group level, but there are likely to be important dynamics in both.

The samples in I/O work–family research tend to be professionals and managers. Thus we know relatively little about laborers, low-income workers, and workers with multiple job. Moreover, research tends to focus on employees' work outcomes and some health outcomes including stress. The outcomes for family members such as spouses or children are seldom considered. Research has yet to delve deeply into work–family issues as related to alternate family structures such as single parents, ethnic differences, cultural differences, and intergenerational dynamics. Work to date also tends to ignore both career and family developmental stage. Research lacks a rich treatment of how these variables influence the work–family interface.

EMERGING TOPICS

Although the conflict perspective has dominated research on the work–family interface to date, there is also a long-standing recognition that multiple role occupancy, such as performing multiple roles in both the work and family domains, can be beneficial to psychological well-being. According to expansionist theory, this is most often the case when the roles are high quality and are experienced as rewarding. Occupying numerous low-quality roles that offer few rewards, however, has a detrimental effect on well-being.

There is an emerging trend toward more positive conceptualizations of the work–family interface. Consistent with the notion of positive spillover, concepts such as *work–family balance, work–family fit, work–family role integration, work–family enrichment,* and *work–family facilitation* all assume more beneficial interactions between the work and family domains. The central thesis is that participation in one domain is facilitated by the skills, resources, and experiences gained through participation in the other domain. Research suggests, for example, that resource-rich jobs (e.g., those characterized by high autonomy, complexity, authority, and variety) produce work–family facilitation. Preliminary work suggests that work–family facilitation may buffer the negative effects of work–family conflict on mental health.

There is widespread agreement that the distinctions and boundaries between the work and family domains are becoming increasingly blurred. Thus, research is beginning to consider the causes and consequences of less boundary distinction. The causes, primarily technological advancements that enable many people to work from virtually anywhere and produce 24-hour accessibility, are perhaps more readily apparent than the consequences. It is important to note that the same technologies that make it possible to work anytime and anywhere also appear to make it easier to maintain ties with family members and to meet family responsibilities. However, the question of whether or perhaps more appropriately under what circumstances these blurred boundaries result in greater work–family facilitation or more pronounced work–family conflict remains a critical future research topic.

The work–family interface is embedded in multiple contexts. Research has primarily focused on the family and organizational contexts in which the interplay occurs. However, the interaction between work and family domains may also be considered in light of a number of additional contexts, including community, societal, political, ethnic, cultural, and national contexts. The frame of reference influences which work–family issues are salient and how they are understood. Cross-cultural work–family research, for example, demonstrates how work–family conflict is influenced not only by characteristics of the work and family contexts but also by features of the cultural and national environments in which the work–family interface occurs.

—Debra A. Major

See also: Quality of Work Life; Role Conflict; Stress, Models and Theories; Telecommuting

FURTHER READING

Allen, T. D. (2001). Family-supportive work environments: The role of organizational perceptions. *Journal of Vocational Behavior, 58,* 414–435.

Barnett, R. C., & Hyde, J. S. (2001). Women, men, work, and family: An expansionist theory. *American Psychologist, 56,* 781–796.

Eby, L. T., Casper, W. J., Lockwood, A., Bordeaux, C., & Brinley, A. (2005). Work and family research in IO/OB: Content analysis and review of the literature (1980–2002) [Monograph]. *Journal of Vocational Behavior, 66,* 124–197.

Frone, M. R. (2003). Work–family balance. In J. C. Quick & L. E. Tetrick (Eds.), *Handbook of occupational health psychology.* Washington, DC: American Psychological Association.

Grzywacz, J. G., & Butler, A. B. (2005). The impact of job characteristics on work-to-family facilitation: Testing a theory and distinguishing a construct. *Journal of Occupational Health Psychology, 10,* 97–109.

Kossek, E. E., & Lambert, S. J. (2005). *Work and life integration: Organizational, cultural, and individual perspectives.* Mahwah, NJ: Lawrence Erlbaum.

Major, D. A., Cardenas, R. A., & Allard, C. B. (2004). Child health: A legitimate business concern. *Journal of Occupational Health Psychology, 9,* 306–321.

Major, D. A., & Germano, L. M. (in press). The changing nature of work and its impact on the work–home interface. In F. Jones, R. Burke, & M. Westman (Eds.), *Work–life balance: A psychological perspective.* London: Psychology Press.

Parasuraman, S., & Greenhaus, J. H. (2002). Toward reducing some critical gaps in work–family research. *Human Resource Management Review, 12,* 299–312.

WORK MOTIVATION

Work motivation is one of the most central and highly researched topics in industrial/organizational (I/O) psychology. Even the earliest textbooks in I/O psychology addressed motivation and topics related to it, such as morale, job attitudes, productivity, and job performance. Several definitions have been offered, but the one adopted here was first advanced by the author in 1984: Work motivation originates within and beyond the individual to initiate and determine work-related behavior.

The focus of most attention on work motivation has been on the *effort* people expend at working, the *intensity* component of the definition. Yet it is critical to keep the other components in mind to fully understand work motivation. Although an individual may not be working very hard toward the goals others set, the person may have plenty of motivation to achieve goals other than those prescribed by managers or critics (the *form* and *direction* components).

It is also important to distinguish between motivation and its antecedents and its consequences, particularly the latter. Observers often conclude that a person's motivation is low (usually implying not enough effort) or misguided (inappropriate goals) on the basis of observing low standards of *performance,* which is the accomplishment of some standard or criterion. This conclusion is often false, resulting in what social psychologists refer to as the fundamental attribution error—attributing low judged performance to low motivation, a characteristic of the individual. Considerable research and theory show that performance is a multiplicative function of motivation *and* individual ability as well as the constraints or opportunities offered by the context in which work is occurring. These distinctions are more than a matter of theoretical or conceptual semantics: They have real, important applied implications if one is to understand job performance, employee withdrawal (in its various forms), creativity at work, career choices, and myriad other work-related phenomena. The source of the poor performance is frequently the context or the person's ability to do the job.

SOME POPULAR THEORIES

There are many popular and well-known theories of work motivation, most of which were first proposed during the 1960s and 1970s. Among managers, they are certainly well-known, some more than others, and some believe that they may be more valid (in terms of their capacity to predict individual work-related attitudes, emotions, and behaviors) than current social scientific methods can demonstrate.

The various theories of work motivation are all predicated on a few fundamental models of human functioning, that is, on a few basic ontological assumptions about human nature. Perhaps the most widely known of these theories are those based on the premise that people are fundamentally need-driven creatures. Hedonism is a central tenet of these models, which share the view that people strive to seek pleasure and avoid pain. Henry Murray developed an insightful definition of human needs during the 1930s that is still in use today. Building on that tradition, Abraham Maslow offered the best known of these theories in the 1940s. He believed that human needs are arranged in hierarchical categories, such that some needs are more *prepotent* than others. For example, as the more basic needs are becoming satisfied, other less urgent needs increase in relative importance. Maslow's theory is frequently oversimplified in interpretation. A key concept in thinking about work motivation and behavior is *overdetermination,* which indicates that most human behavior, except that related to the most basic biological functions, are instigated and directed by more than a single motive (or need). Too frequently, textbooks, teachers, and consultants claim that Maslow believed that behavior was determined by the forces of single needs, one at a time, and that the particular need in force at any given time followed the structure of his famous hierarchy.

More recent versions of need theory have been offered by David McClelland, a student of Henry Murray, who made major contributions in our understanding of three particular needs that have considerable importance for work motivation—the needs for achievement, power, and affiliation—and Clayton Alderfer, who offered a simplified version of Maslow's hierarchy.

Frederick Herzberg and his colleagues advanced a controversial theory of job satisfaction and work motivation in 1959. The theory was heavily criticized for methodological and other reasons, but it was instrumental in spawning later theories of job design that have many implications for work motivation. Indeed, the meaningfulness factor appearing in these later theories (from the 1980s) is enjoying attention now as part of the *positive organizational scholarship* movement.

There are a variety of theories that rest on the assumption that humans are basically information-processing creatures. Collectively, they are the most significant class of current theories. In the 1960s J. S. Adams offered a theory that claimed that work motivation could be understood in terms of people's perceptions of the exchange relationship they have with the employer. Social comparison processes with other individuals played a huge role in the dynamics of this theory, which has evolved over the past 15 years to diverse and more advanced thinking about justice. In fact, justice theories are, as a group, one of the freshest and most progressive bodies of theory to emerge in recent times.

A variety of expected value theories emerged in the late 1960s and early 1970s. The common theme among them is that work motivation is a decision-making process by which people choose among alternatives to maximize their expected utility. Perceptions about the expected value of outcomes associated with alternatives and the perceived probability that those outcomes will accrue are the major parameters of the model.

Popular behaviorist models from the 1960s and 1970s have given way to modified forms that admit cognitive elements. Currently, Albert Bandura's social cognitive theory is one of the most viable approaches of this new generation. The central tenet of this approach is that psychosocial functioning results from three-way interactions among people, their behavior, and the environment.

Edwin Locke and Gary Latham's goal-setting theory is probably the most successful of current contenders. Based on the information processing model, it enjoys the most scientific validity and applied value for practitioners. In a nutshell it claims that people are motivated to pursue goals, based on intentions. Difficult, specific goals are the most motivating, as long as they are accepted by the individual, particularly when they are accompanied by feedback.

Participation, rewards, deadlines, and other incentives enhance goal striving only to the extent that they influence goal acceptance.

A survey of the leading theories published in the *Annual Review of Psychology* in 2005 concluded that, as a group, theories of work motivation have advanced considerably over the previous 30 years, largely by becoming more fully articulated and refined with the inclusion of mediating and moderating effects. Also as a group, work motivation theories have recently been judged as one of the two most valid and useful bodies of knowledge in the organizational sciences. Aside from a sharp increase in research and theory involving human affect, there have been few *fundamentally new* models offered in three decades. Future progress will most likely require the exploitation of other basic models of human functioning, such as spirituality.

—*Craig C. Pinder*

See also Expectancy Theory of Work Motivation; Intrinsic and Extrinsic Work Motivation; Motivational Traits; Need Theories of Work Motivation; Reinforcement Theory of Work Motivation; Self-Concept Theory of Work Motivation

FURTHER READING

Bandura A. (1991). Social cognitive theory of moral thought and action. In W. M. Kurtines & J. L. Gerwitz (Eds.), *Handbook of moral behavior and development* (Vol. 1, pp. 45–103). Hillsdale, NJ: Lawrence Erlbaum.

Locke, E. A., & Latham, G. P. (1990). *A theory of goal setting and task performance.* Englewood Cliffs, NJ: Prentice Hall.

Maslow, A. H. (1943). A theory of human motivation. *Psychological Review, 50,* 370–396.

McClelland, D. C. (1975). *Power: The inner experience.* New York: Halstead.

Murray, H. A., & Shneidman, E. S. (Eds.). (1981). *Selections from the personology of Henry A. Murray.* New York: Harper & Row.

Pinder, C. C. (1998). *Work motivation in organizational behavior.* Upper Saddle River, NJ: Prentice Hall.

WORKPLACE ACCOMMODATIONS FOR THE DISABLED

Workplace accommodations for the disabled are those practices, policies, and procedures put into place by employers to assist in the integration of and participation by disabled people in the workplace. These accommodations are necessitated by national, state, or provincial legislation, such as the Americans With Disabilities Act in the United States or the federal Human Rights Act in Canada, that require employers to provide employment opportunities to disabled individuals who traditionally have been underrepresented in the workforce. Workplace accommodation is important to industrial/organizational (I/O) psychologists and human resources managers (HRMs) because many aspects of the personnel systems that they develop, implement, and evaluate are affected when an accommodation is made.

WHAT ASPECTS OF THE PERSONNEL SYSTEM ARE SUBJECT TO THE ACCOMMODATION REQUIREMENT?

All parts of the personnel system can come under scrutiny of courts and regulators who are tasked with enforcing legislation that prohibits employment discrimination against disabled individuals. These individuals can be impaired either physically or mentally. An example of an accommodation for a visually impaired person in the hiring process would be the provision of employment test materials in double-size print. A person in a wheelchair could be provided with a workstation that is suited to wheelchair access. A person with attention deficit disorder might be provided with detailed written instructions, so they do not miss a step in completing their assigned task. The elements of the personnel system that require attention, as well as the subsequent accommodations made, will depend on the nature of the disability, the effect of that disability on worker behavior and performance, and the conditions currently existing in the workplace.

WHO DECIDES ON WHAT ACCOMMODATIONS ARE REQUIRED AND HOW THEY SHOULD BE IMPLEMENTED?

Workplace accommodation often is a straightforward and intuitively obvious matter that can be resolved quickly, inexpensively, and effectively through discussion between the employer and the disabled individual. For example, a claims adjuster who works most of the day at a computer might be provided with a larger screen as simple job redesign to accommodate a visual impairment. This may be the only workplace accommodation required for that person to succeed on the job. At other times, however, a workplace accommodation is more complex and may require the combined expertise and efforts of a multidisciplinary team, including the disabled person, an I/O psychologist, a health care provider, a human resources manger, and a line supervisor or manager. This is especially true for persons with mental disabilities (e.g., depression, autism, dyslexia) that are *invisible* but still present formidable obstacles to the disabled person who wishes to enter and succeed in the workplace. In these cases it is not apparent whether it is the disability per se or the lack of ability to perform the job requirements that is at the bottom of the person's difficulties in adapting to and functioning in the workplace. Disentangling and resolving these issues may take considerable time and effort.

Where a multidisciplinary team undertakes the identification of a workplace accommodation, the team members should bring distinct, but complementary, talents and perspectives to the task. The I/O psychologist will bring skills and experience in identifying the essential job duties through the use of job analysis and, as needed, assessing the job skills of the disabled individual. The health care provider (e.g., psychiatrist, neuropsychologist, clinical psychologist) will bring insight into the etiology of the disorder, its likely effects on behavior and performance in the workplace, and a prognosis for recovery. The human resources manager will bring an in-depth knowledge of the personnel system of the employer, especially organization policies and procedures (related to hiring and promotion, for example) with which the workplace accommodation will have to articulate. The line supervisor or manager will be able to determine whether an individual accommodation is practicable to achieve within the unit under supervision (it is futile to propose an accommodation that realistically cannot be implemented in the office or on the shop floor). The disabled person also should contribute to team discussions and decisions about how the disability should be accommodated. Other technical experts or stakeholders—such as an occupational therapist, a rehabilitation psychologist, or a union representative—might be asked to participate in the multidisciplinary team to identify and recommend the workplace accommodation, depending on the nature of the disability; the prognosis for recovery of the disabled person; or the labor-management climate within the organization.

In complex cases of workplace accommodation, the team members should use a structured decision process to help guide their discussions and decisions. Steven Cronshaw and Brenda Kenyon proposed a model to guide team members through four steps of identifying and implementing an individual accommodation in the workplace. Whatever the workplace accommodations identified and recommended for implementation, management will be responsible for putting the accommodation in place. Prior participation of the line manger or supervisor in identifying the required workplace accommodation will make informed and successful implementation of it much more likely.

HOW FAR MUST AN EMPLOYER GO TO PROVIDE WORKPLACE ACCOMMODATION?

Some employers feel trepidation that workplace accommodation may interfere with organizational productivity or their ability to compete in the global economy. Typically, legislators have considered this possibility and have sought to balance the rights of the disabled worker for gainful employment with the need of the employer for a productive workplace and reasonable control of costs associated with implementing workplace accommodation. The Americans With Disabilities Act, for example, states that a worker must be able to perform the essential duties of the position and that it is not a reasonable accommodation to excuse a disabled worker from the performance of these essential duties. The I/O psychologist can help the employer identify the essential functions of the job through job or task analysis and differentiate them from nonessential duties from which a disabled person might be excused as part of an individual accommodation. As well, workplace accommodations usually are not required beyond the point where financial or other costs would place an undue or unreasonable burden on the employer. What is *unreasonable* for a given employer will depend on the size of the organization and its ability to absorb the costs associated with the workplace accommodation.

SUMMARY

The need for workplace accommodation engendered by disability legislation offers an opportunity for I/O psychologists to bring their science into application for the benefit of disabled workers and their employing organizations. The goal is to make available the workplace affordances that will enable the entry of disabled workers into full workforce participation while ensuring that their success also makes the needed contribution to the efficiency, effectiveness, and productivity of the organization. Social movements in many countries are providing the impetus to greater inclusion of disabled persons in all spheres of life, including employment. As a result, workplace accommodation, and the involvements of I/O psychologists in providing accommodation to disabled individuals, will grow in importance for the foreseeable future.

—*Steven F. Cronshaw*

See also Americans With Disabilities Act

FURTHER READING

Cronshaw, S. F., & Kenyon, B. L. (2002). An application model relating the essential functions of a job to mental disabilities. In J. C. Thomas & M. Hersen (Eds.), *Handbook of mental health in the workplace.* Thousand Oaks, CA: Sage.

WORKPLACE INCIVILITY

Workplace incivility refers to behaviors that people experience at work that are rude and discourteous, and that generally go against norms for mutual respect and dignity. Examples of incivility include being berated for an action in which one played no part, being excluded from a meeting, and having one's credibility undermined in front of others. Neglecting to greet one another, interrupting others while speaking, failing to return borrowed supplies, and spreading rumors and gossiping constitute incivil acts. Incivility is considered a subset of counterproductive work behaviors (CWBs), employee deviance, and workplace aggression. However, incivility only includes behaviors that are relatively mild (e.g., verbal, passive, and indirect), whereas CWB, deviance, and aggression also include behaviors that are physical, active, and direct. Although incivility is less intense than other forms of CWB or deviance, it is far more common. Unlike employee deviance or aggression, incivility is characterized by an ambiguous intent to harm. That is, an act of incivility may be perceived by the instigator or target as a deliberate attempt to cause harm or it may be attributed to more benign causes. For example, the instigator may claim the behavior was because of ignorance or an oversight on his or her part or may accuse the target of misunderstanding the behavior or being overly sensitive. Incivility is also distinct from mobbing, bullying, and social undermining in that these constructs generally refer to a recurring pattern of deliberately injurious behavior wherein an individual may be systematically targeted by one or more individuals at work. The unique contribution that is made by including incivility alongside these distinct albeit related constructs is the idea that behaviors do not necessarily have to be clearly and deliberately hostile to negatively affect an individual or organization.

Interest in workplace incivility has grown recently as interest in uncivil behavior in society at large such as cell phone use and road rage has increased. The common perception is that incivility is on the rise, but no empirical data are available to substantiate this view. However, several changes in the way we work may have contributed to a relaxing of social norms and a concurrent increase in incivility. For example, organizations have loosened formal rules for dress and behavior as companies become flatter and less formal to increase responsiveness and encourage innovation and creativity. The absence of these formal cues for behavior may be contributing to an increase in incivility. Modern communication technology may also be a factor as electronic communication such as e-mail and instant messaging is more susceptible to misinterpretation because it is unable to convey the subtleties of nonverbal communication including body language and voice intonation that can mean the difference between a statement interpreted as gentle ribbing or a provocative insult. Moreover, the increasing racial and ethnic diversity of the workforce means employees are more likely to encounter others with different cultural norms and expectations regarding what is acceptable and courteous behavior. Finally, the increase in corporate downsizing, restructuring, and mergers coupled with a heightened emphasis on short-term profitability often means that workers are expected to do more with less. All these factors translate into a more complex and fast-paced working environment that leaves little time for niceties and proper manners.

SOCIAL INTERACTIONIST PERSPECTIVE

Incivility is generally characterized as occurring within an interactive social exchange dynamic described as an incivility spiral wherein an act of workplace incivility on the part of one individual leads to an act of incivility by a second party (the original target) that may be of equal or increasing intensity. In the former case, the exchange is nonescalating, but these exchanges may have cumulative negative consequences for organizations by altering norms about such behavior and increasing emotional fatigue among participants and observers of the exchange. The latter case, however, results in an escalating spiral of incivility wherein each act of incivility is followed by an increasingly negative act. Situations such as these have the potential to lead to more intense forms of CWB, perhaps resulting ultimately in aggression or violence wherein the intent to inflict harm is indisputable.

INSTIGATORS AND TARGETS

Instigators of workplace incivility are more likely to be male, and some are also high performers at work. Instigators do not discriminate based on gender or age when choosing a target; however, they are more likely to target individuals who hold lower status positions than themselves. Thus, incivility is more likely to be perpetrated by individuals in positions of power and aimed at individuals with less power. Research indicates that being the target of incivility can lead to increased job stress and job dissatisfaction. Targets often respond by withholding effort or other citizenship behaviors, avoiding the instigator, performing other counterproductive behaviors, or leaving the organization. The effects of incivility may also extend beyond the original involved parties to affect other individuals who may witness uncivil exchanges by creating a stressful working environment, changing organizational norms about how people treat each other at work, and potentially leading to spillover uncivil behavior.

PREVENTION

There are many steps that organizations can take to reduce the occurrence of workplace incivility. Perhaps the most important is to set and clearly communicate expectations and standards for employee behavior to build a culture that will not tolerate rudeness or incivility. To be effective, it is critical that these policies are supported and modeled at all levels of the organization, particularly by those in top management. The selection

and recruitment process should also align with the organization's policies on civil interpersonal treatment. Companies should take care to inform potential hires of behavioral expectations and standards and use the interview process and reference checking to identify individuals with a higher propensity to instigate incivility. Organizations can also provide training to employees to provide them with more productive ways of interacting with others and to make them more aware of the negative effects of incivility. Employee performance appraisals and evaluations should also reflect these standards for behavior. Finally, individuals who violate policies against incivility should incur consequences regardless of status. Because many instigators are in positions of power and possess valuable knowledge and skills, organizations may be reluctant to take action; however, the costs of tolerating incivility are too great to be ignored.

—Lisa M. Penney

See also Counterproductive Work Behaviors, Interpersonal Deviance

FURTHER READING

Cortina, L. M., Magley, V. J., Williams, J. H., & Langhout, R. D. (2001). Incivility in the workplace: Incidence and impact. *Journal of Occupational Health Psychology, 6*(1), 64–80.

Johnson, P. R., & Indvik, J. (2001). Rudeness at work: Impulse over restraint. *Public Personnel Management, 30*(4), 457–465.

Pearson, C. M., Andersson, L. M., & Porath, C. L. (2000). Assessing and attacking workplace incivility. *Organizational Dynamics, 29*(3), 123–137.

Pearson, C. M., & Porath, C. L. (2005). On the nature, consequences, and remedies of workplace incivility: No time for "nice"? Think again. *Academy of Management Executive, 19*(1), 7–18.

Penney, L. M., & Spector, P. E. (in press). Job stress, incivility, and counterproductive work behavior (CWB): The moderating role of negative affectivity. *Journal of Organizational Behavior.*

WORKPLACE INJURIES

The term *workplace injury* refers to any wound or damage to the human body as a consequence of an event or a series of events in the work environment.

Events in this definition refer to the manner in which the injury was produced, such as a fall from a ladder or a series of events such as repetitive strain. Workplace injuries are often referred to in different ways—for example, industrial injuries, occupational accidents, unsafe working, and incidents—a number of which implicitly presuppose no causality (accidents), blame the victim (unsafe working), or communicate a façade of unbiased detachment (incidents). We use the term *workplace injuries* here because it most accurately describes the phenomenon.

In this entry we first provide a simple way of classifying workplace injuries and draw some examples from prevalence data summarized by the Bureau of Labor Statistics (BLS), a division of the United States Department of Labor. With this as background, we then describe two strands of research in industrial/organizational (I/O) psychology that have worked toward understanding the predictors of workplace injuries.

CLASSIFICATION AND PREVALENCE

Taxonomies for classifying workplace injuries vary considerably, and often correspond to how governmental agencies (e.g., BLS, Occupational Safety and Health Administration [OSHA]) classify information on both workplace injuries and the industries in which they occur. Each year in the United States, for example, the BLS collects workplace injury data from thousands of work establishments. Instead of adopting a particular classification system here, however, we classify workplace injuries on two dimensions that refer to the nature of the injury and transcend industry sector: *timing* (acute or chronic) and *physical severity* (minor or major). Acute workplace injuries have sudden onset, and examples of these include cuts and bruises, sprains, needlesticks, and burns. A chronic injury persists for a longer period of time and may include a category of injuries including carpal tunnel syndrome attributed to repetitive strain (e.g., keyboarding, some assembly-line tasks). Within this definition of chronic injuries, we do not include workplace illnesses that characterize longer-term exposure to harmful substances, including poisoning and radiation, or possible interactions between these harmful substances and social contagion like sick building syndrome. Alongside injury timing, the physical severity of injuries ranges from negligible irritation to death. The consequences of a minor injury might be

some on-the-job first aid, little suffering for the victim, and no significant loss of work, whereas a more major injury might involve hospitalization, more widespread suffering for the victim and family, and prolonged and even total loss of life and work.

Although workplace injuries can occur in any employment situation and wide variation does exist in workplace injuries by industry, a number of occupations and workplaces consistently rank among the most dangerous as measured by worker fatalities. For example, at the time of this writing, fishing and logging ranked as the two most dangerous occupations in America, with death rates nearly 18 and 30 times, respectively, that of a typical American workplace (i.e., 4.0 per 100,000 workers). Thus in terms of events in dangerous workplaces, falling trees in forests, drowning in open water, traveling to or from high altitudes (69.8 deaths per 100,000 workers for pilots and navigators and 69.8 deaths per 100,000 workers for structural metal workers), and car crashes on highways (drivers and sales workers such as pizza delivery drivers face 37.9 deaths per 100,000 workers) are, on average, the most dangerous work situations facing U.S. workers. Data reported in the BLS's annual Survey of Occupational Injuries and Illnesses suggest that millions of nonfatal workplace injuries occur in workplaces every year. Private industry, for example, reported approximately 4.4 million nonfatal injuries and illnesses in 2003. We believe that figures for nonfatal workplace injuries are conservative at best, and leave it up to the reader to explore the injury classification system, industrial and occupational rates, and systemic threats to reliable and valid workplace injury data relevant to their context.

RESEARCH ON PREDICTING WORKPLACE INJURIES

Psychological research on the prediction of workplace injuries has two broad strands, with the first having more of a historical foothold in psychology as it has been applied to workplace injuries. The first strand of research attempts to predict the occurrence of workplace injuries from individual differences such as *accident proneness* and personality traits. Studies of workers in munitions factories during World War I described accident-prone individuals as people who had a natural propensity to be injured on the job. Researchers at the time attributed this to inadaptability on the part of the worker and went as far as suggesting that encouraging accident-prone workers to work more safely was a waste of time, perhaps even a source of unnecessary apprehension. With the enthusiastic uptake of scientific management principles at the time, the rather vague notion of accident proneness was ironically swept into industrial practice and became a popular albeit unreliable way of selecting workers for manufacturing settings. The legacy of accident proneness unfortunately pervades even modern selection approaches for safety-critical settings and deserves explicit mention here given the pervasiveness of the myth and the lack of systematic evidence of its nature.

A more methodical approach to understanding the individual differences perspective on predicting workplace injuries involves personality traits. Although the notion that workplace injuries are caused by personal characteristics is unfounded, there is moderate evidence that certain personality characteristics are correlated with injury occurrence. Empirical evidence suggests modest correlations between workplace injury occurrence and some Big Five personality traits such as neuroticism and negative affectivity. Despite this, we note that little variation in workplace injury can be uniquely explained by these variables. From a practice perspective, it appears to be of little value to exclude the proportion of the working population that scores highly on these personality traits to avoid the possibility of workplace injuries. In the face of correlational evidence, we argue that deselecting, for example, highly neurotic employees from a workforce would make no practical difference in the number and type of injuries actually experienced; and we believe instead that a more fruitful line of inquiry should focus on the *interaction* between personality traits and characteristics of the work situation, the latter of which we discuss next.

The second strand of research in the prediction of workplace injury focuses on how people perceive their work environment, including the nature of the tasks they are required to perform such as work design and salient workplace relationships including supervisor influence. Of the two, research on the link between work design and injuries is the less definitive. Although most existing studies on this topic suggest that work characteristics are correlated with injuries, there is little consistency regarding which work characteristics are most important. For example, across a number of studies, high job control, moderate job demands, high role clarity, and low physical hazards

are four important situational predictors of injury occurrence; however, other studies have found less significant relationships for all these work characteristics. In sum, although recognition of work design factors in the prevention of injury is growing, the evidence is far from clear and not causal. Although evidence of the relationship between work characteristics and injuries suffers the same lack of causal data as does the personality and injury relationship discussed earlier, we suggest that changing work design is more instructive than selecting (or deselecting) personnel for three reasons. First, the correlations between work characteristics and injuries are, on average, larger than those of personality and injuries. Second, there is considerable evidence of the potential of work redesign in improving other indicators of well-being such as job-related mental health. Third, redesigning work (e.g., increasing timing and method control, increasing role clarity) to promote healthy work is more within the control of managers for an existing workforce with a range of personality traits.

Among situational factors that are related to workplace injury occurrence, the role of high-quality leadership presently seems to provide the most compelling findings. Across a range of different theories of leadership behavior (e.g., transformational leadership, leader–member exchange theory), there are moderate correlations reflecting that the presence of a high-quality supervisor is related to lower injury occurrence among the supervisor's workers. High-quality leadership could affect the occurrence of injury through a number of mechanisms. For example, a caring and stimulating supervisor might heighten the general sense of how important workplace safety is and increase awareness and attentiveness, thereby reducing the risk of injuries. In contrast, a supervisor with poor leadership behaviors might not communicate concern for subordinates' well-being or generate a disaffected climate that encourages shortcuts to be taken, thereby increasing the chance of injuries. Although existing research suggests a qualitative difference between the preventative effects of high-quality leadership and the detrimental effects of poor leadership, research on the mechanisms linking leadership and workplace injuries more generally is less clear.

—*Nick Turner and Julian Barling*

See also National Institute for Occupational Safety and Health/Occupational Safety and Health Administration; Occupational Health Psychology; Workplace Safety

FURTHER READING

Barling, J., & Frone, M. R. (Eds.). (2004). *Psychology of workplace safety.* Washington, DC: American Psychological Association.

Barling, J., Loughlin, C., & Kelloway, E. K. (2002). Development and test of a model linking safety-specific transformational leadership and occupational safety. *Journal of Applied Psychology, 87,* 488–496.

Frone, M. R. (1998). Predictors of work injuries among employed adolescents. *Journal of Applied Psychology, 83,* 565–576.

Hemingway, M. A., & Smith, C. S. (1999). Organizational climate and occupational stressors as predictors of withdrawal behaviours and injuries in nurses. *Journal of Occupational and Organizational Psychology, 72,* 285–299.

Landen, D. D., & Hendricks, S. (1995). Effect of recall on reporting of at-work injuries. *Public Health Reports, 110,* 350–354.

Nichols, T. (1997). *Sociology of industrial injury.* London: Mansell.

WORKPLACE ROMANCE

The subject of workplace romance is hardly a new one; Robert E. Quinn published his groundbreaking article on the formation, impact, and management of workplace romances in 1977. In 2004 it was estimated that nearly 10 million workplace romances develop annually in organizations throughout the United States. Highly publicized examples include the illicit relationship between Boeing's CEO Harry Stonecipher and executive Debra Peabody and the genuine relationship between Microsoft's Chairman Bill Gates and manager Melinda French.

A workplace romance is a dating or marital relationship that involves mutually desired sexual attraction between two members of the same organization. Workplace romances are classified as one of the following five types:

1. *Companionate:* Both employees are genuinely in love with one another and seeking a long-term companion or spouse.

2. *Passionate:* Both employees are genuinely in love with one another and seeking adventure, ego satisfaction, excitement, or sexual gratification.

3. *Fling:* Both employees are seeking adventure, ego satisfaction, excitement, or sexual gratification.

4. *Mutual User:* Both employees are seeking advancement, financial rewards, increased vacation time, lighter workloads, power, security, or other job-related benefits and resources.

5. *Utilitarian:* One employee (e.g., a subordinate) is seeking advancement, financial rewards, increased vacation time, lighter workloads, power, security, or other job-related benefits and resources, whereas the other employee (e.g., a supervisor) is seeking adventure, ego satisfaction, excitement, or sexual gratification.

One study revealed that 36% of workplace romances are passionate, 23% are companionate, 22% are utilitarian, and 19% are flings. Workplace romances are also described in terms of each participant's organizational rank. Lateral romances occur between employees who have equal rank such as two peers, whereas hierarchical romances occur between employees who have unequal rank, for example, a supervisor and a subordinate.

Workplace romances can affect vital organizational variables such as participants' job performance and motivation to work. In addition, dissolved workplace romances can foster sexually harassing behavior between former relational participants. Accordingly, scholars in fields such as industrial/organizational (I/O) psychology, organizational behavior, and human resource management have conducted research aimed at providing an understanding of the formation, impact, and management of workplace romances.

FORMATION OF WORKPLACE ROMANCES

Explanations for how workplace romances develop are based on social psychological theories of repeated exposure, interpersonal attraction, love, emotion, attitudes, social exchange, group dynamics, and impression management. The main antecedent factors proposed to explain the formation of romances between two employees include their degree of physical and functional proximity to one another, repeated social interactions with one another, similarity of work- and nonwork-related attitudes, physiological arousal in one another's presence, physical attraction to one another, favorability of attitudes toward workplace romance, and job autonomy. Another antecedent factor proposed to explain whether employees decide to partake in workplace romances is the nature of their organization's culture with respect to workplace romance. An organization's culture is determined in part by whether or not it has a formal workplace romance policy and, if so, whether the policy prohibits workplace romances altogether or instead stipulates conditions under which workplace romances are acceptable versus unacceptable. The culture is also determined in part by whether it has workgroup norms that disapprove versus approve of workplace romances.

With respect to formation factors, recent studies have shown that employees who have more favorable attitudes toward workplace romance are more likely to participate in workplace romances than are employees who have less favorable attitudes toward workplace romance. Recent studies have also shown that employees who have the opportunity to make decisions about their own and others' work, and who have the freedom to move around physically and interact with others at work, are more likely to participate in workplace romances than are employees who do not have this degree of autonomy in their jobs.

IMPACT OF WORKPLACE ROMANCES

Workplace romances can affect, both positively and negatively, participants' work-related attitudes and behavior. Examples of proposed impact factors include romance participants' levels of job performance, work motivation, job satisfaction, job involvement, and organizational commitment. Coworkers can also be affected by observing workplace romances. For example, a workgroup's morale may be lowered by observing a hierarchical romance wherein the higher-rank participant exhibits job-related favoritism toward the lower-rank participant.

With respect to impact factors, recent studies have produced mixed results such that participating in a workplace romance has been shown to be both positively associated with and not associated with participants' levels of job performance. One study also showed that employees' participation in a workplace romance is positively associated with their levels of job satisfaction and, to a lesser degree, their levels of commitment to the organization.

Finally, dissolved workplace romances can foster sexually harassing behavior between former relational participants. Indeed, federal cases have dealt with dissolved workplace romances that led to sexual harassment claims supported by the courts. A prior history of workplace romance between a plaintiff and defendant may, however, sway investigators' decisions about the plaintiff's sexual harassment claim. Studies have shown that investigators' knowledge of a prior history of workplace romance, and knowledge of specific features of the dissolved romance, affects how they respond to an ensuing harassment claim.

MANAGEMENT OF WORKPLACE ROMANCES

Considering the impact of workplace romances, organizations typically must manage these liaisons. For example, depending on the level of work disruption caused by a romance, managerial interventions may entail either no action; positive action such as counseling; or punitive action such as a reprimand, suspension, transfer, or termination for one or both participants. Recent studies conducted by the Society for Human Resource Management indicate that about 70% of organizations do not have a formal workplace romance policy. However, those that do (e.g., IBM, Pfizer, Wal-Mart, Xerox) typically permit but discourage lateral romances and prohibit hierarchical romances. Finally, some organizations advise workplace romance participants to sign a consensual relationship agreement. Also known as *love contracts,* these written agreements are used to stipulate terms and conditions of the romance and to prevent costly sexual harassment lawsuits. Unfortunately, the advantages and disadvantages of using consensual relationship agreements have not been studied empirically.

—*Charles A. Pierce, Ivan S. Muslin,*
and Tobias M. Huning

See also Sexual Harassment at Work

FURTHER READING

Foley, S., & Powell, G. N. (1999). Not all is fair in love and work: Coworkers' preferences for and responses to managerial interventions regarding workplace romances. *Journal of Organizational Behavior, 20,* 1043–1056.

Pierce, C. A., & Aguinis, H. (2003). Romantic relationships in organizations: A test of a model of formation and impact factors. *Management Research, 1,* 161–169.

Pierce, C. A., Broberg, B. J., McClure, J. R., & Aguinis, H. (2004). Responding to sexual harassment complaints: Effects of a dissolved workplace romance on decision-making standards. *Organizational Behavior and Human Decision Processes, 95,* 66–82.

Powell, G. N. (2001). Workplace romances between senior-level executives and lower-level employees: An issue of work disruption and gender. *Human Relations, 54,* 1519–1544.

Quinn, R. E. (1977). Coping with cupid: The formation, impact, and management of romantic relationships in organizations. *Administrative Science Quarterly, 22,* 30–45.

WORKPLACE SAFETY

It is probably reasonable to assume that most employees in the developed world go to work each day in the belief that they can return home safely at the end of their workday. Yet the available data from a number of industrialized countries over the last 15 years suggests that this assumption is questionable. Workplace fatalities continue at an alarming rate. In 1995 and 1998, in the United States of America, there were more than 6,000 fatal work injuries. By 1999 there were approximately 833 fatal workplace injuries in Canada. The frequency of disabling work injuries is also staggering. For example, in 1995 there were approximately 3.6 million injuries requiring time off work in the United States, with approximately 1.1 million employees injured at work each year between 1993 and 1996 in the United Kingdom.

But these data only speak to the extent of the problem. The social meaning of these data can perhaps best be appreciated by comparing the number of people who die in workplace safety incidents with those who die from other causes. First, more people are killed each year in workplace safety incidents than are murdered each year in Canada. Others have extended this focus to show that workers are substantially more likely to be injured or killed on the job than they are to experience the same consequence at the hands of a criminal. Second, despite the understandable public attention given to illnesses, injuries, and fatalities from breast, prostate, or colorectal cancer, vehicular-related deaths, firearms, and AIDS, more people are still injured and killed each year in workplace safety incidents in the United Sates.

Despite the magnitude of these data, the issue of workplace safety has largely escaped the focus of psychological research. In this entry we consider three issues. We will first consider the nature and measurement of workplace safety. Thereafter, we address psychological factors at work that promote or detract from workplace safety. Last, we focus on some of the psychological consequences of workplace safety infractions.

THE NATURE AND MEASUREMENT OF WORKPLACE SAFETY

Debate continues as to the most appropriate way to conceptualize and operationalize workplace safety. Most frequently, workplace safety is measured as the number of workplace fatalities, injuries, and lost time from work—broadly speaking, accidents. Perhaps by default, then, workplace safety is usually conceptualized as the absence of injuries and fatalities, or accidents. Although acknowledging that it is not advisable to offer a definition of a construct by stating what it is not, we begin this section with a strong caution against the use of the term *accident*. Terminologically, *accident* implies an event that is random, hence neither predictable nor preventable with no plausible assignment of blame. Yet most postaccident workplace investigations reveal that the event in question was both predictable and preventable. As such, continued use of the term *accident* is not only descriptively inaccurate; it might also impede theorizing and empirical research, and potential misspecification will certainly detract from any comparison of preventive efforts.

Conceptualizing workplace safety in terms of accidents has other problems, too. It does not account for the fact that there are realistic concerns about the accuracy of workplace safety data, the fact that different jurisdictions define incidents and accidents differently (e.g., what constitutes an injury), and that these data are not normally distributed. Taken together, these problems make it difficult to conduct reliable and valid research that is likely to enhance both theory and practice.

A different way of conceptualizing and measuring workplace safety that would enhance theory and research is possible by focusing on safety-related behaviors rather than the consequences of not behaving safely. Three behaviors are worthy of attention. First, some research has concentrated attention on the proximal behaviors that precede injuries. In the restaurant industry, for example, cuts and lacerations are frequent injuries, and the most proximal behaviors that might constitute working safely include being in contact with broken glass or having a knife slip while working in the kitchen. Second, research has focused on employee compliance, such as with safety regulations and supervisory requests, and might be important in the extent to which injuries and fatalities and lost time from work are reduced. Still, it is unlikely that safety compliance would enhance safety (as opposed to limit injuries). The third behavior, referred to as safety participation or safety initiative, reflects a set of behaviors that employees enact when they go beyond compliance with normal safety regulations to assist the organization and its members in improving safety. Employees demonstrate safety initiative when they engage in voluntary behaviors such as agreeing to serve on safety committees or discuss and implement ways to work safely with their colleagues. Together, these three behavioral aspects constitute safety performance; turning the focus in workplace safety to safety performance as opposed to workplace injuries alone might well benefit prevention-oriented research and practice.

PSYCHOLOGICAL FACTORS THAT PROMOTE WORKPLACE SAFETY

There has been a considerable amount of research on the causes of workplace safety. In this respect we acknowledge that a large body of knowledge has accumulated on ergonomics, or human factors engineering, which is generally concerned with the optimal design of machines, equipment, and the physical environment. Although some psychological research has contributed to the field of ergonomics, such as cognitive psychology and perception, we choose to focus in this section on those aspects that are more clearly psychological, namely leadership, psychological climate, and high-performance work systems.

Leadership and Workplace Safety

Organizations typically accept without question that leadership makes a difference. Yet this belief has not been applied to the understanding and management of workplace safety; instead, a command-and-control style of management has been more likely to be implemented to achieve greater levels of employee compliance. Three streams of research now indicate that workplace safety may well benefit from high-quality leadership.

First, perhaps the longest standing approach to understanding the effects of leadership on workplace safety has examined leaders' commitment to safety. Findings across several decades have demonstrated consistently that when leaders manifest a high commitment to workplace safety, organizations enjoy better safety records, their supervisors are more likely

to use a participative style in managing safety, and employees are more motivated to work safely.

A second stream of research is based on leader–member exchange theory, within which it is assumed that when leaders enact behaviors for the benefit of employees such as employees' safety, employees will reciprocate because of a feeling of mutual obligation. Research findings show that leader–member exchanges do indeed influence safety but that this effect is indirect. In one research study, high-quality leader–member exchanges resulted in better safety communications between supervisors and team members, and it was enhanced communication that influenced safety. In another study, high-quality leader–member exchanges resulted in what the authors called *safety citizenship,* which itself may parallel safety initiative.

The third stream of leadership research is based on transformational leadership, which may be especially suited to workplace safety. Transformational leadership reflects behaviors that tangibly show concern for employees, are value based, and inspire employees to go beyond what they previously thought was unattainable and think for themselves. Several findings have emerged from research on transformational leadership and workplace safety. First, paralleling research on leader–member exchange theory, effects of transformational leadership on safety seem to be indirect. Second, transformational leadership influences safety (and reduced injuries) in the extent to which it enhances perceptions of the safety climate, raises individuals' awareness of safety, and increases interactions with employees in which safety issues are discussed. Third, one research study on teenage supervisors shows that transformational leadership behaviors can be taught, which has important preventive implications.

Psychological Climate and Workplace Safety

Safety climate reflects shared perceptions regarding policies, procedures, and practices and can exist at both the organizational and team levels. Research spanning at least three decades has primarily investigated the consequences of group-level safety climate on various aspects of safety performance. The results of this research are both consistent and impressive. In positive safety climates (for example, when employees believe that management offers safety training because they want to rather than because they have to), safety performance is enhanced and injuries are reduced in a variety of different contexts, such as private sector organizations and military units, and at different levels, including organizational, team-level, and individual safety performance.

Research has also investigated the factors that predict positive safety climates across different levels. Although there is less research on the predictors than the outcomes of safety climates, research has demonstrated the importance of high-quality leadership (within both leader–member exchange and transformational leadership frameworks). Given the importance of safety climate to subsequent safety performance, a greater research focus on the development of safety climate is certainly warranted.

High-Performance Work Systems and Workplace Safety

In different ways research has addressed the effects of leadership and climate on workplace safety for decades. By contrast, research assessing the effects of high-performance work systems is certainly more recent. High-performance work systems reflect a group of separate but interrelated practices that together attract, recruit, select, train, develop, motivate, and retain employees. These systems enhance conditions that encourage employees' pride in their work, extra effort, and identification with the organizations' goals. Over the past 15 years, research findings have continued to demonstrate strong links between high-performance work systems and both employee attitudes and performance such as productivity, sales, and turnover.

Recent research has shown that organizations' injury rates are associated with the extent to which a high-performance work system was in place, even after controlling for critical variables such as the organizational size, organization age, and union status. However, although impressive, such studies at the organizational level cannot provide information on how employees are affected by a high-performance work system such that their safety is enhanced. A separate study conducted at the individual level of analysis enables us to understand how this takes place. Using a sample of Canadian employees in the petroleum and telecommunications industries, the extent to which employees believed a high-performance work system was in place was indirectly associated with the number of safety incidents reported as well as

their own personal safety orientation (which included employee compliance with safety regulations, willingness to take the initiative on safety issues, safety knowledge, and safety motivation). More important, this study identified how these effects emerged: Employees who believed they had access to a high-performance work system manifested high trust in management and held more positive perceptions of the company's safety climate, which in turn affected self-reported safety incidents and personal safety orientation.

The high-performance work system research just described focuses on the system as a whole. Other research has investigated individual components of high-performance work systems, and two examples of the more specific focus will suffice. First, it would avail little to implement high-performance work systems if individuals were still left with boring, meaningless work over which they believed they had no control. Research shows that having a high-quality job (one in which training has been available and provides opportunities for autonomy) influences employee morale, which in turn affects workplace safety. In addition, having a high-quality job also exerts direct effects on workplace safety, presumably because autonomy promotes the learning, proactivity, and problem solving that enables preventive action.

Second, teams are an integral part of high-performance work systems and should enhance safety for several reasons: for example, they enhance cohesion, information sharing, and the extent to which individuals feel more responsible for each other's well-being. In studies in the coal mining and railway industries, employees working in teams that are more autonomous had better safety performance than their counterparts who worked less interdependently. Perhaps more tellingly, as the familiarity between team members decreased because of absenteeism, safety infractions increased.

PSYCHOLOGICAL CONSEQUENCES OF WORKPLACE SAFETY INFRACTIONS

Not surprisingly given the enormous personal, organizational, and societal costs of safety infractions, research has long focused on factors that cause workplace injuries and fatalities. Where research has focused on the consequences of safety incidents and infractions, most studies have addressed its financial consequences, or the consequences for the organization in terms of the number of workdays lost.

There are now some data from which we can begin to understand the psychological or attitudinal consequences of being injured at work. Specifically, suffering an injury of sufficient severity to require time away from work is associated with heightened distrust of management and feelings of a lack of influence, both of which result in job dissatisfaction. In turn, this job dissatisfaction results in employees thinking about quitting the organization. It remains for research to investigate this issue further because of the *hidden* attitudinal consequences of suffering a workplace injury both to the affected employees and to the organization. As well, research will need to focus on employees indirectly affected by injuries, such as those who might have seen the fatality or injury occur, or who might identify closely with friends or colleagues who are killed or injured on the job.

—Julian Barling and Nick Turner

AUTHORS' NOTE: The authors acknowledge Jenni Carson for comments on an earlier version of this entry.

See also National Institute for Occupational Safety and Health/Occupational Safety and Health Administration; Workplace Injuries

FURTHER READING

Barling, J., & Frone, M. R. (Eds.). (2004). *Psychology of workplace safety*. Washington, DC: American Psychological Association.

Barling, J., Loughlin, C., & Kelloway, E. K. (2002). Development and test of a model linking safety-specific transformational leadership and occupational safety. *Journal of Applied Psychology, 87,* 488–496.

Goodman, P. S. (1979). *Assessing organizational change: The Rushton quality of work experiment.* New York: Wiley.

Pearson, C. A. L. (1992). Autonomous workgroups: An evaluation at an industrial site. *Human Relations, 45,* 905–936.

Zacharatos, A., Barling, J., & Iverson, R. D. (2005). High performance work systems and occupational safety. *Journal of Applied Psychology, 90,* 77–93.

Zohar, D. (2000). A group-level model of safety climate: Testing the effect of group climate on microaccidents in manufacturing jobs. *Journal of Applied Psychology, 85,* 587–596.

WORK SAMPLES

Work samples, in the strictest sense, are hands-on performance tests or simulations of the job, which are used to estimate current or predict future performance on similar tasks. Uses of work samples include the following:

- *Selection:* Work samples can be used to decide which applicants to hire. This is the most typical use of work samples.
- *Performance measurement and evaluation:* Work samples are sometimes used to estimate an individual's current level of job performance when other measures are unavailable. This is discussed at greater length in a following section.
- *Vocational assessment of disabled workers:* Work samples are commonly used to determine whether applicants with disabilities can perform the duties required on different types of jobs. These types of work samples are used to provide career counseling and vocational guidance to disabled workers.
- *Trainability measure:* Work samples are sometimes used after a short training session to decide whether the person should be selected to continue in a lengthier training program. In these cases the work sample is intended measure trainability to predict how successful the person will be in the training program.
- *Training evaluation:* Work samples are commonly used at the completion of a training program to determine whether the training was effective at improving performance.

The defining feature of work samples is physical replication of the critical tasks performed on the job; however, many other selection tools that do not replicate the work environment can also be considered work samples. Consequently, certain types of simulations fit more squarely under the *work sample* label than others. In the broadest sense of the term, any tests assessing specific skills, knowledge, or aptitudes that are critical for performance on the job in question may, in some cases, be characterized as work samples.

WORK SAMPLE CHARACTERISTICS

All work samples are based on the concepts that the test samples behaviors instead of measuring traitlike constructs and that those behaviors sampled are similar to those elicited on the job. Therefore, work samples are job specific. Although one work sample could be used to predict the same job at multiple organizations, the same test may no longer qualify as a work sample if used to predict a different type of job. To illustrate: A test measuring speed and accuracy of identifying number transcription errors could serve as a work sample for data entry clerks. However, the same test is not a work sample for a quality control position in a candy factory even if the test is a valid predictor of performance for both jobs. In the first instance, the test measures behavior similar to that required on the job (checking numbers); in the second instance, the test is likely an indicator of the construct *attention to detail*. Therefore, researchers cannot determine if a test is a work sample without knowledge of the job to be predicted.

Fidelity to the Job

Work samples can range from high fidelity (an exact duplication of job tasks) to low fidelity (having a measurement format that differs from the job tasks). Examples of high-fidelity work samples from a broad range of jobs include flight simulators, dragging a fire hose and climbing a ladder, blueprint reading tests, typing and filing tests, dental carving tests, sewing tests, tests of microscope use, driving tests, assessment center simulations (i.e., in-basket tests, leaderless group discussions, business games, subordinate simulations), police report writing tests, computer programming tests, and so on.

Low-fidelity work samples fall into one of two main categories:

1. *Physical ability tests* such as manual dexterity tests, optical exams, and strength tests

2. *Paper-and-pencil tests* such as job knowledge measures (e.g., farming knowledge test), situational judgment tests, and job-specific skills or aptitude tests (e.g., math tests)

As such, some researchers have used the term *work sample* to refer to a variety of selection tools commonly used by industrial/organizational (I/O) psychologists.

WORK SAMPLE DISADVANTAGES

Although work samples are often useful tools, there are three occasions when their usefulness may be limited:

Cost of Work Samples

The first disadvantage is concerned with the cost or utility of the tool. Development and maintenance of a simulation can be expensive. High-fidelity work simulations must be tailored to tasks performed on the job, and personnel must be trained to administer and score the work sample. In some cases the expense of work samples may outweigh the potential incremental validity of work samples over other tests. For example, when hiring a carpenter it might not be cost-effective to ask 30 applicants to actually build a cabinet. The expenditure of time and materials for a high-fidelity cabinet-building simulation may be excessive. Instead, low-fidelity simulations of the job such as situational judgment tests or job knowledge measures may be more utilitarian. However, the cost of a high-fidelity simulation can vary greatly depending on the complexity of the simulation. For example, with low-complexity repetitive jobs in manufacturing such as assembling computer chips, a high-fidelity work sample soldering wire connections may be quite cost-efficient.

Work Samples as Measures of Current Performance

Work samples are sometimes used to estimate current employee job performance when other measures such as supervisor ratings are unavailable. In these instances, the work samples no longer serve as predictors but rather as proxy criterion measures for a variety of human resource (HR) practices including the following: validating other selection tools, evaluating training outcomes, assessing individual or workforce training needs, giving performance appraisals, or even making promotion and pay decisions. However, the cautions against using work samples as criterion measures are with good reason. Even work samples with point-to-point correspondence to the job can differ from day-to-day performance. Levels of motivation in work samples are high. However, typical levels of motivation in day-to-day performance can vary greatly across individuals. This means work samples measure what an individual *can* do (maximal performance) but not necessarily what an individual typically *will* do (typical performance). In other words, motivation on the job that is a direct determinant of performance is not necessarily measured in a work sample. Therefore care should be taken in assuming work samples are accurate measures of current job performance.

Trainable Knowledge and Skills

Using work samples as a selection tool may not be feasible or appropriate when the work sample measures knowledge or skills that are easily trainable. In entry-level positions, applicants are expected to learn on the job. In addition, some applicants may have experience, making them appear to be better performers than those who do not. But if a small amount of training would change someone's score on the work sample, many inexperienced but future high performers would be falsely rejected when using the work sample. This limits the usefulness of a work sample for two reasons. First, it lowers the criterion-related validity of the work sample. Second, members of protected classes may differ in their opportunities to gain experience in certain jobs (e.g., women in construction). If this is the case, the work sample would result in adverse impact, and awareness of the work sample may further have a *chilling effect* on those who would otherwise apply. Although adverse impact of work samples can often be defended on the basis of content validity, if the skills are easily trainable at low cost to the organization, the work sample could be subject to legal challenge.

WORK SAMPLE ADVANTAGES

Despite the disadvantages just mentioned, work samples that assess skills that applicants *cannot* easily acquire on the job can offer several advantages over other commonly used selection tools including good legal defensibility, realistic job previews, and positive applicant reactions. Well-designed work samples have clear content overlap with the job; therefore they are usually legally defensible on the basis of content validity alone. This type of validity evidence tends to be well accepted by the courts. In addition, most work samples are also face valid, or *look like* the job. Although face validity is not a legally defensible type of validity, it does lead to more positive reactions and perceived *fairness* by applicants when compared with other common selection tests. Work samples also offer a realistic preview of the job allowing applicants to better judge their own qualifications for and interest in the position. As a result of the perceived fairness and ability to self-assess their own performance, applicants may be less likely to quit shortly after hire. Both the content validity and face validity of work samples make work samples typically the least legally challenged and most legally defensible of all commonly used selection tools.

In addition to positive reactions and legal defensibility, research has also shown that work samples can have positive criterion-related validities that match or even exceed those of other selection tools. On average, the meta-analytic estimate of work sample validity for predicting job performance is .46, and training performance is .42. Why do they predict so well? One explanation is that work samples are based on the tenet that past performance is the best predictor of future performance. However, proper work sample design plays a central role in whether a work sample measures up to that tenet. Critical design features include job analysis emphasizing behaviors and tasks, content validity (i.e., bandwidth and fidelity to the job), rater training to increase accuracy and reduce bias (i.e., leniency, severity, and halo), standardization of administration and scoring, assessment of interrater reliability, and emphasis on rating of behaviors. The presence of these features in a work sample increases the likelihood of, but does not guarantee, significant criterion-related validity. Moreover, because some jobs are easier to simulate than others, work samples may better predict performance in jobs with clearly defined and short-duration tasks that do not change over time (e.g., clerical or manufacturing jobs) than in jobs with less structured and longer-duration tasks that do change over time (e.g., project managers and engineers).

WORK SAMPLES: PAST, PRESENT, AND FUTURE

Published research on work samples began as early as the 1930s; however, research interest in work samples has slowed through last 30 years. Instead, research has turned to more specific types of work samples, including situational judgment tests and assessment centers. But despite the lull in academic research, actual use of all types of work samples has continued in applied settings. Technological innovations continue to make simulations less expensive and more realistic. Virtual reality, voice recognition software, and computerized scoring are just a few of the new technologies incorporated in work sample design. Yet research on work samples has not kept pace with these changes. Questions about whether this new technology can improve work sample predictive validity remain unanswered. Because technology limits our ability to create complex simulations, the utility of work samples in the future is unknown. Nevertheless, one thing is certain—work samples are as much a tool of the future as they are of the past.

—*Chaitra M. Hardison*

See also Adverse Impact/Disparate Treatment/Discrimination at Work; Americans With Disabilities Act; Assessment Center; Job Analysis; Job Knowledge Testing; Job Performance Models; Situational Judgment Tests; Validation Strategies

FURTHER READING

Asher, J. J., & Sciarrino, J. A. (1974). Realistic work sample tests: A review. *Personnel Psychology, 27,* 519–533.

Callinan, M., & Robertson, I. T. (2000). Work sample testing. *International Journal of Selection and Assessment, 8,* 248–260.

Hardison, C. M., Kim, D. J., & Sackett, P. R. (2005). *Meta-analysis of work sample criterion related validity: Revisiting anomalous findings.* Paper presented at the Twentieth Annual Conference of the Society of Industrial Organizational Psychology, Inc., Los Angeles.

Robertson, I. T., & Kandola, R. S. (1982). Work sample tests: Validity, adverse impact and applicant reaction. *Journal of Occupational Psychology, 55,* 171–183.

Smith, F. D. (1991). Work samples as measures of performance. In A. K. Wigdor & B. F. Green, Jr. (Eds.), *Performance assessment for the workplace: Vol. 2. Technical issues* (pp. 27–52). Washington, DC: National Academy Press.

Terpstra, D. E., Mohamed, A. A., & Kethley, R. B. (1999). An analysis of federal court cases involving nine selection devices. *International Journal of Selection & Assessment, 7,* 26–34.

WORK VALUES

Individuals hold central beliefs about two broad aspects of work. First, they have beliefs regarding how they ought to behave in work-relevant contexts (working hard, acting with integrity, respecting others). Second, they have preferences regarding what the work environment will provide for them (a challenging job, high pay). Although authors have usually focused on one or the other of these different approaches to work values, they are, in fact, related. Work values defined as generalized beliefs about modes of conduct at work form a primary component of the self-schema, the *ought* self, whereas work preferences compose a part of the *desired* self. Self-relevant beliefs tend to be the most deeply held and influential of cognitions, and thus values are stable and central beliefs, having powerful influences on other cognitions, motivation, and action in the workplace. Work values are not merely evaluative responses; they are embedded within self-identity.

Based on the preceding definitions, work values defined in the ought frame are a powerful influence on preferences regarding objects or organizational characteristics. Work values, as they address one of a very few primary domains in life, act as an organizing structure for much of the rest of our system of cognition. Perceptions, motivation, attitudes, and opinions are all subject to this structure. Many concepts thought of as factual are influenced by work value systems, for example, the belief that jobs that require more responsibility also require more pay.

STRUCTURE AND ORIGIN OF WORK VALUES

Most authors conceptualize the structure of individual work value systems as ordered in terms of their impact on evaluations of objects, events, and behavior at work; but others have disagreed with such a ranking approach. Because values are socially desirable, individuals tend to learn them in an all-or-nothing fashion as children (always be honest, always achieve the highest possible level of performance). As individuals mature, they integrate these beliefs into a value system. This leads to the necessity of choosing one value over another when they come into contact with conflict; but over time, individuals may try to represent multiple values in their behavior.

Several general categories of work values are commonly identified; these typically include extrinsic or instrumental values (high pay), intrinsic or cognitive values (a challenging job), relational or social values (respectful relationships between coworkers), and power or self-enhancement values (gaining promotion or status). They are seen as more specific manifestations of general life values, but it may be argued that work values also affect life values over time. Evidence tends to support this *spillover* relationship between life and work values; however, it has also been proposed that a compensatory model may represent the relationship between different domains. For example, if individuals are particularly driven to achieve extrinsic outcomes at work, they may focus on relationships in their personal lives. This conceptualization has received minimal support to date.

Differences in work values may also be traced to cultural values based on the developmental history of particular nations or regions. A small number of value dimensions seems to generalize across national cultures; thus such values are pivotal in understanding differences in such work-related cognition and behavior as communication, conflict resolution, and status organizing processes. Research on cultural values indicates that general clusters of these values revolve around basic problems that all human societies must solve:

- The nature of the relationship of the individual to the collective
- The use of hierarchy versus egalitarianism as a means to ensure societal order
- The nature of the relationship to the natural and social world (mastery or control versus harmony or adaptation)

These cultural patterns influence work values in that some cultural values are compatible with certain work values, whereas others conflict. For example, hierarchical approaches to social order are consistent with power and self-enhancement work values, and egalitarianism and harmony as cultural values are consistent with a strong emphasis on relationships at work.

In addition to cultural context, work values are acquired from other societal institutions (family, economic, and political). Besides these contextual influences, individual differences, such as personality, also play a role in the development of an individual's work value system. Work values and personality tend to be related, but they both also contribute uniquely to variance in occupational preferences. Because life values are learned early and relate to relatively stable factors such as culture and personality, they are difficult to change during adulthood. Such change requires a change in an entire system of related beliefs, attitudes, and perceptions. Direct conflict of values may produce change, and having violated a value once, individuals may find it easier over time to violate that value until it has lost its importance. Repeated failure of value-related behavior to produce positive outcomes may also produce change. These processes are likely to explain long-term, cross-situational value changes in adults. Overall, the finding of a tendency toward a desire for increased balance of work and nonwork values provides support for the idea that work ethic values in the United States have tended to erode as related behaviors, or lack thereof, have failed to significantly change lifestyles. Evidence indicates not only that generational differences in work values exist but that values also change as employees age.

Organizational socialization is one important process through which work values are conveyed to employees. Cultural attributes of the organization, such as myths, stories, repetition, and more formal socialization processes, are used to teach employees what they should value in the work context. Leaders or founders may propagate the values of the organization among employees. To be internalized, however, a value must be functional at the individual level or be presented as the sole course of action available. Work values that are stated or espoused by the organization will eventually lose their priority if reward systems do not support them. In such situations employees learn that what they should say is substantially different from what they should do (enacted values). Employees bring values to the organization, and so at times may influence those of the organization, especially if large numbers or particularly powerful employees are hired.

WORK VALUE EFFECTS AND OUTCOMES

Work values influence perceptions regarding what occurs in the work environment, in particular, in highly uncertain contexts. They also act as an influence on behavioral decisions. In general, values lead to goals, which in turn lead to behavior. In addition to the mediating effect of goals, moderators (such as having discretion over action) and the labeling of an action as value relevant can determine whether values will predict behavior in specific situations. Work values act as motivational elements in that they indicate which behaviors are more desirable to perform than others from an ideal perspective, either because the behavior itself is valued, or because the behavior moves the actor toward a valued object or event. Acting on values may or may not fulfill innate needs.

Certain values play important roles in influencing particular behaviors. For example, a dominant honesty value produces more ethical decisions. These relationships between work values and behavior are often small at any one point in time but stronger over time, as with other individual differences. Additionally, in some instances, individuals use value statements (espoused, as opposed to enacted, values) to provide legitimacy for behavior that has already occurred. In these cases we might argue that the behavior is generating espoused work values, as opposed to work values leading to behavior.

Shared value systems, or work value congruence, has received a substantial amount of research attention. Several types of congruence have been identified; for example, supplementary fit, in which similarity with others in the work environment is the basis for congruence, and complementary fit, in which different attributes may be brought to the aggregate by different individuals to *round out* the unit or organization. With regard to work values, supplementary or similarity-based congruence has received the most attention. Shared work values have been shown to influence internal processes positively. Common patterns of cognition lead to reduced conflict and uncertainty; shared goals; and more predictability, trust, and satisfaction. This view is consistent with the Attraction–Selection–Attrition framework, which states that organizations tend to attract and retain similar people, and thus become more homogeneous over time. Value congruence has been explored at multiple levels (individual–organization, supervisor–subordinate, between coworkers, within teams).

Although sharing enacted work values tends to produce positive affective responses by way of common processing, the ability to articulate espoused values congruent with organizational management may relate more consistently to individual performance evaluations. A related view of value sharing, drawn from the organizational culture literature, is represented by the fragmentation perspective, which argues that shared beliefs are temporary because of the existence of multiple belief systems in any complex and uncertain environment.

Although evidence consistently shows that work value similarity generates more positive attitudes, the relationship between value sharing and performance remains unclear. One option is that positive affect generated by value congruence will lead to higher performance. Other areas of research (i.e., the cross-cultural and group decision-making literatures) suggest that too much homogeneity may reduce performance in creative or changing situations and that constructive conflict should be generated by a diversity of task-relevant perspectives. If so, this conflict must be managed carefully to positively influence effectiveness.

—*Elizabeth C. Ravlin*

See also Attitudes and Beliefs; Motivational Traits; Organizational Culture; Person–Organization Fit

FURTHER READING

Kristof, A. L. (1996). Person–organization fit: An integrative review of its conceptualizations, measurement, and implications. *Personnel Psychology, 49,* 1–49.

Meglino, B. M., & Ravlin, E. C. (1998). Individual values in organizations: Concepts, controversies, and research. *Journal of Management, 24,* 351–389.

Roe, R. A., & Ester, P. (1999). Values and work: Empirical findings and theoretical perspective. *Applied Psychology: An International Review, 48,* 1–21.

Schwartz, S. H. (1999). A theory of cultural values and some implications for work. *Applied Psychology: An International Review, 48,* 23–47.

Smola, K. W., & Sutton, C. D. (2002). Generational differences: Revisiting generational work values for the new millennium. *Journal of Organizational Behavior, 23,* 363–382.

Appendixes: Pursuing a Career as a Successful Industrial and Organizational Psychologist

We gratefully acknowledge the Society for Industrial and Organizational Psychology (SIOP) for providing content for these appendixes. As a division of the APA and an organizational affiliate of APS, the society seeks to enhance human well-being and performance in organizational and work settings by promoting the science, practice, and teaching of industrial-organizational psychology through education, public awareness, and opportunities for information exchange among members of the field. To learn more about the society, we direct you to their Web site: www.SIOP.org.

To pursue a successful career in industrial and organizational (I/O) psychology, a graduate degree is recommended. A master's degree takes, on average, two years to complete. **Appendix 1** describes the educational approach and topics studied in this type of degree program. A doctorate takes substantially longer to complete, five years on average. The range of topics studied is quite similar to that for the master's degree; however, the depth of study and focus on conducting applied research are the distinguishing characteristics of a doctoral program. **Appendix 2** provides a detailed summary of the education and training usually found in a doctoral program.

Once you have decided on a degree type, you must pick a graduate school. A complete listing of graduate programs in I/O psychology (and related areas) can be found in **Appendix 3**. To help navigate this list and learn about graduate program rankings, please visit http://siop.org/GTP/.

A common denominator across almost all graduate programs is a reliance on a scientist-practitioner training model. The hallmark of this approach is using science and research to understand and work to improve individual and organizational health, well-being, and effectiveness. You will read from and perhaps even attempt to publish research in a wide range of scientific journals. **Appendix 4** provides a comprehensive listing of the journals you will be seeing in your graduate education.

Upon graduation, your career options will be terrifically diverse. You can pursue a career in academia or become a practitioner. **Appendix 5** outlines the most common academic and practitioner job titles for I/O psychologists.

To find a good job, many prospective candidates choose to network in professional groups. Appendix 6 provides a thorough listing of such groups throughout the world. Membership in one or more of these groups is also a terrific way to gather current information, stay in touch with colleagues, benchmark problems and solutions, and feel part of a special community of professionals dedicated to studying and working to improve the world of work.

Appendix 1. Guidelines for Education and Training at the Master's Level in Industrial and Organizational Psychology

PURPOSE OF THE GUIDELINES

These guidelines have been written to aid faculty and curriculum planners in the design and change of master's-level graduate programs in industrial/organizational (I/O) psychology. Master's-level training in I/O psychology is widespread. Lowe (1993) identified 55 programs designed to award a master's degree in I/O psychology as a stand-alone degree, but she acknowledged that this was a conservative estimate. The large majority of these programs are not affiliated with a doctoral program (Koppes, 1991).

The impetus for these guidelines is threefold. First, the Society for Industrial and Organizational Psychology, Inc. (SIOP) is interested in providing guidance to, and supporting, such programs. Second, the National Conference on Applied Master's Training in Psychology (1990) has recommended the adoption of specialty guidelines such as this. Finally, this is a companion document to the *Guidelines for Education and Training at the Doctoral Level in I/O Psychology* (SIOP, 1985)[1] that called for the creation of guidelines for master's-level education. As the content of this document is an outgrowth of the work that was done for the doctoral-level guidelines, there is much similarity between the two sets of guidelines.

These guidelines were not written to provide the basis for graduate studies program certification, determining eligibility for specialty licensing as an I/O psychologist, establishing eligibility for membership in the Society, or highlighting the continuing education and training needs of the profession. In addition, these guidelines were not designed to be a set of recommendations for education in related fields (e.g., labor and human resources, organizational behavior). Although it is recognized that many academic disciplines or specialties are concerned with developing related subject matter and skills, these related areas are beyond the scope of the guidelines.

PERSPECTIVE OF THE GUIDELINES

These guidelines list, categorize, and describe competencies that should guide curricular and pedagogic decisions by faculty responsible for training I/O

These guidelines were prepared by the Master's Education Subcommittee of the Education and Training Committee of the Society for Industrial and Organizational Psychology, Inc.

EDITOR'S NOTE: Information for this appendix was graciously provided by the Society of Industrial and Organizational Psychology.

students at the master's level. Because almost all of the competencies listed here are also contained in the doctoral guidelines, the reader might ask the obvious question: What distinguishes master's-level and doctoral-level education? The distinctions are described in the following sections.

BREADTH OF TRAINING

Master's-level students will typically receive a narrower breadth of training than will doctoral students. This stems largely from the fact that fewer hours are required for the master's degree. Thus, the competencies listed in Table A.1.1 may not be covered as fully at the master's level as they might be at the doctoral level. As a result, there may be considerable variability in program content among master's-level I/O programs (e.g., one program may emphasize "organizational" issues, while another emphasizes "industrial" issues). Lowe (1993) provides evidence of the variability of master's-level I/O programs.

DEPTH OF TRAINING

Master's students are expected to demonstrate basic-level competencies (e.g., regression analysis, classical test theory), but only to be exposed to higher-level concepts (e.g., causal modeling, generalizability theory). For example, whereas a doctoral student may take several courses in statistical analysis, the master's student may have just one or two courses. Besides fewer hours, master's education is typically delivered with a lower faculty-to-student ratio than is true of doctoral-level training (Lowe, 1993). This type of training is consistent with the generalization that master's-level students will typically be consumers of I/O knowledge rather than producers of new knowledge. As such, they are engaged in applying this knowledge to issues involving individuals and groups in organizational settings. Those involved in research usually do so under the guidance of a doctoral-level psychologist.

CAREER OPTIONS

The career options are different for master's-level versus doctoral-level graduates. Schippmann, Schmitt, and Hawthorne (1992) reviewed the work roles of I/O students whose terminal degree is the master's degree

versus the PhD. They concluded that there are "substantive differences between the kinds of work" performed by these two groups. There were very few master's graduates in academic roles, whereas master's graduates were more highly represented in jobs such as compensation, training, data analysis, and generalist human resource management positions compared with doctoral graduates.

FURTHER EDUCATION

Some master's-level students are interested in continuing to doctoral study. Master's programs may be designed to serve students who want either (a) predoctoral training, (b) practitioner-oriented training (terminal master's degree), or (c) both. Since doctoral-level education in I/O psychology is based on the scientist-practitioner model, programs that provide predoctoral training should also have a scientist-practitioner focus. Thus, when designing such programs, research skills probably should be weighted more heavily (category II competencies) compared with specific content issues (category III competencies). This type of program would also be appropriate for master's-level I/O practitioners who work in research settings. Programs designed to meet the needs of students for whom the master's degree will be their highest degree may opt to place greater weight on content issues relative to research skills.

These and other distinctions between master's-level and doctoral-level training lead to substantial differences in the two levels of training. However, none of the differences highlighted earlier suggests that the basic content of the field changes as a function of the level of education. Thus, the competencies in this document and the companion guidelines for doctoral programs are similar. The perspective of these guidelines is that the competencies identified in Table A.1.1 (particularly sections II and III) are ideals that probably no program will meet completely. They are provided to aid faculty and curriculum planners as they start new programs or try to improve their current programs.

TITLE

A semantic difficulty is encountered in a document such as this. What is the appropriate title, or label, for persons who have completed a master's degree in I/O

Table A.1.1   Areas of Competence to Be Developed in Master's-Level I/O Psychology Programs

This table lists the recommended areas of competence to be developed in students in master's-level I/O programs. Competencies listed in Section I may be obtained as part of the student's psychological training at the undergraduate level. Competencies listed in Section IV are optional.

   I.   Core Psychological Domains (may be acquired at the undergraduate level)
      A. History and Systems of Psychology
      B. Fields of Psychology

  II.   Data Collection and Analysis Skills
      A. Research Methods
      B. Statistical Methods/Data Analysis

 III.   Core I/O Domains
      A. Ethical, Legal, and Professional Contexts
      B. Measurement of Individual Differences
      C. Criterion Theory and Development
      D. Job and Task Analysis
      E. Employee Selection, Placement, and Classification
      F. Performance Appraisal and Feedback
      G. Training: Theory, Program Design, and Evaluation
      H. Work Motivation
      I. Attitude Theory
      J. Small Group Theory and Process
      K. Organization Theory
      L. Organizational Development

 IV.   Additional I/O Domains (educational experiences in these domains are considered desirable but not essential)
      A. Career Development Theory
      B. Human Performance/Human Factors
      C. Consumer Behavior
      D. Compensation and Benefits
      E. Industrial and Labor Relations

psychology? The term "psychologist" is inappropriate because the use of that term is regulated by law in some states and is usually restricted to persons who have completed doctoral training and/or have been licensed. Further, the employment settings in which these graduates work are so diverse that a job-based title is also inappropriate (e.g., human resource manager, trainer, organization consultant). Titles assigned to other psychological subdisciplines at the master's

level (e.g., mental health specialist, caseworker, school counselor) are inappropriate.

The following title is used in this document: "master's-level I/O practitioner." While it is descriptive, it is both unwieldy and, in some cases, misleading. A shorter title would be preferable (e.g., MBA), but the fact that many people are presently unfamiliar with the discipline of I/O psychology makes the use of a very short acronym inappropriate (e.g., MIOP). Further, some master's-level graduates will work in research and/or educational settings, which makes the use of the word "practitioner" problematic. However, since most master's-level graduates work in applied settings (Ekeberg, Switzer, & Siegfried, 1991; Schippmann et al., 1992), "practitioner" is often an appropriate term.

Admittedly, a document such as this cannot mandate the use of a particular title. Nor is it the committee's desire to do so. If, and when, a different title achieves popular acceptance, these guidelines should be changed to reflect that fact. Meanwhile, it is important for students in master's-level I/O programs to be identified with the discipline. The title "master's-level I/O practitioner" serves that purpose.

COMPETENCIES

A competency-based approach is adopted here (as it is in the doctoral guidelines) as opposed to recommendations about specific curriculum designs and educational experiences. These guidelines focus on the outcomes of training, and on the knowledge, skills, behavior, and capabilities necessary to function as a master's-level I/O practitioner. The primary rationale for this approach is contained in the concept of "equifinality." It is frequently the case that several alternative curriculum arrangements are equally effective at producing competent graduates. There are several means to the same end. Focusing on curriculum design loses sight of this.

The competencies presented in Table A.1.1 are taken largely from the doctoral-level guidelines. However, there are some significant dissimilarities. First, they are grouped into four major categories. These categories are meant to make some molar distinctions among the competencies. Category I competencies are those that any person who obtains a graduate degree in any field of psychology should possess (see also National Conference on Applied Master's Training in Psychology, 1990). Many students will acquire a substantial portion of this information in an undergraduate psychology program.

Master's-level I/O programs should ensure that their students have exposure to the broad field of psychology. Category II competencies relate to data collection and analysis. These competencies are important even to "consumers" of knowledge because they enable them to make informed judgments about new research. This training can be very useful to organizations in a variety of applications. Category III competencies are at the "core" of the I/O discipline. Ideally, these should receive substantial coverage by any program. However, of necessity an entire course may not be devoted to each of these competencies, but they could be grouped together in a variety of ways. Category IV competencies are beneficial, but are not at the "core" of the discipline. Many programs might find that other departments or colleges can provide the training for these competencies (e.g., consumer behavior in a marketing department).

A second difference is that some of the competency descriptions have been rewritten to reflect a lower level of sophistication. For example, the statistical methods/ data analysis competency description notes that students should be familiar with (as opposed to competent in) path analysis, factor analysis, and so on. Third, two doctoral-level competencies (decision theory and individual assessment) were eliminated completely. Decision theory is partially subsumed under other competencies (the cognitive-affective bases of behavior section under Fields of Psychology, Employee Selection, Human Performance). Within I/O psychology, the practice of Individual Assessment is generally conceded to require licensure, and thus a doctorate. Finally, two competencies have been added (both in Category IV), namely, Compensation and Benefits and Industrial and Labor Relations. These are areas for which many master's-level I/O practitioners are responsible (Schippmann et al., 1992).

The additions, deletions, and changes described earlier were based on four sources of information. First, SIOP sponsored a survey of I/O and organizational behavior programs, and specifically extended this survey to include master's programs (SIOP, 1992). The second source was the personal experience of the committee members as master's-level educators and their exposure to a variety of master's-level I/O programs. Third, the job analysis information reported by Schippmann et al. (1992) and by Ekeberg et al. (1991) was consulted. Finally, each of the committee members asked several of their colleagues, in both industry and academics, to critique a draft of these guidelines, and their suggestions and comments were incorporated as appropriate.

Related Competencies

The bulk of this document describes the areas or domains recommended specifically for training in I/O psychology. However, before presenting them, it is useful to comment on other areas considered, but judged not to be appropriate as part of this document.

One such set of competencies that had been suggested might be termed "personal skills." These include effective oral and written communication skills, facility at developing interpersonal relationships, effective work habits, critical analytic thinking ability, and so forth. It is quite clear that success in graduate school depends on possessing these attributes. They are also needed for success in one's career. Yet these personal skills are of universal importance, and thus are not included in the domains list.

A second set of issues was suggested by the National Conference on Applied Master's Training in Psychology (1990). All graduate students in psychology should possess these competencies. These include library research skills and sensitivity to social and cultural diversity. These are important skills, but they do not merit inclusion in this list because they are byproducts of quality graduate study and are not specific to I/O training.

Another cluster of competencies that was not explicated involves areas in which it would be desirable, but not necessary, to have training to ensure career success in I/O psychology. A list of these areas could easily be expanded to include much of the social sciences and business (e.g., content mastery in Economics, Marketing, Labor and Human Resources, and even Accounting). Potentially important process skills would include those needed for employee counseling or individual rehabilitation. Competencies in all these areas would be appropriate and desirable, but they are not made part of these guidelines.

Finally, some think that a good graduate program provides guidance to students in their own career planning and in the use of career enhancement strategies.

Table A.1.2   Curriculum Options Considered in the Guidelines

1. **Formal coursework** is classroom instruction common to university settings in which material pertinent to the domains is covered. This method itself can involve a variety of different techniques including lectures, discussion, presentations, case analysis, experiential exercises, and so forth.

2. **Independent reading/study** is nonclassroom instruction in which the student, in consultation with qualified faculty, assumes responsibility for and commitment to the accomplishment of domain objectives. This method includes all forms of nonclassroom instruction for which self-initiated effort is of central concern and for which such effort can successfully result in the achievement of relevant domain objectives. Examples would include self-initiated effort through reading; generating appropriate review manuscripts, proposals, or reports; designing and conducting a research investigation; and acquiring interactive computer skills.

3. **Supervised experience (internships, practicums)** is nonclassroom instruction in which the student is actively engaged in projects under the direct supervision of qualified personnel. Such projects would be aimed at fulfilling specific training objectives mutually agreed to by the student, the supervisor, and program faculty with special emphasis given to the acquisition of skills. Participation would not be motivated primarily for compensation. This method will often be characterized by in vivo learning opportunities such that the student learns skills that will transfer to settings in which the student will eventually be working.

   In all cases, however, there is meaningful professional supervision of the training experience. Although internship supervisors may not be I/O psychologists, their skill and knowledge base, job duties, scope of practice, and ethical principles should be congruent with those of I/O psychology. Students are also supervised by a faculty member who is an I/O psychologist. Examples would include practicum and internship experiences, fieldwork teaching/training, thesis/dissertation research, and so forth.

4. **On-the-job training** is nonclassroom instruction in which capabilities are learned through "hands-on" experience with applied tasks under the explicit guidance of a professionally qualified task expert. Such training is typically done in conjunction with one's "job," and participation involves compensation. On-the-job training provides firsthand knowledge of how the skills and knowledge within the domains of I/O psychology can be used to address problems and allows for the opportunity to focus on solutions that will have an impact on the setting in which the student is working.

5. **Modeling/observation** is nonclassroom implicit instruction that is obtained as a result of studying under, working with, and paying attention to professionally qualified personnel in the daily conduct of their jobs and special projects. This method implies that the learning of important skills might well be obtained without explicit instructional intent on the part of the model. On the other hand, modeling may also be done in a purposeful and self-conscious manner. Modeling/observation, because of its personal nature, cuts across several of the training methods described earlier.

Such activities help a student in drawing together personal information and experiences in a formal effort to make a career decision and to map out a suitable career path. Once a decision has been made, appropriate developmental experiences could then be provided in a systematic way. Many schools already incorporate such planning, often using a variety of mechanisms (e.g., assigning formal advisers). However, once again, while this was viewed as a desirable feature of a graduate program, it is not considered to be a competency that graduates ought to possess.

STRATEGIES FOR BUILDING COMPETENCE

Program designers and faculty may develop a student's capabilities in a competency domain by using one or more methods or techniques. For many (or most) competencies, multiple means are preferable. A given course is likely to touch upon more than one area, particularly in comparison to doctoral-level training. Moreover, the resources and capacities of a given program also will shape curriculum design. For these reasons, the guidelines do not detail a specific curriculum plan.

Table A.1.2 describes curriculum options identified by the Master's Education Subcommittee as useful methods for master's-level training. While other approaches and variations do exist, the list in Table A.1.2 is reasonably inclusive. It would be consistent with the spirit of these guidelines for a program to develop skill or knowledge in several domains using a single particular educational experience (e.g., a seminar, a supervised field project, or an assigned reading list).

COMPETENCIES ARE DYNAMIC

The competency-based approach of these guidelines is advantageous for several reasons. It maintains a focus on what is to be taught and learned, provides desirable flexibility to curriculum planners, and recognizes the multiple paths to developing most important skills. Nonetheless, it also is true that the recommendations based on such an approach might become dated. Therefore, the present guidelines should be reevaluated regularly. They must be kept up-to-date by continuous reference to the nature of work and conditions surrounding the I/O practitioner at work.

COMPETENCY DESCRIPTIONS
I. CORE PSYCHOLOGICAL DOMAINS

(See preceding discussion, especially the Competencies section, for distinctions among the four domains.)

I.A. History and Systems of Psychology

If I/O students know how the discipline of psychology developed and evolved into its present configuration, then each generation will share the common bonds and language of the discipline. They will also possess a knowledge of the intellectual heritage of our field. Such common knowledge is important for the pragmatic functional role it plays in communication and in preventing frequent repetitions of the mistakes and dead ends of the past. Many historical schools and systems of psychology have a contemporary representative, in either a pure or a diluted form; a knowledge of the roots of these different theoretical positions is important. For example, many contemporary debates about theoretical perspectives appear dysfunctional when viewed against the background of historical developments in our field. A knowledge of our history enables us to appreciate these different approaches both for their unique contribution to psychology and for the alternatives they provide for an understanding of observable phenomena. Finally, an understanding of history and systems of psychology allows integration of I/O psychology into the broader discipline by tracing our roots back to American functionalism, radical

behaviorism, views of Freud, Titchener, Tolman, Spearman, and Cattell and other perspectives that have shaped our thinking about psychology. As consumers of current and future psychological research, master's-level I/O practitioners should understand the relationship of these findings to the broader discipline of psychology.

I.B. Fields of Psychology

I/O psychology is basically the study of behavior of individuals that occurs in a particular setting, that is, organizations of almost any kind. This focus differentiates it from fields of psychology that study basic processes (perception, memory, learning); from fields that study particular populations of individuals (children, mentally disturbed, developmentally challenged); from fields that study analytic procedures or assessment procedures (psychometrics); and from fields that study mechanisms of behavior (physiological psychology, brain research). Although the populations of individuals and the locations are diverse, in this emphasis on behavior in a special setting we are eclectic. Because we borrow ideas, procedures, and paradigms from the other fields of psychology, it is important that we have an understanding of the strengths, weaknesses, and sources of our often unacknowledged borrowings.

While we draw freely from other fields of psychology, we do not borrow equally from all fields. We share a great deal with social psychology, psychometrics, motivation, learning, and personality. In our current work (as a group), we borrow less from clinical, developmental, and physiological-sensory psychology. The importance of these fields of psychology to the I/O area changes over time and varies with the particular interests of the individual I/O practitioner. It is difficult to predict which of the related fields will develop research in the near future that will have an impact on I/O psychology.

In any event, to be consistent with American Psychological Association (APA) and Council for Applied Master's Programs in Psychology (CAMPP) recommendations, students should be exposed to the following broad areas:

1. Biological bases of behavior: physiological psychology, comparative psychology, neuropsychology, sensation and perception, psychopharmacology

2. Acquired or learned bases of behavior: learning, thinking, motivation, emotion
3. Social bases of behavior: social psychology, group processes, organizational and systems theory
4. Individual differences: personality theory, human development, abnormal psychology

Master's-level I/O practitioners should be familiar with the relevant perspectives and applications from these areas.

II. DATA COLLECTION AND ANALYSIS SKILLS

II.A. Research Methods

The domain of research methods includes the methods, procedures, and techniques useful in the conduct of empirical research on phenomena of interest in I/O psychology. The specific topics encompassed by research methods include the scientific method (with attention to issues in the philosophy of science), inductive and deductive reasoning, problem statements and research questions, hypotheses, study designs (experimental, quasi-experimental, and nonexperimental), the nature and definition of constructs, the manipulation of variables (in experimental research), the concepts underlying and methods used for the assessment of the reliability and validity of measures, the administration of various specific types of measures (questionnaires, interviews, observations of behavior, projective measures, etc.), the use of various sampling procedures (probability and nonprobability types) especially as applied to survey research, the conduct of research with various specific strategies (field study, laboratory experiment, field experiment, sample survey, simulation, case study, etc.), the use of statistical methods to establish relationships between variables, the formulation of research-based conclusions, and the ethical standards that govern the conduct of all research involving human participants. Specific knowledge about relative strengths and weaknesses of different research strategies as well as a tolerant appreciation of the benefits of alternative strategies must be developed. While master's-level I/O practitioners will need more expert guidance in using these methods and procedures in complex applications, they should develop the skill to use them in less complex applied situations (such as training evaluation and attitude surveys) and the ability to interpret and evaluate others' research.

II.B. Statistical Methods/Data Analysis

This domain has to do with the various statistical techniques that are used in the analysis of data generated by empirical research. The domain includes both descriptive and inferential statistical methods; it spans both parametric and nonparametric statistical methods. Among the specific competencies, issues and techniques encompassed by the domain are estimates of central tendency; measures of variability; sampling distributions; point and interval estimates; inferences about differences between means, proportions, and so forth; univariate analysis of variance; linear regression and correlation; and multiple regression. These topics are likely to be particularly useful in mainstream organizational research settings such as survey analysis and program evaluation. Knowledge of this domain implies a basic understanding of the statistical foundation of such methods, asymptotic sampling variances of different statistics, the assumptions underlying the proper use of the same methods, and the generalizations, inferences, and interpretations that can legitimately be made based on statistical evidence. In addition, familiarity with the following techniques would be useful to students in their role as consumers of research: multivariate analysis of variance, nonlinear regression and correlation, path analysis, factor analysis, meta-analysis, and causal modeling.

Students should be skilled in using at least one of the major statistical software packages designed for social science research so they can perform appropriate analyses for applied research projects in work organizations.

III. CORE I/O DOMAINS

III.A. Ethical, Legal, and Professional Contexts

This domain has to do with the ethical, legal, and professional contexts within which the master's-level I/O practitioner will operate. I/O master's graduates should have knowledge of, and should behave in accord with, relevant ethical guidelines (e.g., *Ethical Principles of Psychologists and Code of Conduct;* APA, 1992). I/O master's students should know relevant federal, state, and local laws, statutes, regulations, and legal precedents (e.g., the Equal Employment Opportunity Commission's *Uniform Guidelines on Employee Selection Procedures,* 1978). Since a fair amount of professional work done in organizations is covered by negotiated labor contracts, competency in this domain would also include an awareness of opportunities and constraints imposed by such agreements as well as an appreciation of the labor/management dynamics associated with them. Finally, all master's-level I/O practitioners should have knowledge of the various professional norms, standards, and guidelines relevant to the profession (e.g., *Specialty Guidelines for the Delivery of Services by Industrial-Organizational Psychologists APA,* 1981; *Principles for the Validation and Use of Personnel Selection Procedures,* SIOP, 1987; and *Standards for Educational and Psychological Testing* APA, 1985).

III.B. Measurement of Individual Differences

I/O psychology emphasizes the importance of individual differences in the study of individual behavior. This topic is foundational to many applied issues, such as employee selection, performance appraisal, employee attitude surveys, and training evaluation. A sound background in classical measurement theory is essential (e.g., reliability, validity), and exposure to modern measurement theories and their respective areas of application is highly desirable (e.g., generalizability theory, item response theory, causal modeling). The areas of measurement that are relevant include all knowledge, skills, abilities, and other personal characteristics that affect behavior in work contexts. Master's-level I/O practitioners would not typically be involved in the creation of new measures except under the direction of a PhD-level psychologist. Much of what master's-level I/O practitioners do in this area is subject to close scrutiny by courts of law, civil rights groups, and professional colleagues. Because of these external and internal pressures, master's-level I/O practitioners should be competent to monitor practice and to apply measurement principles in conformance to the highest standards of the discipline.

III.C. Criterion Theory and Development

Almost all applications of I/O psychology (e.g., selection, human resources planning, leadership, performance appraisal, organization design, organization diagnosis and development, training) involve measurements against criteria (standards) of effectiveness for individuals, groups, and/or organizations. The selection of criteria is not a simple issue and represents a significant area of concern for I/O psychologists. The knowledge base of this domain incorporates understanding the theoretical and practical issues such as single versus multiple criteria, criterion dynamics, the characteristics of good and acceptable criteria (relevance, reliability, practicality), and criteria as a basis for understanding human behavior at work and in organizations. Beyond this knowledge, the master's-level I/O practitioner should have the skills necessary for developing valid criteria and methods of measuring them. These necessarily include skills in many other domains identified in the document (e.g., job analysis, measurement).

III.D. Job and Task Analysis

This domain encompasses the theory and techniques used to generate information about what is involved in performing a job or task, the physical and social context of this performance, and the attributes needed by an incumbent for such performance. Tasks are basic units of activity, the elements of which highlight the connection between behavior and result. A job is a grouping of tasks designed to achieve an organizational objective.

The fundamental concern of job and task analysis is to obtain descriptive information to design training programs, establish performance criteria, develop selection systems, use job evaluation systems, redesign machinery or tools, or create career paths for personnel. The specific steps taken and the type of information gathered will vary depending on the purpose of the job and task analysis. Relevant information that should be considered includes the worker behaviors involved; the knowledge, skills, and abilities required; the standards of performance wanted; the tools, machines, and work aids used; the sources of information available to the incumbent; the social, environmental, and physical working conditions; and the nature of supervision. Similarly, some steps involved in job and task analyses include identifying the purpose of the analysis; preparing, designing, or selecting a job analysis system; collecting job or task information; summarizing the results; and documenting the steps taken for future reference. The individual competent in this domain should have a knowledge of the different approaches to job and task analysis, as well as skill in applying these techniques in the field.

III.E. Employee Selection, Placement, and Classification

This domain consists of the theory and techniques involved in the effective matching of individual needs, preferences, knowledge, skills and abilities with the needs and preferences of organizations. An organization's needs are defined by the jobs assigned to positions in the organization. More specifically, this domain encompasses theory and research in human abilities; test theory development and use; job analysis; criterion development and measurement; classical and decision theory models of selection, placement, and classification; alternative selection devices (e.g., interviews, assessment centers); and legal and societal considerations that affect selection, placement, and classification. In particular, the individual must keep current with the legislation and court decisions related to these issues as well as with responses of the Society to laws and their interpretations. This domain also includes various specialized statistical techniques.

The level of knowledge of the master's-level I/O practitioner should be sufficient to (a) determine the most appropriate selection procedure for measuring knowledge, skill, ability, and/or personal characteristics and the appropriate validation strategies; (b) recognize when a higher level of expertise is necessary to develop and evaluate a selection system; and (c) work under the direction of a PhD psychologist when conducting criterion-related and/or construct validation studies. In addition, the individual should be skillful in applying the theory and techniques of this domain to develop content-valid selection procedures typically found in an employment setting (e.g., interviews, work samples).

III.F. Performance Appraisal and Feedback

Performance appraisal and feedback have a knowledge and skill base. This area centers on the methods of measuring and evaluating individuals as they perform organizational tasks and on taking action (administrative and/or developmental) with individuals based on such appraisals. The knowledge base includes a thorough understanding of rating scale construction and use, as well as understanding of the relative advantages of different rating sources (e.g., supervisory vs. peer). Also relevant are the areas of measurement theory, data analysis, criterion theory and development, motivation theory, and the factors that underlie interpersonal perception and judgment. The skill base includes procedures for communicating performance evaluations to job incumbents and counseling them in appropriate means of improving their performance. Also, skill in designing a complete performance appraisal and feedback system that meets organizational needs while maintaining and/or enhancing worker motivation and/or performance is desirable.

III.G. Training: Theory, Program Design, and Evaluation

This domain includes theory and techniques used to design, conduct, and evaluate instructional programs. The instructional process begins with a needs assessment, including organizational, job, and task analyses to determine the goals and constraints of the organization and the characteristics of the job and trainees. Familiarity with basic phenomena of learning (e.g., modern learning theory, principles of adult learning, conditioning principles) as well as knowledge of the different approaches to training (e.g., computer-assisted instruction, simulation, behavior modification) are necessary for designing programs. Transfer of training to the desired setting is an important consideration. For programs to be conducted as planned, the instructors must have good instructional skills. Thus, training the trainers may be necessary.

Both the process and the outcome of the program may be evaluated to determine if it has been conducted as planned and whether it has had any effect. Knowledge of design issues such as pre- and posttesting and control groups, as well as organizational constraints, is necessary for planning an evaluation strategy.

III.H. Work Motivation

Work motivation refers to the conditions within the individual and his or her environment that influence the direction, strength, and persistence of relevant individual behavior in organizations when individual abilities and organizational constraints are held constant. Master's-level I/O practitioners need to have a sound background in work motivation at three levels. First, they must be familiar with the theories of human motivation including (but not limited to) need theories, cognitive theories, and reinforcement theories. In all cases, there must be a good understanding of the extensive research and theory that exist outside the domain of work in the basic psychological literature.

At the second level, there must be an understanding of the research and theory in relevant domains of I/O psychology that represent general applications of one or more motivational perspectives (i.e., general strategies for work motivation such as goal setting, job design, incentive systems, and participation in decision making). Finally, there must be an awareness of very specific practices that adapt motivational constructs to specific cases. An example of the latter is the use of management-by-objectives—a combination of goal-setting principles with participation.

III.I. Attitude Theory

Attitudes, opinions, and beliefs are extremely important in organizational settings. They are important in their own right because of humanitarian concerns for the quality of working life of those who are employed in organizations. They are also important for diagnosing problems in organizations. Finally, they are important because they relate to the behavioral intentions and to the behavior of individuals at work. In particular, master's-level I/O practitioners should be aware of the extensive literature on the determinants, consequences, and measurement of job satisfaction and related constructs such as involvement and commitment.

III.J. Small Group Theory and Process

Much of human activity in organizations takes place in the presence of other people. This is particularly true of work behavior. The pervasiveness of interpersonal relationships and task interdependencies in organizations demands that master's-level I/O practitioners have a good understanding of the behavior of people in social groups. Such an understanding requires that they be familiar with research and theory related to interpersonal behavior in small groups. This body of theory and research draws from social psychology, organizational psychology, sociology, and organizational behavior. A suitable background in group theory involves an understanding of leadership and power, interpersonal influence, group effectiveness, conformity, conflict, role behavior, and group decision making.

III.K. Organization Theory

It is well accepted that the structure, function, processes, and other organizational level constructs have an impact on the behavior of individuals in organizations. Therefore, it is necessary that master's-level I/O practitioners have a good understanding of the nature of complex organizations. This understanding should include, but is not limited to, classical and contemporary theories of organizations, organizational structure, organizational design, technology, and the process of organizational policy formation and implementation.

III.L. Organizational Development

This domain encompasses theory and research about facilitating change in individuals, groups, and organizations to improve their effectiveness. This body of theory and research draws from such related fields as social psychology, counseling psychology, educational psychology, vocational psychology, engineering psychology, and organizational theory. More specifically, this domain concerns theory and research related to individual change strategies including training, socialization, attitude change, career planning, counseling, and behavior modification; interpersonal and group change strategies, including team building and group training, survey feedback, and conflict management; role or task oriented change strategies, including job redesign, role analysis, management by objectives, and temporary task forces; and organizational system directed change strategies, including survey feedback, open systems oriented change programs, human resource accounting, flexible working hours, structural changes, control system changes, sociotechnical systems, and quality circles.

IV. ADDITIONAL I/O DOMAINS

IV.A. Career Development Theory

Theories and empirical research on career development are concerned with the interplay between individuals and environments and attempt to describe the nature of the patterns of positions held and resultant experiences during an individual's working life. Included in this domain are models and explanations of the origin and measurement of individual aptitudes and interests; how individual, social, chance, and environmental factors shape educational and training experiences; specific skill training and development; early work history, occupational choice, organizational/job choice, and change; the sequence of jobs taken after organization entry; and preretirement planning.

Knowledge in this area would reflect an understanding of these interactional processes, developmental events, and phenomena as they are considered both by the individual employee and from the perspective of the employing organization. Knowledge of how organizational practices such as recruitment, selection, job placement, training, performance appraisal, and career planning programs enhance or retard career development is also necessary.

IV.B. Human Performance/ Human Factors

Human performance is the study of limitations and capabilities in human skilled behavior. Skill is broadly construed to include perceptual, motor, and cognitive activities, and the integration of these into more complex behavior. Emphasis is on the interaction of human behavior and the task environments, ranging from detection and identification of simple events to problem solving, decision making, and control of complex environments. Included among the variables that affect human performance are individual differences, organismic variables, task variables, environmental variables, and training variables.

Competency in this area assures awareness of issues of experimental design, some knowledge of computer programming, and quantitative modeling based on techniques from mathematical psychology, engineering, and computer science. Familiarity in the subject areas of basic experimental psychology is combined with an awareness of applied research in such areas as workstation design, workload measurement, control systems, information display systems, and person-computer interactions.

IV.C. Consumer Behavior

The focus of this area is the systematic study of the relationship between the producers (and distributors) and actual or potential consumers of goods and services. This involves many of the following concerns: consumer preferences for product features, product testing, consumer attitudes and motivation, buying habits and patterns, brand preferences, media research (including the effectiveness of advertisements and commercials), packaging design and features, estimating demand for products or services, and the study of the economic expectations of people. There is a substantive or content basis to this domain because there is a body of theory and data amassed dealing with the antecedents and correlates of consumer behavior that can be learned. There is a skill component as well, since the area is built on the appropriate application of a variety of social science research methodologies (e.g., sampling theory, questionnaire and survey protocol design and execution, individual and group interviewing, stimulus scaling, and mathematical model building).

IV.D. Compensation and Benefits

The reward system for employees can be critical to the success or failure of an organization, and is of intense interest to individual employees as well. Employee benefits constitute a substantial proportion of labor costs. Retirement plans, medical plans, family and parental leave, vacation time, and alternative work schedules are but a few of the issues that an organization must address. This is an applied domain that incorporates many of the competencies identified earlier including job and task analysis, work motivation (e.g., equity and expectancy theory), attitudes (e.g., job satisfaction), and legal and regulatory contexts. In addition, there are specific methods or approaches to the design and implementation of a reward system that should be well understood (e.g., point system of job evaluation).

IV.E. Industrial and Labor Relations

The presence of a union, either formal or informal, in an organization strongly influences human resource management activities. Particularly relevant are the limitations imposed by seniority and job security rules, grievance and arbitration procedures, wage and benefit administration, and union versus management rights regarding job assignments, promotion, discipline, training, attendance, and termination. In addition, the role of unions in supporting systemwide organizational change is critical to the functions of employee and organizational development. Competency in this domain includes familiarity with major labor legislation and with contractual obligations that affect human resource policy implementation, as well as familiarity with labor contract administration processes, with the effects of union-management relationships on disciplinary systems, job and employee evaluation systems, recruitment, selection, placement and training systems, motivation and reward systems, and processes for effecting organizational change.

NOTE

1. A revised version was approved by the American Psychological Association in August 1999.

REFERENCES

American Psychological Association. (1977). *Standards for providers of psychological services.* Washington, DC: Author.

American Psychological Association. (1981). Specialty guidelines for the delivery of services by industrial-organizational psychologists. *American Psychologist, 36,* 664–669.

American Psychological Association. (1985). *Standards for educational and psychological testing.* Washington, DC: Author.

American Psychological Association. (1992). *Ethical principles of psychologists and code of conduct.* Washington, DC: Author.

Ekeberg, S., Switzer, F., & Siegfried, W. D., Jr. (1991, April). What do you do with a master's degree in I/O psychology? L. L. Koppes (Chair), *I/O psychology master's level training: Reality in search of legitimacy.* Symposium conducted at the sixth annual conference of the Society for Industrial and Organizational Psychology, St. Louis, MO.

Equal Employment Opportunity Commission. (1978, August 25). Uniform guidelines on employee selection. *Federal Register, 43*(166), 38290-38315.

Koppes, L. L. (1991). I/O psychology master's-level training: Reality and legitimacy in search of recognition. *The Industrial-Organizational Psychologist, 29*(2), 59–67.

Lowe, R. H. (1993). Master's programs in industrial-organizational psychology: Current status and a call for action. *Professional Psychology: Research and Practice, 24,* 27–34.

National Conference on Applied Master's Training in Psychology. (1990). *Executive summary: Resolutions and standards on education and training for applied master's programs in psychology.* (Available from Rosemary H. Lowe, Department of Psychology, The University of West Florida, Pensacola, FL 32514).

Schippmann, J. S., Schmitt, S. D., & Hawthorne, S. L. (1992). I/O work roles: Ph.D. vs. master's level practitioners. *The Industrial-Organizational Psychologist, 29*(4), 35–39.

Society for Industrial and Organizational Psychology, Inc. (1985). *Guidelines for education and training at the doctoral level in industrial-organizational psychology.* Arlington Heights, IL: Author.

Society for Industrial and Organizational Psychology, Inc. (1987). *Principles for the validation and use of personnel selection procedures* (3rd ed.). Arlington Heights, IL: Author.

Society for Industrial and Organizational Psychology, Inc. (1992). *Graduate training programs in industrial-organizational psychology and related fields.* Arlington Heights, IL: Author.

Appendix 2. Guidelines for Education and Training at the Doctoral Level in Industrial/ Organizational Psychology

These guidelines were prepared by the Education and Training Committee of the Society for Industrial and Organizational Psychology, Inc., Janet Barnes-Farrell, chair. Members of the Committee were Debra A. Major (subcommittee chair), Jeffrey Reed, Kecia Thomas, Lisa Scherer, and Kathleen Lundquist.

PURPOSE OF THE GUIDELINES

These guidelines replace an earlier version published in 1985 by the Society for I/O Psychology (SIOP; Division 14 of the American Psychological Association). The last version was developed by the members of the 1982 Education and Training Committee of the Society for I/O Psychology (i.e., Klimoski, Hulin, Ilgen, Neumann, Peters, Schneider, and Stone). These guidelines have been written to aid faculty and curriculum planners in the design of doctoral-level graduate programs in industrial/ organizational (I/O) psychology. They may also be useful to potential doctoral students in the discipline by providing a preview of doctoral training, suggesting criteria that may be used to select a doctoral program, and giving students an overview of the

competencies they are responsible for mastering during the course of their doctoral education.

The term *guidelines* refers to pronouncements, statements, or declarations that are suggestions or recommendations. Guidelines differ from "standards" in that standards may be mandatory and may be accompanied by an enforcement mechanism. Thus, as guidelines, this document is not intended to be either mandatory or exhaustive or a substitute for appropriate professional judgment, and it may not always be applicable in all situations. The aspirational intent of the guidelines is to facilitate the continued development of I/O psychology.

Although such guidelines have implications for several other related concerns of the Society members, these other concerns will not be addressed here. Specifically, these guidelines were not written for the purpose of providing the basis for graduate studies program certification, determining eligibility for specialty licensing as an I/O psychologist, establishing eligibility for membership in the Society, or highlighting the continuing education and training needs of the profession. Those interested in training at the master's level are referred to the *Guidelines for*

EDITOR'S NOTE: These guidelines represent the views and expertise of the Society for Industrial and Organizational Psychology, Inc., Division 14 of the American Psychological Association and Organizational Affiliate of the Association for Psychological Science. In issuing these guidelines, SIOP is not speaking for APA, APS, or any other division or unit of APA or APS.

Education and Training at the Master's Level in Industrial/Organizational Psychology (SIOP, 1994). Finally, it should be reiterated that the focus of this document is the training of I/O psychologists. These guidelines are not designed to be a set of recommendations for education in related fields (e.g., labor and human resources, organizational behavior). Although it is recognized that a large number of academic disciplines or specialties are concerned with developing related subject matter and skills, these related areas are beyond the scope of the guidelines.

PERSPECTIVE OF THE GUIDELINES

In many respects, the perspective taken in the current guidelines is consistent with that expressed in the 1985 version. In particular, this revision adheres to the scientist-practitioner model and takes a competency-based approach. In other respects, this version is substantially different from the 1985 guidelines (e.g., our treatment of "personal skills"). Both the similarities and differences are discussed in more detail the following sections.

The scientist-practitioner. Consistent with the traditional orientation and philosophy of the members of the Society, the underlying theme embedded in these training guidelines is that the I/O psychologist is frequently both the generator of knowledge and the consumer/user of such knowledge. As a scientist, he or she develops and evaluates theory using research and empirical skills. As a practitioner, he or she applies and evaluates theory and research under specific conditions. Thus, the I/O psychologist frequently provides psychological services to individuals and groups in organizational settings.

Taking the scientist-practitioner model seriously means that doctoral education needs to focus on both the theory and application associated with all content areas. In preparing for the current version of the guidelines, many I/O psychologists, especially those employed outside the academic setting, have expressed concern that previous guidelines have been too focused on theory. We recommend that theory and practice both receive consideration as students learn about the content of I/O psychology. The relevance of theory to practice and applied research should be emphasized. I/O practitioners working in the field can facilitate the development of doctoral students' practical knowledge by offering internship and research opportunities and sharing their own practical experiences.

This dual emphasis on theory and practice is needed regardless of a student's intended career path. Those interested in academic careers need to understand both theory and practice to develop sound research, the findings of which should have a meaningful applied impact. Academicians will also be charged with teaching new generations of I/O psychologists about the theory and applications associated with each content area. I/O practitioners in industry, government, and consulting are required to use their knowledge and skills to deliver products. Thus, students not only need to know each topic in a theoretical sense; they also need to know how to develop and implement associated products. For example, a student should know how to design and conduct a job analysis or conduct and report on the results of a test validation. Learning about a topic in a theoretical sense is not equivalent to the experience of doing it. Doing it and having firsthand familiarity with the pitfalls, limits, and constraints of a technique is different from, and as critical as, theoretical knowledge.

Competencies

As emphasized in the 1985 *Guidelines,* the goal of graduate training is developing competencies. Taking a competency-based approach, these guidelines focus on the skills, behaviors, and capabilities one needs to function as a new member of the profession. One of the committee's primary goals was to update the competency list to reflect current content thought to be important for I/O psychologists.

The description of each competency area was amended as needed to reflect the current state of the discipline. In some cases competency titles were altered or reorganized to reflect new content and more appropriate groupings within a domain. The current guidelines include four additional competency areas (i.e., Business and Consulting Skills, Health and Stress in Organizations, Job Evaluation and Compensation, Leadership and Management). Consistent with the emphasis on the scientist-practitioner model, every opportunity to emphasize both theory and practice related to a competency has been seized in this revision of the guidelines. The word *theory* was deleted from many of the competency titles to emphasize the point that both the theory and practice related to a competency are important.

Just as both science and practice are inherent in each competency, we also feel that an appreciation of diversity can be applied to each area. Although the concept has only received theoretical and scientific attention within our field in recent years, the significance of diversity has been long recognized. Thus, graduate training in I/O psychology should take every opportunity to emphasize working with all types of people and developing an appreciation of diverse views.

The 1985 *Guidelines* included a thorough discussion of the efficacy of the competency-based approach over the previously used multiple curricula models of the 1973–1974 *Guidelines* (Schneider, Carlson, Lawler, & Pritchard, 1974). As argued in 1985, we also believe that the competency-based approach allows for a more integrated training model, recognizes the possibility of "equifinality" in the methods used to produce competent graduates, and allows for a broader application of the guidelines regardless of individual program capacities and resources.

Identifying Competencies

A number of sources were consulted in updating the content of existing competency areas and developing new ones. As mentioned previously, we relied most heavily on the 1985 version of the guidelines, only departing from it as deemed necessary. We also found Schippmann, Hawthorne, and Schmitt's (1992) analysis of the doctoral-level I/O psychologist's work role particularly helpful. Several discussions of the education and training of I/O psychologists in *The Industrial-Organizational Psychologist* were consulted (e.g., Greguras & Stanton, 1996; Maahs & Major, 1995; Sebolsky, Brady, & Wagner, 1996). Various other sources supplied a sense of where we have been and where we are going as a discipline (e.g., Dunnette, 1990; Howard, 1990). In addition, numerous I/O psychologists in academia, industry, consulting, and the government provided input, as did students at various stages of graduate training.

The 1985 *Guidelines* purposely excluded "personal skills" (e.g., oral and written communication skills, facility at developing interpersonal relationships, effective work habits, critical/analytic thinking ability, etc.). The argument for exclusion was that such skills are of universal importance and should constitute a common concern of graduate training in any field. In this version of the guidelines, many of these skills have been included in a new competency labeled *Consulting and Business Skills*. Our contention is that these skills are critical to competence and success as an I/O psychologist. While such skills are indeed universally important, they are applied by I/O psychologists in some unique and consistent ways (e.g., to apply for funding, to communicate with executives and constituents outside the discipline). Although we agree with the 1985 *Guidelines* that such skills could presumably be used as selection criteria in the screening of applicants for graduate study, we also recognize that these skills may need to be further developed through graduate training.

Related Competencies

The bulk of this document describes the areas or domains recommended specifically for training in I/O psychology. However, before presenting them, it would be useful to comment on domains considered, but judged not to be appropriate as part of this document.

One cluster of competencies that was omitted involves areas in which it would be desirable, but not necessary, to have training to ensure career success in I/O psychology. A list of these areas could easily be expanded to include much of social science and business (e.g., content mastery in economics, marketing, labor relations, and even accounting). Potential important process capabilities (skills) would include those needed for organizational development efforts, employee counseling, or individual rehabilitation. Competencies in all these areas would indeed be appropriate and desirable, but they are not made part of these guidelines.

Other aspects of graduate training have not been formally incorporated into these guidelines. Any quality graduate program should provide students with a realistic preview particular to that program. Expectations and requirements should be clear and explicit from the outset, beginning with the recruiting process. If a program has a particular emphasis (e.g., training academicians or training practitioners), it is also reasonable to expect that emphasis to be clearly communicated. While these are things that we encourage graduate programs to do, we have not developed specific guidelines for them.

There is a belief that a good doctoral program provides guidance to students in their own career planning and in the use of career enhancement strategies. Such activities assist a student in drawing together personal information and experiences in a formal effort to make a career decision and to map out a suitable career path. Once a decision has been made, appropriate developmental experiences could then be provided in a systematic way. Many schools already incorporate such planning, often using a variety of mechanisms (e.g., assigning an adviser; establishing a guidance committee). While this is viewed as a desirable feature of a graduate program, it is not expressed as a competency.

Finally, if a primary aim of graduate education is to produce responsible professionals, it seems reasonable that this notion be reinforced throughout graduate training. Helping students understand the ways in which they are responsible for their own education and career development is highly appropriate and desirable. Though we believe that taking responsibility for one's own professional development should be emphasized (e.g., developing a professional network, communicating with peers, participating in the field, etc.), a relevant competency has not been formally articulated.

The Recommended Domains

Table A.2.1 lists the areas identified by the committee as relevant to the training of I/O psychologists at the doctoral level. The competencies were organized into two groups. The first (competencies 1–6) reflects the more general knowledge and skill areas deemed appropriate in the training of I/O psychologists. The second group (competencies 7–25) contains those competencies that reflect substantive content in the field of I/O psychology. The entries are presented alphabetically within their group. Neither the presentation order of the two groupings nor the individual entries should be construed to reflect importance or priority in training at the doctoral level.

In describing the knowledge and skills to be developed, the committee endeavored to stay at the appropriate level of specificity. Our goal was to highlight the key components of each domain well enough to be of help to curriculum designers. We do not describe the totality of the domain. It is also clear that domains are not always easily differentiated. In some cases it may be argued that (analytically/taxonomically) one area could be subsumed within another. Similarly, it is clear that competencies in one domain facilitate mastery or performance in another. These points notwithstanding, the areas listed in Table A.2.1 were all felt to be sufficiently discrete and important to warrant their separate places on the list.

Table A.2.1   Areas of Competence to Be Developed in Doctoral-Level I/O Psychology Programs

1. Consulting and Business Skills
2. Ethical, Legal, and Professional Contexts of I/O Psychology
3. Fields of Psychology
4. History and Systems of Psychology
5. Research Methods
6. Statistical Methods/Data Analysis
7. Attitude Theory, Measurement, and Change
8. Career Development
9. Consumer Behavior
10. Criterion Theory and Development
11. Health and Stress in Organizations
12. Human Performance/Human Factors
13. Individual Assessment
14. Individual Differences
15. Job Evaluation and Compensation
16. Job/Task Analysis and Classification
17. Judgment and Decision Making
18. Leadership and Management
19. Organization Development
20. Organization Theory
21. Performance Appraisal and Feedback
22. Personnel Recruitment, Selection, and Placement
23. Small Group Theory and Team Processes
24. Training: Theory, Program Design, and Evaluation
25. Work Motivation

The presentation of the domain attempts both to define and to suggest ways to measure or to index achievement. That is, there is frequent reference to indicators or possible ways that skills in a domain are manifested. Many of these might be used by educators to decide whether or not a person is indeed proficient in an area. This is not to imply that those which are presented are the only indicators of proficiency.

Recommended Areas of Competence

Table A.2.1 lists the areas recommended by these guidelines for inclusion in doctoral-level programs in I/O psychology. The majority of these competencies were included in the 1985 version of the guidelines. The description of each competency area was updated as appropriate. In some cases competency titles were altered to reflect new content. In addition, four new competency areas (i.e., Consulting and Business Skills, Health and Stress in Organizations, Job

Evaluation and Compensation, Leadership and Management) were added to the list. Each competency area is described in the following sections.

1. Consulting and Business Skills

Success as an I/O psychologist requires development of a variety of consulting and business skills. Communication, business development, and project management represent broad categories capturing some of the most essential business and consulting skills.

Effective business communication is critical and encompasses a variety of writing, presenting, and interpersonal skills. Business writing is characterized by its brevity, action orientation, attention to the audience, and link to the organization's bottom line. Business presentation involves the development and presentation of information to a business audience that clearly articulates key messages in terms the audience can understand, along with skills in presenting and responding to questions. Effective communication and interpersonal skills are required to interact with and influence organizational members. These skills are particularly important in team contexts. An understanding of how individual efforts facilitate group performance and the ability to contribute as a member of a group are essential.

Effective business development depends on the ability to package ideas, proposals, and requests in a fashion that leads to their acceptance and movement of the organization in desired directions. Many good ideas are rejected because they are poorly communicated or inadequately justified in terms of their benefits. A practical problem-solving approach is frequently required in a business or consulting setting. Relevant content and methodological skill or knowledge, regardless of its source or discipline, along with creative "outside-the-box" thinking, is often required to address and solve practical business problems. This involves understanding how elements relate to a larger whole (e.g., effect of a change in compensation on employee productivity, satisfaction, turnover).

Project management skills focus on the details of organizing work in a business setting, whether as an internal or external consultant. This may include budgeting, scheduling, and managing others so that work is accomplished in an efficient and effective manner. Project management often requires the integration and utilization of information from several sources. Success is contingent on being able to attend to detail while maintaining a view of the "big picture."

2. Ethical, Legal, and Professional Contexts of I/O Psychology

This domain has to do with the ethical, legal, and professional contexts within which the I/O psychologist operates. The I/O psychologist should have knowledge of and should behave in accord with relevant ethical guidelines (e.g., *Ethical Principles of Psychologists,* APA, 1981, 1992; and the *Ethical Principles in the Conduct of Research With Human Participants,* APA, 1973, 1982). The I/O psychologist should also have knowledge of relevant federal, state, and local laws, statutes, regulations, and legal precedents (e.g., the Equal Employment Opportunity Commission's *Guidelines on Employee Selection Procedures*). Since a fair amount of professional work done in organizations is covered by negotiated labor contracts, competency in this domain would also include an awareness of opportunities and restrictions imposed by such agreements, as well as an appreciation of the labor/management dynamics associated with them. Finally, all I/O psychologists should have knowledge of the various professional norms, standards, and guidelines relevant to their profession (e.g., *Specialty Guidelines for the Delivery of Services by Industrial/ Organizational Psychologists,* 1981; *Standards for Providers of Psychological Service,* APA, 1979; *Principles for the Validation and Use of Personnel Selection Procedures,* APA, 1987; and *Standards for Educational and Psychological Testing,* National Council on Measurement in Education, 1985).

3. Fields of Psychology

I/O psychology is basically the study of behaviors of individuals or groups of individuals that occur in a particular type of location—organizations of almost any kind. I/O psychology is a context-centered discipline. This focus differentiates it from fields of psychology that study basic processes (e.g., perception, memory, learning), from fields that study particular populations of individuals (e.g., children, mentally disturbed), from fields that study analytic procedures or assessment procedures (e.g., psychometrics), and from fields that study mechanisms of behavior (e.g., physiological psychology, brain research). Although the populations of individuals and the locations are different, in this emphasis on behavior in a set of locations we are like educational psychologists in our eclecticism. Because we borrow concepts, procedures, and paradigms from the other fields of psychology, it is important that we have an understanding of the strengths, weaknesses, and sources of our often unacknowledged borrowings.

While we draw freely from other fields of psychology, we may not borrow equally from all fields. We share a great deal with social psychology, psychometrics, motivation, learning, and personality. Historically, the discipline has borrowed less heavily from clinical, developmental, and physiological-sensory psychology. The importance of these fields of psychology to the I/O area changes over time and obviously varies with the particular interests of the individual I/O psychologist. It is difficult to predict which of the related fields will develop research leads and findings in the near and distant future that will have an impact on I/O psychology. In any event, to be consistent with APA recommendations (American Psychological Association Committee on Accreditation, 1996), exposure should reflect competency in the following broad areas:

a) Biological Bases of Behavior: Physiological Psychology, Comparative Psychology, Neuropsychology, Sensation and Perception, Psychopharmacology.

b) Cognitive-Affective Bases of Behavior: Learning, Thinking, Motivation, Emotion.

c) Social Bases of Behavior: Social Psychology, Group Processes, Organizational and Systems Theory.

d) Individual Differences: Personality Theory, Human Development, Abnormal Psychology.

Students in doctoral programs in I/O psychology should be able to read and to comprehend the issues and controversies involved in basic research published in journals in at least a subset of these related areas. The specific fields of competency and journals read will vary among individuals; but awareness, interest, and reading in several areas seem crucial to both initial doctoral training and continuing education.

4. History and Systems of Psychology

If students in graduate programs in I/O psychology know how the discipline of psychology developed and changed into its present configuration, then each

generation will share the common bonds and language of the discipline. They will also possess a knowledge of the intellectual heritage of our field. Such common knowledge is important for the pragmatic functional role it plays in communication and in preventing frequent repetitions of the mistakes and dead ends of the past. Many historical schools and systems of psychology have contemporary representatives, either in a pure or a diluted form; a knowledge of the roots of these different theoretical positions is important. For example, many contemporary debates about theoretical perspectives appear dysfunctional when viewed against the background of historical developments in our field. A knowledge of our history enables us to appreciate these different approaches both for their unique contributions to psychology and for the alternatives they provide for an understanding of observable phenomena.

An understanding of history and systems of psychology allows integration of I/O psychology into the broader discipline by tracing our roots back to American functionalism, radical behaviorism, views of Freud, Titchener, Tolman, Spearman, and Cattell and other perspectives that have shared the thinking of psychology. Such integration is important to foster an attitude among I/O psychologists that places high value on the development of theoretical approaches to the I/O problems that are well integrated with psychology as a whole. In addition, there is the specific history of the field of I/O psychology to consider. Understanding one's "roots" as an I/O psychologist and our more recent past is essential.

5. Research Methods

The domain of research methods includes the methods, procedures, techniques, and tools useful in the conduct of empirical research on phenomena of interest in I/O psychology. At a general level, the areas encompassed by research methods include the scientific method (with attention to issues in the philosophy of science), inductive and deductive reasoning, problem statements and research questions, hypotheses, the nature and definition of constructs, and study designs (experimental, quasi-experimental, and nonexperimental). At a more operational level, research methods includes, but is not limited to, the manipulation of variables (in experimental research), the concepts underlying and methods used for the assessment of the reliability and validity of measures, the administration of various specific types of measures (questionnaires, interviews, observations of behavior, projective measures, etc.), the use of various sampling procedures (probability and nonprobability type) especially as applied to survey research, the conduct of research with various specific strategies (field study, laboratory experiment, field experiment, sample survey, simulation, case study, etc.), the use of statistical methods to establish relationships between variables, and the formulation of research-based conclusions. Specific knowledge about relative strengths and weaknesses of different research strategies, an understanding of qualitative research methods, as well as a tolerant appreciation of the benefits of alternative strategies must be developed. Computer literacy has become increasingly important, and programming skills may be particularly useful. Finally, an understanding of the ethical standards that govern the conduct of all research involving human participants is essential.

6. Statistical Methods/Data Analysis

This domain has to do with the various statistical techniques that are used in the analysis of data generated by empirical research. The domain includes both descriptive and inferential statistical methods; it spans both parametric and nonparametric statistical methods. Among the specific competencies, issues and techniques encompassed by the domain are estimates of central tendency; estimates of variability; sampling distributions; point and interval estimates; inferences about differences between means, proportions, and so forth; univariate and multivariate analyses of variance (fixed, random, and mixed effects models); linear and nonlinear regression and correlation; path analysis; multiple discriminant function analysis; multiple and canonical regression; factor analysis; components analysis; cluster analysis; pattern analysis; and structural equation modeling. Knowledge of this domain implies a basic understanding of the statistical foundation of such methods, asymptotic sampling variances of different statistics, the assumptions underlying the proper use of the same methods, and the generalizations, inferences, and interpretations that can legitimately be made on the basis of statistical evidence.

7. Attitude Theory, Measurement, and Change

Attitudes, opinions, and beliefs are extremely important in organizational settings. They are important in their own right because of humanitarian concerns for the quality of working life of those who are employed in organizations. They are also important for diagnosing problems in organizations. Finally, they are important because they relate to the behavioral intentions and the behaviors of individuals at work. Some of the job attitudes typically studied by I/O psychologists include, but are not limited to, job satisfaction (general and various facets), job involvement, organizational commitment, and perceptions of fairness.

It is also important that I/O psychologists be aware of the extensive literature on attitude theory, attitude measurement, and attitude change. In particular, I/O psychologists must know how attitudes are formed and changed and how they are related to behaviors. With respect to the latter, a knowledge of the literature on the relationship between attitudes and behavior is important if for no other reason than to know the limitations of the connections between these two constructs.

8. Career Development

Theory and research regarding career development are concerned with the interplay between individuals and environments, and they attempt to describe the nature of the patterns of positions held and resultant experiences during an individual's life span. Included in this domain are models and explanations of the origin and measurement of individual aptitudes and interests, how individual, social, chance, and environmental factors shape educational and training experiences, specific skill training and development, early work history, occupational choice, organizational/job choice and switching, the sequence of jobs taken after organizational entry, work/family issues, midcareer plateaus, and retirement planning.

Knowledge in this area would reflect an understanding of these processes, events, or phenomena as they are considered both by the individual employee and from the perspective of the employing organization. Knowledge of how organizational practices such as recruitment, selection, job placement, socialization, training, performance appraisal, and career planning programs enhance or retard career development is also necessary, as is an understanding of the special career issues and challenges faced by particular groups (e.g., women, ethnic minorities, the disabled).

9. Consumer Behavior

The focus of this area is the systematic study of the relationship between the producers (or distributors) and consumers (actual or potential recipients) of goods and services. Usually this involves many of the following concerns: consumer preferences for product features, consumer attitudes and motivation, buying habits and patterns, brand preferences, media research (including the effectiveness of advertisements and commercials), estimating demand for products or services, and the study of the economic expectations of people. Closely allied to those areas of market research that focus on personal consumption, there is a substantive or content basis to this domain insofar as there is a body of theory and data amassed dealing with the antecedents and correlates of consumer behavior that should be learned. There is a skill component to be mastered as well, inasmuch as the area is built on the appropriate application of a variety of social science research methodologies (e.g., sampling theory, questionnaire and survey protocol design and execution, individual and group interviewing, stimulus scaling, and mathematical model building).

10. Criterion Theory and Development

Almost all applications of I/O psychology (e.g., selection, human resources planning, leadership, performance appraisal, organization design, organization diagnosis and development, training) involve measurements against criteria (standards) that indicate effectiveness on the part of individuals, groups, and/or organizations. The selection of criteria is not a simple issue and represents a significant area of concern for I/O psychologists.

The knowledge base of this domain incorporates understanding the theoretical issues such as single versus multiple criteria, criterion dynamics, the characteristics of good and acceptable criteria (relevance, reliability, practicality), and criteria as a basis for understanding human behavior at work and in organizations. Knowledge of past research in this area, which is quite extensive, is also necessary.

Beyond this knowledge, the I/O psychologist should have the skills necessary for developing valid criteria and methods of measuring them. These necessarily include skills in many of the other domains identified in the document (e.g., Job Analysis, Psychometrics).

11. Health and Stress in Organizations

Job performance and effective organizational functioning can be affected by health and safety factors in the workplace that result in suboptimal working conditions and reduced productivity. This competency area requires the study of interactions between human physical capabilities and problematic conditions in the workplace in an attempt to understand the limits of performance and negative effects on workers. Among the factors considered are hazardous environmental conditions induced by toxic substances (e.g., chemical, biological, nuclear), loud noises, blinding lights, and noxious odors. Other factors considered are related to organizational structure and job design, such as shiftwork or the requirements of particular tasks. Additional sources of organizational stress that may affect performance, commitment, and attitudinal variables include downsizing, harassment, work–family pressures, and outsourcing. There should be some familiarity with government standards relating to the workplace (e.g., OSHA).

12. Human Performance/Human Factors

Human Performance is the study of limitations and capabilities in human skilled behavior. Skill is broadly construed to include perceptual, motor, memory, and cognitive activities, and the integration of these into more complex behavior. Emphasis is on the interaction of human behavior and tools, tasks, and environments, ranging from detection and identification of simple events to problem solving, decision making, human errors, accidents, and control of complex environments. Included among the variables that affect human performance are individual differences, organismic variables, task variables, environmental variables, and training variables.

Competency in this area assures awareness of issues of experimental design, a grounding in perception, cognition, and physiological psychology, some knowledge of computer programming, and quantitative modeling based on techniques from mathematical psychology, engineering, and computer science. Familiarity in the subject areas of basic experimental psychology should be combined with an awareness of applied research in such areas as workstation design, workload measurement, control systems, information display systems, health and safety, and human–computer interactions.

13. Individual Assessment

This domain refers to a set of skills that are needed for assessing, interpreting, and communicating distinguishing characteristics of individuals for a variety of work-related purposes. The two primary purposes of individual assessment can be defined broadly as selection (e.g., hiring, promotion, placement) and development (e.g., career planning, skill and competency building, rehabilitation, employee counseling). Individual assessment may help attain multiple goals, many of which are aimed at achieving some form of person–environment fit, including assessee fit to a specific job or career track and assessee fit within a specific organizational context (e.g., department, work group).

Individual assessment incorporates skill in individual testing, interviewing, and appraisal techniques for the purpose of evaluating ability, personality, aptitude, and interest characteristics. Individual assessment also requires identifying, developing, selecting, and/or using the appropriate means for such assessment, and communicating the results and interpretation of assessment accurately in both face-to-face and written form.

A knowledge of the fact that individual assessment focuses on the whole person is required. In addition, a knowledge of the manner in which environmental and contextual factors shape the purpose and use of the accumulated information of individual assessments is necessary.

14. Individual Differences

I/O psychology emphasizes the importance of individual differences in the study of individuals' behaviors. Because this emphasis requires accurate assessments of unobservable psychological traits, a sound background in both classical and modern measurement theories and their respective areas of application is essential. The domain of measurement includes theory and assessment of individual differences in skills and abilities. This exposure would cover the nature of construct measurement and the philosophy of science assumptions underpinning many of our approaches to scale development. Other topics which might be covered are the measurement of attitudes (e.g., job satisfaction) and product preferences by scaling procedures, measurement of performance on complex jobs, and measurement of comparable worth of individuals to organizations.

A great deal of what I/O psychologists do in this area is subjected to close scrutiny by courts of law, civil rights groups, and professional colleagues. Because of these external and internal pressures, students must be trained to conduct research and to apply measurement principles in conformance to the highest standards of our discipline. Students may also need skills to help communicate their research methods and findings to interested parties outside the discipline.

It is important to recognize the limitations of classical true score theory. Questions about item and scale bias, test equating, minimum competence assessments, mastery testing, tailored testing, and appropriateness measurement raise issues for which classical true score theory can provide only approximate solutions. Although these areas of application were originally studied in relation to ability measurement, they have been generalized to attitude scales, surveys, questionnaires, and rating scales. Thus, it is increasingly important that students in I/O psychology be prepared to use and to conduct research on both classical measurement procedures and more contemporary procedures (e.g., Item Response Theory).

15. Job Evaluation and Compensation

This competency area focuses on determining the appropriate compensation level for skills, tasks, and/or jobs. Job evaluation is a processes by which the relative value of jobs is determined and then linked to commensurate compensation. Job evaluation is closely tied to and usually predicated upon sound job/task analyses. In general, job evaluation and compensation involves identifying compensable factors, attending to perceptions of fairness and equity, and considering issues of comparable worth. Proficiency in this competency area is demonstrated by a theoretical and applied understanding of various job evaluation techniques, compensation strategies (e.g., pay for skills, team-based pay, etc.), and the legal and social issues surrounding compensation.

16. Job/Task Analysis and Classification

This domain encompasses the theory and techniques used to generate information about what is involved in performing a job or task, the physical and social context of this performance, and the attributes needed by an incumbent for such performance. Tasks are basic units of activity, the elements of which highlight the connection between behavior and result. A job is an arbitrary grouping of tasks designed to achieve an organizational objective. It is common for jobs to be grouped or classified on the basis of a variety of criteria, depending on the purpose and goals of the classification system.

The fundamental concern of job and task analysis is to obtain descriptive information to design training programs, establish performance criteria, develop selection systems, implement job evaluation systems, redesign machinery or tools, and create career paths for personnel. The specific steps taken and the type of information gathered will vary depending on the purpose of the job and task analyses and the classification system. Relevant information includes, but is not limited to, the worker behaviors involved; the knowledge, skills, and abilities required; the standards of performance desired; the tools, machines, and work aids used; the sources of information available to the incumbent; the social, environmental, and physical working conditions; and the nature of supervision. Similarly, some of the steps involved in job and task analyses include identifying the purpose of the analysis; preparing, designing, or selecting a job analysis system; collecting job or task information; summarizing the results; and documenting the steps taken for future reference. The classification of jobs typically entails identifying the purpose and goals of the classification system; designing a classification scheme; categorizing jobs according to the established scheme; and documenting the classification process and outcomes.

The individual competent in this domain should have a knowledge of the different approaches to job/task analysis and classification, as well as skill in applying these techniques to real-world situations. This competency area is likely to continue to evolve as the nature of work in our society continues to change.

17. Judgment and Decision Making

Judgment and decision making encompasses an area of research and knowledge that is both prescriptive and normative in its emphases. This area is important because *judgment and decision making under conditions of uncertainty* probably describes the majority of the decisions managers, psychologists, market forecasters, and budget/policy planners make during the course of their work and research. A knowledge of decision theory, judgment, and problem solving research is important to understanding the critical processes that influence how information is processed and the quality of the decision outcomes.

Many different content areas within the broad area of I/O psychology can be studied explicitly as applications of decision and judgment theory. Such areas as vigilance behavior, employee selection, choice behavior, and human performance in complex environments can be integrated by principles of decision theory that may require fewer concepts than are necessary when each content area is considered distinct and unique. Applications of decision theory to the policies of decision makers, judges, and clinicians allow greater understanding of inferential procedures used by individuals. Approaches for describing and predicting judgment and decision making include Brunswik's lens model, Bayesian inference, subjective expected utility, prospect theory, and the cognitive information processing paradigm. A knowledge of these approaches and an ability to integrate across the different approaches are indicative of breadth as well as depth of training in judgment and decision theory.

18. Leadership and Management

Management and leadership can be approached at different levels. The study of management and leadership at the macro level involves the influences senior-level individuals have in the larger organizational context: setting strategy, directing change, and influencing values. Theory and research may focus on characteristics of leaders, leader style, leader–member interactions, behaviors of leaders, and related phenomena. At a more micro level, leadership and management involve the day-to-day exchange between leaders and followers. This includes challenges faced by line managers in their relationships with subordinates in the assignment of tasks, evaluation of performance, coaching and counseling for improvement, resource planning, and related tasks. Related to many other areas, effective leadership and management involves task analysis, motivation, decision making, career planning, selection, performance appraisal, interpersonal communication, and listening and related skills in a supervisor–subordinate context. Increasingly, attention is placed on team leadership and self-leadership (especially in relation to empowerment) and horizontal leadership (i.e., peer influence processes).

19. Organization Development

This domain encompasses theory and research relevant to changing individuals, groups, and organizations to improve their effectiveness. This body of theory and research draws from such related fields as social psychology, counseling psychology, educational psychology, vocational psychology, engineering psychology, and organizational theory.

More specifically, this domain concerns theory and research related, but not limited, to individual change strategies including training, socialization, attitude change, career planning, counseling, and behavior modification; interpersonal and group change strategies, including team building and group training, survey feedback, and conflict management; role or task-oriented change strategies, including job redesign, role analysis, management by objectives, and temporary task forces; and organization system–directed change strategies, including survey feedback, open systems–oriented change programs, human resource accounting, flexible working hours, structural changes, control system changes, and quality circles.

20. Organization Theory

It is well accepted that the structure, function, processes, and other organizational-level constructs have an impact on the behavior of individuals in organizations. Therefore, it is necessary that I/O psychologists have a thorough understanding of the nature of complex organizations. This understanding should include, but is not limited to, classical and contemporary theories of organizations, organizational structure, organizational design, technology, and the process of organizational policy formation and implementation. Much of this theory and research is generated by sociologists and those students of organizational behavior who choose as their unit of analysis constructs not primarily within the individual or within the immediate group environment of the individual. Integration of organizational and individual constructs is an important area of study within I/O psychology. Such an integration obviously requires a knowledge of organizational theory.

21. Performance Appraisal and Feedback

Performance appraisal and feedback have both a knowledge and a skill base. This area centers on the methods of measuring and evaluating individuals as they perform organizational tasks and on taking action (administrative and/or developmental) with individuals on the basis of such appraisals.

The knowledge base includes a thorough understanding of rating scale construction and use. Also relevant are the areas of measurement theory, data analysis, criterion theory and development, motivation theory, and the factors that underlie interpersonal perception and judgment. An understanding of the similarities, differences, and inconsistencies among the perceptions of performance and feedback supplied by peers, subordinates, and supervisors is essential.

The skill base includes procedures for communicating performance evaluations to job incumbents and counseling them in appropriate means of improving their performance. Also, skill in designing a complete performance appraisal and feedback system that meets organizational needs while maintaining or enhancing worker motivation or performance is required.

22. Personnel Recruitment, Selection, and Placement

This domain consists of the theory and techniques involved in the effective matching of individual needs, preferences, skills, and abilities with the needs and preferences of organizations. An organization's needs are defined by the jobs assigned to positions in the organization.

More specifically, this domain encompasses theory and research in human abilities; test theory, development, and use; job analysis; criterion development and measurement; recruitment; classical and decision theory models of selection and placement; alternative selection devices (e.g., interviews, assessment centers); and legal and societal considerations that affect recruitment, selection, and placement. In particular, the individual must keep current with the legislation and court decisions related to these issues, as well as with responses of the Society to laws and their interpretations.

23. Small Group Theory and Team Processes

Much of human activity in organizations takes place in the presence of other people. This is particularly true of work behavior. The pervasiveness of interpersonal and task interdependence in organizations demands that I/O psychologists have a good understanding of the behavior of people in work groups. Though the labels *group* and *team* are often used interchangeably, it is also critical to have a familiarity with the growing teamwork literature. This requires an understanding that extends beyond familiarity with research and theory related to interpersonal behavior in small groups. The body of theory and research concerning groups and teams draws from social psychology, organizational psychology, sociology, and organizational behavior. A good background in group theory and team processes includes, but is not limited to, an understanding of leadership, motivation, interpersonal influence, group effectiveness, conformity, conflict, role behavior, and group decision making.

24. Training: Theory, Program Design, and Evaluation

This domain includes theory and techniques used to design, conduct, and evaluate instructional programs. The instructional process begins with a needs assessment, including organizational, job and task, and person analyses, to determine the goals and constraints of the organization and the characteristics of the job and trainees. Familiarity with basic phenomena of learning (e.g., modern learning theory, conditioning principles), as well as knowledge of the different approaches to training (e.g., computer-assisted instruction, simulation, behavior modification), are necessary for designing programs. An ability to develop meaningful and appropriate training objectives is essential. Transfer of training to the desired setting is an important consideration. For programs to be conducted as planned, the instructors must have good instructional skills. Thus, training the trainers is necessary.

Both the process and the outcome of the program may be evaluated to determine if it has been conducted as planned and whether or not it has had any effect. Knowledge of appropriate training evaluation criteria and design issues, such as pre- and posttesting and control groups, as well as organizational constraints, is necessary for planning an evaluation strategy.

25. Work Motivation

Work motivation refers to the conditions within the individual and his or her environment that influence the direction, strength, and persistence of relevant individual behaviors in organizations when individual abilities and organizational constraints are held

constant. Increasingly, work motivation is a concern at the group level as well.

I/O psychologists need to have a sound background in work motivation in at least three respects. First, they must have a thorough understanding of the theories of human motivation including, but not limited to, need theories, cognitive theories, and reinforcement theories. In all cases there must be a thorough understanding of the extensive research and theory that exist outside the domain of work in the basic psychological literature. At the second level, there must be an understanding of the research and theory in motivationally relevant domains of I/O psychology that represent general applications of one or more motivational perspectives. Such general strategies for work motivation as goal setting, job design, incentive systems, and participative decision making are relevant here. Finally, there must be an awareness of and ability to apply very specific, motivationally oriented practices that adapt motivational constructs to specific cases. For example, understanding and implementing management by objectives involves an application of goal setting principles and participation.

STRATEGIES FOR BUILDING COMPETENCE

Program designers and faculty may develop a student's capabilities in a recommended area by using one or more methods or techniques. In some cases it is likely that multiple means might actually be preferred. A given course may touch on more than one area. Moreover, the resources and capacities of a given program will also shape decisions in this area. For these reasons the guidelines will not detail a specific curriculum plan. However, suggested strategies are provided.

Table A.2.2 describes curriculum options identified as useful methods for doctoral-level training. While other approaches and variations do exist, the list in Table A.2.2 is reasonably inclusive. Table A.2.3 summarizes the recommendations of the guidelines by relating the goals of training to the methods or techniques identified. The entries in this table should be viewed as suggestions of reasonable and appropriate approaches to educating students in the desired knowledge and skill domains. Though the techniques identified are not necessarily the only ones available, an effort was made to match each competency area with the techniques most likely to be effective for development in that domain. The fact that there are multiple entries for training in a skill area should not imply that all techniques listed are required to promote

Table A.2.2 Curriculum Options Considered in the Guidelines

1. **Formal coursework:** Classroom instruction common to university settings in which material pertinent to the domains is covered. This method itself can involve a variety of different means, to include lectures, discussion, presentations, and so forth. While taking courses, students also have the opportunity to work together with peers, taking advantage of the benefits of cooperative peer learning.

2. **Independent readings/study:** Nonclassroom instruction in which the student, in consultation with qualified personnel, assumes basic responsibility for and commitment to the accomplishment of domain objectives. This method includes all forms of nonclassroom instruction for which self-initiated effort is of central concern and for which such effort can successfully result in the achievement of relevant domain objectives. Examples would include self-initiated effort aimed at covering defined domains through reading; generating appropriate review manuscripts, proposals, or reports; designing and conducting a research investigation; and acquiring interactive computer skills.

3. **Supervised experience (and field research):** Nonclassroom instruction in which the student is actively engaged in projects under the direct supervision of qualified personnel (e.g., faculty, senior students, I/O practitioners). Such projects would be aimed at fulfilling specific training objectives with special emphasis given to the acquisition of skills. Participation would not be motivated primarily for compensation. This method might often be characterized by in vivo learning opportunities such that the student learns in settings similar to those to which transfer can be expected. Research experience should begin during the first year of graduate education with small projects and be expanded in later years as the student gains skill and knowledge in the field.

   In all cases, however, there must be meaningful professional supervision of the training experience. Examples would include practicum and internship experiences, fieldwork teaching/training, thesis/dissertation research, and so forth. An extensive (even yearlong) supervised internship performing the work of an I/O psychologist in a business, consulting, or government organization is strongly recommended as an essential component of doctoral preparation, especially for those who intend to become practitioners.

4. **On-the-job training:** Nonclassroom instruction in which capabilities are learned through "hands-on" experience on applied tasks under the explicit guidance of a professionally qualified task expert. Such training is typically done in conjunction with one's "job," and participation involves compensation. In any event, on-the-job training provides firsthand knowledge of the problems associated with particular I/O domains and allows for the opportunity to focus on solutions which will have an impact on the setting in which the student is working.

5. **Modeling/observation:** Nonclassroom implicit instruction that is obtained as a result of working with and paying attention to professionally qualified personnel in the daily conduct of their jobs or projects. This method implies that learning of important skills might well be obtained without explicit instructional intent on the part of the model. On the other hand, modeling may also be done in a purposeful and self-conscious manner. Modeling/observation, because of its general nature, cuts across several of the training methods described earlier.

a level of mastery deemed appropriate by a program's faculty. Finally, it would be consistent with the spirit of these guidelines for a program to develop skills or knowledge in several of the domains using a single particular educational experience (e.g., a seminar, a supervised field project, or an assigned reading list).

Though the guidelines are most specifically intended for curriculum development, they also serve as a guide for students in ensuring the adequacy of their education. It is our firm belief that students are every bit as responsible for their education as faculty are. In some cases this means students must take advantage of presented opportunities (e.g., taking a needed class, participating in a research project, attending conferences). It may also mean that students need to be proactive in developing their own opportunities (e.g., independent study, finding an internship, developing a professional network, reading appropriate journals).

Furthermore, we encourage practitioners to continue to play an active role in the development of I/O psychologists. Giving students opportunities to work on applied projects, offering internships, and taking an active role in the education and training of doctoral students (e.g., serving on the E&T Committee, contributing to doctoral consortia, visiting and speaking at graduate programs). In some respects, no one is more aware of the most current knowledge, skills, and abilities required of I/O psychologists than those practicing the discipline in the field.

Table A.2.3   Means of Training the Recommended Capabilities

	A	B	C	D	E
1. Consulting and Business Skills	*		*	*	*
2. Ethical, Legal, and Professional Contexts of I/O Psychology	*		*	*	*
3. Fields of Psychology	*	*			
4. History and Systems of Psychology	*	*			
5. Research Methods	*	*	*		*
6. Statistical Methods/Data Analysis	*	*	*		*
7. Attitude Theory, Measurement, and Change	*	*		*	
8. Career Development	*	*	*	*	
9. Consumer Behavior	*	*	*		
10. Criterion Theory and Development	*	*	*	*	
11. Health and Stress in Organizations	*	*	*		
12. Human Performance/Human Factors	*	*	*	*	
13. Individual Assessment	*		*	*	*
14. Individual Differences	*	*	*		
15. Job Evaluation and Compensation	*	*	*	*	
16. Job/Task Analysis, Job Evaluation, and Compensation	*	*	*	*	
17. Judgment and Decision Making	*	*			
18. Leadership and Management	*	*	*		*
19. Organization Development	*	*	*	*	*
20. Organization Theory	*	*	*		
21. Performance Appraisal and Feedback	*	*	*	*	*
22. Personnel Recruitment, Selection, Placement, and Classification	*	*	*	*	
23. Small Group Theory and Team Processes	*	*	*		*
24. Training: Theory, Program Design, and Evaluation	*	*	*	*	*
25. Work Motivation	*	*	*	*	

A = formal coursework; B = independent reading/study; C = supervised experience (and field research); D = On-the-job training; E = modeling/observation.

SUMMARY

The competency-based approach of these guidelines has much to recommend it. It maintains a focus on what is to be taught and learned, provides desirable flexibility to curriculum planners, and recognizes the multiple paths to developing most skills of importance. Nonetheless, it is also true that the recommendations based on such an approach might become dated or irrelevant to the field. Therefore, the present guidelines should be reevaluated on a regular basis. They must be kept up-to-date by continuous reference to the nature of work and conditions surrounding the I/O psychologist at work.

Doctoral education in I/O psychology must employ multiple methods of education and training. All of the foregoing approaches have value and should be integrated into a complete program of education and training. This program should ensure that the graduate will possess an appreciation of the roles of both theory and practice; will be able to develop new ideas and also to apply relevant information to solve real-world problems; and will possess the research, methodological, statistical, and measurement knowledge and skills to enable conduct of appropriate research and problem solving.

FURTHER READING

American Psychological Association. (1973, 1982). *Ethical principles in the conduct of research with human participants.* Washington, DC: Author.

American Psychological Association. (1979). *Standards for providers of psychological service* (Rev. ed.). Washington, DC: Author.

American Psychological Association. (1981, 1992). *Ethical principles of psychologists.* Washington, DC: Author.

American Psychological Association Committee on Accreditation. (1996, January). *Guidelines for the review of doctoral and internship programs.* Washington, DC: Author.

American Psychological Association Committee on Professional Standards and Committee on Psychological Tests and Assessment. (1986). *Guidelines for computer-based tests and interpretations.* Washington, DC: American Psychological Association.

American Psychological Association, Division of Industrial and Organizational Psychology. (1987). *Principles for the validation and use of personnel selection procedures.* Washington, DC: Author.

Dunnette, M. D. (1990). Blending the science and practice of industrial and organizational psychology: Where are we and where are we going? In M. D. Dunnette & L. M. Hough (Eds.), *Handbook of industrial and organizational psychology* (2nd ed., Vol. 1, pp. 1–27). Palo Alto, CA: Consulting Psychologists Press.

Greguras, G. J., & Stanton, J. M. (1996). Three considerations for I/O graduate students seeking academic positions: Publish, publish, publish. *The Industrial-Organizational Psychologist, 33*(3), 92–98.

Howard, A. (1990). *The multiple facets of industrial-organizational psychology: Membership survey results.* Washington, DC: Society for Industrial and Organizational Psychology.

Maahs, C. J., & Major, D. A. (1995). Does your graduate program fully prepare you to enter the professional world? *The Industrial-Organizational Psychologist, 32(4),* 90–93.

National Council on Measurement in Education. (1985). *Standards for educational and psychological testing.* Washington, DC: Authors.

Schippmann, J. S., Hawthorne, S. L., & Schmitt, S. D. (1992). Work roles and training needs for the practice of industrial-organizational psychology at the master's and Ph.D. level. *Journal of Business and Psychology, 6,* 311–331.

Schneider, B., Carlson, R., Lawler, E., & Pritchard, R. (1974). *Guidelines for education and training in industrial and organizational psychology.* Washington, DC: APA Division of Industrial and Organizational Psychology.

Sebolsky, J. R., Brady, A. L., & Wagner, S. (1996). Want an applied job? Get experience! *The Industrial-Organizational Psychologist, 33*(4), 65–70.

Society for Industrial and Organizational Psychology, Inc. (1985). *Guidelines for education and training at the doctoral level in industrial/organizational psychology.* College Park, MD: Author.

Society for Industrial and Organizational Psychology, Inc. (1994). *Guidelines for education and training at the master's level in industrial/organizational psychology.* Arlington Heights, IL: Author.

Appendix 3. Universities With Master's and/or Doctoral Graduate Programs in Industrial and Organizational Psychology (and Related Fields)

Information about these graduate programs can be found at http://siop.org/GTP/:

Alliant International University

Angelo State University

Antioch University Los Angeles

Appalachian State University

Auburn University

Austin Peay State University

Ball State University

Barry University

Baruch College, City University of New York

Bowling Green State University

California State University, Long Beach

California State University, Sacramento

California State University, San Bernardino

Capella University

Carlos Albizu University

Carnegie Mellon University

Case Western Reserve University

Central Michigan University

Central Washington University

Chapman University

Chicago School of Professional Psychology

Christopher Newport University

Claremont Graduate University

Clemson University

Cleveland State University

Colorado State University

Concordia University

Curtin University

DePaul University

East Carolina University

EDITOR'S NOTE: Information for this appendix was graciously provided by the Society of Industrial and Organizational Psychology.

Eastern Kentucky University

Elmhurst College

Emporia State University

Exeter University

Fairfield University

Fairleigh Dickinson University (Florham-Madison)

Florida Atlantic University

Florida Institute of Technology

Florida International University

George Mason University

George Washington University

Georgia Institute of Technology

Georgia State University

Golden Gate University

Griffith University

Harvard Business School

Hofstra University

Illinois Institute of Technology

Illinois State University

Indiana University–Purdue University Indianapolis

Kansas State University

Kean University

Lamar University

Louisiana State University

Louisiana Tech University

Macquarie University

Marshall University

McMaster University

Michigan State University

Middle Tennessee State University

Minnesota State University

Montana State University

Montclair State University

National University

New Mexico State University

New York University

North Carolina State University

Northern Illinois University

Northern Kentucky University

Northwestern University

Ohio University

Old Dominion University

Pennsylvania State University

Polytechnic University (Brooklyn, NY)

Portland State University

Purdue University

Radford University

Rice University

Roosevelt University

Rutgers–The State University of New Jersey

Saint Cloud State University

Saint Joseph's University

Saint Louis University

Saint Mary's University

San Diego State University

San Francisco State University

San Jose State University

Saybrook Graduate School & Research Center

Seattle Pacific University

Sonoma State University

Southern Illinois University at Edwardsville

Southern Oregon University

Southwest Missouri State University

Springfield College

Stanford University

State University of New York, Binghamton

State University of New York, Buffalo

Stephen F. Austin State University

Teachers College, Columbia University

Temple University

Texas A&M University

Texas Tech University

Tulane University

Union Institute and University

University at Albany, SUNY

University of Akron

University of Arizona

University of Arkansas

University of Baltimore

University of Calgary

University of California, Berkeley

University of California, Irvine

University of Central Florida

University of Connecticut

University of Detroit–Mercy

University of Georgia

University of Guelph

University of Hartford

University of Houston

University of Idaho

University of Illinois at Chicago

University of Illinois at Urbana-Champaign

University of London

University of Maryland

University of Memphis

University of Michigan

University of Minnesota

University of Mississippi

University of Missouri, Columbia

University of Missouri–St. Louis

University of Nebraska–Omaha

University of New Haven

University of North Carolina Chapel Hill

University of North Carolina Charlotte

University of North Texas

University of Northern Iowa

University of Nottingham–UK

University of Oklahoma

University of Oklahoma–Tulsa

University of Sheffield

University of South Carolina

University of Southern Mississippi

University of South Florida

University of Surrey

University of Tennessee at Chattanooga

University of Tennessee, Knoxville

University of Texas–Arlington

University of the Philippines

University of Toronto

University of Tulsa

University of Waikato

University of Waterloo

University of West Florida

University of Western Ontario

University of Wisconsin–Madison

University of Wisconsin–Oshkosh

University of Wisconsin–Stout

University of Witwatersrand–South Africa

Valdosta State University

Villanova University

Virginia Commonwealth University

Virginia Tech

Washington State University

Wayne State University

West Chester University

Western Kentucky University

Western Michigan University

William Carey College on the Coast

Wright State University

Xavier University

Appendix 4. Scientific Journals Publishing Research in Industrial/Organizational Psychology (and Related Fields)

Academy of Management Executive *
Academy of Management Journal **
Academy of Management Review **
Administration and Society
Administrative Science Quarterly **
American Psychologist
Applied Ergonomics
Applied H.R.M. Management
Applied Psychological Measurement *
Applied Psychology: An International Review *
Australian Journal of Management and
    Organisational Behaviour
Basic and Applied Social Psychology *
British Journal of Management
British Journal of Personality
Business Ethics: A European Review
Career Development Quarterly
Conflict Resolution Quarterly
Consulting Psychology Journal: Practice and
    Research
Creativity and Innovation Management
Cross Cultural Management

Educational and Psychological Measurement *
Employee Assistance Quarterly (changing to Journal
    of Workplace Behavioral Health)
Employee Relations
Environment and Behavior
Ergonomics
European Journal of Work and Organizational
    Psychology
European Review of Applied Psychology
Gender, Work, and Organization
Group Decision and Negotiation
Group Dynamics: Theory, Research, and Practice *
Group Organizational Management *
Group Processes and Intergroup Relations
Human Computer Interaction
Human Factors *
Human Performance *
Human Relations *
Human Resource Development Review
Human Resources Development International
Human Resources Development Quarterly
Human Resources Development Review

EDITOR'S NOTE:

* A journal that would generally be considered as a more common outlet for I/O psychology research in the United States.
** A journal ranked as one of the top 10 journals in I/O psychology: Zickar, M. J., & Highhouse, S. (2001). Measuring prestige of journals in industrial-organizational psychology. *The Industrial-Organizational Psychologist, 38,* 29–36.

Information for this appendix was gathered and organized by Andrew Smith, Grove City College.

Human Resources Management *
Human Resources Management: International Digest
Human Resources Management Journal *
Human Resources Management Review *
Human Resources Planning
Industrial and Corporate Change
Industrial and Labor Relations Review
Industrial Relations: A Journal of Economy
    and Society
Intelligence
International Journal of Cognitive Ergonomics
International Journal of Conflict Management
International Journal of Cross Cultural Management
International Journal of Human Resources
    Management
International Journal of Industrial Ergonomics
International Journal of Organization Theory and
    Behavior
International Journal of Organizational Analysis
International Journal of Productivity and
    Performance Management
International Journal of Selection and Assessment *
International Journal of Social Research
    Methodology
International Journal of Stress Management
International Journal of Testing
International Journal of Training and Development
International Organization
International Review of Industrial and
    Organizational Psychology
Journal for the Theory of Social Behavior
Journal of Applied Behavioral Science *
Journal of Applied Business Research
Journal of Applied Measurement
Journal of Applied Psychology **
Journal of Applied Social Psychology*
Journal of Behavioral Decision Making
Journal of Business and Psychology *
Journal of Business Research
Journal of Career Assessment
Journal of Career Development
Journal of Change Management
Journal of Communication
Journal of Communication Management
Journal of Community and Applied Social
    Psychology
Journal of Computer Mediated Communication
Journal of Conflict Resolution
Journal of Counseling Psychology
Journal of Economic Behavior and Organization

Journal of Economic Psychology
Journal of Employment Counseling
Journal of Environmental Psychology
Journal of Experimental Psychology: Applied *
Journal of Experimental Social Psychology
Journal of Human Resources: Education, Manpower,
    and Welfare Economy
Journal of Individual Differences
Journal of Leadership and Organization Studies
Journal of Management **
Journal of Management and Education
Journal of Management Development
Journal of Management Studies
Journal of Managerial Issues
Journal of Managerial Psychology
Journal of Occupational and Organizational
    Psychology *
Journal of Occupational Health Psychology *
Journal of Occupational Science
Journal of Organizational Behavior **
Journal of Organizational Behavior Management
Journal of Organizational Change Management
Journal of Organizational Excellence
Journal of Personality
Journal of Personality and Social Psychology
Journal of Psychology:
    Interdisciplinary and Applied
Journal of Social Psychology
Journal of Vocational Behavior **
Journal of Vocational Rehabilitation
Journal of Workplace Learning
Journal of World Business
Law and Human Behavior
Leadership
Leadership and Organizational
    Development Journal *
Leadership Quarterly *
Learning and Individual Differences
Learning and Motivation
Management and Organization Review
Management Learning
Management Science
Measurement: Interdisciplinary Research and
    Perspectives
Military Psychology
Motivation and Emotion
Negation Journal
Organization Science *
Organization: The Interdisciplinary Journal
    of Organization, Theory, and Society

Organizational Analysis
Organizational Behavior and Human Decision Processes **
Organizational Development Journal *
Organizational Dynamics *
Organizational Research Methods **
Organizational Studies
Personality and Individual Differences
Personality and Social Psychology Bulletin
Personality and Social Psychology Review
Personnel Psychology **
Personnel Review
Professional Psychology: Research and Practice
Psychological Assessment
Psychological Bulletin *
Psychological Methods *
Psychological Review *
Psychology and Marketing
Psychology, Public Policy and Law
Public Administration: An International Overview
Public Administration Review
Public Opinion Quarterly

Public Personnel Management
Quality and Quantity: International Journal of Methodology
Representative Research in Social Psychology
Risk, Decision, and Policy
Small Group Research *
Social Behavior and Personality
Social Psychology Quarterly
Strategic Change
Strategic Management Journal
Strategic Organization
Strategy and Leadership
Stress and Health: Journal of the International Society for the Investigation of Stress
Stress: The International Journal on the Biology of Stress
Work and Occupations
Work and Stress *
Work, Employment, and Society
Work: Journal of Prevention, Assessment, and Rehabilitation

Appendix 5. Job Titles of Industrial/Organizational Psychologists

Corporate Vice President, Director, Manager, Staff Member of

Organizational Development, Management Development, Human Resources Research, Employee Relations, Training and Development, and Leadership Development

President, Vice President, Director of

Private research, consulting companies, and organizations

Full, Associate, Assistant Professor of

Psychology, Management, Organizational Behavior, and Industrial Relations

---

EDITOR'S NOTE: Information for this appendix was graciously provided by the Society of Industrial and Organizational Psychology.

Appendix 6. Groups and Organizations That Have Industrial/Organizational Psychologists as Members

ASAP (Atlanta Society of Applied Psychology)
For more information, visit www.asapatlanta.org

ASTD (American Society of Training and Development)
The major, national training association. For more information, visit www.astd.org

BAAP (Bay Area Applied Psychologists)
For more information,
visit http://www.baaponline.net

Brunswik Society
Informal association of researchers who are interested in understanding and improving human judgment and decision making. For more information, visit http://brunswik.org/

Central Florida I/O Interest Group
An informal I/O interest group. For more information, please contact Paul Spector spector@chuma.cas.usf.edu

CIOP (Chicago I/O Psychologists, formerly GCAIOP)
For more information, visit http://www.ciop.net

CODESP (Cooperative Organization for the Development of Employee Selection Procedures)
A consortium of classified personnel departments in Nevada and California public school districts. For more information, visit www.codesp.com/

Consortium for Research on Emotional Intelligence in Organizations
Founded in 1996 to aid advancement of research and practice related to emotional intelligence in organizations. For more information, visit www.eiconsortium.org

Competency Consortium
Consortium providing a forum for organizations to share competency models, applications, lessons learned, and benchmark best practices. For more information, please contact Mariangela Battista at 914-640-2686 or Mariangela.Battista @starwoodhotels.com

COP (College of Organizational Psychologists, Australia)
This group is affiliated with the Australian Psychological Society. For more information, visit

EDITOR'S NOTE: Information for this appendix was graciously provided by the Society of Industrial and Organizational Psychology.

www.aps.psychsociety.com.au/units/colleges/
organisational/

CSIOP (I/O Division of the Canadian Psychology Association)

For more information, visit www.ssc.uwo.ca/
psychology/csiop/

CWAIOP (Colorado-Wyoming Association of I/O Psychologists)

For information, visit http://www
.cwaiop.colostate.edu/

DAIOP (Dallas Area I/O Psychologists)

For more information, visit www.daiop.org

EAWOP (European Association of Work and Organizational Psychologists)

A network linking together I/O groups from several
European nations. For more information, visit
www.eawop.org

GIOP (Gateway I/O Psychologists)

Members-only discussion list at groups.yahoo.com/
group/gioptalk

HAIOP (Houston Area Industrial and Organizational Psychologists)

For more information, visit www.haiop.org
or e-mail info@haiop.org

HFES (Human Factors and Ergonomics Society)

5,000 members and in existence since 1957. For
more information, visit www.hfes.org

HRPS (Human Resource Planning Society)

National group for senior HR consultants,
academics, and Fortune 500 practitioners.
3,000 members. For more information, visit
www.hrps.org/home/index.shtml

IPMA (International Personnel Management Association)

For more information, visit www.ipma-hr.org/

IPMA–Assessment Council

A subset of IPMA. Focuses on recruitment, selection,
and assessment issues primarily in the public sector.
For more information, visit www.ipmaac.org/

ISIR (International Society for Intelligence Research)

A scientific society for researchers in human
intelligence; sponsors an annual conference
focused on all aspects of intelligence research.
For more information, visit www.isironline.org

ISPI (International Society for Performance Improvement)

A 39-year-old group of "performance technology"
individuals. 10,000 members. For more
information, visit www.ispi.org

ITC (International Testing Commission)

Founded in 1978, an association of psychological
associations, test commissions, and other
organizations committed to promoting effective
testing and assessment policies and to the proper
development, evaluation, and uses of educational
and psychological instruments. For more
information, visit www.intestcom.org

ITSG (Information Technology Survey Group)

A consortium of about 15 companies (e.g., IBM,
Intel, Sun, SAP, Microsoft) in the IT industry.
For more information, visit www.itsg.org

MAIOP (Michigan Association of I/O Psychologists)

For more information, visit www.maiop.org

MAPAC (Mid-Atlantic Personnel Assessment Consortium, Inc.)

An association of mid-Atlantic public sector
agencies interested in assessment. For more
information, visit www.ipmaac.org/mapac/

Mayflower Group

Founded in 1971, consortium of blue-chip
companies employing at least 10,000 U.S.-based
employees. Dedicated to employee opinion
surveys. For more information, visit
www.mayflowergroup.org

METRO (Metropolitan New York Association for Applied Psychology)

For more information, visit http://www
.MetroApp Psych.com/

MPPAW (Minnesota Professionals for Psychology Applied to Work)
For more information, visit www.mppaw.org

NCIOP (North Carolina Industrial and Organizational Psychologists)
For more information, visit http://www.ncsu.edu/ psychology/graduate/conc/iov/organizations/ ncio/index.htm

NESAP (New England Society for Applied Psychology)
For more information, visit www.NESAP.org

Northwest Conversations
An informal association of assessment professionals in the Pacific Northwest. For more information contact Leta Danielson at letad@dop .wa.gov

NYSPA IOP Division (New York State Psychological Association's Industrial, Organizational & Personnel)
For more information, visit www.NYSPA.org/ specialty/pio.htm

ODI (Organization Development Institute)
For more information, visit http://members.aol.com/ odinst/membinfo.htm

ODN (Organization Development Network)
3,200 members. For more information, visit www.ODNetwork.org/

OH-IO (Ohio I/O Psychologists)
For more information, please contact Jim Austin at 614-292-9897 or austin.38@ osu.edu; or David Kriska at 614-645-8008 or dkriska1@csc.cmhmetro.net

PAI (People Assessment in Industry, South Africa)
Focuses on marketing and educating people about psychological assessment, validation studies, and ethics of use. For more information, visit www.pai.org.za

Performance America
Learning network devoted to assessing and improving government performance through organizational assessment and development. For more information, visit www.opm.gov/ employ/html/perf_am.htm

PIOPA (Portland Industrial & Organizational Psychology Association)
For more information, visit www.piopa.org

PSAIOP (Puget Sound Association of I/O Psychologists)
For more information please contact Peter Scontrino at 425-392-5694 or mpscontrino@aol.com

PTC/A (Personnel Testing Council of Arizona)
For more information, visit www.ipmaac.org/ptca/ index.html

PTC/MW (Personnel Testing Council of Metropolitan Washington, DC)
For more information, visit www.ptcmw.org

PTC/NC (Personnel Testing Council of Northern California)
For more information, visit www.ipmaac.org/ptcnc/

PTC/SC (Personnel Testing Council of Southern California)
For more information, visit www.ipmaac.org/ptcsc/

SCIP (Society for Computers in Psychology)
For more information, visit http://141.225.14.239/ scip/index.php

SCPMA (Southern California Personnel Management Association)
For more information, please contact Bill Osness at 714-536-5586 or fax to 714-374-1571.

SHRM (Society for Human Resource Management)
National group focusing on the needs of HR generalists. For more information, visit www.shrm.org

SIOP (Society for Industrial and Organizational Psychology)

Over 6,000 members. Principal professional association for I/O psychologists in the United States. For more information, visit www.siop.org

SJDM (Society for Judgment & Decision Making)

For more information, visit www.sjdm.org

SPIM (Society of Psychologists in Management)

For more information, visit www.spim.org

TIOP (Texas I/O Psychologists)

For more information, please contact Clyde Mayo at 713-667-9251 or mpsmayo@aol.com

WRIPAC (Western Regional Intergovernmental Personnel Assessment Council)

A consortium of public sector agencies in California, Nevada, and Arizona with an interest in assessment. For more information, visit www.wripac.com/

Index

Abilities assessment instruments, **1:**67
Ability rating scale, **2:**530, 530 (figure)
Ability-to-cope perspective, **2:**669
Abraham, L. A., **1:**270
Abridged Job Descriptive Index (AJDI), **1:**143
Absenteeism, **1:**2, 88
    flexible work schedules and, **1:**254
    hardiness and, **1:**304
    incentives and, **1:**340
    job characteristics and, **1:**393
    job satisfaction and, **1:**409–410
    mood effects and, **2:**487
    older workers and, **2:**532
    organizational commitment and, **2:**550
    performance appraisals and, **2:**599–600
    terrorism at work and, **2:**796
    See also Withdrawal behaviors, absenteeism
Abusive supervision, **1:**1–3
    antecedents of, **1:**3
    consequences of, **1:**2
    coping mechanisms and, **1:**3
    empirical inquiry, obstacles to, **1:**1
    epidemiological studies on, **1:**1
    organizational response to, **1:**3
    outcomes, moderating factors in, **1:**2–3
    See also Leadership and supervision;
        Machiavellianism; Workplace incivility
Academy of Management, **1:**4–5, 218, 318
    career development/job placement service and, **1:**5
    divisions/interest groups in, **1:**4
    electronic communications and, **1:**5
    functions of, **1:**4–5
    membership of, **1:**4
    mission of, **1:**4
    publications of, **1:**5
    See also American Psychological Association;
        Association for Psychological Science;
        Society for Industrial and Organizational
        Psychology
Acceptance theory of management, **1:**328
Accident rates, **2:**600, 902
Accommodation:
    positive accommodation factors, **2:**583
    reasonable accommodation requirement, **1:**24

    See also Americans with Disabilities Act (ADA) of 1990;
        Workplace accommodations for the disabled
Accomplishment striving, **2:**475
Achievement need (nAch), **2:**506–507, 893
Achievement-oriented leadership, **2:**596
Achievement tests, **2:**755
Ackerman, P. L., **1:**347
Acquisitions. *See* Mergers, acquisitions, and strategic alliances
Act-frequency approach to traits, **2:**609
Action. *See* Action-research paradigm; Action-state
    orientation; Action theory; Theory of action
Action theory, **1:**5–7
    action regulation, hierarchical levels of, **1:**5–6
    action sequence, phases of, **1:**5
    applications of, **1:**6
    integrative nature of, **1:**6–7
    operative image system and, **1:**6
    test-operate-test-exit units and, **1:**6
    theoretical foundations of, **1:**5
    See also Goal-setting theory; History of
        industrial-organizational psychology in Europe
        and the United Kingdom; Job performance models;
        Performance feedback; Theory of action
Action-research paradigm, **1:**311, **2:**565, 649
Action-state orientation, **2:**491
Active coping, **1:**3
Active management-by-exception (MBE-A), **2:**835
Adams, J. S., **1:**212, **2:**893
Adaptability constructs, **2:**728, 767, 770–771
    See also Trainability and adaptability
Adaptive testing, **1:**90, 373–374
Adjustment. *See* Adjustment heuristic; Fit; Theory of work
    adjustment (TWA); Work adjustment model
Adjustment heuristic, **1:**430
Adjust-replace-drop decisions, **2:**641
Adkins, J. A., **2:**527
Adult development theories, **1:**347
Advanced education/training. *See* Doctoral level
    education/training; Master's level education/training
Advanced manufacturing technology (AMT), **1:**42
Adverse (disparate) impact, **1:**10, 194
    disparate impact lawsuits, **1:**10
    evidence, forms of, **1:**10
    organizational burden of proof and, **1:**10

See also Adverse impact/disparate treatment/discrimination at work; Americans with Disabilities Act (ADA) of 1990; Bona fide occupational qualifications (BFOQ); Civil Rights Act of 1964; Civil Rights Act of 1991

Adverse impact/disparate treatment/discrimination at work, 1:7–9

allowable discrimination and, **1:**8, 9
bona fide occupational qualification and, **1:**9
discrimination, definition of, **1:**7
disparate treatment claims, **1:**9
employment discrimination law and, **1:**8–9
pattern-and-practice claim, McDonnell Douglas/Burdine framework and, **1:**9
perceptual forces, discriminatory practices and, **1:**7–8
See also Adverse (disparate) impact; Affirmative action

Advice. *See* Judgment and decision-making process: advice giving and taking

Affective circumplex model, **1:**186
Affective commitment scale (ACS), **2:**549
Affective communication, **2:**769

Affective events theory (AET), **1:10–12**, 106

affect-driven vs. judgment-driven behaviors and, **1:**11, 12
affective reactions and, **1:**11
appraisal process in, **1:**12
assumptions of, **1:**11
event, definition of, **1:**11
events, appraisal of, **1:**11–12
job behaviors, cognitive processes and, **1:**10–11
time element and, **1:**11
See also Affective traits

Affective organizational commitment, **2:**548, 549, 550

Affective traits, 1:13–15

attitudes, affective basis of, **1:**37
expectancy theory and, **1:**14
job performance and, **1:**14–15
job satisfaction and, **1:**14
measurement instruments for, **1:**13–14
stressor-strain relationship and, **1:**15
trait affect, definition of, **1:**13
trait-positive vs. trait-negative affects, affective response and, **1:**13
See also Applicant/test-taker reactions; Emotion regulation; Emotions; Job satisfaction; Mood; Stress, coping and management

Affiliation need, **2:**507–508, 893

Affirmative action, 1:15–18

consequences of, **1:**17–18
diversity in the workplace and, **1:**158
empirical research on, **1:**16–17, 18
federal government regulations and, **1:**16, 17
legal issues and, **1:**15–16
private sector organizations and, **1:**16
public attitudes on, **1:**18
set-aside vs. organization-specific programs, **1:**16
See also Adverse impact/disparate treatment/discrimination at work; Affirmative action programs (AAPs); Attitudes and beliefs; Banding; Civil Rights Act of 1964; Civil Rights Act of 1991; Diversity in the workplace; Race

norming; Recruitment; Sexual discrimination; *Uniform Guidelines on Employee Selection Procedures*

Affirmative action programs (AAPs), **1:**15
federal government regulation and, **1:**16, 17
opinion variables in attitude and, **1:**18
organizational performance and, **1:**17
perceiver variables in attitude and, **1:**18
private sector organizations and, **1:**16
psychological mediators and, **1:**18
public attitudes and, **1:**18
set-aside vs. organization-specific programs and, **1:**16
stigmatization of individuals and, **1:**17
structural predictors of attitudes, **1:**18
target groups, effects on, **1:**17
White male population and, **1:**17
See also Affirmative action

AFSCME v. State of Washington, **1:**81

Agate Club, **1:**313

Age Discrimination in Employment Act (ADEA) of 1967, **1:**9, **19–20**, 58, 218, 315, **2:**533

bona fide occupational qualification standard and, **1:**19
direct vs. circumstantial evidence of violation, **1:**20
disparate impact discrimination, **1:**20
disparate treatment theory and, **1:**19–20
impact of, **1:**20
mandatory retirement policy and, **1:**20
prohibited practices, **1:**19
reasonable factor other than age standard and, **1:**20
remedies for violations, **1:**20
violations of, **1:**19–20
See also Adverse impact/disparate treatment/discrimination at work; Older worker issues

Agency theory, **1:**84, **2:**732–733, 746

Aggregation principle, **2:**611, 613

Aging workers. *See* Age discrimination in Employment Act (ADEA) of 1967; Older worker issues; Retirement

Agreeableness trait, **1:**52, **2:**609

Agricultural Centers Program, **2:**502

Ahearne, M., **1:**286

Ahmedabad Textile Industry Research Association (ATIRA), **1:**319

Air Force Human Resources Laboratory (AFHRL), **1:**315

Ajzen, I., **1:**39, **2:**806

Alcohol abuse. *See* Drug and alcohol testing; Substance abuse

Alcoholics Anonymous (AA), **1:**188

Alderfer, C., **2:**893

Alderfer, H., **2:**510

Alignment model, **1:**331

Allport, G. W., **1:**53

Alpha reliability, **1:**56

Altruistic love, **2:**752–753

Amabile, T., **1:**127

Amason, A. C., **1:**95

Ambiguity, **1:**96
tolerance of, **1:**3
See also Role ambiguity

American Association of Applied Psychology (AAAP), **1:**314, 315, **2:**694

American College Testing Program (ACT), **1:**422, **2:**755, 756

American Educational Research Association, **2:**860
American Federation of Labor (AFL), **2:**851–852
American Institutes for Research, **1:**315
American Management Association, **1:**147
American Psychological Association (APA), **1:**xxxvi, **21,**
215, 218, 219, 221, 313, 315, 343, **2:**505, 526,
630, 641, 747
  description of, **1:**21
  education guidelines, **2:**918
  executive coaching certification, **1:**226
  functions of, **1:**21
  healthy workplaces and, **2:**652
  integrity testing and, **1:**359
  membership in, **1:**21
  mission of, **1:**21
  occupational health psychology training programs, **2:**527
  scientist-practitioner model and, **2:**694
  validation approaches, **2:**860
  See also Academy of Management; Association for
      Psychological Science (APS); Society for
      Industrial and Organizational Psychology (SIOP)
American Psychological Association Committee on
      Accreditation, **2:**930
Americans with Disabilities Act (ADA) of 1990, **1:**8–9, **22–25,**
58, 72, 194, 218, 316, **2:**895
  application/employment process and, **1:**24–25
  daily life, coverage of, **1:**22
  defense litigation and, **1:**23
  disability statute, application standards, **1:**23
  employer policy and, **1:**25
  essential/nonessential functions of a job and, **1:**23–24
  Family and Medical Leave Act and, **1:**248
  infectious diseases/HIV-positive status and, **1:**24
  public/private sector organizations and, **1:**22–23
  reasonable accommodation requirement of, **1:**24
  substance abuse and, **1:**24
  See also Civil Rights Act of 1964; Civil Rights Act of 1991;
      Drug and alcohol testing
American Society for Training and Development (ASTD), **2:**819
American Staffing Association, **2:**593
American Telephone & Telegraph (AT&T), **1:**30–31,
315, 342, **2:**766
Amplification, **1:**151
Analysis of variance (ANOVA) models, **1:**152,
266–267, 314, 351, 452, **2:**495, 630, 654
Anchoring heuristic, **1:**430
Anderson, N., **1:**311
Angoff standard-setting procedure, **2:**756
Angoff, W. H., **2:**756
Animated communication style, **1:**367
Antecedent-focused coping, **1:**183
Antecedent-monitor-consequence (AMC) sequence, **2:**675
Anticipatory socialization, **2:**582
Apparent sincerity, **2:**576
Apple Computer, **1:**40
Applicant/test-taker reactions, 1:25–28
  computer-based assessment and, **1:**91
  consequences of, **1:**26–27
  distributive justice rules and, **1:**26

  justice rules and, **1:**26
  perceived job relatedness and, **1:**26
  pre-/post-test reactions and, **1:**27–28
  procedural justice rules and, **1:**26
  race differences in, **1:**28
  receptivity, factors in, **1:**25–26
  research, practical implications of, **1:**28
  self-serving bias and, **1:**27–28
  test performance and, **1:**27
  test-taking motivation and, **1:**27
  types of measures, reaction comparison and, **1:**27
  See also Army Alpha/Army Beta; Individual differences;
      Organizational justice
Applied behavior analysis, **2:**672
Appraisal model of stress, **2:**767
Approach goals, **2:**714
Approach motivation, **2:**490
Aptitude area assessment, **2:**627–628
Aptitude tests, **2:**755
Arbitration. *See* Negotiation, mediation, and arbitration
Architect Registration Examination (ARE), **2:**756
Argyris, C., **1:**449, **2:**620, 803, 804
Armed Forces Qualification Test (AFQT), **2:**627
Armed Services Vocational Aptitude Battery (ASVAB),
1:67, 316, **2:**627, 628, 642, 643, 755–756
Army Alpha/Army Beta, 1:29–30, 314
  administration/use of, **1:**29
  controversy over, **1:**29–30
  formats of, **1:**29
  hereditarian perspective and, **1:**30
  intelligence testing and, **1:**29, 30
  psychological testing, value of, **1:**30
  validity/utility of, **1:**30
  See also Cognitive ability tests; Individual differences;
      Selection strategies
Army General Classification Test (AGCT), **1:**314, **2:**755
Army Research Institute (ARI), **2:**642
Aronson, E., **1:**240
Aronson, J. A., **2:**760
Arvey, R. D., **1:**270
Ashford, S. J., **1:**250, **2:**604
Ashforth, B. E., **1:**153
Ashkanasy, N. M., **2:**559, 561
Ashworth, S., **2:**590
Assembly-line workers, **1:**2, 188
Assessment center, 1:30–33, 447
  collateral benefits of, **1:**32
  complexity/cost of, **1:**33
  construct validity and, **1:**33
  criterion-related validity and, **1:**32
  criticisms of, **1:**33
  feedback experience in, **1:**33
  growth of, **1:**33
  guidelines for, **1:**31–32
  historical foundation of, **1:**30
  initial business application of, **1:**30–31
  integrated total/continuous simulations and, **1:**33
  management competency profiling and, **1:**31, 32
  ongoing assessment, career development and, **1:**33

participant acceptance of, **1:**32–33
research base on, **1:**32–33
technology, assessment process and, **1:**33
validity generalization and, **1:**32
See also Assessment center methods; Computer
    assessment; Leadership development
Assessment center methods, **1:**34–37
cognitive ability testing, **1:**34
complexity/cost issues and, **1:**36–37
criterion-related validity and, **1:**37
fidelity of simulations and, **1:**36
in-basket method, **1:**34–35, 37
individual-differences assessment and, **1:**34
individual/group activities, **1:**34–36
interviews, **1:**34
leaderless group discussion, **1:**35
ongoing assessment and, **1:**37
personality feedback and, **1:**34
presentations, **1:**36
role-play method, **1:**35–36, 37
self-assessment, **1:**36
structured meetings, **1:**36
technology and, **1:**35, 36
360-degree feedback and, **1:**36
written analyses, **1:**36
See also Assessment center; Computer assessment
Association for Behavior Analysis Conference, **2:**538
Association coefficient. *See* Measures of
    association/correlation coefficient
Association for Psychological Science (APS),
    1:21–22, 316, **2:**747
description of, **1:**22
formation of, **1:**21–22
functions of, **1:**22
membership in, **1:**22
mission of, **1:**22
See also Academy of Management; American
    Psychological Association (APA); Society for
    Industrial and Organizational Psychology (SIOP)
Associative learning experiences, **1:**64
Associative storage/retrieval, **1:**77
Aston Group, **1:**311, 312
AT&T Managerial Progress Study, **2:**766
At-risk pay, **1:**83
Attentive communication style, **1:**367
Attitudes and beliefs, **1:**37–39
affective basis of attitude, **1:**37
affirmative action, public attitudes on, **1:**18
ambivalence in attitude, **1:**37–38
attitude, definition of, **1:**37
attitude structure and, **1:**37–38
behavioral basis of attitude, **1:**37
behavioral outcomes and, **1:**39
belief, definition of, **1:**37
bivariate vs. bipolar perspective on, **1:**37–38
classical conditioning and, **1:**38
creativity research and, **1:**127
direct experience and, **1:**38
formation of attitudes, **1:**38

genetic determinants of, **1:**38
implicit/explicit attitudes, **1:**38, 39
indirect methods of measurement, **1:**39
measurement of attitudes, **1:**38–39
operant conditioning and, **1:**38
persuasion, message processing models and, **1:**39
self-report measures of, **1:**38–39
See also Affective events theory (AET); Emotion regulation;
    Employee attitude; Measurement scales; Theory of
    reasoned action/theory of planned behavior
Attitudinal integrity, **1:**356–357
Attraction-selection-attrition (ASA) model, **1:**39–41, **2:**558
attraction process in, **1:**40
attrition process and, **1:**41
micro/macro organizational behaviors and, **1:**39–40, 41
organizational behavior theory and, **1:**41
organizational consequences of, **1:**41
organizational goals, attainment of, **1:**40
overview of, **1:**40–41
person-organization fit and, **2:**616, 620
person-vocation fit and, **2:**623
selection procedures in, **1:**40
value congruence and, **2:**910
See also Employee selection; Organizational
    development; Person-environment (PE) fit;
    Prescreening assessment methods for personnel
    selection; Recruitment; Selection strategies
Attribute preference assessment, **2:**669
Attribution bias, **2:**661–662, 762
Attribution error, **2:**874, 892
Attributional Style Questionnaire (ASQ), **2:**535
Attrition process, **1:**41
Auditory processing, **1:**77
Australia, **1:**320–322
Australian Council for Educational Research (ACER), **1:**321
Australian Institute of Industrial Psychology (AIIP), **1:**321
Australian Psychological Society, **1:**322
Authentic leadership, **2:**632
Authoritarianism, **1:**360
Autism, **2:**538, 540
Automatic text processing, **1:**175
**Automation/advanced manufacturing technology/
    computer-based integrated technology**, **1:**42–44
advanced manufacturing technology, **1:**42
automation, definition of, **1:**42
computer-based integrated technology, **1:**42, 43
deskilling/upskilling and, **1:**43
effective implementation, industrial/organizational
    psychology and, **1:**43–44
enterprise resource planning systems and, **1:**42
globalization and, **1:**43
impacts of technology, **1:**42–43
industries, development of, **1:**43
motivation for adoption of technology, **1:**42
practice guidelines and, **1:**43–44
See also Human-computer interaction (HCI)
Autonomy. *See* Autonomy orientation; Empowerment; Flexible
    work schedules; Intrinsic and extrinsic work motivation;
    Job characteristics theory (JCT); Machiavellianism

Autonomy orientation, **1:**88, **2:**492
Availability heuristic, **1:**430
Aviation Psychology Program, **1:**135, 314
Avoidance goals, **2:**714
Avoidance motivation, **2:**490
Avoidant coping, **1:**3, **2:**767, 768
Avoidant style of conflict management, **1:**98, 99
Avolio, B., **2:**834
Awareness building, **1:**161, 449–450

Ba, S. L., **2:**873
Baer, D. M., **2:**538
Balanced scorecard, **1:**B45–46
    benefits of, **1:**46
    business process perspective and, **1:**45
    challenges of, **1:**46
    creation/implementation of, steps in, **1:**45–46
    customer perspective and, **1:**45
    financial aspects of organizations and, **1:**45
    financial performance, focus on, **1:**45
    learning/growth perspective and, **1:**45
    organizations, perspectives on, **1:**45
    See also Measurement scales; Performance
        appraisal; Total quality management (TQM)
Baldrige Award, **2:**754, 814
Banding, **1:**46–48
    creation of bands, **1:**47, 83
    cutoff scores and, **1:**46
    effectiveness of, **1:**48
    fixed bands, **1:**47
    grouping scores, equivalent scores
        and, **1:**46
    hiring decisions and, **1:**46, 196, **2:**698
    legality of, **1:**48
    purpose of, **1:**46–47
    sliding bands, **1:**47–48
    standard error of the difference and, **1:**47
    top-down selection strategy and, **1:**46, 47
    types of bands and, **1:**47–48
    workforce diversity and, **1:**47
    See also Adverse impact/disparate treatment/
        discrimination at work; Selection
        strategies
Bandura, A., **2:**705, 879, 893
Banks, C., **1:**210
Bar-Hillel, M., **1:**281
Bar-On EQ-i measure, **1:**181
Barki, H., **1:**94
Barnard, C., **1:**328
Barrett, G. V., **1:**132
Barrick, M., **1:**55
Bass, B., **2:**834
Batch selection, **1:**196, **2:**628
Baumrind, D., **1:**222
Bedaeian, A., **1:**328, **2:**692
Beehr, T. A., **2:**769, 772
Behavior:
    attitudes and, **1:**39
    charismatic leadership and, **1:**71

person-situation debate, **1:**41
    See also Behavioral approach to leadership; Construct; Theory
        of reasoned action/theory of planned behavior
Behavior analysis, **2:**538, 539
Behavior genetics, **1:**269–270
Behavior-based conflict, **2:**683
Behavior-outcome links, **1:**132
Behavioral activation system (BAS), **2:**490
Behavioral approach to leadership, **1:**48–50
    consideration behaviors, **1:**49
    contribution of, **1:**50
    ineffective leadership, characteristics of, **1:**49
    initiation of structure behaviors, **1:**49
    Leader Behavior Description Questionnaire and, **1:**49
    leader behavior, work outcomes and, **1:**49
    Leadership Grid and, **1:**50
    limitation of, **1:**50
    Ohio State Leadership Studies, **1:**48–49
    relationship-oriented/employee-oriented behaviors, **1:**50
    situational theories of leadership and, **1:**50
    Supervisory Behavior Description Questionnaire and, **1:**49
    task-oriented/production-oriented behaviors, **1:**50
    trait-oriented leadership research and, **1:**48
    University of Michigan studies, **1:**49–50
    See also Big Five taxonomy of personality; Situational
        approach to leadership; Trait approach to leadership
Behavioral checklists, **2:**603
Behavioral diaries, **2:**603
Behavioral event interviews, **1:**85
Behavioral inhibition system (BIS), **2:**490
Behavioral integrity, **1:**356
Behavioral observation training, **1:**257
Behavioral Systems, Inc., **2:**538
Behaviorally anchored rating scales (BARS), **2:**601–602, 662
Belmont Report, **1:**220
Ben-Abba, E., **1:**281
Ben-Shakhar, G., **1:**281
Benchmark organizations, **1:**307–308
Benchmarking, **1:**B50–52
    benchmark databases, value/quality of, **1:**51
    benefits of, **1:**51
    best practices and, **1:**51
    economic/cultural differences and, **1:**51
    external benchmarking and, **1:**52
    global employee surveys, question comparability and, **1:**51
    internal benchmarking and, **1:**51–52
    See also Measurement scales; Performance appraisal
Beneficence, **1:**216
Benefits. *See* Compensation; Compressed workweek; Incentives
Benefits Survey (Society for Human Resource
        Management), **1:**87
Bennett, R., **1:**120, 123, 125
Berle, A. A., **1:**115
Berry, J. W., **1:**139, 140
Berry, L., **1:**143
Best alternative to a negotiated agreement (BATNA), **2:**512
Best practices, **1:**51, 331, **2:**591
Bethlehem Steel, **2:**692
Beyer, J., **2:**547

Bies, R. J., **2:**838
Big Five taxonomy of personality, 1:13, **52–55,**
        111, 187, 270, 311, 414
    broadside approach to testing and, **1:**55, **2:**613
    challenges to, **1:**53–54
    five-factor theory of personality and, **1:**13, 34, 54
    industrial/organizational psychology and, **1:**54–55
    integrity trait and, **2:**610
    networking and, **2:**515
    personality-performance relationship and, **1:**55, **2:**613
    theoretical foundations of, **1:**53
    traits in, **1:**52–53, 54, 55, **2:**609
    See also Factor analysis; Individual differences;
            Personality; Personality assessment
Bikson, T. K., **2:**557
BILOG program, **1:**374
Binding arbitration, **2:**513
Bingham, W. V., **1:**313, 314
Binning, J. F., **1:**132
Biodata. *See* Biographical data
Biographical data, 1:56–57
    applicant reactions to, **1:**57
    configural scoring and, **1:**57
    criterion-keying scoring and, **1:**56
    cross-validation of samples and, **1:**57
    item attributes in, **1:**56
    personality/temperament measures and, **1:**56–57
    personality vs. situation orientation of, **1:**56
    premises behind, **1:**56
    race differences and, **1:**57
    rational/empirical methods of scoring and, **1:**57
    scoring methods and, **1:**56–57
    stability of scores and, **1:**56
    subject matter expert item-sorting procedure and, **1:**57
    test-retest reliability/alpha reliability and, **1:**56
    See also Individual assessment; Individual differences;
            Person-job (PJ) fit; Prescreening assessment methods
            for personnel selection
Biographical questionnaires, **2:**636
Biserial correlation, **2:**473
Bisexual population. *See* Gay/lesbian/bisexual (GLB) issues at work
Blachard, A., **1:**146
Black-box process, **1:**354
Blanchard, K., **1:**457
Blau, G., **2:**734, 735
Bloom's taxonomy, **1:**400
Blum, Y., **1:**281
Blurred retirement, **2:**680
Bolino, M., **1:**106
Bona fide occupational qualifications (BFOQ), **1:**9, 19, **58–60**
    defense, required elements of, **1:**58–60
    direct relationship requirements and, **1:**58–59
    essence of business requirements and, **1:**59
    general defense guidelines and, **1:**59–60
    legally protected characteristics and, **1:**58, 59
    stereotypes and, **1:**59
    See also Age Discrimination in Employment Act (ADEA) of
            1967; Americans with Disabilities Act (ADA) of 1990;
            Civil Rights Act of 1964; Civil Rights Act of 1991

Bonnardel, R., **1:**310
Boredom at work, 1:60–61
    boredom, definitions of, **1:**60
    causes of, **1:**60–61
    consequences of, **1:**60
    flow and, **1:**60
    job rotation/job enrichment or redesign and, **1:**61
    reduction of, **1:**61
    task-performer interactions and, **1:**61
    work environment and, **1:**61
    work tasks and, **1:**60–61
    See also Intrinsic and extrinsic work motivation; Job
            characteristics theory; Job satisfaction; Role
            overload and underload
Borman, W., **1:**103, 104
Bottom-up/top-down phenomenon, **2:**294
Bouchard, T. J., **1:**270
Boundary-spanning roles, **2:**686
Bowen, D., **2:**620
Brainstorming, **1:**127, 289–290
Branching technique, **2:**590
Brandeis, L., **1:**115
Braverman, E. P., **2:**635, 729
Bray, D., **1:**30
Break-even analysis, **2:**857
Breenfield, D., **1:**147
Bridge employment, **2:**533, 534, 680, 843
Bridges, W., **2:**544
Broadband system, **1:**83
Broadside approach to testing, **1:**55, **2:**613
Brodbeck, F. C., **1:**275
Brogden, H. E., **2:**856–857
Brogden-Cronbach-Gleser utility model, **2:**856–857
Brown, C. W., **1:**315
Brown, S., **1:**64, 67
Brown v. Topeka Board of Education, **1:**315
Brunswik, E., **1:**452, **2:**628, 629
Buffering effect, **2:**743
Bullying behavior, **1:**311, **2:**719
Burden of proof, **1:**10
Bureaucratic structure, **2:**588, 692
Bureau of Labor Statistics (BLS), **1:**422, **2:**525, 898
Bureau of Personnel Research, **1:**313
Bureau of Salesmanship Research (Carnegie Institute of
        Technology), **2:**613
Burke-Litwin model of organizational
        performance/change, **2:**566
Burnout. *See* Emotional burnout
Burns, J. M., **2:**834
Burt, C., **1:**309, 310
Burt, R. E., **2:**848
Burtt, H., **1:**327
Business Environmental Risk Intelligence (BERI), **1:**320
Business process perspective, **1:**45
Business process reengineering (BPR), **2:**815

Cacioppo, J., **1:**39
Caldwell, D. F., **2:**619, 620
California Psychological Inventory, **1:**67, **2:**612

Campbell, D. T., **2:**497, 498, 499, 500, 655, 657, 822
Campbell Interest and Skill Survey, **1:**67
Campbell, J. P., **1:**240, 316
Campion, J. E., **1:**199
Campion, M. A., **1:**199, **2:**635, 729
Canadian Psychological Association, **1:**218, **2:**747
Capitalist economy, **1:**315, 349
Caplan, R. D., **2:**619, 623
Career development, 1:63–65
    application of theories and, **1:**65
    career development theory and, **1:**63–64
    family-needs considerations and, **1:**65, 67
    flattened organizational structures and, **2:**533
    immigrant workers and, **1:**65
    onging assessment and, **1:**33
    pathways of, variations in, **1:**65
    social cognitive career theory and, **1:**64–65
    social learning theory of career decision
        making and, **1:**64, 65
    See also Academy of Management; Career development
        theory; Careers; Employment issues;
        Industrial/organizational psychology
        careers; Networking
Career development theory, **1:**63, 67
    application of, **1:**65
    career choices, self-concept and, **1:**64
    disengagement stage and, **1:**64
    establishment stage and, **1:**63
    exploration stage and, **1:**63
    growth stage and, **1:**63
    life-career rainbow and, **1:**63
    lifespace and, **1:**63
    life span/time and, **1:**63
    maintenance stage and, **1:**63–64
    recycling through stages and, **1:**64
    See also Career development; Careers
Career Force project, **2:**641
Careers, 1:66–67
    career assessment/counseling and, **1:**67
    career development theory and, **1:**67
    career satisfaction, well-being and, **1:**66–67
    concept of career, history of, **1:**66
    occupation health psychology and, **1:**66–67
    pathways of, **1:**65, 66
    plateaus in, **2:**533
    social cognitive career theory and, **1:**67
    theories of, **1:**67
    vocational interest personality types and, **1:**67
    work adjustment theory and, **1:**67
    work-family balance and, **1:**65, 67
    See also Career development; Industrial/organizational
        psychology careers
Carlsmith, J. M., **1:**240
Carnegie Institute of Technology (CIT), **1:**313
Carr, J. Z., **2:**545
Carroll, A. B., **1:**115
Carroll, J. B., **1:**76, 77, 181, 345
Cartwright, D., **1:**49
Caruso, D. R., **1:**181

Carver, C., **2:**534
Cascio, W. F., **1:**25
Case studies for training, **2:**824
Case study method, 1:68–69, 2:649
    collective cases, **1:**68
    collective instrumental case, **1:**68
    data analysis in, **1:**68–69
    data collection in, **1:**68
    flexible nature of, **1:**68, 69
    generalizability of findings and, **1:**69
    general types of cases, **1:**68
    instrumental/illustrative cases, **1:**68
    intercoder reliability and, **1:**69
    internal validity and, **1:**69
    intrinsic cases, **1:**68
    strengths of, **1:**69
    subjectivity of, **1:**69
    thick descriptions and, **1:**69
    weaknesses of, **1:**69
    See also Cross-cultural research methods
        and theory; Naturalistic observation
Cathode ray tubes (CRTs), **1:**323
Cattell, J. M., **1:**313, 314
Cattell, R. B., **1:**53, **2:**612
Causal attribution, **1:**111, **2:**590, 762
Causal modeling, **2:**775
Cautious optimists, **2:**536
Cedi, E. L., **2:**492
Ceiling effect in job evaluation, **1:**396
Censured Job Performance scale, **1:**270
Census surveys, **2:**780–781
Census of Women Corporate Officers and
    Top Earners, **1:**271
Center for Creative Leadership, **1:**316
Center for Effective Organizations (University
    of Southern California), **1:**204
Center of Leadership Studies, **2:**727
Centers for Disease Control and Prevention, **2:**501
Central tendency, **1:**149
Central tendency error, **2:**661
Centralization of organizational structure, **2:**586
Certification examinations, **2:**756
    See also Credentialing
Certified Employee Assistance Professional (CEAP), **1:**189
Chaiken, S., **1:**39
Champy, J., **2:**815
Chan, D., **2:**547, 729
Change. *See* Change communication; Improvement
    initiatives; Organizational change
Change communication, **2:**554
Chaparral Steel Company, **2:**527
Charismatic leadership theory, 1:70–71
    behaviors of charismatic leadership and, **1:**71, **2:**467, 468
    charismatic nature, elements of, **1:**70
    influence processes and, **1:**70–71
    leader characteristics, **1:**70
    leader motivation/commitment and, **1:**70
    limitations of, **1:**70–71
    research on, **1:**70

turbulent/stressful times and, **1:**70
See also Leadership development; Leadership and
    supervision; Machiavellianism; Transformational and
    transactional leadership
Chatman, J. A., **2:**616, 620
Checks and balances, **2:**468
Chemers, M. M., **1:**451, 452
Chi-square statistic, **1:**152
Chokkar, J., **1:**275
Christal, R. E., **1:**53
Christie, R., **2:**467
Chronic fatigue, **2:**721
Circadian rhythm, **1:**87–88, **2:**721
Citizenship behaviors:
    facets of citizenship and, **1:**104
    See also Contextual performance/prosocial
        behavior/organizational citizenship behavior;
        Corporate social responsibility; Organizational
        citizenship behaviors (OCBs)
Civil Right Act of 1866, **1:**72
Civil Rights Act of 1964, 1:8, 16, 22, **71**, 82, 84, 218,
    315, **2:**482, 613, 714, 716, 718, 846
Civil Rights Act of 1991, 1:16, 22, **71–74**, 218, 316
    additional provisions of, **1:**74
    disparate impact cases and, **1:**72–73
    employment discrimination cases, required proof in, **1:**72–73
    fair employment law extension and, **1:**72, 84
    impact of, **1:**74
    jury trial, right to, **1:**73–74
    make-whole relief and, **1:**73
    mixed-motive disparate treatment cases and, **1:**73
    race norming and, **2:**659–660
    same-decision defense and, **1:**73
    successful plaintiffs, damages available to, **1:**73
    See also Adverse impact/disparate treatment/discrimination at
        work; Human resource management (HRM); Human
        resources strategy; Labor law; Sexual discrimination
Civil rights movement, **1:**315
Civil Service Commission, **2:**846
Civil Service Selection Board, **1:**310
Civil War (USA), **2:**557
Claparède, E., **1:**309
Classical conditioning, **1:**38
Classical free enterprise model of business, **1:**115
Classical measurement theory, **1:**75
Classical reliability theory, **1:**75
Classical test theory (CTT), **1:75–76**, 371, 400, **2:**677
    adaptive testing and, **1:**373–374
    assumptions of, **1:**75
    limitations of, **1:**76
    measurement error and, **1:**75
    meta-analysis and, **2:**482
    reliability, parallel tests and, **1:**75–76
    strengths of, **1:**76
    test scores, properties of, **1:**75
    true score and, **1:**75
    validity vs. reliability and, **1:**76
    See also Generalizability theory; Item response theory
        (IRT); Reliability; Validity

Classification. *See* Placement and classification
Climate for safety, **2:**546
Climate for service, **1:**144, **2:**546
Climate strength, **2:**545, 547
Climate of trust, **1:**263
Cloquitt, J., **2:**547
Cluster sampling, **2:**690
Coaching. *See* Coaching leadership; Executive coaching;
    High-performance organization model
Coaching leadership, **2:**725–726
Coding. *See* Computer assessment; Content coding;
    Naturalistic observation
Coeffents of equivalence and stability, **2:**676–677
Coercive power, **1:**443
Cognitive abilities, 1:76–78
    auditory processing and, **1:**77
    cognitive processing speed and, **1:**77
    creative processes and, **1:**126–127
    crystallized intelligence and, **1:**77
    fluid intelligence/reasoning and, **1:**77
    general verbal ability and, **1:**77
    g factor of, **1:**77–78
    job-specific knowledge/skills and, **1:**78
    long-term associative storage/retrieval and, **1:**77
    mood effects and, **2:**486
    narrow abilities and, **1:**77, 78
    predictive validity of, **1:**77–78
    psychometric structure of, **1:**76–77
    quantitative reasoning/skills and, **1:**77
    short-term memory and, **1:**77
    visual-spatial processing and, **1:**77
    See also Cognitive ability tests; Factor analysis;
        Individual differences; Practical intelligence
Cognitive ability tests, 1:34, **79–81**
    concerns about, **1:**80
    industrial environments and, **1:**79–80
    pre-employment selection and, **1:**80
    prevalence of, **1:**80
    validity/fairness of, **1:**80–81
    workplace outcomes, general mental ability and, **1:**79–80
    See also Cognitive abilities; Computer assessment; Factor
        analysis; Individual differences
Cognitive bias. *See* Judgment and decision-making process:
    heuristics, cognitive biases, and contextual influences
Cognitive distortion, **1:**213–214
Cognitive process validity, **2:**866
Cognitive processing speed, **1:**77
Cognitive task analysis, **1:**207, **2:**828
Cognitive work analysis, **1:**207
Cohen, L., **1:**210
Cohen's kappa, **1:**69
Cohort studies, **1:**463
Colella, A., **1:**211, 212
Collaborative work, **1:**35, 70
Collective bargaining, **1:**349, 437, **2:**851, 853
Collective case study, **1:**68
Collective effort model (CEM), **2:**737–738
Collective instrumental case study, **1:**68
College admission tests, **1:**373, **2:**755, 757, 760

Collins, J., **2:**561
Command language, **1:**325
Commensurate measures, **2:**618
Commission salespeople, **1:**2, 84
Commitment. *See* Organizational commitment;
    Psychological contract
Committee on Classification and Personnel, **1:**314
Common fate concept, **1:**261, 262–263
Common Metric Questionnaire, **1:**171
Common Rule, **1:**220, 221
Common sense. *See* Practical intelligence
Commonwealth Department of Labour and
    National Service, **1:**321
Communication. *See* Communications technologies;
    Interpersonal communication
Communications technologies, **1:**43, 362, 365–366, **2:**732, 896
Communism, **1:**315, 316
Comparable worth, 1:81–82
    conducting studies on, **1:**82
    criticisms of, **1:**82
    definition of, **1:**81
    legal status of, **1:**81–82
    pay equity and, **1:**81, 82, 211–212
    sex bias and, **1:**81
    See also Compensation; Equal Pay Act (EPA)
        of 1963; Job evaluation
Compensation, 1:83–84
    base pay rates, **1:**83
    benefits and, **1:**84
    broadband system and, **1:**83
    comparable worth/pay equity debate and, **1:**84
    competitive advantage and, **1:**84
    components of, **1:**83
    creative jobs and, **1:**83
    e-compensation and, **1:**172–173
    executive pay, agency theory and, **1:**84
    expatriates and, **1:**233
    gender inequities in, **2:**715
    globalization and, **1:**84
    incentive pay systems and, **1:**83
    legal issues in, **1:**84
    morale and, **2:**489
    new pay movement and, **1:**83
    pay for performance and, **1:**83
    pay raises and, **1:**83
    pay satisfaction and, **1:**84
    pay satisfaction measurement and, **1:**84
    psychology of pay and, **1:**84
    retail salespeople and, **1:**84
    system design, **1:**83
    total compensation movement and, **1:**83
    underpayment and, **2:**843
    variable pay/at-risk pay and, **1:**83
    virtual companies/e-jobs and, **1:**84
    See also Age Discrimination in Employment Act (ADEA)
        of 1967; Americans with Disabilities Act (ADA) of
        1990; Civil Rights Act of 1963; Civil Rights Act
        of 1991; Incentives
Compensatory model of selection, **1:**195–196

Compensatory scoring strategy, **2:**696
Competence development:
    action theory and, **1:**6
    management competency profiling and, **1:**31, 32
    See also Competency modeling
Competency modeling, 1:85–86
    applications of, **1:**86
    behavioral event/critical incident interviews and, **1:**85
    competencies, definition of, **1:**85
    competency model and, **1:**85–86
    core competencies and, **1:**85
    focus groups and, **1:**85
    job analysis processes and, **1:**85–86
    job requirements and, **1:**85
    job-specific competency models, **1:**86
    organizational change and, **1:**86
    organization-wide model, **1:**86
    outcomes of, **1:**86
    processes of, **1:**85–86
    process modeling and, **1:**85–86
    questionnaires and, **1:**85
    stretch competency model, **1:**86
    talent management systems and, **1:**86
    See also Job analysis; Job performance models
Competitive advantage:
    citizenship behaviors and, **1:**2
    compensation structures and, **1:**84
    coopetition concept and, **2:**592–593
    multinational companies and, **1:**276–277
    organizational image and, **2:**569
    See also Strategic planning
Complemenatry fit, **2:**615
Complexity of organizational structure, **2:**586
Compound traits, **2:**609–610
Comprehensive Test of Basic Skills, **2:**755
Compressed workweek, 1:87–89
    absenteeism and, **1:**88
    alternative work schedules and, **1:**87
    benefits/drawbacks of, **1:**87–88
    circadian rhythm approach to, **1:**87–88
    discretionary time and, **1:**88
    employee autonomy and, **1:**88
    employee perspective on, **1:**87, 88
    employer perspective on, **1:**87, 88
    fatigue factor and, **1:**88
    job characteristics model and, **1:**87, 88
    job satisfaction and, **1:**88
    legal limitations and, **1:**87
    manufacturing organizations and, **1:**87
    performance/productivity levels and, **1:**88
    research on, **1:**88–89
    types of, **1:**87
    See also Flexible work schedules
Compromising style of conflict management, **1:**98, 99
Computer adaptive testing (CAT), 1:89–91, 373–374, **2:**757
    adaptive test concept and, **1:**90
    advantages of, **1:**90
    individual response patterns and, **1:**90
    item response theory and, **1:**90

linear nature of, **1**:90
process of, **1**:90
scoring of, **1**:90
test-taker reaction to, **1**:91
See also Computer assessment
Computer assessment, 1:89–91
advantages of, **1**:90
content-coding/text-mining tools and, **1**:102
critical issues in, **1**:91
definition of, **1**:89
interactive assessments and, **1**:89
measurement equivalence and, **1**:91
multimedia elements in, **1**:89
organizational surveys and, **2**:590–591
page-turner tests and, **1**:89
personality trait testing, **2**:611
test security measures and, **1**:91, **2**:799
test-taker reactions to, **1**:91
Web-based assessment, **1**:89, 90, 91
See also Adverse impact/disparate treatment/discrimination
    at work; Applicant/test-taker reactions; Computer
    adaptive testing (CAT); Human-computer interaction
    (HCI); Selection strategies
Computer simulation. *See* Simulation, computer approach
Computers in daily life. *See* Human-computer interaction (HCI)
Computer-based integrated technology (CIT), **1**:42, 43
Computer-based training. *See* Distance learning
Computerized adaptive testing. *See* Computer
    adaptive testing (CAT)
Concept mapping, **2**:789
Concurrent validation, **2**:642, 861
Confidence intervals/hypothesis testing/effect sizes, 1:91–94
application of confidence intervals, **1**:93
confidence intervals, **1**:92, 93, 351
d metric and, **1**:93
effect sizes, **1**:93–94
hypothesis testing, **1**:92–93
inferential statistics and, **1**:91–92
null hypothesis testing and, **1**:92–93
parameters and, **1**:92
r metric and, **1**:94
sampling distribution and, **1**:92
standard deviation and, **1**:92, 93
standard error and, **1**:92
standardized difference and, **1**:93
statistic and, **1**:92
z-score metric and, **1**:93
Confidentiality, **1**:176, 221–222, 343
Configural scoring, **1**:57
Confirmation bias, **1**:430
Confirmatory factor analysis (CFA), **1**:245–246,
    2:498, 500, 653, 773
See also Factor analysis
Confirmatory rater bias, **2**:661
Conflict at work, 1:94–95
conflict, definitional framework for, **1**:94–95
conflict measurement, methodological issues in, **1**:95
multiple-theme perspective and, **1**:94
personality, experience of conflict and, **1**:95

relationship conflict and, **1**:95
task conflict and, **1**:95, 96, 97
See also Conflict and its outcomes; Conflict management; Least
    preferred coworker (LPC) theory; Work-life balance
Conflict emergence studies, **1**:97
Conflict and its outcomes, 1:95–96
organizational outcomes and, **1**:95–96
personal well-being and, **1**:95
positive outcomes and, **1**:96
stress and, **1**:96
See also Conflict at work; Conflict management
Conflict management, 1:97–99
avoidant style of, **1**:98, 99
compromising style of, **1**:98, 99
conflict emergence studies and, **1**:97
conflict measurement and, **1**:97
conflict resolution and, **1**:97
definition of, **1**:97
dispositional influences on, **1**:99
dominating style of, **1**:98, 99
employee training and, **1**:99
five-style model of, **1**:98–99
integrating style of, **1**:98–99
intervention development and, **1**:97
obliging style of, **1**:98, 99
relationship conflict and, **1**:97
styles of, **1**:97–99
task conflict and, **1**:97
three-/four-style models of, **1**:98
See also Conflict at work; Industrial relations; Negotiation,
    mediation, and arbitration; Work-life balance
Conflict resolution, **1**:97
Congress of Industrial Organizations (CIO), **2**:852
Congressional Office Technology Assessment, **1**:176
Conscientiousness scale, **1**:34, **2**:611
Conscientiousness trait, **1**:52, 54, 55, 105, 357, **2**:609, 746
Consequentialist perspective, **1**:215
Consideration behaviors, **1**:49
Constrained parameters, **2**:774
Construct, 1:99–101
behavioral domains, summarization of, **1**:100
definition of, **1**:100
hypothetical nature of, **1**:100
performance domains, covarying behaviors and, **1**:100–101
psychological constructs and, **1**:100
scientific systems of constructs and, **1**:99–100
theory development and, **1**:100
See also Validation strategies
Construct validity, **1**:238–239, 358–359, **2**:728–729, 861
See also Nomological networks
Construct validity inferences, **2**:865
Contact hypothesis, **1**:361–362
Content analysis of verbatim explanations (CAVE), **2**:535
Content coding, 1:101–103
cautions/recommendations for, **1**:102–103
content-coding/text-mining tools and, **1**:102
qualitative approach and, **1**:101, **2**:650, 651
quantitative approaches and, **1**:101
sampling results and, **1**:102

techniques of, **1:**101–102
thematic structures and, **1:**101–102
utility of, **1:**101
write-in questions and, **1:**101
See also Qualitative research approach; Quantitative research approach; Verbal protocol analysis
Content models of turnover, **2:**883–884
Content validity inferences, **2:**865
Content-based validation strategies, **2:**862
Contentious communication style, **1:**367
Contextual fallacies, **2:**493
Contextual influences. *See* Judgment and decision-making process: heuristics, cognitive biases, and contextual influences
Contextual knowledge constructs, **2:**728
Contextual performance/prosocial behavior/organizational citizenship behavior, 1:103–106, 401
actor-recipient relationship and, **1:**106
affective events theory and, **1:**106
counterproductive work behavior and, **1:**105
dispositional constructs and, **1:**104–105
employee-directed behaviors and, **1:**104
facets of citizenship and, **1:**104
happy/productive worker hypothesis and, **1:**103
job-related appraisals/attitudes and, **1:**104, 106
job satisfaction and, **1:**103, 104, 105
motivation for behaviors and, **1:**106
norm of reciprocity and, **1:**104
organizational citizenship behavior, **1:**103–106, **2:**519, 550, 572, 735
organizational performance and, **1:**106
organization-directed behaviors and, **1:**104
performance constructs and, **1:**105
predictors of citizenship behaviors and, **1:**104
psychological contract theory and, **1:**104
required/expected citizenship behavior and, **1:**106
situational strength and, **1:**103
structure of organizational citizenship behavior and, **1:**104
task performance and, **1:**103, 105
typology of citizenship and, **1:**104
Contingency model of leadership, **1:**450
Contingency theory, **2:**586–587, 588
Contingent labor, **2:**593–594
Contingent reward (CR), **2:**835
Continuance commitment scale (CCS), **2:**549
Continuance organizational commitment, **2:**548, 549, 550
Continuous employee selection, **1:**196
Continuous learning, **1:**446–447, 449, **2:**541
Continuous selection, **1:**196
Contract violation, **1:**197–198, **2:**563, 647–648
Contrast effects, **2:**661
Contributions-based model, **1:**163–164
Control orientation, **2:**492, 573, 586
See also Control theory; Locus of control
Control theory, 1:107–110
complex dynamic nature of, **1:**109
controversies about, **1:**109–110
cybernetics and, **1:**107
feedback effects and, **1:**108

feedback-seeking behavior and, **1:**108–109
feedback-standard comparison process and, **2:** 606
feed-forward process and, **1:**109
goal effects and, **1:**108, 109
homeostasis and, **1:**107
incentives and, **1:**339
industrial/organizational psychology and, **1:**108
mechanisms in, **1:**107
motivation theory and, **1:**108–109
negative feedback loops and, **1:**107
perceptions-goals discrepancies, reduction of, **1:**108–109
psychological systems and, **1:**107–108
self-efficacy and, **1:**109
self-regulation theories and, **1:**107, 109
simulations and, **1:**109–110
variables, perception/state of, **1:**107
See also Engineering psychology; Feedback seeking; Goal-setting theory; Locus of control; Self-Efficacy; Self-regulation theory
Convenience samples, **2:**691
Convergent evidence, **2:**861
Convergent validity, **2:**497, 498, 865
Cook, T. D., **2:**655, 657, 822
Cook, T. M., **2:**518
Cooksey, R. W., **1:**453
Cooper, C. L., **1:**462
Coopetition concept, **2:**592–593
Coping and management. *See* Coping mechanisms; Stress, coping and management
Coping mechanisms:
abusive supervision and, **1:**3
active coping, **1:**3
antecedent-focused coping, **1:**183
avoidant coping, **1:**3
core self-evaluations and, **1:**112
cynicism and, **2:**563
defensive coping strategies, **2:**623
dirty work and, **1:**153–154
hardiness and, **1:**304
See also Affective traits; Emotion regulation; Stress, coping and management
Copper, C., **1:**284, 285, 286
Core competencies, **1:**85, **2:**915–916, 917 (table), 926–927
Core self-evaluations, 1:14, **110–112, 2:**704
causal associations and, **1:**111
coping skills and, **1:**112
expectancy motivation and, **1:**111–112
indirect/direct measures and, **1:**111
individual self-assessments and, **1:**111
job performance and, **1:**111
job satisfaction and, **1:**111
personality traits and, **1:**110–111
structure/measurement of, **1:**110–111
work and, **1:**11–112
See also Job satisfaction; Job satisfaction measurement; Self-efficacy; Self-esteem
Cornell model, **1:**408
Corporate ethics, 1:112–114
avoidance of ethics breaches and, **1:**113, 114

control of ethical behavior and, 1:113–114
culture, ethical conduct and, 1:114
definition of, 1:112
disciplinary approaches to, 1:112–113
moral philosophy and, 1:112, 113
perceptions of fairness and, 1:114
proactive/reactive ethics policies/procedures and, 1:113–114
social scientific inquiry and, 1:113
whistleblowers and, 1:114
See also Corporate social responsibility; Cross-cultural
    research methods and theory; Organizational behavior;
    Organizational citizenship behaviors (OCBs);
    Organizational culture; Organizational justice
Corporate social responsibility, 1:114–117
classical free enterprise model of business and, 1:115
classical model, critiques of, 1:115
constructive performance/proactive activities and, 1:116
critiques of, 1:117
descriptive stakeholder theory and, 1:116
domains of, 1:115
ethical indifference and, 1:115
management role, professionalization of, 1:115–116
moral norms/expectations and, 1:115, 116
normative stakeholder theory and, 1:116
organizational effectiveness and, 1:117
principle of universalism and, 1:116–117
public corporations and, 1:115
revisionist free enterprise model and, 1:115–117
stakeholder theories and, 1:116–117
state/local benefits and, 1:116
strategic/instrumental stakeholder theory and, 1:116
strategic stakeholder approach to management and, 1:116
See also Ethics in industrial/organizational practice; Ethics
    in industrial/organizational research; Organizational
    citizenship behaviors (OCBs)
Correlation analysis, 2:654
Correlation coefficient. See Measures of association/
    correlation coefficient
Correlation matrix, 2:497
Correlational errors, 2:661
Cost accounting, 2:693
Cost-reduction efforts, 1:86
Costa, P., 1:54, 346
Council for Applied Master's Programs in Psychology
    (CAMPP), 2:918
**Counterproductive work behaviors (CWBs),
    1:118–119, 2:800, 896**
antecedents of, 1:119
consequences of, 1:119
definitional features, controversies over, 1:118–119
interpersonal deviance and, 1:118
organizational deviance and, 1:118
specific/unique construct of, 1:118–119
umbrella conceptualization of, 1:118
See also Abusive supervision; Counterproductive work
    behaviors/interpersonal deviance (CWB-I);
    Counterproductive work behaviors/organizational
    deviance (CWB-O); Organizational retaliatory behavior;
    Workplace incivility

**Counterproductive work behaviors/interpersonal
    deviance (CWB-I), 1:118, 119–122**
antecedents of, 1:120–121
environmental antecedents of, 1:120–121
frustration aggression model of, 1:120
job stress model of, 1:120–121, 122
justice theories and, 1:121, 122
measurement of, 1:120
personal antecedents of, 1:121
reduction strategies and, 1:121–122
study of, rationale for, 1:120
See also Counterproductive work behaviors (CWBs);
    Counterproductive work behaviors/organizational
    deviance (CWB-O)
**Counterproductive work behaviors/organizational
    deviance (CWB-O), 1:118, 122–125**
antecedents of, 1:123–124
categories of, 1:123
control factor and, 1:124
deviant behavior model and, 1:125
emotion-centered stress model of, 1:124–125
environmental antecedents of, 1:123–124
frustration-aggression model of, 1:125
interpersonal conflict and, 1:124
justice theories and, 1:123–124, 125
locus of control issues and, 1:124
models/theories of, 1:124–125
negative affectivity and, 1:124
personal anger and, 1:124
personal antecedents of, 1:124
prevention/control of, 1:125
production deviance and, 1:123
property deviance and, 1:123
psychological contract and, 1:124
role conflict/ambiguity and, 1:123
self-control, insufficiency of, 1:124
See also Counterproductive work behaviors (CWBs);
    Counterproductive work behaviors/interpersonal
    deviance (CWB-I)
Covariance parameters, 2:775
Cragg, W., 1:116
Creativity at work, 1:126–129
brainstorming and, 1:127
cognitive processes and, 1:126–127
compensation and, 1:83
diversity at work and, 1:158
domain-relevant skills/knowledge and, 1:127
fostering creativity, 1:128–129
idea generation and, 1:127
implementation planning/monitoring and, 1:127
individual creativity and, 1:126–127
job/team characteristics and, 1:128
leadership role and, 1:128
motivation effects and, 1:127
organizational creativity and, 1:128, 129
outcomes of, 1:128
personality factors and, 1:127
reward systems and, 1:129
See also Innovation; Social cognitive theory

Credentialing, **1:129–131**, **2:**756
  absolute standards and, **1:**131
  business organizations, competence assessments and, **1:**131
  content validity, occupational analysis and, **1:**130
  credentialing exam content, identification of, **1:**129–130
  credentialing exam, development of, **1:**130
  normative standards and, **1:**131
  performance standards and, **1:**131
  subject-matter experts and, **1:**130
  trends in, **1:**131
  See also Doctoral level education/training; Job analysis;
      Job knowledge testing; Master's level education/training;
      Selection strategies
Criterion theory, **1:131–134**
  behavior-outcome links and, **1:**132
  biases and, **1:**134
  criterion deficiency/contamination and, **1:**133–134
  criterion, definition of, **1:**131–132
  criterion problem and, **1:**132–133
  criterion reliability and, **1:**133–134
  individual dimensionality and, **1:**133
  observational reliability, lack of, **1:**134
  operational criterion, **1:**132, 133
  static dimensionality and, **1:**133
  temporal/dynamic dimensionality and, **1:**133
  ultimate criterion and, **1:**132
  See also Counterproductive work behaviors (CWBs);
      Employee selection; Job performance models;
      Training methods
Criterion-keying scoring, **1:**56
Criterion-related validity, **1:**200, 336, **2:**613–614, 728, 861
Criterion-related validity inferences, **2:**865
Critical incident checklist, **2:**603
Critical incident interviews, **1:**85, 135
Critical Incident Stress Debriefing (CISD), **2:**797
Critical incident technique (CIT), **1:134–136**, **2:**634
  analyzing data/stage four, **1:**136
  applications of, **1:**136
  collecting critical incidents/stage three, **1:**135–136
  critical incident interviews, **1:**85, 135
  establishing aims/stage one, **1:**135
  five-stage process of, **1:**135–136
  history of, **1:**135
  interpreting and reporting findings/stage five, **1:**136
  specifying plans and conditions/stage two, **1:**135
  See also Job analysis; Job analysis methods;
      Qualitative research approach
Critical specification, **2:**750
Cronbach, L. J., **1:**268, **2:**519, 856–857
Cronshaw, S. F., **2:**895
Cross-cultural research methods and theory, **1:136–142**
  analysis/interpretation phases and, **1:**142
  construct contamination/deficiency and, **1:**140
  constructs of interest, assessment of, **1:**140–141
  cross-level direct effect models and, **1:**137, 139
  cross-level moderator effects models and, **1:**137, 140
  culture differentiation, dimensions in, **1:**137, 138–139 (table)
  emic instrument and, **1:**141
  imposed etic constructs and, **1:**140, 141

  levels of analysis in, **1:**137–140, 137 (figure)
  pilot studies/feedback and, **1:**141, 142
  rival hypotheses, assessment of, **1:**142
  sampling methods and, **1:**141
  sampling participants and, **1:**140
  translation of materials and, **1:**141–142
  See also Factor analysis; Qualitative research
      approach; Quantitative research approach
Cross-cultural training, **2:**826
Cross-job worker movement, **1:**282–283
Cross-level direct effect models, **1:**137, 139
Cross-level fallacies, **2:**493
Cross-level moderator effects models, **1:**137, 140
Cross-products matrix, **2:**471, 471 (table)
Crystallized intelligence, **1:**77
Csikszentmihalyi, M., **1:**464, **2:**631
Cullen, J., **2:**546
Culturally endorsed implicit leadership theory (CLT), **1:**274, 275
Culture. *See* Globalization; Multinational companies
      (MNCs); Organizational culture; Organizational
      Culture Profile (OCP)
Cummings, L. L., **1:**250, **2:**604
Customer satisfaction with services, **1:**45, 86, **143–145**
  causality, employee/customer outcomes and, **1:**145
  climate for service and, **1:**144
  future service paradigms and, **1:**145
  linkage research and, **1:**144–145
  marketing, user-based approach, **1:**143, 144
  measurement issues and, **1:**144
  operations management and, **1:**145
  organizational behavior, industrial/organizational
      psychology and, **1:**144–145
  organizational climate for service and, **1:**144, **2:**546
  service profit chain and, **1:**144
  service quality, customer satisfaction/loyalty and, **1:**144
  services research, multidisciplinary evolution and, **1:**143–145
  SERVQUAL model and, **1:**143, 144
  unmet expectations gap model and, **1:**144, 145
Cut scores, **1:**46, 196, **2:**659, 696–697, 756
Cyberloafing at work, **1:146–147**
  disciplinary measures for violators, **1:**147
  management of, **1:**146–147
  monitoring/filtering software and, **1:**147
  prevalence of, **1:**146
  problems associated with, **1:**146
  reasons for, **1:**146
  use policies and, **1:**147
  See also Counterproductive work behaviors (CWBs);
      Integrity at work; Organizational retaliatory behavior
Cybernetic model, **2:**767, 772–773
Cybernetics, **1:**107, 339
Cynical hostility, **2:**562
Cynicism. *See* Coping mechanisms; Cynical hostility;
      Emotional burnout; Organizational cynicism

d Metric, **1:**93
Daniels, A., **2:**538
Data sampling. *See* Sampling techniques
Davis, R. A., **1:**147

Dawis, R. V., **1:**67, 347, **2:**616, 622
Day, D., **1:**334
Dearborn Conference Group, **1:**315
Deci, E. L., **2:**840
Decision making:
    affective traits and, **1:**14
    item response theory and, **1:**374
    psychological testing and, **1:**29, 30
    structured decision making, stereotyping and, **2:**763
    unfair procedures in, **1:**3
    See also Judgment and decision-making (JDM) process;
        Judgment and decision-making process: advice giving
        and taking; Judgment and decision-making process:
        heuristics, cognitive biases, and contextual influences
Decision making meetings, **2:**474
Decision making styles scales, **1:**425
Declarative knowledge, **1:**399
Decoy effects, **1:**431–432
Defensive coping strategies, **2:**623
Defensive pessimism, **2:**535, 536
Defensive Pessimism Questionnaire (DPQ), **2:**535
Delegating leadership, **2:**726
Delphi technique, **1:**291
Demand-control model, **1:**407, **2:**722
Demands-abilities fit, **2:**615, 619
Demands-control-support (DCS) model, **2:**772
Deming, W. E., **2:**814
DeNisi, A. S., **1:**248, 249, **2:**517, 606
Deontic justice, **2:**574
Deontological standards, **1:**215, 219
Department of Defense, **2:**641
Department of Health, Education and Welfare (DHEW), **1:**220
Department of Health and Human Services (DHHS), **1:**219, 220
Department of Justice, **1:**23, **2:**846
Department of Labor, **1:**164, 210, 247, 271, 382,
        2:528, 715, 756, 846, 898
Department of Transportation, **1:**23
Depersonalization phenomenon, **1:**178
Depressive realism effect, **2:**486
Descriptive norms, **2:**739
Descriptive stakeholder theory, **1:**116
Descriptive statistics, 1:149–150
    central tendency and, **1:**149
    frequency distributions and, **1:**149
    graphical representation and, **1:**149, 150
    kurtosis and, **1:**150
    platykurtic data and, **1:**150
    range and, **1:**149
    skew and, **1:**149–150
    standard deviation and, **1:**149
    variance and, **1:**149
    See also Inferential statistics; Qualitative research approach;
        Quantitative research approach; Statistical power
Design. *See* Engineering psychology; Job design
Deskilling process, **1:**43
Deutero learning, **1:**449
Deutsch, M., **1:**97
Developmental disabilities, **2:**540
Development dimensions International, **1:**316

Deviant behavior model, **1:**123, 125
de Vries, R., **1:**334
Dewey, J., **2:**803
*Diagnostic and Statistical Manual of Mental
        Disorders, 4th Edition* (DSM-IV), **1:**266
Dickson, M. W., **2:**546
Dictionary of Occupational Titles (DOT), **1:150–151,**
        314, 382, 391, 421, 422, **2:**528
    alternate titles, **1:**150
    definition trailer, **1:**151
    drawbacks of, **1:**150
    history of, **1:**150
    industry designation, **1:**150
    job analysis application and, **1:**151
    lead statements, **1:**150
    listings, components of, **1:**150–151
    may items, **1:**150
    occupational code numbers, **1:**150
    occupational titles, **1:**150
    task element statements, **1:**150
    undefined related titles, **1:**150–151
    See also Occupational Information Network (O*NET)
Difference scores, **2:**617
Differential Aptitude Tests, **1:**67
Differential bundle functioning (DBF), **1:**151
Differential functioning of items and tests (DFIT), **1:**152
Differential item functioning (DIF), **1:151–152**
    analysis of variance and, **1:**152
    bundles and, **1:**151
    detection strategies, **1:**152
    differential bundle functioning and, **1:**151
    differential test functioning and, **1:**152
    impact/between-group difference and, **1:**151
    item-level effects and, **1:**152
    levels of analysis and, **1:**151–152
    p-value differences and, **1:**152
    parametric/nonparametric techniques and, **1:**152
    standardized tests and, **1:**151
    summative effect/amplification and, **1:**151
    See also Item response theory
Differential psychology, **1:**344
Differential test functioning (DTF), **1:**152
Dipboye, R. L., **1:**211, 212
Directed graphs, **2:**774
Direct estimate of attribute preference, **2:**669
Direct experience, **1:**38
Direct observation, **1:**378–379
Directive leadership, **2:**595, **2:**725
Dirty work, 1:152–154
    breadth of taint and, **1:**153
    classifications of, **1:**152–153
    coping strategies and, **1:**153–154
    depth of taint and, **1:**153
    industrial/organizational psychology and, **1:**154
    moral taint and, **1:**153
    normalization process and, **1:**154
    occupational ideology tactics and, **1:**154
    physical taint and, **1:**153
    prestige level of occupation and, **1:**153

social taint and, **1:**153
social weighting strategies and, **1:**153–154
stigma of, **1:**152–153
strength of occupational culture and, **1:**153
See also Emotions; Job satisfaction; Organizational image;
    Self-esteem; Stress, coping and management; Theory
    of work adjustment
Disabled individuals, **1:**17
legal protection for, **1:**22–25
See also Americans with Disabilities Act (ADA) of
    1990; Workplace accommodations for the disabled
Discretionary rewards, **2:**791
Discriminant evidence, **2:**861
Discriminant validity, **2:**497–498, 865
Discrimination:
allowable discrimination, **1:**8, 9
cognitive ability tests, four-fifths rule and, **1:**10, **2:**846
definition of, **1:**7
employment discrimination law, **1:**8–9
restricted policy, evidence of, **1:**10
workforce utilization analysis and, **1:**10
See also Adverse (disparate) impact; Adverse impact/disparate
    treatment/discrimination at work; Affirmative action;
    Affirmative action programs (AAPs); Age Discrimination
    in Employment Act (ADEA) of 1967; Sexual
    discrimination
Disparate impact, **1:**10, 20, 72–73, **2:**715
Disparate treatment, **1:**9, 19–20, 73, **2:**714
Disposition. *See* Personality
Disproportionate stratified sample, **2:**690
Distance learning, 1:155–157
advantages of, **1:**155–156
content of, **1:**155
convenience/cost factors and, **1:**156
environmental distractions and, **1:**156–157
feedback from, **1:**156
individualized instruction and, **1:**155
interpersonal contact and, **1:**156
issues with, **1:**156–157
learner self-efficacy and, **1:**156
needs assessment/training evaluation and, **1:**155
performance tracking and, **1:**156
psychological fidelity of, **1:**155
research on, **1:**156
scope of, **1:**155
sophistication of, **1:**155
standardization of content/delivery and, **1:**156
technological infrastructure and, **1:**156
training time reduction and, **1:**156
See also Computer assessment; Training; Training
    evaluation; Training methods; Training needs
    assessment and analysis; Transfer of training
Distortion practices:
communication and, **2:**552
impression management and, **1:**336–337, 338, **2:**614
individual assessment and, **1:**343
pre-employment screening and, **2:**636–637
Distress. *See* Eustress; Psychological distress
Distributional errors, **2:**660–661

Distributive justice, **1:**26, 121, **2:**571, 577, 783
Diversity in the workplace, 1:157–160
accommodations and, **1:**160
affirmative action and, **1:**158
attraction-selection-attrition model and, **1:**41
banding procedure and, **1:**47
business opportunity approach to, **1:**159
consequences of, **1:**157–158
creativity at work and, **1:**158
diversity, definition of, **1:**157
diversity paradigms and, **1:**159
diversity practices and, **1:**159–160
equal opportunity/fair treatment approach to, **1:**159, 160
group performance potential and, **1:**158
groupthink and, **1:**158
history/development of, **1:**157
learning approach to, **1:**159
management of, **1:**158–160
multinational companies and, **1:**277
networking and, **2:**516
positive/negative outcomes and, **1:**158
recruitment strategies and, **1:**159, **2:**671
sexual orientation diversity and, **1:**263–265
virtual teams and, **2:**873
See also Affirmative action; Affirmative action programs
    (AAPs); Diversity training; Group decision-making
    quality and performance; Group dynamics and
    processes; Stereotyping; Work-life balance
Diversity training, 1:159, 160–163
awareness building and, **1:**161
definition of, **1:**160–161
diversity self-efficacy and, **1:**162–163
effectiveness of, **1:**162–163
integrated training and, **1:**162
motivation to learn and, **1:**162
objectives of, **1:**161
potential of, **1:**163
skill building and, **1:**161–162
strategies of, **1:**161–162
training group composition and, **1:**162
See also Diversity in the workplace;
    Gay/lesbian/bisexual (GLB) issues at work
Division of Applied Psychology, **2:**613
Division of Applied Research and Technology, **2:**501
Division of Respiratory Disease Studies, **2:**502
Division of Safety Research, **2:**502
Division of Surveillance, Hazard Evaluations and
    Field Studies, **2:**501
Dixon, W. J., **1:**305
DMAIC (define/measure/analyze/improve/control)
    improvement model, **2:**815
Doctoral level education/training:
attitude theory/measurement/change and, **2:**931
career development and, **2:**931
competencies, identification of, **2:**927
competency development and, **2:**926–927
consulting/business skills and, **2:**929
consumer behavior and, **2:**931–932
criterion theory/development and, **2:**932

curriculum options/means of training and,
    2:936–937, 937–938 (tables)
equifinality concept and, **2:**927
ethical/legal/professional contexts and, **2:**929
fields of psychology and, **2:**929–930
formal coursework and, **2:**937
guidelines, purpose of, **2:**925–926
health/stress in organizations and, **2:**932
history/systems of psychology and, **2:**930
human performance/human factors and, **2:**932
independent readings/study and, **2:**937
individual assessment and, **2:**932–933
individual differences and, **2:**933
instructional programs, theory/program
    design/evaluation and, **2:**936
job evaluation/compensation and, **2:**933
job/task analysis and classification, **2:**933–934
judgment/decision making and, **2:**934
leadership/management and, **2:**934
modeling/observation and, **2:**937
on-the-job training and, **2:**937
organization development and, **2:**934–935
organization theory and, **2:**935
performance appraisal/feedback and, **2:**935
personnel recruitment/selection/placement and, **2:**935
perspective of the guidelines, **2:**926–929
recommended areas of competence and,
    2:928–936, 928 (table)
recommended domains and, **2:**928
related competencies and, **2:**927–928
research methods and, **2:**930–931
scientist-practitioner model and, **2:**926
small group theory/team processes and, **2:**935–936
statistical methods/data analysis and, **2:**931
supervised experience/field research and, **2:**937
title/positions and, **2:**946
university programs for, **2:**940–942
work motivation and, **2:**936
See also Industrial/organizational psychology careers;
    Master's level education/training
Dominant communication style, **1:**366–367
Dominating style of conflict management, **1:**98, 99
Donaldson, T., **1:**115, 116
Dooley, D., **2:**845
Dorman, P. W., **1:**275
Dornan, J. M., **1:**85
Double-loop learning, **1:**449
Downs, S., **1:**311
Downsizing, 1:163–165, 418, **2:**777, 896
contributions-based model and, **1:**163–164
employee morale and, **2:**489
employment downsizing and, **1:**163
extent of, **1:**64
implementation guidelines for, **1:**165–166
organizational justice and, **2:**572
organizational rightsizing and, **1:**163–164
psychological/financial toll of, **1:**165
rationale for, **1:**165
research on, **1:**164

resizing and, **1:**164
survivors of, **1:**165, **2:**782–784
See also Work motivation
Dramatic communication style, **1:**367
Drori, G., **1:**277
Drucker, P., **2:**541
Drug abuse. *See* Drug and alcohol testing; Substance abuse
Drug and alcohol testing, 1:166–169, 2:636
arguments against, **1:**168
behavior of applicants/employees and, **1:**166–167
benefits of, **1:**166
cheating on drug tests and, **1:**169
employee assistance programs and, **1:**167
legal issues with, **1:**168–169
Medical Review Officers and, **1:**168, 169
rationale for, **1:**166
recruitment process and, **2:**669
testing methods in, **1:**167
testing protocols and, **1:**167–168
training and, **1:**169
types of testing and, **1:**168
utility of, **1:**167
See also Employee Assistance Program (EAP); Pre-screening
    assessment methods for personnel selection; Workplace
    injuries; Workplace safety
Dual-process models, **1:**39
Dugan, S., **1:**139
Dukerich, J. M., **1:**333
Dunnette, M., **1:**316
Dustbowl empiricism, **2:**831
Dutton, J. E., **2:**581
Dweck, C., **2:**490
Dwyer, D. J., **2:**525
Dynamic dimensionality, **1:**133

e-compensation, **1:**172–173
e-job analysis, **1:**171
e-jobs, **1:**84
e-learning, **1:**172
e-performance management, **1:**172
e-recruitment, **1:**171, **2:**668
e-selection, **1:**172
Economic exchange relationships, **2:**734–735
Economic self-interest, **2:**573, 769
Edison T. A., **2:**705
Education and Information Division, **2:**502
Education programs. *See* Doctoral level education/training;
    Master's level education/training; University programs in
    industrial/organizational psychology
Education and Research Centers (ERCs), **2:**502
Educational achievement tests, **2:**755
Educational mismatch, **2:**843
Educational Testing Service, **1:**373
Edwards, J. R., **2:**617, 619, 772
Effect parameters, **2:**775
Effect sizes (ES), **1:**93–94
Effort-reward-imbalance model, **2:**772
Ego defense motive, **1:**251
Egocentric advice discounting, **1:**427–428

Ehrhart, M., **2:**546
Ehrlich, S. B., **1:**333
Eigenvalues, **1:**244
Eisenberg, E. M., **2:**551
Ekeberg, S., **2:**916
Ekman, P., **1:**186
Elaboration likelihood model, **1:**39
Electronic human resources management
    (eHR), 1:171–172
    e-compensation and, **1:**172–173
    e-job analysis and, **1:**171
    e-learning and, **1:**172
    e-performance management and, **1:**172
    e-recruitment and, **1:**171
    e-selection and, **1:**172
    functional/dysfunctional consequences of, **1:**173
    impact of technology and, **1:**171–173
    See also Human resource management (HRM);
        Virtual organizations
Electronic mass media, **2:**730
Electronic performance monitoring, 1:173–177, 2:599
    automatic text processing and, **1:**175
    contemporary organizational applications of, **1:**174–175, 177
    electronic sweatshop and, **1:**176
    implications of, **1:**176
    Internet use monitoring techniques and, **1:**175
    networking technology and, **1:**175, 176
    older monitoring technology and, **1:**173–174
    organization's rights vs. workers' rights and, **1:**176
    privacy law and, **1:**176
    protection function of, **1:**175–176
    techniques of, **1:**173–176
    worker health/stress and, **1:**176
    See also Performance appraisal; Virtual organizations
Electronic sweatshop, **1:**176
Elkind, H., **2:**526
Ellsworth, P. C., **1:**240
Emery Air Freight, **2:**672
Emery, F., **2:**749
Emic instrument, **1:**141
Emotion, 1:185–187
    affective circumplex model and, **1:**186
    boredom, **1:**60
    definition of, **1:**185–186
    dimensional view of, **1:**186–187
    discrete primary emotions and, **1:**186
    emotional expressivity and, **1:**187
    emotion regulation and, **1:**187
    emotion-response tendencies and, **1:**187
    feelings/affect and, **1:**186
    individual differences, experience/expression
        of emotions and, **1:**187
    industrial/organization psychology and, **1:**187
    See also Affective events theory; Affective traits;
        Applicant/test-taker reactions; Dirty work;
        Emotional labor; Emotion regulation; Mood
Emotion regulation:
    action theory and, **1:**6
    core self-evaluations and, **1:**14

high-Mach leaders and, **2:**467
    See also Affective events theory (AET); Affective traits
Emotion-centered stress model, **1:**124–125
Emotional burnout, 1:177–180, 303
    causes/consequences of, **1:**179
    cynicism and, **1:**178
    depersonalization phenomenon and, **1:**178
    emotional exhaustion and, **1:**177–178
    facets of, **1:**177–179
    individual difference and, **1:**179
    job-related consequences of, **1:**179
    job satisfaction and, **1:**409
    measurement of, **1:**177, 178, 179–180
    reduced personal accomplishment feeling and, **1:**178
    reduction of, **1:**180
    research on, **1:**178–179
    stress/occupational burnout and, **2:**705–706, 766, 767
    See also Morale; Stress, consequences; Type A
        and Type B personalities
Emotional Competency Inventory (ECI), **1:**181
Emotional dissonance, **1:**184, 185
Emotional intelligence (EI), 1:180–182
    competency-based approaches to, **1:**181
    definitions of, **1:**180–181
    emotion and, **1:**181
    evaluating models of, **1:**181
    intelligence and, **1:**181
    measurement of, **1:**181
    predictive validity of, **1:**181–182
    training programs for, **1:**182
    trait-based approaches to, **1:**181
    See also Big Five taxonomy of personality; Emotion
Emotional labor, 1:182–185
    antecedent-focused coping and, **1:**183
    antecedents of, **1:**183–184
    customers/organizations, outcomes for, **1:**185
    definition of, **1:**182
    display rules and, **1:**183
    emotional dissonance and, **1:**184, 185
    expressive behaviors and, **1:**183
    felt emotions and, **1:**184
    job settings for, **1:**182–183
    organizational feeling rules and, **1:**183
    outcomes of, **1:**184–185
    process of, **1:**183
    response-focused coping and, **1:**183
    situational demands and, **1:**183–184
    stress outcomes and, **1:**184–185
    surface acting vs. deep acting and, **1:**183
    See also Customer satisfaction with services; Emotion
Emotional quotient. *See* Emotional intelligence (EI)
Emotional stability, **2:**746
Emotional support, **2:**741, 742
Empirical research, **1:**1
    affective traits-job performance relationship, **1:**14
    affirmative action policy, **1:**16–17, 18
    charismatic leadership theory and, **1:**70
    See also Experimental designs
Employee Assistance Professionals Association (EAPA), **1:**189

Employee Assistance Program (EAP), **1:**167, **188–189**
  blended-model of, **1:**189
  effective program, components of, **1:**189
  employee enhancement programs and, **1:**189
  formal/written policies and, **1:**189
  historical development of, **1:**188–189
  mass production requirements and, **1:**188
  occupational alcoholism programs and, **1:**188
  preventative measures and, **1:**189
  program models for, **1:**189
  purpose of, **1:**188
  staff education/training and, **1:**189
  terrorism response and, **2:**797
  unions, member assistance programs and, **1:**189
  within-organization model of, **1:**189
  workplace safety issues and, **1:**188
  See also Drug and alcohol testing; Stress, consequences;
     Stress, coping and management; Withdrawal
     behaviors, absenteeism
Employee attitude:
  affirmative action policy and, **1:**18
  citizenship behaviors, abusive supervision and, **1:**2
  interpersonal discrimination and, **1:**7–8
  negative-affectivity employee, **1:**3, 124
  See also Affective events theory (AET); Attitudes and beliefs;
     Content coding; Dirty work; Emotion regulation
Employee attitude surveys, **1:**101
Employee behaviors:
  citizenship behaviors, **1:**2
  retaliation behaviors, **1:**2–3
  See also Affective events theory (AET); Employee
     development; Employee training
Employee comparison methods, **2:**602
  feedback-standard comparison process, **2:**606
  forced distribution, **2:**603
  paired comparisons, **2:**602–603
  rank ordering, **2:**603
Employee development:
  competence development, action theory and, **1:**6
  utility of, **2:**857
  See also Employee Assistance Program (EAP)
Employee enhancement programs (EEPs), **1:**189
Employee evaluation:
  core self-evaluations and, **1:**14
  social categorization and, **1:**7–8
  stretch competency model and, **1:**86
Employee grievance systems, 1:190–192
  complaints, exit vs. voice method of reporting and, **1:**190
  grievance filing, predictors of, **1:**191
  grievance system characteristics and, **1:**191
  grievance system outcomes and, **1:**191–192
  individual outcomes and, **1:**191–192
  organizational/economic characteristics and, **1:**191
  organizational outcomes and, **1:**191
  perceived fairness of the system and, **1:**190–191
  rationale for, **1:**190
  research, theoretical foundations of, **1:**190–191
  See also Conflict at work; Conflict management;
     Industrial relations; Unions

Employee involvement (EI) interventions, **2:**814–815
Employee opinion-business performance relationship, **1:**459
Employee Polygraph Protection Act of 1988, **1:**357
Employee selection, 1:192–196
  adverse impact and, **1:**194
  banding and, **1:**196
  batch selection, **1:**196
  bias study and, **1:**195
  cognitive ability testing and, **1:**80
  compensatory model of, **1:**195–196
  content-oriented strategies and, **1:**195
  continuous selection and, **1:**196
  criterion-oriented approaches and, **1:**195
  cutoff scores and, **1:**196
  documentation of research/procedures and, **1:**195
  job analysis process and, **1:**195
  judgment and decision-making process and, **1:**426
  knowledge/skills/abilities/other characteristics and,
     1:193, 194, 195
  legal environment and, **1:**193–194
  multiple hurdles approach to, **1:**195–196
  objectives of, **1:**193
  piece of information approach to, **1:**196
  selection instruments and, **1:**193
  selection procedure results, use/interpretation of, **1:**195–196
  selection procedure, validation of, **1:**194–195
  selection procedures, choice of, **1:**194
  sources of candidates, **1:**192–193
  top-down hiring and, **1:**196
  utility of, **1:**196
  validation study and, **1:**195
  validity generalization strategies and, **1:**195
  See also Executive selection; Placement and classification;
     Prescreening assessment methods for personnel selection;
     Recruitment; Selection, occupational tailoring; Selection
     strategies; *Uniform Guidelines on Employee Selection
     Procedures*
Employee training:
  balanced scorecard system and, **1:**45
  competency models and, **1:**86
  conflict management and, **1:**99
  creativity, encouragement of, **1:**128
  error management, action theory and, **1:**6
  general mental ability and, **1:**79–80
  See also Distance learning; Training; Training
     evaluation; Training methods
Employee well-being:
  accomplishment striving and, **2:**475
  career satisfaction and, **1:**66–67
  conflict and, **1:**95
  deskilling, concerns over, **1:**43
  emotional dissonance and, **1:**184, 185
  emotional labor and, **1:**184
  family-work balance and, **1:**65, 67, 88
  job insecurity and, **1:**417–418
  merger syndrome and, **2:**479
  organizational commitment and, **2:**550
  stress outcomes and, **1:**184–185
  See also Abusive supervision; Dirty work

Employee-oriented behaviors, **1:**50, 104
Employment at will, **1:197–198**
  changing law on, **1:**198
  covenant of good faith/fair dealing and, **1:**197
  employee handbooks/manuals and, **1:**198
  implied contract, breach of, **1:**197–198
  limitations on, **1:**197
  public policy, violation of, **1:**197
  See also Whistleblowers
Employment interview, **1:198–202**
  alternative methods of, **1:**201–202
  applicant/interviewer reactions and, **1:**201
  criterion-related validity and, **1:**200
  equal opportunity criterion and, **1:**201
  face validity and, **1:**201
  incremental validity and, **1:**200–201
  interviewer effects and, **1:**199
  interviewer ratings, construct-related validity of, **1:**201
  knowledge/skills/abilities/other characteristics and, **1:**198, 199
  method of, **1:**201–202
  outcomes of, **1:**200–201
  purposes of, **1:**198
  reliability and, **1:**200
  social/cognitive factors in, **1:**198–199
  structured interviews, elements of, **1:**199–200
  See also Realistic job preview (RJP)
Employment issues:
  absenteeism, **1:**2
  job satisfaction, **1:**2
  retention rates, **1:**2
  temporary work, **2:**593–594
  See also Adverse (disparate) impact; Adverse impact/disparate
    treatment/discrimination at work; Affirmative action;
    Careers; Discrimination; Productivity
Employment life cycle, **1:**230
Empowerment, **1:202–205**
  employee experience of, **1:**203–204
  empowerment of leadership, **1:**449
  high-involvement systems/practices and, **1:**203, 204
  linking perspectives on, **1:**204–205
  perspectives on, **1:**202–205
  psychological empowerment, **1:**203–204
  research on, **1:**204–205
  social-structural empowerment, **1:**203, 204
  worksite empowerment practices and, **1:**205
  See also Leadership development; Organizational
    culture; Quality of work life (QWL); Training
Enactive self-mastery, **2:**706
Engagement, **2:**632
Engineering psychology, **1:206–209**
  cognitive task analysis and, **1:**207
  cognitive work analysis and, **1:**207
  historical foundations of, **1:**206
  human-centered engineering and, **1:**206, 207, 209
  knowledge elicitation methods and, **1:**207
  model-based approaches and, **1:**207
  needs analysis and, **1:**207
  participatory ergonomics and, **1:**208
  process design and, **1:**207–208

  sociotechnical systems approach and, **1:**208
  system design and, **1:**208
  systems approach and, **1:**206–207
  task analysis and, **1:**208
  traditional system design and, **1:**208
  user-centered design and, **1:**208
  user interaction/usability and, **1:**208–209
  workflow analysis and, **1:**208
  See also Person-environment (PE) fit
Enhancement motive, **1:**251
Enlightened ethical egoism, **1:**155
Enron, **1:**355
Enterprise resource planning (ERP) systems, **1:**42
Entrepreneurship, **1:209–210**, **2:**703
  ecological approaches to, **1:**210
  entrepreneurial orientation and, **1:**209
  human capital and, **1:**209
  interpersonal variables in, **1:**209
  proximal variables in, **1:**209–210
  psychological model of, **1:**209
  research on, **1:**210
  social dimension of, **1:**210
  training programs and, **1:**210
Environmental factors. *See* Boredom at work; Contextual
    performance/prosocial behavior/organizational citizenship
    behavior; Person-environment (PE) fit
Environmental scan, **2:**764
Equal Employment Opportunity and Affirmative Action
    (EEO/AA), **1:**xxxv
Equal Employment Opportunity Commission (EEOC),
    1:7, 8, 9, 10, 15, 210, 211
  assessment center methodology and, **1:**32
  disabled workers and, **1:**23
  employee selection and, **1:**194
  guidelines publication, **2:**845–846
  sexual discrimination and, **2:**715
  sexual harassment and, **2:**718
  See also Affirmative action
*Equal Employment Opportunity Commission v.
    Arabian American Oil Co.*, **1:**72
Equal Pay Act (EPA) **of 1963**, **1:**81, 82, 84, **210–212**
  antidiscrimination laws and, **1:**210–211
  auditing for fairness and, **1:**211–212
  comparable worth concept and, **1:**211–212
  equal work, definition of, **1:**211
  job evaluation systems and, **1:**211
  provisions of, **1:**210
Equality allocation rule, **2:**571
Equality theory, **1:**84
Equifinality concept, **2:**750, 927
Equity allocation rule, **2:**571
Equity theory, **1:**84, **212–215**, **2:**783
  altering one's own inputs and, **1:**213
  altering one's own outcomes and, **1:**213
  basis of comparison, change in, **1:**214
  cognitive distortion, one's own outcomes/inputs
    and, **1:**213–214
  components of, **1:**212
  current status of, **1:**215

inequity reduction, modes of, **1:**213–214
leaving the field and, **1:**214
other's outcome/inputs, alteration/distortion of, **1:**214
research and, **1:**214
states of equity/inequity and, **1:**212–213
underpayment/overpayment inequity and, **1:**213
See also Organizational justice; Work motivation
Equivalence in measurement, **1:**91
Equivalence in ratings, **1:**403
Ergonomics. *See* Engineering psychology; Physical
    performance assessment
Erikson, E., **1:**319
Error management:
    action theory and, **1:**6
    See also Rating errors and perceptual biases;
        Reliability; Type I/type II errors
Error variance, **2:**677
Espoused theory, **2:**803
Esprit de corps, **1:**300
Esteem needs, **2:**510
Ethical climate, **2:**546, 553
Ethical dilemmas, **1:**216–217
Ethical indifference, **1:**115
*Ethical Principles in the Conduct of Research with
    Human Participants,* **2:**929
*Ethical Principles and Guidelines for the Protection
    of Human Subjects of Research,* **1:**220
*Ethical Principles of Psychologists and Code of
    Conduct,* **1:**219, 220, 359, **2:**919, 929
Ethical well-being, **2:**753
Ethics. *See* Corporate ethics; Ethics in industrial/organizational
    practice; Ethics in industrial/organizational research;
    Socialization; Theft at work
Ethics in industrial/organizational practice, 1:215–218
    attributes of the dilemma and, **1:**217–218
    beneficence and, **1:**216
    contextual/organizational influences and, **1:**218
    cultural influences on, **1:**217
    deontological standards and, **1:**215
    ethical dilemmas and, **1:**216–217
    ethical reasoning and, **1:**215
    ethical/unethical behavior, determinants of, **1:**217–218
    fairness/justice and, **1:**216
    individual difference variables and, **1:**217
    moral action, domain of, **1:**216–218
    moral virtue/character and, **1:**216
    nonmaleficence and, **1:**216
    problems, preventions of, **1:**218
    professional ethics and, **1:**215
    respect ethic and, **1:**216
    theft at work and, **2:**802
    utilitarian perspective and, **1:**215
    See also Corporate ethics; Corporate social responsibility;
        Ethics in industrial/organizational research;
        Whistleblowers
Ethics in industrial/organizational research, 1:219–222
    basic components of, **1:**221–222
    beneficiaries of, **1:**219
    Common Rule and, **1:**220, 221

complaints about, **1:**220–221
current regulations and, **1:**221
deception and, **1:**222
deontological principles and, **1:**219
institutional review boards and, **1:**220, 221
nature of, **1:**219
privacy/confidentiality/informed consent and, **1:**221–222
protection of human subjects and, **1:**220
regulations, history of, **1:**219–221
utilitarian analyses and, **1:**219
waiver of rights and, **1:**221–222
See also Ethics in industrial/organizational practice
Ethnographic research, **2:**649
Etic constructs, **1:**140, 141
Eugenics movement, **1:**30
European Community, **1:**276
European Network of Organizational and Work
    Psychology (ENOP), **1:**311
European Work and Organizational Psychology
    (EAWOP), **1:**311
Eustress, 1:222–223, 462
    See also Stress, consequences; Stress, coping and
        management; Stress, models and theories
Evaluation. *See* Assessment center; Employee evaluation;
    Evaluation potential; Measurement theory
Evaluation potential, **2:**737
Eveland, J. D., **2:**557
Event-contingent studies, **1:**464–465
Exchange theory. *See* Leader-member exchange
    (LMX) theory; Social exchange theory
Executive coaching, 1:223–226, 447
    areas of psychology in, **1:**224
    behavioral approach to, **1:**224
    certifications for, **1:**226
    coach competencies and, **1:**225
    coaching focus, areas of, **1:**224
    cognitive-behavioral approach to, **1:**224–225
    common characteristics of, **1:**224
    definition of, **1:**223
    differing viewpoints in, **1:**224
    duration of, **1:**226
    history of, **1:**223
    intervention strategies, theoretical orientations and, **1:**224–225
    methods/tools in, **1:**226
    process in, **1:**225–226
    psychodynamic approach to, **1:**225
    rational-emotive behavioral approach to, **1:**225
    referral sources and, **1:**225
    therapy and, **1:**225
    See also Emotional intelligence; Global leadership and
        Organizational Behavior Effectiveness (GLOBE) project;
        Individual assessment; Leadership development;
        Organizational culture; Personality; Positive psychology
        applied to work; Social cognitive theory
Executive Order 11246, **1:**16, **2:**846
Executive pay, **1:**84
Executive selection, 1:227–229
    assessment centers and, **1:**228
    decision makers in, **1:**229

executive assessment strategies and, **1:**228–229
executive competencies and, **1:**227
executive recruitment and, **1:**227–228
external recruitment sources and, **1:**228
individual difference measures and, **1:**228–229
internal executive recruitment and, **1:**228
past performance effectiveness measures, **1:**228
simulated leadership scenarios and, **1:**229
top management teams and, **1:**229
See also Attraction-selection-attrition (ASA) model;
    Employee selection; Prescreening assessment methods
    for personnel selection; Selection, occupational tailoring;
    Selection strategies; *Uniform Guidelines on Employee
    Selection Procedures*
Existence/relatedness/growth model, **2:**510
Exit survey (exit interview), 1:, 230–232
    administration method and, **1:**230–231, 231 (table)
    employee attitude/feedback, tracking of, **1:**230
    exit interviews, **1:**231
    Internet-based surveys, **1:**230–231
    populations voluntarily leaving and, **1:**230
    reporting results, **1:**232
    response rates and, **1:**231–232
    survey content and, **1:**230, 231 (table)
    See also Withdrawal behaviors, turnover
Expanded Attributional Style Questionnaire (EASQ), **2:**535
Expatriates, 1:232–235
    anticipatory factors and, **1:**234
    benefits/compensation for, **1:**233
    characteristics of, **1:**232–233
    compensation for, **1:**233
    distal predictors of success, **1:**234
    economic globalization and, **1:**234–235
    general adjustment of, **1:**234
    global employee surveys, **1:**51
    individual factors and, **1:**234
    interaction adjustment of, **1:**234
    job factors and, **1:**234
    job performance of, **1:**233
    non-work factors and, **1:**234
    organizational factors and, **1:**234
    predictors of success, **1:**234
    premature return of, **1:**233–234
    proximal predictors of success, **1:**234
    success, criteria of, **1:**233
    work adjustment of, **1:**234
    See also Globalization; Job performance models;
        Theory of work adjustment
Expectancy methods of selection, **2:**697
Expectancy theory, **1:**14, 27, 387
    absence decisions and, **2:**880
    decision making models and, **2:**670
    See also Expectancy theory of work motivation;
        Path-goal theory
Expectancy theory of work motivation, 1:111–112, **235–238**
    criticisms/variations/assessed value of, **1:**237–238
    elements of, **1:**235
    expectancy and, **1:**237
    instrumentality and, **1:**236, 237

multiplicities of outcomes and, **1:**237
preliminary working example of, **1:**235–236
successes/failures of the theory, **1:**237
valence/expected value of outcomes and, **1:**236–237
See also Intrinsic and extrinsic work motivation; Motivational
    traits; Need theories of work motivation; Reinforcement
    theory of work motivation; Self-concept theory of work
    motivation; Work motivation
Expectations, **2:**534, 670
Expected utility theories, **1:**424
Expected value theories, **2:**893
Experience sampling method (ESM), **1:**463, 464–465
    See also Longitudinal research/experience sampling technique
Experimental designs, 1:238–241, 2:654
    construct validity and, **1:**238–239
    extraneous/confounding variables, control over, **1:**240
    factorial experiments and, **1:**239
    internal validity and, **1:**239
    manipulation checks and, **1:**240
    manipulation of variables and, **1:**239
    measurement of dependent variables and, **1:**240
    random assignment of units to conditions and, **1:**240
    randomized experiments, attributes of, **1:**239–240
    research settings vs. experimental design types
        and, **1:**240–241
    statistical conclusion validity and, **1:**239
    statistical power considerations and, **1:**239
    training evaluation and, **2:**823
    validity of research-based inferences, **1:**238–239
    See also Nonexperimental designs;
        Quasi-experimental designs
Expert power, **1:**443
Experts, **1:**57, 85, 130, 400, 428, **2:**470
Explicit attitudes, **1:**38
Exploratory factor analysis (EFA), **1:**245, **2:**653
    See also Factor analysis
Extended Life Orientation Test (ELOT), **2:**535
Extroversion scale, **1:**34
Extroversion trait, **1:**52, 55, 187, **2:**609, 746
Exxon Oil Company, **2:**777
Eysenck, H. J., **1:**54, **2:**609

Face validity, **1:**201
Faces Scale, **1:**412
Facet-Specific Job Satisfaction (F-SJS) measure, **1:**412–413
Factor analysis, 1:243–246
    basic factor model and, **1:**243–245, 244 (tables)
    biographical data and, **1:**57
    confirmatory factor analysis, **1:**245–246, **2:**498, 500, 653
    exploratory factor analysis, **1:**245, **2:**653
    personality assessment and, **2:**612
    purposes of, **1:**243
    See also Cognitive abilities; Construct; Measures of
        association/correlation coefficient; Personality;
        Reliability; Validation strategies; Validity
Factorial experiments, **1:**239
Fair employment law, **1:**72, 84
Fair Labor Standards Act (FLSA) of 1938, **1:**84, 210, 211, **2:**852
Fairness in decision-making, **1:**425–426

Faking. *See* Distortion practices
Family and Medical Leave Act (FMLA) **of 1993**,
    1:246–248, 339
    Americans with Disabilities Act and, **1:**248
    coverage offered, **1:**246
    enforcement of, **1:**247–248
    leave eligibility and, **1:**246–247
    serious health condition, definition of, **1:**247
    timing requested leave and, **1:**247
    See also Americans with Disabilities Act (ADA) of 1990
Family-work balance, **1:**65, 67, 88, 160, 408
    family-supportive policies and, **2:**769, 890–891
    glass ceiling phenomenon and, **1:**272
    organizational commitment and, **2:**551
    shiftwork and, **2:**722
    telecommuting and, **2:**794
    work-family interface models, **2:**889
    work-family role conflict and, **2:**683, 765, 889–891
    See also Work-life balance
Farmer, E., **1:**309
Fayol, H., **2:**537, 588
Feather, N., **1:**321
Federal Policy for the Protection of Human Subjects, **1:**219
Feedback, **1:248–250**
    computer-based assessment and, **1:**90
    constructs, missing elements of, **1:**141
    delivery of, **1:**248–249
    distance learning and, **1:**156
    feedback intervention theory and, **1:**248–249
    feedback-seeking behavior, **1:**108–109
    interpersonal communication and, **1:**363
    negative feedback loops, **1:**107
    personality feedback, **1:**34
    positive feedback, **1:**370–371
    reactions to, **1:**249
    receptivity to, **1:**249
    recipient expectations and, **1:**249
    reward systems and, **1:**339, 370
    self-regulation and, **2:**713
    See also Feedback seeking; Job characteristics theory;
        Performance appraisal; Performance feedback;
        360-degree feedback
Feedback intervention theory (FIT), **1:**248–249, **2:**605–606
Feedback seeking, **1:**108–109, **250–252**
    contextual issues in, **1:**251–252
    ego defense/enhancement motives and, **1:**251
    future research on, **1:**252
    impression management motive and, **1:**251
    inquiry strategy and, **1:**250
    instrumental motive and, **1:**250
    monitoring strategy and, **1:**250
    strategies of, **1:**250
    See also Feedback; Performance feedback;
        360-degree feedback
Feedback-seeking behaviors (FSBs), **1:**108–109, **2:**604–605
Feedback-standard comparison process, **2:**606
Feed-forward process, **1:**109, 280
Felfe, J., **1:**334
Festinger, L., **1:**284

Fiedler, F. E., **1:**450, 451, 452
Field research methods, **1:**306
File drawer problem, **2:**481
Financial performance:
    balanced scorecard system and, **1:**45–46
    organizations, financial aspects of, **1:**45
Finnegan, E. B., **2:**635, 729
First-impression error, **2:**661
Firzgerald, L. F., **2:**717, 718
Fishbein, M., **1:**39
Fisher, R., **1:**93
Fiske, D. W., **1:**53, **2:**497, 498, 499, 500
Fit:
    attrition process and, **1:**41
    complementary fit, **2:**615
    demands-abilities fit, **2:**615
    fit-derived performance expectations, **2:**716
    fit indexes, **2:**775
    fit statistics, **2:**775
    long-term viability in organizations and, **1:**41
    needs-supplies fit, **2:**615, 618–619
    recruitment, selection procedures and, **1:**40
    sampling error/model misspecification and, **2:**775
    supplementary fit, **2:**615
    See also Engineering psychology; Linkage research and
        analysis; Person-environment (PE) fit; Person-job
        (PJ) fit; Person-organization (PO) fit
Five-factor model of personality, **1:**13, 34, 54, 346–347, **2:**746
Five-style model of conflict management, **1:**98–99
Fixed bands, **1:**47
Fixed parameters, **2:**774
Fixed pie perceptions, **2:**513
Flanagan, J. C., **1:**135, 136, 314, **2:**634
Flattened organizational structures, **2:**533, 586, 871
Flexible optimism, **2:**536
Flexible organizational structures, **1:**449, **2:**750
Flexible work schedules, **1:**87, 160, **252–255**
    absenteeism and, **1:**254
    access to, **1:**253
    characteristics of, **1:**252–253
    job autonomy and, **1:**253
    job characteristics theory and, **1:**253
    lateness and, **2:**882
    organizational commitment and, **2:**551
    perceived benefits of, **1:**253–254
    positive job attitudes and, **1:**254
    research on, **1:**254
    retirement and, **2:**534
    role conflict and, **1:**254
    temporary work and, **2:**593–594
    work adjustment model and, **1:**253
    worker demand for, **1:**253
    See also Compressed workweek; Job design; Job rotation;
        Job sharing; Shiftwork; Telecommuting
Flow, **1:**208, **2:**631–632
Fluid intelligence/reasoning, **1:**77
Focus groups, **1:**85, **255–257**
    applications of, **1:**256–257
    consistent conditions, maintenance of, **1:**256

content coding and, 1:256
discussion guides for, 1:255–256
facilitator skill and, 1:256
fluidity/unexpectedness in, 1:256
group composition and, 1:256
process of, 1:255–256
structured/unstructured focus groups, 1:255
See also Organizational surveys; Qualitative research
approach; Survey approach
Folger, R., 1:125
Follett, M. P., 1:327
Follower development, 2:725
Follower motivation, 2:835–836
Follower-leader trait differences, 2:830
Forced choice item formats, 1:337
Forced choice scales, 2:524, 602, 662
Forced distribution, 2:603, 662
Forced distribution performance appraisal systems, 2:662
Ford, J. K., 2:821
Ford Motor Company, 1:42
Foreign investment, 1:276
Foreign-local subsidiary model, 2:593
Forensic graphoanalysis, 1:281
Forethought capability, 2:730
Formalization of organizational structure, 2:586
Formative evaluation, 2:638, 821
Fortuitous events, 2:732–733
Four-fifths rule, 1:10, 2:846
Fournier, G., 1:461
Four-style model of conflict management, 1:98
Fox, M. L., 2:525
Fragmentation perspective, 2:910
Frame-of-reference (FOR) training, 1:257–259, 2:663
behavioral observation training and, 1:257
components of, 1:257–258
effectiveness of, 1:258
performance dimension training and, 1:257
rater accuracy training and, 1:257
rater error training and, 1:257
rater variability training and, 1:257
research on, 1:258–259
See also Performance appraisal; Performance appraisal,
subjective indexes; Performance feedback; Physical
performance assessment
Framing effects, 1:431
Free enterprise model of business, 1:115–117
Free market perspective, 1:81, 82, 115
Free riding. See Social Loafing
French, J. R. P., Jr., 2:616, 619, 623
Frequency distributions, 1:149
Freud, S., 1:317
Friedman, M., 1:115
Friendly communication style, 1:367–368
Frustration aggression model, 1:120, 125
Functional foremen concept, 2:693
Functional interdependence, 1:360–361
Functional organizational communication, 2:553–554
Functional support, 2:741
Functionalism, 1:313

Funnel shaped design, 2:651
Furnham, A., 2:645

g cognitive ability factor, 1:77, 181
predictive value of, 1:77–78
See also Cognitive abilities; General cognitive ability (GCA)
g factor, 1:77–78
Gagne, M., 2:840
Gainsharing (GS) and profit sharing (PS), 1:83, 261–263
climate of trust and, 1:263
common fate concept and, 1:261, 262–263
effectiveness of, 1:261
effects of, 1:263
enhanced organizational performance, mechanisms for, 1:262
improved efficiency and, 1:261
organizational profits and, 1:261, 263
participative management and, 1:261, 262
pay-for-performance program and, 1:262–263
performance gains, evaluation of, 1:261–262
planning/implementation process and, 1:262
profit sharing criteria and, 1:262
profit sharing effectiveness and, 1:262–263
return on assets and, 1:261, 262
return on investment and, 1:262
team-based rewards, 2:790
See also Compensation; Team-based rewards
Galatea effect, 2:711
Galton, F., 1:313
Ganster, D. C., 2:525
Gantt, H., 2:692
Gardner, J. W., 2:831
Gates, B., 1:40
Gay/lesbian/bisexual (GLB) issues at work, 1:263–266
civil liberties/legal rights and, 1:265–266
concealability factor and, 1:264
controllability factor and, 1:264
disclosure dilemma and, 1:264–265
discriminatory treatment and, 1:264, 265
fear of contagion and, 1:264
improved treatment strategies, 1:265
negative employee/organizational attitudes
and behaviors, 1:264
sexual orientation diversity, organizational
management of, 1:265
stigma framework and, 1:263–264
workplace challenges and, 1:264–265
See also Diversity training; Diversity in the workplace
Geis, F., 2:467
Gelfand, M. G., 1:139
Gemelli, A., 1:309
Gender-based issues:
affirmative action programs and, 1:17, 18
banding procedure and, 1:48
career pursuit and, 1:65
comparable worth, market wages and, 1:81, 2:715
cyberloafing and, 1:146
job evaluation, gender bias and, 1:82
job insecurity and, 1:418
leadership traits and, 2:831

letters of recommendation and, 1:456
mentoring processes and, 2:476–477
physical performance ability and, 2:625
retirement decisions and, 2:679
stereotyping and, 2:715–716
top management positions and, 1:271–272
work-life balance and, 2:891
See also Gay/lesbian/bisexual (GLB) issues at work;
    Glass ceiling phenomenon; Sexual discrimination;
    Sexual harassment at work
General adaptation syndrome (GAS), 2:767, 770–771
General Aptitude Test Battery (GATB), 1:67, 314,
    422, 2:659, 756
General cognitive ability (GCA), 1:270, 283, 345, 2:633, 817
General Electric Company, 1:315, 2:777
General mental ability (GMA), 1:78, 79–80, 181,
    341, 2:701, 702
General verbal ability, 1:77
Generalizability theory (G-theory), **1:266–268**, 2:677
    absolute error and, 1:267
    analysis of variance and, 1:267–268
    criterion-referenced comparisons and, 1:267
    decision study and, 1:268
    fundamentals of, 1:266–268
    generalizability study and, 1:268
    inconsistency errors and, 1:267
    interaction effects and, 1:267
    limitations in measurement designs and, 1:267–268
    main effects of facets of measurement and, 1:267
    measurement designs in, 1:266, 267–268
    partitioning variance in, 1:266–267
    process of, 1:268
    relative error and, 1:267
    scores, true/error components in, 1:266
    true variance/error variance in, 1:267
    universe score variance and, 1:267
    variance components and, 1:267
    See also Classical test theory (CTT); Construct;
        Experimental designs; Reliability; Validity
Generalizations:
    case study method and, 1:69
    representative research design and, 1:452
    self-observation generalizations, 1:64
    validity generalization strategies, 1:195
Generalized self-efficacy, 2:710
Genetics and industrial/organizational psychology, **1:268–271**
    attitude factor and, 1:270
    attitude formation and, 1:38
    behavior genetics methodology and, 1:269
    behavior genetics research/organizational behavior, 1:269–270
    general cognitive ability and, 1:270
    heritability values and, 1:269, 270
    leadership factor and, 1:270
    mediation/interaction models and, 1:270–271
    nature vs. nurture debate and, 1:270
    performance behaviors and, 1:270
    personality factors and, 1:270, 2:609
    research on, 1:271
    work values and, 1:270

Gerhart, B., 1:261
Gersick, C. J., 1:294
Gerstner, C., 1:334
Ghiselli, E. E., 1:315
Gilbreth, F., 1:306, 313, 2:537, 692
Gilbreth, L., 1:313, 2:537, 692
Gilliland, S., 1:25, 26
Gioia, D. A., 2:581
Giverson, T., 2:560
Glass Ceiling Commission, 1:74
Glass ceiling phenomenon, **1:271–273**, 2:715
    ethnic minorities and, 1:272
    organizational factors in, 1:272
    recent gains made, 1:272–273
    research on, 1:271
    structural barriers and, 1:272
    theoretical perspectives on, 1:272–273
    women in top management, 1:271–272
    work-family differences and, 1:272
    See also Adverse impact/disparate treatment/discrimination at
        work; Mentoring; Networking; Sexual discrimination
Glass, G. V., 2:481
Gleser, G. C., 2:856–857
Glick, J., 1:142
Global construct, 2:728
Global employee surveys, 1:51
**Global Leadership and Organizational Behavior
    Effectiveness** (GLOBE) **project**, **1:273–275**, 334, 2:561
    conceptual model of, 1:273–274, 273 (figure)
    culturally endorsed implicit leadership theory and, 1:274
    data analysis/phase three, 1:275
    data sources in, 1:273
    integrated theoretical model of, 1:274, 275
    leadership dimensions and, 1:274, 275
    literature on, 1:275
    organizational practices and, 1:275
    scale development/phase one, 1:274
    societal/organizational cultural dimensions and, 1:274
    testing the integrated model/phase two, 1:274–275
    See also Globalization
Global teams, 2:794
Globalization, **1:43, 65, 276–278**
    compensation structures and, 1:84, 233
    competition and, 1:276–277
    cultural convergence and, 1:277
    cultural diversity, acceptance of, 1:277
    expatriate research and, 1:234–235
    flexibility/openness to change and, 1:277
    global corporate culture and, 1:276–277
    global identity/local-national identity and, 1:277
    global organizations and, 1:276
    high interdependence and, 1:277
    international trade/foreign investment and, 1:276
    job design and, 1:393, 394
    local/global managerial roles and, 1:277
    myths about, 1:276
    negative effects of, 1:277
    organizational flexibility and, 2:589
    positive effects of, 1:277–278

trust building and, **1:**277

unionization, decline in, **2:**852

virtual teams and, **2:**872

See also Global Leadership and Organizational Behavior
Effectiveness (GLOBE) project; Multinational
companies (MNCs)

GLOBE project. *See* Global Leadership and Organizational
Behavior Effectiveness (GLOBE) project

Goal-based rewards, **2:**790, 791

motivation and, **1:**108, **2:**490–491

See also Goal-setting theory; Goal sharing

Goal-setting theory, 1:278–280, 2:893–894

ability/motivation, worker performance and, **1:**278

anticipatory/feed-forward effect and, **1:**280

assigned goals, **1:**280

behavioral goals and, **1:**280

goal commitment and, **1:**280

goal intensity and, **1:**279

goals, attributes of, **1:**278–279

high goals vs. easy goals and, **1:**279

individual self-efficacy and, **1:**279

needs-action relationship and, **1:**278

participatively set goals, **1:**280

performance, motivational mechanisms and, **1:**279

performance vs. learning goals, instruction
framing and, **1:**279–280

self-set goals, **1:**280

specific/difficult goals, level of performance and, **1:**279

values/beliefs and, **1:**278

See also Incentives; Path-goal theory

Goal-sharing, **1:**83

Goffman, I., **1:**152, 153

Goldberg, L. R., **1:**52, 53, 54, 346

Golden Rule, **2:**753

Goldstein, A. P., **2:**517, 518

Goleman, D., **1:**180

Golem effect, **2:**711

Gomersall, E. R., **2:**518

Gompers, S., **2:**851

Gonzalez, M. H., **1:**240

Goodall, H. L., Jr., **2:**551

Gordon, M. E., **2:**848

Gottfredson, L. S., **1:**345, **2:**634

Government. *See* Legal environment; Public sector organizations

Graduate Management Aptitude Test (GMAT), **2:**755

Graduate programs, **2:**940–942

See also Doctoral level education/training; Master's
level education/training

Graduate Record Examination (GRE), **1:**373, **2:**755, 757, 760

Granovetter, M. S., **2:**516

Grapevine communication, **2:**556–557

Graphical representation, **1:**149, 150

Graphical representations of correlations, **2:**472–473, 472 (figure)

Graphical user interface, **1:**323, 324 (figure)

Graphic metaphors, **1:**324, 324 (figure)

Graphic rating scales, **2:**601

Graphology, 1:281–282

appeal of, **1:**282

forensic graphoanalysis and, **1:**281

methodology of, **1:**281–282

structural characteristics of handwriting and, **1:**281

validity of analyses and, **1:**282

writing fluency/clarity of expression and, **1:**281–282

See also Counterproductive work behaviors (CWBs);
Integrity testing; Selection strategies

Graves, L. M., **1:**334

Gravitational hypothesis, 1:282–284

general cognitive ability and, **1:**283

mobility process and, **1:**283

person-job match and, **1:**283–284

Peter Principle and, **1:**283

underemployment and, **1:**283

worker movement across jobs and, **1:**282–283

See also Cognitive ability tests; Person-environment
(PE) fit; Person-job (PJ) fit; Person-organization
(PO) fit; Recruitment; Theory of work adjustment

Gray, J., **2:**490

Great Depression, **1:**66, 150, 305, 327, **2:**776, 852

Great man approach, **2:**830

Grievance systems. *See* Employee grievance
systems; Unions

Griggs v. Duke Power Co., **1:**10, 316

Grojean, M., **2:**546

Gross, J. J., **1:**187

Grounded theory, **2:**651

Group cohesiveness, 1:284–286

applied psychology fields and, **1:**284

dimensions of, **1:**284–285

group affect and, **2:**487

group norms, role of, **1:**286

group performance and, **1:**285–286

measurement of, **1:**285

multidimensional construct of, **1:**285

organizational performance, commitment to, **1:**286

task performance/goal achievement, commitment
to, **1:**284, 285, 286

value of group membership and, **1:**285

See also Group decision-making quality and performance;
Group development; Group dynamics and processes;
Groups; Team mental model

**Group decision-making quality and
performance, 1:286–289**

advantages of, **1:**287

collective solutions and, **1:**287

conflict, role of, **1:**288

decision rule and, **1:**288

effectiveness assessment, **1:**287–288

effectiveness, factors in, **1:**288

group outcomes and, **1:**286–287

groupthink and, **1:**287

hierarchical decision making and, **1:**287

individual biases and, **1:**287

limitations of, **1:**287

minority influence on, **1:**288

organizational context and, **1:**288–289

social decision-making schemes and, **1:**288

types/stages of, **1:**287

See also Group decision-making techniques; Groupthink

Group decision-making techniques, 1:289–292
  brainstorming, 1:289–290
  Delphi technique, 1:291
  effective group decisions and, 1:289
  nominal group technique, 1:290–291
  stepladder technique, 1:291–292
  See also Group decision-making quality and
      performance; Group dynamics and processes;
      Groups; Meetings at work
Group development, 1:293–295
  integrated models of, 1:294
  punctuated equilibrium model of, 1:294
  stage model of, 1:293–294
  systems-oriented approaches to, 1:294–295
  task work/team work capability coordination and, 1:293
  team compilation phenomenon and, 1:295
  top-down/bottom-up phenomenon and, 1:294
  See also Groups; Team-based rewards; Team building
Group dynamics and processes, 1:295–297
  group affect and, 2:487
  group conflict and, 1:297
  group efficacy, perceptions of, 1:297
  group/group tasks, reactions to, 1:297
  input-process-output framework and, 1:296
  issues in, 1:296–297
  knowledge-intensive work and, 1:296–297
  management of group process and, 1:297
  See also Group cohesiveness; Group decision-making quality
      and performance; Group decision-making techniques;
      Group development; Groups
Group interviews, 1:379
Group mental model. *See* Team mental model
Groups, 1:298–299
  definition of, 1:298–299
  group affect and, 2:487
  organizational utilization of, 1:298
  small-group socialization perspective, 2:746
  teams and, 1:298
  See also Group cohesiveness; Group decision-making quality
      and performance; Group decision-making techniques;
      Group development; Group dynamics and processes;
      Groupthink; Input-process-output (IPO) model of team
      effectiveness; Intergroup relations; Justice in teams;
      Social norms and conformity; Team-based rewards; Team
      building; Team mental model
Group tasks, 2:736
Groupthink, 1:158, 287, 299–301
  antecedents of, 1:299
  avoidance strategies and, 1:300
  esprit de corps and, 1:300
  group decision-making failure and, 1:299
  merger syndrome and, 2:479
  null/contradictory experimental results and, 1:301
  research on, 1:300–301
  self-esteem and, 2:710
  symptoms of, 1:299–300
  See also Group cohesiveness; Group decision-making quality
      and performance; Group decision-making techniques;
      Social norms and conformity

Group-value model of justice, 2:573, 574
Growth curve models, 2:496
Growth need strength (GNS), 1:385
G-theory. *See* Generalizability theory (G-theory)
Guide for Occupational Exploration, 1:422
*Guidelines for Education and Training at the Doctoral
      Level in I/O Psychology,* 2:913, 925–929
*Guidelines for Education and Training at the Master's Level in
      Industrial/Organizational Psychology,* 2:925–926
Guidelines on Employee Selection Procedures, 2:929
Gupta, V., 1:275
Gutman, A., 1:210, 211
Guttman, L., 1:318

Hackett, G., 1:64, 67
Hackman, J. R., 1:384, 393, 2:840
Hall, E. T., 1:139
Halo errors, 2:661
Hammer, M., 2:815
Hammond, K. R., 1:453
Handbook of Industrial and Organizational Psychology, 1:316
Handbook of Organizational Culture and Climate, 2:561
Handwriting characteristics, 1:281
Hanges, P. J., 1:275
Happy/productive worker hypothesis, 1:103, 2:488
Hardiness, 1:303–304
  absenteeism and, 1:304
  adaptive coping strategies and, 1:304
  burnout and, 1:303
  challenge and, 1:303
  commitment and, 1:303
  control and, 1:303
  hardiness belief systems and, 1:303
  health-related outcomes and, 1:303
  individual differences and, 1:304
  job attitudes/behavior and, 1:303–304
  social networks and, 1:304
  stress, adverse consequences of, 1:304, 2:766
  stress management programs and, 1:303
  unresonlved issues about, 1:304
  See also Personality; Stress, consequences; Stress,
      coping and management; Stress, models and theories
Harrington-O'Shea Career Decision-Making System, 1:67
Hartke, D. D., 1:451
Hartwick, J., 1:94
Hawthorne, S. L., 2:914, 916, 927
Hawthorne Studies/Hawthorne effect,
      1:305–306, 314, 327, 2:488, 537, 555
  genesis/growth of, 1:305
  industrial/organizational psychology and, 1:306
  key findings of, 1:305–306
  myths about, 1:306
  social relationships, importance of, 1:305–306
  systematic field research methods and, 1:306
  See also Human relations movement; Scientific management
Hay Guide Chart-Profile Method, 1:395
Health Effects Laboratory Division, 2:502
Healthy workplace concept, 2:652
Heath, R. L., 1:364

Hedonism, **2:**893
Heider, F., **1:**212
Hellweg, S. A., **1:**363
Hemphill, J. K., **1:**48
Henle, C., **1:**146
Hereditarian perspective, **1:**30
Heritability values, **1:**269, 270
Hersey, P., **1:**457
Herzberg, F., **1:**392, 407, **2:**839, 893
Heslin, P. A., **2:**707
Heuristics. *See* Judgment and decision-making process:
 heuristics, cognitive biases, and contextual influences
Heuristic-systematic model, **1:**39
Hierarchical decision making, **1:**287
Hierarchical linear modeling (HLM), **2:**495–496, 495 (figure)
Hierarchical multiple regression (HMR), **1:**340
Hierarchical structures, **2:**492–493, 586, 588, 589
Hierarchies of goals, **2:**713–714
Hierarchy of needs, **2:**509, 510, 608, 893
Higgins, E. T., **2:**491
Higgs, C., **2:**589
Higher education. *See* Doctoral level education/training;
 Master's level education/training
High interdependence, **1:**277
High-involvement management, **1:**350
High-involvement systems/practices, **1:**203, 204
High-Mach leaders, **2:**467
High-performance organization model, 1:306–308
 benchmark organizations, elements in, **1:**307–308
 business environment, shifts in, **1:**307
 coach/facilitator roles and, **1:**308
 high-performance approach and, **1:**307
 historical development of, **1:**306–307
 human relations/employee satisfaction and, **1:**307
 industrial efficiency and, **1:**307
 information sharing and, **1:**307
 Japanese revolution in manufacturing and, **1:**307
 literature on, **1:**308
 quality of work life and, **1:**307, 308
 team concept and, **1:**307
 titles/roles, changes in, **1:**307–308
 workplace safety and, **2:**904
 See also Quality of work life (QWL)
Hiring. *See* Attraction-selection-attrition (ASA) model;
 Employee selection; Employment interview;
 Recruitment; Selection strategies
Hirschman, A. O., **1:**190
History of industrial/organizational psychology in Europe
 and the United Kingdom, 1:309–312
 early years, development psychotechnics and, **1:**309–310
 industrial democracy experiments and, **1:**311, **2:**749
 mobbing/bullying behaviors, **1:**311–312
 recent contributions of European
  work/organization psychology, **1:**311–312
 work/organization psychology, postwar Europe and, **1:**310–311
 See also History of industrial/organizational psychology
  in North America; History of industrial/organizational
  psychology in other parts of the world;
  Industrial/organizational psychology careers

History of industrial/organizational psychology
 in North America, 1:312–316
 beginning of, early 20th century, **1:**313–314
 capitalist-communist divisions and, **1:**315
 modern era, 1980s to present time, **1:**316
 post World War I, 1920s and 1930s, **1:**314
 post World War II, 1940s and 1950s, **1:**315
 pre-modern,1960s and,1970s, **1:**315–316
 roots of, late 19th century and, **1:**313
 World War I, 1917–1919, **1:**314
 World War II, **1:**314
 See also American Psychological Association; Association
  for Psychological Science; Industrial/organizational
  psychology careers; Occupational Information Network
  (O*NET); Project A; Society for Industrial and
  Organizational Psychology
History of industrial/organizational psychology in
 other parts of the world, 1:317–322
 ancient time, **1:**318–319
 Australia, **1:**320–322
 early 20th century, **1:**317, 319, 320–321
 India, **1:**318–319
 Israel, **1:**317–318
 late 20th century, **1:**321–322
 post World War I, **1:**321
 post World War II, **1:**317–318, 319, 321
 Singapore, **1:**320
 See also History of industrial/organizational psychology
  in Europe and the United Kingdom; History of
  industrial/organizational psychology in North America
HIV-AIDS contagion, **1:**264
Hoffman, P. J., **2:**628
Hofstede, G. H., **1:**138, **2:**591
Holland, J. L., **1:**67, **1:**345, 346, 422, **2:**616, 622
Homeostasis, **1:**107
Homo reciprocus, **2:**733
Homoscedasticity assumption, **2:**472, 473
Honesty testing. *See* Integrity testing
Horn effects, **1:**661
Hosking, D., **1:**452
Hostility. *See* Abusive supervision; Victim-precipitation perspective
Hot desking, **2:**872
Hough, L. M., **1:**336, 337
House, R. J., **1:**273, 275
Hovland, C., **1:**39
Hubris, **2:**707
Hughes, E., **1:**152, 153
Human capital, **1:**209, 230, **2:**666
Human factors. *See* Engineering psychology;
 Human-computer interaction (HCI)
Human performance intervention (HPI) process, **2:**830
Human performance technology (HPT), **2:**830
Human relations movement, 1:305, **327–328,** **2:**537
 genesis and growth of, **1:**327–328
 Hawthorne Studies and, **1:**327
 key concepts/practices of, **1:**328
 models of cooperation and, **1:**327–328
 role of, **1:**328
 theory X/Theory Y and, **1:**328

See also Hawthorne Studies/Hawthorne effect;
    History of industrial/organizational psychology
    in North America; Scientific management
Human resource management (HRM), **1:**B329–330
    certification to practice and, **1:**330
    compensation/benefits and, **1:**330
    employee relations and, **1:**330
    equal employment opportunity laws and, **1:**329
    health and safety programs and, **1:**330
    high-performance organization model and, **1:**308
    human resource planning and, **1:**329
    job analysis and, **1:**329
    job involvement and, **1:**398–399
    labor relations and, **1:**330
    orientation programs and, **1:**330
    performance appraisals and, **1:**330
    purposes of, **1:**329
    realistic job preview and, **2:**665
    recruitment and, **1:**329
    selection processes and, **1:**330
    training programs and, **1:**330
    See also Adverse impact/disparate treatment/discrimination
        at work; Compensation; Electronic human resources
        management (eHR); Employee selection; Human
        resources strategy; Job analysis; New employee
        orientation; Performance appraisal; Recruitment;
        Succession planning; Training; Unions;
        Workplace safety
Human resources strategy, **1:**B331–332
    alignment model, **1:**331
    best practices model, **1:**331
    issues in, **1:**331
    job involvement and, **1:**398–399
    mediating factors in, **1:**332
    resource-based model, **1:**331–332
Human-centered engineering (HCE), **1:**206–207, 209
Human-computer interaction (HCI), **1:322–326**
    cathode ray tube and, **1:**323
    challenges in, **1:**326
    command language and, **1:**325
    direct manipulation and, **1:**325, 326
    efficient interactions and, **1:**326
    error reduction and, **1:**326
    everyday life applications, **1:**322
    form filling and, **1:**325–326
    graphical user interface and, **1:**323, 324 (figure)
    graphic metaphors/visual language and,
        324 (figure), **1:**324
    historical perspective, character-based to graphical
        interfaces and, **1:**323–325
    interaction design and, **1:**326
    menu selection and, **1:**325
    object orientation and, **1:**324–325
    questions and answers, **1:**325
    satisfactory use experience, **1:**326
    standard query language and, **1:**325
    user-computer dialog/interaction styles and, **1:**325–326
    user interface and, **1:**322–323
    what you see is what you get feature and, **1:**323–324

windows/icons/mouse/pull-down menus and, **1:**324
    See also Automation/advanced manufacturing
        technology/computer-based integrated technology
Hunter, J. E., **1:**345, **2:**481, 482, 483
Hunt, M. D., **1:**364
Huselid, M. A., **1:**398
Hygienes, **2:**839
Hypermedia systems, **2:**825
Hypernetwork method, **2:**691
Hypothesis testing, **1:**92–93, 351, 758, 759 (figure)
Hypothetical construct. *See* Construct

IBM, **2:**777, 901
Idea evaluation process, **1:**127
Idea generation, **1:**127
Idealized influence (II), **2:**835
Identifiability model, **2:**737
Identification with aggressor syndrome, **2:**784
Identity construction, **2:**580
Idiographic science, **2:**608
Idiosyncracy credits, **2:**740
Ilgen, D. R., **2:**525
Illustrative case study, **1:**68
Image. *See* Impression management; Organizational image
Imitation strategy, **2:**587
Immigrant workers, **1:**65
Impersonal orientation, **2:**492
Implicit Association Test, **1:**39
Implicit attitudes, **1:**38
Implicit followership theories, **1:**334
Implicit leadership theory (ILT), **1:**274, 275, **333–335**
    effects of, **1:**334
    future theoretical development and, **1:**334–335
    generalizability of, **1:**334
    See also Global Leadership and Organizational Behavior
        Effectiveness (GLOBE) project; Leadership
        development; 360-degree feedback
Implicit motivation theory, **1:**274
Implicit organizational theories, **1:**335
Implicit relationship theories, **1:**334
Impression-leaving communication style, **1:**367
Impression management, **1:**106, 251, **335–338**
    criterion-related validity and, **1:**336
    detection/correction of distortion and, **1:**337
    distortion practices and, **1:**336, 337, **2:**614
    first-impression error and, **2:**661
    high-Mach leaders and, **2:**467
    hiring decision and, **1:**336–337, 338
    intentional distortion, effects of, **1:**336–337
    multidimensional forced-choice item formats and, **1:**337
    personality assessments and, **2:**614
    prevention of distortion and, **1:**337
    remedies for intentional distortion and, **1:**337, 338
    self-descriptions, distortion of, **1:**335
    See also Big Five taxonomy of personality;
        Personality; Personality assessment
Improshare Plan, **1:**262
Improvement initiatives, **1:**45, 52, 261, 265
Improvisation, **2:**468

In-basket method, **1:**34–35
Incentive pay systems, **1:**83
Incentives, 1:338–340
 evaluation of, **1:**339–340
 influence over behavior and, **1:**338
 monetary incentives and, **1:**338–339
 non-monetary incentives and, **1:**339
 praise as incentive and, **1:**339
 psychological theories and, **1:**339
 types of, **1:**338–339
Incivility. *See* Workplace incivility
Income. *See* Compensation
Incremental validity, **1:**200–201, **340–341**
 applications of, **1:**340–341
 complications with, **1:**341
 estimation of, **1:**340
 hierarchical multiple regression and, **1:**340
 predicting job performance and, **1:**341
 predictive power of a model and, **1:**340
 utility analyses and, **1:**341
 See also Inferential statistics; Measures of
  association/correlation coefficient; Utility
  analysis; Validation strategies; Validity
India, **1:**318–319
Indian Council of Social Science Research, **1:**319
Indian Institutes of Management, **1:**319
Individual assessment, 1:341–344
 alternate assessment processes and, **1:**341–342
 assessment information, integration of, **1:**343
 assessment information, interpretation of, **1:**342–343
 decision making and, **1:**425
 design/implementation of, **1:**342
 distortion practices and, **1:**343
 ethical issues in, **1:**343
 feedback in, **1:**342
 interviews, uses of, **1:**342
 knowledge/skills/abilities/personal characteristics and, **1:**341
 legal issues in, **1:**343–344
 organizational decision-making and, **1:**344
 origins of, **1:**342
 psychometrics of, **1:**343
 utility of, **1:**343
 See also Assessment center; Assessment center methods;
  Computer assessment; Personality assessment; Physical
  performance assessment; Prescreening assessment
  methods for personnel selection
Individual differences, 1:344–347
 abusive supervision, effects of, **1:**2–3
 accomplishment striving and, **2:**475
 action theory, personality enhancement and, **1:**6
 cognitive abilities and, **1:**345
 creativity at work and, **1:**126–127
 data vs. ideas dimension and, **1:**346
 differential psychology and, **1:**344
 emotional burnout and, **1:**179
 emotions, experience/expression of, **1:**187
 ethical behaviors and, **1:**217
 fit, attraction/attrition processes and, **1:**40, 41
 five-factor model of personality and, **1:**346–347

general intelligence and, **1:**345
intergroup relations and, **1:**360
major dimensions of, **1:**344–347
measurement methods and, **1:**344
organizational socialization and, **2:**583
people vs. things dimension and, **1:**346
personality factors and, **1:**346–347
preference dimensions and, **1:**345–346
relationships among attributes and, **1:**347
RIASEC (realistic/investigative/artistic/social/
  enterprising/conventional) model and, **1:**346
time management and, **2:**813
trainability/adaptability and, **2:**817–818
values exploration and, **1:**346
victim-precipitation perspective and, **1:**3
work events, affective reactions and, **1:**11, 14
See also Affective events theory (AET); Affective traits;
  Applicant/test-taker reactions; Assessment center
  methods; Cognitive abilities; Core self-evaluations;
  Emotion regulation; Factor analysis; Personality
Individual differences hypothesis, **2:**671
Individual dimensionality, **1:**133
Individualized consideration (IC), **2:**835
Industrial democracy, **1:**311, **2:**749
Industrial engineering approach, **1:**392, **2:**693
Industrial/organizational psychology:
 advice giving/advice taking and, **1:**428–429
 Big Five taxonomy of personality and, **1:**54–55
 customer satisfaction, organizational behavior and, **1:**144–145
 dirty work and, **1:**154
 emotions, dimensional view of, **1:**187
 gay/lesbian/bisexual issues and, **1:**263
 Hawthorn Studies/effect and, **1:**306
 hierarchical linear modeling and, **2:**495–496
 industrial relations and, **1:**350
 integrated systems practice guidelines and, **1:**43–44
 intrinsic/extrinsic work motivation and, **1:**370
 judgment and decision-making process and, **1:**425, 426
 multitrait-multimethod matrix and, **2:**497
 occupational health psychology and, **2:**525
 personality and, **2:**608–609, 610–611
 personality assessment and, **2:**612, 613, 614
 scientific management concepts and, **2:**693
 sociotechnical thinking, new technologies and, **1:**43
 succession planning and, **2:**776–779
 unions and, **2:**853
 See also Cross-cultural research methods and theory; Genetics
  and industrial/organizational psychology; History of
  industrial/organizational psychology in Europe and the
  United Kingdom; History of industrial/organizational
  psychology in North America; Industrial/organizational
  psychology careers
Industrial/organizational psychology careers, 912
 Doctoral level education/training guidelines, **2:**925–938
 job titles and, **2:**946
 Master's level education/training guidelines, **2:**913–923
 professional groups/organizations and, **2:**947–950
 scientific journals on industrial/organizational
  psychology research, **2:**943–945

university programs in industrial/organizational
   psychology, **2:**940–942
Industrial relations, 1:348–350
   academic study of, **1:**348–349
   broadened field of, **1:**350
   collective bargaining and, **1:**349
   high-involvement management and, **1:**350
   human resource management, new forms of, **1:**350
   industrial/organizational psychology and, **1:**350
   monopoly face of a union and, **1:**349
   partnership approach and, **1:**349
   public policy, transformation of industrial
      relations and, **1:**349–350
   trade unions, role of, **1:**349–350
   voice face of a union and, **1:**349
   See also Conflict at work; High performance organization
      model; Human resource management (HRM); Job
      security/insecurity; Union commitment; Unions
Industrial Relations Research Association, **1:**350
Industrial Revolution, **1:**66
Inferential statistics, 1:91–92, **351–352**
   confidence intervals and, **1:**351
   hypothesis testing and, **1:**351
   information requirements for, **1:**351–352
   meta-analysis and, **2:**481
   probability and, **1:**351
   sampling and, **1:**351
   See also Confidence intervals/hypothesis testing/effect
      sizes; Descriptive statistics; Meta-analysis;
      Sampling techniques
Informal training methods, **2:**823–824
Information engineering approach, **2:**552
Information integration theory, **2:**630
Information overload, **2:**552
Information processing. *See* Cognitive abilities;
   Information technologies
Information seeking behaviors, **2:**585
Information technologies, **1:**43
   See also Electronic performance monitoring
Information Technology Survey Group, **2:**591
Information transfer model, **2:**552
Information-giving meetings, **2:**474
Informed consent, **1:**221–222, 343, 358–359
Ingelhart, R., **1:**138
In-group leadership, **1:**445
In-group members, **1:**360, 361, 364
Initial screening. *See* Prescreening assessment
   methods for personnel selection
Initiative, **1:**2
Injunctive norms, **2:**739
Innovation, 1:352–353
   antecedents to, **1:**352–353
   change and, **2:**541
   external environment and, **1:**352–353
   individual factors and, **1:**352
   organizational climate and, **1:**352
   organizational structure and, **2:**587, 588
   outcomes and, **1:**353
   Pygmalion effects and, **2:**712

role innovation, **2:**745
   See also Creativity at work; Social cognitive theory
**Input-process-output (IPO) model of team
   effectiveness, 1:**296, **353–355**
   dynamic group performance and, **1:**355
   group research and, **1:**353
   inputs and, **1:**353
   limitations of, **1:**354
   linear progression, fallacy of, **1:**354
   outputs and, **1:**354
   processes and, **1:**353–354
   Steiner's formula and, **1:**354
   validity of, **1:**354
   See also Groups; Justice in teams; Team-based rewards;
      Team building; Team mental model; Virtual teams
Inspirational motivation (IM), **2:**835
Institute for Social Research (ISR), **1:**328, **2:**771
Institutional review boards (IRBs), **1:**220, 221
Institutionalized norms, **1:**3
Instituto Nacional de Psicotecnia, **1:**310
Instrumental coping, **2:**767, 768
Instrumental/illustrative case study, **1:**68
Instrumental learning experiences, **1:**64
Instrumental stakeholder theory, **1:**116
Instrumental support, **2:**741
Integrated technology. *See* Automation/advanced
   manufacturing technology/computer-based
   integrated technology
Integrating style of conflict management, **1:**98–99
Integrity at work, 1:355–357
   assessment of, **1:**356
   attitudinal integrity and, **1:**356–357
   behavioral integrity and, **1:**356
   conceptualization of integrity, **1:**355–356
   counterproductive behaviors and, **1:**355
   low integrity, costs of, **1:**355–356
   norms and, **1:**356
   operationalization of integrity, **1:**356–357
   trait integrity and, **1:**357
   See also Integrity testing; Organizational culture;
      Personality; Theft at work
Integrity testing, 1:357–359, 2:636
   assessment of, **1:**359
   common features in, **1:**357–358
   construct validity of, **1:**358–359
   evidence of validity and, **1:**358
   improvements in, **1:**359
   informed consent and, **1:**358–359
   overt tests and, **1:**358
   personality-based tests, **1:**358
   polygraph tests and, **1:**357
   score reporting and, **1:**359
   scoring tests and, **1:**359
   validity of, **1:**358–359
   See also Counterproductive work behaviors (CWBs);
      Graphology; Integrity at work; Personality
      assessment; Selection strategies; Theft at work
Integrity trait, **2:**610
Intellectual stimulation (IS), **2:**835

Intelligence, **1:**54, 76
  crystallized intelligence, **1:**77
  fluid intelligence, **1:**77
  individual differences and, **1:**345
  intelligence testing, **1:**29, 30
  job-specific knowledge/skills and, **1:**78
  organizational citizenship behavior and, **1:**103
  taxonomic categorization and, **1:**142
  See also Cognitive abilities; Cognitive ability
      tests; Emotional intelligence (EI);
      Practical intelligence
Intelligence quotient (IQ), **1:**29, 30, 34, 54, 181–182, 270
Intentions, **1:**39
Interaction model, **1:**270–271, **2:**620
Interactional justice, **2:**571–572, 577
Interactional psychology, **2:**618
Interactive assessments, **1:**89
Intercoder reliability, **1:**69
Interdependence, **1:**277, 360–361, **2:**586
Interest inventories, **1:**67
Intergroup relations, **1:**359–362
  authoritarianism and, **1:**360
  bias and, **1:**359, 360, 362
  competition and, **1:**361
  contact hypothesis and, **1:**361–362
  cooperative interaction and, **1:**360, 362
  functional interdependence and, **1:**360–361
  group conflict theory and, **1:**361
  group status and, **1:**361
  individual differences and, **1:**360
  intergroup boundaries, **1:**360
  intergroup orientation and, **1:**361
  Robber's Cave study and, **1:**361
  social categorization and, **1:**360, 361–362
  social dominance theory and, **1:**360
  superior-subordinate relationships, research on, **1:**364
  See also Attitudes and beliefs; Diversity training; Group
      cohesiveness; Stereotyping
Internal consistency reliability coefficient, **2:**676
Internal validity, **1:**239
Internal-External Locus of Control Scale, **1:**461
International Association of Applied Psychology, **1:**309, 318
*International Guidelines on Computer-Based and
    Internet-Delivered Testing,* **2:**799
International Monetary Fund (IMF), **1:**276
International Organizational Development Code of Ethics, **2:**566
International Organization for Standardization (ISO), **1:**276, 277
International Personality Item Pool-NEO (IPIP-NEO), **1:**347
International Personnel Management Association, **1:**218
International Task Force on Assessment Center
    Guidelines, **1:**31–32, 34, 37
International Testing Commission (ITC), **2:**799
International trade, **1:**276
Internet:
  company Web sites, **2:**665
  computer assessment and, **1:**89, 90, 91
  cyberloafing at work, **1:**146–147
  exit surveys, **1:**230–231
  Internet use monitoring, **1:**175

recruitment and, **1:**171, **2:**668, 670, 671–672
structural equation modeling resources, **2:**776
Interpersonal communication, 1:362–366
  affective communication, types of, **2:**769
  channels and, **1:**363
  employee morale and, **2:**489
  encoding and, **1:**363
  feedback process and, **1:**363
  goal-driven nature of, **1:**362
  leader-member exchange theory and, **1:**364
  mediated communication, communication
    technologies and, **1:**362, 365–366
  message in, **1:**363
  noise and, **1:**363
  organizational context and, **1:**365
  peer communication and, **1:**364–365
  process of, **1:**363
  receiver in, **1:**363
  sender in, **1:**363
  superior-subordinate communication and, **1:**363–364
  trust issues and, **1:**365
  See also Globalization; Interpersonal communication styles;
    Organizational communication, formal; Organizational
    communication, informal; Trust
Interpersonal communication styles, 1:366–368
  animated communication style, **1:**367
  attentive communication style, **1:**367
  contentious communication style, **1:**367
  descriptions of, **1:**366–368
  dominant communication style, **1:**366–367
  dramatic communication style, **1:**367
  impression-leaving communication style, **1:**367
  open communication style, **1:**367
  relaxed communication style, **1:**367
  research on, **1:**366
  See also Impression management;
    Interpersonal communication
Interpersonal conflict model, **1:**96
Interpersonal influence, **2:**576
Interpersonal relationships:
  affective traits and, **1:**14
  counterproductive behaviors and, **1:**118, 124
  distance learning and, **1:**156
  relational conflict and, **1:**95, 97
  virtual teams and, **2:**873–874
  See also Discrimination; Intergroup relations;
    Workplace romance
Interpretive bias, **2:**762
Interpretive qualitative paradigm, **2:**649
Interrater reliability coefficient, **2:**677
Interval-contingent studies, **1:**464
Interval scales, **2:**469–470
Intervention studies, **1:**463
Interviews:
  assessment center methods, **1:**34
  situational interviews, **1:**34
  See also Employment interview; Exit survey
    (exit interview); Job analysis methods
Intrarater reliability coefficient, **2:**677

Intrinsic case study, **1:**68
Intrinsic and extrinsic work motivation, 1:368–371, 407
    autonomy, social context and, **1:**369–370
    externally regulated activity and, **1:**368, 369–370
    identification with regulation and, **1:**369
    industrial/organizational psychology and, **1:**370
    informationally administered rewards and, **1:**370
    integrated regulations, autonomous regulation and, **1:**369
    intrinsic motivation and, 369, **1:**370
    introjection and, 368–369
    motivation assessment and, **1:**369
    rewards, motivation and, **1:**370–371
    self-determination continuum and, **1:**368–369
    See also Motivational traits; Work motivation
Introversion trait, **2:**609
Iowa Test of Basic Skills, **2:**755
Ipsative measurement, **2:**524, 612–613
Ishikawa, K., **2:**814
Israel, **1:**317–318
Israel Defense Forces (IDF), **1:**318
Israel Institute of Applied Social Research, **1:**318
Israel Psychological Association(IPA), **1:**318
Item bias. *See* Differential item functioning (DIF)
Item response function (IRF), **1:**371–373, 372 (figure)
Item response theory (IRT), **1:**90, 152, **371–374**, 400, **2:**653
    applications of, **1:**373–374
    classical test theory and, **1:**371
    computerized adaptive tests and, **1:**373–374
    future of, **1:**374
    information concept in, **1:**373
    item response function and, **1:**371–373, 372 (figure)
    latent traits and, **1:**371
    location/threshold parameters and, **1:**372
    option response functions and, **1:**373
    polytomous models and, **1:**373
    Rasch model and, **1:**373
    two/three parameter logistic models and, **1:**372–373

Jago, A., **2:**521, 522, 523
Jamison, C. L., **1:**4
Janis, I. L., **1:**299, 300, 301, **2:**479, 517, 664
Japanese revolution in manufacturing, **1:**307
Jaques, E., **1:**311
Jares, S. M., **1:**364
Javidan, M., **1:**275
Jeanrie, C., **1:**461
Jehn, K. A., **1:**95
Job advertisements, 1:375–376
    effectiveness of, **1:**376
    impact of, **1:**375
    informational dimensions of, **1:**375–376
    physical attributes of, **1:**376
    purpose of, **1:**375–376
    return on investment measures and, **1:**376
    set size effect and, **1:**376
    See also Recruitment; Recruitment sources
Job analysis, 1:377–380
    abilities and, **1:**378
    competency modeling and, **1:**85–86

    critical incidents and, **1:**378
    Dictionary of Occupational Titles and, **1:**151
    duties and, **1:**378
    e-job analysis and, **1:**171
    employee selection process and, **1:**195
    generalized work activity and, **1:**378
    information sources for, **1:**379–380
    job analysis methods and, **1:**378–379
    knowledge requirements and, **1:**378
    licensure/certification requirements and, **1:**378
    personality characteristics and, **1:**378
    purposes of, **1:**377
    relevant information for, **1:**377–378
    skill requirements and, **1:**378
    tasks and, **1:**377
    tool development, action theory and, **1:**6
    work activity information and, **1:**377
    work environment information and, **1:**378
    worker requirements and, **1:**378
    See also Critical incident technique; Job analysis
        methods; Job description
Job analysis methods, 1:378–379, 380–382
    direct observation and, **1:**378–379
    group interviews and, **1:**379
    hybrid methods, **1:**381–382
    individual interviews and, **1:**379
    Occupational Information Network
        (O*NET) and, **1:**382
    Position Analysis Questionnaire and, **1:**381
    surveys and, **1:**379
    task analysis, steps in, **1:**380–381
    worker-oriented methods, **1:**381
    work-oriented methods, **1:**380–381
    See also Job analysis; Job description; Occupational
        Information Network (O*NET)
Job behavior. *See* Affective events theory (AET); Boredom at
    work; Organizational behavior; Workplace incivility
Job characteristics theory (JCT), **1:383–386**, 393, 407
    context satisfaction and, **1:**385
    creativity at work and, **1:**128
    experienced meaningfulness and, **1:**383–384
    experienced responsibility, autonomy and, **1:**384
    flexible work schedules and, **1:**87, 88, 253
    growth need strength and, **1:**385, 386
    individual conditions and, **1:**385
    internal psychological states and, **1:**383
    job design and, **1:**393–394
    Job Diagnostic Survey and, **1:**385
    knowledge of results, feedback and, **1:**384
    knowledge and skill and, **1:**385
    Motivating Potential Score and, **1:**385, 386
    outcomes measurement and, **1:**384–385
    principles of, **1:**383, 384 (figure)
    research results and, **1:**385–386
    skill variety and, **1:**383
    task identity and, **1:**383–384
    task significance and, **1:**384
    See also Empowerment; Job design;
        Person-job (PJ) fit

Job choice, 1:386–390
   choice set, development of, 1:387–388
   decision process research and, 1:389–390
   expectancy and, 1:387
   final decision process and, 1:387
   instrumentality and, 1:387
   job assessment processes and, 1:387
   job attributes, outcomes and, 1:388
   judgment and decision-making process and, 1:426
   matching models and, 1:388–389
   Organizational Culture Profile and, 1:389
   personality/job preferences and, 1:388–389
   prospect theory and, 1:387
   RIASEC (realistic/investigative/artistic/social/
      enterprising/conventional) model and, 1:389
   valences and, 1:387, 388–389
   See also Career development; Job search; Realistic job
      preview (RJP); Recruitment
Job control. *See* Empowerment
Job description, 1:391–392
   essential duties/work activities and, 1:391
   identifying information and, 1:391
   job summary and, 1:391
   knowledge/skills/abilities/other characteristics
      requirements and, 1:392
   position description and, 1:391
   structure/length of, 1:391
   See also Job analysis; Job analysis methods
Job Descriptive Index (JDI), 1:413
Job design, 1:392–395
   future complexity in work environments and, 1:393–394
   globalization and, 1:393, 394
   individual workers and, 1:392–394
   industrial engineering and, 1:392
   interdisciplinary framework and, 1:392
   job characteristics theory and, 1:393–394
   job enrichment, vertical loading and, 1:392
   motivator-hygiene theory and, 1:392–393
   Multiple Job Design Questionnaire and, 1:394
   older workers, occupational stress and, 2:532–533
   role underload and, 2:687
   scientific management and, 1:392
   team-based work and, 1:394–395
   See also Job characteristics theory (JCT); Scientific
      management; Work design
Job Diagnostic Survey (JDS), 1:385, 393, 412
Job embeddedness construct, 2:885
Job evaluation, 1:395–397
   ceiling effect and, 1:396
   compensable factors and, 1:396
   criticisms of, 1:396–397
   grading/slotting of jobs and, 1:83
   Hay Guide Chart-Profile Method and, 1:395
   job elements and, 1:395
   methodology in, 1:395–396
   point assignment and, 1:396
   point-factor system and, 1:396
   Position Analysis Questionnaire and, 1:395
   rational approach to weights of factors and, 1:396

   statistical approach to weights of factors and, 1:396
   See also Comparable worth; Job analysis
Job in General (JIG) measure, 1:413
Job insecurity. *See* Job security/insecurity
Job involvement, 1:397–399
   hiring selectivity and, 1:398
   human resource policies/practices and, 1:398–399
   individual work performance and, 1:397
   information sharing and, 1:399
   job-involved individual, profile of, 1:397–398
   meaningfulness and, 1:398
   promotion strategies for, 1:398
   psychological climate and, 1:398
   psychological safety and, 1:398
   reward systems and, 1:398–399
   self-managed teams and, 1:399
   status differences and, 1:399
   training and, 1:398
   See also Job design; Work-life balance
Job knowledge testing, 1:399–401
   Bloom's taxonomy and, 1:400
   classical test theory and, 1:400
   computer-based tests and, 1:401
   credentialing testing, 1:400
   declarative knowledge, 1:399
   item response theory and, 1:400
   measurement of, 1:399–400
   performance measurement and, 1:400–401
   performance prediction and, 1:400
   performance tests and, 1:400–401
   procedural knowledge, 1:399
   skill, 1:399
   test blueprint and, 1:400
   See also Job performance models; Practical intelligence
Job maturity, 2:725
Job mobility, 1:2
Job modeling, 2:778
JobNet program, 2:748
Job performance:
   affective traits and, 1:14–15
   compressed workweek and, 1:87–88
   core self-evaluations and, 1:111
   expectancy theory and, 1:14
   general mental ability and, 1:79–80
   high-Mach leaders and, 2:468
   interactional justice and, 2:572
   job-specific knowledge/skills and, 1:78
   organizational commitment and, 2:550
   See also Boredom at work; Conflict at work;
      Job satisfaction; Organizational performance
Job performance models, 1:401–404
   contextual performance and, 1:401
   criterion dynamicity and, 1:403–404
   equivalency of ratings/raters and, 1:403
   general factor of job performance and, 1:402
   job performance assessment, definition of, 1:403
   job performance assessment, measurement
      issues in, 1:403–404
   job performance, content domain of, 1:401–402

literature/research on, **1:**402, 404
multisource assessments and, **1:**403
organizational research/interventions and, **1:**404
reliability issues and, **1:**404
task performance and, **1:**401
taxonomies of job performance and, **1:**402–403
temporal relationships across dimensions and, **1:**403, 404
See also Criterion theory; Performance appraisal; Performance
 appraisal, objective indexes; Performance appraisal,
 subjective indexes; 360-degree feedback
Job rotation, 1:404–406
involvement in, **1:**405
knowledge enlargement and, **1:**405–406
lateral movement within a company and, **1:**405
objectives of, **1:**405
outcomes of, **1:**405–406
physical demands/repetitive tasks and, **1:**404–405
position/department rotation, **1:**, 405, 406
task enlargement and, **1:**406
task rotation, **1:**405–406
See also Career development; Engineering
 psychology; Job characteristics theory (JCT)
Job satisfaction, 1:2, 406–410
absenteeism and, **1:**409–410
affective traits and, **1:**14, 408
burnout and, **1:**409
causes of, **1:**407–409
compressed workweek and, **1:**88
core self-evaluations and, **1:**111
Cornell model and, **1:**408
definition of, **1:**406–407
demand-control model of strain and, **1:**407
demographic variables and, **1:**408
job characteristics model and, **1:**407
job dissatisfaction, negative behaviors and, **1:**409
job performance/organizational behaviors and, **1:**409–410
leader behaviors and, **1:**49
life satisfaction/health and, **1:**409
Machiavellianism and, **2:**468
measurement of, **1:**407
older workers and, **2:**532
organizational citizenship behavior and, **1:**103, 104, 105, 409
outcomes of, **1:**409–410
pay satisfaction and, **1:**84
personal causes of, **1:**408
person-by-situation causes of, **1:**408–409
situational causes of, **1:**407–408
stability of, **1:**408
value-percent theory and, **1:**408–409
See also Affective events theory (AET); Attitudes and beliefs;
 Boredom at work; Dirty work; Employee well-being; Job
 design; Job performance; Job performance models; Job
 satisfaction measurement; Withdrawal behaviors,
 absenteeism; Withdrawal behaviors, lateness; Withdrawal
 behaviors, turnover
Job satisfaction measurement, 1:410–413
Abridged Job Descriptive Index and, **1:**413
appropriate measures and, **1:**411
compendia of satisfaction measures and, **1:**411–412

exemplar measures of job satisfaction, **1:**412
Faces Scale and, **1:**412
facet measures, **1:**411
Facet-Specific Job Satisfaction measures and, **1:**412–413
general vs. occupation-specific measures and, **1:**411
good measures, elements of, **1:**410–411
Job descriptive Index and, **1:**413
Job Diagnostic Survey and, **1:**412
Job in General measure, **1:**413
Job Satisfaction Survey and, **1:**413
measures, quality of, **1:**410–411
Mental Measurement Yearbook and, **1:**411
Minnesota Satisfaction Questionnaire and, **1:**412
overall measures, **1:**411
quantitative vs. qualitative measures and, **1:**411
single vs. multiple item measures and, **1:**411
sources of measures, **1:**411–413
test publishers and, **1:**412
World Wide Web and, **1:**412
See also Attitudes and beliefs; Customer satisfaction with
 services; Job satisfaction; Morale; Organizational surveys
Job Satisfaction Survey (JSS), **1:**413
Job search, 1:414–416
active search behavior and, **1:**414
context of, **1:**414
duration of, **1:**415
intensity of, **1:**415
job alternatives and, **1:**414
job search behavior and, **1:**414
market attributes and, **1:**415
measurement of, **1:**414
outcomes of, **1:**415–416
person attributes and, **1:**414
predictors of, **1:**414–415
preparatory search behavior and, **1:**414
situational attributes and, **1:**414–415
successful outcome and, **1:**413
voluntary turnover, traditional turnover
 model and, **1:**415–416
See also Big Five taxonomy of
 personality; Self-efficacy
Job security/insecurity, 1:416–419
antecedents of, **1:**418
cognitive vs. affective insecurity and, **1:**417
consequences of, **1:**417–418
definition of, **1:**416
gender and, **1:**418
global vs. multifaceted insecurity and, **1:**417
job/organizational attitudes and, **1:**417
measurement of, **1:**418–419
moderators of, **1:**418
objective job insecurity, measures of, **1:**418–419
occupational status and, **1:**418
organizational change and, **1:**418
physical/psychological well-being and, **1:**417–418
social support and, **1:**418
subjective job insecurity, measures of, **1:**419
subjective vs. objective insecurity and, **1:**417, 418–419
taxonomy of, **1:**416–417

work-related behavior and, **1:**418
See also Downsizing; Outsourcing; Quality of work life
(QWL); Stress, consequences
Job sharing, 1:419–421
costs/benefits research and, **1:**420–421
employee costs/benefits of, **1:**420–421
employer costs/benefits of, **1:**420
history/prevalence of, **1:**419–420
See also Career development; Flexible work
schedules; Work-life balance
Job stress model, **1:**120–121, 122
Job titles, **1:**307–308, **2:**914–941, 946
See also Dictionary of Occupational Titles (DOT)
Job typologies, 1:421–423
content model and, **1:**422
Dictionary of Occupational Titles and, **1:**421, 422
General Aptitude Test Battery and, **1:**422
Guide for Occupational Exploration and, **1:**422
job classification/grouping, benefits of, **1:**421
Minnesota Occupational Classification System III and, **1:**422
North American Industry Classification System and, **1:**423
Occupational Information Network and, **1:**421–422
Occupational Aptitude Patterns Map and, **1:**422
Occupational Employment Statistics and, **1:**423
Occupational Outlook Handbook and, **1:**422–423
RIASEC (realistic/investigative/artistic/social/enterprising/
conventional) model and, **1:**422
Standard Occupational Classification System and, **1:**422
World-of-Work Map and, **1:**422
See also Occupational Information Network (O*NET)
Job-specific competency models, **1:**86
Job-specific knowledge/skills, **1:**78
Jobs, S., **1:**40
John, O., **1:**54
Johnson, L. B., **1:**16
Joint Committee on Standards for Educational Evaluation, **2:**641
Joint optimization, **2:**749–750
Joint-Service Job Performance Measurement/Enlistment
Standards (JPM) Project, **2:**, 641, 642
Journal of Applied Behavior Analysis, **2:**538
Journal of Applied Psychology, **2:**538
*Journal of Organizational Behavior
Management* (JOBM), **2:**538
Journals list, **2:**943–945
JPM Project. *See* Joint-Service Job Performance
Measurement/Enlistment Standards (JPM) Project
Judge-advisor system (JAS), **1:**427
Judge, T. A., **1:**13
Judgment analysis, **1:**453, **2:**630
Judgment and decision-making (JDM) **process, 1:424–426**
decision analysis and, **1:**424
decision making styles scales and, **1:**425
emotions/motivation and, **1:**425
expected utility theories and, **1:**424
fairness issues and, **1:**425–426
heuristics and biases approach and, **1:**424
individual differences and, **1:**425
industrial/organizational psychology and, **1:**425, 426
job choice/employee selection and, **1:**426

multiattribute utility theory and, **1:**424
organizational justice and, **1:**425–426
policy-capturing methodology and, **1:**426
prospect theory and, **1:**424–425
time discounting and, **1:**425
ultimatum game and, **1:**426
See also Judgment and decision-making process: advice
giving and taking; Judgment and decision-making
process: heuristics, cognitive biases, and contextual
influences; Situational judgment tests (SJTs)
**Judgment and decision-making process: advice giving and
taking, 1:427–429**
advice, definition of, **1:**427
advice giving and, **1:**428
advice taking and, **1:**427–428
confidence in decisions and, **1:**428
egocentric advice discounting and, **1:**427–428
employment decisions and, **1:**429
industrial/organizational psychology and, **1:**428–429
interpersonal work relationships and, **1:**428–429
judge-advisor systems and, **1:**427
postadvice decision accuracy and, **1:**428
See also Group decision-making quality and performance;
Judgment and decision-making (JDM) process; Judgment
and decision-making process: heuristics, cognitive biases,
and contextual influences
**Judgment and decision-making process: heuristics,
cognitive biases, and contextual influences, 1:B429–432**
anchoring/adjustment heuristic and, **1:**430
availability heuristic and, **1:**430
confirmation bias and, **1:**430
context effects and, **1:**431–432
decoy/phantom effects and, **1:**431–432
framing effects and, **1:**431
heuristics/biases and, **1:**429–431
industrial/organizational psychology and,
1:429–430, 431, 432
organizational decision-making, improvement
strategies for, **1:**432
representativeness heuristic and, **1:**430
selection vs. rejection and, **1:**432
sunk cost fallacy and, **1:**430–431
See also Employee selection; Group decision-making quality
and performance; Judgment and decision-making (JDM)
process; Rating errors and perceptual biases
Judgment methods of selection, **2:**697–698
Juran, J., **2:**814
Justice. *See* Justice in teams; Organizational justice
Justice climate studies, **1:**434
Justice in teams, 1:432–434
generalizing study results to team members and, **1:**433
justice climate studies and, **1:**434
literature/research on, **1:**433, 434
teammate treatment, individual justice
reaction and, **1:**433–434
See also Groups; Organizational climate; Organizational
justice
Justice theory, **1:**121, 122, 123–124, 125, **2:**577–578, 893
Just-identified model, **2:**774, 775

k-means analysis, **1:**57
Kahn, R. L., **1:**49, 363, **2:**526
Kahneman, D., **1:**429, 431
Kanfer, A., **2:**581
Kanfer, R., **2:**491
Kanter, D. L., **2:**563
Kaplan, R., **1:**45
Karasek, R., **2:**772
Karau, S. J., **2:**736, 737
Katz, D., **1:**49, 363
Keller, T., **1:**334
Kenyon, B. L., **2:**895
Kiesler, S., **2:**557
Kim, D. -O., **1:**263
Kimmel, A. J., **1:**219
King, N., **2:**873
Kirkpatrick, D. L., **2:**821, 822
Kluckhohn, C., **1:**138, **2:**608
Kluger, A. N., **1:**248, 249, **2:**606
Knowledge elicitation methods, **1:**207
Knowledge enlargement, **1:**405–406
Knowledge intensive work, **1:**296–297
Knowledge/skills/abilities (KSAs), **2:**615, 616,
    617, 819, 823, 824, 843, 847
Knowledge/skills/abilities/other characteristics
    (KSAOs), **1:**193, 194, 195, 198, 392
Knowledge/skills/abilities/personal characteristics
    (KSAPs), **1:**341
Knowledge transfer, **1:**278, 450, **2:**873
    See also Transfer of training
Knowles, E. S., **2:**505
Komaki, J. L., **2:**539, 674, 675
Kornhauser, A., **1:**310, 327, **2:**526, **2:**849
Kraiger, K., **2:**821, 822
Kreiner, G. E., **1:**153
Krueger, R. A., **1:**255
Krumboltz, J., **1:**64, 65
Kruse, D. L., **1:**262
Kugelmass, S., **1:**318
Kuhl, J., **2:**491
Kurtosis, **1:**150

Labor and Employment Relations Association, **1:**350
Labor law, 1:437–439
    comparable worth wage laws, **1:**81, 82
    Railway Labor Act and, **1:**437
    See also National Labor Relations Act (NLRA);
        Union commitment; Unions
Labor market:
    comparable worth concept and, **1:**81, 82
    contingent labor, **2:**593–594
    See also Compensation
Labor unions. *See* Unions
Laffey v. Northwest Airlines, **1:**211
Lahy, J. M., **1:**309
Laissez-faire (LF) leadership, **2:**835
Larsen, R. J., **1:**13
Lateness. *See* Withdrawal behaviors, lateness
Latent continuous variables, **2:**773

Latent growth curve models, **2:**774
Latent trait theory. *See* Item response theory
Latham, G. P., **1:**278, **2:**839, 893
Lawler, E. E., **1:**262, 263
Lawrence, P. R., **2:**588
Law School Admission Test (LSAT), **2:**755, 760
Laws. *See* Labor law; Legal environment
Layoffs. *See* Downsizing
Lazarus, R. S., **2:**767
Leader Behavior Description Questionnaire (LBDQ), **1:**49
Leader-member exchange (LMX) **theory, 1:**364, **440–442**
    antecedents of, **1:**441
    consequences of, **1:**441
    developmental testing and, **1:**441
    employee retaliatory behavior and, **2:**578
    exchanges, underlying dimensions of, **1:**441
    future of, **1:**442
    leader-member exchange model and, **1:**440–442
    leader-member relationships, nature of, **1:**440–441
    leadership-making model and, **1:**441–442
    maintenance evaluation and, **1:**441
    relationship development and, **1:**441–442
    role making, reciprocity/social exchange and, **1:**441
    vertical dyad linkage model and, **1:**440
    work outcomes and, **1:**441
    workplace safety and, **2:**903
    See also Leadership development; Leadership
        and supervision; Social exchange theory
Leaderless group discussion, **1:**35
Leadership development, 1:445–448
    assessment centers and, **1:**447
    continuous learning and, **1:**446–447
    developmental assignments an, **1:**447
    executive coaching and, **1:**447
    feedback discussions and, **1:**447
    individual perspective and, **1:**447
    manager development programs and, **1:**448
    managerial competency and, **1:**31, 32
    mentoring and, **1:**447
    methodology for, **1:**447–448
    multisource performance ratings and, **1:**447
    off-site leadership development programs and, **1:**447–448
    organizational perspective and, **1:**446–447
    programs, assessment of, !:448
    role modeling and, **1:**447
    short courses/workshops and, **1:**448
    simulations and, **1:**447
    See also Assessment center; Executive selection; Managerial
        leadership; Performance appraisal; Succession planning
Leadership Grid, **1:**50
Leadership and supervision, 1:442–445
    coercive power and, **1:**443
    creativity at work and, **1:**128
    early leadership research and, **1:**443
    expert power and, **1:**443
    in-group leadership and, **1:**445
    leader behavior and, **1:**444
    leader power and, **1:**443–444
    leadership vs. supervision and, **1:**442–443

organizational culture and, **2:**560–561
reward power and, **1:**443
situational leadership theories and, **1:**444–445
task vs. relationship focus of, **1:**444
transactional leadership and, **1:**445
Transformational leadership and, **1:**445
See also Abusive supervision; Behavioral approach to
        leadership; Charismatic leadership theory; Leadership
        development; Life-cycle model of leadership; Managerial
        leadership; Path-goal theory; Situational approach to
        leadership; Trait approach to leadership
Leadership-making model, **1:**441–442
Learning goal orientation (LGO), **2:**491
Learning organizations, **1:**449–450
    change orientation and, **1:**450
    continual individual development and, **1:**449
    definition of, **1:**449
    deutero learning and, **1:**449
    empowerment of leadership and, **1:**449
    flexible organizational structures and, **1:**449
    internal/external environment, awareness of, **1:**449–450
    issues in, **1:**450
    knowledge-sharing mechanisms and, **1:**450
    models of, common features in, **1:**449–450
    shared vision and, **1:**450
    single-loop/double-loop learning and, **1:**449
    strategic alignment and, **1:**450
    systematic approaches to knowledge processing and, **1:**449
    teamwork and, **1:**449
    See also Group development; High-performance
        organization model; Organizational change; Strategic
        planning; Training
Least preferred coworker (LPC) **theory**, **1:**450–452
    contingency model of leadership and, **1:**450
    leader esteem measures, least preferred coworkers and,
        1:450–451
    leader match and, **1:**452
    leader position power and, **1:**451
    leader-member relations and, **1:**451
    practical implications of, **1:**451–452
    situational control and, **1:**451
    situation grid/octants and, **1:**451
    task structure and, **1:**451
    See also Leader-member exchange (LMX) theory;
        Leadership and supervision; Transformational and
        transactional leadership
Leavitt, H., **1:**328
Lectures, **2:**824
Lee, J., **1:**364
Lefkowitz, J., **1:**115
Legal environment:
    affirmative action programs, **1:**15–16
    age discrimination in employment and, **1:**19–20
    banding procedure and, **1:**48
    civil rights protections, **1:**8, 16, 71–74
    comparable worth and, **1:**81–82, 84
    disabled population and, **1:**22–25
    disparate impact lawsuits, **1:**10
    employee selection and, **1:**193–194

employment discrimination law, **1:**8–9
fair employment laws, **1:**71–74
prescreening assessment practices and, **2:**637
privacy, electronic monitoring and, **1:**176
See also Bona fide occupational qualifications
        (BFOQ); Labor law
Leniency errors, **2:**660, 662
Leniency in letters of recommendation, **1:**455
Lens model, **1:**452–454
    industrial/organizational psychology and, **1:**454
    judge/environment modeling and, **1:**454
    judge-environment relationship and, **1:**454
    judgment analysis, cues and, **1:**453
    lens model analysis and, **1:**454
    lens model equation and, **1:**454
    orthogonal/multivariate research designs and, **1:**452
    perceptual analogy of, **1:**453
    principles of, 453 (figure), **1:**453
    representative research design, generalizability and, **1:**452
    See also Policy-capturing (PC)
Lent, R., **1:**64, 67
Lesbian population. *See* Gay/lesbian/bisexual
        (GLB) issues at work
Letters of recommendation, **1:**455–456, **2:**636
    components of, **1:**456
    definitions, **1:**455
    ethical issues in, **1:**456
    evaluation of, **1:**456
    future performance, prediction of, **1:**455
    legal issues and, **1:**456
    leniency and, **1:**455
    problems with, **1:**455–456
    reference checks and, **1:**455
    references and, **1:**455
    reliability of, **1:**455–456
    resumé details, confirmation of, **1:**455
    sex/race differences and, **1:**456
    See also Employment interview; Prescreening
        assessment methods for personnel selection
Leung, K., **1:**138, 142
Levine, J. M., **2:**746
Levy, P. E., **2:**606
Lewicki, R. J., **2:**838
Lewin, K., **1:**5, 311, 315, 328, **2:**541, 560,
        561, 565, 615, 692
Lewis, J. L., **2:**852
Leymann, H., **1:**311
Licensure examinations, **2:**756
    See also Credentialing
Lieblich, I., **1:**281
Lie scales, **2:**637
Life-career rainbow, **1:**63
Life course widening, **2:**680
Life-cycle model of leadership, **1:**457–458, **2:**725
    adaptability tenet, empirical demonstration of, **1:**458
    human development and, **1:**457–458
    leader effectiveness, situational attributes and, **1:**457
    managerial dynamics vs. true leadership and, **1:**458
    military leadership training and, **1:**457

optimal leader behavior, follower maturity and, **1:**457
research outcomes, mixed results and, **1:**458
situational leadership theory and, **1:**457–458
See also Leadership and supervision; Situational
    approach to leadership
Life experience. *See* Biographical data
Life Orientation Test (LOT), **2:**535
Lifespace, **1:**63
Life span studies, **1:**63, **2:**532
Life-stage psychology, **1:**63
Likelihood ratio technique, **1:**152
Likert, R., **1:**49, 328, 331
Likert scale, **1:**38, 373, **2:**523, 590, 612, 780
Lim, V., **1:**146
Lincoln, A., **2:**705
Linearity assumption, **2:**472
Line-of-sight problem, **2:**791
Linkage research and analysis, 1:144–145, **459–460**
assumptions of linkage research, **1:**460
cause-and-effect conclusions, reasonableness of, **1:**460
employee opinion-business performance
    relationship and, **1:**459
employee surveys, design of, **1:**459–460
measures of business performance and, **1:**460
survey content, linkage relationships and, **1:**460
variance of perceptions, meaning of, **1:**460
within-unit agreement and, **1:**460
See also Feedback; Organizational climate;
    Person-environment (PE) fit; Person-organization (PO) fit
Linkage research models, **2:**590
Link, H., **1:**314
L'Institut d'Orientation Profesionnelle, **1:**310
Lipmann, O., **1:**309, 310
Lippitt, R., **2:**560
Locke, E. A., **1:**278, **2:**692, 893
Locke, J., **1:**115
Locus of control, 1:124, 303, 397, **461–462**, **2:**710
cross-cultural studies of, **1:**462
eustress and, **1:**462
Internal-External Locus of Control Scale and, **1:**461
measurement of, **1:**461
misconceptions about, **1:**461
positive health psychology and, **1:**462
primary control and, **1:**461
secondary control and, **1:**461
socioinstrumental control beliefs and, **1:**462
stress moderator function of, **1:**461–462, **2:**766, 767
Vocational Locus of Control Scale and, **1:**461
Work Locus of Control Scale and, **1:**461, 462
See also Control theory
Loehlin, J. C., **1:**270
Lofquist, L. H., **1:**67, 347, **2:**616, 622
London, M., **2:**606
**Longitudinal research/experience sampling
    technique, 1:462–465**
cohort studies, **1:**463
data collection over time and, **1:**463
event-contingent studies and, **1:**464–465
experience sampling, **1:**463, 464–465

experience sampling, advantages/disadvantages of, **1:**465
interval-contingent studies and, **1:**464
intervention studies, **1:**463
longitudinal research, **1:**463–464
longitudinal research, advantages/disadvantages, **1:**464
panel studies, **1:**463
retrospective studies and, **1:**463–464
signal-contingent studies and, **1:**464
trend studies, **1:**463
types of experience sampling studies, **1:**464–465
types of longitudinal research, **1:**463
See also Experimental designs; Hawthorne Studies/Hawthorne
    effect; Quantitative research approach;
    Quasi-experimental designs
Longitudinal validation, **2:**642
Long-term associative storage/retrieval, **1:**77
Loo, G. L., **1:**146
Lord, R., **1:**152, 333, **2:**560
Lorsch, J. W., **2:**588
Lovell, H. T., **1:**321
Low-base-rate phenomenon, **1:**1
Lowe, R. H., **2:**913, 914
Lowman, R. L., **1:**218
Lubin School of Business, Academy of Management, **1:**4–5
Lubinski, D., **1:**345
Luthans, F., **2:**631

Ma, J., **1:**462
Macan, T. H., **2:**813
Machiavellianism, 2:467–468
charismatic leaders and, **2:**467, 468
checks and balances and, **2:**468
definition of, **2:**467
high-Machs and, **2:**467, 468
influence tactics and, **2:**468
job autonomy and, **2:**468
managerial positions and, **2:**468
organizational impact of, **2:**468
personal gain and, **2:**468
research on, **2:**467
See also Abusive supervision; Charismatic
    leadership theory; Workplace incivility
MacKenzie, S. B., **1:**103, 286
Macro organizational behaviors, **1:**39–40, 41
Mael, F. A., **1:**56
Majchrzak, A., **2:**873
Make-whole relief, **1:**73
Malcolm Baldrige National Quality Award
    (MBNQA), **2:**754, 814
Malhotra, A., **2:**873
Malpass, R. S., **1:**142
Management by exception, **2:**835
Management by objectives, **2:**603
Management competency profiling, **1:**31, 32
Management Progress Study, **1:**30–31
Manager development programs, **1:**448
Managerial leadership:
    affective traits and, **1:**14
    autonomous management, **1:**115

executive pay, agency theory and, **1:**84
management competency profiling and, **1:**31, 32
strategic stakeholder approach to, **1:**116
technology and, **1:**35
See also Abusive supervision; Leadership
    development; Leadership and supervision
Managerial Progress Study, **2:**766
Manager rating scale, **2:**727
Mandatory retirement policy, **1:**20
Manifest continuous variables, **2:**773
Mann, L., **2:**517
Mantel-Haenszel method, **1:**152
Manufacturing technology. *See* Automation/advanced
    manufacturing technology/computer-based
    integrated technology
Marketing, **1:**143
Marks, M. L., **2:**479
Martin, A., **1:**321
Maslach Burnout Inventory (MBI), **1:**177, 178, 180
Maslow, A., **2:**509, 510, 608, 893
Mass media, **2:**730
Mass production, **1:**2, 188
Master's level education/training:
    additional industrial/organizational domains, **2:**922–923
    areas of competency, descriptions of, **2:**917–923
    attitude theory and, **2:**921
    breadth of training and, **2:**914
    career options and, **2:**914
    compensation/benefits and, **2:**922–923
    consumer behavior and, **2:**922
    core competencies in, **2:**915–916, 917 (table)
    core industrial/organizational domains and, **2:**919–922
    core psychological domains and, **2:**917–918
    criterion theory/development and, **2:**919
    curriculum options and, **2:**916, 923 (table)
    data collection/analysis skills and, **2:**918–919
    depth of training and, **2:**914
    doctoral studies and, **2:**914
    dynamic nature of competencies and, **2:**916
    employee selection/placement/classification and, **2:**920
    ethical/legal/professional contexts and, **2:**919
    fields of psychology and, **2:**917–918
    formal coursework and, **2:**923
    guidelines, purpose of, **2:**913
    history/systems of psychology and, **2:**917
    human performance/human factors and, **2:**922
    independent reading/study and, **2:**923
    industrial/labor relations and, **2:**923
    instructional programs, theory/program design/
        evaluation and, **2:**920–921
    job/task analysis and, **2:**919–920
    measurement of individual differences and, **2:**919
    modeling/observation and, **2:**923
    on-the-job training and, **2:**923
    organizational development and, **2:**921–922
    organization theory and, **2:**921
    performance appraisal/feedback and, **2:**920
    perspective of the guidelines and, **2:**913–914
    related competencies and, **2:**916

research methods and, **2:**918
small group theory/process and, **2:**921
statistical methods/data analysis and, **2:**918–919
supervised internships/practica and, **2:**923
title/position and, **2:**914–915, 946
university programs for, **2:**940–942
work motivation and, **2:**921
See also Doctoral level education/training;
    Industrial/organizational psychology careers
Matching models, **1:**388–389
Matter, C. F., **2:**505
Mayer, J. D., **1:**180, 181
Mayer, Salovey, Caruso Emotional Intelligence
    Test (MSCEIT), **1:**181
Mayflower Group, **2:**591
Maynard, H. B., **2:**693
Mayo, G. E., **1:**305, 321, 327, **2:**537, 555
McAdams, D. P., **2:**608
McAllister, D. J., **2:**838
McClelland, D., **1:**85, **1:**319, **2:**509, 893
McCrea, R., **1:**54, 346
McDaniel, M. A., **2:**635, 729
McDonald, R. A., **1:**810
McDonnell Douglas/Burdine framework, **1:**9
McGregor, D., **2:**560
Meaning-centered organizational communication, **2:**554–555
Meaningfulness, **1:**398
    See also Organizational sensemaking
Measurement equivalence, **1:**91
Measurement error, **1:**75
Measurement scales, 2:468–470
    career assessment, **1:**67
    conflict measurement, **1:**95
    interval scales, **2:**469–470
    nominal scales, **2:**469
    ordinal scales, **2:**469
    pay satisfaction measurement, **1:**84
    ratio scales, **2:**470
    See also Classical test theory (CTT); Inferential statistics; Item
        response theory (IRT); Measures of association/correlation
        coefficient; Reliability; Statistical power; Validity
Measurement theory:
    true component/error component in scores, **1:**266
    See also Generalizability theory (G-theory);
        Measurement scales; Statistics
Measures of association/correlation coefficient, 2:470–474
    alternate types of correlations, **2:**472, 473, 473 (table)
    biserial correlation, **2:**473
    correlation matrix, 471 (table), **2:**471
    correlations, features of, **2:**472
    cross-products matrix, **2:**471, 471 (table)
    graphical representation of correlations,
        2:472–473, 472 (figure)
    homoscedasticity assumption and, **2:**472–473
    linearity assumption and, **2:**472, 473
    numerical representation of correlations and,
        2:470–472, 472 (tables)
    Pearson product-moment correlation, **2:**472
    phi coefficient, **2:**473

point-biserial correlation, **2:**473
raw score formula and, **2:**471
Spearman's rho correlation, **2:**473
standard score formula and, **2:**471
statistics and, **2:**473–474
tetrachoric correlation, **2:**473
variance-covariance matrix, **2:**471, 471 (table)
See also Factor analysis
Mechanistic models of organizational structure, **2:**587, 588
Mediation model, **1:**270–271
See also Mediator variables; Negotiation, mediation, and arbitration
Mediator variables, **2:**484
Medical College Admissions Test (MCAT), **2:**755
Medical Review Officer (MRO), **1:**168, 169
Meehl, P. E., **2:**519, 612
Meetings at work, 2:474–475
accomplishment striving, meeting demands/employee well-being and, **2:**475
effectiveness of, **2:**475
impromptu meetings, **2:**474
information-giving meetings, **2:**474
monitoring/decision-making meetings, **2:**474
problem-solving meetings, **2:**474
recognition meetings, **2:**474
reporting structures/power differentials and, **2:**474
research on, **2:**475
socialization/relationship-building purposes and, **2:**474
time element in, **2:**474
training meetings, **2:**474
types of, **2:**474
See also Group decision-making quality and performance; Group decision-making techniques; Group dynamics and processes; Groups
Meglino, B. M., **2:**517
Meindl, J. R., **1:**333
Member assistance programs (MAPs), **1:**189
Member-2-Member program, **2:**748
Mental Measurement Yearbook (MMY), **1:**411
Mental model similarity, **2:**788–789
See also Concept mapping; Team mental model
Mentoring, 1:7, 447, 2:475–478
benefits of, **2:**476
definition of, **2:**475
employee proactive socialization and, **2:**746
formal mentoring, **2:**478
functions of, **2:**476
gender and, **2:**476–477
measurement of, **2:**476
mentor attributes, **2:**477
mentoring processes, factors in, **2:**476–478
organizational benefits of, **2:**476
organizational factors in, **2:**478
perceived mentor-protégé similarity and, **2:**477
protégé attributes and, **2:**477
psychosocial mentoring and, **2:**477
race and, **2:**477
stages in, **2:**476
telecommuting and, **2:**793–794

**Mergers, acquisitions, and strategic alliances,
2:478–480**, 777, 896
acquisition, definition of, **2:**478–479
cultural signs of merger syndrome, **2:**479–480
effectiveness of, **2:**479
merger, definition of, **2:**478
merger syndrome and, **2:**479–480
organizational signs of merger syndrome, **2:**479
personal signs of merger syndrome, **2:**479
strategic alliance, definition of, **2:**479
successful outcomes of, **2:**480
transition management and, **2:**480
Merit rewards, **2:**791
Message processing models, **1:**39
Meta-analysis, 2:480–483
artifacts, influence of, **2:**483
behavioral science research and, **2:**481
file drawer problem and, **2:**481
inferential statistics and, **2:**481, 483
limitations of, **2:**483
moderator variables, presence of, **2:**483
narrative review process and, **2:**481
null hypothesis and, **2:**481
number of studies in, **2:**483
sampling errors and, **2:**482–483
significance testing and, **2:**480–481
steps in, **2:**481–482
target populations and, **2:**482
test statistic, value of, **2:**482–483
type I/type II errors and, **2:**481, 482
See also Descriptive statistics; Inferential statistics; Statistical power
Meta-analytical techniques, **2:**654
Met-expectations theory, **2:**669
Metropolitan Achievement Test, **2:**755
Meyer, J. W., **1:**277
Micro organizational behaviors, **1:**39–40, 41
Microsoft Corporation, **1:**40
Microsoft Disk Operating System (MS-DOS), **1:**325
Microworld simulations, **2:**723, 724
Middlemist, R. D., **2:**505
Midvale Steel Company, **2:**692
Miles, G., **1:**309
Milgram, S., **1:**220
Military applications, **1:**29–30, 34, 457,
2:517, 518, 613, 627–628, 755–756
Miller, D., **1:**68
Miner, J. B., **2:**509, 839
Minimalist model of business, **1:**115
Minnesota Importance Questionnaire (MIQ), **1:**67, **2:**622
Minnesota Multiphasic Personality Inventory
(MMPI), **2:**612, 860
Minnesota Occupational Classification System, III, **1:**422
Minnesota Satisfaction Questionnaire (MSQ), **1:**412, **2:**622
Minorities. *See* Adverse impact/disparate
treatment/discrimination at work; Diversity training;
Diversity in the workplace; Race; Race norming
Mira, E., **1:**309, 310
Mirvis, P. H., **2:**479, **2:**563

Mischel, W., **2:**613
Mission statements, **2:**764
Misspecificaiton fallacies, **2:**493
Mitchell, W. N., **1:**4
Mitra, S. K., **1:**319
Mixed-determinants model, **2:**496
Mixed standard scales (MSS), **2:**602
Mobbing behavior, **1:**311
Model Employment Termination Act (META), **1:**198
Modeling. *See* Job modeling; Multilevel modeling; Social
    cognitive theory; Strategic performance modeling
Moderator and mediator variables, 2:483–485
    mediator variables and, **2:**484
    meta-analysis and, **2:**483
    moderator variables, **2:**484–485
Modernist qualitative paradigm, **2:**649
Moede, W., **1:**309
Monitoring feedback, **1:**250
Monitoring meetings, **2:**474
Monopoly face of a union, **1:**349
Monte Carlo simulation, **2:**723, 724
Mood, 2:485–487
    absenteeism/withdrawal behaviors and, **2:**487
    attention to detail/vigilant information processing and, **2:**487
    cognition and, **2:**486
    decision-making and, **2:**487
    depressive realism effect and, **2:**486
    group affect and, **2:**487
    influences on, **2:**486
    job performance and, **2:**487
    performance and, **2:**486–487
    performance appraisals and, **2:**487
    personality and, **2:**486
    prosocial behaviors and, **2:**486–487
    research methodologies and, **2:**485
    theoretical models of, **2:**485
    See also Affective traits; Contextual performance/prosocial
        behavior/organizational citizenship behavior; Group
        dynamics and processes; Withdrawal behaviors
Moore, B. V., **1:**314
Moral action, **1:**216–218
Morale, 2:488–489
    customer satisfaction and, **2:**488
    definition of, **2:**488
    dimensions of attitudes and, **2:**488
    downsizing and, **2:**489
    employee-management relations and, **2:**488
    happy/productive worker concept and, **2:**488
    improvement strategies, **2:**489
    research on, **2:**488–489
    See also Attitudes and beliefs; Job satisfaction;
        Organizational climate; Organizational commitment
Moral obligation, **2:**574
Moral philosophy, **1:**112, 113, 215
Moral standards, **1:**115, 116, **2:**731
Moral taint, **1:**153
Moral virtue, **1:**216
Moreland, R. L., **2:**746
Morgeson, F. P., **2:**635, 729

Morris, R., **1:**256
Motivating Potential Score (MPS), **1:**385
Motivation:
    control theory and, **1:**108–109
    creativity at work and, **1:**127
    emotion regulation, action theory and, **1:**6
    expectancy motivation, **1:**111–112
    goals and, **1:**108
    race differences, test-taking motivation and, **1:**28
    test-taking motivation, applicant reactions and, **1:**27
    valence-instrumentality-expectancy theory of test-taking, **1:**27
    See also Compensation; Expectancy theory of work
        motivation; Intrinsic and extrinsic work motivation; Job
        design; Motivational traits; Work motivation
Motivational Trait Questionnaire, **2:**491
Motivational traits, 2:489–492
    action-state orientation and, **2:**491
    approach/avoidance motivations and, **2:**490, 491
    behavioral activation system and, **2:**490
    behavioral inhibition system and, **2:**490
    conceptualizations of, **2:**490–492
    distal influence, work behaviors and, **2:**490
    goal orientation and, **2:**490–491
    learning goal orientation and, **2:**491
    motivational trait theory and, **2:**491
    performance goal orientation and, **2:**491
    regulatory focus theory and, **2:**491
    self-determination theory and, **2:**492
    stable/nonability nature of, **2:**492
    See also Need for achievement, power, and
        affiliation; Work motivation
Motivator-hygiene theory (MHT), **1:**392–393
Motorola Company, **2:**815
Motowidlo, S. J., **1:**103, 104, **2:**727
Mount, M., **1:**55
MULITLOG program, **1:**374
Mullen, B., **1:**284, 285, 286
Multiattribute judgment, **2:**629, 630
Multiattribute utility theory (MAUT), **1:**424, **2:**630
Multidimensional forced-choice (MFC) item formats, **1:**337
Multilevel appeal systems. *See* Employee grievance systems
Multilevel modeling, 2:492–494
    contextual fallacies and, **2:**493
    cross-level fallacies and, **2:**493
    emergence process/properties and, **2:**493–494
    hierarchical structures and, **2:**492–493
    ignoring multilevel structures and, **2:**493
    misspecifiction fallacies and, **2:**493
    multilevel relationships, types of, **2:**494
    See also Multilevel modeling techniques
Multilevel modeling techniques, 2:494–496
    applications of, **2:**496
    hierarchical linear modeling and, **2:**495–496, 495 (figure)
    longitudinal research questions and, **2:**496
    mixed-determinants model and, **2:**496
    nested data, statistical consequences of, **2:**495
    See also Multilevel modeling
Multimethod Job Design Questionnaire, **1:**382
Multinational companies (MNCs), **1:**232–233, 276–277

Multiple hurdles strategy, **1:**195–196, **2:**695–696
Multiple indicator/multiple cause models, **2:**773–774
Multiple Job Design Questionnaire (MJDQ), **1:**394
Multiple regression, **2:**629
Multisource/multirater feedback systems, **2:**567, 592, 597, 605
Multitrait assessment tools, **2:**613
Multitrait-multimethod (MTMM) **matrix, 2:497–500**, 809
    computation of, **2:**497
    confirmatory factor analysis and, **2:**498, 500
    convergent validity and, **2:**497, 498
    correlation matrix and, **2:**497
    discriminant validity and, **2:**497–498
    industrial/organizational psychology and, **2:**497
    method effects and, **2:**497
    quantification of criteria and, **2:**498
    random errors of measurement and, **2:**498
    statistical evaluation of, **2:**498, 499 (table)
    validity, evaluation of, **2:**498
    See also Quantitative research approach
Multivariate research design, **1:**452
Mumford, M., **1:**126
Münsterberg, H., **1:**309, 313, **2:**526
Murray, H. A., **1:**30, 34, **2:**508, 608, 893
Muscio, B., **1:**321
Mutual obligation, **2:**549, 645, 740
Myers, C., **2:**692
Myers, M. S., **2:**518
Myers-Briggs Type Indicator, **1:**67, **2:**613

N concept, **2:**483
Narrative performance appraisals, **2:**603
Narrative review process, **2:**481
Narrow cognitive ability factors, **1:**77
    predictive validity of, **1:**78
    See also Cognitive abilities
National Association of Temporary and Staffing Services, **2:**593
National Board of Health, **1:**309
National Board of Occupational Safety and Health, **1:**311
National Center for O*NET Development, **2:**530
National Commission for the Protection of Human Subjects of Biomedical and Behavioral Research, **1:**220
National Conference on Applied Master's Training in Psychology, **2:**913, 915, 916
National Conference of Commissioners on Uniform State Laws, **1:**198
National Council on Measurement in Education, **2:**641
National Council of Measurement Used in Education, **2:**860
National Institute of Industrial Psychology, **1:**309
National Institute for Occupational Safety and Health (NIOSH)/**Occupational Safety and Health Administration** (OSHA), **2:501–504**, 771
    employees/divisions in, **2:**503
    functions of, **2:**502, 503–504
    mission of, **2:**502, 503
    occupational health psychology training programs, **2:**527
    organizational structure, **2:**501–502
    quality of work life and, **2:**652
National Institutes of Health (NIH), **1:**220

National Labor Relations Act (NLRA) of 1935, **1:**437, **2:**852
    administration of, **1:**438–439
    appropriate bargaining unit principle, **1:**437
    basic principles of, **1:**437–438
    employee choice principle, **1:**437
    exclusive representation principle, **1:**437
    implications for individuals and organizations, **1:**439
    majority rule principle, **1:**347
    National Labor Relations Board and, **1:**438
    rights under, **1:**438
    union/management determination of terms/conditions of employment principle, **1:**438
    See also Union commitment; Unions
National Labor Relations Board (NLRB), **1:**438
National Labor Union, **2:**851
National Longitudinal Survey of Youth (NLSY), **2:**844
National Occupational Research Agenda (NORA), **2:**501, 502
National Personal Protective Technology Laboratory, **2:**502
National Research Council, **1:**219
National Safety Council, **2:**525
National Training Laboratories (NTL), **1:**328
Naturalistic observation, 2:504–505
    advantages/disadvantages of, **2:**505
    coding process, collaboration in, **2:**504
    data analysis in, **2:**505
    focus/nature of observation and, **2:**505
    participant observation and, **2:**504
    reliability/validity of, **2:**505
    research, elements of, **2:**504–505
    researcher/observer involvement levels and, **2:**504
    time element in, **2:**504
    See also Qualitative research approach;
        Quantitative research approach
Natural language processing, **1:**175
Natural rights theory, **1:**115
Nature vs. nurture debate, **1:**270
Navy Personnel Research and Development Center (NPRDC), **1:**315
Navy Training Systems Center, **1:**316
Naylor, J. C., **2:**856
Naylor-Shine index of utility, **2:**856
Nazi Germany, **1:**317
Need for achievement, power, and affiliation, 2:506–508
    achievement needs, **2:**506–507
    affiliation need and, **2:**507–508
    implicit motives and, **2:**506
    power need and, **2:**507
    self-attributed need and, **2:**506
Need allocation rule, **2:**571
Need fulfillment, **2:**620
Need satisfaction, **2:**509
Need theories of work motivation, 2:508–511, 893
    current research on, **2:**510–511
    esteem needs and, **2:**510
    existence/relatedness/growth needs and, **2:**510
    hierarchical theories of, **2:**509–510
    love needs and, **2:**510
    need, behavior and, **2:**508–509
    need, definition of, **2:**508

need satisfaction and, **2:**509
prepotent needs and, **2:**509–510
self-actualization need and, **2:**510
typologies of needs and, **2:**509
See also Motivational traits; Need for achievement, power, and affiliation; Personality; Work motivation
Needs analysis, **1:**207
Needs assessment. *See* Training needs assessment and analysis
Needs-supplies fit, **2:**615, 618–619
Negative-affectivity employees, **1:**3, 124
Negative feedback loops, **1:**107
Negative reinforcement, **2:**674
Negotiation, mediation, and arbitration, 2:511–514
best alternative to a negotiated agreement and, **2:**512
binding arbitration and, **2:**513
cognitive/behavioral perspectives on, **2:**512
distribution task and, **2:**512
hybrid processes of, **2:**513–514
imposition of settlement and, **2:**514
information sharing and, **2:**513
integration tasks and, **2:**512
joint problem solving and, **2:**512
mediation/arbitration, **2:**513–514
mixed-motive negotiations and, **2:**513
mythical fixed pie perceptions and, **2:**513
negotiation, **2:**511–513
negotiator interests and, **2:**512
Olympian negotiators and, **2:**511–512
psychologically-oriented perspective on, **2:**512
reservation point and, **2:**512
tasks of negotiation, **2:**512–513
third-party processes and, **2:**511, 513–514
See also Conflict management; Judgment and decision-making process
Neisser, U., **2:**634
Nelson, D., **1:**222
NEO Personality Inventory, **1:**346
Nested data, **2:**495
Networking, 1:7, 2:514–516
analysis of, **2:**516
behaviors in, **2:**515
career outcomes and, **2:**515
definition of, **2:**514–515
diversity among contacts and, **2:**516
hardiness and, **1:**3–4
individual employment status/career mobility and, **2:**515
networking comfort/intensity and, **2:**515
political skill and, **2:**576
power/influence of contacts and, **2:**516
size of networks and, **2:**515
strength of ties in, **2:**515–516
structural characteristics in, **2:**515–516
technology for, **1:**175, 176
See also Career development; Job search
Neuroticism trait, **1:**52, 110, 187, **2:**609, 710
Newcomer orientation. *See* New employee orientation
New employee orientation, 2:516–518
control of thoughts/feelings and, **2:**518
definition of, **2:**516–517

emotion-focused method and, **2:**517–518
organizational socialization and, **2:**517
program design, **2:**517–518
rehearsal of actions and, **2:**518
role modeling and, **2:**518
ROPES (Realistic Orientation Programs for new Employee Stress) approach to, **2:**517
short-term process of, **2:**517
targeting specific stressors and, **2:**518
See also Organizational socialization; Organizational socialization tactics; Realistic job preview (RJP); Training
Newman, J., **2:**772
New pay movement, **1:**83
Niederhoffer, A., **2:**563
Nisbett, R., **1:**142
Nishii, L. H., **1:**139
Noise, **2:**653
Nominal group technique, **1:**290–291
Nominal scales, **2:**469
Nomological networks, 2:518–519
description of, **2:**519
example of, **2:**519
prediction testing and, **2:**519
research based on, **2:**519
See also Construct; Criterion theory; Job performance models; Validation strategies
Nomothetic science, **2:**608
Nonaka, I., **1:**449
No-Name Group, **1:**315
Nonexperimental designs, 2:519–521
assumed causes, measurement of, **2:**520
assumed dependent variables, measurement of, **2:**520
attributes of, **2:**520–521
causal inference and, **2:**521
extraneous/confounding variables and, **2:**520–521
nonrandom assignment of participants/absence of conditions and, **2:**520
See also Experimental designs; Quasi-experimental designs
Nonmaleficence, **1:**216
Nonparametric techniques, **1:**152
Nonprobability sample, **2:**689, 691
Nord, W. R., **2:**672
Norm of reciprocity, **1:**104, 441, **2:**549, 733–734, 753
Normalization process, **1:**154
Norman, W. T., **1:**53
Normative assessment, **2:**612–613
Normative commitment scale (NCS), **2:**549
Normative models of decision making and leadership, 2:521–523
balanced scale conceptualization of, **2:**521–522, 522 (figure)
managerial application of, **2:**522, 523
practical implications of, **2:**523
scientific implications of, **2:**522–523
See also Judgment and decision-making process; Leadership and supervision
Normative organizational commitment, **2:**548, 549, 550
Normative stakeholder theory, **1:**116

Normative vs. ipsative measurement, 2:523–524
  forced-choice technique, 2:524
  ipsative measurement, 2:524
  normative measurement, 2:523–524
  See also Individual differences; Integrity testing; Measurement
    scales; Personality assessment
Norming. *See* Race norming
Norms. *See* Institutionalized norms; Norm of
    reciprocity; Social norms and conformity
North American Free Trade Agreement
    (NAFTA), 1:276, 316, 423
North American Industry Classification
    System (NAICS), 1:423
Norton, D., 1:45
Novaco, R. W., 2:518
Null Hypothesis, 1:92–93, 351, 2:481, 654, 758
Numerical representation of correlations,
    2:470–472, 472 (tables)
Nuremberg Code, 1:220
Nye, J. L., 334

O*NET. *See* Occupational Information Network (O*NET)
Obliging style of conflict management, 1:98, 99
O'Brien, G., 1:321
Observation. *See* Naturalistic observation
Occupational alcoholism programs (OAPs), 1:188
Occupational Aptitude Patterns (OAP) Map, 1:422
Occupational Employment Statistics (OES), 1:423
Occupational health psychology (OHP), 1:66–67, **2:525–528**
  definition of, 2:526
  future challenges in, 2:527–528
  historical roots of, 2:526
  inclusive/interdisciplinary nature of, 2:526, 527
  industrial/organizational psychology and, 2:525, 527, 528
  occupational stress and, 1:66–67
  preventive management concept and, 2:526
  primary prevention and, 2:526
  research/practices, survey of, 2:526–527
  secondary interventions and, 2:526
  tertiary preventions and, 2:526
  training programs, North America/Europe, 2:527
  See also Quality of work life (QWL)
Occupational ideology tactics, 1:154
Occupational Information Network (O*NET),
    1:316, 379, 382, 421–422, **2:528–531**
  ability rating scale and, 530 (figure), 2:530
  career exploration tools and, 2:530–531
  content of, 2:529–530
  data sources in, 2:520
  descriptors, content model and, 2:529–530
  Dictionary of Occupational Titles and, 2:528–529
  job-oriented variables and, 2:529–530
  O*NET OnLine, 2:530
  occupations taxonomy and, 2:529
  system components in, 2:530–531
  worker-oriented variables and, 2:529
  See also Dictionary of Occupational Titles; Job analysis;
    Person-vocation (PV) fit; Work values
Occupational Outlook Handbook (OOH), 1:422–423

Occupational Safety and Health Act (OSHA)
    of 1970, 1:330, 2:502, 525
Occupational Safety and Health Administration
    (OSHA), 1:xxxv, 2:502–504, 898
Occupational stress theory, 1:179
Occupational tailoring. *See* Selection, occupational tailoring
Occupations. See *Dictionary of Occupational
    Titles* (DOT); Dirty work
Odbert, H. S., 1:53
Office of Federal Contract Compliance
    Programs (OFCCP), 1:15, 194, 2:846
Office for Human Research Protections (OHRP), 1:220
Office of Personnel Management, 1:247
Office for Protection From Research Risks (OPRR), 1:220
Office of Strategic Services (OSS), 1:30, 31, 314, 342
Off-shoring, 1:277
Off-site leadership development programs, 1:447–448
Ohio State Leadership Studies, 1:48–49, 458
Older worker issues, **2:531–534**
  absenteeism and, 2:532
  age discrimination and, 1:533
  bridge employment and, 2:533, 534
  career/work-life issues and, 2:533
  chronic health conditions and, 2:532, 534
  cognitive abilities and, 2:532
  job satisfaction and, 2:532
  normal aging, changes due to, 2:531–532
  occupational stress and, 2:532–533
  performance/motivation, declines in, 2:532
  personality traits and, 2:532
  retirement decisions and, 2:533–534
  retirement policies and, 2:531
  training/retraining and, 2:533
  workforce demographics and, 2:531
  See also Age Discrimination in Employment Act (ADEA)
    of 1967; Careers; Retirement; Stereotyping; Stress
Oldham, G. R., 1:384, 393, 2:840
Olson, R., 1:306
Olympian negotiators, 2:511–512
Ones, D. S., 1:347
On-the-job training (OJT), 2:824
Open communication style, 1:367
Open systems perspective, 2:749
Open-ended data collection approaches.
    See Content coding; Survey approach
Openness trait, 1:52, 2:609, 746
Operant conditioning, 1:38, 2:672
Operational criterion, 1:132
Operationalization of integrity, 1:356–357
Operative image system, 1:6
Optimism and pessimism, **2:534–536**
  background issues on, 2:534–535
  dimensionality of, 2:535–536
  expectations, predictors of success and, 2:534
  measurement instruments for, 2:535, 536
  organizational cynicism and, 2:563–564
  work setting and, 2:536
  See also Positive psychology applied to work
Option response functions (ORFs), 1:373

Ordinal scales, **2:**469
Ordinary least squares regression, **2:**629
O'Reilly, C., III, **2:**619, 620
Organ, D., **1:**103, 104, 106
Organic models of organizational structure, **2:**587
Organization Development Institute, **2:**566
Organization-directed behaviors, **1:**104
Organization-wide competency model, **1:**86
Organizational behavior (OB), **2:**537
    affirmative action programs and, **1:**16
    current research topics in, **2:**537
    history of interest in, **2:**537
    individual core self-evaluations and, **1:**14
    micro/macro organizational behavior, **1:**39–40
    subfields of, **2:**537
    See also Attraction-selection-attrition (ASA) model;
        Hawthorne Studies/Hawthorne effect; Human relations
        movement; Human resource management (HRM);
        Organizational citizenship behavior; Organizational
        development; Scientific management
Organizational behavior management (OBM), **2:**538–540
    appraisal/motivation, behavioral approach to, **2:**539
    behavior analysis and, **2:**538, 539
    injury reduction, measuring safety performance and, **2:**540
    positive reinforcement programs, work productivity
        and, **2:**538–539
    scientist-practitioner model and, **2:**538–539
    specifying/measuring performance, steps in, **2:**539–540
    teaching techniques, student success and, **2:**540
    See also Reinforcement theory of work motivation
Organizational change, **2:**541–543
    analysis of, **2:**541
    asymmetry of change and, **2:**543
    attitudes toward change and, **2:**542
    competency models and, **1:**86
    conflict management and, **1:**97
    content of change and, **2:**541–542
    context of change and, **2:**542
    cynicism and, **2:**564
    diverse experiences of, **2:**541
    environmental level change and, **2:**541
    episodic change and, **2:**543
    individual level change and, **2:**541
    learning organizations and, **1:**450
    linearity of change and, **2:**542
    merger syndrome and, **2:**479
    nature of, **2:**542–543
    organizational level change and, **2:**541
    outcomes of change and, **2:**542
    pace of change and, **2:**542
    process of change and, **2:**542
    sequence of changes and, **2:**542
    shock/anger/resistance/acceptance model of
        change and, **2:**543, 544
    themes of, **2:**541–542
    three-stage model of change and, **2:**541
    turbulence and, **2:**543
    See also Organizational change, resistance to;
        Organizational development

Organizational change, resistance to, **2:**543–544
    clear/consistent/timely communication and, **2:**544
    communication strategy, delineation of, **2:**544
    employee input/reactions and, **2:**544
    models of reactions to change, **2:**543–544
    reasons for resistance, **2:**543
    shock/anger/resistance/acceptance model of
        change and, **2:**543, 544
    three-stage model of transition, **2:**544
    training/support for, **2:**544
    See also Downsizing; Morale; Organizational change;
        Organizational climate; Organizational culture;
        Organizational cynicism; Organizational development;
        Organizational retaliatory behavior; Survivor syndrome
Organizational citizenship behaviors (OCBs),
    1:103–106, **2:**519, 550, 572, 735, 742
    See also Contextual performance/prosocial
        behavior/organizational citizenship behavior;
        Corporate social responsibility
Organizational climate, **2:**545–548
    climate for safety and, **2:**546
    climate for service and, **1:**144, **2:**546
    climate strength and, **2:**545, 547
    definition of, **2:**545
    ethical climate and, **2:**546–547
    existence of, **2:**547
    organizational culture and, **2:**561
    research data and, **2:**547
    sharedness criterion and, **2:**547
    strategic organizational focus and, **2:**547–548
    See also Organizational culture
Organizational commitment (OC), **1:**2, **2:**548–551
    absenteeism and, **2:**550
    affective commitment, **2:**548, 549, 550
    commitment profile and, **2:**549
    conceptualization of, **2:**548–549
    consequences of, **2:**549–550
    continuance commitment, **2:**548, 549, 550
    cultural factors and, **2:**550
    development of, **2:**549
    employee retention and, **2:**550
    employee well-being and, **2:**550
    employee work behavior and, **2:**550
    future research topics and, **2:**550
    job performance and, **2:**550
    measurement instruments for, **2:**549
    normative commitment, **2:**548, 549, 550
    organizational citizenship behaviors and, **2:**550
    reciprocity norm and, **2:**549
    three-component model of, **2:**548–549
    training costs and, **2:**549
    virtual organizations and, **2:**871–872
    work experiences and, **2:**549
    See also Job satisfaction; Organizational justice;
        Withdrawal behaviors, turnover
Organizational Commitment Questionnaire (OCQ), **2:**549
Organizational communication, formal, **2:**551–555
    ambiguity in interpretation and, **2:**552, 553
    change function and, **2:**554

definition of, **2:**551
distortion in communication and, **2:**552
ethical issues in, **2:**553
expected communication patterns in, **2:**556
formal organizations, characteristics of, **2:**555
functional approach to, **2:**553–554
informal vs. formal organizational communication
    and, **2:**555–556
information overload and, **2:**552
information transfer process and, **2:**551–552
meaning-centered approach to, **2:**554–555
message function and, **2:**553–554
organizing function and, **2:**554
relationship function and, **2:**554
research on, **2:**551–553
shared meaning and, **2:**553
SMCR (sender/message/channel/receiver) model of, **2:**552
strategic control function and, **2:**553
transactional process of communication and, **2:**552–553
See also Organizational communication, informal
Organizational communication, informal, **2:**555–557
actual communication patterns in, **2:**556
current research topics in, **2:**557
formal organizations, characteristics of, **2:**555
formal vs. informal organizational communication
    and, **2:**555–556
grapevine communication, **2:**556–557
informal organizational practices and, **2:**555
perspectives on, **2:**556
rationally specified communication and, **2:**555
rumor mills and, **2:**557
study of, rationale for, **2:**556
traditional formal communication and, **2:**556
virtual organizations and, **2:**871–872
See also Organizational communication, formal
Organizational culture, **2:**558–562
definition of, **2:**558
feedback-oriented culture, **2:**606
leadership role in, **2:**560–561
measurement of, **2:**558–560
organizational climate and, **2:**561
qualitative/anthropological approach to, **2:**559
quantitative/standardized approach to, **2:**559–560
significance of, **2:**561–562
societal culture and, **2:**561
See also Attraction-selection-attrition (ASA) model;
    Global Leadership and Organizational Behavior
    Effectiveness (GLOBE) project; Organizational
    climate; Organizational cynicism
Organizational Culture Profile (OCP), **1:**389, **2:**619, 620
Organizational cynicism, **2:**562–564
command cynics and, **2:**563
contract violation framework for, **2:**563
cynical hostility and, **2:**562
definitions of, **2:**562
flavor-of-the-month change initiative and, **2:**562
hard-bitten cynics and, **2:**563
individual psychology/social processes and, **2:**563–564
organizational change processes and, **2:**564

origins of, **2:**562
personality trait perspective and, **2:**562–563
research on, **2:**562–563
self-fulfilling prophecy and, **2:**562
squeezed cynics and, **2:**563
targets of, **2:**563
types of, **2:**563
work/occupations perspective on, **2:**563
See also Organizational change; Organizational
    change, resistance to
Organizational development (OD), **1:**315, **2:**564–568
action research paradigm and, **2:**565
Burke-Litwin model of organizational
    performance/change and, **2:**566
change process and, **2:**541, 564, 565
consulting approach, phases of, **2:**566–568
data-driven nature of, **2:**565
definition of, **2:**565
external organizational environment and, **2:**566
systems perspective and, **2:**565–566
transactional factors in, **2:**566
transformational factors in, **2:**566
values-based approach of, **2:**566
See also Human resource management (HRM);
    Organizational behavior (OB)
Organizational image, **2:**568–570
applicant attraction and, **2:**569
competitive leverage and, **2:**569
components of, **2:**569
consequences of, **2:**569–570
consumers' product choices and, **2:**569
definition of, **2:**568–569
development of, **2:**569
employee attitude/behavior and, **2:**569–570
objective attributes and, **2:**569
organizational performance advantages and, **2:**570
organizational reputation and, **2:**570
organization's perceived identity and, **2:**570
recruitment and, **2:**668
related constructs, **2:**570
stakeholders/corporate audiences and, **2:**568–569
trait-related inferences and, **2:**569
See also Person-organization (PO) fit;
    Self-concept theory of work motivation
Organizational justice, **2:**570–574
control model and, **2:**573
counterproductive work behaviors and, **1:**121,
    122, 123–124, 125
current research on, **2:**574
definition of, **2:**570
deontic justice and, **2:**574
distributive justice rules and, **1:**26, 121, **2:**571
economic self-interest and, **2:**573
equality allocation rule and, **2:**571
equity allocation rule and, **2:**571
group-value model of, **2:**573, 574
interactional justice rules and, **2:**571–572
interactions among types of justice and, **2:**572–573
judgment and decision-making process and, **1:**425–426

main effects of justice and, **2:**572
multifoci model of effects and, **2:**572
need allocation rule and, **2:**571
procedural justice rules and, **1:**26, 121, **2:**571
referent other and, **2:**5712
significance of, **2:**573–574
social exchange theory and, **2:**573–574
two-factor model of effects and, **2:**572
types of, **2:**570–572
worker attitudes/behavior and, **2:**570
See also Justice in teams; Organizational retaliatory
    behavior; Social exchange theory
Organizational performance:
affirmative action programs and, **1:**17
conflict and, **1:**96
organizational citizenship behaviors and, **1:**106
organizational improvement and, **1:**45, 52
See also Benchmarking; Organizational culture;
    Performance appraisal
Organizational politics, 2:574–576
apparent sincerity and, **2:**576
interpersonal influence and, **2:**576
networking ability and, **2:**576
perceptions of, **2:**575
political behavior research and, **2:**575
political skill and, **2:**575–576
reactions to, **2:**575
social astuteness and, **2:**576
theory/research on, **2:**575
work-related outcomes and, **2:**575
See also Person-environment (PE) fit
Organizational retaliatory behavior, 2:576–579
definition of, **2:**576–577
justice theory and, **2:**577–578
leader-member exchange theory and, **2:**578
legitimization of, **2:**577–578
positive outcomes of, **2:**578
prevention strategies, **2:**578–579
situational context and, **2:**577
social exchange theory and, **2:**578
unfair treatment at work and, **2:**577
See also Counterproductive work behaviors (CWBs);
    Leader-member exchange (LMX)
    theory; Organizational justice; Social
    exchange theory; Workplace incivility
Organizational sensemaking, 2:579–581
action-driven processes of, **2:**581
basic process recipe for, **2:**580–581
belief-driven processes of, **2:**581
correct viewpoints and, **2:**579
definitions of, **2:**579–580
emerging reality and, **2:**579–580
enacted environments and, **2:**580
extracted/partial knowledge and, **2:**580
identity construction and, **2:**580
ongoing/negotiated process and, **2:**580
plausible explanation vs. scientific
    discovery and, **2:**580
properties of, **2:**580

research in, **2:**581
retrospection/reflection and, **2:**580
social process of, **2:**580
Organizational socialization (OS), **2:**517, **581–583**
content approaches to, **2:**582–583
definition of, **2:**581–582
individual differences and, **2:**582
insider actions and, **2:**582
newcomer actions and, **2:**582
newcomer learning and, **2:**582
newcomer role orientations and, **2:**582
organizational culture and, **2:**558
pre-entry/anticipatory socialization and, **2:**582
process approaches to, **2:**582
proximal/distal outcomes and, **2:**582–583
work values and, **2:**909
See also Feedback seeking; Group development;
    New employee orientation; Organizational
    socialization tactics; Socialization; Socialization,
    employee proactive behaviors
Organizational socialization tactics, 2:583–585
change process in, **2:**582–584
cultural information and, **2:**583
definition of, **2:**583
dimensions of, institutional vs. individual
    approaches, **2:**584–585
information seeking actions and, **2:**585
insiders, categories of, **2:**584–585
intersection of outsider/insider forces and, **2:**583
newcomer learning and, **2:**585
personality factors and, **2:**585
positive accommodation factors and, **2:**583
research on, **2:**583–585
social information and, **2:**583
task information and, **2:**583
typology of, **2:**584
unsuccessful socialization and, **2:**583
See also New employee orientation; Organizational
    socialization (OS); Socialization, employee
    proactive behaviors; Training methods
Organizational structure, 2:585–589
bureaucratic structure and, **2:**588
centralization and, **2:**586
citizenship behaviors and, **1:**2
complexity and, **2:**586
conceptualizations of, **2:**587–588
contingency theory and, **2:**586–587, 588
definition of, **2:**585–586
departmentalization and, **2:**586
elements of, **2:**586
environmental factors and, **2:**587, 589
factors relevant to, **2:**586–587
flat organizations and, **2:**586
formalization and, **2:**586
globalization and, **2:**589
height/hierarchical levels and, **2:**586, 588
interdependency/integration and, **2:**586
measures of, **2:**588
mechanistic models of structure and, **2:**587, 588

operating process of an industry and, 2:588
organic models of structure and, 2:587
physical dispersion and, 2:586
role of, 2:588–589
size of an organization and, 2:587
span of control and, 2:586
specialization requirements and, 2:586
strategies of an organization and, 2:587
technological factors and, 2:587, 589
unity of direction concept and, 2:588
See also Groups; Organizational climate; Organizational
    communication; Organizational culture
Organizational surveys, 1:101, **589–592**
branching techniques and, 2:590
causal relationships, testing of, 2:590
close-ended questions and, 2:590
content of, 2:590
electronic versions of, 2:590–591
linkage research models and, 2:590
methodology of, 2:590–591
normative data and, 2:591
organizational development, action taking and, 2:591–592
pulse surveys, 2:591
purpose/history of, 2:589–590
response rates for, 2:591
service-profit chain and, 2:590
See also Feedback; Organizational development;
    360-degree feedback
Organizing communication, 2:554
Orthogonal research design, 1:452
Oslo Work Research Institute, 1:311
Oswald, F. L., 1:337
Otis, A., 1:29
Out-group members, 1:360, 361, 364
Outsourcing, 1:277, 2:551, **592–594**
advantages/disadvantages of, 2:593
best-of-class processes and, 2:593
coopetition concept and, 2:592–593
development of, 2:592–593
foreign-local subsidiary model and, 2:593
international outsourcing and, 2:593
lack of control and, 2:593
military applications of, 2:592–593
out-tasking and, 2:593
temporary work and, 2:593–594
virtual teams and, 2:872
weakened economic power and, 2:592
Overidentified model, 2:774
Overpayment, 1:213
Overt integrity measures, 2:636

p-values, 1:152
Pace University, Academy of Management, 1:4–5
Page-turner tests, 1:89
Paired comparisons, 2:602–603, 662
Palmer, D. K., 1:199
Panel studies, 1:463
Parallel tests, 12:75–76
Parametric techniques, 1:152

Parasuraman, A., 1:143
Parks, L., 1:261
Parry, J., 1:310
PARSCALE program, 1:374
Parsons, F., 2:621
Parsons, T., 1:115
Participant observation, 2:504
Participative leadership, 1:261, 262, 2:595–596, 726
Participatory ergonomics, 1:208
Passive management-by-exception (MBE-P), 2:835
Pasteur, L., 2:733
Past experience, 2:818
Path analysis, 2:773
Path diagrams, 2:774
Path-goal theory, 2:B595–596
definition of, 2:595
empirical support for, 2:596
leader behaviors in, 2:595–596
reformulated theory, 2:596
situational moderators in, 2:596
success of, 2:596
Paton, D., 2:581
Patrick, W. D., 2:526
Pattern-and-practice claim, 1:9
Pay equity, 1:81, 82
    See also Compensation; Equal Pay Act (EPA)
        of 1963; Pay Equity Act of 1988
Pay Equity Act of 1988, 1:82
Pay-for-performance, 1:83, 262–263, 339, 2:692, 693
Pay satisfaction measurement, 1:84
Pay schedules. *See* Compensation
Pearson, K., 1:313
Pearson product-moment correlation, 2:472, 473 (table)
Peer communication, 1:364–365
Pelto, P. J., 1:139
Peng, K., 1:142
Perceived organizational support (POS), 2:883–884
Perceptions-goal discrepancies, 1:108–109
Perceptual biases. *See* Rating errors and perceptual
    biases; Stereotyping
Performance appraisal, 2:597–598
history of, 2:597
performance management systems and, 2:598
purpose of, 2:597
rater sources and, 2:597–598
rating content/format and, 2:598
system characteristics and, 2:598
variations in approaches of, 2:597–598
See also Criterion theory; Electronic performance monitoring;
    Job analysis; Job knowledge testing; Organizational
    performance; Performance appraisal, objective indexes;
    Performance appraisal, subjective indexes; 360-degree
    feedback
Performance appraisal, objective indexes, 2:598–601
absenteeism monitoring and, 2:599–600
deficient indexes and, 2:600
effectiveness of, 2:600, 601
electronic performance monitoring systems and, 2:599
employee accident rates and, 2:600

ineffective feedback and, **2:**600
personnel data and, **2:**599–600
production measures and, **2:**599
quality of work measures and, **2:**599
quantity of work measures and, **2:**599
situational factors and, **2:**600, 601
turnover rates and, **2:**600
types of, **2:**598–600
See also Job analysis; Performance appraisal,
    subjective indexes
Performance appraisal, subjective indexes, 2:601–604
alternative techniques and, **2:**603
behaviorally anchored rating scales and, **2:**601–602
comparison of approaches and, **2:**603–604
employee comparison methods and, **2:**602–603
forced-choice scales and, **2:**602
forced distribution and, **2:**603
graphic rating scales and, **2:**601
methodology in, **2:**601–603
mixed standard scales and, **2:**602
paired comparisons and, **2:**602–603
rank ordering and, **2:**603
See also Criterion theory; Critical incident technique;
    Frame-of-reference (FOR) training; Performance
    appraisal; Performance appraisal, objective indexes
Performance dimension training, **1:**257
Performance feedback, 2:604–607
dynamic approach to, **2:**607
effectiveness of, **2:**606
feedback environment, facets of, **2:**607
feedback intervention theory and, **2:**605–606
feedback-oriented culture and, **2:**606
feedback-seeking behavior and, **2:**604–605
feedback-standard comparison process and, **2:**606
improved performance and, **1:**108
multisource feedback and, **2:**605
pay for performance, **1:**83
person-environment aspects of, **2:**606–607
social context of, **2:**606–607
utility of, **2:**604
See also Control theory; Feedback; Feedback seeking; Job
    performance; Organizational performance; Performance
    appraisal; 360-degree feedback
Performance goal orientation (PGO), **2:**491
Performance standards, **1:**86, 131
Per-piece pay rate, **2:**693
Personal identity, **2:**703, 740
Personal norms, **2:**739
Personal standards, **2:**730–731
Personal well-being:
conflict and, **1:**95
See also Employee well-being
Personality, 2:607–611
act-frequency approach to, **2:**609
affective responding and, **1:**13
aggregation principle and, **2:**611
application of, **2:**610–611
behavior genetics research and, **1:**270
compound traits and, **2:**609–610

computer-based testing and, **2:**611
conflict, experience of, **1:**95
conflict management style and, **1:**99
creativity at work and, **1:**127
cynical hostility and, **2:**562
definition of, **2:**607–608
five-factor model of, **1:**13, 34, 54
genetic influences on, **2:**609
idiographic vs. nomothetic scientific study and, **2:**608
industrial/organizational psychology and, **2:**608–609, 610–611
integrity trait and, **2:**610
internal mechanisms, behavior and, **2:**609
introversion/extroversion and, **2:**609
job satisfaction and, **1:**408
measurement instruments for, **1:**13–14, 34
mood effects and, **2:**486
multitrait personality inventories and, **1:**54
organizational citizenship behavior and, **1:**104–105
personality feedback, **1:**34
pre-employment testing and, **2:**610–611
research on, **2:**610, 611
stress consequences and, **2:**766
trait-situation debate and, **2:**611
traits, perspectives on, **2:**609
traits, structure of, **2:**609
vocational interest personality types, **1:**67, **2:**622
work-related behaviors, prediction of, **2:**610–611
See also Affective traits; Assessment center; Big Five
    taxonomy of personality; Core self-evaluations;
    Individual differences; Motivational traits; Personality
    assessment; Type A and Type B personalities
Personality assessment, 2:612–615
aggregation principle and, **2:**613
broadside approach to, **2:**613
content approach, factor analysis and, **2:**612
criterion-related validity and, **2:**613–614
empirical scale development and, **2:**612
historical development of, **2:**613
impression management/faking and, **2:**614
industrial/organizational psychology and, **2:**612, 613, 614
life-data and, **2:**612
normative vs. ipsative assessment and, **2:**612–613
selection contexts and, **2:**614
self-report measures and, **2:**612
test-data and, **2:**612
trait-situation debate and, **2:**613, 614
utility of, **2:**613–614
See also Big Five taxonomy of personality; Impression
    management; Individual assessment; Personality;
    Reliability; Validity
Personality-based integrity measures, **2:**636
Personality-performance relationship, **1:**55, **2:**613
Person-environment (PE) fit, 1:396, 2:615–618, 771
attraction-selection-attrition model and, **2:**616
complementary fit and, **2:**615
demands-abilities fit and, **2:**615
difference scores and, **2:**617
direct measures of, **2:**617
environment characteristics and, **2:**615

environment, levels of, **2:**615–617
fit, definition of, **2:**615
indirect measures of, **2:**617–618
knowledge/skills/abilities and, **2:**615, 616, 617
measurement of, **2:**617–618
needs-supplies fit and, **2:**615
person characteristics and, **2:**615
person-group fit and, **2:**617
person-job fit and, **2:**616
person-organization fit and, **2:**616–617
person-vocation fit and, **2:**616
polynomial regression and, **2:**617–618
research on, **2:**618
statistical interactions and, **2:**617
stress theory and, **2:**623
supplementary fit and, **2:**615
See also Careers; Individual differences; Person-job (PJ) fit;
    Person-organization (PO) fit; Person-vocation (PV) fit
Person-environment typology, **1:**67
Person-group (PG) fit, **2:**617
Person-job (PJ) fit, **1:**283–284, **2:**616, **618–619**
commensurate measurement and, **2:**618
consequences of, **2:**619
definition of, **2:**618
demands-abilities fit and, **2:**619
interactional psychology and, **2:**618
misfit, conditions of, **2:**619
needs-supplies fit and, **2:**618–619
research on, **2:**619
See also Person-environment (PE) fit; Person-organization
    (PO) fit; Person-vocation (PV) fit
Person-organization (PO) fit, **2:**616–617, **620–621**
attraction-selection-attrition framework and, **2:**616, 620
consequences of, **2:**621
definition of, **2:**620
history of, **2:**620
individual/organizational value congruence and, **2:**620, 621
interactionist perspective and, **2:**620
need fulfillment and, **2:**620
organizational culture profile and, **2:**619, 620
research on, **2:**621
theoretical underpinnings of, **2:**620–621
See also Person-environment (PE) fit; Person-job
    (PJ) fit; Person-vocation (PV) fit
Person-situation debate, **1:**41, **2:**611, 613, 614
Person-vocation (PV) fit, **2:**616, **621–623**
attraction-selection-attrition model and, **2:**623
definition of, **2:**621
stress, person-environment fit theory of, **2:**623
vocational personality types and, **2:**622
work adjustment theory and, **2:**622–623
See also Person-environment (PE) fit; Person-job
    (PJ) fit; Person-organization (PO) fit
Personnel Research Laboratory, **2:**628
Persuasion, **1:**39, **2:**706
Pessimism. *See* Optimism and pessimism
Peter Principle, **1:**283
Peters, L. H., **1:**451
Peterson, M. F., **2:**561

Petty, R., **1:**39
Pfeffer, J., **1:**398
Pfizer, **2:**901
Phantom effects, **1:**431–432
Phased retirement, **2:**680
Phi coefficient, **2:**473
Philanthropy, **1:**115
Phillips Industries, **1:**311
Phillips, R., **1:**113
Philpot, J. W., **2:**848
Physical performance assessment, 2:623–626
basic ability tests, **2:**624, 625
development/validation of, **2:**625
ergonomic parameters and, **2:**625
gender differences and, **2:**625
job analysis data and, **2:**625
physical abilities and, **2:**624
physically demanding jobs and, **2:**623
types of, **2:**624–625
utility/applications of, **2:**624
validity of, **2:**625
working conditions information and, **2:**625
work/job simulation, **2:**624–625, 625
See also Prescreening assessment methods
    for personnel selection
Physical taint, **1:**153
Physical violence. *See* Terrorism and work
Piece of information approach to hiring, **1:**196
Pilot studies, **1:**141
Pinder, C. C., **2:**510, 839
Pinkley, R. L., **1:**95
Piorkowski, C., **1:**309
Pittsburgh Research Laboratory, **2:**501
Pizzoli, U., **1:**309
Placement and classification, 2:626–628
aptitude area composites and, **2:**627–628
batch selection and, **2:**628
classification efficiency and, **2:**627, 628
classification process and, **2:**626
future trends in, **2:**628
military example of, **2:**627–628
placement process and, **2:**626, 627–628
predicted performance scoring and, **2:**626–627
selection process and, **2:**626, 627
See also Army Alpha/Army Beta; Employee selection;
    Project A; Selection strategies
Planned behavior. *See* Theory of reasoned action/theory of
    planned behavior
Plasticity patterns of behavior, **2:**710
Platykurtic data, **1:**150
Ployhart, R., **1:**26
Podsakoff, P. M., **1:**103, 286
Pohlmann, J. F., **1:**451
Point-biserial correlation, **2:**473
Point-factor job evaluation system, **1:**396
Policy. *See* Policy-capturing (PC); Public sector organizations
Policy-capturing (PC), 1:426, 2:628–630
data analysis and, **2:**629
data collection and, **2:**629

decisional tasks and, **2:**629
history of, **2:**628–629
information integration theory and, **2:**630
job choice and, **2:**669–670
judgment analysis and, **2:**630
multiattribute judgment and, **2:**629, 630
multiattribute utility theory and, **2:**630
multiple regression and, **2:**629
performance indexes and, **2:**629–630
typical results of, **2:**630
See also Lens model
Political behavior. *See* Organizational politics
Polygraph tests, **1:**357
Polynomial regression, **2:**617–618, 619
Polytomous models, **1:**373
Porac, J. F., **2:**581
Porras, J., **2:**561
Porter, L. W., **2:**672
Porter, M. E., **2:**764
Position Analysis Questionnaire (PAQ), **1:**381, 395
Positive feedback, **1:**370–371
Positive health psychology, **1:**462
Positive and Negative Affect Schedule (PANAS), **1:**13–14, 187
Positive organizational scholarship movement, **2:**893
Positive psychology applied to work, **2:630–633**
authentic leadership and, **2:**632
engagement and, **2:**632
flow and, **2:**631–632
happiness and, **2:**631
positive institutions and, **2:**632
positive organizational psychology, **2:**631–632
positive psychology, development of, **2:**630–631
positive subjective states and, **2:**631–632
satisfaction and, **2:**631
state-like characteristics, emphasis on, **2:**631
virtuous organizations, **2:**632
work design and, **2:**632
See also Intrinsic and extrinsic work motivation; Job design;
Job involvement; Transformational and transactional
leadership
Positive reinforcement, **2:**538, 673, 674
Postmodern qualitative paradigm, **2:**649
Powell, G. N., **1:**334
Power issues:
abusive supervisors and, **1:**3
leader power typology, **1:**443–444
power differentials, **2:**474
Power need, **2:**507, 893
Practical intelligence, **2:633–635**
approaches to, **2:**633–634
critical incident technique and, **2:**634
definition of, **2:**633
future research on, **2:**634–635
know-how and, **2:**633
laboratory testing of, **2:**634
mathematical calculations and, **2:**633
measurement of, **2:**634, 635
planning/organizational abilities and, **2:**633–634
presupposition/concept learning and, **2:**634

prototypes of, **2:**634
research on, **2:**634–635
simulations and, **2:**634
social judgment and, **2:**634
tacit knowledge inventories and, **2:**634
See also Assessment center; Cognitive abilities; Critical
incident technique (CIT); Job knowledge testing;
Situational approach to leadership
Practical intelligence construct, **2:**728
Praise as incentive, **1:**339
Prause, J., **2:**845
Predicted performance method of selection, **2:**697
Predictive validation studies, **2:**861
Prejudice. *See* Discrimination; Sexual discrimination;
Stereotyping
Premack, D., **2:**673
Premack principle, **2:**673
Preoccupation, **2:**491
**Prescreening assessment methods for personnel
selection**, **2:635–637**
biographical questionnaires and, **2:**636
cognitive ability testing and, **1:**80
common forms of, **2:**635
drug testing and, **2:**636
integrity/honesty tests and, **2:**636
legal issues in, **2:**637
letters of recommendation and, **2:**636
lie scales and, **2:**637
methodology in, **2:**635–637
misinformation/distortion, reduction of, **2:**636–637
reference checks and, **2:**636
training and experience evaluations and, **2:**635–636, 637
validation procedures and, **2:**637
weighted application blanks and, **2:**635–636
See also Biographical data; employee selection; Employment
interview; Integrity testing; Letters of recommendation;
Placement and classification; Selection strategies;
Uniform Guidelines on Employee Selection Procedures
Prestige level of occupations, **1:**153
Preston, L. E., **1:**116
Preventive management, **2:**526
Principles of Scientific Management, **2:**692
*Principles for the Validation and Use of Personnel Selection
Procedures*, **2:**637, **2:**799, 919, 929
Principle of universalism, **1:**116–117
Prior knowledge, **2:**818
Privacy rights, **1:**176, 221–222
Private sector organizations:
affirmative action programs and, **1:**16
disabled workers and, **1:**22–23
See also Public sector organizations
Proactive behaviors. *See* Socialization, employee proactive
behaviors
Proactive ethics policies/procedures, **1:**113–114
Proactive socialization taxonomy, **2:**745
Probability samples, **2:**689
cluster sampling, **2:**690
disproportionate stratified samples, **2:**690
proportionate stratified samples, **2:**690

sample designs, **2:**690–691
sample size and, **2:**691
simple random samples, **2:**690
stratified samples, **2:**690
systematic samples, **2:**690
Probability of success method, **2:**697
Problem-solving meetings, **2:**474
Problem-solving process, **1:**126–127
Procedural justice, **1:**26, 121, **2:**571, 577, 783
Procedural knowledge, **1:**399
Process models of turnover, **2:**884–885
Procrastination, **2:**813
Production-oriented behaviors, **1:**50
Productivity:
    abusive supervision and, **1:**2
    minority workers, interpersonal discrimination and, **1:**7
    See also Job performance; Job performance models;
        Performance feedback
Professional ethics, **1:**215
Professional organizations, **2:**947–950
Profile matching method of selection, **2:**697–698
Profit chain. *See* Service-profit chain
Profit sharing. *See* Gainsharing (GS) and profit sharing (PS)
Program evaluation, 2:638–641
    adjust-replace-drop decisions and, **2:**641
    communication of findings/insights, phase five, **2:**640
    data analysis/interpretation, phase four, **2:**640
    data collection, phase three, **2:**640
    evaluation planning, phase two, **2:**639
    formative evaluation and, **2:**638
    historic use of, **2:**638
    identification of stakeholders/evaluators/evaluation
        questions, phase one, **2:**639
    published guidelines for, **2:**641
    results utilization, phase six, **2:**640–641
    six-phase approach to, **2:**638–641
    summative evaluation and, **2:**638
    See also Compensation; Organizational communication,
        formal; Organizational communication, informal;
        Recruitment; Succession planning; Team building;
        Training; Work-life balance
Programmer Aptitude Test (PAT), **2:**856
Project A, 1:316, 2:641–643
    Armed Services Vocational Aptitude Battery and, **2:**642
    background on, **2:**641–642
    criterion measures and, **2:**642–643
    findings of, **2:**643
    JPM Project and, **2:**641, 642
    predictor measures and, **2:**643
    study design, **2:**642
    See also Job performance models; Selection
        strategies; Validation strategies; Work samples
Project B, **2:**642
Projective test of leadership, **1:**35
Proportionate stratified samples, **2:**690
Prosocial behavior. *See* Contextual performance/prosocial
        behavior/organizational citizenship behavior; Organizational
        behavior management (OBM)
Prospect theory (PT), **1:**387, 424–425

Protection of human subjects, **1:**220
Protégé attributes, **2:**477
Protestant work ethic (PWE), **2:643–645**
    antecedents of endorsement, **2:**644
    consequences of endorsement, **2:**644
    interindividual variation in endorsement and, **2:**644–645
    measures of, **2:**643
    multifaceted construct of, **2:**645
    positive work-related outcomes and, **2:**644
    prejudicial attitudes and, **2:**644
    psychological study of, **2:**643–644
    psychological well-being and, **2:**644
    See also Work motivation; Work values
Pruitt, D. G., **1:**97
PsycARTICLES, **1:**21
PsychINFO, **1:**21, 412, **2:**708–709
Psychodynamic approach, **1:**225
Psychological construct. *See* Construct
Psychological contract, 1:104, 124, 2:645–648, 783
    automatic processes and, **2:**646
    citizenship behaviors and, **2:**648
    definition of, **2:**645
    employment status/job categories and, **2:**647
    features of, **2:**645–646
    human resource practices and, **2:**646
    hybrid/balanced form of, **2:**647
    incompleteness of, **2:**645–646
    individual actions and, **2:**648
    manager role in, **2:**648
    multiple contract makers and, **2:**646
    perceived mutuality of, **2:**645, 647
    relational psychological contracts and, **2:**646–647
    reliance losses and, **2:**646
    transactional psychological contracts and, **2:**647, 648
    types of, **2:**646–648
    violation of, **2:**647–648
    voluntariness of, **2:**645
    See also Withdrawal behaviors, turnover
The Psychological Corporation, **1:**314
Psychological distress, **1:**2
    abusive supervision and, **1:**2
    negative-affectivity employees and, **1:**3
Psychological empowerment, **1:**203–204
Psychological safety, **1:**398
Psychologists Full-Time in Industry, **1:**315
Psychologists Law, **1:**318
Psychosocial mentoring, **2:**477
Psychotechnology concept, **1:**309–310, **2:**692
Publications, **2:**943–945
Public sector organizations:
    affirmative action programs and, **1:**16
    assessment center methodology and, **1:**32
    disabled workers and, **1:**22–23
    ethical responsibilities of, **1:**115
    See also Private sector organizations
Pugh, D. S., **2:**588
Pulse surveys, **2:**591
Punctuated equilibrium model, **1:**294
Purcell, T. V., **2:**849

Purposive samples, **2:**691
Pygmalion effect. See Self-fulfilling prophecy, Pygmalion effect

Qualitative research approach, 2:649–651
  action research and, **2:**649
  analysis strategies in, **2:**650–651
  case study research, **2:**649
  content coding and, **1:**101, **2:**650, 651
  deductive orientation in, **2:**651
  dynamic process-oriented models of, **2:**651
  ethnographic research and, **2:**649
  funnel shaped design in, **2:**651
  grounded theory approach and, **2:**651
  interpretive paradigm in, **2:**649
  job satisfaction measures and, **1:**411
  modernist paradigm in, **2:**649
  open-ended design in, **2:**651
  operational practices in, **2:**649–650
  postmodern paradigm in, **2:**649
  thick descriptions and, **2:**653
  See also Case study method; Content coding; Focus groups; Verbal protocol analysis
Quality circles, **2:**651
Quality of life concerns, **2:**679–680
Quality of work life (QWL), **1:**307, 308, **2:651–652**, 814
  definition of, **2:**651
  healthy workplace concept and, **2:**652
  interventions for, **2:**651–652
  job satisfaction and, **2:**652
  organizational responsibility for, **2:**651
  outcomes of, **2:**652
  work context and, **2:**652
  See also Workaholism; Work-life balance
Quality of work measures, **2:**599
Quantitative reasoning skills, **1:**77
Quantitative research approach, 2:652–655
  analysis of variance approach and, **2:**654
  confirmatory factor analysis and, **2:**653
  content coding and, **1:**101
  correlation/regression analysis and, **2:**654
  current trends in, **2:**654–655
  data/measurement scales and, **2:**653
  definition of, **2:**652–653
  experimental/quasi-experimental designs and, **2:**654
  exploratory factor analysis and, **2:**653
  item response theory and, **2:**653
  job satisfaction measures and, **1:**411
  measurement of psychological variables and, **2:**653–654
  meta-analysis techniques and, **2:**654
  noise and, **2:**653
  null hypothesis and, **2:**654
  relationship issues and, **2:**653, 654
  reliability and, **2:**653
  significance tests and, **2:**653–654
  surveys/questionnaires and, **2:**654
  true effect size and, **2:**654
  validity and, **2:**653

  See also Descriptive statistics; Experimental designs; Factor analysis; Generalizability theory; Inferential statistics; Item response theory (IRT); Measurement scales; Multitrait-multimethod (MTMM) matrix; Structural equation modeling
Quantity of work measures, **2:**599
Quasi-experimental designs, 2:654, 655–657
  attributes of, **2:**655
  confounding/extraneous variables, control over, **2:**657
  control condition/no pretest design, **2:**655
  control conditions/pretest design, **2:**655
  definition of, **2:**655
  dependent variables, measurement of, **2:**656–657
  independent variables, manipulation of, **2:**656
  nonrandom assignment of units to conditions and, **2:**656
  regression discontinuity designs, **2:**656
  single-group/no control condition design, **2:**655
  time series designs, **2:**656
  training evaluation and, **2:**823
  types of, **2:**655–656
Questionnaires, **1:**85, **2:**654
  See also Survey approach
Quick, J. C., **2:**526, 527
Quinn, R. E., **2:**900
Quota samples, **2:**691

r metric, **1:**94
Race:
  affirmative action, attitude toward, **1:**18
  applicant reaction to test-taking and, **1:**28
  banding procedure and, **1:**48
  biodata items and, **1:**57
  glass ceiling phenomenon and, **1:**272
  letters of recommendation and, **1:**456
  mentoring processes and, **2:**477
  See also Race norming; Discrimination; Racism
Race norming, 1:74, 2:659–660
  Civil Rights Act of 1991 and, **2:**659–660
  cutoff scores and, **2:**659
  process of, **2:**659
  test score adjustment, legality of, **2:**659
  within-group norming procedures, **2:**659
Racism. *See* Adverse (disparate) impact; Adverse impact/disparate treatment/discrimination at work; Affirmative action; Discrimination; Race norming; Stereotyping
Rahim, M. A., **1:**95, 98
Railway Labor Act, **1:**437
Random errors of measurement, **2:**498
Random response error, **2:**675–676
Randomized experiments. *See* Experimental designs
Range, **1:**149
Range restriction error, **2:**660–661
Rank ordering, **2:**603
Rasch model, **1:**373
Rate-of-exchange interpretation, **2:**775
Rater accuracy training, **1:**257
Rater error, **2:**676
Rater error training (RET), **1:**257, **2:**662–663

Rater variability training, **1:**257
Rating errors and perceptual biases, **2:**660–663
   accuracy of performance ratings and, **2:**661
   attribution bias and, **2:**661–662
   behaviorally anchored rating scales and, **2:**662
   central tendency error and, **2:**661
   confirmatory rater bias and, **2:**661
   consequences of rating errors and, **2:**662
   contrast effects and, **2:**661
   correlational/halo errors and, **2:**661
   distributional errors and, **2:**660–661
   first-impression error and, **2:**661
   forced-choice instruments and, **2:**662
   forced-distribution performance appraisal systems and, **2:**662
   horn effects and, **2:**661
   leniency/severity errors and, **2:**660, 662
   paired comparison performance rating methods and, **2:**662
   performance ratings and, **2:**660
   range restriction error and, **2:**660–661
   rater error training and, **2:**662–663
   recency effect and, **2:**661
   remedial measures and, **2:**662–663
   similar-to-me error and, **2:**661
   stereotyping and, **2:**662
   types of, **2:**660–662
   See also Performance appraisal; Performance
      appraisal, objective indexes; Performance
      appraisal, subjective indexes
Rational trust, **2:**837
Rational-emotive behavioral approach, **1:**225
Rationally specified communication, **2:**555
Ratio scales, **2:**470
Raver, J. L., **1:**139
Raw score formula, **2:**471
Raymond, J. S., **2:**526
Reactive ethics policies/procedures, **1:**113–114
Reagan, R. W., **1:**17, 349
Realistic information hypothesis, **2:**671
Realistic job preview (RJP), **2:**663–666
   alternate recruiting sources and, **2:**665
   boundaries of, **2:**664–665
   candidate-interviewer conversation and, **2:**664
   company Web site and, **2:**665
   definition of, **2:**663
   design/use guidelines for, **2:**664
   human resource management and, **2:**665
   impact of, **2:**665
   information content in, **2:**663
   information dissemination and, **2:**663–664
   inside sources/referrals and, **2:**665
   newcomer retention and, **2:**664
   purpose of, **2:**663
   recruitment sources, retention/performance
      outcomes and, **2:**665
   selection methods in, **2:**666
   See also Job advertisements; Organizational
      socialization; Recruitment; Recruitment sources
Realistic Orientation Programs for New Employee
   Stress (ROPES), **2:**517

Reasonable accommodation requirement, **1:**24
Reasonable factor other than age (RFOA), **1:**20
Reasoned action. *See* Theory of reasoned action/theory of
   planned behavior
Reber, R. A., **2:**540
Recency effect, **2:**661
Reciprocity norm, **1:**104, 441, **2:**549, 733–734, 753
Recognition meetings, **2:**474
Recruitment, **2:**666–670
   ability-to-cope perspective and, **2:**669
   applicant reactions to, **2:**668–669
   applicants, generation of, **2:**667
   definition of, **2:**666
   direct estimate, attribute preference assessment and, **2:**669
   disabilities protections and, **1:**24–25
   diversity in the workplace and, **1:**159
   early recruitment communications, **2:**667–668
   effective practices of, **2:**666
   employment interviews and, **1:**198
   e-recruitment and, **1:**171, **2:**668
   executive recruitment, **1:**227–228
   expectancy-based decision making and, **2:**670
   final job offer negotiations and, **2:**670
   hiring process and, **2:**666
   honesty and, **2:**669
   human capital, importance of, **2:**666
   job choice, content issues and, **2:**669–670
   job choice, process issues and, **2:**670
   maintenance phase of, **2:**668–669
   met-expectations theory and, **2:**669
   organizational image and, **2:**668
   outcomes of, **2:**666–667
   phases in, **2:**666
   policy capturing studies and, **2:**669–670
   realistic job previews and, **2:**669
   recruiters and, **2:**668
   recruiting sources, **2:**667
   recruitment materials content and, **2:**667–668
   recruitment materials design and, **2:**667
   recruitment source effects and, **2:**667
   selection devices, applicant reaction to, **2:**668–669
   See also Age discrimination in Employment Act (ADEA) of
      1967; Applicant/test-taker reactions; Attraction-selection-
      attrition (ASA) model; Employee selection; Job
      advertisements; Job choice; Job search; Older worker
      issues; Realistic job preview (RJP); Recruitment sources;
      Selection strategies; *Uniform Guidelines on Employee
      Selection Procedures*
Recruitment sources, **2:**667, **670–672**
   contingency perspectives on source effects and, **2:**671
   definition of, **2:**670
   diversity of workforce and, **2:**671
   formal sources, **2:**670
   individual differences hypothesis and, **2:**671
   informal sources, **2:**670, 671
   initial research on, **2:**670–671
   Internet-based recruitment, **1:**171, **2:**668, 670, 671–672
   post-hire outcomes and, **2:**671
   realistic information hypothesis and, **2:**671

source effects and, **2:**667, 671
    See also Job search; Realistic job preview; Recruitment
Recursive/nonrecursive models, **2:**774
Reductions-in-force (RIFs), **1:**216
Reference checks, **2:**636
Referent power, **1:**443
Referrals, **1:**225
Reflective practice, **2:**731–732
Regression analysis, **2:**654
    See also Structural equation modeling (SEM)
Regression discontinuity designs, **2:**656
Regulatory focus theory, **2:**491
Rehabilitation Act of 1973, **1:**16, 22–23
Reichers, A., **2:**561
Reid, D. R., **2:**540
Reinforcement theory of work motivation, **2:**538, **672–675**
    activity consequences and, **2:**673
    antecedent-monitor-consequence sequence and, **2:**675
    antecedents, secondary role of, **2:**673–674
    applied behavior analysis and, **2:**672, 673
    consequences as motivators and, **2:**672–673
    definition of, **2:**672
    development of, **2:**672
    explanatory power of, **2:**674–675
    generalized consequences and, **2:**673
    improvement initiatives at work and, **2:**672–674
    informational consequences and, **2:**673
    leadership effectiveness, monitoring and consequences, **2:**674–675
    negative reinforcement and, **2:**674
    organizational consequences and, **2:**673
    positive reinforcement and, **2:**673, 674
    Premack principle and, **2:**673
    response cost and, **2:**674
    social consequences and, **2:**673
    token economy program and, **2:**672
    See also Feedback; Organizational behavior management (OBM)
Relational communication, **2:**554
Relational psychological contracts, **2:**646–647
Relational trust, **2:**837
Relationship conflict, **1:**95, 96, 97
Relationship-building:
    meetings at work and, **2:**474
    relationship-oriented behaviors, **1:**50
    See also Interpersonal relationships
Relaxed communication style, **1:**367
Reliability, **2:**653, **675–678**
    classical test theory and, **1:**75–76, **2:**677
    coefficients of equivalence and stability and, **2:**676–677
    constructs being measured and, **2:**677–678
    definition of, **2:**675
    employment interviews and, **1:**200
    estimates of reliability, influential factors in, **2:**677–678
    estimation of reliability coefficient and, **2:**677
    generalizability (G) theory and, **2:**677
    heterogeneity of a sample and, **2:**678
    intercoder reliability and, **1:**69
    internal consistency reliability coefficient and, **2:**676
    interrater reliability coefficient and, **2:**677

job performance assessment and, **1:**404
    measurement design limitations and, **2:**677
    measurement error, sources of, **2:**675–676
    naturalistic observation and, **2:**505
    random response error and, **2:**675–676
    rater error and, **2:**676
    reliability coefficients and, **2:**676–677
    specific factor error and, **2:**676
    test length and, **2:**678
    test-retest reliability coefficient and, **2:**676
    transient error and, **2:**676
    See also Classical test theory (CTT); Generalizability theory (G-theory); Validity
Repetitive tasks, **1:**404–405
Replacement planning, **2:**776
Reporting structure, **2:**474
Representativeness heuristic, **1:**430
Research:
    linkage research, **1:**144–145
    low-base-rate phenomenon and, **1:**1
    See also Case study method; Cross-cultural research methods and theory; Empirical research; Experimental designs; Qualitative research approach; Quantitative research approach
Research Bureau of Retail Training, **1:**314
Research Center for Group Dynamics (MIT), **1:**315
Resilience, **2:**732
Resistance, **1:**2–3, **2:**736
Respect ethic, **1:**216, **2:**489
Response cost, **2:**674
Resumés, **1:**455
Retail salespeople, **1:**2, 84
Retaliation behaviors, **1:**2–3, **2:**578
    See also Organizational retaliatory behavior
Retention rates, **1:**2, **2:**550
Retention strategies. *See* Older worker issues; Retirement
Retirement, **2:678–680**
    aging workforce trends and, **2:**678
    blurred/phased retirement and, **2:**680
    bridge employment and, **2:**533, 534, 680, 843
    chronic health problems and, **2:**534
    decisions about, **2:**533–534
    definition of, **2:**678
    demographic trends and, **2:**678–679
    demographic variables and, **2:**679, 680
    evolving conceptualizations of, **2:**680
    familial variables and, **2:**679
    flexible work arrangements and, **2:**534
    gender-based issues and, **2:**679
    individual retirement decisions and, **2:**679–680
    life course, widening trajectory of, **2:**680
    longevity, increase in, **2:**679
    mandatory retirement policy and, **1:**20
    normal retirement age, **2:**534
    organizational level losses and, **2:**679
    quality of life concerns and, **2:**679–680
    retirement policies, **1:**20, **2:**531
    workforce participation trends and, **2:**678–679
    See also Older worker issues

Retributive loafing, **2:**736
Retrospective studies, **1:**463–464
Return on assets (ROA), **1:**261
Return on investment (ROI), **1:**262, 376, **2:**822, 833
Reverse buffering effect, **2:**743
Revised Life Orientation Test (RLOT), **2:**535
Revisionist free enterprise model of business, **1:**115–117
Reward power, **1:**443
Reward systems:
    contingent rewards, **2:**835
    creativity, encouragement of, **1:**129
    informationally administered rewards, **1:**370
    intrinsic motivation and, **1:**370–371
    See also Compensation; Gainsharing (GS) and profit
        sharing (PS); Incentives; Team-based rewards
RIASEC (realistic/investigative/artistic/social/enterprising/
    conventional) model, **1:**346, 389, 422, **2:**616
Rice, A. K., **1:**319
Rice, R. E., **2:**557, 873
Richardson, Bellows, Henry, & Company, **1:**315
Rightsizing. *See* Downsizing
Risk behaviors, **2:**707
Risley, T., **2:**538
Robber's Cave study, **1:**361
Robbins, A. S., **2:**887
Roberts, R., **1:**85
Robertson, I., **1:**311
Robinson, S., 1, **1:**120, 123, 125
Roethlisberger, F. J., **1:**305, 327
Rogelberg, S. G., **1:**255, 256
Role ambiguity, **1:**123, 179, 250, **2:680–682**
    attitudinal consequences and, **2:**681–682
    causes of, **2:**681
    consequences of, **2:**681–682
    health consequences of, **2:**681
    leader behaviors and, **2:**681, 682
    research on, **2:**682
    role clarity and, **2:**680
    role conflict and, **2:**681
    role theory and, **2:**681
    strains and, **2:**681
    stressors and, **2:**681
    terrorism at work and, **2:**796
    treatments for, **2:**682
    work environments and, **2:**681
    See also Role conflict; Role overload and underload; Stress,
        consequences; Stress, coping and management; Stress,
        models and theories
Role conflict, **1:**96, 123, 179, 254, **2:**681, **682–684**
    behavior-base conflict and, **2:**683
    causes of, **2:**683–684
    consequences of, **2:**684
    interrole conflict, **2:**683
    intrarole conflict, **2:**683
    managerial behaviors and, **2:**683
    organizational policies and, **2:**683–684
    role overload and, **2:**683
    role theory and, **2:**682
    simple/unenriched jobs and, **2:**684

simultaneous roles and, **2:**684
strain-based conflict and, **2:**683
stressors and, **2:**682
time-based conflict and, **2:**683
treatments for, **2:**684
types of, **2:**682–683
work-family role conflict and, **2:**683
work-school role conflict and, **2:**683
See also Occupational health psychology; Role ambiguity;
    Stress, consequences; Stress, coping and management;
    Stress, models and theories
Role innovation, **2:**745
Role making, **1:**441
Role modeling, **1:**447, **2:**518, 706
Role overload and underload, **2:**683, **685–687**
    boundary-spanning roles and, **2:**686
    consequences of, **2:**686, 687
    explanations for, **2:**685–686, 687
    job design and, **2:**687
    qualitative perspective on, **2:**685, 686–687
    quantitative perspective on, **2:**685, 686
    role overload, **2:**685–686
    roles, development of, **2:**685
    role size and, **2:**686
    role theory perspective and, **2:**685–686
    role underload, **2:**686–687
    See also Boredom at work; Empowerment; Job
        characteristics theory; Job satisfaction; Occupational
        health psychology (OHP); Role ambiguity; Role
        conflict; Stress, models and theories
Role theory, **1:**179
    role ambiguity and, **2:**681
    role conflict and, **2:**682
    role overload and, **2:**685–686
Role-play method, **1:**35–36, 37, **2:**825
Romantic relationships. *See* Workplace romance
Ronen, S., **2:**510
Roosevelt, F. D., **2:**852
Root, B., **1:**85
ROPES (Realistic Orientation Programs for new
    Employee Stress) approach, **2:**517
Rosen, H., **2:**849
Rosenberg, M., **1:**710
Rosenberg Self-Esteem Scale, **2:**710
Rosenthal, R., **2:**481, 483
Rotation. *See* Job rotation
Rothbaum, F., **1:**461
Rotter, J. B., **1:**461
Rousseau, D., **2:**558, 559
Routinization of activities, **1:**812
Rucker Plan, **1:**262
Rumor mills, **2:**557
Russell, J. T., **2:**855–856
Ryan, A. -M., **1:**26
Ryan, R. M., **2:**492
Rynes, S. L., **1:**261

Salas, C., **1:**306
Salas, E., **2:**821

Salgado, J., **1:**311, 462
Salkind, N., **1:**68
Salovey, P., **1:**180, 181
Same-decision defense, **1:**73
Sample surveys, **2:**781
Sampling distribution, **1:**92
Sampling techniques, 2:689–691
    cluster sampling and, **2:**690
    convenience samples and, **2:**691
    cross-cultural research and, **1:**141
    hypernetwork method and, **2:**691
    nonprobability sample, **2:**689, 691
    probability samples and, **2:**689, 690
    purposive samples and, **2:**691
    quota samples and, **2:**691
    sample size and, **2:**691
    sampling frame and, **2:**690, 691
    simple random samples and, **2:**690
    social network analysis and, **2:**691
    stratified samples and, **2:**690
    systematic samples and, **2:**690
    target populations and, **2:**689–690
    unit of analysis and, **2:**689
    See also Descriptive statistics; Experimental designs;
        Focus groups; Inferential statistics; Longitudinal
        research/experience sampling technique;
        Nonexperimental designs; Quantitative research
        approach; Quasi-experimental designs; Statistical power
Sanchez, J. I., **1:**462
Santos, L., **1:**306
SARA (shock/anger/resistance/acceptance) model of
    organizational change, **2:**543, 544
Sarason, I. G., **2:**518
Scanlon Plan, **1:**262
Scatterplot diagrams, **2:**472, 473
Scheier, M., **2:**534
Schein, E. H., **2:**517, 558, 559, 560, 582, 584
Schein, V., **1:**333
Schippmann, J. S., **2:**914, 916, 927
Schmidt, F. L., **1:**345, 347, **2:**481, 482, 483
Schmitt, N., **1:**337, **2:**729
Schmitt, S. D., **2:**914, 916, 927
Schneider, B., **1:**40, 41, 144, 460, **2:**545, 547,
    558, 561, 616, 620, 623
Scholastic Aptitude Test (SAT), **2:**755, 757, 760
Scholastic Aptitude Test II (SAT II), **2:**755
Schön, D. A., **2:**803, 804
Schriesheim, C. A., **1:**451, 452
Schuster, M., **1:**262
Schwartz, S. H., **1:**138
Schyns, B., **1:**334
Scientific management, 1:305, 313, 327, 331, 392, **2:692–693**
    cost accounting and, **2:**693
    current impact of, **2:**693
    functional foremen concept and, **2:**693
    genesis/growth of, **2:**692
    industrial/organizational psychology and, **2:**693
    key concepts of, **2:**692–693
    pay-for-performance and, **2:**692, 693

per-piece pay rate and, **2:**693
soldiering/restriction of output and, **2:**693
task performance and, **2:**692–693
time studies and, **2:**693
See also Hawthorne Studies/Hawthorne effect; History of
    industrial and organizational psychology in North
    America; Human relations movement
Scientific systems of construct, **1:**99–100
Scientist-practitioner model, 2:538–539, **694,** 926
    acceptance of, **2:**694
    definition of, **2:**694
    development of, **2:**694
    training standards and, **2:**694
    See also American Psychological Association (APA);
        Association for Psychological Science (APS); Society for
        Industrial and Organizational Psychology (SIOP)
Scott Company, **1:**314
Scott, W. D., **1:**313, 314, **2:**692
Segal, N. L., **1:**270
Seifert, C. F., **2:**810
Selection, occupational tailoring, 2:695–698
    considerations in, **2:**695
    contextual behavior and, **2:**695
    contextual behavior-work proficiency overlap and, **2:**696
    existing human resource processes/systems and, **2:**696
    general mental ability and, **2:**695, 696
    organizational culture and, **2:**696–697
    organizational outcomes and, **2:**695–696
    organization fit considerations and, **2:**697–698
    selection procedure classification/design and, **2:**696, 697
    work behavior considerations and, **2:**695–697
    work content analysis and, **2:**696–697
    work proficiency and, **2:**696–697
    See also Employee selection; Selection strategies
Selection strategies, 1:40, **2:698–702**
    banding method and, **2:**701
    cognitive ability testing and, **1:**82
    compensatory scoring strategy and, **2:**698
    competency modeling and, **1:**88
    computer-based assessment and, **1:**91–93
    cut scores strategy and, **2:**698–699
    decisional strategies and, **2:**697–700
    employment contexts, strategy evaluation, **2:**700–702, 701 (table)
    e-selection and, **1:**176
    expectancy methods and, **2:**699
    judgment methods and, **2:**699–700
    legal risk and, **2:**697
    multiple hurdles strategy and, **2:**697–698
    pre-employment selection, **1:**82
    probability of success method and, **2:**699
    profile matching method and, **2:**699–700
    top-down selection strategy, **1:**48, 50
    variety of, **2:**697
    See also Attraction-selection-attrition (ASA) model; Banding;
        Employee selection; Executive selection; Placement and
        classification; Prescreening assessment methods for
        personnel selection; Selection, occupational tailoring;
        Succession planning; *Uniform Guidelines on Employee
        Selection Procedures*

Self-actualization need, **2:**510
Self-categorization theory, **1:**360
Self-concept theory of work motivation, 2:703–704
    congruence needs, self-concept/performance
        feedback and, **2:**704
    core self-evaluations and, **2:**704
    feared/desired selves and, **2:**704
    internal/external basis of motivation and, **2:**704
    personal identity, self-categorization and, **2:**703
    self-concept, structure of, **2:**703
    self-concept/work motivation, relationship
        between, **2:**703–704
    social identity, self-definition through relationships and, **2:**703
    work goals and, **2:**704
    working self-concept and, **2:**703, 704
    See also Job involvement; Work motivation
Self-determination theory (SDT), **1:**368–369, **2:**492, 840
Self-Directed Search, **1:**67
Self-efficacy, 1:14, 64, 65, 67, **2:705–707**
    continuous learning/performance improvement and, **2:**705
    control theory and, **1:**109
    destructive behaviors/messages and, **2:**707
    distance learning and, **1:**156
    diversity training and, **1:**162–163
    enactive self-mastery and, **2:**706
    goal setting and, **1:**279
    managerial efficacy building behaviors and,
        2:707, 707 (figure), 708 (table)
    measurement of, **2:**706
    nature of, **2:**705
    performance/well-being and, **2:**705–706
    regulation of human functioning and, **2:**731
    resilience and, **2:**732
    risk taking/hubris and, **2:**707
    role modeling and, **2:**706
    sources of, **2:**706–707
    stress/occupational burnout and, **2:**705–706, 766, 767
    transformational leadership and, **2:**632
    verbal persuasion and, **2:**706
    See also Social cognitive theory
Self-esteem (SE), **2:708–710**
    abusive supervisors and, **1:**3
    behavioral patterns and, **2:**709–710
    core self-evaluations and, **1:**14, 110
    discriminant validity and, **2:**710
    evaluations, neutrality/variability of, **2:**709
    job performance and, **2:**710
    job satisfaction and, **2:**710
    leadership behavior/efficacy and, **2:**710
    plasticity patterns of behavior and, **2:**710
    research on, **2:**710
    significance of, **2:**708–709
    stress mediator factor of, **2:**766
    subjective well-being and, **2:**710
    theoretical/measurement issues and, **2:**709–710
    voice behavior and, **2:**710
    See also Core self-evaluations
Self-evaluation theory, **2:**738
    See also Core self-evaluations

Self-fulfilling prophecy, **2:**562
Self-fulfilling prophecy, Pygmalion effect, **2:**B711–712
    communication of expectations and, **2:**711–712
    Galatea effect and, **2:**711
    Golem effect and, **2:**711
    group-level expectancy effect and, **2:**711
    high expectations, subordinate satisfaction and, **2:**712
    leader expectations, subordinate performance and, **2:**711, 712
    organizational innovations and, **2:**712
    Pygmalion-at-work model and, **2:**711
    Pygmalion effect, definition of, **2:**711
    Pygmalion effect research and, **2:**712
    See also Leadership and supervision; Training
Self-interest motivation, **1:**18, **2:**573
Self-monitoring, **2:**713
Self-observation generalizations, **1:**64
Self-reflective capability, **2:**731–732
Self-regulation theory, 1:107, 109, **2:713–714**
    affective reactions and, **2:**714
    approach vs. avoidance goals and, **2:**714
    definition of, **2:**713
    feedback/self-monitoring and, **2:**713
    goal hierarchies and, **2:**713–714
    goals/goal setting and, **2:**713
    See also Feedback; Goal-setting theory; Path-goal theory
Self-regulatory capability, **2:**730–731
Seligman, M. E., **2:**535, 630
Selling leadership style, **2:**725–726
Selye, H., **1:**222, 223, **2:**770, 771
Semantic differential, **1:**38
SEMNET e-mail list, **2:**776
Sender/message/channel/receiver (SMCR) model
    of communication, **2:**552
Senge, P., **1:**449
Sensemaking. *See* Organizational sensemaking
Separate-but-equal doctrine, **1:**315
September 11, 2001, **2:**795, 796
Service climate, **1:**144, **2:**546
Service-profit chain, **1:**144, **2:**590
SERVQUAL model, **1:**143, 144
Severity errors, **2:**660
Sexual discrimination, 2:714–717
    antecedents of, **2:**715–716
    compensation and, **2:**715
    disparate impact and, **2:**715
    disparate treatment and, **2:**714–715
    evidence of, **2:**715
    expectations-based discrimination and, **2:**716
    fit-derived performance expectations and, **2:**716
    gay/lesbian/bisexual workers and, **1:**265
    gender inequity and, **1:**81, **2:**715
    gender stereotyping and, **2:**715–716
    legal definitions of, **2:**714–715
    legal protections against, **2:**714
    See also Adverse impact/disparate treatment/discrimination
        at work; Civil Right Act of 1964; Discrimination;
        Glass ceiling phenomenon; Sexual harassment
        at work; Stereotyping
Sexual Experiences Questionnaire (SEQ), **2:**718

Sexual harassment at work, 1:1, **2:717–720**
 behavioral consequences of, **2:**719
 causes of, **2:**718–719
 consequences of, **2:**719
 definition of, **2:**717
 forms of, **2:**717–718
 gender harassment and, **2:**717
 legal protections from, **2:**718
 measurement of, **2:**718
 nonsexual aggression, job
  satisfaction and, **2:**720
 offender characteristics and, **2:**719
 outcomes of, **1:**717
 physical consequences of, **2:**719
 psychological consequences of, **2:**719
 sexual coercion and, **2:**717–718
 unwanted sexual attention and, **2:**717
 work context and, **2:**719
 workplace incivility/aggression and, **2:**719–720
Sexual orientation diversity, **1:**263–265
Shadish, W. R., **2:**655, 657
Shakow, D., **2:**694
Shannon, C., **1:**363
Shared beliefs, **2:**732
Shared meaning, **2:**553, 873
Shared moral understanding, **2:**739
Shared value system, **2:**910
Shared vision, **1:**450, **2:**547, 558
Shartle, C. L., **1:**48
Sherif, M., **2:**739
Shiftwork, 2:720–722
 cardiovascular disease and, **2:**721
 chronic fatigue and, **2:**721
 circadian rhythm disruption and, **2:**721
 design recommendations for, **2:**720–721
 gastrointestinal problems and, **2:**721
 individual differences and, **2:**722
 negative effects of, **2:**721–722
 physical ill-health and, **2:**721–722
 psychological ill-health and, **2:**721
 social/domestic disruption and, **2:**722
 social support and, **2:**722
 types of shiftwork systems and, **2:**720
 See also Flexible work schedules
Shine, L. C., **2:**856
Shock/anger/resistance/acceptance (SARA) model of
  organizational change, **2:**543, 544
Shockley-Zalabak, P., **2:**554
Shop Management, **2:**692
Short-term memory, **1:**77
Shrinkage, **2:**801
SIBTEST (simultaneous item bias test), **1:**152
Siegfried, W. D., Jr., **2:**916
Siegrist, J., **2:**772
Signal-contingent studies, **1:**464
Significance tests, **2:**480–481, 653–654
Similar-to-me error, **2:**661
Simmons, B., **1:**222
Simple random samples, **2:**690

Simulation:
 assessment center methodology and, **1:**33, 36
 control theory complexity and, **1:**109–110
 credentialing process and, **1:**130
 executive assessment and, **1:**229
 job knowledge testing and, **1:**401
 leadership development and, **1:**447
 physical performance assessment and, **2:**624–625
 practical intelligence, measurement of, **2:**634
 training and, **2:**826
 work sample and, **2:**817
 See also Simulation, computer approach
Simulation, computer approach, 2:723–724
 advantages of, **2:**724
 disadvantages of, **2:**724
 microworld simulations, **2:**723, 724
 Monte Carlo simulation, **2:**723, 724
 virtual reality simulation, **2:**723, 724
 See also Human-computer interaction; Judgment and
  decision-making process; Quasi-experimental designs;
  Simulations; Virtual organizations; Virtual teams
Simultaneous item bias test, **1:**152
Singapore, **1:**320
Singapore Psychological Society (SPS), **1:**320
Single-loop learning, **1:**449
Sinha, D., **1:**319
Situational approach to leadership, 1:50,
  444–445, 457–458, **2:724–727**
 behavioral approach and, **2:**725
 coaching leadership style, **2:**725–726
 commitment and, **2:**725
 definition of, **2:**724–725
 delegating leadership style, **2:**726
 directive leadership style, **2:**725
 extensions/applications of model, **2:**726
 follower development level and, **2:**725
 job maturity and, **2:**725
 measurement of, **2:**727
 span of control and, **2:**726
 supportive leadership style, **2:**726
 training model of, **2:**726–727
 work groups/teams and, **2:**726
 See also Leadership development
Situational interviews, **1:**34
Situational judgment tests (SJTs), 2:727–729
 adaptability constructs and, **2:**728
 construct validity, **2:**728–729
 contextual knowledge constructs and, **2:**728
 criterion-related validity of, **2:**728
 development of, **2:**727–728
 instructional/response format for, **2:**727
 modes of administration, **2:**727
 practical intelligence construct and, **2:**728
 psychometric tests of, **2:**727
 relevancy of, **2:**727
 tacit knowledge and, **2:**727
 work-related constructs and, **2:**727
 See also Critical incident technique; Practical
  intelligence; Selection strategies; Validity

Situational leadership theory, **2:**725
Situational strength, **1:**103
Siu, O. L., **1:**462
Six Sigma approach, **2:**815, 816
Skarlicki, D., **1:**125
Skew, **1:**149–150
Skills evaluation. *See* Assessment center
Skinner, B. F., **2:**538, 672
Sliding bands, **1:**47–48
Slotting of jobs, **1:**83
Small-group socialization perspective, **2:**746
SMCR (sender/message/channel/receiver) model of
    communication, **2:**552
Smith, P. B., **1:**139
Smith, A., **1:**115
Smith, A. F., 363
Smith, D. B., **2:**546
Smith v. City of Jackson, Mississippi, **1:**20
Sniezek, J. A., **1:**427
Snyder, S. S., **1:**461
Social astuteness, **2:**576
Social categorization, **1:**7–8, 360
Social cognitive career theory (SCCT), **1:**64, 67
    application of, **1:**65
    interests, cognitive process of career choice and, **1:**64–65
    self-evaluation, continuous process of, **1:**65
    See also Career development
Social cognitive theory, **1:**109.**2:729–733**, 893
    creative innovation and, **2:**730
    cultural contexts and, **2:**732
    description of, **2:**729
    electronic mass media and, **2:**730
    forethought capability and, **2:**730
    fortuitous events, personal agency and, **2:**732–733
    modeled judgments/actions and, **2:**730, 732
    moral standards and, **2:**731
    personal efficacy beliefs and, **2:**731–732
    personal standards and, **2:**730–731
    resilience and, **2:**732
    self-reflective capability and, **2:**731–732
    shared beliefs and, **2:**732
    symbolizing capability and, **2:**729
    vicarious capability and, **2:**729–730
Social comparison processes, **2:**893
Social compensation, **2:**736
Social contract theory, **1:**112, 115, 116
Social decision-making schemes, **1:**288
Social dominance theory, **1:**360
Social exchange theory, **1:**104, 441, **2:733–735**, 850
    anthropological/sociological models of, **2:**734
    conceptual point of view, **2:**733
    economic exchange relationships and, **2:**734–735
    exchange rules/norms and, **2:**733–734
    financial/material benefits and, **2:**734
    interpersonal relationships and, **2:**734–735
    leader-member exchange relationships and, **2:**735
    negotiated rules and, **2:**734
    organizational citizenship behaviors and, **2:**735
    organizational justice and, **2:**573–574

organizational retaliatory behavior and, **2:**578
reciprocity norm and, **2:**733–734
resources for, **2:**734
social exchange relationships and, **2:**734, 735
socioemotional benefits and, **2:**734
transactional basis of behavior and, **2:**733
trust/loyalty and, **2:**735
vulnerability/risk and, **2:**735
workplace incivility and, **2:**896–897
See also Contextual performance/prosocial
    behavior/organizational citizenship behavior
Social identity theory, **1:**360, **2:**703, 740, 761
Social impact theory, **2:**737
Social influence network theory, **2:**739–740
Social judgment, **2:**629, 634
Social justice, **1:**216
Social learning theory of career decision
    making (SLTCDM), **1:**64
    application of, **1:**65
    associative learning experiences and, **1:**64
    instrumental learning experiences and, **1:**64
    self-observation generalizations and, **1:**64
    task approach skills and, **1:**64
    See also Career development
Social loafing, **2:736–738**
    collective effort model and, **2:**737–738
    collective tasks and, **2:**737
    consequences of, **2:**736
    definitions of, **2:**736
    evaluation potential/identifiability model and, **2:**737
    free riding and, **2:**736
    group cohesiveness and, **2:**737
    group tasks and, **2:**736, 737
    individual performance, visibility of, **2:**737
    reduction strategies, **2:**736–737
    research on, **2:**736, 737
    retributive loafing and, **2:**736
    self-evaluation theory and, **2:**738
    social compensation and, **2:**736
    social impact theory and, **2:**737
    See also Expectancy theory of work motivation; Group
        dynamics and processes; Groups
Social network analysis, **2:**691
Social norms and conformity, **2:738–741**
    aberrant behavior and, **2:**740–741
    active/passive transmission of, **2:**739
    benefits of, **2:**739
    breaches of, **2:**741
    compliance motive and, **2:**738–739
    conformity motive and, **2:**739
    definition of, **2:**738
    descriptive norms and, **2:**739
    formalized norms, **2:**738
    group membership domains and, **2:**738
    identification motive and, **2:**739
    idiosyncrasy credits and, **2:**740
    individual motivations and, **2:**738–739, 740
    injunctive norms and, **2:**739
    mutual obligation and, **2:**740

norm formation and, **2:**739–740
norm misperceptions and, **2:**740
personal norms and, **2:**739
reasoned action theory and, **2:**739
social influence network theory and, **2:**739–740
socialization process and, **2:**740
subjective norms and, **2:**739
types of norms and, **2:**739
workplace context/work behavior and, **2:**738
Social psychology, **1:**113, 212
Social responsibility. *See* Corporate social responsibility
Social role psychology, **1:**63
Social Sciences Citation Index, **2:**497
Social stereotypes, **2:**761–762
Social-structural empowerment, **1:**203, 204
Social support, **1:**418, **2:741–744**
    affective communication, types of, **2:**769
    antecedents of, **2:**742
    buffering effect and, **2:**743
    consequences of, **2:**743
    emotional support and, **2:**741, 742
    friendships among coworkers and, **2:**742
    functional support and, **2:**741
    instrumental support and, **2:**741
    leaders, considerate behaviors of, **2:**742
    negative work aspects, conversations about, **2:**742
    organizational citizenship behaviors and, **2:**742
    organizational support and, **2:**743–744
    reverse buffering effect and, **2:**743
    stressor-strain relationship and, **2:**743, 766, 768–769
    structural support and, **2:**741
    workplace social support, **2:**741
    See also Interpersonal communication;
        Occupational health psychology (OHP)
Social systems theory, **2:**565–566
Social taint, **1:**153
Social weighting strategies, **1:**153–154
Socialization:
    action theory and, **1:**6
    advice giving and, **1:**429
    ethical behavior and, **1:**217
    meetings at work and, **2:**474
    organizational cynicism and, **2:**564
    social norms/conformity and, **2:**740
    See also Organizational socialization (OS); Socialization,
        employee proactive behaviors
Socialization, employee proactive behaviors, **2:744–747**
    adjustment and, **2:**745–746
    agency and, **2:**746
    coworker relationships and, **2:**746–747
    five-factor model of personality and, **2:**746
    information seeking and, **2:**745, 746
    interpersonal sources of socialization and, **2:**746–747
    mentoring relationships and, **2:**746
    newcomer proactive behavior and, **2:**745, 746
    orientation programs and, **2:**744–745
    personality and adjustment, **2:**745–746
    proactive socialization taxonomy and, **2:**745
    role innovation and, **2:**745

small-group socialization perspective and, **2:**746
social environment tasks and, **2:**745
turnover rates and, **2:**745
See also Organizational socialization (OS); Socialization
Society for Human Resource Management (SHRM), **1:**87,
    1:218, 330, **2:**901
Society for Industrial and Organizational Psychology (SIOP)
    1:xxxv, 40, 218, 316, 318, 343, **2:**525, 694, **747–749**
    academic resources from, **2:**748
    annual conference of, **2:**749
    functions of, **2:**748–749
    information dissemination and, **2:**748–749
    JobNet program, **2:**748
    Member-2-Member program, **2:**748
    membership of, **2:**747–748
    mission of, **2:**748
    structure of, **2:**747
    test security and, **2:**799
    See also Academy of Management; American
        Psychological Association (APA); Association for
        Psychological Science (APS); Industrial/organizational
        psychology careers
Society for Occupational Health Psychology (OHP), **2:**526
Socioinstrumental control beliefs, **1:**462
Sociotechnical approach, **2:749–750**
    change as norm and, **2:**749
    criticisms of, **2:**750
    effectiveness of, **2:**750
    equifinality concept and, **2:**750
    flexible work design and, **2:**750
    future of, **2:**750
    industrial democracy and, **2:**749
    joint optimization and, **2:**749–750
    minimum critical specification and, **2:**750
    open systems perspective and, **2:**749
    principles/assumptions of, **2:**749–750
    problem solving process and, **2:**750
    publications of, **2:**748
    stakeholder input and, **2:**750
    strategic management and, **2:**750
    teamwork and, **2:**750
    See also Engineering psychology; High-performance
        organization model; Quality of work life (QWL)
Soldiering, **2:**693
Sorcher, M., **2:**517, 518
Span of control, **2:**586, 726
Spearman's rho correlation, **2:**473
*Specialty Guidelines for the Delivery of Services by Industrial-
    Organizational Psychologists,* **2:**919, 929
Specific factor error, **2:**676
Spector, P. E., **1:**96, 461, 462
Spence, J. T., **2:**887
Spielrein, W., **1:**309
Spiller, W. E., **2:**848
Spirituality and leadership at work, **2:751–754**
    altruistic love and, **2:**752–753
    ethical well-being and, **2:**753
    performance excellence and, **2:**751, 752 (figure), 753–754
    religion/denominational politics, spirituality and, **2:**751–753

research on, **2:**754
rule of reciprocity and, **2:**753
spiritual leadership and, **2:**753
spiritual well-being and, **2:**753
strategic management process and, **2:**752 (figure), 753
transcendence/community and, **2:**751
workplace spirituality, **2:**751
See also Leadership development; Leadership and supervision
Spokane Research Laboratory, **2:**501
Staffing issues. *See* Careers; Employment issues
Staff rating scale, **2:**727
Stage model of group development, **1:**293–294
Stagner, R., **2:**849
Stakeholder theory, **1:**112, 116–117, **2:**750
Standard deviation (SD), **1:**92, 93, 149
Standard error (SE), **1:**92
Standard error of difference (SED), **1:**47
Standardized difference, **1:**93
Standardized testing, **1:**151, **2:**754–758
    Angoff standard-setting procedure and, **2:**756
    computerized adaptive tests and, **2:**757
    current/future issues in, **2:**756–757
    cut scores and, **2:**756
    definition of, **2:**754–755
    development of, **2:**754
    educational achievement/aptitude tests and, **2:**755
    fairness issues in, **2:**756
    licensure/certification exams, **2:**756
    military/civil service classification tests, **2:**755–756
    passing rates and, **2:**756
    rater effects and, **2:**756
    scope of measurement in, **2:**757
    stereotype threat and, **2:**760
    subtest development and, **2:**757
    utility of, **2:**757–758
    validity issues in, **2:**757
    See also Prescreening assessment methods
        for personnel selection
Standard Occuapational Classification
    System (SOC), **1:**422
Standard Oil Company, **1:**315
Standard query language (SQL), **1:**325
Standard score formula, **2:**471
Standards for Educational and Psychological Testing,
    1:358–359, **2:**799, 919, 929
Standards for Providers of Psychological Services, **2:**929
Static dimensionality, **1:**133
Statistic, **1:**92
Statistical conclusion validity, **1:**239
Statistical power (SP), **1:**239, **2:**758–759
    definition of, **2:**758
    effect size and, **2:**759
    factors in, **2:**758–759
    hypothesis testing and, **2:**758
    null hypothesis and, **2:**758
    sample size and, **2:**759
    type I/type II errors and, **2:**758–759, 759 (figure)
Statistical process control, **2:**692
Statistically equivalent models, **2:**775

Statistics. *See* Descriptive statistics; Inferential statistics;
    Measurement theory; Measures of association/correlation
    coefficient; Statistical power
Steele, C. M., **2:**760
Steiner, I. D., **1:**354
Steiner's formula, **1:**354
Stepladder technique, **1:**291–292
Stereotype threat, **2:**760–761
    boundary conditions for, **2:**760
    empirical evidence of, **2:**760
    employment settings and, **2:**760–761
    fear factor and, **2:**760
    origin of, **2:**760
    standardized tests, performance gap and, **2:**760
    underlying mechanisms in, **2:**761
    See also Stereotyping
Stereotyping, **1:**59, **2:**662, **761–763**
    categorization process of, **2:**761–762
    causal attributions and, **2:**762
    contextual salience and, **2:**762
    evaluation methods, ambiguity in, **2:**762–763
    gender stereotypes and, **2:**715–716
    information processing, impact on, **2:**762
    interpretive bias and, **2:**762
    memory function and, **2:**762
    multiple function of, **2:**761–762
    organizational factors and, **2:**762–763
    perceiver motivation and, **2:**763
    perceptual bias and, **2:**762
    performance outcomes, ambiguity in, **2:**762
    prejudicial attitudes and, **2:**761
    source of performance, ambiguity about, **2:**763
    structured decision making and, **2:**763
    See also Adverse impact/disparate treatment/discrimination at
        work; Affirmative action; Civil Rights Act of 1964; Civil
        Rights Act of 1991; Diversity training; Sexual
        discrimination; Stereotype threat
Stern, W., **1:**309
Sternberg, R., **2:**727
Stevens Institute of Technology, **2:**692
Stigma:
    dirty work and, **1:**152–153
    gay/lesbian/bisexual identity and, **1:**263–264
Stogdill, R. M., **1:**48
Stone-Romero, E. F., **1:**240, **2:**657
Strain and stress, **1:**15, **2:**743, 766, 768–769
Strain-based conflict, **2:**683
Strategic alliances. *See* Mergers, acquisitions,
    and strategic alliances
Strategic control with communication, **2:**553
Strategic human resources. *See* Human resources strategy
Strategic optimists, **2:**536
Strategic performance modeling, **2:**778
Strategic planning, **2:**763–764
    basis for development of, **2:**763–764
    current state analysis and, **2:**764
    environmental scan and, **2:**764
    future state, definition of, **2:**764
    implementation of, **2:**764

mission statements and, **2:**764
purpose of, **2:**763
steps in, **2:**764
strategy formulation and, **2:**764
vision statement and, **2:**764
white space in the marketplace and, **2:**763
Strategic stakeholder theory, **1:**116
Strategic talent management, **2:**777
Stratified samples, **2:**690
Street smarts. *See* Practical intelligence
Stress:
    abusive supervisors and, **1:**3
    action theory, stressor taxonomy and, **1:**6
    affective traits, stressor-strain relationship and, **1:**15
    charismatic leadership and, **1:**70
    compressed workweek and, **1:**88
    conflict at work and, **1:**96
    counterproductive work behaviors and, **1:**120–121, 124–125
    demand-control model of strain and, **1:**407
    electronic monitoring and, **1:**176
    emotional labor and, **1:**184–185
    hardiness and, **1:**304
    occupational stress and, **1:**66–67, **2:**532–533
    older workers and, **2:**532–533
    person-environment fit theory of, **2:**623
    self-efficacy and, **2:**705–706
    See also Stress, consequences; Stress, coping and
        management; Stress, models and theories
Stress, consequences, **2:**764–766
    behavioral consequences, **2:**766
    emotional consequences, **2:**765
    locus of control and, **2:**766
    occupational stressors, **2:**765
    personality/dispositional characteristics and, **2:**766
    physiological consequences, **2:**765
    role stressors and, **2:**765
    self-efficacy and, **2:**766
    self-esteem and, **2:**766
    social support and, **2:**766
    stress reactions, factors in, **2:**766
    work-family conflict and, **2:**765
    work-related stress effects and, **2:**764–765
    See also Emotional burnout; Empowerment; Job satisfaction;
        Occupational health psychology; Stress; Stress, coping
        and management; Stress, models and theories
Stress, coping and management, **2:**767–769
    affective communication and, **2:**769
    appraisal/transactional model of stress and, **2:**767, 769
    context-specific coping strategies and, **2:**768
    coping strategies and, **2:**767–768
    cybernetic model of stress and, **2:**767
    economic costs of stress and, **2:**769
    emotion-focused vs. problem-focused coping, **2:**767–768
    family networks and, **2:**769
    family-supportive policies/programs and, **2:**769
    feedback loops and, **2:**769
    general adaptation syndrome and, **2:**767, 770–771
    hardiness, training and, **1:**303
    improved coping at work and, **2:**769

locus of control and, **1:**461–462, **2:**767
personality traits and, **2:**769
research on, **2:**767
self-efficacy and, **2:**767
self-image/self-confidence, job performance and, **2:**768
social support and, **2:**768–769
strain and, **2:**767, 768–769
supervisor/coworker reactions and, **2:**768
See also Person-environment (PE) fit; Stress; Stress,
    consequences; Stress, models and theories
Stress, models and theories, **2:**770–773
    cybernetic model and, **2:**772–773
    demands-control model and, **2:**772
    effort-reward-imbalance model and, **2:**772
    general adaptation syndrome and, **2:**770–771
    general models and, **2:**770, 771–772
    generic frameworks and, **2:**770–771
    individual/work-environment characteristics,
        interaction of, **2:**772
    Institute for Social Research model and, **2:**771–772
    model, definition of, **2:**770
    occupational stress models, **2:**770–773
    person-environment fit concept and, **2:**771
    stress process, temporal framework of, **2:**772
    testable theories and, **2:**770, 772–773
    theory, definition of, **2:**770
    See also Emotional burnout; Empowerment; Occupational
        health psychology; Role overload and underload; Stress;
        Stress, consequences; Stress, coping and management
Stressor-strain relationship, **1:**15, **2:**743, 766, 768–769
Stretch competency model, **1:**86
Strodtbeck, F.,**1:**138
Strong Interest Inventory, **1:**67
Structural contingency theory of organizational form and
    effectiveness, **1:**274
Structural equation modeling (SEM), **2:**773–776
    alternatives to, **2:**776
    causal modeling with, **2:**775
    confirmatory factor analysis and, **2:**773
    description of, **2:**773
    effect parameters, rate-of-exchange interpretation and, **2:**775
    effect size estimation, measurement error and, **2:**773
    experimental data analysis and, **2:**775
    fit statistics/fit indexes and, **2:**775
    fixed/constrained parameters and, **2:**774
    just-identified model and, **2:**774, 775
    latent continuous variables and, **2:**773
    latent growth curve models and, **2:**774
    manifest continuous variables and, **2:**773
    misspecification and, **2:**775
    model fit and, **2:**774–775
    model interpretation and, **2:**775
    model specification and, **2:**774
    multiple indicator/multiple cause models and, **2:**773–774
    multiple regression and, **2:**773–774
    overidentified/underidentified models and, **2:**774
    parameter estimation and, **2:**774
    passive observation applications of, **2:**775
    path analysis and, **2:**773

path diagrams/directed graphs and, **2:**774
patterns of associations and, **2:**773
recursive/nonrecursive models and, **2:**774
resources for, **2:**775–776
sampling error and, **2:**775
statistical modeling with, **2:**773–775
statistically equivalent models and, **2:**775
See also Construct; Experimental designs; Factor analysis;
      Item response theory (IRT); Moderator and mediator
      variables; Multilevel modeling; Multitrait-multimethod
      (MTMM) matrix; Nomological networks;
      Nonexperimental designs; Quantitative research
      approach; Quasi-experimental designs; Reliability;
      Statistical power; Survey approach; Validity
Structural support, **2:**741
Structured decision making, **2:**763
Structures. See Organizational structure
Study of Values, **1:**346
Subjective expected utility theory (SEUT), **1:**424
Subjective norms, **2:**739
Subject-matter experts, **1:**57, 85, 130, **2:**470
Substance abuse:
    workplace protections, rehabilitated abusers and, **1:**24
    See also Drug and alcohol testing
Succession planning, 2:776–779
    assessment tools/processes for, **2:**778
    components of a comprehensive process, **2:**777–778
    development of, **2:**776–777
    industrial/organizational psychology and, **2:**776–779
    interdisciplinary approach to, **2:**779
    job modeling/strategic performance modeling and, **2:**778
    leaders as corporate assets and, **2:**777
    learning design/organizational development fields and, **2:**778
    organizational upheaval and, **2:**777
    principles of, **2:**778–779
    rationale for, **2:**776
    replacement planning and, **2:**776
    secret process of, **2:**777
    strategic talent management and, **2:**777
    succession management and, **2:**776–777
    talent inventory components and, **2:**778
    wars for talent and, **2:**777
    See also Executive selection; Selection strategies
Suk Jang, Y., **1:**277
Summative effect, **1:**151
Summative evaluation, **2:**638
Sum of the squared loadings (SSL), **1:**244
Sunk cost fallacy, **1:**430–431
Super, D., **1:**63, 64, 65, 67
Superior-subordinate communication, **1:**363–364
Supervision. See Abusive supervision; Leadership development;
      Leadership and supervision; Managerial leadership;
      Workplace incivility
Supervisory Behavior Description Questionnaire, **1:**49
Supplementary fit, **2:**615
Supportive leadership, **2:**595, 725, 726
Survey approach, 1:379, 2:654, 779–782
    administration of, **2:**780, 781
    census surveys and, **2:**780–781

closed-ended questions and, **2:**780
communication of the survey and, **2:**781
design of surveys, **2:**780–781
incentives for participation and, **2:**781
open-ended questions and, **2:**780
presentation of results and, **2:**782
pretest of items and, **2:**780
purpose/goals of surveys, **2:**780
results analysis and, **2:**781–782
sample surveys and, **2:**781
survey action planning and, **2:**781
survey, definition of, **2:**779–780
taking action and, **2:**782
timing of a survey and, **2:**781
See also Job satisfaction; Linkage research and analysis;
      Organizational surveys; Quantitative research approach
Survivor syndrome, 2:782–784
    antecedents of, **2:**783
    coping mechanisms and, **2:**784
    definitions of, **2:**783
    distributive justice and, **2:**783
    downsizing and, **2:**782–783
    equity theory and, **2:**783
    explanations for, **2:**783
    identification with aggressor syndrome and, **2:**784
    job insecurity, work efforts and, **2:**783–784
    long-term effects and, **2:**784
    outcomes of, **2:**783
    procedural justice and, **2:**783
    psychological contracts and, **2:**783
    research on, **2:**783–784
    symptom clusters in, **2:**783
    See also Downsizing; Psychological contract
Switzer, F., **2:**916
SWOT analysis, **2:**764
Symbolizing capability, **2:**729
Systematic field research methods, **1:**306
Systematic samples, **2:**690
Systems-4 management framework, **1:**328, 331

t tests, **1:**351
Tacit knowledge, **2:**634, 727
Tailoring occupations. See Selection, occupational tailoring
Talent management systems, **1:**86
Tarkenton, F., **2:**538
Task approach skills, **1:**64
Task conflict, **1:**95, 96, 97
Task enlargement, **1:**406
Task performance, **1:**103, 401
    abusive supervision and, **1:**1
    boredom at work and, **1:**60–61
Task rotation, **1:**405, **2:**405–406
Task work/team work capability coordination, **1:**293
Task-oriented behaviors, **1:**50
Tavistock Institute of Human Relations, **1:**311, 312, 315, **2:**749
Taxonomy of needs, **2:**608
Taylor, F. W., **1:**188, 305, 306, 313, 392, **2:**537, 692–693, 750
Taylor, H. C., **2:**855–856
Taylorism, **1:**188, 306, **2:**692

Taylor-Russell utility model, **2:**855–856
Team-based rewards, 2:785–786
  categories of, **2:**785–786
  definition of, **2:**785
  discretionary rewards, **2:**786
  effectiveness of, **2:**788
  full- vs. part-time teams and, **2:**786
  gainsharing/profit sharing, **2:**785
  goal-based rewards, **2:**785, 786
  line-of-sight problem and, **2:**786
  measurable performance standards and, **2:**786
  merit rewards, **2:**786
  organizational context factors and, **2:**786
  research on, **2:**786
  team composition and, **2:**786
  team interdependence and, **2:**786
  team skill rewards, **2:**786
  See also Compensation; Gainsharing (GS) and profit sharing
      (PS); Group cohesiveness; Groups; Incentives; Intrinsic
      and extrinsic work motivation; Performance appraisal;
      Social loafing
Team-based training, **2:**821
Team building, 2:787–789
  evaluation/adjustment of teams and, **2:**788
  launching teams, pilots of team structure and, **2:**788
  organizational level team-building, **2:**787–788
  preparing the organizations and, **2:**788
  problem-solving/planning skills and, **2:**789
  selection of team members/leaders and, **2:**788
  skill development, team members/leaders and, **2:**788
  systems support for, **2:**788
  team-building efforts, characteristics of, **2:**787
  team health monitoring and, **2:**789
  team level team-building, **2:**790
  training for, **2:**789
  See also Group cohesiveness; Group development;
      Group dynamics and processes; Groups
Team compilation phenomenon, **1:**295
Team development. *See* Group Development
Team discretionary rewards, **2:**791
Team mental model, 2:788–790
  antecedents to, **2:**789
  concept mapping and, **2:**789
  definition of, **2:**788
  function of, **2:**788
  importance of, **2:**788
  measurement of, **2:**789
  mental model similarity and, **2:**788–789
  nature of, **2:**788–789
  origin of, **2:**788
  outcomes of, **2:**789
  quality of mental models and, **2:**789
  research on, **2:**789
  task-focused models, **2:**788
  team-focused models, **2:**788
  See also Group dynamics and processes; Groups;
      Team-based rewards; Team building
Team skill rewards, **2:**791
Team task analysis, **2:**828–829

Teams, **1:**298, 307
  See also Groups; Justice in teams; Team building; Team mental
      model; Team-based rewards; Teamwork; Virtual teams
Teamwork:
  creativity and, **1:**128
  learning organizations and, **1:**449
  self-managed teams, job involvement and, **1:**399
  skills training and, **2:**826
  sociotechnical approach and, **2:**750
  task work/team work capability coordination, **1:**293
  telecommuting and, **2:**794
  top management teams, **1:**229
  See also Groups; Justice in teams; Team
      mental model; Virtual teams
Technology, **2:**777
  assessment center process and, **1:**33, 35, 36
  communications technologies, **1:**43, **2:**732
  content-coding/text-mining software tools, **1:**102
  mediated interpersonal communication, **1:**362, 365–366
  migration of workers and, **1:**65
  organization structure and, **2:**587
  training and, **2:**825
  See also Automation/advanced manufacturing
      technology/computer-based integrated technology;
      Computer assessment; Distance learning; Electronic
      human resources management (eHR); Human-computer
      interaction (HCI); Sociotechnical approach;
      Telecommuting; Virtual organizations; Virtual teams
Telecommuting, 1:366, 2:792–795
  absence/lateness and, **2:**882
  advantages of, **2:**793
  challenges of, **2:**793–794
  formal telecommuting programs and, **2:**793
  future concerns with, **2:**794–795
  future workforce practices and, **2:**793
  global teams and, **2:**794
  home-based telecommuting and, **2:**792
  informal telecommuting, **2:**792–793
  mentoring/developmental relationships and, **2:**793–794
  organizational socialization and, **2:**795
  teamwork and, **2:**794
  types of, **2:**792
  virtual teams and, **2:**792
  See also Job design; Organizational communication, informal;
      Virtual organizations; Virtual teams; Work-life balance
Teleworking, **2:**792
Tellegen, A., **1:**54
Temporal dimensionality, **1:**133
Temporary work agencies, **2:**593
Temporary workers, **2:**593–594
  underemployment and, **2:**843
  See also Outsourcing; Retirement
Teo, T., **1:**146
Tepper, B. J., **1:**451
Terman, L., **1:**29
Termination decisions, **2:**662
Terrorism and work, 2:795–797
  absenteeism and, **2:**796
  definition of, **2:**795

disorganized work environment and, **2:**796
employee assistance programs and, **2:**797
feelings of vulnerability/fear and, **2:**796
financial losses and, **2:**796
individual outcomes and, **2:**796
leadership practices and, **2:**797
onsite interventions and, **2:**797
organizational outcomes and, **2:**795–796
organizational practice/policy and, **2:**796–797
role ambiguity and, **2:**796
September 11, 2001 and, **2:**795, 796
See also Violence at work; Workplace safety
Testing:
broadside approach to, **1:**5
differential item functioning and, **1:**151–152
See also Applicant/test-taker reactions; Army Alpha/Army
Beta; Banding; Classical test theory (CTT); Cognitive
ability tests; Computer assessment
Test-operate-test-exit (TOTE) units, **1:**6
Test-retest reliability coefficient, **1:**56, **2:**676
Test score properties, **1:**75
Test security, 1:91, **2:797–800**
breaches, effects of, **2:**798
common forms of security breach, **2:**798
confidence in test results and, **2:**798
definition of, **2:**798
ensuring security of test materials, **2:**798–799
financial/social implications of breaches, **2:**800
ineffective selection procedures and, **2:**798
knowledge base on security, **2:**799–800
legal/regulatory action and, **2:**799
methods for, **2:**799–800
organizational performance, compromise of, **2:**798
security compromise, consequences of, **2:**798
social awareness of, **2:**799
validity/reliability concerns and, **2:**798
See also Ethics in industrial/organizational practice;
Selection strategies; Standardized testing; Validity
Tetlock, P. E., **1:**300
Tetrachoric correlation, **2:**473
TETRAD Project, **2:**776
Tetrault, L. A., **1:**451
Text-mining software, **1:**102
Theft at work, 2:800–802
aggregate measures of, **2:**801
antecedents to, **2:**801–802
control systems and, **2:**802
counterproductive work behaviors and, **2:**800
demographic factors in, **2:**801
employee theft, **2:**800
ethics programs and, **2:**802
integrity tests and, **2:**801, 802
interventions for, **2:**802
measurement of, **2:**800–801
organizational culture and, **2:**802
organizational justice and, **2:**802
person antecedents to, **2:**801
person-oriented interventions and, **2:**802
self-report measures and, **2:**801

shrinkage and, **2:**801
situation antecedents to, **2:**802
situation-oriented interventions and, **2:**802
See also Counterproductive work behaviors (CWBs)
Thematic Apperception Test (TAT), **2:**506
Theory, X, **1:**3, 328
Theory of action, 2:803–804
actionable knowledge and, **2:**804
espoused theory vs. theory-in-use and, **2:**803
Model I actions, automatic nature of, **2:**803–804
Model I socialization and, **2:**803
Model II, governing variables of, **2:**804
practicing the theory of action, **2:**804
single-loop/double-loop learning and, **2:**804
See also Learning organizations; Organizational change;
Organizational change, resistance to; Organizational
development (OD)
**Theory of reasoned action/theory of planned
behavior, 1:**39, **2:**739, **805–807**
actual behavior and, **2:**805–806
application of theory of reasoned action, **2:**806
behavioral intentions and, **2:**805
behavior, prediction/explanation of, **2:**806–807
limitations of theory of reasoned action, **2:**805
perceived control determinant and, **2:**806
subjective norms, normative beliefs and, **2:**805
theory of planned behavior, **2:**806
theory of reasoned action, **2:**805–806
See also Attitudes and beliefs; Judgment and
decision-making (JDM) process; Occupational
health psychology (OHP)
Theory of vocational personality types, **2:**622
Theory of work adjustment (TWA),
1:67, **2:**622, **807–809**
abilities and, **2:**807
adjustment behavior and, **2:**808
adjustment style variables and, **2:**808
environment requirements/tasks and, **2:**807
environment style variables and, **2:**808
maintenance behavior and, **2:**808
person-environment correspondence and, **2:**807–808
person-environment interaction and, **2:**807
person-environment symmetry and, **2:**808–809
person requirements/needs and, **2:**807
person style variables and, **2:**808
satisfaction, situation evaluation and, **2:**808
skill requirements and, **2:**808
values and, **2:**807
See also Person-environment (PE) fit; Person-job
(PJ) fit; Person-organization (PO) fit;
Person-vocation (PV) fit
Theory Y, **1:**328
Theory-in-use, **2:**803
Thick descriptions, **1:**69, **2:**653
Third-person processes. *See* Negotiation, mediation, and
arbitration
Thomas, H., **2:**581
Thompson, C. A., **2:**848
Thoresen, C. J., **1:**14

360-degree feedback, **1:**33, 36, 68, 86, 249–250, 334, **2:**605, **809–812**
    advantages of, **2:**810, 811
    decision making and, **2:**810, 811
    definition of, **2:**809
    development of, **2:**809–810
    evaluation of, **2:**811–812
    leadership development and, **1:**447
    organizational development and, **2:**567
    organizational surveys and, **2:**592
    problems with, **2:**810–811
    rating sources and, **2:**810–811
    recommendations for, **2:**811
    research on, **2:**809
    typical 360-degree systems, **2:**810
    See also Multitrait-multimethod (MTMM) matrix;
        Performance appraisal; Performance feedback
Three-component model (TCM) of organizational
    commitment, **2:**548–549
Three-dimensional surface plot analysis, **2:**619
Three-stage model of change, **2:**541
Three-style model of conflict management, **1:**98
Thurstone, L. L., **1:**314, 328
Thurstone scale, **1:**38
Tiffin, J., **2:**526
Time discounting, **1:**425
Time management, **2:812–813**
    goal-setting/goal achievement, dynamic conditions and, **2:**812
    individual differences and, **2:**813
    perceived control of time and, **2:**813
    problem-solving focus of, **2:**812
    procrastination and, **2:**813
    research on, **2:**813
    self-management strategy of, **2:**812
    standardization/routinization of activities and, **2:**812
    task content/social influences and, **2:**813
    See also Goal-setting theory; Self-regulation theory
Time series designs, **2:**656
Time studies, **2:**693
Time-based conflict, **2:**683
Title, I, **1:**8–9, 22–25
Title, VII, **1:**8, 58, 59, 71–74, 84, 197, 211, 315, **2:**613, 714, 715, 718, 846
Titles. *See Dictionary of Occupational Titles* (DOT); Job titles
Token economy program, **2:**672
Tompkins, P. H., **2:**555
Top management teams (TMTs), **1:**229
Top-down/bottom-up phenomenon, **1:**294
Top-down selection strategy, 1;46, 47, 196
Total compensation movement, **1:**83
Total quality management (TQM), **2:**692, **814–816**
    business process reengineering and, **2:**815, 816
    definition of, **2:**814
    employee involvement interventions and, **2:**814–815
    employee training and, **2:**815
    evolution of, **2:**814
    legitimacy of, **2:**814
    monitoring progress in, **2:**816
    organizational change and, **2:**541

principles/assumptions of, **2:**814
quality of work life interventions and, **2:**814
results of, **2:**816
rewarding results and, **2:**816
senior management commitment/training and, **2:**815
Six Sigma approach to, **2:**815, 816
standardized improvement model and, **2:**815
See also Organizational development; Training
Total shareholder return (TSR), **2:**819
Trade unions. *See* Unions
Trainability and adaptability, **2:817–818**
    adaptive performance dimensions and, **2:**817
    behavioral scales and, **2:**817
    general cognitive ability and, **2:**817
    individual differences and, **2:**817–818
    noncognitive characteristics and, **2:**818
    past experience/prior knowledge and, **2:**818
    performance measurement and, **2:**817
    prediction of, **2:**818
    training for, **2:**818
    work samples/simulations and, **2:**817
    See also Individual differences; Job performance models;
        Training; Training evaluation; Training needs
        assessment and analysis
Training, **2:819–820**
    aptitude area assessment and, **2:**627–628
    constructive feedback and, **2:**820
    delivery of, **2:**819
    development of, **2:**819
    effectiveness principles of, **2:**819–820
    employee development and, **2:**819
    evaluation of, **2:**819
    formal learning contexts, **2:**819
    frame-of-reference training, **1:**257–259, **2:**663
    knowledge/skills/attitudes and, **2:**819
    motivation levels and, **2:**819
    needs assessment and, **2:**819
    occupational health psychology, **2:**527
    older workers and, **2:**533
    organizational changes and, **2:**544
    practice opportunities and, **2:**820
    rater error training, **2:**662–663
    situational leadership model and, **2:**726–727
    supportive environments and, **2:**820
    team-building training, **2:**787
    total quality management implementation and, **2:**815
    training meetings, **2:**474
    transfer of training and, **2:**820
    utility of, **2:**857
    value of, **2:**819
    violence prevention strategies and, **2:**868–869
    See also Diversity training; Doctoral level education/training;
        Frame-of-reference (FOR) training; Master's level
        education/training; Training evaluation; Training
        methods; Training needs assessment and analysis;
        Transfer of training
Training evaluation, **2:820–823**
    affective learning and, **2:**822
    benefits analysis and, **2:**822

causal chains across levels and, **2:**822
cognitive learning and, **2:**822
data collection and, **2:**822
effectiveness of training and, **2:**820
efficiency of training and, **2:**820
formative/process evaluation, **2:**821
global satisfaction construct and, **2:**821
hierarchy of reactions and, **2:**821
knowledge base for, **2:**820
learning, multidimensional nature of, **2:**821–822
levels of evaluation and, **2:**821
measurement of outcomes and, **2:**822
outcomes of, **2:**821–822
pre-experimental designs and, **2:**823
process of, **2:**820–821
purpose of, **2:**821
quasi-experimental designs and, **2:**823
research design strategies and, **2:**822–823
return on investment analysis and, **2:**822
skill-based learning and, **2:**822
targets of, **2:**821
utility analysis and, **2:**822
See also Quasi-experimental designs; Training;
　　Training methods; Training needs assessment and
　　analysis; Utility analysis
Training and experience evaluations (T&Es), **2:**635–636, 637
Training methods, **2:823–827**
case studies and, **2:**824
cross-cultural training and, **2:**826
effective methods, characteristics of, **2:**826–827
formal training and, **2:**824
hypermedia systems and, **2:**825–826
informal training and, **2:**823–824
intelligent tutoring and, **2:**825
knowledge/skills/attitudes and, **2:**823, 824
lectures and, **2:**824
on-the-job training and, **2:**824
other-directed instruction and, **2:**824–825
role plays and, **2:**825
self-assessment tools and, **2:**825
self-directed instruction and, **2:**825
simulations and, **2:**826
team-based training and, **2:**826
technology-assisted instruction and, **2:**825–826
workbooks and, **2:**825
See also Distance learning; Diversity training; Employee
　　training; Leadership development; Team building;
　　Training; Transfer of training
Training needs assessment and analysis, **2:**819, **827–830**
cognitive task analysis and, **2:**828
data collection in, **2:**827, 828
employee selection for training and, **2:**829
environment factors and, **2:**828
evaluation-needs assessment relationship and, **2:**829
human performance intervention process and, **2:**830
human performance technology and, **2:**830
non-training/training needs, performance
　　interventions and, **2:**829
objectives for training programs and, **2:**829

organizational strategy and, **2:**827–828
organization analysis and, **2:**827–828
person analysis and, **2:**829
reactive needs assessment and, **2:**829–830
readiness for training and, **2:**829
task analysis and, **2:**828–829
task information sources and, **2:**828
team task analysis and, **2:**828–829
work environment characteristics and, **2:**828
See also Job analysis; Job analysis methods; Trainability and
　　adaptability; Training; Training evaluation
Training Project Grants, **2:**502
Training Systems Center, **1:**316
Trait approach to leadership, **2:830–832**
early research on, **2:**830
gender differences and, **2:**831
great man approach and, **2:**830
leader-follower differences and, **2:**830
leadership capacity, acquisition of, **2:**831
leadership traits and, **2:**831
limitations of, **2:**831
problems with, **2:**831
recent research on, **2:**831
situational variables and, **2:**830
utility of, **2:**831–832
See also Behavioral approach to leadership; Big Five
　　taxonomy of personality; Leadership and
　　supervision; Situational approach to leadership
Trait integrity, **1:**357
Trait-negative affect (TNA), **1:**13
Trait-oriented leadership research, **1:**48
Trait-positive affect (TPA), **1:**13
Trait-positive/trait-negative affective responses, **1:**13
Trait-situation debate, **2:**611, 613, 614
Traits. See Affective traits; Individual differences;
　　Motivational traits; Personality
Transactional communication, **2:**552–553
Transactional leadership. See Transformational and
　　transactional leadership
Transactional model of stress, **2:**767
Transactional psychological contracts, **2:**647
Transfer of training, **2:**820, **832–834**
adaptability and, **2:**832
definition of, **2:**832–834
enhancement strategies for, **2:**833–834
factors contributing to, **2:**833
generalization and, **2:**832
learning approaches and, **2:**833
maintenance issues and, **2:**832
motivation/capability to learn and, **2:**833
organizational barriers to, **2:**833
post-training implementation plans and, **2:**834
pre-training interventions and, **2:**833–834
return on investment concerns and, **2:**833
work-related case studies/practice
　　opportunities and, **2:**834
See also Trainability and adaptability; Training;
　　Training evaluation; Training methods;
　　Training needs assessment and analysis

Transformational leadership, **1:**70, 128, 445, **2:**596
  authentic leadership, **2:**632
  definition of, **2:**834
  development of, **2:**836–837
  effectiveness, conditions for, **2:**836
  four I's of, **2:**835
  leader characteristics in, **2:**835
  organizational change and, **2:**541
  workplace safety and, **2:**903
  See also Transformational and transactional leadership
Transformational and transactional leadership,
    1:70, 445, **834–837**
  active management-by-exception and, **2:**835
  contingent reward and, **2:**835
  forms of leadership in, **2:**834–835
  idealized influence and, **2:**835
  individualized consideration and, **2:**835
  inspirational motivation and, **2:**835
  intellectual stimulation and, **2:**835
  laissez-faire leadership and, **2:**835
  leadership styles, follower motivation and, **2:**835–836
  organizational effectiveness, recommendations for, **2:**836–837
  outcomes of, **2:**836
  passive management-by-exception and, **2:**835
  research on, **2:**834
  transactional leadership, **1:**445
  transformational leader effectiveness and, **2:**836
  transformational leaders, characteristics of, **2:**835
  transformational leadership, **2:**834
  See also Charismatic leadership theory; Leadership
    development; Life-cycle model of leadership; Team
    building; Transformational leadership
Transient error, **2:**676
Transition management, **2:**480
Transition stages, **2:**544
Transmission model of communication, **2:**552
Trend studies, **1:**463
Triandis, H. C., **1:**139
Trice, H., **2:**547
Trist, E. L., **2:**749
Trompenaars, F., **1:**139
True score theory, **1:**75
True score variance, **2:**677
Trust, 2:837–838
  climate of trust, **1:**263
  distrust/dissolution of trust and, **2:**838
  formation/evolution of, **2:**838
  higher-level/lower-level referents and, **2:**837
  individual level of, **2:**838
  interpersonal communication and, **1:**365
  outcomes of, **2:**837
  proximal/distal factors in, **2:**838
  rational trust, **2:**837
  relational trust, **2:**837
  situational level of, **2:**838
  types of, **2:**837
  See also Organizational cynicism; Organizational
    justice; Psychological contract
Trust building, **1:**2, 263, 277, 365, **2:**871

Tuckman, B. W., **1:**293
Tupes, E. C., **1:**53
Turnover, **1:**2, 96, 230
  advice giving/taking and, **1:**429
  new hires and, **2:**745
  performance appraisal and, **2:**600
  traditional turnover model, voluntary turnover and, **1:**415–416
  See also Withdrawal behaviors, turnover
Tuskegee Study, **1:**220
Tversky, A., **1:**429, 431
Two-factor theory, 2:839–840
  attribution theory and, **2:**839
  hygienes/job context factors and, **2:**839
  job design/redesign and, **2:**839–840
  job satisfaction/dissatisfaction, continuum of, **2:**839
  motivators-hygienes overlap and, **2:**839
  motivators/job content factors and, **2:**839
  self-determination theory and, **2:**840
  tests of the theory, **2:**839
  work motivation theory and, **2:**839–840
Type A and Type B personalities, 2:840–842
  achievement striving component and, **2:**840, 841
  employee-job fit and, **2:**841–842
  health status and, **2:**840–841
  impatience-irritability component and, **2:**840, 841
  work-related variables and, **2:**841
  See also Personality; Person-job (PJ) fit; Stress, consequences;
    Stress, coping and management; Time management
Type I/Type II errors, **2:**481, 482, 758–759
Typology of Deviant Workplace Behavior, **1:**120, 123

Uhl-Bien, M., **1:**334
Ultimate criterion, **1:**132
Ultimatum game, **1:**426
Underemployment, 1:283, **2:843–845**
  consequences of, **2:**844
  demographic correlates of, **2:**844
  educational mismatch and, **2:**843
  employee withdrawal and, **2:**845
  involuntary nature of, **2:**843–844
  job attitudes and, **2:**844
  job performance and, **2:**844
  measurement of, **2:**844
  overqualification and, **2:**843
  part-time/temporary employment and, **2:**843
  prevalence of, **2:**844
  psychological/physical well-being and, **2:**845
  types of, **2:**843
  underpayment and, **2:**843, 844
  See also Job satisfaction; Organizational commitment;
    Person-job (PJ) fit; Quality of work life (QWL);
    Withdrawal behaviors, turnover
Underidentified model, **2:**774
Underpayment, **1:**213, **2:**843
Uniform Guidelines on Employee Selection Procedures,
    1:218, **2:**637, **845–848**, 919
  adverse impact, definition/documentation of, **2:**846
  alternative validation strategies and, **2:**847
  background of, **2:**845–846

four-fifths rule and, **2:**846
impact/validity evidence, documentation of, **2:**847–848
implications of, **2:**848
knowledge/skills/abilities, job analysis and, **2:**847
purpose of, **2:**846
technical standards for validation studies and, **2:**847
topics covered in, **2:**846–848
topics omitted from, **2:**848
validity studies, general standards for, **2:**846–847
See also Adverse impact/disparate treatment/discrimination at
    work; Civil Rights Act of 1964; Civil Rights Act of 1991
Union commitment, 2:848–850
belief in unionism and, **2:**849
closeness of fit indexes, factor model vs.
    observed model and, **2:**849
components in, **2:**848
definition of, **2:**848
early commitment to unions and, **2:**850
exchange theory and, **2:**850
four-factor union commitment scale and, **2:**849
meta-analysis results and, **2:**849–850
predictor-outcome models and, **2:**849–850
responsibility to the union and, **2:**849
socialization process and, **2:**849
union commitment construct, conflicting
    interpretations of, **2:**849
union instrumentality perceptions and, **2:**849–850
union loyalty and, **2:**849
willingness to work for the union and, **2:**849
See also Attitudes and beliefs; Industrial relations;
    Organizational commitment; Organizational
    socialization; Unions
Union law. *See* Labor law
Unions, 1:349, **2:**850–854
American labor union history, **2:**851–852
collective bargaining and, **1:**349, 437, **2:**851, 853
commitment to, **2:**853, 854
compensation systems and, **1:**82, 84
craft unions, **2:**851
decline of, **1:**349–350
decline of unions, **2:**852
grievance systems and, **1:**190
history of, **2:**851–852, 854
industrial/organizational psychology and, **2:**853
industrial unions, **2:**851
instrumentality beliefs and, **2:**853
job dissatisfaction and, **2:**853
joining rationale, **2:**853–854
legal status of, **2:**851
lobbying activities and, **2:**851
member assistance programs and, **1:**189
private vs. public sector unions and, **2:**852
purpose of, **2:**852–853
socialization practices and, **2:**853–854
strike action and, **2:**851
See also Labor law; National Labor Relations
    Act (NLRA); Union commitment
Unitary concept of validity, **2:**863, 864
United National Global Compact, **1:**116

United States Congressional Office of
    Technology Assessment, **1:**176
United States Employment Service (USES), **2:**659
United States Public Health Service (USPHS), **1:**220, **2:**694
Unity of direction, **2:**588
Universalism principle, **1:**116–117
Universe score variance, **1:**267, **2:**677
University of Aston (England), **2:**588
University of Michigan, **1:**48, 49–50, **2:**771
University of Minnesota, **2:**622
University programs in industrial/organizational
    psychology, **2:**940–942
    See also Doctoral level education/training;
        Master's level education/training
Unmet expectations gap model, **1:**144, 145
Upskilling process, **1:**43
User-based marketing approach, **1:**143, 144
User-computer dialog, **1:**325–326
Utilitarian perspective, **1:**215, 219
Utility analysis, 2:854–857
break-even analysis, **2:**857
Brogden-Cronbach-Gleser utility model, **2:**856–857
definition of, **2:**854–855
multiattribute utility theory and, **1:**424
Naylor-Shine index of utility, **2:**856
subjective expected utility theory and, **1:**424
Taylor-Russell utility model, **2:**855–856
training/development activities, utility of, **2:**857
Utility theory, **1:**84, 115, 215, 340, 424

Valence-instrumentality-expectancy (VIE) theory
    of motivation, **1:**27, 237–238
Validation strategies, 2:859–863
concurrent validation studies and, **2:**642, 861
construct-based strategies, **2:**861–862, 863
content-based strategies, **2:**862, 863
convergent evidence and, **2:**861
correlational validity and, **2:**861
criterion-related strategies, **2:**861, 863
cross-validation, **2:**629
discriminant evidence and, **2:**861
employment decisions, validation of, **2:**863
evidence, generation of, **2:**860
experimental/quasi-experimental research and, **2:**861
focus of, **2:**859
general approaches to, **2:**860–862
inferences, conceptual framework for, **2:**859–860,
    860 (figure)
longitudinal validation, **2:**642
performance domain-psychological construct
    relationship and, **2:**861–862
performance domains, personnel selection and, **2:**859–860
predictive validation studies and, **2:**861, 862
predictor-development processes and, **2:**862–863
predictors-critera isomorphism and, **2:**862
systematic job analysis/competency modeling
    and, **2:**861–862
unitary concept of validity and, **2:**863
See also Construct; Criterion theory; Validity

Validity, 2:653, **864–865**
  classical test theory and, **1:**76
  common misconceptions of, **2:**864–865
  construct validity, **1:**238–239, 358–359, **2:**728–729
  construct validity inferences and, **2:**865
  content validity inferences and, **2:**865
  convergent validity, **2:**865
  criterion-related validity, **1:**200, 336, **2:**613–614, 728
  criterion-related validity inferences and, **2:**865
  definition of, **2:**864
  discriminant validity, **2:**865
  employee selection instrument and, **1:**194–195
  employment interviews and, **1:**200–201
  evidence-generation, approaches to, **2:**864–865
  face validity, **1:**201
  g factor, predictive validity of, **1:**77–78
  graphological analysis and, **1:**282
  incremental validity, **1:**200–201, 340–341
  inferences, validity of, **2:**864
  internal validity, **1:**239
  narrow cognitive ability factor, predictive validity of, **1:**78
  naturalistic observation and, **2:**505
  research-based inferences and, **1:**238–239
  standardized test and, **2:**757
  statistical conclusion validity, **1:**239
  types of, evidence-generation strategies and, **2:**864–865
  unitary concept of, **2:**863, 864
  See also Construct; Criterion theory; Incremental validity;
      Multitrait-multimethod (MTMM) matrix; Nomological
      networks; Validation strategies
Validity generalization strategies, **1:**195
Value and belief theory of culture, **1:**274
Value congruence, **2:**616, 620, 621, 910
Value measures, **1:**67
Value-percent theory, **1:**408–409
Values Scale, **1:**67
Van de Vijver, F., **1:**142
van Gelder, J. -L., **1:**334
Van Harrison, R., **2:**619, 623
Van Maanen, J., **2:**582, 584
Variable-based pay, **1:**83, 339
Variance, **1:**149, 266–267
Variance parameters, **2:**775
Variance-covariance matrix, **2:**471, 471 (table)
Verbal persuasion, **2:**706–707
Verbal protocol analysis (VPA), **2:866–867**
  cautions/limitations and, **2:**867
  definition of, **2:**866
  organizational sciences applications of, **2:**866
  process of, **2:**866
  psychological sciences applications of, **2:**866–867
  utility of, **2:**867
  See also Content coding; Qualitative research approach
Verley, J., **1:**306
Vernon, P., **1:**310
Vertical dyad linkage (VDL) model, **1:**440
Veterans, **1:**16, 17
Veterans Administration (VA), **2:**694
Vicarious capability, **2:**729–730

Victim-precipitation perspective, **1:**3
Victimization, **1:**1, 3
Victor, B., **2:**546
Videoconferencing technology, **1:**89
Vietnam Era Veterans' Readjustment
      Assistance Act of 1974, **1:**16
Vietnam War, **1:**315
Violence at work, 2:868–869
  employee training and, **2:**868–869
  environmental risk reduction strategies and, **2:**869
  increased visibility and, **2:**868
  industrial policies/practices, aggression prevention and, **2:**869
  prevalence of, **2:**868
  prevention of Type I violence and, **2:**868–869
  prevention of Type II violence, **2:**869
  reward-reduction strategies and, **2:**868
  target-hardening strategies and, **2:**868
  Type I violence, **2:**868
  Type II violence, **2:**868, 869
  See also Abusive supervision; Counterproductive
      work behaviors (CWBs); Workplace safety
Virtual organizations, 1:84, **2:869–872**
  challenges to, **2:**871–872
  characteristics of, **2:**870
  cohesion/identity/commitment, maintenance of, **2:**871–872
  definition of, **2:**869–870
  degrees of virtuality, dimension of, **2:**870
  efficient/precise communication and, **2:**870
  electronic communication in, **2:**870–871
  electronic vs. face-to-face communication and, **2:**870, 871
  flat structure, multiple communication partners and, **2:**871
  human resource management tasks and, **2:**872
  norms of technology use and, **2:**871
  partner relationships and, **2:**870–871
  task management and, **2:**871
  trust building and, **2:**871
  See also Organizational commitment; Organizational
      communication, informal; Telecommuting; Virtual teams
Virtual reality (VR) simulation, **2:**723, 724
Virtual teams, 1:366, **2:**792, **872–874**
  cohesiveness within, **2:**874
  communications technology, modes of, **2:**872
  conflict, attribution error and, **2:**874
  diversity in, **2:**873
  global organizations, outsourcing and, **2:**872
  hot desking and, **2:**872
  knowledge exchange and, **2:**873
  literature on, **2:**872–874
  recommendations for, **2:**874
  relationship issues and, **2:**873–874
  shared understanding and, **2:**873
  technology mediation and, **2:**873
  telecommuting and, **2:**872
  text-based media and, **2:**873
  trust levels in, **2:**874
  See also Telecommuting; Virtual organizations
Virtuous organizations, **2:**632
Viscerogenic needs, **2:**608
Vision, **1:**450

Vision statement, **2:**764
Visual language, **1:**324, 324 (figure)
Visual-spatial processing, **1:**77
Viswesvaran, C., **1:**347
Viteles, M., **1:**314, 315, 327, **2:**526, 692
Vocational counseling:
   personal abilities, work requirements and, **1:**78
   vocational interest personality typing and, **1:**67, **2:**622
Vocational Guidance Bureau, **1:**321
Vocational Guidance Council, **1:**321
Vocational interest personality types, **1:**67, **2:**622
Vocational Locus of Control Scale, **1:**461
Voice behavior, **2:**710
Voice face of a union, **1:**349
Volunteer Emergency Psychology Service, **1:**321
Volvo Company, **1:**311
von Bertalanffy, L., **2:**749
Vroom, V. H., **2:**521, 522, 523

Waclawski, J., **1:**255, 256
Wages. *See* Compensation
Wagner Act of 1935, **2:**852
Waiver of rights, **1:**221–222
Waldron, V. R., **1:**364
Wallin, J. A., **2:**540
Wal-Mart, **2:**901
Wanberg, C. R., **2:**515
Wanous, J. P., **2:**517, 665
Wards Cove Packing Co. v. Atonio, **1:**72
War Office Selection boards, **1:**310
The Washingtonians, **1:**188
Waterhouse v. Hopkins, **1:**73
Watson, D., **1:**13
Waung, M., **2:**518
Weaver, W., **1:**363
Web-based assessment. See Computer assessment
Weber, M., **2:**537, 588, 643, 645
Weber, Y., **2:**561
Weick, K. E., **2:**554, 579, 580, 581
Weighted application blanks, **2:**635–636
Weighted checklists, **2:**603
Weiner, N., **1:**107
Weisz, J. R., **1:**461
Well-being. *See* Employee well-being; Personal well-being
Western Collaborative Group Study, **2:**840–841
Western Electric Company studies, **1:**305, 314, **2:**488, 537
Whistleblowers, **1:**114, **2:**802, **875–878**
   contextual factors associated with, **2:**876
   description of, **2:**875
   organizational encouragement of, **2:**877–878
   personal characteristics of, **2:**875–876
   predictors/correlates of, **2:**875–876
   predictor whistleblower characteristics,
      retaliation actions and, **2:**876–877
   retaliation against, **2:**876–877
   retaliation, contextual factors and, **2:**877
   whistleblower actions, response to retaliation and, **2:**877
   wrongdoing characteristics, retaliation behaviors and, **2:**877
   wrongdoing/wrongdoer characteristics and, **2:**876

See also Corporate ethics; Corporate social responsibility;
   Counterproductive work behaviors (CWBs); Integrity
   at work; Organizational justice
White, J. K., **1:**262
White, R., **2:**560
White space in the marketplace, **2:**763
Whitehead, T. N., **1:**305
Wichita Jury Study, **1:**220
Wiebe, R., **2:**692
Wilderom, C. P. M., **2:**561
Wiley, C., **1:**217
Williams, K. D., **2:**736, 737
Williams, K. J., **2:**517
Williams, W., **1:**327
Wilson, F., **2:**581
Winchester Repeating Arms Company, **1:**314
Winter, D. G., **2:**509
Withdrawal behaviors, absenteeism, 2:878–880
   causes of, **2:**878
   construct of, **2:**878
   description of, **2:**878
   expectance theory framework and, **2:**880
   external locus of control and, **2:**879, 880
   framework development for, **2:**879–880
   personality characteristics, absence proneness and, **2:**879
   postdictive research design and, **2:**880
   process theory of absence and, **2:**879
   time, importance/mistreatment of, **2:**880
   variance theory and, **2:**878–879
   work attitude-absence hypothesis and, **2:**879
   See also Withdrawal behaviors, lateness;
      Withdrawal behaviors, turnover
Withdrawal behaviors, lateness, 2:881–883
   antecedents of lateness, **2:**881–882
   attitudinal measures and, **2:**881–882
   characteristics of, **2:**881
   description of, **2:**881
   employee lateness, conceptualization of, **2:**881–882
   extraorganizational variables and, **2:**882
   future research directions and, **2:**882–883
   group/organizational variables and, **2:**882
   job embeddedness dimensions and, **2:**882
   management of, **2:**883
   new work environment and, **2:**882–883
   personality indicators and, **2:**882
   See also Attitudes and beliefs; Withdrawal behaviors,
      absenteeism; Withdrawal behaviors, turnover
Withdrawal behaviors, turnover, 2:883–886
   avoidability of, **2:**883
   content models of, **2:**883–884
   demographic variables in, **2:**883
   description of, **2:**883
   economic models of, **2:**885
   employee intention to quit and, **2:**884
   functionality of, **2:**883
   intermediate linkage models of, **2:**884
   job embeddedness construct and, **2:**885
   motivational forces model of, **2:**885–886
   multiple decision paths in, **2:**884–885

new research directions and, **2:**885–886
perceived desirability of movement and, **2:**884
perceived ease of movement and, **2:**884
perceived organizational support and, **2:**883–884
practical recommendations for, **2:**886
process models of, **2:**884–885
shocks to the system and, **2:**884–885
two-factor approach to, **2:**884
unfolding model of, **2:**885
voluntariness of, **2:**883
work attitudes and, **2:**883
See also Turnover; Withdrawal behaviors,
    absenteeism; Withdrawal behaviors, lateness
Wolf, M., **2:**538
Wong, N., **1:**142
Wood, D. W., **2:**526
Woodward, J., **2:**588
Woodworth Personal Data Sheet, **2:**613
Work adjustment model, **1:**253
    See also Theory of work adjustment (TWA)
Work design:
    action theory and, **1:**6
    critical specification and, **2:**750
    positive psychological principles and, **2:**632
    See also Affective events theory (AET); Older worker
        issues; Sociotechnical approach; Work-life balance
Work ethic. *See* Protestant work ethic
Work groups, **2:**726
Work Locus of Control Scale, **1:**461, 462
Work motivation, 2:892–894
    achievement/power/affiliation needs and, **2:**893
    expected value theories and, **2:**893
    goal-setting theory and, **2:**893–894
    hedonistic/need-driven nature of humans and, **2:**893
    justice theories and, **2:**893
    needs hierarchy and, **2:**893
    overdetermination of motives and, **2:**893
    positive organizational scholarship movement and, **2:**893
    research on, **2:**892–893
    social cognitive theory and, **2:**893
    social comparison processes and, **2:**893
    theoretical models of, **2:**893–894
    See also Expectancy theory of work motivation; Intrinsic
        and extrinsic work motivation; Motivational traits; Need
        theories of work motivation; Reinforcement theory of
        work motivation; Self-concept theory of work motivation
Work samples, 2:905–907
    advantages of, **2:**907
    characteristics of, **2:**905–906
    content/face validities and, **2:**907
    cost of, **2:**906
    criterion-related validity of, **2:**907
    current performance, measure of, **2:**906
    definition of, **2:**905
    design features of, **2:**907
    disadvantages of, **2:**906–907
    fidelity to work tasks and, **2:**906
    history/future of, **2:**907
    legal defensibility of, **2:**907

perceived fairness of, **2:**907
trainable knowledge/skills and, **2:**906–907
uses for, **2:**905
See also Adverse impact/disparate treatment/discrimination at
    work; Americans with Disabilities Act (ADA) of 1990;
    Assessment center; Job analysis; Job knowledge testing;
    Job performance models; Situational judgment tests;
    Validation strategies
Work schedules. *See* Compressed workweek
Work values, 2:908–910
    behavior decisions and, **2:**909
    conflict of values, change and, **2:**909
    cultural values and, **2:**908–909
    definitions of, **2:**908
    effects/outcomes of, **2:**909–910
    erosion processes and, **2:**909
    fragmentation perspective and, **2:**910
    individual differences and, **2:**909
    motivational elements of, **2:**909
    organizational socialization and, **2:**909
    origin of, **2:**908–909
    self-relevant beliefs and, **2:**908
    self-schema and, **2:**908
    societal institutions and, **2:**909
    structure of, **2:**908
    value congruence and, **2:**910
    work preferences and, **2:**908
    See also Attitudes and beliefs; Motivational traits;
        Organizational culture; Person-organization (PO) fit
Work-life balance, 1:65, 67, 88, 160, 408, 2:888–892
    antecedents of work-family conflict and, **2:**889–890
    behavior-based conflicts and, **2:**889
    consequences of work-family conflict and, **2:**890
    description of, **2:**888–889
    directionality of conflict and, **2:**889
    emerging topics on, **2:**891–892
    family-friendly policies and, **2:**769, 890–891
    flexible work schedules and, **2:**890
    gender-based experience of, **2:**891
    industrial/organizational research limitations and, **2:**891
    older workers and, **2:**533
    organizational commitment and, **2:**551
    reduction of work-family conflict an, **2:**890–891
    telecommuting and, **2:**794
    time-based conflicts and, **2:**889
    work-family interface models, **2:**889, 891–892
    work-family role conflict, **2:**683, 765, 889–891
    See also Quality of work life (QWL); Role conflict; Stress,
        models and theories; Telecommuting; Workaholism
Work-school role conflict, **2:**683
Workaholism, 2:887–888
    attitudes/value-based characteristics of, **2:**887
    definitional issues in, **2:**887
    job involvement and, **2:**887
    negative organizational outcomes and, **2:**888
    quantitative boundaries and, **2:**887
    secondary addictions and, **2:**888
    self-report measure of, **2:**887
    significance of, **2:**887–888

workaholism syndrome, **2:**888
work-life balance and, **2:**888
See also Quality of work life (QWL); Work-life balance
Workflow analysis, **1:**208
Workforce utilization analysis, **1:**10
Working self-concept (WSC), **2:**703, 704
Workplace accommodations for the disabled, **2:894–896**
decisional process in, **2:**894–895
description of, **2:**894
employer responsibility for, **2:**895
legal protections and, **2:**895–896
multidisciplinary team decision and, **2:**895
personnel system accommodations and, **2:**894
structured decision process and, **2:**895
See also Americans with Disabilities Act (ADA) of 1990
Workplace incivility, **2:**719, **896–897**
comparative levels of, **2:**896
counterproductive work behaviors and, **2:**896, 897
description of, **2:**896
instigators of, **2:**897
modern communication technology and, **2:**896
organizational behaviors/structures and, **2:**896
prevention of, **2:**897
racial/ethnic diversity and, **2:**896
social interactionist perspective and, **2:**896–897
social norms, relaxation of, **2:**896
targets of, **2:**897
See also Counterproductive work behaviors/interpersonal
    deviance (CWB-I); Machiavellianism
Workplace injuries, **2:897–899**
accident proneness and, **2:**898
classification of, **2:**898
definition of, **2:**897–898
individual differences/personality traits and, **2:**898–899
industry-specific risks and, **2:**898
prediction, research on, **2:**898–899
prevalence of, **2:**898
situational predictors of injury and, **2:**899
timing/physical severity dimensions of, **2:**898
work design factors and, **2:**899
See also National Institute for Occupational Safety and
    Health (NIOSH)/Occupational Safety and Health
    Administration (OSHA); Occupational health
    psychology (OHP); Workplace safety
Workplace romance, **2:900–901**
definition of, **2:**900
formation of, **2:**900–901
impact of, **2:**901
management of, **2:**901
organizational variables and, **2:**900

types of relationships within, **2:**900
See also Sexual harassment
Workplace safety, **2:902–905**
accident-focus and, **2:**902
employee compliance and, **2:**902–903
fatal injuries and, **2:**902
high-performance work systems and, **2:**904
leader commitment to safety and, **2:**903
leader-member exchange theory and, **2:**903
leadership and, **2:**903
measurement of, **2:**902–903
nature of, **2:**902
prevention-oriented research and practice, **2:**540, 903
proximal behaviors preceding injury and, **2:**902
psychological climate and, **2:**903–904
psychological factors in safety, **2:**903–904
safety infractions, psychological consequences of, **2:**904–905
safety initiative/participation and, **2:**903
safety-related behavior focus and, **2:**902–903
teamwork and, **2:**904
transformational leadership and, **2:**903
See also National Institute for Occupational Safety and Health
    (NIOSH)/Occupational Safety and Health Administration
    (OSHA); Terrorism and work; Workplace injuries
Workplace social support, **2:**741
Worksite empowerment practices, **1:**205
World Health Organization (WHO), **2:**525
World Trade Center, **2:**795, 796
World War I, **1:**29, 30, 66, 314, 342, **2:**613
World War II, **1:**30, 34, 48, 66, 135, 206, 219, 314–315, 328,
    342, **2:**597, 616, 630, 694
World Wide Web, **1:**89, 90, 91, 155, 412, **2:**665
WorldCom, **1:**355
World-of-Work Map, **1:**422
Wrege, C., **2:**692
Wren, D., **1:**328, **2:**692
Wundt, W., **1:**313

Xerox, **2:**901

Yerkes, R. M., **1:**29, 314
Yetton, P. W., **2:**521, 522, 523
Yin, R. K., **1:**68
Youngblood, S. A., **2:**517
Yukl, G., **2:**810

z score, **1:**93, **2:**856
Zeithaml, V., **1:**143
Zohar, D., **2:**546
Zottoli, M. A., **2:**665